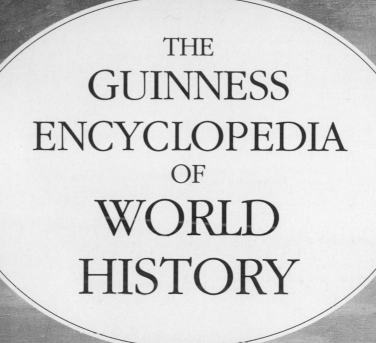

THE
GUINNESS
ENCYCLOPEDIA
OF
WORLD
HISTORY

GUINNESS PUBLISHING

First published 1992

© Guinness Publishing Ltd. 1992

Published in Great Britain by Guinness Publishing Ltd., London Road, Enfield, Middlesex

Colour reproduction by Bright Arts (HK) Ltd., Hong Kong

Printed and bound in Italy by New Interlitho SpA, Milan

British Library Cataloguing in Publication Data:
A catalogue record for this book is available from the British Library.

ISBN 0–85112–994–3

Project Editor

Richard Milbank

Design

Amanda Sedge
Sarah Silvé

Systems Support

Alex Reid
Kathy Milligan

Picture Editing

P. Alexander Goldberg

Additional Picture Research

James Clift

Illustrators

Robert and Rhoda Burns
Peter Harper
Chris Forsey

Art Director

David Roberts

Editorial Director

Ian Crofton

CONSULTANT EDITORS

Dr Tim Cornell .... Senior Lecturer in Ancient History, University College London

Dr Colin McEvedy .... Author of the *Penguin Atlas of History*

John Gillingham .... Senior Lecturer in Medieval History, London School of Economics

Professor Matthew Anderson.... Professor Emeritus of International History, London School of Economics

Professor Robert O'Neill .... Chichele Professor of the History of War, All Souls College, Oxford

CONTRIBUTORS

BB   Bryan Bridges
CM   Dr Colin McEvedy
CS   Dr Christopher Storrs, University of St Andrews
DB   David Bell, University of Leeds
DM   Dr David Morgan, School of Oriental and African Studies, University of London
FT   Dr Francis Toase, The Royal Military Academy Sandhurst
GR   Dr Gowher Rizvi, Nuffield College, Oxford
GW   Greg Woolf, Magdalen College, Oxford
HF   Hamish Forbes, University of Nottingham
IDC   Ian Crofton
JG   John Gillingham, London School of Economics
JP   Dr J.L. Pimlott, The Royal Military Academy Sandhurst
JS   John Schofield, Museum of London
JSp   Dr John Springhall, University of Ulster
LF   Lin Foxhall, University College London
LR   Louis Rawlings, University College London
LW   Dr Linda Walker
MB   Matthew Bennett, The Royal Military Academy Sandhurst
MD   Dr Malcolm Deas, St Anthony's College, Oxford
MH   Michael Hurst, St John's College, Oxford
MO   Margaret Oliphant
MP   Mark Pegram

MW   Matthew Wyman, University of Birmingham
ND   Nicole Douek, The British Museum, London
NF   Dr N.R.E. Fisher, University of Wales, Cardiff
NH   Nick Hooper
NP   Neil Parsons
PD   Dr Peter Denley, Queen Mary and Westfield College, University of London
PDS   Philip de Sousa, University of Leicester
PO   Pat Owen
RC   Dr Robert Cook, University of Sheffield
RJ   Richard Jones
RK   Dr Randolph Kent
RM   Richard Milbank
SL   Seán Lang, University of Exeter
SS   Dr S.J. Salter, University of Sheffield
TC   Dr Tim Cornell, University College London
TK   Dr Tim Kirk, Polytechnic of Newcastle-upon-Tyne
ViD   Dr Virginia Davis, Queen Mary and Westfield College, University of London

TIMECHARTS

Clive Carpenter

CARTOGRAPHIC CONSULTANT

Dr Colin McEvedy

The Guinness Encyclopedia of World History presents a general introduction to world history from humanity's earliest beginnings to the present. Roughly three-quarters of the book follows the thematic approach of the *Guinness Encyclopedia*, and is devoted to a series of chronologically arranged articles and features focusing on key historical periods and topics; the remainder of the book consists of an A-to-Z 'Factfinder' section, providing quick information about rulers, statesmen, wars, treaties, ideologies, religions, countries and many other topics. This dual format allows the reader to exploit the book in two different but complementary ways. The thematic section gives an overview of the broad sweep of history, in which the people and events of the past are placed in a wider context; the Factfinder gives access to more detailed information about these people and events, and is useful for finding a quick reference or checking a fact.

Using the Thematic Section

The thematic section of the Encyclopedia is divided up into six chapters, preceded by introductory articles on the nature of history and archaeology. The first chapter, **The Ancient World**, deals with human prehistory, the empires of the ancient Near and Middle East, and the civilizations of Greece and Rome. The pre-colonial history of Africa, Asia, the Americas, Australasia and Oceania is treated under **Other Worlds**, while the history of Europe and the Mediterranean from the fall of Rome to the coming of the Renaissance is covered in **The Medieval World**. **Broadening Horizons** is concerned with the voyages of discovery, European expansion overseas, and the struggle for power in Europe and elsewhere from the Reformation to the French Revolution. **Revolution, Industry and Empire** reviews the age of Napoleon, the rise of the USA, the growth of European imperialism, and the economics, politics and society of the 19th century. The major conflicts, issues and ideologies of the 20th century – from World War I to the collapse of Communism – are treated in **The Modern World**. Each chapter opens with a double-page timechart listing key events and their dates.

Within the thematic section, the pages are colour-coded to indicate to which chapter they belong. The reader will quickly become familiar with these colours and be able to flick from chapter to chapter with ease. Most of the topics within the thematic section are in the form of double-page spreads, though some subjects of particular importance and complexity are dealt with in four-page articles. Within each article there is a 'See Also' box to related spreads within the same section or elsewhere. There are also cross-references within the text itself to guide the reader to pages where further relevant details will be found. If the user wishes to find out more about a ruler, battle or other subject to which only passing reference is made in the text, the appropriate entry can easily be found in the Factfinder section at the end of the book.

Using the Factfinder

The Factfinder consists of some 3000 alphabetically arranged entries providing at-a-glance information on a range of items of historical importance. Many of the entries relate to topics that receive some treatment in the main text; such entries tend to be brief, providing basic details such as the dates of a monarch's rule or the date and outcome of a battle, together with a page reference to the relevant article in the thematic section. The Factfinder also contains numerous entries for items for which there was insufficient room to do justice in the main text, as well as entries providing further details on important topics and people to which only brief allusion was made in the thematic section.

The Factfinder is linked with the main thematic section by means of a simple cross-referencing and indexing system. The references at the end of the entries refer to specific mentions of the headword in the main text: where there is a string of page references, the main one is indicated by means of bold type; italic type indicates a reference to an illustration or illustration caption. The words in small capital letters refer the user to important related entries within the Factfinder itself.

CONTENTS

Contents

5. REVOLUTION, INDUSTRY AND EMPIRE

The battle of Preussisch-Eylau, 7/8 February 1807.

6. THE MODERN WORLD

The funeral of Ayatollah Ruhollah Khomeini, Teheran 1990.

FACTFINDER

Title page illustration: The surrender of Ulm to Napoleon by the Austrians, 20 October 1805; painting by Charles Thevenin (1764–1838).

Illustration opposite: The Mogul emperor Akbar crossing the Ganges; Mogul miniature, c. 1600.

THE
GUINNESS
ENCYCLOPEDIA
OF
WORLD
HISTORY

What is History?

For a subject that commands strong public interest, history has come in for a lot of criticism. The US industrialist Henry Ford famously dismissed it as 'bunk'. More recently, the English historian Christopher Hill feared that it might sometimes degenerate into 'lies about crimes'. The very word 'history' means 'story' (in several languages – French and German for example – the two words are identical), and if its narrative aspect has always attracted people to the subject, it also arouses suspicion about just how much of history is truth and how much is fiction.

It is important to be clear on the difference between 'history' and 'the past'. Everything that has ever happened is now in the past and can never be retrieved. However, a vast number of human actions leave behind them some sort of trace – whether in people's memories or in some concrete form, which may be anything from a diary entry to entire cities – from which a picture of the past can be reconstructed. It is this reconstruction of the past that is described as history.

Even the best historical reconstruction, however, is imperfect and to some extent conjectural. This is because for most of the past the evidence available is incomplete, and for more distant periods, or for

Clio, the muse of history, portrayed by an artist of the Umbrian school, 16th century.

areas of the globe with no written tradition, it can be very patchy indeed. Even recent periods, which have left an abundance of evidence of all sorts, can never be reconstructed exactly as they were. Not only is the past ephemeral by its very nature, but historians also inevitably present the past in the light of their own views and concerns. History is a highly subjective activity, and no historical account, however full, can ever be complete or wholly objective.

What is history for?

If the past is irrecoverable, why should anyone try to reconstruct it? There is no simple answer to this question. Clearly, however, any society that has advanced beyond a relatively low level of life and complexity *needs* history. A view of how the present emerged from the past helps us to understand, or at least to feel that we understand, the world and our own place in it. In early societies myths, legends, even genealogies, performed some of these functions. In modern ones they are performed by an elaborate apparatus of research and publication. The writing of history has often been distorted by political or religious prejudice or by the need to defend the position of some ruling group, but it is a fundamental element of the intellectual life of humanity. The 12th-century English historian, Henry of Huntingdon, wrote that 'history distinguishes rational beings from brutes – for brutes, whether animals or men, neither know nor wish to know anything about their origins or their history'.

Greek and Roman historians

The earliest histories were inspirational epics such as Homer's *Iliad*, perhaps loosely based on fact, but so intertwined with myth and invention that they cannot count as history (▷ pp. 7, 25 and 44).

However, it was among the ancient Greeks that historical writing as we recognize it started. Herodotus (?484–?420 BC) wrote a history of the Persian Wars whose facts he tried to check by travelling through Greece, talking with people who remembered the events (▷ p. 44). Although he wanted his *History* to show the magnitude of the Greek achievement in defeating the Persians, his account was so even-handed that he was accused of a pro-Persian bias by later writers (▷ p. 26). His careful approach to his sources, and his attempt at an objective, balanced approach, have led to his being called 'the Father of History'.

Thucydides (c. 455–c. 400 BC) followed Herodotus' approach in his *History* of the Peloponnesian Wars between Athens and Sparta, refraining from lofty judgement, and recounting the events with relative detachment (▷ p. 30).

The Romans inherited their historical tradition, like so much else, from the Greeks. However, they also kept an official record of state events, the *Annals*, which provided a body of 'official facts' on which Roman historians based their work. Their history was often unashamedly propagandist: Livy (?59 BC–AD ?19)

praised the virtues of the Roman Republic (▷ p. 36), though he embellished his sources with a considerable number of his own invention. Under the Empire, Roman historians turned increasingly to biography, usually of emperors, of which the best known example is Suetonius' (AD c. 69–140) *Lives of the Twelve Caesars*. The first of his subjects, Julius Caesar (100–44 BC), himself wrote a series of suitably immodest *Commentaries* on his own campaigns, particularly in Gaul (▷ p. 37). It was left to Tacitus (AD c. 56–120), probably the greatest Roman historian and certainly one of the most readable, to point out in his *Annals* the iniquities of the Empire and to bemoan the loss of the Republic.

From chroniclers to critics

For many centuries the Roman historical tradition survived more vigorously in the East than in the West. In the 12th century the Byzantine Princess Anna Comnena (1083–1153) wrote a life of her father, the Emperor Alexius I (▷ p. 81). In the West the critical scholarship and brilliant historical vision of the *History of the English Church and People* by the Northumbrian monk Bede (673–735) remained unsurpassed for 400 years.

The 12th-century Renaissance witnessed a historical revival. The works of writers such as William of Malmesbury (c. 1095–c. 1143), Orderic Vitalis (c. 1075–c. 1142), Otto of Freising (c. 1115–1158) and William of Tyre (c. 1130–c. 1184) were far more than mere chronicles of events. The revival even produced a spoof history, the *History of the Kings of Britain* by Geoffrey of Monmouth (?–c. 1154). In skilful hands, such as those of Matthew Paris (c. 1200–59) and Jean Froissart (c. 1337–c. 1410), the more straightforward chronicle form could provide a lively and exciting narrative.

Niccolò Machiavelli (1469–1527) used Roman history in his *Discourses* to give lessons in kingship for contemporary rulers (▷ p. 101). The idea that history was a storehouse of examples from which the correct course of action in any situation could be deduced – an idea that had classical roots, particularly in the work of the Greek biographer Plutarch (AD c. 46–120) – was to remain important until the 19th century. Some see a similarly instructive function in the 'history plays' of Shakespeare. The latter provide a distinctly biased account of late medieval English history, based as they were on the chronicles of Raphael Holinshed (died c. 1580), a Tudor propagandist. During the Reformation, history was scoured for ammunition for the bitter polemic that Catholics and Protestants hurled at each other (▷ p. 110). Not surprisingly, the lives of martyrs were considered most useful for this sort of propagandist writing. John Foxe's (1516–87) *Actes and Monuments*, better known as his 'Book of Martyrs' – a history of Christian martyrdom focusing especially on the English Protestant martyrs – remains the classic example of this particular use of the past.

But if history could be used to fuel argument between Christians, it could also be used to criticize Christianity itself, as the writers of the 18th-century Enlightenment showed (▷ p. 134). Already in 1685 a Frenchman, Richard Simon, in his *Critical History of the Old Testament*, had made the first important effort to apply the principles of historical criticism to the Bible, while about the same time in France the Benedictine monks of St Maur introduced hitherto unknown standards of thoroughness and accuracy into historical writing – although they remained devout Catholics. Voltaire (1699–1778) used history to compare Christianity with the religions of China and India, pointing out that the latter had sustained civilized life every bit as well as Christianity had done in Europe. Edward Gibbon (1737–94) went even further in his *Decline and Fall of the Roman Empire*, in which he blamed Christianity for eroding the martial spirit that had built the Empire up, and also for strengthening a spirit of intolerance, thereby contributing greatly to the Empire's collapse (▷ p. 41).

Underlying the Enlightenment approach was the search for the causes – the rationale – behind historical events. Gibbon's analysis was an attempt to explain why the Roman Empire fell, and in this he followed the example of the French Enlightenment thinker Montesquieu (1689–1755; ▷ p. 135), whose *Considerations on the Causes of the Greatness and the Decadence of the Romans* had stressed the important point that the historian's task is not just to chronicle events, but to seek to explain them.

'As it really was'

The German historian Leopold von Ranke (1795–1886) took this idea a stage further by saying that the historian's task was not to praise patrons, nor to treat the past as a depository of instructive examples or debating material, but to present it *wie es eigentlich gewesen ist*' ('as it really was'). Ranke believed that objective analysis, to reveal both what people did and what they thought they were doing – the element that is nowadays known as 'empathy with the past' – would provide the explanations of the past that Montesquieu sought.

Although later historians have taken Ranke's dictum as a touchstone for their work, history in modern times has still been used in order to make a point about the present. Many 19th-century historians, such as the Englishman George Babington Macaulay (1800–59), confident of the superiority of the institutions and society of their own day, used history to explain and thereby justify the development of that society. To them, the past appeared to be a journey towards a fixed end, with each event and even each character allotted a particular role in history's inexorable progress towards its 19th-century terminus. Those who at any period wanted to set off in a different direction, notably Royalists and Catholics, were presented as either wicked or stupid for wishing to go against the clear-

Historians are dependent on the source material that the past has left behind: it is as important to ask 'How do we know?' as it is to ask 'What happened and why?' Historians rely most heavily on written evidence, but there are also other important sources. Pictures, film, artefacts, literature, bones, discarded rubbish, even fairy stories – anything, in fact, can provide a clue as to what people in the past did and thought.

Historians usually draw a rough distinction between 'primary' evidence, which comes from the period they are studying, and 'secondary' evidence, which is more recent and normally includes other historians' accounts of past events. Historical writing itself, of course, fits into both categories. Macaulay's *History of England* (1848) is a secondary source for the 17th century, but a very good primary source for the beliefs and ideas of Macaulay's own day.

It is often assumed that primary sources are more accurate or more objective than secondary accounts. This is by no means necessarily the case. A primary source, by its very nature, will normally only give one point of view, which may be limited by circumstance or by ignorance, or may be highly partisan. Diaries and memoirs, for example, are often carefully written with an eye to future publication. Historians frequently use soldiers' eye-witness accounts to construct a picture of battles in the past, but it would be unrealistic to expect any one account – even that of a general – to give a full and definitive account of the whole battle. Napoleon, undoubtedly a primary source, altered the official version of the Battle of Marengo (1800; ▷ p. 146) so as to show him winning comfortably, when in fact he was only saved from disaster by General Desaix. The historian fits the different accounts and sources together like pieces of a jigsaw, except that in history there is no limit to the number of pieces the picture can contain – and there are always countless pieces missing.

Nor should all sources, even primary ones, necessarily be trusted. Pieces of the jigsaw can be tampered with. Under Stalin, historical material, including photographs, was sometimes 'doctored' to conform to the prevailing orthodoxy. Certain individuals, notably Trotsky (▷ p. 181), were airbrushed in and out according to their standing in the Party at any one time (▷ picture). Some 'pieces' turn out to be fakes. In a much publicized case in 1983, the German magazine *Stern* bought the rights to what it mistakenly thought were Adolf Hitler's diaries. Failure to check the authenticity of the primary source material cost the magazine dear.

True and false versions of the past, reflected in two images of Lenin addressing Russian troops in Petrograd before their departure for the Polish front, 5 May 1920. The figure of Leon Trotsky, visible to the right of the podium in the first photograph (top), was subsequently removed from the picture (above) when he fell out of favour under Stalin in the mid-1920s (▷ p. 181).

cut 'course of history'. This approach later became known, rather misleadingly, as the 'Whig version of History', though it was far from being confined to the English political party of the same name, and it is far from dead even today.

Hegel and Marx

This 'determinist' approach to the past was taken a stage further by the Marxist school, which also remains influential to this day. Although Karl Marx (1818–83) was strictly speaking a political economist rather than a historian, his view of history underpinned his philosophy. 'Dialectical materialism', as Marx's political and economic philosophy is known, owed its philosophical basis to the system of thought devised by the German idealist philosopher Georg Wilhelm Friedrich Hegel (1770–1831). Hegel held that historical change could only be explained in terms of contradiction; human history, like philosophy, displays a process of

**Alexander the Great's
victory** at Issus (▷
p. 32), as seen through
the Renaissance eyes of
Albrecht Altdorfer
(1529). Just as historians
inevitably see the past in
the light of present-day
concerns, so painters –
until the later 18th
century – tended to dress
up historical subjects in
contemporary costumes.

'dialectic', whereby a 'thesis' comes into conflict with an 'antithesis', producing a 'synthesis'.

Translated into Marxist 'historical materialism', human history – a process of gradual technological advance – has seen the existence of a number of progressive 'modes of production', each of which is characterized by class conflict and exploitation. Marx believed that the ruling class of each mode of production, who controlled the state, would be challenged and replaced by a new ruling class once their rule ceased to advance the progress of material production. Changes in modes of production – for example from feudalism to capitalism (▷ p. 130) – occurred through 'class struggle' and were always signalled by revolution (▷ p. 168). Marx claimed that by tracing the story of class struggle through past ages it was possible to project into the future and see the inevitable path that events were bound to follow (for him this meant towards a 'classless' Communist society).

Marx's views had considerable effect, especially after the Russian Revolution of 1917. Whole tracts of history were reinterpreted in the light of Marxist analysis: this has meant a much heavier emphasis than in the past on economic and social history and on changing societies as opposed to the actions of rulers, statesmen and military commanders.

In France, the *Annales* school of historical writing, led by Marc Bloch (1886–1944) and Fernand Braudel (1902–), sought to widen the scope of historical writing by providing 'photographs' of societies in the past in considerable detail, with particular emphasis on the experiences of ordinary people. The *Annales* approach had considerable influence, and sometimes – as with Emmanuel LeRoy Ladurie's analysis of the French medieval village of Montaillou (1978) – it met with great popular success.

History for all

The 20th century has seen an explosion in public interest in history. Membership of historical societies is by no means confined to professional historians, and recently there has been a tremendous increase in public interest – and participation – in the writing of local and family history. History books and periodicals aimed at a mass audience continue to sell, and television documentaries can provoke great debate.

One indication of public interest in history has been the growth of history for young people. Since time began children have learned tales of their people's glorious past, usually as a series of military victories with the occasional (unfair) defeat – a kind of history that is particularly susceptible to manipulation by totalitarian regimes. More recently history teaching has moved towards developing in children the critical approach towards historical evidence employed by professional historians.

Historiography and the philosophy of history

Historiography is the study of the development of historical study. A good many historians turn to it at some point in their careers (though not always with much enthusiasm). The English historian A.J.P. Taylor said that 'like Goering with culture, I reach for my revolver when offered philosophies of history'.

Historiography uses historians and their writings as clues both to the times in which they were writing and to an understanding of the nature of history itself. The English historian E.H. Carr, in *What is History?* (1961), drew a distinction between 'facts' and 'historical facts'. Facts, according to Carr, abound, but they only become historical facts when they are rescued from obscurity by a historian and used to illustrate something – or, even better to prove it. Some facts, like Caesar's crossing of the Rubicon, are inherently more likely to be employed as historical facts than others, though even the most obscure incident can be used by a historian to illustrate a wider trend, and can be given an importance that would astound those who witnessed it. While many historians have taken issue with Carr's distinction, few would disagree that it is possible for previously neglected people or factors to soar in importance if they find the right champion. The English Levellers of the 17th century, the sans-culottes of the French Revolution (▷ p. 144), the pre-Columbian natives of America, and women from almost any period of history have all to some extent been 'promoted' from the background to the forefront of our historical conscious-ness by historians' reassessments of the past.

The philosophy of history also addresses the issue of causation. Historians are seldom short of reasons explaining why events happened: their task is to sort those reasons into some sort of order, separating long-term causes from short-term ones, and ultimately deciding which were the more important. Nor has there ever been any shortage of people ready to apply the 'lessons' of causation to the contemporary world. The British historian Paul Kennedy's best-selling study of *The Rise and Fall of the Great Powers* (1988) was widely studied by Americans who saw in his analysis of the causes of the fall of European empires a worrying model for the future of contemporary America. This is a good illustration of the continuing deep-rooted tendency to see history as a storehouse of lessons and examples.

Types of history

The English historian, Thomas Carlyle (1795–1881) held that 'The history of the world is but the biography of great men'. Since history from the Ancient Greeks on was intended to record the deeds of gen-erals and statesmen for the edification of rulers, it is not surprising that Carlyle's judgement should have held good for so long. But political, diplomatic and mili-tary history have never been the sole concern of historians.

Biography is an art related to history, though it demands a slightly different approach to its writing, and historians are not always the most successful biogra-phers. Another related field whose de-mands are different from those of history is archaeology (▷ pp. 6–7). Archaeo-logists use highly developed skills of exca-vation and dating to try to make sense even of the most fragmentary remains, and archaeological evidence can be used to construct whole narratives of history; nevertheless, the two disciplines remain distinct, and are usually taught sepa-rately.

The fact that during the Middle Ages history was written predominantly by churchmen, and the bitter controver-sies that later raged during the Reforma-tion and Counter-Reformation (▷ pp. 110–13), meant that for centuries the his-tory of religion remained a very promi-nent branch of the subject. Growing

---

DOES HISTORY REPEAT ITSELF?

Many features of the past seem to suggest that there is a pattern to events that tends to repeat itself. Wars, coups, famines, trade booms and slumps, all seem to feature with depressing regula-rity in all periods and societies. Karl Marx was convinced that history re-peated itself – 'the first time as tragedy, the second as farce'.

Politicians frequently state an intention either to avoid the mistakes of the past or to relive its glories. In the Falklands War of 1982, the British Conservative government of Margaret Thatcher was determined not to appear like Neville Chamberlain, who pursued a policy of 'appeasement' towards Hitler and Mussolini in the years leading up to World War II (▷ p. 188). Mussolini him-self based his political programme on an attempt to revive the glories of the Roman Empire. A particularly bizarre example was the attempt by Jean Bedel Bokassa (1921–) to recreate the empire of Napoleon in Central Africa, a feat that had even eluded Napoleon's great-nephew, Napoleon III (1808–73), when he tried to do the same thing in France.

Historians often do attempt to see gen-eral causes for wars and revolutions. The French historian Alexis de Tocque-ville (1805–59) argued in his work on the French Revolution that autocratic regimes are at their most vulnerable when they begin to reform themselves, a point that some later experience has reinforced, notably in the examples of Russia in 1917 (▷ p. 180) and the Soviet Union in 1991 (▷ p. 224).

Nevertheless, there are few historians who would take this argument very far. Circumstances in any two cases, how-ever similar they may appear at first, are usually so unlike each other that, even if the outcomes are similar, the causes are nearly always significantly different. Moreover, placing too heavy a stress on repetition in history is to underestimate the important role played by chance in determining human events. There are indeed lessons to be gained from the past – but the past provides us with general principles, rather than examples to be followed too closely.

---

concern about social conditions in the industrial society of the 19th century helped give rise to the writing of social history, notably in the work of Englishman G.M. Trevelyan (1876–1962), who described it as history 'with the politics left out'. The influence of Marx was seen in the development of economic history, which does not just look at the working of economies in the past, but looks for economic factors in other fields of the subject as well. Economic his-torians have in recent decades been keen exponents of quantitative methods and statistical analysis in the study of history, and have also been pioneers in the use of computers in their research.

Computerized data is also increasingly being used in local history, which relies heavily on such sources as census mater-ial or tax returns. Local history (which has a strong overlap with social history) is an important concern of any historian, cautioning against simplistic assump-tions based on wide-ranging theories. A lot of valuable work in local history is also carried out by amateur historians, who usually have a personal link to the locality. An offshoot of local history, family history or genealogy has seen an explosion of interest in recent years.

There are plenty of other spheres within which historians can operate. The history of art is a well-established field in its own right, as is the history of music or litera-ture, and other aspects of life, such as education, medicine or business, have also attracted their own historians. A crucial growth area in recent years has been women's history, which is sometimes treated as a separate field and sometimes integrated into other fields of historical research. Much the same is true of black history. Both of these relatively new fields have been largely pioneered in the USA.

Mention should also be made of the impor-tant contributions to history made by other disciplines, such as literary studies, geography, psychology, sociology (parti-cularly the work of Max Weber; 1864–1920), anthropology and economics.

History around us

We live surrounded by our history. Buildings, street plans, place-names, field structures – all reflect an inheritance from the past. Many institutions – includ-ing those of law and government – often also have their roots in the actions and thoughts of earlier generations.

The history that surrounds us can lead to controversy. As anniversaries of histori-cal events come up, we look back on them with a fresh and critical eye. The 50th anniversary of the Munich agreement of 1938 (▷ p. 189) prompted a reappraisal that went some way towards rehabili-tating Neville Chamberlain's reputation; in 1992 the 500th anniversary of Columbus' voyage to America (▷ p. 109) prompted heated debate over the impact of Europeans on the indigenous culture they found there.

People's sense of their own historical identity can be surprisingly strong. Old national sentiments, even old flags, which many had thought long disappeared, re-emerged in the wake of the anti-Communist revolutions of 1989 in Eastern Europe, and again in 1991 as the different nationalities of the mighty Soviet Union (▷ p. 224) pulled it apart. The long-running conflicts in Northern Ireland and the Middle East (▷ p. 210), as well as the civil war that broke out in Yugoslavia in 1990, are all to a large extent battles arising from the past and sustained by rival interpretations of it. In the end, history is far too dangerous to be dis-missed as bunk.   SL

SEE ALSO

● ARCHAEOLOGY p. 6
● ARCHAIC AND CLASSICAL GREECE p. 28
● MEDIEVAL AND RENAISSANCE CULTURE p. 100
● THE ENLIGHTENMENT p. 134
● THE FRENCH REVOLUTION p. 144
● THE RISE OF MASS POLITICS p. 168
● THE RUSSIAN REVOLUTIONS p. 180

Archaeology

Some of the most spectacular discoveries about our past
have come not from written records but from archaeological
finds. Archaeological investigation is crucial to historians
not only for the study of periods for which no written
records exist, but also for later periods where the written
records are scarce or fragmentary.

The sort of evidence uncovered by
archaeologists is of a entirely different
kind from that normally studied by historians: buildings, artefacts, and so on
require very different methods of recovery
and interpretation from written documents, often involving the application of
scientific techniques. Compared to history – which in its broad sense of a study
of humanity's past has been written since
the time of the ancient Greeks (▷ pp. 2
and 28) – archaeology is a relatively new
discipline.

The history of archaeology

Before the 18th century humanity's origins were obscured in myth and legend, or
discussion was based on the Bible.
Although the classical civilizations of
Greek and Rome prompted much interest
during the Renaissance (▷ p. 101), true
archaeological investigation only began
in earnest with French, German and
English travellers in the late 18th
century. Collection and description was
followed by excavation, a notable example being the uncovering of the Roman
towns of Pompeii and Herculaneum,
buried since the eruption of Vesuvius in
AD 79. These particular discoveries had a
great influence on contemporary art, as
seen for example in Josiah Wedgwood's
Neoclassical vases.

Gradually archaeology became a discipline. Stone implements, previously
thought to be the work of fairies and
elves, were acknowledged as man-made.
In 1819 C.J. Thomsen arranged prehistoric artefacts in the Copenhagen
Museum on the basis of a 'Three-age
System' – the Stone, Bronze and Iron Ages
(▷ p. 12) – which were stages of development of materials technology. From the
new science of geology came the notion
that stratification of layers gave a readable chronology, enabling an item in any
one layer to be dated in relation to other
layers.

During the 19th century recording of
monuments and excavation spread rapidly through Egypt and Mesopotamia,
uncovering the spectacular civilizations
of Babylon and other Biblical cities
(▷ pp. 16, 20 and 22). From 1860, excavat-
ing at Pompeii and Herculaneum, the
Italian Giuseppe Fiorelli stressed that all
evidence was important enough to collect. In the eastern Mediterranean the
German Heinrich Schliemann revealed
the ancient cities of Troy (modern Hissarlik, in Turkey) and Mycenae in Greece,
and the Minoan civilization was discovered in Crete by Sir Arthur Evans
(▷ p. 24). While these spectacular finds
caught the public imagination, rigorous
and careful new methods of investigation
were being developed by such scholars as
A.H. Pitt-Rivers on his Dorset estates and
William Flinders Petrie in Egypt.

In the 20th century the main developments have been in the application of
scientific dating techniques, the study of
ancient environments, and the realization that the archaeological heritage
of every country should be recorded
before it is destroyed by human activities.
Some archaeological work involves tar-
getted research to answer specific questions, but much of it involves 'rescue
techniques' to preserve the record of what
was there before the site is destroyed by
new buildings, deep ploughing, quarry-
ing, and so on.

Archaeological evidence

Artefacts such as pottery, glass and most
metals survive well (though usually in
fragments), while objects made of organic
substances (wood, leather and textiles)
often only survive in waterlogged sites
such as ports or rivers or in exceptionally
arid conditions, as in Egypt (▷ p. 17).

Saving the evidence. Rescue archaeologists uncover the *caldarium*, or hot room, of a Roman bath
house in the City of London dating from the 1st century AD. The stacks of tiles (*pilae*) formed part of the
heating system (or hypocaust) of the baths. After full recording, the remains of the bath house were
reburied to ensure their long-term survival.

Heinrich Schliemann, the German archaeologist who discovered the site of the ancient city of Troy in northwestern Anatolia. Excavations carried out by Schliemann between 1870 and 1890, and continued by others since, have revealed evidence of ten cities built on the site between the early Bronze Age and the Roman period. The seventh city, which was probably destroyed by fire in the mid-13th century BC, may be the city whose ten-year siege by the Greeks is decribed in Homer's *Iliad*.

The ancient Canaanite city of Ugarit (modern Ras Shamra) on the Mediterranean coast of Syria. A cosmopolitan port town, Ugarit flourished as a trading centre between c. 1450 and c. 1200 BC (▷ p. 22). Excavation of the ruins – first uncovered by a farmer's plough – began in 1929, and has revealed a wealth of ancient records not only in Babylonian cuneiform script, but also in an early form of alphabetic writing.

When objects are found in their original (primary) position in buildings, as opposed to being thrown away somewhere else (secondary), we can reconstruct the functions of rooms or spaces – how they were used for industrial, ceremonial, or domestic purposes.

Human bones provide details of the age- and sex-structure of the population, congenital disorders, famine, weather conditions, blood types and diseases of the skeleton. Animal bones, shells and dried excrement furnish information on diet and farming techniques. Environmental factors such as climate or pollution can be studied by looking at seeds, pollen counts, insects and the remains of microscopic organisms.

Excavation

The first question every archaeologist is asked is 'How did you know where to dig?' There are two kinds of helpful evidence: previous written records (including maps) of what stood on the site and what it was used for, and prospecting methods such as aerial photography (which, with the use of specialist techniques, can also identify monuments beneath the ground) or remote sensing on the ground.

The main task of archaeological recording is to note even the smallest evidence of past human activity – a layer, a ditch, a wall. These are called 'contexts', and they are given numbers so that information about them, and the artefacts from them, can be stored separately (▷ box). The context will be surveyed and probably photographed before it is removed to uncover the one below; it may also be sampled for environmental or industrial residues.

The contexts are ordered to show the succession of layers representing the history of the site – construction, occupation, destruction, decay – and natural actions such as river flooding or erosion. The 'stratigraphy' of a site is the record of its various layers, which can be shown in a scale drawing and in diagrammatic form as a 'matrix' (▷ box). The stratigraphy is the basis of all future research. Once the dates are established, these are then added to the matrix.

Methods of dating

Dates may be established by examining historical records, or by comparing the finds with similar finds of known date – a method known as 'typology'.

Various scientific techniques are also used. Radiocarbon dating is based on the fact that all living material (such as wood) absorbs small amounts of radioactive carbon-14, which reduces by a known amount over time once the material is dead. In general this method is useful only for prehistoric periods, because of its margin of error.

Dendrochronology (tree-dating) is far more precise, being based on the annual growth rings in trees, and is especially useful for the Roman and later historic periods. Variations in the width between rings correspond with climatic changes,

and so timber used in a building can be compared with other timber of known age.

The range of archaeology

Archaeologists, particularly those working on the prehistoric period, have looked at very wide factors over large regions, giving rise to conflicting theories as to whether cultures spread by invasion – the 'invasion hypothesis' – or by autonomous development – the 'continuity hypothesis' (▷ p. 35 for an example). Today, in addition, the archaeologist is interested in identifying small groups within communities – village, town or city – and working out how these groups rose and fell, interacted with each other, and disappeared from view.　　　JS

SEE ALSO

● WHAT IS HISTORY? p. 2
● HUMAN PREHISTORY p. 12
● CIVILIZATIONS OF THE ANCIENT NEAR EAST pp. 16–23 and 26
● MINOANS AND MYCENAEANS p. 24
● GREEK AND ROMAN CIVILIZATION pp. 28–33 and 36–41
● EARLY CIVILIZATIONS OF ASIA, AFRICA, AUSTRALASIA, OCEANIA AND THE AMERICAS pp. 52–4, 58–60 and 64–72

ANALYSIS OF AN ARCHAEOLOGICAL DIG

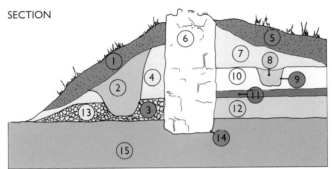

SECTION

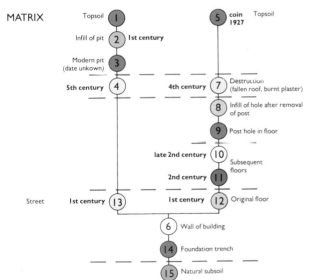

MATRIX

Topsoil — 1
Infill of pit — 2 — 1st century
Modern pit (date unkown) — 3
5th century — 4 — 4th century — 7 — Destruction (fallen roof, burnt plaster)
8 — Infill of hole after removal of post
9 — Post hole in floor
late 2nd century — 10 — Subsequent floors
2nd century — 11
Street — 1st century — 13 — 1st century — 12 — Original floor
6 — Wall of building
14 — Foundation trench
15 — Natural subsoil

5 — coin 1927 — Topsoil

This diagram shows how the archaeologist analyses strata in the ground, as shown by a section (vertical cut) through the wall of a building. The layers or contexts are numbered as they are excavated, and their stratigraphic links shown in the matrix. The sequence of construction, use and destruction of the building can be reconstructed using the matrix. The latest dates from each layer – from artefacts or dating mechanisms such as carbon-14 – will be added to the matrix, to find out the overall dates for the phases shown. Note that some layers have no finds.

The above example shows a Roman street and building laid out in the 1st century AD, with internal floors renewed in the 2nd century. The street and building were destroyed in the 5th century: note how layer 4 has later material than layer 7, and therefore the destruction is dated by the later material. Note also the misleading finds in layer 2, filling the pit 3; this pit was dug after the 5th century, but contains residual 1st-century finds (probably from layer 13).

THE
ANCIENT
WORLD

NEAR EAST	EGYPT AND NORTH AFRICA
4000–3000 BC Development of the world's first known cities in Mesopotamia **c. 3300 BC** Earliest surviving Sumerian texts **before 3000 BC** Emergence of several city-states in Sumer **c. 3000 BC** Rise of the Assyrian cities of Nineveh and Ashur **c. 2900–2370 BC** Early Dynastic Period in Sumeria **c. 2370 BC** Conquest of Sumer by Sargon of Akkad **c. 2200 BC** Akkad overrun by the Gutians **c. 2113–2006 BC** Third Dynasty of Ur **2006 BC** Elamites sacked Ur; end of Sumerian dominance of Mesopotamia	**3100–2725 BC** Early Dynastic Period (1st–3rd dynasties) began with the unification of Upper and Lower Egypt **2575–2134 BC** Old Kingdom in Egypt (4th–8th dynasties) – a period of centralized administration; construction of the Great Pyramids at Giza **2134–2040 BC** First Intermediate Period (9th–11th dynasties) **2040–1640 BC** Middle Kingdom (11th–13th dynasties) – Egypt reunited under Mentuhotep II
c. 1900 BC Amorite dynasty established in Babylon **by 1800 BC** Amorite kingdoms established in Syria and Palestine **c. 1792–1750** Hammurabi unified Mesopotamia under the hegemony of Babylon **c. 1650 BC** Foundation of the Hittite Empire **c. 1595 BC** Babylon sacked by the Hittite king Mursilis I **c. 1500–c. 1157 BC** Kassite rule in Mesopotamia **1430–1350 BC** Hurrian kingdom of Mitanni reached its greatest extent **c. 1380–1350 BC** Under Suppiluliumas I, the Hittite Empire reached its greatest extent **c. 1230 BC** Israelite conquest of Caanan **before 1200 BC** Collapse of the Hittite Empire	**1640–1552 BC** Second Intermediate Period (14th–17th dynasties) – Hyksos rule; Theban dynasty liberated Egypt **1555–1070 BC** New Kingdom (18th–20th dynasties) – Egyptian empire extended from Syria to southern Sudan **c. 1450–1425 BC** The campaigns of Amenophis II against Mitanni extended the Egyptian Empire in the Near East **c. 1313 BC** Hittite invasion of Egypt **1285 BC** Egypt clashed with the Hittites at Kadesh in Palestine
c. 1000 BC Foundation of the kingdom of Israel **9th century BC** Medes and Persians occupied western Iran **883–824 BC** Expansion of the Assyrian Empire under Ashurnasirpal II and Shalmaneser III **after 824 BC** Rise of the kingdom of Urartu **745–727 BC** Major expansion of the Assyrian Empire under Tiglath-Pileser III; Assyria conquered Babylon in 729 BC **732 BC** Aram-Damascus conquered by Assyria **721–705 BC** The Assyrian Sargon II overthrew Urartu **704–681 BC** Assyrian invasion of Palestine under Sennacherib; Assyrian capital moved to Nineveh **668–627 BC** Reign of Ashurbanipal – Assyrian Empire attained its greatest extent **625–605 BC** Babylon regained its independence under Nabopolassar **612 BC** Nineveh sacked by the Medes	**1070–712 BC** Third Intermediate Period (21st–24th dynasties) – Egypt divided **814 BC** Traditional date of the foundation of Carthage **712–332 BC** Late Period (25th–30th dynasties) – Egypt reunified under the 26th dynasty **675 BC** The Assyrians, under Esarhaddon, attacked Egypt and took Memphis **c. 630 BC** Greek colony founded at Cyrene
605–562 BC Nebuchadnezzar II extended the Neo-Babylonian empire, capturing Jerusalem in 597 BC and taking the Jews into the Babylonian Captivity **585–550 BC** Astyages, last king of the Medes, overthrown by the Persians **549 BC** Cyrus I united the Medes and Persians and founded the Persian Achaemenid Empire **539 BC** Cyrus I took Babylon and acquired the Neo-Babylonian Empire **521–486 BC** Reign of Darius I; Persian Empire reached its greatest extent **486–465 BC** Reign of Xerxes I **333 and 332 BC** Darius III defeated by Alexander the Great at Issus and Gaugamela **312 BC** Foundation of the Hellenistic Seleucid Empire by Alexander the Great's general Seleucus Nicator	**526–525 BC** Persians under Cambyses II invaded Egypt **480 BC** Carthaginian expedition to Sicily defeated by Gelon, tyrant of Syracuse, at the battle of Himera **c. 470 BC** Hanno of Carthage navigated down the coast of West Africa, probably as far as Sierra Leone **406 BC** Egypt revolted against Persian rule **332 BC** Alexander the Great invaded Egypt and founded Alexandria-in-Egypt **305 BC** Ptolemy, Alexander the Great's general, declared himself ruler of Egypt, founding the Ptolemaic dynasty
247 BC Foundation of the Parthian dynasty by Arsaces **198 BC** The Seleucid Anthiochus III took Palestine from Egypt **191 BC** Anthiochus III defeated by the Romans at Thermopylae – decline of the Seleucid Empire began **153–63 BC** Independent Maccabaean Jewish state **133 BC** Asia (western Anatolia) became a Roman province **120–63 BC** Reign of Mithridates VI of Pontus **101 BC** Cilicia (southern Anatolia) became a Roman province	**241 BC** Carthage defeated by Rome in the First Punic War **238 BC** The Carthaginians under Hamilcar began the conquest of Spain **202 BC** Hannibal defeated by Scipio at Zama **149–146 BC** Third Punic War – Carthage was destroyed and 'Africa' became a Roman province **110–105 BC** Jugurthian War in Numidia **96 BC** Cyrenaica (eastern Libya) became a Roman province **41 BC** Antony went to Egypt and ruled the Egyptian region with his mistress Cleopatra VII until defeated in the naval battle of Actium (31 BC) **30 BC** Ptolemy XVI, son of Cleopatra VII and Julius Caesar, deposed and executed; last of the pharaohs; Egypt became a Roman province
AD 70 Jewish revolt against Rome **1st century AD** Christianity spread rapidly from Palestine **226** Foundation of the Sassanian dynasty in Persia **240–272** Sassanian Empire greatly expanded by Shapur I **260** Sassanians overran Syria and captured the Roman emperor Valerian **395** Anatolia and the Roman provinces in the Near East included in the Eastern Empire when the Roman Empire was divided	**AD 41** Mauretania (Morocco) became a Roman province **395** Egypt and Cyrenaica (Libya) included in the Eastern Empire when the Roman Empire was divided **395** St Augustine became bishop of Hippo **5th century** Vandals overran Roman provinces in North Africa

GREECE AND THE HELLENISTIC WORLD	ROME AND WESTERN EUROPE
c. 3000 BC Neolithic settlements in Crete **c. 2200** Minoan pottery appeared in Greece; Minoan script (Linear A) appeared **2200–1450 BC** Minoan civilization in Crete reached its peak in the Middle and Late Bronze Age	**c. 4000 BC** Neolithic culture flourished in most of Europe; earliest Neolithic sites in Britain date from c. 4000 BC **3000–2000 BC** Bronze Age culture in southeastern Europe spreading to northern and western Europe; bronze artefacts **c. 2500 BC** Burial barrows constructed in Britain; construction of Stonehenge **c. 2000 BC** Stone circles of Carnac (Brittany) erected
from c. 1700 BC Construction of the Palace of Minos at Knossos **c. 1600 BC** Start of Mycenaean civilization **1550–1500 BC** Minoan civilization hit by destructive earthquakes **c. 1500–1150 BC** Height of Mycenaean civilization on mainland Greece **1400–1300 BC** Minoan (Linear A) script adapted as Linear B to write an early form of Greek **c. 1200–1100 BC** Collapse of Mycenaean civilization; Greece entered a 'dark age'	**2nd millennium BC** Iron-Age agricultural systems established in present-day France, Britain and their neighbours; construction of hillforts in much of western Europe **15th century BC** Beginnings of Urnfield culture in eastern and central Europe **by 1000 BC** A village settlement existed on the site of Rome
c. 800 BC Beginning of the Archaic period in Greece **8th century–650 BC** Greek colonies founded around the Aegean, Adriatic and Black Seas **8th century BC** Sparta gained control of most of the southern Peloponnese **c. 750 BC** Reintroduction of literacy into Greece **c. 750–700 BC** The poems traditionally attributed to Homer were written down in their final form **mid-7th century** Major revolt of the helots (state serfs) against Sparta	**900–500 BC** Hallstatt art flourished in central Europe and then spread through much of northern and western Europe **8th century** Rise of the Etruscan civilization in Italy **by 600 BC** Rome had developed into a substantial city **6th century** Etruscan colonies founded in northern and southern Italy **6th and 5th centuries** Etruscan monarchies replaced by republics
594 BC Solon appointed 'archon' at Athens; established legal code **6th century** Sparta founded the Peloponnesian League **545–510 BC** Athens ruled by the tyrant Peisistratos and his sons **507 BC** The reforms of Cleisthenes in Athens **490 BC** Battle of Marathon – defeat of the Persians by the Greeks **480 BC** Persians defeated by the Greeks in the naval battle of Salamis **479 BC** Battle of Plataea – end of the Persian threat to Greece **478 BC** Athens assumed the leadership of the Delian League, which by the 440s had evolved into an Athenian 'empire' **462–429 BC** Athenian politics dominated by Pericles **431–404 BC** The Peloponnesian War between Athens and Sparta and their allies **378/7 BC** Athenian power re-emerged in the Aegean Confederacy **338 BC** Defeat of the Greek city-states at Chaeronea gave Philip II of Macedon control of Greece **336–323 BC** Alexander the Great (of Macedon) conquered the whole of the Persian Empire	**509 BC** The Roman republic established – power exercised by two annually elected consuls **5th–4th centuries** Decline of Etruria **450 BC** Celtic La Tène art flourished in much of Europe, reaching as far as Ireland in the west and Hungary in the east **415 BC** Athens attempted to conquer Sicily **390 BC** Rome sacked by the Celts **4th century BC** The plebeians gained access to political office in Rome **275 BC** Battle of Beneventum – defeat of Pyrrhus by Romans ended Greek attempt to conquer Italy **264 BC** Roman conquest of the Italian peninsula completed **264–241 BC** First Punic War; Rome challenged Carthage for the control of Sicily
from c. 240 BC Two federations of city-states, Aetolia and Achaea, dominated Greece **238 BC** Foundation of the kingdom of Pergamum by Attalos I **167 BC** Macedon conquered by the Romans **147 BC** War between Sparta and Achaea; Romans invaded Greece and destroyed Corinth **146 BC** Most of Greece came under Roman rule	**218–202 BC** Second Punic War – Hannibal crossed the Alps and invaded Italy **216 BC** Hannibal defeated the Romans at Cannae **by 167 BC** Rome dominated the western Mediterranean **133 BC** Tiberius Gracchus murdered after introducing land reforms **121 BC** Southern Gaul became a Roman province **91–88 BC** Revolt of the Italian allies **81 BC** Sulla established himself as dictator of Rome **60 BC** The 'First Triumvirate' – political alliance between Pompey, Caesar and Crassus **49 BC** Caesar crossed the Rubicon and began the civil war against Pompey **48 BC** Pompey defeated at Pharsalus; Julius Caesar became consul and dictator for life – assassinated in 44 BC **42 BC** Roman Empire effectively divided between Octavian and Antony (the Second Triumvirate) **31 BC** Octavian defeated Antony at Actium **27 BC** Octavian proclaimed emperor by the Roman Senate, and given the title 'Augustus'
AD 123 and 128–34 Hadrian visited Greece **267** Barbarian Herulians invaded Greece, and sacked Athens, Spartan, Argos and Corinth **286** An 'eastern' Roman emperor established over Anatolia and Greece by Diocletian **324–37** Constantine I (the Great) reunited Roman Empire but moved the capital to Constantinople (Byzantium) **395** Division of the Roman Empire into eastern and western parts – the East, based on Constantinople, became the Byzantine Empire	**AD 9** Loss of the Roman provinces in Germany between the rivers Rhine and Elbe **43–7** Britain became a Roman province **79** Destruction of Pompeii **98–117** Roman Empire enjoyed peace and stability under Trajan **101–6** Dacia (modern Romania) became a Roman province **122–6** Construction of Hadrian's Wall in Britain **192–7** Period of civil war after the assassination of Commodus **235** Empire entered a period of chaos at the end of the Severan dynasty **284** Diocletian reorganized the Roman Empire **313** Constantine I issued the Edict of Milan, tolerating Christianity **395** Division of the Roman Empire **5th century** Germanic barbarians overran Gaul, Spain and Italy

Human Prehistory

'Prehistory' is the period of time before written documents, the normal means by which historical events are recorded and dated. Before the development of scientific dating methods – especially radiocarbon dating – after World War II, dating methods were largely relative – in other words, definite dates were not assigned, but instead it was simply indicated whether a period came before or after certain important technological developments of unknown date.

The Olduvai Gorge in northern Tanzania. The 51 km (31 mi) long gorge has yielded a wealth of fossil evidence of early man dating back over more than 2 million years. Research since 1935 has revealed fossil remains of three types of hominid – australopithecines, *Homo habilis* and *Homo erectus* – as well as animal bones and stone artefacts.

The division of human prehistory into the Stone Age, Bronze Age and Iron Age, based on the materials used for tools, was introduced in the early 19th century by two Danes, C.J. Thomsen and J.J.A. Worsaae. This 'Three Age System' was further developed in the late 19th century by subdividing the Stone Age into the Palaeolithic ('Old Stone'), Mesolithic ('Middle Stone'), and Neolithic ('New Stone') Ages. These technologically based divisions remain useful for European prehistory, but they are not always valid in other parts of the world.

The Palaeolithic

Most of the Palaeolithic developments in Europe, and in Asia outside the tropics, occurred against a background of periods of much colder climate – the 'Ice Ages' – associated with the growth of vast ice-sheets in northern latitudes, and extensive glacier development in more southerly latitudes, including the Alps and the Balkans.

The causes, and exact number, of the cold periods, which were separated by warmer phases, are not clearly understood; nor is their age well established, since scientific methods have as yet not been very successful in dating this geological time span. However, the last cold phase ended about 10 000 years ago and the different warm and cold phases can be recognized archaeologically because of the preservation of the bones of characteristic animals and even the pollen of particular trees, which indicate warmer or colder periods. They thus provide a useful relative chronology in which to place human developments. Archaeologists also use changes in stone-tool types to subdivide the Palaeolithic into Lower (i.e. earliest), Middle, and Upper phases.

The Lower Palaeolithic

The earliest hominids – man-like creatures – so far known are the several species of australopithecine. Fossil remains of these upright-walking, small-brained creatures have been found in eastern and southern Africa, and are dated between 4 and 1 million years ago. The earliest species, dating perhaps 4–3 million years ago, may well be a direct human ancestor. But later species, which were contemporary with more advanced human types, were evolutionary sidelines. *Homo habilis* ('handy man') – the name given to human fossil remains found at the Olduvai Gorge in Tanzania and other eastern African sites – is dated from 2–1.5 million years ago. *Homo habilis* had a larger brain than the australopithecines, and appeared at the same period as the oldest stone tools. The following *Homo erectus* stage started about 1·5 million years ago. A very successful species with a larger brain and larger stature than its predecessors, it continued until 200 000 years ago and marks the first appearance of humans outside Africa. However, in Europe and Asia outside the

tropics there is no good evidence for human occupation until well after 1 million years ago. *Homo erectus* fossils have been discovered in France, Germany, China and Java.

The earliest tools date from the period when *Homo habilis* co-existed with the later australopithecines. A few simple flakes were removed from pieces of stone to produce very crude knives and chopping tools. At present it is unclear whether these tools were made by *Homo habilis* alone or by some of the australopithecines as well. The 'industries' (i.e. tool types) used by *Homo erectus* and the earliest members of the following *Homo sapiens* stage also belong to the Lower Palaeolithic. The most characteristic tool is the hand axe, a general-purpose implement made by striking off pieces of stone (flakes) from a lump of stone until the correct shape and cutting edge were produced. Simple tools made of flakes removed from a lump of stone (a core) were also used, sometimes improved by further flaking of the edges. Tools in materials other than stone very rarely survive, but a Lower Palaeolithic wooden spear point has been found in Essex, England. Even at this early stage humans used fire, as exemplified by the fire hardening of the spear.

While Lower Palaeolithic tools continued until about 100 000 years ago, it seems that between 300 000–200 000 and 100 000 years ago *Homo erectus* evolved into a more developed stage, at least in Europe. However, there is little evidence of this stage.

The Middle Palaeolithic

The Middle Palaeolithic stage, from 100 000 to as late as 30 000 years ago, is associated with the remains of Neanderthal man (*Homo sapiens neanderthalensis*; ⇨ box). While *Homo erectus* only occupied Eurasia during relatively warm

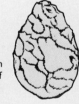

periods, Neanderthals could exploit the arctic environments of the full glacial phases, living in caves and in skin tents held down by mammoth bones.

Middle Palaeolithic stone tools, made mainly from flakes, were more specialized than earlier tools, and included spear heads, knives and scraping tools for wood and hides. Neanderthals were the first humans to bury their dead, and there is evidence that they had a sense of beauty (▷ box).

The Upper Palaeolithic

There is still much scientific debate about the date of the first appearance of anatomically modern humans (*Homo sapiens sapiens*, also called Cro-Magnon man, named after a cave in the Dordogne, France). However, it seems likely that in Europe and northern Asia they appeared relatively late – perhaps as late as 30 000 BC in Western Europe – although in some other parts of the world they had appeared before 40 000 BC.

In Eurasia, Upper Palaeolithic tools, associated with modern humans, have a number of characteristic features: stone tools were now based on blades – long, thin flakes – which were made into an even wider variety of specialized tools than previously. Bone tools also appear regularly for the first time. Another Upper Palaeolithic cultural achievement is 'Ice Age Art' (▷ box, p. 14).

It is tempting to see the life of Upper Palaeolithic peoples in glacially affected Eurasia as harsh and difficult, and to compare their societies with those of simple hunter-gatherers like the San (Bushmen) of southern Africa (▷ p. 66) and the Inuit (Eskimo) of the Arctic (▷ p. 72). However, recent Russian fossil finds suggest the existence of sizeable and complex groups dependent on the herds of large gregarious mammals that existed at the time. The bones of these mammals appear to have been used for fuel, while their meat was stored in pits dug down to the permafrost level which acted as natural freezers.

The achievements of these early modern humans include the peopling of the previously unoccupied continents of Australasia and the Americas (▷ pp. 68 and 70). The lowered sea levels associated with the

last Ice Age shortened the sea journey to New Guinea and Australia, but the peopling of that area as early as 50 000 years ago is evidence of a major achievement in seamanship (▷ box, p. 69). A less positive achievement was the extinction of a number of large mammal species (such as mammoth) both in Eurasia and the Americas before the end of the last Ice Age (about 8000 BC). This was at least partially a result of the efficient hunting methods of Upper Palaeolithic peoples.

The Mesolithic

The end of the Ice Age saw significantly increased temperatures and rainfall in Europe and parts of Asia. A largely treeless environment was replaced by forests, especially in Europe north of the Alps, and mammal species adapted to tundra and steppe environments were replaced by forest species. Humans adapted to these changes by living in smaller groups and exploiting the increased numbers of wildfowl and fish. In Eurasia the bow and arrow became important in this period, but they did not appear in the Americas until later.

The Neolithic

In the Old World the earliest Neolithic cultures, defined by the appearance of agriculture as a way of life, are found in the Near East, in an area between Turkey and Israel in the west and Iran in the east. But agriculture also developed independently in other parts of the world after the last Ice Age. Other centres of domestication, exploiting local species of plants and animals, include Central America, the South American Andes region, east and Southeast Asia and sub-Saharan Africa (▷ box).

In the Near East the wild ancestors of wheat, barley, rye, and of sheep, goat, pigs and cattle all occurred. The earliest Neolithic sites date to the period 9000–7000 BC, contemporary with the Mesolithic period in Europe. But in the Near East the climatic changes associated with the end of the Ice Age were far less marked than in Europe, and population pressure is a more likely explanation for the beginnings of agriculture than climatic change. By 6000 BC some substantial towns existed in the Near East, for instance at Çatal Hüyük in Turkey and Jericho in the Jordan Valley (▷ p. 44).

The spread of agriculture was relatively rapid: Neolithic sites in Greece start before 6000 BC and appear in Britain by 4000 BC. During the 2000–3000-year lifespan of the Neolithic, considerable social distinctions emerged along with increasingly centralized political power. These developments are associated with the building of large burial and ceremonial monuments in earth and stone that began in many parts of Europe at this time. Specialized production of and widespread trade in a variety of objects and materials also developed. For example, flint mining on a large scale was carried out in Poland, Denmark, the Low Countries and England.

The Bronze Age

Copper and gold were the main metals

THE THREE AGES OF NEAR-EASTERN AND EUROPEAN PREHISTORY

AGE	STONE AGE					BRONZE AGE	IRON AGE
	PALAEOLITHIC			MESOLITHIC	NEOLITHIC		
	LOWER	MIDDLE	UPPER				
PERIOD BEGAN (approximately)	1 million years ago	100 000 years ago	30 000 BC	10 000 BC	9000-4000 BC (spreading from Near East to W Europe)	3000-2000 BC (both periods earliest in Near East and SE Europe, spreading to W and N Europe)	1200-500 BC
DOMINANT HOMINID	*Homo erectus*	Neanderthal man (*H. sapiens neanderthalensis*)	Modern man (*Homo sapiens sapiens*)				
TECHNOLOGY	Simple stone tools, e.g. hand axes Use of fire	More specialized stone tools, e.g. spear heads, knives	Development of stone blades and bone tools Beginnings of art	Use of bow and arrow	Beginnings of agriculture First towns in Near East	Bronze artefacts First cities	Iron artefacts

PALAEOLITHIC ART

The Neanderthals' sense of beauty and their use of colourful minerals like red ochre in some burials suggest that they might have practised body-painting, or art-work on perishable materials. However, no trace of Neanderthal art survives (▷ box, p. 13).

The earliest art, contemporary with the Upper Palaeo-lithic in Eurasia, is the work of modern humans (*Homo sapiens sapiens*). It is best known from caves and open sites in Europe (especially Spain and France), and Russia as far east as Siberia, and dates from soon after 16 000 BC (i.e. 18 000 years ago). But new dating methods suggest that Australian cave painting may date from as early as 20 000 years ago. Cave paintings have also been found in other areas of the world, such as Africa. Not all of these paintings have been dated yet, so dates as early as the Australian examples cannot be ruled out, though many are much later.

European Palaeolithic art ('Ice Age art') has been divided into 'mobiliary' art (small portable objects found in caves and open sites), and 'parietal' art (paintings and engrav-ings on the walls of caves. Occasional examples of large clay sculptures of animals do not easily fit into either category.

Since objects of mobiliary art are found in archaeological levels (▷ p. 6), they are easy to date to particular subdivisions of the Upper Palaeolithic. The famous 'Venus' figurines, for instance, are mostly dated to the Gravettian phase, starting about 30 000 BC. These small sculptures, only a few centimetres in height, are carved from various materials, particularly bone, stone and ivory. Many depict nude females with quite detailed depiction of the pubic area, breasts, buttocks and stom-ach. These naked figures are often decidedly obese (notably the Willendorf 'Venus' from Austria). In con-trast, the arms, legs and faces of most figurines are not depicted or are highly stylized. The meaning or functions of these figurines is unclear. Their large breasts and buttocks have been linked with a cult of human fertility among Upper Palaeolithic peoples.

Although a number of different styles of parietal art have been recognized, they are not easy to associate

The Willendorf 'Venus', a limestone figurine dating from c. 25 000 BC. The accentuated breasts and buttocks suggest that the figurine may have had a role in fertility rites.

with specific Upper Palaeolithic phases. It is generally accepted, however, that the most accomplished art comes from the final phase, the Magdalenian. Cave art is mostly found in southern France and northern Spain, sometimes deep within cave systems, and sometimes near cave entrances or in shallow rock shelters. The hunters who created cave art depicted the animals around them, particularly large herbivores such as wild horses, bison, reindeer, wild pig, rhinoceros and mam-moth. While they frequently drew abstract (or uni-dentifiable) shapes, they drew only a few human and semi-human figures, and never trees, plants or land-scapes. Cave art concentrates on individual subjects, which are sometimes superimposed on earlier pictures.

Since cave art began to be accepted as Palaeolithic in the late 19th century, it has been interpreted in many ways. An early theory – 'sympathetic magic' – claimed that many of the animals were shown dead or wounded in order to bring luck in hunting. An alternative approach, using parallels with Australian Aborigines (▷ p. 68), suggests that the animals illustrated tribal mythologies or clan totems.

More recently – and more controversially – it has been suggested that the animals and accompanying abstract shapes are part of an elaborate system of opposed symbols centred on the human differentiation into male and female social spheres (e.g. horse = maleness; bison = femaleness). Subjects with seasonal associations also occur in cave art. These might be related to a theory that some mobiliary art indicates, in the form of small pits and notches, a calendrical notation system.

There is no certainty, however, that all Palaeolithic art – or even all cave-wall art – can be explained in the same way. More generally acceptable explanations of cave art may come from recent detailed research on the contexts of the artwork. For example, certain species are often depicted in association, and tend to be located preferen-tially in particular parts of caves (entrances, middle zones and rear recesses). Ultimately it must be remem-bered that cave art, like any other art, is a form of communication set in a specific cultural context – one that is separated from ours by tens of thousands of years.

The Lascaux caves consist of a main chamber and several steep galleries decorated with painted and engraved animals dating from between 15 000 and 10 000 BC. The animals, many of them depicted leaping and galloping, may have had a ritual significance linked with hunting.

used during the Bronze Age (bronze is an alloy: a mixture of copper with a little tin). The production of metal objects is a complex process, but the discovery of metallurgy probably occurred independently in several places, including the Near East and southeastern Europe. In parts of Europe and the Near East, small numbers of simple copper objects were in use many centuries before the beginning of the Bronze Age: this transitional period is called the Chalcolithic ('copper-stone') Age.

Social distinctions increased as more powerful individuals displayed their status via bronze weapons and gold jewellery. The status and power of certain individuals was particularly marked in the Late Bronze Age in imposing grave-monuments and offerings, such as the Mycenaean shaft graves (▷ p. 25), and bronze weapons and armour in a number of central European graves.

The Late Bronze Age societies of mainland Greece and Crete were in contact with the literate civilizations of the Near East, such as the Hittites (▷ p. 22) and the Egyptians (▷ p. 17), and may have been important cultural influences on neighbouring regions of Europe. Certainly the Late Bronze Age societies of Europe north of the Alps were far more sophisticated than their Neolithic predecessors. Production and distribution of certain materials – particularly salt and copper – were now carried out on an industrial scale. Returns from the substantial salt mines at Hallstatt in the Austrian Alps provided grave-goods for the cemetery there (▷ p. 34). Similarly, the organization and technology of the deep Mitterberg copper mines in Austria are comparable to late medieval operations. Heavily fortified hill-top communities ('hillforts'), often considered typical of the succeeding Iron Age, also start to appear at this time.

The Iron Age

The development of iron working in the Near East and its spread, starting at about 1000 BC, had little immediate effect on Late Bronze Age cultures. The recognizably Celtic societies of Iron Age temperate Europe (▷ p. 34) developed directly out of Late Bronze Age cultures. European Iron Age societies had increasing contacts with the Greeks and Phoenicians (▷ p. 23), and later on with the Romans (▷ p. 36). In earlier phases these contacts were primarily via trade. In the central and western Mediterranean, the Greeks and Phoenicians set up communities ('colonies') that traded with native peoples (▷ p. 28). They were also springboards for Greek trading expeditions into Europe north of the Alps. Here the most visible items of Mediterranean origin are associated with wine-drinking: wine-amphorae, drinking vessels, mixing bowls, and strainers. Closer contact between Europe and Greece is indicated at the Heuneberg, a hillfort in Germany, where a mud brick wall in the Greek manner was constructed, quite different from the normal Celtic type. It is pre-

THE BEGINNINGS OF AGRICULTURE

The most widely grown domesticated food plant today is wheat, and the most important food animals are sheep, goats, pigs and cattle. These, along with barley and beans, were all domesticated from their wild ancestors in the Near East between 9000 and 6000 BC. Other crops on which millions now depend – maize, rice, sorghum and the potato – were also domesticated in the period since the last Ice Age, in Central America, southern China and Southeast Asia, Africa and South America respectively. The path to a dependence on agriculture is best understood in the Near East, but it is clear that different patterns occurred in other parts of the world.

In the Near East, the domestication of the staple cereals (wheat and barley) and sheep and goats occurred first, at the same time as the establishment of permanent settlement. Crops and animals of secondary importance (such as olives, grapes, horses, donkeys and camels) did not appear until much later.

In the New World the appearance of cultivated maize in Mexico around 3600 BC is predated by the domestication of plants of lesser importance to the diet such as gourds, peppers and possibly types of cucumber. Permanent villages of full-time farmers seem to have appeared only around 1500 BC. Maize may also have been independently domesticated along with several other plant species, including the potato, in South America (▷ p. 70). Animal domestication in the Americas was less important than in the Near East: apart from the dog, it consisted of the domestication of the turkey in North America and the llama, alpaca and guinea pig in the Andean zone of South America.

The domestication of the wide range of native African domesticated plants is as yet poorly understood. Different species of cereal, root and tree crop may well have been domesticated over a wide range of environments and areas in sub-Saharan Africa. Nevertheless, many crops, such as sorghum, pearl millet and African rice, are known to have originated in the low-rainfall grasslands north of the equatorial forests. Even the yam and the oil palm, now staples in the high-rainfall forest zone, may have originated in the forest margins.

The history of domestication in East and Southeast Asia is also poorly known. In central and northern China, the earliest well-known phase of domestication started before 5000 BC (▷ p. 52). Village communities depended on domestic animals and the cultivation of millet. It is thought that millet was domesticated locally, but the animals – cattle, sheep, pigs and horses – are believed to have originally come from the Near East. The appearance of the same types of domesticated millet in Neolithic Europe may also indicate early contacts between Europe and China, but separate domestication cannot be ruled out.

The wild ancestors of rice are found from southern China to India. Domesticated rice appeared in several parts of this zone around 5000 BC. However, evidence discovered recently in Thailand suggests that wild rice may have been exploited long before this. Permanent settlements dependent on gathering and fishing had been established in coastal areas of Indochina by 6000 BC. These communities are known to have harvested rice, but it may well have still been wild (▷ p. 60).

sumed that Mediterranean traders mainly received raw materials and possibly slaves in exchange for their goods. The invasion of much of Celtic Europe by the Romans put an end to prehistory in those areas. However, the peripheries of Europe (Ireland, Scotland, Scandinavia, and northern Germany) were never colonized by the Romans. The emergence of these areas from prehistory only occurred gradually, within the last 1500 years, after their conversion to Christianity.   HF

The Dolmen of Kereadoret at Locmariaquer in Brittany, northwestern France. Dolmens are megalithic ('giant stone') tomb structures of the Neolithic period, consisting of a horizontal stone supported by several vertical stones.

Sumer and Akkad

The world's first known cities developed between 4000 and 3000 BC in the southern part of the floodplain between the Tigris and Euphrates rivers. This region, known as Mesopotamia (a Greek word meaning 'the land between the rivers'), is today in Iraq. The southernmost part of Mesopotamia was the ancient land of Sumer, where several city-states had emerged by 3000 BC. Following the conquest of these cities by Sargon of Akkad, they became part of the short-lived Akkadian Empire, which was itself succeeded by a Sumerian renaissance under a dynasty at Ur.

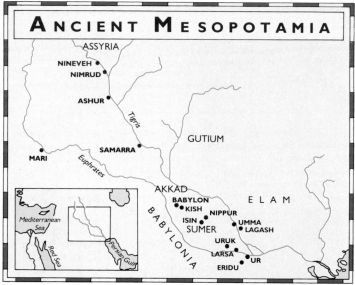

ANCIENT MESOPOTAMIA

ASSYRIA
NINEVEH
NIMRUD
ASHUR
Tigris
GUTIUM
SAMARRA
MARI
Euphrates
AKKAD
BABYLON
KISH
ELAM
NIPPUR
ISIN
UMMA
SUMER
LAGASH
URUK
LARSA
BABYLONIA
UR
ERIDU

Mediterranean Sea
Red Sea
Persian Gulf

SEE ALSO

● BABYLONIA AND ASSYRIA p. 20
● SYRIA AND THE LEVANT p. 22

The Tigris and Euphrates flooded their banks during the spring and made the surrounding plain extremely fertile. To control these floods the Mesopotamian farmers had to build a complex system of dykes and reservoirs. This required a great deal of organization and co-operation. Variations in the fertility of the soil led to differences in individual wealth – and hence to the emergence of social classes. Another factor in this latter process was the growing pursuit of occupations other than farming. Food surpluses allowed some people to give up farming and become craftsmen, labourers, merchants and administrators. These developments created a need for centralized decision-making, regulation and control: the beginnings of urban civilization.

The Sumerians

Scenes of Sumerian life (right), depicted on the 'peace side' of the 'Standard of Ur', c. 2500 BC. The standard is inlaid with shell, lapis lazuli and red limestone.

Much of the evidence for Sumerian cities comes from the remains of temples. These may have been the cities' main economic centres, but as little is known about the surrounding urban areas it is impossible to say whether this was in fact the case. At Uruk, the best known of the early cities,

the White Temple enclosed the remains of earlier religious buildings. Its 'high temple', on an 18-metre (60-foot) terrace, typifies the ever larger and more elaborate structures being built in these cities between c. 3500 and 3000 BC. The increase in wealth and technical skills can also be seen in the mosaic wall decorations and superb limestone and marble carvings found at this site.

At about this time the first writing developed. The earliest texts, dated around 3300 BC, are economic records from Uruk in a pictographic script. By 2800 BC a syllabic script had evolved which could express not only objects, but also ideas and actions. The picture signs had become abstract symbols representing the sounds of the Sumerian language. This system was later adapted for the Semitic languages Eblaite and Akkadian, and subsequently for other languages of the ancient Near East (▷ p. 6). This form of writing is known as cuneiform, from the Latin word for the wedge shapes impressed on the clay tablet by a reed stylus.

In the Early Dynastic period (c. 2900–2370 BC) the Sumerian city-states were constantly at war with each other. Large city walls were built and military equipment was developed, such as war chariots, shields, spears and metal helmets (▷ p. 44). The contents from the Royal Tombs of Ur, dating from about 2500 BC, include weapons and equipment as well as numerous items of gold, silver, lapis lazuli and other precious stones. These finds reveal the wealth of the Sumerians and show the extent to which they had access, either by trade or conquest, to precious raw materials from Afghanistan, Iran and elsewhere. The later Sumerian 'king list', which records the early dynasties, reflects the changing status of the various cities, as first one, and then another, became the most important, or the holder of 'kingship'. The king or *lugal* ('great man') may have originally been a war leader appointed by his peers to be the arbiter in boundary disputes and the like. In time this function became permanent

and hereditary. At Eridu – one of the earliest cities – kingship was first 'lowered from heaven', according to the king list. It was next taken to Kish, another early site, and then to Uruk. Other cities involved in these early struggles were Lagash, Ur and Umma. The ruler of Umma, Lugalzaggesi, became 'king of the land of Sumer', heading a confederation of 50 cities.

The Akkadians

This short-lived political unity ended with the conquest of Sumer by Sargon of Akkad around 2370 BC. According to the legend of his birth, Sargon – a foundling – rose to the position of cup-bearer to the king of Kish, whom he later overthrew. Sargon conquered Mesopotamia, parts of northern Syria, and Elam to the east. He founded as his capital the city of Akkad, which has not yet been discovered. At this time, also, the Sumerian cuneiform script was adapted to write Akkadian (or ancient Babylonian) – the language of Sargon and his successors.

In spite of Sargon's achievements and those of his grandson Naram-Sin, this dynasty did not last. In about 2200 BC, Akkad was overrun by the Gutians, a mountain people from the east. It is possible that others, such as the Elamites and Lullubi, also from the east, as well as Hurrians from the north (▷ p. 22), also played a part in the demise of Akkad.

The third dynasty of Ur

After 100 years of anarchy, the Third Dynasty of Ur (c. 2113–2006 BC) was founded by Ur-Nammu. He and his successors were great warriors, but this was also a century of prosperity. The kings ruled Mesopotamia either directly or through provincial governors, created an efficient administration and encouraged a renaissance in Sumerian art and literature. But incursions of Semitic Amorites from the west, together with famine and loss of provincial support, made Ur vulnerable. In 2006 BC, the Elamites sacked the city and carried off its king, Ibbi-Sin (▷ p. 20).   MO

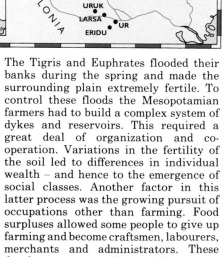

Ancient Egypt

'Concerning Egypt itself, I shall extend my remarks to a great length, because there is no country that possesses so many wonders.' So wrote the Greek writer Herodotus in the 5th century BC. Egypt's ancient civilization has continued to interest and fascinate. Geographically isolated by deserts and sea, it developed a unique and self-contained culture that lasted three thousand years. Its dry climate has contributed to the preservation of a wealth of monuments: ancient cities, pyramids, temples and sumptuous artefacts that are a source of wonder today, as they were in antiquity.

With the decipherment of hieroglyphic script in 1822 by the French scholar Jean-François Champollion, it became possible to read and understand the written documents of the ancient Egyptians: religious and historical texts, literary compositions, and the many documents that illustrate aspects of their daily lives.

Geography and resources

Ancient Egypt consisted of the Nile

THE PERIODS AND DYNASTIES OF ANCIENT EGYPT

Dates (BC)	Period	Dynasties	Main events
3100–2725	Early Dynastic Period	1–3	Unification of Upper and Lower Egypt under Menes. Foundation of Memphis. Building of Step Pyramid.
2575–2134	Old Kingdom	4–8	Centralized administration. Building of Great Pyramids at Giza.
2134–2040	First Intermediate Period	9–11	Egypt divided. Political fragmentation. Control by local monarchs.
2040–1640	Middle Kingdom	11–13	Reunification under Mentuhotep II. Foundation of Itj-towy. Administrative reforms. Co-regencies. Conquest of Nubia.
1640–1552	Second Intermediate Period	14–17	Hyksos rule. Theban dynasty liberates Egypt.
1552–1070	New Kingdom	18–20	Imperial Egypt: empire extends from Syria to southern Sudan. Capital at Thebes. Great building programme.
1070–712	Third Intermediate Period	21–24	Egypt divided: priesthood of Amun rule in Thebes, while pharaohs rule in Tanis.
712–332	Late Period	25–30	Reunification of Egypt under 26th Dynasty. Persian invasion. Conquest by Alexander the Great: end of the line of native pharaohs.

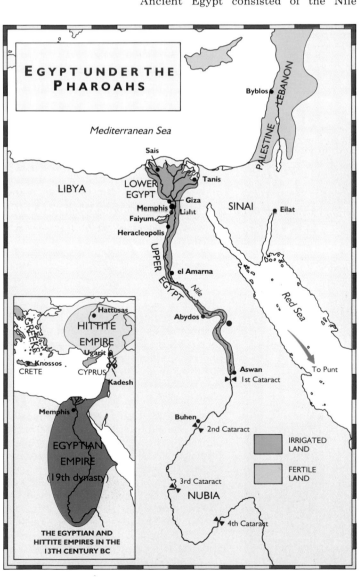

EGYPT UNDER THE PHARAOHS

Mediterranean Sea

Byblos
LEBANON
PALESTINE
LIBYA
Sais
LOWER EGYPT
Tanis
Memphis
Giza
Light
SINAI
Eilat
Faiyum
Heracleopolis
UPPER EGYPT
el Amarna
Nile
Red Sea
Abydos
Aswan
1st Cataract
To Punt
Buhen
2nd Cataract

IRRIGATED LAND

FERTILE LAND

3rd Cataract
NUBIA
4th Cataract

HATTIAS
HITTITE EMPIRE
GREECE
Ugarit
Knossos
CRETE
CYPRUS
Kadesh
Memphis
EGYPTIAN EMPIRE (19th dynasty)

THE EGYPTIAN AND HITTITE EMPIRES IN THE 13TH CENTURY BC

Valley – a long and narrow strip of land extending some 600 miles from Aswan to the area south of modern Cairo, where the river opened up into the Delta. On either side of the valley stretched vast expanses of desert. The Nile was not only the unifying feature of the country, it was also its main source of life. In Egypt rainfall is negligible, but in antiquity the regular annual inundation of the Nile between July and October covered most of the land in the valley and in the Delta, laying down a rich layer of fertilizing silt. Agriculture involved careful management of the waters of the river through the creation of irrigation basins and channels. The main crops were cereals, but pulses, vegetables and fruit were also grown. Flax was used for clothing, sails and ropes, and the pith of the papyrus plant to produce a type of paper. The Egyptians also kept cattle, pigs, goats and sheep, and hunting and fishing provided some additional variety to their diet.

Ancient Egypt was rich in mineral resources – gold, copper, and turquoise – and building and semi-precious stones were also quarried (▷ box, p. 18). Trading expeditions brought to Egypt the resources that the country lacked: wood from the Lebanon; oil, wine and silver from western Asia; lapis lazuli from Afghanistan; and incense, ebony, ivory, precious stones and exotic animals from the semi-mythical land of Punt, situated somewhere in the area of modern Eritrea or Somalia.

The Early Dynastic Period and the Old Kingdom

It is customary to divide the history of ancient Egypt into thirty dynasties of pharaohs (as the kings of ancient Egypt were known; ▷ table). The history of Pharaonic Egypt begins around 3100 BC with the unification of Upper and Lower Egypt under a king known to history as Menes. Though it is impossible to trace the events leading to the unification of the country, evidence suggests that the Delta area was conquered by rulers from the south.

During the Early Dynastic (or Archaic) Period, a considerable administrative organization of the state took place. A new capital, Memphis, was founded at the junction of Upper and Lower Egypt. There was a dramatic development in the science of writing, no doubt to keep pace with the requirements of a centralized bureaucratic government. Burial customs had become increasingly complex, and the first pyramid was built – the Step Pyramid at Saqqara.

This formative period led to the tremendous achievements of the Old Kingdom, the great pyramid age of Egypt. Written records indicate that all aspects of government and administration were controlled by the pharaoh from the royal residence at Memphis. The monumental size of the Great Pyramids at Giza clearly shows that the pharaoh was the dominant figure of the state, acting as an intermediary between the gods and mankind. The construction of these enormous monuments is also evidence of the degree of state organization that the Egyptians had achieved. At the same time the horizons of the Egyptians expanded, with trading expeditions to Nubia, Sinai, Libya and the Levant all recorded.

A relaxation of the strong personal

The temple of Queen Hatshepsut at Dayr al-Bahri. The temple – designed as a funerary monument to Hatshepsut and her father Thutmose I – is decorated with reliefs recording the major events of her 20-year reign (c. 1540– c. 1481 BC).

Queen Nefertari (19th dynasty) makes an offering of vases to the goddess Hathor, represented by a woman wearing a cow's headdress.

authority of the pharaohs towards the end of the 5th and during the 6th dynasty resulted in a complete breakdown of royal power during what has been called the First Intermediate Period. For about a hundred years, a number of rival princes claimed the kingship of Upper and Lower Egypt. Civil wars broke out and there is evidence of famine.

The Middle Kingdom

The accession of Mentuhotep II of the 11th dynasty, the first Theban pharaoh, ended 90 years of conflict. Mentuhotep took control of the whole country, restored order and consolidated the borders. Trading expeditions were sent to the Levant, Nubia and the land of Punt. The period that followed the reunification of Egypt is known as the Middle Kingdom. It was regarded in later tradition as the 'classical' period of Pharaonic civilization.

Under the strong kings of the 12th dynasty, Egypt once again became a highly centralized and well-administered state and a new capital, Lisht (Itj-towy), was founded south of Memphis by Amenemhat I. The practice of a co-regency was instituted at the very beginning of the dynasty, whereby the ruling pharaoh nominated his successor as co-regent and reigned with him for the last years of his rule.

Administrative reforms removed from the

MINERALS, MINING AND METALLURGY

The Egyptians had access to extensive mineral resources. From the Aswan quarries came granite for the huge obelisks, which were carved *in situ*, and then transported downriver by boat. Close to the Nile valley were quarries of alabaster and quartzite, whilst the eastern desert yielded several semi-precious and building stones. The desert was also rich in copper, iron and lead ores, but these were not exploited until Roman times.

Mining was a state monopoly, and large-scale expeditions, with military escorts, were sent regularly to work the more distant mines and quarries. Turquoise was mined in Sinai from the 3rd dynasty to the end of the New Kingdom. Copper also came from Sinai, but was probably acquired by trade. At Timna, near Eilat, the extensive copper mines were worked by local people, perhaps under Egyptian control.

Egypt fully exploited its large deposits of gold. Much of the earliest ancient gold was alluvial. Later more advanced mining methods were developed. Areas of quartz rock were heated and then quenched in order to fracture their gold-bearing veins. The broken portions then had to be pounded and ground, before being panned to separate the heavier metal particles. The ore was then smelted and refined in a refractory pot. By the 19th dynasty the more accessible supplies had been exploited, and mines were opened deeper in the eastern desert. Here water – perhaps from subterranean wells – would have had to be found for the washing of crushed ore, and for the workers.

From this period dates the only extant ancient Egyptian map. It probably shows the Wadi Hammamat, an area where there were gold mines and grey-wacke quarries. An 18th-dynasty tomb painting, showing all the stages of smelting and casting for a pair of copper doors, is one of the earliest records of metal working.   MO

provincial nobility much of the power they had acquired during the First Intermediate Period. In foreign affairs, contacts with the Levant were re-established and in Nubia a series of fortresses were constructed along the Nile, to secure the southern boundaries and to regulate all trade into Egypt.

The end of the 13th dynasty was followed by the Second Intermediate Period, when political control of the land was again fragmented. Of the four dynasties assigned to this period, two are native Egyptian (the 14th and 15th), whilst two are allotted to foreign Asiatic rulers, the Hyksos kings (the 15th and 16th dynasties). The Hyksos ruled from Avaris in the eastern delta. Later tradition, probably based on propaganda, claimed that there was anarchy under the Hyksos, who were accused of burning temples and cities, but there is no evidence for this and they appear to have adopted and respected Egyptian culture. Several innovations were now introduced into Egypt, including the vertical loom, the lyre and lute, the horse-drawn chariot and new weapons (▷ p. 44). Whatever the true nature of Hyksos rule, they were remembered later as hated foreign usurpers, and were eventually expelled by a new dynasty ruling from Thebes in Upper Egypt.

The New Kingdom

The memory of Hyksos domination of Egypt was largely responsible for shaping the policies of the New Kingdom rulers. Egypt now became an expansionist power with a standing army. Under a series of able 18th-dynasty rulers, Egypt established control over Syria, Palestine and Nubia, and became the largest empire in the Near East. Diplomatic contacts were established with other great powers of the period – the Hittites, Babylonians and Assyrians (▷ p. 21) – and peace treaties were concluded between them, often cemented by dynastic marriages between the pharaohs and foreign princesses.

Provincial governors – often local princes – were placed in charge of the newly conquered Asian territories and in some states Egyptian garrisons were installed. The sons of local princes were taken to Egypt, where their education ensured that they would become pro-Egyptian. The provinces paid annual tribute. Egyptian control of Nubia extended to beyond the 4th cataract, and walled towns, each with a temple, were constructed, replacing the earlier fortresses.

Enormous wealth from booty, trade and tribute poured into Egypt from the various regions of the empire. This wealth and the increasing contacts with other countries stimulated cultural life and introduced new fashions and customs. From their ancient capital at Memphis and their new religious centre of Thebes, the New Kingdom pharaohs undertook a large number of building projects. The grandiose temple complex of Karnak was built not only as the main cult temple for the state god Amun-Ra, but also as the treasury of the state. The royal tombs were situated, for security reasons, in the 'Valley of the Kings', a remote canyon on the west bank of the Nile opposite Thebes. Vast mortuary temples, palaces and shrines were erected.

During the reign of Amenophis IV, Egyptian influence in the conquered Asian territories lapsed. The Amarna letters (▷ p. 21) reveal the extent to which Amenophis neglected the requests for help from his loyal vassals. He abandoned the worship of Amun, and claiming divine guidance from the Aten or sun's disc, changed his name to Akhenaten (meaning 'beneficial to the sun disc'). A new capital, Akhenaten ('the horizon of the sun disc', now known as el-Amarna), was built north of Thebes. However, the

new religion – based on the cult of the sun disc – was opposed by the powerful priests of Amun. After the accession of the young Tutankhamun, there was a return to traditional policies.

The early rulers of the 19th dynasty did much to restore Egypt's prestige and Palestine was once again brought under control. Conflict with the Hittites in Syria culminated in the battle of Kadesh in 1285 BC (▷ pp. 22 and 44). In spite of Ramesses II's claims of a great victory, the result was indecisive. Both sides withdrew and sixteen years later signed a peace treaty. During the reign of Ramesses II, a new capital city was founded at Per-Ramesses in the Delta. The artistic output of the New Kingdom is unsurpassed, both in quantity and in the quality of the craftsmanship.

The Late Period

Under the successors of Ramesses II, Egypt entered a long period of decline. Invaders from Libya and the 'Sea Peoples' from the eastern Mediterranean were among those the 20th-dynasty pharaoh, Ramesses III, claimed to have repulsed. Egypt's control over her empire disintegrated, and a series of weak kings resulted in much of the royal power being usurped by the high priest of Amun at Thebes.

The final collapse of the new kingdom saw once more the division of the country into two halves, with Upper Egypt ruled by the priesthood of Amun in Thebes, whilst pharaohs of the 21st dynasty, descended from the vizier of Lower Egypt, governed from their new capital of Tanis in the Delta. This period is usually referred to as the Third Intermediate Period.

During the 25th dynasty, Egypt was taken over by Nubian pharaohs. Their involvement in the affairs of Palestine led to invasion by Assyria and finally to an attack upon Thebes, which was plundered.

The Assyrian king had appointed vassals loyal to himself, but as Assyria's power declined, Egypt regained its independence under a dynasty from Sais in the delta. Under the strong 26th-dynasty Saite pharaohs, the country was reunited and enjoyed a last period of splendour. There was an artistic renaissance with a revival of earlier art forms. Trade was active and Greek traders now began to settle in Egypt.

But in 525 BC the Persians under Cambyses invaded Egypt. The conquest by the Achaemenid Persians meant the end of independence. Egypt was now ruled as a Persian province by a Persian satrap, or governor (▷ p. 26). In 332 BC Alexander the Great invaded Egypt and the satrap surrendered without a struggle. He was welcomed by the Egyptians and accepted as pharaoh (▷ p. 32). At his death, his general Ptolemy took control of the country, founding a line of kings who were to rule for some three hundred years until Egypt was annexed as a province of the Roman Empire (▷ box).   ND/MO

PTOLEMAIC EGYPT

A painted linen shroud from the Ptolemaic period, depicting Osiris (the Egyptian god of the dead), and Anubis (jackal-headed god of the necropolis), flanking a dead man. The painting, dating from c. 180 BC, is Hellenistic in style and execution but Egyptian in subject-matter.

In 305 BC, Alexander's general, Ptolemy, declared himself ruler of Egypt. Ptolemy had brought the king's body to Alexandria, the new capital, for burial, thus symbolically associating himself and his successors with the divine pharaoh and founder of the city. In taking pharaonic titles and paying honour to Egyptian gods, the Macedonian Ptolemies also linked themselves to the ancient dynasties and gained the support of the priesthood. The prosperous city of Alexandria became a great centre of Hellenistic learning and culture, endowed with the world's first museum and largest library. One reason for the city's prosperity was the excellence of its two harbours, which became the busiest in the Mediterranean.

But this cosmopolitan trading city, with its large Greek and Jewish population, was part of Egypt only in name. The economic development of Alexandria hindered improvement elsewhere in the country. Under the early Ptolemies there was some agricultural progress; the introduction of two harvests a year, for example, increased the country's wealth. However, while in some areas of Greek settlement – particularly in the Faiyum – land was reclaimed from the marshes, the Egyptians were subjected to heavy taxes and became increasingly poor. The state regulated the type and quantity of crops grown, and then bought part of the crop at a fixed price and took part as tax. Discontent began to manifest itself in strikes, widespread unrest and rural depopulation.

Greek was the language of the ruling class, and of the Ptolemies; only Cleopatra VII, the last of the Ptolemies, spoke Egyptian. Some inscriptions were now written in Greek and Egyptian, including a priestly decree of 196 BC. This bilingual document, known as the Rosetta Stone, was to be the key to deciphering the hieroglyphs – the classic script of the lost Egyptian language (▷ p. 6).   MO

Babylonia and Assyria

The sack of Ur by the Elamites in 2006 BC marked the end of Sumerian rule in Mesopotamia. The centre of political gravity moved northwards, and in the first half of the 2nd millennium BC Babylon became pre-eminent. Ancient Babylonian (or Akkadian) replaced Sumerian as the spoken language of the region, but Mesopotamian culture retained its Sumerian roots. Over the centuries there was a constant influx of new peoples, but the ancient traditions of Mesopotamia remained intact and absorbed those of the new arrivals.

Even when Assyria became the dominant power in the region after 1000 BC – and Aramaic became widely spoken in both Assyria and Babylonia – the culture and religion of both north and south was still stamped with the imprint of Mesopotamia. Following the defeat of Assyria in the 7th century BC, Babylon briefly regained her former might.

The Amorites and the rise of Babylon

During the century of peace that followed the sack of Ur, a dynasty based at Isin – having expelled the Elamites – claimed control of the reduced but still sizeable domains of Ur. From about 1900 BC Isin's dominance was challenged by an Amorite dynasty based at Larsa, and for more than a century there was political turmoil, during which a number of petty Amorite states emerged.

The Amorites – a nomadic people from the Syrian desert – had gradually infiltrated

Hammurabi praying to the god Umurru. The discovery of the Code of Hammurabi in 1901 established his prominence in ancient history, but it is likely that other Babylonian kings contributed equally important (but as yet unknown) achievements.

Mesopotamia from the west and eventually took control of several centres. Prominent amongst these were Ashur in the north, Mari on the upper Euphrates, and Babylon, where an Amorite dynasty ruled from around 1900 BC. Until the reign of Hammurabi (c. 1792–1750 BC), Babylon was a small provincial city. Known to posterity for his law code – which specified individual rights as well as punishments – Hammurabi unified Mesopotamia for a short time under the hegemony of Babylon.

A cache of letters found at Mari has illuminated the international situation during the first 30 years of Hammurabi's long reign. There appear to have been constantly shifting allegiances, which Hammurabi exploited. By about 1750 BC he had destroyed the prosperous city of Mari, which had grown rich from tolls levied on the river-borne trade between Syria and the cities of the south. Another set of documents, from the Assyrian trading colony of Kanesh in Anatolia, gives an insight into the trading activities of merchants from Ashur, the Assyrian capital in northern Mesopotamia. Between c. 1950 and 1750 BC, textiles and tin were sent from Ashur to Anatolia. The profits, in gold and silver, were sent back to Ashur. Textiles were also a major commodity of the southern cities of Mesopotamia (▷ p. 42).

The successors of Hammurabi continued to hold Babylon and the surrounding provinces for about 150 years. But the territories he had gained were now much reduced in size as independent dynasties began to establish themselves. To the north, in Anatolia, the Hittites (an Indo-European people; ▷ p. 22) held sway and reigned from their capital at Hattusas (modern Boghazköy). After conquering northern Syria, the Hittite king Mursilis I marched down the Euphrates and sacked Babylon around 1595 BC. Little is known of events in Mesopotamia for the next 100 years, which were followed by some four centuries of rule by the Kassites.

The Kassites

A people of obscure origin, the Kassites first appear in Mesopotamian texts as expert handlers of horses. Although not originally from Mesopotamia, the Kassites adopted local custom, religion and language. Their capital was at Dur Kurigalzu to the northwest of Babylon. The long and largely peaceful rule of the Kassite dynasty was accompanied by considerable social change. There was also increasing conflict with Assyria, which lasted until the 7th century. A royal archive of the 14th century BC, found at Amarna in Egypt, shows that the Kassites and the other 'Great Powers' of the time maintained the existing balance of power by means of diplomacy (▷ box).

With the death of the last Kassite king around 1157 BC, Babylon entered an extended period of political instability. Between this time and the Assyrian conquest in the 8th century BC the country was ruled by six dynasties. There seem to

DIPLOMACY IN THE ANCIENT NEAR EAST

Between c. 1600 and 1200 BC, the Great Powers of the Near East were Egypt, Hatti (in Anatolia), Babylonia, Mitanni (in northern Syria), and – to a lesser extent – Assyria. For much of this period these states tried to achieve their ends by diplomacy, though occasionally they resorted to force. Egypt, which had long been dominant in the Syria/Palestine region, was the major power in the Near East (▷ p. 18). The emergence of the Hurrians (Mitanni) and then the Hittites threatened Egyptian hegemony in Syria/Palestine. Similarly, Babylonia felt threatened by Assyrian and Hurrian power.

By the 2nd millennium, cuneiform (▷ p. 16) was the international script and Akkadian the international language of the Near East. In 1887 an archive of cuneiform tablets was found at El-Amarna in Egypt. It proved to be the correspondence between the Pharaohs Amenophis III (c. 1417–1379 BC) and Akhenaten (c. 1379–1362 BC) and the other powers of the region. The archive also included letters from Egypt's vassals in Palestine. Through the tablets it is possible to follow the international political developments of the age, such as the demise of Mitanni, the growth of Hittite power and the anxieties of the Babylonian ruler in the face of Assyrian aggression. The tablets reveal that alliances between states were often sealed with dynastic royal marriages. Gift exchange between rulers was important as a measure of status and loyalty, as is shown by this *cri de coeur* from Burnaburiash of Babylon – a vassal of Egypt – to Akhenaten: 'Now behold Assyria has arrayed against me. Did I not send to you, as to their thoughts about your land? Why do they send against me? If you have pity on me it will never be done. I have sent to you precious stones, fifteen pairs of horses . . . . '

have been a number of border skirmishes with Assyria. But from 1100 BC pressure from the nomadic Aramaean tribes of the west encouraged the Babylonians and Assyrians to forget their differences for a while.

Assyria

The Assyrian heartland was in northern Mesopotamia, on the Tigris river. Since about 3000 BC there had been sanctuaries at Nineveh and Ashur, the capital. Assyria lay on important trade routes to Anatolia and until c. 2000 BC was dominated by Sumer. Assyrian control over northern Mesopotamia was first established by the Amorite ruler, Shamshi-Adad I. With the emergence of Babylonian power under Hammurabi, this independence was lost and Assyria was later dominated by Mitanni (▷ p. 22).

The unsettled conditions in the Near East at the end of the Bronze Age (▷ p. 22) created a political vacuum. Assyria now emerged as an expanding power after regaining territory lost to the Aramaeans. During the reigns of Ashurnasirpal II (883–859 BC) and his successor Shalmaneser III (858–824 BC), the remaining Aramaean states within Assyria's former domains were conquered and the boundary was established at the Euphrates. Several northern Syrian kingdoms became vassal states. Ashurnasirpal moved his capital from Ashur to Nimrud, where a great palace was built. At the end of Shalmaneser's reign there was a revolt in Assyria, and during the succeeding period of relative Assyrian weakness, the kingdom of Urartu, to the northeast, expanded. For a time the Urartians controlled the eastern trade routes and the Syrian vassals, who were important as suppliers of metals and horses from Asia Minor.

The Neo-Assyrian empire

With the accession of the usurper Tiglath-Pileser III (745–727 BC), the imperial expansion of Assyria began. Gradual Assyrian encroachment on Babylonian territory to the south culminated in the conquest of Babylon in 729 BC. In the west the Syrian states were reconquered and placed under direct Assyrian rule. The Aramaean kingdom of Damascus and outlying parts of Israel were seized and turned into provinces. Tiglath-Pileser III also campaigned against Urartu, which was not eliminated until the reign of Sargon II (721–705 BC). Under Sargon's son Sennacherib (704–681 BC) – during the reign of Hezekiah of Judah – the Assyrians entered Palestine. They defeated the coastal cities, repelled an Egyptian force, and overran Judah. Some towns – such as Lachish – were captured, but Jerusalem was not taken depite being besieged. In the east there was trouble in Babylonia and in 689 BC Sennacherib sacked Babylon after a nine month siege.

Sargon II had moved the Assyrian capital from Nimrud to the newly built site of Dur-Sharrukin ('the fort of Sargon'), which was more convenient for his frequent campaigns to the north. However, Sennacherib returned the royal centre to the Tigris, selecting as his capital the ancient town of Nineveh. There he built his great 'Palace without Rival', which was laid out with sumptuous gardens watered by streams from a newly built aqueduct. Adorned with the booty and tribute from conquered territories, Nineveh became famous for its wealth and splendour.

Babylon was rebuilt under Sennacherib's son, Esarhaddon (680–669 BC), who made vassal treaties with peoples to the east, including the increasingly powerful Medes. Esarhaddon attacked Egypt in 675 BC and captured Memphis. He proclaimed himself king, but following his departure, the Nubian pharaoh Taharqa returned. Under his successor Ashurbanipal (668–627 BC), the Assyrian empire reached its largest extent (⊳ map). In Egypt,

Thebes was captured, sacked and looted, and to the east, Elam was conquered.

The Assyrians developed a highly organized system of imperial administration. Provincial governors collected taxes and tribute, raised conscripts for the standing army and provided the supplies for campaigning Assyrian armies. They had also to provide forced labour for road building and maintenance of the road system. Whole populations were deported and resettled as punishment for rebellion.

These harsh conditions led to frequent rebellions, the quashing of which further stretched the empire's resources. A combination of external pressure and internal strife rendered Assyria too weak to resist an alliance of the Babylonians and the Medes, whose forces sacked Nineveh in 612 BC (⊳ p. 26). The Assyrian empire was now divided between the Babylonians and their Median allies.

The Neo-Babylonian empire

Under Nabopolassar (625–605 BC), first of a dynasty of Chaldaean kings, Babylon regained its independence and defeated Assyria with the help of the Medes and Scythians. In 605 BC, Nebuchadnezzar II (605–562 BC) defeated an Egyptian force at Carchemish and campaigned extensively in Syria and Palestine. In March 597 BC he captured Jerusalem and took thousands of Jews, including the king, Jehoiakin, and members of his elite, into exile in Babylon (the Babylonian Captivity).

The Neo-Babylonian empire survived for less than a century, although Babylon – which had been rebuilt by Nabopolassar and Nebuchadnezzar – survived to be recorded by Herodotus (⊳ p. 2). Excavation has borne out his account of the city's magnificence. The city was surrounded by huge outer and inner walls and had several gates, including the great Ishtar Gate leading to the sacred way.

The last king, Nabonidus, spent several years of his reign at Teima in Arabia. The Babylonian priests resented his neglect of the temple of the god Marduk and his absence from Babylon. In 539 BC, the city fell without resistance to the Persian ruler, Cyrus, of the Achaemenid dynasty (⊳ p. 26). MO

Assyrian archers during the siege of a town by the forces of Ashurnasirpal II. The lengthy campaigns of Ashurnasipal – among the first to use cavalry and battering rams – greatly enlarged the Assyrian empire.

SEE ALSO
● SUMER AND AKKAD p. 16
● ANCIENT EGYPT p. 17
● SYRIA AND THE LEVANT p. 22
● THE PERSIAN EMPIRE p. 26

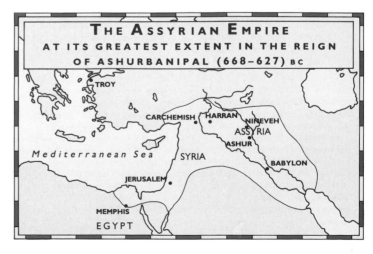

THE ASSYRIAN EMPIRE
AT ITS GREATEST EXTENT IN THE REIGN
OF ASHURBANIPAL (668–627) BC

Syria and the Levant

To the west of Mesopotamia, beyond the Euphrates, lay Syria, Palestine and the coast of the Levant. This region was neither geographically nor culturally homogeneous. In some areas there were plentiful natural resources such as timber and metals, whereas others, bordering the desert, were less richly endowed. The main trade routes between the Mediterranean and the interior ran through northern Syria, where a number of prosperous city-states emerged in the 3rd millennium BC. It was in the Levant that there evolved – in the latter part of the 2nd millennium BC – the scripts from which the modern Roman alphabet would develop.

Akkadian texts of the 3rd millennium listed Ebla, south of Aleppo, as one of the Syrian city-states. The archive from Ebla, written in cuneiform Eblaite – the earliest known form of written West Semitic – shows that around 2500 BC the city was a prosperous trading centre. Part of its wealth came from felling timber and transporting it to Mesopotamia.

Amorites, Hurrians and Canaanites

In about 2000 BC, Ebla was sacked by nomadic Amorites from the Syrian desert. The Amorites, who spoke a West Semitic dialect, also settled in Mesopotamia. By about 1800 BC there were a number of Amorite kingdoms in Syria and Palestine. The largest was the kingdom of Aleppo, which reached from the Taurus Mountains to the Euphrates, and controlled the main east–west trade routes. Other important Amorite cities were the ports of Ugarit and Byblos.

In the 2nd millennium BC, the Hurrians – a non-Semitic people, possibly from eastern Anatolia – also settled in Syria. Some time later the Hurrian kingdom of Mitanni was formed in northern Syria and absorbed part of Aleppo's territory. At its greatest extent, between 1430 and 1350 BC, Mitanni reached from the Zagros to the Mediterranean. Its capital, Washukani, has not yet been found. Although its population was mainly Hurrian, the ruling aristocracy seems to have been Indo-Aryan. The prominence of Mitanni at this time was due to its effective use of the two-wheeled horse-drawn war chariot (▷ p. 44). In the mid-14th century BC, the Hittites (▷ below) defeated Mitanni and her vassals, taking control of Syria. Among the centres they now controlled was the coastal trading city of Ugarit, which had expanded considerably under Mitannian hegemony. Much of its wealth came from the copper trade with Cyprus and from metalworking. Ugarit also had close links with the Aegean world (▷ p. 24).

Although the Canaanites of Palestine and the Levant spoke virtually the same language as the Amorites, there were cultural differences between the two peoples. The Canaanites, descended from earlier Amorite settlement in the region, had assimilated elements of Egyptian culture. Trading contacts between the Levant and Egypt are documented as early as c. 2950 BC – when cedars of Lebanon were sent to Egypt – and continued through most of the Bronze Age.

The Hittites

The Hittites of Anatolia were an Indo-European-speaking people whose empire was founded in about 1650 BC, with its capital at Hattusas (modern Boghazköy) in central Anatolia (modern Turkey). Control of northern Syria was of great importance to the Hittites, because of its trade routes and the access it gave to ports such as Ugarit. Under Suppiluliumas I (c. 1380–1350 BC), the Hittite Empire reached its greatest extent. In northern Syria the main centres of power were Carchemish and Alalakh. A series of 'vassal treaties' – notably one with Ugarit – institutionalized Hittite control of the region.

First Mitanni and then the Hittites came into conflict with Egypt in Syria (▷ p. 19). Egypt had established control of Palestine, the Levant and part of Syria, reaching the Euphrates around 1525 BC. Peace was established with Mitanni after the campaigns of Amenophis II (c. 1450–1425 BC), and the resulting alliance was later sealed by a marriage between a princess of Mitanni and the Egyptian pharaoh. Egypt controlled its territories in the Near East mainly through loyal vassals.

The 'status quo' was maintained through diplomacy until the Hittites challenged Mitanni for control of Syria. Mitanni eventually fell to attacks by its former Assyrian vassals and by the Hittites. Although Mitanni was allied to Egypt, this was to no avail. While the Hittites were ably led by the formidable warrior-king Suppiluliumas I, Mitanni received no assistance from Egypt's pharaoh, Akhenaten, who was absorbed in religious reforms (▷ p. 19). Not only did the Hittites acquire Mitanni's Syrian territory, they also began intriguing with Egypt's Syrian vassals. Much of this region was now irrevocably lost to Egyptian control. The Amarna Letters (▷ p. 21), which contain the diplomatic correspondence between the various great kings of the period, also include letters from Egypt's loyal vassals, who unsuccessfully requested help from the pharaoh to counter the threat posed by cities who transferred their allegiance to the Hittites.

Egypt regained control over Palestine under the first rulers of the 19th dynasty. Ramesses II (▷ p. 19) clashed with the Hittites at Kadesh on the Orontes c. 1285 BC. The outcome of this encounter was indecisive, but 16 years later a peace treaty was signed and a Hittite princess was married to the pharaoh.

The Kadesh treaty lasted until the demise of the Hittite Empire shortly before 1200 BC. The reasons for the sudden eclipse of the Hittite Empire are not fully understood, but are probably connected with the appearance of the Sea Peoples (raiding tribes from the north), and with internal disturbances.

THE BOOKS OF THE OLD TESTAMENT

The main written source for the history of Israel and Judah is the Old Testament. The absolute conviction of the Israelites in the power of their god Yahweh, above all others, led them to preserve their books of history and law through their many vicissitudes. The tradition was originally transmitted orally from generation to generation, before being written down from the 8th century BC onwards.

There are different traditions behind the Old Testament stories, which account for some of the duplications and variations. The Pentateuch (the first five books), containing the divine laws, gives the account of Yahweh's people from Abraham's departure from Ur and arrival in Canaan to the death of Moses. It is impossible to reconstruct a history from these stories, but they reflect in a general way certain elements of the Near Eastern world of the 2nd millennium. The historical books – particularly the Books of Kings and Chronicles – provide the history of the kingdoms of Judah and Israel.

Most of the books of the Old Testament were written down in Hebrew, although some of the later books were written in Aramaic. The earliest complete extant manuscript dates from the 9th century AD. Roughly 1000 years older are the Dead Sea Scrolls, a collection of Hebrew and Aramaic manuscripts discovered between 1947 and 1956. They include fragments of nearly every book in the Old Testament and a complete text of the Book of Isaiah. The earliest translation is the Greek Septuagint of the 2nd and 3rd centuries BC, so called because it was believed to be the work of 70 scholars. The Septuagint was later translated into Aramaic, Syriac and Latin, and was used by the early Christian Church.

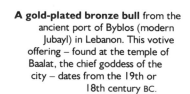

A gold-plated bronze bull from the ancient port of Byblos (modern Jubayl) in Lebanon. This votive offering – found at the temple of Baalat, the chief goddess of the city – dates from the 19th or 18th century BC.

The Sea Peoples

At about the same time, many cities of the eastern Mediterranean coast were laid to waste and some – such as Ugarit – were never inhabited again. These disturbances were probably caused by marauders known as the 'Sea Peoples', who were eventually defeated by the Egyptian pharaohs Merneptah and Ramesses III (▷ p. 19).

The disturbances of c. 1200 BC changed the face of the Near East. Egypt, Babylonia and Assyria lost much of their former strength. One of the groups of the Sea Peoples – the Peleset – settled around Gaza in southern Canaan. Known later as the Philistines, they gave this region its name – Palestine. Their battles against the Israelites are recorded in the Old Testament, and the remains of their iron weapons bear out the biblical accounts.

Aramaeans and Neo-Hittites

The Aramaean tribes, who had formerly been nomadic, occupied Syria and the lands along the Euphrates river, spreading into Assyria and Babylonia. They formed numerous small kingdoms and frequently fought the Assyrians and the Israelites. The kingdom of Aram-Damascus, which became the most powerful of these states, was finally conquered by Assyria in 732 BC (▷ p. 20). Aramaic became the international language of the Near East, being spoken over an area stretching from the Mediterranean to Iran. A simple alphabetic script displaced cuneiform, and was widely used until it was replaced by the Arabic script in the 7th century AD. Aramaic was the original language of some of the later books of the Old Testament (▷ box).

Beyond the Aramaean domains were seven Neo-Hittite states in northern Syria. The name 'Neo-Hittite' has been given to them because of the characteristics they shared with the earlier Hittites. Carchemish, from where a junior branch of the Hittite royal family once ruled Syria, was one of the main Neo-Hittite centres. The Neo-Hittites fought successfully against the Aramaeans, but were conquered by the Assyrians in the 9th and 8th centuries BC.

The Israelites

The Old Testament records the exodus of the Jews from Egypt under Moses and their conquest of Canaan (Palestine) under Joshua. The Israelites destroyed many Canaanite towns, including Ai and ancient Jericho. This conquest is usually dated around 1230 BC. However, the archaeological evidence for the settlement of Canaan by these tribes does not confirm the biblical version of events. The process of settlement was probably more complex than that described in the Bible, with different tribes coming into possession of the land at different times and in a variety of ways.

Following their conflicts with neighbouring peoples, the kingdom of Israel came into being around 1000 BC, with Saul and David as its first kings. David's son and successor, Solomon, employed Phoenician craftsmen to build the temple at Jerusalem. After his death, the kingdom divided into the separate states of Israel in the north and Judah in the south. From the 8th century BC the laws and history of these peoples were written down and have been partly preserved in the Old Testament (▷ box).

About 50 years after the division, Omri became king of Israel. His son, Ahab, married Jezebel, a Tyrian princess. Ahab fought in alliance with Aramaean and other kings against the Assyrians in 853 BC. Within a few years of taking Damascus, the Assyrians captured Samaria, the capital, and Israel became an Assyrian province. Judah remained independent until the Babylonian captivity in 587 BC (▷ p. 21).

The Phoenicians

The people of the Levantine coastal cities called themselves Canaanites. The word 'Phoenician' comes from *Phoi-*

THE FOUNDING OF CARTHAGE

The colonies that the Phoenicians founded on the coast of North Africa and in the western Mediterranean were established for various reasons (▷ map, p. 29). Some were founded as trading posts, some for mining activities – as at Gades (Cadiz) in Spain – and others for victualling, as in the case of Carthage.

Traditionally Carthage (near the site of modern Tunis) was founded from Tyre in 814 BC, on a site chosen for its good harbour. In fact it was probably founded somewhat later, for no artefacts earlier than c. 750 BC have been found there. According to one tradition it was founded by Elissa (Dido), sister of the Tyrian king Pygmalion, from whom she fled after he had killed her husband.

More prosaically, the new colony provided anchorage and supplies for ships trading in the west for minerals, and for about two centuries remained dependent on Tyre. But in time it outstripped the other Phoenician colonies because of its position and excellent harbour. The Carthaginians traded with Spain and the tribes of their African hinterland, exchanging wine, cloth and cheap manufactured goods for metals. They also developed prosperous farms inland and from the 4th century exported agricultural products.

As the city grew more powerful, it gained control of the sea routes to the west. Carthage was surrounded by a huge wall 22 miles long, and equipped with an artificial harbour basin. The city came into conflict with the Greek colonies of Sicily and later with Rome, which destroyed the city in 146 BC (▷ p. 36).

nikes – meaning 'the purple men' – the name the Greeks gave them on account of the famous Tyrian purple dye that they made from the murex sea snail.

Although the Phoenicians had always traded their cedarwood and precious oils, particularly with Egypt, it was not until the 1st millennium BC that they became great seafaring traders. The Mycenaeans, who had formerly controlled the sea lanes, had disappeared at the end of the Bronze Age (▷ p. 25). At about this time the keel is thought to have come into use, making possible longer voyages on the open sea.

Most ancient of the coastal cities was Byblos (ancient Gubla), but Tyre was to become the greatest and wealthiest. As well as dye and textiles, the Phoenicians exported glassware, carved ivory, jewellery and metal goods. From the 10th century they went searching for metals, and on Cyprus – the 'copper island' – founded the colony of Kition. They sailed to Britain to obtain tin from Cornwall, and in Spain founded the colony of Gades (modern Cadiz) to extract its rich silver deposits. Carthage, their most famous colony, developed into a major maritime power (▷ box and p. 36).

The Phoenician cities remained prosperous through the various political changes wrought in the Near East. The Assyrians took generous tribute from them – large quantities of Phoenician ivories have been found at Nimrud (▷ p. 20). The Phoenicians' great legacy to posterity was the alphabetic writing system. Canaanite alphabetic systems were used to write Semitic languages such as Phoenician, Hebrew and Aramaic. From the Phoenicians the system was adopted by the Greeks, who made changes to it to suit their own language. The system continues to be used today, in the Greek and Latin scripts.   MO

SEE ALSO

- ANCIENT EGYPT p. 17
- BABYLONIA AND ASSYRIA p. 20
- MINOANS AND MYCENAEANS p. 24
- THE RISE OF ROME p. 36
- THE ANCIENT ECONOMY p. 42
- WARFARE IN THE ANCIENT WORLD p. 44
- ANCIENT RELIGIONS p. 46

A Neo-Hittite relief (left) from the 8th century BC. Later Hittite stone sculpture shows the influence of Syrian, Assyrian and – less frequently – Phoenician and Egyptian motifs.

Minoans and Mycenaeans

Long before the classical era two great civilizations flourished in the area of the Aegean Sea. The existence of the Minoans and the Mycenaeans was unknown until late in the 19th century. The Minoans were named after the legendary King Minos, and the Mycenaeans take their name from one of the major centres of their culture, the city of Mycenae, home of Agamemnon, the mythological king who led the Greeks against Troy.

Boxing children in a fresco from the Minoan site found at Akrotiri on the island of Thera (modern Santoríni).

Minoan civilization, based on the island of Crete, reached its peak in the Middle and Late Bronze Age between 2200 and 1450 BC. The height of the Mycenaean culture of mainland Greece is slightly later – about 1500 to 1150 BC.

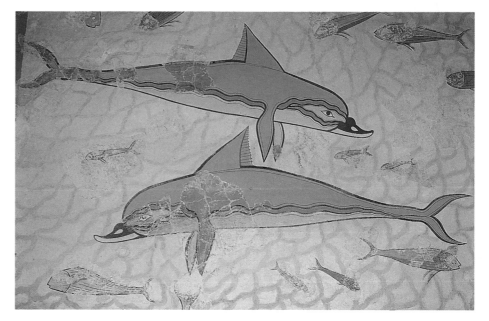

The rise of Minoan civilization

Early in the Middle Bronze Age, about 2200 BC, the first palaces began to be built on Crete, most notably at the sites of later palaces at Knossos and Phaistos. At this time writing also appeared in the Aegean region. The script, called Linear A, was mostly impressed on unbaked clay tablets, but signs painted or scratched on vases are also common. The language is as yet undeciphered, and practically all that can be determined is that the Minoans were not Greek-speakers. Some writing appears in religious contexts, although mostly it seems to have been used for administrative purposes.

It is not clear whether there was one great Minoan 'king' or several smaller leaders ruling on Crete. There are several important palace sites – for example, Phaistos, Aghia Triadha and Mallia – but the palace at Knossos is by far the largest, so perhaps the most important king resided there. Another indication of centralized power is the fact that there is little local variation in Minoan, especially late Minoan, pottery, which may suggest it

A fresco with dolphins from the palace of Knossos, the greatest of the Minoan palaces on Crete. The palace was excavated and partially restored between 1899 and 1935 by the British archaeologist Sir Arthur Evans, the first man to discover the remains of Minoan civilization. The complex floor-plan of the palace may have given rise to the later Greek myth of the labyrinth, in which the Minotaur – a bull with a man's head – lurked in wait for Theseus.

was controlled by (if not made in) a single centre.

The Minoans were great seafarers, and there is evidence of some Minoan presence on the Aegean islands. There are many representations of ships and other marine motifs on pottery and wall paintings, and the palaces are full of beautiful things brought back from abroad. Crete is also mentioned in ancient Egyptian documents as 'Kheftiu'.

The palace at Knossos

The palace, along with the luxurious houses that surrounded it, reveals much about the life of the Minoan elite. The palace alone covers about 1.3 ha (3 acres). There is a large central courtyard, and the

THE ERUPTION OF THERA

The small island of Thera (modern Santoríni) is the Pompeii of the Aegean Bronze Age. The remarkable site of Akrotiri, once a Minoan port town whose ancient name is unknown, was buried by a gigantic volcanic eruption around 1500–1450 BC. The force of the blast blew away an entire section of the island, accounting for its present-day crescent shape. Houses with brightly coloured wall paintings, pottery, tools and all the implements of everyday life have been discovered at Akrotiri in a well-preserved state. Extensive finds of food, animal bones and seeds have allowed archaeologists to reconstruct the diet and economy of the Minoan period.

There has been much speculation about how widespread the effects of the Thera

eruption were. Some scholars have speculated that it might have contributed to the decline of Minoan civilization. Some identify it with the myth of the lost island of Atlantis, which Plato described in the 4th century BC. Dust from the eruption has been found on Cretan sites. However, although at the time the dust must have darkened the sky for several days at least, it does not seem to have caused any long-term problems for Crete. The biggest mystery surrounding the eruption of Thera is its precise date. Carbon-14 dating (⇨ p. 7) does not seem to work properly on Theran material, probably because of the effects of the volcano on radioactive carbon levels in the atmosphere.

floor-plan is very complicated, with hundreds of rooms.

Little is known about the upper storeys of the palace – there was at least one – but the ground floor and the basement rooms, which are probably not the grandest, are better preserved. Most striking are the large numbers of storage rooms, some filled with enormous storage jars, probably to hold wine and olive oil. Other rooms probably contained metals, textiles and dry foodstuffs like grain. Such remains show that the rulers who lived here had the power to collect tribute and to redistribute it to their allies and friends.

In many rooms of the palace at Knossos the walls are beautifully painted with scenes from Minoan life. Most are of people – beautiful young men in kilts and women in elegant, topless dresses. There are also scenes vividly depicting plant and animal life.

The palace suffered several phases of destruction, but it is not known for certain what caused any of these events, and the chronology is shaky. It has been suggested that the damage around 1500 BC might be related to earthquakes occurring between 1550 and 1500, when the great eruption of Thera occurred (▷ box), but this is only a remote possibility. Since palace records after a destruction around 1450 BC are in Mycenaean Linear B script (▷ below), it has been suggested that Mycenaean invaders might have been responsible.

Minoan religion

Some wall paintings from Knossos and elsewhere seem to depict religious scenes, such as those of young men and women performing acrobatics over charging bulls. It has been suggested that the arena for these extraordinary games might have been the courtyard of the palace itself. Some of the women may be goddesses and some religious symbols are present, like the sign of the double axe or the bulls' horns.

The true complexity of Minoan religion is still beyond the reach of archaeologists. There are no Minoan 'temples' as such, but there are a few shrines, one of which is in the basement of the palace at Knossos. Perhaps, given its underground location, it was dedicated to an earth deity. Some sites, like that of Aghia Triadha, seem to have had special religious significance.

The Mycenaeans

The Mycenaeans, who replaced the Minoans as the dominant power in the Aegean from about 1450 BC, were based in citadel cities with great palaces throughout mainland Greece. The most important sites include Mycenae, Tiryns, Pylos, Thebes, Gla and Athens. It is unlikely that any one king controlled the whole of Greece in this period, although some palaces are clearly much richer than others.

The earliest evidence of a powerful Mycenaean nobility comes from the shaft graves of Mycenae, which are arranged in

---

THE TROJAN WAR: FACT OR MYTH?

It has long been asked if the later Greek tradition of the Trojan War preserves memories of the glorious Mycenaean past and the destruction of Mycenaean civilization. It is certainly true that some elements of the *Iliad* and the *Odyssey* belong in the Bronze Age, although the poems – traditionally attributed to Homer – were probably written down in their final form around 750–700 BC (▷ p. 44).

It is difficult to relate these epics to the archaeological remains of Mycenaean civilization with any certainty. Clearly, there were Mycenaean contacts with Troy (probably the mound at modern Hissarlik in northwest Turkey). There is more Mycenaean pottery from this site than from any other site in Anatolia, but Mycenaean pottery still represents only a minute proportion of the total pottery found there. Perhaps the Homeric traditions contain genuine memories from the troubled times at the end of the Bronze Age. But if they do, it is impossible for historians to dissect the poetry to find the truth.

---

two circles outside the city walls and which date from c. 1600 BC (▷ picture). The large amounts of gold and other metals deposited in them provide an awesome reminder of the wealth and strength of the city's rulers.

Mycenaean cities and palaces

The cities themselves were massively fortified, the walls made of huge, irregular blocks. The actual palaces were much simpler than in Crete, the most important feature being the *megaron*, a hall with a central hearth flanked by two columns.

From the records at Pylos, Mycenae, Thebes and other sites, we know that Mycenaean palaces, like those of the Minoans, were centres of political and economic control. These records were written on unbaked clay tablets in a script called Linear B, which is similar to Minoan Linear A, but the language is a form of Greek.

It is clear from these records that the Mycenaean kings had control of vast amounts of land, full of flocks and crops, and worked on by great numbers of slaves. The palaces seem to have supervised the manufacture and trade of many crucial commodities, such as metals.

Like the Minoan palaces, Mycenaean palaces were full of treasures and works of art commissioned by the nobility. Walls were painted, but not usually so elaborately as in Crete. Many luxury items were imported from abroad, and Mycenaean pottery is found in Syria, Palestine, Egypt and elsewhere.

Mycenaean religion

The Linear B tablets reveal that the Mycenaeans worshipped many of the gods and goddesses familiar from later Greek religion (▷ p. 46). There were priests and priestesses who received offerings for the deities at their shrines. The remains of several Mycenaean shrines, with religious statues, have been found.

The end of the Greek Bronze Age

Around 1200–1100 BC several of the palaces seem to have been destroyed, and it is still a mystery why such rich and powerful civilizations suddenly declined at this period. Many suggestions have been made, including internal dissent and revolution, climatic change, and foreign invaders – the Dorians – from the north. It is probable that the true reasons for their decline are complex, and possible that all the suggestions made are partially right in some way. It has been securely established now that at least some Mycenaeans settled on Cyprus at this time. Whatever the cause of Mycenaean decline, Greece at this time entered a 'dark age' from which it did not emerge until the beginning of the Archaic period, in about 800 BC (▷ p. 28). LF

SEE ALSO

● ARCHAEOLOGY p. 6
● HUMAN PREHISTORY p. 12
● ARCHAIC AND CLASSICAL GREECE p. 28
● ANCIENT WARFARE p. 44
● ANCIENT RELIGIONS p. 46

The shaft graves at Mycenae, the principal late Bronze Age site on mainland Greece. Heinrich Schliemann (▷ p. 7), the German archaeologist who first uncovered the treasures of the site in 1876, believed that he had found the city of Agamemnon, the Mycenaean king who led the Greek forces in the Trojan War. However, subsequent research has revealed that he had discovered the tombs of kings who reigned around 1600 BC, about 400 years before the commonly accepted date for the fall of Troy.

The Persian Empire

For some two hundred years, from the 6th until the late 4th century BC, the empire of the Persian Achaemenids was the largest that the Near East had seen. From their Iranian homeland, Cyrus the Great and his successors conquered the whole of the Near East including Anatolia, Egypt and part of northwest India. In 330 BC, the last Achaemenid was murdered and Alexander the Great became ruler of this vast empire.

Indo-European Aryans are thought to have entered Iran from a homeland in southern Russia in the latter half of the 2nd millennium BC (▷ p. 58). These people gave their name to Iran, meaning 'land of the Aryans'. Among their descendants were the Medes and Persians, who are known from Assyrian texts to have occupied western Iran from the mid-9th century BC.

The Medes and Persians

In the 9th century the Medes were probably a loose tribal confederation, but by the 7th century BC they had united, and controlled, a large area around their capital, Ecbatana (modern Hamadan in Iran). By the end of the century, the Medes were attacking Assyrian cities. They formed an alliance with the Babylonians, and in 612 BC their combined forces besieged and captured Nineveh (▷ p. 21). As part of the spoils, the Medes received Assyria's northern domains, reaching to central Anatolia, where they came into conflict with the Lydians. Peace was made in 585 BC, and the Halys river became the boundary between Lydia and Median territory.

By the 7th century BC, the Persians, now settled in the south west of Iran, were subjects of the Medes. The Assyrian defeat of Elam allowed the Persians to settle in this region, which became known as Parsa (modern Fars). From Parsa (*Persis* in Greek) comes the name 'Persia', which the Greeks were the first to give to the whole of Iran.

Astyages (585–550 BC), the last king of the Medes, was overthrown by Cyrus II ('the Great'), of the ruling Achaemenid dynasty of Persia (Fars), who had succeeded his father Cambyses I in 559 BC. Having established good relations with various Persian and other Iranian groups, he rebelled against Astyages and defeated him in 549. This made him ruler of both the Medes and the Persians, and by according equal status to the former, he gained their support.

Foundation of the empire

Cyrus now turned west to Anatolia (modern Turkey), where Croesus, the wealthy king of Lydia, was attempting to expand his territory beyond the Halys boundary. Having consulted the Delphic Oracle, which told him that if he crossed the Halys a great empire would fall, Croesus – interpreting the ambiguous prophecy to his own advantage – advanced beyond the river. After an inconclusive battle, the Lydians returned to their capital, Sardis, which was attacked and captured by Cyrus in 546 BC.

Leaving one of his generals to complete the conquest of Anatolia, Cyrus returned to Iran. It was probably at this time that he took Bactria and Sogdiana in the northeast, reaching the Jaxartes river (modern Syr Darya). Meanwhile, Lycia, Caria and the Greek cities of the Ionian coast had been added to the newly formed empire. Following his eastern campaigns Cyrus advanced to Babylon. After a battle at nearby Opis, Cyrus entered Babylon without opposition in October 539 BC (▷ p. 21).

With the capture of Babylon, Cyrus acquired the Babylonian Empire, which reached to the borders of Egypt. But he did not seize the Babylonian throne as a conqueror, instead taking Babylonian titles and ruling according to local custom. Foreign exiles were repatriated, amongst them the Jews of Jerusalem (▷ pp. 21 and 23). Having returned to Iran, he was killed in battle on the northeastern frontier in 530 BC and was buried at Pasargadae, the capital he had founded in Persia.

The Achaemenid Empire

Cambyses II (530–522 BC) succeeded his father and four years later, in 526 BC, conquered Egypt. He advanced beyond the first cataract of the Nile and also made gains to the west, beyond Cyrene. The Persian Empire now reached from the Nile to the borders of Central Asia. Greek tradition portrayed Cambyses as a madman and a tyrant, but there is no other evidence for this (▷ box). In fact, so effective was his consolidation of Persian rule in Egypt that there was no rebellion there until 486 BC, shortly before the death of his successor. In 522 BC, Cambyses left Egypt to return to Persia, where revolt had broken out, possibly led by his brother Bardiya. However, he died before reaching home.

It took Darius I (521–486 BC), an Achaemenid of a junior branch of the family and spearbearer to Cambyses, almost two years to put down this widespread rebellion and restore peace. His version of the defeat of the rebels is recorded on a large trilingual inscription at Bisitun. On it he also stated his justification for taking the throne, which he claimed was his right through his pater-

PERSIA IN GREEK LITERATURE

In 472 BC, eight years after the Greek victory over the Persians at Salamis, Aeschylus's play, *The Persians*, was produced. His theme, the victory of Athens at Salamis (▷ p. 30), is presented as the focal point in Persia's defeat. This event was of undoubted importance in Greek history, and in their literature it came also to be seen as a turning point for the Achaemenid Empire. In Greek tradition before this time, particularly under Cyrus II, the Persians were portrayed as having good qualities: they were strong, energetic, tolerant and truthful. But thereafter, the Greeks had little good to say of them: their government was weak, they were corrupt and effete, and ruined by wealth and luxurious living. Implicit in this view of the Persians was the idea that as Orientals (and therefore barbarians) they were the opposite of all that was good and Greek.

Such was the standard portrayal of the Persians by Greek authors. However, in his great *History*, Herodotus (c. 490/80–c. 425 BC), whose views were less simplistic, wrote about Greeks who were far from perfect, and Persians who were not all worthless. Sadly, Herodotus's view was to be discredited after the publication of Ktesias's *Persika*, whose inaccurate account of the Eastern world became the accepted version. In Xenophon's historical romance *The Education of Cyrus*, the tradition of the virtuous Persians of Cyrus' time is continued. But in complete contrast to the rest of the book, the final chapter relates the decline of virtually every aspect of Persian civilization since the age of Cyrus. It was probably a later addition to Xenophon's work and written to counteract his positive image of the Persians. According to its author – whose account of contemporary Persians may be regarded as a paradigm for the representation of Persia in Greek literature – 'As soon as Cyrus was dead, his children fell into dissension . . . and everything began to deteriorate.'

nal ancestors. In fact, it would seem that he had the support of a group of nobles who were opposed to the rebellion, as well as that of much of the army.

In the early years of his reign, Darius campaigned in northwest India, further extending the Empire. He also fought against the nomadic Scythians, north of the Black Sea, but without success. Under Darius, the Achaemenid Empire reached its greatest extent, reaching from the Nile to the Indus.

The organization of the Empire

Darius, a brilliant administrator, divided the Empire into provinces or 'satrapies'. The governor, or 'satrap', was usually a loyal Persian noble or member of the royal family. Within each satrapy, a separate official was responsible for the army and for collecting the annual tribute, which was paid in kind, as well as in gold or silver. The reliefs of the tribute-bearers at Persepolis (▷ below) show that a wide

A vase handle in the form of a winged ibex, from Samsun on the southern shore of the Black Sea. Achaemenid metalworking, especially in gold, reached a sophisticated level of development.

range of products were offered as tribute, including ivory, incense, textiles, honey, and even giraffes and camels.

Darius also reorganized the army and built a fleet. A canal was cut from the Red Sea to the Nile, enabling ships to travel between the Mediterranean and the Indian Ocean. Most importantly, he built a great system of roads, which made travelling faster and easier. Taking advantage of the staging posts and fresh horses along the way, a royal courier could travel the Royal Road from Susa to Sardis – some 2700 km (1670 mi) – in a week. Other innovations introduced by Darius included a postal system and coinage. His subjects also had recourse to a legal system.

Under Darius the capital was moved from Pasargadae to Susa, which became the main administrative centre. The other capitals were used for ceremonial functions or as summer quarters. Darius carried out extensive building works both at Susa and at Persepolis. The function of Persepolis is not known for certain, for there are no surrounding dwellings and it does not seem to have been lived in continuously. It is possible that the tribute was submitted here, perhaps at the time of the New Year celebrations.

The conflict with Greece
Nothing of the conflict between the Greeks and the Persians (⮞ p. 29) is known from Persian sources, although it has achieved fame from the great history of Herodotus, an Ionian Greek (⮞ box). The war began with a revolt of Persia's subject Ionian cities, which was put down in 494 BC. Four years later Darius attacked Athens, but the Persians were defeated at Marathon. Darius was succeeded by his son, Xerxes (486–465 BC), who crushed a rebellion in Egypt shortly after his accession and three years later put down a revolt in Babylon. Xerxes reversed the Persian tradition of tolerance, ignoring local traditions and pursuing ruthless policies after his victories.

In 480 BC Xerxes invaded the Greek main-

land at the head of a large army. After initial successes, the campaign foundered with defeats at Salamis and Plataea, before which time Xerxes had returned to Persia, leaving his general Mardonius in charge. The rest of his reign was spent attending to his building programme at Persepolis and dealing with harem intrigues, which were to lead to his assassination in 465.

Persian involvement in the affairs of Greece continued through the reigns of the next three kings. Persia temporarily relinquished her interest in the Aegean with the Peace of Callias (449–8 BC) and, in return, Athens promised not to intervene in the Greek cities of Asia Minor (Ionia). But during the Peloponnesian War between Athens and Sparta (⮞ p. 29), Persia once again intervened, and gave assistance to whichever side would favour her interests.

The decline of the Empire
In 405 BC, Egypt revolted and was lost, to be regained only very briefly a few years later. Henceforth there was almost constant strife or rebellion in some part of the empire. Three years after the loss of Egypt, the brother of Artaxerxes II (405–359 BC), Cyrus the Younger, hired 10 000 Greek mercenaries and marched east to depose his brother and seize the throne, but was killed in battle (401 BC) at Cunaxa. One of the Greek generals, Xenophon, described these events, and the long homeward journey across Anatolia, in his *Anabasis*. The Greeks' achievement in reaching home safely was a measure of the weakness of the Persian Empire at this time. Artaxerxes put down the satraps' revolt (373 BC) only with difficulty, and was obliged to give back provinces to satraps who had rebelled.

By now harem conspiracies and assassinations were endemic, and the reigns of the last Achaemenid kings all began or ended with murders. Artaxerxes III, who had murdered his way to the throne and imposed a reign of terror, was himself slain by his minister, the powerful eunuch

Bagoas. The man who owed his elevation to Bagoas' scheming – Darius III, the last Achaemenid – was defeated by Alexander of Macedon at Issos and Gaugamela and finally murdered by his own nobles (⮞ p. 32). After Alexander's death, his generals fought each other for control of this vast region, and for a time Iran itself became part of the Hellenistic world.

For all the problems of the later Empire, Persian rule was in general tolerant and not repressive. In the satrapies conquered peoples were able to keep their own customs and religions and benefited from efficient administration and local courts of law. The quality of Persian imperial rule can perhaps be judged by the behaviour of its subject peoples at the time of the Macedonian invasion. Apart from Egypt and some, but by no means all, of the Ionian cities, they did not rise up against their Persian rulers. Indeed, many of them fought steadfastly and with valour on the side of Persia. MO

Persian archers (left) in an enamelled brick relief from the palace of Darius at Susa. Darius undertook an ambitious programme of construction after making Susa his administrative capital in 521 BC. The architectural style that developed under Darius remained unchanged until the demise of the Achaemenid Empire.

SEE ALSO
● BABYLONIA AND ASSYRIA p. 20
● ARCHAIC AND CLASSICAL GREECE p. 28
● ALEXANDER THE GREAT AND THE HELLENISTIC WORLD p. 32
● ANCIENT RELIGIONS p. 46
● THE RISE OF ISLAM p. 82

PARTHIANS AND SASSANIANS

Parthia, a satrapy in northeast Iran, seceded from the Hellenistic Seleucid kingdom in the mid-3rd century BC. The Parthian dynasty was founded by Arsaces in 247 BC. Mithridates I (171–138 BC) gained control of Iran c. 148–7 BC, and Mesopotamia in 141 BC. Under Mithridates II (124–87 BC), who campaigned as far east as the Euphrates in Syria, Parthia reached its greatest extent. In 53 BC the Parthians defeated Rome at Carrhae (Harran) in northern Syria. But by the 2nd century AD, much territory had been lost to Rome, and Parthia was in decline. The last Parthian king, Artabanus V, was overthrown in AD 226 by Ardashir, first ruler of the Sassanian dynasty.

The Sassanian Shapur I (AD 240–272) expanded the borders north and east to Central Asia and Pakistan, and southwest to the eastern coast of Arabia. Rome, and later the Byzantine Empire, were the traditional enemies of Sassanian Persia (⮞ p. 80), but in the end the Sassanians were defeated by the armies of Islam (⮞ p. 83). In 637 their capital, Ctesiphon (modern Baghdad), was captured and Yazdigird III, the last Sassanian king, was murdered by his nobles.

Both the Parthians and Sassanians saw themselves as the successors of the Achaemenids. The rejection of the Greek past began under the Parthians. They used the ancient Achaemenid title 'King of Kings' on their coins, and reliefs echoing ancient motifs were placed at the ancient sites. The Sassanians – particularly in their devotion to Zoroastrianism (which they turned into a state religion) – exceeded the Parthians in their claims to be the preservers of the Iranian and Achaemenid traditions.

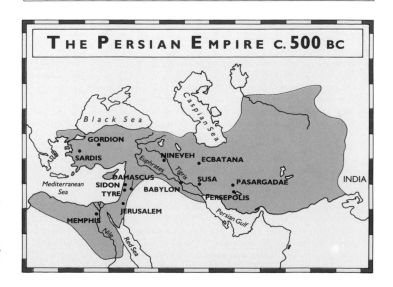

THE PERSIAN EMPIRE C. 500 BC

Archaic and Classical Greece

The typical unit of political and social organization in ancient Greece was the *polis* or independent city-state. City-states arose in many parts of the Greek-speaking world during the 8th century BC at the beginning of the so-called Archaic period (c. 800–500 BC). This development marked the end of a long period of poverty that had followed the collapse of Mycenaean civilization (▷ p. 25). In the Archaic period, and still more in the following Classical period (c. 500–338 BC), the Greeks made radical experiments in the conduct of politics, which gave large numbers of citizens a significant role in the making of decisions, and created a general openness and freedom of political argument. This atmosphere of rational debate encouraged the exploration of new ideas in many other areas of life, including art, literature and philosophy (▷ box, p. 30). All of these developments have had a lasting impact on Western civilization.

The geography of Greece, with many small plains and valleys surrounded by high mountains, encouraged the formation of many small states. However,

THE SOCIAL LIFE OF THE CITY STATE

For all its political experimentation, and encouragement of debate, the Greek city-state often failed to achieve internal stability, and Classical Greece did not achieve political unity. The more successful states tended to win prosperity for their citizens by exploiting other cities: through empire, league or confederacy. However, their dominance over other city-states was often short-lived.

Furthermore, the Greek city-states were all 'male clubs'; women were excluded from all political rights and participation, and regarded as intellectually and emotionally inferior to men. Respectable women – the wives and daughters of citizens – were 'protected' from the dangerous attentions of other men and from their own supposedly more wicked natures. A high value was placed on their chastity, and their prime duty was to marry and produce children.

Finally the Greek city-state was a club dominated by a privileged elite of 'club-members' – the citizens – and was to a greater or lesser extent economically dependent on the labour of subject classes. Sparta had its helots (▷ text and p. 42), and some other cities had comparable serf-like labour forces. But more commonly the Greeks used 'chattel-slaves', purchased or captured from non-Greek communities. The extent to which Athens, and Athenian democracy, depended on slave-labour is a subject of much debate. A crucial question is whether ordinary peasant-citizens – as well as the richer land-owners and manufacturers – used slave-labour on their farms in addition to family labour and mutual help between neighbours. The political freedom and democracy of peasant-citizens could certainly not have been created and maintained without the existence of an alternative, relatively cheap, source of labour for the rich and the better-off. Slavery was a fundamental and unquestioned part of Greek society, and the distinction between slave and free citizen was of central importance in the ways Greek male citizens conceived of their identities and their social and moral values.

factors other than geographical remoteness were probably more important in creating and maintaining such states, each with its own powerful sense of individual identity. A city-state usually consisted of an agricultural territory (in which the vast majority of its citizens worked), and a fortified town, at the centre of which were open areas for temples and other public buildings, communal meetings and trading activity. The identity of each city-state was reinforced by the development of religious rituals for their protective gods and heroes, and by a shared involvement in the making of political and legal decisions.

The Archaic city-state

Initially the government of these city-states was mainly aristocratic. Though decisions might be put to assemblies of all citizens, small groups of noble families tended to monopolize political, religious and cultural life. However, from about 750 BC on this aristocratic dominance was progressively undermined. Firstly, the reintroduction of literacy into Greece (c. 750 BC) led to the public display of written versions of the laws, enabling citizens to question, and perhaps to change, what had previously been under the strict control of the aristocrats. Secondly, from around 800 BC there was a considerable expansion of trade with other lands, and many new Greek city-states webe established around the Mediterranean and the Black Sea (▷ box and map, p. 29). The setting up of new cities, with new laws and a fresh distribution of land, also encouraged questioning of the distribution of power and wealth at home. Thirdly, the gradual introduction of hoplite armour and tactics – which relied on massed ranks of heavily armed infantrymen (hoplites), rather than on a small number of nobles on horses or in chariots – gave the ordinary people a greater potential power and self-confidence (▷ p. 44).

Thus new laws began to restrict the power of the nobles. In a number of cities government by hereditary nobles was replaced, for a generation or two, by the rule of a 'tyrant', a usurper who seized power with the support of the hoplites. As a result of such upheavals, in many city-states power came to be held by a small group (an oligarchy), defined now by wealth rather than by birth, although important issues might still be put to the citizens.

Archaic Sparta

By the end of the Archaic period, two city-states, Sparta and Athens, had become particularly important. They developed in very different ways. In the 8th century the Spartans gained control of most of the southern Peloponnese (the large peninsula in southern Greece). Some of the defeated peoples (the *perioikoi*, or 'neighbours') were left to run their own communities but were required to provide troops. However, the majority (the 'helots') became 'state serfs', compelled to work the fields of the Spartans under brutal conditions (▷ p. 42). Sparta was thus faced with the need to control a large subject population of Greeks who remembered their former

A hoplite warrior, part of the frieze on the the neck of the krater of Vix, a huge (1.64 m/5 ft 5 in high) bronze wine-mixing vessel dating from the late 6th century BC. Probably of Spartan origin, its discovery in the burial mound of a Gallic princess in eastern France indicates the existence of direct trading links between Archaic Greece and the Celtic world. Such artefacts may have been offered to non-Greek chiefs to win their approval for trade with the Greeks, especially in metals.

freedom, and did in fact revolt at regular intervals.

In the mid-7th century BC a major helot revolt occurred, and at about the same time Spartan citizens – now organized in a hoplite army – won more political rights and a more equitable distribution of land. Socially, however, Sparta was transformed into a tightly regimented and authoritarian state, with a high respect for authority, hierarchy and the officials of the state (two kings, a council of elders appointed for life, and five annually appointed 'ephors', or judicial and executive magistrates).

All Spartan boys, from the age of seven onwards, were subjected to a rigorous educational and training programme, and all adult males who completed this programme were organized into life-long and uniform 'messes' (*syssitia*) of about 15–20. Membership of a mess was a qualification for citizenship, and Spartans were expected to spend more time with their mess-mates than with their own families.

During the 6th century BC the reorganized Sparta, through military and diplomatic means, created the 'Peloponnesian League', a network of alliances throughout the Peloponnese, and became the most powerful state in Greece.

Archaic Athens

The first steps towards democracy in Athens were made by Solon, who was appointed in 594 to create new laws after a period of serious unrest between rich and poor, especially over the use of land. Solon's reforms freed many peasant-citizens from various forms of dependence on richer landowners and debts (▷ p. 42), and did much to establish the peasants in ownership of their lands. His laws encouraged all citizens to participate in the assembly, in the prosecution of legal cases, and as jurors in a new people's court of appeal. He introduced a division of all citizens based on wealth, but restricted the various offices to the better-off classes (where previously they had been restricted to certain noble families).

Political discontent continued, and the leader of the poorer peasants, Peisistratos, established himself as tyrant. He and his sons ruled Athens from about 545 to 510 BC. Like Solon they helped to secure the peasants on their lands, and their building and religious programme helped to unify the city-state as a whole; but the regime became unpopular and cruel in its later years. This period of one-man rule had the effect – not wholly intended – of discrediting both the former domination of the aristocrats and the idea of tyranny itself.

After further conflict new reforms proposed by Cleisthenes in 508–7 BC created more democratic means of decision-making at local and city level, and a more unified Athens. At local level, 139 newly defined 'demes' – local villages or divisions of the city – were created. These became the units into which all citizens had to be enrolled, and were run by an open assembly and annually elected officers. The demes were linked, through a complex structure, to 10 'tribes', in such a way that every tribe had members from each of the three regions of Attica (coastal, inland and city). 'Tribal' contingents fought together in the hoplite army, and tribal representatives were selected by lot to serve in the new 'Council of Five Hundred'. The Council prepared business for the assembly and performed an increasing number of administrative activities. Cleisthenes also introduced the curious institution of ostracism, whereby Athenians could vote for a politician to be banished from the city for ten years; its purpose was probably both to avoid another tyranny, and to resolve serious political disputes by exiling an advocate of the less popular policy. Helped by these reforms, Athens became a more effective military power, and fought off attempts by Sparta to destroy the new style of government.

The Persian Wars

The growing power of the Persian Empire (▷ p. 26) had led by c. 500 BC to its dominance over the Greek cities of western Anatolia (modern Turkey). Athenian support for an unsuccessful revolt against Persian rule by these cities (500–494 BC) led in 490 BC to the first invasion by the Persians of the Greek mainland. This was repulsed by the Athenians in the land battle at Marathon.

A much more serious invasion followed in 480 BC, under the new Persian king, Xerxes. An anti-Persian alliance was formed under the leadership of Sparta, which provided the most powerful infantry. Athens had the largest fleet, which had recently been expanded using the

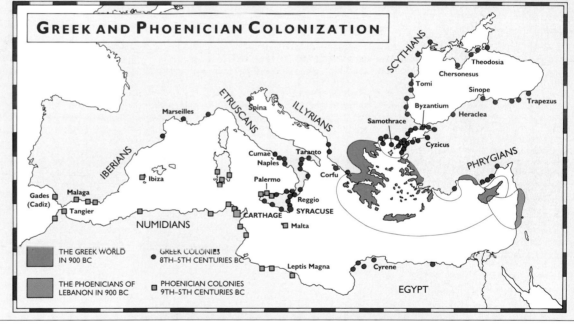

profits of the silver mines in southern Attica. After the initial heroic defeat at Thermopylae, the combined Greek forces defeated the Persians at sea at Salamis (480), and on land the next year at Plataea. These victories (▷ map, p. 31) helped to keep Greece free from external domination for a further 150 years, and confirmed Sparta and Athens as the two major Greek powers. They also greatly heightened the Greeks' sense of their superiority – military, political, and cultural – over all foreigners, whom they called 'Barbarians' (▷ box, p. 26). The fact that the Athenian fleet was manned by the poorest citizens (▷ p. 44) was a crucial factor in the development of Athenian democracy. One Athenian, Themistocles, as well as being the main driving force behind the development of the Athenian navy and the strategy adopted in 480–79 BC, also recognized that naval

dominance could lead to greater political dominance for all Athenian citizens.

Athenian empire and Athenian democracy

The Greek fleet pursued the Persians across the Aegean and 'liberated' the Greek cities from Persian rule. In 478 BC Athens assumed leadership of a new alliance, the Delian League (based on the island of Delos). A number of victories were won under the dynamic leadership of Cimon, and by c. 465 BC the Persians had been pushed back as far as Cyprus. Active fighting ceased by c. 450 BC.

Meanwhile the League was increasingly dominated by Athens. Cities were forced to pay tribute, either in ships or money, and any who tried to leave were forcibly brought into line. Athenian interference in the politics and economies of its allies grew. Although measures such as the imposition of garrisons and the confiscation of land for the use of poorer Athenian citizens were unpopular, the introduction of more democratic governments, the increase in trade and reduction of piracy were welcomed by many in the allied cities. By the 440s the League could more appropriately be described as an Athenian empire.

During this period Athens completed the development of its democracy, under the leadership of Ephialtes and Pericles. The aristocratic council (the Areopagus) lost most of its power: the popular juries – consisting of 6000 citizens appointed by lot each year – heard all law suits except homicide, and the scrutiny of all office-holders and their conduct was shared between the Council of Five Hundred, the assembly, and the juries. Modest payment for juries, the Council and other offices increased the level of participation of the poorer citizens. Finally, Athenian citizenship and its advantages were made a more exclusive privilege. After 451–50, to be registered in a deme as a citizen, a youth had to have an Athenian mother as well as a citizen father. The main reason for this measure was to ensure that all Athenians could find citizen fathers for their daughters.

From 462 BC until his death Pericles took an increasingly influential role in Athenian politics, and particularly from 443 BC he exercised a degree of dominance in policy-making that was quite exceptional, since the democratic system had no fixed position for a single individual. At this time Athens was at its most prosperous, successful and powerful. But its use of power did not lead to the unity of Greece. Many in its empire, especially the rich, resented Athenian control, and Sparta and its rival power bloc of the Peloponnesian League were suspicious of its growing power. Relations between Athens and Sparta became openly hostile in 461 BC, and there was sporadic fighting between 460 and 445, followed by an uneasy peace.

The Peloponnesian War

Lasting from 431 to 404 BC, this major war, as its great historian Thucydides observed (▷ p. 2), was one of the most destructive in Greek history, and had a profound effect on Greek society. Its immediate origins lay in areas where the interests of Athens and the Peloponnesians overlapped, especially Corinth, Megara and Aegina (▷ map). In 431 BC the complaints of the Athenian allies, and the refusal of Athens to compromise, led the Spartans to declare war. The fundamental reason, as Thucydides suggested, may have been Spartan fear of losing control over its own allies.

Sparta was strong on land and Athens strong at sea, and for long each avoided a decisive battle. Since one side tended to support democracies and the other oligarchies, and each tried to win over the other's allies, the war greatly intensified the political and economic struggles inside many Greek cities, and there were many savage outbreaks of civil war. In Athens itself after the death of Pericles, a more populist set of politicians appeared, and as each vied for the sort of dominance Pericles had achieved, political and social tensions increased.

A temporary peace was made in 421 BC, but relations between the states remained unsettled. In 416 Athens committed the most notorious of the acts of atrocity of which both sides were guilty, the total destruction of the small island of Melos, which had refused to join its empire. The following year Athens made the serious mistake of committing large resources to an attack on the democratic city of Syracuse, with the further aim of the conquest of the whole of Sicily; Syracuse responded by appealing for Spartan help. The man behind the Athenian expedition was Alcibiades, an ambitious relative of Pericles. Despite his abilities, democratic Athens was never able for long to tolerate his wild lifestyle and contempt for conventions. In 415 he was implicated in religious scandals (▷ p. 47) and – to avoid trial in Athens – he fled to Sparta, giving the Spartans useful strategic advice. The Sicilian expedition was a major disaster for Athens. Its large forces there were destroyed in 413, and Sparta renewed the war in Greece with enthusiasm, holding a fort in Attica and attacking the Athenian Empire in the Aegean.

What was decisive in the long run was that the Persians increasingly contributed to the expenses of the Spartan fleet.

ATHENIAN CULTURE AND ITS CONTEXT

Athens was the most open and innovative of the Greek city-states, as well as one of the most prosperous. Its varied cultural activities and achievements were on the whole valued highly by the majority of its citizens, and reflected and questioned their political and social concerns. They have had a profound and continuous influence on the subsequent history of Western civilization.

Greek art and architecture focused distinctively on proportion, formal balance, and human scale; Greek figurative art concentrated on human activities, often by presenting scenes from myth. From the mid-6th century on Athenian potters and painters came to dominate the painted pottery market, most of whose products were designed for use at the all-male social gathering of the *symposium,* or drinking party. They painted, often movingly or humorously, scenes from everyday life as well as from myth, and developed a sophisticated 'language' of conventions to connect the two, and to present the concerns of the lives of their clients. Athens' great temples and other public buildings, together with their sculptures, were sponsored by the state at enormous cost. The successes of the Persian Wars were commemorated in the major programme of public buildings on the Athenian acropolis and elsewhere, which was planned by Pericles and his architect-sculptor Pheidias, and paid for by the profits of the Athenian Empire. The buildings attracted artists and craftsmen from all over the Greek world, and reflected Athenian gratitude to the gods for its victories, and its confidence in its own political and cultural superiority (▷ p. 42).

Athenian drama – the entertainment that the Athenian people supported and valued most – still speaks powerfully to us today. Tragedies and comedies were performed in the open-air theatre to audiences of about 15 000, as part of a festival for the god Dionysus (▷ p. 46). The democracy paid some of the costs and persuaded rich men to share in the costs and work of the productions. The 5th-century tragedies of Aeschylus, Sophocles and Euripides explored – through the re-shaping of mythical stories such as those of Oedipus and the Trojan War – the deepest issues of human heroism, wrong-doing and suffering. While the plays, like Athenian public art, often reinforced cultural stereotypes – for example the perceived superiority of Greeks over barbarians, or Athens over Sparta – many plays explored contemporary political issues such as the workings of democracy or the conduct of war, and social issues such as friendship and revenge, sexuality and male–female relationships, and slavery. The 5th-century comedies of Aristophanes combined fantastic and ribald plots with personal abuse and satirical attacks on contemporary policies or other trends.

Athens also became, from the mid-5th century on, a major centre for intellectual debate and the development of philosophy. However, relations between the democracy and the philosophers were often ambivalent and suspicious. The Sophists – innovative thinkers from many different city-states – turned from 'natural philosophy' (what we now call science) to concentrate on issues of politics, rhetoric and ethics, and found many pupils in Athens for their lectures and classes. Some of the Sophists seemed to subvert all ideas and conventions with their radical questioning. Socrates, who developed his own commitment to philosophical enquiry through debate with the Sophists, was executed in 399 BC, having apparently been confused with the Sophists, and held responsible for the political damage done by some of his pupils. His greatest follower, Plato, founded the Academy in Athens as the base for his philosophical teachings. Plato's greatest pupil, Aristotle, after a spell as Alexander the Great's tutor (▷ p. 32), opened his school, the Lyceum, in Athens in 335 BC, but left Athens swiftly in 323, at a time of anti-Macedonian feeling following Alexander's death. Neither Plato nor Aristotle could conceive of any mode of political organization superior to the city-state. Yet these two greatest thinkers of the ancient world – neither of them admirers of Athenian democracy – chose and were permitted to do much of their work in the city that had put their beloved Socrates to death, and established educational institutions there that were to flourish for many centuries.

An Athenian plate (above) depicting a Scythian archer, dating from the late 6th century BC. The signature of Epictetus, the man who made and decorated the plate, is visible to the left of the archer. Scythian archers were maintained as mercenaries in Athens by the tyrant Peisistratos in the 6th century. Vase-painters often portrayed them as a contrast to the model of the hoplite-citizen.

Inside Athens, the democratic system took much of the blame for the defeat in Sicily, and in 411 there was a brief period of non-democratic rule. Despite all these difficulties – and further mistakes – Athens fought on until its final defeat at Aegospotami in the Dardanelles in 404 BC. Thus the great war ended in complete victory for Sparta. However, most of the Greek cities, although liberated from Athenian 'tyranny', found themselves either ruled once more by the Persians, or by narrow, Spartan-backed oligarchies.

In Athens defeat was followed by the brief and savage rule of an oligarchy, the 'Thirty Tyrants' (404–403 BC), but this was overthrown when Sparta withdrew its support from so unpopular a regime. The restored democracy won credit by declaring an amnesty for all except the chief oligarchs. But the conviction and execution of the philosopher Socrates on charges of corrupting the young and of impiety did lasting damage to Athens' reputation (▷ box, Athenian Culture). Socrates was blamed for his associations with young men such as Alcibiades, and the leader of the 'Thirty Tyrants', Critias.

Greece in the 4th century BC

The Athenian defeat did not bring peace. The harsh policies of Sparta, and the reversal of its former policies by attacking Persian rule in Anatolia, led to a coalition against it. This consisted of its former allies, Corinth and Thebes, and its old enemies Athens and Argos, supported by Persian gold. A succession of wars continued until the middle of the century, punctuated by 'Common Peaces' supposedly guaranteed by the king of Persia. Thebes, the leader of the Boeotian Confederacy, gained steadily in military strength from 378 BC onwards, guided by the commanders Epaminondas and Pelopidas, and achieved major victories over Sparta (notably at Leuctra in 371 BC; ▷ p. 44), after which Thebes liberated the Messenian helots. However, Thebes, too, failed to establish a lasting position of dominance. Sparta failed to recover, largely owing to the gradual breakdown of its economic and social system and the unwillingness of the Spartans to reproduce themselves. The gap between rich and poor Spartan citizens increased steadily; many of the poor were thus deprived of citizen-rights, while the rich preferred to have fewer children than see their wealth diminish. Athens did recover some of its former power, and from 378–7 created a new Aegean Confederacy. However, this was less extensive than the Delian League had been, and more suspicious of Athenian dominance. Internally, Athens' restored democracy operated with a greater respect for moderation and social consensus, rather than the uncontrolled power of the assembly.

The emergence of Macedon

The main Greek states thus became weaker, a weakness often exacerbated by conflicts between rich and poor and by ensuing civil wars – which broke out, for example, in the 360s in many Peloponnesian cities. Various outside powers began to take advantage of the weakness of the Greek states and of the Persian

ATHENS AND SPARTA c.450 BC

ILLYRIANS
KINGDOM OF MACEDON
THRACIANS
Byzantium
Selymbria
Perinthus
Chalcedon
Thasos
Abdera
Aenus
Acanthus
Samothrace
Cyzicus
Imbros
Lampsacus
Poitidaea
Lemnos
Mende
Torone
Scione
EPIROTES
THESSALY
AND
DEPENDENCIES
ATHENIAN
Methymna
PERSIAN
Ambracia
EMPIRE
Mytilene
EMPIRE
Leucas
Anactorium
AETOLIANS
Cyme
BOEOTIANS
EUBOEA
Delphi
Orchomenus
Chalcis
Chios
Erythrae
Thespiae
Eretria
Thebes
Teos
Plataea
ACHAEANS
Megara
Zacynthus
Elis
Sicyon
ATTICA
Carystus
Ephesus
Olympia
Phlius
Corinth
ATHENS
ARCADIANS
Epidaurus
Aegina
Andros
Samos
Argos
Troezen
Delos
Miletus
Hermione
MESSENIANS
Paros
Naxos
SPARTA
Cos
Melos
Cnidus
Camirus
Ialysus
Thera
Lindus
CRETANS

ATHENIAN EMPIRE

SPARTA and ALLIES

OTHER GREEKS

Battlesites of the Greek–Persian wars (490–479BC)

1 MARATHON 490 BC   3 SALAMIS 480 BC
2 THERMOPYLAE 480 BC   4 PLATAEA 479 BC

Empire. The most important of these powers was Macedon, a previously backward kingdom in northeastern Greece. In 359 BC Philip II became king, and immediately undertook a total reorganization of the army and the kingdom, and the extension of its boundaries and resources. He benefited from the continuing wars in Greece, for example the 'Social War' between Athens and some of her Aegean allies, and the 'Sacred War' in central Greece between the Phocians and the Thebans. By a cunning blend of diplomacy and force Philip achieved a position of dominance in mainland Greece, winning

final victory at the battle of Chaeronea (338) over a coalition of Greek states led by Athens (inspired by Demosthenes) and Thebes. Philip was assassinated in 336, leaving his son Alexander to carry out his plan to invade Persia (▷ p. 32). Although the Greek city-states were to maintain their cultural identities – and a degree of self-government – for centuries, from now on power in Greece was to depend ultimately on outsiders: the Macedonian kings Philip and Alexander, then the successor kingdoms founded after Alexander's death, and finally the Roman Empire (▷ p. 37).   NF

The temple of Apollo at Corinth, c. 550 BC. The seven columns are examples of the Doric order of architecture – the earliest of the five Classical orders (▷ p. 39) – which developed in the second half of the 7th century BC, probably in Corinth. The preferred order of mainland Greece and the western Greek colonies, it was characterized by simple baseless columns, heavy vertically ridged tapering shafts, spreading capitals and a plain entablature.

Alexander the Great
and the Hellenistic Age

The conquests of Alexander the Great brought the whole of the former Persian Empire under the control of Greek-speaking rulers. The monarchies that were established after his death enabled Greek culture to penetrate through Syria, Mesopotamia and Iran to India. The Hellenistic Age (from the Greek *Hellenistes*, 'an imitator of the Greeks') is the period from Alexander's death (323 BC) until the gradual extinction of these kingdoms, most of which were absorbed by the Roman or Parthian Empires in the 2nd and 1st centuries BC.

Alexander was born in the summer of 356 BC, eldest son of Philip II, king of Macedon (⊳ p. 31). Alexander was educated by – among others – the philosopher Aristotle, and acquired all the skills needed by a future ruler. When Philip won complete control over the Greek city-states at the battle of Chaeronea in 338 BC, Alexander commanded the Macedonian army's victorious left wing. On the assassination of Philip in 336 BC he was immediately proclaimed king. Some of the states subject to Macedon tried to take advantage of the new king, but he crushed the uprisings. A series of swift and brutal campaigns in Thrace and Greece culminated in the defeat of the Thebans and the destruction of their city in 335 BC.

The conquest of the Persian Empire

Having secured his position in Europe, Alexander was able to continue the Greek offensive against the Persian Empire. This had been initiated by his father and was portrayed as revenge for the desecrations of Xerxes (⊳ pp. 26 and 28) and liberation for the Greeks of Asia Minor (or Anatolia; modern Turkey). In practice this meant replacing Persian rule with Macedonian rule by right of conquest.

Alexander crossed into Asia Minor in 334 BC with an army of 32 000 infantry and 5000 cavalry. He engaged the massed forces of the western Persian provinces at the River Granicus and defeated them. He proceeded through Asia Minor, entering some cities as a welcome deliverer and others as a resisted conqueror. When he came to the edge of Asia proper he was faced by a larger Persian army commanded by Darius III himself, the Achaemenid king of Persia (⊳ p. 27). At the battle of Issus in 333 BC Alexander won a brilliant victory, personally leading his cavalry into the heart of the battle. Darius fled, leaving his family to be captured, while Alexander entered Egypt and was accepted as its new ruler by the Egyptian priests.

A final stand by Darius ended in total defeat at Gaugamela in 332 BC. The fleeing king was eventually murdered by his own nobles, only hours before Alexander caught up with him. Alexander became his successor, although it took a great deal more campaigning before Alexander had subdued all of the Persian Empire. He led his army across Asia to the edge of the Himalaya and the northern provinces of India. As he progressed further away from Greece he began to use Persian soldiers and appoint Persian nobles to positions of authority, much to the dismay of the Macedonians. After a mutiny by his tired army in 324 BC he turned back towards the west, only getting as far as Babylon, where he fell ill and died in 323 BC.

In ten years Alexander had created the largest empire that the world had ever known, stretching from the Greek mainland to the River Indus, incorporating all or part of 17 modern states. His outstandingly successful career made him the ideal king, against whom all others were judged and whose deeds all tried to emulate. Just before his death he may have planned further campaigns against the powerful states of the western Mediterranean – after his conquest of the Persian Empire anything was possible.

The successors of Alexander

There was no clear rule of succession for Macedonian kings. Alexander's wife Roxane was pregnant when he died and a regent was appointed. Both the child and his mother were murdered in the disputes which followed. The leading Macedonian generals immediately fought amongst themselves over who should govern the various parts of the empire and several tried to set themselves up as kings. Three main dynasties were eventually established – by Ptolemy (Egypt), Seleucus (Asia) and Antigonus (Macedon and Greece). Smaller vassal kingdoms and city-states existed within their terri-

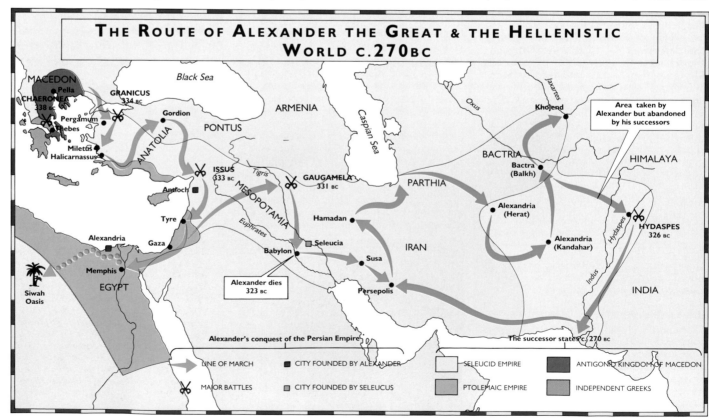

THE ROUTE OF ALEXANDER THE GREAT & THE HELLENISTIC WORLD C.270BC

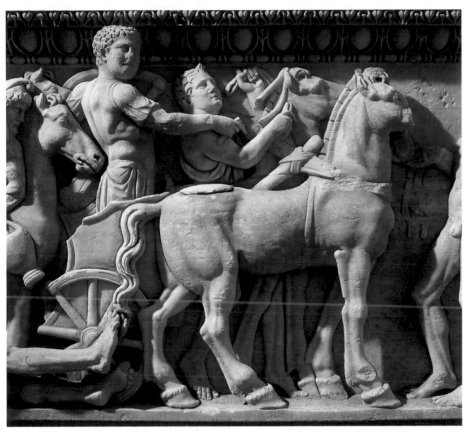

A scene from the Trojan War, depicted on a Hellenistic tomb from the city of Tyre. Hellenistic art differs markedly from Greek art of the 4th and 5th centuries BC, being characterized by greater emotionalism and technical display.

SEE ALSO

- PTOLEMAIC EGYPT p. 19
- THE PERSIAN EMPIRE p. 26
- ARCHAIC AND CLASSICAL GREECE p. 28
- THE RISE OF ROME p. 36
- THE ANCIENT ECONOMY p. 42
- ANCIENT WARFARE p. 44

rivals on a grand scale in war and politics. They fought each other for the control of people and places, sometimes with force, sometimes diplomacy. Vassals and cities competed for a monarch's favour and protection. Citizens tried to amass larger fortunes than their fellows through agriculture and trade. They showed off their riches by financing splendid buildings or festivals for their cities, and were rewarded with extravagant honours and titles. Most public works were paid for by private wealth, and official posts were occupied by men, and occasionally women, who could afford to be generous. Wealth determined how easy or hard life was. If a person was captured by the ubiquitous pirates, for example, whether they were sold into slavery or ransomed depended on how rich they or their patrons were.

The decline of the Hellenistic world

Competition was not always beneficial. The Hellenistic monarchies weakened each other through constant wars, and fell victim to outsiders. Macedon was conquered by the Romans in 167 BC, and Greece became a Roman province in 146 BC. Attalos III of Pergamum bequeathed his kingdoms to Rome in 133 BC to avoid further internal strife. The Seleucid family quarrelled over an ever-shrinking kingdom as the provinces rebelled under local leaders, overthrowing Greek rule in favour of native rulers. Egypt was the longest lived of the Hellenisitic kingdoms, thanks largely to the speed with which Macedonian rule was assimilated into the traditional pattern of Egyptian monarchy. It was at the battle of Actium in 31 BC that the Hellenistic Age came to a close, with the defeat of Cleopatra VII, last of the Hellenistic monarchs (⊳ pp. 19 and 37).   PDS

tories, especially in parts where their authority was weakest. In time some of these became more powerful and achieved independence from the main dynasties.

In Macedon the kingship was to a limited degree elective – the king was approved by his subjects, especially the army, and he ruled by consent. The Antigonids retained this idea, so that their monarchy closely resembled that of Philip II and Alexander, before the conquest of Persia. In Egypt and Asia, however, native concepts of absolute monarchy and the divine nature of the king's authority produced monarchies more like those of the pharaohs and the Achaemenids. The Seleucids and the Ptolemies were worshipped as gods, supposedly descended from Apollo and Dionysus or their local equivalents. Divine nature was also attributed to their families. All over the Hellenistic world Alexander was honoured as a god, from whom all kings claimed descent.

Kingdoms and cities

The nature of the Hellenistic kingdoms varied greatly. The Antigonids ruled Macedon securely, but their control over central and southern Greece was not always so firm. Two federations of city-states, Aetolia and Achaea, were dominant from c. 240 BC onwards. The Ptolemaic kingdom was limited to Egypt and some coastal areas of the eastern Mediterranean (⊳ p. 19). It had the most effective navy and the least rebellious population. The Seleucid kingdom included many peoples spread over a huge area. Much of their original territory fragmented into ethnic kingdoms, such as Bactria, Armenia, Bithynia and Pontus. Those areas which they did retain were controlled like the Achaemenid Empire by local governors (*satraps*).

The basic social and political unit of the Hellenistic world was the city, made up of an urban centre and surrounding countryside. Alexander founded many cities bearing his name as part of the process of spreading Greek culture and ideas throughout his empire. He even named one city after his horse, Bucephalus. Some of these cities, like Alexandria in Egypt, have endured to the present day. His successors copied this idea (e.g. Antiochia, Seleucia). Cities were centres of wealth and power, to be controlled and exploited. Many were free to administer their own affairs and to behave almost as independent states, although this could lead to rebellion.

Eumenes, the governor of Pergamum, transformed the city from a Seleucid fortress and treasury into an independent state. In 238 BC his son Attalos I became a king. The territory of Pergamum was small, but favourable circumstances and location enabled it to develop into one of the most prosperous and beautiful of all the Hellenistic cities.

The competitive spirit

The Hellenistic Age was marked by a highly competitive spirit affecting individuals at all levels of society. Kings were

HELLENISTIC ARMIES

All the Hellenistic kings were generals first and rulers second. It was possible to be a king without a kingdom, but not without an army. Wars were fought for booty and prestige as much as for territory. The basic infantry unity of Hellenistic armies was the *phalanx*, 1000 or more men standing close together in lines 16 deep. They were armed with a sword, a shield and a spear, the *sarissa*, about 4 m (13 ft) long. The spear points of the first five rows made an impenetrable barrier ahead and the others held their spears overhead to ward off missiles. Cavalrymen in squadrons of 200 protected the wings. Both Philip II and Alexander used the strong but unwieldy *phalanx* to engage the enemy and break up his line. The cavalry would then charge on the flanks and win the battle. Later monarchs employed elephants for a shock effect. The early *phalanx* was composed of Macedonian peasant soldiers. In the second and first centuries BC mercenaries from all over the Hellenistic world served together in the armies of the various monarchs (⊳ p. 45).

The Celts

Prehistoric Europe was populated by a large number of different groups. Most of them are quite obscure to us now, but the way of life of those societies, located on the fringe of literate Mediterranean cultures, may be reconstructed in some detail. Best known of all are the late Iron-Age inhabitants of present-day France and Britain and their neighbours.

Archaeologists have no way of knowing either the languages spoken by most of these peoples or even their own names for themselves. Greek explorers and Roman conquerors (▷ box) referred to them all as Gauls or Celts, and more recently the term Celtic has been applied to a group of languages. But it is a modern (and mistaken) idea that the Celts were a single people with a common language and a common culture, who shared a history extending from prehistory to the present day.

Europe in the first millennium BC

Temperate Europe is a land of rolling hills and wide plains and plateaux. Most of this landscape was covered in woodland until a few thousand years ago, when groups of settled farmers began to clear large areas for cultivation. With the discovery of iron technology (▷ p. 15), the rate of clearance accelerated. Marshes were drained, hillsides were deforested, and the fertile river valleys supported dense populations long before the Roman invasions.

Iron-Age agricultural systems were fairly sophisticated. Most areas depended on a variety of grains – emmer, spelt, barley and millet being the most important. Stock breeding was also used to develop valued traits in cattle, pigs and sheep. Regional specialities developed – cattle in the Low Countries for example – but most communities were probably self-sufficient in basic foodstuffs.

Most of the population lived in villages. Traces of scattered farmsteads are found in some regions, and at some periods massive fortifications were constructed – the hillforts that still dominate the landscape of many parts of the countryside. But we cannot be sure that all these fortifications were permanently inhabited, and, except in mountainous areas like Scot-

land or the Alps, hillforts were built and used only for brief periods of prehistory.

Iron-Age society was village based. Most people were peasant farmers who lived with their relatives near to the land they farmed. Villages may have had headmen, but kinship was probably equally important in organizing daily life.

By the time the Romans invaded, many areas were also organized into larger political units. Hereditary nobles owned much of the land, and dominated society with their bands of followers. Noble society was violent – young men won

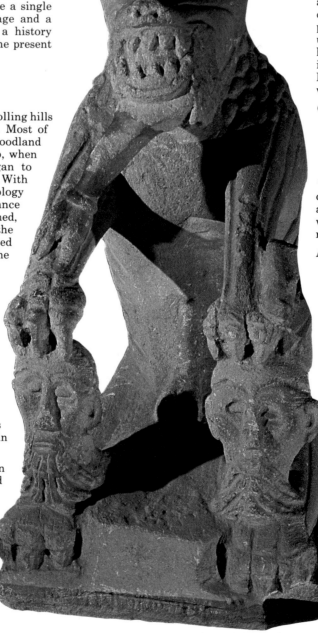

A Celtic monster from the south of France, an example of La Tène art. This style was characterized by the use of human and animal masks such as those seen on the knees of this sculpture.

praise and wealth by raids, duels and in war (▷ p. 45). Iron-Age groups were probably no more warlike than any other ancient society, but they have acquired a reputation for ferocity both from the accounts of Roman generals who fought them and from the splendid weaponry found by archaeologists in noble graves.

Material culture and art

Archaeology allows us to reconstruct a detailed picture of everyday life in late prehistoric Europe. Houses were built of wood and wickerwork and coated in mud to weatherproof them. Food was stored, cooked and served in pottery vessels, most of them coarse by modern standards but some brightly painted or covered in a shimmering coat of graphite. Bone was used to make needles, and clothes were woven on looms from flax and wool.

But it is the metalwork of prehistoric Europe that has most excited the admiration of recent generations. Weapons, ornaments and drinking equipment show a high degree of metallurgical proficiency. A great quantity of iron was produced: the largest hillfort ramparts used hundreds of tons merely for nails to hold timbers together. The quality of ironworking was also very high: some late Iron-Age swords will still spring back when bent.

Gold and silver were used to make necklaces (torques) and brooches decorated with stylized artwork. Animals and religious motifs combine with graceful curves and elaborate decoration to form wonderfully balanced overall designs. The interests of the nobility are graphically illustrated by the beautiful weapons and drinking equipment with which they were buried or which they threw into rivers as offerings to the gods.

Art historians have identified two widely used styles, now known after the sites at which they were first observed. *Hall statt* art (named after an Austrian village), which flourished between 900 and 500 BC, originated in central Europe and spread widely across continental Europe. *La Tène* art (named after a part of Lake Neuchâtel, Switzerland) developed around 450 BC under the influences of civilizations of the south and east. The style first appears in the Rhineland, but spread even further than Hallstatt art, reaching Ireland and Spain in the west and Hungary in the east.

The invasion hypothesis

Archaeologists used to imagine that particular styles of material culture (tools, weapons, pots, etc.) corresponded to particular peoples, with distinctive beliefs, languages, customs and identities. They believed that movements of peoples could be traced through the archaeological records by looking for key artefacts. This theory is known as the 'invasion hypothesis'.

SEE ALSO

● HUMAN PREHISTORY p. 12
● ANCIENT WARFARE p. 44
● THE BARBARIAN KINGDOMS p. 78

So the spread of Hallstatt and La Tène styles and artefacts used to be interpreted as migrations of Hallstatt people or La Tène warrior bands. One or both groups were thought to be the ancestors of 'the Celts'. The case seemed to be proved by Greek and Latin accounts of 'barbarian invasions' (▷ box).

Modern archaeology and anthropology have shown that the relationship between material culture and particular peoples is more complex. Firstly, the same kind of material culture is often used by individuals who think of themselves as belonging to quite different groups. Secondly, the whole idea of fixed 'peoples' is now seen to derive from ideas of race developed during the 1930s and long discredited in most parts of the world.

Most anthropologists prefer to talk of 'ethnicity', the sense of identity created for itself by a group in a particular time and place. Ethnicity, unlike race, is culturally defined and changes over time, just as individuals can change their ethnicity by becoming part of another group.

No doubt there were population movements in prehistoric Europe (although they may be invisible to archaeologists), but ethnicities must have been continually forming and breaking up and reforming just as they do today.

What happened to the Celts?

Who are today's Celts? After the Roman conquest of much of Europe, Iron-Age cultures fed into the Romanized culture of the empire. Local traditions remained, but the overwhelming influence was Mediterranean.

Celts appear again on the fringes of the Roman world after the fall of the empire. Modern scholars have used the term to refer to the early medieval groups who inhabited present-day Scotland, Ireland, Wales, Cornwall and Brittany. Many contemporary inhabitants of these areas now think of themselves as 'Celtic' – that is they have adopted a Celtic 'ethnicity'.

The creation of the modern Celts has to be seen in the context of the rise of nationalism in the 19th century (▷ p. 150). All over Europe, disadvantaged minorities in the new nations adopted new ethnicities, often based on linguistic divisions. In fact, no Classical writers ever speak of Celts in Ireland. But the myth of the Celts has become a powerful symbol in the struggle of many groups for autonomy and independence from the larger political units in which they are embedded.   GW

A bronze disc with enamel inlay displaying the graceful curves and elaborate decoration typical of the La Tène style. The Celts were the first people in Western Europe to use enamel in place of coral or cut-stone inlay.

GREEK AND ROMAN IMAGES OF THE CELTS

Northern Europe was the 'Dark Continent' of the Classical World. Unclear of its size or shape, Classical writers described a land of forests and mountains populated by barbarians and monsters. Herodotus, writing in the 5th century BC, reported rumours that beyond the Black Sea lived the human Issedones, beyond them the one-eyed Arimaspians, and beyond them griffins who guarded hoards of gold. Elsewhere he writes that no one knows whether there is sea to the north or east of Europe. As Greek explorers travelled on the Atlantic, and as Rome's conquests expanded, northern Europe became better known, but it always remained a mysterious land, rather as Africa was to early European explorers.

Fear played a great part in Greek and Roman images of the barbarians. Migrating northerners sacked the Greek oracle at Delphi in the 3rd century BC and Galatian tribes then established themselves on the Anatolian plateau (in modern Turkey), from where they terrorized neighbouring Greek cities and kingdoms. Gauls provided mercenaries in most Mediterranean wars in the Hellenistic period (▷ pp. 33 and 45). Rome itself was sacked by Celts in 390 BC and – despite the suppression of the Gauls of northern Italy – the '*terror Gallicus*' obsessed Romans until Julius Caesar's conquest of Gaul (modern France; ▷ p. 37).

Classical unease concerning the barbarians also had its roots in fear of the unknown. The Greek historian Polybius wrote, 'They lived in villages without walls and had no other possessions, for they slept on leaves, ate meat and cared for nothing except warfare and farming – their only wealth was in herds or in gold, as these were the only things they could carry about with them easily.' What could be more different from the settled urban lifestyles of ancient Mediterranean civilization? Not all descriptions were hostile, however. Barbarians were seen by some as 'noble savages', lacking the improving aspects of civilized men, but untainted by their more degenerate traits. Their priests – the Druids – were credited with a sophisticated natural philosophy, but also with practising human sacrifice. Caesar wrote that the Gauls who lived furthest from civilization were the bravest, having fewer of those southern luxuries that induced effeminacy, and Tacitus contrasted the chastity of the Germans with Roman decadence. On the other hand, barbarians were ridiculed for their dress (trousers), their language, and their hairstyles (long hair and moustaches).

Greek and Roman ambivalence about 'barbarians' mirrored ambivalence about their own civilization. Likewise, Greek and Roman ethnographers often tell us more about what they considered 'normal' than about the realities of Iron-Age Europe. But it is important to understand how Greeks and Romans imagined the barbarians, as it influenced the way they treated them, just as Western ideas about 'primitives' influenced the ways in which European empires were ruled in the 18th and 19th centuries (▷ pp. 160–3).

The Gundestrup Cauldron, a ritual silver vessel dating from the 1st century BC. This detail shows a human sacrifice by drowning.

The Rise of Rome

The beginnings of Rome are lost in legend. According to the story, the city took its name from Romulus, a shepherd king who founded a settlement on the banks of the Tiber after killing his twin brother Remus, traditionally in 753 BC. Romulus was the first of seven kings of Rome, the last of whom, Tarquin the Proud, was expelled in 509 BC when a republic was set up.

It is difficult to know how much truth there is in the legends of early Rome. Archaeologists have established that one or more villages existed on the site from the end of the Bronze Age (c. 1000 BC), and that by 600 BC the settlement had developed into a substantial city.

At the time of the overthrow of Tarquin, Rome possessed an extensive territory, a strong army and a wide network of commercial and diplomatic contacts, not only with other Latin-speaking towns, which it dominated, but with the powerful Etruscan states to the north (▷ box), the Greek colonies in the south, and even with distant Carthage, a Phoenician trading city on the North African coast (▷ p. 23).

The early Republic

Under the republic that was established in 509 BC power was exercised by two annually elected consuls, who ruled the city and commanded the army. They were advised by a council of elders (the Senate), and in the course of time were assisted by more junior officials, who were also elected annually. Only in emergencies was a single dictator appointed, for a maximum of six months.

At first these posts were held almost exclusively by the patricians, a hereditary elite of obscure origin. But in the 4th century BC other wealthy citizens, representing the rest of the population (the plebeians), also obtained access to high office. The plebeians had formed their own assembly and elected their own officials, called tribunes, to represent them. In 287 BC the plebeians obtained the right to pass laws in their assemblies, and at this point the struggle between the patricians and plebeians was finally ended.

The growth of the Empire

In the 4th century BC, after a temporary setback in 390 when the city was sacked by Gallic raiders from northern Italy, the Romans gradually expanded their power. The neighbouring peoples whom they conquered were obliged to become allies and to fight alongside them in subsequent

THE ETRUSCANS

In ancient times the Etruscans inhabited an area on the west coast of Italy bounded by the Tiber and the Arno. The problem of who they were and where they came from is tied up with the puzzle of their language, which is not Indo-European and has no similarity to any other known language. Its presence in a region of central Italy that was neither backward nor remote is extremely mysterious. The most likely explanation is that it was brought from elsewhere, a theory deriving some support from an ancient legend that the Etruscans had migrated to Italy from the Near East. But any such migration must have occurred in prehistoric times (certainly before 1000 BC), since archaeologists are convinced that Etruscan civilization was formed in Italy and developed from a preceding Iron-Age culture known as Villanovan (from Villanova, a village near Bologna, where the first discoveries of this culture were made in 1853).

Etruscan civilization reached its zenith in the archaic period (8th to 5th centuries BC), when a number of powerful city-states emerged. These are conventionally divided into a southern group, including Veii, Caere, Tarquinii and Vulci; a northern group, comprising Volaterrae, Populonia, Vetulonia and Rusellae; and an inland group, including Arretium, Cortona, Perusia, Clusium and Volsinii. Our knowledge of these centres is based on archaeological evidence (particularly finds from their rich cemeteries), information in the work of Greek and Roman historians, and Etruscan inscriptions, of which around 13 000 (mostly brief epitaphs) are now recorded. Although the language is not properly understood, the texts are written in the Greek alphabet, and the basic meaning of most of them can now be made out.

In the 6th century BC the Etruscans colonized other parts of Italy, and Etruscan settlements were established in the Po Valley and in Campania. But the Etruscans never attempted to unify Italy; their city-states were fiercely independent, and there was intense rivalry – and sometimes armed conflict – between them. Little is known of the political organization and social structure of the cities, but there is evidence that in some of them, as in Rome, monarchical regimes were replaced by republics in the 6th and 5th centuries, and that wealth and power were concentrated in the hands of powerful aristocratic clans comparable to the Roman patricians. In many ways early Rome was very like its Etruscan neighbours, and had close (though not always friendly) links with them. However, the theory that Rome was subjected to Etruscan rule in the 6th century is not supported by historical evidence.

In the 5th and 4th centuries Etruria was hit by economic recession and social crisis, and gradually fell victim to the growing power of Rome. The defeat and capture of Veii in 396 BC was the first stage in the Roman conquest of Etruria, which was finally completed when Volsinii was destroyed in 264 BC. Even so, the remaining Etruscan cities preserved much of their ancient culture and distinctive social organization well into the Roman period. Their language continued to be spoken at least until the 1st century BC, when it gave way to the universal spread of Latin.

A wall painting showing musicians and a servant, from an Etruscan tomb in Tarquinia, Italy (5th century BC). Flute music is thought to have played an important ritual role in many aspects of Etruscan life, from hunting to food preparation. Music was also used in elaborate religious ceremonies that emphasized the afterlife and the practice of divination.

wars (⊳ p. 45). Part of the land they conquered was colonized by the poor (allies as well as Romans), while the rest was left to its original owners, who were enrolled as allies and invited to share in future conquests. By 272 BC the conquest of peninsular Italy was complete.

Shortly afterwards the Romans became involved in a major overseas war, when in 264 BC they challenged the Carthaginians for the control of Sicily. In spite of immense losses the Romans finally emerged as victors in 241 BC in what is known as the First Punic War (from *Punicus*, 'Carthaginian'), and Sicily became the first Roman province. The Second Punic War began in 218 when the Carthaginian general Hannibal sought revenge by crossing the Alps and invading Italy with an army of 26 000 men and several war elephants. In spite of some spectacular victories at Trasimene and Cannae, Hannibal failed to won over Rome's Italian allies and was gradually worn down by the tactics of Quintus Fabius Maximus. Hannibal withdrew from Italy in 204 BC and was finally defeated at Zama in Africa by Scipio Africanus in 202 BC.

As a result the Romans obtained further provinces from the former Carthaginian possessions in Spain, and in the following decades they decisively defeated the major Hellenistic kingdoms in Greece and Asia Minor (⊳ p. 33). By 167 BC Rome dominated the whole Mediterranean. After the Third Punic War (149–146 BC) Carthage was destroyed and 'Africa' (i.e. roughly modern Tunisia) became a Roman province. Greece was made a province at the same time; Asia (i.e. western Turkey) followed in 133, and then southern Gaul (Provence) in 121, Cilicia (southern Turkey) in 101, and Cyrenaica (eastern Libya) in 96.

The consequences of Roman imperialism

These overseas successes vastly increased the power and wealth of the upper classes, who hastened to invest their gains in large landed estates, worked by war captives imported as slaves. Slave labour replaced the small peasant proprietors, who formed the backbone of the Roman army but found that prolonged military service in distant lands made it increasingly difficult to maintain their farms. Many peasants were thus driven off their land to a life of penury and unemployment. One result of this was a problem in military recruitment, since the law laid down a property qualification for service in the army. Social tensions thus began to build up, and the earlier consensus came under increasing strain.

Meanwhile the rich began to adopt luxurious and increasingly sophisticated habits. The influence of Greek culture became pervasive, as Romans began to imitate the leisured style of the great centres of the Hellenistic world (⊳ p. 33).

The breakdown of the Republic

The widening gulf between rich and poor

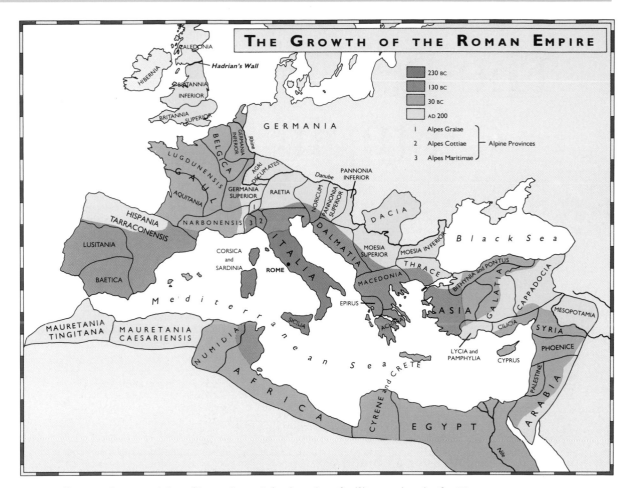

eventually gave rise to social conflict and political breakdown. In 133 BC a tribune, Tiberius Gracchus, introduced a land reform that proposed to redistribute among the poor the state-owned land that had been annexed by the rich. There was immense opposition, and Gracchus was murdered in a furious outbreak of political violence. Ten years later, his brother Gaius attempted to bring in a series of popular reforms, and suffered the same fate.

In the following generation Rome faced hostile military threats in every part of the Empire, including a serious revolt by the Italian allies (91–88). The ruling oligarchy showed itself corrupt and incompetent in attempting to respond to these crises, which were only overcome by allowing able and ambitious individuals to take control of the government, and by creating a professional army from the proletariat (⊳ p. 45).

These measures solved the military problems, but had fatal political consequences, becaused they provided the poor with a means to redress their grievances, and ambitious nobles with the chance to gain personal power by means of armed force. The first civil war was between the successful general Gaius Marius and Lucius Sulla. Both men marched against the city and massacred their political opponents, and in 81 BC Sulla set himself up as dictator. His attempts to reform the political system were ineffectual, however, and the same lethal trends continued.

A fresh series of military crises in the 70s enabled the popular general Pompey (Gnaeus Pompeius) to gain a position of pre-eminence in the state. But he was unable to prevent other leaders from doing the same thing, and in 60 BC he joined Marcus Crassus and Julius Caesar in the First Triumvirate. Following his conquest of Gaul (modern France) Caesar invaded Italy and once again plunged the Empire into civil war. After defeating Pompey at Pharsalus in 48 BC Caesar became consul and dictator for life.

Caesar's monarchical tendencies went against republican tradition and offended the nobles. On 15 March (the 'Ides of March') 44 BC, he was stabbed to death by a group of senators led by Marcus Junius Brutus and Gaius Cassius Longinus. The conspirators were unable to restore the Republic, however, because Caesar's chief aides, Mark Antony (Marcus Antonius) and Marcus Lepidus, joined together with Caesar's heir, the 19-year-old Caesar Octavian (the future Augustus; ⊳ p. 38), to form the Second Triumvirate, and in the following year Brutus and Cassius were defeated at Philippi in Macedonia, and committed suicide.

Lepidus was soon squeezed out of the Triumvirate and the Empire was uneasily divided between Octavian and Antony until 31 BC, when the issue was decided in Octavian's favour at the battle of Actium, off the west coast of Greece. Mark Antony and his mistress, the Egyptian queen Cleopatra, committed suicide, leaving Octavian in complete control of the Roman Empire.   TC

The Roman Empire

After his victory at Actium (▷ p. 37) Octavian was faced with the problem of retaining the loyalty of the army while at the same time establishing a position of permanent power that would be acceptable to traditional opinion. Octavian's great achievement was to find a lasting solution to this problem. The name Augustus (meaning 'revered') was an honorary title conferred on him in 27 BC, when his position was formalized by the grant of special powers by the Senate and the people. He later took on other powers, but made sure that they were voted to him, so as not to offend republican sentiment.

The Senate effectively became a branch of the administration and lost all political independence. The resentment caused by this loss of power was never entirely eliminated, and was the source of much political conflict during the century that followed.

The work of Augustus

In general, however, the new regime was welcomed by the upper classes, since it brought peace, stability and a chance to prosper. In the provinces, which had suffered dreadfully from civil war, Augustus was hailed as a saviour and universal benefactor. Throughout the Empire formal cults of the emperor were established and became a focus for the loyalty of his subjects.

Augustus obtained the enthusiastic support of the people of Rome with free rations of grain, cash hand-outs, games and shows ('bread and circuses'; ▷ box). He also secured the loyalty of the army by settling veterans in colonies in the provinces and establishing a permanent standing force, with fixed terms of service and regular wages (▷ p. 45). This reform had the effect of taking the army out of politics, and guaranteeing its loyalty to the state.

Under Augustus the army was kept busy in wars of conquest. Northwest Spain, the Alpine regions and the Balkans were overrun by Augustus' generals, although the plan to extend Roman rule in Germany east of the Rhine had to be abandoned after the annihilation of three legions under Varus in the Teutoburger forest in AD 9.

Victories abroad and peace at home were the hallmarks of Augustus' long reign. Agriculture and trade benefited, city life prospered, and literature and the arts flourished in what came to be regarded as Rome's 'Golden Age'. On the negative side, political debate was suppressed and freedom of thought was discouraged. This trend intensified under Augustus' successors, with sinister results.

The imperial succession

Augustus was succeeded by his stepson Tiberius, whose long and peaceful reign (AD 14–37) was marred by conflicts with the Senate, treason trials, and palace conspiracies. These traits became more pronounced under the later rulers of the Julio-Claudian dynasty: the insane Caligula (37–41), the feeble and pedantic Claudius (41–54), and the colourful but vicious Nero (54–68).

Nero's suicide left the throne with no legitimate heir, and opened the way to civil war as the various provincial armies backed the claims of their generals. The chaos was finally ended by Vespasian, the commander of the eastern legions, who fought his way to power in late 69 and established the Flavian dynasty. This too became a reign of terror under Domitian (81–96), who was eventually murdered.

The Senate replaced him with the weak and ineffectual Nerva (96–98), who only averted the possibility of renewed civil war by adopting a popular general, Trajan, as his successor. Trajan (98–117) was a successful military ruler who also won over the Senate, which regarded him as an ideal emperor. The atmosphere of stability and concord continued under Hadrian (117–138), Antoninus Pius (138–161) and Marcus Aurelius (161–180). Each of these beneficent rulers was adopted by his predecessor in the absence of a natural heir; the sequence was broken by Marcus' son Commodus (180–192), who turned out to be a maniac, thus confirming the Senate's worst suspicions of dynastic succession.

The assassination of Commodus ushered in a period of turmoil which resembled the events of 68–9 and from which Septimius Severus emerged as the final victor. Severus' reign (193–211) was a naked military despotism, and the army became politically dominant under his successors. When Alexander Severus was murdered by his soldiers in 235, the Severan dynasty came to an end and the Empire lapsed into anarchy.

State and subject

The Roman Empire embraced the territory of some 25 modern countries, and had a population of over 50 million people. Nevertheless, its administrative organization was rudimentary. The *Pax Romana* ('Roman Peace') was maintained in spite of – or perhaps rather because of – the inertia of the central government. The state made only a minimal impact on the daily lives of its subjects. The emperor, who worked with a tiny secretarial staff of domestic slaves and freedmen, delegated his authority to the provincial governors and lesser administrators called procurators, none of whom had any significant clerical staff to assist them. There was no bureaucracy or civil service.

Two soldiers, on a fragment of a provincial Roman bas-relief from Mogontiacum (Mainz), Germany. The soldiers are equipped with the oblong shield, helmet, short stabbing sword and spear typical of the Roman legionary.

— THE ROMAN ARMY — AND FRONTIERS

By the late Republic the Roman army had become a fully professional fighting force, noted for its tactical skills and ruthless discipline. Augustus made it into a regular standing army, permanently stationed in the outlying provinces of the Empire. It numbered some 300 000 men in all, divided roughly half and half between the legions (units of c. 5000 men), recruited from Roman citizens, and 'auxiliaries', soldiers of provincial origin who received Roman citizenship as a reward after 25 years of service (▷ p. 45).

Conquest was still the army's principal task under Augustus, but under his successors it was organized for defence behind fixed frontiers. Even so, it still retained its potential as a fearsome instrument in the field, for example during the conquest of Dacia (modern Romania) in AD 101–6.

Under the Flavian and Antonine emperors the frontiers began to be marked by permanent fortifications, the most famous of which is Hadrian's Wall, constructed in AD 122. The wall stretched across northern England for 130 km (80 mi) from the Tyne to the Solway. Its precise strategic function is still not properly understood, but many experts believe that it was designed to separate and control turbulent populations on both sides of the wall, rather than to withstand full-scale invasions from outside the province.

ECONOMY, SOCIETY AND CULTURE

Although trade and manufacture reached significant levels in the Roman Empire, growth was hindered by backward technology, low investment and poor demand. Agriculture was always the most important sector of the economy, and engaged most of the population. Land was the chief focus of investment, and the most respectable form of wealth. There was no significant class of businessmen or entrepreneurs.

Society was sharply divided between the rich landowners and the mass of rural peasants and urban poor, who were heavily dependent on the patronage of the well-to-do. Finally, there were the slaves. In the cities slaves were used largely as domestic staff in the houses of the rich; but slave labour was also used in quarries and mines, where conditions of work were inhuman, and sometimes in the fields, although the large-scale use of agricultural slavery was probably not common outside Italy. The Romans regularly freed their slaves, who thereby obtained Roman citizenship, a considerable privilege. Many of them prospered, and well-off freedmen became an important social group.

A notable feature of Roman society was its uniformity and ease of movement. People could travel without a passport from York to Alexandria, or from Ankara to Tangier, get by with just Latin and Greek, and always find themselves in familar surroundings. The large cities were especially cosmopolitan and open to outside influences.

In these circumstances new ideas spread rapidly. Especially important were new

Banqueting scene from a fresco of the 1st century AD. Rich Romans were able to enjoy a remarkable variety of food from provinces overseas. Oysters were imported from Britain, wheat from North Africa and dates from the Near East. Poultry, fish and eels were bred for the table, and meat was cured for the winter. Honey was used as a sweetener, but although the Roman diet was rich in fruit and meat, relatively few vegetables were consumed.

religious beliefs, including the so-called oriental mystery cults, which offered converts a chance of personal salvation through direct communion with divine powers. The most important cults were the worship of the Phrygian goddess Cybele, the Egyptian Isis, the Persian Mithras, and above all the Palestinian-Jewish cult of Christianity, which ultimately triumphed over all its competitors (▷ p. 46).

on the Balkan provinces and made seaborne raids on Greece and Asia Minor (northern Turkey). In the east a new and aggressive power arose in the shape of the Sassanian Persians, who made frequent attacks on eastern provinces (▷ p. 27). In 260 they overran Syria and captured the emperor, Valerian.

Military difficulties made increasing demands on the Empire's finances, which the taxpayers were unable to meet. The government responded by depreciating the currency, which resulted in galloping inflation. By the 250s the coinage was worthless and the monetary system of the Empire had collapsed. Taxes and payments to soldiers and officials began to be paid in kind, and the requisitioning of supplies became a form of organized looting by the armies.

In these circumstances trade and agriculture suffered, land became deserted, and banditry flourished. Famines and epidemics reduced the population, and cultural activity virtually ceased. Public buildings in the towns fell into disrepair, and the only new constructions were fortifications and city walls. Rome itself was surrounded by defensive walls under Aurelian (271–5), a clear sign of the weakness of the Empire – in earlier times an attack on the city would have been unthinkable.

Recovery under Diocletian and Constantine

The first signs of recovery occurred in the 270s with a series of significant military successes and a perceptible upturn in the economy. Political stability returned with Diocletian, who took office in 284 and managed to stay in power for 20 years. Recognizing that he could not rule the whole Empire on his own, Diocletian chose a colleague, Maximian, to whom he entrusted the management of the western provinces, while he took charge of the east. Shortly afterwards the two emperors (Augusti) each took on an assistant

The Empire functioned thanks to the active cooperation of its subjects, who largely governed themselves. The provinces formed a patchwork of self-governing cities, each with its surrounding territory, whose local elite was responsible for day-to-day administration and collection of taxes. Each city was a miniature version of Rome, with its own senate and annual office holders, elected from the wealthiest citizens. These men attained status and prestige by spending lavishly from their own fortunes on public amenities, charities, and festivals. The civic spirit shown by this local munificence is a key feature of Roman civilization.

The beginnings of decline

In the middle years of the third century AD the Roman Empire was plagued by civil war, foreign invasion and economic breakdown. The political system collapsed, as emperors succumbed one after another to assassination or military revolt. In the 50 years to the accession of Diocletian (284) there were at least twenty emperors who could claim some sort of legitimacy, as well as countless usurpers who were proclaimed by the armies in different parts of the Empire.

The increased political significance of the army arose from the fact that the Empire

now depended on it for survival. Pressure from German tribes beyond the Rhine and Danube became intense as Gaul and Germany were ravaged by the incursions of two newly formed tribal groups, the Franks and the Alemanni. Meanwhile the Goths on the lower Danube pressed hard

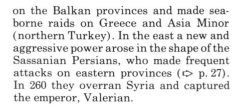

The library of Celsus at Ephesus, a Greek city in Asia Minor (modern Turkey), which contains some of the most impressive Roman remains outside Italy. Even provincial centres boasted impressive public buildings. Roman architecture developed the three Greek orders of columns – particularly the most flamboyant order, Corinthian – and added a fourth, Tuscan.

The emperor Marcus Aurelius (169–80) offering a sacrifice in front of the temple of Jupiter on the Capitol in Rome. As well as worshipping a panoply of gods, the Romans elevated the reigning emperor himself to divine status. Emperor worship was officially encouraged as a means of uniting a multilingual empire and may be regarded as a political gesture rather than an act of religious devotion. After the death of an emperor, the Senate decided whether he would be posthumously deified and, therefore, the object of a continuing cult.

(*Caesar*). This tetrarchy ('rule of four') was intended to be a permanent institution, but when Diocletian retired in 305 civil war erupted between the various heirs. Constantine, son of Maximian's Caesar, was victorious in the west in 312, and in 324 defeated the eastern emperor. He thus reunited the Empire under his sole rule, which lasted until his death in 337.

Under Diocletian and Constantine the Empire was completely reorganized. The army was enlarged and divided between frontier guards and a mobile field army, concentrated in fortified cities and ready to strike back against invaders. Commanders were professional soldiers appointed from the ranks.

The provinces were subdivided into areas of more manageable size, and their governors relieved of military command. The currency was reformed and attempts made to combat inflation. Diocletian also reformed the tax system and it was he who invented the idea of an annual budget.

These measures reimposed order, but at a price. The central government became more oppressive, and a vast bureaucracy was established. This was self-serving, inefficient and corrupt – an intolerable burden on the taxpayer. Peasants and other workers found it increasingly difficult to make a living and to meet the demands of the state, which in turn attempted to prevent desertion and declining output by compelling workers and their descendants to remain in their jobs. Society thus became more rigid, and the peasants were gradually reduced to serfdom.

The rise of Christianity

From its beginnings in Palestine in the early 1st century Christianity spread rapidly. By the 2nd century the new faith had won adherents in all parts of the Empire. At this early stage most people were hostile to Christianity, which was seen as a weird and irrational cult,

focused as it was on a man who had been executed as a common criminal in the relatively recent past, rather than on a 'normal' god. The Christians were also considered antisocial atheists since they refused to believe in pagan gods or to take part in their festivals. The government was largely indifferent, however, and made no attempt to stamp out the cult – the earliest persecutions were spontaneous outbreaks of popular hatred.

The 3rd-century troubles swelled the membership of the Church but at the same time fuelled popular hostility. Official persecutions began at this time, and were intensified under Diocletin in 303. These persecutions were ruthless and bloody, but the courage of the martyrs served only to increase the prestige and strength of the Church. The point was not lost on Constantine, who issued an edict of toleration in 313.

Constantine's personal attitude is uncertain, since he continued to endorse pagan cults and was only baptized on his deathbed. However, he honoured the Church and its leaders, and used his authority to settle theological disputes, which from now on become matters of political importance. All subsequent emperors were nominally Christians – with the exception of Julian the Apostate (360–3), who staged an abortive pagan revival – and Christianity became the officially established religion of the Empire.

The Eastern and Western Empires

In 330 Constantine inaugurated a new capital at Constantinople (modern Istanbul). This move symbolized the declining importance of Rome and the growing separation of the eastern and western halves of the Empire. From the later 4th century they had separate emperors and their histories diverged. The West was menaced by foreign invaders, and at the start of the 5th century German barbarians overran Gaul, Spain, Africa and Italy (⊳ pp. 78 and 80). In 410 Rome itself was sacked by the Visigoths under Alaric. After these disasters things were patched up, and the Western Empire limped on until 476 when the last Roman emperor, Romulus Augustulus, was deposed and replaced in Italy by the Gothic king, Odoacer.

The East survived, however, partly because it faced fewer military problems. Thrace (a region of the eastern Balkans) was continually attacked by Goths and Huns in the 5th century, and by Avars and Bulgars in the 6th, but these threats were dealt with relatively easily, and diplomacy secured peace with the Persians in the east. The Byzantine Empire, as the Eastern Empire became known, although steadily reduced by Arab and then Turkish conquests, was to survive until the 15th century (⊳ p. 80).

Why did Rome fall?

Historians have long puzzled over the causes of the decline and fall of the

BARBARIAN INCURSIONS IN THE 5TH CENTURY AD

ANGLES
JUTES
SAXONS
FRANKS   LOMBARDS
BURGUNDIANS   OSTROGOTHS
ALAMANNI   VANDALS
VISIGOTHS
ROME   CONSTANTINOPLE
HUNS
SASSANIAN EMPIRE

EAST — WEST DIVIDING LINE in c.395

SAXONS, ANGLES & JUTES
FRANKS
BURGUNDIANS   OSTROGOTHS
VANDALS   HUNS
VISIGOTHS

EXTENT of the ROMAN EMPIRE in c.395

ROMAN ENTERTAINMENT AND LEISURE

SEE ALSO
● THE RISE OF ROME p. 36
● ANCIENT WARFARE p. 44
● THE BARBARIAN KINGDOMS p. 78
● THE BYZANTINE EMPIRE p. 80

No society before modern times has been more obsessed with sport, entertainment and organized leisure than the Roman Empire. In Rome entertainments were provided by the emperor (and placed in importance alongside food subsidies in Juvenal's famous jibe about 'bread and circuses'), while in provincial cities annually elected officials were obliged to put on shows at their own expense as part of their duties. The emperor was expected to appear in public at the races or the theatre, where the crowd was able to express its approval or disapproval of him, and even to make demands, for example for lower taxes.

Roman society expended much time, energy and above all money on leisure and entertainment. The amphitheatres, theatres and public bath houses in Rome and every major provincial city are among the finest achievements of Roman architecture, and the most evident sign of the importance of sport and leisure in Roman life.

The most popular form of mass entertainment was chariot racing. Huge crowds attended the races – the Circus Maximus, only one of several racetracks in Rome, could hold an estimated 250 000 spectators. The four teams, the Reds, Whites, Blues and Greens, had fanatical followings throughout the Empire. The outcome of a race depended on the skill and bravado of the charioteers, some of whom became wealthy celebrities. As in modern horseracing, the spectacle was only part of the excitement; an equally important ingredient was betting – a Roman obsession.

The thrill of the arena also attracted enormous crowds, whose enthusiasm had a more pathological character. The Colosseum in Rome (which could hold between 50 000 and 70 000 people) and its many provincial imitations were devoted to blood sports involving wild animal hunts, fights to the death between gladiators, and public executions of criminals, who were mercilessly torn to pieces by wild beasts. These sadistic spectacles were on an unimaginable scale. Under Augustus regular shows occurred about twice a year in Rome, and the emperor decreed that no more than sixty pairs of gladiators could take part on each occasion; but it is doubtful if these restrictions were enforced, and they were certainly exceeded at the shows staged to mark special occasions, such as a victory or the accession of a new emperor. The games given by Trajan to celebrate the conquest of Dacia (modern Romania) in AD 108–9 lasted for 123 days, and entailed the slaughter of 11 000 animals and combats between 10 000 gladiators.

Gladiators themselves were mostly slaves, convicts and desperadoes, who could sometimes achieve fame and fortune in the course of a successful – though usually short – career. Such was the glamour that surrounded them that Roman aristocrats, and

Three gladiators and a bear are depicted in this mosaic from the Roman villa at Nennig an der Mosel, Germany. The Ancient Greeks used mosaic as an art form, but the Romans transformed it into a common decorative medium for floors. Many Roman mosaics were functional, sometimes monochrome. However, complex and detailed mosaics adorned palaces and major public buildings, while mythological representations and vivid pictorial mosaics eventually replaced religious statuary as the principal decoration of Roman temples.

even some emperors, were tempted to try their hand, to the great distaste of their peers. Educated people sometimes expressed disgust and disapproval of the shows (though they did nothing); others unconvincingly affected boredom. In fact the games appealed to people of all classes throughout Roman history. St Augustine (AD 354–430) tells the story of a friend who went along to see how awful it was, but was so excited by the sight of blood and the roar of the crowd that he instantly became an addict. The more extreme practices of the arena were gradually abolished by Christian emperors in the 5th and 6th centuries, but some aspects lived on. Echoes of Roman-style entertainment still survive in parts of the former Roman empire, most notably in the Spanish bullfights.

Other popular entertainments included the theatre, which offered a wide variety of performances, from literary plays, music and dance, to crude popular comedies, which the well-to-do denounced as obscene, and which were sometimes banned by the authorities. Professional actors were glamorous figures who achieved immense popularity as well as the envious disapproval of upper-class intellectuals.

Mass spectator sports and popular theatrical performances thus turned the inhabitants of the Roman empire into an audience of passive consumers. But they also had opportunities for active social recreation. The most important of these leisure activities was visiting the baths. The baths ranged from small privately owned establishments containing little more than a pool and a hot room, and charging a small fee, to the great thermal complexes of Rome and other large cities, which offered a sophisticated variety of hot and cold baths, steam rooms, and so on, and were provided at public expense. The baths were devoted to social recreation as much as to washing. Complexes such as the Baths of Caracalla in Rome provided exercise space for gymnastics and ball games, conversation, board games and gambling. They were also, as our sources make clear, places where one could find sexual partners. In all respects the daily visit to the baths was the central feature of Roman social life.

Western Empire, and have offered a bewildering variety of explanations. Excessive taxation, military weakness and population decline were all relevant factors, but were themselves symptoms of the condition that needs to be explained, and cannot be considered causes in their own right. The same is true of such explanations as moral corruption, while supposed environmental factors such as climate

change or poisoning from lead water pipes seem contrived and unconvincing.

Much depends on the subjective view of the historian. For instance, Edward Gibbon (1737–94) in his monumental *Decline and Fall of the Roman Empire* deeply lamented the disappearance of an enlightened and rational culture, swept away on a tide of barbarism and superstition. Christians have not unnaturally

challenged this view of the triumph of their faith. Modern academic historians are more neutral. They tend to emphasize the prosaic fact of the German invasions, which arose from external causes. Barbarian pressure on the frontiers had not existed under the early Empire, but built up in the 3rd century and became irresistible in the 5th (⊳ p. 78). The conclusion of this view is that the Roman Empire did not fall – it was pushed. **TC**

The Ancient Economy

Some of the familiar economic institutions of the modern world, such as money and banks, already existed in antiquity. Ancient economies were by no means 'primitive' or 'underdeveloped', but they were certainly very different from the world of stock exchanges and credit cards we know today. Economic activity in the ancient world had a closer relationship with the social, political, and religious aspects of life than it has in our own society. For example, institutions such as temples and households were involved in the production and distribution of goods and services, the mobilization of labour and the cultivation of land.

Warfare had a crucial impact on ancient economies. Individuals made war to gain booty, while imperialist states such as Assyria and Rome fought to acquire tribute-paying territories, whose payments filled the coffers of the state (⊳ p. 44). In all ancient societies economic activity was centred upon households, temples and governments, but their role and importance varied considerably. Ancient societies solved the basic problems of how to supply labour for the land, how to distribute food and manufactured goods, and the related problems of borrowing, lending and trading, in strikingly different ways.

Labour and power

In a world with no petrol engines or electricity all work was done by humans and animals. Acquiring wealth meant gaining control of the labour-power available. Since most ancient societies found it difficult to conceive of labour as an abstract commodity that could be separated from the person of the labourer, hiring people to work for a wage (that is, buying people's work) was not the most common way of mobilizing labour. Wage labour was very important for some tasks, but salaried workers were not the mainstay of the ancient economy as they are today. Hired labourers did mostly seasonal or short-term jobs such as harvesting cereals, or undertook contract labour, such as the monumental rebuilding of the centre of Athens undertaken by Pericles in the 5th century BC (⊳ p. 31).

Early Greek coins often used animal motifs with cult or symbolic associations. This Athenian coin of the 5th century BC portrays the owl of wisdom, luck and victory, the olive spray of peace and prosperity, and the moon – possibly symbolizing victory over the Persians at the battle of Marathon. Coin-portraits depicting reigning monarchs were first introduced by Alexander the Great, prior to which only the heads of gods had appeared on coins.

Slaves

The ancient economy made extensive use of slave labour. However, 'chattel slaves' of the type who worked the plantations of Jamaica and America in the 18th and 19th centuries (who were bought and sold as property, and had no rights and no hope of ever gaining their freedom) were rare in antiquity. Most chattel slaves in the ancient world were initially acquired through war or conquest, and piracy provided another important source of supply.

In ancient Sumer slaves are known to have worked in the cities as domestics, and in the fields and mines in large groups. 'Chattel slavery' was an accepted fact of life throughout Greek and Roman civilization. In Athens many families owned domestic slaves, and slaves and masters often worked side by side in small businesses. But private slaves were also employed in the silver mines, where they toiled in unpleasant and unhealthy conditions.

Slavery existed in Rome from early times. The expansion of the Empire in the 2nd and 1st centuries BC brought a vast increase in the ownership of slaves. After the annihilation of the Macedonian army by Rome at Pydna in 167 BC, Epirus was sacked and 150 000 of its inhabitants sold into slavery by the victorious Roman general Aemilius Paullus. Slaves were used on a large scale in mining enterprises in the Roman provinces. The historian Polybius describes how 40 000 slaves were employed in the silver mines of Cartagena in Spain in the mid-2nd century BC. In Italy slaves were also widely employed in agriculture during this period, working in gangs on the great estates of the Roman upper classes. Slavery continued to flourish during the Roman Empire. During this period the slave market appears to have been supplied from internal sources and by an extensive slave trade with areas outside the borders of the Roman provinces.

Slaves could sometimes attain their freedom. Some were freed for good service by benevolent masters, some were able to purchase their freedom by accumulating savings, while others were freed after their master's death by provision in his will. In Athens, where there was no formal procedure for 'manumission' (the act of freeing a slave), freed slaves did not become citizens, and were liable to certain taxes and restrictions of privilege. In Rome manumission was often performed in a legal ceremony in front of a magistrate. Roman freedmen acquired Roman citizenship, subject to certain restrictions.

Ancient societies also included various classes of dependent labourers, i.e. people who were forced to work for others through birth or other circumstances, such as debt. Dependent labourers were not slaves, but neither were they free in a modern sense. They could be described as tenants with no right to cancel the rental agreement. Many of the workers who cultivated temple lands in ancient Mesopotamian cities were dependent labourers They had to pay a portion of the crop to the temple, and had no freedom to move away from the land they worked. The 'helots' of Sparta (⊳ p. 28) were a class of dependent, serf-like labourers. Around 700 BC the Spartans conquered the territory of their neighbour, Messenia, and forced the Messenians to work as state-owned helots. Every year the helots paid a set percentage of what they grew to a Spartan master, and lived off what was left. Helots were used in domestic service as well as in agricultural labour, but they were always owned by the state. Some wealthy Spartans also personally owned chattel slaves. Helots did not have the political rights of Spartan citizens, and, since they outnumbered the Spartans themselves, were kept under tight military control.

Another category of dependent labour was that of debt-bondsmen. The *hektemoroi* (or 'sixth parters') of archaic Athens were a group who had accepted loans of seed-corn and other resources in hard times. Their obligation forced them to pay one-sixth of their produce to the lender, and few seem ever to have been able to pay off the debt. If they defaulted on their payments, they could be sold into slavery. The plight of the hektemoroi was alleviated by the reforms of Solon after 594 BC (⊳ p. 28). The debt-bondsmen of early Rome, tied to their creditors by a complex relationship called *nexum*, were similarly forced to work for others.

Agriculture and the land

Agriculture was the most important sector of the ancient economy, and most people worked on the land. Given the technological limitations of farming, storage and transport systems, and the high risks inherent in food production itself, the primary aim of individual households, city-states, palaces – and even empires – was to be self-sufficient in food production. Without airlifts and convoys of trucks, the scope for famine was immense. No ancient city could have existed for long without being able to feed itself. Whatever political and social relationships linked the small farmer to the rulers, it was ultimately the business of individual households to feed themselves and to produce a surplus to feed priests, government officials, craftsmen and traders.

In ancient Egypt, for example, small-scale farmers grew food for themselves, as well as for the complex Egyptian bureaucracy. Theoretically the Pharaoh owned all the land. He sometimes made grants of land to temples and court officials, but in return expected to receive a proportion of the produce grown, which he then used to pay tomb-builders, metalworkers, scribes, and others. The portion the Pharaoh received was ultimately exacted from the peasant families who worked the land, and the amount of 'tax' thus collected depended on how much the Nile had flooded, since this affected the size of the crop. The inundation was carefully measured annually, since the Pharaoh's income depended on it directly.

Elsewhere, even where temples or states were closely involved in the administration of agricultural land, as in Mesopotamian city-states or Mycenaean Greek palaces, land could usually be bought, sold and leased by private individuals. Such transactions often had no formal legal status, and the sale of a field, for example, might be disguised as a gift.

Few ancient cities imported food staples. Rome, the largest city in the ancient world with a population of around 1 000 000 in the age of Augustus, was an exceptional case, but even so much of its food was supplied by Italy and the areas close to the city itself. Some Classical Greek cities also imported wheat (most notably Athens at the height of its power in the 5th and 4th centuries BC), but none ever stopped producing their own staple food. Only when a city or a palace had a secure food supply from territory that it firmly controlled could it afford to support other non-subsistence economic activities, such as craft production and trade (▷ p. box).

Craft production and manufacturing

In the ancient Near Eastern and Mediterranean world craft production was usually based at palace or urban centres. In the Mycenaean palaces and the Old Babylonian palace at Mari (▷ p. 20), the royal court tried to monopolize certain types of craft production, such as bronze-working. The fact that an essential commodity like bronze could only be obtained through the palace increased the prestige and political power of the royal family. Mining was a state monopoly in ancient Egypt (▷ p. 18).

Manufacturing, like farming, often operated at household level, with the members of a family, perhaps helped by a few dependants or slaves, running a small enterprise. This may have been the case even within the political structures of royal palaces, as is suggested by Mycenaean records of bronze workers and their products (▷ p. 25).

Many different manufacturing processes and retail trades are documented in ancient texts: goldsmiths and silversmiths, ivory workers, garment makers, glass-workers, perfumers, leather-workers, butchers, bakers, brewers, and so on. Many craftsmen were highly specialized, and worked on only part of a process, such as fulling (i.e. putting special finishes on textiles). Many made luxury goods – such as ivory-inlaid furniture (a Phoenician speciality) – for wealthy or royal clients. Some craftsmen – notably sculptors and stonemasons – were itinerant, travelling from place to place to practise their trades. The Jewish Old Testament describes how a craftsman – 'a man of great skill and ingenuity, versed in every kind of craftsmanship in bronze' – was brought from the Phoenician city of Tyre to build King Solomon's temple and palace in Jerusalem. A craftsman's livelihood was uncertain, however. Unless they also had direct access to land for growing crops, as was the case in some Mesopotamian societies, craftsmen were dependent on the patronage of the wealthy and the activi-

---

ANCIENT TRADE

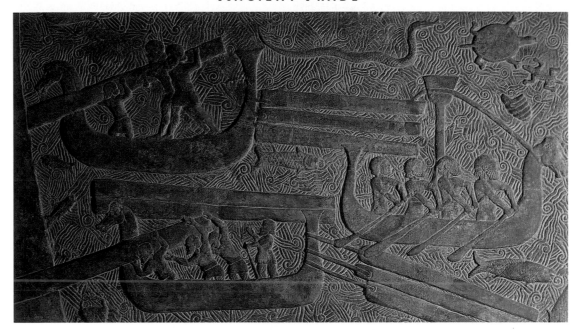

A cargo of timber is unloaded after a sea voyage in this Assyrian relief dating from between 721 and 705 BC.

Food staples and other necessities were the least important items of trade in antiquity. Long-distance trade was dominated by luxury goods. Transport by sea (around the Mediterranean) and by river (especially in Mesopotamia and Egypt) was faster and easier than overland caravans. But sea travel was a risky undertaking. 'Bottomry' loans were a crucial aspect of sea trade in ancient Athens, where they were developed to a fine art. Before a merchant ship embarked on a journey, the owner solicited loans from a number of different people to outfit the ship, hire the crew and sometimes pay for the cargo. If the ship went down at sea, the 'investors' lost their money – but if it returned safely, their loans were repaid at a high rate of interest. This provided a means of spreading the risks so that no one person lost everything in a shipwreck. Normally, a trader would not put all his merchandise in one ship, but would put a little bit in each of a number of ships, so as not to risk losing

everything if the ship was captured by pirates or wrecked. Shipwrecks were frequent, and those that have been discovered have provided archaeologists with valuable evidence for ancient trade.

But prestigious and valuable commodities could also travel long distances overland. A remarkable set of cuneiform tablets unearthed at the city of Kanesh in Turkey and dating from c. 1900 BC documents the activities of a community of Assyrian traders living there. The tablets record the business contracts, loans, credit arrangements, payments, and correspondence relating to the lucrative trade in textiles and tin carried on between Kanesh and the Assyrian city of Ashur (▷ p. 20). The traders – whose donkey caravans had to traverse c. 650 km (c. 400 mi) of wild, mountainous country – were private entrepreneurs, but their activities were encouraged by the Assyrian state.

---

ties of traders for the necessities of life (▷ box).

Money and banking

The date of the invention of coinage is hotly debated, but is unlikely to have been before the 6th century BC. However, the idea of money is much older than the invention of coins. As early as c. 2000 BC the kings and temples of Ur paid for goods and services by chopping set weights of silver rings off large coils. The use of set weights of silver (and later gold) as a standard of value had a long and well-established history in ancient Mesopotamia.

The first proper coins appear to have come from Lydia c. 650 BC and were discovered in the foundation deposit of the Temple of Artemis at Ephesus in western Anatolia. They probably date from the period when restoration work on the temple was carried out by Croesus, the wealthy king of Greek legend. These early coins were large and valuable – small change was not invented until much later – and bear the Lydian royal symbol of a lion. They were made of electrum, a

natural alloy of gold and silver. It is not clear what they were used for, besides foundation deposits, though paying armies is one possibility.

Soon after this, the rulers of neighbouring Ionian Greek cities and the Great King of Persia begin to issue their own coins. These were as much an expression of political authority as a means of purchase. It was only late in the 6th century BC that the Greek city of Aegina (▷ map, p. 31) developed a silver coinage that was used widely in trade.

Since each Greek city-state minted its own coins to different standards, bankers who would change money became essential in port towns. In Athens bankers not only changed money but also made loans on the security of property, and accepted deposits of money on which they paid interest. But except in the case of mining, few loans were put to use as business investments. Most businesses, including farms, were small family ventures contained within households. The idea of a larger 'company' in the modern sense would have been incomprehensible in the ancient world.   LF

Ancient Warfare

The earliest wars were fought before history was written. No details remain of campaigns or individuals; the only evidence is archaeological and consists of remains of settlements, weapons and human bones. With the development of agriculture and the change from nomadic hunting to farming during the early Neolithic period (⊳ p. 15), fortified sites spread throughout the Near East and the Mediterranean region.

As early as 7000 BC Jericho had been encircled with walls three metres thick. Bows and spears that had been used to hunt animals were now turned on men. Stone maces, knives and slings – obvious mankillers – occurred for the first time.

Near Eastern warfare

With the emergence of the first urban civilizations in southern Mesopotamia in the 4th millenium BC, there appeared two innovations that had enormous implications for the history of warfare: metalworking and the wheel. The new technology enabled men to fashion swords, spears, axe heads and helmets. Four-wheeled chariots or 'battle-wagons' drawn by wild asses first appeared in Sumer around 2800 BC, and were an important component of the large standing army of Sargon of Akkad (⊳ p. 16).

The greatest exponents of the chariot were the Egyptians. The highly efficient armies of New Kingdom pharaohs such as Thutmose III and Ramses II (⊳ p. 19) fielded thousands of light, two-wheeled horse-drawn chariots. Their two-man crews comprised a charioteer and an armoured warrior wielding a bow and a javelin. With heavy infantry armed with spears and shields, and light infantry equipped with bows, slings and axes in support, the chariot spearheaded Egyptian imperial expansion into Nubia and Palestine. At Kadesh (c. 1280 BC) – one of the earliest recorded battles – the Egyptians clashed with the Hittites of Anatolia (⊳ p. 22), who used heavier, less manoeuvrable chariots to penetrate enemy lines.

Soon afterwards the Hittite empire collapsed, but the traditions of Near Eastern military organization continued through the later empires of Assyria and Persia (⊳ pp. 20 and 26). The Assyrians were responsible for a revolution in the use of cavalry. Their armoured horsemen – equipped with spears and bows and capable of charging to close combat – hastened the demise of the war-chariot.

Mycenaean warfare

The warlike Mycenaean civilization in Greece also crumbled at the end of the Bronze Age (⊳ p. 25). Homer's *Iliad* tells of a great expedition against Troy led by the Mycenaean king Agamemnon. But Homer's epic – composed centuries after the destruction of Mycenae – contains elements that belong to a much later period. The poem describes 'aristocratic' war, in which kings and princes rode into battle in chariots, dismounting to engage in single combat with opponents of equal social status. The motivation for such war was the acquisition of booty such as slaves, livestock and valuables, and not the conquest of territory. Homer may be describing the warfare of his own day rather than that of the Bronze Age, but without contemporary accounts we cannot tell whether Mycenaean warfare was aristocratic or Near Eastern in character.

Classical Greek warfare

In Greece, around 750 BC, aristocratic raiding was supplanted by 'hoplite war'. In a Greek city-state those who owned land had the rights to vote, to become magistrates, and to serve in the army as heavily armed citizen-soldiers or 'hoplites'. Military service was an important part of any Greek citizen's life. It was both a duty and a privilege to fight in a phalanx – a tightly packed formation of pike-armed infantrymen, typically eight men deep. Each hoplite provided his own arms and armour of spear, short sword, round shield, breastplate and greaves (shin-pads). He received no pay except a share in the booty, and had to rely on the income from his farmland to support himself and his family. The hoplite's farming responsibilities limited the campaigning season to a few weeks in summer before the harvest. In Sparta citizens spent all their time in hoplite training, while the 'state serfs' (or *helots*; ⊳ p. 28) had to farm to support them.

Great courage was required to fight in a hoplite battle. Often one side would waver and break before their opponents' onslaught. If both sides kept their nerve a grim struggle would ensue, with the rear ranks pushing with all their strength, while the front ranks jabbed at the necks and faces of their opponents over the rims of their shields. Most casualties occurred in pursuit, after an enemy's phalanx had become disordered and broken. To escape the slaughter a hoplite had to drop his heavy shield, the loss of which was a mark of great dishonour. Against other types of army the phalanx was almost unstoppable. The Greek historian Herodotus describes how the hoplites frustrated the Persian invasions of Greece (490 and 480–79 BC; ⊳ pp. 26 and 29), shattering the largely missile-armed forces of their opponents at the battles of Marathon (490) and Plataea (479).

Another crucial factor in the Greek victory was the role of the recently created Athenian navy. Although the Greeks had used warships before the Persian Wars, the Athenians, in response to the Persian attacks, constructed several hundred triremes (galleys powered by three banks of oars) and manned them with crews from the lower classes who could not afford hoplite arms. Victory over the Persians at Salamis (480 BC) enabled the Athenians to build an empire in the Aegean based on naval superiority.

The Peloponnesian War between Athens and Sparta (431–404 BC; ⊳ p. 30) broke the power of the Athenian navy and undermined the supremacy of the phalanx. Athenian hoplites were defeated by light troops in Aetolia in 426 BC, and even Spartan hoplites had to surrender after lengthy skirmishing with unarmoured infantry on the island of Sphacteria in 425 BC. Defeat at the hands of the Thebans at Leuctra (371 BC) finally ended the myth of the invincibility of the Spartan hoplite.

Alexander the Great

Philip II of Macedon transformed Greek warfare, reforming his army and integrating the striking power of cavalry with steady infantry (see box 'Hellenistic Armies'; ⊳ p. 33). His crushing defeat of the Greek city-states at Chaeronea in 338 BC rang the death-knell of hoplite pre-eminence and brought mainland Greece under his control. Philip's son Alexander continued the offensive against Persia begun by his father. To overcome the vast

An Elamite chariot advances to do battle with Ashurbanipal's Assyrians in this 7th-century BC relief from Nineveh. But the Elamites had no answer to the cavalry and heavier chariots of the Assyrian invaders.

Achaemenid empire an efficient logistics organization was essential. To provide for the needs of a 60 000-strong army forays had to be made into regions where supplies were readily available. If an army lingered for a long time in one place, the local people could be faced with famine.

Alexander was a master of strategy and tactics, and those who came after him studied his campaigns and battles in great detail. Alexander's successors fought each other initially with armies composed of veterans of his expedition, but, as time passed, the Hellenistic kings turned to other sources. Constant wars had produced a large number of dispossessed and landless men, who were prepared to serve as mercenaries for the warring kings. The Ptolemies of Egypt (▷ p. 19) used mercenaries extensively because they could not trust their subject native populations; other kingdoms and cities used them to spare their own peoples the burden of military service. Mercenaries were fairly reliable provided pay was forthcoming. One of the bloodiest wars in ancient history broke out when the mercenaries Carthage had employed in the First Punic War against Rome (264–241 BC) mutinied in protest at not being paid on their return to Africa from Sicily.

Roman warfare

At the time of the First Punic War Rome had already conquered Italy (▷ p. 36). Unlike the rulers of the Greek city-states, the Romans were willing to extend citizenship to those who migrated to Rome, to freed slaves, and to conquered populations. This gave them large resources of manpower for military purposes. The Romans had also developed a system of alliances with the neighbouring towns and tribes of Italy. These allies were bound to help Rome in the event of attack and were forbidden to have dealings with one another. Allies who revolted could expect to be attacked by the rest of the Roman alliance. Rome was also willing to adopt the best military ideas from her neighbours, borrowing the phalanx from the Etruscans, and during the 4th century BC changing to a looser 'manipular' formation – based on small units of footsoldiers – to fight in the hills against the Samnites.

Roman society was geared to war. Servius Tullius, the semi-legendary king of Rome, is said to have created the system by which different classes voted according to their wealth and contribution in war. Under the Republic the consuls had command of both civil and military affairs, although it was the people who voted for war or peace. A general had the right to dispose of any booty as he saw fit, and so being a consul in wartime could bring large profits. The chance to win glory in war and celebrate a triumph led to great competition amongst the aristocracy for the consulship.

The Roman army was paid – traditionally as early as 406 BC, and this enabled the Romans to conduct wars outside the normal seasonal restrictions. However, it had the side-effect of eroding the class of peasant-farmers (the main recruiting-ground for the professional army) who were unable to maintain their land.

Rome's extensive manpower resources, based on the contributions of its Italian allies, provided great resilience in times of crisis. Hannibal (▷ p. 36) was dismayed by the Romans' ability to replace losses and to continue to fight not only in Italy but also in Spain, Sicily and Macedonia, and to maintain a large fleet. The Second Punic War (218–202 BC) thus became a Mediterranean-wide conflict, and victory enabled Rome to become overlord of the whole Mediterranean region.

The opponents that the Romans feared above all others were the Celts (▷ p. 34). Celtic warriors were renowned for their ferocity and reckless courage, running into battle naked and collecting the heads of their enemies. Celtic warfare was aristocratic in character, concerned mainly with raiding neighbouring tribes, although the tribes were capable of forming large alliances. Tribal loyalty was strong, but Celts also served as mercenaries for both Mediterranean states and other Celtic tribes. Their mastery of metallurgy allowed them to develop chainmail and the shortsword – innovations that the Romans are believed to have adopted from them. The Celts sacked Rome in 390 BC and periodically defeated its legions. Julius Caesar conquered Gaul (58–51 BC) by exploiting the rivalries of various tribes, but his army's tactics had been shaped by three centuries of conflict with the Celts.

Roman veterans increasingly demanded land as a reward for long service, and they relied on their generals to put their case to the senate. Ambitious generals like Caesar could create armies of veterans loyal not to the state but to themselves, and thus could aim at domination of the Empire. After decades of civil war Augustus emerged in control of all the Roman armies (▷ p 38). He initiated a programme of settling colonies of veterans in the provinces. He also introduced a regular standing army, in which legionaries served for a fixed term of 20 years. On discharge they received either a lump sum in cash or a land grant. The troops were permanently stationed in the outlying provinces of the empire.

In the later empire the army became two-tiered. Frontier units had the task of limiting the damage of foreign incursion, while a high-quality reserve army, consisting mainly of cavalry and allied barbarian troops (▷ p. 78), accompanied the emperor on campaign. Rome's long-standing opponent at this time was the empire of the Sassanid Persians (▷ p. 27), who used cavalry armies composed of horse archers and cataphracts – lancers so heavily armoured that both horse and rider were covered in mail. However, it was the large migrations of Germanic peoples into the Western Empire that eventually broke its cohesion and set the tone for the military development of medieval Europe (▷ p. 102).

LR

SEE ALSO

- CIVILIZATIONS OF THE ANCIENT NEAR EAST pp. 16–27
- ARCHAIC AND CLASSICAL GREECE p. 28
- ALEXANDER THE GREAT p. 32
- THE RISE OF ROME p. 36
- THE ROMAN EMPIRE p. 38
- THE MONGOL WARRIOR p. 55
- THE BARBARIAN KINGDOMS p. 78
- MEDIEVAL AND RENAISSANCE WARFARE p. 102

ROMAN SIEGECRAFT

Siegeworks such as those used by Julius Caesar to crush the Gallic chieftain Vercingetorix and his 80 000-strong army at Alesia in 52 BC testify to Roman mastery of military engineering. Caesar first surrounded the hilltop town with a 16 km (10 mi) line of walls and trenches. When Gallic allies attempted to march to the rescue of Vercingetorix, Caesar threw a second line of fortifications around his own army to repel them. Each line consisted of a number of different elements. The ramparts were fortified with towers at regular intervals, and water-filled ditches and booby-traps of sharpened branches completed a formidable system of obstacles. When besieging an isolated enemy, with no risk of attack from the rear, a single line of fortifications sufficed.

The Romans had an imposing arsenal of siege weaponry at their disposal. The battering-ram – consisting of a roofed shed with a long metal-headed beam suspended from the ridge-piece – was used to breach walls and gates. Layers of clay or soaked hides protected the machine from fire or bombardment. The key Roman artillery weapons were the arrow-firing *catapulta* and the stone-throwing *ballista*. Some ballistae were capable of hurling boulders weighing up to 40 kg (88 lb). Mobile siege towers with elevated platforms facilitated missile attacks by archers and artillery. When approaching the walls, legionaries would adopt the *testudo* (or 'tortoise') formation, locking their shields over their heads in a 'shell' to protect them from enemy arrows and spears.

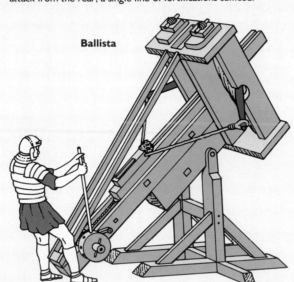

Ballista

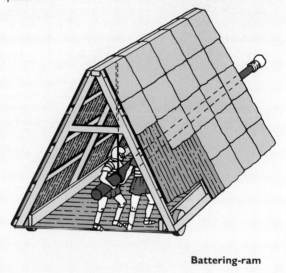

Battering-ram

Ancient Religions

Despite wide variations over time and space, all known human societies have had religions. However, before the spread of 'world' religions such as Christianity and Islam, attitudes toward religion as well as religious beliefs themselves were rather different. Most religions in the ancient Near Eastern and Classical worlds were specific to a people and place, but they were by no means exclusive. Even Judaism, which was exceptional, did not become exclusive until relatively late in its history.

By modern standards, religious intolerance was not a major problem in the ancient world. When people travelled to or conquered another territory, they accepted as valid – at least for that place – the religious beliefs and the gods of the people they met. Frequently they combined them with their own, as when the Greeks and the Phoenicians both met a powerful, native female deity on Cyprus. The Phoenicians identified her with their own goddess Astarte, while the Greeks worshipped her (often in the very same sanctuaries) as Aphrodite.

Gods and human lives

The supernatural embraced all areas of human life, and was every bit as real to people as the natural world. Gods dwelt in the heavens and under the earth. The streams, mountains, woods and other features of the natural landscape might also be inhabited by lesser supernatural beings – for example the nymphs of Greek religion. Some gods were themselves

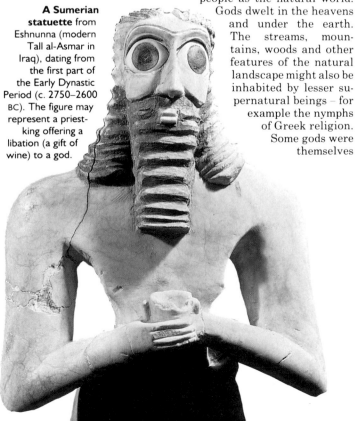

A Sumerian statuette from Eshnunna (modern Tall al-Asmar in Iraq), dating from the first part of the Early Dynastic Period (c. 2750–2600 BC). The figure may represent a priest-king offering a libation (a gift of wine) to a god.

manifestations of natural forces – Teshub, the northern Mesopotamian and Anatolian storm-god; Baal, the Canaanite god of rain and fertility; Shamash, the Mesopotamian sun-god; or Poseidon, the Greek god of the sea and of earthquakes.

Deities, demons and spirits involved themselves in human lives in several different ways. They could both help and harm people. Some evil spirits were thought to harm babies and small children, so special measures had to be taken to protect them. In ancient Mesopotamia lists of magic spells and rituals gave protection against the demons causing physical or mental illness, bad dreams and other misfortunes. Lead tablets from the Temple of Asclepius at Epidaurus in Greece dating from the 4th century BC describe how the god appeared to patients in their dreams while they slept in the Temple, and miraculously healed them.

Gods also helped people to pass through crucial life stages (or 'rites of passage'). In ancient Athens young men ritually entered adulthood at a festival of Apollo known as the Apatouria, at which their long hair was cut short. Young girls dedicated their toys to Apollo's twin sister – the goddess Artemis – on the night before they were married, to symbolize the fact that they were leaving childhood behind. Deities who took special charge of birth, death and marriage featured in almost all ancient religions.

Sanctuaries and temples

Temples and shrines could be the homes of a particular god, but more often they served as locations where the human and the divine realms met. Generally they were places where special rituals and festivals to a god or gods were performed. (Although in Greece rituals nearly always took place outside the temple itself, close to the altar.) But temples and shrines also sometimes had more worldly interests. In Egypt, Mesopotamia and the Levant, temples often controlled large amounts of wealth both in the form of offerings to the god, and in terms of agricultural land. These resources were normally managed by the priests, though in Egypt they belonged in theory to the Pharaoh (▷ p. 42). In ancient Greece and Rome temples were often repositories of dedications (votive offerings) given by worshippers either to thank the god for a service rendered, or to request the granting of a wish. Most of these dedications were modest offerings of items such as pots or clay figurines, but some were very lavish indeed, and included gold, silver and bronze vessels and marble statues.

Shrines and sanctuaries took many different forms. The gigantic, stone-built royal temples of Egypt, the tall mud-brick ziggurats of ancient Mesopotamia and the gleaming colonnaded marble temples of Greece and Rome are some of the best-known places of worship of the ancient world. But many sacred places bore no such monuments. In Minoan Crete and Mycenaean Greece there seem to have

been no large free-standing temples, though there were shrines in palaces and sacred deposits are often found in caves and on mountain tops (▷ pp. 24–5). The Jews of the Levant did not have a large monumental sanctuary site until King Solomon built his temple at Jerusalem (▷ pp. 23 and 43). Even Greek sanctuaries often consisted only of an altar, and on all Greek temple sites the altar predated the temple.

Animal sacrifice was a central feature of much ancient worship at temples and religious festivals. In ancient Greece virtually all meat eaten was first sacrificed on the altar of a god. The fat and the bones were burned for the god (who was nourished by the smoke), while the sacrificer and his friends and relations enjoyed the meat.

Religion and political structures

Some of the best documented aspects of ancient religion are those connected with royalty. In many ancient societies the king held a special place in religious beliefs. Some kings were considered to be divine, as in the case of the Egyptian Pharaoh, who was thought to be the incarnation of the god Horus on earth (▷ p. 17). Much later, in the 4th century BC, some evidence suggests that Alexander the Great was worshipped as a god during his lifetime (▷ p. 32). Roman emperors were normally deified (i.e. made into gods) after their death (▷ picture, p. 40). At the funeral of a Roman emperor, an eagle – symbolizing the soul of the emperor flying up to heaven to join the gods – was released as the funeral pyre burned. The claim that a king was a god (rather than an ordinary mortal), or was going to become a god when he departed from the earth, legitimized the power and authority he wielded over others.

In Mesopotamia the king was not a god, but instead was perceived as having a unique relationship with the gods, because he ruled in accordance with divine will and was the special recipient of divine favour. Often he was the nominal high priest of one or more gods. As an intermediary between ordinary mortals and the gods, the king's role was to recreate divine order and justice on earth. This is reflected in the art, literature and ritual of the region. For example, on Assyrian palace reliefs the king is often shown wearing the symbols of the gods, or with the god Asshur floating above him in the same pose as the king.

Religion and military conquest

Kings, in turn, were often dependent on their professional priests to interpret signs and messages from the divine world. Often this was done by inspecting the entrails of sacrificially slaughtered animals. The liver in particular was inspected for colour, size and shape, and for unusual lumps and bumps. Such features were thought to predict good or bad fortune, or to convey certain messages. The omens derived from 'extispicy' – as

THE DELPHIC ORACLE

A few shrines gained international repute in the ancient world. One of the most famous was the oracle of Apollo at Delphi in central Greece. Delphi belonged to no single city but was run by a committee – the Delphic Amphyction – with representatives from several cities. Many cities built small structures there known as treasuries, where dedications from that city were deposited, and where the city's representatives stayed and entertained when they came to consult the oracle. Many non-Greeks also dedicated offerings and made enquiries of the oracle at Delphi.

At Delphi Apollo supposedly spoke through the voice of his priestess, the Pythia. Frequently Greek city-states came with questions, and the oracle seems to have ratified many overseas colonizing ventures (▷ box, p. 29). It is thought that most of the questions simply required 'yes' or 'no' answers, but the oracle gained a reputation for giving ambiguous oracles in verse. When the Lydian king Croesus, based at Sardis in Anatolia, enquired whether he should go to war with the Persians, he was told that if he did, 'he would destroy a great empire'. When he was defeated by the Persians in 546 BC, he realized that the 'great empire' to be destroyed was his own (▷ pp. 26 and 43).

this technique is called – were often related to the fate of kings who had lived long ago. In ancient Mesopotamia, for instance, a lucky king might receive an omen that had previously occurred for Sargon of Akkad, who became a superhero of Mesopotamian royal tradition. A less fortunate king might receive an omen that had been vouchsafed to Ibbi Sin of the Third Dynasty of Ur (▷ p. 16), who – probably unjustly – acquired a reputation as a disastrous ruler. In Rome a special group of priests known as 'haruspices' interpreted the will of the gods as revealed through animal entrails and phenomena such as thunder and lightning.

Extispicy was especially important when kings undertook military campaigns. Priests travelled with the army and examined sacrificial victims before any important military decision was taken. They also kept an eye out for and interpreted any natural phenomena that might be an omen of divine will, such as bizarre dreams, flocks of birds, earth tremors, or solar or lunar eclipses. No military action was taken until the omens were favourable. If a slaughtered animal was found to contain bad omens, then further victims would be killed at regular intervals until good results were obtained. These practices, with minor variations, were virtually universal in the ancient world. Both the Greeks and Romans were particularly sensitive about omens. A loud thunderclap at an unexpected moment could close down the whole city of Rome for the day. The Athenian expedition to Sicily during the Peloponnesian War (413

BC; ▷ p. 31) was almost not sent out because the mutilation of the faces and phalluses of the many small statues of Hermes in the city was felt to be a bad omen for the fate of the campaign. (The Athenian general Alcibiades was later accused of having vandalized them, and of having parodied the rituals of the Athenian cult of the Eleusian mysteries.) No army wanted to fight unless they felt the gods were on their side. When major losses occurred, they were often attributed to a misinterpretation of the omens.

Religion in other ancient societies

In societies without a strongly centralized kingship, the political role of religion was very different from that in ancient Egypt and Mesopotamia, Hellenistic Greece and Imperial Rome. In the city-states of Classical Greece, or in 'tribal' societies such as pre-monarchic Israel, religion often served to emphasize community solidarity. The Jewish Passover, for example, not only remembers the plight of the Jews in Egypt, but emphasizes that as a people they are the chosen ones of the god Yahweh.

In Greece each city had its own civic festivals. Many activities that we consider to be purely secular, such as drama and sport, were in Greece performed as part of religious festivals. In Athens tragedies and comedies were staged as part of important festivals in honour of Dionysus, the wine-god, and there was a prize for the best play (▷ box, p. 30). The Panathenaia, held in the summer in honour of the goddess Athena, also included athletic competitions.

Even the festivals that were common to a number of Greek cities – such as the autumnal festival of Thesmophoria (▷ below), dedicated to Demeter, the corn-goddess, and her daughter Kore (Persephone) were celebrated by cities individually. Each city had its own special god or goddess who was believed to look after the interests of that particular community. Athena Polias and Zeus Polieus ('Athena and Zeus of the Acropolis') were celebrated annually as the guardians of Athens. Sparta's protecting deities were Apollo of Amyklai and Artemis Orthia ('Upright Artemis'), while in Argos Hera guarded the city from her temple on the Argive plain. Similarly, in Celtic Britain different places, groups and natural features were felt to be under the protection of specific gods.

Religion and the agricultural year

Throughout the ancient world, many religious festivals were associated with crucial points of the agricultural year. This is hardly surprising, since almost everyone depended on farming for a livelihood, either directly or indirectly (▷ p. 42). One of the most important roles of the gods was to look after the well-being of the crops.

In societies with a strong kingship, such as in Egypt and Mesopotamia, it was often

the responsibility of the king to mediate with the gods on behalf of his people for a good harvest. In Egypt, this depended on how well the Nile flooded, and the king was annually involved in celebrations aimed at ensuring a good inundation. In Mesopotamia too, the just rule of the king was thought to ensure the fertility of the land, and the king was a central figure in sowing and harvest festivals. On Sumerian cylinder seals the king is sometimes shown performing ritual ploughing. On Assyrian palace reliefs it is common to see the king fertilizing or sprinkling holy water on a Sacred Tree, with bird headed genies standing behind him.

In Classical Greece, in contrast, many of the most important festivals associated with the agricultural year were performed by women, and men were excluded. The Thesmophoria, which lasted for several days just before the beginning of the sowing season, was the most widespread of these. In Athens, the women took over the city, made sacrifices of animals and held their own assembly, in contrast to their normal exclusion from public and political life (▷ box, p. 28). Interestingly, all of the agricultural rituals performed by women celebrated work that was usually done by men. Women's religious and men's practical contribution were both seen as crucial for the fertility of the land and the well-being of the community.

In all ancient societies, the existence of the gods and the supernatural world was never questioned. People took it for granted that they shared the universe with a huge number of invisible beings who could influence their lives for good or ill. Although their beliefs might seem odd and superstitious to us today, they were real for them. Religion frequently provided the most important motives for action in the ancient world.   LF

A Ptolemaic entrance to the Temple of Amun-Ra at Karnak in Egypt, one of a number of additions made to the Great Temple by the Macedonian dynasty that ruled Egypt from 323 to 30 BC. The Ptolemies honoured the Egyptian gods – indeed, in Ptolemaic Egypt Greek gods were only known as names applied to native Egyptian deities.

SEE ALSO
- ANCIENT EGYPT p. 17
- BABYLONIA AND ASSYRIA p. 20
- SYRIA AND THE LEVANT p. 22
- MINOANS AND MYCENAEANS p. 24
- ARCHAIC AND CLASSICAL GREECE p. 28
- ALEXANDER THE GREAT p. 32
- THE ROMAN EMPIRE p. 38
- THE ANCIENT ECONOMY p. 42

OTHER
WORLDS

CHINA AND KOREA	INDIAN SUBCONTINENT	SOUTHEAST ASIA	JAPAN
c. 4000 BC Neolithic farming established in the Yellow River basin **c. 2500 BC** Farming spread to the Yangtze basin **c. 2000 BC** Bronze working in the Yellow River valley **1480–1050 BC** Shang dynasty ruled the first Chinese kingdom **1122–256 BC** Zhou dynasty **551–479 BC** Kongfuzi (Confucius)	**c. 5000 BC** Neolithic farming established in the Indus valley **c. 2300–1700 BC** Harappan civilization flourished in the Indus Valley **c. 2000 BC** Neolithic farming spread to southern India **c. 1500 BC** Bronze Age culture established in the Ganges basin **c. 800 BC** Hindu Iron Age culture established in the Ganges basin	**before 7000 BC** Foodgatherers settled in Indochina **c. 5000 BC** Malay speakers moved from Taiwan into Indonesia **c. 1500 BC** Rice farming established in Indochina **c. 900 BC** Indian traders established links with Southeast Asia	**c. 10 000 BC** Pottery developed in Japan **10 000–c. 250 BC** Neolithic Jomon culture – use of polished tools
481–221 BC 'Warring States' **221–210 BC** Shi Huangdi became China's first emperor, began to build Great Wall **202 BC–AD 220** Han dynasty **221–206 BC** Qin dynasty **107 BC** China invaded Korea	**c. 563–483 BC** Prince Gautama, the Buddha **543–491 BC** Kingdom of Magdalha emerged as a major power in north India **c. 500 BC** Indian agriculturalists colonized Sri Lanka **326** Alexander the Great conquered the Indus valley **c. 300 BC** Sri Lanka converted to Buddhism **272–232 BC** Ashoka, founder of the Mauryan Empire **2nd century BC** Indo-Greek civilization in the Indus valley	**207 BC** Tongking conquered by a Chinese warlord **111 BC** Tongking incorporated into the Chinese Empire	**c. 400 BC** Rice farming reached Japan from Korea **c. 250 BC–AD 250** Yayoi culture – use of metals
AD 265–316 Jin dynasty **1st–7th centuries** Korea divided into three kingdoms – Koryo, Paikche and Silla **383–533** Wei dynasty in the Yellow River valley	**1st–5th centuries AD** Indus valley dominated by the Kushans from Central Asia **c. AD 320–540** Gupta period in northern India **c. 460–550** Invasion of northern India by the Huns	**AD 39** Vietnamese revolt against Chinese rule **1st century** Cambodian state of Funan founded	**AD 57** Japanese state of Wu sent tribute to the emperor of China **2nd century AD** Civil war in Japan **c. 360–400** Unification of Japan
589–618 Sui dynasty **596–649** The reforms of Emperor Taizong **618–907** Tang dynasty **668** Korea united by the Silla kingdom as a tributary of China **907–960** Disintegration of the Chinese Empire **918–1392** Korea united by the Koryo dynasty **960–1127** Song dynasty	**606** Harsha established a Buddhist kingdom in northern India **6th–8th centuries** Calukya kingdom in the Deccan **711** Sind conquered by an Arab army **c 780–c. 927** Rastrakuta kingdom in the Deccan **c. 900** Tamils from southern India began to settle in Sri Lanka **970–13th century** Cola kingdom in southeastern India **before 1000** Dravidian kingdoms established in southern India	**c. 590** Cambodian kingdom of Chenla overthrew Funan **c. 700–c. 850** Sailendra kingdom in Java **849** Burmese kingdom of Pagan founded **939** Vietnam gained independence from China	**c. 538–52** Buddhism introduced **646** Centralized *ritso-ryu* system of government established **710–84** Chinese-style imperial court established at Nara **794** The court moved to Kyoto **857–1160** Government dominated by the Fujiwara family **10th century** Japanese script developed
11th century 'The Reformists' – Wang Anshi and Fan Zhongyan **Early 13th century** Ghenghis Khan began conquest of Jin Empire of northern China, the first step in the creation of a pan-Eurasian Mongol Empire **1127–1279** Song dynasty in power only in southern China	**1001–1027** Mahmud of Ghazni raided northern India from Afghanistan **1185** Muhammad of Ghur invaded the Punjab from Afghanistan and took Lahore **1206** Islamic sultanate of Delhi founded	**1150** Angkor Wat temples completed **1177** The Cambodians overthrew the empire of the Chams **1238** Thai principality of Sukhothai established	**by 1000** Real power passed from the emperor to the Fujiwara family **11th century** Rise of the samurai **1159** Minamoto Yoritomo established the shogunate **1199–1333** Kamakura period – shogunate held by the Hojo family
1260–94 Reign of Kublai Khan **1271–1368** Yuan (Mongol) dynasty **1368** Mongols fled from Beijing **1368–1644** Ming dynasty **1392–1910** Yi dynasty in Korea	**1336** Foundation of the city and empire of Vijayanagar **1347–1518** Bahmani sultanate in the Deccan **14th century** Muslim conquest of northern India completed **1398** Delhi sacked by Timur (Tamerlane) **1451–1526** Lodi kingdom in the Punjab	**1290** Thai principality of Chiang-Mai founded **end of 13th century** Islam arrived in northern Sumatra and began to spread throughout the East Indies **1369** Angkor Wat sacked by the Thais **1471** Kingdom of Annam founded	**1274–81** Attempted invasions by the Mongols **1333–1537/8** Ashikaga shogunate **1333–92** Rival northern and southern courts **1467–77** Civil war – the *Onin* war **15th–16th centuries** Feudal anarchy – the period of the 'Warring Country'
1592 Unsuccessful Japanese invasion of Korea **1644–1911** Qing (Manchu) dynasty **1689** Chinese border with Russia defined by Treaty of Nerchinsk **1662–1722** Enlargement of the Chinese Empire into Central Asia and Tibet under Emperor Kangxi **1682** End of civil war in southern China **1715** Christianity banned	**1489–1686** Adil Shahi dynasty made Bijapur a major power **1518–1611** Sultanate of Golconda, the most powerful state in the Deccan **1526** Babur of Kabul overthrew the Delhi sultanate and established the Mogul Empire **1565** Muslim forces routed Vijayanagar **1658–1707** Aurangzeb made the Mogul Empire a Muslim state, discriminating against Hindus **1674–1802** Maratha Empire in the Deccan **before 1700** The Mogul Empire covered all of India except the far south	**16th century** European exploration of Southeast Asia began **before 1600** Burmese kingdom of Ava gained control of most of modern Burma **1620–1802** Division of Vietnam into rival states	**1549** Francis Xavier, first Christian missionary to Japan **1550–60** Civil war between factions of samurai **1582–1600** Japan reunified by Toyotomi Hideyoshi **1600–1868** Tokugawa shogunate established by Tokugawa Ieyasu **1612** Christianity banned **1630s** Beginning of *Sakoku* – policy of national seclusion
1839–42 First Opium War **1851** The Taiping Movement took up arms **1851–1908** Discontent grew in China as the Dowager Empress Cixi resisted reforms **1851–64** The Taiping Rebellion **1856–60** Second Opium War **1894–5** Sino-Japanese War; Taiwan annexed by Japan **1900–1** Boxer Rebellion against Western influence **1911** Army rebellion toppled the Qing dynasty	**18th century** Provincial governors and other local rulers took power, effectively destroying the Mogul Empire **1757** Battle of Plassey – British rule firmly established in much of India **1818** The settlement of India – the subcontinent was divided between British-ruled and protected states **1857–8** The Indian Mutiny **1885** Indian National Congress founded	**1802** Vietnam reunited by Nguyen Anh **1819** Re-foundation of Singapore **1825–30** Java War **late 1850s–1890s** French colonization of Indochina **1867** Rubber introduced into Malaya **1873–1903** Acheh War	**c. 1750** Tokyo became the world's largest city **1853** US fleet forced Japan to open to trade **1867–9** Tokugawa shogunate toppled; Emperor Meiji gained executive power and instituted Western-style reforms **1894–5** Sino-Japanese War

SUB-SAHARAN AFRICA	AUSTRALASIA	THE AMERICAS	EUROPE
before 3000 BC Farming spread from Egypt to the Middle Nile valley **c. 1000–100 BC** Village communities emerged in West Africa **c. 800 BC** Nubian kingdom established	**c. 40 000–25 000 BC** Australian Aborigines arrived in the subcontinent **c. 3000 BC** First settlement of Micronesia **c. 2500–2000 BC** Settlement of the Solomon Islands, Vanuatu and New Caledonia **c. 1500–1250 BC** Settlement of Fiji and Tonga	**c. 10 000 BC** First settlement of North America across the Bering Strait from Asia **before c. 2500 BC** Farming established in Mexico and Central America **c. 2000 BC** Great Plains tribes began to hunt bison **c. 1500 BC** Domestication of the potato in the Andes **c. 1000 BC** Maize farming established in the North American Great Basin	**c. 2200–1450 BC** Minoan civilization **c. 1500–1150 BC** Mycenaean civilization **8th century** Emergence of Greek city-states **8th–5th centuries BC** peak of Etruscan civilization in Italy
c. 400–100 BC Nok culture in West Africa	**c. 300 BC** First settlement of Samoa **c. 100 BC** First settlement of the Marquesas	**c. 300 BC–AD c. 300** Olmec civilization flourished in western Mexico **c. 100 BC** Foundation of Teotihuacán in central Mexico	**509 BC** Foundation of the Roman republic **499–479 BC** Greek-Persian wars **336–323 BC** Empire of Alexander the Great **27 BC** Augustus became the first Roman emperor
c. AD 50 Rise of the kingdom of Axum **c. AD 100** Negro (mainly Bantu) farmers spread east and south from West Africa **4th century** Abyssinia adopted Christianity **c. 500** Bantus reached east coast of southern Africa	**c. AD 300** First settlement of Tahiti and the Society Islands **c. 400** First settlement of the Cook Islands and Easter Island	**c. AD 300** Rise of the Mayan civilization **c. 400–c. 700** Zapotec civilization in Mexico	**AD 284** Roman Empire reorganized under Diocletian **313** Edict of Milan – Christianity tolerated in the Roman Empire **410** Rome sacked by the Visigoths
6th century Three separate black Christian Nubian kingdoms founded **8th century** Rise of the kingdom of Kongo (Angola and Zaire) **8th century** Arabs established trading links with West Africa across the Sahara **8th–12th centuries** Kingdom of Ghana flourished	**c. 750** First settlement in New Zealand	**c. 600** Beginning of the Ayamará civilization in modern Bolivia **c. 700** Teotihuacán abandoned by the Mayas **9th–12th centuries** Huari state flourished in Peru **c. 900** Rise of the Toltec civilization based on Tula **985** Viking settlements in Greenland	**535** Byzantine conquest of much of Italy **711** Muslim invasion of Spain **800** Charlemagne crowned emperor
11th century Islam reached the Sahel **13th–14th centuries** Kingdom of Mali flourished in the Sahel **13th–15th centuries** Kingdom of Zimbabwe flourished	**11th–16th centuries** Easter Island statues erected	**after 1000** Temple Mound culture in North American Great Basin **11th–16th centuries** Pueblo culture flourished in modern southwestern USA **12th century** Toltec Empire collapsed into warring states **c. 1200** Foundation of the Inca dynasty	**1054** Schism between Roman Catholic and Greek Orthodox churches **1066** Norman conquest of England **1096–9** First Crusade **1241** Mongols overran eastern Europe
14th century Rise of the Muslim emirate of Bornu (Nigeria) **15th century** Nubian Christian states extinguished **15th–17th centuries** The (Ibo) kingdom of Benin flourished in Nigeria **1460s–1591** Empire of Songhay in the Sahel **late 15th century** The Portuguese explored much of the African coast	**1432** Probable Chinese landing on northern coast of Australia	**1345** Foundation of Tenochtitlán (modern Mexico City) by the Aztecs **before 1350–1476** Chimú Empire based on Chan Chan (Peru) **c. 1440–76** Major expansion of the Inca Empire	**1337** Hundred Years War began **1340s** The Black Death ravaged Europe **1450** Gutenberg's printing press **1469** Union of Aragon and Castile **1492** Moors expelled from Spain
c. 1500 Beginning of the slave trade on the West African coast **1625** Foundation of kingdom of Abomey **c. 1650–1750** The (Yoruba) Oyo Empire flourished in West Africa **1652** Dutch colony founded at the Cape	**c. 1500** Beginning of the Maori civil wars **1642** Abel Tasman discovered Tasmania and the south island of New Zealand	**1500** Peak of the Aztec Empire **1519–21** Spain conquered the Aztec Empire **1532–5** Spain conquered the Inca Empire **late 16th century** First permanent European settlements on the eastern seaboard of North America **1572** Last Inca state ceased to exist **1598** Pueblo culture disrupted by Spanish colonization	**1517** Luther's '95 Theses', the start of the Reformation **1618** Start of the Thirty Years War **1700–21** The Great Northern War **1740–8** War of the Austrian Succession
c. 1700/50–1901 Kingdom of Ashanti flourished in West Africa **1835–7** The 'Great Trek' of the Boers in South Africa **1875–1900** The 'scramble for Africa' – colonial division of the continent	**1788** First British settlement in Australia **1860–70** Maori Wars against European settlement **1867** End of transportation of convicts to Australia **1901** The Commonwealth of Australia established	**1750** White settlement crossed the Appalachians **c. 1800** White settlement west of the Mississippi **1830** Indian Removal Act (USA) **1850–90** Indian wars on the western Plains **1884** Araucanians defeated by Chile after 350 years' resistance **1887** US legislation on reservations	**c. 1750** Start of the Industrial Revolution **1789** Start of the French Revolution **1799–1814/15** Napoleon in power **1861** Italian unification **1871** German unification **1878** Congress of Berlin **1914–18** World War I

China to the Mongol Conquest

Since the fall of the Roman Empire, China has been the largest state on earth and, until the European Renaissance, technologically the most advanced. The Chinese continue to call their country the Middle Kingdom, and for long they thought of it as the centre of the world. Beyond the limits of its power were only outer darkness and barbarity.

SEE ALSO

● EMPIRES OF THE STEPPE p. 54
● CHINA FROM THE MONGOLS TO THE MANCHU p. 56
● SOUTHEAST ASIA TO THE 19TH CENTURY p. 60
● JAPAN TO THE 20TH CENTURY p. 64

The historic core of China was the area around the middle reaches of the Yellow River (Hwang He), in what is now the northern part of Henan. There, on the fertile, easily worked soil that colours the river, the domestication of millet resulted in well-established Neolithic farming by 4000 BC. From this heartland, farming spread out in all directions, reaching the other great river basin, that of the Yangtze (Chang Jiang), by 2500 BC. As agriculture reached the warmer south, it adopted a more suitable local staple crop: rice. By 1500 BC, fully developed rice farming had spread south into Indochina and, by 500 BC, northeast into Korea.

Early civilization in the Chinese heartland

In the Yellow River heartland, the scale and organization of the farming communities increased and their technology improved. By 2000 BC, they had developed bronzeworking and ceremonial centres of some size, even a shadowy dynasty, the Xia. Around 1500 BC, the first historical rulers emerged, the kings of the Shang dynasty. The remains of Shang cities and tombs reveal a civilization clearly ancestral to classic Chinese culture. Its script was of the ideographic type still used by the Chinese today, and its capital cities were laid out on a grid system oriented to the points of the compass, as all subsequent Chinese capitals have been. In addition, its bronze, pottery, jade and silk artefacts conformed to a style that the Chinese have held to ever since.

Civilization gradually spread outwards from the core area ruled by the Shang. To the west, the rulers of the Zhou acquired its essentials efficiently enough to displace the Shang as overlords of the Chinese heartland around 1000 BC. The Zhou expanded their hegemony north as far as Manchuria and south over the Yangtze basin. Within those boundaries, advances in agriculture (irrigation) and technology (ironworking) made it possible to support powerful local rulers, their courts and warriors. As the centuries passed, power devolved to these smaller states, which eventually – from the mid 5th century BC – became the 'Warring States'.

When they were not making war, the rulers of the fiefs of Zhou China found time to consider the nature of power and government. At their courts, the essentials of Chinese views on the good society were developed. The most prominent administrator-philosopher was Kongfuzi (Confucius; 551–479 BC), who, around 500 BC, set out the basis of an ethic of civilized life – based on hierarchies of family and state, culminating in the emperor – that was to influence Chinese society down to the 20th century.

The beginnings of empire

The westernmost of the Warring States – Qin – emerged as the final victor. In 221 BC, its ruler became Shi Huangdi (259–210) – 'the First Emperor' – and in the 11 years of his reign established the framework of the greatest state the world had so far seen. His empire spread out to touch the South China Sea and Central Asia. In the north, its boundary with the nomads was defined by the largest single human artefact ever made: the Great Wall. Within these borders, the inhabitants were conscripted to build a massive road system as well as the Wall. The laws, administration, script, currency, weights and measures of the Empire were all reorganized and standardized.

Qin rule did not long outlast Shi Huangdi, but the foundations of empire had been firmly laid. Under the succeeding Han dynasty, the Chinese Empire defined its traditional bounds. At the end of the 2nd century BC, it spread west into Central Asia, south into Vietnam and east into Korea. However, these lands were too far away to be held for long and, although they remained under strong Chinese influence, they subsequently went their own way politically.

One result of the expansion of the Han Empire and its contacts with other soci-

IMPERIAL DYNASTIES OF CHINA

Shang	1480 BC–1050 BC
Zhou	1122 BC–256 BC
(Warring States	481 BC–221 BC)
Qin (Ch'in)	221 BC–206 BC
Han	202 BC–AD 220
Jin (Tsin)	265–316
Sui	589–618
Tang	618–907
Song (Sung)	960–1127
(in south only	1127–1279)
Yuan (Mongol)	1271–1368
Ming	1368–1644
Qing (Manchu)	1644–1911

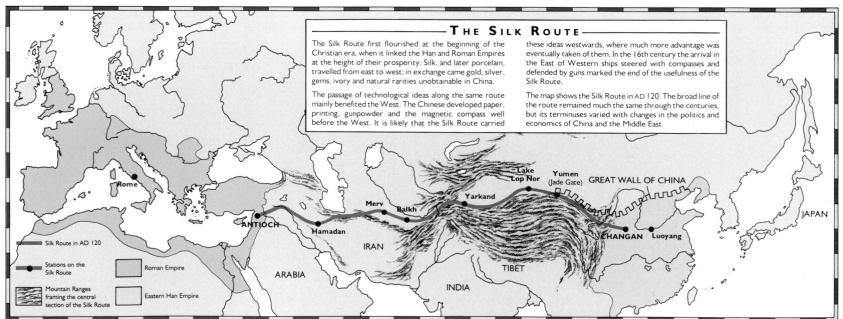

THE SILK ROUTE

The Silk Route first flourished at the beginning of the Christian era, when it linked the Han and Roman Empires at the height of their prosperity. Silk, and later porcelain, travelled from east to west; in exchange came gold, silver, gems, ivory and natural rarities unobtainable in China.

The passage of technological ideas along the same route mainly benefited the West. The Chinese developed paper, printing, gunpowder and the magnetic compass well before the West. It is likely that the Silk Route carried these ideas westwards, where much more advantage was eventually taken of them. In the 16th century the arrival in the East of Western ships steered with compasses and defended by guns marked the end of the usefulness of the Silk Route.

The map shows the Silk Route in AD 120. The broad line of the route remained much the same through the centuries, but its terminuses varied with changes in the politics and economics of China and the Middle East.

Silk Route in AD 120

Stations on the Silk Route

Mountain Ranges framing the central section of the Silk Route

Roman Empire

Eastern Han Empire

Rome — ANTIOCH — Hamadan — IRAN — ARABIA — Merv — Balkh — INDIA — TIBET — Yarkand — Lake Lop Nor — Yumen (Jade Gate) — GREAT WALL OF CHINA — CHANGAN — Luoyang — JAPAN

2nd century AD. For much of the 3rd century, China was divided between three kingdoms before the ruler of the northernmost conquered the others and restored the Empire under the Jin dynasty. Then a massive nomad invasion in 316 again destroyed the unity of imperial China. For nearly 300 years, the Yellow River valley – the heartland of Chinese culture – remained under the rule of nomad dynasties, notably the Wei (386–533), while Chinese dynasties, at first the surviving Jin, continued to rule the Yangtze valley and the south.

Unity was again restored in the late 6th century, when a Turco-Chinese general (Yang Jian) first seized power in the north and then conquered the south, founding the short-lived Sui dynasty. After a short period of chaos, the Tang dynasty took power. The man who established the dynasty and became its second emperor – Taizong (596–649) – was one of the greatest of the Chinese emperors. He reformed the administration of the Empire, restoring the supremacy of the civil service and establishing the principle of selection for office by examination. Under the Tang, the Empire rose to a classic perfection, ruled with rigid efficiency from Changan (modern Xi'an), a city of perhaps half a million inhabitants and the most crushingly magnificent of the imperial capitals.

In its decline, the Tang Empire displayed the classic recurring features of Chinese imperial history. Each dynasty started with a period of just and efficient government and imperial expansion. Then, slowly and inevitably, decline and disintegration set in. In the provinces, generals and governors built up separate local centres of power. Peasants rebelled as the burdens of tax and conscription weighed more heavily. Nomads pressed on the northern frontiers and sometimes broke through.

The fall of the Tang dynasty in 907 was followed by half a century of disintegration before most of the old area of the empire was reunited under the Song dynasty. Under the new dynasty, China rose to a new peak of imperial grandeur. Song China, between the 10th and 12th centuries, had a more complex economic and social structure than previous empires. It was larger, too, containing over 100 million subjects at its peak. Among its most prosperous parts were the great new commercial cities along the Yangtze and the southern and eastern coasts, with trading links well beyond the traditional bounds of empire. These cities marked a drift of the centre of gravity of imperial China away from the Yellow River and towards the south.

In 1126, yet another nomad invasion – of the Jin from Manchuria – again split China. The Jin ruled in the Yellow River basin and the north; the Song retreated to the Yangtze basin, ruling a reduced southern Song Empire for another century and a half, until it too succumbed to the greatest of all nomad invaders – the Mongols (▷ pp. 54 and 56).   RJ

A tower of glazed pottery (below) from the Han dynasty, showing typical Chinese architectural features that remained largely unchanged for the next two thousand years.

eties was the arrival of Buddhism. Buddhism spread from India (▷ p. 58) along the Central Asian trade routes that flourished in this period. Although it never displaced native philosophies such as Confucianism, Buddhist belief became and remained a major component of popular religion and culture in China.

The Han Empire also set the pattern of Chinese government. At the centre was the emperor and his court, ruling through a rigorously educated bureaucracy (▷ box). The emperor also had a religious role: the welfare of the Empire and its people was bound up with his well-being and correct performance of ritual duties. The carefully planned imperial city was the focus of ritual, bureaucracy, wealth and culture. The Chinese capitals – with populations of up to half a million – were easily the largest and most magnificent cities in the world between the fall of Rome and the rise of London (▷ p. 131).

A pattern of dynasties

Han China fell apart from the end of the

Empires of the Steppe

The Roman and Chinese Empires, large though they were, occupied only the extremities of the Eurasian land mass: between them was a half-empty world of desert and steppe, inhabited by nomadic pastoralists who lived by herding. These nomads spent much of their time on horseback, moving their flocks from one pasture to another as the seasons changed. When they fought among themselves, which they did frequently, their armies consisted entirely of mounted men.

The earliest groups to practise this lifestyle were of Iranian stock and lived at the western end of the Central Asian steppe. By 550 BC the Scythians and Sakas who occupied this area had developed most of the items of equipment that characterized the mature nomadic culture: short but powerful compound bows (▷ box), elaborate horse trappings, and felt blankets and tents. Still to come were the lance (3rd century AD) and the stirrup (5th century AD).

From the Scythians and Sakas the new culture spread to the Huns, Turks and Mongols of the eastern half of the steppe. These peoples belong to a quite different ethnic and linguistic group, being Altaians (a name taken from the Altai mountain range in Central Asia) as opposed to Iranians. Gradually the Altaians gained the upper hand. By the end of the 4th century AD they had made themselves masters of all the grasslands between the Danube in eastern Europe and the Yellow River (Huang He) in China.

The impact of the nomads

For the settled agrarian communities of east and west, the Altaians proved fearsome neighbours. They were hard to beat on the battlefield and recovered quickly after defeat, simply returning to the steppe until they had rebuilt their strength. In victory they were pitiless, massacring out of hand the settled farmers whose land they coveted. China suffered particularly badly. In the course of the 4th century AD the entire Yellow River valley passed under nomad control, and in the 5th century it became the centre of a Turkish empire that the Chinese refer to as the Northern Wei (▷ p. 52). At the same time the Huns of the Volga steppe moved west, setting in train the tribal movements that brought the Western Roman Empire to ruin (▷ pp. 41 and 78). Attila, the king who carried this Hun Empire to its peak, was to raid as far west as Orleans in France.

During the next five hundred years the nomads often attempted to repeat these early triumphs. The Avars, a Mongol tribe, achieved a passable imitation of Attila's European dominion at the end of the 6th century AD. The Magyars, ancestors of the Hungarians, did much the same in the 10th century. But off the steppe the power of the nomads tended to be short-lived: there were simply too few of them against too many peasants. There was, however, one permanent gain. In 1071 the Seljuk Turks won a great victory over the Byzantines at Manzikert, in eastern Anatolia (modern Turkey) (▷ pp. 81 and 83). Following this battle Turkish tribes flooded into the area, which has remained Turkish ever since.

The Mongol empire

Of all the nomad empires by far the greatest was the creation of a Mongol chieftain named Temujim. In twenty years of unremitting warfare he united all the tribes of present-day Mongolia. This achievement was celebrated at a great *kuliltai* (tribal gathering) held in 1206. In the course of this, Temujim took a new title, Genghis Khan ('Lord of the Earth'), and unfolded a plan for the conquest of the world beyond Mongolia.

Genghis first set his sights on two rival nomad states in northern China, the Tangut Kingdom of Gansu in the upper Yellow River valley, and – more important – the Jin Empire centred on the fertile flood plain of the river. By 1215 he had brought both to their knees, and had become the effective ruler of the northern half of China.

Next, Genghis turned his attention westward. In 1219 he launched a massive attack on the Shah of Khwarizm, a Turkish ruler whose empire took in most of Afghanistan and all of Iran. The Mongol armies quickly overwhelmed the Shah's forces, and the eastern half of his dominion was incorporated into the Mongol Khanate.

Genghis died in 1227. He had allocated fiefs to each of his sons but he had also made provision for one of them, Ogodei, to succeed him as Great Khan. During Ogodei's reign and those of his two successors the Mongol Empire was to remain united and its expansion continued at a ferocious rate.

The advances in the west were truly remarkable. In 1238 a Mongol army crossed the Volga and began a series of annual campaigns that brought all European Russia under Mongol control. Another westward thrust brought the Turks of Anatolia into the empire. Finally, in the late 1250s, the Mongol prince Hulagu completed the conquest of Iran and added Iraq. A chill ran through the world of Islam as the last Caliph of Baghdad was trampled to death by Hulagu's victorious cavalry.

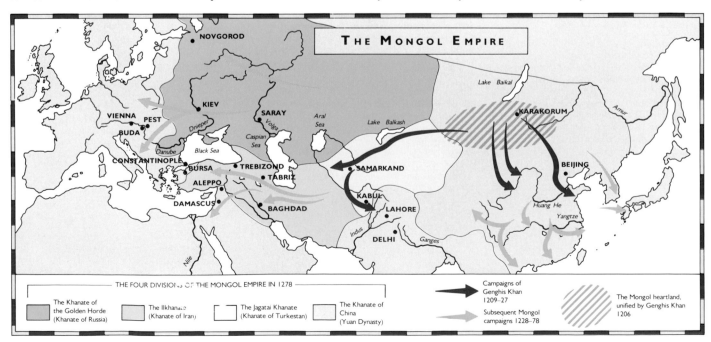

THE FOUR DIVISIONS OF THE MONGOL EMPIRE IN 1278

The Khanate of the Golden Horde (Khanate of Russia) — The Ilkhanate (Khanate of Iran) — The Jagatai Khanate (Khanate of Turkestan) — The Khanate of China (Yuan Dynasty)

Campaigns of Genghis Khan 1209–27
Subsequent Mongol campaigns 1228–78
The Mongol heartland, unified by Genghis Khan 1206

THE MONGOL WARRIOR

The peoples of the steppe fought as they lived, on horseback. They did not engage in close combat like infantry armies, but constantly advanced and retreated, wheeled and turned, like a swarm of bees – and like bees they stung. Their favoured weapon was the bow, which they used to equal effect whether pursued or pursuing.

The steppe tribes did not play much part in the wars of the ancient world: their numbers were too few and they had not, as yet, developed all the equipment needed to turn man and horse into an integrated fighting machine. But by the medieval period they had both the numbers and the technology. It is largely because of their impact – initially on the Roman Empire, later on Eastern Christendom and Islam – that Western historians refer to the era from the late 4th century to the late 15th century as 'the Cavalry Age'. The phrase can be applied with equal justice at the other end of the steppe, in China.

Huns, Turks and Mongols all campaigned in the same way. Their armies consisted exclusively of mounted men and each had several spare mounts in tow. Both men and horses were tough, inured to the harsh conditions of the steppe. They covered vast distances extremely quickly, and their speed of movement enabled them to take their opponents by surprise. Sometimes an enemy would be overwhelmed before he had even had time to assemble his forces. The nomads were at their most successful when the enemy did not know what had hit him or where it had come from.

If speed of attack was not enough to disrupt their opponents and the nomads found themselves facing a well-marshalled army, they immediately surrendered the initiative, lurking around their opponents' front and flanks and firing off their arrows from a safe distance. If the enemy's main force advanced, they feigned retreat. When it halted, they resumed their initial tactics. Most armies started to come apart after a few hours of this treatment. Then the nomads would grow bolder. They would cut off any regiments that got separated from the main body and shower them with arrows until they either broke or turned and made a stand. If they ran, they became targets for the lancers who formed the elite of the nomad army; if they stood, they would be blockaded until thirst and continuing losses forced a surrender.

Few armies – not even those supported by the type of heavy cavalry favoured in the West – ever found an effective answer to these tactics. The Huns, Turks and Mongols were able to chalk up a formidable string of victories, often at very little cost to themselves.

The Mongol warrior – unglamorous fighting man though he was – dominated the medieval battlefield. His horse was no bigger than a modern pony. Over his shoulder was a recurved compound bow – constructed from several carefully shaped pieces of wood that massively enhanced its propellant qualities; at his back a quiver of 50 arrows. He wore a felt greatcoat, a leather jerkin and a fur-trimmed hat, but – unless he was one of the Khan's bodyguard – he had neither armour nor lance. He used his bow to unhorse his enemy, his sword to fell him, and his dagger to finish him off. He looked like a part-time soldier – which he usually was – and he very nearly conquered the world.

In the east the Song Empire of southern China was conquered by Hulagu's brother Kublai in the 1270s. Kublai had become Great Khan in 1260, but his concentration on eastern affairs and the sheer scale of his achievement there meant that the other princes of the blood were allowed to go their own ways. Kublai had effectively turned his back on the rest of the empire by the mid-1260s, when he moved his capital from Karakorum in Mongolia to Beijing (Peking) in northern China. In 1271 he adopted a Chinese name, Yuan, for his dynasty, which subsequently became purely Chinese in style (▷ p. 56).

The rest of the Mongol Empire divided into three Khanates. Hulagu's descendants, while retaining his relatively modest title of Ilkhan (subordinate Khan), became sovereigns of Anatolia, Iran and Iraq. A line descended from Genghis Khan's eldest son became Khans of the Golden Horde on the Russian steppe. Another lineage, founded by Genghis Khan's second son Jagatai, acquired Turkestan.

The longevity of these successor states varied. The Ilkhanate disintegrated half way through the 14th century, and the Golden Horde went the same way at the end of the 15th, but the Jagatai Khanate lasted, in a much reduced form, until 1678. The Mongol rulers of China were expelled by the first Ming emperor in 1368 and the final representative of the dynasty succumbed to a local revolt in Mongolia in 1399.

The last nomad empires

In the later 14th century the western half of the Jagatai Khanate was taken over by a Turkish chieftain, Tamerlane (or Timur the Lame) who claimed descent from Genghis Khan. Tamerlane proved to be a conqueror on a scale that rivalled Genghis. In virtually every year of his long reign (1369–1405) he added another major city to the list of places he had plundered. These included Delhi, Saray (the capital of the Golden Horde), Baghdad, Aleppo, Damascus and Bursa (the capital of the Ottoman Sultans of Anatolia). At the time of his death he was busy with preparations for an invasion of China that would doubtless have brought a great deal of misery to the people of that long-suffering land. Where Tamerlane was no match for Genghis was in longer-term planning. He took little interest in administration and his empire began to contract within a few years of his death.

In this respect it is arguable that the most successful nomads ever were the Manchu. This clan, from which Manchuria takes its name, conquered first China, then the areas of the steppe that bordered it: inner and outer Mongolia and eastern Turkestan – as well as Tibet. The dynasty that they founded, the Qing, ruled China from 1644 to 1911 (▷ p. 57). It is because of the Manchu's military prowess that the present-day Chinese state has the extensive inner Asian possessions that make up such a large part of its area.

By modern times the nomadic lifestyle had become an anachronism. Because their form of husbandry is capable of only limited expansion, nomadic peoples have been left behind by the population explosions of the 19th and 20th centuries. Well before that they had seen their traditional military advantage rendered obsolete by the development of firearms: mounted bowmen had no place in wars waged with artillery and muskets. In the 16th century the Russians had little difficulty in conquering the khanates into which the Golden Horde had split. The only nomadic peoples who continued to be successful were the ones who abandoned their lifestyle and adopted the new weaponry, as did the Ottomans in Anatolia (▷ p. 120) and the Moguls (Mongols) in India (▷ p. 68).   CM/RJ

Savagery and destructiveness were the hallmarks of the military campaigns waged by Genghis Khan and his successors and imitators. This 16th-century Mogul miniature shows the troops of Tamerlane sacking the fort of Mikrit in the Hindu Kush. Tamerlane left a trail of devastated towns and cities from the Indian seaboard to the Volga, and in their place his warriors built towers of severed heads.

SEE ALSO

● CHINA TO THE MONGOL CONQUEST p. 52
● CHINA FROM THE MONGOLS TO THE MANCHU p. 56
● MUSLIM INDIA p. 62
● THE OTTOMAN EMPIRE p. 114
● THE EMERGENCE OF RUSSIA p. 126

China from the Mongols to the Manchu

The Mongol Empire ruled by Kublai Khan between 1260 and 1294 was unique (⊳ p. 54), but the Chinese Empire incorporated within it belonged very much to the traditional pattern of Chinese history. Under its new Mongol dynasty – the Yuan – the Chinese Empire was reunited for the first time since the early 12th century, and it was never again to lose that unity.

Kublai had plans for an even greater empire. His generals conquered Upper Burma, his admirals extracted tribute from the nearer parts of Indochina and even attempted to do so from Java. He also launched two unsuccessful invasions of Japan. But these enterprises were of little significance beside what inevitably became his main business – governing the 100 million Chinese who constituted the bulk of his subjects. And this Kublai did, in Chinese imperial style. Once the horrors of invasion were past, the normal patterns of Chinese agriculture and economy were re-established. No attempt was made to turn any part of China over to the nomadic pastoralism favoured by the Mongols (⊳ p. 54).

Cranes in the waves, a painting of the Ming dynasty. During this period, artists developed strong personal styles within the limitations of two schools. The 'scholar-artists' of the Wu school painted with great subtlety, and largely for their own amusement. The professional painters of the Zhe school executed large, decorative works that echoed earlier styles.

At the same time, Kublai's rule denied the traditional exclusiveness of Chinese thought and government. The top ranks of the administration were recruited from far and wide within the Mongol Empire and even from beyond its boundaries. The Empire was ruled from Beijing in the north, close to the steppe where the Great Khan kept his summer camp. Buddhism in its Central Asian form was encouraged, and contacts with western Asia and Europe along the Silk Route were nurtured (⊳ map, p. 52).

The system worked well under a great ruler such as Kublai Khan; under less brilliant successors and long minorities, Mongol control over China began to disintegrate. By the mid-14th century, nationalist rebellion was being raised in the provinces. A rebel army took the southern capital of Nanjing in 1356 and gradually extended its power over China until the Mongols fled from Beijing in 1368. The rebel leader, Zhu Yuanzhang – a beggar turned bandit, was proclaimed Hongwu, the first emperor of the Ming dynasty.

Ming China

The collapse of the Mongols was so comprehensive that the Ming were once more able to set Chinese imperial boundaries well into Central Asia and control the nomads who had dominated northern China for so many centuries. The influence of the Ming Empire as an Asian power was further reinforced under Hongwu's son, Yongle (reigned 1403–24). Between 1405 and 1433, a court eunuch, Zheng He, took Chinese fleets to explore the old trade routes to the Spice Islands, Arabia and Africa. The possibilities opened up by these voyages were never exploited (⊳ p. 108). The interests of Ming China turned inward and northward; it was in this period that the capital was moved from Nanjing back to Beijing, from where it was easier to keep an eye on the nomads.

The next significant contact with the outside world was to come about as a result of European rather than Chinese initiative. At the beginning of the 16th century Portuguese fleets moved eastward along the trade routes sailed by Zheng He a century before. European contacts with the late Ming Empire took two forms: a Portuguese trading post was maintained at Macao from the mid-16th century and a Roman Catholic presence established at the imperial court with the residence of the Italian Jesuit missionary Matteo Ricci at the beginning of the 17th century.

For the late Ming Empire, these contacts with Europe were of relatively little significance; the Portuguese were but one more set of barbarian traders anxious to acquire the famed silk and porcelain of China, while the missionaries were a useful source of knowledge of the latest European advances in science and technology, which had begun to overtake those of the East. But the Chinese Empire remained by far the largest and wealthiest state on earth; under the Ming its population grew to 150 million, boosted in

part by the settlement of previously underpopulated areas on the fringes of the Empire.

The Ming Empire entered a period of instability in the first half of the 17th century. At first, it looked as if the birth pangs of the Ming dynasty were to be repeated. A rebel leader of peasant origins seized power in the south and marched on Beijing in 1644, where Ming resistance collapsed. In the confusion that followed, northern China was seized by the Manchu, who had consolidated a nomad-ruled state north of the Great Wall in the first half of the 17th century. But this was not the end of the upheaval; only in 1682 did civil war in south China come to an end, enabling the Qing dynasty of the Manchu to establish an unchallenged hold over the whole Empire.

The last empire

Under the Qing, particularly under its most able emperors, Kangxi (reigned 1662–1722) and Qianlong (reigned 1735–95), China rose to new heights of power and prosperity. Areas on its borders that had formerly paid tribute – such as Tibet and Turkestan – were taken under effective control. In the north, as firearms turned the balance of power against the nomads, China was able to reach agreement with Russia to fix a boundary across the steppes of Central Asia as far as the Pacific Ocean (the Treaty of Nerchinsk, 1689).

Within these boundaries, the Qing dynasty ruled in traditional Chinese ways through the old-established bureaucracy. Only in the army and in court dress and ceremonial were vestiges of its nomadic origins still visible. A century and a half of peace and prosperity under the Qing pushed the Chinese population to new levels; it rose past the 400 million mark in the 18th century (more than ten times that of Napoleonic France and the Russian Empire, the next most populous states on earth). The capital, Beijing, with a population approaching a million, remained the largest city in the world until the end of the 18th century.

The late 18th century was the turning point, the moment it became clear that – in terms of technology at least – China was standing still in an increasingly fast-moving world. At first the decay and collapse of Qing authority in the 19th century was in part a repetition of the old cycle of imperial decline, as population pressure, official corruption and increased taxation made peasant life a misery and revolt an attractive alternative.

It was once more a time for barbarians from beyond the frontier to take advantage of an empire in chaos. But this time the barbarians pressing on the Empire were different: they were Europeans. The Europeans did not want to seize power; they wanted to trade at a profit. The Chinese Empire, however, was unwilling to expand its trade with the West, partly from a desire to remain self-sufficient and partly out of incomprehension.

An attack on Shanghai (left) during the bloody Taiping Rebellion (1851–64). The Christian ideas adopted by the authoritarian Taiping Movement emphasized the Old Testament concepts of order, obedience and a vengeful God. Their social teachings – which bore a resemblance to modern Chinese Communism – included sexual equality and an equal distribution of land.

The refusal of the Chinese to trade seriously with Europe led to an imbalance in trade with Britain in the early 19th century. The Western demand for Chinese goods such as tea, silk and porcelain was growing, but the Chinese had no great need for imports in return. The British decided to create a demand by unloading Indian opium on the Chinese market. Although there was a demand for drugs in China, drug-taking was officially discouraged and the imperial government acted to prevent British opium imports. The subsequent Opium War (1839–42) revealed the weakness of Chinese military power and enabled the British government to impose the first of the 'Unequal Treaties', regulating trade on European terms and securing European control over five 'Treaty Ports' (▷ p. 163).

In the middle of the century the power of the Qing dynasty was seriously challenged by rebellion. The Taiping ('heavenly peace') Movement took up arms in 1851 and controlled a large part of the south for over a decade, ruling between 1853 and 1864 from the old southern capital of Nanjing. Under its messianic leader, Hong Xiuquan – who claimed to be the younger brother of Jesus Christ, the movement developed an ideology that mixed peasant egalitarianism with elements of Christianity borrowed from Western missionaries. The rebellion eventually succumbed to government armies revitalized by Western arms and military advice. The strength of the Taiping Movement – and the brutality of its suppression – was reflected in a death toll estimated to have run into millions.

While supporting the imperial court against rebellion, the Western powers continued to push it into further trading concessions. A second Opium War (1856–60) saw an Anglo-French army march on Beijing and occupy the seat of imperial government, the Forbidden City. Further unequal treaties followed, with Treaty Ports conceded to all the Western powers. At the end of the century, a rapidly modernizing Japan got in on the act, seizing control of Korea and Taiwan in the Sino-Japanese War of 1894–5 (▷ p. 65).

The outcome of the Sino-Japanese War prompted attempts from within the imperial court to learn from Japan and react to the modern world by reform and reconstruction. These attempts, like previous ones, were defeated by the power of the Empress Dowager, Cixi (Tz'u-hsi; reigned 1862–1908). Her control of the imperial court between 1851 and her death in 1908 kept China locked in a largely negative reaction to the pressures of Western expansion.

The Chinese people themselves could only react blindly to the decay of the Middle Kingdom. The bloody and xenophobic Boxer Rebellion (1900–1) was directed – with the connivance of the imperial court – against Westerners and those Chinese who adopted Western ideas. The rising was suppressed by a joint military operation by the Western powers. There now followed a second occupation of Beijing and further trade and diplomatic concessions. These included the payment by China of an annual indemnity, the stationing of troops on its territory, and foreign control of Beijing's diplomatic quarter.

A badly frightened imperial court began to consider reform, but it was too little and too late. China entered the 20th century still the largest nation on earth but with only a shadow of the power and prestige that should have gone with its size. Ten years later, in 1911, the Qing dynasty itself fell to army rebellion (▷ p. 196).   RJ

German cavalry – part of the Western forces of occupation after the collapse of the Boxer rebellion (1901) – arriving at the Forbidden City in Beijing. The Forbidden City – containing the imperial palaces – lay at the heart of the Imperial City, itself a walled enclosure in the Inner City. Alongside lay the Outer, or Chinese, City with walls 22 km (14 mi) long. The plan of Beijing displays remarkable symmetry and – through the additions of succeeding dynasties – reflects Chinese history.

India before Islam

The history of civilization in the Indian subcontinent begins in the northwest, in the Indus Valley (now Pakistan). This region formed an extension of the Middle-Eastern/Iranian cultural zone and it was from that direction that it acquired Neolithic farming techniques by 5000 BC (▷ p. 14). The techniques spread on, first to central India and then to the far south by 2000 BC.

The citadel of Mohenjo-daro ('the mound of the dead'). The mounds of Mohenjo-daro, on the right bank of the River Indus in Sind, Pakistan, have been excavated since 1922 to reveal what was once the largest city in the Indus Valley. The size of the site, and the richness of the artefacts discovered there, have encouraged the theory that the city was the capital of a substantial kingdom.

The Indus Valley civilization evolved in much the same way as its Mesopotamian parent (▷ p. 16). Settlements became larger, bronze working was introduced, and ruling elites – probably priestly – emerged. The high point was reached with the Harappan civilization, which flourished in the Indus Valley between 2300 and 1700 BC, focused on the two cities of Harappa and Mohenjo-daro. In these cities the full repertoire of a Bronze Age urban society was displayed: a literate elite, carefully organized and controlled water and food supplies, and densely packed artisan quarters. The detail of the town planning of Harappa and Mohenjo-daro reflects a society of rank and order. This urban civilization flourished for 600 years and then collapsed for reasons that remain unclear, although the arrival of the Aryans probably had something to do with it. Life in the villages went on much as before.

The northeast of the subcontinent developed in a very different way. It, too, formed part of a wider zone, that of tropical Southeast Asia. As in other tropical areas, the development of settled farming took forms that were more horticultural than agricultural, with rice eventually emerging as its staple crop. By 1500 BC, this part of India, the Ganges basin, had evolved a Bronze Age culture of its own and succeeded the Indus Valley as the core area of Indian civilization.

The shift from the Indus to the Ganges broadly coincides with the entry into the subcontinent of the Aryans – Indo-European pastoralists from the Iranian steppe. The Aryans imposed themselves on the native Dravidians, and the resulting amalgam became the Hindu society that has been the majority community of India ever since. One of the Aryan contributions was an Indo-European language, which became known in its literary form as Sanskrit. This was the language from which the major languages of northern India developed. The body of Sanskrit religious literature originating in this period was collected in a corpus known as the *Vedas* ('wisdom'). This forms the basis of both Hindu religious thought and Indian literature.

Kingdoms and empires

By 800 BC, the Hindu society of the Ganges Valley had entered the Iron Age. It was a period of intensifying agriculture, rapidly developing towns, and a wide expansion of trade. It also saw the development of the social structures that were to dominate the subsequent history of Hindu India. Tribes evolved into republics or kingdoms, and society became increasingly hierarchical.

Hindu kingship carried with it the additional power of religion: the person of the king was sacred in life and his spirit was elevated to the ranks of the gods after death. Ranked beneath the king were priests, warriors and lords, then the ordinary farmers and craftsmen, then those who lived in bondage or on the fringes of society. It was the typical hierarchy of an Iron Age society. But in India, strengthened both by religious sanctions and strict rules of hereditary descent, it has survived down to the present day in the form of the caste system.

By this period, too, the complex and colourful hierarchy of the gods of Hinduism was fully established. The middle of the first millennium BC saw Hinduism challenged by a number of sects preaching a more abstract spirituality and individualistic ethic. Of these sects, the Jains survive to this day. More important, both for the subcontinent and the whole world, was the influence of one of history's great religious teachers, Prince Gautama, the Buddha ('Enlightened One'). Buddhist thought was to play a major role in Indian society for the next thousand years, but its influence in its homeland then waned. However, in the interim it had spread through Central and Eastern Asia. It played a significant part in the cultural development of China and Japan (▷ pp. 52 and 64) and a dominating one in several peripheral nations: Tibet, Mongolia, Burma, Thailand, and Sri Lanka (▷ p. 60).

The political history of India begins with the emergence of the kingdom of Magdalha in the middle of the Ganges Valley. The reign of its first important king, Bimbisara (543–491 BC) overlaps the lifetime of the Buddha. Under the Nanda dynasty (362–321 BC), Magdalha rose to new heights and, under Chandragupta (321–297 BC), founder of the Mauryan dynasty, it became the centre of the first Indian empire.

Chandragupta Maurya exercised control over most of the kingdoms of northern and central India; his grandson, Ashoka (272–232 BC), consciously moulded them into an empire. This involved the development of a central bureaucracy and central system of taxation, and also the promulgation of a philosophy of 'state-Dhamma'. Based on the Buddhist beliefs that Ashoka had adopted, Dhamma emphasized the ruler's moral and social responsibility for the welfare of all his subjects. The pillars and rock-hewn inscriptions that Ashoka placed throughout his empire, as far apart as Afghanistan and the southern Deccan, proclaimed not just the extent of his domain but also the philosophy of his rule.

An Indian empire of the extent of Ashoka's was exceptional, however. Most of the Indus Valley belonged to empires that lay to the west – to Persia between the late 6th and 4th centuries BC (▷ p. 26) and to Alexander the Great at the end of the 4th century BC (▷ p. 32). After

One of the five rathas (monolithic temples) at Mahabalipuram in Tamil Nadu, India. The temples – the survivors of seven rathas that gave the city its name 'Seven Pagodas' – formed the religious centre of a Hindu kingdom in southeastern India in the 7th and 8th centuries AD. The coastal city, founded by King Mamalla, is known to have traded with Persia and China.

Ashoka, the Greeks returned to the upper Indus basin and a rich Indo-Greek society developed in the area; they in their turn were supplanted by nomad rulers from Central Asia (▷ p. 54), notably the Kushans (1st to 5th centuries AD).

The expansion of Hindu culture

The decline of the Mauryan dynasty after Ashoka saw the north and centre of the subcontinent revert to a glittering mosaic of regional kingdoms. The spread of north Indian influence then became the work of traders rather than warriors. As merchants from the north of the subcontinent built up their coastal trade, tribal societies in the south of India as well as far beyond, in Southeast Asia and Indonesia (▷ p. 60), came under the influence of Hindu religion and culture, and tribal chiefdoms were replaced by kingdoms on the Hindu model. By the end of the first millennium BC the Dravidian peoples of the south of the subcontinent had acquired the same pattern of local kingdoms as the north.

Further south, the island of Ceylon (Sri Lanka) had a somewhat different history. The original hunter-gatherer inhabitants were mostly displaced by northern Indian agriculturalists who arrived by sea around 500 BC. These settlers, the Sinhalese, who adopted Buddhism around 300 BC, remained the dominant power on the island. However, they came under increasing pressure from expansionist Hindu kingdoms in southern India. From the 10th century AD, Tamils from southeast India established a substantial presence in the northern part of the island.

More kingdoms and empires

The basic political units of Hindu India in the first millennium AD remained the regional kingdoms. These were not so much organized states as areas within which kings exercised lordship over other powerful families. There was much scope for local rivalry and warfare, and also for the development of complex hierarchies of power, maintained by the giving and receiving of homage and tribute.

Few regional kingdoms aspired to wider power. In the 4th century AD, another Magdalhan dynasty, the Guptas, created an empire that briefly lorded it over most of the kingdoms and republics of northern and central India. Two centuries later, Harsha, a Buddhist monarch whose centre of power was in the Delhi region, brought much of the north under his sway. But in the main, Indian political units were local, with strictly limited horizons. It was partly because of this that the Hindus of northern India put up such a poor showing against the Muslim raiders who first pillaged and then conquered the entire northern half of the subcontinent (11th–14th centuries AD; ▷ p. 62).

The southern Hindus fared better. To some extent this was simply because it was more difficult for the Muslims to get at them, but the southerners did manage to create one relatively large and relatively stable empire, Vijayanagar. Named after its capital ('City of Victory'), it was the personal creation of its first ruler, Harihara.

However, it did have staying power, and it was only in 1565, after sustaining the Hindu cause for more than 200 years, that Vijayanagar was finally vanquished by a coalition of neighbouring Muslim rulers.   RJ

A statue of Buddha at the Ajanta caves, in Maharashtra, India. Vigorous sculpture and colourful wall paintings distinguish the 30 sanctuaries and temples hewn from the granite cliffs of Ajanta between the 1st century BC and the 7th century AD.

SEE ALSO

● SOUTHEAST ASIA TO THE 19TH CENTURY p. 60
● MUSLIM INDIA p. 62

Southeast Asia to the 19th Century

Southeast Asia is made up of two different worlds, a continental portion that is sandwiched between India and China, and which – for obvious geographical and cultural reasons – is often referred to as Indochina, and the peninsula and islands that together form the Malay (or Indonesian) archipelago. In neither region are the native peoples of Indian or Chinese stock; they belong to a distinct 'Austric' ethnolinguistic group, of which Thai, Viet-muong and Malay are the most important members. The Burmese, who moved into the region relatively late, are an exception: they are related to the Tibetans, and through them to the Chinese.

In Southeast Asia, food-gatherers settled down early – by 7000 BC at the latest. They lived along rivers and coastlines, cultivating gardens and drawing on the rich resources of nearby waters, building villages and developing pottery and the other crafts of settlement.

As methods of cultivation grew more sophisticated and populations expanded – particularly in China – whole peoples were periodically set in motion across Southeast Asia. One series of movements – spread over several millennia after 5000 BC – took Malay speakers from southern China on a course through the islands, starting with Taiwan and moving on through the Philippines to Borneo, Sulawesi and the other islands of the archipelago, where they replaced an aboriginal population of Papuan type.

The Chinese connection

The settled tribal peoples of the north of Indochina were open to remote influences from the developing Chinese civilization further north. Around 1500 BC, they acquired the skill of bronze-working; iron-working followed a millennium later. By then, the Viets of the Red River delta in Tongking were developing, in their Dong Son culture, all the usual features of early civilization: dependence on a staple food crop – in this case, irrigated 'wet rice' – wealthy elites, and carefully planned ceremonial cities.

Tongking was the first part of Southeast Asia to enter the historical record, when it was conquered by a Chinese warlord in 207 BC and incorporated into the Han Empire in 111 BC (▷ p. 52). It remained under Chinese rule for the next thousand years, only recovering its independence in the 10th century AD. Further south, native kingdoms developed that showed surprisingly little awareness of China. These states – Champa on the coast, and Chenla and Funan in the Mekong valley – looked west rather than east, deriving their ideas on kingship and cosmology from the Indian subcontinent.

The Indian connection

The Indian civilization of the Ganges valley was only on rare occasions imperialist. It spread its influence through traders who, by the end of the first millennium BC, had established links with the tribal peoples of Southeast Asia. These traders took with them the full panoply of Indian culture: its literacy, its religious ideas, both Hindu and Buddhist, and its art and architecture. They also brought with them a particular concept of the state: rule by a semi-divine king who ascended to full divinity at death. In the Mekong basin, where the Khmers of Chenla conquered Funan around AD 550, producing a unified Cambodian kingdom, the large labour force normally employed in wet rice cultivation was available to give this concept of kingship monumental expression. The result was the series of grandiose 'temple cities' built by the Khmers, of which the most famous is Angkor Wat (▷ box).

India in the archipelago

Indian contacts with Indochina were sustained by a trade route that passed across the Bay of Bengal and through the Straits of Malacca. From there vessels had a straight run across the South China Sea to Cambodia and Champa. Most traders, however, took a different direction: they threaded their way through the Malay archipelago to the Moluccas (the Spice Islands) at its far end. On their way they passed Java, the most populous of the Indonesian islands, and when Indian-style states emerged in this region it was on Java that they made their first appearance (around AD 700). The best known of them is the Saliendra kingdom of central Java, which constructed a monument that rivals Angkor Wat in scale – the temple-mountain of Borobudur. This is a representation of the Buddhist vision of the universe, translated into stone. Like Angkor Wat it marks the apogee of the dynasty, which lost power in Java shortly afterwards (around 850). This was not the end of the Saliendras, however, for the line was continued in the kingdom of Srivijaya, which was to rule over southern Sumatra and the region of the Straits for a further 300 years (9th–12th centuries). The dominant position of Srivijaya in the region eventually passed to the Javanese kingdom of Majapahit (14th–15th centuries).

North versus south

In the 10th and subsequent centuries a new political trend appeared in continental Southeast Asia, a polarization between north and south. The northerners, whether native peoples like the Viets, or intruders like the Burmese, began to press on the peoples to the south, the Chams (in central Vietnam), the Khmers (in Cambodia) and the Mons (in southern Burma and Thailand). One of the casualties of this process was the kingdom of Champa, which was overthrown by the Viets of Tongking in 1471. It was replaced by a new Viet kingdom, Annam, which continued the advance southwards, chasing the last Cham king into Cambodia in 1720 and taking the Mekong delta from the Khmers towards the end of the 18th century. By 1802 the whole of the coastline from the Red River

---

ANGKOR AND ANURADHAPURA

Angkor, the temple-city of the Khmer abandoned to the jungle in the 15th century.

Hindu kingship left its most haunting relics in the deserted temple-cities of southern Asia, above all, Angkor in Cambodia and Anuradhapura in Sri Lanka. The kings of these Hindu (and later Buddhist) kingdoms took on divine characteristics at their accession to power. In their lifetime, their palaces intermingled with the temples of their fellow gods; after death, their shrines were added to those of the other deities. Because they were the residences of gods, the cities symbolized the universe in microcosm, with temple-topped mounds and artificial lakes re-creating the mountains and seas of the real world.

The god-king was responsible for the spiritual and material well-being of his people. If he failed in that responsibility, he and his city had failed to please the other gods. The solution to a national disaster was therefore to start again with a new and auspicious capital. We can understand what happened in earlier centuries from what we know of the movement of capitals in 18th- and 19th-century Burma. When the capital was moved from Ava to Amarapura in 1783 or from Amarapura to Mandalay in 1857, the rejected city was deserted almost overnight. Wooden palaces and houses were moved from the discarded city to the new site and most of the inhabitants went with them.

Anuradhapura failed to protect the Sinhalese against Tamil invaders from southern India and was discarded in favour of Polonnaruwa in the 8th century AD (itself abandoned in the 13th century). The divine protection embodied in Angkor failed to protect the Khmer against Thai invaders in the 15th century and the city was abandoned to be replaced by Phnom Penh.

For all their splendour, the temple-cities we see today were – in the end – magnificent failures.

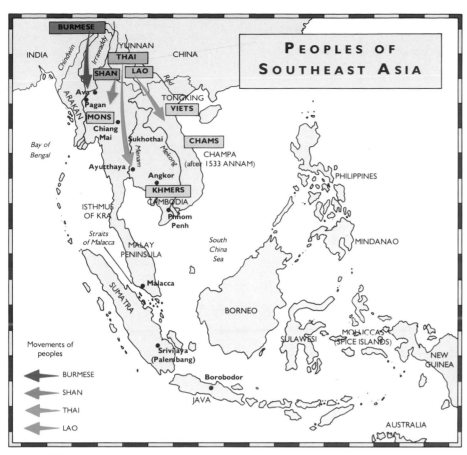

PEOPLES OF SOUTHEAST ASIA

Muslims and Christians

By this time India itself was increasingly under the influence of another religion – Islam (▷ p. 62). Following a familiar pattern, Indian Muslims carried their faith with them as they travelled the same trade routes as their Hindu and Buddhist predecessors. By the end of the 13th century Islam was established among the merchants of the ports of northern Sumatra. From there it spread steadily eastward, reaching the Moluccas at the eastern extremity of the archipelago, and the southern Philippines to the north of it in the course of the 15th century.

There were two keys to the spice trade. One was the Spice Islands themselves, the sole source of cloves and nutmeg. The other was the Straits of Malacca, the bottleneck through which the established trade route was funnelled. In the 15th century both keys were in Muslim hands, but in 1497–8 Vasco da Gama's voyage round Africa put Portugal in contention (▷ p. 109). In 1511 the Portuguese gained control of Malacca, and a few years later they were building a strong position in the Spice Islands as well. There was a brief altercation with the Spanish, who, following Magellan and del Cano's circumnavigation of the globe in 1519–22 (▷ p. 109), attempted to tap into the spice trade from the Americas. However, in 1529 a treaty between the two Iberian powers awarded the Spice Islands to Portugal, Spain getting the Philippines in compensation.

The progress of the European powers in the next two and a half centuries was slow. There were only two major colonial enterprises: the Spanish conquest of the Philippines (excepting Muslim Mindanao) in the late 16th century, and the Dutch seizure of Java in the mid-18th century. Elsewhere the Dutch, who succeeded the Portuguese as the dominant trading nation in the archipelago, relied on a series of outposts stretching from Malacca (taken from the Portuguese in 1641) to the Spice Islands themselves (brought into the Dutch orbit in the later 17th century). The rest of Southeast Asia remained under its native rulers until well into the 19th century, Hindu rajahs and Muslim sultans in the archipelago, and nation states – Burma, Thailand, and Annam – in Indochina.   CM/RJ

SEE ALSO
● CHINA TO THE MONGOL
   CONQUEST p. 52
● INDIA BEFORE ISLAM p. 58
● MUSLIM INDIA p. 62
● THE AGE OF DISCOVERY
   p. 108

to the Mekong was under the rule of a self-proclaimed 'Emperor of Annam'.

The Khmer kingdom of Cambodia came under equal pressure from another group of northerners, the Thai. The original focus of the Thai peoples was in the highlands of Yunnan on the present-day Chinese–Burmese border; the main thrust of their expansion was to the south, into the valley of the Menam river, where the first Thai principalities appeared in the course of the 13th century (Sukhothai 1238, Chiang-Mai 1290). By the middle of the 14th century the entire Menam valley was in Thai hands and Sukhothai had been abandoned in favour of a new capital, Ayutthaya, 320 km (200 mi) to the south. In 1369 and again 20 years later, Thai armies sacked Angkor, forcing the Khmers to withdraw to Phnom Penh. The remnant Khmer state became a satellite of the Thai kingdom, whose writ now ran from the Mekong to the Isthmus of Kra.

Tribes of the same family as the Thai – the Lao and the Shan – were on the move at the same time, the Lao on the eastern flank of the main Thai thrust, the Shan to the west of it. The Lao movement through the highlands east of the Mekong created the precursor of the present-day state of Laos. The Shan contested the control of the upper Irrawaddy valley with the Burmese but eventually lost the struggle; they now form part of the Burmese state.

The Burmese were the most successful of all these northern invaders. The original axis of their advance seems to have been the Chindwin river, which brought them to the central Irrawaddy, where – at a date that is traditionally given as AD 849 – they founded the kingdom of Pagan. This

Burmese kingdom was badly jolted by the Mongols who, as part of Kublai Khan's imperialist programme, invaded upper Burma in 1287 (▷ p. 54). Recovery was long delayed and it was only in the 15th century that the Burmese began to get the measure of the Mons (close relatives of the Khmers) who ruled lower Burma. By the 17th century the Burmese kingdom of Ava (successor to Pagan) was in effective control of most of present-day Burma, and was usually the winner in the wars that flared up from time to time with the neighbouring kingdom of Thailand. The politics of this century, as of the next, were hectic, with frequent rebellions and assassinations, but underneath all the turmoil there seems to have been a steady strengthening of the central government. Arakan, the last province needed to complete the outline of the modern state, was annexed in 1784.

A Thai chariot with attendant demons, from an 18th-century fresco in the Grand Palace, Bangkok. Unlike the rest of Southeast Asia, Thailand never fell under the rule of European powers.

Muslim India

Between the 13th and the 18th centuries, the rulers of the empires that dominated the Indian subcontinent were Muslims, usually of Turkish or Mongol ancestry. The influence of this originally alien faith reached its peak in the Mogul Empire of the 16th and 17th centuries, and has remained an important element in the politics and culture of the subcontinent ever since.

The first Muslim invasion of India was launched less than a hundred years after the death of the Prophet Muhammad (⊳ p. 82). An Arab army marched from the east of Iran to the mouth of the Indus and conquered the province of Sind (711). This area remained Muslim thereafter, but no further expeditions were undertaken by this route, and the rest of north India remained undisturbed for another 300 years.

In the early 11th century a new Muslim offensive began, organized by Mahmud of Ghazni, a Turk who had inherited an Islamic principality in Afghanistan. He led his followers on a series of raids into northern India which yielded a huge booty, but did not lead to any permanent conquests. The first step in this direction was taken in the late 12th century, when Muhammad of Ghur, another Turkish ruler with an empire centred on Afghanistan, overthrew the kingdom of Delhi and brought all of north-central India under his rule.

The Delhi Sultanate

The Ghurid empire did not survive Muhammad's assassination in 1206, but independent rulers of Turkish and Afghan origin remained in control of northern India. Delhi itself was ruled for most of the 13th century by 'Slave' dynasties, so called because the Mameluks, Turkish soldiers of humble origin, exercised most of the power at court. The Delhi Sultanate was the most powerful of the Indo-Islamic states and, under

The Agra Fort, built by the emperor Akbar in the late 16th century. The fortress-palace is surrounded by a massive enclosure wall 2·5 km (1·5 mi) in length.

The emperor Shah Jahan hunts deer in this 18th-century Mogul miniature.

Muhammad ibn Tughluq (1324–51) made a strong bid to create a wider empire. However, by the 15th century major centres of Muslim power had also appeared in Bengal and Gujarat.

The Turco-Afghan rulers of northern India belonged to a wider western Asian world. They shared in its dominant Perso-Islamic culture and were threatened by its traditional enemies – as in the Mongol raids of the 13th century and the sack of Delhi by Timur (Tamerlane) in 1398 (⊳ p. 55). But Islam also began to put down roots in northern India. The faith was adopted by native land-owning families and by merchants and other townsmen. In eastern Bengal and the Punjab,

state-sponsored settlement in agriculturally underdeveloped areas created regions inhabited by Muslim peasants (and marked out the political boundaries of the subcontinent for the second half of the 20th century; ⊳ pp. 200–3).

The Mogul Empire

Northern India was thus already substantially Islamicized when Mogul power was established there in the 16th century. Like their Muslim predecessors, the new rulers had their origins in Afghanistan and its Turkish governing families. In 1526, Babur of Kabul, a descendant of Timur and therefore nominally a Mongol or 'Mogul', invaded northern India and overthrew the Delhi Sultanate.

Babur's attempt to carve a wider Indian empire for himself was incomplete at his death in 1530. His son, Humayun, was unable at first to maintain his conquests in northern India against local Muslim rulers, notably the Suris of Bengal. It was only shortly before his death in 1556 that Humayun was able to re-establish Mogul rule over a wide area of northern India.

From the base established by his grandfather and father, Akbar, the greatest of the Moguls, was able to extend his power over the whole of northern India in the next half-century. Akbar sought to bring unity to the diversity of the subcontinent. In order to bind together the previously independent Muslim states now under his control, he removed power from existing local elites and put it into the hands of subordinates drawn both from elsewhere in India – including Hindus such as the Rajputs – and from other parts of western Asia.

Akbar rationalized and made uniform the administration and law of the empire. He attempted to bring unity to an empire containing peoples of many faiths – although the large majority remained Hindu – by actively pursuing religious tolerance and by claiming to rule with divine mandate that embraced all creeds and sects.

Under Akbar's successors in the first half of the 17th century – Jahangir and Shah Jahan – the Empire continued to flourish. Its boundaries were edged forward, particularly in the south. The economy flourished, providing a base on which the artists of Mogul India could produce the works that still maintain its fame.

In the second half of the 17th century, under Aurangzeb, the momentum of territorial expansion was maintained. By 1700 the Mogul Empire covered all the subcontinent except its southernmost tip. Yet, as it expanded, the Empire changed its nature and the basic imperial ideals of Akbar were discarded. Under Aurangzeb the Mogul Empire became a much more exclusively Muslim state, discriminating against its Hindu majority. The unity and administrative efficiency of the Empire began to decline, being replaced by a looser, more traditionally Indian structure embracing a hierarchy of local powers.

The decline of empire

In the 18th century, the Mogul Empire became decentralized. Strong rule from the centre had always been essential to resist the centrifugal tendencies of the subcontinent. The Mogul dynasty in the 18th century did not produce rulers with the necessary resolution, and their actual power was increasingly transmuted into symbolic overlordship as regional powers began to assert themselves.

Weakness at the centre produced a political situation of great complexity. Provincial governors of the Mogul Empire in Bengal, Avadh (Oudh) and Hyderabad effectively took power for themselves. Elsewhere, with the abandonment of conciliatory religious policies, resurgent Hindus – notably the Marathas and Rajputs – took control. At the same time, in the areas of the south that had been brought relatively late into the Empire, the Islamic faith and culture of later Mogul India were still gaining ground.

Much of the prosperity of the increasingly autonomous regions of 18th-century Mogul India was linked to the growth of overseas trade, particularly the export of fine cotton goods to Europe. The ports of India had always been stopping-off points on the trade routes between the Far East and Arabia. Between the 8th and 15th centuries, the main influence on trade between India and the West was Arab and Islamic. From the end of the 15th century, however, the Arab role was increasingly taken over by the Portuguese (▷ p. 114). Then, in the 17th century, Dutch, French and British traders pushed the Portuguese into the background (▷ p. 128).

For a long time, the European traders seemed no different from those of previous centuries. Then, soon after 1750, the relationship between Mogul India and the Europeans suddenly went sour. In 1750, the Europeans were still just traders, confining their activities to the coasts. However, by 1800, the British had become a major political power on the subcontinent (▷ p. 129). The East India Company exercised direct rule over Bengal, the most prosperous region of Mogul India, and 'protected' several of the major princely states within the Mogul Empire.

Increased European intervention in the internecine quarrels of the coastal states – partly to pursue European, mainly Anglo-French, rivalries, partly to try to establish local political stability – only produced greater instability. It became easier for Britain to use superior European arms to impose direct control than to continue its indirect manoeuvring of the affairs of a diversity of states within the Mogul Empire. In the end, the long-established – and often successful – pattern of diffused local political power in India had proved its undoing.   RJ

WONDERS OF INK AND STONE

Mogul art was a product of the cosmopolitan world of southwest Asia under Islam. The Moguls and most of the other rulers of Islamic India were in origin Central Asian nomads who had established their power over the settled peoples to the south of the steppe. By the time they entered India they had accepted the dominant culture of this region, both its faith, Islam, and its arts, which derived from the ancient civilization of Persia.

Initially the Moguls imported their artists, and their paintings and buildings were purely Persian. As time passed, local artists and craftsmen made an increasing contribution, and the mature Mogul style is a blend of Indian and Persian elements.

The Mogul court took particular delight in miniature paintings. Among the finest are those depicting the deeds of the Mogul emperors in war and peace. The example opposite shows the emperor Shah Jahan pursuing one of the arts of peace. The firearms are not the only signs in the miniature of European influence on the Mogul court; the emphasis on the landscape and the art of perspective used to establish its depth are indications of the distant influence of contemporary European art on the Mogul painter.

The influence of native Indian traditions can be seen in the colour and the intricate patterning of the detail in the miniature. These characteristics are also marked on a much larger scale in the splendid buildings that survive in and around the Mogul capitals of Agra, Delhi and Fatehpur Sikri (▷ picture, bottom left). There, colour and pattern, light and shade are emphasized by the intricacy of carved surfaces, alternating white marble and red sandstone, deeply recessed entrances and overhanging roofs.

Robert Clive, the representative of the British East India Company, receives sovereign rights over the prosperous territory of Bengal from the Mogul emperor in 1765.

Japan
to the 20th Century

Japan was first peopled from Asia in one of those periods in the last Ice Age when lowered sea levels joined offshore islands to the mainland. Over tens of thousands of years, hunting and gathering communities thrived on the Japanese islands. They were among the earliest societies in the world to develop pottery, probably around 10 000 BC, and, for much of the next ten thousand years, the pottery of the Jomon culture showed what could be achieved in material terms by a society living on the proceeds of hunting, gathering and perhaps some horticulture.

The techniques of fully developed rice farming reached the southern island of Kyushu from Korea, the nearest point on the Asian mainland, around 400 BC and spread up the island chain to reach the east coast of the central island of Honshu by AD 100. Progress further north was much slower: the northern island of Hokkaido was not brought into the farming zone until the 19th century, and the hunting-gathering culture of the Ainu survived there until recently.

Links with the Asian mainland were maintained and strengthened by the early farming communities of Japan. It is possible that considerable numbers of immigrants arrived; and certainly technical skills and cultural ideas were borrowed, including the Chinese script, Confucianism and the then popular Chinese form of Buddhism. These were added to Shinto, the traditional Japanese ancestor worship, to form a trio of often interrelated systems of belief.

Imperial Japan

By the 7th century AD, Chinese concepts of government were being put into practice in the southern Yamato Plain of Honshu, whose rulers dominated much of central and western Japan by this time. A Chinese-style emperor was established at Nara (710–784) in a Chinese-style imperial city, and the main features of the Chinese system of government were imitated. The court was moved to Heian (modern Kyoto) in 794, and the 9th century saw an elaboration of the imperial system there.

Having borrowed from China, the Japanese absorbed and transformed their borrowings. At the same time, contacts with China diminished. The imperial system, too, was transformed. The emperor became a religious figurehead, power being held by members of an aristocratic court family, the Fujiwara. Then power in turn slipped away from the Fujiwara and the court, and into the hands of provincial governors and landowners.

Feudal Japan

By the 12th century, much of the real power in Japan was exercised by provincial barons (*daimyos*) through bands of warriors (*samurai*; ▷ box). In the mid-12th century, the head of one baronial family, Taira Kiyamori, seized power as a military dictator. His successor, Yorimoto, leader of the Minamoto family, took the logic of the separation of real power and imperial dignity to its conclusion. He ruled Japan after 1185 from Kamakura (near present-day Tokyo), eventually under the title of *shogun*, in the name of a powerless emperor who remained in courtly isolation at Kyoto.

The Kamakura shogunate lasted a century and a half. For much of that time, the shogun himself was a figurehead, the real power being exercised by regents from the Hojo family. In the 14th century, the Ashikaga family instituted a new shogunate based at Kyoto. This lasted in name until 1578, but long before that date Japan had once again fallen apart into warring provincial baronies. An emperor and a shogun still nominally ruled in Kyoto, but real power was contested by the provincial daimyos and their military forces.

This was the Japan that came into contact with European (mainly Portuguese) traders and missionaries from the 1540s. During the 16th century, Western ideas, particularly Christianity, made a significant impact on Japan, but the impact that really mattered was that of European firearms. Three military leaders in turn – Odo Nobunaga, Toyatomi Hideyoshi and Tokugawa Ieyasu – used muskets to fight their way out of the impasse of feudal anarchy and into control of a united Japan.

Tokugawa Japan

Under Ieyasu, the shogunate was established at Edo (Tokyo) in the control of the Tokugawa family. The emperor, with some dignity restored, remained at Kyoto.

The Tokugawa shogunate was built on feudal concepts but governed as a military bureaucracy. In particular, the daimyos were subject to close supervision from Edo and their local power diminished by long periods of compulsory residence at the court of the shogun. Their families remained there the whole time as potential hostages.

Loyalty to the regime was further encouraged by excluding foreign influences. Christianity was suppressed; and the only foreign traders permitted were the Dutch, who were restricted to Nagasaki harbour. Firearms, having done their work, were limited to the use of the government.

Hermetically sealed from outside influences, Japan went its own way between the mid-17th and mid-19th centuries. Tokugawa Japan was a stable and, in many ways, a prosperous pre-industrial

Himeji Castle in western Honshu, Japan. Known as 'the Castle of the White Heron', the fortress at Himeji was constructed in the 14th century, when the Ashikaga shogunate rose to power. It was refashioned and strengthened during the anarchy of the 16th century and extensively renovated in 1967.

society, able to sustain great cities and a complex bureaucracy – and also, when the crunch came, able to face the challenges of the 19th century.

Japan transforms

The industrial West arrived with Commodore Perry and an American fleet in 1853. Japan was forced into the global trading system. The loss of face and the impact of the outside world destabilized an already weakening Tokugawa regime. In 1867–8, power was seized at Kyoto by a group representing daimyos from western Japan together with reforming imperial courtiers.

The prestige of the emperor was restored, the last Tokugawa shogun was overthrown and, in 1869, Emperor Mutsuhito was installed with executive power at Edo, renamed Tokyo ('the eastern capital'). The emperor adopted 'Meiji' ('enlightened government') as his throne name, and the term is also applied to the period of his reign (1867–1912).

The group of privy councillors who exercised power on behalf of the emperor then proceeded to transform Japan. Within ten years, virtually all vestiges of feudalism had been removed. The daimyos and samurai were pensioned off and the peasants given ownership of the land they worked (and then heavily taxed). Western systems of law, administration and taxation were introduced, followed in 1889 by a constitution and parliament along Western lines.

The Meiji reformers saw that survival in the modern world demanded not just Western institutions but also a Western-

style economy. This took longer to achieve, but industrialization, sponsored by the state, was well underway by the beginning of the 20th century.

By then, Japan was sufficiently well-established in the world to be accepted as an equal by the Western powers, who relinquished their unequal treaty rights.

Japan even began to fight and win Western-type wars, against China in 1894–5, and Russia in 1904–5 (▷ p. 180), coming away with the beginnings of a colonial empire in Taiwan, Korea and the south of Manchuria. The world career of Japan as a major power had begun (▷ pp. 187, 194 and 222).   RJ

Samurai crossing the 'Bridge of Boats' during the battle of Nagaragawa (1347), as depicted by the artist Kuniyoshi in the 19th century.

KOREA – THE HERMIT KINGDOM

In 108 BC the northwestern part of Korea was conquered by the Chinese (▷ p. 53), and became a colony of the Western Han. Direct Chinese rule only lasted a century or two, but it spawned no fewer than three Chinese-style Korean kingdoms: Koguryo in the north, Paikche in the southwest, and Silla in the southeast. These three kingdoms lived and fought together in relative isolation for several centuries until Chinese imperial ambitions in the 7th century AD brought the armies of the Sui dynasty and then the Tang into Korea.

For 200 years from 668 AD a united Korea was ruled by the Silla as a tributary state of China. After a period of civil war, the Koryo kingdom (918–1392) emerged supreme. Koryo bowed to the inevitability of Mongol overlordship from 1259, but the fall of the Yuan in China (▷ p. 56) enabled Yi Song-gye to seize power with the support of the Ming. Korea was to be greatly influenced by Ming China in the early years of the Yi dynasty (1392–1910).

United Korea lived as an outlying tributary kingdom of the Chinese Empire until the 19th century. Most of the time it paid its dues to the Empire and got on with its own life: Chinese in its broad patterns, Korean in its local detail.

But across the sea to the east the power of Japan was growing. The Korean peninsula – always the main stepping stone between China and Japan – now became a battlefield. In 1592 Korea was invaded by the armies of the Japanese warlord, Hideyoshi, intent on conquering

the Chinese Empire. Initial Japanese successes were halted by fierce Korean resistance before Chinese armies finally saw off the Japanese, exacting recognition of Chinese overlordship in return.

In the 17th and 18th centuries, Korea was left alone by its larger neighbours. Like them, it reacted to probings from European traders by retreating into its shell. Trade with the outside world – except a minimal amount with China and Japan – was banned, and any contact with the West discouraged. The 'Hermit Kingdom' was added to Western travellers' tales.

However, the outside world could not be kept out indefinitely. The shell was broken not by the Europeans, but by Japan, which traded with Korea from 1876. By now Japan was looking for a Western-style empire to go with its Western-style state and economy. The Asian mainland was the focus for Japanese imperialist ambitions, and Korea its first target.

The fact that Korea was still officially part of the Chinese Empire made the challenge to expansionist Japan all the more attractive. China was heavily defeated by Japan in the Sino-Japanese War of 1894–5 and obliged to grant Korean independence in the Treaty of Shimonoseki, which marked the beginning of Japanese domination in the region. This was reinforced by Japanese victory in the Russo-Japanese War of 1904–5 (▷ p. 180), when Korea was again a battleground; it was subsequently 'protected', then annexed by Japan in 1910.

Africa
to the Colonial Age

Africa south of the Sahara is the cradle of the human race: the first man-like creatures evolved there as did the first men (▷ p. 12). The earliest form of man, *Homo habilis*, known from remains at the Olduvai Gorge in Tanzania, emerged some 2 million years ago, evolving into *Homo erectus* around 1.6 million years ago. *Homo erectus* spread from Africa to Europe and Asia, and gave rise to modern man, *Homo sapiens*. In sub-Saharan Africa, various groups established themselves in different areas: the Negroes in the West African bush, the Pygmies in the equatorial rain forest, the Nilo-Saharans in the middle Nile, and the Bushmen in the open lands in the east and south.

The relatively small area of Africa north of the Sahara belonged, then as now, to a different world; its peoples, sometimes referred to as Hamites, are related ethnically and linguistically to the Semites of the Middle East. They can be divided into three main groups: the Berbers of the Maghreb (Morocco, Algeria and Tunisia), the Egyptians, and the Cushites of the Red Sea coast. The history of these peoples belongs largely to that of the Mediterranean and the Middle East.

The first farmers
The Nilo-Saharans of the Nile valley had

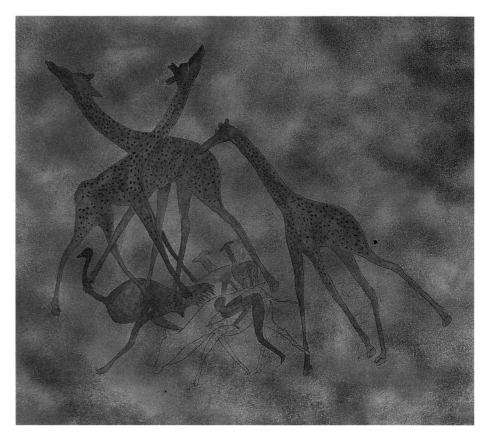

A rock painting from the Sahara Desert, showing a man hunting giraffes and an ostrich (c. 3500 BC). Paintings on the walls of Saharan rock shelters are the earliest known African art. Early examples of Saharan rock art depict animals now extinct in the region – such as hippopotamuses and buffalo – that were able to live in the region during the wetter climate of the period. Later, less naturalistic, paintings show only those animals able to survive a drier climate – mainly camels, goats, antelope and oryx.

the closest contact with the Mediterranean and Middle Eastern world to the north. The practice of farming spread from the Middle East through Egypt to the middle Nile valley sometime before 3000 BC. When it spread beyond the Nile valley, it encountered an environment that favoured pastoral farming. Soon Nilo-Saharans and Cushites and their herds were moving west along the Sahel, the area of open savannah to the south of the Sahara, and into West Africa.

In West Africa the land was more suited to settled farming. In the course of the final millennium BC, village communities began to appear in this zone and the Negro peoples who lived in them subsequently developed other skills too, notably the ability to smelt iron. The first of these West African Iron Age communities recognized by the archaeologists is known as the Nok culture; it has been dated to the last few centuries BC.

The combination of agriculture and iron created a potent force in prehistoric society. Around AD 100, Negro farmers – mainly Bantu – began to spread east and south out of West Africa, settling areas previously roamed by hunter-gatherers. By AD 500 they had reached as far as the east coast of southern Africa, leaving only the deep rain forest to the Pygmies and the Kalahari Desert to the Bushmen.

Africa and the wider world
Settled, agricultural Black Africa of the

Iron Age had several major links with the wider world. That world – to the north and east – offered trade in exchange for Africa's gold, ivory and slaves, and was eventually to offer monotheistic religion as well. Egypt had always been in touch along the Nile with Nilo-Saharan Nubia (northern Sudan, known to the Ancient Egyptians as 'Cush'). By 800 BC, the Nubians had learned their lessons from Egypt sufficiently well to establish a powerful kingdom there in their own right, one that actually supplied Egypt with a dynasty, the 25th, in the century around 700 BC (▷ p. 19).

The Pharaonic model of a powerful ceremonial kingship was widely influential. Early in the first millennium AD, kings had established themselves over the area between Nubia and the Red Sea, ruling from an Egyptian-style ceremonial city at Axum. At first the kingdom also had close contact with the Arab societies on the other side of the Red Sea, but its centre of gravity later moved inland, into the Ethiopian highlands, where it became known as Abyssinia.

In the 4th century, the kingdom of Abyssinia became the first state outside the influence of the Roman Empire to adopt Christianity. It was followed in the 6th century by the three separate kingdoms into which Nubia was then divided. Once established, the black Christian kingdoms of the upper Nile and Abyssinia

GREAT ZIMBABWE

When Europeans explored distant lands they liked to make a mystery of the cultural evidence – particularly the deserted ruins – they found there. Who built them and why? The questions always carried the implication that, whoever was responsible, it was not the ordinary and 'inferior' peoples who still lived their daily lives around the ruins.

At Great Zimbabwe – as elsewhere – the mystery-makers were wrong. The massive and magnificent ruins had been the palace of powerful local rulers, perhaps wealthier than many other African rulers of prehistory but otherwise no different from them. The people who had built the existing palace in the 14th and 15th centuries AD still lived locally; they are represented by the modern Shona.

Zimbabwe was built as a result of the coming together of three factors. The first – and the reason for its spectacular survival – was a good local supply of building stone. Most African rulers had to make do with mud or bricks. Their buildings, although they could be large, made less of an immediate visual impact and had shorter lifespans.

The second factor was the power and wealth of its rulers at the time. This had its roots in their control over the supply of local gold to the east coast of Africa and its Arab traders. To move beyond ruling a small collection of villages from a small palace, an African ruler needed to possess outstanding military skills or to have some non-agricultural source of income, usually trade in a scarce natural resource such as gold. To have both was even better.

The third factor in the building of a palace such as Zimbabwe was the desire to emphasize the prestige of the ruler. This was not just a matter of military power or wealth. The person of the ruler was sacred and his palace was designed to secure his ritual sanctity. The ruler lived a largely secluded life, surrounded and shielded by elaborate ceremonial and taboos. His wives and the usually powerful queen-mother, as well as court officials, lived in other compounds within the surrounding walls, all leading separate but interlocking lives.

Africans did not expect their rulers just to provide community leadership and physical protection, they expected religious benefits as well. A good ruler dealt with all who could secure the well-being of the community – gods and spirits as well as other rulers and traders from outside. Safe in his palace, his ritual purity as well as his political skill protected the people from evil.

---

proved tenacious, despite being cut off from the rest of the Christian world by the expansion of Islam in the 7th century. Christian kingdoms survived in Nubia into the 14th and 15th centuries, while Abyssinia continued to assert its existence – at times tenuous   against all comers into the 20th century (⇨ p. 163).

The eastern coast of Africa, too, had its contacts with the wider world: longstanding ones with the Arabian peninsula, and occasional ones with lands further to the east. It was, however, probably an accident that brought the Malagasy people from Indonesia to settle Madagascar around AD 500. Arab expansion (⇨ p. 82) brought Islam to the northeast coast, as far south as Somalia by the 12th century, and the Arabs also established trading settlements along the coast down to Mozambique between the 9th and 13th centuries. In West Africa, trade began to reach across the Sahara from Muslim North Africa in the 8th century, and Islam followed into the Sahel in the 11th century.

African kingdoms

African contact with the Arab world reveals for the first time something of the political history of Africa south of the Sahara and of the rise and fall of its kingdoms. The profit from that contact – particularly from the gold trade – enabled some African kingdoms to establish themselves on a much more lavish scale than before. In West Africa, the kingdoms of Ghana (8th–12th centuries) and Mali

(13th–14th centuries) dominated the routes between the goldfields and the desert trails to North Africa. Similarly, the eastern kingdom of Zimbabwe (13th–15th centuries; ⇨ box) controlled that region's goldfields and its trade with the coastal Arabs.

From the 13th century, West African links with the Islamic world became even stronger. The kings of Mali were Muslims, as were those of all the major states of the Sahel in the following centuries – states such as Songhay, which succeeded Mali as the major power in the western Sahel in the 15th and 16th centuries, and Bornu, the dominant power in the central Sahel in the 17th century.

New sea routes

A new strand was added to the pattern of contact between Africa and the wider world with the arrival of the Portuguese, who opened up a route along the west coast in the late 15th century and circumnavigated the continent in 1497–8 (⇨ p. 108). These and other voyages, including the discovery of the Americas, led to a vast increase in the slave trade. In this operation the Portuguese were succeeded by the Dutch (in the 17th century) and the French and English (in the 18th; ⇨ p. 128).

Inland African kingdoms – such as Benin (17th century), Oyo (18th century) and Ashanti (18th and 19th centuries) in West Africa – lived in symbiosis with the coastal traders, supplying them with gold and slaves to work the plantations of the

Americas in exchange for textiles, iron goods and guns (⇨ p. 128).

In the far south was there a different type of development: Dutch colonists, the Boers, began to settle the Cape in the second half of the 17th century. By the end of the 18th century, Boer expansion had led to clashes with the southernmost of the Bantu kingdoms, destabilizing the whole of southern Africa and leading to the emergence of a powerful new Zulu state. A pattern of European invasion and colonization was begun that was to bring about the fall of all the kingdoms of Black Africa except Abyssinia by the end of the 19th century (⇨ p. 161).

At first, the inland thrust of the Boers remained untypical. Before the mid-19th century, most Europeans kept to the coast. The interior remained the 'Dark Continent', its peoples and kingdoms protected from European expansion by lack of material incentive and deadly tropical diseases. In the second half of the century, the geographical darkness was dispersed by a combination of explorers, missionaries and traders. Natural resources such as gold in southern Africa began to be exploited, and palliatives for major tropical diseases such as malaria were discovered. Geography had been the only formidable defence of the kingdoms of Black Africa; they could not hope to match the firepower of advanced Western nations. Once the European scramble for Africa got under way in the last quarter of the 19th century (⇨ p. 160), however valiant the Africans' defence was in the short term, their longer-term fate was sealed. RJ

SEE ALSO

- ANCIENT EGYPT p. 17
- THE ANCIENT ECONOMY p. 42
- THE RISE OF ISLAM p. 82
- THE AGE OF DISCOVERY p. 108
- THE SPANISH AND PORTUGUESE EMPIRES p. 116
- COLONIAL EXPANSION IN THE 17TH AND 18TH CENTURIES p. 128
- THE PEAK OF EMPIRE p. 160
- SOUTHERN AFRICA IN THE 20TH CENTURY p. 220

A bronze head from the city of Ife, Nigeria (?13th century). Hollow-cast heads representing dead kings are typical of the Nigerian sculpture that flourished from the 12th to the 19th centuries. Traditionally referred to as 'bronzes', many pieces – especially early works – were in fact made of brass.

Australasia and Oceania to the Colonial Age

Compared to Africa and Eurasia, human beings settled in Australasia relatively recently. The first inhabitants arrived in New Guinea and Australia around 50 000 BC, when the last Ice Age lowered the sea level sufficiently to make island-hopping along the Indonesian archipelago relatively easy. And, for a long time, that was as far as they got.

Aborigine cave paintings in Arnhem Land, Northern Territory, Australia. Each Aboriginal cultural area developed its own distinctive style of art. 'X-ray art' – showing the skeletons and internal organs of subjects – is unique to Arnhem Land.

Even relatively close Oceanic island groups like the New Hebrides (Vanuatu) and New Caledonia were not colonized much before 2000 BC, and Hawaii and New Zealand were still undiscovered and uninhabited when the Christian era began.

Australia

At the end of the last Ice Age, the waters gradually rose to their present levels. One result was the flooding of the Torres Strait, which divided Australia from New Guinea around 5000 BC. The Stone Age Aboriginal culture of Australasia was largely isolated from this time. Isolation did not mean an unchanging culture, but neither internal pressures nor sporadic contacts with the outside world – one resulting in the introduction of the dingo, perhaps around 2000 BC – led to the development of agriculture.

Instead, roving hunter-gathers reacted in sophisticated ways to a wide variety of environments. They took full advantage of the seasonal patterns of growth in fruits, vegetables, fish and animals to develop a rich and varied diet. They even managed their environment to a significant degree, regularly firing large areas of ground to restrict the growth of less useful vegetation and encourage more nutritious plants and the animals that fed on them. Where the environment was particularly favourable, along some of the coasts and rivers, roving decreased and more settled communities developed.

Because the hunter-gathering economy of the Aboriginal Australians was so successful, its practitioners had ample time for leisure. However, partly owing to their largely nomadic lifestyle, and partly owing to the destructive impact of European settlement, few physical relics are left of the rich cultural life that resulted. Neither are there any vestiges of the great feasts and ceremonies held when the small family groups – which formed the basic units of Aboriginal society – met together. Some rock art does remain, but there is little else to see and touch.

It is only in the minds of contemporary Aborigines that the interpretation of life encapsulated in prehistoric art and ritual still survives – in the elaborate mythology of the 'Dream Time', with all its reminders of the native Australians' successful adaptation to time and space.

Melanesia

By the time that Australia went its separate way, the Melanesian inhabitants of New Guinea had begun to acquire new methods of food production from Southeast Asia (▷ p. 60). Once an advanced Stone Age economy had been established in New Guinea, it persisted with relatively little change well into the 20th century. As in Australia, the lack of persistent contact with the outside world and the successful balance achieved between man and nature reduced the chances of further major upheavals.

The basis of the economy of New Guinea was a tropical horticulture concentrating on root crops such as yams and taro. The sweet potato was introduced at a relatively late stage, probably not until the 16th century. On this horticultural foundation there developed a rich variety of village and tribal cultures, moulded into a wide range of forms by the complex geography of New Guinea. Each valley was an enclosed world, sometimes with its own language, art and culture.

With their particular brand of food production fully developed in New Guinea, Melanesian horticulturalists began to settle the islands to the east, reaching the New Hebrides and New Caledonia by 2000 BC. At the same time, other peoples – originally of east Asian stock – were moving east from the Philippines and surrounding islands to settle the northern and eastern fringes of Melanesia and, eventually, much of Micronesia to the north as well.

Polynesia

These newcomers to the area brought with them a different language and culture from those previously developed in Melanesia. But they also brought a similar Neolithic horticulture which, combined with fishing, was well suited to the smaller islands of the Pacific. Settlers from such a background had reached Fiji by 1500 BC, spreading from there to Tonga and Samoa. It was in this central Pacific area over the next millennium that the language and culture of the islanders developed the traits we recognize as Polynesian.

An outstanding aspect of Polynesian culture was a magnificent tradition of seafaring (▷ box). Time and again, Polynesians set out into the unknown on outrigger canoes loaded with the essentials of their life – coconut, taro, yam, banana, breadfruit, pig and chicken, none of which was native to the area – and used their considerable navigational skill – and perhaps some luck – to colonize islands all over the vastness of the Pacific.

Once settled on their islands, the Polynesians lived in societies that were neces-

Maori chiefs in the 19th century. Members of each Maori tribe (*iwi*) owed allegiance to a chief (*ariki*) and traced a common ancestry to the mythical 'great fleet' that arrived in New Zealand from the land of 'Hawaiki'. The subtribe (*hapuu*) – a group exercising shared land rights – was the most significant unit in Maori society.

sarily small in scale but still highly complex. Hereditary chiefs played a powerful economic and social role in these communities. Major islands were divided between several chiefdoms, whose relationships gave much scope for rivalry and warfare.

Religion, too, developed its own complexities. On the eastern Polynesian islands it focused on large open-air courtyards with statues or other symbolic representations of gods and ancestors. On Easter Island, the cult of stone statues developed to a unique extent between AD 1000 and 1600. The massive, standardized statues of Easter Island (some up to 12 m/40 ft in height), with their long heads and diminutive torsos, have puzzled outsiders since the first European contacts of the 18th century. They were erected on platforms all around the coast by a population of probably no more than 10 000. But the carving appears to have suddenly stopped. The half-finished statues were left in the quarries and many of the standing statues were toppled. A possible explanation is that the statues were cult objects, and that the cult was ended suddenly by a brutal civil war.

New Zealand

In the south Pacific, the two main islands of New Zealand were much larger than the other Polynesian islands and lay in the temperate zone. In this different environment, which was settled late in the first millennium AD, Maori culture developed its own variations. At first, the peculiar fauna of New Zealand, particularly the flightless moa, made hunting an important part of life. When there were very few moas left, the Maori turned to a

horticulture founded on the cultivation of sweet potatoes and fern rhizomes, although many on the colder South Island remained largely hunter-gatherers.

For reasons perhaps to do with climatic change and competition for resources, Maori society in New Zealand developed particularly warlike traits in the period after 1500. Tribal refuges were fortified on hilltops and along the coastline, war taking the form of seasonal raids on these forts by bands of warriors. On the coast, these raids were seaborne, the warriors travelling in highly ornamented war canoes.

The coming of the Europeans

This warrior culture enabled the Maoris to become the only Pacific people to offer armed resistance to European advances in the 19th century. Peace between the Maoris and the British colonists was only finally achieved in 1871, 30 years after the first colony was founded.

The earlier British colonization of Australia, starting in 1788, had been a walkover (▷ p. 129). The disparity between Western technology and a Stone Age hunter gatherer society was such that the Aborigines were quickly driven from all the best lands and survived only on the fringes of society or in the more remote corners of the continent.

Most of the other peoples of this area – of New Guinea and the smaller Pacific islands – were not brought within the Western political orbit until a century later than Australia. Their settled cultures were better able to retain some integrity in the face of colonization. Some societies in New Guinea were so sheltered and remote that only recently have they been forced to move in one step from the Stone Age to the 20th century. RJ

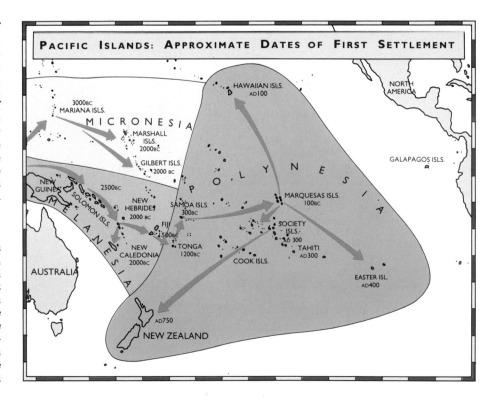

PACIFIC ISLANDS: APPROXIMATE DATES OF FIRST SETTLEMENT

NORTH AMERICA

3000BC MARIANA ISLS.

MICRONESIA

MARSHALL ISLS. 2000BC

GILBERT ISLS. 2000 BC

GALAPAGOS ISLS.

HAWAIIAN ISLS. AD100

2500BC

NEW GUINEA

MELANESIA

SOLOMON ISLS.

NEW HEBRIDES 2000 BC

FIJI 1500BC

SAMOA ISLS. 300BC

POLYNESIA

MARQUESAS ISLS. 100BC

SOCIETY ISLS. AD 300

TAHITI AD300

NEW CALEDONIA 2000BC

TONGA 1200BC

COOK ISLS.

EASTER ISL. AD400

AUSTRALIA

AD750

NEW ZEALAND

SEE ALSO

● COLONIAL EXPANSION IN THE 17TH AND 18TH CENTURIES p. 128
● THE PEAK OF EMPIRE p. 160

The Americas before Columbus

The Americas were the last of the habitable continents to be colonized by man, an event that occurred during the last Ice Age. Two opposing geographical changes made it possible. First the sea level fell because of the amount of water locked up in the icecaps; this led to the appearance of a land bridge connecting Asia and Alaska. Then the melting of the North American icecap removed the barrier to movement between Alaska and the rest of North America. There was just enough time for a few families of Siberian mammoth hunters to make the journey before the rising sea level obliterated the land bridge.

Current thinking is that this happened around 10 000 BC or perhaps a little before. Earlier dates have been proposed, but the scientific evidence is insecure and a relatively late date still fits best into the history of settlement on both sides of the Bering Straits. What happened next is well supported by evidence. Within a few hundred years, the descendants of these few families had spread over North America and some had already moved further south. Their hunting methods were so efficient – and their quarries so unused to man – that by the 7th millennium BC many of the big game animals – including both mastodon and mammoth – had been hunted out of existence.

The great pyramid (the 'Castillo') at Chichén Itzá, from the 10th to the 12th centuries the main Toltec city of Yucatán. Stepped pyramids were built by various Meso-American cultures, including the Mayans, Toltecs amd Aztecs, and were often the site of human sacrifices.

New world agriculture

As the climate got warmer and many of the bigger animals were hunted to extinction, the early Americans found it increasingly difficult to support themselves by big-game hunting alone. As a result, many of them turned to the hunting of smaller game and the gathering of edible seeds and fruits.

By about 2500 BC, experiments with the domestication of *teosinte*, a type of grass ancestral to modern maize, had led to the appearance of fully developed agricultural communities in Meso-America (Mexico and Central America). Parallel developments took place in the central Andean region of South America (now Equador, Peru and Bolivia). In Meso-America the staple crop was always maize. In the Andes and on their western side, a number of crops were domesticated, including the potato, but there too – after 1500 BC – maize became a major crop. By 1000 BC, a third area of farming – relying largely on manioc (cassava) – had developed in the tropical area now covered by Colombia and Venezuela.

By AD 500, the whole western part of the

Pottery figurines from southern Mexico, made by either the Mixtec or Zapotec peoples and dating from the 12th–13th centuries.

continent between Mexico and northern Chile was occupied by maize farmers, while tropical farmers had settled on river banks along the whole length of the Amazon river system and had reached the Caribbean islands as well. Tropical farming continued to spread after this, reaching south to the Paraná basin by AD 1000 and then moving north up the Brazilian coast.

Not all Americans turned to agriculture, however. Along the coastline, on the open plains in the far north and in the deep tropical jungle of the Amazon basin, specialist fishers, hunters and gatherers maintained rich and varied ways of life up to the 19th or 20th centuries.

The development of civilization

As in the Old World, the acquisition of agriculture was only the beginning of a sequence of social developments. Settled farmers can support settled places of worship. After a while, by coming together in sufficient numbers, they can build temples of some size and maintain the priestly elites to go with them. This development took place separately by 1500 BC in both of the core areas of temperate agriculture, Meso-America and the Central Andes.

The steps in the organization of society beyond tribal farming and local religious centres were taken only in Meso-America and the central Andes. The initial focus of the development of civilization in these two areas was religious, centring on the building of increasingly grandiose temples and then temple-cities. This phase reached its peak in the Maya cities of lowland Meso-America, at Teotihuacán

in the Mexico valley and at Tiahuanaco high up in the Andes, all of which were at the height of their spendour in the first millennium AD.

At the heart of the American ceremonial cities were great artificial temple mounds (pyramids) set within rigid geometric layouts that had astronomical significance. In Meso-America an obsession with the calendar led to complex mathematical calculations and the development of hieroglyphic means of record. Another obsession of Meso-American religion was human sacrifice, intended to appease the gods and maintain the patterns of the seasons.

These temple-cities were not primarily the capitals of political states. They were the religious and social centres of agricultural peoples – organized into tribes and chiefdoms – who periodically went to their temples to worship and celebrate. By far the largest of these temple-cities was Teotihuacán, which does seem to have exercised a power and influence in Meso-America in the period around AD 500 that was more than purely religious and cultural. It is known that the rulers of the city dispatched armed embassies far afield; their purpose can only have been to enforce the acknowledgement of supremacy and the collection of tribute.

In the 7th century, Teotihuacán was abandoned and the same fate gradually overtook all the other pyramid cities of Mexico and Yucatán in the next two centuries. No one knows why – perhaps the rituals had simply become too onerous to sustain. The setback was not permanent, however, and by 900 new cities were under construction, notably Tula, the capital of the Toltecs, just to the north of present-day Mexico City.

Toltecs and Aztecs

From their headquarters at Tula, the Toltecs came to dominate a large part of central Mexico between the 10th and 12th centuries. They imposed their rule on the Yucatán from their base at Chichén Itzá. Toltec dominance was established on a more secular basis than that of Teotihuacán. The ruling elite had religious functions but they ruled through the power of a warrior tribe.

The period that followed the collapse of Toltec power in the 12th century was one of warring local states, none of which established more than a brief regional dominance. Then from the mid-14th century the Aztecs, based on their island city of Tenochtitlán in Lake Texcoco (the site of Mexico City), spread out to bring a large part of Meso-America under their rule.

The Aztec empire was another warrior empire, founded on the subjugation of neighbouring tribes and local states. These kept their separate identities but paid homage and rendered tribute – and human sacrificial victims – to the victorious Aztecs. The tribute – and the victims – flowed to the capital, Tenochtitlán, which by the early 16th century had reached

a magnificence unparalleled in the Americas, its temples and palaces rising proudly above the causeways and reclaimed garden lands that spread out across the surrounding lake.

The Incas

In South America, the first military hegemony of some size was that established from Huari, in highland Peru, between the 9th and 12th centuries AD. It was succeeded, after a period in which regional states reasserted themselves, by the coastal power of Chimu, ruling from its capital at Chan Chan from the late 14th to the mid-15th centuries, and then by the highland domination of the Incas of Cuzco (in modern-day Peru).

By the end of the 15th century, Inca power spread over virtually the whole of the area from modern Ecuador to northern Chile. Although Inca rule was again based on the military dominance of a warrior elite over many tribes and regional powers, the Inca empire became the most unified of the American states. Central power was reinforced by a system of excellently built roads and forts, and its efficiency is symbolized by the *quipu*, an accounting system based on knotted cords that to some degree took the place of writing, a skill never fully developed in the Americas.

The coming of the Spanish

The young and still evolving empires of the Incas and the Aztecs were brought to a violent end by Spanish invasion in the early 16th century, by Cortez in Meso-America and by Pizarro in Peru (▷ p. 116). The Aztec and Inca empires fell in unequal struggles. They were at a cultural level roughly equivalent to the Old World Bronze Age (▷ p. 15). They had built their first proper cities and had begun to organize themselves to collect tribute efficiently from the tribes and chiefdoms they dominated. But with their flint knives and wooden clubs, their simple battle-lines and uncertain strategies they could not long resist the arquebuses, armoured knights and steel swords of the conquistadores. RJ

A gold toucan, part of the ransom paid in 1533 by Atahualpa, the last Inca king, to the Spanish conquistador Pizarro. However, the ransom failed to save him, and Pizarro had the king strangled.

SEE ALSO

● NATIVE PEOPLES OF NORTH AMERICA p. 72
● THE SPANISH AND PORTU-GUESE EMPIRES p. 116

INCA WALLS

The cyclopean stone walls found in the Inca capital of Cuzco and the lost Inca city of Machu Picchu high in the Andes, as well as in the great pre-Inca religious centre of Tiahuanaco, are among the most impressive remains of pre-Columbian American civilization.

These walls were clearly built to impress: the perfect jointing of the great blocks was carefully outlined with bevelled edges, just to emphasize what a good job had been done. Only the best was due to the gods or to the semi-divine rulers for whose use the walls were constructed.

However, the walls were not built just for show; they were practical in every detail. The great unmortared stone walls, tapering upwards from wide bases and held together only by the force of gravity and the skill of their jointing, have repeatedly shown a capacity to withstand earthquakes while more modern buildings have crumbled around them.

But a mystery surrounds the building of these walls. How were such feats of engineering possible in societies that apparently had only the most primitive technology?

Shifting large stones some distance was a problem solved quite commonly at an early stage of civilization. The requisite tools were rollers (tree trunks were quite adequate), ramps, simple levers, ropes and a large amount of manpower.

Shaping the masonry demanded an awareness of the effects of heat and cold in splitting stones, the use of wedges, frequently sharpened tools, and abrasives such as sand and water for more exact shaping. Also necessary were simple but robust systems of measurement, and a very large amount of time.

Time and manpower are the keys to the mystery. A comparatively unlimited supply of both could be found in Inca society, which demanded periodic labour service – *mita* – from all its householders, and lifetime work for the state from its most skilled craftsmen.

These walls were not built in a day. They are monuments, not to slick technology, but to slowly acquired skills, to months or years of patient labour and to a devotion to the sacred power of the gods and the rulers who deputized for them. Who is to say how far that devotion was compelled, how far freely given?

Native Peoples of North America

The native inhabitants of North America never quite attained the degree of social and cultural complexity reached by their cousins who had moved further south into Mexico and Peru. But they achieved many other things instead: above all, a successful adaptation to life in a wide variety of environments.

In the Great Plains of Central North America, the Plains bison – the buffalo – avoided the fate that overtook most of the other American big-game animals soon after the arrival of man, and, for the next 10 000 years, men continued to live as the first Americans had done, as hunters on the plains. Their way of life was not unchanged over this period, however. The skills needed to follow the herds of buffalo and to drive selected animals to kill sites became ever more sophisticated, as did the weaponry employed, which from the second millennium BC included bows and arrows.

In the heart of the Plains, tribes of big-game hunters such as the Blackfoot, Crow and Sioux remained predominantly nomadic throughout their history. But on the fringes of the Plains, where contacts with other cultures were maintained, many eventually settled in villages and only followed the herds on a seasonal basis.

The sea, too, was a rich hunting ground. In the northwest in particular, hunter-gatherers settled along the coasts and rivers and exploited their resources to the full. These resources gave tribes such as the Chinook, Kwakiutl and Tlingit the leisure to build solid villages of wood-

Plains Indians stalking buffalo. A lithograph by George Catlin, who made extensive studies of North American Indians in the mid-19th century.

framed houses, to produce richly carved canoes and totem poles, and to maintain a complex society and culture, in which rank was marked and maintained by feasting and the exchange of gifts.

The far north

In the whole of the far north, human society remained based on hunting and fishing until modern times. The Aleuts of the Pacific coast of Alaska and the islands of the Bering Straits, the Eskimo of the frozen north, and the Athapascan-speaking tribes such as the Chipewyan who roamed the subarctic zone to the south, all spoke related languages and shared characteristics with peoples living in northwest Asia. These features show them to be relative late-comers to North America, perhaps arriving by boat up to 5000 or 6000 years after the big-game hunters.

At first, the Eskimo and the Aleuts were nomadic, hunting the land animals of the Arctic fringe, particularly the caribou and musk ox. It took them time to develop the complex skills necessary for settling down in one place and exploiting the resources of the cold seas. Only early in the first millennium AD, with the Thule culture, did the full modern Eskimo way of life develop successfully in the far northwest of America. The Thule culture and its practitioners, the Inuit, spread rapidly eastward, reaching as far as

Greenland by the 10th century AD and coming to dominate the whole Arctic zone.

In Greenland, there was a strange meeting between the Inuit and the Norse settlers (➡ p. 86) who had been moving westward as the Inuit moved east. For 200 years – until the climate turned too harsh for the Norse – Inuit and Norse occupied parts of the same territory from Greenland down to Newfoundland. The fact that archaeologists find it hard to distinguish Norse and Inuit settlement in the area shows the degree of adaptation necessary for settlement in the far north.

Early Americans of the southwest

North America exhibits better than anywhere else the capacity of human beings to survive at the extremes. Early Americans lived in the southwestern deserts as well as the frozen north. Some, particularly those dwelling along the west coast and in the Great Basin, remained hunter-gatherers throughout their history; the Shoshone are an example. By 1000 BC, others had acquired maize-farming from Meso-American civilization to the south (➡ p. 70).

The farmers of the southwest – tribes such as the Hopi and the Zuni – lived in a particularly hostile and arid environment. The history of their settlements is erratic, the result perhaps of both climatic swings and periodic hostility from surrounding nomads such as the Apache – Athapascan speakers from the north who seem to have arrived in the area around the 10th century AD. At times, the farmers of the area settled in large adobe or stone-built villages – pueblos – which were at their largest between the 11th and 13th centuries; at other times, they scattered to live in much smaller settlements elsewhere.

The eastern American farmers

To the east of the Great Plains, in the Mississippi basin and the woodlands beyond, there were rich pickings for hunter-gatherers once the days of big-game hunting were over. Those who lived close to the well-stocked lakes and rivers such as the Mississippi and the Ohio were best placed, and it was there that the most complex societies evolved, based on wooden villages and tribal ceremonial centres.

After AD 700 these eastern societies became increasingly dependent on maize-farming for their staple food, although the woods, lakes and rivers still contributed much to their diet. With the additional resources of agriculture, eastern cultures grew more complex and tribal religion more ambitious, culminating after AD 1000 in the great ceremonial centres of the Temple Mound Culture. These incorporated groups of temple-topped mounds where sacrificial rites similar to the death cults of Meso-America (⯈ p. 70) were practised.

The temple mounds are now the only visible remains of the maize-farmers who lived in the whole area from west of the Mississippi to the Great Lakes and the east coast. They are the most tangible reminder of the lives of the Cherokee, Chickasaw, Choctaw, Creek, Huron, Iroquois, and other, smaller tribes who lived there.

Members of each of these tribes shared a local language and culture and often claimed a common descent. They were governed by meetings of tribal elders and came together from time to time to worship and socialize – and to wage war with other tribes. War called for individual leadership and this led to the grouping of some tribes into more permanent confederations under the rule of powerful chiefs.

The European impact

Tribal society in general was dynamic rather than static; tribes could be reformed or regrouped, sometimes moving from one area to another. This dynamism was an important advantage when the native North Americans experienced the pressure of European invasion from the late 16th century onwards. The pressure came mostly in the east, although the pueblo farmers of the southwest were incorporated into Spain's Mexican empire as early as 1598 (⯈ p. 116).

The Europeans brought disease, war and dispossession. Of the three, disease – and the population decline that resulted from

it – was initially the most damaging to native society; dispossession of land was the most destructive in the longer term. But the native Americans had time to react to these pressures; white settlement did not reach beyond the Appalachians before 1750 and beyond the Mississippi before 1800.

As the line of settlement advanced, tribes depleted by disease or dispossessed of their land migrated and regrouped. The most successful case of this was the expansion of the Iroquois Confederation in the first half of the 18th century. These remodelled tribes of the east fought a long rearguard action throughout the 17th and 18th centuries, waging war, negotiating concessions and exploiting divisions between the British and the French and then between the colonists and their mother country (⯈ pp. 129 and 142).

Further west, the hunters of the Great Plains constructed a new way of life for themselves in this period. The southernmost tribes acquired horses from the Spanish colonists; by the mid-18th century, tribes all over the Great Plains possessed them. By that time, too, firearms had found their way westward. Horse-riding, rifle-toting tribes such as the Blackfoot soon found they had the advantage over both the buffalo and the neighbouring settled tribes. They were joined on the Plains by migrants from the east who had previously been settled farmers.

For nearly a hundred years, until the arrival of railroads and settlers in the mid-19th century, this violent Horse Indian society dominated the Great Plains. Some of the eastern tribes, too, had constructed a new way of life by the early 19th century. The extreme example was that of the Cherokee, who welcomed Christian missionaries, adopted an alphabet, printed books in their own language, and established a constitution and legislature. None of this prevented the dispossession of all the remaining tribes east of the Mississippi in the first half of the 18th century and their resettlement further west. The 'Five Civilized Indian Nations' of the southeast – Creek, Cherokee, Choctaw, Chickasaw and Seminole – were all removed to Oklahoma by more or less legal means in the 1830s. The Cherokee went last. They were evicted by the army in 1838 and lost a quarter of the tribe on the journey west. By the end of the 19th century the only native American peoples still pursuing more or less traditional life styles and living in the areas that they had inhabited before the Europeans came, were the pueblo farmers of the southwest and the hunters and fishers of the northwest and the far north.   RJ

MAJOR TRIBES OF NORTH AMERICA AD 1500

ESKIMO HUNTERS AND FISHERS	PLAINS HUNTERS AND GATHERERS	DESERT HUNTERS AND GATHERERS
FOREST HUNTERS AND GATHERERS	PLAINS FARMERS	PUEBLO FARMERS
SETTLED FISHERS AND GATHERERS	MISSISSIPPIAN FARMERS	PENINSULAR AND ANTILLEAN FARMERS AND FISHERS

A medicine man of the Chilkat tribe performs a ritual ceremony in this photograph taken in 1895. The Chilkat are one of the tribes of the Tlingit, the northernmost Indians of America's Pacific coast. The prosperity and sophistication of Tlingit culture were reflected in its 'potlatches' – elaborate ceremonies in which property and gifts were distributed by an heir or successor to affirm his new social position.

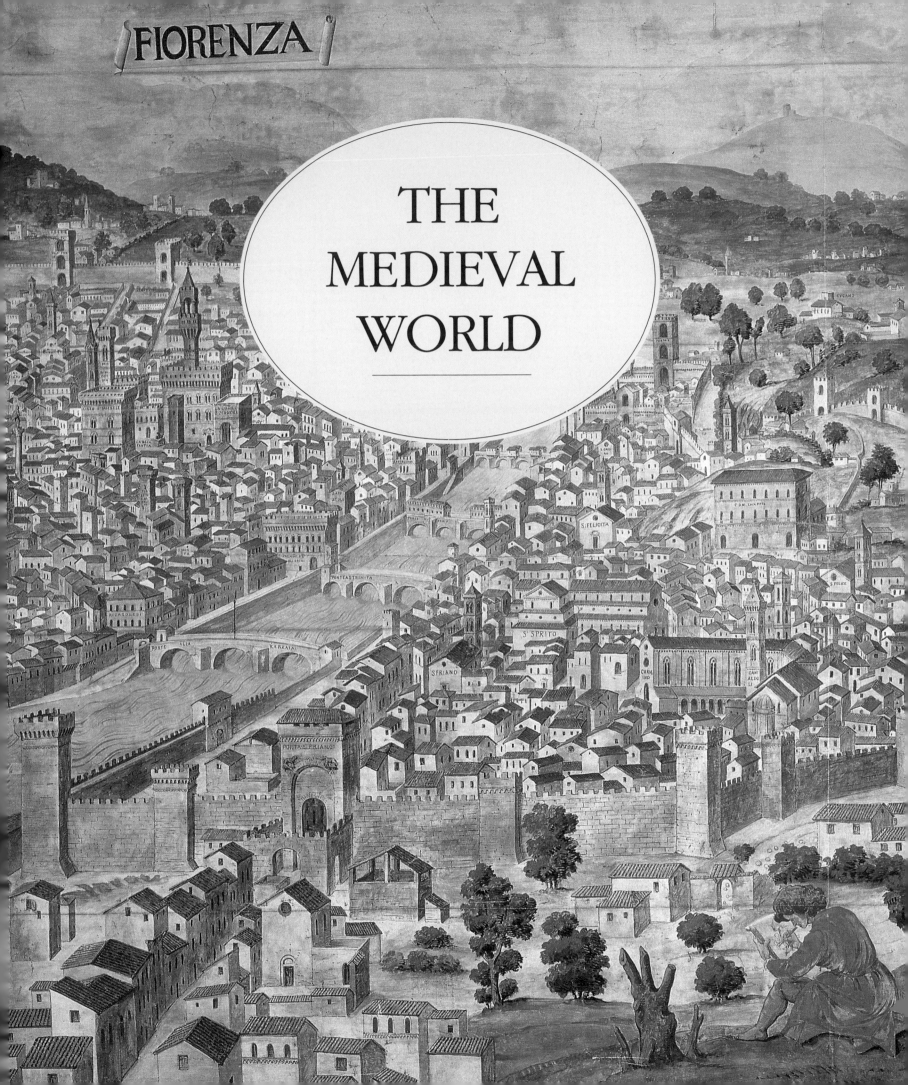

NORTHWESTERN EUROPE	CENTRAL AND EASTERN EUROPE	THE CHURCH	BYZANTINE EMPIRE
406 Alans, Vandals and Sueves invaded Gaul across the Rhine **407** Withdrawal of the last Roman troops from Britain **412** Visigoths crossed the Alps into Gaul **418** Foundation of the Visigoth kingdom of Toulouse **5th century** Anglo-Saxons settled in Britain **451** Combined force of Romans, Visigoths and Burgundians defeated Attila the Hun at the Catalaunian Fields **476** Accession of the Frankish king Clovis **c. 500** Ethelbert, king of Kent **507** Clovis defeated the Visigoths at Vouillé	**375** The Huns arrived in Europe from Central Asia **378** Visigoths defeated the Romans at Adrianople **433–53** Attila the Hun conducted an offensive throughout Central Europe **453** Death of Attila the Hun **570s** Slavs launched attacks on the Byzantine Empire's Balkan frontiers	**354–430** Augustine of Hippo **mid-5th century** Patrick began his mission to Ireland **496** Compilation of the first Missal **c. 529** Benedict founded Monte Cassino **590–604** Pontificate of Gregory the Great **597** Augustine sent to convert the English to Christianity	**527–65** Reign of Emperor Justinian **530s** Belisarius reconquered North Africa and Sicily for the Byzantine Empire **by 551** Belisarius recovered most of Italy for the Byzantine Empire
613 Frankish lands reunited under Chlotar II **639** Death of Dagobert, the last powerful Merovingian king **732** Battle of Poitiers – Charles Martel defeated an Arab raiding army **751** Carolingian dynasty founded in France **757–96** Reign of Offa of Mercia **787** Viking raids on Britain began **768–814** Frankish Empire ruled by Charlemagne	**7th century** Slav conquest of the Balkans **8th century** Moravian empire flourished in Central Europe **772–96** Most of the German lands united under the Frankish Empire by Charlemagne, who conquered Saxony, the Avars and Bavaria	**7th century** Lombards converted to Christianity **720s** Beginning of the iconoclast movement in the Byzantine Church **c. 750** Boniface evangelized Germany	**626** Constantinople besieged by the Persians and Avars **628** Heraclius defeated the Persians **630s and 640s** Byzantines lost Syria, Palestine, Egypt and North Africa to the Muslims **674–8 and 717–18** Arab sieges of Constantinople **c. 750** Byzantine Empire confined to Greece and Anatolia
9th century Viking settlements made in Ireland **800** Charlemagne crowned Emperor of the West **843** Treaty of Verdun – Frankish Empire divided into three **c. 843** Kenneth MacAlpine united the Scots and Picts **874–930** Vikings settled in Iceland **878** Alfred halted Danish advance at battle of Edington **911** Vikings granted the duchy of Normandy **c. 960** Unification of England by Wessex **987** Beginning of the Capetian dynasty in France	**9th century** Foundation of Kiev Rus **c. 900** Magyar invasion of Central Europe **924** Height of the Bulgarian Empire; Simeon I threatened Constantinople **936–73** Otto the Great extended his power throughout Germany **955** Battle of Lechfeld – Germans defeated the Magyars **960–92** Reign of Mieszko I, founder of Polish kingdom **962** Coronation of Otto I as Emperor of the Romans **997–1038** Reign of Stephen, first king of Hungary	**9th century** Bulgars, Serbs and Magyars converted to Christianity **910** Foundation of Cluny Abbey **960s** Danes and Poles converted to Christianity **970s** Christianity spread to Bohemia **988** Orthodox Christianity established in Kiev Rus	**811** Byzantine Empire defeated by the Bulgars **867–86** Revival of Byzantine Empire under Basil I **960s** Nicephorus II destroyed the Arab fleet in the Aegean **976–1025** Reign of Basil II
1014 Defeat of the Vikings in Ireland by Brian Boru **1016–35** Cnut's Anglo-Danish empire **1066** Norman conquest of England **1154** Henry II established a Plantagenet empire in England and France **1171** Henry II of England invaded Ireland and claimed sovereignty	**1024** First Salian king in Germany **1075–1122** The Investiture Contest between Empire and papacy **1152** Frederick I 'Barbarossa' established the Hohenstaufen dynasty	**1048–54** Pontificate of Leo IX; papal reformation began **1054** East–West Schism between the Churches of Rome and Constantinople **11th century** Conversion of Sweden to Christianity completed **1096** Urban II preached crusade against Islam **1098** Cîteaux, first Cistercian foundation	**1040s** Byzantine campaigns in Sicily **1071** Battle of Manzikert – Seljuk Turks crushed the Byzantine army **1081–1118** Revival of Byzantine power under Alexius I Comnenus
1215 Magna Carta **1283–4** English conquest of Wales completed **1302** Matins of Bruges, popular revolt in Flanders **1314** Victory at Bannockburn ensured Scottish independence **1328** Extinction of Capetian dynasty in France; Philip VI (Valois) challenged by Edward III of England **1337–1453** The Hundred Years War **1340** Battle of Sluys **1346** Battle of Crécy **1358** The Jacquerie, popular revolt in France **1360** Treaty of Brétigny temporarily halted the Hundred Years War **1381** The Peasants' Revolt against the poll tax in England **late 14th century** Rise of the duchy of Burgundy **1397** Union of Kalmar – Eric of Pomerania crowned king of Norway, Sweden and Denmark **1399** Richard II deposed in England; House of Lancaster usurped the throne	**1237–41** Mongols overran Russia and eastern Europe **1240–63** Alexander 'Nevski' established a Russian state based on Vladimir **1276** Rudolf of Habsburg became duke of Austria and established his dynasty in Vienna **1291** Independence of the Swiss cantons from Habsburg rule **1316–41** Creation of the Lithuanian Empire by Gediminas **c. 1350** Foundation of the Hanseatic League **1356** The 'Golden Bull' of Charles IV regularized the election of the Holy Roman Emperor **1386** Union of the crowns of Poland and Lithuania **1389–93** Ottoman Turks annexed Serbia and Bulgaria **1399** Defeat of Poland-Lithuania by the Mongol Golden Horde	**1209** Foundation of the Franciscan friars **1209–29** Albigensian Crusade against the Cathars **1215** Fourth Lateran Council – major pastoral reforms; foundation of the Dominican friars **1229** Teutonic Knights began to convert the Prussians to Christianity **1307–14** Destruction of the Order of Knights Templar **1309–77** Avignon papacy **late 14th century** Lollard heresy in England **1378–1417** The Great Schism **1387** Lithuania accepted Christianity	**1204** Constantinople besieged and sacked by a Crusader army; foundation of the Latin Empire **1261** Restoration of the Byzantine Empire in Constantinople under the Palaeologan dynasty
1400–8 Welsh rebellion led by Owen Glendower **1415** Battle of Agincourt **1425–30** Expansion of the duchy of Burgundy under Philip the Good **1429** Joan of Arc relieved Orléans in the Hundred Years War **1439** End of Scandinavian union **1450–3** Loss of Normandy and Gascony by the English **1455–85** Wars of the Roses in England **1477** Battle of Nancy – Charles the Bold killed in battle **1485** Henry Tudor defeated Richard III of England at Bosworth	**1410** Battle of Tannenberg – the Teutonic Order defeated by the Poles and Lithuanians **1419–36** Hussite Wars in Bohemia **1437** Beginning of the period of Habsburg dominance of the office of Holy Roman Emperor **1466** Western Prussia restored to the Teutonic Knights by Poland **1478** Hungary gained Lusatia, Moravia and Silesia from Bohemia **1480** Ivan III of Moscow defeated the Mongols	**1412** Jan Hus excommunicated for condemning indulgences in Bohemia **1414–17** Council of Constance ended the Great Schism **1478** Establishment of the Spanish Inquisition	**by 1400** All the territories surrounding Constantinople had been conquered by the Ottoman Turks **1453** Constantinople was besieged and taken by Ottoman Sultan Mehmet II; end of the Byzantine Empire **1460** The Ottoman Turks captured Morea (the Peloponnese)

SOUTHERN EUROPE	MIDDLE EAST	CULTURE AND SOCIETY	REST OF THE WORLD
402–3 Visigoths invaded Italy **410** Alaric sacked Rome **411** Kingdom of Galicia founded by the Sueves **476** Romulus Augustus, the last Roman emperor, deposed **493–526** Reign of Theodoric the Great in Italy **c. 500** Visigoth states established in Spain **563** Ostrogoth kingdom overthrown in Italy **568** Lombards invaded Italy	**525** Yemen conquered by Abyssinia **530–79** Period of Persian expansion and conquest **c. 570** Birth of Muhammad	**4th and 5th centuries** Development of iconography **c. 439** Theodosian code of Roman law **529** Justinian's code of civil law **542–94** Pandemic of plague across Europe	**c. 300** Rise of the Maya civilization in Central America **429** Vandals crossed into Africa, taking Carthage by 439 **c. 550** First migration of Turkic peoples from Central Asia
711 Islamic Berbers invaded Spain and soon conquered most of the Iberian Peninsula **718** Foundation of the Christian kingdom of Asturias in northern Spain **720** Muslim armies invaded Sardinia **722** Asturias defeated the Moors in the Battle of Covadonga **754–6** The pope gained temporal powers in central Italy; foundation of the Papal States **774** Charlemagne conquered Lombardy	**622** The *Hijra* – Muhammad left Mecca for Medina **632** Death of Muhammad **630–50** Arabia, Syria, Egypt and Mesopotamia taken by the Muslims **661–750** Umayyad dynasty ruled from Damascus **750** Beginning of the Abbasid dynasty	**620s–630s** Isidore of Seville compiled an encyclopedia **c. 731** *Ecclesiastical History of the English People* by Bede (c. 673–735) **from 8th century** Reception of Classical learning by Islamic scholars	**618–907** Tang dynasty in China **640–50** Arab conquest of North Africa **711** Arab armies conquer parts of northwestern India **c. 750** First Maori settlement in New Zealand
827–32 Arab conquest of Sicily **846** Rome sacked by Arabs **849** Arab fleet defeated by a papal fleet at Ostia **928** Foundation of the Umayyad caliphate in Spain **951** Otto I conquered Italy (crowned Emperor of the Romans in 962)	**969** Fatimid caliphate founded in Egypt	**c. 800** Carolingian court became the centre of a cultural renaissance **890s** Beginning of the *Anglo-Saxon Chronicle* **9th–10th centuries** Slow economic, commercial and population development in Europe	**857** Fujiwara family came to power in Japan **c. 900** Rise of the Toltec Empire **10th century** Japanese script developed **960–1127** Song dynasty in China **985** Viking settlements in Greenland
1031 Caliphate of Córdoba collapsed **by 1035** Castile, Aragon and Navarre began the Reconquista in Spain **1040s** The Normans began to carve out territories in southern Italy **1085** Toledo captured from the Muslims in Spain **1091** Roger completed the Norman conquest of Sicily **1138–9** Foundation of the kingdom of Portugal **c. 1150–1200** Rise of the early Italian city-states	**1040s** Seljuk Turks entered the Middle East **1098/1103–1268** Crusader states of Antioch and Tripoli **1099** Jerusalem taken by the Crusaders; foundation of kingdom of Jerusalem **1187** Jerusalem recaptured by the sultan of Egypt, Saladin	**11th and 12th centuries** Spread of Romanesque architecture in Europe; proliferation of horizontal looms for weaving cloth **11th century** Beginning of an economic boom in Europe **12th century** Spread of the ability to read among the upper classes; more schools founded; spread of vernacular literature; development of Gothic-style pointed arch revolutionizes building construction **12th–13th centuries** Discovery of new sources of silver led to a great increase in coinage **12th century** Rapid growth of the cloth industry in Flanders	**after 1000** Temple Mound culture in North American Great Basin **11th century** Islam reached the Sahel **1126** Manchu invasion of northern China **12th century** Peak of the Khmer Empire of Cambodia
after 1204 Great expansion of Venetian territory and commerce in the eastern Mediterranean **1249** Moors expelled from Portugal **1266** Angevin French gained control of Sicily **1282** The Sicilian Vespers – French expelled from Sicily **1378–1402** Giangaleazzo Visconti led Milan to control much of northern Italy **1380** Venetian defeat of Genoa removed Genoese influence from the eastern Mediterranean **1383** Establishment of the House of Avis in Portugal **1385** Portuguese defeat of Castile ensures Portuguese independence	**1219–60** Successive Mongol attacks on Persia, Iraq and Anatolia, initially led by Genghis Khan **1250** Mamluks seized power in Egypt **1258** Last Abbasid caliph killed when the Mongols sacked Baghdad **1260** Battle of Ain Jalut – defeat of the Mongols by the Mamluks **c. 1300** Foundation of the first Ottoman Turkish state in Anatolia	**c. 1200** Foundation of universities at Oxford, Paris and Bologna **13th century** Spread of Gothic architecture; emergence of finance houses in Italy **1225–74** St Thomas Aquinas – developed comprehensive theological system, synthesized Aristotelian philosophy and Christian doctrine **c. 1265–1321** Dante Alighieri, author of *The Divine Comedy* **14th century** Renewed interest in the literature of ancient Greece and Rome; beginnings of humanism and the Renaissance; Florentine painters (such as Giotto) developed the naturalistic style of Renaissance art; guns began to be used in warfare in Europe; proliferation of mechanical clocks **1315–17** Major famine in Europe **1346–7** Arrival of the Black Death in Europe **1387–1400** Chaucer's *Canterbury Tales*	**c. 1200** Foundation of the Inca dynasty **1206** Genghis Khan acknowledged as ruler of all the Mongols **by 1215** Genghis Khan conquered northern China **1271–1368** Yuan (Mongol) dynasty in China **14th century** Movable wooden type in China **c. 1362–1405** Empire of Tamerlane (Timur) in Asia **1345** Foundation of Tenochtitlán (modern Mexico City) by the Aztecs **14th century** Muslim conquest of northern India completed
1434 The Medici family came to power in Florence **1442** All of southern Italy came under Spanish rule **1454** Peace of Lodi, end of Italian wars **1469** Marriage of Ferdinand II (king of Aragon after 1479) to Isabella I (queen of Castile after 1474) led to the unification of Spain **1492** Granada, the last Muslim state in Spain, fell to Ferdinand and Isabella **1494–5** French invasion of Italy	**1402** Tamerlane (Timur) defeated and captured Ottoman Sultan Bajezid I **1444** Timurid state established in Baghdad **1447** Persia regained independence upon the breakup of the Timurid Empire **1476** Timurids lost control of Mesopotamia	**early 15th century** increasing secularization of music at the court of Burgundy – start of the Renaissance in music **15th century** Renaissance architecture superseded the Gothic in Italy; development of more efficient ocean-going ships (carracks and caravels) **1440s** Portuguese traders in West Africa **1450** Gutenberg set up his printing press in Mainz **c. 1450–1521** Josquin Després, Flemish composer of sacred polyphony **from 1450** significant growth of European trade **1452–1519** Leonardo da Vinci, painter, sculptor and inventor	**c. 1440–76** Major expansion of the Inca Empire **1488** Dias rounded the Cape **1492–3** Columbus's first voyage to the New World **1494** Treaty of Tordesillas divided the New World between Spain and Portugal **1497** Cabot's first voyage to North America **1498** Vasco da Gama reached India

The Barbarian Kingdoms

Although the image of the Goths sacking Rome in 410 is a powerful one, the act was more symbolic than significant. Germanic peoples had been pressing on Roman borders for centuries and had already broken through once, in the 3rd century. However, the conquest of the 5th century marked the final collapse of the political structure of the Roman Empire in the West. By around 500, successor states had been established by the Visigoths in Spain, the Vandals in North Africa, the Ostrogoths in Italy, and the Franks in Gaul (France).

It was the Franks who were to survive and attempt to re-create Rome's Empire. The others fell either to Justinian's 'reconquest' in the mid-6th century (▷ below and p. 80), or to Islam (▷ p. 83).

Who were the 'barbarians'?

The term 'barbarian' was used by the Romans and their Latin-speaking subjects to describe peoples outside their Empire whose language they considered uncivilized: the word derives from the Greek *barbaros* ('non-Greek'), originally an imitation of incomprehensible speech. Among them were those Germanic peoples who occupied the lands north and east of the Rhine–Danube frontier (▷ map, p. 78). Their tribal names – Visigoths, Ostrogoths, Vandals, Franks, and so on – were Roman titles of convenience and their political structure was not as neat as might appear on the map. But they were not primitives. Their leaders had long been attracted by the Roman way of life and they and their followers had been recruited to serve as mercenaries in an increasingly beleaguered Roman army. As a consequence, Roman economic and cultural penetration was deep.

Entering the empire

The arrival in Europe of the formidable nomadic Huns from Central Asia in 375 pushed the Germans out of their homelands and into the Empire. Visigothic refugees, harshly treated by the Romans, rebelled and defeated a Roman army at Adrianople in 378 – a battle in which the Eastern emperor, Valens, was killed. Under Alaric, the Visigoths moved into Epirus and went on to attack Italy (402–3). In 410 Alaric sacked Rome. Pressures were mounting elsewhere in the Empire. In December 406 a decisive crossing of the frozen Rhine by Alans, Vandals and Sueves opened the whole of Gaul to their ravages. In 412 the Visigoths crossed the Alps into Gaul, where they became Roman allies – *foederati* – and were allowed to settle in Aquitaine, where, in 418, they founded the kingdom of Toulouse, the first Germanic kingdom to be established in Roman territory.

Other tribes ventured still further afield. The Sueves went on into the Iberian Peninsula and established a kingdom in Galicia (411). The Vandals crossed over into Africa in 429, and by 439 had taken Carthage and its hinterland. Equipped with a naval base they built fleets and captured the Balearic Islands, Sardinia and Corsica, and established a bridgehead in Sicily. Their king, Gaiseric, an Arian Christian, was recognized by Rome in 442. In 455, however, his forces sacked Rome itself.

Defeat of the Huns

Under Attila (433–53) the Huns renewed their offensive in Europe. They attacked the Burgundians (another German tribe) who had sought refuge within the Western Empire and were settled as *foederati* around Lake Geneva (443). Attila brought all German tribes east of the Rhine under the rule of the Huns, but his raid on Gaul in 451 was defeated at the Catalaunian Fields (near Châlons-sur-Marne) by a combined force of Romans and Visigoths under a Roman general, Aetius. The battle was no more than a check for Attila, who went on to penetrate and plunder Italy in the following year. But his authority was undermined and his German subjects rebelled. Attila's death in 453 generated a succession dispute and enabled the subject Germans to overthrow their new masters.

The first kingdoms

The late 5th and early 6th centuries saw the creation of four main power blocs in what had been the Western Empire. The Vandals held sway in North Africa; the Visigoths occupied most of Spain and Gaul south of the Loire; the Ostrogoths under Theodoric the Great occupied Italy; and the Franks under Clovis controlled lands in northern France and on both sides of the Rhine. In 507 Clovis defeated the Visigoths at Vouillé, near Poitiers, and extended his territories as far as the Pyrenees. When Clovis chose to be baptized a Catholic it meant that the Franks adopted the religion of the Gallo-Romans. Elsewhere in the West, the Germanic conquerors had opted for the Arian form of Christianity. In the eyes of their subjects they were heretics – and were there to be an imperial revival this would make them vulnerable in ways the Franks were not.

Imperial recovery?

The reign of the Eastern emperor Justinian (527–65; ▷ p. 80) saw a remarkable recovery of imperial fortunes. A series of expeditions from Constantinople seemed to promise a complete restoration of the old frontiers. The Vandals were overwhelmed in a single campaign (533). There were successes in Italy, too, follow-

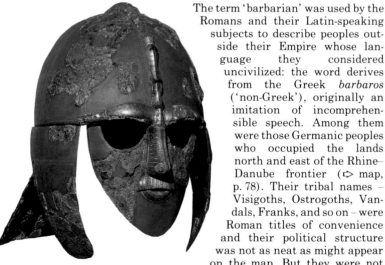

A reconstruction of an Anglo-Saxon helmet from Sutton Hoo in Suffolk, England – the site of an Anglo-Saxon ship burial discovered in 1939. Comprising a boat 24 m (80 ft) in length and 4·3 m (14 ft) across at its widest beam, the tomb at Sutton Hoo housed a wealth of artefacts, including Byzantine spoons, Swedish weaponry, Merovingian coins and Anglo-Saxon jewellery.

THE BARBARIAN KINGDOMS
AT THE DEATH OF CLOVIS, KING OF THE FRANKS AD 511

IRISH

DANES

BRITISH

ANGLO-SAXONS

FRISIANS

ANGLES

SAXONS

SLAVS

THURINGIANS

KINGDOM OF THE FRANKS

BAVARIANS

LOMBARDS

HUNS

BRETONS

NEUSTRIA

AUSTRASIA

Vouillé

Poitiers

KINGDOM OF THE BURGUNDIANS

KINGDOM OF THE GEPIDS

KINGDOM OF THE SUEVES

AQUITAINE

Pavia

Ravenna

KINGDOM OF THE OSTROGOTHS

EASTERN ROMAN EMPIRE

GALICIA

BASQUES

Toulouse

Rome

Benevento

KINGDOM OF THE VISIGOTHS

CORSICA

SARDINIA

BALEARIC ISLANDS

KINGDOM OF THE VANDALS

SICILY

Carthage

ing an invasion in 536, but the Ostrogothic kingdom showed more resilience. It was not finally overthrown until 563, after long years of war. Very soon afterwards, in 568, the Lombards swept into Italy, establishing themselves around Pavia in the north and Benevento in the south, although Rome and Ravenna remained in Byzantine hands (⊳ map, p. 81). Justinian's generals also made short-term gains in Visigothic Spain between 554 and 585. By the latter date the Visigoths had recovered sufficiently to annex the Suevic kingdom of Galicia and confine imperial troops to the southern littoral of the peninsula.

The triumph of the Franks

The chief beneficiaries of these wars were the Franks. During the 6th century, under rulers of the Merovingian dynasty, their territories were expanded to include the whole of Gaul north of the Alps. In accordance with the Frankish system of partible inheritance (division amongst heirs), on his death in 511 Clovis' kingdom was divided between his four sons. One of these, Chlotar, was briefly king of all the Frankish lands (558–61). They were to be reunited again under Chlotar II from 613.

For all the family rivalries and sometimes bloody hostilities that typify Merovingian history, the Frankish realms survived the vicissitudes of divided inheritance remarkably well. In 623, when Chlotar II gave his eastern territories (Austrasia) to Dagobert I, whilst retaining Neustria in the west, he recognized a difference that outlasted the Middle Ages – between Romance-speaking France and Teutonic Germany. After the death of Dagobert I in 639, effective power in the Frankish lands passed to the 'mayors of the palace' – originally heads of the royal household who came to control the political, social and commercial life of the Franks. The later Merovingians were often mere puppets in the hands of the mayors.

In 711, Islamic Berbers invaded the Visigothic kingdom from North Africa (⊳ p. 87), and within a few years had conquered the entire Iberian Peninsula save for the mountain strip in the extreme north, where the Asturians and native Basques hung on. The Muslims were able to push across the Pyrenees, but Charles Martel's victory near Poitiers in 732 marked the end of their northward expansion.

Charles Martel was a member of an aristocratic Frankish family who held the post of mayor of the palace. In 751, his son and successor, Pepin the Short, ousted the last token Merovingian, Childeric III, and was crowned king of the Franks. The Carolingian dynasty that he established created the largest political unit in the West since the last Roman emperors. Pepin's son Charlemagne (768–814) believed he was re-creating the Roman Empire and had himself crowned emperor at Rome to make the point (⊳ p. 84). The 'barbarian kingdoms' had become the Empire reborn.   MB

SEE ALSO
● THE ROMAN EMPIRE p. 38
● THE BYZANTINE EMPIRE p. 80
● THE RISE OF ISLAM p. 82
● THE HOLY ROMAN EMPIRE p. 84
● VIKINGS AND NORMANS p. 86

THE ANGLO-SAXONS

ANGLO-SAXON & SCOTTISH INVASIONS 5TH–7TH CENTURIES

PICTLAND · SCOTS · STRATHCLYDE · IRELAND · NORTHUMBRIA · ANGLES · JUTES · SAXONS · WALES · MERCIA · EAST ANGLIA · ESSEX · FRISIANS · KENT · CORNWALL · WESSEX · SUSSEX · FRANKS

SCOTS and IRISH
PICTS
BRITONS
ANGLO-SAXONS

Following the great barbarian invasions that had destroyed the western part of the Roman Empire, further movements of people continued in Europe, especially in the northwest. Between the 5th and 11th centuries AD, Britain in particular was the target of a series of invasions that fundamentally changed its culture, language, institutions and history. The sea, which subsequently proved Britain's main defence, was used as a highway by many invaders – Celtic and Germanic peoples, Vikings, and finally the Normans (⊳ p. 87).

For 400 years the Romans had colonized Britain south of the Solway. The native Britons, who were Celts (⊳ p. 34), had been largely Romanized, and Christianity had been established. But in 407, pressure from barbarians on other parts of the Empire led to the final withdrawal of Roman forces from Britain, leaving a power vacuum that other peoples were eager to exploit.

The northern Britons were threatened by raids from the Picts – who occupied what is now Scotland – and from the Scots, who originated in Ireland, but some of whom had established themselves in southwestern Scotland. The chief threat to southern Britain came from pagan Germanic invaders – principally Angles, Saxons and Jutes, but also Frisians and Franks (⊳ map). Collectively, these peoples are known as Anglo-Saxons, and it is from their language that modern English derives.

An account by the British priest Gildas, written a century later, indicates that in c. 450 British leaders hired Saxon mercenaries to help repel the Picts, but that the Saxons sent for reinforcements and turned on their former employers. Gildas goes on to describe how the British fought back, winning a great victory at 'Mount Badon' (whose date and location are not known).

Although later Welsh legends associate King Arthur with this phase of British resistance, there is no secure evidence that he existed at all.

The Anglo-Saxon advance resumed in the later 6th century. In the first half of the 7th century Anglo-Saxon control reached the Firth of Forth in the north and the borders of Wales in the west. However, in the southwest (Cornwall) and northwest (Strathclyde) the British retained their independence.

Throughout the 7th and 8th centuries there was a fluctuating number of Anglo-Saxon kingdoms, sometimes as many as a dozen. Gradually, however, a 'big three' emerged: Northumbria, Mercia and Wessex – the three kingdoms that were the cutting edge of expansion northwards and westwards.

Yet it is clear that relations between native British and Anglo-Saxon invaders were not exclusively hostile. In Wessex and Mercia some kings bore British names, and in their western parts many British place names survive. It is possible that Wessex, Mercia and Northumbria were mixed British and Anglo-Saxon societies in which Anglo-Saxon (English) culture came to be dominant – except in one respect: Christianity, the religion of the Britons, had been re-introduced. In 597 St Augustine had been sent from Rome to convert the English and to bring the British Churches under Roman authority. Augustine founded the church at Canterbury, but further north the main work of conversion was carried out by Scottish monks.

During the 7th and 8th centuries Anglo-Saxon kings were more concerned with a struggle for supremacy over each other than further expansion at the expense of the Welsh. This internal struggle was interrupted by raids carried out by fierce seafarers from across the North Sea – the Vikings (⊳ p. 86).   NH

The Byzantine Empire

In 324, the eastern Roman emperor created a new capital and named it after himself: the city of Constantine or Constantinople (modern Istanbul). It was built on the site of the Greek city of Byzantium, and its territories became known as the Byzantine Empire. But its inhabitants and rulers, although speaking Greek, never thought of themselves as anything but Roman, carrying on the old traditions of Rome in a new Christian context.

Constantinople itself withstood attacks by Persians, Arabs, Slavs and Russians, only succumbing to conquest by Crusaders in 1204 (⊳ pp. 88 and 96). Even then it recovered, surviving for another 250 years before finally falling to the Ottoman Turks in 1453 (⊳ p. 114). The cultural inheritance of Byzantium – in art, architecture, literature, law and monasticism – still lives on.

Revival under Justinian

Secure within the massive walls of Constantinople, the Eastern emperors weathered the storm of the 5th century. During the remarkable reign of Justinian (527–65) the Empire underwent an intellectual, administrative, architectural and military revival. A new law code, the great church of Hagia Sophia and an attempt to enforce religious uniformity set the tone for the rest of Byzantine history.

Justinian's most ambitious project was to reconquer the Empire's lost western provinces, and so turn the Mediterranean once again into a 'Roman lake'. In the 530s his great general Belisarius achieved some remarkable triumphs: the reconquest of North Africa, Sicily and most of Ostrogothic Italy. But in 542 bubonic plague struck. This and subsequent epidemics may have reduced the Empire's population by as much as one-third. While Justinian wrestled with the devastating economic and financial consequences, the Ostrogoths took the opportunity to fight back. Remarkably, by the early 560s Justinian's armies had once again gained control of Italy and reconquered southern Spain. At the time of the emperor's death his greatly extended empire was still intact (⊳ p. 78).

Crisis and survival

New invaders soon threatened the Empire's borders. The Slavs, with the help of the nomadic Avars, launched devastating attacks on the Empire's Balkan frontier from the 570s, making significant inroads across the Danube and into Macedonia, Thrace and Greece.

Avar pressure on Pannonia (⊳ p. 37) had pushed the Lombards into Italy in 568 (⊳ p. 78). Conceivably they might have been thrown out, but Justinian's overconfident successors chose this moment to break with Rome's ancient enemy, Sassanid Persia (⊳ p. 27), and quickly found themselves embroiled in what was to be a long and debilitating war. By the time Heraclius seized the throne in 610 it was a war the Empire was losing. In 626 the Persians, in alliance with the Avars, laid siege to Constantinople itself. But Heraclius launched a stunning counterattack on the Persian heartlands, and while Constantinople's walls held firm, the Persian Empire crumbled. The great soldier-emperor's conjuring trick was, however, in vain. In the 630s and 640s his exhausted empire was unable to prevent the loss of its richest provinces – Syria, Egypt, Mesopotamia and then Africa – to the Arabs (⊳ p. 82). The tax revenues of Egypt alone were about one-third of those of the whole Empire. This was a blow from which the Empire never entirely recovered.

The 7th century also saw the Lombards make further advances in Italy, while the Danube frontier collapsed as Slavs moved in and settled the Balkans in increasing numbers. This was the century that left its mark on the map: from now on the Middle East was to remain a Muslim preserve, and the Balkans largely a Slav one.

Heraclius responded to the challenges of the 7th century by militarizing Byzantine society. The surviving provinces of Asia Minor were organized into large military zones known as 'themes', each headed by a 'strategos' as military governor. Their forces were composed of soldier-farmers, representing a free peasantry. Central government was hard-pressed to maintain this structure against the demands of powerful land-owners who wished to force lesser men into dependence. The theme system was gradually introduced to all Byzantine lands as a defensive measure, and was later imposed in the territories conquered in the 10th century.

For the moment, however, these measures were enough to hold the line. Fortress towns took the place of the old 'open' cities of antiquity. This was the Byzantine 'dark age' as trade stagnated, city populations dwindled and literacy declined. But the military imperative was achieved; the Empire withstood the incessant pressure of Arab raids into Anatolia from the mid-7th to the mid-8th century, and, most notably, the Arab sieges of Constantinople in 670 and 717–18.

Iconoclasts and missionaries

The Empire was also wracked by an inter-

The Byzantine Emperor Justinian occupies centre stage in this mosaic from the church of San Vitale at Ravenna, in northern Italy. He is flanked – from left to right – by bodyguards, nobles, the archbishop Maximian, and Orthodox deacons. The mosaic was completed shortly after the recapture of Ravenna from the Ostrogoths by Byzantine forces in 540. Ravenna remained the capital of Byzantine Italy until 751.

nal crisis. The feeling that God had forsaken them led the Byzantines to a radical questioning of religious practices, notably the veneration of icons (images of Christ and the saints). The result was an iconoclast ('icon-breaker') movement which disturbed Byzantine society from the 720s until the final restoration of the icons in 843. Yet several 'iconoclast' emperors were able soldiers, and, within its reduced borders, the Empire survived.

The iconoclastic controversy split the Eastern Church into factions and worsened tensions between Byzantium and Rome. However, the second half of the 9th century was to witness a revitalization of the Orthodox Church. Successful missions among the Bulgars, Slavs and Russians led by the Greek monks St Cyril and his brother St Methodius (probable inventors of the Cyrillic alphabet – an adapted form of the Greek alphabet for the writing of Slavonic languages) spread literacy and Christianity in Slavic lands.

The 10th-century revival

Under the Macedonian dynasty, founded by Basil I in 867, the Byzantine Empire enjoyed a golden age. Its armies had begun to reassert their power in the east with notable victories over the Arabs in the 850s. What had long been a struggle for survival now became a confident offensive. First Armenia and the passes leading into Asia Minor above Syria and Antioch were wrested from Muslim control. Then, in the reign of Romanus I (920–944), Byzantine armies pressed on into Mesopotamia, penetrating the territory of the Abbasid caliph (⊳ p. 82). Romanus typifies a pattern that was crucial to Byzantine success at this period. A soldier-emperor, he both campaigned effectively and protected the rights of the legitimate heir Constantine VII (913–59) during the latter's minority.

In the 960s Nicephorus II (963–9), having destroyed the Arab fleet that had terrorized the Aegean for 150 years, recovered Crete and Cyprus. However, an attempt to recapture Sicily (in Arab hands since 902) ended in failure. The campaigns of John I Tzimiskes (969–76) thrust deep into Syria and Palestine. Jerusalem – and even the Abbasid capital of Baghdad – looked to be there for the taking, but John's successor, Basil II (976–1025), concentrated his efforts on conquering the kingdom of Bulgaria, bringing it within Orthodox Christian jurisdiction. Overall, the period up to 1025 was a triumph for Byzantine military leadership, diplomacy and Christianizing colonization.

The East–West Schism

But the 11th century was also a time of religious upheaval. Tensions between the Eastern and Western Churches had existed since the demise of the Western Roman Empire, and were exacerbated by doctrinal disputes and by the fact that the papacy tended to seek the support of the Holy Roman Empire rather than the

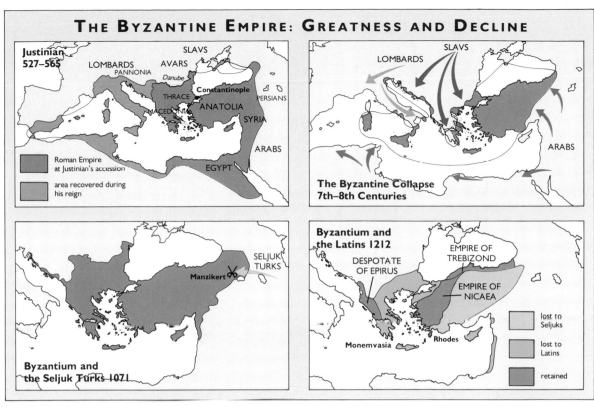

THE BYZANTINE EMPIRE: GREATNESS AND DECLINE

Justinian 527–565 / LOMBARDS / PANNONIA / AVARS / SLAVS / Danube / THRACE / Constantinople / MACEDONIA / ANATOLIA / PERSIANS / SYRIA / ARABS / EGYPT

Roman Empire at Justinian's accession

area recovered during his reign

The Byzantine Collapse 7th–8th Centuries / LOMBARDS / SLAVS / ARABS

Byzantium and the Seljuk Turks 1071 / SELJUK TURKS / Manzikert

Byzantium and the Latins 1212 / DESPOTATE OF EPIRUS / EMPIRE OF TREBIZOND / EMPIRE OF NICAEA / Monemvasia / Rhodes

lost to Seljuks

lost to Latins

retained

Byzantine Empire. In 1054 a state of schism was declared between the Churches of Rome and Constantinople – a turning-point in East–West relations (⊳ p. 90).

The Seljuk threat

Even after Basil's death the Empire continued to expand, with campaigns in Muslim Sicily in the 1040s launched from the Italian themes. But Basil's successors were unable to provide dynamic leadership. The reigns of two elderly and childless empresses (1028–56) undermined imperial authority as rival noble families vied for power. As a result the Empire was ill-equipped to face the threat posed by the arrival of new enemies on its eastern frontier. The Seljuk Turks gave notice of their intention of reversing the regional balance of power by crushing the imperial army at Manzikert in 1071 – a victory that paved the way for a concerted Turkish assault on Anatolia.

The later empire

In Alexius I Comnenus (1081–1118) the Byzantine Empire again found a vigorous leader for a time of crisis. A gifted military strategist and diplomat, he repulsed barbarian assaults on the Empire's northern frontier, checked the Norman challenge in the Mediterranean (⊳ p. 87) and founded the Comnenian dynasty, which survived for a century. But Alexius owed some of his success to outside assistance. His victory against the Normans was achieved with Venetian naval help, and in exchange he granted Venice extensive trading privileges in the Byzantine Empire. From this period Byzantine armies increasingly had recourse to mercenaries – it was Alexius's request for papal help in recruiting them that

sparked the First Crusade (⊳ p. 88). Italian mercantile cities took over the profitable Mediterranean trade routes during the 12th century. Economic domination by the West became territorial conquest with the disastrous events of 1204, when Constantinople was besieged and sacked by a Crusader army, and a Latin Empire established (⊳ pp. 88 and 97). Although this lasted only until 1261, the re-established Byzantine Empire was to be only a shadow of its former self.

The emperors of the restored Greek dynasty – the Palaeologans – sought assistance from the Latin West, and tried to mend the doctrinal breach of the 1054 Schism against popular wishes. Meanwhile the Ottoman Turks slowly closed in on Constantinople, and had conquered all the surrounding territories by the end of the 14th century. By now the Empire was little more than a glorified city-state, hemmed in by enemies on all sides. Only the defeat and capture of Sultan Bayezid I by Tamerlane in 1402 (⊳ pp. 55 and 83) provided a respite. When Sultan Mehmet II brought his big guns and huge forces to seize the city in 1453, it was a case of an elephant crushing a flea (⊳ p. 114). Only then did the West wake up to what had been lost.

The legacy of Byzantium

Yet Byzantium had always meant more than merely its territories. It created Orthodox Christianity and it preserved Greek culture. For centuries this preservation of Greek culture was to be a source of inspiration to the West, either directly or indirectly through the Arabs (⊳ p. 85). In the end its Turkish conquerors were themselves captured by the image of Byzantium. They chose to rule, in Byzantine manner, from the place they called simply 'Stamboul' – the city.   MB

SEE ALSO

- THE ROMAN EMPIRE p. 38
- THE BARBARIAN KINGDOMS p. 78
- THE RISE OF ISLAM p. 82
- THE CRUSADES p. 88
- MEDIEVAL AND RENAISSANCE WARFARE p. 102

The Rise of Islam

The great powers of the Near East around AD 600 were the Byzantine Empire (▷ p. 80), whose rule extended from modern Turkey down through Syria to Egypt and North Africa, and the Sassanian Empire of Persia (▷ p. 27), whose homeland was in Iran but whose capital was at Ctesiphon in Iraq, not far from modern Baghdad. These empires were to spend the next quarter century fighting each other, and utterly exhausting one another in the process. Neither paid much attention to the barren wastes of the Arabian peninsula, though it was from there that their fate was to be decided. For in Arabia a charismatic new prophet emerged; his name was Muhammad, and his religion was Islam (meaning 'submission' to the will of God).

In the name of Islam, Muhammad's people – the Muslim Arabs – were to embark on conquests that within a hundred years would carry them to Spain in the west and to Central Asia in the east. A new civilization was about to be founded on the ruins of the old empires.

Muhammad and the birth of Islam

Muhammad, born in about AD 570, was a native of Mecca, a shrine city and perhaps a trading centre in western Arabia. The religion that dominated Mecca, and on which its prosperity as a shrine depended, was a form of polytheistic paganism – the cult of the Kaaba, the Black Stone. Elsewhere in Arabia, Judaism and Christianity – both monotheistic religions – were widely known.

From 610 Muhammad received what he believed were revelations from God, mediated to him by the angel Gabriel. These revelations eventually formed the basis of the holy book of Islam, the Qur'an (Koran), which most Muslims hold to be the very word of God, co-eternal with God

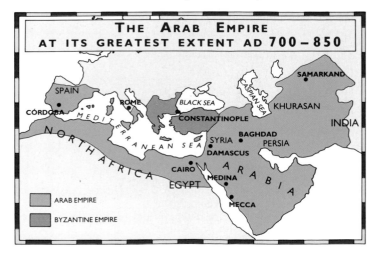

THE ARAB EMPIRE AT ITS GREATEST EXTENT AD 700–850

SPAIN · CÓRDOBA · ROME · BLACK SEA · CASPIAN SEA · SAMARKAND · KHURASAN · MEDITERRANEAN SEA · CONSTANTINOPLE · INDIA · NORTH AFRICA · SYRIA · BAGHDAD · DAMASCUS · PERSIA · CAIRO · ARABIA · EGYPT · MEDINA · MECCA

☐ ARAB EMPIRE
☐ BYZANTINE EMPIRE

ISLAMIC CULTURE

Medieval Islam formed a community defined essentially by its faith and, secondarily, by a common cultural language, Arabic. The fact that the Qur'an (Koran), God's own word, was written in Arabic gave the language a unique status which it still retains for writings on theology and law. The main intellectual effort of Islam in the Middle Ages was concentrated not on theology, as in Christendom, but on the elaboration of law. The holy law of Islam (the *Sharia*) was principally based on the Qur'an. It also drew on the sunna – the tradition of Muhammad found in *hadith* (stories relating what Muhammad and his companions were believed to have said or done), on *ijma'* – the consensus of the learned (there being no priests in Islam), and *qiyas*, argument by analogy. The resulting body of law covered all aspects of life, not just matters which would in the West be regarded as 'legal': so it is that Islam is claimed to be a way of life rather than 'just' a religion. There was room for differences: four schools of law grew up, all differing from the others in emphasis, but mutually recognizing each others' orthodoxy. In the 14th century Ibn Battuta, a *qadi* (judge) of one of these schools, could travel from Morocco to India and beyond, finding both acceptance and employment in the local judiciary wherever he went.

Speculative theology and philosophy also had their place, though it was a lesser one. Here the legacy of ancient Greek thought, cherished by many early Islamic thinkers, was of formative importance. Other forms of intellectual and literary activity flourished, including geographical studies, the writing of history and the composition of poetry. From the 13th century the dominant cultural strand in the Islamic lands of both the Middle East and India, in matters not strictly religious or legal, was

A decorated Qur'an (Koran) from the 12th century.

Persian rather than Arabic; and poetry occupied a central place in it. Much of the feeling underlying Sufism, the mystical dimension of Islam, found its most eloquent expression in Persian poetry. There was much suspicion of Sufism; it was the 11th-century Persian thinker al-Ghazali who did most to reconcile Sufism with orthodox scholastic Islam.

Painting, insofar as it involved the representation of the human form, was also seen as dubious: hence the great elaboration of non-representational art in Islam (the Arabic script itself providing an ideal medium for this). In later centuries, however, concentration on the art of the book brought with it a development of painting in the form of miniatures, especially Persian and Turkish. Architecture too, from the building of the Dome of the Rock in Jerusalem in the first Islamic century, flourished throughout the lands of Islam.

Considered overall, Christian Europe was for most of the Middle Ages a cultural and intellectual backwater compared with the world of Islam, though this situation was to change from the 14th century onwards (▷ p. 100).

---

himself. Muhammad did not see his religion as something new. For him it was the uncorrupted completion of the true monotheistic revelations of the past, those of Judaism and Christianity: a return to the religion of Abraham.

Muhammad denounced idolatry, and preached the oneness of Allah – 'the God', and the inevitability of judgement. His preaching made little headway in Mecca, and in 622 he and his followers were invited to emigrate to another city, Medina. This migration (*hijra*) marks the beginning of the Islamic era and thus of the Muslim calendar. In Medina Muhammad's message was more sympathetically received, and he was able to found his Islamic community. In 630, after years of sometimes violent struggle, Mecca capitulated to Muhammad. The Kaaba was cleared of idols and became a shrine of Islam. By the time of Muhammad's death in 632 he was the effective ruler of all Arabia. Before he died, Muhammad urged a *jihad* ('holy war') against unbelievers.

Islamic expansion

Four of Muhammad's followers in succession were appointed *Caliphs* ('successors' or 'representatives' of the Prophet), to take on his role as head of the Muslim community, though there was to be no successor to his prophethood. Under these 'Rightly Guided' Caliphs (632–61) the Arabs burst out of Arabia in a series of devastatingly effective military campaigns, seizing Syria and Egypt from the Byzantines (▷ p. 80) and Iraq and Persia from the Sassanians. The Arab cause was helped by the fact that many of the peoples of the areas they attacked were disenchanted – mainly for religious reasons – with their central governments. For much of the population of Syria, Egypt and Iraq, rule by the Arabs, who were tolerant of Judaism and Christianity of whatever theological complexion, was preferable to persecution by the Greek Orthodox Byzantines or the Zoroastrian Sassanians.

The Umayyad dynasty

Tensions were already showing themselves in the infant state. The last of the first four Caliphs, Muhammad's cousin and son-in-law Ali, had to fight a civil war with the relatives of his predecessor Uthman. When Ali was murdered in 661, his principal enemy, Mu'awiya, seized control, moved the capital of the Islamic empire from Medina to his own power-base, Damascus in Syria, and founded the first Islamic dynasty, the Umayyads. The party of Ali (*Shi'at 'Ali*), however, survived him, and its members formed the nucleus of the major sectarian division in Islam, that of the Shiite (or Shia) sect. The majority party later became known as the Sunnis, after the *sunna*, the tradition of the Prophet Muhammad. Despite these troubles, expansion continued under the Umayyads, especially into Central Asia and, to the west, along the coast of North Africa and into Spain.

The Abbasid dynasty

According to the Arabic sources (all of them written after the fall of the Umayyads), the Umayyad dynasty was widely resented precisely because it was a dynasty: a hereditary kingdom after the traditional Near Eastern pattern rather than an Islamic Caliphate. This, together with opposition from Shiites and resentment among non-Arab converts to Islam of their inferior status, eventually led to revolt against the Umayyads and their replacement in 750 by the Abbasid dynasty. The Abbasids moved the capital of the Caliphate eastwards from Damascus to the newly-founded city of Baghdad in Iraq. Persian influence on the Caliphate became much stronger.

In the 9th century, however, the real political power of the Abbasid Caliphs began to wane. Throughout the empire, local rulers, though usually careful to secure a diploma of appointment as governor from the Caliph, became in effect independent. In the 10th century Abbasid rule in North Africa and Egypt was overthrown (969) by a rival Caliphate, that of the Shiite Fatimids (who claimed descent from Ali and Muhammad's daughter Fatima). In 945 political power in Baghdad had been seized by a Shiite people from northern Persia, the Buyids. The Abbasid Caliphs, although they survived until 1258, were hardly more than nominal rulers of the Islamic community.

Turks and Crusaders

In the early 11th century it looked as if Shiite Islam might become the dominant form of the religion. The salvation of Sunnism came in the unexpected form of the nomadic Seljuk Turks. Converted to Sunni Islam before they left their ancestral pastures in Central Asia, they swept through the eastern Islamic world from the 1040s. They drove the Buyids from Baghdad, and restored the Abbasid Caliph to a position of honour, though they retained much of the actual power in their own hands. They were unable, however, to destroy the Fatimid Caliphate. From the end of the 11th century they and the other Muslim powers of the region had also to reckon with the Crusaders from Western Europe, who mounted holy wars against Islam with the aim of restoring the Holy Land to Christian rule (⊳ p. 88). Jerusalem was captured in 1099 and a number of Crusader states set up in Syria and Palestine. The Crusaders never penetrated very far into Muslim territory, however, and were not a serious threat to Islam: the Crusades are more important in European than in Islamic history. Jerusalem was recaptured by the Kurdish Sultan Saladin in 1187, though Crusader rule lingered on the coast for a further century.

The Mongols

Much more threatening to Islam were the Mongol invasions of the 13th century. The Mongols, like the Seljuk Turks, were Central Asian nomads; but unlike them they arrived still adhering to their ancestral paganism – and in large numbers. The Mongol invasions of the Middle East were part of a vast enterprise which resulted in the establishment of the largest land empire known to history (⊳ p. 54).

Between 1219 and 1260 successive assaults, first under Genghis Khan and then led by his generals and descendants, conquered Persia, Iraq and much of Anatolia. Baghdad was sacked in 1258, and the last Abbasid Caliph killed. But the Mamluk Sultans of Egypt and Syria held out and by the end of the century the Mongols in the Middle East had become Muslims and were gradually tamed.

In the 1330s the Mongol regime collapsed, to be revived briefly by the conquests of Tamerlane (or Timur, c. 1336–1405; ⊳ p. 55). Meanwhile in the far west of Anatolia, at the extreme edge of Mongol influence, a small Turkish principality was beginning to form around 1300. It would develop into the last and greatest of the Muslim empires – that of the Ottomans – and would survive until the end of World War I (⊳ p. 114).   DM

SEE ALSO

● EMPIRES OF THE STEPPE p. 54
● THE BYZANTINE EMPIRE p. 80
● THE CRUSADES p. 88
● THE OTTOMAN EMPIRE p. 114

ISLAMIC SPAIN

As the Muslim Arabs advanced westwards across North Africa, they encountered and converted the local people, the Berbers. It was a Muslim Berber general, Tariq, who led the first Islamic invasion of Spain in 711. He crossed from North Africa by way of Gibraltar (*Jabal Tariq*). The country was soon conquered and formed into an Arab province, al-Andalus, with its capital at Córdoba. In the mountains of the extreme northwest, however, small Christian principalities survived. These would be the nucleus of the kingdoms that ultimately reconquered Spain for Christendom. The furthest point of the Arab advance was reached in 733, when an expeditionary force (not an attempt at conquest) met and was defeated by the Frankish Charles Martel at Poitiers in central France (⊳ p. 78). After the fall of the Umayyads in 750, an Umayyad prince, 'Abd al-Rahman, fled to Spain and was accepted as ruler. In 928 his descendant and namesake declared himself Caliph, in opposition to both the Abbasids of Baghdad and the Fatimids of Cairo.

Muslim power in Spain declined from the mid-11th century – in 1031 the Caliphate of Córdoba collapsed – but was periodically reinforced by the armies of Berber dynasties (the Almoravids and the Almohads) from North Africa. Most of Spain had been lost to the Christian *Reconquista* by the middle of the 13th century (⊳ p. 89). The last Muslim state to survive, until it fell to Ferdinand of Aragon and Isabella of Castile in 1492, was Granada in the south. There the rulers' palace, the Alhambra, remains as evidence of the cultural splendours of Spain's Islamic centuries. Those centuries had been important, too, in intellectual history. In its early period Islamic Spain had provided, by the standards of the time, a distinctly tolerant environment in which Christians, Jews and Muslims co-existed fruitfully, despite the non-Muslims' status as second-class citizens. This resulted in a remarkable degree of intellectual cross-fertilization. For example, much of the philosophy of ancient Greece was first made known to medieval Europe through Latin translations made in Muslim Spain from Arabic translations of the originals. All the more ironic, then, that Catholic Spain after 1492 should have become one of the least open and least tolerant of early modern societies (⊳ pp. 112 and 116).

The interior of the Great Mosque of Córdoba. The Mosque was founded by 'Abd al-Rahman in the 8th century.

The Holy Roman Empire

Although the term 'Holy Roman Empire' was not coined until the 13th century, the imperial dignity to which it referred was very much older. It was established in an epoch-making ceremony in Rome on Christmas Day in the year 800, when Charlemagne ('Charles the Great') was crowned Emperor of the West by Pope Leo III. For the next thousand years those rulers who saw themselves as Charlemagne's successors were to cling to the imperial title.

But these emperors did not rule an empire in the manner of the Roman emperors of antiquity. Nor did they possess authority or jurisdiction over the other kings of Europe in the way that the pope was to have over the whole Latin Church. They were simply kings with a fancy title and with an unusually close and, at times, tense relationship with the papacy (⇨ p. 90).

The Carolingian Empire

The Frankish ruler Charlemagne (768–814) built on the political and military achievements of his father Pepin the Short (751–68) and of his grandfather Charles Martel (⇨ p. 79). During the course of a long and vigorous reign he organized and directed a remarkably sus-

tained series of campaigns of aggression against neighbouring peoples. Although he was able to present himself as the champion of Christianity against both pagans (Saxons and Avars) and infidels (the Muslims of Spain; ⇨ p. 83), some of his victims were in fact fellow-Christians (Bavarians of southern Germany and Lombards of northern Italy; ⇨ p. 78). But as the most powerful warlord in Europe his claim to be the protector of the shrine of St Peter could not be gainsaid. Hence his coronation as emperor.

Charlemagne's palace at Aachen (Aix-la-Chapelle) became the focal point of a Carolingian court culture that did much to preserve classical learning. His political dominance was, however, personal. In 806, in accordance with the Frankish system of partible inheritance (division amongst heirs), he planned to divide his territories between three sons. Only the fact that two of them died before their father, enabled the surviving son, Louis the Pious (814–840), to succeed to an undivided Carolingian Empire. (The name comes from *Carolus*, the Latin version of Charles.) In the next two generations a combination of the system of partible inheritance and frequent external attacks threatened the Empire's survival. Louis divided it between his three sons, and quarrels between these three kings led to the formalization of this division in the Treaty of Verdun (843). In the late 9th century imperial leadership proved ineffective against Muslim, Viking and Magyar (Hungarian) raids. As a result, power slipped into the hands of regional aristocracies. After 887 the West Frankish (French) and East Frankish (German) lands increasingly went their own ways, while the imperial crown

became little more than a meaningless bonus awarded to the most powerful magnate in Italy.

The German Empire

The East Frankish aristocracy became particularly prominent. In the early 10th century its leaders replaced the Carolingians as kings east of the Rhine. At first the disputed succession of Henry, duke of the Saxons (919–936) seemed to mark just another stage in the disintegration of the Carolingian world, for his power barely extended beyond southeastern Saxony. But precisely because his power was so limited he was unable to elevate all his sons to kingship. Thus this power passed, weak but undivided, to his eldest son Otto I (936–973). By determination, skill and good fortune Otto 'the Great' decisively extended his influence over the other German duchies (Bavaria, Franconia, Lorraine and Swabia), defeated the Magyars at the battle of Lechfeld (955) and conquered the kingdom of Italy. In 962 he was crowned emperor in Rome.

Otto I was survived by only one son, Otto II (973–983), who succeeded to his father's rights both north and south of the Alps. He in turn had only one son, Otto III (983–1002). Indeed, owing to an extraordinary series of dynastic accidents, not until 1190 was an emperor (Frederick I) survived by more than one son. By this date an undivided German Empire encompassing Germany, northern Italy and, since 1033, Burgundy (⇨ p. 95) had existed for so long that partitioning it had become unthinkable. In the early 11th century Italian magnates occasionally resisted the rulers thrust upon them from the north, but after 1037 they acquiesced in a convention that accepted the German king as ruler of northern Italy and the only possible candidate for emperor. Thus this Empire was to last until the end of the Middle Ages and beyond.

When the Saxon (Ottonian) dynasty died out (1024), another German princely family – the Salians – took over. But they were less fortunately placed than the later Ottonians. Otto I's acquisitions had enabled his successors to stay in palaces on their own estates as they travelled the length and breadth of their kingdom. But as the inexorable pressure to be generous to their followers took its toll, so the Salians increasingly found themselves reliant on the hospitality of the Church. The resulting close relationship between king and Church rendered the Salians particularly vulnerable on the question of Church reform. The war cry of the Gregorian reform movement was that the Church should be freed from the shackles of secular domination (⇨ p. 91). Of particular concern to churchmen was the issue of lay investiture (the right of lay rulers to grant Church officials the symbols of their authority). During the reign of the Salian Henry IV (1054–1106) the increasingly bitter dispute over the claims of Church and state erupted into the Investiture Contest (1075–1122). This reached a theatrical climax when Henry tried to depose Pope Gregory VII, was excommu-

Otto III (Holy Roman Emperor 983–1002) depicted in a portrait miniature dated c. 1000. Hoping to re-create the power of the Roman Empire in a state uniting the whole of Christendom under the Holy Roman Emperor, Otto installed his tutor as pope, established an elaborate court in Rome, and took the titles 'Servant of the Apostles' and 'Emperor of the World'. Otto's ambitions were frustrated by rebellions in Italy, and ended by his early death.

nicated, and was then forced to go in penance to Canossa (1077). The quarrel undermined the emperor's claim to be the papacy's protector; it also led popes to try to secure kings whom they could trust, and hence contributed to the emergence of the theory that the German king (or, as he was now called, 'the king of the Romans') owed his crown not to hereditary right but to election. After the Salian dynasty died out (1125), this theory became the generally accepted one. In practice, however, Frederick I 'Barbarossa' (1152–90) was able to establish his family – the Hohenstaufen – so firmly on the throne that they were able to retain it until 1254.

Throughout this period Italy was significantly richer than Germany, and the Hohenstaufen were determined to retain control there. This led to a series of quarrels with the increasingly wealthy and independent cities of northern Italy (⊳ p. 96). Continuing involvement in Italy provoked further quarrels with the popes, as a result of which emperors insisted on the God-given dignity of their own position. Thus in the 12th century they started to use the term 'Holy Empire'; then in the next century, 'Holy Roman Empire'. In addition, Henry VI's conquest of the kingdom of Sicily (1194) meant that he and his son Frederick II were able to maintain the imperial tradition of being the richest rulers in Europe – and the most over-extended.

The Holy Roman Empire

The demise of the Hohenstaufen was followed by a period of approximately a hundred years during which no one family was able to secure a firm hold on the German throne; instead the crown circulated among a number of princely houses: Habsburg, Nassau, Luxembourg and Wittelsbach. In these circumstances no ruler felt himself well enough established in Germany to be able to intervene decisively in Italy. From now on the Italian cities and their rulers went their own way, occasionally applying to the emperor for some special privilege, but otherwise realizing they could perfectly well ignore him. The Empire became ever more clearly a German institution, and in the 15th century came to be known as 'The Holy Roman Empire of the German Nation'.

In 1356 Charles IV (1346–78) issued the Golden Bull (⊳ picture). It formalized the convention, observable since the mid-13th century, by which the king – the emperor-to-be – was elected by a majority of the votes of a college of seven electors. This was to remain the *Grundgesetz*, the 'fundamental law', of the Empire until its dissolution in 1806 (⊳ p. 125). Yet although the Golden Bull constituted a clear-cut statement of the electoral principle, ironically the Empire became hereditary again in practice. Charles IV's successor turned out to be his young son Wenceslas, and at subsequent elections the electors were generally content to elect the dynastic heir. When Charles IV's Luxembourg dynasty died out in the

male line in 1437, it was succeeded by its heirs, the Habsburgs. From then on until its end, the Holy Roman Empire remained an essentially Habsburg affair. By far the most prominent of the Habsburg emperors was Charles V (1519–56). Combining in his hands the Habsburg, Burgundian and Spanish inheritances, he ruled the largest European empire since Charlemagne (⊳ p. 116).

Yet the fact that this Luxembourg-Habsburg empire remained theoretically an elective monarchy was to have important consequences. No one could claim to be emperor on the grounds that it was his hereditary right. No disappointed candidate could pass on his claim to his heirs. Thus Germany never suffered in the way that France did during the Hundred Years War as a result of the Plantagenet claim to be the rightful heirs to the crown of France (⊳ p. 94). Not until the wars of Catholic against Protestant in the 16th and 17th centuries would Germany become a battleground (⊳ pp. 110–13). JG

The Golden Bull of Emperor Charles IV (1356) formalized the election of the Holy Roman Emperor by seven electors and effectively removed papal interference from the choice of candidates. The seven electors – the archbishops of Cologne, Mainz and Trier, the duke of Saxony, the margrave of Brandenburg (later king of Prussia) and the king of Bohemia (later the head of the Habsburg family) – were later joined by the electors of Bavaria (1623), Hanover (1708), Württemberg (1802), and Baden and Hesse-Cassel (both 1803).

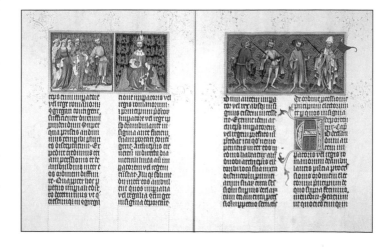

Vikings and Normans

In the 9th century a group of Scandinavian seafarers and traders made their appearance on the European stage, embarking on one of the most remarkable periods of expansion in history. The Vikings (or 'Norsemen') came from three distinct parts of Scandinavia – Norway, Sweden and Denmark. They were brilliant seamen, their longships taking them as far as the Black Sea in the east and North America in the west in the quest for trade and plunder. Although the original meaning of 'Viking' may have been 'men who go to trading places' (*wics*), it is for their destructive raids on France, Britain and Ireland that they are chiefly remembered.

VIKING AND NORMAN INVASIONS

Viking armies were small, usually to be numbered in hundreds, and not militantly anti-Christian – by the end of the 11th century they had all been converted to Christianity. The Vikings shared many values with the rulers of the societies they attacked in western Europe, and when they turned to conquest and colonization they found it easy to stay as settlers.

Viking expansion

The Norwegians were active on both shores of the Irish Sea, ultimately settling in eastern Ireland, western Scotland, the Isle of Man and northwest England, as well as the Orkney, Shetland and Faeroe Islands. They also sailed the Atlantic to colonize Iceland. It was from Iceland that Eric the Red sailed west to discover Greenland (c. 896), where a settlement survived into the 15th century. In around 1000 the Norwegians, under Leif Eriksson, also briefly settled in northeast North America, which they called Vinland (possibly Newfoundland).

The Swedes went east into Russia where they formed the first organized states (▷ p. 126). Their search for materials to trade took them to the shores of the Baltic, around which they established a network of trading places, and then along the River Neva to Novgorod. They sailed down the rivers of western Russia such as the Dnieper and the Volga as far as the Black Sea and the Caspian Sea and established trading contacts with the Byzantine Empire (▷ p. 80) and the Arab Abbasid Empire (▷ p. 82). As in the west, the *Rus* (as the Swedes were known) were never mere traders. In 860 Viking armies joined forces to mount an assault on Constantinople, and although this was unsuccessful it did not deter them from future attempts. In the late 9th century a group under Oleg took over Kiev. By the end of the 10th century Kiev had become the most important Russian principality, stretching from the Baltic almost to the Black Sea.

The Danes directed most of their energies against the Anglo-Saxon and Frankish kingdoms (in the latter concentrating on what is now northern France and the Low Countries). The raids started in the 790s, when groups of Norwegians and Danes launched small-scale, hit-and-run attacks on the Irish, English and French coasts. In the 830s larger raiding parties began to penetrate further inland. A sign of growing Viking boldness was the seizing of winter-bases – the first was the island of Noirmoutier at the mouth of the River Loire in France in 843. The Vikings were quick to take advantage of civil discord – they stepped up their incursions into France after the death of the Frankish emperor Louis the Pious in 840. When Charles the Bald began to organize effective resistance in northern France, the Vikings turned their attention to England.

The Vikings in England

The destructive activities of the Vikings were at their greatest in England. By now they were no longer operating in small bands but had come together into one 'great host' (as their victims called it) under several royal leaders. They moved far inland, increasing their mobility by seizing horses, and exploiting new regions from fortified bases each campaigning season. Within 15 years of the host's arrival in 865 the kingdoms of Northumbria, East Anglia and Mercia had been overwhelmed. Only Wessex (England south of the Thames) survived the onslaught, under a remarkable king, Alfred the Great (871–899). In 878 he narrowly held off a Danish onslaught under Guthrum, and in 886 reached agreement with Guthrum on the boundaries between Wessex and the Danelaw (those parts of England settled and

administered by the Vikings). By building a network of fortresses, increasing the mobility of his army and organizing a fleet, Alfred was able to end the Viking threat to Wessex by 896. By 960 his successors had conquered the rest of England, forming one kingdom for the first time. Ironically the elimination of Wessex's Anglo-Saxon rivals had paved the way for the unification of England.

In England the era of Viking conquests was followed by a period of stability during which there was considerable settlement of Vikings in the Danelaw, to which the hundreds of Scandinavian place-names in northern and central England are witness. One of the greatest Viking achievements in England was the establishment of a new centre of workshops and small industries at York (Jorvik). In the 10th century York boasted trading links with the Byzantine Empire and the Muslim east, as well as the Scandinavian towns of Ireland and the Baltic.

Viking attacks on England were renewed during Ethelred II's reign (978–1016). After prolonged resistance the English kingdom finally capitulated to the Danish king Cnut in 1016. However, this conquest did not involve a major new settlement of Scandinavians in England, and in 1042 Ethelred's son, Edward the Confessor (1042–66), recovered his throne. Two more unsuccessful attempts were made to conquer England, in 1066 (▷ below) and 1069–70, but by the last years of the 11th century the Viking threat to England was over.

The origins of the Normans

When the Viking 'great host' split up in 896 some of its members crossed the Channel again to invade northern France. In 911 one of their leaders, Rollo, was granted control of the lower Seine valley by the West Frankish king, Charles the Simple. In the following decades Rollo's descendants and their followers extended their grip on the Channel coast. Thus they created the duchy of Normandy, 'the land of the Northmen'.

Contacts with Scandinavia were maintained until the early 11th century, but the Viking settlers rapidly merged into the aristocracy of northern France. The 'Norman' armies that operated in Italy, Spain and England consisted of men from all over northern France. By the 11th century, when they had become one of the most successful peoples in Europe, the Normans had lost their Viking character.

The Norman Conquest of England

Under Duke William II (later known as 'the Conqueror'), Normandy was forged into a powerful principality, William harnessing the forces of internal disorder to wage a successful war of conquest against England. William claimed that he had been made heir to the English throne by his childless cousin, Edward the Confessor. However, when Edward died in 1066 his most powerful subject, Harold Godwinson, earl of Wessex, also claimed he had been designated heir, and was duly acclaimed king by the English. Harold's defence of his crown was complicated by the need to repel a Norwegian invasion under Harold Hardrada, which he crushed in a great battle at Stamford Bridge near York. Meanwhile William, with all the resources of his duchy behind him, landed on the south coast. In a daring and well-planned campaign (September–December 1066), he displayed his superior military skill, defeating and killing Harold at the Battle of Hastings. He was crowned king on Christmas Day 1066.

William had seized control of a richer and more powerful kingdom by a bold and well-organized coup. Until 1071 the Norman grip on England was severely tested by revolts and Danish invasions, but this opposition hastened the destruction of the English ruling class and its replacement by a new Norman-French nobility.

For their own safety, and in order to overawe the English, the Normans built castles throughout the country. Cheap and easy to build, the timber and earthwork castle (⊳ p. 103) was the perfect instrument of colonization. William himself planted castles in all the major English towns, some of them in stone, notably the White Tower in London. The Normans also introduced the Romanesque style of church architecture into England, which in its English form is known as 'Norman'.

The Normans in Italy

Other Normans, in acts of private enterprise, were active in Spain fighting the Muslims, and in southern Italy, where, having started as mercenaries, they began to carve out territories for themselves from the 1040s. The most successful of the newcomers were Robert Guiscard and his brother Roger, sons of Tancred de Hauteville. By 1071, Guiscard had conquered the Byzantine provinces of Apulia and Calabria. In 1091 Roger, after 30 years of almost continuous campaigning, completed the conquest of Sicily from the Arabs. Eventually Roger's son, Roger II, ousted his kinsmen and took control of all the Norman possessions in southern Italy. On Christmas Day 1130 he was crowned king. However, Norman control in southern Italy was to be short-lived: by the end of the century it was in the hands of the Hohenstaufen emperors (⊳ pp. 84–5). In the meantime Bohemund, Guiscard's disinherited son, one of the leaders of the First Crusade (⊳ p. 88), had seized the principality of Antioch in the Levant.

Norman adaptability

The states the Normans established in Normandy, England and Italy reveal their genius for adaptation. In southern Italy a Norman élite ruled over a population of Lombards, Greeks and Arabs. Their administration was based principally on Byzantine and Islamic models, and was characterized by toleration of the religions of all their subjects.

The Norman Conquest of England initially involved only some 10 000 newcomers. There were many things the settlers could not, indeed did not, wish to change. The more sophisticated administrative structures of Anglo-Saxon England were taken over virtually unchanged, and these formed the framework of English government not just in the Middle Ages, but down to the present day. Domesday Book, a vast survey of property, land and tax liability, testifies to the efficiency and attention to detail the Normans brought to government, though it was largely based on pre-Norman administrative records.

Intermarriage between Normans and Anglo-Saxons, the modification of existing institutions, and the co-existence of Norman French and the Old English language led in the long-term to a hybrid administration and culture. If Norman adaptability contributed to their successes it also meant that in southern Italy, Antioch and even England soon only the continuing use of the French language testified to the 'Norman' character of these regimes. In England this was to have a lasting impact on the English language.

In addition to their cultural legacy, the establishment of Norman kings in England who still held vast possessions in France was to create conflicts between the two countries for centuries to come, culminating in the Hundred Years War (⊳ p. 94).   NH

THE BATTLE OF HASTINGS

Norman cavalry assaulting English footsoldiers (from the Bayeux Tapestry).

Within a few days of his decisive defeat of the Norwegians at Stamford Bridge (25 September), Harold heard of the Norman landing on the south coast. Without delay he marched his English army nearly 400 km (250 miles) southwards, arriving near Hastings on 13 October. Although all his forces may not have been assembled, Harold seems to have been intent on mounting a surprise attack. However, William learnt of the proximity of the English, and decided to strike first. It was a great risk – the English were in a powerful position on top of a sharp ridge – but William had everything to play for.

Early on the morning of 14 October the English, on foot, organized themselves into the traditional shieldwall on top of their ridge. The first two lines of Norman infantry were repelled with spears, clubs and axes, as was an attack by Norman heavy cavalry, whose momentum foundered on the steep slope. The Normans and their Breton allies began to waver, but in this crisis William's superior generalship came to the fore. He ordered his cavalry to feign a retreat, drawing some of the English down from their hill and into a vulnerable position. He then put his archers into action, and these, combined with renewed cavalry and infantry attacks, began to wear down English resistance. The morale of the English finally crumbled with the death of Harold, hit in the face by an arrow and cut down by Norman knights. By the end of the year William had had himself crowned king of England.

The Crusades

The era of the Crusades saw Christian Europe once more on the offensive. Inspired by a reformed and revitalized papacy, knights flocked eastwards to rescue Jerusalem from Islam. Even though in the long run the Crusader states that they set up in the Holy Land were to prove vulnerable to the Muslim 'counter-crusade', elsewhere the crusading spirit was to have more lasting consequences.

In Eastern Europe missionaries and warrior monks extended Christendom into previously pagan areas. In a process known as the *Reconquista*, Spain was recovered from the Islamic Moors after four centuries of conflict. And in the motives of men like Henry the Navigator, organizer of the Portuguese exploration of Africa, the crusading outlook moved out into a wider world (▷ pp. 109 and 116). For better or for worse the Crusades marked the beginning of Western attempts to dominate the other peoples of the world.

The First Crusade and the Crusader states

No sermon has ever had greater impact than that delivered by Pope Urban II at Clermont in 1095. It set in motion the whole crusading movement. All that had been intended was to send some military assistance to the Byzantine emperor, Alexius I, who was battling against nomadic Seljuk Turks in Asia Minor (▷ p. 81). In the West, however, men believed that these Turks were making life intolerably difficult for pilgrims on their way to Jerusalem – the Holy City – and in consequence the response to Urban's preaching was on a totally unexpected scale. In 1096 several huge armies set out on the long march to Jerusalem, intending to free the Christian churches in the east and recapture the Holy City, which had been in Muslim hands since the 7th century (▷ p. 82).

At the time the movement was seen as an armed pilgrimage, and those warriors who took up their swords on the pope's behalf were promised the rewards of heaven. No kings commanded these armies. Instead, prominent princes took the lead: Raymond of St Gilles, count of Toulouse; Robert, duke of Normandy; the Norman Sicilian Bohemond, son of Robert Guiscard (▷ p. 87); and Godfrey of Bouillon, duke of Lorraine, who became the first ruler of the Latin Kingdom of Jerusalem.

These diverse forces battled through the deserts and mountains of Anatolia, capturing the heavily fortified city of Antioch after a long siege during the bitter winter of 1097/8. On July 15 1099, Jerusalem itself fell to the Crusaders, who proceeded to slaughter its Muslim and Jewish inhabitants in an orgy of bloodletting. The Crusaders established a handful of small states along the coastal strip of the Levant: the Kingdom of Jerusalem, and its three fiefdoms – the counties of Antioch, Tripoli and Edessa.

The Crusader states had only a precarious existence. Edessa fell to the Turks in 1144, and when Saladin (?1137–1193, sultan of Egypt and Syria) succeeded in mobilizing the much greater Muslim resources, he recaptured the Holy City in 1187. This prompted the sending of a Third Crusade led by the German emperor and the kings of France and England. It achieved some successes – notably the capture of Acre by Richard the Lionheart in 1191 – but Jerusalem was not recovered. Further military attempts to recapture the city proved futile. Only the diplomacy of Emperor Frederick II brought about its temporary recovery (1228–44).

The decline of the crusading movement

For much of the 13th century the Crusaders held on to the coast of Palestine and Syria, but this gradually fell into the hands of the powerful Mamluk sultans of Egypt. When the port of Acre fell in 1291 the Crusaders lost their last base in the Holy Land. Other crusades, directed against Egypt, became bogged down in the Nile Delta and ended ingloriously.

Political and military turmoil in Europe in the 14th century, epitomized by the Hundred Years' War and the Schisms that eroded the authority of the papacy (▷ pp. 90 and 94), undermined the schemes for crusades that idealists continued to produce. Those that did get off the ground were easily defeated by the Turks. The last one, in 1396 – which took a French and Burgundian army as far as Nicopolis (on the Danube) – was ignominiously defeated by the Ottoman sultan.

Although the primary motive of the Crusaders was religious fervour, there was a good deal of self-interested adventurism involved. At times quarrels broke out between the various European contingents, and their progress to the Holy Land was marred by indiscriminate pil-

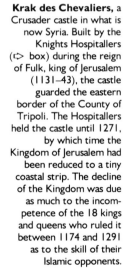

Krak des Chevaliers, a Crusader castle in what is now Syria. Built by the Knights Hospitallers (▷ box) during the reign of Fulk, king of Jerusalem (1131–43), the castle guarded the eastern border of the County of Tripoli. The Hospitallers held the castle until 1271, by which time the Kingdom of Jerusalem had been reduced to a tiny coastal strip. The decline of the Kingdom was due as much to the incompetence of the 18 kings and queens who ruled it between 1174 and 1291 as to the skill of their Islamic opponents.

— PRINCIPAL CRUSADES AGAINST ISLAM —				
Crusade	Dates	Region	Principal leaders	Results
First	1096–99	Holy Land	Counts and dukes of France, Germany and southern Italy	Capture of Jerusalem and establishment of Crusader states
Second	1146–49	Holy Land	Louis VII, king of France (1137–80) Conrad III, German emperor (1138–52)	Failed siege of Damascus
Third	1189–92	Holy Land	Emperor Frederick I 'Barbarossa' (1152–90; died en route) Richard I 'the Lionheart', king of England (1189–99) Philip II, king of France (1180–1223)	Capture of Acre, defeat of Saladin at Arsuf (1191), failure to take Jerusalem
Fourth	1200–4	Intended for Holy Land	Boniface, marquis of Montferrat Baldwin, count of Flanders Dandolo, doge of Venice	Capture of Constantinople and establishment of Latin empire of Constantinople (until 1260)
Fifth	1216–21	Egypt	Pelagius, papal legate	Failed attack on Cairo
Sixth	1228	Holy Land	Emperor Frederick II (1215–50)	Recovery of Jerusalem by treaty (until 1244)
Seventh	1248–52	Egypt	Louis IX (St Louis), King of France (1226–70)	Failed attack on Cairo; all Crusade leaders captured

laging and slaughter of Christians and Jews in Europe. The Fourth Crusade of 1200–4, summoned by Pope Innocent III, followed a particularly bizarre and destructive course. Its mainly French participants never even reached the Holy Land. Instead, at the instigation of Venice, they captured and sacked Christian Constantinople, the capital of the Byzantine Empire, Venice's rival in the eastern Mediterranean. This, and the establishing by the Crusaders of the Latin (Western) Empire of Constantinople – which lasted until 1260 – widened the breach between the Eastern and Western forms of Christianity (▷ pp. 81 and 90).

In the 13th century crusades were also mounted within Christendom, both against heretics (such as the Cathars of southern France; ▷ p. 90), and against the papacy's political enemies, such as Emperor Frederick II. In the 15th century crusading became limited to Eastern Europe, against the Turks or the Hussite heretics of Bohemia (▷ p. 90) – generally without success.

The Reconquista

In the Iberian Peninsula the forces of Christendom fared rather better. In the mid-11th century the small Christian kingdoms of northern Spain, principally Castile and Aragon, began to expand at the expense of the Muslim states that had long dominated the peninsula (▷ p. 83); this was the start of what became known as the Reconquista ('reconquest'). The conquest of Toledo by Alfonso VI in 1085 recovered for Christian Spain one of its most important centres. The war in Spain was considered by some as a distraction from the serious business of crusading in the Holy Land, and it only occasionally received direct papal support. Despite this, the reconquest prospered and in 1139 the kingdom of Portugal was established.

But initially the progress of reconquest was by no means irreversible. On two occasions Islam was reinforced by waves of Berber tribesmen from North Africa – a potent threat when united under inspired religious leadership. Invasions by the Almoravids in 1086 and the Almohads in 1145 inflicted significant defeats on Christian forces, as at Alarcos in 1195. Despite such reverses, by 1200 the tide was turning inexorably in favour of the Reconquista. The Castilian victory at Las Navas de Tolosa in 1212 set the seal on this process and swift advances followed. The port of Cadiz was reclaimed from the Moors in 1265.

By the mid-13th century Muslim rule was confined to the Emirate of Granada (▷ map, p. 85). In the 14th century Aragonese seapower secured the Mediterranean coast and the Balearic islands. A Muslim attack across the Straits of Gibraltar was defeated by Castile at Salado in 1340. This – together with the siege and capture of Algeçiras (1342–4) – ended the threat of Islamic invasion. Granada survived as a dutiful client-state until 1492, when it was finally snuffed out by the dual monarchy of Ferdinand of Aragon and Isabella of Castile (▷ p. 116).   MB

SEE ALSO
● THE BYZANTINE EMPIRE p. 80
● THE RISE OF ISLAM p. 82
● POPES, SAINTS AND HERETICS p. 90
● THE SPANISH AND PORTUGUESE EMPIRES p. 116

THE MILITARY ORDERS

The Hospitallers prepare to defend Rhodes against the Turks in this illustration from a late 15th-century manuscript. Founded before 1099 to maintain a hospital for sick pilgrims in Jerusalem, the order reverted to purely humanitarian works after its expulsion from Malta in 1798. It continues to the present day as the Sovereign Order of the Knights of Malta, whose grand master is internationally recognized as a head of state.

The reformed papacy's call for knights to serve Christ and the pope led to the creation of a new type of warrior: the soldier monk. In 1128, St Bernard of Clairvaux (?1090–1153) devised a 'Rule' by which men might live as trained knights devoted to fighting a holy war, while simultaneously sharing the monastic obligations of poverty, chastity and obedience (▷ p. 90).

The first order to be created was the Knights Templar, named after the Temple of Solomon, their base in Jerusalem. Soon afterwards the Knights of St John, or Hospitallers, were converted from a purely medical to a military role. Both orders were predominantly French in composition. In imitation and competition German knights formed the Teutonic order, and Spain provided several other groups, such as the Knights of Calatrava.

The military orders were the cutting edge of the Crusader states and on all the borders of Christendom. Donations of land in Europe gave them great wealth, enabling them to carry out their military role.

The Templars also became great bankers. But after the fall of Acre they were rich men without a cause. This proved too much of a temptation for Philip IV of France (▷ p. 94): in 1306 he had the Order of the Temple dissolved and profited from its riches.

The other orders survived and adapted to changed circumstances. The Teutonic Order returned to its homeland and headed the drive to the east into Slav lands, creating a Baltic empire in what later became Prussia. After playing a large part in the warfare and politics of Eastern Europe, they were defeated by the Poles at Tannenberg in 1410.

The Hospitallers established themselves on Rhodes. From there they harried Muslim coasts and shipping for two centuries. Chased off the island by the Ottoman Turks in 1522, they defended Malta against the same enemy in 1565. There they survived, although with declining military significance, until overrun by Napoleon's forces on their way to Egypt in 1798.

Popes, Saints and Heretics

The Middle Ages saw the expansion of the power of the popes over the Church and people of Western Christendom. Initially papal influence derived from the fact that the pope was based in the capital of the Roman Empire, but this influence diminished after the collapse of the Western Empire in 476 and had to be gradually reasserted.

Papal power peaked in the high Middle Ages, but from the late 13th century the increasing politicization of the papacy, its rivalry with the Holy Roman Emperor (▷ p. 84), and scandals such as the Great Schism, all served to undermine papal authority, and gave impetus to reformist movements.

The early papacy

Early Christian tradition identified St Peter as the first bishop of Rome, whose authority over the Church had been given to him by Christ. Subsequent popes were heirs of this tradition, and adopted the keys of St Peter as a symbol. After the Roman Empire moved to Constantinople, the pope gradually emerged as the spiritual leader of Christendom. Gelasius I (492–496), the first pope to be called 'vicar of Christ', developed the influential idea of two complementary powers governing the world – one centred in the pope, the other centred in the emperor, of which the spiritual power was superior.

The personal piety, political acumen and missionary work of Gregory the Great (590–604) – the first monk to be elected pope – enhanced the status and power of the papacy. The links forged with the emergent Carolingian Empire, especially between Charlemagne and Leo III (795–816), weakened the ties between the papacy and Constantinople and directed the energies of successive popes towards the West. Differences of language and culture exacerbated the split between Eastern and Western forms of Christianity, and by the 11th century the break had hardened, with Roman Catholicism holding sway in the West and Orthodox Christianity in the East (▷ p. 81).

Papal reform

By the 11th century many people felt that the popes were becoming corrupt and inward-looking, dominated by local Roman affairs. Emperor Henry III (1039–56) responded to this by initiating a wide-ranging reform of the papacy. Attempts were made to eradicate widespread abuses such as simony (the buying of ecclesiastical offices), and to insist on clerical celibacy, which emphasized the special nature of priests.

Emperor Henry IV (1056–1106) resented papal interference in the appointment of bishops and senior clergy within the empire. He engaged in a long struggle with a papacy equally anxious to free Church affairs from interference by laymen (the Investiture Contest; ▷ p. 84). This period of reform and strife – often called the Gregorian Reform, after its most forceful exponent, Pope Gregory VII (1073–85) – witnessed a great leap forward in papal assertion of its leadership of Western Christendom.

The new pre-eminence of the papacy was reflected in a number of major initiatives. In 1095 Urban II (1088–99) summoned the First Crusade (▷ p. 88). Another reforming pope, Innocent III (1198–1216), took steps to improve the quality of the clergy. The Fourth Lateran Council, which he called in 1215, resulted in decrees on pastoral affairs that affected the lives of every Christian in Europe.

Continuing attempts by successive popes to assert the supremacy of spiritual over temporal power throughout Europe were resented by secular rulers, and led to frequent disputes, such as that between Pope Boniface VIII (1294–1303) and Philip IV of France (1285–1314) concerning that king's right to tax the clergy.

The Avignon period

Feuds among the Italian cardinals and their allies in the Roman nobility persuaded Pope Clement V (1305–14) to stay in southern France. This led to a preponderance of Frenchmen in the College of Cardinals, which ensured a line of French popes resident at Avignon. Their policies became increasingly influenced by the interests of the French crown.

Concerned Christians, who believed the pope's place was in Rome, were reproachful; the poet Petrarch referred to the Avignon period as the 'Babylonish captivity'. Criticism was heightened by the extravagance and growing bureaucracy of the Avignon papacy. But a number of factors – political disturbances in Italy, the convenience and comfort of Avignon, and the influence of the French cardinals – combined to prevent a return of the papal court to Rome until 1377.

The Great Schism

Ironically the return to the city of St Peter plunged the papacy into yet deeper turmoil in the form of the Great Schism. In 1378 Urban VI (1378–89) – the first Italian pope for 75 years – was elected amidst tumultuous scenes in Rome. His obstinacy and unwillingness to compromise alienated many non-Italian cardinals who would have preferred to remain in Avignon; they responded by electing a rival pope. Christian Europe was scandalized. The reputation of the papacy plummeted further as two (and, from 1409, three) rival popes vied for political support from the rulers and peoples of Europe. Churchmen, canon lawyers and political theorists attempted various means of settling the dispute. General councils of the Church were called to express the wishes of Christendom. At the Council of Constance (1414–17), with the backing of the Emperor Sigismund (1411–37), the rivals were deposed and Martin V (1417–31) elected as unopposed pope.

Monasticism

The earliest monks were the desert hermits who lived on top of tall pillars. Hermits continued to exist throughout the Middle Ages, but increasingly a communal lifestyle devoted to God rather than an isolated one became popular. Monasteries were founded where devout men or women lived under a 'rule' (code of conduct) that governed their daily routines. The most influential of all rules was that laid down by the 'father' of Western monasticism, St Benedict of Nursia (c. 480–c. 550). The Benedictine rule, reformed and systematized by St Benedict of Aniane in the 9th century, divided the day into periods of work and devotion; it required humility, prayer and obedience. Benedictine monasteries were repositories of books and learning, institutions of great wealth and considerable artistic patronage. The Burgundian abbey of Cluny, founded in 910 under the protection of the papacy, became the mother house of a large and wealthy order. Cluniac monks influenced both secular rulers and papal policy.

The Cistercians, who derived their name from their first foundation at Cîteaux in central France (1098), turned away from the lavishness of the Cluniac lifestyle to a more ascetic path. The Cistercians built their houses in remote areas and placed great emphasis on the importance of physical labour. The use of 'lay' brothers allowed an involvement in monasticism by lower classes not hitherto possible. Bernard of Clairvaux, the most influential churchman of his age, inspired

St Francis of Assisi renounces his family and material possessions to embrace a life of poverty, prayer and care for the needy. The teachings of St Francis reflect his deep love of the natural world, which he saw as the mirror of God. This fresco – one of a cycle in the upper church of S. Francesco at Assisi depicting scenes from the saint's life – was long attributed to Giotto.

recruitment to the order; by his death in 1153 there were hundreds of Cistercian monasteries all over Europe.

Canons and friars

This period of flourishing monasticism also saw the growing popularity of the Augustinian canons, who followed a rule supposedly laid down by the early Church father, St Augustine of Hippo (354–430). Augustinian canons lived together like monks, but were more outward-looking than other orders, serving society in direct ways by preaching, teaching and running hospitals.

A new form of religious life emerged in the early 13th century – that of the mendicants or friars, who were determined to follow Christ's example by living a life of devout poverty among the sick and the needy. Pope Innocent III encouraged the development of two major orders of friars: the Franciscans – followers of St Francis of Assisi (1182–1226; ⇨ picture), and the Dominicans – who were originally formed to preach against the spread of heresy. The friars worked actively among the people and enjoyed considerable popularity throughout Europe, especially in urban areas.

Heresy and anticlericalism

The Catholic church condemned any who held beliefs at variance with Church orthodoxy as heretics. Some heresies were simply beliefs held by isolated intellectuals, others attracted a mass following. Arianism, which denied the divinity of Christ, was widespread in early medieval Europe, but after its decline in the 6th century, there was remarkably little heresy for several centuries in the West.

In the 11th century the lack of pastoral care for a growing population and the religious enthusiasm inspired by radical reformers combined to create an explosion of heretical movements. It was interest in the Church and ways of salvation, not disregard of religion, that led to anticlericalism and heresy. These movements were seen as threats by the Church authorities, but those condemned as heretics were usually seeking ways to live a more perfect Christian life. Most widespread, particularly in northern Italy and southern France, was Catharism – a dualist heresy whose adherents believed the material world was evil, and that only the spiritual was good. Church authorities tried to eradicate heresy using a variety of methods. These included extensive preaching, the use of inquisitors (⇨ p. 113), the invocation of military aid from secular rulers, and, as a last resort, crusades. In 1209 Innocent III launched the Albigensian Crusade against the Cathars in southern France, and by 1229 they had largely been crushed.

However, a century later the Avignon period led to a growing disillusionment with the wealth and worldliness of the established Church, and inspired a surge of anticlericalism. During the Great Schism two new heresies surfaced. In England the Oxford theologian John

Wyclif (?1330–84) based his criticism on a study of scripture, rejecting the authority of the papacy and the doctrine of transubstantiation in the Eucharist. His followers – insultingly known as Lollards – stressed the importance of individual action for salvation in contrast to the Church's emphasis on the mediatory role of the priesthood. They circulated extracts from the Bible and other religious texts, written in English (rather than the orthodox Latin) so that they were more easily understood by the laity.

Wyclif's writings influenced the Bohemian reformer, Jan Hus (?1372–1415), whose followers led a revolution in Bohemia in the early 15th century. Hus was condemned and burnt at the Council of Constance in 1415 for refusing to recant his beliefs. His ideas became far more of a threat than Wyclif's owing to their connection with Bohemian nationalism. Under the able command of John Zizka, the Hussites defeated crusaders from Germany, Austria and Hungary. The Compact of Prague of 1436 recognized their distinctive beliefs and granted many of their demands.

But not all communities of devout lay folk were hostile to the established Church. Some – the Netherlandish Brethren of the Common Life, for example – remained within the Church's fold. All of them in their different ways contributed to the diversity of religious experience that existed by the end of the Middle Ages, a diversity that was to pave the way for the reform movements of the 16th-century Protestant Reformation (⇨ p. 110).   ViD

SEE ALSO

- THE ROMAN EMPIRE p. 38
- THE BARBARIAN KINGDOMS p. 78
- THE BYZANTINE EMPIRE p. 80
- THE RISE OF ISLAM p. 82
- THE HOLY ROMAN EMPIRE p. 84
- THE CRUSADES p. 88
- CRISIS IN EUROPE p. 92
- MEDIEVAL AND RENAISSANCE CULTURE p. 100
- THE REFORMATION p. 110

A BENEDICTINE MONASTERY

With minor variations, Benedictine monasteries were built to the same plan all over Europe during the Middle Ages. The different sections of the monastery shown here reflect St Benedict's prescription that everything necessary for the religious life should be found within the buildings of the community.

At the centre of the monastery is the abbey church (1) with the altar end (2) facing east (towards Jerusalem). Next to the abbey is the cloister (3), which links together the important elements of the monastery and provides the monks with a place to walk, study, and meditate. On the side of the cloister adjoining the church is the scriptorium (for the writing and copying of manuscripts) and the library (4). On the upper floor of the eastern side of the cloister, built over the refectory or dining-room (5), is the monks' dormitory or dorter (6). This is linked to the church by a night-stair, giving direct access to the church for night services. The north transept (7) of the abbey church continues into a passage leading to the chapterhouse (8), where meetings were held.

On the western side of the cloister is the cellarer's range (9), including storerooms for food. On the northern side of the cloister are the kitchens (10), brewhouse (where ale was brewed) and buttery (where it was stored) (11), and workshops for smiths, shoemakers and saddlers (12). Sewage from the lavatories, or rere-dorter (13), would be carried downstream. The infirmary (14) has its own chapel (15), kitchen (16), refectory (17) and garden (18).

The buildings around the courtyard (19) provide for dealings with the outside world. There is the almonry (20), where food and clothing would be distributed to the poor, and guest-houses for wealthy travellers (21) and poor pilgrims (22), and stables (23). The abbot's house (24) is positioned near the gatehouse (25).

Many religious orders practised intensive agriculture. The land and buildings associated with this include the farm (26), barn (27), mill (28), garden (29), and fish ponds (30).

Crisis in Europe

In the 14th century, Europe was dealt a series of blows that made it the most calamitous century before our own. Early in the century appalling weather resulted in harvest failures and famine. Then, in mid-century, bubonic plague – the Black Death – wiped out a significant proportion of the population. As a consequence demand for basic foodstuffs contracted sharply; for many landowners, accustomed to seeing their products eagerly sought after, this was a rude awakening.

In some regions the miseries of war (▷ p. 102) added to the sense of confusion. Criticism of the Church, the appearance of new heresies (▷ p. 90) and a series of popular uprisings all added to the fundamental challenges faced by medieval society.

The end of expansion
From the 11th to the end of the 13th century Europe experienced an economic boom (▷ p. 98). Areas that were wild and forested in 1000 were brought under cultivation in the two centuries that followed. Colonization and cultivation of new land and an increase in its total production was accompanied by population expansion – a European population of 40 million in 1000 rose to 60 million over the next two centuries. However, this growth was checked at the beginning of the 14th century when food supplies became insufficient for the population. The fragility of the medieval economy – in particular its dependence on favourable weather – were exposed by the setbacks of 1315–17, when three bad harvests caused famine throughout northern and eastern Europe. The cloth town of Ypres in Flanders lost 10% of its population in the summer of 1316. Elsewhere the bodies of the poor who died from hunger and illness lined the roads.

The Black Death
The setbacks of the early years of the century turned into demographic disaster with the arrival in the middle of the century of the Black Death. Bubonic plague originated in the Far East, and was brought to Europe in 1346–7 by Italian merchant ships from the ports of the Crimea on the Black Sea. As well as Ukrainian grain they carried the rats whose fleas spread the disease. The plague spread rapidly from the Mediterranean ports, reaching southern England in 1348 (▷ map). Victims developed fever and hard black buboes (swollen lymph nodes in the groin and armpits); more than half of those infected died. The pneumonic strain affected the lungs and

THE SPREAD OF THE BLACK DEATH 1346–53

INITIAL FOCUS 1346

CRIMEA Kaffa

Constantinople

Genoa

Marseilles

Messina

Alexandria

INFECTED AREAS

SPREAD

1347

1348 1350 1352

1349 1351 1353

© Colin McEvedy 1991

was spread by coughing, making it more virulent in winter when the bubonic form was less active. This strain, and the rare septicaemic variety – which attacked the bloodstream and brought death before symptoms could develop – were almost always fatal.

Contemporary medicine knew no treatment for this terrifying affliction. Clean living and the avoidance of sin was advanced as one means of escaping infection, as was the avoidance of 'pestilential' air – believed to be the cause of the disease. This meant shunning baths (which opened the pores), keeping windows shut when the weather was cold or misty, and purifying the air by burning aromatic substances, including the quack concoctions of apothecaries. If people had to venture out, one treatise recommended carrying a block of costly drugs, another a sponge soaked in vinegar, to prevent contaminated air from entering the body. For those already afflicted, bleeding was prescribed.

Death rates are difficult to calculate in the absence of population statistics. In some pockets mortality was light, while most of Bohemia, Silesia and Poland escaped the Black Death altogether. The undernourished, overcrowded poor were hit badly, and the clergy suffered most of all, as a consequence of its duties to the sick. The rich derived some protection from their better living conditions, but the plague was no respecter of rank – and

princes and great lords, including Alfonso XI of Castile, died as well as the poor. A conservative estimate is that one-quarter of the European population perished in the epidemic of 1348–9.

An age of population decline
Recovery from even this severe blow might have been quick had it not been for recurrent epidemics in the 1360s and 70s. The serious outbreak of the winter of 1361–2, and renewed epidemics in 1369 and 1375 attacked children in particular, so reducing the future breeding stock. An era of population decline set in. Over the 14th century as a whole, it is reckoned that up to 40% of the population died as a consequence of plague, other illnesses and famine. Only towards the end of the 15th century did the population slowly begin to grow again. But plague became a fact of European life for more than three centuries. In England the last outbreak was the London plague of 1665 (▷ p. 119), and in Europe it persisted until the 18th century.

Economic effects
The first onslaught of the Black Death was followed by labour shortages and disruption of production. Wages and prices both rose sharply. Ruling classes and governments reacted by passing labour legislation to maintain their grip on economic power. In England the government panicked and introduced the Ordinance of Labourers (1351), designed

to freeze wages at pre-plague levels. However, in the 1350s there was a respite from the plague and the population began to recover. While unproductive marginal fields were abandoned there was no shortage of takers for vacant tenancies, an indication of overpopulation on the eve of the pestilence. Landlords also vigorously enforced their legal rights over tenants. For some decades these measures were successful, and the incomes of employers remained buoyant.

The long-term effects of plague were more marked. Consumption and production of basic foodstuffs declined as the population did. Within a few decades acute labour shortages meant that serfdom (⊳ p. 98) had to be abandoned and that real wages and living standards for rural and urban labourers reached levels unmatched for centuries to come. For the surviving peasantry the plague was thus a blessing, inaugurating a golden age of improved conditions and relative plenty. Landlords suffered severe falls in their incomes and were forced to rent out their land, or to convert them into pasture.

Psychological effects

The immediate psychological effect of the Black Death was to encourage survivors to live for the day. When it became clear that this was not the end of the world there were varied reactions. Penitential processions were organized to mollify the anger of God and included displays of self-flagellation. Among those singled out as scapegoats were the Jews, who were subjected to pogroms, and witches and heretics, who were burnt. The ever-present threat of pestilence may be responsible for a mood of pessimism in the literature and art of the period, where images of death and damnation abound. It may also have encouraged a questioning of authority and religious teachings and given rise to a new spirit of religious enquiry (⊳ p. 90). Equally, however, there was a new mood of piety, which may have been inspired by the plague.

Popular revolts

Economic change, the burdens of warfare, resentment at foreign domination and hostility to the small ruling elites all inspired widespread challenges to authority in the late 13th and 14th centuries.

In the Sicilian Vespers of 1282 the population rose up and successfully drove out the hated Angevin French who had ruled Sicily since 1266 (⊳ p. 96). The French government and the patrician rulers of the Flemish textile cities were the targets of the 'Matins of Bruges' in Flanders (1302), which scored initial success when the Flemish infantry defeated the French knights at Courtrai, but was defeated by 1305. However, popular opposition to the French crown continued intermittently for much of the century, and for some years after 1340 the weaving towns of Ghent, Ypres and Bruges recognized Edward III as king of France (⊳ p. 94). In the case of Flanders, economic distress caused by English wool embargoes was one reason why the artisans and their rulers favoured different policies. After the first onslaught of the plague, economic grievances were sharpened.

In northern France the peasantry laboured under twin afflictions – the devastation caused by marauding English armies, and a heavy burden of taxation to pay for the Hundred Years War. A popular rebellion broke out there in 1358, following the humiliating defeat of the French aristocracy at the battle of Poitiers. This revolt was known as the 'Jacquerie', after 'Jacques Bonhomme', the aristocrats' contemptuous nickname for a French peasant. Armed bands attacked the nobility and castles were demolished and looted. The threat to the existing social order caused the feuding French factions to sink their differences, and the disorder was suppressed.

The last decades of the century – when the long-term economic effects of plague were beginning to bite – saw a wave of popular uprisings caused by the refusal of the ruling classes in town and country to allow urban and rural labourers the opportunities for improvement that seemed to have opened. The 1370s witnessed popular unrest in several central Italian cities. In Florence the wool workers (ciompi) briefly seized power in 1378. As daily-paid workers they were particularly vulnerable to economic fluctuations, but it was the heavy burden of taxation to pay for war with the papacy which brought their grievances to a head. Chief among their demands was that they be allowed to organize their own guilds. There were risings in southern France in the 1380s and the Flemish towns rebelled again in 1382–4.

The weight of taxation (at a time when the Hundred Years War was going badly for the English) was a contributory cause of the English Peasants' Revolt in 1381. The main revolt in Kent and Essex was sparked off by the bungled collection of the third poll tax – which hit the poor particularly – in an area that had recently suffered from French raids. Under the leadership of Wat Tyler and John Ball, the men of Kent and Essex marched on London, attacking the property of tax collectors, burning tax records, and lynching members of the government. The demands by the rebels to Richard II – namely the abolition of serfdom and the charging of moderate rents – reveal that the deep-seated causes of rebellion concerned the often successful measures the ruling classes had taken to keep down wages and counteract the effects of the Black Death. Nor was this simply a rebellion of peasants. In London workers took advantage of the disorder to massacre Flemings, who were accused of taking away their work, and many private scores were settled. Copycat risings elsewhere in the kingdom reveal local grievances: in St Albans, Bury St Edmunds and Cambridge the townspeople rose up against their landlords – respectively the abbots and the university.

The English 'Great Rebellion', like the other popular uprisings, was suppressed with relative ease. Despite their numbers, the rebels were disorganized and their leaders could be separated from one another. The ruling classes controlled military force and the law, and always succeeded in restoring order. But they could not cheat the economic pressures that the plague had induced. Although the risings themselves achieved little change, competition for the services of a declining labour force did lead to improvement in the working conditions of the labouring classes.

A century of calamities?

It is important not to exaggerate the effect of the 14th-century crisis. It has already been said that life may have been better for the survivors of the shocks of the 14th century. They almost certainly enjoyed a more varied diet; this was because farmers, faced by a declining demand for grain as the numbers of mouths fell, grew vegetables instead, or turned to livestock. In the wake of natural and man-made calamities European society was to show great powers of recovery in the 15th century – the century of the printing press and of overseas exploration and expansion (⊳ pp. 101 and 108). NH

The triumph of death, a Pisan fresco of the 1340s. The Black Death – the subject of many medieval paintings and engravings – also gave fresh impetus to the *danse macabre* or 'dance of death'. Originally performed in churchyards – without the blessing of the clergy – the dance began in the 11th and 12th centuries. A later German form, the *Totentanz*, involved a dramatic element in which the character of Death seized spectactors.

The Hundred Years War

In the 14th and 15th centuries, rivalry between the kingdoms of France and England became the dominant political feature of northwestern Europe. From 1337 until 1453 the two states fought out an irregular succession of wars. At issue was the English king's claim to the French crown, as well as control of lands the English kings held in France. This conflict is known as the Hundred Years War.

The battle of Sluys, 24 June 1340, as depicted in Froissart's chronicles. Massed English archers gave notice of the threat they would pose at the later battles of Crécy and Poitiers by defeating a force of French, Genoese and Castilian ships off the coast of Flanders. Victory gave England control of the English Channel.

During the course of the 13th century a series of powerful rulers belonging to the Capetian dynasty, Philip Augustus (1180–1223), Louis IX – Saint Louis – (1226–70), and Philip IV – the Fair – (1285–1314), had made France the outstanding kingdom in Europe. They could raise taxes and muster armies on a grander scale than any other European ruler. Even so their success depended on the cooperation of the great and independent-minded nobles of France. These nobles owed allegiance to the king, shared in the profits of taxation and enjoyed wide-ranging rights of justice over their extensive lands. One of these nobles held the title 'Duke of Aquitaine'. He was also the king of England.

The origins of the conflict

Ever since 1066, when the duke of Normandy took the English throne as William I, the Norman kings and their Plantagenet successors had continued to enjoy possession of huge territories in France (⊳ p. 85). This straddling of the English Channel reached its height in the 12th century with Henry II, whose marriage to Eleanor of Aquitaine established a Plantagenet Empire that incorporated most of western France. However, King John's incompetence meant that in a few years between 1203 and 1206 most of these territories were lost to Philip Augustus, and by the 1330s only Gascony (the southwest of Aquitaine; ⊳ map, p. 85) was still retained by the English king. Yet even these much reduced dominions continued to provide ample cause for conflict.

As duke of Aquitaine the king of England owed formal allegiance to the French crown. Moreover his Gascon subjects were only too willing, whenever it suited their own private interests, to appeal from the duke's court to the court of the king of France.

Tension in the 1330s

What added spice to the long-standing wrangling between the two monarchies was that when the Capetian dynasty died out in the direct male line in 1328, then the Plantagenet Edward III (1327–77), as a maternal grandson of Philip the Fair, had an excellent claim to the French throne. In fact, however, the crown passed to a nephew, Philip of Valois, who became Philip VI (1328–50). Soon the two kings were fighting a kind of border war, the initial phases of the struggle being confined to Scotland and Flanders.

From the 1290s, when Edward I of England had attempted to conquer Scotland, the Scots had found common cause with France in the 'Auld Alliance' against England. But more significantly, the merchants and workers in the thriving Flemish cloth towns – Bruges, Ghent and Ypres (⊳ p. 98) – found themselves drawn by economic self-interest to the English side, for it was from England that they imported the raw material, wool, indispensable to their industrial prosperity. Yet the county of Flanders 'belonged' to France, and so they owed allegiance to Philip VI. It would therefore ease their consciences if Edward III proclaimed himself the true French king. At Ghent in January 1340 Edward duly assumed the title 'king of England and France', which was to be borne by his successors for nearly five centuries, until 1801.

The first phase: 1337–60

Initially Edward's claim to the French crown may have been a bargaining counter by which he hoped to obtain French recognition of English sovereignty over Gascony. He built up an alliance with the towns and nobles of the Low Countries (including Flanders), and took an army there in 1338–9. In 1340 an English naval victory at Sluys, off the Flemish coast, put an end to a threatened French invasion of England.

France was a much richer country than England, however, and at this stage the war was proving an immense strain on Edward's resources. Not until some Breton and Norman nobles deserted the Valois cause did the fortunes of the war on land begin to go Edward's way. In 1346 the main French army was routed by the firepower of English archers at Crécy. In 1347 Edward captured Calais, which was to remain in English possession until 1558. At the battle of Poitiers, ten years after Crécy, the English archers, this time under the command of Edward, Prince of Wales (the 'Black Prince'), repeated their slaughter of the over-confident French knights. At Poitiers the French king, John II (1350–64), was taken prisoner, and after four years of ransom negotiations the French agreed at Brétigny to hand over no less than a third of the land of France in full sovereignty. In return Edward was to renounce his claim to the throne.

French recovery

But the Treaty of Brétigny was never quite ratified in full. Both sides preferred to leave loopholes that might be exploited later if opportunity arose. Meanwhile Edward rapidly occupied his new terri-

THE DUCHY OF BURGUNDY

Charles 'the Bold', duke of Burgundy, and his wife Isabelle of Bourbon, portrayed by an unknown 15th-century Flemish painter.

Burgundy (named after a Germanic tribe, the Burgundians, who settled in what is now eastern France in the 5th century) was conquered by the Merovingian Franks (▷ p. 78) in the 6th century. In the late Middle Ages, under a series of strong dukes, it became a powerful state in its own right, and the most affluent in Europe.

For almost a century, from 1384 to 1477, the four Valois dukes of Burgundy, Philip 'the Bold' (1363–1404), John 'the Fearless' (1404–19), Philip 'the Good' (1419–67) and Charles 'the Bold' (1467–77), were dominating figures in the political and cultural life of northwestern Europe. During this period both the French and English monarchies were often in acute difficulties, suffering either from civil war or from inept rulers. Burgundy by contrast was governed by four competent dukes in succession. As rivals and allies of kings – yet not quite their equals – the dukes adopted a lifestyle of imperial splendour. As rulers of the most urbanized and prosperous region in northern Europe, they could afford to do so. The patronage they offered attracted the finest artists (such as Jan van Eyck), the most forward-looking composers (such as Guillaume Dufay) and the most enthusiastic chroniclers of chivalry and the courtly life (such as Olivier de la Marche and Georges Chastellain).

The key to Burgundian prestige lay in the marriage (1369) that Charles V of France arranged between his younger brother, Philip duke of Burgundy, and Margaret, the heiress to the counties of Flanders and Artois. In 1384 Philip's father-in-law died and he took possession of his wife's inheritance. From then on, as the wealthiest of the French princes, ruling towns that were as important to England's prosperity as to France's territorial integrity, the dukes of Burgundy were destined to play a central role in the violent politics of the Hundred Years War.

Between 1425 and 1430 Philip 'the Good' took advantage of the Anglo-Burgundian alliance to add Hainault, Holland and Brabant to his list of territories. Prosperous economic centres such as Amsterdam, Antwerp, Bruges, Brussels, Ghent and Lille were now among the towns he ruled (▷ p. 98). In 1430 he founded a chivalric order, the Order of the Golden Fleece. His workaholic son Charles 'the Bold' conquered Lorraine in 1475, but his further attempts to extend Burgundian power by military means ended in defeat at the hands of the Swiss and then his own death at the Battle of Nancy (1477). Little wonder that the outstanding historians of the age, from Froissart to Commynes, should have been fascinated by the spectacular triumphs of Burgundian history, and by its sudden end.

unleashed a ferocious struggle for control between the dukes of Burgundy (▷ box) and Orleans, both of them representatives of junior branches of the royal house. Here was a situation which the English warrior-king, Henry V (1413–22), was ideally equipped to exploit. This marked the opening of the third phase of hostilities, and after his stunning victory at Agincourt in 1415 Henry launched a full-scale war of conquest.

On the French side things became even more chaotic when in 1419 the heir to the throne (the dauphin, later Charles VII) became implicated in the murder of Duke John 'the Fearless' of Burgundy on the bridge at Montereau. As a result John's son, Duke Philip 'the Good', determined to throw all his weight behind the English cause. Within a year of the murder at Montereau, Charles VI had agreed, in the Treaty of Troyes, to name Henry V as his successor. The Anglo-Burgundian regime took control of Paris and much of northern France. As it turned out, however, Henry V died two months before Charles VI.

Victory for France

In the early years of his reign Charles VII (1422–61) was confined to the lands south of the Loire (the kingdom of Bourges), but in 1429 a French revival, in part inspired by Joan of Arc, recaptured the initiative. By 1435 Duke Philip had swung back to the French royal side. For more than a decade the English held on stubbornly. Then suddenly, between 1450 and 1453, both Normandy and Gascony were lost forever.

From now on the monarchies of France and England, bound together in a troubled relationship since 1066, went their separate ways. In England the shock of the unexpected defeat led to civil war, with the Wars of the Roses (1455–85) between the houses of Lancaster and York (▷ p. 118). In France the monarchy garnered the rewards of victory, and of the reorganization of government that victory had entailed. Following the break-up of the Burgundian state after the death of Duke Charles 'the Bold' (1467–77), the French kings once again enjoyed unrivalled power in France. JG

SEE ALSO
● VIKINGS AND NORMANS p. 86
● MEDIEVAL AND RENAISSANCE CULTURE p. 100
● THE MAKING OF BRITAIN p. 118

Joan of Arc, the national heroine of France, rides into battle in this 15th-century woodcut. Born the daughter of a peasant in around 1412, she claimed to have heard the voices of Saints Michael, Catherine and Margaret urging her to rid France of the English invaders. She led the French army that relieved the besieged town of Orleans in 1429, and went on to crown the dauphin as Charles VII in Reims cathedral. Captured by the English, Joan was burnt as a heretic in 1431. She was made a saint in 1920.

tories and created his eldest son 'prince of Aquitaine'. But the Black Prince's stern rule aggravated a number of the leading Gascon nobles and they appealed for help to the new king of France, Charles V (1364–80). In 1369 Edward formally resumed his French title and war broke out anew. Under the shrewd leadership of Charles V and of captains such as Bertrand du Guesclin, the French avoided pitched battles. Instead they settled down to use their greater resources in the piecemeal reconquest of territory. Generally the English found themselves outmanoeuvred and in 1396 the English king, Richard II (1377–99), was happy to agree to a 28-year truce.

Henry V and the Burgundian alliance

Charles VI of France (1380–1422) suffered recurrent bouts of mental illness. This

Italy of the City-States

From the end of the Roman Empire to the mid-19th century Italy was a patchwork of separate political units, frequently fought over by rival foreign powers. In the High Middle Ages and early Renaissance, however, fragmentation was turned to advantage with the rise of dynamic independent city-states governed by communes or princes. Despite constant internecine warfare, these city-states achieved much in political, economic and cultural life, developing sophisticated forms of republican government, building up huge commercial and financial empires, and producing the great cultural flowering of the Renaissance (⊳ p. 100).

Lorenzo de' Medici ('the Magnificent'; 1449–92), one of the most celebrated members of the wealthy family that ruled Florence virtually without interruption from 1421 to 1737. This 16th-century portrait includes a view of the city in the background. Like his grandfather Cosimo, Lorenzo was a generous and enthusiastic patron of the arts.

For much of the High Middle Ages Italian territory was the subject of dispute. The Holy Roman Emperor laid claim to the north and some of central Italy, while the papacy – based in Rome – attempted to extend its influence northwards and carve out a territorial base in the centre (⊳ map, p. 85). Both powers were too unstable to impose control with any continuity. At most they played the roles of magnets for the warring factions of northern and central Italy – the 'Guelphs', who adhered to the papal line, and the 'Ghibellines', who supported the emperor.

The rise of the city-state

The beneficiaries of this stalemate were

the towns of northern and central Italy. Lack of effective authority gave them virtual independence, provided they could defend themselves from outside interference. The northern Italian towns also profited from the economic upturn of the High Middle Ages (⊳ p. 98). With access to both the eastern and the western basins of the Mediterranean, as well as to transalpine routes to northern Europe, Italian towns were in a uniquely favourable position. The ports of Pisa, Amalfi, Genoa and Venice spearheaded the recovery of long-distance trade, which soon also began to benefit the inland towns of the fertile Po valley and Tuscany, such as Milan, Florence and Lucca.

In the course of the High Middle Ages a number of northern Italian towns resorted to self-government. By the end of the 12th century these independent 'communes' had triumphed all over Lombardy and Tuscany. The controlling class within the communes varied considerably from town to town – in Pisa, for example, the merchant class held sway – but the early city-states tended to be dominated by the aristocracy.

The term 'city-state' implies more than just the city. To establish its independence successfully a city had to gain and retain control over the surrounding countryside – the *contado*. This involved the subjugation of the rural aristocracy, many of whom subsequently moved into the city. That move, however, brought its own problems. Powerful landowners suddenly found themselves living cheek by jowl with their equals and inferiors. Clans of extended families and their supporters formed and aligned themselves in mutual opposition, often driven by blood-feuds. The towns became endemically violent and factional.

For much of the 13th century the towns struggled to contain these tendencies. As economic prosperity grew and town populations increased, the rule of the aristocracy in the communes began to be challenged. In Florence, as in many other towns, an alliance of guildsmen and other citizens (the *popolo*) eventually gained control. New forms of communal government with elaborate constitutions were evolved. Various layers of committees were established, with an outsider – the *podestà* – in the chief judiciary role, an inner council as the main executive body, and a broader general council to oversee and check the work of the elected officials. Methods of election, while complex and sophisticated, were never immune to corruption. The world of the city-state was one of endless experimentation and instability.

The achievements of these city-states were, however, considerable. Town and countryside were both subjected to intensive development and planning provisions. Italy's Gothic cathedrals and civic building programmes date mostly from this period. The towns legislated in great detail on every aspect of their citizens' lives. They provided for education – municipal schools and universities were often founded and supported from the public purse – as well as governing the

religious and moral life of their subjects. And they were intensely aware – and proud – of what they were doing.

Control of the south

A very different pattern is evident in southern Italy. Norman adventurers arrived in the mid-11th century, and soon took the territory south of Rome, including the island of Sicily, as a papal fief. From then on, southern Italy – known as 'Sicily' or, simply, the *Regno* or kingdom – was almost permanently in foreign hands. From 1220 to 1250 it was ruled by the half-Sicilian, half-German Hohenstaufen emperor, Frederick II. However, the papacy had always regarded the Hohenstaufens as dangerous neighbours. In 1265 pope Urban IV offered the kingdom of Sicily to a French prince, Charles of Anjou, who defeated and killed the last Hohenstaufen. This initiated French interest in the peninsula, and for the next century the French played a prominent part in the 'Guelph' alliance. To the French Angevin presence was soon added the Spanish: in 1282 the people of Palermo rose up against Angevin tyranny (in the uprising known as the 'Sicilian Vespers') and invited Peter III of Aragon to be their king.

The war of the Sicilian Vespers lasted twenty years and ended in the partition of 'Sicily' into the Angevin kingdom of Naples and the Aragonese kingdom of Trinacria (the island of Sicily). In the mid-15th century the increasingly ineffective Angevins were ousted by the Aragonese; by 1442 all the territory of the former *Regno* was in Spanish hands.

What all these foreign rulers of southern Italy had in common was a lack of interest in the economic well-being of their lands. They used Sicily as a resource for their ambitions elsewhere, taxing it heavily and exploiting its natural resources until they were irreversibly weakened. The impoverishment of southern Italy – once the 'granary of Europe' – is largely a result of this exploitation.

Communes and despots

Perennial factional violence, the dangers from more powerful rival towns, and collective political processes that were cumbersome and ineffective began to take their toll on the city-states. These problems were exacerbated by the strains of the mid-14th century – famine, warfare, plague – which affected Italy at least as gravely as the rest of Europe (⊳ p. 92), and the political instability brought about by the removal of the papacy to Avignon (⊳ p. 90), which weakened the Guelph alliance.

All this combined to make the idea of one-man rule increasingly attractive. From the late 13th century through to the early 15th, there was a steady process of recourse to the 'despot', the single ruler who might sweep aside these weaknesses. Yet the significance of this trend can be exaggerated. Recently it has been shown that the two styles of government were not so different. Communes, where they survived, did so by becoming increasingly oligarchical (i.e. concentrating power in

The waterfront at Venice forms a sumptuous backdrop for Vittore Carpaccio's depiction of the meeting of the betrothed and the departure of the pilgrims (c. 1495) – one of a cycle of scenes he painted from the legend of St Ursula. The wealth, architectural grandeur and civic ceremonial that characterized Venice at the height of its power and influence are all evident in Carpaccio's painting.

VENICE
THE MOST SERENE REPUBLIC

When northeastern Italy was invaded by the barbarians in the 5th century (▷ p. 78), its inhabitants – the *Veneti* – took refuge on the islands and mudflats of a lagoon at the head of the Adriatic. Venice – the town they founded there – was to become a powerful independent republic and a great commercial and maritime power (▷ map, p. 85).

Venice soon built up a trading empire extending across the Mediterranean and beyond. Venice began as a fief of the Byzantine Empire – initially its main trading partner – but by the 11th century the relationship between the two was on a more equal footing. In 1204, at Venice's request, the Fourth Crusade was diverted to sack Constantinople (▷ pp. 80 and 88), and the roles were virtually reversed. After 1204 Venice gained many crucial territories and trading posts throughout the Byzantine Empire, which it continued to exploit until the Turkish conquests of the 15th century (▷ p. 114).

By the late 13th century Venetian trading stretched from the Far East to the Atlantic. Profiting from new navigational techniques, Venetian convoys made twice-annual sailings to the Black Sea (where they established a colony), the North African coast, Marseilles, Barcelona, and through the Straits of Gibraltar. The Venetian Arsenal was Europe's biggest shipyard, and the Venetians had an effective monopoly of the grain trade in the eastern Mediterranean. The Venetians pioneered the introduction of glass to the West, as well as a number of innovations in commercial techniques. Their only serious rival was Genoa, against which Venice fought five naval wars in two centuries. The Venetian defeat of Genoa in 1380 eliminated Genoese influence from the eastern Mediterranean.

From early on, Venice fascinated outsiders. Its fabulous wealth (much of which was treasure plundered from the Byzantine Empire), its unusual waterways and layout, and the picture of stability it was so careful to present to the outside world, made it a unique city. With its *doge* – a ruler appointed for life – its all-important Council of Ten, and its stress on civic ceremonial, Venice gained a reputation for constitutional perfection. The fact that Venice was the only Italian city-state to keep its independence until the end of the 18th century shows that this reputation was to some extent merited. However, the 'myth of Venice' required much nurturing. Secrecy of government, and a geographical position that protected it from the aspirations and depredations of other powers, played their part as well.

the hands of a few); despots, who usually had no title, at least at the outset, had to carry support, be consultative, and distribute jobs, offices or favours to their supporters or potential adversaries. The real development over the 14th century was a shift towards fewer but larger territorial states.

A fragile stability
The early 15th century saw Italy in the grip of large-scale power struggles. Five powers had come to dominate the peninsula. Under Giangaleazzo Visconti (1351–1402), Milan briefly acquired control of most of northern and much of central Italy. In the late 14th century Venice had turned its attention to expansion on the mainland, and for the first time became a major force in Italian politics. In Tuscany, Florence extended its hegemony and settled into increasingly oligarchical government; in 1434 there began the unofficial but powerful rule of the Medici family. The least stable of the five powers were in the south: the papacy, whose policies and allegiances fluctuated; and Naples, which was exper-

iencing the final phase of the Angevin–Aragonese struggle.

From the 1420s, much of Italy was in an almost permanent state of war. By the early 1450s, exhaustion, stalemate, and the growing Turkish threat (▷ p. 114) prompted peace initiatives that culminated in the Peace of Lodi (1454) and the formation of the Italic League (1455), to which all the main powers were signatories.

There followed forty years of precarious balance. In this 'twilight of Italian independence', potential eruptions of violence were contained by the major powers and by fear of outside attack. By this time the rulers of Italy were also increasingly bound by what they had in common. Republican government was largely a thing of the past – in Florence the Medici retained it only in name – and the courts of Italy now shared assumptions about the nature of government and the methods of conducting it. 'Italy of the courts' evolved a common culture, and its rulers settled into more civilized forms of competition – diplomacy, intellectual and artistic patronage. The flourishing of

Renaissance culture (▷ p. 100) owes much to this brief period of comparative tranquillity.

The end of independence
However, storm-clouds were gathering. Two major powers, France and Spain, had developed rapidly over the 15th century, and had built up powerful standing armies. Both had long traditions of territorial claims in Italy, and both were ready to intervene in Italian politics if the alliance of city-states cracked. In the wars that erupted with the French invasion of Italy in 1494 Italy found itself the battleground not because the city-states were of primary importance, but because they were no longer powerful or large enough to survive in a world of developing nation-states. The consequence was over three centuries of foreign occupation.

By 1550 much of the Italian peninsula had been subjugated by the Emperor Charles V (▷ p. 85), through whom Italy passed to the Spanish Habsburgs. They were to hold sway until the Austrians gained control of much of northern Italy in the first half of the 18th century (▷ p. 124).   PD

Medieval and Renaissance Economy and Society

The medieval world was essentially a rural one. It depended on a hard-working peasantry, fair weather and good harvests. At first, in the centuries after the fall of Rome, both people and money were in short supply. There then followed a long period of economic, commercial and population growth. This growth was slow at first – in the 9th and 10th centuries – but then accelerated through the 12th and 13th centuries. The catastrophe of the Black Death brought a century of uncertainty before expansion was resumed in the later 15th century.

Even though the population of Europe in 1600 may have been little greater than in 1300, the basic fact remains that for most of the Middle Ages the population of Europe was a growing one. This meant pressure to bring more land into cultivation and to improve the processing and distribution of basic necessities: food, fuel and clothing. Water mills proliferated, and in the 12th century a new invention, the windmill, provided a supplementary source of power. Bulk-carrying ships were developed and, on land, improved harness design enabled the much faster horse cart to replace the ox cart.

Slaves, serfs and freemen

Throughout these centuries the greater part of the work was done by small tenant farmers (i.e. peasants) and their servants though initially, as in the ancient world, slave labour was employed on many estates. By 1200, however, slavery and the slave trade had both died out in Europe north of the Alps. Some tenants were obliged by the terms of their tenure to work their lord's land as well as their own: those whose obligations were particularly burdensome tended to be called 'serfs' or 'villeins', and after the demise of slavery it was these men who were regarded as 'unfree'. Then the long period of labour shortage following the Black Death in the 14th century (⊳ p. 92) led to the end of serfdom. From then on virtually all tenants either owed a share of their harvest or a money rent; as the volume of coinage in circulation increased, the latter became more common. Thus in northwestern Europe the Middle Ages witnessed the end of both slavery and serfdom – two important moments in the history of liberty.

Medieval farming practices illustrated in a wall painting depicting rural life in the month of April. Medieval farming was characterized by the 'open-field' system in which fields were divided into long strips separated by ridges or furrows. Individuals worked a number of strips scattered in the two or three large fields into which each village's holdings were typically divided. The length of a strip – which usually occupied 0.4 hectare (1 acre) – is believed to be have been determined by the distance an ox could pull a plough without resting.

The 'feudal system'

Most of Europe was dominated by landlords throughout these centuries. Small local landlords owed rent or service or both to greater landlords, and so on all the way up the social hierarchy to the ruler. At each level tenants owed the kind of service – financial, administrative or military – appropriate to their status. Thus tenants of knightly status might be expected to perform 'knight service' in return for 'fiefs', estates granted them by their lords. Historians have often called this kind of society 'feudal' – from the latin *feudum* meaning a fief – though neither the word nor the concept 'feudal' existed in the Middle Ages.

Moreover the 'feudal system' was not a static one. From the 12th and 13th centuries onwards lords increasingly secured men's service by paying them in cash. At the same time the demand for administrators rose sharply – for men who were literate and numerate. To meet this demand schools were founded all over Europe (⊳ p. 100). For men who gave their lords good service there were plenty of opportunities to rise in the world. The economic effect of the adoption of an aristocratic life style by the richer landlords – consuming conspicuously and spending and giving freely – was to redistribute the wealth that otherwise might have accumulated in their hands.

Town life

From the 11th century onwards a rising population led to a massive growth in the number and size of towns through Europe, most of them functioning principally as local markets. Most towns were small by today's standards – though by 1300 London may have had a population of 40 000 and Paris perhaps twice as many. (To put this in perspective, at this period in China there were several cities with populations of a quarter of a million or more; ⊳ p. 53.)

Townspeople struggled to win certain freedoms, notably the right to supervise their own markets and to elect their own magistrates. Successful towns obtained charters from the king – in England and

Scotland such towns became known as boroughs. A characteristic feature of towns everywhere was the existence within them of a number of associations and clubs, known variously to contemporaries as guilds, fraternities, companies or crafts. Some of them were based on particular trades or crafts and were responsible for regulating their members' economic activities, but they also performed a wide range of social, religious and charitable functions.

In the more urbanized parts of Europe many towns – such as Milan, Florence, Cologne and Bruges – were able to become communes, self-governing municipalities capable of independent political action. This was particularly so in northern Italy where a fiercely competitive society of rival city-states, not unlike the society of Classical Greece, had emerged by the 13th century (▷ p. 96). This was the seedbed of the Italian Renaissance (▷ p. 100).

The cloth industry

In the earlier Middle Ages weaving was an essentially small-scale domestic occupation that could be carried on virtually anywhere. But when the vertical loom gave way to the horizontal loom with foot-operated treadles – a technological advance that required permanent housing and skilled workers – cloth-making became an urban industry. In the major towns, especially in the Low Countries and northern Italy, large numbers of wage-earning weavers constituted an urban proletariat, which in periods of recession added to the vigour and turbulence of political life.

The rapidly growing cloth industry of the 12th and 13th centuries required high-quality wool, and this meant prosperity for countries – such as England – that produced it. Flemish and Italian businessmen flocked to England, English wool exports soared, and there was a corresponding demand for luxury woollen cloths from Flanders and Tuscany rather than the local home-spun variety. In the late 13th and 14th centuries – and particularly when they were at war with France (▷ p. 94) – the kings of England levied an increasingly heavy customs duty on wool exports. At times as much as two-thirds of total royal revenue came from this source alone. One – probably unintended – result of this tax regime was to favour the growth of the domestic cloth industry, and consequently to promote the rise of those businessmen who dealt in finished cloth – the Merchant Adventurers. Conversely the once flourishing company of English wool exporters (the Company of the Staple) went into relative decline.

The commercial revolution

Between the 1160s and the early 14th century new sources of silver were discovered in Germany, Sardinia and Bohemia, enabling unprecedented volumes of bullion to be coined and put into circulation. In England, where mint accounts survive from the 13th century, the weight of silver generally minted each year during this period was not regularly exceeded until the 19th century. Local and inter-regional trade expanded.

In 13th-century Italy a critical volume of trade was reached, and a division of labour became possible. The merchant no longer had to accompany his goods wherever they went. It made sense for him to employ specialist carriers for this purpose – both on land and sea – and also to employ resident agents in the places where he regularly did business; this allowed him to stay at home and give all his attention to financial operations. Italian businessmen developed an array of sophisticated financial practices and institutions – double-entry book-keeping, credit finance, stocks and shares, and local and international banking. The creation of negotiable paper had the effect of increasing the money supply yet further. As commercial investments became more routine, so interest rates dropped, from 20% or more at the beginning of the 13th century to 7–10% a hundred years later. Great financial houses, like the Bardi and Peruzzi companies of early 14th-century Florence, were doing business on a scale not to be surpassed for centuries. In the mid-14th century, however, the whole banking system fell into crisis. Banks had been unable to resist the temptation of lending to governments at attractive rates of interest, notably to Edward III of England to finance his attack on France (▷ p. 94). His failure to repay his debts plunged his Italian creditors into bankruptcy and precipitated a collapse of confidence that was then exacerbated by the demographic shock of the Black Death (▷ p. 92). When recovery came it was on a more modest scale. The dealings of even the greatest 15th-century banking house, the Medici of Florence, never matched those of the Bardi and Peruzzi.

Nor indeed did Italian merchants of the 15th century travel as far afield as Marco Polo's father (and others) had done during the course of their 13th-century business trips to China (▷ p. 109). Throughout these centuries the republics of Venice, Pisa and Genoa fought out an intensely competitive struggle for control of the highly lucrative commerce of the Mediterranean (▷ p. 97). In the 12th and 13th centuries the fairs of Champagne played an important role in mediating trade between the south and north of Europe. This trade was boosted by the opening up of the Atlantic route between the Mediterranean and the Channel. Maritime contacts between northern and southern Europe then stimulated those improvements in ship design that made possible the exploration of the Atlantic: the re-discovery of the Canaries, the discovery of the Azores, and the exploration of the West African coast. By the 1440s cargoes of West African gold were being shipped back to Portugal, a portent of the European conquest of the seas of the world in the later 15th and 16th centuries (▷ p. 108). JG

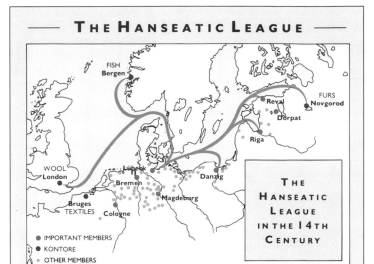

THE HANSEATIC LEAGUE

THE HANSEATIC LEAGUE IN THE 14TH CENTURY

● IMPORTANT MEMBERS
◇ KONTORE
· OTHER MEMBERS

Although they never developed the advanced business methods of the Italians, groups of German merchants from towns such as Lübeck, Hamburg, Cologne and Danzig (now Gdansk in Poland) took advantage of 12th- and 13th-century economic expansion in the Baltic and North Sea areas to establish major trading posts (later known as *Kontore*) at Novgorod, Bergen, London and Bruges. Raw materials from the east (including furs, timber, grain and fish) were exchanged for processed products from the west (such as cloth and wine).

Trade disputes in which the Kontore engaged often had damaging repercussions for the home towns of the merchants concerned. To offset these, in around 1350 the strategically placed Baltic city of Lübeck took the lead in subjecting the Kontore to the authority of a league of towns, the Hansa. At times of crisis, when its domination of Baltic trade was threatened, the Hanseatic League proved capable of organizing naval campaigns as well as economic boycotts and blockades. In its heyday well over 100 towns were members. But changing patterns of trade and, in the 17th century, the rise of Sweden led to its demise (▷ p. 126). The last assembly of a rump of nine Hansa towns met at Lübeck in 1669.

Cloth merchants depicted in a wall painting at Castello Issogne, in the Val d'Aosta, Italy. Associations of merchants and traders – merchant guilds – began to appear in Dutch towns in the 11th century and had spread throughout Western Europe by the end of the 12th century. In England, the Merchant Staplers controlled the export of wool from the 13th to the 16th centuries, although in most of Europe craft guilds – associations of smaller crafts and trades – had eclipsed merchant guilds by the 15th century.

Medieval and Renaissance Culture

After the fall of the western Roman Empire, people in Western Europe gradually lost touch with the centres of culture in the eastern Mediterranean. Much of the learning of the ancient world was lost. What survived the 'Dark Ages' – the 7th to 10th centuries – did so because it was preserved in monasteries. For centuries formal education was not much more than a by-product of religion.

In the 12th and 13th centuries all that changed. Through a variety of channels, classical learning (in philosophy, law and the sciences) was recovered. Schools and universities, medical schools and hospitals were founded. At the same time there was a new architecture – Gothic – and a remarkable flowering of vernacular literature. In the most urbanized region in Europe – northern Italy (▷ p. 96) – a rather different style took root, and by the 16th century Renaissance Italy was setting the fashion for the rest of Europe, a development assisted by a powerful new invention: the printing press.

The monastic centuries

Christianity was adopted as the official religion of the Roman Empire in the 4th century AD, and Christians found that they had become part of the imperial establishment – an experience which was not to the liking of all of them. Many preferred to turn their backs on the material comforts and pleasures that society now offered. In Egypt and Syria – the most urbanized and prosperous parts of the Roman world – so many followed this course that hundreds of new communities dedicated to religious self-denial were established, often in the desert. These were the first monasteries. During the 5th and 6th centuries this style of religious life caught on in the West, and while the Roman cultural world collapsed, monasteries survived, islands of stability, quiet, and traditional learning (▷ p. 90).

For four or five hundred years there were few men (except in Italy, where there always seem to have been town schools) who learned to read and write anywhere but in a monastery school. Moreover, the accumulation of pious gifts over the centuries meant that many monasteries became great landowning corporations, and could afford to employ the finest builders, sculptors and artists. In these circumstances it was probably inevitable that early medieval culture should come to have a distinctly ecclesiastical tinge.

Schools and universities

By the 12th century Western Europe was a more populous and more complex society (▷ p. 98). All over Europe, teachers began to set up new schools, including some in quite small towns and villages. The 'lost' learning of the ancient world was translated out of Arabic into Latin and so made generally available to European scholars (▷ p. 82).

It was in this receptive and expansionist educational environment that the earliest universities – Paris, Bologna and Oxford – were established (by around 1200), and they set a trend that was to last for centuries. By 1500 more than 70 more universities had been founded, among them Cambridge, Prague, Heidelberg and St Andrews. Most students were clerks – in other words, they were nominally churchmen. Relatively few, however, chose to become theologians or parish priests. Most studied for the 'arts' degree; of those who went on to take a higher degree most chose one of what were known as the 'lucrative sciences' – law or medicine. Their ambitions were professional and worldly.

Chivalry and secular culture

Outside the Church there had always of course been another culture – even in the 'Dark Ages'. The Church might have been a rich patron, but the nobles were even richer. However, in the early Middle Ages the culture of the European aristocracy was essentially an illiterate one. Except in Anglo-Saxon England, its ideas and values were rarely fixed in writing and in consequence we know little about them.

But the vernacular literature of the 12th and 13th centuries throws a whole new flood of light on the upper levels of secular society. It shows us the world of chivalry – a society that valued knightly prowess, courage, loyalty, generosity and courtesy (particularly when in the company of ladies). It was a very courtly world. The ideal nobleman was expected not only to be a warrior and huntsman, but also a fine musician, a graceful dancer, an eloquent and shrewd speaker in several languages, and to possess polished manners. The idea of the all-round 'Renaissance man' embodied in *The Book of the Courtier* by Baldassare Castiglione (1478–1529) had in fact been around long before the Renaissance, and one of the reasons for the book's success across Europe was that it was preaching – and with rare eloquence – to an audience that had been converted for centuries.

In the 12th and 13th centuries it became normal for members of the upper classes – gentry as well as business people, women as well as men – to be able to read. Many of them employed clerks to do their writing for them, just as businessmen today employ secretaries. By the 15th century a reading public existed that was large enough to absorb the enormous increase in books produced by the new printing presses (▷ below).

Humanism and the Renaissance

In the 14th century, the Italian poet Petrarch (1304–74) inspired a new kind of enthusiasm for the writings of ancient Greece and Rome – an enthusiasm for their style as well as for their content. Following this lead, a diverse group of scholars, known as the humanists, came to regard classical texts as models for public speaking, writing and conduct. Initially based in northern Italy, by 1500 humanist ideas began to spread to northern Europe, where Erasmus (▷ below and box) was the most important scholar.

Because the humanists laid weight on being able to speak and write like the Roman orator and writer Cicero, this tended to make them contemptuous of all

The Garden of Love was a recurring allegory in medieval literature. In the 12th century a number of writers 'discovered' nature, linking Christian belief with natural beauty in romances of courtly love. Many of these works have a seasonal theme, celebrating the arrival of a new springtime in the garden of love. The garden – as represented in the poem *The Romance of the Rose* by Guillaume de Lorris and Jean de Meung in the 13th century – was portrayed as an enclosed castle garden where an ideal knight wooed his lady. The theme is also pursued in English literature, notably in original works by Chaucer as well as in his translation of *The Romance of the Rose*.

those who had not even tried to do so. Thus they popularized the idea of the 'Dark Ages', a period of supposed barbarism stretching between the ancient world and their own time.

Undoubtedly their enthusiasm for antiquity led them to discover previously unknown classical texts, notably some works by the Greek philosopher Plato. By translating such texts into Latin – for knowledge of Greek remained rare throughout the Renaissance – they made them more widely available. Whether their enthusiasm for classical models led them to a new or 'modern' view of the world and of man's place within it is a question that historians still debate. In 15th-century Florence, humanist language was used to encourage active citizenship and loyalty to the state – but these were qualities of which rulers everywhere approved. Although humanism did not involve a rejection of Christian doctrine, it did undoubtedly focus on man's – as opposed to God's – role in the world, but so also did the 'old-fashioned' secular ideals of chivalry and good lordship.

The importance of printing

In 1450 the first printing press was set up at Mainz in Germany by Johannes Gutenberg. The new technique spread rapidly, particularly in the urbanized regions: 90% of European book production before 1500 was concentrated in Italy and the Rhineland. In 1475 William Caxton introduced the technique into England. Print-

ERASMUS

Desiderius Erasmus (1466–1536), the illegitimate son of a Dutch priest, became an Augustinian canon in 1492 (▷ p. 90). He studied in the Low Countries, England, Italy, Basel and Paris, where he first encountered the humanism that he so eagerly adopted. His *Adagia* – a collection of over 3000 proverbs culled from Greek and Roman writers – established his reputation as the finest Renaissance scholar in northern Europe. Although Erasmus won patronage in several countries, lectured at Cambridge and was awarded a benefice in Kent, he pursued the life of a wandering scholar, seeking the financial means to study in comfort. His edition of the New Testament appeared in 1516, with an elegant Latin version alongside. On the basis of this translation – and his appended critical notes – Erasmus is often cited as the first New Testament scholar. In 1517 – after an absence of over 20 years – he was recalled to his order, but obtained a dispensation from Pope Leo X allowing him to live in the world. Although Erasmus had criticized the Church, he attempted to act as a mediator between Rome and Luther (1519–21; ▷ p. 110). However, he became increasingly alienated from the reformers, many of whom had initially supported him. In old age Erasmus turned down the belated offer of high clerical office.

Erasmus, as portrayed by the Flemish painter Quentin Massys.

ing – pictures as well as words – meant that writers could reach a much larger international audience than ever before.

When the Florentine, Niccolò Machiavelli, argued in his book *The Prince* that the need to ensure the survival of the state justified acts that otherwise might be regarded as immoral, he was not doing much more than laying bare the way governments had always acted – but in the new world of the printed book this was

enough to make his name synonymous with duplicity. More importantly, when the Dutch scholar Desiderius Erasmus edited the Greek New Testament, and when in letters and tracts such as *In Praise of Folly* he called for Church reform, his words, now in print, reached minds and hearts that earlier writers had failed to reach. This anticipated the way in which printing was to play a crucial role in the spread of the Reformation (▷ p. 110). JG

The Procession of the Magi, part of a fresco cycle in the chapel of the Medici-Riccardi Palace in Florence, by Benozzo Gozzoli (1420–97). The confidence and detail of Gozzoli's work reflects the growing interest in nature and landscape. This series of frescos also illustrates the development of the art of portraiture in the 15th century. Various members of the Medici family, including Gozzoli's patron, Lorenzo the Magnificent (▷ p. 96) – in pride of place at the head of the procession – appear in the picture. The inclusion of the artist's patrons in historical roles was a form of flattery that gained considerable currency during the period.

SEE ALSO

● POPES, SAINTS AND HERETICS p. 90
● ITALY OF THE CITY-STATES p. 96
● MEDIEVAL AND RENAISSANCE ECONOMY AND SOCIETY p. 98
● THE REFORMATION p. 110

Medieval and Renaissance Warfare

The medieval period was an age of military innovation, reflected in major developments in fortification, weaponry, protective armour and shipbuilding. Technological advances produced superior siege artillery and gunpowder weapons; huge bombards forced military architects to change from tall to thick walls; ships developed from shallow Viking longships and Mediterranean galleys to towering galleons deploying broadsides of cannon.

In theory, warfare was fought in accordance with internationally accepted codes, but it was always the peasantry who suffered. War was characterized as one of the 'Four Horsemen of the Apocalypse' and often brought the other three – death, disease and starvation – in its wake.

Warfare and social structures

The political structure of early medieval Europe dictated the type of warfare that was practised. There was no large, centralized state on the lines of the Roman Empire, and the rulers of its successor kingdoms relied upon the loyalty of individual magnates to provide them with forces in time of need.

However, effective rulers could harness

A 15th–century knight. The main weapon used during charges would have been a lance. When riding into battle, a shield would probably not have been carried as the development of such effective plate armour had by this time made it superfluous.

Labels (clockwise): Crinet, Bascinet, Chanfron, Pavloron, Flanchard, Couter, Vambrace, Sword, Shield displaying coat of arms, Sabaton, Greave, Poleyn, Cuisse, Tasset, Breastplate

such resources for both conquest and defence. The conquests of Charlemagne (778–814) were not to be surpassed until Napoleonic times (▷ p. 146). It used to be thought that the introduction of the stirrup into Western Europe was the motor for Carolingian expansion, on the grounds that it provided them with an irresistible cavalry in the form of mounted knights. This technological explanation now seems unlikely. The 'couched lance' technique that stirrups made possible did not develop until as late as the 11th century. Exaggeration of the effectiveness of the mounted knight is part of the 'chivalric myth'; it underplays the significance of other resources such as infantry, engineers and logistical support. Charlemagne's victories were made possible by central direction and organization of wagon trains of supplies, allied to a careful fortress policy – not by the rash charges of paladins.

In subsequent centuries control of fortifications descended to local level. In 864 the Frankish king forbade the construction of castles without royal consent. Despite this, in 10th- and 11th-century France lords of castles enjoyed a high degree of local independence and power. In the 12th century, principally in England and France, but also elsewhere in Europe, administrative reforms made possible much larger armies and impressive programmes of fortification. Edward I's armies, for example, were larger than any raised by the Tudors. His achievement in conquering Wales (permanently) and Scotland (temporarily) shows what could be done. His grandson, Edward III, used small but professional armies to conquer large parts of France, and Henry V achieved similar successes at a later stage of the Hundred Years War (▷ pp. 94–5). However, once the French kings gained a closer grip on their country's resources they regained control. Philip II (1180–1223) had begun this process, and his grandson Louis IX (1226–70) was able to pursue a crusading career as a result (▷ p. 88). But the loosely organized French kingdom, still dependent upon feudal troops, remained vulnerable to English attack in the 14th and early 15th centuries. Reorganization under Charles VII and Louis XI in the mid-15th century, especially using artillery and fortification, helped the French to victory in the Hundred Years War and pointed the way to 16th-century developments.

Battle tactics and chivalry

The idea that medieval warfare was dominated by the charge of mounted knights is a false one. The knights' superiority was social rather than tactical. Good cavalry, well used, could be a battle winner, but more often than not wise commanders dismounted their knights. The English did this frequently in the 12th century, and it was an almost universal practice on both sides in the Hundred Years War. Missile power in combination was also much sought after – the bow and crossbow were the preferred long-range weapons. The English bowmen of the 14th and 15th centuries were effective because of their massed and disciplined shooting rather

than because the bow was in itself a 'super-weapon'. The power of massed archers prefigured the fire of arquebus and musket, which developed from early handguns to be the dominant force on battlefields after 1600.

Chivalry was a code of conduct that laid down how men were expected to behave when at court or when jousting (▷ p. 100). However, on the field of battle the leaders of the cult of chivalry were as professional and as ruthless as soldiers anywhere. Chivalry, especially as represented by the pageantry of heraldry, was practised at times, and there were accepted 'laws of war' that restrained behaviour and laid down conventions for the surrender of fortresses. But this was no more than a gloss on the realities of warfare, which were as brutal then as now.

Castles

A castle might be no more than an enclosure surrounded by a ditch, bank and palisade. The motte-and-bailey type had the additional security of a tall, man-made mound topped by a timber tower (▷ illustration). They were especially popular at the time of the Norman Conquest, as the English countryside still bears witness, but they continued in use long after 1066 (▷ p. 87). Nor was the transition from early use of timber to later use of stone entirely clear-cut. Tall stone towers known as 'donjons' were already being constructed in 10th-century Anjou – the 11th-century White Tower in the Tower of London is a good example of this type of keep. In the 12th century outer, or 'curtain', walls were built to provide another line of defence. The rebuilding that took place in the 12th and 13th centuries replaced basic earthwork and timber fortifications with vastly more expensive stone walls. High stone walls and towers were designed to counter the high-trajectory siege catapults of the period.

Some of the finest examples of medieval military architecture are found in the Levant, where the beleaguered Crusaders had to make stones do the work of men. Krak des Chevaliers, in northern Syria, was built with all the enormous resources of the Knights Hospitaller (▷ pp. 88 and 89). A further development came in the form of the concentric castles built by Edward I of England to hold down the Welsh. Castles needed to be as invulnerable as possible, partly because garrisons were small, but also to allow defenders to hold off besieging armies until the arrival of relieving forces. Battles were often brought about by such a clash.

Castles were not just means of defence, but also huge storehouses and bases for raids – for the role of the households of knights was to ravage an enemy's territory and destroy his political authority. Medieval states did not always have well-defined borders in the modern sense, but were often separated by areas known as 'marches', where raiding activity was practised by both sides. The Vexin between Normandy and France and the Border country between England and Scotland are examples of this kind of disputed land.

Chevauchée

The 'chevauchée', or ride through enemy lands, was a destructive raid in which crops and villages were burnt and movable booty looted. The Black Prince engaged in a chevauchée from Bordeaux to the Mediterranean in 1355. In the following year he marched north to Tours but was caught by the French at Poitiers. The ensuing battle ended in a significant victory for the English, but such encounters were not generally sought after. For all that battle was celebrated in chivalric literature it was usually avoided by medieval commanders.

Siege warfare

The network of fortification – castles, walled towns and defended ports – usually dictated the course of a campaign. The preferred method of capturing a stronghold was blockade and starvation of the defenders. But sometimes more immediate action was required. A great deal of ingenuity went into devising ways of breaking down the stone walls of the defender. The three means of attack were 'over' (by assault), 'under' (by mining), or 'through' (by battery) – often used in combination. However, bribing a traitor within – the crucial factor in the Norman leader Bohemond's capture of Antioch in 1098 (⊳ p. 88) – was to be preferred to all of these.

Before an assault it was first necessary to make a breach. Mines were dug underneath walls or towers, shored up with timber and filled with combustibles. As the supports burnt away the stonework crashed into the void. Counter-mining by the defenders and water-filled ditches often neutralized this form of attack. Stone-throwing engines were used for battering walls. Many were of the classical type: single-armed machines worked by torsion or functioned like giant crossbows. In the 12th century the trebuchet – a huge sling hanging from a beam counterweighted at its base – was introduced from China via the Islamic world.

In the 14th century gunpowder weapons began to appear. They rapidly developed into huge bombards such as the Ottoman Turks used to destroy the previously invulnerable walls of Constantinople in 1453 (⊳ pp. 81 and 114). Old-style walls – which depended upon height for their effectiveness – began to be replaced by

lower, immensely thick defences with 'bastion' towers of rubble and brick that absorbed the impact of the shot. Bastions were also gun platforms, enabling the defenders to hit back at any attacker. They were first developed in Italy around 1400 and soon spread to northern Europe. They were the basis of the 'scientific fortification' devised by Louis XIV's military engineer Vauban and others in the 17th century.

War at sea

Medieval fleets could not control the seas – the size of the ships and their technical limitations would not allow this – but they were still of great strategic importance. The Mediterranean was dominated by the galley fleets of the Italian city-states (⊳ p. 96). Venetian, Pisan and Genoan vessels transported men, horses and supplies to the Holy Land. Italian and Iberian fleets also traded with Flanders, where Castilian ships were employed by the king of France against England during the Hundred Years War. In northern waters, the Norman Conquest of England was made possible by an amphibious assault using Viking longships (⊳ p. 87). In the 12th and 13th centuries northern shipwrights developed two- and three-deck roundships or 'cogs' capable of carrying up to 1000 men. When equipped with cannon in the 15th century it was ships of this type that were to dominate the sea-lanes of the world until the 19th century.   MB

The battle of Nájera, 3 April 1367, as depicted in Froissart's chronicles. An English army under Edward the Black Prince, in alliance with Peter the Cruel of Castile, routed the forces of Peter's usurping half-brother. Contrary to popular opinion – and images such as this – medieval commanders found it most effective tactically to dismount their knights.

FORTIFICATION

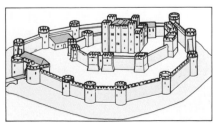

11th century: motte and bailey

12th–13th centuries: stone castle

14th century onwards: bastion

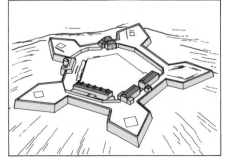

SEE ALSO

- ANCIENT WARFARE p. 44
- THE BARBARIAN KINGDOMS p. 78
- THE BYZANTINE EMPIRE p. 80
- VIKINGS AND NORMANS p. 86
- THE CRUSADES p. 88
- THE HUNDRED YEARS WAR p. 94

BROADENING HORIZONS

NORTHWESTERN EUROPE	CENTRAL EUROPE	EASTERN EUROPE	THE CHURCH
1500 France conquered the Duchy of Milan **1511** England, Aragon, the papacy and Venice formed a Holy League against France **1513** English army under Henry VIII invaded France **1513** Scotland defeated by the English at Flodden Field **1523** Gustavus Vasa elected as king of Sweden **1529** Peace of Cambrai between France and Spain temporarily halted the Habsburg–Valois Wars **1533–5** The English Reformation began – Henry VIII broke with Rome and made himself Head of the Church in England	**1512** Diet of Cologne established Ten Circles as the basis for the government of Holy Roman Empire **1519** Charles V became Holy Roman Emperor **1525** German Peasants' War crushed by German princes **1529** Vienna besieged by the Turks **1531** The Protestant German states formed the League of Schmalkalden against Charles V **1534–5** Anabaptist rule in Münster, Germany **1538** Catholic German princes formed the League of Nuremberg	**by 1500** Ottoman (Turkish) conquest of Bosnia, Albania and the Peloponnese completed **1512–20** Ottoman Empire doubled in size under Selim I **1520–66** Suleiman the Magnificent Ottoman sultan **1522** Knights of St John expelled from Rhodes by the Turks **1526** Battle of Mohács – Ottoman army defeated and annexed Hungary	**1517** Luther nailed the 95 Theses to the door of Wittenberg church **1520** Luther excommunicated **1533–5** The English Reformation began **1534** Foundation of the Jesuits **1536** Calvin's first radical Protestant treatise published **1541–63** Council of Trent launched the Counter-Reformation
1558–1603 Elizabeth I, queen of England **1559–98** French Wars of Religion **1567** Revolt of Protestant Dutch against Spanish rule began **1572** St Bartholomew's Day Massacre of French Huguenots **1581** Dutch declared independence from Spain **1584** Assassination of William the Silent **1587** Execution of Mary, Queen of Scots **1588** Spanish Armada attempted to invade England **1589** Henry of Navarre became the first Bourbon king of France	**1552** War between Saxony and Charles V **1555** Peace of Augsburg recognized Lutheranism **1556** Abdication of Charles V **1561** Baltic lands of the Teutonic Order secularized **1597–1651** Maximilian I, elector of Bavaria, founder of the Catholic League in the Thirty Years War	**1533–84** Ivan IV (the Terrible) **1553** Chancellor reached Moscow via the North Cape **1566–74** Selim II annexed Venetian possessions in the Aegean **1571** Fleet of the Holy League defeated the Ottomans at Lepanto	**1559** Church of England re-established on the basis of the 39 Articles **1596** Catholic influence in Poland and the Ukraine extended by the Union of Brest-Litovsk **1598** Edict of Nantes recognized rights of the Huguenots in France **by 1600** Most of northern and parts of Central Europe had become Protestant
1603 James VI of Scotland became James I of England **1605** Catholic Gunpowder Plot against James I **1611–32** Gustavus Adolphus, king of Sweden **1624–42** Cardinal Richelieu, chief minister of France **1635** Outbreak of Franco-Spanish war **1641–9** Catholic Irish revolt suppressed by Cromwell **1642–9** Civil War in England – Parliamentarians deposed and beheaded Charles I and declared a republic **1643** Spain defeated by France at battle of Rocroi **1648** Dutch independence recognized	**1618–48** Thirty Years War – a complex series of struggles resulting from political and religious tensions in Central Europe **1620** Bohemia reconquered by the Habsburgs at the battle of the White Mountain **1630** Swedes under Gustavus Adolphus invaded Germany **1632** Battle of Lützen – Gustavus Adolphus killed **1640–88** Frederick William (The Great Elector) created a centralized state in Brandenburg **1648** Peace of Westphalia intensified the political divisions of Germany	**1613** Romanov dynasty came to power in Russia **early 17th century** Beginning of the administrative and social decay of the Ottoman Empire **1640s–60s** Rapid decline and disintegration in Poland **1645–69** Crete taken from the Venetians by the Ottomans	**early 17th century** Roman Catholic Church sought to suppress Copernicanism **after 1605** Increase in anti-Catholic legislation in England **1611** The Authorized Version of the Bible published in English **1623** Protestant worship forbidden in Bohemia **1648** Society of Friends (Quakers) founded
1643–1715 Louis XIV of France created an absolute monarchy and pursued an aggressive foreign policy **1652–4, 1664–7 and 1672–4** Anglo-Dutch naval wars **1653–8** Oliver Cromwell, Lord Protector of England **1659** Peace of the Pyrenees ended Franco-Spanish war **1660** Restoration of the monarchy in England under Charles II **1688–9** The 'Glorious Revolution' marked beginning of constitutional monarchy in England **1688–97** Nine Years War – English-led alliance against Louis XIV	**1657** Brandenburg acquired Duchy of Prussia **1683** Last Turkish attack on Vienna **1686** The Emperor Leopold I, Saxony, Bavaria, Spain and Sweden formed the League of Augsburg against France **1687** Battle of Mohács – Habsburgs defeated the Ottoman Turks to take control of Hungary	**1667** Russian annexation of Kiev **1674** Jan Sobieski became king of Poland **1682–1725** Peter the Great modernized Russia **1691** Habsburgs conquered Transylvania **end of 17th century** Ottoman Empire ruled by Köprülü grand viziers	**1653** Jansenism declared a heresy **1656** Pascal in his *Provincial Letters* attacked casuistry and the Jesuits **1666** Great Schism in Russia **1685** Edict of Nantes revoked in France
1701–13 War of the Spanish Succession **1706** Marlborough defeated the French at Ramillies and conquered the Spanish Netherlands **1707** Act of Union between England and Scotland **1713** Treaty of Utrecht ended the War of the Spanish Succession **1714** George, elector of Hanover, succeeded to the British throne **1715 and 1745–6** Jacobite rebellions in Britain **1721–42** Sir Robert Walpole was effectively the first 'prime minister' of Britain	**1704** Anglo-Austrian force defeated the French at Blenheim **1713** Pragmatic Sanction of Charles VI declared that all Habsburg lands were to pass undivided to his daughter **1713–40** Frederick William I, king of Prussia – Prussian army reformed **1740** Prussia seized Silesia from Austria – beginning of the War of the Austrian Succession **1740–86** Frederick the Great expands Prussian territory in Germany and Poland **1740–80** Maria Theresa, ruler of Austria **1748** War of the Austrian Succession ended in Treaty of Aix-la-Chapelle	**1700** Start of the Northern War between Russia and Sweden **1703** Peter the Great began the construction of St Petersburg **1709** Russia defeated Sweden in the battle of Poltava **1718** Austria took northern Serbia from the Ottomans **1721** Treaty of Nystad ended Northern War – Swedish Baltic lands ceded to Russia	**1713** Papal bull *Unigenitas* condemned Jansenist doctrines **1730s** John and Charles Wesley began to found Methodism in England **1722–31** Expulsion of Protestants from Archbishopric of Salzburg
1756–63 Seven Years War **1756–7, 1757–61 and 1766–8** Pitt the Elder in power in Britain **1770** The Parlements temporarily abolished in France **1772** Gustavus III of Sweden broke the power of the nobles and established an autocracy **1778–83** Anglo-French War **1780** Armed Neutrality of the North formed to protect neutral ships from Britain **1783–1801** Pitt the Younger, British prime minister **1785–7** Republican Dutch Estates in revolt against the stadholders **1787** French Assembly of Notables dismissed **1789** Beginning of the French Revolution	**1753–92** Kaunitz, chancellor of Austria **1756** The Diplomatic Revolution – alliance between Austria and France **1756** Prussia invaded Saxony – start of the Seven Years War **1759** France defeated by Britain and Hanover at Minden **1763** Prussia confirmed as a great power by the Treaty of Paris **1780–90** Enlightened despotism of Joseph II, ruler of Austria **1785** Prussia formed League of German Princes against Austria	**1762–96** Catherine II 'the Great' reformed Russia and annexed territory from the Ottoman Turks and Poland **1772** First partition of Poland between Austria, Prussia and Russia **1774** Russia gained an outlet to the Black Sea by the Treaty of Kuchuk Kainardji **1783–4** Russia annexed the Crimea	**1764** Jesuits expelled from France **1767** Jesuits expelled from Naples and Spain **1769** Dissolution of many monasteries in Austria **1773** Suppression of the Jesuits **1770s and 1780s** Threats of schism from Catholic Church in Austria and Germany

SOUTHERN EUROPE	THE AMERICAS	CULTURE AND SOCIETY	REST OF THE WORLD
1500 Treaty of Granada – France and Spain partitioned Italy **1508** League of Cambrai concluded between Aragon, France and the Holy Roman Empire against Venice **1512** France defeated at Ravenna and driven from Italy **1515** France defeated the Holy League at Marignano **1525** Francis I of France defeated and captured by Charles V at Pavia **1527** Army of Charles V sacked Rome **1530** Knights of St John installed on Malta	**1500** Cabral discovered Brazil **1502** Vespucci explored the eastern coast of South America **1519–21** Cortez overthrew the Aztec Empire in Mexico **1531–3** Pizarro subdued the Inca Empire in Peru **1534** Cartier's first voyage to the St Lawrence	**c. 1466–1536** Erasmus, humanist and leading scholar of the northern Renaissance **1475–1564** Michelangelo, Florentine sculptor, painter and poet **1510–46** Peak of prosperity of the Fugger family of German bankers **1513** Machiavelli's *The Prince* **1526** Tynedale's English translation of the Bible printed **1531** Foundation of the Antwerp bourse **1543** Copernicus argued that the sun was at the centre of the universe	**c. 1500** Start of West African slave trade **1510** Portuguese captured Goa **1514** Ottoman Turks defeated the Safavid Persians at Chaldiran **1516–17** Syria and Egypt conquered by the Ottomans **1519–22** First circumnavigation of the world by Magellan and Del Cano **1534** Ottomans annexed Mesopotamia
1556 Philip II became ruler of the Spanish Empire after the abdication of his father, Charles V **1565** Ottoman Turks besieged Malta **1580** Portugal annexed by Spain **1596** English force sacked Cadiz **by 1600** The Spanish Empire comprised the Iberian Peninsula, most of Latin America, parts of Italy and the Netherlands, and the East Indies	**late 16th century** Spanish and Portuguese settlements established in many coastal areas of South and Central America **1562–7** Hawkins' voyages to the West Indies **1583** Gilbert attempted to found an English colony in Newfoundland **1585–7** Unsuccessful attempts to found an English colony in Virginia	**16th century** Flourishing of Venetian art, including that of Titian (c. 1487/90–1576); apogee of sacred polyphony in the music of Palestrina (c. 1525–84) **Late 16th–mid-17th century** Cultural golden age in England – dramas of Shakespeare (1564–1616), music of Byrd and Dowland, poetry of Donne and Milton **1569** Mercator invented navigation charts based on the projection that bears his name **late 16th century** Galileo Galilei (1564–1642) investigated the motion of objects falling freely in air **c. 1580** Potatoes first imported into Europe from South America	**1550–60** Samurai civil war in Japan **1556–1605** Akbar raised Mogul Empire in India to its highest pitch of success **1557** Portuguese established in Macao **1565** Destruction of the Indian empire of Vijayanagar **1574** Ottomans ousted Spain from Tunis **1595** Dutch trading posts established in the East Indies
17th century Naples and Sicily under Spanish rule **1610** Moriscos (Christian Moors) expelled from Spain **1640** Portuguese and Catalans rebelled against centralized rule from Madrid **1647–8** Revolt in Naples against Spanish rule **1652** Catalan revolt suppressed	**early 17th century** Spanish colonies in Latin America became self-sufficient; colonial trade declined **1607** Foundation of the English settlement at Jamestown **1608** Foundation of the French colony of Quebec **1625** Dutch colony of New Amsterdam (later New York) **1624–54** Dutch occupation of part of Brazil	**17th century** In music, modes gave way to modern tonality **early 17th century** Dutch painting flourished; High Baroque art and architecture in Italy; rise of Classicism **1607** Monteverdi's opera, *Orfeo* **1609** Janssen invented the microscope **1618–48** 30–60% of the population of Germany perished during the Thirty Years War **1628** Harvey published his discovery of the circulation of the blood **c. 1620–c. 1670** Period of economic recession in Europe **1637** Descartes's *Discourse on Method*	**1600** English East India Company founded **1600** Tokugawa shogunate established in Japan **1602** Dutch East India Company founded **1642** Tasman discovered Tasmania and New Zealand and explored the coasts of Australia **1644** Qing (Manchu) dynasty came to power in China
1668 Independence of Portugal recognized **1694–1700** Venetian campaigns against the Ottomans – last period of Venetian power **1700** Philip, duke of Anjou, inherited the Spanish throne as the first Bourbon king of Spain **2nd half of 17th century** Marked political, economic and military decline of Spain	**1670** Hudson's Bay Company chartered **1675–6** Indian war against New England settlers **by 1700** Chain of French forts and trading posts established from Quebec to Louisiana	**1651** Hobbes's treatise on government, *Leviathan* **from c. 1637** Flowering of Neoclassical French literature – dramas of Corneille, Molière and Racine **1665 and 1666** Great Plague and Great Fire of London **1670–1700** Transformation of the palace of Versailles **1687** Newton formulated laws of motion and gravitation in the *Principia* **1690** Locke's two *Treatises on Government*	**c. 1650–1750** Oyo Empire flourished in West Africa **1652** Dutch Cape Colony founded **1658–1707** Decline of the Mogul Empire in India under Aurangzeb **1689** Russo-Chinese Treaty of Nerchinsk, first between China and a European state
1704 English forces took Gibraltar **1718** Foundation of the kingdom of Sardinia **1727–0** Spanish siege of Gibraltar **1737** Tuscany came under Habsburg rule **1748** Kingdom of Sardinia made territorial gains by Aix-la-Chapelle peace settlement	**1689–1763** Anglo-French colonial wars in North America **1713** France ceded Nova Scotia to Britain **1729** North and South Carolina became Crown colonies **1746** Britain captured Louisburg **1751** Georgia became a Crown colony	**18th century** Boom in colonial trade; increase in size and wealth of the middle class in Western Europe **early 18th century** Growth of popularity of the novel **1709** Darby produced coke and used it to smelt iron **1712** Corelli's *Concerti Grossi* published – concerto grosso spread throughout Europe **c. 1730** Townshend introduced four-crop rotation **1734** Voltaire's *Lettres philosophiques* **1740** Hume's *Treatise of Human Nature* further developed empiricist philosophy **1741** Handel's *Messiah*	**c. 1700/50–1901** Kingdom of Ashanti flourished in West Africa **early 18th century** Local rulers took power in India, destroying the Mogul Empire **1720s–40s** Rise of the Marathas in India **1739** Nadir Shah, ruler of Persia, defeated the Mogul Empire and sacked Delhi
1755 Beginning of Paoli's Corsican rebellion against Genoa **1755–77** Chief Minister Pombal carried out reforms and curbed the power of the Church in Portugal **1761** Treaty of Ildefonso, Franco-Spanish Bourbon family pact **1779–82** Unsuccessful Franco-Spanish siege of Gibraltar **1780** British fleet under Rodney defeated the Spanish fleet off Cape St Vincent **1789** Accession of the last doge of Venice	**1759** British force under Wolfe captured Quebec from France **1760s–80s** Great growth of French West Indian trade **1763** Britain acquired Canada and Louisiana east of the Mississippi **1772** Boston Assembly threatened secession from Britain **1774** Continental Congress issued the Declaration of Rights **1776** American Declaration of Independence **1776–83** American War of Independence **1783** Peace of Paris recognized American independence **1787–9** American Constitution drawn up	**c. 1750** The peak of the Enlightenment; beginning of the Industrial Revolution in Britain **from 1750** Development of sonata form – spread of the Classical symphony **1751–72** Diderot's *Encyclopédie* **1755** Lisbon earthquake; Johnson's *Dictionary of the English Language* **1762** Rousseau's *Social Contract* **1769** Watt improves the steam engine **1774** Crompton's spinning mule **1776** Adam Smith's *Wealth of Nations* **late 18th century** Spread of idealist philosophy in Germany (originating with Kant) – roots of the Romantic movement; *Sturm und Drang* movement in literature dominated by Goethe (1749–1832) and Schiller **end of 18th century** Growth in parts of Western Europe of religious and humanitarian opposition to slavery	**c. 1750** Tokyo became the world's largest city **1751** British force under Clive captured Arcot and weakened French power in India **1756–63** Seven Years War – Britain acquired vast new territories in India **1756** The 'Black Hole of Calcutta' **1757** Battle of Plassey – British rule began to be established in Bengal **1768–71, 1772–5 and 1775–9** Cook's voyages of discovery in the Pacific **1788** First British settlement in Australia

The Age of Discovery

In 1400 Western Europe was by no means the most advanced of the world's cultures. Despite trade and other links with Asia and North Africa, Europeans were either ignorant of, or lacked contact with, most other civilizations. However, in the 15th and 16th centuries Europeans – in particular the Spanish and Portuguese – took the lead in undertaking ambitious voyages overseas, discovering hitherto unknown lands and civilizations, and establishing new links with known ones.

This process was crucial for the long-term development of a relationship between Europe and the rest of the world that persisted almost to the present day (▷ p. 200).

European exploration to 1400

Individuals had always attempted to advance beyond the limits of the known world. In the 11th century, a group of Vikings had briefly settled in North America (▷ p. 86). The main spur to exploration was trade. Merchants particularly wished to reach the East (the Indies), whose goods – above all spices – were in great demand in Europe and a source of enormous profit to those who sold them. Merchants, particularly from Genoa in Italy, and from Catalonia in the Spanish kingdom of Aragon, played a leading part in overseas exploration.

At the end of the 13th century the Venetian Marco Polo travelled overland to China (▷ box). The Genoese (and later

Marco Polo leaving Venice with his father, Niccolo, and his uncle, Maffeo, in 1271. Their journey took them through the Middle East, Iran, Afghanistan and Central Asia to China, where they stayed for 16 or 17 years. Marco's account of his travels – *Il milione* (better known in English as *The Travels of Marco Polo*) – came to be popularly regarded as romance rather than a serious historical and geographical work. For example, Samuel Taylor Coleridge turned the description of the Mongol capital Shang-tu into the fable of Xanadu.

the Venetians; ▷ p. 97) also began to send ships regularly from the Mediterranean into the Atlantic (and so to northern Europe). Henceforth, European ships made regular voyages down the Atlantic coast of Africa. The Canary Islands were discovered in 1341, while a Catalan expedition may have reached Senegal as early as 1346. However, partly due to the effects on the European economy of the Black Death (▷ p. 92), these successes were hardly followed up before 1400.

Chinese voyages

Sophisticated maritime skills, technological superiority and trading connections made early Ming China (▷ p. 56) rather better equipped to embark on ambitious voyages of discovery than late 14th- and early 15th-century Europe. Ming China was particular well-placed to open up the Indian Ocean and to establish trading contacts with the eastern coast of Africa. The Chinese were more advanced than Europe in shipbuilding and in navigational techniques, and had a tradition of trade with India, southern Arabia, and parts of east Africa. At the end of the 14th century the Chinese government initiated an ambitious programme of military and trading voyages overseas (▷ box).

The abrupt ending of this policy after 1431 was probably due to the triumph at the imperial court of the mandarins (scholarly officials). They believed that the promotion of trade for profit was unnecessary as China was so rich in resources and – above all – that trade was an inferior activity which the emperor should not engage in. The mandarins advocated that the emperor should devote himself to a high-minded pursuit of moral and spirit-

ual excellence in government and that the money spent on the voyages would be better used to improve the landward defences of the Chinese empire. The triumph of the mandarins reinforced a sense of Chinese superiority over foreigners. As a result, China became more inward-looking and less sympathetic to overseas exploration.

The renewal of the European advance

The abandonment of further exploration by the Chinese left the field to Europe, which was politically and socially very different from Ming China. European merchants often influenced government policy, and competing princes were eager to seize the opportunities offered by trade and conquest.

The breakup of the Mongol empire and the expansion of the Ottomans in the 14th century (▷ pp. 55 and 114) made overland trade and travel between Europe and Asia much harder. Venetian merchants were able to obtain spices through Egypt and Syria, establishing a monopoly that contributed to the enormous wealth and power of the Venetian republic in the 15th century (▷ p. 97). But their Spanish and Portuguese trading rivals sought alternative routes to the wealth of the Indies. Believing that it was possible to sail around Africa, they turned their attention to the Atlantic.

The Iberian contribution

The Iberian realms of Portugal, Castile and Aragon were well placed to explore the Atlantic because of their geographical position, their maritime strength, and the role of Genoese and Catalan merchants who provided a ready market

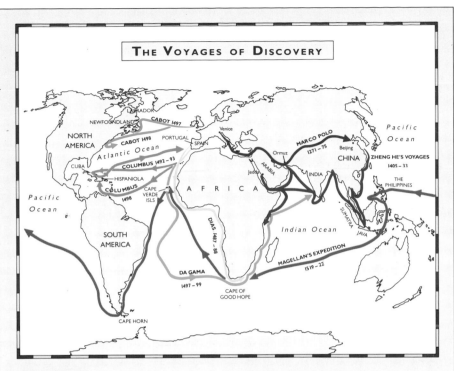

THE VOYAGES OF DISCOVERY

Marco Polo (c. 1254–1324)
Trade between Europe and China along the Silk Route (⊳ p. 56) had long been established, and in 1260–9 Marco Polo's father and uncle made a trading expedition there. Marco Polo accompanied them on their second expedition, reaching China in 1275. There he entered the service of the emperor, Kublai Khan, and remained in China until 1292.

Zheng He (or Cheng Ho; died c. 1433)
In the early 15th century China was also expanding its horizons and Admiral Zheng He led several expeditions to India, Arabia and the coast of East Africa. At this point, however, the Chinese government decided against further exploration.

Bartolomeu Dias (?1450–1500)
In 1488 the Portuguese navigator Bartolomeu Dias rounded the Cape of Good Hope and could report that a sea route to the spices and other wealth of the East now lay open.

Vasco da Gama (1469–1524)
Setting out from Portugal in 1497, da Gama followed a slightly different course to that of Dias and reached Calicut on the southwest coast of India, returning home in 1499. The route from Portugal to the East was now confirmed.

Christopher Columbus (1451–1506)
Because the Italian navigator Christopher Columbus believed that the world was much smaller than it is, he was confident that he could reach the East by sailing west. It had been known for centuries that the world was round, but for a long time Columbus' schemes were rejected by experts who had a much more accurate idea of the actual size of the globe. Not until 1492 was he given the backing of the Spanish Crown. His flotilla of three ships led by the *Santa Maria* reached the Bahamas in 33 days. On subsequent voyages Columbus reached the American mainland. He died still convinced, however, that he had reached the East, or the Indies, hence the name 'West Indies'.

John Cabot (c. 1450–?98)
An Italian navigator in the service of Henry VII of England, Cabot discovered Cape Breton Island in 1497, and is sometimes credited with the discovery of North America – though the Vikings had reached there, via Iceland and Greenland, five hundred years earlier.

Ferdinand Magellan (c. 1480–1521)
A Portuguese navigator sponsored by Spain, in 1519 Magellan set off with five ships to seek a western route to the East Indies. He negotiated the strait later named after him between Tierra del Fuego and the South American mainland. The expedition crossed the Pacific and reached the East Indies in 1521, where Magellan was killed. Only one ship returned to Spain in 1522, so completing the first circumnavigation of the world.

used as slaves to work the developing sugar plantations of the Canary Islands and the Azores (discovered in 1427). In North Africa European cloth and wheat were exchanged for gold brought from the Sudan by the caravans of the Sahara. This gold helped finance Europe's unfavourable trade balance with the East.

Henry's ships had discovered Africa to be much bigger than expected. Despite this apparent difficulty, John II of Portugal (1481–95) continued to sponsor voyages of exploration down the west coast of Africa in the hope of finding a sea route to India and breaking the Venetian spice monopoly. This aim was to be realized by Vasco da Gama (⊳ box).

The Portuguese expeditions provided training in Atlantic navigation for men like the Genoese Christopher Columbus. After a decade of unsuccessful attempts to find sponsorship, he found patrons in the rulers of the recently united kingdoms of Aragon and Castile (⊳ p. 116). Portuguese achievements had convinced Ferdinand and Isabella of the possibilities offered by voyages of exploration. Columbus's initial successes stimulated further Spanish efforts (⊳ box, and p. 116).

The achievement

By the early 16th century, Europeans had established sea links with India and the Americas, and charted lands and seas hitherto unknown. Some parts of the world remained undiscovered, and the process of exploration would continue into subsequent centuries (⊳ p. 128). European domination of the world was not yet inevitable, but the first steps towards it had unquestionably been taken.   CS

SEE ALSO
● CHINA FROM THE MONGOLS TO THE MANCHU p. 56
● MEDIEVAL AND RENAISSANCE ECONOMY AND SOCIETY p. 98
● MEDIEVAL AND RENAISSANCE CULTURE p. 100
● THE SPANISH AND PORTUGUESE EMPIRES p. 116
● COLONIAL EXPANSION IN THE 17TH AND 18TH CENTURIES p. 128

The *Victoria*, the only one of Magellan's fleet of five ships to return to Spain after circumnavigating the world. The ship returned with only 17 survivors from the expedition, but with its hold full of spices from the Moluccas. More importantly – by rounding the tip of South America on the outward voyage and returning by the Cape of Good Hope – the expedition had proved that the world was round.

for the goods brought back by the first explorers. Portugal, which had recently asserted its independence from Castile, took the lead for most of the 15th century. The main force behind Portuguese exploration in the early part of the century was Prince Henry the Navigator (1394–1460), younger son of John I of Portugal. Patron of a succession of Portuguese voyages down the west coast of Africa (⊳ box), Henry was motivated by both material and religious ambitions.

As well as seeking to spread Christianity (by continuing the crusade against the Moors into North Africa), Henry sought wealth for himself and his followers, while Portuguese merchants hoped to find new markets for their goods. Henry's ships captured native Africans, who were

The Reformation

The Reformation was the outcome of dissatisfaction with abuses within the Roman Catholic Church, and also with the role of the clergy and with the direction of the Church. The close link which often developed between Protestant reformers and secular rulers resulted in the development of national churches and the appropriation of Church property. The publication of the Bible in various national languages was also a very important effect of the Reformation.

The Catholic Church made a determined effort to reverse the success of the Reformation in the late 16th and early 17th centuries (▷ p. 112), but with only partial success. Protestantism for its part had lost much of its dynamism by 1650 – but had survived.

The background

The desire for reform was not new. The weakness of the papacy in the late 14th and early 15th centuries had stimulated the progress of Lollardy in England and Hussitism in Bohemia, both of which anticipated the Protestant Reformation (▷ p. 91). However, their success was limited and the late 15th century saw a revival of papal authority.

The popes had St Peter's rebuilt so that Rome should be a fitting capital, and they paid for this and other projects by exploiting their headship of the Church to raise money throughout Europe. They sold indulgences (remissions of the penance imposed on confessed sinners), dispensations and cardinalships, and at the same time resisted calls for reform in an increasingly corrupt and secular Church. In Germany this provoked a strong anti-Italian feeling based on the belief that the papacy was extorting great sums from the Germans.

The humanists new scholarly work on the texts of the Bible (▷ p. 100) drew attention to the great gulf between the early and contemporary Church, and gave added strength to the growing hostility to the clergy and the papacy. The invention of printing played a crucial role in the spread of the ideas both of the humanists and of the new reformers (▷ p. 100).

Martin Luther and Protestantism

In 1517 Martin Luther, a German monk and theologian, published his opposition to indulgences and other abuses in the Church. Attempts to silence him only clarified his ideas. Luther believed that the foundation of all faith must be the Bible, and that all peole should have access to it, not just those who understood Latin. Those religious doctrines and practices not founded in Scripture, such as monastic orders, the cult of Mary and the saints, he regarded as abuses; only faith in God brought salvation. Luther also denied the special status of the clergy administering the sacraments. To him the priesthood comprised all true believers, and each believer stood alone and equal before God. Following his excommunication in 1520 Luther rejected papal authority.

Luther's protest, spread by the new printing presses and by preachers, was popular in Germany. The poor thought it meant freedom from some of their burdens. However, Luther urged the brutal suppression of the Peasants' War (1525) by the German princes (▷ box), whom he needed to defend the Reformation against the hostility of Charles V, the Holy Roman Emperor (▷ p. 85). Yet Charles's commitments elsewhere prevented him from having time or strength enough to root out Protestantism in Germany. In 1555 he had to agree to the Peace of Augsburg, which allowed each prince, Lutheran or Catholic, to decide the religion of his subjects.

By that time Lutheran churches had been established in a number of states in Germany, and in Sweden and Denmark, while the new state church emerging in England (▷ p. 118) was influenced by Lutheran doctrines. A number of rulers ordered Reformation in their states because they profited from the seizure of church property, and increased their authority by creating a clergy subject to them and not to Rome.

Calvin and Calvinism

Reform was also effected in Zurich by Ulrich Zwingli (1484–1531). Zwingli agreed with Luther on the role of the authorities (in Switzerland the city magistrates) in carrying out the Reformation. However, whereas Luther sometimes allowed what the Bible did not reject, Zwingli would only permit what it specifically mentioned. The Zwinglian church therefore tended to be simpler, and a more radical break with past practice, than the Lutheran. These differences prevented the two churches from presenting a common front against their Catholic opponents.

The most influential of the other reformers, however, was John Calvin (1509–

The French Holy League marches in Paris. Formed in 1576 under the leadership of Henry, duke of Guise – one of the instigators of the St Bartholomew's Day Massacre – the militant Catholic League opposed the concessions granted to Protestants by Henry III, and played a major role in the French Wars of Religion.

The torture of John of Leiden, leader of the Anabaptists of Münster, in 1535.

THE RADICAL REFORMATION

The Lutheran and Calvinist attacks on the Church were accompanied by more radical religious movements. These often had their roots in medieval millenarian tradition: the belief (based upon the Book of Revelation) in the Second Coming of Christ, after which would follow the millennium, a period of a thousand years when Christ would reign on earth. It was believed that the millennium would be preceded by the reign of the Antichrist, a period of great disorder. People looked for signs of this era in war, plague, famine, and extraordinary phenomena such as comets. Millenarian ideas had always attracted some support from the less well off in society, who looked forward to the millennium as an improvement on their present material life.

Radicalism also drew those who felt that Luther (and Zwingli) were too ready to compromise with authority and to settle for a less than perfect church. Thomas Müntzer (1489–1525) conceived of the millennium as a state in which all would be equal, and property held in common. Rejecting Luther's faith in the princes, he preached that the poor were God's chosen, and should hasten the imminent Second Coming by violent action. Müntzer encouraged the German Peasants' War, and was executed when it was bloodily crushed by the forces of the Swabian League under Philip of Hesse.

The most successful radical movement was Anabaptism, which emerged in Zurich in the 1520s. Although rejecting the idea of a single organized Church, Anabaptists shared certain beliefs. Taking biblical fundamentalism to its limit, they insisted that the true Church consisted only of those who freely entered it, and that adult baptism alone was valid. Anabaptists saw themselves as a community of saints on earth, who did not need magistrates or law. They reserved the right in conscience not to bear arms, swear oaths, or participate in government. Although in practice Anabaptists were often law-abiding, believing that they must patiently bear the tribulations imposed on them by sinners and the state, governments inevitably saw them as a threat. However, persecution ensured that Anabaptism spread throughout Europe.

In 1534 Anabaptists sought to turn the city of Münster, in northwest Germany, into a new Jerusalem. In what soon became a reign of terror, they enforced mass baptisms, the expulsion of Lutherans and Catholics, common ownership of property, the banning of all books but the Bible, polygamy, and the execution of opponents. The Anabaptist leader, John of Leiden, finally declared himself king in Münster, inspiring his followers with the belief that in the imminent destruction of the world they alone would be saved. In the face of such revolutionary ideas and practices, Lutheran and Catholic princes joined forces to destroy the Anabaptist kingdom in 1535.

Thereafter, in the face of continuing persecution, and under the influence of men like Menno Simmons (1496–1561) – founder of the Mennonites – Anabaptism became a quieter, more withdrawn movement. In subsequent centuries, Anabaptists and other Protestant radicals sought to establish a more peaceful earthly paradise in America. That political and religious turbulence could still throw up religious radicalism was evident, however, in the appearance of extreme Puritan sects such as the Ranters, millenarian Fifth Monarchists and Diggers during the English Civil War (▷ p. 118).

1556) a French lawyer. Calvinism was also based firmly on Scripture, but differed from Lutheranism in believing that only those were saved who had been predestined or chosen by God, and that the efforts of individual men and women could play no part in their salvation. Calvin also went further than Luther in rejecting religious ceremonial and imagery. Like Zwingli, but unlike Luther, Calvin placed great emphasis on the supervision of the behaviour of church members.

Calvin reformed both the Church and government of Geneva, ensuring a closer link between the two and a greater supervision of the religious and moral life of its citizens. The consistory – a body of ministers (or pastors) of the church and members of the town council – was responsible for church discipline. Officials (elders) reported to the consistory on the behaviour of the people of Geneva. The consistory enabled the Calvinist church to direct the lives of church members and other citizens. Geneva offered a new intellectual inspiration and organizational model to those eager for church reform. Calvinists took the lead in the

reform movement in the later 16th century. However, their different beliefs often meant conflict with other reformers as well as with Catholics.

In Scotland, a successful revolt against the Catholic Mary Queen of Scots was followed by reform of the Church on Calvinist lines by John Knox (?1514–72). In France the Huguenots (as French Calvinists were known) became involved in the rivalries of the noble factions in the French Wars of Religion (1559–1598). Huguenot strength fell considerably after the St Bartholomew's Day massacre of their leaders (1572), ordered by the Queen Mother, Catherine de Medici. Yet they were strong enough to obtain toleration in 1598 under the Edict of Nantes.

Calvinist resistance contributed to the success of the Dutch revolt against Philip II (▷ p. 120), a Calvinist church being set up in the Dutch Republic. Calvinist churches were also established in Bohemia, Hungary, Poland, and parts of Germany (where Calvinism was not included in the settlement of 1555). Not surprisingly, Calvinism was associated with rebellion.

By 1600, the religious map of Europe had

been transformed. Although Catholicism retained the allegiance of much of Europe, a variety of 'Protestant' or 'Reformed' churches had attracted away from Rome a number of princely and city states. Protestantism was, in one form or another, the official religion in half the European continent. CS

DIVIDED EUROPE
RELIGIOUS FAITHS IN 1650

LUTHERAN • ROMAN CATHOLIC • REFORMED/CALVINIST • ORTHODOX • ANGLICAN • ISLAM

SEE ALSO

- THE HOLY ROMAN EMPIRE p. 84
- THE CRUSADES p. 88
- POPES, SAINTS AND HERETICS p. 90
- MEDIEVAL AND RENAISSANCE CULTURE p. 100
- THE COUNTER-REFORMATION p. 112
- THE SPANISH AND PORTUGUESE EMPIRES p. 116
- THE MAKING OF BRITAIN p. 118
- THE DUTCH REPUBLIC p. 120

The Counter-Reformation

Before and during the Protestant Reformation (▷ p. 110) there were strong reforming currents within the Catholic Church, associated with humanists and others (▷ p. 101). The success of the Reformation stimulated and transformed this internal movement for reform, and from the late 16th century a revitalized Catholic Church was making great efforts to recover lost ground.

However, the success of the Counter-Reformation – as this Catholic revival is known – depended ultimately on the power of Catholic rulers, such as Philip II of Spain (▷ p. 116). In the early 17th century they made determined attempts to resist the spread of Protestantism, achieving some success. By 1650 Roman Catholicism had regained much ground, especially in central Europe.

The Council of Trent

The success of the Reformation increased the pressure for a council to reform the Catholic Church from within. Such a council met in three sessions at Trent (now Trento) in northern Italy between 1541 and 1563. The Council reformed some abuses but made few concessions to Protestant criticisms. Instead it restated traditional doctrine regarding the sacraments, the Bible and papal supremacy, making clear the differences between Catholics and Protestants. The Council declared that Catholics should be better instructed in their faith, and that they should attend mass and confession more regularly. In order to ensure that the clergy were better trained, bishops were urged to establish seminaries in their dioceses. The Council's decrees shaped Catholic doctrine and practice until the second Vatican Council or Vatican II (1962–5).

Enforcement of the decrees of the Council of Trent greatly depended upon the local clergy. St Charles Borromeo (1538–84; archbishop of Milan 1560–84) – who had attended the final sessions of the Council of Trent – worked tirelessly to put its reforms into practice. He called provincial and diocesan synods (as ordered by the Council of Trent) to inform his clergy of its decrees, and made frequent visits to the parishes of his archdiocese to see that the reforms were carried out. He also established seminaries, and founded a college to provide missionary priests for Switzerland. Not all bishops were as zealous as Borromeo, however, and the decrees of the Council of Trent were not fully enforced in all dioceses of the Roman Catholic Church until long after 1563.

The Jesuits

Even before the Council of Trent, some of the older religious orders had been reformed and new ones established. Most of these new foundations were active in the world rather than enclosed in a monastery or a convent, and this trend continued after the Council of Trent. Many religious orders and lay organizations set up in the 16th and 17th centuries – such as the Sisters of Charity founded by St Vincent de Paul (1581–1660) – were concerned to help the poor, sick and needy. Women played an important part in such charitable activities.

The Council of Trent was also followed by a great missionary effort to recover the areas lost to Protestantism. A leading part in this sometimes dangerous activity was played by the Jesuits (the Society of Jesus). The Order was founded by a Spaniard, St Ignatius Loyola (1491–1556), whose strict standards ensured that the Order was well disciplined and composed of capable men. The Jesuits worked both as missionaries and as teachers in Europe, America and Asia. Their teaching methods, combining firm discipline with an understanding of the need to harness rather than repress youthful energy, earned the Jesuit schools an exalted reputation. By 1640, there were more than 500 of them throughout Europe – educating at least 150 000 children (all of them boys) – together with a number of Jesuit universities. In these institutions the Jesuits helped mould successive generations of Catholic princes. As royal confessors they urged Catholic rulers to ignore Protestant rights as a limitation on their power.

The Counter-Reformation and the princes

The progress of the Counter-Reformation depended greatly on the support of monarchs such as Mary I of England (1553–8), who tried to recatholicize her kingdom, and Philip II of Spain (▷ p. 116). Although determined to restrict papal authority in his territories, Philip was firm in his Catholic faith – the religion of the overwhelming majority of his subjects. His efforts to root out heresy in the Low Countries contributed to the outbreak of the Dutch Revolt (▷ p. 120). Philip was also an enthusiastic sponsor of the Catholic Holy League in its struggle with the Huguenots during the French

St Ignatius Loyola chases out devils in this painting by Peter Paul Rubens. Although the Council of Trent had decreed that sensuality, profanity and excessive elegance should be avoided in the arts, from the early 17th century religious painting in Catholic countries became dominated by the emotional exuberance and sensual extravagance of the Baroque style.

Wars of Religion (⇨ p. 111). Spanish money and troops bolstered the League's efforts to halt the spread of Protestantism during the reign of Henry III of France (1574–89) and – after the latter's assassination – to exclude the Protestant Henry of Navarre (later Henry IV) from the succession to the throne. Philip's intervention in the French Wars of Religion, together with his struggles against the United Provinces and Protestant England (⇨ p. 118), made him the secular champion of the Counter-Reformation in the later 16th century.

The Thirty Years War (1618–48)

The religious tensions that had built up in western Europe over half a century finally erupted in a complex series of struggles known as the Thirty Years War. The war began with a revolt in Bohemia (1618) against the anti-Protestant and centralizing policies of the Habsburg Emperor Ferdinand II, when Catholic councillors were thrown out of a window of the royal palace in Prague (the 'Defenestration of Prague'). By 1620 the revolt had been crushed. However, the struggle quickly became entangled with wider European conflicts.

In 1620, Spain, the ally of the Austrian Habsburgs, occupied the Rhenish Palatinate (in western Germany) whose ruler had led the Bohemian revolt and had subsequently been elected king of Bohemia (Frederick V). The following year, Spain resumed its war with the Dutch (⇨ p. 120). By 1629 Habsburg power seemed dominant in Germany, and in that year Ferdinand II attempted to reimpose the religious settlement of 1555, thus ending the unofficial toleration of Calvinism. Fear of Habsburg and Catholic power led Gustavus Adolphus, Protestant king of Sweden (1611–32), to invade Germany in 1630. A string of brilliant successes brought most of northern Germany under the control of the Swedes and their allies. Only Gustavus' death at the battle of Lützen in 1632 halted his further progress. However, a subsidy from France and military assistance from German Protestants enabled the Swedes to fight on for financial compensation and territorial concessions in northern Germany.

The entry of France (1635), the greatest anti-Habsburg power, changed the character of the war into an essentially political struggle. The growing difficulties of both the Spanish and Austrian Habsburgs led in 1648 to the Peace of Westphalia, which confirmed the 1555 religious settlement, and now included the Calvinists.

In parts of Germany up to one-third – and in a few areas up to two-thirds – of the population may have died during the war, mainly through disease and economic disruption. The struggle between France and Spain went on until 1659, but the age of religious, or partly religious, wars was over. The religious map of Europe (⇨ map, p. 111) was now fixed essentially as it is today.   CS

EUROPE IN 1659

Boundary of the Holy Roman Empire

KINGDOM OF SWEDEN

RUSSIA

KINGDOM OF DENMARK

MINOR GERMAN STATES

BRANDENBURG-PRUSSIA

to Sweden

to Sweden

KINGDOMS OF ENGLAND AND SCOTLAND

UNITED PROVINCES

KINGDOM OF POLAND

SPANISH NETHERLANDS

SILESIA

BOHEMIA

AUSTRIAN DOMINIONS

SPANISH BURGUNDY

AUSTRIA

HUNGARY

KINGDOM OF FRANCE

SWITZERLAND

TYROL

OTTOMAN EMPIRE

to the Papacy

SAVOY

VENICE

KINGDOM OF PORTUGAL

GENOA

PAPAL STATES

to Venice

KINGDOM OF CASTILE

DUCHY OF MILAN

MINOR ITALIAN STATES

to Venice

KINGDOM OF ARAGON

KINGDOM OF THE TWO SICILIES

SPANISH   DOMINIONS

to Venice

to Ottomans

THE INQUISITION

The Counter-Reformation re-activated the ecclesiastical court known as the Inquisition, originally established around 1332 for the detection and punishment of heretics. In the Middle Ages it had been responsible to local bishops, but in the 15th century became part of the secular administration. In most Catholic states the Inquisition was either reformed or newly introduced. In Venice, in the 17th century, it heard nearly 2000 cases, of which 20 resulted in execution.

There were 22 tribunals of the Inquisition in the various realms of the Spanish empire in Europe and overseas, controlled by a royal council in Madrid. Between 1478 (when it was established) and 1500, the Spanish Inquisition – under its Grand Inquisitor Tomás de Torquemada – convicted and executed thousands of Christianized Jews for Jewish practices. They were handed over to the secular authorities for punishment (burning) at elaborate public spectacles known as autos-da-fé ('acts of faith'). After 1550 its activities were less spectacular. Between 1550 and 1700, the tribunals

handled 150 000 cases. About 75% of cases dealt with by the Spanish Inquisition concerned religious 'deviance': witchcraft, Protestantism, Jewish practices, and blasphemy. The remaining cases concerned sexual morality. Only 1% of those tried by the Spanish tribunals between 1550 and 1700 were executed, and another 2% were burnt in effigy (because they had escaped or died). Although only a small proportion of the population of the Spanish empire was brought before the Inquisition, it held terrors for all. Arrest was arbitrary, usually following anonymous denunciation by neighbours of the victim or by one of the many 'familiars' who helped the Inquisition in all areas. Trial was secret, protracted, and often involved torture. Imprisonment (at the expense of the accused) during the investigation and trial was unpleasant and sometimes fatal. Guilt was punished by the confiscation of goods, public humiliation and perpetual infamy. The penitent's gown of a condemned person was displayed in his local church, even after death, and was replaced if it disintegrated.

The Ottoman Empire

In the early 14th century the Ottoman emirate was but one of many small Turkish states in western Anatolia (Asian Turkey). Its rulers were originally steppe dwellers, who had embraced Islam and were devoted to religious war (jihad). The Ottomans became the outstanding holy warriors among the Turks of Asia Minor and emerged as the foremost Muslim power in the centuries that followed. From Anatolia they extended their rule into Europe, Asia, the Middle East and Africa, reaching their zenith in the 16th century.

Suleiman the Magnificent at the siege of Budapest (1541).

Thereafter the Ottoman Empire was in decline. This was not immediately apparent, but had been glaringly exposed by the end of the 18th century. The Ottoman Empire in 1800 remained an extensive one, but with the Turks clearly unable to defend themselves against their European neighbours, the Western powers became increasingly anxious to prevent the collapse of the Ottoman Empire from disturbing the European balance of power (⊳ p. 154).

Early Ottoman expansion

The Ottoman Empire was founded by Osman I, a nomad leader who turned from raiding to a policy of permanent conquest. In 1290 he declared his independence from the Seljuk Turks (⊳ p. 76) and set about extending his territory to the northwest at the expense of the declining Byzantine Empire. More ambitious expansion was undertaken by Orkhan (1326–60), who expelled the Byzantine Empire from Asia Minor (⊳ p. 81). By forging alliances with factions within the Byzantine Empire, the Ottomans gained a foothold in the Balkans, and they rapidly moved into Thrace, Macedonia, Bulgaria and Serbia. Despite exacting financial tribute in all conquered areas, the Ottomans offered the peasant populations of Christian southeast Europe better conditions than had their indigenous rulers. Murad I (1362–89) lost his life in a notable victory over the Serbs at Kosovo in 1389, which paved the way for Turkish expansion into central Europe. Murad's son Bajezid I (1389–1402) consolidated Ottoman rule and was awarded the title of sultan by the caliph of Cairo.

By the end of the 14th century devastating Ottoman raids had reduced the Byzantine Empire to the walls of its capital, Constantinople. The city was saved on this occasion not by the misbegotten crusade of 1396 (⊳ p. 88), which the Turks easily crushed, but by invaders from Central Asia under their fearsome leader, Tamerlaine (or Timur; c.1336–1405), who claimed descent from the Mongol Genghis Khan (⊳ p. 54). From Samarkand he led his armies in an orgy of conquest and destruction across Mongolia, India, Russia and the Middle East, and in 1402 defeated and captured the Ottoman sultan. However, this was merely a stay of execution for Constantinople, which was overwhelmed by Ottoman forces under Mehmed II in 1453. Renamed Istanbul, the city became the capital of the Ottoman Empire. By 1500 the annexation or conquest of Bosnia, Albania, the Peloponnese and Trebizond had completed Ottoman domination of the Balkans and Asia Minor. The Ottomans also ventured north across the Black Sea to the Crimea, where the Tartars fell under their sway. Selim I (1512–20) doubled the size of the empire by taking Syria and Egypt from the Mamelukes. His defeat of the Safavid Persians at Chaldiran in 1514 strengthened Ottoman control of eastern Anatolia and extended the empire into Armenia (1514–16). In 1517 the Hejaz (part of Arabia including the Muslim holy cities of Mecca and Medina) and Yemen were occupied.

Suleiman the Magnificent

The reign of Selim's son and successor, Suleiman the Magnificent (1520–66), was a golden age of Ottoman power and grandeur. In three major campaigns against the Safavid Persians he annexed Mesopotamia. Despite the signing of a peace between Ottomans and Safavids in 1555, religious divisions between the orthodox Sunni Ottomans and the Shiite Persians (⊳ p. 82) contributed to constant and bitter conflict between the two empires well into the 17th century.

Suleiman also established Turkish power in Europe to an unprecedented degree. He occupied Belgrade in 1521, and in 1526 defeated the army of the kingdom of Hungary – hitherto a buffer between the the rest of Christian Europe and the advancing Turks. By 1529 Suleiman was threatening Vienna. The city was saved less by the efforts of German and other Christian princes than by weather and disease, which forced Suleiman to abandon his siege. The Turks were not to advance so far into Central Europe again in the 16th century. But they remained a threat, occupying Transylvania and most of Hungary, which became the warring frontier between Western Christendom (represented by the Austrian Habsburg emperors) and Islam.

The Ottomans also became a formidable naval power. In 1522 they captured the island of Rhodes from the crusading Knights of St John, gaining an important naval base in the eastern Mediterranean. The construction of an Ottoman war fleet enabled the Turks to attack Italy and to challenge the Holy Roman Emperor Charles V (⊳ p. 85) for control of the central and western Mediterranean. From the 1530s the Ottoman fleet was commanded by Khayr ad-Din ('Barbarossa'), one of the corsair leaders of the Barbary Coast of North Africa who had become vassals of the sultan. The Turks were also helped by Charles's Christian enemies, the French, who allowed the Turkish fleet to spend the winter of 1543–4 in Toulon harbour, and by the failure of the West to mount a united naval offensive. Charles's capture of the corsair base at Tunis (1535) was an isolated success. In 1551 the Ottoman fleet ousted the Spaniards from Tripoli, which became an Ottoman vassal state.

By Suleiman's death, the Ottoman Empire extended from Central Europe to the Persian Gulf, dominated the eastern Mediterranean, Adriatic and Black Seas, and included many races, languages, and religions. The Ottoman sultans began to claim authority over all Muslims as caliphs – heirs of the Prophet (⊳ p. 82). They advanced the cause of Islam, but tolerated the Christian and other non-Muslim religions of their subjects. Suleiman gave his empire greater centralized administrative unity – although the provincial governors (pashas) retained considerable autonomy – and a system of law. His reign was a time of economic prosperity associated with the development of town life, and with a flowering of the arts (often promoted by the sultan's court).

Ottoman decline

In 1565 only a determined effort by Philip II of Spain (⊳ p. 116) prevented the Ottomans from capturing the strategically vital island of Malta. This was a crucial blow to Ottoman expansionism in the Mediterranean. Selim II (1566–74) turned his attention to the more vulnerable empire of the Venetian Republic in the Adriatic and eastern Mediterranean. Venice had hitherto preferred to buy peace with the Turks rather than fight them but – following the Ottoman conquest of Cyprus (1571) – Venice agreed to join her forces with those of Spain, Genoa and the papacy in a Holy League, whose fleet defeated the Turks in a great naval engagement off Lepanto in western Greece (1571; ▷ p. 117).

But this was not the end of Ottoman power in the Mediterranean. The Holy League broke up soon afterwards and the Turks ousted the Spanish from Tunis in 1574. Thereafter, Spain was preoccupied with war against England and the Dutch (▷ pp. 118 and 120). This, and other factors, notably Ottoman involvement in the East – where the war against Persia was not ended until 1639 – and the Austrian emperor's role in the Thirty Years War (▷ p. 113), largely halted the struggle between Turks and Christians until the middle of the 17th century.

From the middle of the 16th century the Ottoman Empire showed growing signs of administrative and social decay. Centralized control began to break down, particularly in the 18th century. Provincial governors became more independent, while appointments in the civil administration and the army – previously only for life – became hereditary. The decline was exacerbated by the fact that the sultans after Suleiman were generally of poorer quality than their predecessors. Brought up to do little more than indulge themselves, they had scant understanding of the empire and its complexities. Their position was also undermined by the disruption of the strict line of succession, since the janissaries (▷ p. box) had violently deposed unpopular sultans in 1622 and 1648.

Decline was also evident in the Ottoman economy, which became increasingly dependent on manufactured imports from Western Europe. Despite growing cultural links between the Ottoman Empire and the rest of Europe in the 18th century, the Turks played no part in the intellectual advances associated with the Enlightenment (▷ p. 134) and remained technologically backward. Printing was not introduced into the Ottoman Empire until the 18th century, while the Turks continued to use galleys long after other Mediterranean naval powers had abandoned them.

This conservatism – in striking contrast with the transformation of Russia from the late 17th century (▷ p. 126) – owed much to the entrenched and growing power of conservative Muslim religious institutions. The latter also fed a growing desire among the subject Christian populations of the Balkans – who were becoming more aware of their national identity – to be free of Turkish rule.

The full implications of these defects did not become apparent overnight. The

THE GROWTH OF THE OTTOMAN EMPIRE

Phase I 1290–1402

Ottoman lands under Osman 1290–1326

Additions under Orkhan 1326–1359

Additions under Murad I 1359–1389

Additions under Bajezid I 1389–1402

After Bajezid's overthrow at Ankara in 1402 all the Anatolian territories won since Orkhan's reign were lost. They were gradually won back again, the last of them by Mehmet II in 1471.

Phase II 1451–1566

Aquisitions beyond the frontier during the reign of Mehmet II, the Conqueror 1451–1481

Additions under Selim I, the Grim 1512–1520 (including small gains of Bajezid II 1481–1512)

Additions under Suleiman the Magnificent 1520–1566

Additions under Selim II 1566–74

Extent of Ottoman Empire 1566

SEE ALSO
- THE BYZANTINE EMPIRE p. 80
- THE RISE OF ISLAM p. 82
- THE EASTERN QUESTION p. 154

Empire continued to expand – as far as the Caspian Sea in the east – while a series of vigorous and capable grand viziers (leading court officials) of the Albanian Köprülü family provided the leadership that Mehmed IV (1648–87) could not. The Turks seized Crete from the Venetians (1645–69) and resumed the offensive in Central Europe, again besieging Vienna (albeit unsuccessfully) in 1683. However, the grand viziers who succeeded the Köprülüs were unable to provide the same vigorous leadership. The rapid turnover of grand viziers (some unsuccessful, some reforming) during the 18th century contributed to the domestic instability of the Ottoman Empire.

Despite the Austrian Habsburg conquest of Hungary after 1683, the Turks continued to resist their enemies with some success. Austria, Russia, Venice and Poland were themselves often divided and in as poor a state as the Turks. However, Ottoman deficiencies were clearly exposed in disastrous wars against Russia (1768–72 and 1787–92), which resulted in the loss of Turkish territory around the Black Sea. In the 19th century, the nationalist aspirations of the various peoples under Turkish domination in Eastern Europe were to become linked with attempts by the European powers (notably Austria and Russia) to fill the vacuum created by Ottoman decline (▷ p. 154). CS

The Spanish and Portuguese Empires

The 16th century saw the creation of the first large colonial empires by European powers. The empires of Spain and Portugal resulted from their sponsorship of the great voyages of discovery (▷ p. 108). In the case of Spain its empire would not have been created without the achievement of political unity at home. This came about in 1469, when Isabella of Castile married Ferdinand of Aragon. With his support she restored order and royal authority in Castile. In 1492 they completed the conquest of the Moorish kingdom of Granada, bringing to a conclusion the Reconquista, the reconquest of Islamic Spain (▷ p. 83).

The achievement of Ferdinand and Isabella rested on the co-operation of their two realms. Aragon feared being swallowed up by the far richer Castile and made little contribution to Spain's subsequent greatness. Yet the union was held together, first by Ferdinand and Isabella, and then from 1516 by the Habsburgs, initially in the person of Charles V. Charles inherited both realms and was also elected Holy Roman Emperor in 1519 (▷ p. 85). Spain's incorporation into the Habsburg Empire offered it the opportunity to use its own resources and those of its American empire on a wider stage. Spain assumed the role of leading power in Europe until well into the 17th century.

The division of the world

Following Columbus's successful voyage of 1492, Isabella needed to establish her right to colonize the Americas. After arbitration by the pope, Spain and Portugal came to an agreement at the Treaty of Tordesillas in 1493. All lands west of an imaginary north-to-south line drawn 370 leagues west of the Azores and Cape Verde Islands were to go to Spain, and all those east of it to Portugal. The result of this was that Portugal got Brazil, and Spain virtually all of the rest of South and Central America, and even parts of North America.

The conquistadores

Before settlement of the Americas could begin, the existing native empires (▷ p. 70) had to be subdued. This was the achievement of the conquistadores. In a short time and against vastly greater numbers – but aided by an overwhelming technological superiority – Cortez overthrew the Aztec empire in Mexico (1519–21), Alvarado conquered the Mayas in Yucatán (1524), and Pizarro subdued the Inca empire in Peru (1531–3; ▷ box).

Spanish colonization accelerated, and the native Indians were subjected to a colonial administration headed by two viceroys – in Mexico and Peru – responsible to the king in Spain. The Indians were obliged to work on the Spaniards' lands and in the gold and silver mines. Spanish missionaries destroyed the Indians' temples and idols, established mission churches, and began a process of wholesale, sometimes forcible, conversion. The Roman Catholic Church thereby acquired massive numbers of believers in the Americas. The disruption of the Indians' way of life, together with the introduction of diseases to which they were not immune, contributed to a massive decline in their numbers – from perhaps 25 million in Mexico alone in 1519 to just over 1 million in 1600.

Trade, gold and silver

Gold had been the original attraction of the Americas for the conquistadores, and tales of El Dorado, a fabled city rich in gold, continued to fuel exploration. However, silver soon made up 90% of the precious metals sent back to Spain. These metals went as taxes and to pay for the goods the colonists received from Spain. Spain tried to prevent foreigners trading with their colonies, but this proved difficult. The silver stimulated the Spanish economy, and then that of the whole of Europe, contributing to the general inflation in the 16th century. However, in the 17th century, colonial self-sufficiency and economic recession, combined with a fall in silver exports, all contributed to a depression in the European economy (▷ p. 130).

Portugal in Africa and Asia

Portugal's empire was much more dispersed than that of Spain. Limited to a few coastal settlements in Brazil, the Portuguese also had a handful of forts and 'trading' factories in West Africa and along the Mozambique coast, and a scattering of settlements between India and the Pacific.

This pattern reflected the importance of trade with the East. Portugal drew from the East an impressive range of spices, which then attracted high prices in Europe. The Portuguese also obtained gold from China and silver from Japan. Some of these goods were traded locally, but many were carried back to Lisbon, and on to Antwerp for European distribution. Since the only way to Portugal from the East was round the Cape of Good Hope, the forts and factories along the African coast protected this trade. Africa also provided gold – particularly from the Gold Coast (now Ghana) – and slaves. The latter were especially valued as

A Spanish gold mine. The Spanish settlers used both native Indian and African slaves to mine the vast mineral resources of their new American colonies. Gold and silver from the New World made Spain the richest country in Europe in the 16th century.

The Battle of Lepanto, 7 October 1571, depicted by the Italian painter Giorgio Vasari. It was off Lepanto (the western Greek port of Návpaktos) that a combined Spanish and Venetian fleet defeated the Ottoman Turks, so preventing Turkish expansion into the western Mediterranean. The Christian fleet was commanded by Don John of Austria, the half-brother of Philip II of Spain. The battle was the last great naval engagement involving oar-powered galleys.

labour on the developing sugar plantations of Brazil (⇨ p. 128).

The number of white settlers in both the Portuguese and Spanish Empires was always far inferior to the number of non-whites, but many whites, including missionaries, were attracted to the colonies. The Portuguese, like the Spanish, condoned conversion of the native populations by force, so it is not clear how genuine the conversions were.

Spanish power in Europe

In 1556 Charles V abdicated. His brother had long ruled the Habsburg lands in Austria, and now kept them. Everything else went to Charles's son, Philip II (who ruled 1556–98). Spain now dominated much of Italy and therefore the whole of the western Mediterranean. It also surrounded France – and threatened England – through its possession of the Netherlands. Spain also led the Christian fight against the Turks at sea: it was a largely Spanish fleet that defeated the Turks at Lepanto in 1571, although this did not end Turkish power in the Mediterranean (⇨ p. 114).

Following the death of the king of Portugal in battle in Morocco in 1578, Philip added the Portuguese Empire to that of Spain. Apart from making Spain a major power in the East, this made Philip much stronger in Europe. The Spanish Empire in 1600 was the biggest the world had ever seen.

Spain's great military strength was used in a long struggle to suppress the revolt of the Protestant Netherlands from 1567 (⇨ p. 120). However, Philip was unable to devote himself wholly to ending the revolt, and his enemies aided the rebels in order to weaken Spain. The failure of Philip's Armada against England in 1588 (⇨ p. 118) meant that these distractions continued. Warfare on this scale was too expensive even with the silver of the Americas, and Spain was unable to beat the Dutch rebels.

The decline of Spain

The recovery of France from the weakness inflicted by the Wars of Religion (⇨ p. 111) proved disastrous for Spain. Spanish troops proved very successful in the first half of the Thirty Years War (⇨ p. 113), but their victories ended after France's entry into the war in 1635. At the same time Castile was less able to carry the cost of empire alone, largely owing to decline in its population, agriculture and industry, and to the American recession. Yet the non-Castilian realms refused to shoulder more of the costs. Catalonia revolted in 1640 when Castile attempted to pass on some of the burden, as did Portugal, whose empire Spain had proved incapable of defending.

Spain recovered Catalonia but was obliged to recognize Dutch (1648) and Portuguese (1668) independence. Portugal then rebuilt its colonial empire around Brazil. Although Spain continued to decline, the support of other states, now concerned to resist France rather than Spain, meant that the Spanish Empire was still vast enough to be worth fighting over when the last Habsburg king of Spain died (the War of the Spanish Succession; ⇨ pp. 123 and 124). CS

The Making of Britain

Between the end of the 15th and the middle of the 18th centuries England became Great Britain. By 1763 Britain had emerged as a leading power in Europe and the world, with a vast colonial empire (▷ p. 128). This achievement rested on the achievement of political stability after the upheavals of the 16th and 17th centuries. Stability was associated with the establishment of a Protestant, parliamentary monarchy from 1688. The achievement of effective control over the previously independent realms of Scotland and Ireland (Wales had been subjugated in the 13th century) contributed to the success of that new system.

Henry VIII arrives in France for a showpiece meeting with his rival Francis I in 1520. Henry's wars with France achieved little and were ruinously expensive, but he did succeed in creating a powerful English navy. (Musée de la Marine, Paris)

England's future success was not obvious when Henry Tudor defeated Richard III at Bosworth in 1485, so becoming Henry VII (1485–1509). It remained to be seen whether Henry could end the cycle of civil war known as the Wars of the Roses, which had started in 1455. These wars did little real damage to the wealth of England, but reduced the prestige and authority of the Crown, which had often proved incapable of enforcing obedience from the great nobles. The Crown had become the plaything of factions, being claimed by the Houses of York (the white rose) and Lancaster (the red rose). Scotland remained an independent kingdom inclined to ally with France against England (▷ p. 94).

The early Tudor achievement

Henry married Elizabeth, daughter of Edward IV, ensuring that their children were heirs of both Lancaster and York.

Oliver Cromwell, commander of the Parliamentary forces in the English Civil War, and Lord Protector of England. For all Cromwell's undoubted administrative skills, the 'Protectorate' he ruled over from 1653 to 1658 was never popular. Within two years of his death the people were celebrating the restoration of the monarchy.

OLIVERIVS   CROMWEL
ANGLICÆ REIP. PRO-   TECTOR. EIVSDEMQ,
EXERCITVM DVX   GENERALIS. ETC.

He defeated Yorkist attempts to seize his throne, and gained foreign support by a policy of marriage alliances and peace. Henry had no police or army and could restore royal authority only by channelling patronage (grants of land and offices) to those who obeyed him.

Henry VII's success was such that Henry VIII (1509–47) succeeded without question to a rich and powerful Crown, financially independent thanks to Henry VII's careful exploitation of the Crown's extensive landed estates. Henry VIII revived the traditions of the Hundred Years War (▷ p. 94), invading France in 1513. In his absence the Scots invaded England, but were defeated at Flodden. The man who organized the French expedition, Cardinal Thomas Wolsey (1473–1530), became Henry's chief minister.

The English Reformation

Henry VIII's wife, Catherine of Aragon, had five children, but only Princess Mary survived. The security of the Tudor dynasty required that Henry be followed by a son. The pope, not wishing to offend Catherine's uncle, Emperor Charles V, refused Henry a divorce. Henry therefore declared himself Supreme Head of the Church in England, which then granted him a divorce. Henry and his new chief minister, Thomas Cromwell (1485–1540), then dissolved the monasteries – thereby increasing the landed revenue available to the Crown – and reformed the Church. Opposition to Henry's policies was brutally suppressed. In the interests of security, Wales was incorporated into the English Crown (1536, 1543), Henry was declared king of Ireland (1541), and efforts were made in the 1540s to subject the Scots.

Under Edward VI (1547–53), Henry VIII's son by his third wife, Jane Seymour,

the Reformation continued. However, Edward was succeeded by his half-sister, Mary (1553–58), who hoped to restore Catholicism and papal authority in England, burning nearly 300 Protestants in the process. Mary might have been successful, but died in 1558 leaving no children to carry on the work. She was succeeded by Elizabeth I (1558–1603), Henry's daughter by his second wife, Anne Boleyn.

Elizabeth re-established the Church of England (also known as the Anglican Church) on the basis of the Thirty-Nine Articles (1559), disappointing those 'Puritans' who wished for a purer Protestant Church. Fear of Spanish power led her to support the Dutch rebels against Philip II (▷ pp. 117 and 120). Following the discovery of plots against Elizabeth's life by Philip and Mary Queen of Scots (held prisoner by Elizabeth since 1568), Mary was executed in 1587. In 1588 Philip attempted the conquest of England by means of the Armada. It failed, but Philip continued to threaten Elizabeth, aiding the Catholic Irish chiefs, who rebelled against Elizabeth in 1599. Ireland was not reconquered until 1603, the year of Elizabeth's death (▷ box). Elizabeth never married and so left no heir. Instead she left the Crown to her Stuart relative, James VI of Scotland, who became James I of England (1603–25).

Parliament, the Stuarts, and the English Civil War

Elizabeth's wars, and the great inflation of the 16th century, eroded the financial achievement of the early Tudors. The Crown sought Parliamentary help since Parliament's consent was necessary for full-scale taxation. This gave MPs the opportunity to criticize the Crown, and to attempt to influence its policy. The ending of the war with Spain by James I did not end these problems, but the situation was far worse under James's son Charles I (1625–49).

Charles expected to be obeyed, and after fierce arguments over his efforts to pay for an expensive foreign policy, he ruled without Parliament from 1629, raising money on his own authority. This, and the religious policies of Archbishop Laud – which seemed to threaten the return of Catholicism – were unpopular. However, Charles succeeded until in 1639 Presbyterian Scotland rebelled against his efforts to impose an English-style Church there. The Scots invaded England, and Charles's need for money obliged him to call Parliament. Parliament's distrust of Charles and its efforts to obtain a share of government led him to begin the Civil War in 1642. The creation of the successful New Model Army helped Parliament to victory by 1649.

The Parliamentarians felt that Charles could not be trusted. He was therefore beheaded, and England was declared a republic (1649). The Parliamentary commander, Oliver Cromwell (1599–1658), then asserted by force the authority of the Parliamentary regime in Ireland and Scotland. English foreign policy in the 1650s was more aggressive and successful than under the Stuarts. However, the problem of a permanent replacement for the monarchy proved insoluble. Cromwell ruled as 'Lord Protector' (1653–8), but on his death the only solution seemed to be the restoration of the Stuart monarchy, stripped of the powers that had proved so offensive under Charles I.

The Glorious Revolution and parliamentary monarchy

Exploiting the widespread fear of another civil war, Charles II (1660–85) advanced towards an absolute monarchy, supported by a small standing army. He also used this fear to defeat attempts to exclude his Catholic brother James from the succession. However, the efforts of James II (1685–8) to recatholicize England led supporters of the Anglican Church to invite William of Orange, husband of James's daughter Mary, to come to save them. William and his army landed in England in November 1688, and James fled to France. No blood was spilt, and the 'Glorious Revolution' had been achieved.

In the Bill of Rights of 1689 Parliament declared some of the royal powers used by James illegal, and offered the Crown jointly to William (1689–1702) and Mary (1689–94), obliging them to call Parliament regularly. Aided by Louis XIV, James led a revolt in Ireland, but was defeated by William at the Battle of the Boyne (1690). This laid the foundations of effective British control of Ireland (▷ box). Scotland also rejected James's political and religious policies in 1688–9, offering the Scottish Crown to William and Mary, but retaining its own parliament. Under William and Mary, and then Anne (1702–14), England's growing army and navy played a major part in defeating Louis XIV (▷ p. 123), obliging him to recognize the Revolution settlement.

These wars required enormous loans – often raised by the Bank of England, founded in 1694 – which in turn contributed to the growth of the national debt. These loans were secured by regular grants from Parliament, to which governments became more accountable for their policies. Ministers controlled Parliament by the use of patronage (basically a form of bribery), a system perfected by Sir Robert Walpole, the first 'Prime Minister' (1721–42).

Anne, the last Stuart monarch, left no surviving heir, so the Elector George of Hanover, in virtue of his descent from a daughter of James I, became king as George I. The most obvious threat to the new Hanoverian dynasty came from the Jacobites, supporters of the son (Prince James Francis Edward Stuart, the 'Old Pretender') and grandson (Prince Charles Edward Stuart, the 'Young Pretender') of the exiled James II. In Scotland – which had lost its separate parliament by the 1707 Act of Union – Jacobite sympathies remained strong, particularly in the Highlands. These sympathies broke out in two major revolts, in 1715 and 1745–6, which were, however, defeated. The final defeat of the Jacobites was followed by the collapse of the old Gaelic-speaking society and culture of the Scottish Highlands.

Secure at home, Great Britain had triumphed abroad by 1763 with its victories in the Seven Years War and acquisition of vast new colonial territories (▷ p. 128). This stability, combined with its growing empire, enabled Britain to embark on a process of industrialization that was to make it the world's most powerful country in the 19th century (▷ pp. 140, 160 and 164). CS

BRITAIN AND IRELAND

The independence of Gaelic Ireland came to an end in 1171, when its disunited kingdoms succumbed to invasion by Henry II of England. But the Anglo-Norman settlers soon lost their identity and were absorbed into Gaelic Irish culture. Over the next 400 years English monarchs made successive attempts to quell Irish resistance to their authority. By 1500 only a small area around Dublin (the Pale) remained loyal to English culture and administration. Beyond the Pale most land was in the hands of native Irish, who looked to their Gaelic chieftains for leadership. In the 16th century the racial and cultural hostility between English and Irish was exacerbated by the Reformation (▷ p. 110), which also divided the English in Ireland along confessional lines.

These tensions – together with efforts made to increase the authority of the English Crown at the expense of the chieftains – contributed to a number of Catholic Irish rebellions. Most threatening was the revolt in Ulster (1595–1603) led by the chieftains O'Neill (Earl of Tyrone) and O'Donnell. Despite early successes and some support from Philip II of Spain, their rebellion was eventually suppressed by a concerted English effort. The flight of the earls of Tyrone and Tyrconnel to Spain in 1607 meant the departure from Ireland of the last of the great Gaelic chieftains.

Under Mary I and Elizabeth I 'plantations' of English settlers had been established in Munster, Leinster and Ulster. James I continued this policy with a more ambitious plantation of Ulster. Native Catholic landowners were dispossessed and replaced by (generally Protestant) settlers from England and southwest Scotland. In 1641 the embittered Catholics of the north of Ireland rose up and slaughtered thousands of Protestant settlers. The Irish rebellion was not suppressed until the arrival in Ireland of Oliver Cromwell in 1649. The Parliamentary army waged a ruthless campaign against the Irish, storming the towns of Drogheda and Wexford and massacring their civilian populations. Cromwell sought to prevent further uprisings by encouraging increased Protestant settlement. The lands of those involved in the revolt were given to Englishmen, many native Irish being forcibly resettled on less fertile land elsewhere.

William III's victory at the battle of the Boyne (1690; ▷ text) ensured the triumph of British rule and the Protestant ascendancy in Ireland. Thereafter, new 'penal laws' further discriminated against Irish Catholics, while revolt was discouraged by the presence of large numbers of English troops. The disastrous history of 17th-century Ireland established a tradition of national and sectarian hostility that has persisted to the present day.

A view of London around 1760. The city survived the depredations of fire and plague to enjoy a massive boom in trade and population during the 17th century. By the mid-18th century it was the commercial and political hub of Britain's expanding empire.

SEE ALSO

● VIKINGS AND NORMANS p. 86
● THE HUNDRED YEARS WAR p. 94
● THE REFORMATION p. 110
● COLONIAL EXPANSION IN THE 17TH AND 18TH CENTURIES p. 128
● THE ENLIGHTENMENT p. 134
● THE AGRICULTURAL AND INDUSTRIAL REVOLUTIONS p. 140
● THE REVOLUTIONARY AND NAPOLEONIC WARS p. 146
● THE PEAK OF EMPIRE p. 160

The Dutch Republic

One of the most striking features of 16th- and 17th century-Europe was the achievement of the United Provinces of the Netherlands – a small, predominantly Calvinist state popularly known as the Dutch Republic. After throwing off Spanish rule, the Dutch became Europe's leading commercial power in the 17th century and played an important part in international affairs.

Their commercial successes were accompanied by a high cultural achievement reflecting the distinctive social structure of the United Provinces. However, Dutch power declined in the 18th century, and in 1795 the Republic fell to the French.

The Habsburg Low Countries

In the Middle Ages the Low Countries were fragmented into numerous provinces, many of which (notably Flanders, Holland and Brabant) were acquired by the Valois Dukes of Burgundy in the 14th and 15th centuries (▷ p. 95). Through the marriage in 1477 of Mary, daughter of Duke Charles the Bold, to the Holy Roman Emperor Maximilian I, these provinces passed to the Habsburgs and formed part of the empire of Charles V (▷ p. 85). Charles added the remaining provinces of the Low Countries, including Gelderland and Friesland, creating a relatively compact bloc of Habsburg territory.

DUTCH ART

The distinct character of Dutch society was reflected in its culture in the 17th century. Elsewhere in Europe writers and artists depended upon the patronage of princes, aristocrats and great churchmen, and were often restricted by Academies and other bodies (notably the Inquisition; ▷ p. 113). In the United Provinces, however, princely patronage, apart from that of the House of Orange, did not exist, while the nobility were generally poor. The Dutch Calvinist Church had neither the wealth nor the desire to patronize the arts, while the fragmentation of authority reduced the constraints on artists and writers.

The vitality and diversity of Dutch culture (in particular its art, and – to a lesser extent – literature) depended upon the wide demand from a broad social spectrum of rich merchants and humbler (but relatively prosperous and generally literate) social groups, particularly in the maritime provinces. Artisans, shopkeepers and farmers spent substantial sums on their own small private collections of pictures, and on printed literature.

Dutch culture reflected these differences in its style and subject matter. There was a demand for representations of all aspects of Dutch life, from calm middle-class interiors to rowdy peasant drinking sessions, all depicted with a concern for naturalistic detail very alien to the idealizing art of southern Europe, where religious and mythological themes held sway. Dutch artists concentrated on very different genres from their Italian or Spanish counterparts: still lifes, portraits and landscapes (including marine and urban subjects) were particularly popular, reflecting as they did the quiet and orderly prosperity of the new, bourgeois state.

The provinces of the Habsburg Low Countries had little in common, and each jealously defended its own privileges. Charles experienced difficulties in maintaining his authority; his attempts to introduce greater centralization triggered a serious revolt in the traditionally independent town of Ghent in 1539.

The Dutch Revolts

The reforming and strongly Catholic policies of Charles' son, Philip II of Spain (▷ p. 116), helped to provoke the struggle for independence from Spain known as the Dutch Revolts. Philip alienated the local nobles by denying them their traditional role in government. Prominent among the aristocratic opponents of Philip's centralizing absolutism was the Lutheran prince of Orange, William the Silent (1533–84) – formerly a trusted servant of Charles V, and stadholder (provincial governor) of Holland, Zeeland and Utrecht.

Such opposition made it harder for Philip to enforce Charles V's anti-heresy laws in the Low Countries, and Calvinism spread. After the widespread destruction of images in churches in 1567, Philip ordered Spanish troops to the Low Countries to restore order. Their commander, the Duke of Alba (1507–82), began a notoriously brutal reign of terror.

In 1572 the Sea Beggars – a well-organized force of privateers licensed by William the Silent – seized control of most of the towns of Zeeland and Holland. The Beggars had some support in the town councils and among the inhabitants. Most councillors, although Catholic and loyal to Philip, detested Alba's rule. The Beggars wrested power from the royalists and imposed a Calvinist reformation, though they did not challenge the domination of the towns by privileged merchant oligarchies.

Under William the Silent, who negotiated military and financial help from abroad, the rebels offered resourceful resistance to the Spanish. Philip's campaigns against the Turks in the Mediterranean and North Africa stretched his resources (▷ p. 115). The sack of Antwerp by unpaid Spanish troops in 1576 led to the temporary union of the whole Netherlands, the southern provinces making their own peace with Holland and Zeeland (the Pacification of Ghent) and obliging Philip to withdraw his troops from the Low Countries in 1577.

The Catholic nobles of the southern provinces of Flanders and Brabant remained loyal to Philip and were horrified at the progress of Calvinism in the north. Following popular disturbances in the south, they welcomed the Spaniards back as a guarantee of order. Philip II pledged to respect their privileges in the Union of Arras of 1579. Henceforth, those provinces south of the rivers Rhine, Maas, and Lek were an integral part of the Spanish empire.

The northern provinces formed their own league, the Union of Utrecht, in 1579, and declared their independence of Spain in 1581. Free of commitments elsewhere, Philip II's forces renewed their offensive against them. The assassination in 1584 of

William the Silent was a great loss to the Dutch. With their finances stretched by constant warfare, the rebels began to lose ground to the Spanish.

The Dutch were saved from defeat by supplies of men and money from England (from 1585), the diversion of Spanish efforts against England in the Armada of 1588 (▷ p. 118), and Philip's intervention in the French Wars of Religion in the 1590s (▷ p. 111). William the Silent's son, Count Maurice of Nassau (1566–1625), reformed the Dutch army and its tactics, and cleared the Spaniards from the northern provinces. An exhausted Spain was unable to take advantage of peace with France (1598) and England (1605) to crush the Dutch. In 1609 both sides agreed to a truce, but war was resumed in 1621. Fighting on many fronts in the Thirty Years War, Spain again could not defeat the Dutch. At the Peace of Westphalia in 1648 (▷ p. 113), Spain recognized the independence of the seven United Provinces – Holland, Zeeland, Friesland, Utrecht, Gelderland, Gronigen and Overissel.

Dutch politics and society

The United Provinces differed greatly from their neighbours. Having revolted to defend their privileges, they refused to surrender them to a strong central government of their own. Power lay with the merchants who dominated those towns with votes in the seven provincial assemblies. The merchant class was particularly powerful in the western maritime provinces, Holland and Zeeland, where there were numerous densely populated towns. Only in the poorer eastern provinces of Gronigen and Overissel did the nobility have much influence.

This system worked well in the 17th century. The main internal threat to it was the desire of successive princes of Orange in the 17th and 18th centuries to increase their authority. Their most consistent opponent was Amsterdam, the most powerful of the towns of Holland, which contributed a quarter of the total annual budget of the Republic.

The United Provinces was a remarkably tolerant society. Although officially Calvinist, much of its population remained Catholic. The merchants who dominated the maritime provinces recognized that toleration was good for business. They offered a refuge to Flemish Protestants, Portuguese Jews, and French Huguenots. Some of these, including the Jewish philosopher Baruch Spinoza (1632–77), made significant contributions to thought and learning, and helped to make the Republic an important intellectual centre.

The Dutch economy

The Dutch dominated Europe's trade and financial life in the 17th century. Their economic success was primarily concentrated in Holland (and to a lesser degree Zeeland and Friesland) and underpinned the independence and power of the merchants and towns of those provinces.

The Low Countries were not naturally wealthy, but were well placed to act as a channel of trade between the Baltic and the rest of Europe. Holland and Zeeland already dominated the North Sea fisheries and the carriage of bulky goods in and out of the Baltic before the Dutch Revolt. The enormous growth of Baltic trade in the 16th and 17th centuries mainly benefited the Dutch, whose merchant fleet by 1670 totalled more than those of all their rivals combined (▷ p. 128).

Overseas, the Dutch East India Company (founded 1602) broke the Portuguese monopoly of trade with the East Indies, and then conquered most of Portugal's East Indian and African trading empire. By 1680 a Dutch East Indian empire had been created, and the Dutch monopolized the profitable supply of eastern spices to Europe. The Dutch West India Company (founded 1621) temporarily wrested control of Brazil from the Portuguese (1630–45), and took permanent possession of the Caribbean island of Curaçao. From there they supplied African slaves to the plantations of Brazil, the West Indies, and America (▷ p. 128), and in turn purchased colonial goods for shipment to Holland and Zeeland, where they were processed and re-exported.

The United Provinces was also the financial centre of Europe (▷ p. 130). The remarkable commercial and financial services available in Amsterdam – through the Stock Exchange (1608), and the Loan and Exchange Banks (1609 and 1614) – encouraged investment and helped to keep interest rates low. Dutch expertise and capital played a crucial part in the development of agriculture, trade and industry elsewhere in Europe. Low interest rates benefited both agriculture and industry. The large urban population was a market for locally produced goods and provided a cheap supply of labour for the merchant fleet and for the shipbuilding yards and other occupations. Manufacturers were able to produce goods more cheaply than their foreign rivals.

The Dutch staunchly defended their commercial pre-eminence. They had destroyed the trading power of Antwerp in Spanish Flanders from 1585 with a blockade that the Spaniards were obliged to maintain after 1648. Dutch fleets intervened to prevent Sweden or Denmark from controlling the entrance to the Baltic, and successfully fought off England's attempts to destroy the Republic's European and colonial trade in the Anglo-Dutch Wars (▷ p. 128). In the later 17th century, the Dutch faced the commercial and territorial aggression of Louis XIV, whose attack in 1672 almost destroyed the Republic. Thereafter, under the leadership of William III of Orange (1672–1702), the Dutch played a leading role in the wars against France (▷ p. 123).

Dutch decline

By 1713 the Dutch economy was in difficulty, although serious decline did not set in until the later 18th century. Dutch trade was greatly disrupted by the War of the Spanish Succession (▷ p. 123) and the Great Northern War (▷ p. 126). Thereafter the Dutch avoided war, abandoning the vigorous foreign policy that had underpinned their earlier success. They continued to profit from the East Indies trade but played a much smaller role in Atlantic trade, where the biggest profits were made in the 18th century. These went to Britain and France, whose governments aggressively supported their merchants (▷ p. 128).

The growth of the merchant fleets of France and above all Britain freed these states from dependence on the Dutch, whose share of Baltic trade fell drastically. Deprived of their overseas markets, and lacking the domestic resources to sustain industrial development, Dutch industry declined. The Republic remained the financial centre of Europe, but Dutch investment was increasingly diverted abroad. Many Dutch towns stagnated, and the growing number of poor overwhelmed the charitable institutions that had been the envy of foreigners in the 17th century.

The political system blocked much-needed reforms, resulting in the emergence of a 'Patriot' movement that urged constitutional change. The 'Patriots' welcomed the invasion by French Revolutionary forces in 1794–5 and the collapse of the United Provinces in 1795. In the 1815 settlement following the Napoleonic Wars (▷ p. 147), the Republic was not restored, and instead, the entire Low Countries became the independent Kingdom of the Netherlands. CS

The elegant architecture, flourishing commerce and bourgeois solidity of Harlem as depicted by Gerrit Berckheyde in the late 17th century. A major artistic centre and a refuge for Huguenots, Harlem – and the Dutch Republic as a whole – was at the peak of its economic and cultural vigour during this period.

Louis XIV

Between the end of the Thirty Years War and the French Revolution the most characteristic form of government in Europe was absolute monarchy. In this style of government not only were kings unhindered by the need to refer to representative assemblies, but they also developed ways of controlling their states more firmly. The archetype of the absolute monarch was Louis XIV, king of France (1643–1715), whom many other rulers took as their model. Despite practical limitations on his absolutism, Louis was able to threaten Western Europe with French domination.

For much of the first half of the 17th century, France had been ruled by two chief ministers. Louis XIII (1610–43) had given great power to Cardinal Richelieu, and when Louis died his widow acted as regent for his son Louis XIV – then a child – though much power was in the hands of another chief minister, Cardinal Mazarin. Resentment of Mazarin's influence contributed to the outbreak of civil war in France (the so-called 'Frondes') in 1648–53.

Louis' personal rule in France

When Mazarin died in 1661, the 22-year-old Louis declared that henceforth he would rule personally. He did so until his death in 1715. His persistence owed a great deal to his belief (commonly held at that time) that kings ruled by divine right, receiving their power from God, and so must rule justly and in person. This belief is summed up in the famous words attributed to Louis, '*L'état c'est moi*' ('I am the state').

Louis had a number of very capable ministers, notably Jean Baptiste Colbert (minister of finance 1661–83) and the marquis de Louvois (war minister 1662–91), but made it clear that they were his servants and dependent on his favour. He also adopted the Sun as his personal emblem and commissioned artists and writers to glorify him as the Sun King (*le roi soleil*).

Royal academies were set up to promote and direct the arts and sciences. Colbert set up state trading companies and state-subsidized factories in order to stimulate the economy. This growing regulation and Colbert's efforts to increase tax revenue greatly stimulated the development of a centrally controlled bureaucracy.

Efforts were also made to end disorder. The nobles, who had been so unruly during the Frondes, were encouraged to attend Louis' court at Versailles (▷ box). Far away from their power bases in the provinces, and under the watchful eye of the king, they were less likely to cause mischief.

At the same time the king's power to suppress dissent was increased once Louvois had completed the creation of a large standing army. Religious division was strongly disapproved, and in 1685 Louis revoked the Edict of Nantes (▷ p. 111), which had declared toleration for Protestantism in France. Louis also asserted his authority over the Church in France against the pope, but subsequently allied with him to suppress the Jansenists, a radical and anti-papal school of thought within the French Church.

Louis and Europe

Louis' identification of himself with the state was most evident in his foreign policy. He was always jealous of his personal reputation, or *gloire* ('glory'), which he considered to be inseparable from that of France. One of Louis' main concerns, however, was France's vulnerability, and for this reason he had great fortresses built along the eastern and northeastern borders. Louis also believed in dynastic right, and asserted his claim to the Spanish empire that ringed France (▷ p. 116). Skilled French diplomacy was backed by the army, and by a large navy built by Colbert.

Between 1667 and 1713 Louis fought a series of increasingly large-scale and expensive wars in an effort to strengthen France's frontiers and assert his own prestige and dynastic rights (▷ box). As time went on the fear he aroused led to the formation of large coalitions against him; and the fact that after the Glorious Revolution of 1688 (▷ p. 119) England finally joined his enemies was a very serious setback. The peace of Ryswick (1697) saw Louis forced for the first time to return some of his previous gains, while the War of the Spanish Succession (1701–13) brought France close to collapse. When Louis died in 1715, he left France with much stronger defences, but at heavy economic and social cost – and with the other major European powers suspicious of French ambitions to dominate Europe.

VERSAILLES

The palace of Versailles remains the most enduring monument to Louis XIV's absolute rule. Louis had a great passion for building, and he also had unpleasant memories of Paris during the Frondes. He therefore built the greatest of his palaces at Versailles, outside Paris.

Originally a hunting lodge, it was transformed between 1670 and 1700 by the addition of two wings in an ornate rococo style designed by J.H. Mansart, and the laying out of extensive formal gardens by André Le Nôtre. The interior was redesigned by Charles Le Brun, with much gilt and glass, and many tapestries. These were often supplied by subsidized factories, such as the famous Gobelins tapestry factory. Paintings celebrated Louis' military successes in the Dutch War and his achievements within France. The image of the Sun – Louis' personal emblem – was everywhere.

Louis personally directed much of the works, which employed 36 000 men in the 1680s and cost 70 million livres. They were still unfinished when he and his court took up residence from the 1670s. Eventually 15 000 people lived there and in the adjacent town.

Versailles remained the residence of the absolute monarchy until 1789. Here Louis saw his ministers, gave his orders, and received foreign princes and ambassadors. Spectacular entertainments stressed the king's magnificence, many of these being contrived by the playwright Molière and the composer Lully. Life at Versailles revolved around Louis' daily routine: it was claimed that the time could be told simply by knowing what Louis was doing.

The greater nobles were expected to attend the court as a sign of loyalty, and did so, competing with each other to perform menial tasks around Louis, since that was the means to royal favour. Banishment from Versailles and the king's presence became a severe punishment. In this way Louis reduced the independence of the nobility and reinforced his own power.

The Palace of Versailles, as depicted in 1722 by Pierre Denis Martin. As well as being Louis XIV's greatest memorial, Versailles was also to become the scene of Britain's recognition of American independence (1783), the crowning of Wilhelm I as the first emperor of Germany (1871), and the signing of the main peace treaty after World War I.

Yet French influence remained great. Other rulers in Europe envied Louis' authority in France and his success abroad. Those who had not already introduced absolutist measures copied his bureaucracy, his tax system, his standing army, his academies, and his style of personal rule. Many set up court in great new palaces away from their capitals in imitation of Versailles. The fashions, craftmanship, manners and neoclassical literature of France's *Grand Siècle* ('great century') were widely imitated.

The limits of absolutism

Yet despite greater central control, a large number of individuals, groups and provinces enjoyed privileges restricting Louis' authority. Since Louis had neither the resources nor the inclination to end these privileges, the administration of France was by no means completely centralized or uniform. Much of it remained in the hands of independent officials. Louis therefore depended on the cooperation of the privileged groups, and their desire for order. His government also depended increasingly on huge loans from private financiers.

These limits were made clear in the 1690s and 1700s, when Louis' wars demanded more money. More offices were sold, and the tax burden and government debt vastly increased. The growing burden on the mass of the population became even heavier when accompanied, as in 1693–4 and in 1709, by harvest failure and famine.

Nevertheless absolute monarchy was still intact in 1715. It declined under Louis XIV's successors because neither Louis XV nor Louis XVI had the same capacity to run the machine. Even so, its survival until the Revolution in 1789 (➪ p. 144) contributed to the long-term centralization of French government. CS

EUROPE IN 1715

— Boundary of Holy Roman Empire

FINLAND occupied by Russia 1744 returned to Sweden 1721

RUSSIAN EMPIRE

KINGDOM OF SWEDEN

KINGDOM OF DENMARK

to Denmark

HANOVER

to Denmark

PRUSSIA

KINGDOM OF POLAND

KINGDOM OF GREAT BRITAIN

UNITED PROVINCES

KINGDOM OF

SAXONY

AUSTRIAN NETHERLANDS

Minor German States

LUXEMBURG

LORRAINE

Versailles ● Paris

AUSTRIAN DOMINIONS

KINGDOM OF FRANCE

Franche-Comté

BAVARIA

HUNGARY

MILAN (to Austria)

SWITZER-LAND

SAVOY

VENICE

to Papacy

to Venice

OTTOMAN EMPIRE

GENOA

CORSICA (to Genoa)

Minor Italian States

to Venice

RAGUSA (modern Dubrovnik)

PAPAL STATES

NAPLES (to Austria)

KINGDOM OF PORTUGAL

KINGDOM OF SPAIN

MINORCA (to Britain)

SARDINIA (to Austria)

SICILY (to Savoy)

to Venice

CEUTA (to Spain)

GIBRALTAR (to Britain)

MELILLA (to Spain)

KINGDOM OF MOROCCO

REGENCY OF ALGIERS

BEYUK OF TUNIS

THE WARS OF LOUIS XIV

In 1667 Louis invaded the Spanish Netherlands (➪ map, p. 113), invoking a dubious legal claim that it was part of his wife's inheritance. This move marked the beginning of the War of Devolution (1667–8), the first of a series of wars that were to occupy a considerable part of Louis' long reign.

Alarmed at French aggression against a declining Spain, England, the United Provinces and Sweden formed a defensive alliance, obliging Louis to retreat. In the Treaty of Aix-la-Chapelle (1668) Louis was forced to restore the land he had seized, and was allowed to retain only a small number of towns in the Spanish Low Countries.

For Louis the Dutch represented a threat to his long-term designs on the Spanish Netherlands. His next move was to isolate the United Provinces by diplomatic means, before invading them in 1672. The Dutch War (1672–8) brought the United Provinces close to collapse, but they were saved by forming a coalition with England, Spain, and Austria. Yet Louis' resources proved the greater, and in 1678 his diplomats succeeding in separating the Dutch from their allies. In the Treaty of Nijmegen (1678–9) Louis acquired Franche Comté (a region of eastern France) from Spain. The Truce of Ratisbon (1684) – which concluded a further short war with Spain – forced Spain to cede Luxemburg to France, and brought

Louis to the peak of his power in Europe.

A new cause of concern for Louis was the growing power of Austria, which achieved some notable victories against the Turks in the Balkans in the 1680s (➪ p. 124). Anxious about the implications for his own power and security of these Habsburg successes, Louis launched a pre-emptive attack on the Rhineland in 1688. His aggression led to the formation of a 'Grand Alliance' of England, the United Provinces, Austria, Spain, and Savoy, and marked the start of the Nine Years War (also known as the War of the Grand Alliance, 1688–97). A leading role in directing the alliance was played by William III, king of England and effective ruler of the United Provinces since 1672. Louis waged successful campaigns in northern Italy and Catalonia, and managed to detach Savoy from the alliance, but the war in the Spanish Netherlands degenerated into a debilitating stalemate. The greater financial resources of England and the United Provinces ultimately decided matters in the alliance's favour. In the Treaty of Ryswick (1697) Louis was obliged to recognize William III as king of England, end his occupation of Lorraine, and restore Luxemburg to Spain.

In 1700 the childless Charles II of Spain died, bequeathing his empire to Louis' grandson, Philip of Anjou (the future Philip V of Spain). Louis – who had

previously agreed to divide the Spanish empire between France and Austria in the event of Charles' death – could not resist the opportunity of preventing Spain from falling into the hands of the Austrian Habsburgs (who also claimed to have inherited the right to rule the Spanish empire); he accepted Charles's will, and began to intervene in Spanish affairs. To counter the renewed threat of French domination of Europe, William III of England formed a grand alliance of England, the United Provinces, Austria and Savoy, with the intention of putting the rival Austrian candidate – the Archduke Charles – on the throne of Spain. In the ensuing War of the Spanish Succession (1701–13) the resources of the allies, and the superiority of their generals – notably the Duke of Marlborough and Prince Eugène of Savoy – brought France near to collapse. The Treaties of Utrecht (1713) and Rastadt (1714) represented a defeat for Louis. He surrendered his gains on the right bank of the Rhine, and ceded valuable colonial concessions to Britain. Philip remained on the Spanish throne, but had to renounce his claim to the French throne and was obliged to give up Spain's European possessions. The Austrian Habsburgs gained the Spanish Low Countries and also became the dominant power in Italy (➪ map). France remained a great power, but its domination of Europe had been significantly checked.

Central Europe: The Struggle for Power 1648–1806

Although Germany's economy had prospered in the 16th century, Germany took little part in the great voyages of discovery and was poorly placed to exploit the trading possibilities associated with them. German firms such as the Fuggers and Welsers of Augsburg and the Hanseatic League (▷ pp. 99 and 130) could not compete with the growing rivalry of government-backed foreign merchants. Consequently, the German economy was already in relative decline before 1618. The Thirty Years War exacerbated these difficulties, Germany's population being reduced from 20 to about 16 million (▷ p. 113).

This war also confirmed the breakdown of the authority of the Holy Roman Emperor over the German princes, thus hastening the political fragmentation of Germany. Nevertheless the imperial office remained a source of prestige and limited power to the Austrian Habsburgs (in which family it was virtually hereditary; ▷ p. 85). The political division of Germany also left Austria as the most potent force there, since the Habsburgs had now increased their control of their own territories (▷ map, p. 113) and established a standing army. The German princes remained suspicious of Habsburg and imperial power after 1648. Preoccupied with the reconstruction of their devastated lands, many looked to France for protection (▷ p. 123).

The Austrian empire 1660–1740

Leopold I (1658–1705) wished to pursue political and dynastic ambitions in western Europe, notably the Habsburg claim to the Spanish Succession, which brought him into conflict with Austria's chief rival, Louis XIV (▷ below). However, he faced a number of domestic problems. The tighter grip he exerted over the Habsburg territories – Austria, Bohemia and that part of Hungary not in Turkish hands – had not established real unity. This was supplied only by their common subjection to the same ruler and, to a lesser extent, by Counter-Reformation Catholicism (▷ p. 112). Nor did Leopold's resources match those of France. Leopold achieved little against Louis XIV in the wars of the 1670s and 1680s (▷ p. 123).

However the 1680s and 1690s saw a number of brilliant Habsburg successes in the Danube valley. These were facilitated by the formation in 1684 of a Holy League, which allied the Holy Roman Emperor with Poland and the papacy and was later joined by Russia. The great Austrian general Prince Eugène of Savoy ended the war with the Turks by decisively defeating them at Zenta (1697); and the Treaty of Carlowitz in 1699 ceded Hungary and Transylvania to Austria.

When the Holy Roman Emperor Charles VI (1711–40) renewed the war in the Balkans in 1716 Prince Eugène gained further victories. In 1718 northern Serbia, including Belgrade and Temesvár (now Timisoara in Romania), were ceded by the Ottoman Empire. The Habsburgs also made impressive gains in the Netherlands and Italy during these decades. They played an important role in the Nine Years War with Louis XIV (1689–97; ▷ p. 123), and at the end of the War of the Spanish Succession (1701–13/14; ▷ p. 123) Charles VI received the Spanish Netherlands as well as the Duchy of Milan, the Kingdom of Naples and Sardinia (which was exchanged for Sicily in 1719; ▷ map, p. 113). Austria was now the dominant power in Italy.

By 1720 the Austrian Habsburgs had acquired a European empire, most of it outside the Holy Roman Empire. Yet it remained united by little more than the Habsburg dynasty. This, and the inability to extract from their generally poor domains the revenues needed to pay for large armies, made Austria weaker than most of the other great powers. Austria was defeated by France, Spain and Sardinia in the War of the Polish Succession (1733–8), and by Turkey in the war of 1736–9, losing some of its recent territorial gains.

A more serious problem arose over the succession to the Emperor Charles VI. Charles's Pragmatic Sanction of 1713 decreed that all Habsburg territories were to pass undivided to his children. By 1720, lacking a male heir, Charles feared the destruction of the Austrian empire after his death. He sought to prevent it by obtaining a promise from the European powers to respect the succession of his eldest daughter, Maria Theresa (or Theresia), to all her father's lands (▷ below).

The battle of Olmütz, 30 June 1758. Frederick the Great was forced to abandon his siege of the Moravian town when the Austrians destroyed the Prussian supply column of 4000 wagons. Despite inflicting many such defeats on Frederick during the Seven Years War, Austria was unsuccessful in its attempts to wrest its lost province of Silesia from Prussian hands.

Brandenburg-Prussia to 1740

Brandenburg and Prussia were the largest and most important of the widely scattered territories ruled by the Calvinist Hohenzollern Electors (the duchy of Prussia had passed under the control of the Electors of Brandenburg in 1618). Brandenburg-Prussia had suffered greatly in the Thirty Years War. Frederick William, the Great Elector (1640–88), encouraged foreign – including Huguenot – settlement as part of its reconstruction. He also established a standing army and efficient bureaucracy, and eroded the power of the representative assemblies in his territories.

Prussia's administration and army were perfected by the reforms of King Frederick William I (1713–40). Thereafter a centralized bureaucracy united his scattered provinces and ensured a regular supply of conscripts for an army of 80 000 men. This represented a larger proportion of the country's population (2.25 million) than in any other European state. Bureaucratic efficiency helped finance the army by maximizing revenues. Royal authority was tempered only by an alliance with the Prussian nobility (Junkers), who were given effective control over the peasantry in return for their support and service, particularly as army officers.

Prussia showed her military potential by defeating the Swedes at Fehrbellin in 1675. She was also a member of the alliances against Louis XIV in the 1690s and 1700s – for which the Elector received the title of King of Prussia (1701) from the Emperor – and the alliance against Sweden in the Great Northern War (⊳ p. 127). Military successes in 1720 brought Prussia new territories in Pomerania. However, since Frederick William I was unwilling to use his army in an independent foreign policy, Prussia remained a second-rank power. It was neither feared nor respected and by no means the superior of the other large German states – Bavaria, Saxony and Hanover; it was certainly not yet the rival of Austria.

The wars of Frederick the Great

Frederick II (the Great) of Prussia (1740–86) transformed the position of his state and was in many respects the most successful of the 'enlightened despots' (⊳ p. 134). He believed that foreign policy should be based upon the interests of the state rather than on morality and dynastic right, and that war should be an instrument of this policy. A military pragmatist, he fought only when necessary and sought the rapid defeat of his opponents (even if they outnumbered his own forces). His military strategy – involving rapid movement and offensive battle tactics – contrasted with the general preference of 18th-century armies for siege warfare and almost leisurely manoeuvre.

In 1740, without declaring war, Frederick seized Silesia from Maria Theresa of Austria (1740–80). Frederick's action – a signal for other states to renege on their promises to Charles VI – precipitated the War of the Austrian Succession. The war's central issue was the right of Maria Theresa to succeed to her father's lands. This was challenged not merely by Frederick but by the Elector Charles Albert of Bavaria, who ruled as Holy Roman Emperor in 1742–5 and was supported by Frederick and Louis XIV of France. After Charles Albert's death, however, Maria Theresa secured the imperial title for her husband, Francis of Lorraine, who became Francis I (1745–65). The conflict was complicated by a number of related disputes, notably Spanish-Austrian rivalry in Italy, the British challenge to Franco-Spanish domination of the Mediterranean, and the continuing struggle between Britain and France over colonial possessions in America and India (⊳ p. 129).

In 1741, invaded by French and Bavarian forces, the Austrian empire seemed about to collapse. However, due largely to the loyalty of Hungary and the support of Britain (ruled since 1714 by the Electors of Hanover and closely involved in German affairs; ⊳ p. 119), the Austrian empire survived intact except for the loss of Silesia to Frederick. This was confirmed at the general peace of Aix-la-Chapelle (1748).

Eager to recover Silesia and to remedy the weaknesses exposed by the war, Maria Theresa introduced reforms based partly on Prussian models. These transformed the Austrian empire, establishing greater centralized coordination of – and unity between – her Austrian and Bohemian realms. Increased revenues financed a larger army. The enmity between Austria and France was replaced by an alliance between the two – the so-called Diplomatic Revolution of 1756.

Those issues left unresolved at Aix-la-Chapelle – Austro-Prussian rivalry in Germany and the Anglo-French colonial struggle – were continued in the Seven Years War (1756–63; ⊳ also p. 129). A wide-ranging conflict fought in Europe, India, and North America, it pitted Prussia, Britain and Hanover against Austria, France, Russia, Sweden and Spain.

Frederick made the opening move with an invasion of Saxony (1756), but he faced overwhelming odds. Despite his alliance with Britain, and victories over much larger opposing forces, Frederick's territories were severely pressed, particularly by the Russians, who devastated East Prussia. Near collapse, Prussia was saved by the accession of Tsar Peter III (1762), whose admiration for Frederick undermined the coalition. Frederick kept Silesia at the Peace of Paris (1763). Prussia's heroic resistance confirmed its new status as a great power, and a rival to Austria in Germany.

Reform and reconstruction

The decades after 1763 saw greater stability in Germany and Austria. War had again exposed Austria's weaknesses, prompting further reforms by Maria Theresa and her more radical son, Joseph II (1780–90; ⊳ p. 134). His measures to establish greater centralized control over Hungary and the Low Countries provoked resistance and had to be withdrawn. In Prussia the devastation of Frederick's territories during the Seven Years War required a period of reconstruction. Peace did not prevent further Prussian territorial gains (⊳ box). It also contributed to greater economic prosperity and cultural achievement.

This situation was transformed after 1789. The victorious armies of republican and imperial France again exposed the weaknesses of the Austrian empire and also defeated the Prussians. In 1806 Napoleon abolished the Holy Roman Empire, and it was not restored at the general peace settlement in 1815 (⊳ p. 147). Austro-Prussian rivalry continued, while French domination spurred the growth of German national feeling (⊳ pp. 150 and 153).   CS

The Empress Maria Theresa with her husband the emperor Francis I at Schönbrünn Palace in Vienna. Among their many children are the future emperor Joseph II, and Marie Antoinette, the future queen of France.

THE PARTITIONS OF POLAND

In the 18th century Poland-Lithuania was a very large state, but its monarchy – elective since 1572 – was weak. Real power lay with the nobles, who resisted efforts at administrative and military reform similar to those in neighbouring states. Polish social and economic life was extremely backward.

Russia's successes against the Turks in the Balkans (1768–72) alarmed Austria, which threatened to enter the war against Russia. Frederick the Great feared that a general war would be disastrous for Prussia and was anxious to calm Austro-Russian relations by shifting the focus of Russian territorial expansion away from the Ottoman provinces. Thus he proposed that Austria, Prussia and Russia divide up considerable portions of Polish territory between them. All would gain without upsetting the balance of power between them. Poland, then in the grip of civil war, was ill-equipped to withstand territorial seizures. In the First Partition (1772) it lost one-third of its territory and population to the three powers.

Reforming Poles hoped to prevent further losses by establishing a strong constitutional monarchy (1791). Catherine II of Russia saw this as a threat to her gains and as a sign of the arrival of revolutionary radicalism in eastern Europe. With Prussia she effected a Second Partition (1793), in which Poland lost half of its remaining territories. A Polish revolt against Russian rule was suppressed and a Third Partition carried out by Austria, Prussia, and Russia (1795). With this final partition Poland disappeared from the map of Europe. It would not regain independent sovereign statehood until the end of World War I, when Poland was finally restored as a republic (see p. 182).

The Emergence of Russia

There was little contact between Russia and Western Europe in the earlier Middle Ages. Between the 14th and 17th centuries, however, cultural and commercial links between Europe and Russia were growing. Great changes in many aspects of Russian life were introduced or accelerated by Peter the Great in the late 17th and early 18th centuries, while victory over Sweden during his reign helped Russia become politically part of Europe.

However, certain aspects of Russian society – notably the role of serfdom – still marked it as different from that of Western Europe, while Russia's continued expansion in the later 18th century created new international tensions.

The rise of Muscovy

The town of Moscow was founded in the 12th century by Slavs who had settled European Russia in the 9th century and subsequently converted to Christianity. It formed part of Kiev Rus, a feudal state ruled by the Rurik dynasty from the 9th to the 13th centuries (▷ p. 86). Kiev Rus was at its peak in the 10th and 11th centuries, but declined thereafter, collapsing in the face of the Mongol onslaught in the 13th century. Kiev was destroyed in 1240 and Rus became part of the Mongol (or Tartar) Empire (▷ p. 54).

Moscow benefited from a good defensive and trading position, and also from a succession of able rulers who cultivated good relations with their Tartar overlords. Ivan I (1325–40) obtained the title of 'Grand Prince' from the Mongol khan. He also formed a close alliance with the metropolitan (head) of the Russian branch of the Orthodox Church, whose seat was transferred to Moscow in 1326. By the middle of the 15th century Muscovy had asserted its independence of the Mongol Empire (which had broken up into a number of independent states; ▷ p. 55) and was the most powerful of the Christian Slav principalities of Russia. Ivan III ('the Great'; 1462–1505) incorporated most of these into Muscovy, greatly expanding its territory, and laid down the foundations of the centralized Russian state.

Ivan IV ('the Terrible'; 1533–84), a ruthless autocrat, adopted the title of tsar (from the Latin *Caesar*, or emperor) of all Russia. His conquest of Tartar Kazan (1552) and Astrakhan (1556) extended his rule to the Caspian Sea, and opened the way for a Russian advance into Siberia in the later 16th century. Further progress to the south was blocked by the Ottoman Turks (overlords of the Crimean Tartars since 1475). To the west Muscovy was faced by the enormous and still powerful state of Poland–Lithuania and the nascent Swedish Empire (▷ box). Ivan made a number of legal and administrative reforms and significantly reduced the power of the boyars (the highest class of Russian aristocracy).

The rule of Ivan's son, Theodore I (1584–98), the last of his dynasty, and that of the elected Tsar Boris Godunov (1598–1605) was challenged by boyar families. During the 'Time of Troubles' (1605–13) there were a number of rival candidates for the throne. The difficulties created by these pretenders were exploited by Sweden and Poland. Following the election of Tsar Michael Romanov (1613–45), and the concession of territory to both Sweden and Poland, Muscovy recovered stability and prosperity and resumed its advance, reaching the Pacific by 1700. In the west, Alexis I (1645–76) exploited Poland's growing weakness to gain much of the Ukraine (1667).

Serfdom

Constant warfare greatly reduced Muscovy's peasant population, depriving the landowners of the labour to work their lands and the tsar of soldiers and taxpayers. To prevent further losses by peasant emigration, a growing body of laws tied much of the peasantry to the land in the 16th century. These peasants became 'unfree' serfs. This legislation was consolidated and tightened up as part of a general codification of Russian law in 1649. Henceforth landlords were absolute masters of a growing serf population, and collected the taxes paid by the latter.

For 200 years after 1649 serfdom was the dominant feature of Russian society. Many peasants sought to escape. Some fled to join the Cossacks – runaways and frontiersmen who lived in the borderlands between Muscovy, Poland and the Ottoman empire and were employed as irregular troops by those states (whose rulers nevertheless sought to reduce their independence). Others revolted, sometimes aided by the Cossacks. These rebellions were crushed by landowners and governments who found serfdom too useful to be abolished.

Peter the Great

Growing trade with Europe brought foreigners and new intellectual influences to Moscow in the 17th century. However, with no coastline except in the far north, and much power in the hands of the highly conservative Orthodox Church, Muscovy was still largely isolated from Western Europe.

Peter I ('the Great'; joint tsar with Ivan V 1682–96, sole tsar 1696–1725) transformed Russia and its international position. Often gross and brutal, he was also forward-looking and immensely energetic. Peter captured Azov from the Turks in 1696, hoping by this to obtain an outlet on the Black Sea. He toured Western Europe in 1697–8 – he was the first tsar to go there – to obtain support for further efforts against the Turks. Excluded from the Treaty of Carlowitz (1699) by his Austrian, Polish and Venetian allies, Peter had to conclude his own peace with the Turks in 1700 (the Treaty of Constantinople).

Peter now turned his attention to the Baltic, hoping to recover a secure outlet to the sea with the help of Denmark, Saxony and Poland (▷ box). After defeat by a smaller Swedish force at the battle of Narva (1700), Peter accelerated reform of the Russian army. Henceforth all Russian regiments were organized along Western lines. Evidence of the effectiveness of these reforms was provided by the Russian defeat of the Swedes at the decisive battle of Poltava (1709).

In 1703 Peter had begun the building of St Petersburg, which he modelled on Western cities. In 1712 he moved his capital there from Moscow. Situated at the mouth of the river Neva, St Petersburg gave easier access to the Baltic and Western Europe. Russia's new Baltic fleet, which Peter built up from nothing, made Russia an effective power on both sea and land for the first time.

To mobilize the resources needed for war, Peter established a more bureaucratic and centralized government, which also made his power more effective in Russia. He created a senate (1711) to provide overall direction, and replaced the numerous overlapping government departments with a smaller number of administrative colleges (1718–19) with well-defined duties. Below these were the provincial governments (also reformed by Peter) and

Ivan the Terrible, tsar of Russia, depicted in a 16th-century engraving. An assiduous reformer in his early years, from 1564 he embarked on a reign of terror, partly as a result of his deteriorating mental condition. In 1580 he killed his son and heir in a fit of rage, and spent the rest of his life in penance.

a growing body of local officials. Many of these innovations copied the practices of Russia's European neighbours.

Peter used Church revenues to pay for the war and broke the political power of the Orthodox Church in Russia. He replaced the Patriarchate (set up at the end of the 16th century to give the Russian Church greater independence from Constantinople) with the Holy Synod (1721). A layman appointed by Peter himself ran the Synod, and was responsible for Church affairs in general.

Since Russia lacked the private enterprise necessary for the provision of vital war supplies, Peter set up state-owned industries and subsidized private initiatives. He also intensified the burden of serfdom. Serfs were forced to pay a poll tax (introduced to pay for the war) and were conscripted into the army. These were to remain features of Russian life until the late 19th century. To provide officers and bureaucrats for the growing army and administration, Peter insisted that all landowners must serve the state, and granted hereditary nobility to senior soldiers and civil servants (the Table of Ranks, 1722). He sent Russians to the West to learn practical skills, contributing to the spread of Western influence in Russia.

A disastrous war against the Turks in 1711 resulted in the loss of Azov. But in the west Peter's armies established Russian influence in Poland, reduced the independence of the Cossacks of the Ukraine, and conquered Estonia, Latvia, and Ingria. The latter were formally ceded by Sweden in the Treaty of Nystad in 1721. Peter adopted the Western title of emperor, having gained enormous prestige in Europe for himself and his country.

Twenty years of war had produced major changes in Russia, but the Westernized face of St Petersburg was hardly an accurate reflection of Russian society. Apart from the impositions of fresh burdens of taxation and conscription, life for the mass of Russia's preponderantly peasant society changed little under Peter the Great.

Russia after 1725

Under Peter's successors some of his innovations, notably the navy, were neglected, and Russia did not play a major part in European affairs until the Seven Years War (▷ p. 125).

Distance made military intervention in Europe difficult, but Russia's inactivity also owed something to the weakness of Peter's successors. The obligation of the nobility to serve the state was eroded, and eventually abolished in 1762. The Charter to the Nobility (1785) issued by the reforming Empress Catherine II ('the Great', 1762–96; ▷ p. 134) recognized the nobility as a privileged order in Russian society with a role similar to that of its counterpart nobilities elsewhere in Europe. The nobles also benefited from grants of serfs from the empress, who extended serfdom to the Ukraine (1783).

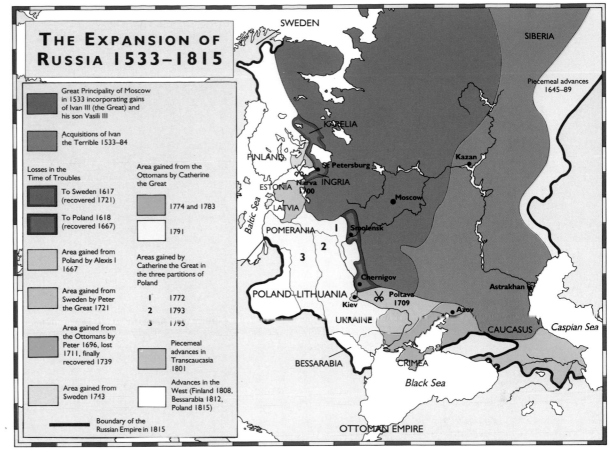

THE EXPANSION OF RUSSIA 1533–1815

Great Principality of Moscow in 1533 incorporating gains of Ivan III (the Great) and his son Vasili III

Acquisitions of Ivan the Terrible 1533–84

Losses in the Time of Troubles

To Sweden 1617 (recovered 1721)

To Poland 1618 (recovered 1667)

Area gained from Poland by Alexis I 1667

Area gained from Sweden by Peter the Great 1721

Area gained from the Ottomans by Peter 1696, lost 1711, finally recovered 1739

Area gained from Sweden 1743

Area gained from the Ottomans by Catherine the Great

1774 and 1783

1791

Areas gained by Catherine the Great in the three partitions of Poland

1   1772
2   1793
3   1795

Piecemeal advances in Transcaucasia 1801

Advances in the West (Finland 1808, Bessarabia 1812, Poland 1815)

Boundary of the Russian Empire in 1815

Under Catherine Russia resumed its territorial advance. A successful war against the declining Ottoman Turks (1768–74) brought substantial gains. The Crimea was freed from Ottoman rule by the Treaty of Kutchuk Kainardji (1774) and seized by Catherine in 1783. With the Crimea in Russian hands, Catherine's gifted administrator Potemkin was able to build a Black Sea fleet and a naval base at Sevastopol. Russia was also the major beneficiary of the Partitions of Poland (▷ p. 125). After suppressing a peasant and Cossack revolt – the Pugachev rebellion (1773–5) – Catherine strengthened central government control by a reform of the provincial administration.

Her successors played a leading role in the Revolutionary and Napoleonic wars (▷ p. 146) and continued the process of expansion. Russia seized Finland from Sweden (1809), Bessarabia from the Turks (1812), gained most of Poland in the peace settlement in 1815, and advanced into the Caucasus. Between 1815 and 1900 Russia made significant gains in Central Asia, securing control of Kazakh territory and a number of khanates to the south. In the Far East the region north of the Amur was conquered at the expense of the Chinese Empire (1856–76). Russia's continued expansion was to be a source of anxiety for the rest of Europe in the 19th century (▷ p. 154).   cs

Colonial Expansion in the 17th and 18th Centuries

European expansion overseas in the 16th century had been limited to Spain and Portugal (⇨ p. 116), and the Spanish colonial empire remained the largest in the world in the 17th and 18th centuries. However, in the 17th century new colonial empires were created by the maritime states of northwest Europe – Britain, France and the Dutch Republic. Much of this expansion was at the expense of Spain and Portugal, but Europeans were also making their presence felt in new areas. These new empires provided Europe with a wide range of colonial products and stimulated the demand for and production of European manufactured goods.

THE ATLANTIC ECONOMY IN THE MID-18TH CENTURY
HUDSON BAY
FURS
CANADA
Louisburg
Quebec
NEWFOUNDLAND
FISH
NOVA SCOTIA
Mississippi
TOBACCO
LOUISIANA
MANUFACTURED GOODS
SUGAR
FLORIDA
WEST INDIES
Caribbean Sea
BARBADOS
WEST AFRICA
COFFEE
SLAVES
'The Middle Passage'
BRAZIL
SPICES
SILKS
COTTONS
TEA and COFFEE
COLONIAL POWERS
BRITAIN
FRANCE
SPAIN
DUTCH REPUBLIC
PORTUGAL

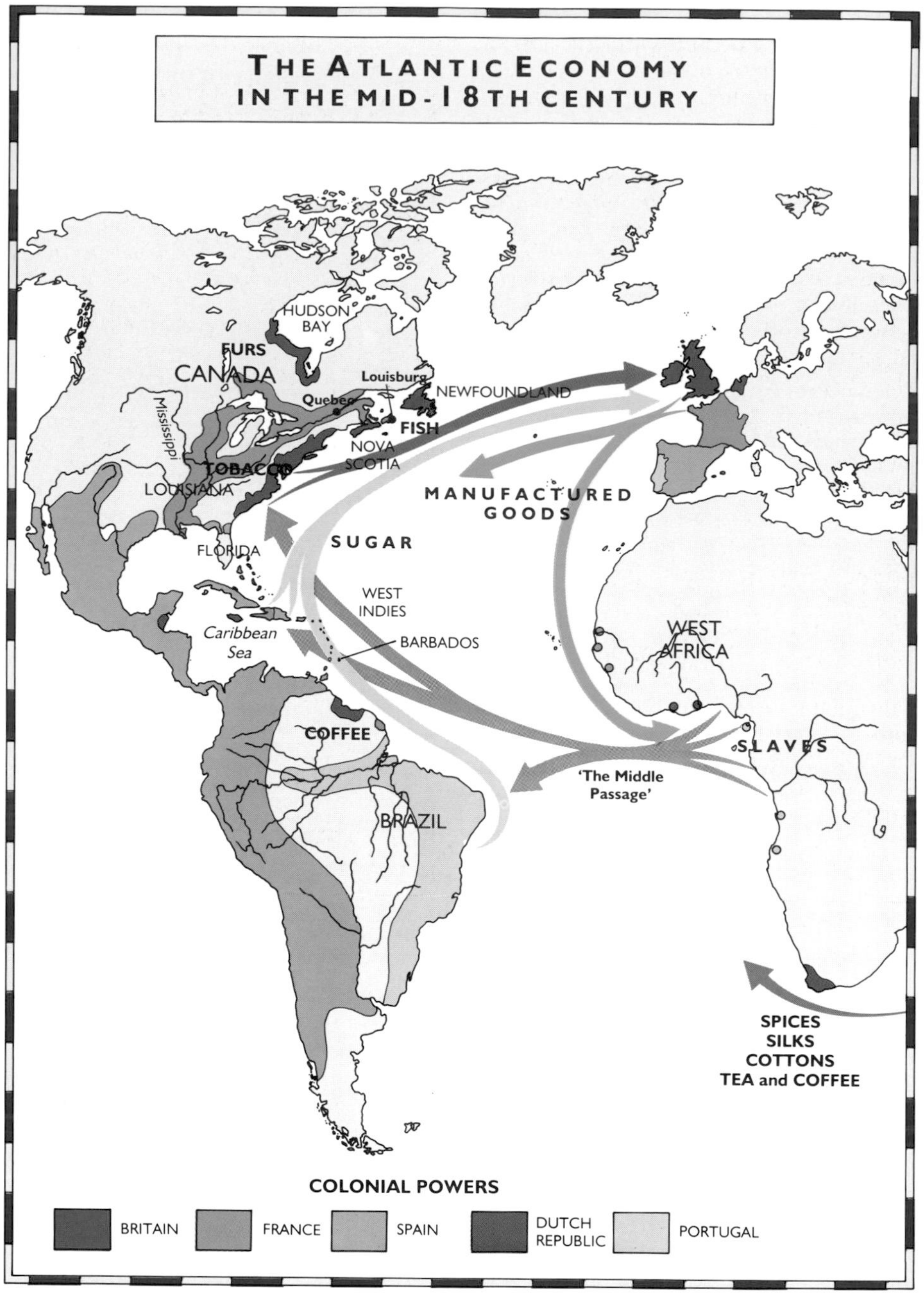

The wealth of their new trading empires increased the importance of Britain and the Dutch Republic in European politics. These states were therefore eager to defend and add to their colonies, and this led to wars that were fought all over the world.

Colonial trade, mercantilism and settlement

Europe's overseas trade boomed in the 17th and 18th centuries owing to growing demand for a wider range of goods: timber and other naval stores, furs, tobacco, rice, and fish (all from North America), tea, cotton and silk (from the East), coffee (from Java, the Americas, and the East), but above all sugar (from Brazil and the West Indies). The sugar, tobacco, and coffee plantations depended on regular supplies of black slaves from West Africa (⇨ box). A trade 'triangle' developed. Traders from Europe bought slaves in West Africa, carrying them to the Americas. There they traded them for colonial products with which they returned to Europe (⇨ map). In Europe, processing industries refined those goods for re-export to other parts of Europe.

The attitude of the governments of the period towards their colonies was influenced by the theories of 'mercantilism'. These theories assumed the amount of wealth in the world to be fixed, and therefore that individual states had to ensure that their subjects achieved the largest share possible of world trade. Since success depended on a favourable trade balance, governments felt that their policies should encourage manufactured exports, and discourage their import. It was thought that a country's trade should be monopolized by its own subjects and that colonies existed only to benefit the mother country.

European governments therefore encouraged production of valuable commodities in their own colonies and the formation of overseas trading companies. These were generally founded by government charter and had a monopoly of the trade of a given area. Typical of these were the British East India Company (1600) – Britain's biggest trading organization in the 18th century – and the Dutch (1602) and French (1664) East India Companies. The British East India Company wielded considerable political influence.

Although mercantilists thought colonial settlement encouraged demand for home exports, colonies were regarded more as sources of profit than as outlets for excess population. Settlement, which was heaviest in the Americas, was often independent of government sponsorship (⇨ p. 142).

The Anglo-Dutch Wars

Profits from the Dutch domination of the maritime trade between the Baltic and southern Europe provided capital for colonial projects. In the first half of the 17th century the Dutch seized most of Portugal's scattered East Indian empire, along with its valuable spice trade. They also captured many of its African forts, and temporarily held part of Brazil. During the English Civil War, the Dutch also gained a hold on England's trade with her North American colonies.

The Dutch were therefore the target for the mercantilist policies of their rivals. From 1651 Navigation Acts reserved the

SEE ALSO

- THE SPANISH AND PORTUGUESE EMPIRES p. 116
- THE RISE OF BRITAIN p. 118
- THE DUTCH REPUBLIC p. 120
- THE RISE OF THE BOURGEOISIE p. 130
- THE BIRTH OF THE USA p. 142
- THE PEAK OF EMPIRE p. 160

produce of England's colonies for England, and their carriage to English shipping. The Acts contributed to a series of Anglo-Dutch Wars (1652–4, 1665–7, 1672–4) fought out – mostly at sea – in many parts of the world. England ousted the Dutch from North America and West Africa – and so from the slave trade (▷ box) – and gradually excluded them from its foreign and colonial trades. Expensive land wars against France overstretched Dutch resources, and by 1713 – when the wars of Louis XIV ended (▷ p. 123) – the Dutch were being overtaken by both Britain and France.

The Anglo-French colonial struggle

Britain and France now increasingly felt that each was the other's natural trading and colonial rival. French colonization had begun in a number of West Indian islands and Canada early in the 17th century, and in Louisiana (which then comprised much of the Mississippi basin) at the end of the 17th century. In 1713 Britain took advantage of her victory in Europe (▷ p. 123) to secure her position in North America, gaining Nova Scotia, Newfoundland, and Hudson's Bay. The two countries were on opposing sides during the War of the Austrian Succession (1740–8), when for the first time the British and French East India Companies fought each other in India, the French taking Madras (1746). British naval supremacy halted France's overseas and colonial trade, and contributed to the capture of the French fortress of Louisburg in North America (1745), but was offset by the French threat in Europe. But neither country had gained a decisive advantage and the struggle continued.

Fighting in North America contributed to the outbreak of the Seven Years War (1756–63; ▷ p. 125). While Prussia distracted France in Germany, the British navy achieved domination over the French at sea in the battles of Lagos and Quiberon Bay (1759). Most of France's main colonies were captured, including Canada, thanks to the victory (1759) of General James Wolfe at Quebec. In India, under the generalship of Robert Clive, the British East India Company achieved military successes against the French and Indians (notably at Plassey; 1757), and emerged as the most powerful trader in India. The next hundred years would confirm British domination of the subcontinent (▷ pp. 63 and 160). In the Treaty of Paris (1763), which ended the Seven Years War, Britain returned France's West Indian islands but gained Florida from France's ally Spain (which received Louisiana as compensation). France renewed the struggle during the War of American Independence (1776–83, ▷ p. 142). Yet, despite Britain's loss of its American colonies, the war did not reverse Britain's long-term victory in the colonial struggle.   CS

THE SLAVE TRADE

The Portuguese discovered that the best way to produce sugar in their new colonial possessions in Brazil was on large-scale plantations. Their success led the English, French, and Spaniards to introduce plantations in their own West Indian and American colonies. By the end of the 17th century the island of Barbados in the West Indies was dominated by a small number of large sugar plantations. Such plantations in the New World – and those in the West Indies in particular – provided their owners, often absent in Europe, with fabulous wealth.

A large labour force was needed to work these enormous estates, the largest of which resembled small towns. Initially, the Portuguese used native Indians, but the decline of the Indian population obliged them to seek an alternative source of labour: black slaves from Africa. The British and French did the same. By 1680 the slave population of the British West Indies totalled more than 60 000, and that of the French West Indies 21 000. In the 1780s there were 100 000 black African slaves in the Spanish Caribbean, 400 000 in the British West Indies, about 500 000 in the French West Indies, 400 000 in the United States, and more than 800 000 in Brazil.

This demand for labour could only be met by the continued transport of slaves across the Atlantic from Africa: 968 000 made the crossing in the later 17th century, and a further 6 million in the 18th century. While many slaves died on the Atlantic crossing,

carriers were concerned that their valuable cargo should reach the West Indies in good condition. In fact more slaves died on the journey from the interior of Africa to the ports than at sea.

By the end of the 18th century religious and humanitarian opposition to slavery and the slave trade was growing in Western Europe. The British slave trade was abolished in 1807, and slavery in the British Empire in 1833. It was not until the end of the Civil War of 1861–5 (▷ p. 158), however, that slavery ceased to exist in the USA, while in Brazil it lingered on until 1889.

A trader bargains for slaves on the west coast of Africa in the 1820s. By 1815 most European countries supported the abolition of slavery, but illegal smuggling of slaves – mainly from Africa – continued for the next half century.

THE OPENING UP OF THE PACIFIC

Captain Cook is clubbed to death by islanders on Hawaii in 1779.

Spanish, Portuguese and Dutch explorers began to explore the Pacific in the 17th century. At first they believed that Australia (then known as New Holland) was part of a larger southern continent. In 1642 the Dutchman Abel Tasman discovered Tasmania and the south island of New Zealand, and by sailing round Australia proved it to be an island. However, the Pacific remained largely unknown, too distant and too poor to attract European trading interest.

France's expulsion from America and India, and the belief that the East offered great wealth, turned European attention to the Pacific in the 1760s. In 1767 the British reached Tahiti, to be followed in 1768 by a French expedition under Louis de Bougainville.

Captain James Cook visited Tahiti on the first (1768–71) of three Pacific voyages. He also charted the New Zealand coasts and landed on the coast of Australia at Botany Bay. On his second voyage (1772–5) Cook revisited Tahiti, charted Easter Island, the Marquesas and Society Islands, the Friendly Islands (Tonga), and the New Hebrides (Vanuatu), and discovered New Caledonia and Norfolk Island (▷ map, p. 69). On his last voyage, in search of a northwest passage from the Pacific to the Atlantic (1775–9), he discovered the Hawaiian Islands, but was killed in a skirmish with islanders on Hawaii on his return journey.

However, the new lands were still too poor to be settled without government intervention. American independence obliged the British government to transport convicts elsewhere. They were sent to Botany Bay, on the eastern coast of Australia, where the first batch arrived in 1788. Another convict settlement was established in Tasmania in 1803.

Further settlement followed the survey of a large part of the Australian coast by Captain Matthew Flinders (1801–3). The government sought to attract free settlers, offering them convict labour, and granted convicts land on completion of their sentence. It also permitted the import of sheep into Australia, laying the foundations of large sheep ranches. The first non-convict settlement was the Swan River Colony, later Western Australia, founded in 1829.

The Rise of the Bourgeoisie

Despite many fluctuations and a long period of stagnation during the 17th century, the European economy was in general expanding between the 15th century (▷ p. 98) and the Industrial Revolution in the 18th century (▷ p. 140). This expansion was associated with a great increase in the facilities for investment, and with a shift of economic primacy from the Mediterranean to the northwest corner of Europe. Commerce and banking – rather than industry – brought wealth and political power to a privileged few in the towns, particularly those of the United Provinces (in what is now the Netherlands), England, and France.

A broader urban middle class also had growing influence during this period. But even in the 18th century European society remained predominantly agricultural, and dominated by the values of the landed nobility.

Jakob II Fugger (the Rich; 1459–1525) – head of the powerful southern German mercantile family from 1510 – with his accountant. Jakob and his two brothers developed a vast business empire based on trade, silver and copper mining, and banking. Lending vast sums to Maximilian I and financing Charles V's candidacy as Holy Roman Emperor in 1519, the Fuggers enjoyed considerable political influence as well as immense wealth.

The growth of capitalism

Europe's trade grew remarkably from around 1450. The recovery of its population after the Black Death (▷ p. 92) stimulated food production and trade in foodstuffs, wool and cloth. Spanish and Portuguese settlements overseas also required European goods (▷ p. 116). The gold and silver obtained in return stimulated European trade with the Far East (mainly the import of expensive spices), which depended upon the export of precious metals. The Fuggers of Augsburg, the most successful of a number of similar enterprises based in southern Germany, developed worldwide interests. They controlled the largest mining enterprises in Central Europe, and had agents in the New World and the Mediterranean.

The increase in trade was facilitated by a range of sophisticated financial services developed by the Italians in the Middle Ages (▷ p. 98) and further refined in the 16th century. These were increasingly provided by bankers, often merchants who had abandoned trade. Cash was rarely used in the settlement of accounts in long-distance trade. Instead merchants used the negotiable bill of exchange – a promise to pay a certain sum, given by one merchant to another, which could then be given to a third party. Such bills of exchange effectively took the place of money.

The trade in bills of exchange was part of an elaborate money market centred in a number of exchanges – or 'bourses'. Here merchants, brokers and bankers met to do business and, increasingly, to speculate in commodities and foreign exchange. It was in the bourses, as well, that the capital of smaller investors (often people who had profited from the price inflation associated with increased supplies of precious metals) was channelled into new enterprises.

The most important bourse was founded at Antwerp in 1531. Antwerp was already the commercial hub of the Burgundian Low Countries by c. 1450 (▷ pp. 95 and 120), and an important centre for dealings in German silver, English cloth, and Baltic grain. The Portuguese marketed their Eastern spices in Antwerp from 1499, and many imported goods were processed there for re-export.

In Antwerp, as in some other great commercial centres – notably Lyons in France – the availability of money and credit attracted rulers who needed financial assistance. Despite a great increase in taxation in the 16th century, governments rarely had enough money to finance the expensive wars that were their main preoccupation. Charles V and Philip II (▷ pp. 85 and 116) both raised large loans in Antwerp on the security of the American bullion reaching Seville. Loans such as these helped Antwerp become the financial capital of 16th-century Europe.

Lending to governments could be very profitable. The Fuggers, whose loans to Charles V were crucial to his military successes, made enormous profits in this way. But lending was also vulnerable to government bankruptcies, which disrupted the entire credit structure. By 1600 the Fuggers had been seriously damaged by Habsburg bankruptcies. A similar fate befell the Genoese and later the Portuguese Jews who replaced them in the 16th and 17th centuries as lenders to the Spanish Crown.

After 1620 a number of factors created uncertainty and discouraged growth. These included the fall in silver imports from America, the monetary instability caused by the debasing of the coinage by a number of governments (▷ picture), and the ravages of the Thirty Years War (▷ p. 113). This recession lasted until about 1670.

The Dutch – and to a lesser extent the English – escaped this downturn, and helped the further development of a Europe-wide credit and financial network. Dutch and English joint-stock trading companies raised capital by issuing shares that were freely traded on the Amsterdam – and later the London – stock exchange. The public exchange bank founded in Amsterdam and that established later in Hamburg became major European clearing banks. The excellence of Amsterdam's financial institutions ensured a continuous supply of cheap capital there (▷ p. 120).

Europe was thus well placed to take advantage of the colonial trade boom in the 18th century (▷ p. 128), which further stimulated its money markets and credit institutions. The number of banks increased, and they expanded the money supply by issuing paper currency. Governments, still in need of loans, encouraged these developments. The growth of the British national debt in the 18th century created a market in government securities (▷ p. 119). The developing money market, and speculation in stocks and shares, were only temporarily affected by the collapse of the stock markets in France in 1719 and in England in 1720 (the 'South Sea Bubble').

The shift to the northwest

In the 16th century Italy and much of Germany had shared fully in Europe's economic success. However, political disunity, stagnant population, weak governments, and above all their geographical location prevented them from profiting similarly from the 18th-century boom. This benefited most the northwest corner of Europe – principally Britain, France and the Netherlands. Hamburg, Genoa and some Swiss towns continued to play an important role in European finance. However, the rest of Europe was increasingly a supplier of raw materials to the northwest, receiving manufactured and colonial goods in return.

The wealth and influence of the bourgeoisie

Throughout Western Europe, but particularly in the United Provinces, Britain and France, trade and finance increased the numbers, wealth and influence of the bourgeoisie – or middle class – in the 18th century. In England, it is believed to have made up 9% of society in 1688 and 15% in 1800. Its share of national income perhaps doubled from about 20% in 1688 to over 40% in 1800. In France, the bourgeoisie grew more rapidly than the population as a whole. In 1789 2.3 million bourgeois made up more than 8% of the population. Their wealth may have trebled since 1660.

A small upper middle class of very wealthy bankers and merchants had great influence in these countries. In the United Provinces the oligarchs of Amsterdam had long enjoyed real power (▷ p. 120). In England, for most of the 18th century, government ministers depended on the financial support of London merchants and bankers – often men of Jewish, Dutch or Huguenot origin – who some-

times had a decisive influence on policy. In France, a smaller but equally influential class of financiers emerged in the latter half of the reign of Louis XIV (▷ p. 122).

Below this 'haute bourgeoisie' was a larger and diverse range of middle-class occupations. Apart from those directly involved in trade and financial services – including shopkeepers and craftsmen – a growing number were employed in the professions: lawyers, doctors, apothecaries, and journalists. The political influence of these professions increased throughout the 18th century. Middle-class influence exerted through political societies and the growing number of newspapers lay behind many of the reforming measures in administration and taxation attempted in Britain from the 1780s. Many of the leaders of the French Revolution were drawn from the bourgeoisie (▷ p. 144).

The bourgeoisie had a striking impact upon the culture of the United Provinces in the 17th century (▷ p. 120). In 18th-century Britain and France the middle class was at the heart of the development of a consumer society. A leisured and moneyed public provided an alternative source of patronage to that of kings and nobles. It ensured the success of a new literary form – the novel – which devel-

oped in England and France in the 18th century, and of the growing number of theatres to which access was gained by purchase of a ticket. The middle class also lay behind the improvement of many towns in the 18th century – for example the great classical urban designs in Edinburgh and Bath – and their flourishing intellectual and social life.

Restraints on the bourgeoisie

Yet the power and self-consciousness of this bourgeoisie remained limited. European society was still overwhelmingly agrarian, and even in Western Europe the nobility remained the most powerful and wealthiest group in society. In Prussia, the Habsburg empire, Russia and Poland – states with few towns, small merchant fleets, and little capital – the bourgeoisie was a far less influential force than in Western Europe.

Even in the United Provinces, Britain and France, many of the middle class depended primarily on the state for their existence and opportunities. Government service employed many of the lower middle class. Others gained a regular income from investment in government debt, which yielded a smaller profit than successful trade, but which was safer and less despised.

Far from being committed to alternative entrepreneurial values, the middle classes shared the contemporary prejudice against trade and in favour of investment in land, and abandoned trade as soon as their financial circumstances allowed. By the late 17th century the oligarchs who dominated the Dutch towns had largely lost their earlier contact with trade. The successful bourgeois ultimately hoped to join the nobility – in France, for example, in the later 18th century nearly 4000 purchaseable offices conferred nobility. Throughout Europe the commercial bourgeoisie was generally outnumbered by a 'noble bourgeoisie' that had severed its links with trade. CS

Coiners at work in a 16th-century print. In medieval Europe, the value of a coin was derived from the weight of the metal that it contained. This led to many abuses, including 'clipping', where the edges of a coin were shaved off. Widespread clipping resulted in inflation as the currency became debased. The coinage was further debased – and inflation fuelled – when from the early 16th century governments began to mint coins that included increasing proportions of base metals.

THE GROWTH OF TOWNS

The rise of the bourgeoisie was reflected in the growth of Europe's towns, both in number and size. In 1500 only five towns in Europe had more than 100 000 inhabitants: Istanbul, Venice, Naples, Milan and Paris. By 1800 there were ten towns with more than 200 000 inhabitants.

The most striking success was London, which lay at the heart of Britain's growing economic and colonial power (▷ pp. 119 and 128). Its population trebled between 1500 and 1600 to 220 000 – about 5% of the population of England. Despite the loss of 10 000 people in the last of the plagues to hit London (1665), its population had more than doubled to 550 000 by 1700 – 10% of the population of England. By 1800, 1 million people lived in London – 11 or 12% of the population of England.

The growth of towns depended upon continual immigration from the country, since urban death rates – particularly among the poor – were high. Immigrants were attracted by the greater opportunities in the towns. The population of those towns involved in the Atlantic trade in the 18th century rose dramatically. The population of Bordeaux doubled to 100 000, while that of Glasgow rose from 13 000 to more than 80 000.

In the less economically advanced eastern part of Europe, the towns were often dominated by government employees. In 1789, more than 55 000 – or one-quarter – of the population of St Petersburg (which had not existed in 1700; ▷ p. 126) were soldiers or their families. Berlin and Vienna showed similar characteristics.

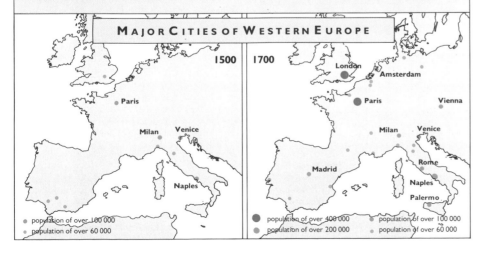

MAJOR CITIES OF WESTERN EUROPE

1500

Paris

Milan · Venice

Naples

● population of over 100 000
● population of over 60 000

1700

London
Amsterdam

Paris · Vienna

Milan · Venice

Madrid

Rome

Naples
Palermo

● population of over 400 000 · ● population of over 100 000
● population of over 200 000 · ● population of over 60 000

SEE ALSO

● MEDIEVAL AND RENAISSANCE ECONOMY AND SOCIETY p. 98
● THE VOYAGES OF DISCOVERY p. 108
● THE SPANISH AND PORTUGUESE EMPIRES p. 116
● THE RISE OF BRITAIN p. 118
● THE DUTCH REPUBLIC p. 120
● CENTRAL EUROPE: THE STRUGGLE FOR POWER 1648–1806 p. 124
● COLONIAL EMPIRES IN THE 17TH AND 18TH CENTURIES p. 128
● THE AGRICULTURAL AND INDUSTRIAL REVOLUTIONS p. 140

The Scientific Revolution

In 1500 European understanding of the natural world and the universe was largely based upon a synthesis of Christian teaching and the intellectual tradition deriving from the Greek thinker Aristotle (▷ p. 30). Only a tiny minority questioned the traditional certainty of a universe centred upon the Earth and subject to the operation of divine power. There was little scientific thinking in the sense of a systematic investigation of reality by observation, experimentation and induction. The 16th and 17th centuries, however, marked the coming of the so-called Scientific Revolution – a period of scientific progress that emphasized experiment, and resulted in a new view of the universe and the Earth's place in it.

A distinction began to be made between natural science – or natural philosophy as it was known – and occult science. The 'new science' and its practitioners acquired great prestige, and contributed to the gradual secularization of European thought.

The Aristotelian orthodoxy

After the fall of Greece to the Roman empire, few important scientific advances were made outside medicine (▷ box); and during the late Roman and early medieval periods science as we understand it today was practically unknown in Europe. Islamic culture alone preserved Greek knowledge of medicine, astronomy and mathematics, and later transmitted it back to the West (▷ p. 82). In the 13th century theologians such as Thomas Aquinas synthesized Aristotelian science and philosophy and Christian doctrine. In the same century the English Franciscan friar Roger Bacon (c. 1214–92) advocated experimentation, did important work in optics and was the first European to describe the manufacture of gunpowder. But few followed his example.

Copernicanism

In his book *Concerning the Movement of Heavenly Bodies* (1543), the Polish mathematician Nicholas Copernicus (1473–1543) revived the heliocentric theory, placing the Sun at the centre of the universe. The theory that the Earth orbits the Sun had been advocated by Aristarchus of Samos as early as the 3rd century BC, but the notion put forward by the Alexandrian scholar Ptolemy in the 2nd century AD that the Earth was at the centre of the universe had subsequently held sway. Copernicus used mathematical calculations to disprove Ptolemy's notion, arguing that the Earth revolved both about the Sun (in a year) and about its own axis (in a day).

Copernicus had no means of testing his theory, however. This was the achievement of Johannes Kepler (1571–1603), the German assistant of the Danish astronomer Tycho Brahe (1546–1601).

Brahe made the most comprehensive and accurate astronomical observations then recorded. His discoveries of a supernova (an exploding star) in 1572 and a comet in 1577 disproved the Aristotelian view of a perfect, unchanging cosmos. From these and his own observations Kepler calculated that the planets moved in elliptical orbits around the Sun (rather than in circles, which the ancients – and Copernicus – had regarded as the perfect mathematical figure).

Brahe was the last great astronomer to rely on the naked eye. Further progress in astronomy depended upon the development of the telescope, invented in 1608. An improved version was devised by the Italian mathematician and physicist Galileo Galilei (1564–1642). Galileo's astronomical observations convinced him of the correctness of the Copernican hypothesis. He also discovered spots on the supposedly perfect Sun, mountains on the Moon, the phases of Venus, the four larger moons of Jupiter, and the rings of Saturn.

But Galileo's work in astronomy was only part of a much greater theoretical project – to discover universal laws of motion and thereby describe the physics that made the Copernican universe possible. Galileo advanced a considerable way towards this, and founded two 'new sciences' – statics and dynamics. However, the physical explanation of the Copernican universe was to be the achievement of Newton (▷ below).

Copernican views conflicted with Biblical accounts and undermined the alliance between Aristotelian philosophy and

The Alchemist by Jan van der Straet (1523–1605).

FROM ALCHEMY TO CHEMISTRY

Throughout the Middle Ages chemistry was largely indistinguishable from alchemy. Alchemy had emerged in China and Egypt by the 3rd century BC. It was revived in the 8th century BC in Alexandria by the Arabs, and reached Western Europe by the High Middle Ages.

Alchemists searched for a secret substance – the 'philosopher's stone' – that would convert 'base' metals into valuable ones such as gold and silver, and for an elixir that would make its possessor immortal. Much of the practice of alchemy – and the writings associated with it – was based on superstition, and became esoteric to the point of obscurity. But medieval alchemy was responsible for some important chemical discoveries, notably those of the mineral acids and alcohol. The experiments of the alchemists – while 'pseudo-scientific' in nature – helped develop techniques that formed the basis of modern chemistry, though they differed fundamentally from the latter in aims and approach.

The colourful 16th-century Swiss-German alchemist and physician Paracelsus (Theophrastus Bombastus von Hohenheim) helped to establish the role of chemistry in medicine. He rejected the medicine of Galen (▷ box) and the medieval Arab teachers, pioneering the idea that specific diseases require specific treatments. Paracelsus introduced the use of chemicals such as opium, mercury and sulphur in medicine.

Robert Boyle (1627–1716), a member of the Royal Society, undermined Aristotelian and Galenic medicine by demonstrating that the old Greek notion that the four elements of air, fire, earth, and water were the constituents of all things was an inadequate account of chemical phenomena. He also established that there were far more elements than those identified by the alchemists. In this way, Boyle, and to a lesser extent Robert Hooke (1635–1703), did much to free serious chemistry from alchemy.

However, chemistry did not truly emerge as a distinct science until the 18th century. Henry Cavendish (1731–1810) discovered hydrogen and its properties and the composition of water, while Joseph Priestley (1733–1804) discovered oxygen, disproving the theory that the hypothetical substance phlogiston was essential to combustion. The naming of oxygen was the work of the French chemist Antoine Lavoisier (1743–94), who created a language and methodology for chemistry that clearly distinguished it from alchemy.

Sir Isaac Newton's discovery of universally valid laws of motion has been acclaimed as one of the greatest advances in the history of science. His reputation in his own day is summed up by the epitaph written for him by Alexander Pope: 'Nature, and Nature's laws, lay hid in night: / God said, *Let Newton be!* and all was light.'

Christianity. They therefore clashed both with the Protestant emphasis on Scripture and with the Counter-Reformation affirmation of tradition. In 1616 Copernicus' book was put on the papal Index of prohibited books. Galileo's continued support of Copernicanism resulted in his denunciation to the Roman Inquisition (▷ p. 112). He was obliged to abjure his Copernicanism (1633), but is said to have muttered as he did so: '*eppur si muove*' ('and yet it [the earth] moves').

Scientific method

Thereafter, scientists in Catholic countries confined themselves to less contentious work. English scientists now began to play a leading part in the progress of science. In part they were responding to the call by the philosopher and politician Francis Bacon (1561–1626) to use the inductive method (the establishing of general principles from precise experimentation) to achieve a true understanding of the world.

An alternative to Bacon's inductive method was outlined by the French mathematician and philosopher René Descartes (1596–1650; ▷ p. 140) in his *Discourse on Method* (1637). Denying the reliability of any knowledge other than that of his own thinking mind – 'I think therefore I am' – Descartes attained absolute certainty by deductive reasoning, drawing conclusions from first or basic principles rather than from experiment. Descartes also contributed to the advance of mathematics (which continued to underpin advances in the other sciences) by developing analytical geometry.

Newton

Science and its trappings became highly fashionable from the later 17th century, and also attracted much royal and state patronage. The founding of the Académie des Sciences by Louis XIV in France and the Royal Society by Charles II in Britain were landmarks in this trend.

A leading figure in the Royal Society was the mathematician and physicist Sir Isaac Newton (1643–1727). A man of almost universal scientific interests, Newton made important contributions to optics and also advanced mathematical method. He and the German mathematician and philosopher Gottfried Wilhelm Leibniz (1645–1716) simultaneously but separately developed calculus.

But Newton's greatest achievement was to complete the revolution begun by Copernicus. Experiment and mathematics enabled him to discover universally valid laws of mechanics. Newton saw the universe as a rigid mechanism held together by three absolute laws of motion and by a law of gravitation, all of which he formulated in the *Mathematical Principles of Natural Philosophy* or *Principia* (1687). Newton had at last produced an explanation of the universe that took account of the discoveries made by his 16th- and 17th-century predecessors in a way in which Descartes' system did not. Newtonian physics was to dominate scientific understanding until the 20th century, and still remains valid except for speeds approaching the speed of light and for dimensions on a subatomic scale.

The impact of the Scientific Revolution

The intellectual impact of the Scientific Revolution of the 17th century was massive. Traditional ways of looking at the universe had been replaced by new ones more firmly based upon a truly scientific approach. The close relationship between religious orthodoxy and discredited old scientific ideas contributed to the breakdown of respect for religious authority. Natural science acquired greater prestige and a growing audience, and more books on scientific subjects were published. Royal and other scientific academies were established throughout Europe in the 18th century, helping to spread knowledge of new discoveries.

But not all branches of science had progressed as much as mathematics, mechanics and astronomy. Chemistry would have to wait until the 18th century , and medicine until the 19th century for decisive advances (▷ boxes). Nor did the Scientific Revolution necessarily undermine religious belief or the hold of the occult – particularly astrology – even among the scientists themselves. Newton devoted his last decades to researching Scriptural prophecy and ancient miracles, and to alchemy.

There was also the danger that, as well as encouraging a more rational view of the universe, the discovery of powerful forces such as gravity might also justify the view that the 'new science' was a 'new magic'. Even for the educated, much science had to be dressed up as entertainment to obtain an audience. Moreover, although there was some awareness of the value of using the new advances in the fields of

MEDICINE

Before the Scientific Revolution medicine in Europe was largely founded upon an erroneous theory of the 'humours', originating with the ancient Greek philosophers Empedocles and Aristotle, and refined four centuries later by Galen of Pergamon. According to this theory there were four elements – air, fire, earth and water, which in the human body combined to form four humours: blood (hot and wet), yellow bile (hot and dry), black bile (dry and cold), and phlegm (cold and wet). Good health depended upon the correct balance of the humours.

After the fall of the Roman Empire, Greek medical knowledge was codified by Arab scholars and later widely diffused in Christian Europe through Latin translations. Medicine was taught in new universities (▷ p. 100) such as Montpellier in France and Bologna in Italy. However, in general medieval medicine remained a mixture of ancient physiology, empirical knowledge of the effects of some drugs, and superstitious incantation. Yet criticism of Greek medicine – based on practical observation – was growing. Physicians such as Paracelsus (▷ box, From Alchemy to Chemistry) questioned Galen's authority on specific points, and after the invention of printing (▷ p. 100) such doubts became widely disseminated. In his book *De Humani Corporis Fabrica*, the Belgian anatomist Andreas Vesalius (1514–54) exposed Galen's inadequacies. It is the first accurate anatomy book, based upon dissection of human corpses, and laid the foundations of modern anatomy.

The main medical event of the 17th century was the discovery by the English physician William Harvey (1578–1677) of the true nature of the heartbeat and the circulation of the blood. Harvey's book *De Motu Cordis* ('On the Movement of the Heart') laid the foundation of all modern physiology. A further aid to physiology, and to medical science generally, was provided by the invention of the microscope in the late 16th century.

During the 18th century a number of great medical schools, including Vienna and Edinburgh, were founded. Surgery was established on firm scientific principles by the Scot John Hunter (1728–93), who also proved the value of experimental surgery. Such developments set the scene for the massive advances to come in the 19th century – the great era of anaesthesia, antisepsis, and the discovery of the role of germs in causing disease.

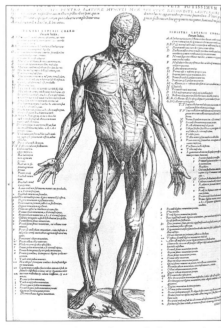

A page from *De Humani Corporis Fabrica* ('on the fabric of the human body'), compiled by Andreas Vesalius. As well as being the first comprehensive textbook of anatomy, the *Fabrica* also attained new standards of printing and illustration.

industry and warfare, their practical application was limited before 1800.

Despite these limitations, the Scientific Revolution was to have a fundamental impact on the Western consciousness in the long term, not least because of its contribution to the 18th-century Enlightenment (▷ p. 134).   CS

SEE ALSO

● ARCHAIC AND CLASSICAL GREECE p. 28
● MEDIEVAL AND RENAISSANCE CULTURE p. 100
● THE ENLIGHTENMENT p. 134

The Enlightenment

In the late 17th century English thinkers provided the foundation for a body of ideas that were developed in France in the 18th century and then spread through Europe. For their adherents these ideas represented an attempt to bring humanity into the light of reason out of the darkness of tradition and prejudice – hence the term the Enlightenment. This 'enlightenment' was to be achieved by the application of critical and rational thought to assumptions hitherto taken for granted.

Joseph II, Holy Roman Emperor and ruler of the Habsburg dominions. Along with the other 'enlightened despots' – Frederick II of Prussia and Catherine II of Russia – Joseph introduced reforms based on the ideas of the Enlightenment (albeit by authoritarian means).

At its peak in the 1750s it seemed that this bold, liberating movement had captured the minds of monarchs – the so-called 'enlightened despots' – and that this explained the major reforms being attempted in many states in the later 18th century. Yet the practical influence of the Enlightenment was never great, and its intellectual impetus declined in the later 18th century. Tradition and the Church, the great enemies of the Enlightenment, survived the attack.

The development of the Enlightenment

The scientific discoveries of the first half of the 17th century undermined traditional explanations of the universe (▷ p. 132). A new explanation was devised by the French philosopher René Descartes (1596–1650). Descartes was sceptical about all knowledge derived from the senses, and saw the universe as a mechanical system ordained by God, a system explicable by abstract mathematical laws. By 1700 Cartesianism – as Descartes' philosophy became known – was the general intellectual orthodoxy in much of Europe. However, the continued progress of experimental science, and Newton's discoveries in physics and optics (▷ p. 133), showed that Descartes' system had no basis in reality.

That system was therefore discredited in favour of an explanation of reality based on experiment (an approach known as empiricism). The English philosopher John Locke (1632–1704; ▷ box) provided an intellectual basis for this empiricism. He argued that ideas were the product of sensation and experience and that people were not born with ideas (not even of God, contrary to what the Church and Descartes himself believed). According to Locke, human behaviour was based on two desires – to avoid pain, and to seek pleasure.

Newton and Locke provided the basis of a sustained critical movement, popularized by a group of French writers known as the Philosophes. The greatest of these was Voltaire (1694–1778), who introduced the ideas of Newton and Locke to France in his *Philosophical Letters on the English* (1734). Encyclopedias and dictionaries were a favourite way of spreading the new ideas. The Philosophe Denis Diderot (1713–84) was largely responsible for the 28-volume *Encyclopédie* (1751–72), which incorporated the latest knowledge and progressive ideas, and which helped to spread the ideas of the Enlightenment in France and in other parts of Europe.

The Enlightenment consensus

There was no single 'Enlightenment' attitude. However, there was a consensus of enlightened opinion in the 1750s, symbolized by the *Encyclopédie*. This concensus was founded on the belief that the combination of reason and personal experience could discover the rules underlying the workings of nature. Such ideas led to a practical humanitarianism. The Italian legal theorist Cesare Beccaria (1738–94) urged the abolition of torture and the reform of penal codes. Some Philosophes

A gathering of intellectuals and artists, including Diderot and d'Alembert – two of the most celebrated names of the French Enlightenment – at the salon of Madame Geoffrin in 1755. Presided over by fashionable and intelligent women, the Parisian salons provided a forum for aesthetic, philosophical and political debate. France retained its cultural pre-eminence in Europe in the 18th century, despite the loss of its political supremacy.

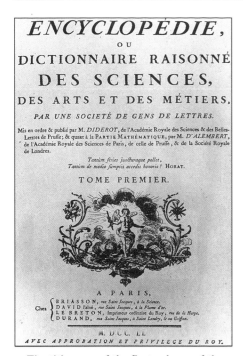

ENCYCLOPÉDIE,
OU
DICTIONNAIRE RAISONNÉ
DES SCIENCES,
DES ARTS ET DES MÉTIERS,
PAR UNE SOCIÉTÉ DE GENS DE LETTRES.

Mis en ordre & publié par M. DIDEROT, de l'Académie Royale des Sciences & des Belles-Lettres de Prusse; & quant à la PARTIE MATHÉMATIQUE, par M. D'ALEMBERT, de l'Académie Royale des Sciences de Paris, de celle de Prusse, & de la Société Royale de Londres.

Tantùm series juncturaque pollet,
Tantùm de medio sumptis accedit honoris ! HORAT.

TOME PREMIER.

A PARIS,

Chez
BRIASSON, rue Saint Jacques, à la Science.
DAVID l'aîné, rue Saint Jacques, à la Plume d'or.
LE BRETON, Imprimeur ordinaire du Roy, rue de la Harpe.
DURAND, rue Saint Jacques, à Saint Landry, & au Griffon.

M. DCC. LI.
AVEC APPROBATION ET PRIVILÈGE DU ROY.

The title-page of the first volume of the *Encyclopédie*, the multi-volume monument to Enlightenment thinking. Masterminded by Diderot, the *Encyclopédie* included Voltaire and Rousseau among its contributors.

were also critical of the way governments inflicted the horrors of war on their peoples.

Morality came to be seen as the product of circumstance, rather than an absolute truth – a view known as relativism. In his *Spirit of the Laws* (1748) the French philosopher Montesquieu (1689–1755; ⇨ box) analysed how different circumstances in different societies produced different laws. The discovery of non-Christian societies by overseas exploration encouraged such relativism. Since there was no monopoly of truth or right, Enlightenment thinkers – notably Voltaire – called for toleration and attacked the Church as a powerful and repressive authority.

In place of established religion many of the Philosophes proposed the 'natural religion' of Deism, which required that religion conform to the workings of the universe as discovered by reason. Miracles and religion dependent on divine revelation were rejected as mere superstition. The Deists proposed a God who was simply a benevolent force. He had endowed individuals with reason and control of their fate, but otherwise played little part in human affairs.

Enlightened despotism

Apart from Montesquieu, Enlightenment writers said little about political theory or organization (⇨ box). Although the Philosophes were generally liberal in outlook, some looked to autocratic rulers to carry out their ideas. Catherine the Great (1762–96; ⇨ p. 127) drew on Enlightenment ideas when initiating reform in Russia. The transformation of Prussia by Frederick the Great (⇨ p. 124), who corresponded with Voltaire, seemed a

triumph of enlightened despotism. Both Frederick and Emperor Joseph II of Austria (1765–90; ⇨ p. 124) saw authority as a trust, to be used to promote the welfare of their subjects.

Yet Joseph's major reform of the Habsburg monarchy was largely a continuation of the reforms begun by his very conservative mother, Maria Theresa. Both wished to make Austria powerful again – the object of reform in most big states. Joseph wished to abolish serfdom mainly so that peasants could pay higher taxes. For the same reason, the humanitarian aspect of the Enlightenment was largely ignored in Prussia. Genuinely enlightened reform was often easier in the smaller states of Germany and Italy. Elsewhere tradition and privilege remained powerful. Most of Joseph II's reforms were eventually withdrawn in the face of the hostility of various privileged groups.

Reform was often forced on governments. The suppression of the Jesuits in 1773 was not the result of Enlightenment influence, but nevertheless obliged governments to establish new educational institutions to replace those previously run by the Jesuits (⇨ p. 112).

The impact of the Enlightenment

The Enlightenment provided some of the ideas and language of the American and French Revolutions (⇨ pp. 142 and 144), but did not cause them. Since the vast majority of Europeans remained uneducated, the number of those directly influenced by the Enlightenment was very small.

In the second half of the 18th century the Enlightenment faced growing competition from irrational movements. The reaction against reason was expressed most forcefully by Jean-Jacques Rousseau (⇨ box). Formerly a Philosophe, Rousseau now rejected the values of the Enlightenment, arguing that natural instinct was the best guide. Individual feeling, not universal reason, was what mattered. This attitude was the core of Romanticism, the movement that was to sweep across Europe at the end of the 18th century (⇨ p. 150). CS

SEE ALSO

- THE RISE OF THE BOURGEOISIE p. 130
- THE SCIENTIFIC REVOLUTION p. 132
- THE BIRTH OF THE USA p. 142
- THE FRENCH REVOLUTION p. 144
- NATIONALISM, LIBERALISM AND REVOLUTION p. 150

POLITICAL AND ECONOMIC THOUGHT

Although the Philosophes had little to say about political or economic theory, the 17th and 18th centuries produced some remarkable advances in both these spheres. The emergence of the idea of the 'social contract' in the 16th century had reintroduced the notion that government rests on the consent of the people. The English political philosopher Thomas Hobbes (1588–1679) described the chaos in which he believed people lived when they did not have a proper government. He claims in his most important treatise, *Leviathan* (1651), that the life of man in his natural, ungoverned state is 'solitary, poor, nasty, brutish and short'. Hobbes's doctrine is that men can only live together in peace if they agree to obey an absolute sovereign, and this agreement he called 'the social contract'. Hobbes's concern about what happened when government broke down, as in the English Civil War (⇨ p. 119) during his lifetime, led him to suggest that considerable power should be placed in the hands of the sovereign.

In his two *Treatises of Government* (1690), the English philosopher John Locke (⇨ text) also made use of the idea of a social contract. However, Locke opposed absolutism, and saw the free consent of the governed as the basis of legitimate government. Obedience depends on governments ruling for the good of the governed, who have the right to rebel if they are oppressed. This idea would appear quite acceptable today, but was seen as radical at the time – being adopted, for example, by the American Revolutionaries of 1776 (⇨ p. 142).

After the Glorious Revolution (⇨ p. 119), Britain was seen as a political model by many foreign thinkers. Typical of these was Montesquieu (⇨ text), although his understanding of the British constitution was imperfect. His *Spirit of the Laws* argued that monarchy was founded on and restrained by laws, and that these laws were protected – and monarchy prevented from becoming despotic – by an 'intermediary' power. According to Montesquieu, in England the intermediary role was fulfilled by Parliament. However, as a nobleman, he believed that in monarchies like France this role should be the responsibility of the nobility (and other privileged groups). Such conservative political ideas were very popular with the privileged classes of Europe. Montesquieu's emphasis on the balancing and separation of the judicial, legislative, and executive powers of the state exerted some influence on the makers of the Constitution of the USA (⇨ p. 143).

The only 18th-century writer to propose a new theory of the state was Rousseau (⇨ text). He elevated the state to a position not suggested by his predecessors, arguing in his *Social Contract* (1762) that it was only in the state that men reached their true potential. Rousseau (unlike his predecessors) placed sovereignty in the hands of the people as a whole, and declared that it could not be divided, separated, or alienated. He believed in a 'General Will' – the good of the community – which all wished for though they might not know it. The authoritarian implications of Rousseau's political theory are evident in this, as they are in his granting the state far more responsibilities in all areas of a citizen's life than any had done before him.

A belief in reason and the duties of sovereigns towards their subjects also influenced economic thinking. A theory known as 'cameralism', which justified government intervention in the economy for the good of the state and society, developed in Germany after the Thirty Years War (⇨ p. 113). Believing that the best foundation of a wealthy, powerful state was a prosperous, happy population, cameralists urged governments to act rationally to improve the welfare and living standards of their subjects. Cameralist ideas were an important source of many reforms in later 18th-century Europe.

Other 18th-century currents were hostile to economic control. The French Physiocrats – at their peak between 1750 and the 1770s – believed that the growth of trade and wealth depended upon agriculture rather than industry. They urged governments to free the market of all restrictions (tolls, privileges, guilds, and export controls).

The Physiocrats had only a limited effect on economic policy, but they influenced two leading figures in Scotland's contribution to the Enlightenment – David Hume (1711–76) and Adam Smith (1723–90). In his *Wealth of Nations* (1776) Smith argued that unregulated labour – whether in agriculture, trade, or industry – was the true source of wealth, and opposed mercantilist regulation (⇨ p. 128) as inimical to wealth creation. Smith's views had few practical consequences in the 18th century, but subsequently became the foundation of free-market ideas, which were to have widespread influence in the 19th and 20th centuries.

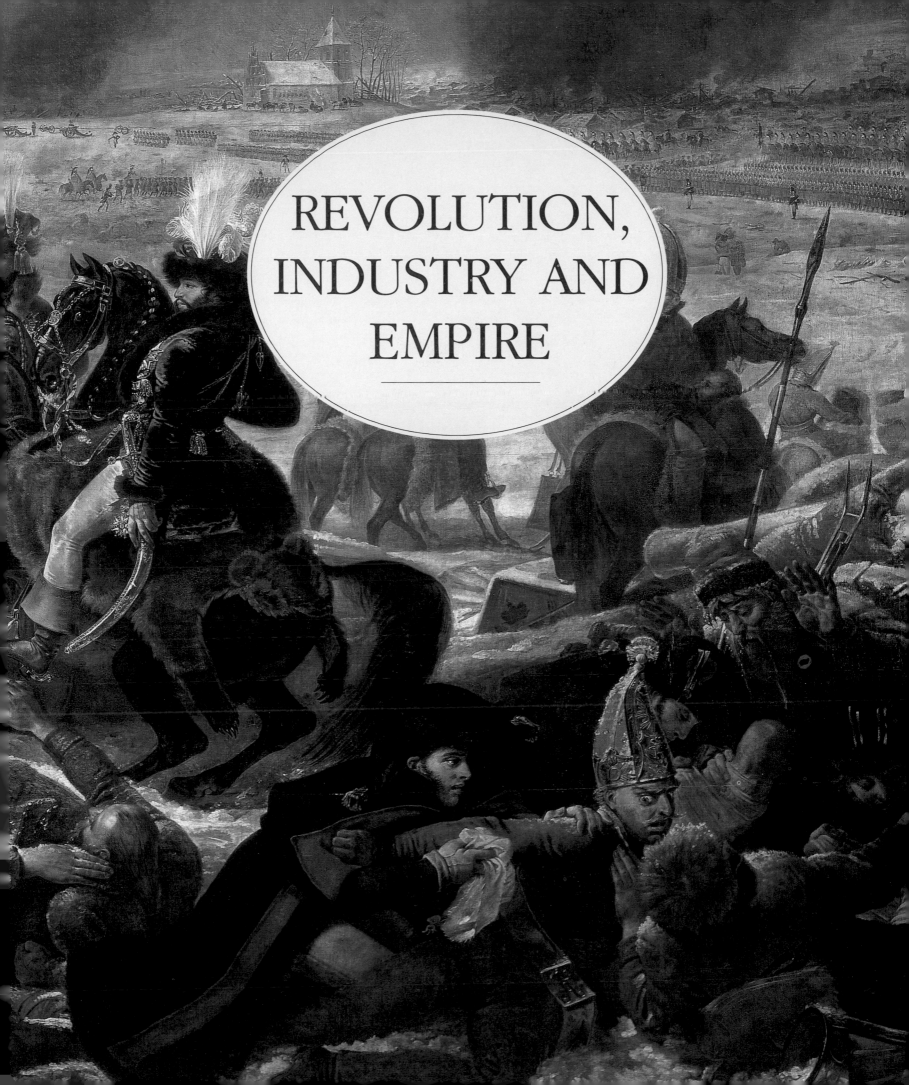

REVOLUTION, INDUSTRY AND EMPIRE

NORTHWESTERN EUROPE	CENTRAL EUROPE	EASTERN EUROPE	SOUTHERN EUROPE
1789 French Third Estate declared itself to be the National Assembly; fall of the Bastille; start of the French Revolution **1792** France became a republic; France defeated Prussia at Valmy – start of the French Revolutionary Wars **1793** Execution of Louis XVI **1794** The Terror; execution of Robespierre **1795** Batavian Republic, a French puppet state, established in the Netherlands **1795–9** France ruled by the Directory **1798** Wolfe Tone's rebellion in Ireland **1799** Napoleon Bonaparte seized power in France	**1797** French army under Napoleon Bonaparte invaded Austria **1798** France invaded Switzerland and established the Helvetic Republic	**1793** Second Partition of Poland between Prussia and Russia **1795** Third Partition of Poland between Austria, Prussia and Russia	**1796–7** Napoleon Bonaparte campaigned against Sardinia and Austria in Italy **1797** French-controlled Cisalpine and Ligurian republics founded in northern Italy; France occupied Venice
1801 Act of Union between Britain and Ireland **1804** Bonaparte crowned himself emperor as Napoleon I **1805** British fleet defeated French and Spanish at Trafalgar **1806–10** Louis Bonaparte, king of Holland **1814** Napoleon defeated and exiled to Elba **1815** Napoleon defeated at Waterloo by Britain and Prussia and exiled to St Helena **1814–15** Bourbons restored in France; kingdom of the Netherlands founded; Sweden gained Norway from Denmark	**1800** France defeated Austria at Marengo and Hohenlinden **1805** France defeated Austria at Ulm, and Russia and Austria at Austerlitz **1806** France defeated Prussia at Auerstadt and Jena; Confederation of the Rhine established; Holy Roman Empire abolished **1809–48** Metternich, foreign minister of Austria (chancellor after 1821) **1814–15** Congress of Vienna – Austria and Prussia enlarged; Germany reorganized	**1804–13** Serbian revolt against Turkish Ottoman rule **1808** France defeated Russia at Eylau and Friedland **1812** Napoleon invaded Russia and defeated Russians at Borodino – campaign ended with the retreat from Moscow **1815** Russian-ruled kingdom of Poland established	**1805** Napoleonic kingdoms established in Italy, Naples and Spain **1807–14** Wellesley (Wellington) defeated the French in the Peninsular War **1808** France annexed the Papal States – restored 1814 **1820** Liberal revolts throughout southern Europe **1821** Greek revolt against the Turks
1829 Catholic Emancipation in the UK **1830** 'July Revolution' in France – Bourbons overthrown; liberal Orleans monarchy established **1830–1** Successful Belgian revolt against Dutch rule **1832** British Great Reform Act – rotten boroughs suppressed **1845–51** Irish Famine **1846** Repeal of the Corn Laws in UK **1848** Orleans monarchy overthrown in France; Second Republic established	**1833** German states formed a customs union (*Zollverein*), the first step towards German unification **1847–8** Swiss civil war – new federal constitution in 1848 **1848–9** Liberal revolts in many German states; Frankfurt Assembly attempted to unite Germany with a liberal constitution **1848–9** Habsburg monarchy shaken by revolts in Budapest (under Kossuth), Vienna and Prague	**1825** Decembrist revolt in Russia **1830** Polish revolt against Russian rule **1832** Poland annexed by Russia **1833** Russo-Turkish Treaty of Unkiar Skelessi **1841** Straits Convention closed the Dardanelles to non-Ottoman warships	**1827** Turkish power in Greece ended at naval battle of Navarino **1829** Greek independence **1830–1** Liberal revolts in Italian states suppressed by Austria **1833–8** Carlist civil war in Spain **1848–9** Liberal revolts in Italian states; Austria defeated Sardinia-Piedmont at Novara
1851 Louis Napoleon came to power in France **1852** Second Empire established in France – Louis Napoleon became Napoleon III **1861** Death of Prince Albert, husband of Queen Victoria **1867** Second Reform Act in UK – electorate doubled **1868 and 1874–80** Disraeli's premierships in UK **1869** Disestablishment of the Church of Ireland **1870** Gladstone's Irish Land Act **1870** Napoleon III defeated at Sedan in Franco-Prussian War; Second Empire overthrown; Commune of Paris set up in French capital besieged by Prussian forces **1871** End of Franco-Prussian War; France ceded Alsace-Lorraine to Germany; French Third Republic established	**1862** Bismarck became chancellor of Prussia **1863–4** Schleswig-Holstein crisis – Prussia and Austria annexed the Danish duchies **1866** Austro-Prussian War – Prussia defeated Austria at Königgrätz – end of Austrian influence in Germany; Prussia annexed Hanover, Nassau and Hesse-Cassel **1867** North German Confederation and Austro-Hungarian Empire established **1871** German unification – German Second Empire founded with Wilhelm I of Prussia as emperor (Kaiser)	**1853** Russia conquered Romania during Russo-Turkish War **1854–6** Crimean War – UK, France, Turkey and Sardinia-Piedmont confronted Russia; battles of Balaclava and Inkerman (1854); siege of Sevastopol (1854–5) **1859** Romania united **1861** Emancipation of Russian serfs **1863** Revolt by Poles and Lithuanians against Russian rule **1867** Turkey withdrew from Serbia	**1859–61** Unification of Italy – French and Piedmontese defeated Austria at Magenta and Solferino (1859); Lombardy, central duchies and Papal States (except Rome) united with Sardinia-Piedmont (1860); Garibaldi's irregular forces conquered Naples and Sicily (1860); Victor Emanuel II became first king of Italy (1861) **1868** Liberal revolt in Spain; Isabella II deposed **1870** Rome occupied by Italian forces
1879 Irish Land League formed with Parnell as president **1880** Anticlericalism in France – Benedictines, Carmelites and Jesuits expelled **1881–2** Parnell imprisoned; Phoenix Park murders sparked off Anglo-Irish crisis (1882) **1884** Third Reform Bill in UK **1886 and 1893** Irish Home Rule Bills failed **1892** Keir Hardie became first independent British Labour MP **1894–1906** Dreyfus Affair in France	**1878** Congress of Berlin **1879** Bismarck abandoned free trade **1880** Church–state conflict ended in Germany with repeal of the May Laws **1882** Germany, Austria and Italy formed the Triple Alliance **1888** William II became emperor (Kaiser) of Germany **1890** Fall of Bismarck **1897** First Zionist Congress at Basel	**1876** The Bulgarian massacre – Turkey savagely repressed a revolt in Bulgaria **1878** Congress of Berlin – Romania, Serbia and Montenegro independent, Bulgaria autonomous **1891** Launch of the reformist Young Turk Movement **1894** Franco-Russian alliance	**1875** Carlists expelled from Catalonia and Valencia **1875** Liberal constitution granted in restored Spanish Bourbon monarchy **1876** End of Spanish Carlist Wars
1901 Death of Queen Victoria **1904** *Entente Cordiale* between UK and France **1905** Norway gained independence from Sweden **1906** Foundation of the British Labour party **1907** Anglo-Russian *entente* **1909** Lloyd George's 'People's Budget' introduced social security measures **1913** Third Irish Home Rule Bill rejected **1914** Militant suffragette demonstrations in London; British Expeditionary Force sent to France at outbreak of World War I	**1907** Germany opposed arms limitations at the Hague Peace Conference **1908** Austria annexed Bosnia and Herzegovina **1914** Assassination of Austrian heir Archduke Franz Ferdinand led to Austrian declaration of war against Serbia; general mobilization; Germany declared war on Russia and France; outbreak of World War I	**1903** Bolshevik/Menshevik split in Russia **1905** 'Bloody Sunday' revolt in Russia – *Duma* established with limited powers **1912** First Balkan War – Balkan states defeated Turkey, which lost most of its European territory; Albania independent **1913** Second Balkan War – Balkan states and Turkey defeated Bulgaria	**1900** Assassination of Umberto I, king of Italy **1908** Assassination of Carlos, king of Portugal **1910** Establishment of a republic in Portugal **1912** Italy seized the Dodecanese from Turkey

THE AMERICAS	SCIENCE AND TECHNOLOGY	CULTURE AND SOCIETY	REST OF THE WORLD
1787 Washington became first US president **1791** Touissaint l'Ouverture's black revolt against French rule in Haiti **1791** Division of Canada into English- and French-speaking provinces – Upper and Lower Canada	**1783** First manned balloon flight **1785** Steam power first used in cotton mills; Cartwright patented power-loom **1795** Metric system adopted in France **1793** Whitney's improved cotton gin in USA **1796** Jenner began immunization against smallpox	**end of 18th century** Large increase in enclosures in England **1782–95** Last symphonies of Mozart and Haydn – peak of the Classical symphony **1787** Mozart's opera *Don Giovanni* **1790s** Emergence of Romanticism in Britain – *Lyrical Ballads* published by Wordsworth and Coleridge (1798) **1795** Speenhamland Poor Law relief began in England	**1794** Foundation of Qajar dynasty in Persia **1795** Britain took Ceylon and the Cape from the Dutch **1797** Bonaparte's campaign in Egypt **1798** Tipoo Sahib defeated by Britain **1799** Discovery in Egypt of the Rosetta Stone
1803 Louisiana Purchase: USA bought Louisiana from France **1810** Revolts against Spanish rule in Colombia, Mexico and Argentina **1811** Venezuela in revolt against Spain **1812–4** Anglo–US War of 1812 **1816** Argentine independence **1817** Independent Venezuelan government set up by Bolívar **1818** Chilean independence **1821** Peruvian independence declared **1822** Brazilian independence from Portugal	**1800** Volta made the first electric battery **1804** Trevithick built the first operative steam engine **1810** Dalton's *New System of Chemical Philosophy* described atomic theory **1814** Stephenson's first steam engine **1821** Faraday conducted pioneer work in electric motors	**from c. 1800** Major growth in religious non-conformism in Britain **early 19th century** Romanticism in art flourished – works of Goya, Turner and Delacroix; network of roads constructed in Britain by Telford, McAdam and others **1799–1823** Beethoven's symphonies **1807** Gas lighting used for London streets **1810–20s** 'Second generation' of English Romantic poets – Byron, Shelley and Keats **1812–14** Hegel (1770–1831) developed his concept of dialectic	**1815** At Congress of Vienna, UK gained the Cape, Ceylon, Ionian Islands, Mauritius, Tobago, St Lucia **1818** Zulu Empire founded by Chaka **1819** Refoundation of Singapore **1820** Foundation of Liberia **1821** Gold Coast became a British colony
1823 Monroe Doctrine warned European powers against further New World colonization **1828** Uruguayan independence **1836–45** Independent republic of Texas **1837** Mackenzie's Rebellion and Papineau's Rebellion (1837–8) in Canada **1846–8** Mexican–American War – USA gained Arizona, California and New Mexico **1846** US–Canadian boundary defined by the Oregon Treaty **1848** Gold discovered in California	**1825** First passenger railway – Stockton to Darlington **1828** Clifton Suspension Bridge designed by Brunel in UK **1835** Darwin studied the origin of species in the Galápagos **1838** Daguerre produced photographs **1839** Goodyear vulcanized rubber **1840s** Railway boom in Europe **1844** First use of Morse's telegraph	**from c. 1825** Spread of Gothic revival architecture – British Houses of Parliament built 1837–60 **1829** Balzac began his novel sequence *La comédie humaine* **1834** Tolpuddle martyrs transported to Australia **c. 1836–60** Transcendentalist movement flourished in the USA – works of Emerson and Thoreau **1837–70** Publication of Dickens's novels, beginning with *Pickwick Papers* (1837) **from c. 1840** Increase in emigration to USA from Europe **from c. 1830** Romantic period in music – works of Berlioz, Chopin and Lizst **1848** Marx and Engels – *The Communist Party Manifesto*	**1830** France annexed Algeria **1833** Slavery abolished throughout the British Empire **1835–7** The 'Great Trek' of Boers in South Africa **1839–42** First Opium War in China **1840** New Zealand became a British colony **1841** Mehemet Ali recognized as hereditary ruler of Egypt
1850 Compromise of 1850 on slavery **1850–90** Indian wars on the western US plains **1854** Kansas–Nebraska Act; formation of US Republican Party **1861** Confederate States of America formed by 11 southern secessionist 'slave' states; start of American Civil War **1863** Union forces defeated the Confederates at Gettysburg, turning point of American Civil War; US emancipation of slaves **1864–7** French military involvement in Mexico – Habsburg prince Maximilian emperor of Mexico **1865** Surrender of Confederate forces at Appomattox – end of American Civil War; US President Lincoln assassinated **1867** Confederation of Canada established **1867–8** US Reconstruction Acts	**1851** First cable laid under the English Channel **1855** Florence Nightingale pioneered modern nursing during the Crimean War **1857** Bessemer's process for converting pig iron into steel **1859** Darwin's *Origin of the Species* published **1863** First underground railway in London **1865** Mendel published his laws of heredity **1869** Completion of Union Pacific Railroad – first transcontinental rail connection in the USA	**1840** First postage stamps in Britain **c. 1840–c. 1880** Flourishing of Realism in art **from c. 1850** Flourishing of the Realist novel in France and Russia (Flaubert, Turgenev, Tolstoy and Dostoevski) **1851** Great Exhibition in London; Melville's novel *Moby-Dick* **1853** Verdi's operas *Il Trovatore* and *La Traviata* **1855** Whitman's collection of poems, *Leaves of Grass* **1857** Baudelaire's collection of poems, *Les Fleurs du Mal* **1865** Wagner's opera *Tristan and Isolde* **1868** Trades Union Congress formed in Britain (unions did not gain legal status until 1871) **1869–86** Knights of Labor flourished – US national trade union federation **late 1860s** Beginning of Impressionist movement in painting, dominated by Renoir and Monet **1870s** Arts and Crafts movement developed, characterized by works of William Morris	**1853** US fleet under Perry forced Japan to open up to Western trade **1856–60** Second Opium War in China **1857–8** The Indian Mutiny **1860–70** Maori Wars against European settlement in New Zealand **1860s–70s** Russia conquered Central Asia **1867–9** Tokugawa shogunate toppled in Japan; Meiji reforms began **1869** Opening of Suez Canal
1876 The Sioux massacred Custer's cavalry at Little Big Horn **1879–84** Chile defeated Peru and Bolivia in the War of the Pacific **1889** Brazil became a republic **1890** Indian wars ended in defeat of the Sioux at Wounded Knee **1893** US settlers overthrew the Hawaiian monarchy – formal annexation of the islands 1898 **1898** Spanish–American War – USA acquired Cuba, Puerto Rica, Guam and the Philippines	**1876** Bell invented the telephone **1879** Edison successfully produced an incandescent electric lamp **1884** Benz announced the first petrol-driven car **1895** Roentgen discovered X-rays **1896** Becquerel discovered radioactivity **1898** The Curies discovered radium	**1877** First cricket 'Test Match' between England and Australia **c. 1880–1905** Post-Impressionism flourished in painting – works of Cézanne and van Gogh **1888** Foundation of the English Football League **1890** Ibsen's drama *Hedda Gabler* **1891** Mahler's first symphony performed **1895** Oscar Wilde imprisoned for homosexuality; films shown in public in France; beginning of the cinema **by end of 19th century** Major improvements had been made in industrial working conditions, housing, public health and free education for children in most industrialized countries	**1875–1900** The 'scramble for Africa' – intensified after the 1884 Berlin Conference **1877** Queen Victoria became Empress of India **1885** Khartoum fell to the Mahdi; General Gordon killed **1895** The Jameson Raid **1898** The Fashoda Incident **1899** Start of the Second Boer War
1901 US President McKinley assassinated: Theodore Roosevelt became president **1902** Cuba became independent republic **1903** USA gained control of the Panama Canal Zone **1903** Panama seceded from Colombia **1910–40** Mexican Revolution **1914** Panama Canal completed	**1901** Marconi transmitted a morse wireless signal across the Atlantic **1903** Wright brothers made first aeroplane flight **1905** Einstein formulated the special theory of relativity **1908** The Model T Ford **1911** Rutherford published his theory of atomic structures	**early 20th century** Beginnings of jazz and ragtime music in the USA; spread of the campaign for women's suffrage; cinema became a form of popular entertainment; beginnings of modernism in the arts, flourishing of artistic experimentation – music of Schoenberg and Webern broke down tonality – Cubism in art originated by Picasso and Braque – literary symbolism flourished in Paris and elsewhere in Europe **1900** Publication of *The Interpretation of Dreams* by Sigmund Freud, the founder of psychoanalysis **1912** The sinking of the *Titanic* **1913** First part of Proust's novel, *A La Recherche du Temps Perdu*, published	**1900–1** Boxer rebellion in China against Western influence **1901** Commonwealth of Australia founded **1902** End of Boer War **1910** Union of South Africa formed **1911** Army rebellion toppled the Chinese Qing dynasty; a republic established

The Agricultural and Industrial Revolutions

A rapid and unprecedented rise in population occurred in Britain during the second half of the 18th century, and later in most other European nations. New and more efficient farming methods had to be found to feed the increased numbers, as traditional farming, based on subsistence methods, could not cope with the rise.

SEE ALSO

● THE RISE OF THE BOUR-
GEOISIE p. 130
● INDUSTRIAL SOCIETY IN THE
19TH CENTURY p. 164

The Industrial Revolution, which also began in Britain during the 18th century, spread to much of the northern hemisphere throughout the 19th and early part of the 20th centuries. The advent of mechanized mass production heralded the transformation of the countries of Europe and North America into predominantly industrial rather than agricultural nations, with their populations increasingly concentrated in the cities.

The Agricultural Revolution

In Britain almost all traces of the ancient 'open-field' system of arable farming disappeared, and between 1760 and 1820 over 20 000 km² (7700 sq mi) of open field and common land were enclosed. Similar processes took place elsewhere. The process of enclosure involved wealthier farmers and landowners taking over land previously farmed by peasants who could not demonstrate legal ownership.

Once fields began to be enclosed, it was possible to keep animals away from others that might be diseased or underweight, and landowners began to experiment with carefully planned selective livestock breeding. Animals could be kept alive during the winter months, as extra fodder crops, such as turnips, were now grown. The introduction of four-field crop rotation made it possible to use all fields to the full every year.

New types of agricultural machinery such

An oval spinning mule. In 1779 Samuel Crompton invented the first spinning mule that simultaneously drew out and twisted cotton yarn, successfully reproducing by machine the actions of hand spinning. The invention revolutionized the textile industry.

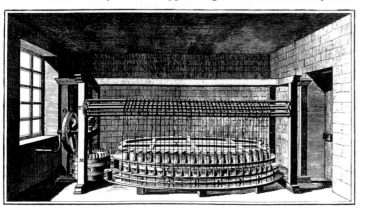

as the seed drill invented by Jethro Tull (1674–1741) in 1730 also led eventually to a great improvement in crop production. But new machines required fewer men to operate them. In some areas, farm workers forced farmers to destroy them, or did so themselves. Enclosures often led to great hardship, and to the eviction of many peasant farmers, which in some places led to riots and revolts, and in Ireland and the Scottish Highlands, for example, to mass emigration.

Throughout Europe the enormous agricultural changes made it possible for a reduced number of people working on the land to produce more food for the growing numbers of people who left the countryside to live in the industrial towns and cities. This process was helped by the increased use of artificial fertilizers and the cultivation of 'new' staple crops: potatoes in northern Europe and maize in the south. More and more potential farmland was put to use, but despite this, by the early 20th century imported North American grain was essential to feed Europe's growing population.

The beginnings of the Industrial Revolution

Why did the Industrial Revolution begin in Britain? Britain had the advantage of being a united country with a relatively stable internal political situation, free from internal customs duties and with well-established banking and insurance facilities (▷ p. 130). In the 18th century Britain became the dominant international trading power (▷ p. 128), and many British merchants had accumulated large sums of capital. In addition, the Agricultural Revolution produced huge profits for some farmers. This made it possible for ambitious new schemes to be financed at very low rates of interest.

Britain's secure position as an island, combined with its proximity to the principal sea routes between northern Europe and the rest of the world, gave it great natural advantages. In addition, Britain's large numbers of natural harbours and navigable rivers – many linked by new canals in the 18th century – meant that internal and overseas trade were easily linked. Acquisition of a colonial empire became vitally important for Britain and later for other powers, so as to provide markets and raw materials (▷ pp. 128 and 160).

Rapid industrial development was also precipitated by a need to tackle Britain's fuel crisis. By the mid-18th century it was apparent that the forests were seriously depleted; opencast and shallow underground coal mines were nearing exhaustion and existing technologies for draining deeper mine shafts were inadequate. The invention of steam pumps as a far more efficient way to drain mines and the discovery of a process for smelting iron using coke made possible a more intense exploitation of Britain's mineral resources. The geology of Britain – with sources of coal and iron ore close to each other – also played its part.

Textiles

Woollen cloth had long been one of Britain's most important products, but as the 18th century progressed, it became difficult to fulfil the greatly increased demand. Inventions such as the spinning jenny produced larger quantities of thread more quickly, especially cotton. Cotton was imported in increasing quantities from the USA, and became vital to the British textile industry. Further mechanical spinning devices such as the water frame and the spinning mule appeared in the 1770s, and in 1785 the introduction of Cartwright's power loom, capable of being operated by relatively unskilled labour, marked the end of hand-loom weaving. The initial development of mechanized textile industries in the USA and much of continental Europe was dependent on many of these British inventions.

Only those with capital could invest in the new machinery, and those without it could not produce thread or cloth as cheaply. Thus mechanization of the textile industry gave rise to the factory system. Instead of being self-employed and working at home, women and children (who had always been expected to work for their living) – and later men as well – went 'out to work' for wages in the factories, where steam engines set the pace. Attempts to destroy the new machinery by disgruntled weavers ('Luddites') were severely repressed.

Iron, steel, steam and coal

The breakthroughs in iron smelting and production in the 18th century were vital to early industrialization. Iron was used for machinery, ships, and railways. Although high-quality cast steel was produced from the 1740s, it was not until 1857 that a cheap method of mass producing mild steel was discovered (the Bessemer process; ▷ picture, p. 164). This process was developed and improved by others, and large-scale production of steel using these techniques was an important factor in the rapid industrial growth of Germany and the USA (▷ p. 164).

Experimental attempts to drain water from mines led to the early steam engines of Thomas Savery (1650–1715) in 1698 and Thomas Newcomen (1663–1729) in 1712. However, it was not until James Watt (1736–1809) redesigned Newcomen's device (patented in 1769) that a cheaper and more efficient steam pump became available. With the addition of rotary motion, achieved by Watt in 1781, steam engines quickly became ubiquitous. As well as pumps, steam engines powered all kinds of factory machinery, railway locomotives, and ships. Without steam many of the later developments of the Industrial Revolution would have been impossible.

Coal production was dramatically increased as a direct result of the availability of practical steam pumps and other technological innovations. However, deeper, more mechanized mining proved more dangerous to the mineworkers, who included children of 4 years old and upwards. Coal was the basic fuel for steam engines, and throughout Europe and the northeast USA heavy industry grew up in areas close to rich coal seams. Such areas included the Scottish lowlands, South Wales, the Ruhr and Silesia.

By the 1880s, the development of electrical energy as a power source, pioneered by Michael Faraday (1791–1867), heralded the introduction of a rival that was eventually to supersede steam. British industries, unlike those in Germany and the USA, were slow to abandon steam engines until well into the 20th century.

Other industries, such as the potteries of Josiah Wedgwood (1730–1795), were transformed during the 18th century by the invention of new chemical processes. Development of accurate and standardized machine tools was also a very important aspect of the Industrial Revolution.

Transport

The need for reliable and cheap access to raw materials and markets made improvements in transport an essential part of the Industrial Revolution.

Road building enjoyed a long overdue revival in the 18th century, pioneered in Britain by such men as John McAdam (1756–1836) and Thomas Telford (1757–1834). Initially more important, however, were canals, which provided the cheapest way of transporting goods and materials in bulk. A massive canal-building programme got under way in the 18th century, and by 1830 there were over 6400 km (4000 mi) of canals in Britain alone, linking all the main industrial areas. However, with the advent of the railways, the canals fell rapidly into disuse.

Following the opening of the first public steam line in 1825 (the Stockton & Darlington line, designed by George Stephenson; 1781–1848), private railway companies in Britain proliferated rapidly, with the result that a national network evolved with little attempt at planning. In continental Europe the railways were subject to a greater degree of state regulation and control. This was especially true of Belgium and Germany.

By providing a rapid means of transporting in bulk both raw materials and manufactured goods, the growth of railway networks greatly assisted the process of industrialization. The railways also provided an impetus for other developments, such as the electric telegraph, and in the USA they played a key role in opening up the interior after the Civil War (⊳ p. 156). The railways also played a social and cultural role: by providing a

means of cheap and swift long-distance passenger transport they opened up a wider world to millions of people.

Industrialization outside Britain

Although Britain initiated the Industrial Revolution, other European nations, notably Belgium, were close behind. In France, industrialization proceeded more slowly, but was still impressive. In the late 19th century superior expertise in the key technologies of electricity and the internal combustion engine would result in Germany overtaking Britain as Europe's leading industrial power (⊳ p. 164). In the USA the difficulties of developing an adequate transport system to cover vast distances held industrialization in check for a while. But rapid growth would make the USA the world's leading industrial power by the beginning of the 20th century (⊳ pp. 157 and 164).

For Russia and Japan, industrialization during the later part of the 19th century was a result of deliberate government policy. In the 1850s both powers were largely agricultural societies dominated by ancient feudal systems, but by the start of the 20th century Japan had emerged as a serious industrial, military and economic rival to the world's industrial giants (⊳ pp. 65 and 164).

Russia's industrialization was hampered

by the country's vast size and poor communications, and even more so by the backwardness of a society still run as a feudal system, and by the inertia of the autocratic rule of the Tsars. A succession of foreign loans and internal reforms gradually made it possible to increase production and build up a railway network, and in the early years of the 20th century state aid was used to encourage growth. Industrialization continued following the Revolution, but under circumstances of extreme difficulty (⊳ p. 181).

The effects of industrialization

Industrialization radically altered the face of European society. The demographic shift away from the countryside led to an explosion of large cities in which slum housing, low wages and the use of child labour created social and economic problems on a massive scale (⊳ p. 164). The growth of industrial capitalism in Western Europe also produced a more complex political society, in which the new social and economic classes spawned by the Industrial Revolution began to organize themselves and to wield greater political influence. The industrial and commercial middle class played a crucial role in the development of 19th-century liberalism (⊳ p. 150), while the new urban proletariat of skilled and semi-skilled workers began to organize themselves in trade unions from the mid-19th century onwards (⊳ pp. 166 and 169). PO

The pithead of an English coalmine (1792). Although a steam engine is used for pumping water out of the mine and for raising the coal by means of a steam-powered windlass (first used in 1770), horsepower is still the means of transporting coal from the pit.

A steam train on the line between Lyon and St Etienne in 1834, two years after its inauguration as the first steam railway in continental Europe. Similar systems were soon in operation in Belgium and Germany (1835), and Austria and Russia (1837).

The Birth of the USA

Continuous European settlement of North America was a product of intense rivalry among the nation-states of early modern Europe. In the 16th century Spain and Portugal capitalized on the discoveries of Christopher Columbus by establishing colonies in Central and South America (▷ p. 116). These yielded vast quantities of precious metals, prompting attacks on Iberian treasure fleets by English and French privateers such as Drake, Raleigh and Hawkins. Seeing rival monarchs profit from their American possessions, the English Crown became convinced that it too could benefit from the vast material resources of the New World.

King James I's decision to permit a group of London merchants to found a 'plantation' on the North American coast set the scene for the founding of thirteen British colonies that would eventually become the United States of America.

Early settlement and growth

The joint-stock company chartered by the Crown founded its first American colony, Virginia, in 1607, with its centre at Jamestown. The original settlers faced appalling hardships: roughly half the population died from disease in 1609 alone. But once the Virginians learned how to cultivate and export an indigenous weed called tobacco, the colony began to mature and prosper – initially on the basis of white indentured labour, then, by the end of the 17th century, with the aid of black slaves imported from Africa and the Caribbean sugar islands.

A second English beachhead, Plymouth, was established in 1620 by Protestant separatists or Puritans. They reached Cape Cod in November after setting out from home in the *Mayflower* two months earlier. In 1630 another group of Puritans under John Winthrop founded the neighbouring colony of Massachusetts Bay. Six years later a religious dispute prompted Roger Williams, a believer in the separation of Church and state, to set up a third New England colony, Rhode Island. White expansion in this region proceeded rapidly after the defeat of local Pequot and Naragansett Indians.

Other British settlements followed, notably the fertile middle colonies of New York (formerly Dutch New Netherland), New Jersey, and Quaker Pennsylvania. By 1750 most of the colonies possessed governors appointed by the Crown and had been integrated into Britain's Atlantic empire. Blessed with a surfeit of agricultural wealth, and enjoying guaranteed markets for their products, the colonies prospered during the first half of the 18th century. Most Americans regarded themselves as loyal subjects of the Crown with all the inherent rights of free-born Englishmen. American troops contributed significantly to the defeat of the French in the Seven Years War (1756–63; ▷ pp. 125 and 129).

Victory in that conflict gave Britain not only Canada, but also mastery of the North American continent. France surrendered Louisiana (then comprising much of the Mississippi basin) to Spain (regaining it in 1800) and Spain yielded Florida to Britain, but retained its own settlements in the southwest. The British victory, however, was a costly one, for the national debt almost doubled during these years. It was time, the British Parliament concluded, that the colonists made a greater contribution to their own defence.

Origins of the Revolution

During the first half of the 18th century Americans became accustomed to a substantial measure of self-government. Wealthy planters, lawyers, and merchants played leading roles in colonial society. Placing great value on rights and sovereignty, they resented their lack of representation in Parliament as well as their economic subordination within the Empire (particularly restrictions on their ability to trade). In 1765 Parliament's imposition of a stamp duty on legal documents and merchandise unleashed the cry of 'no taxation without representation'.

Although widespread opposition to this measure forced the British government to back down – both on this occasion and again in 1767 – Parliament continued to insist that it had full power to make laws for the colonies, and left a tax on tea as proof of its authority. In 1773 it allowed the struggling East India Company to dump its tea on the American market, still retaining the controversial duty. When the first consignment reached Boston, Massachusetts, a group of patriots – as the American radicals now called themselves – disguised themselves as Indians. They proceeded to throw the tea chests into the harbour, in what became known as the 'Boston Tea Party'. America was now ripe for revolution.

First blows

When Britain instituted repressive measures against Massachusetts, Americans reacted by sending delegates to the First Continental Congress in September 1774. This banned the import of goods from Britain, while colonial pamphleteers insisted that traditional freedoms were being threatened by a corrupt and tyrannical enemy. In April 1775, when British troops moved to seize a store of arms outside Boston, they were confronted at Lexington by armed Massachusetts farmers, and retreated without achieving their objective.

The Declaration of Independence

King George III and his government in Britain now regarded the Americans as traitors who must be suppressed. To this end large numbers of British troops and German mercenaries were dispatched across the Atlantic. The Americans themselves were divided as to how they should react. Most of those at the head of the patriot movement, however, believed Britain's policy of coercion had severed the ties of empire. In mid-1776 a Virginia planter, Thomas Jefferson (1743–1826), drafted a formal Declaration of Independence. This also announced the potentially revolutionary new doctrine: 'that all men are created equal, that they are endowed by their Creator with certain unalienable rights, that among these are life, liberty and the pursuit of happiness'.

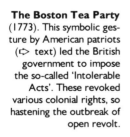

The Boston Tea Party (1773). This symbolic gesture by American patriots (▷ text) led the British government to impose the so-called 'Intolerable Acts'. These revoked various colonial rights, so hastening the outbreak of open revolt.

200 Boston Boys throwing tea into the Harbour

Congress approved the document on 4 July.

The war of independence

In their eight-year-long struggle for independence the Americans had a number of crucial advantages. They were fighting in conditions familiar to them but to which the British had to adapt; and the considerable number of Americans who remained loyal to the British Crown proved a relatively ineffective force. Even more important, the Americans had interior lines of communication, whereas the enemy was dependent on a 5000-km (3000-mi) long supply route from Europe. Moreover the rebels owed much to the leadership of General George Washington (1732–99), a cautious but inspiring commander.

Finally, France's decision to support the American cause after the patriot victory at Saratoga in 1777 diverted much of Britain's resources and threatened the Royal Navy's mastery of the seas. When a British army under Cornwallis found itself besieged by Washington at Yorktown in 1781 a French fleet in Chesapeake Bay cut off the only avenue of escape. Cornwallis surrendered on 19 October, and Yorktown turned out to be the decisive engagement of the war. Two years later, in 1783, Britain recognized American independence. The United States had entered the community of nations.

The Constitution

Until 1788 the only legal basis for the USA was provided by the Articles of Confederation, which delegated very restricted powers to Congress. However, by the mid-1780s Congress's inability to respond effectively to economic pressure from European powers revealed clearly the shortcomings of the Articles. Moreover, many conservatives feared serious social unrest in the aftermath of the war. The Articles, leading figures concluded, would have to be replaced

Fifty-five delegates from 12 of the states

The siege of Yorktown by American and French forces led to the final surrender of the British in 1781. Here the Comte de Rochambeau, the Marquis de Lafayette and General Washington discuss their strategy.

gathered in Philadelphia in May 1787 to draft a constitution for the new federal republic. Although Washington was president of the Convention, it was his fellow Virginian, James Madison (1751–1836), who had most influence on the proceedings. His 'Virginia Plan' proposed to invest substantial powers in a stronger federal government made up of a national executive, judiciary and legislature.

After much debate the Plan was modified, and as it finally emerged was a compromise between the various regional interests in the Convention. In spite of serious flaws it was a remarkably democratic document for its time. 'Anti-federalist' critics who disliked its strengthening of central government were placated by the passage of a Bill of Rights (see box), which formed the first ten amendments to the Constitution. RC

THE US CONSTITUTION AND THE BILL OF RIGHTS

The US Constitution (ratified in 1788) placed the republic on a firmly federal basis. Its main provisions were:

1. A stronger central government divided into three branches – a President chosen by an Electoral College; a Federal judiciary; and a national legislature (composed of a popularly elected House of Representatives and a Senate chosen by the state legislatures).

2. While representation in the House was based on population, each state sent two delegates to the Senate.

3. Congress was given full power to levy import duties and taxes.

4. For representation and tax purposes a black slave was to be enumerated as three-fifths of a white person.

5. The African slave trade was not to be abolished before 1808.

The Bill of Rights (ratified in 1791) formed the first 10 amendments to the Constitution. These ruled against:

1. Abridgement of freedom of religion, speech, the press, petition, and peaceful assembly.

2. The infringement of the right to bear arms.

3. The illegal quartering of troops.

4. Unreasonable searches and seizures.

5. The capital trial of any person for the same offence; deprivation of life, liberty or property 'without due process of law'; self-incrimination; uncompensated seizure of property.

6. Infringement of an accused person's right to a speedy and public trial before an impartial jury.

7. Depriving persons of the right to trial by jury in common-law suits where the value in question exceeded $20.

8. Excessive bail and punishments.

Amendments 9 and 10 declared that the listing of certain rights in the Constitution should not be taken to deny others retained by the people, and reserved to the states all powers not delegated to the Federal government by the Constitution.

Jefferson described these rights as 'what the people are entitled to against every government on earth', and several of them have been enshrined in the constitutions of other democratic countries.

SEE ALSO

● COLONIAL EXPANSION IN THE 17TH AND 18TH CENTURIES p. 128
● THE ENLIGHTENMENT p. 134
● THE EXPANSION OF THE USA p. 156

The French Revolution

Between 1789 and 1791 the political and social institutions that had characterized France for the previous century and more were overthrown. In 1792 France became a republic, and between 1793 and 1794 experienced a revolutionary dictatorship (the 'Reign of Terror'). Thereafter a reaction set in, culminating in the establishment of a military dictatorship under Napoleon Bonaparte (1769–1821). With the overthrow of the republic, many of the institutions and practices of pre-Revolutionary France were reintroduced. In 1815, following Napoleon's final defeat (▷ p. 147), the Bourbon dynasty was restored.

Yet the French revolution remains an event of major importance. It was the first 'modern' revolution, in that it attempted to transform the whole social and political system. It put into circulation modern notions of democracy, nationalism, and even socialism. In these respects, and in its resort to violent dictatorship to effect this programme, the French Revolution was very different from the earlier revolutions in England (▷ p. 119) and America (▷ p. 142).

The background

The France of the *ancien régime* – the term given to the political and social system prior to the Revolution – was a centralized, absolute monarchy ruled by Louis XVI (1774–92) from Versailles (▷ p. 123). Yet it remained a patchwork of privilege with the great mass of taxation being paid by the unprivileged urban poor, and by the peasantry, who had the additional burden of feudal dues. The wealthiest non-nobles (the *bourgeois*), although by no means unprivileged, had fewer legal and social rights than the aristocracy (▷ p. 130).

Some nobles and bourgeois (particularly those influenced by Enlightenment ideas (▷ p. 134) agreed that merit should be the true basis of social status. They were also critical of royal absolutism and the corruption of the court. The monarchy was further undermined by the weak character of Louis XVI, and by the unpopularity of his Austrian queen, Marie Antoinette (▷ p. 124).

The immediate background to the revolution was the government's bankruptcy following French intervention in the American War of Independence (▷ p. 142), and a trade recession coinciding with harvest failure. At a time of growing discontent among the poor, Louis XVI was obliged to call the States-General (a national assembly that had not met since 1614) to consider reform of the tax system, including a reduction in privileges.

The events of 1789

The Third Estate (the commoners) of the States-General declared itself a National Assembly, intending to introduce reform. Louis ordered troops to Paris and Versailles. On 14 July, fearing an attack on Paris and the Assembly, the Paris mob seized the Bastille (a royal fortress and prison) in order to obtain arms. An independent municipal government (*commune*) and National Guard were established in Paris, and other towns followed suit. Since the army was divided and unreliable, royal authority collapsed. The National Assembly survived.

Following a wave of peasant revolts, the Assembly abolished feudal and other privileges in August 1789. This abolition was confirmed in the Declaration of the

Rights of Man. This stated that the natural rights of man and the citizen (liberty, property, security, and the right to resist oppression) could never be given up. All men were free and equal, and equally liable to taxation, and the king derived his authority solely from the will of the people.

France becomes a republic

The Assembly prepared a 'modern' constitutional government. Henceforth legislative power lay with a new elected assembly, and local government and the legal system were completely re-organized. Religious toleration for Protestants and Jews ended the privileged position of the Catholic Church, and the confiscation and sale of Church lands solved the problem of the national debt while a fairer tax system was being devised.

In October 1789 Louis XVI and the Assembly had been forced to leave Versailles for Paris. There the mob, organized by members of political clubs (notably the left-wing Jacobins), could influence events. After a failed attempt to flee the country in 1791, Louis XVI was obliged to approve the new constitution. By the end of 1791 the Revolution had – relatively peacefully – put an end to absolute monarchy and transformed French society.

Yet the Revolution was by no means over. In 1792 foreign powers, anxious to nip the Revolution in the bud before it spread to their own countries, invaded France (▷ p. 146). This stimulated suspicions of plots to betray the Revolution. A thousand suspected counter-revolutionaries

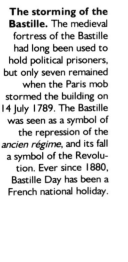

The storming of the Bastille. The medieval fortress of the Bastille had long been used to hold political prisoners, but only seven remained when the Paris mob stormed the building on 14 July 1789. The Bastille was seen as a symbol of the repression of the *ancien régime*, and its fall a symbol of the Revolution. Ever since 1880, Bastille Day has been a French national holiday.

were massacred in the prisons of Paris (September 1792), and France was declared a republic (November). In the following year Louis XVI and Marie Antoinette were tried for treason and guillotined.

The Reign of Terror

Not all Frenchmen supported the Revolution. Many left France (the so-called *émigrés*), but many more remained. In 1793 revolt broke out in the Vendée in the west, and also in Normandy and the south. Against the background of civil and foreign war some people – for example the influential journalist Jean-Paul Marat – called for a revolutionary dictatorship.

This was brought about by the Jacobins in the summer of 1793, following the expulsion from the Convention of the moderate Girondin deputies. The Girondins were so called because they were from the Gironde area of southwest France, and their expulsion was effected by the revolutionary mob known as the *sans culottes* ('without breeches' – working men wore trousers). Marat himself was murdered by Charlotte Corday, a Girondin sympathizer.

Virtually dictatorial powers were assumed by the Committee of Public Safety, of which Maximilien Robespierre was the most prominent member. The Committee unleashed what became known as the 'Reign of Terror' against suspected counter-revolutionaries. All over France at least 300 000 people were arrested, and of these about 17 000 were guillotined.

In the spring of 1794 the Terror intensified. The Committee eliminated its political opponents, including those on the left responsible for a policy of dechristianization. Robespierre – believing that religion was necessary to social stability – introduced a 'Cult of the Supreme Being'.

(⊳ picture). Other victims included the moderate Georges Danton, himself a former head of the Committee. Suspects' rights were reduced and no mercy shown to those convicted. Fearing for their own lives, and that Robespierre's power was too great, his enemies had him arrested on 27 July 1794 (the coup of 9 Thermidor; ⊳ box) and executed. A new regime, a group of five known as the Directory, was established.

The end of the Revolution

The Terror was brought to an end, the Jacobin club closed, and the Paris commune abolished. The more democratic constitution of 1793 was replaced. The Paris mob resented these moves but was powerless against the army, whose support proved crucial to the continuance of the Directory. Frequent military interventions in politics culminated in 1799 in the coup of 18 Brumaire (8 November; ⊳ box) on behalf of General Napoleon Bonaparte. In 1800 Bonaparte became first Consul, and in 1804 Emperor Napoleon I, so ending the First Republic. His military dictatorship saw the restoration of central control of local government, the end of representative assemblies, and the creation of a new aristocracy.

The debate on the Revolution

The Revolution divided informed opinion throughout Europe. The views of its opponents were expressed by the Anglo-Irish Edmund Burke in *Reflections on the Revolution in France* (1790). Burke denied that there was any virtue in destroying established social institutions, and refused to see any evils in pre-Revolutionary France. He predicted that the Revolution would consume itself in violence. He was answered by the Anglo-American radical, Thomas Paine, whose *Rights of Man* (1792) defended the right of the nation to

reform what was corrupt. The British government, afraid of revolution, persecuted Paine and other radicals. Governments elsewhere repressed reform movements, putting an end to the progress of the Enlightenment. CS

A View in Perspective

The Zenith of French Glory; – The Pinnacle of Liberty.
Religion, Justice, Loyalty & all the Bugbears of Unenlightened Minds, Farewell!

A satire on the excesses of the French Revolution by the English caricaturist James Gillray. The French Revolution had a mixed reception in Britain. Progressive Whigs (such as Charles James Fox) and Romantic radicals (such as William Wordsworth) celebrated it, but others – such as Edmund Burke (⊳ text) – saw in it a threat to the Christian social order of Europe.

The Festival of the Supreme Being in Paris, June 1794. Anti-Christian feeling was a feature of the outset of the Revolution. However, within a few years the Revolutionary leadership had come to believe that religion was necessary for social stability, and introduced a cult of the Supreme Being. This cult was based on Deism, the Enlightenment idea of a 'natural religion' founded on human reason (⊳ p. 134).

The Revolutionary and Napoleonic Wars

The French Revolution transformed Europe and the relations of its states with France. From 1792 the French were obliged to defend their Revolution against a series of foreign enemies, who feared the spread of revolutionary ideas to their own countries. For their own part, the French appealed to peoples everywhere to rise up against their rulers. The war became an ideological crusade on both sides. Obliged to wage 'total war' at home and abroad, France was soon on the offensive, and its expansion meant the end of some old-established states.

Napoleon on the bridge at Arcole (right), by Antoine-Jean Gros. Napoleon's whirlwind campaign against the Austrians in Italy culminated in brilliant victories at Arcole and Rivoli, and the capture of Mantua. Dramatic and romanticized depictions such as this all helped to feed the Napoleonic myth.

Napoleon strengthened the imperialist trend in French policy and his empire became the largest in Europe since that of Rome. French domination inspired 'national' resistance, which contributed to the collapse of Napoleon and his empire in 1815. However, Napoleon's downfall was mainly the work of the 'Great Powers' – Russia, Prussia, Austria, and particularly Britain.

The First Coalition 1793–97

Those Frenchmen who fled France after 1789 urged foreign monarchs to suppress the Revolution. Eventually in 1792 the Austrians and Prussians invaded France, but were repulsed, and France went onto the offensive. French success, particularly the conquest of the Austrian Netherlands, alarmed Britain, which declared war in 1793. By offering cash subsidies Britain built up the First Coalition against France. The Coalition included most of Europe and all of France's neighbours, but it lacked an effective strategy.

The French introduced conscription, which gave France the largest army in Europe (750 000 men in 1794), and in 1794–5 French armies carried all before them. French leaders put forward the idea of 'natural frontiers' to justify their first annexations of territory. One by one the allies settled with France. The brilliant French campaign in Italy in 1796–7 – led by a young general, Napoleon Bonaparte – forced Austria to surrender Belgium in exchange for the previously independent state of Venice (▷ p. 97). The French, co-operating with local enthusiasts, established 'sister republics' in the United Provinces, Italy and Switzerland. Napoleon, having secured the Revolution against foreign enemies, set off to conquer Egypt in 1798 (▷ p. 154).

The Second Coalition 1798–1802

Britain's naval power had enabled it to survive, even to score a number of victories against France. However, if it were to defeat France it needed continental allies. Again using subsidies, Britain built up the Second Coalition, consisting of Russia, the Ottoman (Turkish) Empire, Austria, Portugal and Naples. After some initial successes, the allies were weakened by the mutual jealousies of Austria and Russia. Despite the defeat of the French fleet at the Nile (1798) by the British under Admiral (later Lord) Horatio Nelson (1758–1805), Napoleon returned to Europe, and seized political power in France (▷ p. 145).

Having defeated the Austrians at Marengo (1800) in Italy, Napoleon forced them to recognize French domination of Italy. Britain's other allies were soon forced to settle with France. Nelson's destruction of the Danish fleet at Copenhagen (1801) destroyed the threat posed by a league of neutrals resentful of British efforts to end their trade with France. But Britain found it too expensive to carry on alone, and settled with France (the Peace of Amiens, 1802).

The Third Coalition 1805–07

Peace did not end the antagonisms between Britain and France, or put an end to French expansion. In 1803 Britain declared war again. Napoleon declared himself Emperor in 1804 and proceeded to assemble an army to invade England, but his plans were frustrated by Nelson's defeat of the Franco-Spanish fleet at Trafalgar (1805). Yet Britain again depended on European allies. Napoleon's proclamation of himself as king of Italy led Austria, Russia and Naples to join the Third Coalition. Britain again provided subsidies. However, Prussia remained neutral (as it had since 1795), and a number of smaller German states joined Napoleon.

In a lightning campaign, Napoleon's troops left the Channel ports for Germany, marching 800 km (500 mi) in five weeks. Defeating the Austrians at Ulm (October 1805), he occupied Vienna, before defeating an Austro-Russian army at Austerlitz (December). Austria was forced to recognize French supremacy in Italy and Germany.

Prussia decided to restrain Napoleon, but suffered a disastrous defeat at Jena (1806). Prussia lost much territory as Napoleon reorganized Germany: the Holy Roman Empire was abolished and a French satellite organization, the Confederation of the Rhine, was established. In 1807 Russia too was beaten, settling with Napoleon and declaring war on Britain. Austria, having been defeated again in 1809, decided to join France. Napoleon, having divorced Josephine (his first wife), married an Austrian princess.

The Continental System

Napoleon was at the peak of his power in 1807, and determined to destroy Britain by ruining its export trade – the basis of its wealth and so of its continued opposition to France. Napoleon banned the import of British goods into all parts of Europe under French control. This blockade (the *Continental System*) created serious difficulties for Britain, including an inconclusive war in 1812–14 with the USA over the trading rights of neutrals (▷ p. 156). However, the System was not effective. Its unpopularity contributed to growing disillusionment with and resentment of French occupation in many parts of Europe.

The collapse of the Napoleonic Empire 1807–15

In 1808 Napoleon imposed his brother – Joseph Bonaparte – as king of Spain, sparking off a popular revolt. Henceforth large numbers of French troops were tied down in Spain, fighting a savage guerrilla war. Britain sent an expeditionary force to the Iberian Peninsula, and many years of fighting (the Peninsular War) followed. After their victory at Vitoria (1813) under the command of Arthur Wellesley (1769–1852) – later the Duke of Wellington – British troops entered France in 1814.

By that time, French prestige had suffered disastrously in Russia. Relations between the two countries had deteriorated to the

---

NAPOLEON'S MILITARY REVOLUTION

In the 18th century, armies had been relatively small, professional and expensive. Warfare had largely been a matter of siege and manoeuvre, because troops were too expensive to lose in battle. With their massive conscript armies, the French developed – and Napoleon perfected – new formations and tactics.

Napoleon always sought decisive victory, concentrating his troops against his enemy's weakest point. He divided his armies into corps of 25 000–30 000 men. These could be deployed over a wide front (keeping the enemy guessing as to where the attack would come) and then be reunited before the decisive battle. Napoleon was a master of rapid manoeuvre, and developed an appropriately flexible logistic system, including living off the land as his troops marched on. In a poor country such as Russia, however, this system left his troops highly vulnerable.

The success of Napoleon's approach was founded on good communications and supply, a vast reservoir of new conscripts, and on his popularity with his troops. This popularity was helped by a system of promotion through the ranks, and many of Napoleon's generals – such as the great Marshal Ney (1769–1815) – had risen in this way.

THE NAPOLEONIC CODE

One of the most permanent achievements of the Revolution was the Napoleonic Code. Codification of the mass of legislation enacted in France since 1789 had begun in 1792. It was completed in 1804, and renamed the *Code Napoléon* in 1807. The Code restated in legal terms the egalitarian principles of 1789, including religious toleration, and confirmed the abolition of feudal rights. However, it put greater emphasis on the rights of property, reflecting the conservatism of French political life after the Terror. It also stressed the rights of husbands and fathers, reducing the status of women.

This reflected Napoleon's personal views.

The Code, one small volume containing 2251 articles, spread the basic principles of the Revolution across Europe. Many states had little choice, since the Code was often imposed by Napoleon on those states incorporated into his empire. It was also adopted by his satellites and allies. In many states the Code survived the fall of Napoleon, and continued to play a vital part in national life. It contributed to the unification of states that before the wars had been divided by different sorts of law. In this way it ensured the permanent impact of the Revolution.

NAPOLEON'S EMPIRE AT ITS HEIGHT IN 1812

FRENCH EMPIRE

STATES RULED BY NAPOLEON'S FAMILY

OTHER DEPENDENT STATES

BOUNDARY of CONFEDERATION of THE RHINE

French Victories
⚔ MARENGO 1800
⚔ ULM 1805
⚔ AUSTERLITZ 1805
⚔ JENA 1806
⚔ BORODINO 1812

French Defeats
⚔ TRAFALGAR 1805
⚔ VITORIA 1813
⚔ LEIPZIG 1813
⚔ WATERLOO 1815

point that in 1812 Napoleon invaded Russia. Despite defeating the Russians at Borodino and reaching Moscow, Napoleon could not force the Russians to terms, and was himself obliged to retreat. The bitter winter combined with Russian attacks and the inadequacies of the French logistic system took a terrible toll: only 40 000 of the original French army of 450 000 men returned.

The Russian fiasco stimulated the formation of a Fourth Coalition. This included Prussia and Austria, and was again financed by British subsidies. In France itself the constant drainage of manpower led to growing resistance to conscription, and to Napoleon's rule in general. Fighting on two fronts, Spain and Germany, Napoleon was defeated at Leipzig (1813). In 1814, following the capture of Paris by the allies, he abdicated and was exiled to Elba. However, in March 1815 Napoleon exploited the unpopularity of the new Bourbon king, Louis XVIII, to return to France, seize power and renew the war. His 'Hundred Days' ended with his defeat at Waterloo (June 1815) by allied forces under Wellington and the Prussian general, von Blücher. Napoleon was sent to St Helena in the South Atlantic, and Louis XVIII was restored.

The peace settlement

The peace settlement was worked out at Paris and the Congress of Vienna in 1814–15. It was a compromise between restoring pre-Revolutionary Europe, rewarding the victors, and preventing France from again dominating Europe. A ring of strong states was established around France, including a new kingdom of the Netherlands and a Prussian presence in the Rhineland. The Confederation of the Rhine was abolished, but security needs meant that not all the small states were restored. Austria kept Venice, and Russia was rewarded by the acquisition of most of Poland. In order to prevent future threats to their peace settlement, the victorious allies planned to hold regular meetings. The settlement effectively suppressed much radical and nationalist sentiment in Europe, which was to come to the boil in 1848 (⇨ p. 150).   CS

SEE ALSO

● THE FRENCH REVOLUTION p. 144
● LATIN AMERICAN INDEPENDENCE p. 148
● NATIONALISM, LIBERALISM AND REVOLUTION p. 150
● THE UNIFICATION OF ITALY AND GERMANY p. 152

The battle of Waterloo, 18 June 1815. Wellington's Allied army took up a strong position south of the Belgian village of Waterloo and held back repeated French assaults until the timely arrival of Blücher's Prussians. In the general Allied advance that followed, the French were routed. Four days later Napoleon abdicated for the second – and last – time. This painting by Henri Phillipoteaux shows French cuirassiers charging a square formation of Highlanders.

Latin American Independence

Between 1808 and 1826 Spain lost its empire in the Americas, except the islands of Cuba and Puerto Rico. In 1824 the Portuguese colony of Brazil declared itself an empire independent of the mother country (▷ box). These were not the first independence movements in the western hemisphere. The USA had freed itself from British dominion in the American War of Independence (1775–83; ▷ p. 142), and in 1804 the French island of Haiti also attained its liberty after 15 years of rebellion and counter-invasion.

Simón Bolívar enters Caracas in triumph. Having driven the Spanish from Venezuela, Ecuador, Colombia and Peru in a series of brilliant military campaigns, Bolívar established the Confederation of Gran Colombia (consisting of Venezuela, Colombia, Ecuador and Panama) in 1826. However, he was unable to prevent its collapse under secessionist pressures in 1830.

The new states of Latin America covered vast and varied territories, hitherto jealously guarded against foreign intrusion by Spain and Portugal. In some ways they can be seen as the first states to emerge in the 'Third World' from a struggle for national liberation.

The Spanish Empire

At the beginning of the 19th century Spain's possessions in the Americas stretched from Cape Horn in the south to what are now the southwestern states of the USA. The viceroyalty of New Spain – the imperial division that included present-day Mexico – also embraced Texas, Arizona, New Mexico and California, vast territories that Mexico would finally lose in the war with her northern neighbour in 1846. Spain ceded Louisiana back to France in 1800, but held parts of Florida until 1819 (▷ p. 156).

The Spanish American territories had a population of some 17 million. Their racial composition varied considerably according to region. The two oldest viceroyalties – New Spain and Peru – had large indigenous populations, the descendants of the subjects of the Aztec and Inca empires that had fallen to the Spanish conquest in the 16th century (▷ pp. 73 and 116). Throughout Spanish America, during the three centuries of colonial rule, varying degrees of intermarriage of the Spanish immigrant, native American and black African slave populations had occurred.

With its abundance of mineral resources, particularly precious metals, Latin America offered many opportunities for development. It was the world's most important source of gold and silver until the mid-19th century discoveries in California and Australia. Brazil was a leading supplier of sugar. The commercial growth of coffee had spread from the West Indian islands to mainland South and Central America by the late 18th century. Most of the world's chocolate was produced in the Caracas and Guayaquil regions (Venezuela and Equador). The exotic allure of tropical nature added to the region's exciting potential. Between 1799 and 1804 the German explorer and naturalist Wilhelm von Humboldt travelled extensively in the tropical regions of the Spanish empire. His account of his travels did much to convince his contemporaries of the wealth waiting to be tapped.

The Spanish possessions in the New World were settled with a well-rooted and numerous upper class composed of creoles (colonial descendants of Spanish settlers). This was not merely an empire of administrators, soldiers and merchants, but an entire society – with its religion, culture, bureaucracy and law – transposed and adapted to new conditions. Unlike most later European colonial societies in Africa and Asia (▷ pp. 160 and 200), the Spanish roots in Latin America were put down to endure.

However, administration, society and the economy were carefully regulated from Spain. This control was further tightened in the late 18th century, and more officials were appointed from mainland Spain at the expense of Latin American-born creoles. The revenues of the Spanish crown rose, but at the same time Spain found it less and less possible to supply the economic needs of the Empire from its own domestic production. Increasingly Spain and Spanish merchants maintained their monopoly by regulating trade, rather than by supplying goods.

The Revolutionary and Napoleonic Wars (▷ p. 146) exposed Spain's military and naval weakness. Despite efforts to improve its defences against outside enemies, and the need to maintain troops on some frontiers with native American areas, the Empire was never heavily garrisoned. Spanish fortresses had been established to protect the coasts, not to dominate the inhabitants. When there was war in Europe, the Spanish navy could not keep open the lines of communication to the mother country, nor could it maintain effective control of colonial trade. Thus the Battle of Trafalgar (1805; ▷ p. 147) had as much influence on the fate of the Spanish Empire as on the outcome of the Napoleonic Wars.

The first revolts

In 1808 Napoleon forced the Bourbon king of Spain to abdicate and invaded Spain, precipitating a crisis throughout the Spanish dominions. Local notables formed town meetings (or *juntas*) to decide what course they should follow. Feelings of local patriotism and identity – long germinating but previously without political expression – led them to reject Napoleon's emissaries. They pledged local loyalty to the deposed Ferdinand VII, rejected the authority of the Spanish patriot regents, and finally proclaimed their independence.

Many divisions appeared in this first confused period of rebellion. Creoles turned against Spaniards, but they also soon fell out among themselves. Rival towns and provinces rejected each other's pretensions, while some of the native Americans and other less-privileged groups showed more inclination for the continuation of royal rule from Spain than for new masters nearer home.

An exception was the revolt in Mexico of the priest Miguel Hidalgo (1810); this gathered such a degree of native American support that it threatened the social order. Hidalgo was defeated and executed in 1811, but Mexican independence was later to be declared by a conservative elite after liberalism had momentarily triumphed in Spain in 1820.

In the viceroyalty of Rio de la Plata the town of Buenos Aires successfully resisted an abortive British invasion in 1806 – an attempt to subvert the colony against Spain. However, this produced no lasting unity, and for a long time no power emerged that was capable of bringing stability even to the provinces of the coast, let alone to the area that was eventually to become Argentina.

BRAZILIAN INDEPENDENCE

The Napoleonic Wars – the catalyst for Spain's loss of its American empire – also directly led to the independence of the Portuguese colony of Brazil. With a flourishing economy based on sugar, gold and diamonds, Brazil had by 1800 outstripped the mother country in prosperity. In 1808, threatened by French invasion, the Portuguese royal family and government fled to Brazil. The prince regent, Dom John, reformed the administration and abolished Portugal's monopoly of trade with Brazil. Trade and industry flourished. Ministries, courts, and a range of legal, academic and educational institutions were founded, and Brazil's equality with Portugal under the crown was recognized. Dom John became king of Portugal (as John VI) in 1816. However, although the mother country had been freed from French rule, he did not return to Portugal until 1821, when his son Dom Pedro became regent in Brazil. The Portuguese parliament undid John's reforms in Brazil, reduced the country to its former colonial status, and – fearing that Dom Pedro

would lead resistance to these changes – insisted that he return to Portugal, an order that he refused. Supported by an indignant population, he summoned a Brazilian assembly and declared Brazil independent with himself as emperor (1822).

Although Pedro I had little regard for democratic principles, a liberal constitution was introduced in 1824. After a disastrous war against Argentina (1828) Pedro I abdicated in favour of his infant son (1831). Central government was weak during the minority of Pedro II, and the country experienced the most turbulent phase of its history. However, after being confirmed as emperor in 1840 – when he was declared to have come of age – Pedro II guided Brazil through a long period of relative stability and economic growth. Opposition from landowners (angered by the abolition of slavery in 1888) and the military (who were excluded from political power) led to a coup in 1889. Pedro II was forced to abdicate and a republican government was established.

In New Granada the rivalries between cities and regions facilitated Spanish reconquest between 1814 and 1819 (⇨ below). The first Venezuelan republic was likewise divided, and experienced a particularly savage backlash from the royalists. Peru remained largely loyal to Spain, in part through memories of the native Indian rebellion of Tupac Amarú (1780). Under viceroy Abascal, a forthright and effective official, Peru – the oldest viceroyalty – remained for long a seat of substantial Spanish power.

Events in Europe continued to influence the course of the independence struggle. Had Napoleon not invaded Spain, the expeditionary force that Wellington took to the Iberian Peninsula to fight with the Spaniards against the French was to have been sent to 'the Caracas' – as the British then called Venezuela – to raise that colony against Spain. Britain – the paymaster of the anti-French coalitions – was excluded from European trade by Napoleon's Continental System (⇨ p. 146) and was keen to gain access to the silver and new markets of Spanish America. When Spain became its ally against Napoleon, Britain had to be more discreet in its dealings with Latin America.

The wars of independence

In 1815, with the French expelled from the Iberian Peninsula and Napoleon defeated, Spain was able to mount a serious attempt to reconquer its Latin American empire. An expeditionary force was sent to South America under General Pablo Morillo, who had served under Wellington. Morillo rapidly reconquered Venezuela and New Granada. In Mexico José Maria Morelos, successor to Hidalgo, was captured and executed. Outside the viceroyalty of Rio de la Plata, the areas held by Latin American patriots were scattered and insignificant. In Venezuela Simón Bolívar had some fleeting suc-

cesses before Morillo's arrival, but was forced to look for support among the British merchants in Jamaica and from the free black republic of Haiti. This was the low point of patriot fortunes.

But the tide now turned. Morillo had large numbers of patriot leaders executed, exiled or subjected to humiliating punishment. His severity did much to create a sense of identity within the patriot camp which had previously been indifferent and divided. 'Where there are Spaniards, there will be executioners,' Bolívar had said. A further setback for Spain occurred in 1820, when the forces destined to reinforce Morillo in South America mutinied in favour of a liberal constitution for Spain. When the news reached Morillo, he virtually acknowledged defeat.

In 1816 Bolívar had returned to Venezuela to declare a 'war to the death' against the Spanish. Under Bolívar's rules only those who actively embraced the cause of independence were safe from retribution. Between 1816 and 1819 he re-established his presence and command in Venezuela, and mounted an expedition that crossed the eastern Cordillera of the Andes from the plains of the interior and defeated the main Spanish force in New Granada at the battle of Boyacá (August 1819).

This was the second strategic crossing of the Andes during the wars of independence. The first – which crossed into Chile from the Argentine interior – was the masterstroke of the most effective soldier among the liberators of the south, José de San Martín. Previous attempts to strike at Spanish power in Peru from Rio de la Plata had sought a path through the province of Upper Peru (modern Bolivia). San Martín's strategy was to capture the compact province of Chile, form a navy, and move northwards up the coast. He liberated Chile in 1817–18 with victories over the Spanish at Chacabuco and

Maipó, establishing the rule of Bernardo O'Higgins (1817–23). In 1820, with a fleet commanded by the Scottish mercenary Admiral Cochrane, he invaded Peru.

Grand strategic moves and decisive battles were, however, not typical of the wars of independence. Generally, the small and ill-equipped patriot armies engaged in scattered encounters and irregular fighting. Peasants and slaves were recruited by force. Although it was becoming clear by 1820 that the Spanish cause was – in the long term – a hopeless one, it took Bolívar and his lieutenants until 1824 to defeat the Spanish armies in Peru, at the battles of Junín and Ayacucho.

As befitted men who lived in the immodest age of Napoleon and Nelson, and who fought under the historic shadow of Washington, Bolívar, San Martín and many of the protagonists of the Latin American wars of independence were certainly glory-seekers. However, the history of Latin America after independence was somewhat less glorious, and great difficulties were experienced in consolidating the new order.

The poor and war-ravaged republics of Latin America emerged into a world economy that found that it had overestimated their potential wealth. Though their fortunes varied – Chile, Argentina and Uruguay had far outstripped the rest by the close of the 19th century – most had to endure much disappointment and disorder. Even Brazil, whose independence was achieved peacefully (⇨ box), had a turbulent 19th century. Establishing stable governments in these ex-colonial societies proved a long and arduous task, an experience later repeated elsewhere in the world (⇨ p. 218).   MD

SEE ALSO
- THE BIRTH OF THE USA p. 142
- THE REVOLUTIONARY AND NAPOLEONIC WARS p. 146
- NATIONALISM, LIBERALISM AND REVOLUTION p. 150
- THE EXPANSION OF THE USA p. 156

An attack on Valparaiso during the civil war between liberals and conservatives in Chile (1891). Political chaos and violence were recurrent features of Latin American history after independence – particularly up to 1850 – as the new states sought workable political solutions to the problems of the region. From the mid-19th century the new states partially alleviated their difficulties by exporting their natural resources to the USA and Europe (Britain invested heavily in the subcontinent in this period and controlled a large portion of its market). However, instability and military intervention remained a characteristic of South American politics until the late 20th century, holding back the development of democratic forms of government.

Nationalism, Liberalism and Revolution

The 'Restoration Europe' created by the Congress of Vienna of 1814–15 (▷ p. 147) proved to be flawed and fragile. Over much of Europe – but especially in France – the restoration consensus was based on a measure of compromise with the emergent bourgeoisie, and the first half of the 19th century saw increasing pressure for political and economic modernization. In Italy, and particularly in the German Confederation, this pressure was linked with a growing sense of national identity and demands for national self-determination.

Such demands were to threaten the authority of the multi-national Habsburg Empire, not only in the German Confederation and Italy, but in Eastern Europe as well. The seeds of the national unrest that would destabilize the Balkans at the end of the 19th century (▷ pp. 154 and 175) were already evident before the revolutions of 1848.

Liberalism

Liberalism is founded on Enlightenment notions of reason, progress and individual freedom within a constitutional state

under the rule of law. Liberal principles were fundamental to the demands of many of the French revolutionaries of 1789, and reflected the political aspirations of a growing middle class during a period of rapid economic change and political upheaval. European liberals sought to establish governmental accountability in place of the arbitrary rule of kings and their ministers. They opposed the traditional privileges of monarchy, aristocracy and clergy alike, and demanded the establishment of political rights, including freedom of conscience, expression, association and assembly. However, despite their insistence on equality before the law, liberals were opposed to the open-ended democratization of society and restricted the franchise – the vote – to the propertied and educated. It was not until later in the 19th century that some male liberals began to support the growing pressure from women for the vote (▷ pp. 168 and 232). Sovereignty, liberals believed, was invested not in the people, but in representative assemblies, where the will of the 'nation' was exercised by 'notables' on behalf of the community.

Freedom from arbitrary interference – whether by the state or traditional institutions – was also central to liberal economic philosophy, which insisted on a free-market ('laissez faire') economy. The triumph of political liberalism coincided with the extension of industrial capitalism in Western Europe (▷ p. 164).

Nationalism

Nationalism – which initially developed in tandem with liberalism, above all during the French Revolution – is based on a feeling of common identity between people speaking the same language, and sharing the same ethnic origins and cultural history. Modern nationalism is essentially a product of the 19th century, and was an important force in the unification of Italy and Germany (▷ p. 152). While nationalism provided the ideological cement for the construction of powerful new states in central and southern Europe, elsewhere it proved a more volatile force. Eastern European nationalism threatened to replace the ostensible stability of the region's authoritarian imperial states with anarchy (▷ p. 154).

Nineteenth-century European nationalism soon developed a romantic character. It invested national traditions, institutions, languages and arts with a new value, often to the point of mythologizing the national past and inventing its traditions. In its attempt to establish national unity and independence it was to become exclusivist and intolerant of nonconformity in general and of ethnic minorities in particular.

Liberalism, nationalism and revolution

Liberalism and nationalism underpinned the ideology of constitutional movements on the continent of Europe during the early 19th century, and were central to the demands and programmes of revolutionaries from the 1820s to 1848. Liberals

Delacroix's *Greece Expiring on the Ruins of Missolonghi* (1827). Like many other Romantic artists, Delacroix was sympathetic to liberal and nationalist aspirations.

and nationalists were at the forefront of most of the first challenges to established authority, notably in Spain, Portugal and Naples in 1820. The outcome of these southern European uprisings was decided not by the political aspirations of the local population, however, but by European power politics, as was the Greek War of Independence (1821–29; ▷ p. 154), which was followed by the imposition of a Bavarian absolute monarch.

In 1830 revolution broke out again in France, forcing the abdication of Charles X. Moderate liberal members of the propertied bourgeoisie assumed control of the situation, deployed a 'National Guard' to restore order on the streets, and offered the crown to Louis Philippe, duke of Orleans, who became a constitutional monarch at the head of a liberal state. The outcome of the 1830 revolution aptly demonstrates the limitations of early 19th-century liberalism. Under the conservative and authoritarian 'July Monarchy' (1830–48) radicals and republicans were excluded from power and influence and the interests of the propertied bourgeoisie were protected; left-wing insurrections were put down in 1832 and 1834. Louis-Philippe's chief minister, François-Pierre Guillaume Guizot, encouraged the middle classes with the slogan 'enrichissez-vous!' ('enrich yourselves') and presided over the golden age of French industrial capitalism.

The July Revolution was the most spectacular outbreak of a wave of unrest that swept across most of Europe, largely liberal in orientation in the West, and nationalist in the East. An uprising in Brussels against the absolute monarchy of the United Netherlands led to the secession of the southern part of the kingdom as Belgium, which was recognized by the major European powers in 1831. The Polish rebellion of the same year was suppressed by Russian troops.

ROMANTICISM

The revolutionary political upheavals of the late 18th and early 19th centuries were accompanied by a similar assault on the cultural life of Europe by the Romantic movement. Romanticism is broadly defined as a reaction against the French neoclassicism that had dominated 18th-century art and architecture and the faith in human reason that characterized the Enlightenment (▷ p. 134). Its roots lie in a period of great cultural revival in Germany during the late 18th and early 19th centuries and, in particular, in the emergence in Germany of a new type of philosophy, known as idealist thinking, which was to have a profound impact on aesthetics, moral philosophy and political thought.

While the Romantic movement contained contradictory aspects and impulses, its adherents had many features in common. They embraced personal and artistic freedom, celebrated the force of the human spirit, and saw the artist as a figure of heroic stature, dedicated to an idealistic cause; they were for imagination and against reason, for energy and against control, and – in some cases – for revolution and against the old empires.

The artistic expression of the individual's political or philosophical outlook (*Weltanschauung*) was an important feature of the Romantic movement and is reflected in the attachment of many Romantic artists to the ideals of liberty and nationhood. An enthusiasm for the republican ideals of the French Revolution is found in the early poetry of William Wordsworth, amongst others. The visual arts celebrated such ideals in works as diverse as those of Caspar David Friedrich, inspired by German nationalism, and those of Eugène Delacroix, whose celebration of the July Revolution of 1830, *The 28th July: Liberty Leading the People*, combines political allegory with realistic representation.

1848: the 'Springtime of the Peoples'

If the bourgeoisie had largely replaced aristocratic power in much of Western Europe by the 1830s, this did not mean that the threat of further revolution was defused. Moderate liberalism, once established, quickly lost any enthusiasm for further upheaval. However, radical democrats and early socialists, drawing on support from the lower middle classes and the intelligentsia, continued to press for concessions. In some instances the threat of popular revolt was bought off by a judicious dose of further liberal reform: Britain repealed the Corn Laws in 1846 (alleviating hardship to poorer people caused by rises in the price of bread), and Pius IX introduced liberal reforms in the Papal States in 1847. Elsewhere conflict was not so easily resolved. In Switzerland, liberal reforms in some cantons provoked others, dominated by Catholic conservatism, to organize in a separate association (the *Sonderbund*) to protect Catholic interests and preserve the federal status of the cantons. The 'Sonderbund War' of 1847 was followed by the promulgation of a new liberal constitution that ended the virtual sovereignty of the cantons.

By the late 1840s political pressure from below was mounting. It was increased by the economic grievances of large sections of the population in a decade of poor harvests and material deprivation. While political hostility to the 1815 settlement motivated liberals and intellectuals, hunger and unemployment disaffected peasants and urban artisans.

The catalyst to revolution on a European scale was the outbreak of revolution in Paris in February 1848. When Guizot's prohibition of a banquet to be held by liberal reformers led to an armed clash between the government's opponents and armed troops, Guizot himself was forced to resign and Louis-Philippe abdicated. Although the propertied and educated bourgeoisie remained in control, the provisional government of the Second Republic contained two socialists and established 'national workshops' for the unemployed.

Disturbances spread quickly to central Europe, where the political situation had long been volatile. Demonstrations were held throughout the German Confederation and there were uprisings in Berlin, Vienna, Prague and Budapest. Frederick William IV of Prussia was forced to appoint a liberal ministry and promise a national assembly, a constitution and support for German national unity. Further south the Habsburg monarchy seemed to be falling apart. Metternich, the autocratic Austrian Chancellor, was effectively deposed and Vienna – like Berlin – fell into the hands of the revolutionaries. The emperor was forced to promise the Bohemians a diet (assembly) elected on a franchise that included the middle classes. After a short war with Austria, Hungary won virtual independence from Vienna. Austria suffered similar reverses in Italy, where a 'holy war'

was waged against the Habsburgs between March and September. Tuscany, Piedmont and the Papal States received constitutions in February and March, while Venice was declared a republic.

The initial success of the 1848 revolutions was deceptive. In June the dissolution of the French 'national workshops' led to street fighting in Paris followed by government reprisals. Louis Napoleon Bonaparte, elected president in December, was to establish himself as dictator (later emperor) following a coup d'état in 1851, ushering in a period of authoritarian rule. The Habsburgs used armed force to reassert their control in Prague, and Vienna was taken back from the radicals in October. In 1849 Hungary, Piedmont and Venice fell to the forces of counter-revolution. Two years later Austria's constitution was suppressed, initiating a period of 'neo-absolutism' under Emperor Franz Josef. The new regime in Vienna also resolutely opposed German national unification (▷ p. 153). The authority of the Frankfurt parliament – the constituent assembly of the putative German state – was undermined by the refusal of Frederick William of Prussia to accept the crown.

The apparent solidarity between liberals and radicals, and the unity of purpose among bourgeoisie, intelligentsia, urban poor and peasantry, had proved superficial, and was maintained only in the face of common enemies: Church, crown and aristocracy. The wealthier classes, disturbed by the prospect of the more far-reaching changes demanded by the radicals, re-aligned in a coalition of political forces representing both the old order of crown, Church and landed elites, and an emerging new order, represented by a centralizing state bureaucracy and an industrial bourgeoisie. In France the populism of the Bonapartist regime (of Napoleon III) foreshadowed an age of mass politics in which the majority of the population would be mobilized – if not genuinely emancipated (▷ p. 168). Piedmont and Prussia – the most advanced and dynamic states in Italy and Germany respectively – both retained their constitutions, providing them with the constitutional basis for the national unification of those two countries (▷ pp. 152–3). TK

SEE ALSO

- THE FRENCH REVOLUTION p. 144
- THE REVOLUTIONARY AND NAPOLEONIC WARS p. 146
- THE UNIFICATION OF ITALY AND GERMANY p. 152
- THE EASTERN QUESTION p. 154
- INDUSTRIAL SOCIETY IN THE 19TH CENTURY p. 164
- THE RISE OF MASS POLITICS p. 168

EUROPE IN 1848

KINGDOM OF SWEDEN AND NORWAY

RUSSIAN EMPIRE

KINGDOM OF DENMARK

KINGDOM OF GREAT BRITAIN AND IRELAND

HOLSTEIN

KINGDOM OF HOLLAND

HANOVER

P

KINGDOM OF PRUSSIA

Berlin ★

★ Warsaw

SAXONY

★ Cracow

KINGDOM OF BELGIUM

To Prussia

Paris ★

To Holland

To Bavaria

To Holland

BADEN

BAVARIA

WURTTEMBERG

★ Prague

AUSTRIAN EMPIRE

Vienna ★

★ Budapest

MOLDAVIA

The Rebellions of 1848–9

★ MAJOR

★ MINOR

★ ABORTIVE

── Boundary of the German Confederation

P = Independent German Principalities

FRANCE

SWITZER-LAND

KINGDOM OF SARDINIA-PIEDMONT

★ Milan

Parma ★

★ Venice

Florence ★

PAPAL STATES

Rome ★

WALLACHIA

SERBIA

MONTE-NEGRO

OTTOMAN EMPIRE

KINGDOM OF PORTUGAL

KINGDOM OF SPAIN

★ Naples

★ Palermo

IONIAN ISLANDS (To Britain)

KINGDOM OF GREECE

CEUTA (To Spain)

GIBRALTAR (To Britain)

MELILLA (To Spain)

ALGERIA (To France)

MALTA (To Britain)

KINGDOM OF MOROCCO

BEYUK OF TUNIS

The Unification of Italy and Germany

Like modern nationalism itself (▷ p. 150), the urge to form nation-states with clear territorial boundaries was largely a product of the French Revolution. The basis for the creation of such states in Central Europe and the Italian peninsula was laid by Napoleon, who simplified the state system of both regions. The territorial consolidation of Italy and Germany arose from the expansionist ambitions of Piedmont and Prussia, and their respective political leaders Count Camillo di Cavour and Prince Otto von Bismarck.

Neither was a nationalist in the ideological sense, and their policies arose from a combination of political pragmatism (*Realpolitik*) and the necessity of devising constitutional arrangements to accommodate social and economic change without conceding power to radical democrats or nationalists.

The Risorgimento

At the Congress of Vienna in 1815 (▷ p. 147), Napoleonic Italy was divided into 13 separate states, of which only 2 – the Papal States and the kingdom of Sardinia (including Piedmont in northwest Italy) – were ruled by Italians (▷ map, p. 151). The peninsula was dominated by Austria, which had recovered its former Italian possessions in the settlement, and had virtually a free hand in keeping the other Italian states in order. In the south, the kingdom of the Two Sicilies (Naples and Sicily) was ruled by Spanish Bourbons.

The notion of the 'resurrection' (*risorgimento*) of a free and united Italy was fuelled by the political ideology of the French revolutionaries, and the most notable influence on the nationalist Italian intelligentsia was that of the Jacobins (▷ p. 145). From the outset the politics of the secret societies that proliferated in post-Napoleonic Italy bore marked radical and democratic traits. These societies spread nationalist ideas during the 1820s and 1830s, and included the democratic republican *adelfia* of northern Italy, led by Filippo Buonarotti, and the *Carbonari* ('charcoal burners') of the south, who led the Neapolitan revolution of 1820. But perhaps the most notable of the conspiratorial cliques was 'Young Italy', a radical democratic sect led by Giuseppe Mazzini.

The Italian nationalist movement was weak and divided. Nationalist intellectuals such as Mazzini and his more moderate contemporary, Vincenzo Gioberti, were more successful and influential as theorists than as practical politicians. Both in 1820 and in the subsequent upheavals of 1831 and 1848, incipient revolution was rapidly contained by the superior force of Austrian arms, and Mazzini's uprising, planned for 1834, was a shambles.

The leadership of the 1848 revolutions was formed by the moderate middle classes, strengthened by the economic advances of the previous two decades. Italian agriculture had become commercialized, producing increasingly for a market and developing links with trade, business and government. The revolutions themselves unleashed widespread unrest in both town and countryside, revealing marked class divisions. These differences were reflected in the divergent political aspirations of radical republican democrats such as Mazzini and Giuseppe Garibaldi on the one hand and the more moderate liberals on the other.

The rise of Piedmont

Following the failure of the 1848 revolutions, Piedmont – the most industrialized and economically prosperous Italian state – came to the forefront of the movement for national unification. Appointed prime minister of Piedmont in 1852, Camillo di Cavour instituted a series of political and economic reforms. By asserting the authority of the secular state over the influence of the Church, he attracted the support of moderate nationalists throughout Italy. At the same time he solicited foreign support for the Piedmontese cause by means of a concerted diplomatic effort. Piedmontese involvement in the Crimean War gave Cavour an international voice, and enabled him to forge the alliances he needed to expel the Austrians from northern Italy. In secret negotiations with Napoleon III in 1858 Cavour promised Nice and Savoy to France in exchange for a French commitment to intervene in Italy in the event of an Austrian invasion. When the Austrian army went on the offensive in 1859, it was routed by French and Piedmontese troops at the battles of Magenta and Solferino. The brief conflict was followed by uprisings in central Italy and the emergence of a unified northern Italian kingdom led by Piedmont.

In the following year the nationalist guerrilla leader Giuseppe Garibaldi landed in Sicily with an army of 1000 volunteers – his famous 'Redshirts' – and swiftly took control. He crossed to the mainland and swept aside minimal Bourbon resistance in southern Italy. The southern movement was radically democratic, representing the last hope of the Mazzinian opposition to Piedmontese supremacy. Cavour, who was working towards a liberal constitutional monarchy, recognized this and sent an army to the Papal States in order to assert Piedmontese control of the newly united Italy. Garibaldi and his followers were successfully persuaded to accept Victor Emmanuel II of Piedmont as king.

In 1861 the 'kingdom of Italy' comprised the entire peninsula, with the exceptions of Venetia (in the northeast) and Rome. Venetia was eventually acquired from Austria after Italian help had been given to Prussia in the 1866 'Seven Weeks War' (▷ below). Rome itself was acquired with the departure of the French garrison in 1870, leaving the pope – now an embittered opponent of the new Italian state – isolated in the Vatican.

German nationalism

Where the culture of the Risorgimento looked back to the achievements of Rome and the Renaissance for its inspiration, the Romantic poets and thinkers who formed the intellectual leadership of the German national movement in the early 19th century looked back to the Early Middle Ages (▷ p. 84). Reacting against the experience of French occupation during the Napoleonic Wars, they rejected the values of the Enlightenment (▷ p. 134) and stressed the power of historical tradition against rational attempts at progress. The political principles upon which the American and French revolutions had been based were superseded by historically based notions of the cultural uniqueness of the organic 'nation-people' (or *Volk*). German nationalism included other, more liberal, conceptions of the nation as a political community of free individuals, but the former strand remained influential. It was taken up in the universities by aristocratic student associations (*Burschenschaften*) – essentially chauvinistic duelling and drinking clubs – and popularized by the gymnastics movement established by Friedrich Ludwig Jahn.

German unification

Such nationalist ideologues and their followers achieved little in the face of the political structure of the German Confederation – the loosely grouped and weak alliance of 39 German sovereign states established at the end of the Napoleonic

Giuseppe Garibaldi, whose charisma led many to follow him in the cause of Italian unification. With his Redshirts – a band of irregular guerrilla fighters – he was responsible for many of the military successes of the Risorgimento, but his radical republicanism and independent ways often put him at odds with the more conservative Italian leaders.

Wars (⊳ p. 147). The Confederation preserved the vested interests of minor princes, and above all those of the Austrian Habsburgs.

The first real moves towards unification came with the beginnings of industrialization in Germany in the 1830s, and the formation in 1834 of a Prussian-led customs union (*Zollverein*). This both established Prussia's economic domination of the Confederation and isolated protectionist Austria. The customs union was accompanied by practical measures to bring currencies into line and construct a transport infrastructure of roads and railways.

Attempts to establish political unity were less successful: the failure of the 1848 revolutions and the collapse of the Frankfurt Parliament thwarted the hopes of German nationalists and liberals alike (⊳ p. 151). By 1851 Austria – having crushed its own revolutionary unrest – had reverted to the position of dominant power within the German Confederation. Austrian hostility to German unification virtually removed the issue from the political agenda for a decade. The Prussian chancellor (prime minister), Otto von Bismarck, determined to challenge Austrian dominance through a policy of 'blood and iron', which unfolded in three main stages.

The first stage involved Prussia allying with Austria against Denmark over the thorny and complicated question of who should control the duchies of Schleswig and Holstein. In 1864 Prussia invaded and swiftly defeated Denmark, and then took control of Schleswig, while Austria took Holstein.

In the second stage Bismarck isolated Austria by means of skilful diplomacy and then provoked a war with Austria and various north German states in June 1866. This 'Seven Weeks War' culminated in a

SEE ALSO
● THE REVOLUTIONARY AND NAPOLEONIC WARS p. 146
● NATIONALISM, LIBERALISM AND REVOLUTION p. 150
● THE CAUSES OF WORLD WAR I p. 174

THE PARIS COMMUNE

During the Franco-Prussian War (1870–1) Paris was besieged for four and a half months – from 19 September 1870 to 28 January 1871. Inside the city resistance increasingly came to be organized by a radical, 'neo-Jacobin' left, and there was a socialist rebellion in October. Although this was unsuccessful, the material deprivation brought about by the siege caused disaffection to spread, particularly in poorer working-class districts. In national elections in February the rural south and west of France voted resoundingly for the royalists, who supported peace with Prussia. Paris, however, delivered a huge majority for the radical socialists, who favoured a continuation of the war and a return to the principles of the First Republic (⊳ p. 144).

After the fall of the city and the acceptance of peace terms by the royalist-dominated National Assembly in Bordeaux under Adolphe Thiers, the French government instituted a series of measures designed to undermine the Parisian left. In doing so it provoked a popular revolt. With the victorious German forces still encamped on the hills outside Paris, Thiers sent in government troops to disarm the National Guard (largely composed of workers who had fought in the siege of Paris). The government's attempt to remove all cannon from the city provoked fierce resistance, with riots breaking out on 18 March. The insurgents refused to surrender their arms to the troops of the 'Bordeaux government', and instead set up a city administration which they called the Commune – a reference to the Jacobin Commune of 1793 (⊳ p. 145).

In elections to the Commune the socialists increased their share of the city vote from 25% to 80%. Of its 80 members 35 were workers, although the latter were generally artisans rather than industrial workers in the modern sense. The Commune introduced a number of radical measures, including the confiscation of the property of businessmen who had fled the city during the siege, and the establishment of producer cooperatives. Ultimately however, the 'communards' lost their battle to defend the city against French government forces sent to restore order. In the street fighting that ensued (21–28 May) 20 000 people were killed, and tens of thousands of others imprisoned or forced to flee. The bloody suppression of the Commune soured relations between the people of Paris and successive French governments for a generation.

decisive Prussian victory over Austria at Königgrätz in Bohemia. Austria was forced to accept that Prussia was now pre-eminent in north German affairs. The still independent south German states (Bavaria, Württemberg and Baden) were associated with the new, Prussian-dominated North German Confederation in an economic alliance.

In the final stage, the fears of the southern Germans of possible French aggression were exploited by Bismarck as a means of compelling them to draw closer to Prussia. Bismarck manoeuvred France into declaring war on Prussia in 1870 (the Franco-Prussian War). After six months of hard campaigning the French were humiliatingly defeated. The whole of the 'German' area of Europe was finally unified under Prussian control, and Prussia also gained Alsace and Lorraine from France (⊳ pp. 174 and 182). The new German 'Second' Empire was proclaimed on 18 January 1871, with the Prussian king declared Kaiser (emperor) Wilhelm I of Germany.   TK

The battle of Königgrätz, 3 July 1866, in which the Prussian army under Moltke overcame Benedek's Austrian army. The Prussian victory ended the Seven Weeks War and marked the end of Austrian dominance in the German-speaking part of Europe.

The Eastern Question

The struggles for control of the lands and seas in the Near East and the Balkans – the strategic junction of Europe, Asia and Africa – came to be known as the 'Eastern Question'. At its root was the diplomatic and military problem caused by the declining power of the Turkish Ottoman Empire (▷ p. 115) and the rivalry of those powers – particularly Austria and Russia (▷ p. 127) – seeking to benefit from its collapse. The Eastern Question emerged in the 18th century, greatly added to tension between the European powers in the 19th century, and may be seen as a contributory factor to unrest in the Balkans at the close of the 19th century (▷ p. 175).

Mehemet Ali (right), pasha of Egypt (1805–49). His attempts at expansion in the eastern Mediterranean alarmed the Western powers, who forced him to accept the suzerainty of the Ottoman sultan in 1841. By way of compensation, he and his family were granted the hereditary right to rule Egypt. His dynasty held power in Egypt until the middle of the 20th century.

Before 1774 no European power possessed significant territory in the region. Turkish Ottoman authority ruled the roost. However, in the Treaty of Kuchuk Kainarji (1774), the Ottomans ceded to Russia substantial territories north of the Black Sea. The treaty also gave Russia the right to intervene on behalf of Orthodox Christians in the Danubian (Romanian) principalities of Moldavia and Wallachia, and in Constantinople itself.

Russian expansion

Further territorial gains (1783–92) added Jedisan (southwest Ukraine), the Crimea, and all of the region surrounding the Sea of Azov to Tsarist Russia (▷ map, p. 127). These were highly significant gains in strategic terms, since they made it possible for Russia to launch a pincer movement against Turkey down the Caucasus peninsula to the east and through the Balkans to the west. But Russia was not alone in coveting the Ottoman possessions in the Balkans. Even before the Russo-Turkish war of 1768–72, Austria was alarmed by the prospect of an Ottoman defeat, and hesitated between opposition and cooperation as the best means of containing Russian influence in the Balkans.

Another great power, Britain, was concerned at the growth of Russian naval power in the Black Sea. Catherine the Great and her successors (▷ p. 127) sought control of the Straits between the Black Sea and the Mediterranean (the Dardanelles). The Treaty of Kuchuk Kainardji had already given the Russian fleet the freedom to pass through the Dardanelles. With control of the Straits, Russia would be well placed to influence the whole eastern Mediterranean region, including the Levant.

Russia had the option of two paths to its goal. Conquest of the Balkans was one possibility, but this would arouse the opposition not only of Britain and

Austria, but also conceivably Prussia and Sweden. The path through the Caucasus – a patchwork of small states, Ottoman tributaries and Turkish provinces – was the easier option, since no other great power was capable of intervening directly against Russia in the area. For Britain, Russian control of the Caucasus raised the alarming possibility of a Russian push through to the Persian Gulf and the Indian Ocean beyond, threatening British India.

The Napoleonic Wars

Napoleon's foray into Egypt and Syria (1798–9; ▷ p. 146) launched the grandiose notion of total French control of the Ottoman Empire. This would have placed a powerful French presence between India and Britain. Although Britain was briefly ascendant in the region after Napoleon's defeat in Egypt (▷ p. 146), Russia was the principal long-term beneficiary. So preoccupied was Britain with the war against Napoleon in Western Europe, that it was unable to prevent further Russian encroachments on Ottoman territory. By 1812, Russia had acquired Bessarabia (the eastern half of Moldavia) from Turkey, and a number of former Turkish and Persian territories in the Caucasus.

When the great powers met at Vienna in 1815 (▷ p. 147) to shape the post-Napoleonic world, they evaded the Eastern Question, and Turkey was excluded from the 'Concert of Europe'. However, because both Britain and Austria were keen to preserve a friendly and malleable Ottoman Empire as a block to Russia's ambitions, Turkey seemed to have a brighter future.

Serbia and Greece

Riots, rebellions and palace plots were the stuff of life – and death – in the Ottoman Empire. Unrest appeared to be a tradition. More threatening to the survival of the Empire, however, was the revival of national feeling among the Serbs and Greeks. Growing Russian interference in the affairs of the Danubian principalities, together with the rising power of Egypt within the Empire, presented additional challenges.

The Serbian renaissance proved the least dangerous threat. Localized discontent at

Turkish methods of government in Serbia led to Russian-sponsored revolts (1804–13 and 1815–17). However, the situation was defused by the Ottoman recognition of the Serbian nationalist leader, Karageorge, as prince of Serbia (1817), and by the establishment of Serbia as an internationally recognized autonomous principality (1829–30).

Greece was ripe for revolt against Ottoman rule. Greek émigrés were prominent in St Petersburg and Vienna, and European liberals were sympathetic towards the plight of Greece. Actively encouraged by the Orthodox Church, revolt broke out in the Peloponnese in 1821. The following year a National Greek Assembly declared Greece independent, and liberal and nationalist sympathizers from all over Europe pledged their support. Initial Greek successes were ended by the fearsome intervention of the forces of the Ottoman viceroy of Egypt, Mehemet Ali (▷ below). The European powers were outraged by massacres perpetrated by Egyptian troops, and Russia declared its intention to intervene. In 1826, in order to forestall Russian domination in the area, Britain and France put pressure on the Turks to grant a measure of autonomy to Greece, and, when they refused, a joint British, French and Russian naval force sank the Egyptian fleet at Navarino Bay (1827). The following year the Russian army advanced through the Balkans, took Adrianople (Edirne) and threatened Istanbul. At the London Conference of 1829 Turkey was obliged to recognize Greek independence, which was guaranteed by Britain, France and Russia in 1830.

The war between Russia and Turkey was ended by the Treaty of Adrianople (1829), under which Russia tightened its grip on the Danube delta and increased its influence in the Danubian principalities. Turkey was further weakened by continuing pressure from her nominal vassal, Egypt, and in 1833 signed an eight-year defensive agreement with Russia – the Treaty of Unkiar-Skelessi. This increased Russian power in the region and, under the terms of a secret clause, gave Russia the right to close the Straits (the Dardanelles) to the ships of any power during wartime.

Mehemet Ali

A significant player on the Near Eastern stage during this period was Mehemet Ali, pasha (or viceroy) of Egypt from 1805 to 1849. He fought in the Ottoman army against Napoleon and returned to Egypt to sweep the Mamelukes from power in 1811. Although nominally under Ottoman suzerainty, he effectively ruled Egypt as an independent sovereign. His sweeping administrative, agricultural, commercial and military reforms made Egypt the leading power in the eastern Mediterranean. In 1833, under French pressure, the Turkish sultan ceded Syria to Mehemet Ali. By 1839, again with French blessing, he had extended his power as far as Yemen and the Persian Gulf, and constituted a serious threat to the survival of the Ottoman

Empire. Faced with Turkish defeats at the hands of the Egyptians, and the refusal of the French to join a concerted European effort against Mehemet Ali, Britain and Russia grew closer together. In 1840, Britain, Russia, Austria and Prussia coerced Mehemet Ali, obliging him to retreat within Egypt's borders. Joined by France, the powers agreed the Straits Convention (1841), under which the Straits were closed to all non-Ottoman warships in peacetime.

Russia and the Balkans

Although liberal opinion in Britain and France was very much in sympathy with the national aspirations of the Balkan peoples, and appalled by the cruelty with which the Turks put down Slav rebellions, the governments of these two countries were more concerned by Russian territorial ambitions in the region. Russian encroachment on Afghanistan and Persia (present-day Iran) also caused tension with Britain, as it appeared to threaten the security of British India. Austria-Hungary, meanwhile, was alarmed at the prospect of Slav nationalism spreading to its own subject peoples.

British and French fears of Russian ambitions were confirmed when Russia occupied Wallachia and Moldavia in 1853. The following year the Russians sank a Turkish fleet and Britain, France and Turkey sent an expeditionary force to the Crimea, a Russian peninsula in the Black Sea. But the Crimean War (1854–6; ⇨ box) did not in the end forestall Russian ambitions.

At the Congress of Paris (1856), which ended the Crimean War, Russia's rights and territories in the Danubian principalities – gained in the Treaty of Adrianople – were withdrawn. Moldavia and Wallachia now proclaimed themselves independent. In 1862 they united to form Romania – electing a local prince, Alexander Cuza, as ruler – though they remained nominally subject to Turkey. The Congress of Paris also neutralized the Black Sea, denying its utility in war to the Russians. In 1870 Russia denounced this provision, precipitating a crisis that was resolved at the London Conference (1871). Russia was given naval freedom in the Black Sea in return for its acknowledgement that international treaties could not be revised unilaterally.

The rise of nationalism in Bulgaria from 1858 threatened Ottoman rule in another part of the Balkans. Bulgarian nationalism was fuelled by the ideology of Pan-Slavism, the idea of a confederation of all the Slavic peoples under Russian leadership and control. As the largest Slav nation, Russia took upon itself to promote the desires of other Slav peoples for independence. However, help to Balkan nationalists tended to coincide with Russian foreign-policy aims, particularly for power in the eastern Mediterranean. In other areas, where Russia's own interests were not likely to be furthered by the promotion of local nationalist aspirations, any such stirrings were quickly and firmly crushed, as happened in Russian-ruled Poland in 1830 and 1863.

Pan-Slavism intensified in the period 1867–70, when Austrian ambitions in the Balkans increasingly confronted those of Russia. Common causes still allowed the formation of the 'Three Emperors League' (1873) of Russia, Austria and newly unified Germany, who sought to shape the destiny of the Balkans themselves (⇨ p. 174). But revolts in Bosnia-Herzegovina and Bulgaria, and continued attempts by Serbia and the small mountainous state of Montenegro to expand their territory at the expense of Turkey, were forceful reminders of the strength of nationalism in the region.

In 1877 Russia took matters into her own hands. In alliance with Romania, Russia invaded Turkey, winning an important victory at Plevna. The Ottoman Empire was obliged to sign a humiliating peace at San Stefano (March 1878) which recognized the independence of an enlarged Serbia, Romania and Montenegro, autonomy for Bosnia-Herzegovina, the creation of a large Russian-dominated Bulgaria that extended south to the Aegean Sea, and the cession of considerable territory to Russia in the Caucasus.

Such an arrangement appeared to have made Russia the master of the region.

THE CRIMEAN WAR

In 1852 Russia and France fell out over the question of Orthodox and Catholic influence in the Christian 'Holy Places' of Palestine. The following year Russia, having failed to gain equal rights with France, occupied the Danubian principalities of the Ottoman Empire. Turkey declared war on Russia, only to see its fleet destroyed by Russia at Sinope in the Black Sea (November 1853). Britain and France, concerned at this upset in the regional balance of power, also declared war on Russia, and with Turkey despatched an expeditionary force to the Crimea – a peninsula in the Black Sea (⇨ map, p. 127) – with the intention of capturing the strategically vital Russian port and naval base of Sevastopol. The war that ensued, between Russia on one side, and Britain, France, Turkey, Austria and Sardinia-Piedmont on the other, was the first major European conflict since 1815.

After suffering defeat at the battle of the Alma on 20 September 1854, the Russian army retreated to the fortress of Sevastopol, which the Allies forces subjected to a gruelling 11-month siege. The rigours of fighting in the bitter Crimean winter were aggravated by incompetent, senile commanders and a lack of fuel, clothing and supplies for the Allied troops, thousands of whom died in the nightmarish squalor of the barracks hospital at Scutari. At Balaklava on 25 October a mistaken British order led the Light Brigade to charge straight at a Russian artillery position at the end of a long, narrow valley. The battle was indecisive, although on 5 November the Russians were defeated at Inkerman. Convinced of the need to accede to Allied conditions, the Russians finally evacuated Sevastopol in September 1855. Of the 250 000 men lost by each side, over half succumbed to disease. Peace was concluded at the Congress of Paris in 1856 (⇨ text).

However, with the survival of the Ottoman Empire in danger, the European powers cooperated to frustrate Russia. Pressure by Britain and Austria, with the support of France and Germany, overturned the Treaty of San Stefano. A new division of the Balkans was agreed at the Congress of Berlin (June–July 1878). The independence of Serbia, Romania and Montenegro was recognized, but Bosnia-Herzegovina passed under Austro-Hungarian rule. The 'Big Bulgaria' proposed under San Stefano was replaced by two much smaller territories without an Aegean coastline, one of which remained in Ottoman hands. Russia retained some of her gains in the Caucasus.

The Congress also confirmed the transfer of Cyprus from Turkish to British rule. This was one of the more visible aspects of an increasing British presence in the region after the Congress of Berlin. Britain established strong strategic influence in Constantinople, and, through occupation of Egypt, secured control of the Suez Canal (⇨ pp. 163 and 211).

Russia had extended her territory nearer to the Straits, but she was further than ever from controlling them. The bolder the moves made by Russia, the more Britain abandoned the policy of creating buffer zones to contain her, and intervened directly on Russia's borders instead. Russia had encourged Pan-Slavism as the answer to the Eastern Question, aspiring to bring southeast Europe within its orbit. But the Balkan countries were to bring about the end of the Ottoman Empire in Europe themselves in the two Balkan Wars (1912–13), when Serbia, Bulgaria, Greece and Montenegro captured all the remaining Turkish territory except for the area around Constantinople (⇨ p. 174).   MH

SEE ALSO

● THE OTTOMAN EMPIRE p. 114
● THE EMERGENCE OF RUSSIA p. 126
● THE REVOLUTIONARY AND NAPOLEONIC WARS p. 146
● NATIONALISM, LIBERALISM AND REVOLUTION p. 150
● THE CAUSES OF WORLD WAR I p. 174

The siege of Sevastopol (left). This anonymous painting shows French zouaves (Algerian recruits) taking the Malakhov tower, a crucial Russian defensive position, on 8 September 1855. Three days later the Russians scuttled their ships in Sevastopol harbour, blew up the fortifications and evacuated the city.

The Expansion of the USA

The 19th century saw the transformation of the USA from an undeveloped, rural nation into an industrial giant. Population growth combined with economic and geographical expansion to produce by 1900 a dynamic, ethnically diverse republic stretching from the Atlantic Ocean to the Pacific.

This transformation was not accomplished smoothly. While regional strife over the question of slavery and the rights of individual states threatened to destroy the Union in the bitter Civil War of 1861–5 (⏵ p. 158), western settlement, mass immigration from Europe and the growth of large business corporations produced further strains within society. The Founding Fathers' vision of a compact, harmonious republic dissolved under pressure from the forces of modernization.

The early national period

Although a majority of Americans welcomed the creation of a stronger national government in 1787 (⏵ p. 142), the initial unity produced by the Constitution was soon undermined by a debate over the future of the country. This debate brought about the formation of America's first political parties. On the one hand the Federalists, followers of Secretary of the Treasury Alexander Hamilton (1755–1804), demanded a sound system of public finance that would attract capital for commerce and manufacturing. On the other hand Democratic-Republicans, led by President Thomas Jefferson, hailed the virtues of a predominantly agrarian republic in which the states would check the excesses of Federal power.

In 1812 aggressive British naval policy and American hopes of conquering Canada led to a second war between the two countries. But although the British managed a raid on Washington, DC, and the Americans, ably led by General Andrew Jackson, defeated the redcoats at the Battle of New Orleans in 1815, the final result was a military stalemate. Nonetheless, the War of 1812 confirmed American independence, strengthened the forces of American nationalism, and set the scene for 19th-century expansion.

Territorial growth

Relatively few Americans had crossed the Appalachian mountains by the time the Revolution ended in 1783. The Peace of Paris, however, heralded the beginning of the westward movement. Lured by the prospect of cheap, fertile land and rising prices for grain and cotton, white Americans poured into the Mississippi and Ohio valleys, forcing the native Indians to retreat before them. In 1787 Congress passed the Northwest Ordinance to provide a mechanism for the entrance of new states into the Union, and two western states – Tennessee and Kentucky – became full members of the republic in the 1790s.

President Thomas Jefferson provided the real springboard for territorial expansion. In 1803 he negotiated the purchase of Louisiana from Napoleon for $15 million – a small price to pay for a deal that more than doubled the size of the nation and gave it the vital Mississippi River port of New Orleans. Another important addition came in 1819 when Spain ceded the territory of Florida after an illegal incursion by American troops under Andrew Jackson.

These acquisitions fuelled the aggressive notion that white Americans had a semi-religious duty ('Manifest Destiny' they called it) to spread the principles of republican liberty across the continent. New forms of transport such as the steamboat, the canal and the railroad also contributed to the expansionist fervour of the early 19th century. The Federal government responded to public pressure by continually reducing western land prices. The Homestead Act of 1862 actually made western lands free for the taking, although most of the fertile land had already been sold by that date.

After the annexation of Texas in 1845, the final piece in the continental jigsaw was provided by the Mexican War of 1846–8. The Americans' victory in this one-sided contest gave the USA the rich territory of California, together with the future states of New Mexico, Arizona, Nevada, Utah and Colorado. It was the debate over whether slavery should be excluded from this vast region that led ultimately to the Civil War (⏵ p. 158).

As a result of these territorial acquisitions America's geographical frontier moved steadily westwards during the 19th century. At each stage in the process the first arrivals – miners, trappers and loggers – were followed rapidly by European immigrants and farmers migrating in family units from the eastern states.

Purchasing land from a variety of sources – for example, the federal government, railroad companies and local speculators – these later arrivals were intent on securing a homestead that would give them economic independence. Settlement on marginal land and falling crop prices made this goal an increasingly difficult one by the end of the century, but by this time the western movement was over. The renowned historian Frederick Jackson Turner pronounced the frontier closed in 1893.

Economic growth

Economic change went hand in hand with western expansion. As demand grew for foodstuffs and textiles, millions of urban craftsmen and onetime subsistence farmers found their lives transformed by the market. This was particularly the case in the northeastern states, where the first pockets of industrialization began to emerge in the 1820s and 1830s. Southern New England, New York and Philadelphia became centres of the country's buoyant textile industry. Although most of the first factories were small in scale, a few, notably those at Lowell and Waltham in Massachusetts, were large operations employing significant numbers of female and child labourers.

A romantic view of westward expansion. In the wake of the trail-blazing trans-continental expedition of Meriwether Lewis and William Clark in 1804–6 came trappers, traders and surveyors, who in turn were followed by land-hungry settlers in their wagon trains.

Andrew Carnegie (1835–1919) was one of the greatest industrial entrepreneurs of the 19th century. A Scot by birth, he emigrated to the USA in 1848 after his father, a Dunfermline linen worker, had been made redundant by the advent of machine competition. The family settled in the grimy industrial city of Pittsburgh, where the young Carnegie found employment as a telegraph operator. In 1852 he accepted a managerial post with the powerful Pennsylvania Railroad, and it was in this position that he learned many of the modern business techniques that would eventually make him a fortune. Foremost among these was a recognition of the importance of cost-cutting and high turnovers.

By the early 1870s Carnegie had made enough money in share dealings to invest in a Pittsburgh steel manufacturing company. This was a shrewd move, for as the American economy expanded and matured after the Civil War, demand for steel was increasing rapidly. Carnegie's dynamism as an entrepreneur soon revealed itself in his determination to achieve economies of scale, and to control supplies of essential raw materials (especially iron ore). Efficiency led to profit on a massive scale. By 1890 Carnegie himself was worth around $30 million.

Carnegie's aggressive business strategy did not always endear him to his workforce. During the depression of the 1890s his efforts to reduce wages and eliminate trade unions prompted a bitter strike at his famous Homestead works, terminating in a pitched battle between workers and security men.

Although industrial entrepreneurs like Carnegie have been labelled 'Robber Barons' by some critics, there can be no denying that they helped to transform the American economy during the late 19th century. It should also be mentioned that Carnegie used his great wealth to fund a variety of philanthropic enterprises.

Rapid urbanization accompanied these first stirrings of industrialization. New York emerged as the republic's most populous and important financial centre, but other cities such as Philadelphia, Boston, Pittsburgh, and (after mid-century) Chicago grew apace during the century.

Cities, towns and villages across the North competed vigorously for commercial supremacy. This competition contributed to the tremendous surge of railroad construction that occurred after 1840, and by 1890 over 266 000 km (166 000 miles) of track were in operation. The railroads in turn helped to promote western expansion and were the first industrial enterprises to experiment with modern business techniques and corporate structures.

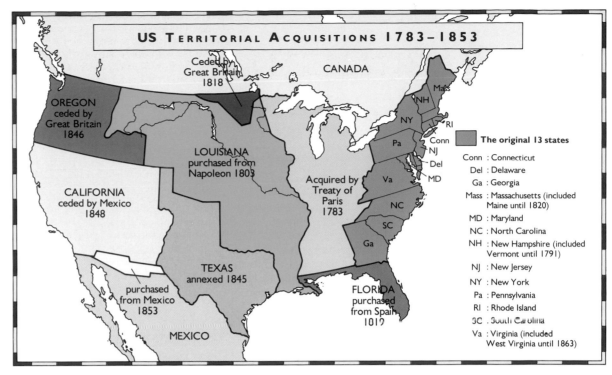

Immigration

Demographic growth was a vital factor in economic modernization. The population of the USA rose from a mere 9.6 million in 1820 to 76 million in 1900. This was a product not only of natural increase, but also of massive immigration from Europe, beginning in the 1830s and reaching a peak in the 1890s. Unlike most of the early inhabitants, the bulk of these newcomers were neither English-speaking nor Protestant. They came first from Ireland, Germany and Scandinavia, then, after the Civil War, from eastern and southern Europe. Although they settled in all parts of the country, they were most conspicuous (not least for their poverty) in the teeming cities of the northeast. Assimilation was far from easy, America's pluralistic traditions notwithstanding. Anti-immigrant fervour was a recurrent feature of 19th-century America.

The politics of growth

Westward migration, industrial growth, urbanization and immigration, by disrupting traditional communities, helped to promote the forces of individualism and democracy in American life. After 1828, when Andrew Jackson was elected president, these forces assumed political form in the shape of the pro-Southern Jacksonian Democratic Party. Claiming to champion the cause of the common man against designing aristocrats and monopolistic capitalists, the Democrats were fervent supporters of western expansion. Vigorously opposed to centralized government, they were finally undone by the sectional crisis (▷ p. 158) that brought the Republican Party to power. The northern-dominated Republicans proved themselves particularly amenable to banks, railroads and other business corporations in the excess-ridden postwar era (dubbed 'the Gilded Age' by Mark Twain and Charles Dudley Warner), thereby providing a healthy climate for the growth of big business.

The industrial giant

By the 1880s American capitalists were seeking to maximize efficiency through consolidation. This resulted in a proliferation of huge corporations, such as US Steel and Standard Oil, which were prepared to take advantage of new markets for manufactures and processed goods. Headed by dynamic entrepreneurs – notably Andrew Carnegie (▷ box), John D. Rockefeller and J.P. Morgan – and run by professional managers, these companies formed oligopolies (i.e. groups of large firms dominating particular markets) and were to form the basis of the modern American economy. Even though they were distrusted by many interest groups in society (notably debtor farmers from the south and west, who formed the backbone of the shortlived Populist Party, and organized industrial workers), the 'trusts' were simply too powerful and too important for the national economy to be cast aside.

The once insignificant republic was now on the threshold of claiming an imperial role. This had been hinted at as early as 1823 by the Monroe Doctrine (enunciated by President James Monroe), which had warned Europeans not to seek further colonies in the New World. In 1867 the USA purchased Alaska from Russia, and in 1898 assumed control over Puerto Rico, Cuba and the Philippines after winning a brief, jingoistic war against Spain. Not all Americans were pleased with their country's aggressive rise to great-power status, but neither they nor the rest of humanity could deny that the USA had finally arrived on the world stage. RC

The American Civil War

The Civil War was by far the bloodiest domestic conflict in American history – and one of the most devastating wars fought in the Western world in the 19th century. Lasting four years and costing over 600 000 lives, it was a tragedy on a massive scale. But appalling though the carnage was, it did at least preserve the American Union intact and set free four million black slaves. The North did not go to war against the South to emancipate the slaves, but the slavery question was bound up with the conflict at every stage.

SEE ALSO

● THE BIRTH OF THE USA
  p. 142
● THE EXPANSION OF THE USA
  p. 156
● THE GREAT AMERICAN
  DREAM p. 216

The Civil War had its origins in the emergence of two distinct systems of labour in the northern and southern parts of the USA. While commercial farming and industry took root in the North on a free labour basis, the agricultural South found itself increasingly dependent on the labour of black slaves. This situation was brought about by two events. In 1793 a New Englander, Eli Whitney (1765–1825), invented an improved cotton gin to separate seeds from the fibres of the cotton plant; and ten years later the USA acquired the territory of Louisiana from France (▷ p. 156). These developments paved the way for the expansion of cotton growing into the fertile southwest and reinforced the demand for slaves to work the plantations.

Notwithstanding the development of a domestic abolition movement in the 1830s, most Northerners were reluctant to endanger the Union by agitating the slavery question. However, the US military defeat of Mexico in 1846–8 added a vast tract of land to the national domain (▷ p. 156), unleashing a bitter debate over whether slavery should be excluded from the new territories (notably California). In 1854 Congress passed the Kansas–Nebraska Act repealing a previous ban on slavery in the northern part of the Louisiana Purchase. This appeared to open up all the new territories to slave labour, and Northern and Southern hotheads then became embroiled in a vicious guerrilla war to make Kansas a state in their own image.

The crisis deepened as Northerners perceived the South's ruling planter class (the 'Slave Power') as a threat to their own freedoms and began voting for the newly formed Republican Party. This organization, which represented Northern evangelical sentiment and economic interests, demanded a Federal government ban on the future expansion of slavery. Southerners, on the other hand, believed their slave-based society to be under attack from abolitionists. When the Democratic party split into Northern and Southern factions over the slavery issue, the Republican candidate, Abraham Lincoln, won the 1860 presidential election. The seven Deep South states responded by seceding from the Union and forming an independent, pro-slavery Confederacy under the presidency of Jefferson Davis.

When Confederates bombarded Fort Sumter – a Federal post in Confederate South Carolina – in April 1861, President Lincoln issued a call for 75 000 troops to put down the rebellion. The Upper South states – Virginia, North Carolina, Tennessee and Arkansas – then opted to join the Confederacy, thereby depriving the Union of some key military men, notably Robert E. Lee. Most Americans thought the resulting conflict would be brief. They could not have been more mistaken.

The war to 1863

Although the North possessed greater economic and military resources than the South, these advantages were not immediately apparent. Indeed, the first two years of the war were extremely bleak ones for the Union cause. In July 1861 the Confederates inflicted a humiliating defeat on the Union at Bull Run, Virginia. The following year Union General George B. McLellan landed troops on the Virginian coast in a lacklustre effort to capture the Confederate capital at Richmond from the southeast. Pinned down by Lee and embarrassed by the cavalry of 'Jeb' Stuart, the Federals were forced to withdraw by sea.

The North's main problem was clear: while the Confederates had only to defend their territory to win, Union generals had to take the offensive if they were to defeat the rebels. Neither McLellan nor many of the other Union commanders during the early years of the war appeared capable of positive action. Until 1863 Southern generalship was markedly superior to the North's, particularly in the vital eastern theatre. Confederate generals Lee and Thomas 'Stonewall' Jackson, in particular, displayed great strategic flair. However, casualty figures for both sides mounted relentlessly during 1862–3. Vicious set-piece battles at Shiloh, Antietam and Fredericksburg highlighted the futility of war and seemed to point towards a military stalemate.

The only real Union successes during 1861–2 were naval ones. Federal gunboats played an important role in Ulysses S. Grant's seizure of Forts Donelson and Henry in Tennessee, and Commodore David Farragut captured New Orleans. The strangest naval engagement, however, was the drawn battle between two ironclad warships, the USS *Monitor* and CSS *Merrimac* (renamed *Virginia*) in Hampton Roads, Virginia. This famous duel heralded the demise of wooden fleets, but it was only the North, with its greater industrial capacity, that built significant numbers of ironclads during the war. These helped to ensure that the US naval blockade of Southern ports remained effective.

The race question

With the Union armies stalled on all fronts, Lincoln found himself under attack from fellow Republicans for what they regarded as his tentative approach to the war, and particularly for his reluctance to alienate the loyal slave states – Delaware, Kentucky, Maryland and Missouri – by tackling the question of abolition. Without slavery, it was argued, the Southern military effort could not be sustained. On 22 September 1862 Lincoln finally gave way on this point by issuing the Preliminary Emancipation Proclamation, which declared all slaves beyond Union lines to be free.

Lincoln had good reason to be wary of the race question. Many Northerners were contemptuous of black capabilities and rejected the notion that abolition was a war aim. However, the pressing need for action to break the military stalemate resulted in not only the Emancipation Proclamation, but also the admission of black troops into the Union army. Segregated in separate 'colored' regiments and officered by whites, American blacks played a crucial role in the Northern war effort from 1863.

Decline and fall of the Confederacy

July 1863 was the turning point of the Civil War. In that month Union forces won two crucial victories. The first of these came at Gettysburg. Aware that

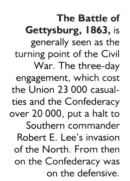

The Battle of Gettysburg, 1863, is generally seen as the turning point of the Civil War. The three-day engagement, which cost the Union 23 000 casualties and the Confederacy over 20 000, put a halt to Southern commander Robert E. Lee's invasion of the North. From then on the Confederacy was on the defensive.

time was running out for the South and that a crushing victory might prompt British recognition of the Confederacy, Robert E. Lee determined to launch a bold invasion of Pennsylvania. His army stumbled across the Army of the Potomac under General George Meade at Gettysburg, and, after a vainglorious Confederate charge against the Union centre, were forced to retreat. The next day, 4 July, saw the surrender of the Southern stronghold of Vicksburg, Mississippi, to the besieging Northern army of General Ulysses S. Grant. This defeat split the Confederacy in two and ended any hopes of diplomatic recognition.

Inferior manpower and industrial resources now began to take their toll of the Confederacy. Its troops were hungry and poorly clad; its economy was ravaged by inflation and the Union blockade; and Confederate politicians squabbled over the rights of the states vis-à-vis the central government. During 1864 Union armies penetrated deep into the Confederacy. One, led by Grant, pushed slowly south into Virginia, where its progress was hampered by fierce enemy resistance at the Battle of the Wilderness. Another, commanded by General William T. Sherman, drove southeast into Georgia. In September 1864 Federal troops took Atlanta. This development meant that a compromise peace was now unattainable for the Confederates, for it guaranteed Lincoln's re-election in the subsequent presidential election.

The South held out for another six months. After taking Atlanta, Sherman cut loose from his supply lines and set off for the coastal town of Savannah. His 'March to the Sea' cut a great swathe of destruction across Georgia, tearing the heart out of the Confederate cause. Sherman's troops then wheeled north into the Carolinas to link up with Grant in Virginia. The war ended before they arrived. Richmond was evacuated on 2 April 1865 and Confederate President Jefferson Davis fled for his life. He was subsequently captured and imprisoned, but eventually survived to write his memoirs. Lincoln was less fortunate. Shortly after Lee's army surrendered at Appomattox Court House on 9 April, he was assassinated by a Southern sympathizer at Ford's Theatre in Washington, DC.

Reconstruction

The North's triumph in the Civil War preserved the Union, ended slavery, and confirmed the primacy of free labour. But it also created new problems: how should the South be reintegrated into the nation and what was to be done with the emancipated slaves (formally liberated by the 13th Amendment to the Constitution in 1865)?

Radical Republicans hoped that after Lincoln's assassination his successor, Andrew Johnson, would help them reconstruct Southern society before readmit-

ting Southern delegates to Congress. In fact Johnson, a Tennessean, proved to be an ally of the defeated planter class. After the war a fierce political struggle evolved during which moderate and radical Republicans united to give the vote to American blacks. More extreme measures such as land redistribution might have followed had not an attempt to impeach the President been defeated by the Senate in May 1868.

Although this period saw the founding of racist Southern organizations like the Ku Klux Klan, Reconstruction was a period

of hope for the emancipated slaves. During the 1870s Deep South states with large black populations (notably Mississippi, Louisiana and South Carolina) sent black delegates to Congress for the first time in US history. However, after the onset of economic recession in 1873, Northern voters finally lost interest in Reconstruction and the Republicans abandoned their Southern allies to the racist white majority. During the 1890s Southern blacks were deprived of the vote by state laws, and they remained second-class citizens until the mid-20th century (⊳ p. 216).   RC

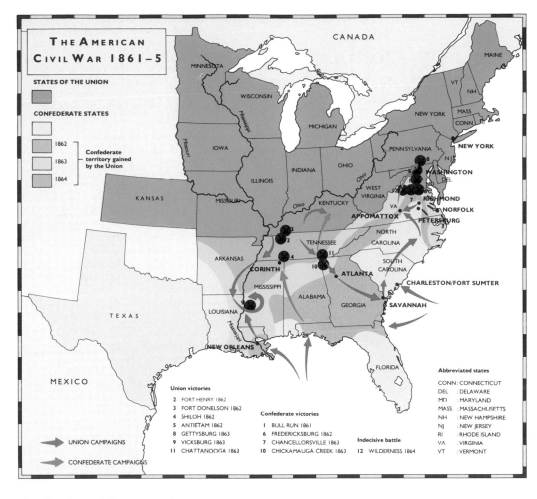

THE AMERICAN CIVIL WAR 1861–5

STATES OF THE UNION

CONFEDERATE STATES

1862
1863   Confederate
1864   territory gained
        by the Union

Union victories

2 FORT HENRY 1862
3 FORT DONELSON 1862
4 SHILOH 1862
5 ANTIETAM 1862
8 GETTYSBURG 1863
9 VICKSBURG 1863
11 CHATTANOOGA 1863

Confederate victories

1 BULL RUN 1861
6 FREDERICKSBURG 1862
7 CHANCELLORSVILLE 1863
10 CHICKAMAUGA CREEK 1863

Indecisive battle

12 WILDERNESS 1864

→ UNION CAMPAIGNS

→ CONFEDERATE CAMPAIGNS

Abbreviated states

CONN : CONNECTICUT
DEL : DELAWARE
MD   : MARYLAND
MASS : MASSACHUSETTS
NH   : NEW HAMPSHIRE
NJ   : NEW JERSEY
RI   : RHODE ISLAND
VA   : VIRGINIA
VT   : VERMONT

The arsenal of the **Confederate capital, Richmond,** destroyed by Union bombardment. The devastation inflicted on civilian populations, together with the impact on the conflict of new technology such as the field telegraph, the long-range rifle and the steam locomotive, have led many to call the US Civil War the first truly modern war.

The Peak of Empire

The 19th century witnessed one of the most remarkable events in world history. In 1800 most people in the world were self-governing. By 1914 about one-quarter of the globe had been taken over as colonies by half a dozen states. At the time many people argued that imperialism was needed to increase trade and find new materials for the economies of Europe. Others wanted to gain more territories to increase their strategic power in relation to other states. In the 19th century the various motives of the imperialists – economic, political and strategic – came together and encouraged the drive for Empire.

By the late 18th century various European empires had been established (▷ pp. 116 and 128), but these had either been in relatively under-populated areas, such as Canada and Australia, or had already shown signs of growing independence, as in the United States (1776; ▷ p. 142) and South America in the early 19th century (▷ p. 148). The one serious exception was the rule of the British East India Company.

The British in India

By 1805 the East India Company was dominant in India. Wars against Nepal (1814–16), Sind (1843) and the Sikh kingdom of the Punjab (1849) extended the frontiers to the natural boundaries of the subcontinent in the north. To the east the British had annexed the Burmese empire by 1886.

Within India the traditional system of landholding was destroyed and the British introduced private ownership. Production of food did not keep pace with the growth in population (some 190 million in 1871) and famine was a continuous threat. As a result the land quickly passed into the hands of relatively few large landowners, creating a large number of landless peasants.

The Indian Mutiny was the last effort of traditional India to oppose British rule. Princes, landlords and peasants were all united by the speed and tactlessness of the changes imposed by the British. The revolt began in 1857 as a mutiny of the Company's Indian soldiers. This spark ignited into rebellion all those who resented the growing British interference in Indian customs and culture. Economic tensions such as those arising out of the increased payment of land tax also played their part. The British brutally ended the revolt in 1858 after 14 months of bitter struggle.

After the Indian Mutiny the British government took direct control of India, and embarked on a programme of modernization. By 1927 92 000 km (57 000 mi) of roads had been built; education in English was introduced; and, most importantly, a railway network was constructed. The railways made possible the exploitation of Indian raw materials and the introduction of cash crops, such as tea. On the other hand, the British refused or failed to modernize industry, destroying, for example, the Indian cotton industry so that it could not compete with the British.

Fears of a Russian threat to the Indian subcontinent led to ill-fated British expeditions to Afghanistan in 1839–42 and again in 1878–80. The fiercely independent Afghan tribesmen managed to oust the British, and their country remained as a buffer between the British and Russian Empires.

European imperialism

After 1870 there was a rush to acquire colonial possessions by the major European powers. Two major areas of the world were almost entirely divided up: Africa and the Pacific. There were a number of reasons for this striking change.

The development of commerce in the 19th century created a global economic system. Many formerly remote areas of the world were being settled and developed: Canada, the USA west of the Mississippi, Australia and New Zealand. Ancient civilizations – such as Persia (Iran), China (▷ p. 57) and Japan (▷ p. 65) – were being opened to European penetration. In Africa and Asia missionaries and traders were arguing the enormous potential value of colonies as a treasure house of souls and raw materials.

The second major factor was the development of new technologies that depended on raw materials found mostly in remote places: for example, the motor car depended on oil and rubber, and copper from Africa and South America was needed for the new electrical industry. In addition the new mass consumption of sugar, tea, coffee, cocoa and fruit led to the development of tropical plantation economies. So the scramble for natural resources provided a fresh impetus for expansion.

In Europe there was increasing competition between the old imperial powers – Britain and France – and the emerging nations, especially Germany and Italy. Each feared being left behind by its rivals. Missionaries, traders, military and naval men and the public came together in the European capitals to press for imperial advances.

The scramble for empire

Before the 1880s the Africans, aided by the climate, had largely resisted European conquest, even forcing the Portuguese out in 1690. Even in the late 19th century the Ashanti, the Zulu and the Abyssinians were capable of strong resistance, but the balance of military technology was now decisively in favour of Europe (▷ p. 67). Large areas of the globe, particularly in Africa and Oceania, were carved up between the Western powers (▷ map, p. 163).

The French gained most of north and west Africa as well as Madagascar and Indochina. Germany acquired an empire in the Cameroons, Togoland, South West Africa, Tanganyika, China, part of New Guinea and some Pacific islands (all lost to the Allies after World War I). Italy obtained Libya, Eritrea and part of Somaliland, but failed in 1896 to conquer Abyssinia. The British made the greatest gains, including Egypt (although it was nominally still part of the Ottoman Empire), the Sudan, Uganda, Kenya, British Somaliland, Nigeria, Ghana, the Rhodesias and Nyasaland, as well as strategically important areas of the Pacific such as Singapore, Malaya and Fiji. The British also consolidated their rule of South Africa with their victory in the Second Boer War (1899–1902; ▷ box,

Highlanders and Gurkhas in action during the relief of Kandahar, 1 September 1880. A British army under General Roberts marched south from Kabul and defeated an Afghan force under Ayub Khan, inflicting heavy casualties. Success in the Second Afghan War was something of a Pyrrhic victory for Britain. The British never managed to establish a firm grip over the whole of Afghanistan, but controlled its foreign policy until it became independent in 1921.

THE IMPERIAL ETHOS

Attempts to interpret the nature of late 19th- and early 20th-century imperialism have tended to concentrate on unromantic political and economic factors. It was the English economist John Hobson (1858–1940) who first drew attention to the 'moral and sentimental' factors exploited by imperialism. He placed hero-worship, the quest for military glory, missionary endeavour and the sporting spirit alongside political chicanery and capitalist greed as key factors in the growth of popular enthusiasm for imperialism. Imperialist heroics such as H.M. Stanley's explorations of central Africa or the crusade-like campaign to rescue General 'Chinese' Gordon from the Mahdi's forces besieging Khartoum were clearly more enticing to the newspaper-reading public than investment prospects and treaty boundaries.

In the late 19th century imperialism ceased to be merely the esoteric faith of a small governing elite. Through the transmutation of popular nationalism into jingoism, imperialism began to appeal to the working classes, culminating in the British propaganda triumphs of the Second Boer War (1899–1902). Thus the term 'mafficking' was added to the English language after the boisterous London street scenes of 18 May 1900, celebrating news of the relief of Baden-Powell's small force surrounded by the Boers in Mafeking (▷ box, p. 163).

The commercial and strategic value of 'opening up' colonies for the white man's civilizing mission was emphasized by politicians anxious to forestall rivals in the 'scramble' for territory in Africa, the Pacific or Southeast Asia. 'Take up the White Man's burden – Send forth the best ye breed,' Rudyard Kipling exhorted the USA in 1899 on its acquisition of the Philippines from Spain. The supposed Anglo-Saxon genius for colonial rule and the French effort to overcome the humiliation of their defeat in the Franco-Prussian War (▷ p. 153) were boosted by the arguments of Social Darwinism. This pseudo-scientific creed asserted not only the rightful duty of the 'superior' white races to dominate and exploit the 'inferior' coloured races, but also encouraged conflict between imperialist nations. These assertions were based on the principle of the 'survival of the fittest', regarded as the key to evolutionary progress. Those who popularized Social Darwinian ideas stressed the necessity for countries to extend their power beyond natural boundaries or face imminent racial decline.

An imperial world view – compounded of patriotic, military and racial ideas, and glorifying violence and a sense of national and racial superiority – was successfully projected through popular culture. Youth movements (such as the Boy Scouts), music hall songs, imperial exhibitions, and 'imperial' lessons in schools all played their part, as did writers such as Kipling, Joseph Conrad and Ernest Psichari at the 'literary' level, and, at a more popular level, H. Rider Haggard, John Buchan, G.A. Henty, Pierre Mille and a host of boys' story papers.

Before 1914 opposition to British imperialism came from progressive writers and politicians on the fringes of the Liberal and Labour parties working to achieve a new radical realignment in British politics. In

The Delhi Durbar of 1903, held to celebrate the coronation of Edward VII. Durbars (the word means 'court' in Persian and Urdu) were originally formal court receptions held by Mogul emperors. Under British rule the term was appropriated to describe lavish imperial gatherings usually connected with important royal events.

France, prime minister Jules Ferry's imperialist ambitions of the 1880s provoked an anti-colonial reaction from many on the left. Anti-imperialist fervour was a strong motivation for the radicals who founded the French Communist Party in 1920 – including the future Vietnamese Communist leader Ho Chi Minh (▷ p. 208). The anti-imperial spirit of British intellectuals was also widely promulgated between the two world wars through a new generation of writers such as Robert Graves, George Orwell, Leonard Woolf and H.G. Wells. (However, the success of feature films like *The Lives of a Bengal Lancer* (1935), *Clive of India* (1935) and *The Four Feathers* (1939) is testimony to the continuing vigour of imperialist notions in popular culture during this period.) The radical anti-imperialism pioneered by Hobson was also taken up by American critics in books on economic imperialism and 'dollar diplomacy'. Despite their best efforts, imperialism probably remained a core ideology in British society well into the 1950s, when a last generation of schoolchildren were raised on the moral certainties of imperial rule through history textbooks, geography lessons, Empire Day, children's literature and popular cinema. JS

p. 163, and pp. 67 and 220) over the Boers (or Afrikaners: settlers of Dutch descent).

The old empire of the Dutch remained in Indonesia, while the Portuguese reasserted control of Angola, Mozambique and Guinea, although their largest colony, Brazil, had become independent in 1822. What remained of the Spanish Empire after the successful wars of independence in its South American colonies (1810–29; ▷ p. 148), however, was largely taken over by the USA after a brief war in 1898. The Americans acquired Puerto Rico, Guam and the Philippines from Spain, and also the Panama Canal, Hawaii and other Pacific bases.

The imposition of colonial rule varied. In the Congo the personal rule of King Leopold II of Belgium led to horrific atrocities (▷ p. 203). In South West Africa the Germans massacred the Hereros to impose their rule. Many Africans revolted against colonial rule: for

example, the Ndebele and Shona rose in rebellion in Rhodesia (1896–7) and the Zulus in South Africa (1906). These movements, while trying to maintain traditional independence, also prefigured future nationalist movements.

China

Once a great empire, by the 19th century China was politically weak and corrupt. It remained closed to outsiders until in the first Opium War of 1839–42 the British forced the Chinese to allow the traffic of drugs into China, and established five British-dominated treaty ports. British and French victory in the second Opium War (1856–60) forced the Chinese to open further ports. China seemed doomed to disappear under colonial rule (▷ p. 57). Russia exercised influence in Manchuria, the Germans carved out bases in the north, Britain enlarged its Hong Kong colony (▷ p. 197), and the rising power of Japan annexed Taiwan in 1894–5 and

Imperial acquisitions 1876-1914

During this period, nearly one fifth of the Earth's land surface was colonized. The shares taken by the various imperial powers are shown in this pie chart.

Total 30 million km² (10·8 million sq mi)

Korea in 1910 after defeating the Russians in the Russo-Japanese War of 1905 (▷ p. 65).

The Western powers were able to unite to put down the Boxer Rising and to occupy and loot Beijing (Peking) in 1900, but they were unable to agree how to divide the immense Chinese Empire. As a result China remained independent, but the strains of foreign interference helped cause the final collapse of the world's most ancient civilization in 1911 (▷ pp. 57 and 196).

Imperial rivalry and World War I

There is no simple connection between imperialism and the outbreak of World War I (▷ p. 176). Colonial disputes – such as the Fashoda Incident in 1898 between the French and British (▷ box), and the crises over Morocco in 1906 and 1911, involving Germany (▷ p. 175) – were successfully defused. Nevertheless, the drive for empire and control of the world economy created new antagonisms between the major powers. The rivalries between the powers, formerly confined to Europe, were now global and imperial.

The legacy of imperialism

Imperialism was both a massive movement and a very brief experience for those involved. The entire experience of colonialism in many parts of the world can be fitted within a single life – decolonization started after World War II, accelerated in the 1960s and was virtually complete by the 1980s (▷ p. 200). For most people the cultural impact of imperialism was very limited, though a minority did have Western education and many of these later became the leaders of anti-imperialist movements.

Perhaps the most significant long-term impact of imperialism is continuing resentment against the imposition of Western ideas and against the economic dominance of the West over large areas of the Third World (▷ p. 218).   MP

THE FASHODA INCIDENT

After his victory over the Mahdi (the Sudanese leader who claimed to be the Islamic Messiah) at Omdurman in early September 1898, British forces under Lord Kitchener pushed into southern Sudan along the White Nile. Kitchener was surprised to discover the French tricolour flying over a battered fortress at Fashoda; it looked as if the French, irritated by British actions in Egypt and Sudan, had laid claim to the strategically vital Upper Nile.

There was, in reality, no danger to British interests. On 10 July 1898, Major Jean-Baptiste Marchand of the French Marines, with seven officers and 120 Senegalese soldiers, had reached Fashoda after a two-year trek from the Atlantic coast of Africa – a 3200 km (2000 mi) trip across some of

the worst terrain imaginable. He was in no condition to withstand Kitchener, who arrived to confront him with two battalions of infantry and a battery of artillery on 19 September. Nevertheless, Marchand refused to lower the flag and, as local negotiations began, telegrams to London and Paris heightened the crisis.

Common sense eventually prevailed. On 4 November the French government, recognizing the futility of war, ordered Marchand to quit, despite the national humiliation involved. Four months later, a convention was signed establishing the watershed of the Nile and the Congo as the boundary between British and French spheres of influence in Africa. But the incident had shown how strained international relations could become over even the most minor event.   JP

Members of the Marchand expedition carrying their dismantled steamer through the brush between the Nile and the Congo. The French expedition, which aimed to thwart British designs on the Upper Nile basin, ended in tense confrontation with an Anglo-Egyptian army at Fashoda in the Sudan.

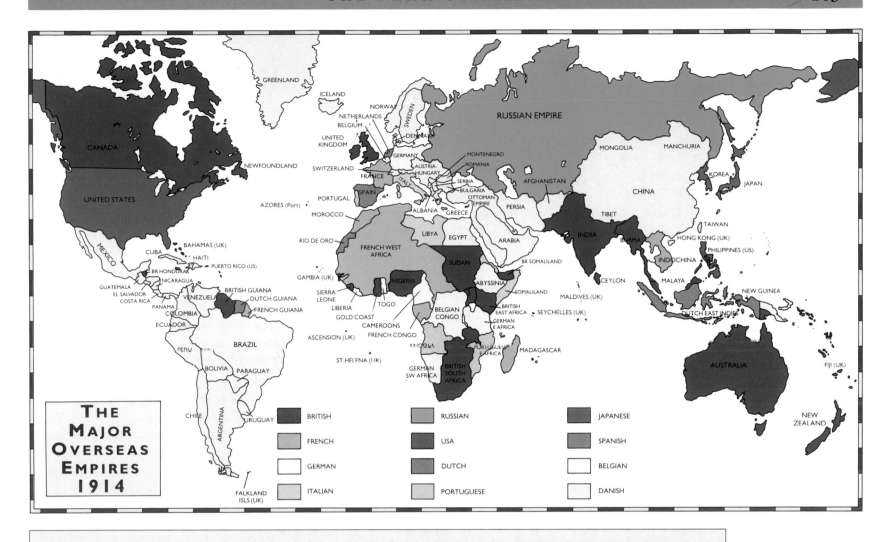

THE MAJOR OVERSEAS EMPIRES 1914

BRITISH — RUSSIAN — JAPANESE
FRENCH — USA — SPANISH
GERMAN — DUTCH — BELGIAN
ITALIAN — PORTUGUESE — DANISH

THE BOER WARS

The British presence in southern Africa led to resentment among the predominantly Dutch (Boer) settlers. To escape British rule, many 'trekked' north from Cape Colony in the 1830s and then, when Britain annexed Natal in 1845, crossed the Drakensberg Mountains to create two independent republics – the Orange Free State and the South African Republic (better known as the Transvaal). But the British followed; in 1877, ostensibly to protect it from marauding tribesmen, they annexed the Transvaal.

The Boers organized resistance, and in December 1880 declared their independence. A British force moved against Boer positions at Laing's Nek, just inside Natal, in January 1881, but was repulsed; a month later a second British attack took Majuba Hill but failed to dislodge the Boers. Negotiations led, in August, to the Pretoria Convention, which restored independence to the Transvaal and ended the war. The First Boer War was a humiliating experience for Britain.

Desire for revenge was reinforced by more pragmatic British emotions, particularly a fear that the gold-rich Boer republics might expand to the west, where German settlers in South West Africa (modern Namibia) were their potential allies. When two small Boer republics (Goshen and Stellaland) were founded in southern Bechuanaland (1884), British expansion northwards was threatened. In response, Britain annexed southern Bechuanaland (1885) and declared

a protectorate over northern Bechuanaland (modern Botswana), isolating the Transvaal from the west. Meanwhile, Cecil Rhodes began to carve out territory to the north (which would later become Rhodesia). More directly, in December 1895 one of Rhodes' chief administrators, Dr L.S. Jameson, led 600 horsemen into the Transvaal, hoping to trigger an anti-Boer insurrection among the *Uitlanders* (non-Afrikaner immigrants in the Transvaal). When the 'Jameson Raid' failed, the initial British reaction was one of disdain, but this quickly turned to anger when the German Kaiser sent a telegram of congratulations to the Transvaal president, Paul Kruger.

As British pressure on Transvaal increased, not least over the question of political rights for the *Uitlanders*, Kruger realized that it was only a matter of time before war began. In October 1899, he demanded a British guarantee of Boer independence; when this was not forthcoming, Boer forces – organized into *ad hoc* groups known as 'Commandos' – invaded Natal and Cape Colony.

The Second Boer War began badly for Britain. Boer offensives caught them unprepared and, although these attacks soon degenerated into sieges at Ladysmith, Kimberley and Mafeking, British counterattacks were poorly conducted. General Sir Redvers Buller, in command of a hastily assembled field force, tried to relieve Ladysmith, only to be repulsed at Colenso. Similar attempts to relieve Kimberley and

to protect the Cape ended ignominiously at Magersfontein and Stormberg respectively. All three battles occurred between 10 and 17 December 1899 – 'Black Week' for British forces.

But the Boers could not exploit their success and, when Lord Roberts arrived with reinforcements, the tables were turned. In February 1900 he forced the surrender of 4000 Boers at Paardeberg Drift before invading the Orange Free State and, in June, taking the Transvaal capital, Pretoria. With Buller advancing from Natal, recovering from defeat at Spion Kop in late January, the Boer republics seemed finished. The sieges of Ladysmith, Kimberley and Mafeking were all lifted, to explosions of British public emotion.

The Boers did not accept defeat. Instead, the Commandos reverted to guerrilla warfare, using their mobility and knowledge of the ground to mount hit-and-run attacks on British positions. In response, the British 'blockaded' the Boer homelands with barbed wire, sent their own mobile forces to destroy farmsteads, and interned Boer families in 'concentration camps', where many died in the appalling conditions. By April 1902, the Boers had suffered enough: at the Peace of Vereeniging they accepted British rule, with a promise of future self-government within a British-dominated federation of South African states. At a cost of 22 000 dead, the British had gained political dominance in southern Africa. JP

SEE ALSO

- CHINA FROM THE MONGOLS TO THE MANCHU p. 56
- MUSLIM INDIA p. 62
- AFRICA TO THE COLONIAL AGE p. 66
- THE SPANISH AND PORTUGUESE EMPIRES p. 116
- COLONIAL EXPANSION IN THE 17TH AND 18TH CENTURIES p. 128
- DECOLONIZATION p. 200
- THE THIRD WORLD p. 218
- SOUTHERN AFRICA IN THE 20TH CENTURY p. 220

Industrial Society in the 19th Century

The 19th century, across much of Europe and the USA, was seen by the prosperous as an 'age of progress' or 'improvement', exemplified by the growth of industry and the emergence of large cities. To describe this protracted and complex development as an Industrial Revolution is considered a misnomer by those economic historians who have become pessimistic about concepts such as 'progress', 'improvement' and economic growth. The process of European industrialization is now seen as a rather limited, gradual and piecemeal phenomenon. Emphasis is placed on the slow rate at which factories spread, new techniques were adopted and steam power was diffused, even in Britain, the first industrial nation.

Nonetheless, for those peasants and farm workers who migrated to cities in search of work, or whose isolated rural lives were disrupted by the advent of rail travel, nothing would ever be the same again. 'It was only yesterday,' wrote the novelist William Thackeray in 1860 of the pre-railway world, 'but what a gulf between now and then.'

The first industrial workforces paid a huge cost in human suffering for the benefits in living standards that accrued to future generations. The initial phases of capitalist manufacture involved long working hours under harsh conditions, the employment of children in factories and mines, as well as the destruction of traditional rural ways of life. People in pre-industrial society had to work long and exhausting hours as well, but often in their own homes, rather than at the impersonal command of factory steam whistles or under the rigid discipline of a workplace overseer. Large numbers of agricultural workers, attracted by higher wages – or in Britain driven off the land by enclosures (▷ p. 140) – crowded into the new factory towns and cities of industrial Lancashire, northern France, Alsace, Switzerland and Saxony, to work in cotton spinning mills.

As industrialization and urbanization spread, the social consequences first experienced in Britain – of class segregation in overcrowded cities, cyclical unemployment, the ravages of cholera, and rising crime levels – were repeated on the continent. More positive effects, such as rising literacy levels, improved living standards, campaigns for universal suffrage (▷ p. 168), and the emancipation of women (▷ p. 232), were also slowly felt across much of 19th-century Europe.

Industrialization and population

A rapid and unprecedented rise in population accompanied industrialization in Britain and subsequently in most other European countries. In 1850 there were roughly 66 million more inhabitants in Europe than there had been in 1815, with Britain and Russia growing faster than any of the other European nations. Paris and Tokyo counted just over one million people, London well over two million, while Vienna, Berlin, Naples and St Petersburg all had well over 400 000 inhabitants. Until the 1860s Belgium was the only European country to keep pace with Britain in industrial growth. More English people were living in urban than rural areas at the 1851 census, whereas only one in three French and German persons lived in towns even by 1871.

The massive extension of industrialization, especially the strong surges of economic activity enjoyed in the 1880s and 1890s by Germany, Russia, Italy, the Scandinavian countries and Japan, saw a decisive shift in industrial power. This second industrial phase, dominated by steel, electricity and the internal combustion engine, saw Germany overtake Britain as the greatest industrial nation in Europe, exploiting the rich mineral resources of the Ruhr, the Saar and – after the 1870 Franco-Prussian War – Alsace-Lorraine. The USA, with its unique combination of having both a populous and a highly industrialized workforce, had by 1900 exceeded both Britain and Germany in terms of its relative share of world manufacturing output (▷ p. 157).

Social adjustments

Wealth and power were unevenly distributed in all European societies, despite the advent in some of more democratic parliamentary forms of government. The threat of political disturbance was correspondingly high, above all in Paris from 1830 to 1851 (▷ p. 150). The breakdown of the old, informal, village controls caused by the unprecedented growth of cities created a major problem for 19th-century ruling elites of how to maintain order. The prison, the church, the workhouse, the factory, the reformatory and the school, whatever their other functions, became concrete symbols of attempts to assert a new sort of discipline and control over the urban masses of industrial towns and cities. In England the political threat of Chartism (a popular reform movement to secure the suffrage) spurred bills to set up police forces in Birmingham, Bolton and Manchester. The Prussian police force acquired a formidable reputation for vindictive petty-mindeness, for example, solemnly recording all the visitors to the graves in a Berlin cemetery of liberal rebels shot during the 1848 revolution. In France the emerging 'police state' of 1848–51 banned even village fetes as potential breeding-grounds of socialist agitation (▷ p. 150).

Northwestern Europe and parts of the USA had by the 1870s acquired many of the symptoms of advanced industrialism, but lacked the necessary machinery to identify and treat the consequent social effects. Housing, sewerage, water supplies and employment opportunities failed to keep pace with the demographic explosion as workers flooded into the cities from the countryside. Repression or control were not the only techniques of social management available to the state in an increasingly urban society. The 19th century was also characterized by a growing, though often inadequate, effort from above to make cities better places in which to live. However, the tenacity of private monopolies and laissez-faire government policies hindered more ambitious reforms because, in liberal capitalist societies, state interference was long considered an anathema. A movement towards the improvement of urban living

Bessemer converters at the Krupp works in Essen, Germany (1900). The Bessemer process was the first to allow high-quality steel to be made at low cost. The large-scale manufacture of steel contributed to the emergence of Germany and the USA as major industrial powers.

The strike by Robert Koehler (1850–1917). The increasingly effective use of strikes was a feature of European labour history from the 1880s. In Germany the Social Democratic party periodically agitated for mass political strikes during the 1890s. In Britain strikes were largely used to achieve better conditions of employment. For example, the London dockers' strike of 1889 secured a wage increase, overtime pay, and the end of piecework. The success of the dockers' strike encouraged 200 000 unskilled British workers to join unions during the following year.

conditions, and the feeling that widespread ill-health, poor housing, crime and drunkenness were nationally shameful as well as politically dangerous, can be seen in a whole series of both public and private initiatives before 1914.

The cholera epidemic of 1831–2 affected places as far apart as Riga, Hamburg, Sunderland, London and Paris. When it was realized that the rich could die from cholera or typhus as easily as the poor, measures were taken by governments to clean up the towns. The reformer Edwin Chadwick was responsible for the English Public Health Board of 1848, but it was largely ineffective. In the second half of the century, municipal authorities in London, Birmingham and Liverpool provided a good supply of water, removed cesspools and pulled down slums. The Public Health Act of 1875 reinforced and codified earlier British legislation. In 1882 the powers of English local authorities were increased, leading to schemes for adequate sewage disposal, water supply and street lighting. There were also some very limited attempts at direct provision of working-class housing by the state, as in the Housing of the Working Classes Act of 1890 in Britain, and French legislation from 1896 onwards to provide government loans for such housing. In Germany the Krupp family was prominent in the building of model settlements for workers near their factories at Essen.

Unlike Britain, where doctrines of minimum state intervention held sway, France was under the paternalist rule of Napoleon III during its years of rapid industrial development in the 1850s. Technological modernization, rail construction and economic growth were all advocated as remedies for France's chronic political instability and class conflict. The 'pint-sized' Emperor was also responsible for the large-scale demolition of slum housing and the extensive rebuilding of Paris under Baron Haussmann, whose wide boulevards had the convenient side-effect of making riot control easier. Several European states developed systems of social security providing for the payment of insurance benefits by the state in the event of illness, accident and old age. Chancellor Otto von Bismarck's state welfare legislation of the 1880s in Germany was the first such scheme (⇨ p. 153). Even in Tsarist Russia industrial workers were encouraged by legislation of 1888 to insure with private companies created for the purpose, but in a peasant society some 80% of the population still derived their livelihood from agriculture (⇨ p. 180). In Japan many cities still remained without amenities such as modern sewage systems, although by 1907 both Tokyo and Osaka had waterworks and other public facilities.

Working conditions

In Britain the protests of the artisans themselves, and the sympathetic support of humanitarian Tory reformers such as Lord Shaftesbury, brought about legislative reforms to improve conditions for factory and other workers. Laws were often limited to women and children – with the side effect of making them more dependent on the male head of the household – whereas adult male workers did not receive the same protection. Althorp's Act of 1833 forbade the employment of children under nine in textile mills, while the Mines Act of 1842 prohibited the employment of women and children underground. In 1847 Parliament passed the Ten Hours Act limiting the working week of women and young people to 58 hours in certain industries, of which no more than ten might be worked in any one day. The working day for men was not limited to 10 hours by law in Britain until 1874.

In the USA a 10-hour day became mandatory in New Hampshire in 1847, and in several other states soon after, but loopholes in the law made it ineffective. By the beginning of the 20th century, many children in the USA still spent 12 to 14 hours a day in the textile mills, and, by the time of World War I, despite being the world's richest industrial state, the USA had far fewer laws than the industrialized nations of Europe for the protection of workers and the regulation of laws and conditions of employment.

In France the Child Labour Law of 1841 fixed the minimum age at which children might be employed in factories at eight years and also limited their hours of work, but it was not until 1874 that more radical and effective legislation was passed. In Prussia a decree of 1839 forbade the employment of children under nine in mines, iron works and factories, and also limited the labour of young people under sixteen to 10 hours a day. In Russia it was not until 1882 that an edict was issued ending employment of children under the age of twelve and restricting the hours worked between twelve and fifteen years to eight. Passing laws was one remedial option, enforcing them through a proper

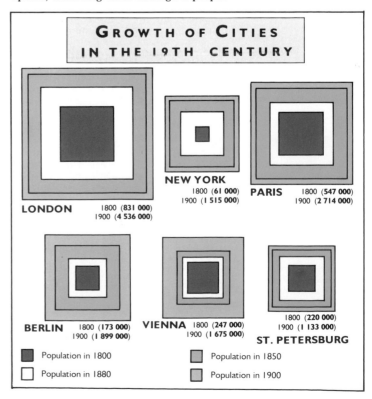

GROWTH OF CITIES IN THE 19TH CENTURY

LONDON 1800 (831 000) 1900 (4 536 000)

NEW YORK 1800 (61 000) 1900 (1 515 000)

PARIS 1800 (547 000) 1900 (2 714 000)

BERLIN 1800 (173 000) 1900 (1 899 000)

VIENNA 1800 (247 000) 1900 (1 675 000)

ST. PETERSBURG 1800 (220 000) 1900 (1 133 000)

Population in 1800
Population in 1880
Population in 1850
Population in 1900

system of inspection was another, and the more reactionary employers often delayed their full implementation.

Trade unions

Trade unions of workers, combined to present a united front to secure better wages and improved conditions, were initially opposed by employers in all of the industrializing countries. In Britain they were prohibited by the Combination Acts of 1799 and 1800, in France by articles in Napoleon's Penal and Civil Codes, and in Russia by the Penal Code of 1845. The repeal of the Combination Acts in 1824–5 permitted trade union activity in certain crafts, but strikes remained illegal. Attempts were made to establish trade unions among factory workers and miners on something more than a purely local basis. The Utopian socialist and factory owner Robert Owen unsuccessfully promoted an all-embracing 'Grand National Consolidated Trades Union' in 1833–4. Government fear of subversive trade union activities was exemplified by the case of the 'Tolpuddle martyrs', the name given to six Dorset farm workers who were transported to Australia for administering an illegal oath to establish a trade union.

Greater prosperity in the 1850s and 1860s led to considerable development of so-called 'new model' unionism on a national scale: the Miners' Association (1841); the Amalgamated Society of Engineers (1851) and of Carpenters and Joiners (1862). British trade unions were still not fully legal and in 1868 the Trades Union Congress (TUC) was founded to coordinate action to secure legal status, which was achieved in 1871. Mass 'new unionism' among unskilled workers developed in the 1880s and was greatly encouraged by the London dockers' strike of 1889. The leaders of these more militant unions believed in political as well as industrial action and were closely associated with the socialist organizations that came together to form the forerunner of the British Labour Party in 1900.

The growth of trade unionism elsewhere in Europe was hampered by legal restrictions. In France, many early workers' associations, driven underground by the hostility of employers and governments, disguised themselves as friendly societies. It was not until 1868 that Napoleon III, facing severe industrial unrest, gave French workers partial recognition of the right to combine to protect their interests. The bloody repression of the Paris Commune of 1871 (⊳ p. 153) was followed by the persecution of socialists and trade unionists and once again workers' organizations were driven underground. The French 'syndicates' had to wait until 1884 before they were allowed to engage in trade union activities, but only a relatively small proportion of all eligible workers actually joined.

The political and industrial sides of the workers' movement did not show signs of revival in Germany until the 1860s. The most important workers' associations were the 'free' unions, which generally adopted model statutes and were closely

RELATIVE SHARES OF WORLD MANUFACTURING OUTPUT

1800

Third World · Rest of Europe · Russia · UK · France · Germany · Habsburg Empire · USA · Japan

1860

Japan · Third World · USA · Rest of Europe · UK · Russia · France · Habsburg Empire · Germany

1900

Japan · Third World · UK · USA · France · Rest of Europe · Germany · Russia · Habsburg Empire

associated with the Social Democratic Party (⊳ p. 169). The 'free' unions survived all attempts to suppress them, such as Bismarck's Socialist Law of 1878. German workers recovered their right to form trade unions after Bismarck's departure from power in 1890 and by 1914 the 'free' German unions, with a membership of over two million, were the most powerful workers' organizations in continental Europe.

In America, 'combinations' of workers had begun to appear at the end of the 18th century, developing into fully fledged unions in the 1820s and 1830s, but working from a weak basis because the industrial working class never formed a

majority of the American population. In 1876, when a mostly Irish secret society, the 'Molly Maguires', attempted to wrest concessions from the mine-owners in western Pennsylvania, ten of their leaders were hanged for murder and conspiracy. Evidence against them was supplied by an undercover agent from the Pinkerton Detective Agency, the industrialists' secret police, which furnished spies, gunmen and strike-breakers on demand.

From the mid-19th century, American unions began to amalgamate in larger federations, including the National Labor Union (1866), the Knights of Labor (1869), the American Federation of Labor (AFL; 1886) and the Industrial Workers of the World (1905) – the 'Wobblies'. With the exception of the AFL these organizations were socialist-inspired. Despite opposition in the courts and from many employers, and the bad publicity resulting from various anarchist-inspired acts of violence (such as the 1886 Haymarket Square riot in Chicago), trade unionism in the USA proved durable and effective, but only the AFL survived into the period following World War I. Socialism in the USA also reached its peak before 1914.

All trade-union activity was banned as subversive in Russia throughout the 19th century, and those unions that did exist were clandestine. For a short period following the revolution of 1905 (⊳ p. 180), unions of a limited kind were permitted, but repression was quickly resumed. Metal workers and railway employees attempted to form unions in Japan in the late 1890s, but early efforts met with repression. The 'Yuaikai', a national labour organization, was set up in 1912. It began as a kind of self-help group, but in 1919, renamed as the Federation of Labour, it rapidly began to expand its membership.

Education

The need for an educated workforce, as manufacturing processes became more complex, led for the first time to state provision of more or less universal and compulsory systems of elementary education in most of the industrialized nations. Mass primary schools were also

A hatting factory (right) in Manchester at the beginning of the 20th century. Women were employed as cheap labour in many such factories, performing repetitive tasks by hand rather than by machine. In North America and Western Europe women represented a small minority of the labour force until World War II. In the USA, under 19% of the female population aged 16 or over was in paid employment in 1900.

expected to teach habits of industry, order and obedience that would help discipline the next generation of factory workers. Literacy rates had been increasing in England and Scotland since the turn of the 19th century, owing to the provision of primary education for the working class by Church schools and Sunday schools. Cheap non-denominational, elementary education did not become widely available in England until the Elementary Education Act of 1870, which required local authorities to provide schools where they were needed, but insisted on attendance only until age ten. Compulsory education from the 1880s met with some working-class resistance or non-attendance in poor areas, where a child's wages were needed to supplement the family income. When the 1899 Education Act was passed, extending compulsory attendance to 12, a loophole allowed children employed as agricultural labourers to complete their full-time schooling at 11.

Serious conflicts over education sometimes arose between Church and state in France and Germany. The French 1833 Guizot law had insisted on a school in every village, yet schooling was neither free nor compulsory. In 1850 the Falloux law extended Church control over education, placing teacher training colleges under tighter supervision. The education ministers of the Second Empire (1852–70) were also compelled to make tactical concessions to the Catholic Church, which many Frenchmen saw as an obstacle to a modern and progressive education system. In the 1880s the Ferry laws, establishing compulsory primary education, banned priests from teaching in public schools and closed all Jesuit schools.

French education nonetheless remained a rigid two-tier system – although primary education was freely available, secondary education was not. Lycée (grammar school) education cost roughly the annual wage of an industrial worker. France instituted state secondary education for girls in 1880, which in Germany did not occur until 1908. German education was largely secularized during the *Kulturkampf* ('conflict of cultures') – a clash between Bismarck's government and the Roman Catholic Church in the 1870s. However, Bavaria continued to give public support to its Catholic schools.

Provision of free education in the USA predated its arrival in much of Europe. A system of free public schools spread across the country from the 1880s, particularly in the North, where children were taught to honour the stars and stripes. Also in the 1880s, the old universities, such as Harvard and Princeton, were reformed. In the private schools (often run by religious bodies) the use of military drill to instil discipline reached a high point of popularity between 1870 and 1910. Under the Meiji regime in Japan (⊳ p. 65), compulsory, state-run elementary schools were set up from 1872, with a curriculum laid down by the government. Schools were strictly segregated above the elementary level and opportunities for women highly restricted.   JSp

THE GROWTH OF LEISURE

Custom, ritual and the rural holiday calendar diminished in importance with the advent of urban-industrial society in Britain. But the erosion of traditional rural recreations by the forces of industrialization, urbanization and evangelism did not leave behind a total vacuum. The decades from 1780 to 1860 actually saw a vigorous growth of popular leisure, particularly the arrival of new organized forms of commercial entertainment for the urban working and lower-middle classes, as well as the introduction of traditional 'blood sports', such as ratting and cockfighting, into urban public houses. The commercialization of the people's leisure in Britain was not confined to the late 19th century, however. Menageries, circuses, the pantomime, dancing saloons, panoramic exhibitions, cheap theatres and fiction were among the forms of commercial entertainment in existence before 1850, and based upon consumer demand.

One of the earliest mass markets to emerge among the newly urbanized 19th-century working class was that for popular fiction published in serial form. Its spread was facilitated by the combination of cheap paper and mechanical printing. In 1836 the first *roman feuilleton* – a serialized novel crammed with sensational events and leaving the reader in suspense at the end of each weekly part – appeared in a French newspaper. In England lurid 'penny bloods' and 'penny dreadfuls' were devoured by a lower-middle and working-class readership with an appetite for simple and sensational reading-matter. 'Dime novels' were an American equivalent of 'penny dreadfuls'. In Germany in the 1870s and 1880s, *Kolportageroman* – serialized fiction sold at the door by wandering book pedlars and consisting of bloodthirsty tales of ghosts, bandits, mysterious scandals and murders – were enormously popular among the working classes.

Touring fairs and circuses, mass circulation newspapers, penny readings and travelling players brought the urban and national culture to ever more remote parts of Europe and the USA, and created a shared national experience of leisure. As the century progressed, the police, and property-owners who paid their wages, became more tolerant of large crowds of working people gathered together for entertainments. Local by-laws were relaxed to allow fairs and spectator sports to take place. Football and other sports were seen as ideal vehicles for bringing together a nation's conflicting regions, faiths and social classes. But in practice sport could reflect rather than obscure internal divisions. In France a Catholic sports federation ran a separate Catholic national football team in a conscious attempt to create a new virile and Christian ethos. By 1899 two-thirds of lycées in the southwest of France had rugby teams. Football was popular in the north, while the new cycle race, the Tour de France, was promoted for both commercial and nationalistic

The Olympia music hall, Paris, in the 1890s. Music halls offered a mixture of low comedy and patriotic, comic or romantic ballads. The outstanding music-hall performers who emerged in the 1880s and 1890s – including Vesta Tilley, Marie Lloyd, Dan Leno, Albert Chevalier, Little Tich and Harry Lauder – were the first popular entertainers to achieve national celebrity in Britain.

motives. Before 1914 spectator sports enjoyed little popularity in Germany. In England the Football Association Cup was won in its first few years by ex-public school teams, but working-class Blackburn Olympic's victory over the amateur Old Etonians in 1883 brought encroaching professionalism closer.

The British mass leisure market took off from the 1870s with Saturday half-holidays, increased spending money, a much expanded urban population and an improved transport system. Music halls, which developed out of public house sing-songs, were, like the Parisian café-concert, a prototype form of mass entertainment. The respectability, patriotism and conservatism of the music halls reflected the homogeneity of their social appeal. During 1896 Marconi arrived in England to demonstrate and patent wireless signals, Alfred Harmsworth (later Lord Northcliffe) started the first halfpenny national newspaper, and the first paid film shows were put on in London and New York by the Lumière brothers from Lyons, who had pioneered a system for taking and projecting moving pictures on a celluloid strip. The wireless, the popular newspaper and the cinema were to be the dominant forms of mass leisure in the first half of the 20th century.

SEE ALSO

● THE AGRICULTURAL AND INDUSTRIAL REVOLUTIONS p. 140
● THE RISE OF MASS POLITICS p. 168

The Rise of Mass Politics

With the exception of revolutionary eruptions such as those of 1830 and 1848–9 (▷ p. 150), politics in early- and mid-19th-century Europe was the preserve of small elites of the noble and non-noble propertied classes. Political opinion within such elites was divided between support for dynastic conservatism and support for moderate liberalism. From the 1860s, however, the extension of the franchise in many European countries led to the emergence of a genuinely mass politics that was to challenge oligarchical control of government and which seemed to many to threaten the political, social and economic status quo.

SEE ALSO

● NATIONALISM, LIBERALISM AND REVOLUTION p. 150
● INDUSTRIAL SOCIETY IN THE 19TH CENTURY p. 164
● THE RUSSIAN REVOLUTIONS p. 180

By the 1870s, electoral systems based on a wide adult male suffrage existed in France, the German Empire, Denmark, and Switzerland. By 1914, the franchise had been widened in much of the rest of Europe. The 1884 Reform Act in Britain almost doubled the electorate. In Belgium the electorate was doubled in 1894, that in Norway in 1898, that in Sweden in 1908. Universal adult male suffrage was introduced in the Austrian half of the Austro-Hungarian Empire in 1907, and in Italy in 1912. In most of eastern and southeastern Europe, however – even in the few states in which national representative bodies existed – the vote was confined to small property-owning elites.

By modern standards, the extension of the franchise fell far short of creating a democratic political system. Even by 1914, only a minority of the adult male population was able to vote in most European coun-

A German socialist poster of 1915 proclaims the message 'Freedom, Justice and Peace'. The red flag first appeared as a revolutionary banner in France in 1792. It was adopted as the flag of the Paris Commune (1871) and became an international symbol of socialism.

Freiheit-Recht-Friede!

tries, and only in Finland and Norway were some women entitled to vote. Manipulation of election results was widespread; unelected upper houses – typically drawn from the aristocracy – checked the power of elected lower chambers; and monarchs retained extensive prerogatives (only France, Switzerland and Portugal were republics in 1914). Nevertheless, the development of mass politics, based on an increasingly wide electorate, was seemingly irreversible in most of Europe by 1914. In the USA all white men had voting rights by the end of the Civil War (1865) and the 14th amendment to the US Constitution sought to extend the vote to all black citizens. However, this had little real effect (▷ p. 159). It was not until 1920 that all women throughout the USA gained the vote.

The decline of liberalism

The advent of mass politics led to a decline in the influence of political liberalism throughout Europe from the 1870s. Liberal politics in mid-19th-century Europe had been dominated by small groups of local or regional notables. Party organization had been rudimentary. With the extension of the franchise, liberals were compelled to try to develop more highly structured party organizations capable of engaging in the intensive campaigning that increasingly characterized elections to representative bodies. Electoral campaigning entailed appealing for the support of the newest members of the political nation – the large body of citizens who were neither educated nor propertied. But liberal politicians proved disinclined to court the masses and were suspicious of the restrictions implicit in the modern party system – notably on the freedom of the individual elected representative to vote as he saw fit. As a result liberal party organization generally remained amateur. Better-organized rivals garnered the votes of the newly enfranchised masses.

The claim of classical liberalism (▷ p. 150) to stand above class or sectional interest and to represent the well-being of all became less plausible in the late 19th century. Liberals took the view that government expenditure and state intervention in the working of a free-market economy should be kept to an absolute minimum. They found it difficult to come to terms with the expanding role of the state dictated by the social problems accompanying rapid urbanization. Another problem was the intensification of class conflict arising from industrialization. This diminished the attractiveness of a creed that preached the virtues of a free market in labour and capital, resisted any interference with employers' freedom of action, and was hostile to the formation of trade unions (▷ p. 166). The economic depression that affected most of central and western Europe from the mid-1870s – and the subsequent general move to protectionism – dealt a severe blow to liberal beliefs in the ability of free-market, free-trade capitalism to promote general material well-being.

The challenge of the Left

The feeble response of liberalism to these new challenges led many newly enfranchised voters to look elsewhere. Socialist parties were the principal beneficiaries. Barely present in 1880, by 1914 socialist parties were a major electoral force wherever the franchise and the law permitted the formation of mass parties based on the working class. Their rapid development rested on the simplicity of their message: declaring themselves to represent the interests of all manual wage-labourers, socialist parties sought to represent workers in their struggles with employers and the state. They promised to create a new society in which exploitation would disappear as economic life was ordered for the promotion of the general good. This vision of society was not new (in the modern period, it had been anticipated by Robert Owen and Saint-Simon amongst others), but belief in the inevitability of its realization certainly was. By 1914, almost all socialist parties looked for their inspiration and theoretical understanding of the new industrialized world to the political and economic doctrines of Karl Marx (1818–83), especially as popularized by the later writings of his collaborator Friedrich Engels (1820–95). In *The Communist Manifesto* (1848), Marx had argued that 'All history is the history of class struggles.' He believed that at each stage of human development, changes in technology and the economic organization of society had led to changes in the balance of power between the different classes. As feudalism had given way to capitalism, so the land-owning nobility had been displaced as the ruling class by that class which owned the new means of production – the factory-owning middle-classes or bourgeoisie (▷ p. 130). The contradictions within the capitalist economic system, he claimed, would inevitably lead to its collapse. A new economic and social order would emerge in which the working class was dominant.

The political strategy adopted by the socialist parties was influenced by the attitude of the middle classes towards the working class and the opportunities – or lack of them – for trade-union organization. But perhaps the most important factor in determining the political complexion of the socialist parties was the attitude of the state towards the labour movement in the different European states. Where the state was tolerant of the emerging labour movement – as in Britain and Scandinavia, working-class parties had the possibility of secur-

SPREAD OF UNIVERSAL SUFFRAGE		
	Men	**Women**
Britain	1918	1918 (over 30)
		1928 (over 21)
France	1871 (briefly in 1848)	1945
Germany	1870	1918
Russia	1917	1917
Japan	1925	1945

ing representation of workers' interests and reforms through a greater parliamentary presence. However, where the state sought to suppress the labour movement – as in Imperial Germany and Tsarist Russia – the revolutionary path seemed the only one open to socialist parties.

The attempt to establish highly organized socialist parties committed to the capture of state power was the norm in northern and western Europe before 1914. In Mediterranean Europe, however, the anarchist and anarcho-syndicalist traditions remained influential. These rejected the idea of the capture of state power by the workers, advocating instead that ordinary workers should organize and run their own lives through local and regional committees. Anarchists and anarcho-syndicalists aimed at the overthrow of all oppressive institutions: anarchists attempted to bring this about through terrorist attacks on representatives of the state; anarcho-syndicalists believed that the existing order could be overturned by a series of general strikes. Anarchism was an influential political ideology in Spain; whilst anarcho-syndicalism remained powerful within the French labour movement up to 1914.

Political Catholicism

Marxist 'scientific' socialism was explicitly atheistic and all the new socialist parties which sprang up in Europe in the decades before 1914 (except the British Labour Party, founded in 1906) were hostile to the power and influence of the Christian Churches. But the Churches' responses to the advent of mass politics were far from insignificant. From the 1870s onwards, the Roman Catholic Church gave its blessing to the establishment of political parties committed to the defence of Catholic interests (in the sphere of education, for instance) in a political environment often dominated by anti-clerical liberals. Such parties based their appeal on a distinctive economic, social and political ideology, which sought to apply Catholic moral teaching to the new industrializing world. They were able to rely on the organizational

presence of the Catholic Church to create an extensive political apparatus. The Popular Association for a Catholic Germany – the mass organization of the Catholic 'Centre' party in Imperial Germany – boasted 865 000 members by the beginning of the 20th century.

The New Right

During the last two decades of the 19th century, a new form of conservative politics emerged in much of Europe – a 'New Right', which differed from traditional conservatism both in its ideology and in its organization.

The 'Old Right' had been dynastic and legitimist, and stressed the virtues of a hierarchical society in which each was allocated his place at birth. It had been hostile towards nationalism, which it saw as a progressive movement bent on destroying the old dynastic order and as a dangerous ally of liberalism (⇨ p. 150). In the early 19th century, nationalism – with its emphasis on the nation-state as the embodiment of the popular will – had indeed seemed a radical force. By 1900, however, a new form of nationalism – 'integral nationalism' – had emerged, which stressed the subordination of the individual to the higher purposes of the nation-state and the inevitability of conflict between nation-states in an era of imperialism. Integral nationalists argued that class conflict, as propagated by the internationalist and pacifist socialist parties, merely divided the national community, which they increasingly defined in cultural and racial terms. The economic and social ills that accompanied industrialization were widely blamed on 'outsider' groups which – it was claimed – did not truly belong to the nation. In France, Protestants, Jews and Freemasons were seen as alien bodies threatening the integrity of the national body; in Imperial Germany, the Catholic population, Jews, and the Polish minority were stigmatized as 'enemies of the Reich'; and so on. The ideology of the New Right in the decades before 1914 was militaristic, chauvinistic and antisemitic; suspicious of – if not openly hostile towards – parliamentary gov-

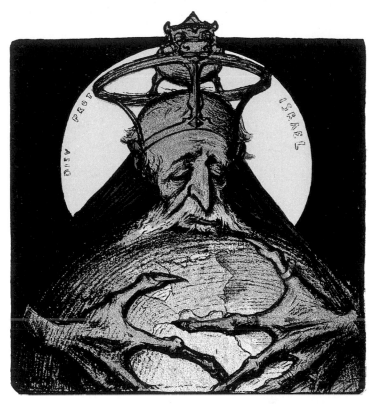

ernment, and rabidly anti-socialist. In many ways it anticipated Fascist ideology of the 1920s and 1930s (⇨ p. 186).

The New Right also broke with traditional conservatism in terms of organization. Traditionally, conservatives had despised the 'masses' and had seen no need to appeal for their support. With the widening of the franchise, however, they were forced to try to mobilize a mass base for conservatism. Rather than seeking to create an extensive party organization, conservatives preferred to mobilize their supporters by means of pressure- and interest-groups with a mass membership, such as the Agrarian League in Imperial Germany. Founded in 1893 to promote the interests of farmers and oppose trade liberalization policies, the League had over 330 000 members by 1914. In establishing such organizations, conservatives in much of Europe were often strikingly successful in mobilizing peasants, artisans and large sections of the 'new' lower middle class of white-collar workers in an anti-socialist bloc committed to the defence of the status quo.

A new political landscape

The political landscape of Europe was transformed by the advent of mass politics after 1870. By 1914, many European governments were confronted by mass socialist parties ostensibly committed to the revolutionary overthrow of the existing order, and even the staunchest conservatives acknowledged the necessity – however disagreeable – of actively seeking popular support for the status quo. The experience of World War I (⇨ pp. 176–9) was to confirm that, under modern conditions, effective government is dependent on at least the notional assent of the governed.   SS

A French anti-Semitic poster (1898) caricaturing the international financial and political influence of the Rothschild family. Anti-Semitism was adopted by some factions of the New Right to widen their popular appeal. In France anti-Semitism reached a peak during the Dreyfus affair (1894), when a Jewish officer, Alfred Dreyfus, was wrongly convicted of treason. The case dominated French politics until he was exonerated in 1906.

Prussian cavalry quell demonstrations by Berlin workers in 1892 (left) after the Prussian premier had called for legislation against the (socialist) Social Democratic Party. In Imperial Germany – as in Tsarist Russia – the authorities sought to suppress socialism, but the attitude of the state towards the labour movement differed in other countries. In Britain and Scandinavia, working-class parties were able to secure reforms through parliamentary representation.

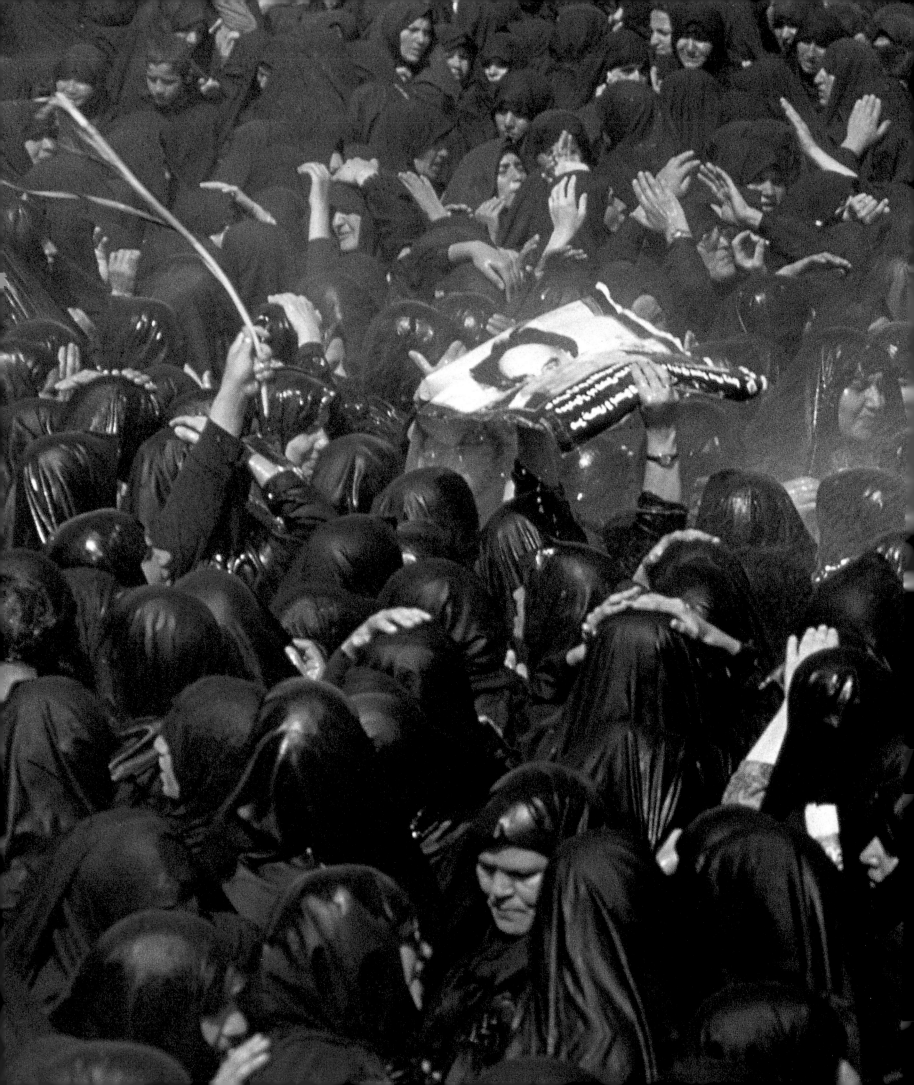

THE
MODERN
WORLD

WESTERN EUROPE	EASTERN EUROPE	AFRICA	ASIA AND THE PACIFIC
1914 Outbreak of World War I – Germany declared war on France and invaded Belgium; UK declared war on Germany; German invasion of France; first battle of Ypres; start of trench warfare **1915** Second Battle of Ypres; Italy joined war against Central Powers **1916** Battle of Verdun; naval battle of Jutland; battle of the Somme; Easter Rising in Dublin against British rule **1917** Battle of Passchendaele; Italy defeated at Caporetto **1918** German defeat in Second Battle of the Marne; revolution in Germany – abdication of the Kaiser; Germany signed armistice on 11 November	**1914** Assassination of Archduke Franz Ferdinand; Austrian ultimatum to Serbia; Austria declared war on Serbia; Austria and Germany declared war on Russia; Turkey entered war allied to Central Powers; Russia defeated by Germany at Tannenberg **1915** Abortive Allied campaign at Gallipoli **1916** Failure of Russian offensive **1917** February Revolution in Russia – abdication of the Tsar and formation of a provisional government; October Revolution – Bolsheviks under Lenin seized power **1918** Russia withdrew from war; Russian Imperial family massacred; Austria-Hungary surrendered and Habsburgs deposed; large-scale Russian industries nationalized by the Bolsheviks	**1914** South Africa entered the war against the Central Powers; German Togo occupied by Franco-British forces **1915** German South West Africa (Namibia) occupied by South Africa **1916** German Cameroon occupied by Franco-British forces; German East Africa occupied by Belgo-British forces	**1914** Australia and New Zealand entered the war against the Central Powers; German territories in the Pacific occupied – Western Samoa by New Zealand, Nauru by Australia, Micronesia and the Marshall Islands by Japan
1919–23 Versailles Peace Settlement – France regained Alsace-Lorraine; Rhineland demilitarized **1921** Partition of Ireland; Irish Free State established **1922** Fascists under Mussolini took power in Italy **1923** Hitler attempted coup in Munich, Bavaria **1923–5** Franco-Belgian occupation of Ruhr when Germany defaulted on reparations; rampant German inflation **1926** General strike in UK **1929** Salazar came to power in Portugal	**1918–21** Russian Civil War **1919** Czechoslovakia, Hungary, Poland and Yugoslavia established as independent states **1920** Independence of Baltic states recognized **1922** Foundation of the USSR **1924** Death of Lenin; Stalin became Soviet leader	**1919** Former German colonies became League of Nations mandates – Cameroon and Togo (UK and France), Ruanda-Urundi (Belgium), South West Africa (South Africa), and Tanganyika (UK) **1923** Southern Rhodesia became a Crown colony	**1923** Sun Yat-sen established Nationalist Chinese government **1927–8** Civil war in China between Nationalists and Communists **1928** Nationalists under Jiang Jie Shi (Chiang Kai-shek) reunited China
1930 French forces left the Rhineland **1930–4** Collapse of German monetary system (1930); rise of the German Nazi party; Hitler became chancellor in 1933 and created a one-party dictatorship; anti-Semitic laws from 1933; Night of the Long Knives (1934) **1936–9** Spanish Civil War – Franco's Falangists defeated the republicans **1937** Sudetenland crisis – Munich Pact allowed Germany to annex German-speaking areas of Bohemia; Irish Free State became the Republic of Eire **1938** Anschluss – Germany annexed Austria **1939** Britain and France declared war on Germany	**1928–38** Land taken from peasants in USSR to create collectives – destruction of the kulak class **1930s** Gradual elimination of democracy in many Eastern European states as virtual dictatorships were established in Poland, Yugoslavia, Romania, Hungary, Albania, Lithuania, Estonia and Latvia **from 1934** Stalin's purges in USSR **1935** Restoration of the Greek monarchy **1935–8** Treason trials in USSR	**1930s** Growth of Afrikaner nationalism in South Africa **1935** Italian invasion of Ethiopia **1936** Italian forces occupied Addis Ababa; Emperor Haile Selassie deposed; Ethiopia annexed	**1930s** Congress Party under Gandhi encouraged a campaign of civil disobedience against British rule in India **1931** Japan invaded Manchuria and established a puppet state **1934** Mao Zedong led Chinese Communists on the Long March **1937** Beginning of Sino-Japanese War – Japanese occupied Beijing and Shanghai
1940 German invasion of Denmark, Norway, the Low Countries; British evacuation of Dunkirk; fall of France; Churchill became British PM; aerial battle of Britain **1941** Extermination of Jews began in German concentration camps **1942** Start of massive Allied air raids on Germany **1943** Mussolini overthrown; Allied invasion of Italy **1944** Germans expelled from northern Italy; D-Day – Allied landings in Normandy; Paris and Brussels liberated; failure of Allied Arnhem campaign; final German offensive – battle of the Bulge; Allied forces entered Germany **1945** Mussolini killed by partisans; Allied defeat of Germany completed; Hitler committed suicide	**1939–40** Russo-Finnish 'Winter' War **1939** Germany invaded Poland – outbreak of World War II **1940** USSR annexed Baltic states **1941** German invasion of Greece, Yugoslavia and USSR – siege of Leningrad; Romania and Bulgaria joined Axis powers **1942** USSR defeated Germany at Stalingrad **1943** German retreat from USSR began; German surrender at Stalingrad; extermination of Jews intensified **1944** Yugoslavia liberated; Soviet offensive in Eastern Europe – Germans pushed back in Poland, Hungary, Romania and Bulgaria **1945** Yalta Conference – Allies decided future division of Europe; Berlin surrendered to Soviet forces	**1939–45** White South African public opinion divided upon participation in World War II in the Allied cause **1940–42** Administration of most of French West Africa by Vichy sympathizers **1940–45** Cameroon and French Equatorial Africa held for the Free French **1942** French West Africa held for the Free French	**1940** Japan invaded Indochina **1941** Japan invaded the Philippines **1942** Japan invaded Malaya, Singapore, East Indies and Burma; Japan defeated by USA in naval battle at Midway **1943** USA forced Japanese to retreat in Pacific **1944** US naval victory over Japan at Leyte Gulf **1945** USA dropped atom bombs on Hiroshima and Nagasaki; Japan surrendered
1945–51 Attlee's Labour governments in UK established the welfare state **1945** Germany divided into four zones of occupation **1948** Berlin airlift to West Berlin **1949** Foundation of NATO, Western military alliance; foundation of Federal Republic of (West) Germany **1952–7** Campaign by Greek Cypriots to end British rule **1957** Treaty of Rome established Common Market (EEC) **1958** de Gaulle established French Fifth Republic	**1945** Beginning of the Cold War – Soviet-imposed Communist regimes began to be established in Eastern Europe **1946** Greek civil war **1948** Communist takeover of Czechoslovakia **1949** Foundation of German Democratic Republic (East Germany) **1953** Stalin died; Khrushchev came to power in USSR **1955** Warsaw Pact formed **1956** Hungarian rising put down by Soviet forces	**1948** Nationalists won power in South Africa; imposition of apartheid **1956** Morocco, Tunisia and Sudan independent **1957** Ghana became the first British black African colony to gain independence	**1946–9** Chinese Civil War; Communist victory in 1949 **1947** India and Pakistan independent **1949** Indonesia independent **1950–1** Chinese invasion of Tibet **1950–3** Korean War **1954** French defeated by Communist Vietnamese
1964 Election of Wilson's Labour government in UK **1967–74** Military junta in Greece – 'The Colonels' **1968** Student unrest in much of West **1969** Start of the 'Troubles' in Northern Ireland – British troops deployed; resignation of de Gaulle as French president **1972** UK imposed direct rule on Northern Ireland **1973** UK, Ireland and Denmark joined EC **1974** Portuguese revolution – authoritarian regime deposed	**1960s** Arms race between USSR and USA intensified despite Nuclear Test Ban Treaty in 1963 **1961** Berlin Wall constructed **1964–82** Brezhnev, Soviet Communist Party leader – Brezhnev Doctrine defined as right of USSR to intervene in affairs of Communist states **1968** Dubcek's attempt to reform Communism in Czechoslovakia crushed by USSR **1970** Unrest in Poland – riots in Gdansk **1974** Turkish invasion and partition of Cyprus	**1960** Sharpeville Massacre in South Africa **1960–1** Belgian Congo independent; Katanga attempted secession **1960s** Independence of majority of British and French African colonies **1962** Algerian independent after eight-year uprising **1965** Rhodesian UDI **1967–70** Nigerian civil war	**1964–73** US military support for South Vietnam against Communist North **1966–76** Cultural Revolution in China **1969** Sino-Soviet border dispute **1971** Pakistan civil war; secession of East Pakistan as Bangladesh; Vietnam war spread to Laos and Cambodia
1975 Death of Franco; democracy restored in Spain **1979–90** Right-wing Conservative premiership of Margaret Thatcher in UK **1981** Mitterrand became French president **1986** Spain and Portugal joined EC **1990** German reunification **1992** Conservatives in UK won fourth consecutive term of office; single European Market established	**1980** Solidarity suppressed in Poland **1981** Greece joined EC **1985** Gorbachov came to power in USSR and began reforms **1989–91** Collapse of Communism in Eastern Europe; former Soviet satellites became multi-party democracies **1991** Attempted coup by Communist hardliners in Moscow; dissolution of USSR into 15 independent republics; Gorbachov resigned **1991–2** Civil war led to breakup of Yugoslavia	**1975** Completion of Portuguese decolonization in Africa **1977** Crackdown on anti-apartheid activity in South Africa **1980** Rhodesia independent as Zimbabwe **1990–2** Dismantling of apartheid in South Africa	**1975** South Vietnam surrendered; end of Vietnam War **1975–9** Khmer Rouge in power in Cambodia – ended by Vietnamese invasion **1979–89** Soviet intervention in Afghanistan **1989** Pro-democracy movement suppressed in China

THE AMERICAS	THE MIDDLE EAST	CULTURE AND SOCIETY	SCIENCE AND TECHNOLOGY
1914 Canada entered the war against the Central Powers **1915** *Lusitania* sunk by German U-boat **1916** US forces occupied Haiti **1916–17** American expedition under 'Black Jack' Pershing into Mexico against Pancho Villa **1917** USA entered war against Germany	**1914** British forces began Mesopotamian campaign against Turkey **1915–16** Siege of Kut – British defeated by Turks **1916–18** T.E. Lawrence played major role in encouraging Arab revolt against Turkish rule **1917** British forces took Baghdad and Jerusalem	**1910–24** Peak of the Expressionist movement in art and theatre **1913** Stravinsky's ballet music *The Rite of Spring* caused a riot **1914** Charlie Chaplin made his first film **1916** D.W. Griffith's film *Intolerance* introduced modern cinematic techniques **1918** Women over 30 granted the vote in UK; worldwide pandemic of influenza	**1914** First Zeppelin air raid on UK **1915** Einstein formulated the general theory of relativity **1916** Typhus isolated; first refrigeration of blood for transfusion
1920 US Senate overrode President Wilson's support for the League of Nations – USA entered a period of isolationism **1920** Prohibition of alcohol throughout USA **1924–30** Persecution of the Church in Mexico **1928–35** Chaco War between Bolivia and Paraguay **1929** Wall Street Crash – beginning of worldwide Depression	**1920** Syria mandated to France; Palestine, Transjordan and Iraq mandated to Britain **1921–2** Turkey repulsed Greek forces; Atatürk deposed the last Ottoman and laid foundations of modern Turkey **1921–7** Saudis united Arabia **1922** Egyptian independence	**1919** Foundation of the Bauhaus art and design school by Walter Gropius **1920s** Dada and Surrealist movements flourished in art; German Expressionist cinema; first plays of American dramatist Eugene O'Neill (1888–1953) **1922** T.S. Eliot's Modernist poem, *The Waste Land*; James Joyce's Modernist novel, *Ulysses* **1925** Kafka's *The Trial*; Fitzgerald's *The Great Gatsby* **1927** *The Jazz Singer*, the first 'talkie'	**1923** Freud's *The Ego and the Id*; Hubble proved the existence of other galaxies **1925** Baird transmitted a television picture **1927** Lindbergh's solo transatlantic flight **1928** Fleming discovered penicillin
1930 President Hoover adopted protectionist policies to protect US industry in the Depression **1930s** Order restored in Mexico by Institutional Revolutionary Party – redistribution of land (1934–9) **1930–45** Vargas's dictatorship (the 'New State') in Brazil **1933–45** F.D. Roosevelt, US president – instituted the New Deal (1933) to relieve economic distress and promote recovery	**1930s** Jewish settlement in Palestine increased **1932** Iraqi independence **1936** Anglo-Egyptian treaty – Britain retained control of Suez Canal	**early 1930s** World trade collapsed, unemployment rose steeply, leading to poverty, homelessness and misery for millions in the Depression **1930s** Brecht's epic theatre – *Mother Courage* (1937) and *The Good Person of Setzuan* (1938–40); rise of the Broadway musical **1936** Keynes's *General Theory of Employment, Interest and Money* **1937** Picasso's Cubist painting *Guernica*, inspired by the Spanish Civil War	**from 1930** Whittle experimented with jet turbines **1932** Chadwick discovered the neutron **1933** Discovery of polythene **1936** Turing published his theories on electronic computing machines **1937** *Hindenburg* destroyed by fire; end of airship development **1938** Creation of nylon
1935–9 US Neutrality Acts preventing US involvement in non-American wars **1941** US 'Lend-Lease' scheme agreed, supplying equipment to UK and its Allies; Japanese attack on Pearl Harbor – USA entered the war on Allied side **1942** US troops arrived in theatres of war in Europe, North Africa and the Pacific	**1941** Start of Allied campaign in North Africa **1942** Montgomery defeated German-Italian forces at El Alamein; Allies captured Tripoli and Tunis **1943** Axis troops evacuated North Africa	**1939** Steinbeck's novel *The Grapes of Wrath*; *Gone with the Wind* – film with Clark Gable and Vivien Leigh; National Service (conscription) introduced in Britain **1939–45** Radio became a popular means of entertainment and source of news **1941** Orson Welles' film *Citizen Kane* **from 1941** Strict rationing in UK **1945** Orwell's *Animal Farm*; Bebop heralded era of 'modern jazz'	**1939** Sikorsky developed the helicopter **1941** First jet aircraft; Zuse developed the first mechanical computer **1942** Splitting of the atom; construction of the first nuclear reactor **1944** German V1 and V2 rockets used in war **1945** First use of atomic bombs in warfare at Hiroshima; development of the COLOSSUS I and ENIAC computers
1946–55 Juan Perón in power in Argentina **1949** Escalation of Cold War between USA and USSR after explosion of first Soviet atomic bomb **1950–4** McCarthy's witchhunt against alleged Communists in USA **mid-1950s** Growth of Civil Rights movement in Southern States of USA led by Martin Luther King **1959** Castro seized power in Cuba and gradually imposed a Marxist regime	**1948** Foundation of Israel; first Arab–Israeli War **1952** Monarchy toppled in Egypt; Nasser came to power in 1954 **1956–7** Nasser nationalized Suez Canal; UK and France invaded Suez; Israel invaded Sinai **1958** Iraqi revolution – fall of the Hashemite monarchy	**1949** Orwell's *1984* **1950s** Spread of television as a medium of entertainment; Modernist architecture characterized by Le Corbusier (1887–1965); emergence of postwar youth cultures in the West – e.g. Beatniks and Teddy Boys; spread of electronic *avant-garde* music – works of Cage and Stockhausen **1952** Beckett's play *Waiting for Godot* **mid 1950s** Rock and roll music became popular **1956** Emergence of mass disarmament movements in West	**1947** Transistors demonstrated **1952** USA exploded first H-bomb **1953** Structure of DNA discovered **1957** USSR launched the first satellite in space – *Sputnik I* **1957–9** Computer languages introduced **1958** First US space satellite
1960s Race riots in many US cities **1961** Abortive 'Bay of Pigs' invasion by Cuban exiles **1962** Cuban Missile Crisis **1963** Assassination of President Kennedy **late 1960s** Growth of French-Canadian separatism **1968** Martin Luther King assassinated **1968–70** Opposition to US involvement in Vietnam intensified **1973** Left-wing Allende government overthrown in Chile by General Pinochet with indirect US support	**1967** Arab–Israeli 'Six Day' War; Israel captured Sinai, West Bank, Gaza and Golan **1970** Jordanian civil war; Palestinians expelled **1973** Arab–Israeli 'Yom Kippur' War; Arab oil embargo of the West **1975** Start of civil war in Lebanon	**1960s** Growth of feminist movement **1960** D.H. Lawrence's *Lady Chatterley's Lover* judged not obscene by UK jury **from 1962** Reforms in Roman Catholic Church **1963** Beatles pop group gained international popularity **from 1963–4** 'The Pill' more easily available in most Western countries **1966** Mao Zedong's 'Little Red Book' **1967** 'Summer of Love' – birth of the hippy movement **1968** Radical youth protest throughout Western world	**1961** Soviet cosmonaut Yuri Gagarin became the first man in space **1962** US telecommunications satellite Telstar **1963** Quasars discovered **1967** First heart transplant **1969** USA landed the first man on the Moon; test flights of Concorde – first supersonic airliner
1979 Somoza overthrown by Sandinistas in Nicaragua **1982** Falklands (Malvinas) War between Argentina and Britain following Argentine invasion of the Falkland Islands **1983** US-led forces invaded Grenada **1980–90** Spread of multi-party democracy to most Latin American countries **late 1980s** Colombia destabilized by drug trade; 'Shining Path' Maoist terrorists active in Peru **1989** US intervention in Panama	**1979** Islamic Revolution in Iran – rise of Islamic fundamentalism **1979–81** Iran hostage crisis **1980–8** Iran–Iraq War **1982** Israel invaded Lebanon **1986** Palestinian *intifada* (uprising) began **1990** Iraqi invasion of Kuwait **1991** Gulf War – US-led coalition defeated Iraq	**from mid-1970s** Hi Tech and Post-Modernist architecture **1976–80** 'Punk' music and fashion **1980s** Increase in relative poverty of Third World; Western aid to counter famine increased; spread of the AIDS virus **from 1980s** Increase in divorce and single-parent families in most Western countries **1988** Rushdie's *Satanic Verses* published	**1978** First test tube baby **1980s** Great improvement in computer performance; microcomputers in general use **1981** USA launched the *Columbia* space shuttle **1982** First commercial compact discs **1986** Chernobyl nuclear disaster in USSR

The Causes of World War I

Many theories have been put forward to account for the conflict that was to tear Europe apart between 1914 and 1918. Some have suggested that the Great Powers stumbled into war almost by accident in a volatile climate of mounting international tension; while others, notably Marxists, have viewed World War I as the inevitable outcome of capitalist and imperialist rivalry between states. Despite differences of emphasis, most analyses are united in focusing on certain key factors. Principal among these was the existence of a complex European alliance system, which heightened the possibility of coalition war, especially in the light of the antagonism between Austria-Hungary and Russia – an antagonism exacerbated by nationalist agitation in the Balkans. The distrust of German ambitions on the part of France, Russia and Britain also played a crucial role.

By 1914, Europe was divided into two armed camps, based on political, territorial and economic rivalries. In the centre of Europe was a recently unified Germany, allied to Austria-Hungary since 1879 and Italy since 1882, fearful of attack by France and Russia (allied since 1894), yet threatening expansion against either or both. Britain, traditionally aloof, viewed German industrial development, naval expansion and colonial ambitions (▷ pp. 160–3) with distrust, and from 1904 was associated with Germany's rivals.

The new Germany

On 18 January 1871, as the Franco-Prussian War was drawing to a dismal close for the French (▷ p. 153), an extraordinary declaration was made in the Hall of Mirrors in the Palace of Versailles. The king of Prussia was proclaimed Kaiser (emperor) Wilhelm I of a unified Germany, stretching from the Baltic to the Danube, from the Vosges to the Vistula. It radically altered the map of Europe, producing a powerful single state where before there had been a host of smaller territories.

The chief instigator of German unity was the Prussian Chancellor, Bismarck (▷ p. 153), and his policies thereafter were dedicated to strengthening and ensuring the survival of the new state. His main worries centred on French ambitions to recover Alsace-Lorraine, annexed by Germany as part of the Treaty of Frankfurt (1871) to ensure that France would be denied territorial access to the Rhine. If Germany was to survive, France had to be kept isolated: in short, a new balance of power in Europe, favourable to Germany, had to be created and maintained.

The alliance system

With this aim in view, as early as 1873

Bismarck negotiated a *Dreikaiserbund* ('Three Emperors' League'), an alliance between Germany, Austria-Hungary and Russia. It did not last, principally because of clashes over policy in the Balkans between Vienna and St Petersburg (▷ pp. 154–5). In 1879 it was effectively replaced by a much firmer Dual Alliance between Germany and Austria-Hungary, aimed at mutual protection against France and Russia respectively. Three years later, in response to French expansion in North Africa, Italy joined them to produce the Triple Alliance (1882).

Although these alliances gave a degree of strength to a Central European bloc, they did little to solve – and, ironically, much to exacerbate – Germany's major strategic problem: that of simultaneous attacks by France and Russia. Bismarck, aware that these two peripheral powers were by no means natural allies, prevented them from coming together. However, after his resignation in 1890, German diplomacy fell into the less capable hands of the new Kaiser, Wilhelm II, and Germany became less sensitive to the concerns of the Russians, particularly in the Balkans. By 1894 it was obvious that the Kaiser was more interested in strengthening ties with Vienna than with St Petersburg, and the Russians, fearful of Austrian expansionism in the Balkans, entered into an alliance with France. The German strategic nightmare began to assume reality, colouring every crisis thereafter with the dark possibility of war.

Militarism and imperialism

But the creation of alliances alone does not produce war; they are merely manifestations of fear and rivalry, centred in this case upon trade, territory and nationalism. In the aftermath of unification, Germany gained enormous economic strength, fuelled by the annexation of already developed industries in Alsace-Lorraine and by a massive cash indemnity

Le Petit Journal
SUPPLÉMENT ILLUSTRÉ

LE NEZ DE LA TRIPLICE
imité du « Laocoön » antique

imposed on the French after the Franco-Prussian War. This, together with the exploitation of resources and skills within the new Germany, ensured the emergence of a dynamic state, capable of using surplus capital and finished products to extend its influence far and wide. At the same time, unification enabled the Prussians to raise and train military forces, equipped with the latest weapons. To the Kaiser, increased military strength was essential as a means of protecting Germany against the threat of concerted attack, but to many outside it smacked of deliberate aggrandizement, designed to spearhead and protect German expansion both within and beyond Europe.

Germany's determination to increase its economic and military strength was manifested also in its search for colonies overseas. Territorial gains could be exploited as resource-centres and markets, but also carried with them the undeniable prestige associated with imperialist expansion. From 1884, Germany acquired an empire consisting of territories in Africa and Oceania (▷ pp. 160–3). In order to ensure free passage to and from the new territories, the Kaiser authorized the creation of an ocean-going navy in 1897–8, enlarging it still further two years later (▷ box).

Britain tilts the balance

Such expansion was guaranteed to antagonize the British, whose aloofness from the alliance system had helped to maintain a rough balance in Europe. As long as the alliance blocs had rough parity, neither could gain an advantage. But were one or the other to be joined by an uncommitted great power, the balance would be destabilized.

Germany tried to tilt the balance by making the alliance with Italy in 1882 and by pursuing ties with Turkey. In 1889, the Kaiser made a well-publicized visit to Istanbul and, ten years later, German engineers were granted a concession to build railways in Turkey, as part of a project to link Berlin and Baghdad. At the same time, German officers helped to train and modernize the Turkish army; although this was offset by British involvement in training the Turkish navy, it was more than enough to alarm the Russians. Nevertheless, neither Italy nor Turkey had 'great power' status: the only contender in the end was Britain.

It took time for Anglo-German antagonism to develop. At first, in the 1880s, Germany's colonial policy was tolerated – indeed, colonial clashes between the great powers were generally settled without recourse to force. This was shown in the aftermath of the Berlin Conference of 1884–5, when unexplored Africa was 'parcelled out' quite amicably, and was still apparent as late as 1898, when British and French claims to Fashoda in the Sudan were settled peacefully (▷ pp. 160–3). But Britain could not ignore German expansion indefinitely; when it began to be coupled to statements that seemed deliberately provocative – as in 1896,

A satirical French allegory (right) from 1896 of the Triple Alliance (Germany, Austria-Hungary and Italy), based on the famous Greek statue of Laocoön and his sons being crushed to death by serpents. France and Russia, apparently more happily matched in their alliance, march blithely by.

when the Kaiser publicly backed the Boers of South Africa against the British (⊳ pp. 160–3) – distrust grew.

Britain was forced out of isolation. In 1902 a treaty was signed between Japan and Britain to counter Russian influence in the Far East and enable Britain to avoid a naval race in the Pacific. Two years later, an *entente* (an 'understanding' short of a formal alliance) was agreed between Britain and France, opening the way to 'informal' military talks that had only one conceivable objective – the containment of Germany. Britain's entry into the Franco-Russian sphere was consolidated in 1907 by the signing of a further *entente* between London and St Petersburg. This was made possible (in British eyes) by the defeat of Russia by Japan in 1904–5 (⊳ pp. 65 and 180) and the subsequent shift of Russian interests away from the Far East. By 1907, therefore, the alliance balance had begun to tilt, to the detriment of Germany and Austria-Hungary, although Britain was still not formally an ally of France and Russia. The Kaiser continued to hope for British neutrality, if not friendship.

The Moroccan crises

Crises now became much harder to 'manage'. In 1905, for example, the Kaiser grew alarmed at reports that the French and Spanish were planning to partition Morocco (still under Turkish suzerainty) and convened an international conference at Algeciras to gain support for Moroccan independence. This was agreed in January 1906, but, unknown to the Kaiser, the Anglo-French *entente* of 1904 had contained an agreement that the British were prepared to tolerate French expansion in northwest Africa if the French reciprocated over British policies in Egypt. The French therefore felt safe to pursue their claims to Morocco, occupying its then capital, Fez, in 1911. The

Kaiser responded by sending a gunboat to Agadir and war was only narrowly averted. Germany was humiliated and the Kaiser aggrieved.

The Balkans

Far from bloodless, however, were another series of simultaneous crises inside Europe. These were centred on the Balkans – a hotbed of nascent Slavic nationalisms caught between a desire to throw off the last vestiges of Ottoman Turkish rule on the one hand and the rival policies of Austria-Hungary and Russia

on the other. This state of affairs was by no means new; as early as 1878, at the Congress of Berlin (⊳ p. 155), the great powers had tried to deal with the problem by affirming the independence of Serbia, Romania and Montenegro, but this merely fuelled the nationalist aspirations of other Slavic peoples, particularly the Bulgarians, who naturally looked to Russia for support. In 1908 the Bulgarians declared their independence. In response, Austria-Hungary annexed Bosnia and Herzegovina, hoping to create a buffer against the spread of political unrest. All it succeeded in doing was to alarm the Balkan states, fearful of Austro Hungarian expansionism.

Serbia, Bulgaria, Montenegro and Greece now formed the Balkan League and displayed their power by declaring war on, and defeating, Turkey (now under the more dynamic leadership of the 'Young Turks') in the First Balkan War (1912–13). Almost immediately, they fell out over the spoils, with Bulgaria demanding more territory than Serbia and Greece were prepared to give. The result was a Second Balkan War (1913), in which Bulgaria was roundly defeated and stripped of its earlier territorial gains. By now the great powers had lost control of the crisis and, as Austria-Hungary grew ever more fearful of Slavic nationalism and the support afforded to it by the Russians, the chances of an escalation to great-power involvement increased. All it needed was a spark to ignite the powder-keg of the alliance system, for once Austria-Hungary and Russia came into conflict they would be sure to drag their allies with them. That spark was provided on 28 June 1914 at Sarajevo. **JP**

Macedonian volunteers during the First Balkan War (1912–13) being issued with arms and equipment to sabotage telegraph wires. Macedonia was claimed by Serbia, Greece and Bulgaria, and divided between them in 1913.

THE ANGLO-GERMAN NAVAL RACE

The German Naval Laws of 1897 and 1898 alarmed the British. By adding 12 battleships and 33 cruisers to a navy that had hitherto been small, the Laws gave notice of the Kaiser's intention to create an ocean-going fleet. He never had the aim of building a navy more powerful than that of the British, but hoped to create a force that, if added to the navy of another great power, would challenge British maritime supremacy and therefore incline Britain to desire Germany as a naval ally. But the expansion plan triggered widespread fears in Britain, particularly since it coincided with similar naval construction in France, Italy, Japan and the USA.

Britain took up the challenge in 1903, after another Naval Law had doubled the projected number of German battleships. Naval rearmament was authorized, and a North Sea fleet established, based at Rosyth in Scotland to cover the main German ports. In 1906 the rivalry intensified with the unveiling by the British Admiralty of the first 'Dreadnought' – a

heavily armed and armoured fast battleship that rendered all previous designs obsolete. The Germans had responded to this development by 1907, their Chief of Naval Staff Admiral Alfred von Tirpitz announcing a programme of construction of Dreadnought-class battleships for the High Seas Fleet. Two years later, public alarm in Britain at the number of new ships being laid down by Germany forced a political crisis over how many new Dreadnoughts should be built to ensure superiority. With the slogan 'We want eight and we won't wait' ringing in their ears, the British government of H.H. Asquith ordered yet another round of construction.

The Agadir crisis of 1911 (⊳ main text) did nothing to calm the situation and, despite periodic attempts at international agreement to limit naval rearmament, the race went on. It may not have caused World War I, but it helped to align Britain with France and Russia, thereby achieving the reverse of the Kaiser's intention.

World War I

On 28 June 1914 the Archduke Franz Ferdinand, heir to the throne of Austria-Hungary, was assassinated in Sarajevo, capital of Bosnia, a region of the Balkans then part of the Austro-Hungarian Empire (▷ p. 175). The Austrians – supported by the Germans, who feared for the disintegration of their ally – blamed the newly independent neighbouring state of Serbia and threatened to attack. The Serbs in turn appealed for aid from their fellow Slavs in Russia, who began to mobilize their vast army.

Fearing attack, Germany put into action a strategy known as the Schlieffen Plan, and declared war on both Russia and France. The Plan was designed to knock out France (Russia's ally) before the Russians completed mobilization, so avoiding a two-front war. As German troops crossed into neutral Belgium as a preliminary to their attack on France, Britain (which had guaranteed Belgian independence) declared war on Germany.

The battle lines were drawn. On the one side were the Allies (Britain, France and Russia), and on the other the Central Powers (Germany and Austria-Hungary). Italy held back. By 4 August Europe had been plunged into a conflict that was to last for over four years, killing an estimated 20 million people.

Opening moves

Everyone expected a short war, but previous military plans soon became irrelevant. The French, intent on recovering the provinces of Alsace and Lorraine (lost to the Germans in 1870; ▷ p. 153), mounted a major attack around Metz on 14 August, only to suffer enormous casualties. Meanwhile the Germans swept into Belgium towards northeastern France, aiming to take Paris in a huge outflanking movement. However, the Germans, with large distances to cover, lost momentum in the broiling heat of summer. This allowed the French to scrape together a new army to defend Paris, counterattacking across the River Marne in early September to force the Germans back. Both sides then tried to outflank the other to the north, but neither could gain advantage. The rival armies dug in and, by October, had created a line of trenches from the Channel to the Swiss border (▷ box, 'Tactics and Weapons').

By then the Germans had been forced to divert armies to the east. The Russians had initially made a ponderous advance into East Prussia in August, but were defeated in a series of battles around Tannenberg. Further south the Russians were more successful, pushing the Austrians back in Galicia, necessitating a German reinforcement to prevent defeat. By Christmas 1914 a two-front war had become a reality for Germany.

The trench nightmare

Warfare on the Western Front was characterized by the trench system. This emerged to a large extent because of new weapons that gave the advantage to the defender (▷ box). If one side wished to attack – as Britain and France did in order to liberate northeastern France and Belgium – their soldiers had to do so through mud, across barbed wire and into the teeth of machine guns and quick-fire artillery. In 1915, as casualties mounted alarmingly, the nature of the war changed, forcing all the major combatants to raise large armies and to mobilize their societies to produce new armaments (▷ box 'The Impact of War'). Anglo-French offensives in Champagne (February), at Neuve Chapelle (March) and Loos (September) failed to break the deadlock in the west, while on the Eastern Front the situation, although more fluid, similarly denied victory to either side.

Instead, the war expanded. In October 1914 the Turks declared war on the Allies, and in May 1915 Italy – in return for Allied promises of territorial gains from Austria-Hungary – declared war on the Central Powers, opening up new fronts that drained resources. In mid-1915 the Germans forced the Russians back through Poland, taking pressure off Germany's eastern border, and in October Bulgaria joined the Central Powers. Only in Serbia was a decisive campaign fought: by December 1915 the country had been conquered by the Central Powers.

The nightmare deepened in 1916. In February the Germans made an attack around Verdun on the River Meuse. The French obliged by pouring in reserves until, by December, the fighting had cost each side about 700 000 men. On 1 July the British tried to break through on the River Somme, losing 57 000 soldiers in the first few hours; by November this figure had risen to 460 000. On the Eastern Front it was even worse: a Russian offensive in June enjoyed initial success near the Carpathian Mountains, only to be turned back three months later at a cost of a million men. The Russian Army came perilously close to collapse.

Things were no better in 1917: after a failed French offensive in Champagne in April, elements of the French Army mutinied, while at Passchendaele in July the British entered a nightmare of mud that cost a further half-million casualties. Only on the Austrian-Italian front was there a break in the stalemate, with the massive defeat of the Italians at Caporetto.

Alternatives to trench deadlock

In such circumstances, alternatives to

French soldiers wearing gas marks prepare to go 'over the top'. In the First Battle of the Somme (June–November 1916), British and French forces attacked from trenches on a 34 km (21 mi) front. Torrential rain in October turned the battlefield into a nightmare of impassable mud. By the time the front stabilized again in November, the new Allied trenches were only 8 km (5 mi) in advance of the old front line, but 460 000 British, 450 000 German, and 200 000 French lives had been lost.

TACTICS AND WEAPONS

In August 1914 all the combatants expected to fight a short, sharp war, based on mobility. On the battlefield this meant an ability to mass troops quickly at the decisive point, to outmanoeuvre the enemy and to advance into his territory, bringing him to battle at times and places he was not expecting. The onus was therefore on cavalry, horse-drawn artillery and supplies, and fast-marching infantry – the latter equipped with magazine-fed, bolt-action rifles and water-cooled machine guns.

As it turned out, the firepower produced by these weapons was sufficient to halt the German advance on Paris at the battle of the Marne in September 1914 (though the French had to resort to the desperate measure of rushing troops from Lorraine to the Marne by taxi to bolster their beleaguered forces north of Paris). The Germans, realizing the rapid victory they had hoped for had been denied them, dug in for a longer campaign. Each side probed the other's flanks, but by October 1914 a defensive line of trenches had been created, stretching from the Belgian coast to Switzerland. The result was a deadlock in which the defender, dug in and secure behind machine guns and barbed wire, held the advantage. It was to last for nearly four years, and was mirrored to a lesser extent on all other fronts (⊳ map, p. 178).

The first and most logical response to the deadlock was to try to punch a hole through enemy trenches using artillery, allowing infantry and cavalry to advance. The Allied commanders Marshal Joffre and Field Marshal Haig pursued this tactic with determination in 1916 when, in the eight days preceding the British attack on the Somme on 1 July, 1·7 million shells were poured onto German positions along a 40 km (25 mi) front. It had little effect: not only did the barrage give warning to the Germans of where to expect the next attack, it also churned up the ground, making it difficult for troops to advance. In addition, the shells proved incapable of destroying barbed wire, while most of the German machine gunners, secure in deep bunkers and pill boxes, survived. The British suffered over 57 000 casualties on the first day alone.

Other methods were tried. In April 1915, for example, the Germans used poison gas to asphyxiate the defending Allied troops in the Ypres salient. The effects of gas – used initially by the Germans against the Russians in January and then widely by both sides – were horrific, but they could be reduced by issuing soldiers with respirators (gas masks). Attempts to tunnel beneath enemy defences, detonating mines to coincide with an advance, could be spectacular – in June 1917 the British detonated nearly a million pounds of high explosives under the Messines Ridge, destroying German trenches – but they were not 'war winners'.

Victory would clearly go to the side that successfully countered the surface defences, enabling infantry to advance without suffering horrendous casualties. To the British, the answer lay in the tank, designed in 1915 as a specific response to the trench deadlock. To enable it to cross trenches, flatten barbed wire and negotiate the mud of no-man's-land, it was designed with a lozenge shape and equipped with tracks; it also needed to overrun machine guns, so was armoured to withstand the bullets. When used for the first time on the Somme in September 1916, the tank had a dramatic effect, creating panic in German lines, but it was mechanically unreliable and vulnerable to any weapon more powerful than a machine gun. Only when used *en masse* at Cambrai in November 1917 did tanks achieve a significant breakthrough, but this was not exploited because the cavalry could not cross 'no-man's-land' in time.

Zensiert
Paul Hoffmann & Co.
Berlin-Schöneberg.

*Zerstörter engl. Tank
in den gestürmten engl. Linien zwischen Bapaume–Arras.*

In contrast, the German response to deadlock was the development of small groups of heavily armed but mobile 'stormtroops', whose job it was to infiltrate enemy defences prior to the main attack, spreading confusion in rear areas. Preceded by short 'hurricane' artillery barrages to preserve surprise, and equipped with weapons such as flamethrowers, light machine guns, mortars and grenades, as well as rifles, the stormtroops achieved outstanding success in March 1918, breaking through British lines with comparative ease. They were halted by a lack of supplies and the deployment of large Allied forces equipped with tanks and supported by ground-attack aircraft. Together, these weapons restored mobility to the battlefield, enabling the Allies to advance, break the stalemate and force the Germans – their resolve broken by political and economic difficulties at home – to surrender by November 1918.

A German propaganda postcard showing a captured British tank. The first tracked armoured vehicle used in World War I was an improvised British 'tank' constructed by mounting an armoured car body on a tracked tractor. By September 1916, 100 British tanks were in service. Over 40 French Schneider tanks entered service the following year. Although the USA and Italy also had tanks before the end of the war, Germany only produced about 20 of these revolutionary weapons.

attritional deadlock were sought. Britain, for example, devoted part of her effort to attacks against the outer edge of the Central Powers, searching for weaknesses. As early as September 1914 British forces had seized many of Germany's colonies in Africa, but a greater opportunity arose when Turkey came into the war.

Already regarded as the 'sick man' of Europe, a knock-out blow against Turkey would, it was argued, open up the southern flank of the Central Powers. In April 1915 a seaborne attack was made on the Gallipoli peninsula, on the Dardanelles Straits between the Aegean and Black Seas, with the main aim of taking Constantinople (now Istanbul). It failed, at a cost of 265 000 Allied troops, many of them Australian and New Zealand volunteers.

British troops resting on the banks of the captured St Quentin Canal. The town of St Quentin – which was almost completely destroyed during World War I – was at the centre of a major German offensive in March–April 1918 when the Germans advanced but overextended their lines.

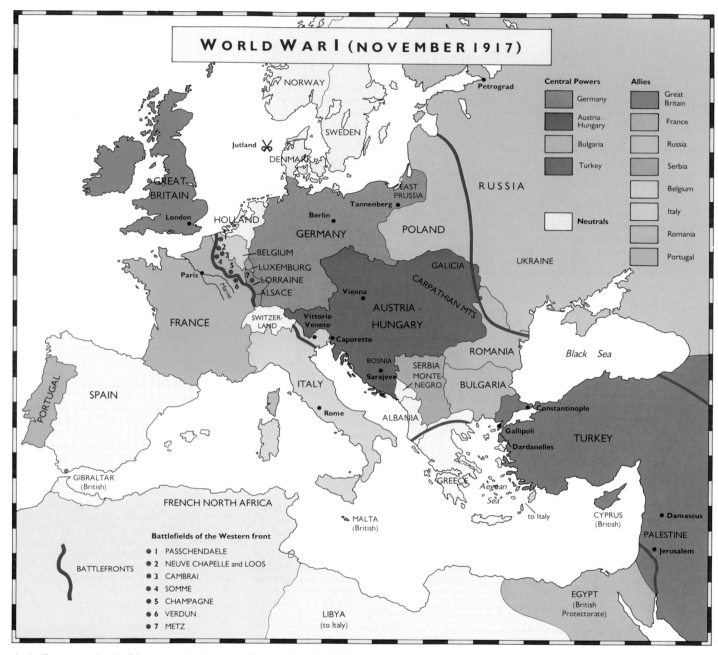

WORLD WAR I (NOVEMBER 1917)

Central Powers
- Germany
- Austria-Hungary
- Bulgaria
- Turkey

Neutrals

Allies
- Great Britain
- France
- Russia
- Serbia
- Belgium
- Italy
- Romania
- Portugal

Battlefields of the Western front
- 1 PASSCHENDAELE
- 2 NEUVE CHAPELLE and LOOS
- 3 CAMBRAI
- 4 SOMME
- 5 CHAMPAGNE
- 6 VERDUN
- 7 METZ

BATTLEFRONTS

A similar campaign in Mesopotamia (now Iraq) ended in disaster at Kut, on the road to Baghdad, in April 1916. Only later, in Mesopotamia and Palestine (the latter aided by an Arab revolt coordinated by T.E. Lawrence), was success achieved, but the costs were high and resources diverted from the war in France.

Other alternatives were also tried, using the sea and air to reinforce the pressures of conflict on land. At sea, fleet actions were rare – the only major engagement between the British and Germans, at Jutland in May 1916, ended in stalemate – but from the start of the war both maritime powers attempted to impose blockades on their rivals. Britain was successful, but Germany was not.

The German U-boat (submarine) offensive caused heavy British losses, but in 1917, with a declaration of unrestricted warfare against any ships suspected of trading with Britain, it helped to trigger a declaration of war against the Central

Powers by the USA. Using protected convoys and new anti-submarine weapons, the British gradually gained the initiative. By late 1918 the British blockade of Germany had led to starvation and social unrest, but that year the Central Powers gained the Ukraine with its rich harvests. Germany mounted bombing raids on England by Zeppelin airships and aircraft, but they had little effect on the war effort. In the end, whoever won the land battles would prevail, and this meant looking to new weapons and tactics to break the trench deadlock (▷ p. 177).

Allied victory

By the end of 1917 the balance of power between the two sides had shifted. In late 1917 Russia dissolved into revolutionary chaos (▷ p. 180) and the Germans took the opportunity to attack, with decisive results: by March 1918 a peace treaty between the two countries had been signed. This enabled the Germans to concentrate their forces in the west for a major assault on the British and French

before American troops arrived in Europe in large numbers.

The German offensive enjoyed some success in March, using new stormtrooper tactics first tried out at Cambrai in 1917 (▷ box, p. 177), but by the middle of April Allied forces had rallied and stopped the advance. In August they moved onto the offensive, using tanks supported by ground-attack aircraft and, significantly, involving the first of the newly arrived American divisions. Elsewhere, the Central Powers began to crumble, first in the Middle East, where British troops took Jerusalem and Damascus and defeated the Turks, then in Italy, where the Austro-Hungarians were defeated at Vittorio Veneto and forced to seek terms. By November the Germans were isolated. With public confidence in the government evaporating, Communism spreading from the east and the Allies closing in, the German Kaiser fled to Holland and an armistice was arranged. At 11 AM on 11 November 1918 the fighting ceased.   JP

VERDUN: THE KILLING GROUND

In an effort to break Allied resolve on the Western Front, the German commander Erich von Falkenhayn decided in early 1916 to mount a major assault on French positions around the town of Verdun on the River Meuse. Although the area was well protected by fortresses, covering an obvious route to Paris, Falkenhayn believed that it was of such strategic importance to the French that they would be sure to respond by pouring in reinforcements. The German plan was to allow this to happen, and then to hit the reinforcements with concentrated artillery fire: the French Army would be 'bled white', leaving the British to face future attacks alone.

The assault began on 21 February along a 12 km (8 mi) front and enjoyed some success: four days later, amid snow-squalls and artillery fire, the key position of Fort Douaumont was taken by a small group of German soldiers, led by a sergeant. The French reacted as expected, sending a stream of reserves to plug the gap. They entered the battlefield along the *Voie Sacrée* ('Sacred Way') in convoys of lorries carrying up to 20 000 men a day into a hell of mud, gas, artillery fire, freezing trenches and continuous fighting. At the same time, however, the Germans were unable to exploit their initial gains, being forced to commit their own reserves to prevent defeat. They attempted a fresh attack on 5 March, only to lose more and more soldiers for less and less gain.

Chances of a German victory slipped away amid hand-to-hand fighting and mounting casualties. Despite the capture of Fort Vaux on 9 June, the Germans found that the French were prepared to accept heavy losses and, in addition, were capable of inflicting crippling damage on the attacking army. The battle lasted until December, by which time nearly one and a half million men had been lost – about 700 000 on each side. It was the epitome of senseless war.

An American recruiting poster invoking the spectre of German militarism. As well as sporting a 'Kaiser Bill' moustache, the ape wears a helmet of the German imperial army, while its bloodstained cudgel bears the German word *Kultur* ('Culture'). Similar images appeared on posters produced by all the opposing states in World War I.

THE IMPACT OF WAR

In order to create and supply the large armed forces needed in World War I, entire societies had to be mobilized. The most pressing demand was for men in uniform, and this necessitated the introduction or extension of conscription. Most European states already had conscription in 1914, but they had to call up their reservists and cast the net wide to keep the ranks filled. In Britain, where pre-war military service was voluntary, the Secretary of State for War, Lord Kitchener, called for 100 000 new recruits in 1914, but succeeded in raising over 1·5 million. However, when they were decimated on the Somme two years later, even Britain had to introduce conscription. By 1918 all able-bodied men between the ages of 17 and 41 were eligible for call-up.

Such demands depleted the industrial workforce and, to begin with, industry did suffer. In France, as reservists were recalled to service in 1914, over 50% of industrial establishments were forced to close, while the rush of 'Kitchener Volunteers' in Britain at the same time left key sectors of the economy seriously short of manpower. There was a crisis in weapons production, particularly of artillery shells, and both Britain and France had no choice but to recall skilled tradesmen from their armed forces and to open industrial work to sectors of the population (especially women) not previously associated with heavy labour. Even then, the problems were not solved easily.

In such circumstances, governments in all combatant states had to intervene to direct labour and legislate control of the war effort. In Britain, under the Defence of the Realm Acts (DORA; 1914, 1915 and 1916), the government took direct control of all aspects of war production, and made it illegal for war-workers to move away from their place of employment. Left-wing activists on Clydeside found themselves forcibly transferred to other parts of the country. The government also placed restrictions on opening hours in public houses and introduced the novel concept of 'summer time', in which all clocks were put forward an hour to give extra daylight for farming. In Germany, similar control was exercised by means of a Law of Siege, introduced in 1914. Other aspects of central control involved the rationing of food and the introduction of press censorship to reflect a positive view of the war.

Not everyone accepted such controls. In industry, trade-union activity increased and, although cooperation with management was generally good, strikes did occur: in 1917, for instance, British engineering workers downed tools in pursuit of better wages and conditions. Moreover, some people refused to bear arms, pleading religious or moral scruples: such 'conscientious objectors' could be imprisoned, fined (as in the case of Bertrand Russell), or forced to work on the land instead. Even within the armed forces, mutiny was not unknown: in 1917 the French Army, sickened by the slaughter at Verdun and elsewhere, suffered a rash of 'combat refusals' that was halted only when the ringleaders were tried and shot.

In response to such unease, governments used propaganda to persuade their people to accept the sacrifices and contribute to the war effort. Posters, newspaper articles and newsreels in the newly popular cinemas portrayed the enemy as evil and spread stories (many of them false) about atrocities. This did not always work – by 1918 many people were cynical about the management of the war – but it was indicative of the ways in which societies had to adapt to the demands of an unprecedented, almost total, conflict.

Nor were the effects confined to the war years. In Britain, France and Germany particularly, it was noticeable that the heavy casualties – concentrated as they were among the young – left countries short of 'natural leaders' in the postwar period. An entire generation had been decimated, and many who survived were so deeply affected by their horrific experiences that it made the solution of later economic and social problems more difficult.

Women working in a munitions factory. World War I affected every part of society in the combatant countries. Many women entered the labour market for the first time, filling the gap left by those men who had been conscripted.

SEE ALSO

- THE PEAK OF EMPIRE p. 160
- THE CAUSES OF WORLD WAR I p. 174
- THE RUSSIAN REVOLUTIONS p. 180
- THE POSTWAR SETTLEMENT p. 182
- THE DEPRESSION p. 184
- THE GROWTH OF FASCISM p. 186

The Russian Revolutions

At the turn of the 20th century Russia was a feudal state. Tsar Nicholas II ruled, as his ancestors had ruled before him, as an autocratic monarch. Nicholas had the backing of a large and inefficient bureaucracy, but remained supreme. His will was enforced by the state police and the army, and his officials controlled education and censored the press. Dissent was ruthlessly crushed. It was a situation ripe for revolution.

The vast majority of Russian subjects were poverty-stricken peasants, controlled through 'land captains' appointed by the government. Although serfdom (virtual ownership of the peasants by the land-owning classes; ▷ p. 126) had been abolished in 1861, the peasants were closely bound to the land by a communal system of landholding.

Nevertheless, increasing numbers migrated to the cities, for Russia began to industrialize rapidly in the first decade of the 20th century with the aid of Western, particularly French, capital. Life for the 15 million or so members of the urban working class was harsh. Housing and conditions in the factories were poor, providing fertile ground for the growth of radical and revolutionary political parties. The two most important such parties were the Social Democrats and the Social Revolutionaries. The effective leader of the former was Vladimir Ilyich Ulyanov, better known as Lenin.

The roots of revolution

In 1904–5 Russia fought and lost a war

The Cossack charge on demonstrators outside the Winter Palace, St Petersburg, in January 1905. The protesters were led by a priest, Georgy Gapon, who was active in one of the official workers' societies. Disorders following 'Bloody Sunday' were most severe in non-Russian parts of the empire where Polish, Latvian, Georgian and Ukrainian nationalism resurfaced.

THE ROOTS OF RADICAL DISSENT

By 1917 the Russian people could look back to over a century of radical – and often violent – opposition to the tsarist regime. It had its immediate origins in the defeat of Napoleon in 1815, when Russian army officers first came into contact with Western liberal traditions. In 1825, when Tsar Alexander I died, a group of such officers, known as 'Decembrists' from the date of their revolt, tried to use the army to force the new tsar, Nicholas I, to introduce reforms, but without success.

Nicholas responded by using repression to preserve the status quo. His will was imposed by the army bureaucracy and police. Dissenting intellectuals were forced underground and organized themselves in secret societies. By the 1840s two distinct and polarized strands of opposition had emerged among the intelligentsia: a 'Slavophile' movement advocating the preservation of Russian culture through the Orthodox church and the village community, and a 'Westernizing' movement (prominent among which were the revolutionaries Alexander Herzen and Mikhail Bakunin) favouring the introduction of Western-style technology and liberal government.

Bakunin was a founder-member of the Populist Movement, a group of agrarian socialists who believed that the only way to achieve reform was from below, by mobilizing the peasant masses through socialist communes to overthrow the tsar and establish a democratic republic. The Utopian dreams of the Populists were not to be realized, however. Although the Russian peasantry were among the most oppressed in Europe – even after Tsar Alexander II's emancipation of the serfs in

1861 – they did not respond to ideas imposed upon them by an alien middle class. Populism reached an extreme in the 1870s when members of the intelligentsia left their homes to live and work among the peasants, hoping to inspire them to revolution, but tsarist repression soon restored order.

Faced with the failure of their attempts to promote social revolution among the peasantry, some radicals turned to terrorism, aiming to force change by instilling fear into the tsarist establishment. In 1879 the revolutionary Populist organization 'Land and Liberty' split after a disagreement over tactics. The extremist faction spawned by this split – the 'People's Will' movement – was responsible for a wave of bombings and shootings, culminating in the assassination of Alexander II on 1 March 1881.

But this did not trigger a mass revolt, partly because of effective repression by the secret police and partly because the ordinary people had not been involved in Land and Liberty. Terrorism was temporarily discredited, although the use of violence as a political weapon did not disappear. By the 1890s two separate strands of revolutionary socialism had emerged in Russia. The first, represented by the Social Revolutionary Party, sought to mobilize the peasantry through village communes on the old Populist pattern. The second, represented by the Social Democratic Party, was more interested in the spread of Marxist ideas among the dispossessed and resentful urban working class. In the event, it was an offshoot of the latter – Lenin's Bolsheviks – that was to seize and hold power in November 1917.

with Japan. Even before this, unrest had been growing in both urban and rural areas. The defeat at the hands of the Japanese precipitated a revolution. On 'Bloody Sunday' (22 January 1905) troops opened fire on a peaceful demonstration

near the Tsar's Winter Palace in the capital, St Petersburg. About 1000 protesters, including women and children, were killed. This was followed by a general strike, peasant uprisings in the countryside, rioting, assassinations and army mutinies. In October 1905 the Tsar agreed to elections to a *Duma*, or parliament. This rallied moderate political reformers to the side of the government, which was able to crush the revolt.

The first two Dumas proved to be too radical for the Tsar's taste, but in 1907 a conservative Duma was elected after electoral changes. Some reforms did take place under the chief minister, Petr Arkadievich Stolypin, who curbed the power of the land captains and helped to create a small class of peasants who owned their own land. However, Stolypin was unpopular with both Left and Right, and was assassinated.

World War I placed Russian society under tremendous strain. After three years of war the army had suffered 8 million casualties and over 1 million men had deserted. Inflation was rife and the peasants began to stop sending their produce to the cities, leading to food shortages. Respect for the imperial government – which was seen to be domin-

ated by the corrupt and debauched monk Grigori Efimovich Rasputin – had crumbled and revolutionary propaganda began to spread among the soldiers and workers.

On 8 March 1917 revolution broke out in Petrograd (as St Petersburg had been renamed in 1914). *Soviets* (councils) of soldiers, workers and peasants were set up all over Russia. On 15 March the Tsar abdicated and a moderate provisional government was set up. In the summer of 1917 Aleksandr Fyodorovich Kerenski became the chief minister, but the powerful Petrograd soviet was controlled by Lenin and his followers. On 7–8 November (25–26 October in the old Russian calendar) Kerenski was ousted in a coup led by Lenin.

Lenin and the Bolsheviks

Lenin had studied the ideas of Karl Marx (⊳ p. 168) and aimed to replace capitalism with a Communist workers' state. He decided that the Russian people needed to be led by a well-educated, dedicated revolutionary elite. His opponents in the Social Democratic Party, who wished to build a mass party, were dubbed *Mensheviks* (or the minority), although in fact it was the followers of Lenin, the *Bolsheviks* (or majority), who formed the smaller group.

When the March revolution began, Lenin was in exile in Switzerland, but in April 1917 he was allowed by the Germans to return to Russia in a sealed train. He immediately began to plot the downfall of the provisional government, which had misguidedly decided to continue the war with Germany and was slow in introducing land reform. Lenin's promise of 'bread, peace and land' won many to the Bolshevik cause. After he seized power in November 1917, Lenin moved against rival socialist groups, using the Cheka (secret police; ⊳ p. 199) as a weapon, and executed the deposed Tsar and his family.

The Bolsheviks were forced to accept a harsh peace with Germany at Brest-Litovsk in March 1918, but this allowed the Bolsheviks to turn their attention to the civil war that had begun in Russia. The 'Reds' were opposed by the 'Whites' – a loose coalition of democrats, socialists and reactionaries, united only by their opposition to Lenin – and by armies sent by Britain, France, Japan and the USA.

However, the various White factions were unable to coordinate their strategy, and they were defeated piecemeal by the Red Army created by Leon Trotsky, a former Menshevik. By mid-1920 it was clear that the Bolsheviks had triumphed. Russia was then attacked by Poland, which was intent on seizing territory in western Russia. The Red Army weathered the attack and then advanced as far as Warsaw before suffering a defeat on the Vistula.

During the civil war the Red Army also reconquered most of the European non-Russian areas of the former Tsarist empire that had formed their own republics in 1917–18. The federal republic of Transcaucasia – Armenia, Georgia and

Azerbaijan – was captured in 1920 and the independent state of the Ukraine – created with German encouragement in 1918 – was not finally suppressed by the Red Army until 1921. The recaptured territories – along with Soviet Central Asia – were reorganized into the Union of Soviet Socialist Republics, which was formally established in 1922.

However, the northwestern borderlands – ceded by Russia at Brest-Litovsk – became the independent states of Finland, Estonia, Latvia and Lithuania. Finland fought a civil war in 1918 to defeat Bolshevik rebels and retained its independence. The Baltic states – which had all established republican democratic constitutions by 1922 – were not reoccupied by the Soviets until 1940.

Economic problems and the NEP

In November 1917 the new Bolshevik government faced many economic problems. Initially, the government gained considerable support from the peasants who received land when the old estates were broken up. In June 1918 Lenin was forced to introduce 'War Communism', by which there was wholesale nationalization and state control of agriculture. This led to the collapse of industrial production and serious food shortages. In March 1921, after a serious naval mutiny at Kronstadt, the New Economic Policy (NEP) was introduced. This returned small businesses to private hands and allowed farmers to sell their crops. Previously, surplus produce had simply been requisitioned by the state, but now a class of *kulaks* (affluent peasant farmers) emerged. The NEP improved both industrial and agricultural output.

The death of Lenin in 1924 initiated a power struggle among his successors. By 1929 Joseph Stalin had emerged victorious and he remained the unchallenged ruler until his death in 1953. His chief rival had been Trotsky, who had advocated spreading revolution across Eur-

ope. In the mid-1920s Trotsky was eased out of power and eventually went into exile in Mexico, where he was murdered in 1940 by a Spanish Communist, probably acting for Stalin. Stalin's policy of building 'socialism in one country' was undoubtedly more realistic, given the weakness of the USSR, but it was one that led to untold suffering for the Soviet people (⊳ p. 198).

The USSR and Europe

Although European governments feared that the USSR was bent on spreading revolution to their countries, the Soviets played relatively little part in European affairs in this period. The 1922 Treaty of Rapallo brought the USSR together with Germany, but with the emergence of Hitler, the Soviets began a bitter war of propaganda against the Nazis.

From 1934 onwards Stalin moved towards Britain and France. However, disillusioned by the policies of appeasement and worried at the prospect of Soviet isolation, Stalin signed a non-aggression pact with Hitler in 1939, agreeing to partition Poland between their two countries (⊳ p. 189). This gave the Soviets a breathing space, but it was only to last until June 1941, when Hitler invaded the USSR (⊳ p. 192). JP

SEE ALSO
- THE EMERGENCE OF RUSSIA p. 126
- THE EASTERN QUESTION p. 154
- INDUSTRIAL SOCIETY IN THE 19TH CENTURY p. 164
- WORLD WAR II: THE EAST p. 192
- THE SOVIET EMPIRE p. 198

A Soviet propaganda poster (1924) portraying the tasks of chemical workers, supplying gas for warfare and fertilizer for agriculture during peacetime.

Bolshevik leaders including Lenin and Trotsky. The Bolsheviks – who were renamed Communists at the Seventh Party Congress in 1918 – established a single-party dictatorship by 1920, in turn banning the conservative parties, the Right and Left Socialist Revolutionaries, and finally the Mensheviks.

The Postwar Settlement

Two months after Germany was forced to ask the Allies for an armistice to end World War I (▷ p. 179), the Paris Peace Conference opened. Although 32 states (but neither Germany nor Russia) sent representatives, most of the major decisions were taken by the 'Big Three' – the British and French prime ministers (David Lloyd George and Georges Clemençeau) and the US president (Woodrow Wilson). What they decided was to lay the foundations for the future of the world.

France had lost 1.4 million men in the war and Clemençeau was determined to weaken Germany so that it could never again threaten French security. Among his demands was a demilitarized 'buffer zone' in the Rhineland. Lloyd George, despite having exploited anti-German hysteria to win the December 1918 election, attempted to moderate the more extreme of Clemençeau's demands. In January 1918 Wilson had announced his 'Fourteen Points', which were to form the basis of a moderate peace based on national self-determination (▷ box). However, during the Conference the idealistic Wilson had to compromise with the demands of the French and British. The terms of the resulting Treaty of Versailles with Germany were severe, including a clause in which Germany accepted responsibility for the war.

Redrawing the map of Europe

The break-up of the German, Russian, Turkish and Austro-Hungarian empires gave the Big Three the opportunity to redraw the map of Europe and to fulfil one of their major aims of building up buffer states around Germany and Russia – the latter because of fears of its Communist revolution (▷ p. 180) spreading to other countries.

Under the Treaty of Versailles (signed on 28 June 1919) the state of Poland was created in the east and awarded the 'Danzig Corridor' – a belt of former

'**The military struggle** is over – now starts the struggle for political power.' A cartoon (1918) by Theodore Heine from the German satirical magazine *Simplicissimus*.

German land that gave the Poles access to the sea and separated East Prussia from the rest of Germany. Danzig (the modern Polish Gdansk) became a free city administered by the newly created League of Nations (▷ below). Germany also lost northern Schleswig to Denmark, and Eupen and Malmedy to Belgium. The provinces of Alsace and Lorraine (seized in 1870; ▷ p. 153) were returned to France. The Saarland was to be governed by an international commission for 15 years, until a referendum to decide its future, and the coalmines of the area given to France. The Rhineland was occupied by Allied troops and a 50-km (31 mi) wide swathe of land east of the Rhine was demilitarized. Control of German colonies overseas passed to the Allies under the guise of mandates from the League of Nations. The size of the German army was limited to 100 000 men, conscription was forbidden, and Germany was banned from possessing tanks, military aircraft and large naval vessels. In addition, heavy reparations were imposed (▷ below).

The victorious powers also signed treaties with Austria-Hungary. By the Treaty of St Germain (10 September 1919) Austria lost Bohemia (including the Sudetenland) and Moravia to the newly created state of Czechoslovakia; Galicia went to Poland; and Trieste, Istria and the South Tyrol to Italy. By the Treaty of Trianon (4 June 1921) Hungary, the other half of the old Dual Monarchy, was stripped of two thirds of its territory to help form Czechoslovakia, the new state of Yugoslavia and Poland. Under the terms of the Treaty of Neuilly (26 November 1919) Bulgaria ceded land to Greece. Austria, Hungary and Bulgaria – like Germany – were all forbidden to build up their troops beyond a certain level.

The Allies were forced to sign two treaties with Turkey. The first, the Treaty of Sèvres in August 1920, gave substantial parts of the old Ottoman Empire as mandates to France (which received 'Greater Syria') and Britain (which gained Palestine, Iraq and Transjordan; ▷ p. 210). However, an attempt by Greece, Britain

EUROPE IN 1922

- - - - - NATIONAL BOUNDARIES
in 1914 (where different)

▢ FREE CITIES

NORWAY
SWEDEN
FINLAND
ESTONIA
LATVIA
LITHUANIA
Memel
Danzig
EAST PRUSSIA
Moscow
SOVIET RUSSIA
DENMARK
NORTH SCHLESWIG
IRISH FREE STATE
GREAT BRITAIN
London
HOLLAND
GERMANY
RUHR
Weimar
SUDETENLAND
POLISH CORRIDOR
POLAND
BELGIUM
LUXEMBURG
RHINELAND
BOHEMIA
CZECHOSLOVAKIA
MORAVIA
GALICIA
Paris
Versailles
LORRAINE
BAVARIA
SAARLAND
Vienna
AUSTRIA
HUNGARY
ROMANIA
ALSACE
SWITZERLAND
Locarno
FRANCE
SOUTH TYROL
Trieste
Fiume
YUGOSLAVIA
BULGARIA
Ankara
ISTRIA
ZARA (to Italy)
ITALY
Rome
ALBANIA
TURKEY
PORTUGAL
SPAIN
GIBRALTAR (to Britain)
GREECE
to Italy
CYPRUS (to Britain)
SYRIA (French mandate)
MALTA (to Britain)
PALESTINE
TRANS-JORDAN (British mandates)
FRENCH NORTH AFRICA
EGYPT (British protectorate)
ITALIAN NORTH AFRICA

THE FOURTEEN POINTS

President Wilson of the USA proposed his 'Fourteen Points' on 8 January 1918. They enunciated the USA's aims in World War 1, and Wilson hoped they would provide the basis of a lasting peace. However, at the Paris Peace Conference, Wilson was forced by Britain and France to give way on many of them.

1. An open peace treaty, with no secret diplomacy.

2. Freedom of navigation in international waters.

3. The removal of international trade barriers.

4. Reduction in the armaments of all countries.

5. Impartial settlement of conflicting colonial claims, taking into account the interests of the colonial populations concerned.

6. The evacuation of foreign troops from Russian territory, and no further interference in Russia's own political self-determination (▷ p. 181).

7. The evacuation of German troops from Belgium, and a guarantee of Belgian sovereignty.

8. The evacuation of German troops from France, and the restoration of Alsace and Lorraine.

9. The adjustment of Italian frontiers on the basis of nationality.

10. Self-determination for all nationalities within the Austro-Hungarian Empire.

11. Removal of occupying forces from Romania, Montenegro and Serbia, and access to the sea for Serbia.

12. Guarantee of sovereignty of the Turkish portion of the Ottoman Empire, and self-determination for other nationalities within the Empire, plus free passage for all nations through the Dardanelles (between the Mediterranean and the Black Sea).

13. An independent Poland with access to the sea. (Poland had been partitioned between Prussia, Austria and Russia in the 18th century; ▷ p. 125.)

14. The formation of a 'general association of nations' – which was to become the League of Nations (▷ main text and box).

strife. Versailles, for example, resulted in ethnic Germans being placed under Polish and Czech rule in the Polish Corridor and the Sudetenland respectively. Italy, which had suffered heavy losses, left the Peace Conference disgruntled at her treatment by the Big Three, having failed to gain all the territory it had been promised when it entered the war on the Allied side. Above all, Germany emerged from the postwar settlement weakened and embittered but still the strongest power in central Europe. With the USA withdrawing into isolationism, France faced the prospect of a resurgent Germany alone, except for the unenthusiastic support of Britain and the weak and vulnerable states of Eastern Europe. The grievances of both Italy and Germany were to help undermine the fragile democratic systems in those countries (▷ p. 186).

The Versailles settlement has often been criticized for being too harsh; it has also been argued – in retrospect – that it was too mild and that only occupation and partition could have prevented future German aggression. One of the most bitterly resented aspects of the Treaty of Versailles was the imposition of monetary reparations (▷ pp. 184 and 186). Britain and France demanded the payment of reparations from Germany both to satisfy their desire for revenge and to pay off their enormous war debts to the USA: Britain owed $5 billion and France about $4 billion.

John Maynard Keynes, the British economist, warned that reparations would be damaging to the economies of the victorious powers as well as Germany, but he was ignored. In 1923, during a period of rampant inflation in Germany, the payment of reparations was unilaterally suspended. The French Army marched into the German industrial area of the Ruhr, which caused the German economy further damage. A promise that reparations would once again be paid induced the French to pull out in September 1923. Reparations were scrapped in 1932 without having been paid in full.

The League of Nations

Some of the events of the 1920s made the international scene appear somewhat brighter. For example, the League of Nations had been created at the Peace Conference in 1920 in an attempt to outlaw war. It was intended that aggressor states would be punished by economic sanctions, or in the last resort by military action by states that were members of the League. Unfortunately for the idea, the US Senate refused in 1920 to ratify the Treaty of Versailles, and the USA did not join the League, thus weakening it from the outset (▷ box).

However, the notion of 'collective security' survived and by the Locarno Treaties of 1925 Germany's western frontiers were guaranteed by Italy and Britain. At this time Germany joined the League. The Kellogg-Briand Pact (named after the US and French foreign ministers who proposed it in 1928) renounced war as a means of settling disputes, and was signed

THE COVENANT OF THE LEAGUE OF NATIONS

On 14 February 1919, President Wilson of the USA outlined the Covenant ('binding contract') of the projected League of Nations, to be established as part of the peace settlement. The Covenant was based on two principles – that 'no nation shall go to war . . . until every other possible means of settling the dispute shall have been full and fairly tried', and that 'under no circumstances shall any nation seek forcibly to disturb the territorial settlement arrived at as a consequence of this peace or to interfere with the political independence of any of the States of the world'. Agreed by 32 states, the League came into existence on 10 January 1920, and was dedicated to the achievement of international security through 'collective action'. The League was crippled from the start by the refusal of the US Senate to ratify the Covenant, thereby keeping the USA out of the major international body for preserving security.

Another problem was that 'collective action' was never adequately defined. The situation was complicated further in 1923 when the League adopted an 'interpretative resolution', which left it to member-states to decide how far they would go to prevent or punish aggression. A Geneva Protocol of 1924 tried to fill in the gaps by defining how the Council of the League reported on disputes, but this was not accepted by all member-states. Such confusions left the League ill-equipped to deal with the new round of international aggression in the 1930s (▷ p. 188).

The impotence of the League of Nations is lampooned in this *Punch* cartoon of July 1920, entitled 'Moral Suasion'. Confronted by the snake, the rabbit remarks: 'My offensive equipment being practically *nil*, it remains for me to fascinate him with the power of my eye.'

and Italy to occupy parts of the Turkish homeland provoked a nationalist revolt led by a distinguished Turkish general, Mustapha Kemal (Kemal Atatürk, 1881–1938). His military and diplomatic successes cleared much of what is now present-day Turkey of foreign troops, and in 1923 he signed the Treaty of Lausanne, which gave Turkey much improved terms (▷ p. 210).

The seeds of future conflict

The seeds of future conflict were sown by these treaties. The various peoples of Europe were too mixed up to be neatly separated into nation-states, and the territorial settlement caused resentment and

by 65 nations. However, like Locarno, it proved to be of little lasting value. Growing rivalry in the Pacific between Japan and the USA appeared to have been defused by the Washington Naval Conference of 1921–2. This established a ratio of tonnage of capital ships (i.e. battleships and heavy cruisers) of 5:5:3 between the fleets of the USA, Britain and Japan. JP

SEE ALSO

● WORLD WAR 1 p. 176
● THE DEPRESSION p. 184
● THE GROWTH OF FASCISM p. 186
● THE ROAD TO WAR p. 188

The Depression

On 24 October 1929 – 'Black Thursday' – the New York stock exchange on Wall Street ceased to function. Amid scenes of chaos and panic, the price of shares plummeted, leading to unprecedented attempts to sell them before they became completely worthless. Altogether, nearly 13 million shares passed through the exchange; by the end of the day, many speculators had lost everything.

The jobless queue (right) in an employment agency in San Francisco in 1938. During the blackest days of the Depression – in the early 1930s – as many as 14 million Americans were out of work (⊳ box).

Before the crash, speculation had increased until the prices paid for shares bore little relation to the economic strength of the companies concerned. As few shares had any real value, the façade of Wall Street soon came crashing down. The impact of the 'Wall Street Crash' was felt particularly by those speculators who bought shares 'on margin', paying a small amount immediately, with the rest borrowed or owed: when trading collapsed they had no 'real' money with which to settle their debts. Many of the banks and insurance companies that had financed the 'margin' system called in their debts and cut credit elsewhere to make up the shortfall.

Money now became 'tight', and prices of commodities such as sugar, rubber and wheat fell, as no one could afford to buy them. The result was that commodity-producing countries suddenly found that their exports dropped in value, undermining national income. This was the beginning of the Depression – a period of economic mismanagement on a global scale that was to last until the late 1930s, creating unemployment, social unrest and radical political change.

Causes of the Depression

But the collapse of a single stock exchange on a single day could only be a symptom of a far deeper international malaise, the roots of which lay in the economic disruption caused by World War I and its aftermath (⊳ p. 182). That conflict had not only been extremely expensive for the combatant states, but had also 'warped' national economies by shifting industrial production to armaments. Traditional trading patterns had been upset, stockpiles of raw materials run down, and factories overused. Although there was a boom in 1919–20 as the victorious powers scrambled to replace goods expended during the war, this soon gave way to recession as production picked up and markets were glutted.

This was particularly true in the domain of agriculture. Once Europe had restored production, prices declined and farmers who had taken advantage of wartime needs by growing extra crops faced disaster. In the USA, where a quarter of total employment was connected with agriculture, farmers resorted to mortgaging their land, yet continued to suffer falling demand. On an international level, food-exporting countries (such as the British dominions) raised loans on the money markets in London or New York, only to find that they could not pay the interest and therefore needed to borrow more. A spiral of inflation set in, in which money came to be worth less and less but debts increased. The fact that the very banks that suffered the major losses on 'Black Thursday' were the same ones that had lent money to farmers and foreign states could only exacerbate the situation. Some banks collapsed, wiping out depositers' savings; others foreclosed on mortgages, causing widespread distress in farming communities. In America's Mid-West, for example, entire families were forced off the land, taking to the roads in a desperate search for work.

In the past, economic problems such as these had been managed at an international level, with richer countries such as Britain or the USA negotiating loans and, by ensuring that their currency remained 'solid', offering stability at the centre of the system. But this did not happen in the early 1930s. Britain, weakened by World War I, was in no position to offer financial help to other countries, while the USA – the only contender for the role of world economic leader – was unwilling to accept responsibility. Another key factor was the deliberate weakening of the German economy by the Western allies under the Treaty of Versailles (⊳ p. 182), most importantly through the crushing burden of war debts (reparations) amounting to 132 billion gold marks. This left a vacuum in the centre of Europe that almost proved fatal. With the USA also insisting on the repayment of all war debts – money lent to allies to fund their war efforts – a massive imbalance was created in the international economy. European resources were poured into debt repayment and interest, thereby cutting the market for industrial goods.

Reparations and war debts

Attempts had been made to ease the burden of reparations when it became obvious that the Weimar Republic was in serious economic difficulties in the early 1920s. By 1923 the German mark had plummeted in value – from 275 to the US dollar in May 1922 to 16 667 to the dollar a year later. An international crisis arose when Franco-Belgian forces occupied the

UNEMPLOYMENT DURING THE DEPRESSION
(percentage of total labour force)

GERMANY | USA | UK

Ruhr to enforce their countries' claims to debt repayment (⇨ p. 186). Consequently, in September 1924 a new repayment scheme – the Dawes Plan – was introduced. It laid down a more manageable schedule of annual payments, introduced a new Reichsmark, and raised a substantial loan for Germany in New York. For a time, this seemed to work, but as the international money crisis deepened, Germany again fell into economic difficulties. The Young Plan of April 1930 arranged another rescheduling of payments and a new loan, but to no avail. As German banks collapsed and unemployment spiralled, the international community had no choice but to cancel all reparations at the Lausanne Conference in July 1932.

However, the Americans refused to negotiate a similar deal with Britain and France over their war debts, insisting on repayment in full. This created resentment at a time when these powerful states could have come together to provide collective leadership. Instead, they viewed each other as economic rivals, raising tariff barriers to trade (by imposing import taxes) and forming economic 'blocs' that deliberately excluded other powers. World Economic Conferences were organized, in 1927 (in Geneva) and 1933 (in London), in an attempt to bring about cooperation, but they failed, helping to push a distrustful USA into isolation rather then world leadership. In the end, responses to the Depression had to come from within individual states – a state of affairs that inevitably lengthened the crisis.

Responses to the Depression

The Depression placed enormous strains on democratic political systems and produced a range of different outcomes. In the USA, Franklin D. Roosevelt was elected President in 1932 promising 'a new deal for the American people'. His priorities were to create jobs and restore business confidence. The 'New Deal' involved centralized regulation of production and prices, government-sponsored 'public works' projects for the unemployed, and large-scale federal industrial developments. With cuts to federal employees' salaries and war veterans' pensions to raise the necessary money, the New Deal was far from popular. Nonetheless, by 1934 unemployment – though still high – was falling, bank reserves were rising, and bankruptcies were in decline.

The widespread extension of federal authority that characterized the New Deal was mirrored in Europe in a general increase in government control of domestic economies. But while the social and political order in the USA was preserved largely intact by Roosevelt's policies, national politics in parts of Europe were to follow an unstable course of radicalization and ideological polarization.

In Britain and France, left-wing governments were in power when the Depression first struck. They initially pursued policies of increased state relief to the unemployed in an effort to stimulate demand and, in the longer term, production. Both were brought down when their policies failed to restore prosperity. In Britain the Labour government collapsed after a damaging split over cuts in public spending and was replaced in 1931 by a Conservative-dominated National Government. In France a right-wing government gained power in 1934.

In Britain, the National Government attempted to stabilize the pound by taking it off the 'gold standard' (meaning that it could no longer be exchanged directly for gold but had to compete with other currencies). To tackle unemployment – totalling nearly 3 million by 1933 – the government boosted new industries such as chemicals, electrical goods and cars. In the process, traditional industries such as shipbuilding, coal and cotton suffered, and unemployment in such areas as the North of England and South Wales remained an acute problem: as late as 1936 the men of Jarrow in County Durham organized a march to London to protest at the lack of jobs. The situation gradually improved, although not without a damaging political debate between those who favoured free trade and government spending and those who advocated protective tariffs and cost-cutting. The prime advocate of government intervention, the British economist John Maynard Keynes (⇨ p. 183), argued that in a depression governments should increase, rather than decrease, expenditure on public works programmes.

Not everyone welcomed government interference, however: to some critics, it constituted an attack on the spirit of free enterprise; to others it seemed to undermine workers' rights. In France, for example, attempts by right-wing political parties to regulate the economy led to the creation by Socialists and Communists in 1936 of a left-wing Popular Front, intent on protecting workers and opposing the spread of Fascism (⇨ p. 187). During its brief spell in power, the Front implemented a programme of radical social and economic reforms, including new laws guaranteeing a 40-hour working week and paid annual holidays. But these proved to be expensive policies that fuelled inflation. In response, the more traditional parties banded together to regain power, compounding a growing polarization of French politics that did little to prepare the country for imminent war.

The totalitarian response

That war was to be against Germany, where – with unemployment falling and prosperity returning – the totalitarian policies of the Nazis were perceived by many as having 'solved' the economic problems caused by the Depression (⇨ p. 186). Totalitarianism did not always produce solutions – in the Soviet Union, for instance, Stalin's successive Five-Year Plans, based on enforced collectivization of agriculture and strict production quotas for industry, caused

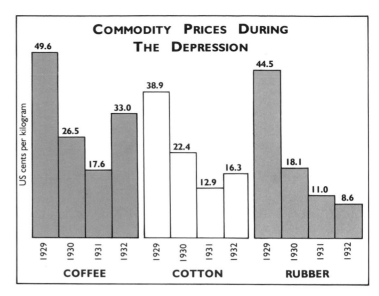

COMMODITY PRICES DURING THE DEPRESSION

US cents per kilogram

COFFEE: 49.6 (1929), 26.5 (1930), 17.6 (1931), 33.0 (1932)
COTTON: 38.9 (1929), 22.4 (1930), 12.9 (1931), 16.3 (1932)
RUBBER: 44.5 (1929), 18.1 (1930), 11.0 (1931), 8.6 (1932)

immense hardship (⇨ p. 198) – but Germany was a different case. As soon as Hitler gained full power in March 1933, he introduced laws to control prices, production quotas and employment, but with a modicum of local and personal responsibility and an emphasis on the restoration of German pride. Conscription, reintroduced in 1935, together with a National Labour Front ensured that everyone had a job to do, while the banning of trade unions undermined opposition. By 1936 Germany seemed to be in good economic shape and, for a time, the National Socialist economic 'miracle' (paralleled in Fascist Italy) was regarded in many countries as an attractive ideal.   JP

SEE ALSO

● WORLD WAR I p. 176
● THE POSTWAR SETTLEMENT p. 182
● THE RISE OF FASCISM p. 186
● THE ROAD TO WAR p. 188

PROHIBITION IN THE USA

On the 16 January 1920 the Eighteenth Amendment to the US Constitution came into force. It prohibited the manufacture, transport, sale or consumption of alcohol throughout the USA. Prohibition represented a victory for those who believed that drinking was a sin and that, without alcohol, crime would decrease. It was the culmination of a campaign that had spread across America during the 19th century. Deriving strength from sources as diverse as evangelical Christianity and the Women's Movement, temperance had become a potent force in US politics.

Prohibition did not prove easy to enforce, for determined criminals saw the provision of illicit alcohol as a sure way to make money. Illegal drinking dens – 'speakeasies' – proliferated, selling illicitly distilled 'bootleg' whisky at inflated prices. New York speakeasies were notorious for stocking whisky contaminated with wood alcohol, and deaths from drinking such 'hootch' reached significant levels – in 1927, for example, 719 people died from alcohol poisoning in the USA. Despite the actions of police and Federal Bureau of Investigation (FBI) agents, who destroyed illegal drink as well as the stills and bottling plants, the appeal of alcohol did not decline.

The situation was made worse by the gangsters who gained profit from it – men like Al Capone and George 'Bugsy' Malone – whose activities received a considerable boost from 'bootlegging'. Gang warfare – epitomized by the St Valentine Day's massacre (1929), in which seven members of Malone's mob were lined up and shot by rival gangsters in a Chicago garage – led to an atmosphere of lawlessness in the major cities. Furthermore, the success of Capone and others led to the corruption of police and local government. By 1933, it was obvious that prohibition had done more harm than good and that it had fostered public disregard for the law in general. The Twenty-First Amendment was ratified and, on 5 December, prohibition ceased, President Roosevelt remarking 'I think this would be a good time for a beer.'

The Growth of Fascism

An ancient Roman symbol of authority, the *fasces*, provides the origin of the name of one of the most significant ideologies of the 20th century – Fascism. Fascism grew out of the unstable political conditions that followed World War I. Its mass appeal derived from its promises to replace weak democratic governments with strong leadership and to rectify the grievances of individuals and states arising out of the postwar settlement (▷ p. 182). In the 1920s Fascist dictators began to gain power in several countries. Once they did, tensions arose between themselves and the democratic states – tensions that would lead eventually to war.

Fascism was not a coherent doctrine like Marxism (▷ p. 169), but all Fascists believed in a strong, nationalist, authoritarian state, ruled by a charismatic dictator backed by a single paramilitary party. Fascists were fanatically opposed to democracy, socialism, Marxism and liberalism, and were often racist and antisemitic. Both in opposition and in power, Fascists made effective use of propaganda and terror to win support and to dispose of political rivals.

Mussolini gains power

Italy appeared to be threatened by Communist revolution after World War I. One of the many extremist right-wing groups that was formed in response was the Fasci di Combattimento (usually shortened to 'Fascists'), led by Benito Mussolini. By 1922, largely through Mussolini's brilliant oratory and shrewd political sense, the Fascists had gained enough support to attempt to seize power. In October, 25 000 Fascist 'Blackshirts' made their 'March on Rome', and King Victor Emmanuel III was forced to ask Mussolini to form a government.

In 1926 Mussolini made himself dictator, awarding himself the title 'Il Duce' ('the Leader'). His most notable achievement was the Lateran Treaty of 1929, which ended the hostility between the Catholic Church and the Italian State. Massive programmes of public works were undertaken, but this did not prevent Italy from suffering badly in the Depression (▷ p. 184).

The rise of the Nazis

In Germany the weak Weimar Republic (▷ box) came under attack in 1919 from Communist 'Spartacist' revolutionaries, and in 1920 right-wing paramilitary units launched an abortive coup – the 'Kapp Putsch'. In 1923 Adolf Hitler, leader of the small National Socialist German Workers' (or Nazi) Party, tried to overthrow the Bavarian government. The 'Beer-Hall Putsch' was unsuccessful and Hitler, a former army corporal, was arrested, serving a short prison sentence. During his imprisonment he wrote *Mein Kampf* ('My Struggle'). In it he set out his beliefs on race: that 'Aryan' Germanic peoples were superior to Slavs, Negroes and, above all, Jews, and that the German 'Master Race' must conquer territory in the east to achieve *Lebensraum* ('living space'; ▷ pp. 188 and 192).

From 1923 to 1929 Germany enjoyed some prosperity and stability, but the Depression rang the death knell of the Weimar Republic. In 1930 a political crisis developed over plans to cut government spending on welfare services, and President von Hindenburg (1847–1934) began to rule by decree. The Nazis were well placed to exploit the crisis. Hitler was a masterly orator and one of his principal lieutenants, Joseph Goebbels, had a genius for propaganda. Hitler denounced democratic politicians for stabbing the undefeated German army in the back at the end of World War I by signing the Treaty of Versailles (▷ p. 182), and blamed the Depression on Jewish financiers. Nazi tactics were ruthless but effective: the brown-shirted 'Stormtroopers' of the SA (*Sturmabteilung*) intimidated and murdered opponents. The Nazis began to receive support from people of all classes who longed for firm government.

In the 1932 election the Nazis won 230 seats, becoming the largest party in the Reichstag (the German parliament), and on 30 January 1933 Hitler became chancellor (prime minister). The move to totalitarianism was swift. The Nazis used the burning of the Reichstag on 27 February 1933 – which was probably the work of the Nazis themselves – as an excuse to arrest opposition politicians. The Nazis also forced through a law giving Hitler dictatorial powers.

Hitler in power

After von Hindenburg's death in August 1934 Hitler became 'Führer' ('Leader') with the powers of chancellor and president. The Nazis outlawed all other political parties, banned trade unions, and tightened their grip on the state by the use

THE WEIMAR REPUBLIC

When Kaiser Wilhelm II abdicated in November 1918, Germany was declared a republic and a Social Democratic government was formed in Berlin. It came under immediate attack from Communist 'Spartacist' opponents, who attempted an uprising in Berlin. As law and order broke down, a National Constituent Assembly was convened at Weimar to draw up a new constitution, with the republic taking its name from the town. At the time, the Weimar Constitution – providing for bicameral (two-chamber) government, proportional representation, a seven-year presidential term of office and federal rights – was seen as remarkably advanced, but it was weakened by Article 48, which allowed the President to rule by decree in times of emergency.

In its early years, the republic came under intense pressure; associated by many Germans with military defeat and with the punitive peace settlement imposed by the Treaty of Versailles, it was vilified by extremists of both left and right. If it had not been for individual politicians such as the moderate socialist Friedrich Ebert (Presi-

'The Profiteer', a satirical cartoon from 1922, the period of German hyperinflation.

dent 1919–25) and Gustav Stresemann (Foreign Minister 1923–9), the Weimar Republic would probably not have survived the hyperinflation of the early 1920s and

occupation of the Ruhr by France and Belgium in 1923 (an attempt to force Germany to comply with reparations demands; ▷ p. 184).

The Republic experienced a recovery of sorts after 1923 with the introduction of a new currency – the Reichsmark – and the rescheduling of reparation repayments under the Dawes Plan (1924). In 1925 a new coalition of rightist parties under the presidency of Field Marshal Paul von Hindenburg offered promise of greater political stability. Internal unrest decreased and industrial production returned to pre-war levels.

But the onset of the Depression in 1929 (▷ p. 184) brought a fresh economic crisis and mass unemployment (6 000 000 by 1932), for which many blamed the Weimar Republic. In March 1930, Hindenburg appointed Heinrich Brüning as Chancellor and allowed him to rule more and more by decree, according to Article 48 of the Weimar Constitution. This was the beginning of moves away from democracy that culminated in Hindenburg's legal but misguided decision to appoint Adolf Hitler as Chancellor in January 1933.

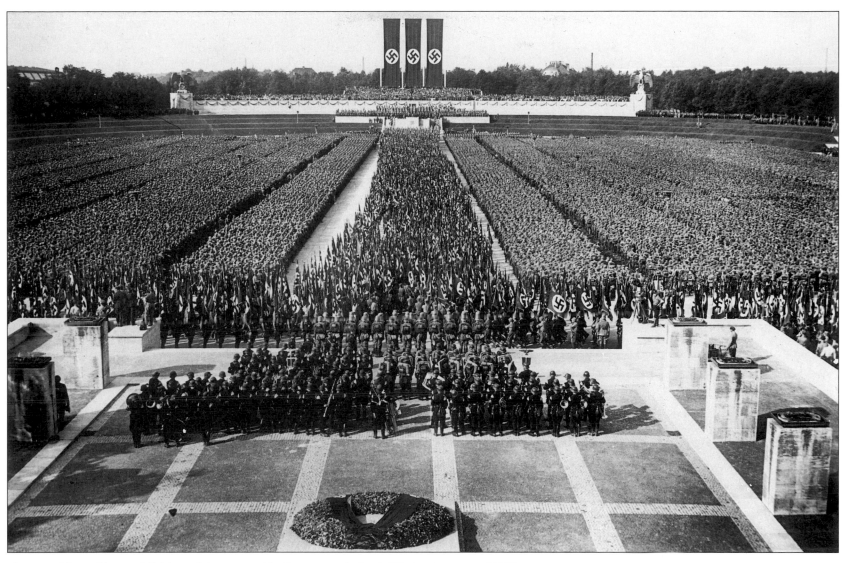

The Nuremberg Rally of 1935, from Leni Riefenstahl's film *The Triumph of the Will*. Such mass gatherings of Nazi party members were a potent propaganda weapon, symbolizing in dramatic terms the subordination of the individual to the state.

of censorship and by establishing a hierarchy of Nazi officials down to the lowest levels. Hitler's will was enforced by the SS (*Schutzstaffel*, 'protection squad') and Gestapo (*Geheime Staatspolizei*, 'secret state police'), both under the authority of Heinrich Himmler. Ernst Röhm, the head of the SA and a potential rival to Hitler, was murdered along with 150 of his followers on the 'Night of the Long Knives' (30 June 1934).

In accordance with Hitler's hatred of the Jews, the 1935 Nuremberg Laws stripped German Jews of their remaining rights; eventually almost 6 million Jews were murdered in concentration camps (▷ pp. 192–3). By reintroducing conscription and rearming in defiance of the Treaty of Versailles, Hitler both reduced unemployment and restored national pride, and was genuinely popular in Germany in the 1930s.

Totalitarianism in Japan

Other European states – notably Hungary, Yugoslavia, Poland and Romania – were also ruled by right-wing dictators during the interwar years. However, the growth of totalitarianism was not confined to Europe. Japanese governments in the 1920s tended to be weak, and even before the Wall Street Crash (▷ p. 184)

the country suffered from serious economic problems. Faced with the power of big business on the one hand and the development of left-wing movements on the other, Fascist-style ideas, combined with a revival of emperor-worship, began to influence army officers. Many sections of Japanese society supported the idea of strong military government and military expansion at the expense of Japan's neighbours – particularly the European colonial powers.

The army began to demonstrate increasing independence from the government. In 1931, following a clash with Chinese troops at Mukden, the army occupied Chinese Manchuria on its own initiative. Four years later it attempted to seize power in Tokyo. Although the coup failed, the army came to have a dominating influence on the government, with General Hideki Tojo becoming prime minister in 1941. Domestic policies began to resemble those of the Fascist states of Europe.   JP

THE RESPONSE TO FASCISM

As Fascism spread in the 1930s, so did a reaction to it in the democracies of Europe, particularly among left-wing and moderate political parties. In France, a Popular Front – a coalition of left-wing parties in defence of democratic forms of government – gained power in 1936 under the leadership of the socialist Léon Blum. It coincided with a similar development in Spain, where a combination of parties on the Republican left won the elections of February 1936.

In both countries, the aims of the Popular Front were to resist Fascism and war and to shore up democracy by mobilizing the people against the threat. Blum, for example, legislated against the 'Fascist leagues' that had appeared in France, and offered improvements in pay and working conditions, including a 40-hour working week, paid annual vacations, and the nationalization of the arms industries. Such policies won elections, but proved extremely difficult to put into practice, not least because of their high cost at a time of economic depression.

But the Popular Fronts faced additional problems. Stalin, following the slogan that Fascism is merely capitalism in its death throes, tried to exploit the situation by ensuring Communist involvement in the Popular Fronts. Not only did this lead to splits on the left – in France, traditional rivalries between Socialists and Communists undermined the effectiveness of the Popular Front – but it also produced a backlash from the right. In Spain, a right-wing coalition of conservatives and monarchists opposed the Popular Front and set the scene for a civil war (▷ p. 189). In France Blum's government, lacking the parliamentary support necessary to carry through its social reforms, fell in 1938, and was replaced by one of a more radical persuasion. But by now time was running out for democracy in Western Europe.

The Road to War

One of the hopes behind the 1919 peace settlement (▷ p. 182) was that war could be avoided in the future through the League of Nations and international 'collective action'. But the League was never strong and, with a lack of consensus over what constituted 'war' and 'collective action', it proved unable to carry out its task. When a League Commission denounced the Japanese attack on Manchuria in 1933, Japan's response was simply to leave the League and pursue its own policies regardless of world opinion – policies that, in 1937, led to all-out war with China. Similarly, in 1935, when Mussolini ordered his troops to invade Abyssinia (Ethiopia), the League did nothing beyond imposing economic sanctions on Italy – which were largely ignored by member-states.

Such weakness coincided with – and fuelled – Hitler's policies of rearmament and expansion. As early as 1934, Germany left the League (she had been admitted in 1925 as part of the Locarno agreement). In March 1935 Hitler openly breached the Versailles settlement by reintroducing conscription to the German armed forces, thereby increasing their size beyond the limits laid down in 1919. In 1936 he sent his troops into the 'demilitarized' zone of the Rhineland – a move that no one attempted to resist, despite the fact that any German military presence there was forbidden by the Treaty of Versailles. The

same year also saw Mussolini and Hitler become Allies in the Rome-Berlin Axis, and Japan join Germany in the Anti-Comintern pact, aimed against the USSR.

Hitler's ultimate aim (outlined in *Mein Kampf*; ▷ p. 186) was the occupation of vast areas of Eastern Europe, whose Slavic peoples were to be subjugated and the land colonized as *Lebensraum* ('living space') for the Nazi 'master race' (▷ p. 186). But he was aware that Germany was not yet in a position to go to war with Britain, France or the Soviet Union. On 5 November 1937 Hitler told his armed forces chiefs that, although 'Germany's problems can only be solved by means of force', it was likely to take until 1940 to create the weapons and services needed for a full-scale conflict. Until then, Germany's aims would have to be achieved by means of diplomacy, political pressure and selective force, the latter to be used only when the circumstances were right and the chances of Anglo-French or Soviet response slim. Between 1936 and 1939, this approach proved effective for Hitler, although inevitably it led to crises that paved the way to war.

Appeasement

Hitler's immediate objective was to assimilate or conquer those states to the south and east – Austria, Czechoslovakia and Poland – which were to open the way to *Lebensraum*. His 'excuse' for action lay in the dissatisfaction expressed by ethnic Germans who found themselves living in these new states following the territorial changes imposed at Versailles. The British and French – desperate to avoid another war and beset with their own domestic crises (the abdication of Edward VIII in Britain, the confrontation

between left and right in France; ▷ p. 187) – were only too willing to accept the 'natural justice' of ethnic-German demands. As long as Hitler took no direct military action – or took it so quickly that it presented a *fait accompli* – the response of the Western powers was muted. This became clear in May 1937 when one of the first foreign-policy decisions by Britain's new prime minister, Neville Chamberlain, was to start negotiations with Hitler. At his meetings with Hitler, he was to make concessions that facilitated German territorial expansion. Chamberlain's policy of accommodating the dictators was largely popular, but was later to be stigmatized as 'appeasement' by its critics.

The annexation of Austria

In such circumstances, it was only a matter of time before Hitler began to exert stronger pressure for change. His first opportunity came in early 1938, and his objective was Austria, where Nazi influence had been growing for some time. In July 1936 the new chancellor of Austria, Kurt von Schuschnigg, had agreed to adopt a foreign policy in line with that of Germany, but this merely whetted Hitler's appetite. In February 1938 he insisted that Nazi sympathizers should be included in the Austrian government. Schuschnigg appeared to agree, then changed his mind, calling for a plebiscite on the question of German-Austrian unification. Afraid that this would be unfavourable, Hitler decided to act. On 12 March 1938 German troops occupied Austria and imposed an *Anschluss* (union of the two countries). Hitler then called a plebiscite in both Germany and Austria, which, it was claimed, backed his actions completely.

Britain and France protested, but the incident had happened so quickly that they could do little without risking war. Instead, they pursued appeasement with new vigour, particularly when it became apparent that Czechoslovakia, now hemmed in on three sides by German territory, was likely to be the next objective. Again, Hitler had a 'built-in' excuse for action, this time in the form of three million ethnic Germans living in the Sudetenland (Czech territory on the German border). Under the leadership of Konrad Henlein, they were already calling for the right to join the Reich.

The fall of Czechoslovakia

Pressure grew on Czechoslovakia in the summer of 1938. As the Czech leader, Eduard Beneš, tried to defuse the crisis by offering concessions, so Henlein (on Hitler's orders) increased the demands, backed by Sudeten Germans now openly in revolt against the Czech government. Chamberlain met Hitler in September, hoping to negotiate a settlement, but the Führer insisted on the right to occupy the Sudetenland immediately. The crisis deepened and, in a desperate attempt to avoid war, a conference was convened in Munich, attended by Hitler, Mussolini, Chamberlain, and the French premier, Edouard Daladier. No Czech represent-

Chamberlain with Mussolini at Munich, 1938: diplomatic persuasion founders on the reef of totalitarian certainty.

SEE ALSO

● THE POSTWAR SETTLEMENT
  p. 182
● THE GROWTH OF FASCISM
  p. 186
● WORLD WAR II pp. 190–95

atives were invited, yet the Munich Agreement, signed on 30 September, effectively dismembered their country: it was agreed that the Sudetenland would be transferred to Germany under international supervision and that the new Czech borders would be guaranteed. Beneš, who later resigned in disgust, had no choice but to accept. The British prime minister returned to Britain announcing that he had achieved 'peace in our time'. But if Chamberlain and Daladier believed that the transference of the last significant group of Germans from foreign rule to that of their homeland represented the summit of Hitler's ambitions, they were soon to be rudely disabused of the notion.

Any hopes of permanent peace were short-lived. Hitler's next move came in March 1939, when he sent troops into Prague, ostensibly to protect ethnic Germans in what was left of independent Czechoslovakia. Slovakia became an independent state, Germany declared a 'protectorate' over Bohemia and Moravia, and the Hungarians occupied Ruthenia: Czechoslovakia ceased to exist, and with it went one of the main barriers to further German expansion. Less than a month later, Hitler formally annexed the district of Memel – Lithuanian territory on the border of East Prussia – while Mussolini, seizing the opportunity of crisis elsewhere, invaded Albania. On 22 May 1939 Hitler and Mussolini concluded a full-scale alliance – the 'Pact of Steel'. Neither the League of Nations nor the British and French governments made any move to stop these events, which had utterly discredited the policy of appeasement. Faced with the prospect of limitless Fascist expansion in Central Europe, Britain and France at last began to change tack. They issued guarantees to Poland, Greece and Romania, promising military assistance if any of them was attacked.

Meanwhile, it was to Poland that Hitler was now turning his attention. But here he had to be very careful indeed. Any direct attack on Poland was likely to trigger an Anglo-French response, partly because there were few ethnic Germans to create an excuse for action but also because of Western promises of support to the Poles. In addition, the Soviet Union had to be taken into account, for any military response by Moscow would recreate the German nightmare of a two-front war. Hitler continued his familiar tactics of pressure and bluff during the summer of 1939, demanding that the 'free city' of Danzig (now Gdansk) and the 'Polish Corridor' (giving Poland access to the sea between the German territories of Pomerania and East Prussia) should be handed over to Germany. But he was aware that, this time, Chamberlain and Daladier would not pursue appeasement.

The Nazi-Soviet Pact

Hitler's solution to the problem was to approach the Soviets to negotiate a non-aggression pact. It was an unlikely move – after all, most of the *Lebensraum* Hitler

THE SPANISH CIVIL WAR

An execution during the Spanish Civil War. Both sides dealt ruthlessly with prisoners and civilians.

By the early 1930s, Spain was politically divided. In 1931 King Alfonso XIII abdicated, leaving his country to become a democratic, if unstable, republic. The first government was weak, and its downfall in 1933 led to elections that revealed the polarization of Spanish politics: the authority of the right-wing government was challenged first by a general strike and then, in October 1934, by an armed revolt in Asturias. Public revulsion at the army's brutal suppression of this uprising led to the election of a Popular Front of socialists, radicals and Communists in February 1936. In the months that followed, Spain was shaken by a succession of strikes, riots, and military plots.

In July 1936 a right-wing coalition of conservatives and monarchists, supported by army officers under General José Sanjurjo, carried out a *coup d'état* in Spanish Morocco. When Sanjurjo was killed in a plane crash he was replaced by General Francisco Franco, who rallied the army in North Africa and, using German-supplied aircraft, invaded mainland Spain. The civil war had begun.

Franco's Nationalists enjoyed distinct advantages in the ensuing struggle – they had experienced forces and were already receiving aid from Hitler and Mussolini – but their rival Republicans did have widespread public support. Although Franco was able to seize much of northern and western Spain (except Asturias, the Basque Provinces and Catalonia) by late July 1936, the Republicans held firm elsewhere. Indeed, despite a Nationalist advance in the autumn that took Madrid, the Republicans were able to counterattack and regain the city.

During this counterattack, the Republicans fielded the first of their 'International Brigades', groups of left-wing volunteers from countries outside Spain, but this was about the extent of their international support. The Soviet Union later provided some equipment, but by then the decision of Britain and France to adopt a policy of non-intervention (at the Noyan Conference in September 1937) had cut off the Republicans' main source of

supply. Fascist support for Franco continued unabated, however, and although the Italians were deterred from carrying supplies by ship to Spain by a British threat to use submarines against them, the flow of supplies to the Nationalists from Germany, Italy and Portugal never dried up. Over 10 000 Germans served in the 'Condor Legion' in Spain, using modern aircraft, tanks and artillery, as Hitler took the opportunity to field-test new methods of warfare.

Despite fighting at a disadvantage, the Republicans were by no means ineffective. In early 1937 they defeated the Nationalists twice – at Jarama and Guadalajara – as Franco tried to retake Madrid, causing him to divert his attention north, into the Basque Provinces and Asturias. On 26 April, the Basque market town of Guernica was razed by aircraft of the Condor Legion and the Republicans lost the port of Bilbao in the land attacks that followed. A similar combination of air and land assaults defeated Republican forces in Catalonia, Aragon and New Castile.

A last-ditch Republican attack across the Ebro in July 1938 led to five months of bitter fighting for no gain. Both Madrid and Barcelona fell to the Nationalists in Franco's offensive of early 1939, and on 1 April he announced that the war was over. It had cost Spain over 800 000 casualties, leaving the country exhausted and embittered by a legacy of internal hatreds.

Franco did little to heal the rifts, preferring to set up a quasi-Fascist state in which the army retained a significant say and opposition was ruthlessly repressed. The war may have persuaded the Fascist powers – Germany and Italy – that, in Franco, they had a natural ally for the future, but as events during World War II were to show, he was determined to consolidate his own powers at home rather than become involved in adventures abroad. In the end, the greatest effect of the Spanish Civil War was that it reinforced Fascist beliefs that their methods of warfare worked, plunging the Western democracies deeper into despair, intent as they were on attempting to avoid future conflict.

wanted lay in western Russia, and the antipathy between Communism and Fascism was deep. But it worked. Stalin, annoyed at not having been consulted by Britain and France over Czechoslovakia and desperate to avoid war while his armed forces were weak, agreed to the pact, which was signed on 23 August 1939. The pact effectively partitioned Poland between Germany and the Soviet Union;

it also allowed Stalin to annex the independent Baltic republics of Estonia, Latvia and Lithuania, which he occupied in 1940. Hitler now had virtually a free hand, secure in the knowledge that whatever he did the British and French could not stop him or call on the Soviets to exert pressure. On 1 September his armed forces invaded Poland (⇨ p. 192). A general war was now inevitable.   JP

World War II: The West

Britain and France declared war on Germany on 3 September 1939, two days after Hitler's invasion of Poland (⊳ pp. 189 and 192). There was little they could do to help the Poles. Instead, they looked to their own defences. British forces were shipped to France and convoys were organized to protect merchant vessels in the Atlantic, where German U-boats (submarines) and surface warships were already active. The Battle of the River Plate, after which the German battleship *Graf Spee* was scuttled off the Uruguayan coast in December 1939, was one of the few incidents in this period of 'Phoney War'.

Hitler turned towards the north in April 1940, invading Denmark and Norway. Anglo-French units were sent to help the Norwegians, but could make little impact, particularly when, on 10 May, a more immediate threat emerged – a German attack on France and the Low Countries. The Germans used classic *blitzkrieg* ('lightning war') tactics, spearheading their attacks with dive bombers and fast-moving tank units. Allied armies were drawn north into Belgium to forestall what they believed to be a repeat of the 1914 Schlieffen Plan, while German panzers (tanks) and aircraft swept through the 'impassable' Ardennes to cut across the Allied rear. Caught in a trap, the British retreated to Dunkirk. Between 26 May and 4 June, over 330 000 troops escaped across the Channel, but nothing could disguise the enormity of the disaster. By late June, France, Belgium, Netherlands and Luxembourg were in German hands. After the French surrender on 22 June the northern part of France was placed under German occupation, while the rest of the country was administered by a pro-German French government set up in the spa town of Vichy.

German bombers over the ruins of Dunkirk, 22 May 1940. The terrorizing and panicking of the civilian population was as much an aim of German tactics in 1939–40 as the rapid disruption of enemy forces.

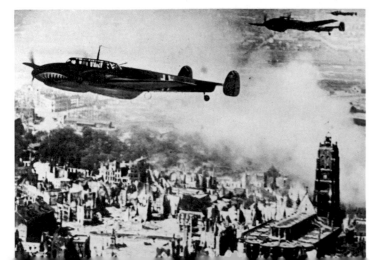

The Battle of Britain

Britain now stood alone and in grave danger. Attacks by German U-boats on British merchant shipping in the Atlantic were already threatening to sever the lifeline with North America; an Italian declaration of war (on 10 June) was opening up new theatres of conflict in Africa; and Hitler's intention to invade the British Isles was clear. In August, massed German bombers began to attack aircraft factories, installations and airfields in southern England in preparation for the invasion (Operation Sea Lion). Despite heavy British losses, they were repulsed by Spitfires and Hurricanes of RAF Fighter Command in the Battle of Britain. On 7 September, the Germans switched to attacks on London, aiming to bomb Britain into submission: it was the beginning of the 'Blitz'. However, although substantial damage was inflicted on cities such as London, Coventry, Liverpool, Glasgow, Southampton and Belfast, public morale did not crack. The Blitz continued until May 1941, but Sea Lion had already been postponed indefinitely as Hitler turned to his impending war against the Soviet Union (⊳ p. 192).

The war spreads

By then, the war had spread to Africa, the Mediterranean and the Balkans. When Italy declared war on the Allies, Mussolini took advantage of their weakness to seize British Somaliland and invade Egypt. In the event, both attacks were defeated: in East Africa, Somaliland was liberated by British-Indian forces in March 1941 and by August the Italians had been destroyed in Abyssinia (Ethiopia); in North Africa, a British counterattack in December 1940 developed into a successful invasion of Cyrenaica (eastern Libya). It looked as if the Italians were about to be defeated in Africa.

This triggered a German response to prevent Italian humiliation. In February 1941 Hitler sent Lieutenant-General Erwin Rommel and his *Afrika Korps* to Libya, where they quickly pushed the British back to the Egyptian border, while in the Mediterranean the key island of Malta came under sustained air attack. In the Balkans, where an Italian invasion of Greece (October 1940) had come close to disaster, German forces overran Yugoslavia and Greece in April–May 1941 before seizing Crete in an audacious (but costly) airborne assault. Britain was in danger of losing access to the eastern Mediterranean and the vital route to the Far East through the Suez Canal, just at a time when Japan was preparing to attack (⊳ p. 194). British fortunes were at a low ebb, boosted only by a growing friendship with the USA. This was to result in the provision of war materials to the UK under the 'lend-lease' programme. A British counterattack in North Africa in November 1941 (Operation Crusader) succeeded in relieving the besieged port of Tobruk and forcing Rommel back, but his riposte in early 1942 caused the British to retreat yet again, this time as far as Gazala.

The tide turns

By then, the war in the Far East had begun, and, despite further British defeats, it represented a turning point, bringing the USA into the conflict (⊳ p. 194). A series of meetings between Prime Minister Winston Churchill and President Franklin D. Roosevelt led to the adoption of a 'grand strategy' in which the defeat of Germany was given priority. The Americans favoured an immediate cross-Channel invasion to liberate Europe, but Churchill was strongly opposed to this. By early 1942, North Africa had still to be cleared and, despite the sinking of the German battleship *Bismarck* in May 1941, Allied shipping was still under heavy U-boat attack in the Atlantic. Churchill persuaded the Americans to concentrate on these areas first, together with a combined bombing campaign against German cities. A raid on Dieppe on 19 August 1942, in which Canadian troops suffered heavy casualties, merely emphasized the lack of Allied expertise in seaborne landings.

The introduction of new tactics and weapons (notably radar) enabled the Allies to defeat the U-boats in early 1943, which in turn allowed a massive build-up of US troops and supplies in Britain to begin. In North Africa, Rommel attacked at Gazala in May 1942, pushing the British back into Egypt, but the tide was turned at El Alamein in late October, when forces under General Bernard Montgomery defeated an overstretched *Afrika Korps*. Anglo-American landings in French North Africa on 8 November (Operation Torch) threatened to take Rommel in the rear. Although the fighting was hard, by May 1943 Tunis had been seized and the North African coast cleared of Axis troops.

The Americans again called for a cross-Channel assault, but the Mediterranean retained priority. In July 1943 Sicily was invaded and, in September, southern Italy. By then Mussolini had been overthrown, allowing the Italians to surrender, although not before German forces had rushed south to fill the breach. The Allied advance from Salerno and Taranto soon stalled in mountains to the south of Rome, especially around Monte Cassino. Despite an amphibious landing at Anzio (January 1944), Cassino was not taken until May. Rome was liberated on 4 June.

The liberation of France

Meanwhile, preparations for Operation Overlord – the liberation of Northwest Europe – had been completed. Allied bombers, having enjoyed some success in their campaign against targets in Germany (including the destruction of Hamburg in a 'firestorm' in late July 1943), were switched to attacks on northern France. On 6 June 1944 (D-Day) Allied forces crossed the Channel under the overall command of General Dwight D. Eisenhower to make amphibious landings on the Normandy coast. Beachheads were seized and, although the fighting in the close hedgerow country was difficult, the Allied armies broke out in August, surrounding substantial German forces in a pocket around Falaise. Paris was liberated on 25 August and, as further Allied formations moved up the Rhône valley from landing beaches in southern France (secured on 15 August in Operation Dragoon), most of France, Belgium, Luxembourg and the southern Netherlands was seized. Montgomery, commanding the British-Canadian 21st Army Group, tried to maintain momentum by using a large parachute force to seize bridges in the northern Netherlands in mid-September (Operation Market Garden), but when this failed at Arnhem on the lower Rhine, the Allied advance stalled. A similar stalemate affected the Italian front, where poor weather prevented a final Allied thrust into the Po valley.

Allied victory

As autumn turned to winter, Allied units in Northwest Europe fought bitterly for small gains around Aachen, in the Hurtgen Forest, and in Alsace-Lorraine, tempting the Germans to mount a counterattack in December 1944 in the lightly defended Ardennes. It took the Allies until mid-January 1945 to win the

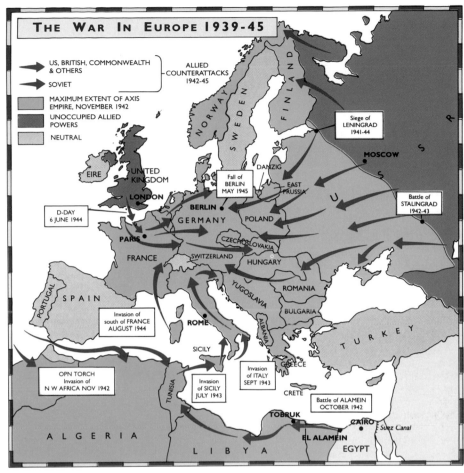

THE WAR IN EUROPE 1939-45

➤ US, BRITISH, COMMONWEALTH & OTHERS

➤ SOVIET

ALLIED COUNTERATTACKS 1942-45

MAXIMUM EXTENT OF AXIS EMPIRE, NOVEMBER 1942

UNOCCUPIED ALLIED POWERS

NEUTRAL

Siege of LENINGRAD 1941-44
MOSCOW
Fall of BERLIN MAY 1945
Battle of STALINGRAD 1942-43
D-DAY 6 JUNE 1944
BERLIN
POLAND
PARIS
GERMANY
CZECHOSLOVAKIA
FRANCE
SWITZERLAND
HUNGARY
PORTUGAL
SPAIN
YUGOSLAVIA
ROMANIA
BULGARIA
Invasion of south of FRANCE AUGUST 1944
ROME
ALBANIA
GREECE
TURKEY
SICILY
Invasion of ITALY SEPT 1943
CRETE
OPN TORCH Invasion of N W AFRICA NOV 1942
Invasion of SICILY JULY 1943
Battle of ALAMEIN OCTOBER 1942
TUNISIA
TOBRUK
CAIRO   Suez Canal
ALGERIA
LIBYA
EL ALAMEIN
EGYPT
NORWAY
SWEDEN
FINLAND
EIRE
UNITED KINGDOM
LONDON
DANZIG
EAST PRUSSIA
U S S R

SEE ALSO

● THE POSTWAR SETTLEMENT p. 182
● THE GROWTH OF FASCISM p. 186
● THE ROAD TO WAR p. 188
● WORLD WAR II: THE EAST p. 192
● WORLD WAR II: THE PACIFIC AND THE FAR EAST p. 194
● THE COLD WAR p. 204
● WESTERN EUROPE SINCE 1945 p. 214

'Battle of the Bulge', but by then the Germans – under heavy attack from the east by the Soviets (⟡ p. 193) – were close to defeat. Massive fleets of British and US bombers intensified their attacks on German cities – destroying Dresden on 13/14 February – while ground units advanced to the west bank of the Rhine in March, preparatory to assault crossings in the north and south. Berlin was left to the Soviets, allowing Eisenhower to commit the bulk of his forces to central and southern Germany. At the same time, as spring weather arrived, Allied armies in Italy pushed towards the Alps; and by early May direct connections had been made between Allied and Soviet units on the Elbe. With Hitler dead in his bunker and Berlin in Soviet hands (⟡ p. 193), the Germans surrendered unconditionally on 8 May.   JP

TOTAL WAR

World War II was a 'total' war – a conflict in which combatant powers fought for the spread of their ideals and for national survival, devoting their full human and material resources to the complete destruction of their enemies. In the process, the fighting spread to almost every continent and ocean, and all the ingenuity of humankind was used to produce new weapons of mass destruction.

As the war escalated, ideological and racial enmities ensured an increasing lack of humanitarian restraint: the Soviet-German conflict was to be a fight to the finish between Communism and Fascism, while the war in the Far East soon took on the appearance of a conflict between the European and Japanese races. Total destruction of the opposing side became the aim, an aim reinforced by increasingly ingenious government-controlled propaganda designed to ridicule and belittle enemy peoples.

Such total aims necessitated total mobilization of resources and effective long-term economic planning. By 1945 both the

USA and USSR had armed forces of more than 12 million, created by conscription, and Germany was not far behind with 10 million. In order to maintain such forces, industries had to be geared up to war production, with governments controlling the allocation of both labour and resources. In addition, rationing of food, fuel and other commodities was introduced to ensure a steady flow. The results were often dramatic: in the USA, for example, over 96 000 aircraft and 60 000 tanks were produced between 1941 and 1945.

All this brought the civilian workforce into the front line, often subject to the effects of naval blockade and aerial bombardment. German bombing of Britain during the 'Blitz' (1940–1) may not have produced collapse, but the Allied riposte against German and Japanese cities – causing the deaths of hundreds of thousands of civilians – was eventually devastating, leading to some public questioning of its morality. Altogether, over 50 million people died in World War II – the costliest and most total war to date.

World War II: The East

Early on 1 September 1939, the Germans invaded Poland. The Luftwaffe virtually destroyed the Polish air force on the ground in the first few hours, allowing tank and infantry units to advance out of Pomerania and East Prussia in the north and Silesia in the south. Polish border defences were encircled and, by 16 September, Warsaw was under attack. Twenty-four hours later, Soviet troops invaded from the east. By the end of the month Poland, split between the victorious powers, had ceased to exist.

Germany and the USSR now shared a long common border and, despite their pact of 23 August 1939 (▷ p. 189), it was inevitable that traditional enmity and ideological differences would lead to war. Indeed, Hitler had always maintained that Communism was his principal enemy

and the conquest of *Lebensraum* his chief aim (▷ p. 188). But he could do nothing until his western flank was secure, so plans for an attack on the Soviet Union were postponed until he had dealt with Britain and France. Nevertheless, he was heartened by the poor showing of the Red Army in its 'Winter War' against Finland; this began on 30 November 1939, the Finns having refused to accede to Stalin's demands for Soviet military bases on their soil. The Soviets won in the end: Finland signed a peace agreement in March 1940 yielding parts of their eastern territory to the USSR. But Soviet tactics and leadership were clearly not strong.

Operation Barbarossa

The German invasion of the Soviet Union (Operation Barbarossa) – delayed by the failure to defeat Britain and the need to send forces into the Balkans (▷ p. 190) – began on 22 June 1941. It was an enormous undertaking. Divided into three Army Groups (North, Centre and South), three million Axis troops aimed to destroy the bulk of the Red Army close to the border in a series of gigantic *blitzkrieg* pincer movements, after which Leningrad, Moscow and the Ukraine would be occupied. The operation almost succeeded.

Army Group North advanced from East Prussia into the Baltic states of Lithuania, Estonia and Latvia (seized by Stalin in 1940), crossing into Russia itself to the southwest of Leningrad on 14 July. By then, Army Group Centre, spearheaded by panzers (fast-moving armoured units), had thrust to the north and south of Minsk on the road to Moscow, trapping over 300 000 Soviet troops. In early July the same panzers repeated the process around Smolensk. Only in the south, where the Soviet defences were stronger and the distances huge, did the Germans encounter problems, and these disrupted the momentum of the campaign. On 19 July, Hitler diverted panzers from their drive on Moscow, ordering half of them north to complete the encirclement of Leningrad (now under attack from Finns as well as Germans) and half of them south to link up with Army Group South to the east of Kiev. The latter move worked well – Kiev fell on 19 September, opening up the Ukraine – but the attack on Moscow was delayed.

When it was renewed on 30 September, the panzers faced problems. The vast distances already covered had led to breakdowns, crews were exhausted and, to top it all, autumn rains soon turned the ground to mud. Although some tanks

---

THE HOLOCAUST

'The Führer has ordered that the Jewish question be solved once and for all . . . Every Jew that we can lay our hands on is to be destroyed.' This shocking statement of policy was made by Heinrich Himmler, head of the SS, in May 1941. It summarizes that most despicable of Nazi acts – the deliberate and systematic destruction of European Jewry. To those who survived, it became known as 'The Holocaust'.

Hitler's hatred of the Jews can be seen in his book *Mein Kampf* (1925; ▷ p. 186), in which he blamed a 'Jewish conspiracy' for Germany's defeat in World War I. His views reflected a long tradition of European anti-semitism, which helps to explain the ease with which he was able to impose repressive legislation after 1933. Jews in Germany (and, after 1938, Austria) were forbidden to practise certain professions, to marry non-Jews, or to join the armed services, and by late 1938 open attacks against Jewish property and persons were being condoned. Many Jews fled to Britain, the USA, Palestine and elsewhere.

It was not just the Jews who suffered. Within Germany, socialists, communists, homosexuals and the mentally ill – in short, anyone who did not match the ideal of a pure, healthy 'Aryan' race – were persecuted and, from as early as 1933, sent to concentration camps. Other 'undesirables' such as gypsies, Slavs and members of religious minorities joined them as German rule spread in Europe, but the Jewish question remained a priority. In Poland, for example, Jews were herded into special ghettos, while in the Soviet Union SS *Einsatzgruppen* ('Special Squads') were created expressly to root out Jews in areas seized by the German Army. (In addition,

Jewish children in the Warsaw Ghetto, 1941. Two years later, after a hopeless uprising, all 100 000 survivors were put to death by the Nazis.

Hitler also issued an order that all political commissars from the Red Army were to be 'disposed of by gunshot immediately'.) Many of the Jews were shot: at Babi Yar outside Kiev in September 1941, for instance, nearly 33 000 were machine-gunned and their bodies thrown into a ravine. Altogether, *Einsatzgruppen* accounted for nearly 500 000 Soviet Jews in 1941–2.

Such methods of extermination were considered 'inefficient', and a search for less

time-consuming solutions began. An alternative was to use gas, which had already been experimented with on the mentally ill. *Einsatzgruppen* were equipped with special vans into which carbon monoxide could be pumped from the engine's exhaust, but a new gas – Zyklon-B – promised 'cleaner' results. In January 1942 a Nazi interdepartmental conference was held at Wannsee (a suburb of Berlin), chaired by Reinhard Heydrich, head of the SD (*Sicherheitsdienst* – the security service of the SS), at which a deliberate extermination programme – the 'Final Solution' – was discussed. To meet the needs of the Final Solution, the existing system of concentration camps was expanded by the setting up of a number of vast new extermination camps in the east, to which Jews and others could be sent by the trainload for gassing. Auschwitz, Belzec, Chelmno, Majdenek, Sobibor and Treblinka were the chosen sites.

Not all those sent to the camps died immediately – some were used as slave labour in Germany's war factories, others as guinea-pigs in horrific medical experiments – but the final statistics of the Holocaust are mind-numbing. By 1945 when, despite last-minute attempts to destroy the evidence by the SS, Allied soldiers discovered the death camps, 5·4 million Jews, nearly 400 000 gypsies and untold thousands of Slavs had been killed. In addition, many others had died at the hands of *Einsatzgruppen* elsewhere: altogether 5·9 million Jews – 67% of Europe's pre-war Jewish population – had been murdered, the population of Poland had been cut by 15%, and 10% of the world gypsy population had ceased to exist.

---

advanced to within 32 km (20 miles) of Red Square, they were stopped by hastily constructed defences. In mid-November the rain turned to freezing snow and the Germans, ill-equipped for winter fighting, stalled. Soviet counterattacks in December retook ground to the west of Moscow before running out of steam, but the capital was secure.

The battle for Stalingrad

In 1942, Hitler altered his priorities. As Army Group North continued the siege of Leningrad, the bulk of the Axis forces were to shift south to take oilfields in the Caucasus. As a preliminary, the Crimea was secured, but the main attack began on 28 June, with forces moving east from Rostov towards the Volga while others pushed south a few days later into the Caucasus. It was an elaborate manoeuvre, made more complex when, on 13 July, Hitler insisted on the capture of Stalingrad (Volgograd) to prevent a Soviet counterattack from east of the Volga. It was a fateful decision.

The German Sixth Army, commanded by General Friedrich Paulus, reached the outskirts of Stalingrad in late August, but found the Soviet defences strong. In response, Hitler diverted panzers from the Caucasus, leaving that advance too weak to make further headway. By September the oilfields were still in Soviet hands, while Paulus was experiencing the nightmare of close fighting in the industrial suburbs of Stalingrad. On 19 November, as winter closed in, the Soviets counterattacked to the north and south of the city, trapping nearly 200 000 German troops. Despite attempts to breach the cordon, the ring tightened around the Sixth Army. On 31 January 1943, Paulus surrendered.

The Soviets push westward

By then, the Soviets had hit back in the Caucasus and along a front between Rostov and Orel. By March they had liberated Kursk and were threatening Kharkov, only to run short of supplies and stall. This left a large salient, centred on Kursk, jutting westwards into German-held territory. Hitler decided to attack the salient from both north and south to 'pinch it out', but delays caused by the weather, and the determination to deploy the latest Panther and Tiger tanks, allowed the Soviets time to build deep defences, guaranteed to enmesh the panzers. 'Operation Citadel' finally began on 5 July 1943 but achieved little: German advances in the north were halted, while in the south the Soviets counterattacked with massive tank forces around Prokhorovka. The battle of Kursk was the biggest tank battle of the war, the Germans losing over 2000 armoured vehicles, 1000 guns, 1400 aircraft and 70 000 men. They also lost the initiative on the Eastern Front.

The Soviets exploited their victory by advancing around Orel and Kharkov: by the end of 1943 they had reached the Dniepr, liberated Kiev and trapped an

entire German army in the Crimea. Nor did they relax the pressure during the winter months. In January 1944 attacks took place in the north, relieving Leningrad from a siege that had lasted nearly 900 days and cost a million civilian lives, and forcing Army Group North back into the Baltic states. At the same time, in the south, Soviet attacks took them to the Dniestr, liberated Odessa, and cleared the Crimea. By the end of May Soviet troops were close to the pre-war Polish border and had entered Romania. There was little the overstretched Germans could do.

Their plight worsened on 22–23 June 1944, when the Soviets opened their main attack ('Operation Bagration') in Byelorussia. Deploying 2·5 million troops, backed by massive armour and artillery, they drove through Army Group Centre with relative ease. As part of the Soviet force swept south towards Lvov, the bulk aimed for Warsaw, crossing the Vistula to the north and south of the city. In response, the Polish Home Army (the main resistance group) rose in revolt in Warsaw in August, overcoming a weak German garrison to take control of the city. The Soviets, having reached the suburbs of Warsaw, then halted, ostensibly because their supplies had run out. They offered no assistance to the insurgents, who were brutally suppressed in a strong counterattack by German SS units, who proceeded to deport Warsaw's inhabitants and razed the city. This refusal of the Soviets to intervene ensured the destruction of a body of Poles who could have provided an organized alternative to postwar Soviet dominance of Poland.

Meanwhile, further Soviet attacks to the

north had defeated the Finns, ending a second round of hostilities – the Continuation War – in September 1944, and trapped the remnants of Army Group North in East Prussia, their backs to the sea. In the south, another offensive took the Soviets deep into the Balkans, forcing both Romania and Bulgaria to switch sides away from the crumbling Axis. Yugoslavia, Albania and Greece were liberated largely by their own resistance fighters, who harried retreating Axis forces (➡ pp. 190–1).

After a pause to build up supplies, the main Soviet attack was renewed on 12 January 1945, seizing Warsaw, trapping most of Army Group Centre around Danzig and thrusting westwards to the Oder, only 65 km (40 miles) from Berlin. The Germans by this time were extremely short of fuel, the Allied strategic bombing offensive (➡ pp. 190–1) having wiped out their synthetic oil plants. Soviet operations continued to the south, with Budapest being taken on 13 February and Vienna two months later. On 16 April, however, the long-awaited attack on Berlin began, preceded by enormous artillery and air strikes. As part of the Soviet force advanced northwest, eventually to link up with the Western Allies on the Elbe, the remainder closed in on Hitler's capital. The fighting was desperate and casualties heavy on both sides, but by 25 April Berlin was surrounded. Hitler committed suicide five days later, and the city was finally secured on 4 May. Although fighting was to continue in Czechoslovakia until 11 May, the war effectively ended with Germany's unconditional surrender on the 8th. It had cost the Soviets some 27 million dead. JP

Stalingrad, October 1942: the remains of a German infantry division assemble prior to a renewed attack on the city. The German defeat at Stalingrad at the hands of Marshal Zhukov's Red Army was perhaps the most decisive battle in the European theatre of war.

World War II: The Pacific and the Far East

Early on Sunday, 7 December 1941, Japanese aircraft attacked the US Pacific Fleet at Pearl Harbor, on the Hawaiian island of Oahu, catching the Americans by surprise. Two hours later, when the last of the attackers flew north to rejoin their aircraft carriers, five US battleships had been knocked out and three more damaged. The Pacific War had begun.

Relations between Japan and the USA had been strained for some time. Japanese expansionism, shown by attacks on Manchuria (1931) and China (1937) (⇨ pp. 187, 188 and 196), alarmed the Americans, who reacted by denying the Japanese access to strategic raw materials. To the Japanese – increasingly dominated by militarist leaders – this was deeply worrying, for without resources such as coal, iron ore and oil, the country could not survive. Pressure on the colonial powers – Britain, France and the Netherlands – to guarantee access to such resources merely caused the Americans to freeze Japanese assets and limit the export of their own oil. A clash became inevitable. Behind a screen of diplomacy, the Japanese planned to destroy US naval power in the western Pacific, in preparation for attacks on British, American and Dutch possessions in the Far East. Their aim was to create a 'Greater East Asia Co-Prosperity Sphere', out of which strategic resources could be exploited. Pearl Harbor was the first step.

US Navy recruiting poster, 1942. The USA's mobilization of manpower and industry during World War II was on an unprecedented scale. Given its huge resources, the defeat of the Axis powers was only a matter of time.

The fall of the Far East

The next few months saw one of the most breathtaking offensives of World War II. As Pearl Harbor was being bombed, Japanese forces attacked Wake Island and Hong Kong, mounted air assaults on the Philippines, and invaded both Thailand and northern Malaya. By Christmas 1941, the Gilbert Islands and Guam had been seized, Borneo and the Philippines invaded, and British naval strength in the Far East destroyed. On 15 February 1942, after a poorly conducted British campaign in Malaya, Singapore surrendered, while in the Philippines the Americans capitulated on 6 May. By then, the Japanese had landed in New Britain and northeast New Guinea (so threatening Australia), had secured the Dutch East Indies (Indonesia), and forced the British to abandon Burma. In less than six months, an immense new empire had been carved out.

The battle of Midway

But the Allies were not about to give in. On 18 April 1942, US bombers flew from the aircraft carrier USS *Hornet* to raid Tokyo. This helped to persuade Japanese leaders that further offensives were needed to create a protective barrier around their new possessions. Attacks against the Aleutian Islands in the north were intended to divert US attention and allow amphibious forces to seize Port Moresby in Papua New Guinea and Midway in the central Pacific.

Unknown to the Japanese, the Americans had cracked their naval codes and were aware of the plan. As an invasion fleet approached Port Moresby, it was intercepted and turned back in the battle of the Coral Sea (7/8 May) by US carrier-borne aircraft (⇨ box). The Japanese responded by mounting an overland attack on Port Moresby, using the Kokoda Trail from Buna (seized on 22 July), but atrocious terrain and dogged Australian resistance forced them back in September. By then, the Americans, ignoring moves against the Aleutians, had concentrated naval forces to meet the main Japanese invasion fleet heading for Midway. On 4/5 June the rival naval-air fleets battered each other in the battle of Midway, during which the Americans lost one carrier but destroyed four Japanese equivalents. It was a turning point of the Pacific War.

The Allied counter-offensive

Victory at Midway allowed the Americans in the southwest Pacific, under General Douglas MacArthur, to mount a counter-offensive in the Solomons. On 7 August, US Marines landed on Guadalcanal and, after hard fighting on land and at sea, the Japanese were forced to evacuate the island in February 1943. By then, Australian and US troops had counter-attacked along the Kokoda Trail and recaptured Buna. This gave MacArthur two axes to exploit – on the left in New Guinea and on the right in the Solomons –

in order to seize the Bismarck Archipelago and neutralize the enemy base at Rabaul (New Britain). It was a long, tough campaign. In New Guinea, the Allies advanced into the Huon peninsula in late 1943 before carrying out a series of amphibious landings along the northern coast to secure the island by July 1944. Meanwhile, US troops had taken Rendova, New Georgia, Bougainville and the Admiralty Islands, leaving Rabaul to 'wither on the vine'.

This coincided with the start of a counter-offensive in the central Pacific under Admiral Chester Nimitz, driving west in a series of 'island-hopping' campaigns. The first, against Tarawa in the Gilberts, began on 13 November 1943: although it lasted only three days, the USA suffered nearly a thousand casualties against fanatical Japanese defenders. Similar difficulties arose in February 1944 when Nimitz moved on to Kwajalein and Eniwetok in the Marshalls, but a momentum was building up. It was further exploited in June, when Nimitz projected forces another 1600 km (1000 miles) westwards

MAXIMUM AREA
OCCUPIED BY JAPAN
AUGUST 1942

US, BRITISH
& COMMONWEALTH   ALLIED COUNTER-
                      OFFENSIVES 1943-45
SOVIET

WAR IN THE PACIFIC & FAR EAST 1941–45

CARRIER WARFARE

A Douglas Dauntless dive bomber circles above its carrier. These planes played a key role at the battle of Midway, the turning point of the Pacific War.

Despite the damage inflicted by Japanese aircraft at Pearl Harbor, the US Pacific Fleet was not destroyed. On 7 December 1941, no US aircraft carriers were in harbour and they remained available as a basis for future naval recovery. They were used to good effect at the battle of the Coral Sea in May 1942 and, a month later, at the battle of Midway. These were the first naval engagements fought entirely by carrier-borne aircraft, with the rival fleets remaining out of sight of each other. Such successes – plus, of course, the Japanese use of carriers in the Pearl Harbor attack – demonstrated that the era of 'grand fleets', centred upon heavily armoured, big-gunned battleships, was over.

Although US battleships played an important role, not least in shore bombardment, throughout the Pacific campaign, the crucial feature of the war against Japan was the development of carrier-based task forces. By 1944 the US Fifth Fleet was built around two new classes of carrier – the 38 000-ton 'Essex' class heavy carrier (equipped with 90 aircraft) and the 14 000-ton 'Independence' class light carrier (equipped with 33 aircraft). Spearheading such a fleet was a Fast Carrier Task Force, which, divided into mutually supporting Task Groups, could thrust deep into Japanese territory to bombard shore installations, destroy enemy aircraft, and prepare the way for amphibious landings on key islands or atolls. By early 1945, Fast Carrier Groups of the US Third Fleet were even bombarding Japan.

---

to attack Saipan in the Marianas. This time, the Japanese responded with naval units, only to suffer heavy defeat in the battle of the Philippine Sea (19/20 June). The Americans went on to take Guam and Tinian by 10 August, using them as bases for B-29 Superfortress bombers in raids against Japan.

Both MacArthur and Nimitz now converged on the Philippines. Landings took place on Leyte Island on 20 October 1944, triggering another Japanese naval commitment. It proved to be their last: on 24/25 October, in engagements known collectively as the battle of Leyte Gulf, the remaining Japanese fleet carriers were sunk. In desperation, Japanese pilots mounted *kamikaze* (suicide) attacks on Allied shipping, but to little avail. Leyte was secured by the end of December.

Elsewhere, the pressure on Japan was growing. In Burma, British-Indian and Sino-American troops slowly recovered from the humiliations of 1942, gaining experience of jungle warfare and assuming the offensive in both Arakan and northern Burma. A Japanese attack towards eastern India in March 1944 was blunted by the British Fourteenth Army under General William Slim at Imphal and Kohima. The broken enemy was then pursued to the Chindwin, where a link was forged with Sino-American and British Chindit forces under Lieutenant-General 'Vinegar Joe' Stilwell, moving

south from Myitkyina. Slim pushed southeast towards Mandalay, achieving a brilliant victory in March 1945 to by-pass the city at Meiktila, before striking down the Irrawaddy and Sittang valleys to take Rangoon. When Rangoon fell to an airborne and amphibious assault from Arakan in May, Japanese resistance in Burma crumbled.

The defeat of Japan

Meanwhile, in the Philippines MacArthur had invaded Luzon on 9 January 1945, aiming for Manila. The fighting was hard – it was early March before the devastated capital was secured, and clearing the rest of the Philippines was to take until August – but the Japanese were clearly in trouble. Casualties on both sides were heavy: the Americans lost 8000 men in the liberation of the Philippines, another 7000 to take the small island of Iwo Jima (February–March) and 12 000 in securing Okinawa (April–June); Japanese casualties were even higher. Such escalating losses made the Allies uneasy about the potential cost of an actual invasion of Japan.

In the event, Japan was defeated by other, more terrible, means. By early 1945 the Japanese navy and merchant fleet had virtually ceased to exist, cutting the Home Islands off from the resources of the southern Pacific. Equally significantly, B-29s from the Marianas had begun to mount devastating raids on Japan's cities – Tokyo was burnt out in a firestorm on

9/10 March. By July the bombers had, quite literally, run out of worthwhile targets. But the Japanese still did not surrender, causing President Harry Truman (Roosevelt's successor after the latter's death in April) to deploy the very latest – and deadliest – weapon. On 6 August an atomic bomb was exploded over Hiroshima, killing 78 000 people in an instant; another was exploded over Nagasaki three days later, killing a further 35 000 (▷ p. 226). By then the USSR had declared war on Japan and invaded Manchuria. On 15 August Emperor Hirohito broadcast to his people, ordering surrender. The Pacific War ended officially on 2 September when Japan signed the documents of capitulation on board the US battleship *Missouri* in Tokyo Bay. On 8 September the Americans under General MacArthur arrived in Japan and set up a US military government (▷ p. 222).   JP

China in the 20th Century

At the beginning of the 20th century China was in turmoil. Despite a remarkable continuity of civilization dating back to at least 2000 BC (▷ p. 52), the authority of the emperor had been weakened in the 19th century by outside powers greedy for trade, and by huge rebellions which had left large areas of the country beyond the control of central government (▷ pp. 57 and 163). In 1911 a revolution, led by the *Guomindang* (*Kuomintang* or Nationalists) under Sun Zhong Shan (Sun Yat-sen; 1866–1925), overthrew the last of the Manchu emperors. Strong in the south (where Sun established a republic in 1916), the Nationalists faced problems in the north, which was ruled by independent warlords resentful of central interference.

Revolutionary soldiers in Hangzhou, Zheijiang province (east-central China) in 1911. The revolution began in Hubei province (central China), where junior officers took possession of the city of Wuhan following a mutiny. Supportive uprisings in other provinces quickly developed into a national revolution, ending 2500 years of imperial rule.

By the time of Sun's death in 1925 it was obvious that if the republic was to be extended to the whole of China, force would have to be used: indeed, Sun's successor, Jiang Jie Shi (Chiang Kaishek; 1887–1975), gained his new position primarily because he commanded the Nationalist armies. Some inroads were made into the north, only to be undermined by the emergence of another, potentially powerful political force – the Communists.

Mao Zedong and the Communist revolution

The Chinese Communist Party (CCP) was formed in Beijing (Peking) in 1921, taking as its model the Bolshevik revolution in Russia four years earlier (▷ p. 180). But the Russian Communists had based their revolution on the discontented urban working class, and this the Chinese – an overwhelmingly peasant people – lacked. By 1928, after a series of disastrous urban uprisings, easily and brutally suppressed by Jiang, the CCP seemed doomed to extinction.

While this was going on, however, a relatively unknown member of the CCP, Mao Zedong (Mao Tse-tung; 1893–1976), had been experimenting with new ideas. Recognizing that any successful revolution needed popular support and that in the China of the time such support could only come from the peasants, he concentrated on the rural areas, setting up 'safe bases' among the people, which would act as a strong foundation for future action against the Nationalist government. Operating initially in his own home province of Hunan, in south-central China, then in the remote and inaccessible mountains of neighbouring Jiangxi, Mao proved so successful that by the early 1930s he was posing a direct challenge to Jiang's authority.

Jiang responded with military action, gradually reducing the Jiangxi base until, in October 1934, Mao was forced to withdraw. During the next 12 months he led his followers on a 9000-km (5600-mi) trek known as the 'Long March', moving from Jiangxi to the even more remote northwestern province of Shaanxi. Jiang, convinced that he could do no more damage, let him go.

The Sino-Japanese War

But by this time Jiang was facing a much more immediate threat – that of Japanese

Mao Zedong, a former teacher and son of a prosperous farmer. By bringing Communist rule to China, he transformed the lives of a quarter of the world's inhabitants.

expansion. This had begun in 1931 with the Japanese seizure of Manchuria (one of the few centres of Chinese industry), and this was followed six years later by an all-out attack that led to the Japanese occupation of Beijing as well as of substantial parts of the Chinese coast (▷ p. 187).

Despite an alliance between Jiang and Mao, the Nationalists (who bore the brunt of the fighting) could do little to counter Japanese aggression. Only after the extension of the war to the Pacific and Southeast Asia in 1941–2 (▷ p. 195) could Jiang be guaranteed the outside support he needed, especially from the USA, but even then the record of the Nationalists was poor. They were still facing the Japanese occupation of large parts of China when Japan surrendered to the Allies in August 1945 (▷ p. 195).

Part of the pressure exerted on Japan in the final days of the war was a Soviet invasion of Manchuria. In its aftermath the Soviets tried to ensure that Mao's Communists took over the area, hoping to accelerate the revolution. During the Sino-Japanese War Mao had extended his influence and gathered strength, waiting for an opportunity to attack the weakened Nationalists. In 1946 he marched into Manchuria.

The civil war and Communist victory

This began a civil war in China that was to last for three years. At first the Nationalists held on to Manchuria, but gradually lost their grip in the face of guerrilla attacks. By 1948 Manchuria was in Communist hands and, when this was followed by attacks on Beijing, Jiang's forces began to collapse. On 1 October 1949 Mao proclaimed a People's Republic in Beijing. Jiang fled to the offshore island of Taiwan, where a Nationalist government was set up. The Communists periodically exerted military and political pressure against the Nationalists, most notably in 1958 when Mao's forces tried to seize the Nationalist-controlled islands of Quemoy

and Matsu. However, the Nationalist government in Taiwan still exists today (⇨ p. 223).

Meanwhile, in 1949 Mao's first priority was to ensure Communist control over the whole of mainland China, sending the newly created People's Liberation Army (PLA) to root out 'class enemies' and the remnants of the Nationalist armies. This led in 1950 to the first of a series of moves beyond the borders of China, when PLA units entered Tibet, an independent state since 1916. Repressive Communist rule alienated the native Tibetans, loyal to their religious leader, the Dalai Lama, and in 1959 they rose in revolt, only to be ruthlessly suppressed. Tibet has remained under Chinese control ever since.

Border wars

Expansion such as this highlights one of the chief priorities of the Chinese Communists – to secure the borders of China against outside interference. From late October 1950 PLA 'volunteers' saw action in Korea, triggered by an advance by United Nations forces into Communist North Korea after the North Koreans had been pushed back from their invasion of the South (⇨ pp. 204–5). As the UN advance seemed to be approaching the Yalu River on the border with China, Mao felt justified in committing his troops, initiating a costly but (in Chinese eyes) ultimately successful campaign that lasted almost three years. At the end of the Korean War in 1953 all of the North had been restored to Communist control and the threat to China's border removed.

Similar intervention in the Himalayan border region against India in 1962 prevented what was seen as a threat from that direction, while in 1979 an incursion into northern Vietnam, albeit less successful militarily, continued the trend.

The Sino-Soviet split

The incursion into Vietnam had its origins in a Chinese fear of Soviet encirclement, for by then Vietnam was supported by the USSR. Such a fear had seemed justified ever since relations between China and the USSR deteriorated in the late 1950s, triggered by ideological clashes over the true nature of Communism and fuelled by border clashes in Manchuria. One of the results was an acceleration of Chinese research into atomic weapons – they test-exploded their first device in 1964 (⇨ p. 226) – but of far more significance was the effects of the split on Chinese domestic and foreign policy. In foreign-policy terms, Mao mended fences with the USA in the early 1970s, playing the West against the East in a new twist to the Cold War (⇨ p. 206), while at home he tried to radicalize the revolution to ensure its ideological strength.

The Cultural Revolution and its aftermath

The process of radicalization had begun in the 1950s, when the PLA (always primarily a political rather than a military

---

HONG KONG

On 26 January 1841, British sailors raised the Union Jack over the tiny, barren island of Hong Kong, off the southern coast of China. The action was in response to the Chinese closure of the nearby port of Canton to British trade – dominated by opium: the First Opium War ended in 1842 (⇨ pp. 57 and 163), when Hong Kong island was ceded to Britain in perpetuity. Eighteen years later, at the end of the Second Opium War, Britain received the tip of the Kowloon peninsula on the mainland, and in 1898 negotiated a 99-year lease over the rest of the New Territories.

When Hong Kong was first seized, the native population was less than 5000, but the island's position as a free port under British rule attracted entrepreneurs and refugees from the rest of China. By 1854 the population had increased to 45 000; by 1919 it stood at over 600 000. Today, the population – 98% of whom are still Chinese – is over six million, placing enormous strain on housing and social services. British troops and the Hong Kong Police try constantly to prevent additional, illegal immigration from China, while the influx of Vietnamese 'Boat People' since 1975 (⇨ p. 209) has done nothing to ease population pressure.

In 1984 Britain negotiated with China over the future of Hong Kong. The lease on the New Territories runs out in 1997 and, although Hong Kong island would theoretically remain British, its position would clearly be untenable. China is scheduled to take over the whole colony in 1997 – a prospect that worries Hong Kong's inhabitants, many of whom were originally refugees from the Communist system on the mainland.

---

instrument) had been sent into the countryside to spearhead the 'Great Leap Forward', an ambitious programme of land collectivization and education. It had largely failed, suggesting to Mao that the PLA had lost its revolutionary zeal.

After appropriate reforms in the PLA, Mao tried again in the mid-1960s, determined to spread more radical revolutionary ideas to the people in the so-called

---

Cultural Revolution. He stirred up a hornets' nest, with militant students forming groups of 'Red Guards' to attack the existing hierarchy, which they regarded as bourgeois, over-Westernized and technocratic. Thousands died, and thousands more bureaucrats and intellectuals were sent to work in the fields. Mao was lucky to survive, having to turn to the PLA for support against the Red Guards when they went out of control. The power struggle that ensued between the militants and the now influential PLA was still being played out when Mao died in 1976.

After Mao's death China – under the leadership of Deng Xiaoping (1904–) – followed a more careful course both at home and abroad. Border disputes were settled more peaceably, and relations with the USSR were cautiously re-established in 1989. Foreign affairs generally were characterized by more open friendship with previously hated enemies. The agreement to negotiate the future of Hong Kong, which is to cease to be a British colony and revert to Chinese control in 1997, is a case in point (⇨ box).

The reason for this opening up to foreign countries was that the Party leadership had recognized the need for industrialization and modernization if China was to compete in the world, and this would be impossible if foreign crises occurred. Western technology was needed, and for this to be available and effective in China, less extreme policies had to be introduced. Economic liberalization and an opening up to Western cultural influences led to internal pressures for political change, culminating in massive pro-democracy demonstrations by students and workers in early 1989. These were brutally repressed by an ageing leadership apparently unwilling to loosen its hold on political power. In the face of an international outcry, China seemed to be turning inwards again.

China is currently at a crossroads: if it succeeds in modernizing its industry it has great potential; if it reverts to repression and international distrust, the record of violence and war so characteristic of its history in the 20th century could continue. JP

SEE ALSO
● CHINA TO THE MONGOLS p. 52
● CHINA FROM THE MONGOLS TO THE MANCHU p. 56
● WORLD WAR II: THE PACIFIC AND THE FAR EAST p. 194
● THE COLD WAR p. 204
● THE RISE OF EAST ASIA p. 222

Pro-democracy demonstrators in Tiananmen Square, Beijing (1989). The visit to Beijing of President Gorbachov for a Sino-Soviet summit (15–18 May) encouraged many dissident students and workers to join the protest that had begun in April. Between 500 and 5000 of the 150 000 protesters camped in the square were killed when the demonstrations were crushed by troops (3–4 June).

The Soviet Empire

The decade of the 1930s saw the Soviet Union transformed. Under the slogan 'building socialism in one country', the Communist Party, led by Joseph Stalin, launched a massive programme of industrialization. A series of 'five-year plans' turned the USSR, in a very short time, into a modern industrial state. New steel mills, tractor factories and power plants were built. The cities grew, and output rose fourfold.

Yet the cost in human terms of this attempt to catch up with the West was incalculable. To pay for the new industries, Stalin ordered that the land be taken away from its new peasant owners (1928; ▷ p. 181) and used to create collective farms, which were supposed to be more efficient as well as egalitarian. In the process the kulak (rich peasant) class was destroyed, with perhaps 10 million deaths in 10 years. Millions starved to death during the 'Harvest of Sorrow' in the Ukraine during the winter of 1932–3. The 'Great Terror' of 1936–8 (▷ box) consumed many millions more, shot by the secret police or dying in the Gulags (▷ box).

In 1928 the first of the five-year plans to improve Soviet heavy industry began. Generally, the targets were too ambitious; nonetheless Soviet industry did begin to catch up with the West. As in pre-revolutionary days, rapid industrial growth caused much hardship. Living standards plummeted as the industrial workforce swiftly doubled to 6 million,

Stalin and Lenin dominate a poster of the Spanish Association of Friends of the Soviet Union (1937). In the 1930s, a more expansive Soviet foreign policy was introduced by Maksim Litvinov, who emphasized the need to cultivate possible allies abroad. The new Popular Front policy encouraged Communists to ally themselves with socialist parties, and Communist-supported Popular Front coalitions took power in both Spain and France in 1936.

and Soviet officials were quick to punish underproduction by imprisonment in labour camps.

The East European empire

World War II saw still more suffering. During what the Soviet people know as the Great Patriotic War, the USSR lost 27 million people – more than the total number of casualties of the Western allies in both World Wars (▷ p. 192). After the defeat of Nazi Germany in 1945, the formerly independent Baltic states of Estonia, Latvia and Lithuania – annexed since 1940 – were absorbed into the Soviet Union. Areas of eastern Poland were annexed by the Soviet republic of the Ukraine, while northern Bukovina and part of Moldavia were taken from Romania. Moscow-dominated regimes were imposed throughout Central and Eastern Europe. And in all the newly 'liberated' countries the Stalinist system of one-party dictatorial rule was introduced.

For the great majority of people throughout the Communist world the postwar years were a time of great hardship. Resources were poured into rebuilding the war-devastated economies of the USSR and her satellites, leaving their citizens with little food, primitive living conditions, and subject to arbitrary police terror and the constant threat of the labour camp. For the lucky few in the party and state bureaucracies, however, a vast system of special privileges was introduced.

Khrushchev and 'de-Stalinization'

Within three years of Stalin's death in March 1953, Nikita Khrushchev had become the dominant leader of the Soviet Union. He embarked upon a policy of reform and attempted to restructure the inefficient planned economy. Increased spending was allocated to the provision of food for the people and the improvement of living conditions. In his 'secret speech' to the 20th Congress of the Soviet Communist Party in 1956, Khrushchev denounced Stalin's crimes. The new mood of 'de-Stalinization' saw an end to mass terror, the closure of the labour camps and much greater freedom of speech.

This was a time of great optimism. The economy was growing, with consequent improvements in living standards for millions of ordinary citizens. Khrushchev's personal diplomacy and informal manner contributed to a brief thaw in the Cold War (▷ p. 204–7) as he pursued a policy of 'peaceful coexistence'. Scientific and technological achievements captured the public imagination. The USSR successfully launched the first artificial satellite, the Sputnik, in 1957, and Yuri Gagarin became the first man in space in 1961. In the same year Khrushchev predicted that the Soviet Union would overtake the USA economically by 1970, and would implement 'full Communism' by 1980, when goods would be distributed according to the Marxist principle 'from each

according to his ability, to each according to his needs'.

However, things rapidly went wrong for Khrushchev. His economic reforms and his unrealistic plan to open up over 250 000 km² (nearly 100 000 square mi) of virgin land for agriculture ended in failure and a return to food shortages. Relations with the West deteriorated after Soviet tanks crushed the Hungarian revolution in 1956, and especially after the Cuban missile crisis of 1962 (▷ p. 206). Khrushchev's cuts in defence spending antagonized the Soviet military and, above all, his political reforms threatened the power and privileges of the bureaucracy. The groups he had offended combined to remove him from power in October 1964.

Brezhnev and the 'period of stagnation'

The new general secretary of the Communist Party was Leonid Brezhnev. By nature a cautious leader, Brezhnev was motivated above all by a desire to avoid Khrushchev's mistakes. After Brezhnev sent Warsaw Pact forces into Czechoslovakia to crush the 'Prague Spring' reform movement in 1968, he formulated what became known in the West as the 'Brezhnev Doctrine' – that is, the right of the Soviet Union to intervene militarily in the affairs of Communist countries to maintain unchallenged ideological and political supremacy.

At home, the Brezhnev leadership relied upon compromise, although dissidents were suppressed. Wages for the working class were raised and many consumer goods, such as colour televisions and refrigerators, could now be found in the shops for the first time. The Soviet armed forces were kept happy by the huge sums poured into defence, and the bureaucrats were assured of jobs and special privileges for life.

This policy worked for as long as there was economic growth. However, by the late 1970s the absence of reform led to a rapid deterioration in industrial and agricultural performance and in the distribution of food. Many goods were now only available on the black market. Corruption, alcoholism and abuse of power were commonplace. Life expectancy fell as hospitals proved unable to cope with the demands placed upon them. But official statistics continued to claim growth and achievements.

Relations with the West were greatly harmed by the Soviet invasion of Afghanistan (1979; ▷ p. 207) and the declaration of martial law to crush the Solidarity movement in Poland (1981). The Cold War intensified as a reassertive USA confronted what American president Ronald Reagan called 'the evil empire' of the Soviet Union. But while the crisis in international relations was obvious, the extent of the USSR's internal problems was not so evident.

The response to the crisis was inactivity. Brezhnev – in his last years incapacitated by illness – effectively ceased to govern, and the remainder of the leadership – isolated from the everyday problems by their privileges, special shops and hospitals – were too preoccupied with the struggle to succeed him. Brezhnev was followed by two weak and ageing leaders – the former head of the KGB Yuri Andropov and the colourless Konstantin Chernenko. These stopgap leaders were either unwilling or unable to make much impact on the crisis. By 1985 the USSR was crying out for change (▷ p. 224).   MW

Soviet leaders, including Leonid Brezhnev (fourth from the right), taking the salute during the traditional May Day parade on Red Square. The precedence given to particular individuals on these occasions – and their apparent state of health – was closely watched by Western 'Kremlinologists' to assess the relative power and influence of various politicians and factions within the Communist Party.

A Soviet tank in the streets of Prague in August 1968, when Soviet bloc forces suppressed the so-called 'Prague Spring'. In April 1968, Czechoslovak Communist Party leader Alexander Dubček initiated an 'action programme' of constitutional, legal and social reforms – 'Socialism with a human face'. Alarmed by the freedom of the Czech press and attempts to re-establish an opposition party, Warsaw Pact forces invaded and occupied Czechoslovakia (20 August). Dubček was replaced by the hardliner Gustav Husák.

GULAG

GULAG in Russian is the acronym for the Chief Administration of Corrective Labour Camps. This was the body responsible for supervising a vast and elaborate system of detention, torture and imprisonment of dissidents – 'enemies of the state' – inside the Soviet Union, chiefly during Stalin's period of rule (1924–53). Those caught up in the system, many for reasons they did not fully understand, usually served their sentences in one of a huge network of camps – the 'Gulag archipelago' – in northern Siberia. Survivors of the camps often remained in 'internal exile' for further terms.

The practice of exiling political dissidents to Siberia dated back to 19th-century Russia, but the precise origins of GULAG lie in the early days of the Russian Revolution of 1917, when Lenin, as leader of the Bolshevik faction (▷ p. 181), ordered the 'merciless suppression of attempts at anarchy on the part of drunkards, hooligans, counter-revolutionaries and other persons'. It was a wide net, and was used over the succeeding years by the Ministry of the Interior (MVD) and its secret police (NKVD) to catch an enormous variety of people and remove them from society. These included political protesters, Christians, Jews, members of ethnic minorities, opponents of agricultural collectivization, intellectuals, teachers, and even ordinary workers who 'sabotaged' the state by failing to complete impossible 'norms' of industrial production. They were joined in the late 1930s by the victims of Stalin's political and military purges (▷ box) and, after 1945, by Soviet soldiers who had surrendered to the Germans in World War II. Estimates of the numbers detained in the camps under Stalin range from 6 to 15 million people.

Under Khrushchev, control of the labour camps was transferred from the security services to the Ministry of the Interior. Many of the Siberian camps – traditionally those with the harshest regimes – were closed, and there began a gradual mitigation of the worst excesses of the network. But the system of corrective labour remained as a harsh but effective method of totalitarian control. Under Brezhnev many distinguished dissidents were imprisoned; among those sent into exile were the novelist Alexander Solzhenitsyn and the physicist Andrei Sakharov. After Gorbachev came to power intellectual dissidents were released as his policy of *glasnost* (▷ p. 224) came to have effect from 1987.   JP

Decolonization

Soviet leader Nikita Khrushchev (centre) with presidents Nasser of Egypt (on his right) and Ben Bella of Algeria (on his left). Khrushchev abandoned Stalin's policy of encouraging African and Asian Communists in favour of supporting nationalist Third World leaders with aid and trade. By supplying arms to Egypt from 1955, the USSR allied itself with radical Arab nationalism in the Middle East.

The process of decolonization, or withdrawal from empire, is by no means a novelty peculiar to the second half of the 20th century. In classical times, for instance, the Persians, Greeks and Romans in turn abandoned their once-expansive empires; in the early 19th century Spain and Portugal proved unable to maintain their colonies in Latin America in the face of an outburst of nationalist feeling. More recently Germany lost its overseas holdings in Africa and the Pacific as a result of defeat in World War I (⊳ p. 182), while both Italy and Japan lost theirs as a result of defeat in World War II. The theme of decolonization is therefore a well-established one and, like the process of setting up and maintaining an empire – imperialism – a recurrent one in world history.

For all that, however, the decolonization process that has taken place since 1945 can be distinguished from previous imperial retreats by the sheer magnitude of what has happened. Whereas the Roman Empire of antiquity was restricted to the Mediterranean basin, Western Europe and parts of the Middle East, the retreat from empire by Western European powers during the modern period has affected virtually the entire world.

It is instructive to contrast the political map of the world in 1945 with its equivalent 30 years later. In 1945 there were some 70 independent sovereign states in existence, and much of the globe – especially vast tracts of Africa, the Indian subcontinent, Southeast Asia and the Middle East – was controlled by European colonial powers, either as colonies and protectorates or 'mandates' from the now defunct League of Nations (⊳ p. 183 and map, p. 163). Thirty years later there were more than 170 independent states on the map, the increase being accounted for almost entirely by decolonization, and there were hardly any non-self-governing areas left. The age of European colonialism was over, the nationalist revolution having wrought a massive change in the international political system.

Pressures for change

That such a transformation came about has been explained by some historians in terms of a 'push-pull' concept – in other words, that the colonial powers abandoned their empires both because of the 'push' provided by the rise and spread of nationalism within their colonies, and because of the 'pull' provided by liberal opinion in the home countries. The two processes coincided with dramatic effect during the second and third quarters of the 20th century to produce the wholesale withdrawal from empire.

The 'push' – rising demand for self-government and independence – may be explained by a number of factors. One of these, the basis for the growth of nationalist sentiment within colonial territories, was the tendency of the colonial powers to provide Western-style education to their colonial subjects, albeit a minority of those subjects only and usually no more than a small elite. Education was provided for reasons of self-interest as well as altruism – an educated elite was a valuable asset in terms of local administration and development. But the consequences were the same: the emergence of a group of people who understood Western ways and who were imbued with notions such as freedom, self-determin-

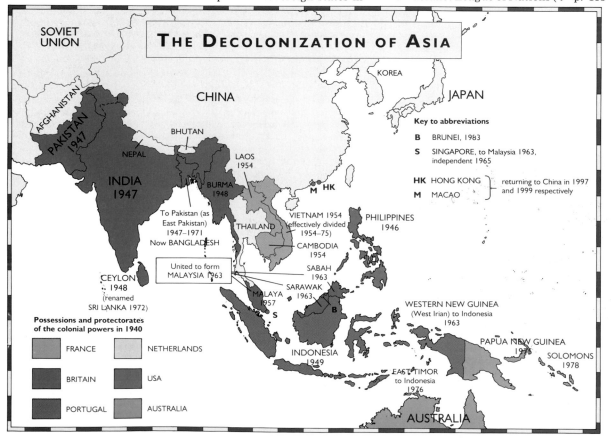

THE DECOLONIZATION OF ASIA

SOVIET UNION

CHINA

KOREA

JAPAN

AFGHANISTAN

PAKISTAN 1947

BHUTAN

NEPAL

INDIA 1947

BURMA 1948

LAOS 1954

To Pakistan (as East Pakistan) 1947–1971 Now BANGLADESH

VIETNAM 1954 (effectively divided 1954–75)

THAILAND

CAMBODIA 1954

PHILIPPINES 1946

United to form MALAYSIA 1963

SABAH 1963

SARAWAK 1963

CEYLON 1948 (renamed SRI LANKA 1972)

MALAYA 1957

S

B

WESTERN NEW GUINEA (West Irian) to Indonesia 1963

PAPUA NEW GUINEA 1975

SOLOMONS 1978

INDONESIA 1949

EAST TIMOR to Indonesia 1976

AUSTRALIA

Key to abbreviations

B   BRUNEI, 1983

S   SINGAPORE, to Malaysia 1963, independent 1965

HK   HONG KONG   } returning to China in 1997
M   MACAO   } and 1999 respectively

Possessions and protectorates of the colonial powers in 1940

FRANCE

NETHERLANDS

BRITAIN

USA

PORTUGAL

AUSTRALIA

ation and equality, and determined to enjoy such advantages themselves.

Another equally significant factor was the development in many colonies of an economic infrastructure (roads, railways, schools, etc.) and even some commerce and industry. This helped to stimulate 'detribalization' (the breaking down of barriers between different groups of people within a colonial area) and, allied to the spread of education, this produced groups of colonial subjects susceptible to the nationalist message.

Finally, the clash of cultures brought about by imperialism created upheaval. The imperialists were alien in terms of race and religion in most cases, and local people – often for the first time – became aware of their own unique characteristics. In the Middle East, for example, the importance of the Islamic religion and the steady growth of an awareness of the Arab race as a distinct social and cultural grouping undoubtedly fuelled the rise of Arab nationalism – a force of some potential as early as the 1920s and 1930s (▷ p. 210).

The myth of White invincibility

If the effect of these factors could be seen from such an early stage, World War II gave a tremendous boost to the growth of nationalist feeling – especially in areas occupied by Axis forces or cut off from the imperial power.

In Southeast Asia, for example, French and British territories were exposed to revolutionary ideas following the Japanese conquests of 1941–2 (▷ p. 194). Having shattered the myth of White invincibility, the Japanese encouraged local anti-colonial movements. After the war, these movements were superseded or enlarged by anti-Japanese nationalists – many of them Communists. Winning considerable popular backing, these elements were able to persuade or coerce the returning imperialists into granting independence – in Burma with minimal violence but in the Dutch East Indies (Indonesia) and French Indochina (Vietnam, Laos and Cambodia) only after prolonged and bloody conflict in the late 1940s and early 1950s (▷ p. 208).

In Africa, too, nationalist sentiment developed rapidly as a result of World War II. Its rise was fuelled by a variety of factors: the humiliation of France and Britain in 1940 and of Italy by 1943; economic and commercial development during the war; and, of course, by inspiration offered by Asian countries such as India and Pakistan, which gained their independence (albeit to the accompaniment of widespread sectarian violence) in 1947. By then, the Philippines had gained independence from the USA (in 1946), Britain had given notice of her intention to withdraw from the mandate of Palestine (in 1947; ▷ p. 210), and Indonesia formally became independent of the Dutch in 1949.

World War II, or more accurately the effects of that war, also encouraged the

INDIAN INDEPENDENCE

India was the key to Britain's colonial empire – a source of raw materials and an enormous market for manufactured goods at the heart of an elaborate trading system. Yet it was a deeply divided state, consisting of a host of different races, many of which had their own fiercely defended language, customs and religion. The most striking religious split – between Hindus and Muslims – produced political and social differences that transcended local boundaries. To complicate the situation further, over 550 separate princedoms still existed under their own rulers (maharajahs), subordinate to the British Viceroy but enjoying a degree of local autonomy. As a result of all this, pressures for Indian independence came from different sources, each of which had different motives and aims.

Attempts had been made to create an all-India independence movement as early as 1885, when Hindus and Muslims together founded the Indian National Congress. Divisions later emerged between moderates under G. K. Gokhale, and a militant faction led by B. G. Tilak, leading to a temporary split in 1907. After Tilak's death in 1920, under leaders such as Mohandas K. Gandhi and Jawaharlal Nehru, the Congress developed a more sophisticated administrative structure, acquired a mass membership, and embarked on a series of co-ordinated political campaigns for independence. An organization representing the interests of Indian Muslims – the Muslim League – had been founded in 1905. Elements within the League sometimes worked in harness with Congress, notably in Gandhi's non-cooperation movement of the early 1920s. But while both Congress and League were campaigning for independence, their demands were clearly contradictory. Whereas the Congress called for the establishment of an independent India within the existing boundaries of the Raj, the League opposed this – chiefly because it guaranteed Hindu rule. Mohammed Ali Jinnah, the leader of the Muslim league since 1934, in 1940 demanded a separate Muslim state of Pakistan. Communal violence, endemic since the 1930s in areas containing Hindu and Muslim populations, increased dramatically after 1945. The British authorities – prepared to offer independence but unsure how to proceed – were caught in the middle.

Field Marshal Lord Wavell, Viceroy since 1944, concluded that no single Indian authority could be created at independence, and advised instead that power should be transferred to a number of smaller states. The British government rejected this and, in 1947, replaced Wavell with Lord Louis Mountbatten. He took with him a new

independence plan: two separate states, one Hindu and one Muslim, would be created in June 1948; the individual princedoms could choose to join one or the other, or, if they preferred, could opt for their own independence. Both Congress and League accepted the proposals, and the Indian Independence Act was passed by the British Parliament in July 1947.

It was, in reality, a formula for mass violence. As soon as the plan was announced, Muslims in Hindu areas fled to either east Bengal or west Punjab (the two widely separated areas of northern India scheduled to become the new Muslim state of Pakistan), while Hindus and other non-Muslims from those regions moved in the opposite direction. Violence reached unprecedented levels as refugees were attacked, trains derailed and property looted. British-Indian troops, unsure of where their future loyalties lay, were loath to act, while a Boundary Commission under Sir Cyril Radcliffe, charged with establishing the borders of the new states, encountered insurmountable local problems. The worst of these were in west Punjab, where indigenous Sikhs fought to prevent their inclusion in Pakistan, and in Kashmir in the northwest, where the Hindu Maharajah, Sir Hari Singh, opted for independence, only to find that his predominantly Muslim population demanded transfer to the new Muslim state. It was a nightmare the British were keen to avoid: the granting of independence was accelerated, coming into effect on 15 August 1947.

In the immediate aftermath, the sub-continent dissolved into violent chaos. By the end of 1947, some 6·5 million refugees had entered Pakistan, with up to 5 million Hindus and Sikhs fleeing from west Punjab alone; in the process an estimated 500 000 Muslims and an undisclosed number of non-Muslims had died. Nor was the territorial settlement secure. Although three princedoms – Travancore, Hyderabad and Kashmir – attempted to gain independence, the new state of India refused to accept the arrangement. Travancore succumbed to political pressure and joined the Indian Federation almost immediately and Hyderabad followed suit in 1949 after an economic blockade. Kashmir, however, proved a major problem, being claimed by both India and Pakistan. Sir Hari Singh called for Indian help against his Muslim subjects in late 1947 and India effectively occupied the state. By early 1948 Pakistani and Indian troops had begun to clash on the border between Kashmir and Pakistan in the first of three wars that were to be fought between the two states. The last of these, in 1971, led to the secession of East Pakistan as Bangladesh.

The historic conference in New Delhi in July 1947 at which Lord Mountbatten (centre), viceroy of India, revealed his partition plan to Jawaharlal Nehru (left), leader of the Congress Party and the future prime minister of independent India, and Mohammed Ali Jinnah (right), leader of the All-India Muslim League and later first governor-general of Pakistan.

THE ALGERIAN REVOLUTION

A French patrol ambushed by FLN Algerian rebels (1958). A French army of over 500 000 was unable to suppress the FLN, who were well armed and trained, and received support from nationalists in adjoining Tunisia and Morocco.

Algeria was not strictly speaking a colony of France – from 1848 to 1962 its coastal region was legally and constitutionally part of 'metropolitan' France. Yet it displayed many of the characteristics of a subject territory. The population was predominantly native Muslim, dominated by a small number of European settlers known as *colons*, who held a virtual monopoly of land and political power.

Pressure for independence came from the Muslim *Front de Libération Nationale* (FLN), which began a campaign of violence in November 1954. Despite a backlash from the colons and French military commitment, the FLN gained support within Algeria and – after their independence in 1956 – from Morocco and Tunisia. By early 1957 the FLN was particularly active in Algiers, where terrorists emerged from the Arab Kasbah to plant bombs in European areas of the city. The French army was deployed in force, gaining the upper hand over the nationalists in a matter of weeks. However, the use of torture to extract information from Muslim suspects alienated moderate Muslim and domestic French opinion, leaving politicians loath to act and the army frustrated.

Elements within the army accused the French government of weakness and, in 1958, publicly sided with the *colons*, demanding *Algérie française* – a French Algeria. In Paris, the government – and with it the Fourth Republic – fell, bringing Charles de Gaulle back to power. By now, with successes against FLN guerrillas in the countryside and the creation of an effective barrier – the Morice Line – along the Tunisian border, the army was convinced it was winning. De Gaulle, however, was aware of public opposition to the war. In September 1959 his call for 'self-determination' for Algeria led extremist *colons* and members of the army to take to the streets in Algiers, threatening a coup. De Gaulle weathered the crisis, but when he sent representatives to talk to FLN leaders in 1960, four of his generals instigated a takeover of power in Algiers. Once again, French opinion backed de Gaulle, forcing the generals to surrender. Extremists now created their own terrorist group, the *Organisation de l'Armée Secrète* (OAS), which initiated a ruthless anti-Muslim campaign and plotted an unsuccessful assassination attempt on de Gaulle in 1967 in a bid to destroy the Fifth Republic. The war degenerated into a bloodbath, characterized by atrocities on both sides. De Gaulle's response was to accelerate independence. He negotiated an end to hostilities in the Évian Agreements, and Algeria was granted independence after a referendum in March 1962.

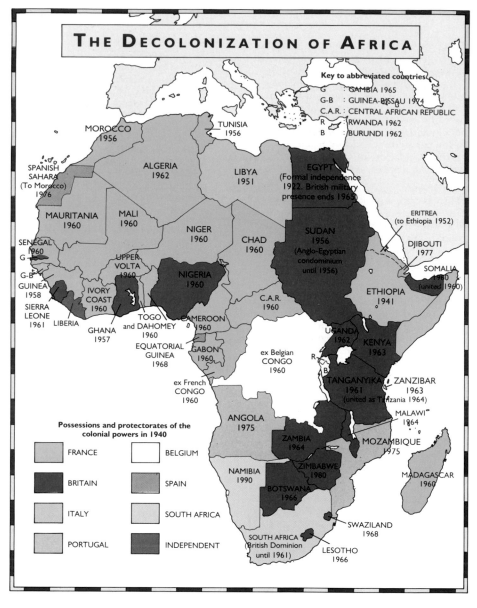

THE DECOLONIZATION OF AFRICA

Key to abbreviated countries:
G : GAMBIA 1965
G-B : GUINEA-BISSAU 1974
C.A.R. : CENTRAL AFRICAN REPUBLIC
R : RWANDA 1962
B : BURUNDI 1962

MOROCCO 1956
TUNISIA 1956
SPANISH SAHARA (To Morocco) 1976
ALGERIA 1962
LIBYA 1951
EGYPT (Formal independence 1922. British military presence ends 1965)
ERITREA (to Ethiopia 1952)
MAURITANIA 1960
MALI 1960
NIGER 1960
CHAD 1960
SUDAN 1956 (Anglo-Egyptian condominium until 1956)
DJIBOUTI 1977
SENEGAL 1960
G
UPPER VOLTA 1960
SOMALIA 1960 (united 1960)
G-B GUINEA 1958
NIGERIA 1960
C.A.R. 1960
ETHIOPIA 1941
SIERRA LEONE 1961
IVORY COAST 1960
LIBERIA
GHANA 1957
TOGO and DAHOMEY 1960
CAMEROON 1960
UGANDA 1962
KENYA 1963
EQUATORIAL GUINEA 1968
GABON 1960
ex Belgian CONGO 1960
R
TANGANYIKA 1961 (united as Tanzania 1964)
ZANZIBAR 1963
B
ex French CONGO 1960
ANGOLA 1975
MALAWI 1964
MOZAMBIQUE 1975
ZAMBIA 1964
NAMIBIA 1990
ZIMBABWE 1980
BOTSWANA 1966
MADAGASCAR 1960

Possessions and protectorates of the colonial powers in 1940

FRANCE
BELGIUM
BRITAIN
SPAIN
ITALY
SOUTH AFRICA
PORTUGAL
INDEPENDENT

SOUTH AFRICA (British Dominion until 1961)
SWAZILAND 1968
LESOTHO 1966

man's burden' of empire. Imperial glory began to feel like imperial strain.

Moreover, the colonial powers began to find themselves overstretched not only economically and militarily but also, in a sense, morally. West European leaders and public opinion in general became responsive to the idea that colonial peoples should be allowed, indeed encouraged, to achieve the same rights of self-determination that Europeans had claimed for themselves long before. In short, the colonial powers began to lose the will, as opposed to just the power, to hang on to their empires indefinitely. The 'push' and the 'pull' thus came together and the imperial powers withdrew from empire in the third quarter of the 20th century almost as systematically as they had rushed into it in the latter half of the 19th. The days of empire, for better or worse, were over.

The end of empire

Setting the pace of decolonization were the British, who had established the largest of the overseas empires. Britain had begun the process long before World War

II, granting independence to the countries of White settlement – Canada, Australia, New Zealand and South Africa – and this was followed in 1947 by the concession of independence to the largest non-White territory, India (split along religious lines into predominantly Hindu India and Muslim Pakistan; ⊳ box).

Then, under successive governments, colonies in Asia, Africa, the West Indies and Oceania followed suit, the process being greatly accelerated by the Suez Crisis of 1956, when Britain, having invaded Egypt (in conjunction with the French and Israelis) in an effort to reverse President Nasser's decision to nationalize the Anglo-French Suez Canal Company, was forced to withdraw under intense diplomatic and economic pressure from the USA (⊳ p. 210). The implication was that, even if Britain wished to maintain an empire, it could no longer do so in a superpower-dominated world.

Decolonization gathered pace in the 1960s, presaged by Prime Minister Harold Macmillan's recognition of a 'wind of change' blowing through Africa. Empire was replaced by the concept of a multira-

growth of anti-imperialist feeling in the mother countries themselves. Many of these countries, notably Britain, France, Belgium and the Netherlands, had been devastated or virtually bankrupted by the war and were finding it difficult to provide the necessary resources to rebuild their shattered economies, provide greater living standards at home and, at the same time, continue to bear the 'White

SEE ALSO

- THE PEAK OF EMPIRE p. 160
- WORLD WAR II: THE PACIFIC AND THE FAR EAST p. 194
- THE WARS IN VIETNAM p. 208
- THE MIDDLE EAST p. 210
- THE THIRD WORLD p. 218
- POPULATION AND HUNGER p. 230

THE CONGO CRISIS

The vast central African territory now known as Zaïre became a Belgian colony in 1908. From 1885, as the Congo Free State, it had been the personal possession of King Leopold II of Belgium, who amassed great personal wealth from its rubber and ivory trade and imposed a brutally repressive regime on its native population. An international outcry forced him to hand over the territory to his parliament in 1908. As the Belgian Congo, the territory became a major exporter of minerals, and developed a relatively advanced system of social services. However, the administration put a strict curb on African political activity, leaving the country inadequately prepared for decolonization.

In the 1950s, as other colonial powers resigned themselves to withdrawal from empire, the Belgians remained intransigent. However, in the late 1950s Belgian complacency received a rude shock from the wave of nationalism that swept across west and equatorial Africa. When political violence spread from Leopoldville (Kinshasa) to a number of other Congolese towns in 1959, a decolonization conference was hastily convened. June 1960 was fixed as the date for the transfer of power.

Little preparation had been made for the independence of a territory containing numerous ethnic groups and tribes, each with different aims and aspirations. A government was installed with Joseph Kasavubu as president and Patrice Lumumba as prime minister, but within two weeks of the declaration of independence on 30 June, the new state had fallen apart. The Congolese army mutinied and most Belgian colonists fled. In the copper-rich province of Katanga, Moise Tshombe, with the backing of the main Belgian mining conglomerate – the Union Minière – as well as a number of Belgian troops and white mercenaries, proclaimed an independent republic. The Belgian government promptly rushed its troops back to the Congo; not solely, as they claimed, to protect Belgian citizens, but also to support Tshombe and protect Belgian mining interests in Katanga.

Lumumba appealed to the UN for help, but the UN force of 20 000 despatched to the Congo merely expelled the Belgians and made no attempt to crush the Katangan revolt. Lumumba made preparations to invade the province, but was sacked by Kasavubu. Central government was plunged into chaos. On 14 September the chief of staff of the Congolese army, Colonel Joseph Mobutu, seized power in a military coup and arrested Lumumba. (Lumumba was to be murdered by Katangan secessionists in February 1961.)

In August 1960 a new government was set up under Cyrille Adoula, but both Lumumbist supporters in Stanleyville (Kisingani) and Tshombe in Katanga continued to defy central authority. The Congo now dissolved into a confused and bloody civil war, characterized by bitter tribal fighting and the use of white mercenaries by the rival factions. At different times independent regimes were established in Stanleyville and Kasai, as well as Katanga. With the major powers aligned with different sides in the conflict, the effectiveness of the UN forces was significantly reduced. UN operations in Katanga forced Tshombe to the negotiating table in December 1961, but Katanga only fell to the UN forces after a year of heavy fighting in December 1962. The UN forces withdrew in June 1964.

It was to take another 18 months for a strong government to emerge. During that time Tshombe – invited back from exile by Kasavubu to take control of central government – used the army and white mercenaries to put down the Lumumbist rebels in Stanleyville, who responded by taking over 1000 white hostages. On 24 November 1964 Belgian paratroopers mounted a rescue mission, but this did nothing to enhance Tshombe's political position. Unable to gain widespread support, he was dismissed by Kasavubu, who, in turn, was overthrown in a second coup by Mobutu in November 1965. Mobutu imposed his authority by force, ending a chaotic and bloody process of decolonization.

---

cial Commonwealth, formed for the most part from states that had gained independence without recourse to violence, although the British did have to fight in places such as Malaya (1948–60), Kenya (1952–60), Cyprus (1955–59), Borneo (1963–66) and Aden (1964–67) to ensure, or try to ensure, the emergence of friendly governments.

The French also withdrew from empire, though only after two protracted and bitter conflicts against nationalists in Indochina (1946–54; see p. 212) and Algeria (1954–62; ⟶ box) had persuaded them to abandon the concept of an indivisible French Union. The Portuguese, too, tried to preserve an indivisible empire, but gave up in 1974–5 after prolonged insurgencies in their three African territories of Angola (1961–74), Mozambique (1964–74) and Guinea-Bissau (1963–74).

In contrast, the Dutch accepted more quickly that they could not reassert their authority in the East Indies (Indonesia), while the Belgians granted independence to their main overseas holding, the Congo (Zaïre), in 1960, although this was followed by a bitter civil war (⟶ box). Even Spain decided to abandon her African colonies, Guinea and the Spanish Sahara, in 1968 and 1976 respectively.

By the late 1970s the world had changed dramatically, producing new political, territorial and economic rivalries as well as new opportunities for alliances and trade. One significant political development was the establishment in 1961 of the non-aligned movement (mostly consisting of African and Asian states), which encouraged foreign policies independent of the Eastern and Western superpower blocs (⟶ p. 204). However, despite the technical independence of Third World states, many of them continue to be influenced strongly – politically and economically – by either the superpowers or a former colonial power – a situation sometimes described as neo-imperialism or economic imperialism (⟶ p. 218). JP

Milton Obote swearing allegiance as prime minister of Uganda at the lavish independence celebrations (10 September 1962). The wig and gown of the lord chief justice of Uganda (left) and the plumed hat of the governor-general (right) symbolize the Westminster-style parliamentary system and institutions unsuccessfully imposed upon Uganda and other former British colonies in Africa.

The Cold War

The Allied victory in World War II was largely due to the massive military involvement of the USA and the USSR. With Europe in ruins, it was these two giants that emerged as the world's superpowers. Two new opposing military alliances emerged in Europe: NATO in the West, and the Warsaw Pact in the East (▷ box). The Cold War is the name that has been given to the confrontation between the superpowers and their respective allies that continued with varying degrees of hostility for four decades after 1945.

The term 'Cold War' derives from the fact that the superpowers themselves were never in direct military conflict, partially for fear of nuclear war. Instead there was a conflict of ideologies – Western capitalism versus Eastern Communism – exacerbated by what each side believed was the other's desire for economic and political domination of the world.

The division of Europe

In February 1945 Roosevelt, Churchill and Stalin met at Yalta to decide on the fate of postwar Europe. It was implicitly agreed that the USSR should maintain its influence in those areas occupied by the Red Army in Eastern Europe. Furthermore, Germany itself was to be divided into four zones of military occupation, with the UK, USA and France in the West and the USSR in the East. Berlin, lying totally within the Soviet sector, was to be split along the same lines.

By 1949 Soviet-dominated Communist governments were in power in East Germany, Romania, Bulgaria, Poland, Czechoslovakia, Hungary and Albania. A Communist government also came to power in Yugoslavia in 1945, but that country was expelled from the Soviet bloc by Stalin in 1948 for failing to toe the Moscow line. Throughout Communist Eastern Europe all opposition was suppressed, and many freedoms curtailed. Europe was effectively divided from the Baltic to the Adriatic, and the so-called 'Iron Curtain' had fallen.

Until 1989, only Yugoslavia, Albania and Romania had managed to break with the Moscow line. When other Eastern European countries tried to implement independent policies the USSR quickly reasserted its domination. For example, the reforming governments of Hungary (1956) and Czechoslovakia (1968) were overthrown by military invasion, and in 1981 martial law was declared in Poland to suppress the independent trade union Solidarity.

What the USSR effectively created in Eastern Europe was a series of buffer states between itself and the West. The fact that in World War II the USSR lost 27 million dead, many of them civilians, contributed to a kind of siege mentality, and in particular a determination to keep Germany divided. This fear of invasion

The Potsdam Conference
(July–August 1945) confirmed that the Soviet Union was to keep eastern Poland, which it had annexed in 1939, while Poland was to receive part of eastern Germany in compensation. The principal delegates were (front row, left to right) Clement Attlee (who replaced Churchill during the conference), Harry S. Truman and Joseph Stalin.

was undoubtedly replenished by periods of virulent anti-Communism in the West. However, it should not be forgotten that Russia even in the 19th century had had extensive imperial ambitions in Eastern Europe and Asia (▷ p. 154), and that all Soviet leaders up to the mid-1980s espoused a doctrine of world revolution.

Early confrontations

Once Hitler had been defeated, the war-

Korean War. US marines held up by advancing Chinese troops during the latter's drive across the Yalu River, December 1950.

NATO AND THE WARSAW PACT

The North Atlantic Treaty Organization (NATO) came into force in August 1949. Members are pledged to come to each other's assistance in the event of armed aggression against them. The 16 members of NATO (with the dates of their entry) are: Belgium (1949), Canada (1949), Denmark (1949), France (1949 – France left the military command structure in 1966 but remains a member of NATO), Germany (1955 as West Germany; 1990 as reunified Germany), Greece (1952), Iceland (1949), Italy (1949), Luxembourg (1949), the Netherlands (1949), Norway (1949), Portugal (1949), Spain (1982), Turkey (1952), the UK (1949) and the USA (1949).

The Warsaw Pact refers to a treaty of friendship and non-aggression signed between the USSR and its East European satellite states in May 1955. The members of the Warsaw Pact were: Bulgaria, Czechoslovakia, the German Democratic Republic (East Germany), Hungary, Poland, Romania and the USSR. Albania began to distance itself from the Pact in 1962 and withdrew in 1968. Political changes in Eastern Europe in 1989–90 weakened the Pact, and it was formally disbanded in March 1991.

time friendship and cooperation between the Allies quickly crumbled, and the old ideological hostility re-emerged.

In 1947 President Truman declared the intention of the USA to resist Communist expansion. This policy, known as the Truman Doctrine, has been pursued by all subsequent US governments. American military and economic aid was sent to the governments of Greece and Turkey, who were both fighting Communist insurrections. In addition, European reliance on the USA was ensured by the Marshall Plan, which pumped $13 billion of aid into Western Europe.

When the Western Allies proposed currency reform throughout occupied Germany, the USSR vetoed the idea. The Western Allies unilaterally instituted the reforms in their own occupation zones. In retaliation, Soviet forces blocked off all land links to West Berlin in June 1948. However, the USA and the UK organized an enormous airlift of supplies, and the blockade was eventually lifted in May 1949.

Anti-Communist feeling in the West was further intensified by the explosion of the first Soviet atom bomb, the Communist victory in China (both in 1949; ⇨ p. 196), and the outbreak of the Korean War in 1950. In the USA the 'Red Scare' came to a head with Senator Joseph McCarthy's witch-hunt of suspected Communists (1950–4; ⇨ box).

McCARTHYISM

Joseph McCarthy, a Republican senator for Wisconsin from 1946, was once described by US president Harry Truman as a 'pathological character assassin'. McCarthy came to prominence at the height of the Cold War in the early 1950s, when he alleged that there existed an orchestrated Communist campaign to infiltrate the US government at the highest level. After declaring that there were 205 Communists in the State Department – none of whom he was able to name – McCarthy embarked on a crusade to root out 'un-American' activities in all walks of life. The notoriety of his methods gave rise to the term 'McCarthyism' to refer to the practice of making unsubstantiated accusations of disloyalty or – more specifically – of Communist leanings.

As chairman of the Senate Permanent Subcommittee on Investigation, McCarthy conducted a series of televised hearings in which people suspected of leftwing beliefs were subjected to hysterical accusations, ranging from Communist sympathies to homosexuality. Those who fought back or against whom no evidence could be found were found guilty 'by association' when they refused to answer questions about friends or colleagues. Many lost their jobs as a result; others fled the USA in fear or disgust.

McCarthyism reflected the shock felt by many Americans at the sudden spread of Communism worldwide. Presented with the evidence of Communist revolts in the Far East in the late 1940s (⇨ p. 208), as well as the imposition of Soviet rule in Eastern Europe and the spate of 'spy trials' in America at the same time (⇨ box; Cold War Espionage, p. 207), McCarthy's conspiracy theory was a convenient interpretation of a complex change in the international political climate. But his methods soon alienated public opinion, especially when the investigations were extended to Hollywood. By December 1954 the Senate had seen enough: in a special vote they censured McCarthy for a 'breach of constitutional privilege', after which he faded into obscurity. His actions had been a reflection of the Cold War mentality, although his methods remain a symbol of the dangers of simplistic political views when held by powerful elected representatives.   JP

The Korean War

Korea, which had been a Japanese territory, was divided in 1945 into two occupation zones, with the Soviets to the north of the 38th parallel of latitude and the Americans to the south. The plan was that the country should eventually be reunified, but in each zone the occupying forces set up governments that reflected their own ideologies.

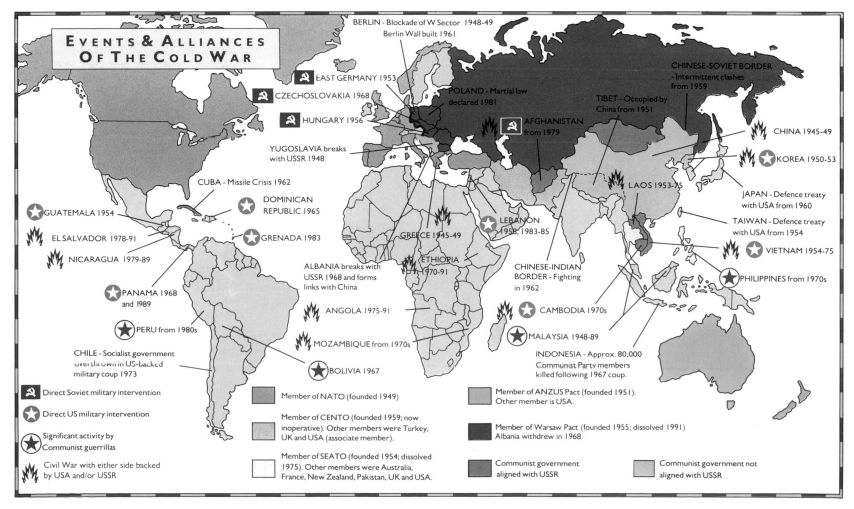

EVENTS & ALLIANCES OF THE COLD WAR

BERLIN - Blockade of W Sector 1948-49
Berlin Wall built 1961

EAST GERMANY 1953

CZECHOSLOVAKIA 1968

HUNGARY 1956

YUGOSLAVIA breaks with USSR 1948

POLAND - Martial law declared 1981

AFGHANISTAN from 1979

TIBET - Occupied by China from 1951

CHINESE-SOVIET BORDER - Intermittent clashes from 1959

CHINA 1945-49

KOREA 1950-53

JAPAN - Defence treaty with USA from 1960

TAIWAN - Defence treaty with USA from 1954

CUBA - Missile Crisis 1962

DOMINICAN REPUBLIC 1965

GUATEMALA 1954

EL SALVADOR 1978-91

NICARAGUA 1979-89

GRENADA 1983

GREECE 1945-49

LEBANON 1958, 1983-85

ALBANIA breaks with USSR 1968 and forms links with China

ETHIOPIA 1970-91

CHINESE-INDIAN BORDER - Fighting in 1962

VIETNAM 1954-75

PHILIPPINES from 1970s

PANAMA 1968 and 1989

ANGOLA 1975-91

CAMBODIA 1970s

PERU from 1980s

MOZAMBIQUE from 1970s

MALAYSIA 1948-89

CHILE - Socialist government overthrown in US-backed military coup 1973

BOLIVIA 1967

INDONESIA - Approx. 80,000 Communist Party members killed following 1967 coup.

Direct Soviet military intervention

Direct US military intervention

Significant activity by Communist guerrillas

Civil War with either side backed by USA and/or USSR

Member of NATO (founded 1949)

Member of CENTO (founded 1959; now inoperative). Other members were Turkey, UK and USA (associate member).

Member of SEATO (founded 1954; dissolved 1975). Other members were Australia, France, New Zealand, Pakistan, UK and USA.

Member of ANZUS Pact (founded 1951). Other member is USA.

Member of Warsaw Pact (founded 1955; dissolved 1991) Albania withdrew in 1968.

Communist government aligned with USSR

Communist government not aligned with USSR

The occupation ended in 1948, and in June 1950 North Korea, encouraged by social unrest in South Korea, launched a massive invasion of the South. The United Nations Security Council, which was then being boycotted by the USSR, sent armed forces to assist the South Koreans. American and South Korean forces under the command of General MacArthur (▷ p. 194) launched a counter-attack at Inchon in September and by the end of October had pushed the North Koreans back over the 38th parallel. They continued to advance northwards, ignoring Chinese warnings.

China now entered the war on the Northern side, responding with a massive attack, that drove south as far as the South Korean capital of Seoul by January 1951. However, the war of rapid movement soon stabilized into virtual stalemate along the border, where fighting continued for another two years. It was not until the USA threatened to use nuclear weapons that an armistice was signed in 1953, restoring the status quo.

Latin America and the Caribbean

Since the formulation of the Monroe Doctrine (▷ p. 157) the USA has regarded the Americas as its sphere of influence. With the onset of the Cold War this policy was adapted to resist Communist penetration of the region. Sometimes this has led to covert American involvement in the overthrow of democratically elected governments that the USA considers dangerously left-wing, as in Chile in 1973. It has also led the USA to support authoritarian governments of the right.

A long-standing irritation to the USA in the area has been Cuba, where in 1959 Fidel Castro's left-wing government came to power. Castro's nationalization of American-owned property led the US government to back an unsuccessful invasion by Cuban exiles at the Bay of Pigs (1961). Castro retaliated by adopting full-blooded Communism, and allowed the USSR to build missile bases on the island in 1962.

Afghan guerrillas resisted Soviet forces in Afghanistan (1979–89) and have continued to wage war against the pro-Soviet government in Kabul. Over 3 000 000 refugees have fled from Afghanistan into Pakistan and Iran since 1979.

THE BERLIN WALL

Under the Brandenburg Gate in Berlin, East German troops erected the first barbed wire barriers between the eastern and western sectors of the city on 13 August 1961.

During the evening of Friday, 10 November 1989, the residents of the Eberswalderstrasse in Berlin were amazed to see East German bulldozers demolishing a sector of the 'Wall' that had divided them from their neighbours in the West for over 28 years. They were aware that, only 24 hours earlier, the East German government had announced that people could pass freely through existing checkpoints in the Wall, but this was a dramatic new development. Because so many East Germans had taken advantage of their unaccustomed freedom, checkpoints had been swamped; earlier on 10 November the decision had been taken to create 18 new crossings, using bulldozers to dismantle the barrier. The Wall had effectively ceased to exist.

It had first appeared on 13 August 1961, when East German troops erected a rudimentary barrier of barbed wire through the centre of Berlin, splitting the Soviet sector of the city from areas under the control of the USA, Britain and France. Within weeks it had become a more permanent structure of bricks and concrete illuminated by floodlights, and equipped with a fearsome array of devices to discourage crossings. Movement between East and West Berlin virtually ceased. West Berlin itself, the object of Stalin's blockade in 1948–9 (▷ text) and over 160 km (100 mi) inside East German territory, became a potent symbol of the Cold War – a capitalist enclave surrounded by Communism.

The reasons for building the Wall were both political and economic. To the East Germans and their Soviet sponsors it represented a physical barrier to Western influence and a crude attempt to force a Western withdrawal from Berlin. On a more practical level, however, it was designed to stop the exodus of East Germans to the West – in the period up to 1961 some 150 000 people a year had fled across the relatively open frontier in Berlin. To the West the Wall was a constant reminder of Communist repression, denying East Germans the basic right of free movement and cruelly dividing families caught on opposite sides of the barrier.

But the Wall did not deter all those from the East who were determined to escape. Some did not survive – by 1989 over 80 people had been killed by East German guards – but those who did displayed remarkable ingenuity. Tunnels were dug beneath the Wall, special hiding places were constructed in vehicles that were allowed through the checkpoints, while some escapers even erected a rope slide from a tall building in the East down into the West.

By the 1970s – the era of détente between the superpowers (▷ text) – some movement between East and West Berlin was officially allowed, but it was to take the glasnost of the late 1980s (▷ p. 224) to produce the real breakthrough. Once the Berlin Wall had been demolished, unification of East and West Germany was not far away. It came on 3 October 1990, by which time the Wall was little more than a painful memory. **JP**

The USA saw this as a direct threat to its security, and told the Soviets to withdraw the missiles or face a nuclear attack. This piece of brinkmanship succeeded, and the missiles were removed.

Cuba subsequently attempted to export its revolution to various Third World countries. Notably active in this effort was Ernesto ('Che') Guevara. In the 1980s Cuba supported the left-wing Sandinista government of Nicaragua, while the USA supplied extensive aid to the right-wing 'Contra' rebels.

Towards détente

Following the Cuban Missile Crisis both the USA and the USSR realized how close they had come to nuclear war and mutual annihilation. Both sides sought thereafter to defuse tensions between them and to try to achieve a measure of 'peaceful coexistence'.

Although the most dangerous phase of the Cold War was over, both sides were to become embroiled in local conflicts, carefully avoiding direct confrontation with the other. Without doubt the worst of these conflicts was in Vietnam (⊳ pp. 208–9). The beginning of the Vietnam peace talks in 1968 coincided with a broader effort at détente – the term applied to a reduction in tensions between states. The USA, China and the USSR all began to adopt a more realistic, less ideologically motivated attitude to world affairs.

One of the first signs of this process was the re-establishment of friendly relations between the USA and Communist China, which by this time had established itself as the third superpower. China had broken with the USSR in the 1950s (⊳ pp. 196–7), since when relations between the two had steadily deteriorated. With China making friends with the USA, the Soviet Union saw the necessity of improving relations with the Americans. There was also the realization by both the USA and the USSR that it would be too risky to intervene militarily in the Arab-Israeli wars of 1967 and 1973 (⊳ pp. 210–3).

The results of détente included the SALT and ABM agreements in the 1970s at which the USA and USSR agreed to limitations in the nuclear arms race (⊳ pp. 226–7). There was also the Helsinki Conference of 1973–75, which was designed to reduce tension and increase cooperation within Europe.

A major setback to détente occurred in 1979 with the Soviet invasion of Afghanistan. The West immediately condemned the invasion and sent military aid to the anti-Soviet Afghani guerrillas in the subsequent civil war. For several years East-West relations were extremely frosty, with both sides accelerating the arms race. Regional conflicts broke out not only in Afghanistan but also in Central America and Africa.

The end of the Cold War

With the advent of Mikhail Gorbachov as the Soviet leader in 1985 the international climate began to change. Gradually Gorbachov initiated liberalizing reforms at home, and made a series of initiatives on arms reductions (for example agreeing the INF Treaty with the USA in 1987; ⊳ pp. 226–7). Like the Americans in Vietnam before them, the Soviets realized they could not win the war in Afghanistan without unacceptable losses, and in 1989 all Soviet forces were withdrawn.

Gorbachov also encouraged change in Eastern Europe, making it clear to the old-guard Communist leaderships that they should give way to reformers. This process was accelerated by massive popular demonstrations in many East European countries in 1989. By the beginning of the 1990s multi-party elections had taken place in all the former Soviet satellites, resulting in the collapse of Communist power in Eastern Europe, epitomized by the destruction of the Berlin Wall and, in October 1990, the unification of West and East Germany. A month later, the Charter of Paris for a New Europe, signed

by 34 states representing the old East-West divide, marked the official end to the Cold War, with agreements on human rights, territorial boundaries and arms reduction.

In September 1991, following the abortive coup by hardliners in the USSR, the Soviet Communist Party was suspended and major political reforms were implemented. However, with the Soviet Union breaking up and Yugoslavia embroiled in civil war (⊳ p. 225), Europe was clearly still subject to internal conflict. Although direct confrontation between West and East is now more remote, lasting peace has yet to be achieved. IDC

Castro's Cuba frequently expressed solidarity with other Communist states and actively supported liberation movements throughout the Third World. However, the upheavals in the USSR and Eastern Europe in 1989–91 left the Cuban government increasingly isolated as a hardline Marxist state.

COLD WAR ESPIONAGE

In September 1945 Igor Gouzenko, a cypher clerk in the Soviet embassy in Ottawa, approached the Canadian authorities with some remarkable documents. They revealed that the Soviets were running large and sophisticated spy rings in Canada, Britain and the USA and that these had been operating throughout World War II, when the Soviet Union was an ally of the Western powers. High-ranking officials, scientists and researchers had been recruited, chiefly through the Western countries' Communist parties. They were providing the Soviets with information on many of the latest developments in radar, explosives and – most significantly – atomic weaponry.

Gouzenko's revelations prompted a 'spy-hunt' in Britain and the USA. In 1946 the British physicist Dr Alan Nunn May was found to have been providing the Soviets with samples of uranium used in atomic-bomb manufacture; four years later the German-born scientist Dr Klaus Fuchs, head of Britain's atomic research centre at Harwell, was also exposed as an 'atom spy'. Both men were sentenced to long periods of imprisonment. In the USA in 1951, Julius and Ethel Rosenberg were caught passing information to the Soviets and sentenced to death; in Britain two Foreign Office officials, Guy Burgess and Donald Maclean, fled to the Soviet Union rather than face trial for similar activities. They had been tipped off by a 'third man', later found to be Kim Philby – a 'mole' in the British secret service, who defected to the Soviet Union in 1963.

Such evidence suggested that Soviet penetration of Western intelligence services was deep, and that no secrets were safe.

The fact that the Soviets had test-exploded their first atomic device in 1949 – far sooner than expected (⊳ p. 226) – tended to reinforce this view. The consequent undermining of Western confidence helped to fuel the growing belief that the Soviet Union was intent on world domination – a factor central to the development of the Cold War and to the hysteria of McCarthyism in the USA (⊳ box). Spying clearly had some effect, but it was perhaps over-emphasized. In the meantime spy rings continued to be exposed – in 1957, for example, Rudolf Ivanovich Abel (alias Martin Collins but actually called William Fischer) was found to have been operating a spy network in New York for nearly 10 years. But other methods of information-gathering were being perfected. By 1960, the Americans were deploying high-flying U2 'spy planes', capable of photographing vast areas of the Soviet Union, and electronic 'bugs' were used to eavesdrop on 'secret' conversations in embassies and elsewhere.

The Soviets were not alone in engaging in espionage. Western organizations such as MI6 in Britain and the Central Intelligence Agency (CIA) in the United States were busy returning the compliment. In 1960, for example, Anatoli Golitsyn, a Polish intelligence officer, defected to the West after having acted as a Western spy for at least 18 months. But as the Cold War progressed, more and more information was gained through spy satellites, reconnaissance aircraft and sophisticated listening posts. The 'cloak and dagger' approach – beloved of novelists and film-makers – may still be used, but it rarely has a decisive impact. JP

The Wars in Vietnam

Indochina, the area of Southeast Asia comprising Vietnam, Laos and Cambodia, has suffered almost continuous conflict since the early 1930s. In the process all three countries have come under Communist rule, and two Western powers – France and the USA – have experienced the humiliation of political and military defeat. Under the Communists conflict has continued, with fighting between differently aligned groups.

French troops defending the airstrip at Dien Bien Phu, March 1954. With the Viet Minh occupying the high ground on all sides of their isolated base, the French could only be supplied by air. The eventual French surrender led to Vietnamese independence, but the wars in Vietnam still had twenty years to run.

Communism in Indochina had its roots in nationalist opposition to French colonial rule. The Vietnamese Communist Party was founded in 1930 by Ho Chi Minh (1892–1969), dedicated to securing independence and political power. When French authority in the region was weakened by Japanese domination (and eventual occupation) during World War II, the Communists – known as the *Viet Minh* – set up 'safe bases' in remote areas and organized a strong political structure. In September 1945, after the Japanese surrender but before the French return, Ho Chi Minh declared independence for Vietnam – only to face French opposition. By 1947 he had withdrawn to the safe bases, determined to wear down his enemy using political subversion and guerrilla warfare.

The First Indochina War

The First Indochina War began in earnest in 1950 with Viet Minh attacks against isolated French outposts, forcing the colonial rulers back to defensive positions around Hanoi. In 1951 the Communists assaulted these positions head on, and were badly defeated. But Ho Chi Minh did not give up. Reverting to guerrilla tactics, he waited for his enemy to make a mistake. This came in November 1953 when, in response to a Viet Minh move into northern Laos, French airborne forces seized the isolated valley of Dien Bien Phu, close to the Laotian border. The Viet Minh surrounded the French base, and, after a 55-day onslaught, forced the French to surrender in May 1954.

Their defeat was reflected in the Geneva Accords, signed in July 1954, which granted independence to Laos, Cambodia and Vietnam. Vietnam was split along the 17th parallel of latitude, with a Communist government in the North and a Western-style government in the South, on the understanding by the North that there would be nationwide elections in 1956. The South refused to cooperate in such elections, and by 1959 the South was facing renewed pressure from the North, intent on reunification under Communist rule.

The start of the Second Indochina War

Communist guerrillas in the South, known as the *Viet Cong* (VC), began to mount attacks in rural areas. They were supported by the North via a network of jungle paths in Laos and Cambodia known as the *Ho Chi Minh Trail*. The Americans – viewing South Vietnam as a bulwark against the spread of Communism in Asia – committed advisers to train the South Vietnamese army (the Army of the Republic of Vietnam, or ARVN). It did little good: by 1963 nearly 60% of South Vietnam was affected by VC activity, and the ARVN was proving ineffectual. In November 1963 there was a military coup and South Vietnam entered a period of political chaos.

American commitment

The Americans were drawn in to fill the vacuum. In August 1964, President Lyndon Johnson claimed that North Vietnamese gunboats had attacked US warships in the Gulf of Tonkin, thereby gaining US Congressional approval for an expanded military commitment to South Vietnam and for retaliatory air strikes against the North. With VC attacks against military bases in the South increasing, and the North Vietnamese Army (NVA) beginning to threaten the borders, US Marines were put ashore to guard Da Nang, just south of the Demilitarized Zone (DMZ) on the 17th parallel (March 1965). The Marines were soon conducting major operations against VC bases, and US Army units began to be sent to the South.

Between 1965 and 1968 the Americans consciously avoided full-scale commitment of their forces, yet found themselves drawn ever deeper into the conflict. The US strategy was to use their own 'main-force' units to guard the most vital regions of South Vietnam against VC and NVA attack, and to deter the North from more active involvement by bombing selected targets beyond the DMZ. The ARVN, with its US advisers and some main-force support, struggled to remain effective. Forces from Australia, New Zealand, the Philippines, South Korea and Thailand also entered the war, but America's NATO allies refused to assist (⊳ p. 204).

Major battles took place on the borders, in which US firepower and technology invariably prevailed, but at heavy cost in casualties and material. US forces were increasingly diverted to the defence of the populated areas, although they also mounted multi-divisional 'search-and-destroy' operations in which vast areas of countryside were cleared using firepower and mobile units – but this did nothing to gain the support of the local people. The VC, adept at living underground in tunnel complexes, merely waited for the operations to end and then re-emerged to continue their activities.

Tet and US withdrawal

Nevertheless by early 1968 American generals were confidently stating that victory was in sight. So when in late January the NVA and VC mounted a series of coordinated attacks throughout the South (the *Tet Offensive*), the sense of shock in the USA was profound. It deepened as TV pictures of the fighting appeared in American homes, leading many people to question the effectiveness of Johnson's policies despite the ultimate defeat of the Tet attackers (⊳ box). Under mounting pressure, Johnson refused to stand for president in the forthcoming elections, called for peace talks (which began that year in Paris) and, as a preliminary, halted the bombing of the North. In November 1968 Richard Nixon was elected in his place, determined to end the US combat commitment (⊳ p. 217). By then, the Americans had over 550 000 troops in Vietnam.

Nixon's strategy was 'Vietnamization' – handing responsibility for the war to the ARVN so that US troops could be withdrawn. The defeat of the Tet attackers allowed the withdrawal to begin, but the NVA was still active, leading to continued fighting and US casualties. American troop morale began to suffer and US public opinion turned even more strongly

A **Chinook helicopter** airlifting members of the US 1st Cavalry Division (Airmobile) during operations near Pleiku, Vietnam, January 1966.

against the war. Nixon had no choice but to continue withdrawals, buying time by permitting air attacks and limited ground incursions into Cambodia (1970) and Laos (1971), aimed at the Ho Chi Minh Trail, by now an elaborate supply route. The pro-US Cambodian army mounted a successful coup against Prince Sihanouk, and abandoned his policy of neutrality. However, these incursions merely spread the war, leaving both countries increasingly vulnerable to pressure from their own indigenous Communist groups, the *Khmer Rouge* in Cambodia and *Pathet Lao* in Laos.

The North Vietnamese exploited the diversion of US and ARVN attention by mounting an all-out invasion of the South in March 1972. They were halted partly by ARVN resolve but more significantly by US airpower, including renewed attacks on the North. The damage was extensive and the North Vietnamese agreed to a ceasefire, signed in Paris in early 1973, which left their forces in place in South Vietnam. The Americans and other allies completed their withdrawal. Over 47 000 US servicemen had been killed without the satisfaction of a clear-cut victory.

Peace stood little chance. Nixon was forced to resign over the Watergate scandal in 1974 (⊳ p. 217) and his successor, Gerald Ford, lacked the political strength to maintain support to the South. When the NVA attacked again in early 1975 the ARVN collapsed and by late April Saigon was in Communist hands. In all, 1.3 million Vietnamese had died. Simultaneously the Khmer Rouge took the Cambodian capital Phnom Penh, and, a few months later, Laos fell to the Pathet Lao. It was a major defeat for US policy.

Continuing conflict

The violence did not end. In Cambodia the Khmer Rouge leader Pol Pot (1925–) initiated a bizarre experiment in 'social re-education', forcibly moving city dwellers to rural areas to work the land. An estimated 1.4 million people died, either of famine or at the hands of the Khmer Rouge. At the same time, Cambodian forces exerted pressure on the border with Vietnam, triggering a Vietnamese invasion in December 1978, which by 1979 had pushed the Khmer Rouge back to the Thai border. China tried to help Pol Pot by launching a four-week punitive attack on northern Vietnam (which was Moscow-orientated), but the Chinese army did not perform well (⊳ p. 197). The Vietnamese remained in Cambodia until 1988–9 when the withdrawal of their forces created a vacuum that Pol Pot attempted to fill. However, in August 1991 Cambodia's warring factions agreed on a UN-supervised peace plan.

Since 1975 there has been a mass exodus of refugees, many braving the open seas and pirates in leaky boats to find landfall in countries such as Malaysia, the Philippines and Hong Kong (⊳ p. 197). The 'Boat People' stretch the resources of their reluctant host countries, most of whom favour the forced repatriation of people they regard as economic, rather than political, refugees. The ripples caused by the violence of Indochina have not yet been calmed. JP

Vietnamese troops taking part in the formal withdrawal across the Cambodia–Vietnam border in 1989. The vacuum created by Vietnam's retreat from Cambodia was not filled until October 1991, when UN troops were deployed under the terms of a peace accord signed between the Vietnamese-installed Cambodian government and three rebel groups.

The Middle East

The Middle East refers loosely to the region around the eastern Mediterranean, stretching from Turkey in the north to Yemen in the south, and from Libya in the west to Iran in the east. In 1900 most of the region, with the exception of Persia (Iran) in the east, belonged to the Ottoman Empire. After World War I the Ottoman Empire ceased to exist (▷ p. 188), and by 1923 a new system of states had come into existence. The history of the Middle East since 1923 has been marked by the efforts of these states to establish themselves, and by their rivalries and internal political and religious struggles.

The system of states that emerged by 1923 came into being as a result of three factors: the ambitions of the victorious Allied powers during World War I, the new ideas of self-determination that flourished at the end of the war, and the resistance mounted by Middle Eastern peoples to the settlement that Europe planned to impose on the region.

After the entry of the Ottoman Empire into World War I the Allies made a number of agreements for the partition of the Ottoman Empire in the event of their victory (notably the Anglo-French Sykes-Picot secret agreement of 1916). After the war these plans were modified in deference to the USA, which regarded protectorates and annexations as old-fashioned and imperialist, and was anxious to promote self-determination for the nationalities within the Ottoman Empire. Allied demands were eventually presented to the Turks in 1920 in the Treaty of Sèvres (▷ p. 189). By that treaty the Turks renounced all their claims over the Arab provinces of the Empire, abandoned Thrace, agreed to the establishment of an

Armenian state and a Kurdish region in eastern Anatolia, a Greek-controlled enclave in Izmir, and an international regime for the Straits of the Bosphorus and the Dardanelles. They also accepted European financial control of the remainder of their territories.

Turkish nationalism

The harsh Allied proposals gave impetus to a Turkish national movement under the dynamic leadership of Mustafa Kemal (later known as Atatürk). A Greek army – originally stationed in Turkey to protect Greek citizens and property – marched inland from Izmir, but was defeated. The Armenian areas of Turkey were reoccupied in 1920. By the Treaty of Lausanne (1923; ▷ p. 182), the Allied powers abandoned their plans for the division and control of Anatolia and eastern Thrace, and in October of the same year the Republic of Turkey was proclaimed. Atatürk, its first president, embarked upon a policy of secular modernization, including the separation of state and religion, the abolition of the caliphate, and the introduction of Western law in place of Islamic.

Arabia and the Fertile Crescent

In the Treaty of Sèvres the former Arab provinces of the Ottoman Empire were treated in different ways. The granting of independence to the Ottoman territories in Arabia gave rise to a power struggle between King Hussein ibn Ali of the Hejaz and Abd al-Aziz ibn Sa'ud of Najd. By 1925 this struggle had ended in victory for al-Aziz. The territories he now controlled formed the Kingdom of Saudi Arabia in 1932. Yemen maintained its isolated independence, while along the coasts of southern and eastern Arabia a number of small states – the Aden protectorates, Oman, Trucial Oman, Qatar, Bahrain and Kuwait – remained under British protection.

The provinces north of Arabia – in the area sometimes called the Fertile Crescent – were re-formed into states under British and French mandates from the League of Nations (▷ p. 183). Mandates were trusteeship agreements and represented a compromise between the old devices of annexation and protectorate and the new concept of self-determination. Iraq, Palestine and Transjordan (modern Jordan) were given to Britain, while France received 'Greater Syria'. By 1948 all were independent, but in the meantime had experienced considerable upheaval as a result of conflict between the mandatory powers and the local populations.

The state system that the Allies imposed on this region meant little to its peoples. The boundaries drawn between the new states were artificial ones, cutting across the cultural, religious and ethnic identity of what many of its inhabitants saw as 'the Arab nation'. The potential unity of the latter was to be a powerful rallying-cry for Arab nationalists in the the 1950s and after (▷ below).

In 1920 it was still unclear what form of government Iraq was to have, or, indeed, whether it would be maintained as a single state. A major Arab uprising in the same year – suppressed only with considerable effort – led Britain to reduce its commitment in Iraq and create an Arab government under King Faisal, a son of King Hussein of the Hejaz. Faisal, a close associate of T. E. Lawrence in the wartime Arab revolt of 1916 (▷ p. 178), had been chosen as king of Syria by the Syrian National Congress, but was expelled by France, the mandatory power. In 1930 Britain substituted a treaty for the mandate and Iraq moved rapidly towards independence, which was achieved in 1932. Following a military coup that brought pro-German officers to power in 1941, Britain occupied Iraq until 1945. Britain retained bases in Iraq, and its influence there remained strong until the demise of the Hashemite monarchy in 1958.

In July 1920 French forces overthrew the Syrian kingdom established under Faisal in Damascus. France created the state of 'Greater Lebanon' by adding territories to the small autonomous region of Mount Lebanon, which had existed under the Ottoman Empire. This action was undertaken under pressure from the Christian Maronite community and was resented by other religious groups, in particular by the Sunni Muslims (▷ p. 82), who wished to remain united with their co-religionists in Damascus. From 1941 to 1945 Lebanon was occupied by the Allies. Compromise between the religious communities was reached in 1943, the resulting National Pact providing for an agreed shareout of political power. Lebanon achieved its independence from France in 1945.

France's aim of dividing Syria into several small states was thwarted by Syrian opposition. A serious uprising in 1925 forced France to seek a political solution. A treaty – similar to the Anglo-Iraqi treaty and providing for the independence of Syria and Lebanon – was agreed in 1936, but never put into force. The fall of France in 1940 and the overthrow of Vichy rule in Syria by British and Free French forces in 1941 paved the way for new demands for independence, which was finally achieved in 1946.

Palestine

Palestine proved to be the most troubled of all the mandated territories because of Britain's support for the establishment in Palestine of a Jewish national home. Political Zionism had emerged at the end of the 19th century under the leadership of the Hungarian Jew Theodor Herzl. Its aim was the creation of a Jewish state in Palestine (based on the 'biblical' lands of Israel and Judah; ▷ p. 22) as a refuge for the persecuted Jewish communities of Eastern Europe and Russia. Before 1914 the Zionist movement had little success. The Ottomans opposed Zionist demands and Zionism found no real support from any Great Power. In addition most Jews preferred to go elsewhere than Palestine

Israeli troops in action near the Suez Canal during the Suez War (October–November 1956).

(in particular to the USA), and many assimilated Jews in Western countries actively opposed Zionism.

But World War I, the projected partition of the Ottoman Empire and British plans for the conquest of Palestine improved Zionist prospects. In November 1917, in an attempt to ensure Jewish support for the war effort, the British foreign secretary Arthur Balfour undertook – subject to certain conditions – to 'view with favour the establishment of a Jewish homeland' in Palestine once the Turks had been defeated. The 'Balfour Declaration' was incorporated into the Palestinian mandate, which came into force in 1923. To the British in the 1920s and 1930s the Balfour Declaration meant little more than permitting restricted Jewish immigration to Palestine. Transjordan (the territories east of the River Jordan, now known as Jordan) was excluded from the scope of the Balfour Declaration. Britain recognized Abdullah, brother of Faisal, as ruler of this territory in 1921.

The opposition of Palestinian Arabs to Zionism was such that they refused to cooperate in constitutional developments within the mandated territory. Arab–Jewish tension was exacerbated by growing Jewish immigration from 1920. In 1936 there began a major Arab uprising against British rule, leading to a commitment of British troops to the area. In 1937 the Peel Commission declared the mandate to be unworkable and recommended partition and the formation of Jewish and Arab states. However, the British government, fearing that it might be sucked into a lengthy campaign in Palestine at a time of mounting tension in Europe, decided to oppose its recommendations. During World War II a decision on Palestine was deferred. The arrival of refugees from the Holocaust from 1946 (⇨ p. 192) heightened pressure for a Jewish state. Violence between Arabs and Jews escalated and British forces were exposed to a campaign of violence by Zionist terrorist groups, notably the Irgun Zvai Leumi and the breakaway Stern Gang. Britain gave notice that it wished to surrender the mandate to the United Nations (the successor organization to the League of Nations). On 29 November 1947 a resolution in favour of partition was passed by the UN General Assembly.

After the UN vote for partition a civil war broke out in Palestine between Jews and Arabs. The Jews eventually gained the upper hand and occupied areas of territory allocated to the Arab state. On 15 May 1948 the British mandate ended. The Jewish state of Israel, proclaimed the previous day, was recognized by the USA, but attacked by all the neighbouring Arab states and Iraq. This first Arab–Israeli war – interspersed with UN ceasefires – lasted from May 1948 to January 1949. Israel survived the conflict and made considerable territorial gains. The Arab state of Palestine – and the proposed international zone of Jerusalem –

completely disappeared, being partitioned between Israel and Transjordan, while Egypt held Gaza. In the course of the conflict some 700 000 or more Arabs fled their homes in Israel and Israeli-occupied territory and became refugees. The war was ended by a series of armistice agreements, the Arab states refusing to sign peace treaties with Israel.

Egypt: independence and revolution

For most of the 19th century Egypt had enjoyed virtual independence as an autonomous province of the Ottoman Empire (⇨ p. 154). The building of the Suez Canal by the French in the 1860s made Egypt strategically important, and in 1882 Britain occupied the country, anxious to control a waterway it considered vital to its imperial communications. In 1914 Britain declared a protectorate over Egypt, but in 1919 Egyptian nationalists led by Sa'd Zaghlul demanded independence. Egypt received nominal independence in 1922, when Britain abolished the protectorate but kept control of defence and communications. The Anglo-Egyptian treaty of 1936 recognized Egyptian independence but allowed Britain to keep troops in Egypt and so retain control of the Canal (by now an 'international waterway'). In 1946 an attempt was made to renegotiate this treaty. Britain agreed to evacuate its troops from Egypt, but the negotiations foundered on the question of the Sudan, which had been administered under an Anglo-Egyptian condominium since 1899.

By 1952 there was widespread unrest in Egypt and government began to disintegrate. A group of army officers, known as the Free Officers, staged a coup in July, forced King Farouk to abdicate, and seized power. One of the leaders of the Free Officers – Colonel Gamal Abdul Nasser (⇨ p. 200) – was to become the dominant personality in the Arab World until his death in 1970.

Radical Arab nationalism

The 1952 Egyptian revolution was the model for what became known as radical Arab nationalism – a movement designed to appeal to Arabs as a whole, not just as citizens of individual states. It was followed by revolutions in Iraq in 1958, Syria in 1963, and in several other Arab countries during the 1960s. The Ba'ath Party, which took power in Syria and Iraq during the 1960s, was to become the dominant political force in these two states. Radical Arab nationalism professed as its objectives Arab unity, socialism, and the defeat of imperialism, although its main accomplishments were to eliminate the power of the old landed classes through land reform and to replace them with a group of military officers and bureaucrats dependent on the enhanced power of the state. In foreign policy, radical Arab nationalism allied with the Soviet Union and challenged the position of monarchical and pro-Western regimes in the Middle East.

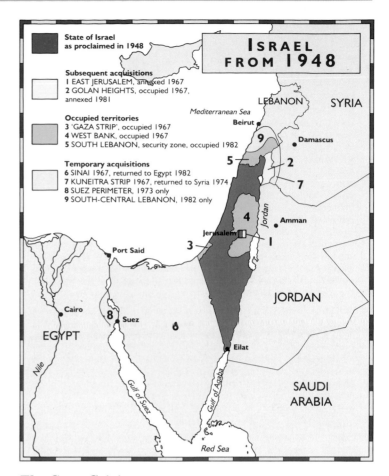

ISRAEL FROM 1948

- State of Israel as proclaimed in 1948
- **Subsequent acquisitions**
  1 EAST JERUSALEM, annexed 1967
  2 GOLAN HEIGHTS, occupied 1967, annexed 1981
- **Occupied territories**
  3 'GAZA STRIP', occupied 1967
  4 WEST BANK, occupied 1967
  5 SOUTH LEBANON, security zone, occupied 1982
- **Temporary acquisitions**
  6 SINAI 1967, returned to Egypt 1982
  7 KUNEITRA STRIP 1967, returned to Syria 1974
  8 SUEZ PERIMETER, 1973 only
  9 SOUTH-CENTRAL LEBANON, 1982 only

The Suez Crisis

European influence in the Middle East received its death blow in the Suez Crisis of 1956, which also established Nasser's position as a pan-Arab leader. The Crisis arose from Nasser's nationalization of the Anglo-French Suez Canal Company in July 1956. Fearful of losing access to the Suez Canal, Britain and France came to a secret agreement with Israel to attack Egypt. In a short, sharp war the Israeli forces occupied Sinai, while British and French forces attacked the area around the Canal. There was an international outcry, and the USA in particular exerted pressure that led to a withdrawal. A UN peacekeeping force moved into Sinai to keep the two sides apart. The Suez Crisis diminished the role of Britain and France in the Middle East. Thereafter the most influential outside powers in the region were the USA and the Soviet Union. Nasser's reputation soared as a result of his defiance of two Western powers, and in 1958 Egypt joined with Syria to form the United Arab Republic, although in 1961 Syria broke away from the union following an army coup.

The 1967 Arab–Israeli War

Nasser also played the most prominent role in the continuing dispute with Israel. The central issue of the legitimacy of the Israeli state, together with disputes over the return of Palestinian refugees, and the question of the division of the Jordan waters, had kept the Arab–Israeli conflict alive in the years after 1949. In 1967 tensions came to a head. Believing that Israel was about to attack Syria, Nasser

THE IRANIAN REVOLUTION

In February 1979 Mohammed Reza Pahlavi, who had been Shah of Iran since 1941, was overthrown and replaced by an Islamic Republic. It was a severe rebuttal for US policy, which had sponsored the Shah as a modernizing, pro-Western force in the Middle East, and as a reliable supplier of oil.

Iran had begun to benefit substantially from its oil revenues from the late 1950s, and during the 1960s the Shah launched an ambitious programme of modernization known as the White Revolution. By the mid-1970s, however, the programme had outrun Iran's ability to manage change. There was a sharp cutback and widespread discontent expressed first by liberals and then by fundamentalist Shiite Muslim groups offended by the Shah's policy of secular modernization. The Shiites came to acknowledge Ayatollah Ruhollah Khomeini, who had been exiled for opposing the Shah's policies, as their leader. From 1978 there were massive demonstrations and strikes in Iranian cities. The Shah's response veered from repression to conciliation, and involved frequent government changes. But the demonstrations increased in size, and demands expanded to embrace the abdication of the Shah and the formation of an Islamic Republic.

On 16 January 1979 the Shah left Iran: on 1 February Khomeini returned and achieved recognition as the religious leader of the revolution. The Pahlavi government collapsed; Islamic radicals took over power and created a new Islamic Republic based on an all-embracing application of Islamic values. The militantly anti-Western nature of the Iranian revolution was shown by the Iran Hostage Crisis (1979–81), in which Khomeiniite students seized the US embassy and took 66 Americans hostage (▷ p. 217).

As Supreme Spiritual Guide, Khomeini dominated Iran and its political factions until his death in 1989. He supported fundamentalist – especially Shiite – Islamic movements throughout the Middle East. His brand of militant Islam had a destabilizing influence on secular Arab nationalist states such as Iraq and Egypt, as well as on the traditional monarchies of the Gulf states. Khomeini's sponsoring of radical Shiites in Lebanon was a significant contribution to that country's political chaos in the 1980s (▷ text).

ordered the UN peacekeeping force stationed in Sinai since 1957 to withdraw from the Israeli frontier. He increased Egyptian forces in Sinai, threatened Israel, and formed a military alliance with Syria and Jordan. At the same time he blockaded the Strait of Tiran at the mouth of the Gulf of Aqaba, thereby preventing shipping from entering or leaving Eilat – the only Israeli outlet to the Red Sea.

Israel's answer was to launch a devastating attack on the air forces of the Arab coalition on 5 June, followed immediately by a rapid land campaign. In six days Israel defeated and captured territory from the Egyptians in Sinai, and did the same to the Jordanians on the West Bank (that part of Jordan west of the River Jordan), and the Syrians on the Golan Heights. Israel also took the whole of Jerusalem, which was later proclaimed as the capital of Israel. Israel's territorial gains placed it behind more defendable borders, but also made Israel less prepared to countenance a negotiated settlement of the Palestinian question. The gradual establishment of Jewish settlements in the newly occupied territories only increased Arab resentment.

The 1967 war was a defeat for radical Arab nationalism and for the Soviet Union, which had supported the radical Arab states. As the power of the radicals declined, that of the oil-rich states around

the Persian Gulf led by Saudi Arabia was enhanced as they used their wealth to subsidize the defeated states. The war also marked the beginning of much closer US involvement in the Middle East. Concern about Soviet friendship with Egypt and Syria had led the USA to back Israel in the conflict, and it came to see Israel as a valuable strategic asset against the twin threats of radical Arab nationalism and the Soviet Union (▷ p. 204). The defeat of the Arab forces also brought to prominence an important new player on the Middle Eastern stage – the Palestine Liberation Organization (PLO). Founded in 1964 virtually as an Egyptian front organization, the PLO was dominated from 1967 by al-Fatah, a guerrilla group led by Yasser Arafat, who advocated a policy of armed struggle against Israel. In the years that followed, the PLO conducted terrorist campaigns against Israel and her alleged supporters throughout the world to promote its cause. Al-Fatah guerrillas established commando bases in Jordan from where they carried out raids on Israel. In 1970 hostilities broke out between the guerrillas – angered by the moderate stance of King Hussein – and the Jordanian government, which felt threatened by their activities. Al-Fatah's military bases were broken up by the Jordanian army, and the PLO moved its forces to Lebanon (▷ below).

The 1973 Arab–Israeli war

The death of Nasser in 1970 brought to power a more pragmatic Egyptian leader in Anwar el-Sadat, who began to distance himself from the close Soviet–Egyptian ties forged by his predecessor. Intent on recovering lost territory, Egypt and Syria attempted to force Israel to the conference table on the terms of UN resolution 242, which called for a return to the borders of 1949. But neither Sadat's diplomatic efforts nor the PLO's terrorist campaign could shift the Israelis from their position.

In an attempt to break the deadlock, in October 1973 Egypt and Syria simultaneously mounted major attacks on Israel, under cover of the Jewish religious holiday Yom Kippur. Caught by war on two fronts, the Israelis were hard pressed, but nevertheless defeated Egypt and Syria after 19 days of hard fighting. During the war, a US nuclear alert – triggered by apparent Soviet moves to commit troops to the support of Egypt and Syria – reminded the world of the volatile nature of the Middle East.

The 1973 war and its immediate aftermath was notable for the impact of other Arab states – most significantly Saudi Arabia – on the crisis, through the so-called 'oil weapon'. Since 1967 the West had become much more dependent on Middle Eastern oil, and the oil price had begun to rise. In December 1973 the Organization of Petroleum-Exporting Countries (OPEC) announced a 70% increase in oil prices – causing severe balance-of-payment problems throughout the industrialized world – and threatened drastically to lower production unless Israel's Western spon-

sors forced it to withdraw from the occupied territories. The move had some diplomatic impact and brought home to the West that it could no longer afford to ignore Arab demands.

The Egyptian–Israeli peace

The 'shuttle diplomacy' of US Secretary of State Henry Kissinger (1974) led to a partial Israeli withdrawal in Sinai and the Golan, but failed to tackle the Palestinian question. In 1977 Sadat made a dramatic move in visiting Jerusalem, an action that led eventually to a peace treaty between Israel (led by the hardliner Menachem Begin) and Egypt in 1978 (the Camp David Accord), by which Israel agreed to evacuate all Egyptian territory in return for the normalization of relations between the two states. Sadat was denounced by the rest of the Arab world for deserting the Palestinians and his former allies, and Egypt was expelled from the Arab League (the main organization of independent Arab states). Sadat himself paid a heavy price for breaking with the Arab mainstream when he was assassinated by militant Islamic fundamentalists in October 1981.

Peace between the two main opposing powers of the Middle East only provided a very partial solution to the problems of the region. Israel took the opportunity of the respite to consolidate its position: in the following years it annexed part of the Golan Heights, drove the PLO from the southern part of Lebanon, and also attempted to create a pro-Israeli leadership on the West Bank, where Jews had settled in increasing numbers since 1967.

Lebanon

The National Pact in force when Lebanon became independent in 1945 enshrined power-sharing between Maronite Christians and Muslims. However, the relative toleration between the various religious groups in Lebanon began to break down in the late 1950s as Muslim numerical superiority failed to be matched by corresponding constitutional changes. Radical Muslim supporters of the union of Syria and Egypt in 1958 clashed with the pro-Western party of Camille Chamoun (president 1952-9), leading to a brief US intervention. The 1967 Arab–Israeli war and the transfer of the Palestinian leadership to Beirut (1970-1) further destabilized Lebanon.

A civil war between Christian and Muslim groups in 1975-6 caused the Syrians (who had never accepted the creation of a separate Lebanon) to intervene, moving forces into the Beqa'a Valley to the east of Beirut. The Israelis regarded this as another threat to their security, exacerbated by increasing attacks by the PLO. In June 1982 Israeli forces invaded southern Lebanon, intent on destroying PLO forces based there. They also aimed to create a buffer of Christian Lebanese between Israel and the Syrian positions.

The Israelis advanced to Beirut in less than six days, but the lack of an immediate UN-sponsored ceasefire condemned

Israel to a war of attrition. A local ceasefire in August allowed the PLO to withdraw from Beirut. However, a subsequent Israeli move into Muslim controlled West Beirut (during which Christian Lebanese forces massacred Palestinian civilians at the Sabra and Chatilla refugee camps) revived the fighting.

By June 1985 the Israelis, weakened by the seemingly endless commitment to Lebanon, had withdrawn, leaving a buffer zone on their border in the hands of the Israeli-backed South Lebanese Army. Lebanon disintegrated into ungovernable chaos, with Maronites, various Sunni and Shiite Lebanese groups (including Iranian-backed fundamentalists), Syrian troops, Druze militia and UN peacekeeping forces all occupying zones of the fragmented country. In 1990, the Christian militia of Michel Aoun was crushed by the Syrians, and the Lebanese government – under Syrian auspices – was able to reassert its authority over the whole of Beirut. However, the Israeli-sponsored forces continue to occupy the south, while Islamic fundamentalist Hizbollah forces control the Beqa'a Valley.

Continuing conflict

From the mid-1970s Israeli control over the Palestinian territories occupied in 1967 was increasingly challenged. On the West Bank, Jordanian leaders were replaced by younger, more radical PLO supporters, and in Gaza a tradition of militant opposition to Israel flourished. At the end of 1987 Palestinian Arabs in the occupied territories began the 'Intifada' – a widespread campaign of mainly peaceful demonstrations against Israeli rule. The often brutal response of the

Israeli armed forces to the Intifada attracted international condemnation. From the late 1980s the large-scale influx into Israel of Soviet Jews, a number of whom have been settled in the occupied territories, has further fuelled the Intifada.

In the Gulf War of 1991 (⊳ box) a number of influential Arab states – notably Syria and Egypt – aligned themselves with the US-dominated coalition. After the war

there was renewed international pressure for a resolution of the Arab–Israeli confrontation. The 'peace process' stuttered unconvincingly into life in October 1991, the initial talks being hampered by deep mutual distrust and arguments over Palestinian representation. No agreements were reached, and the Israelis remained intransigent in the face of Arab demands for their complete withdrawal from the occupied territories.   JP/RM

US helicopters near the Kuwait–Iraq border after the ceasefire in the 1991 Gulf War. The oil fires started by the retreating Iraqi forces took nearly a year to extinguish, and caused considerable damage to the environment of the region.

WARS IN THE GULF

The Islamic revival in Iran led to tensions with other Arab states in the Middle East ruled by more secular Sunni Muslims. In their most dramatic form these tensions led to the Iran–Iraq War, a bloody conflict that lasted eight years, caused one million casualties and ended in stalemate. The main cause of the war was the attempt by the Iraqi president, Saddam Hussein, to take advantage of a weakened Iran by refusing to acknowledge the territorial concessions on the Shatt al-Arab waterway made to Iran by Iraq in 1975. Border skirmishes were followed by a full-scale Iraqi invasion of Iran's oil-producing region (September 1980). Iraq's early military gains were wiped out by 1982 and for the next five years Iraq was forced onto the defensive. Iran strove to capture Basra, while Iraq replied with air attacks on tankers and oil installations in the Gulf. A feature of the war was the attacking of civilian targets by both sides.

Despite their evident interests the superpowers held back from close involvement in the Iran–Iraq War. However, Iraq received military aid from France and pro-Western Arab states such as Saudi Arabia and Egypt, as well as the Soviet Union, which was fearful of the potential effects of a spread of

Islamic radicalism on the Muslim populations of its southern republics. The USA was drawn into the conflict in 1987 when it came to the aid of Kuwaiti merchant vessels that were attacked by Iranian forces because of Kuwait's financial assistance to Iraq. Naval escorts were sent to the Persian Gulf by the USA and other Western nations to protect commercial shipping from Iranian attack.

Following a renewed Iraqi offensive, Iran accepted a UN ceasefire resolution in August 1988. Peace, on the basis of the 1980 situation, was agreed in 1990, ending a war that had resulted in great losses of manpower for both combatants, and had virtually bankrupted Iraq.

On 2 August 1990, in an attempt to restore Iraq's economic fortunes, Saddam Hussein invaded oil-rich Kuwait, formally annexing it on 28 August. Saddam justified his action with the old, but weak, Iraqi claim that Kuwait was historically part of Iraq. The international community was almost unanimous in its condemnation of the invasion. The UN passed a series of resolutions calling for an Iraqi withdrawal, declared the annexation null and void, imposed sanctions, and demanded compensation for Kuwait. An international force drawn from

over 30 countries, but dominated by a huge US contingent, was despatched to the Gulf to prevent an Iraqi invasion of Saudi Arabia. Following Saddam Hussein's failure to respond to repeated UN demands to withdraw from Kuwait, the international coalition launched Operation Desert Storm on 16/17 January 1991, with US and British forces subjecting Baghdad to a massive aerial bombardment with precision weapons. Sustained air attacks on military targets in Iraq and Kuwait wore down Iraq's fighting capability, and on 24 February coalition forces entered Kuwaiti and Iraqi territory. The Iraqi forces were routed, and retreated from Kuwait after setting on fire over 500 Kuwaiti oil wells. Iraq accepted all the UN resolutions regarding Kuwait and agreed to a ceasefire after a ground campaign lasting only 100 hours. However, despite his defeat, Saddam remained in power with his military capability still largely intact, enabling him to suppress revolts by Kurds in the north and Shiites in the south. Although with the liberation of Kuwait the main stated war aim of the coalition had been achieved, the decision not to continue the war may have had as much to do with the West's fear of further destabilizing the region.

SEE ALSO

● THE EASTERN QUESTION p. 154
● THE POSTWAR SETTLEMENT p. 182
● DECOLONIZATION p. 200
● THE COLD WAR p. 204

Western Europe since 1945

A review of Samuel Beckett's play *Waiting for Godot* (1952) described the play as a metaphor for the mood of liberal uncertainty prevailing in postwar Western Europe. Even after the continent was liberated from Nazi rule in 1945, euphoria was tempered with more pessimistic feelings. Europe, once the maker of world history, seemed to have been consigned to the sidelines, as the continent was divided into spheres of influence by the two superpowers, the USA and the USSR (▷ p. 204).

Within a few years, however, new European institutions had been established (▷ box), economic growth had taken off, and the western part of the 'Old Continent' was recognized as a model of political stability and economic progress. Rebuilding after the devastation of World War II, Western Europe transformed itself beyond recognition.

EUROPE: MAIN ECONOMIC GROUPINGS

ICELAND
NORWAY
SWEDEN
FINLAND
RUSSIA
ESTONIA
LATVIA
DENMARK
THE NETHERLANDS
RUSSIA
LITHUANIA
IRELAND
UK
BELARUS
BELGIUM
LUXEMBOURG
GERMANY
POLAND
FRANCE
CZECHOSLOVAKIA
UKRAINE
MOLDOVA
AUSTRIA
HUNGARY
SWITZER-LAND
ITALY
SLOVENIA
ROMANIA
CROATIA
YUGOSLAVIA
BULGARIA
PORTUGAL
SPAIN
BOSNIA-HERZEGOVINA
ALBANIA
GREECE
TURKEY

◻ EUROPEAN COMMUNITY (EC)

◻ EUROPEAN FREE TRADE AREA (EFTA)

◻ ORGANIZATION for ECONOMIC COOPERATION and DEVELOPMENT (OECD)

OECD also includes Australia, Canada, Japan, New Zealand and the USA. Yugoslavia is an associate member of the OECD.

Growth and consensus

Economically the years 1945–75 were decades of unprecedented success in which shattered industries were not merely rebuilt but surpassed previous records of growth. From 1953 to 1973 growth averaged 4.8% in Western Europe, and some countries achieved even higher rates (Spain 6.1%, France 5.3%, West Germany 5.5%). Britain, although growing fast by its own historical standards, only achieved an average rate of 3%. At the same time there was an increase in the number of multinationals – large companies operating across national boundaries.

Rapid economic growth was accompanied by structural changes in Western European economies. Investment grew rapidly (by 16.8% between 1950 and 1970). The number of people working on the land declined – most dramatically in France, Spain and Italy – while the proportion of the labour force working in industry, and particularly in services and commerce, greatly increased. Although peasant farming slowly disappeared, a number of countries, mainly in southern Europe, remain labour-intensive in agriculture. Greece and Portugal have respectively 29.7% and 28.4% of their labour force engaged in agriculture, followed by Ireland (19.2%) and Spain (18.9%).

After 1945 the manual working class in Western Europe diminished as rapidly as the numbers in middle management and 'white-collar' jobs increased. Economic expansion in Western Europe drew in immigrants to work mostly in unskilled jobs during the 1950s and 1960s. Events in Eastern Europe and North Africa in the late 1980s and early 1990s promised to encourage a further wave of economic immigrants.

Economic growth was accompanied by an expansion of health care, pensions, sickness and unemployment benefit, and other provisions of the 'welfare state'. Because this redistribution of wealth took place in a growing economy, conflicts of interest were largely avoided, but the growth of government intervention and the power of the state was a feature of postwar Western Europe. The welfare state was part of a consensus approach to economic management (often referred to as 'Keynesian', after the British economist John Maynard Keynes; ▷ pp. 183 and 185). In many Western European states, trade unions, management and government worked in harness to plan the future growth of wages, prices and output. If in certain countries, such as Sweden and Austria, this system was institutionalized, in some (notably Britain) it did not work, while in others (Greece, Ireland, Portugal) it was hardly tried.

Economic slow-down

In the 1970s inflation and sharply rising oil prices caused the Western nations to perform below capacity. They experienced a recession in which their average rates of growth were much lower than in the 1950s and 1960s (2.4% from 1973 to 1979). Unemployment also began to rise.

Any residual optimism about the future was dissipated in the 1980s, as confidence in the techniques of government intervention that had worked so well in the past began to wane. In Britain in the early 1980s the Conservative government of Margaret Thatcher – reacting strongly against Keynesian interventionism – experimented with the policy of 'monetarism', whereby governments restrict their involvement in the economy to management of the money supply as a means of controlling inflation. However, the UK's combination of poor economic performance (low growth, high inflation and high unemployment) and extreme balance of payments problems was not experienced elsewhere.

The major economies of Western Europe suffered from persistent unemployment in the 1970s and 1980s. At the beginning of the 1990s even Sweden, formerly a byword for economic success, began to falter, apparently no longer willing to sustain such an extensive welfare state.

Newly industrializing countries such as South Korea and Taiwan had been dangerous competitors in 'low-tech' industries (such as textiles) in the 1960s (▷ p. 222). In the 1980s and 1990s they also moved into machine tools, motor manufacture and electronics. Competition from Japan also continued to grow alarmingly, Japanese enterprises moving into highly advanced sectors of the economy, and acquiring substantial companies and real estate in Western Europe. There were calls for protection from such 'unfair' competition, as Europe's ability to stay ahead in the 'product cycle' (by moving on to more sophisticated products as the simpler ones were increasingly produced elsewhere) began to be questioned.

Security

In security terms the principal threat was perceived as coming from the Soviet Union (▷ p. 198). American backing against the Soviet threat was provided through NATO (▷ p. 204). NATO served as a guarantee of US commitment to Western Europe, but its role was never precisely defined. There were too many troops for NATO to be a mere 'trip wire', alerting the West to Soviet strategic moves, but too few troops for it to be able to depend on conventional forces alone. For all the 'Atlantic' rhetoric of successive US presidents, American doubts about its military presence in Europe have never been entirely absent, and some groups in Western Europe have had their own worries about American leadership of the Western Alliance. When the Soviet threat appeared to diminish in the late 1980s (▷ p. 224), NATO was left without a clear rationale.

Politics: the centrist orthodoxy

Politically, Western Europe drew confidence from its economic success, consolidating and extending its own democratic regimes. Parliamentary democracies were established in West Germany and Italy after World War II. The extension of democracy to the old dictatorships

THE EUROPEAN COMMUNITY

The establishment of the European Coal and Steel Community (ECSC) in 1952 paved the way for a measure of economic and political integration in Europe. Encouraged by its success, its members – the 'six' (West Germany, France, Italy, Belgium, Luxembourg and the Netherlands) – negotiated the Rome Treaties to create the European Economic Community (or Common Market) and the European Atomic Energy Authority (EURATOM). The Community sought to end customs duties and trade restrictions between members, and to establish a common commercial policy and common tariff. In addition to the free trade in capital, services and goods and the free movement of people, the Rome Treaties pledged to aim for improvements in living standards and working conditions, and 'an ever closer union among the peoples of Europe'.

The Community's programme was the most ambitious undertaken by any international institution; it provoked hostility in most European societies, although by conventional diplomatic standards it made very healthy progress. By July 1968 all customs duties between the 'six' had been removed, a common tariff had been established and the harmonization of industrial standards went ahead. A competition policy that would equalize the market was also slowly established, and the EC emerged as the largest trading bloc on the world economic stage.

For political rather than economic reasons, EC membership became increasingly attractive to non-member states. The 'six' were joined by Denmark, Ireland and the UK in 1973, by Greece in 1981, and by Portugal and Spain in 1986. The majority of the remaining countries of Europe – including most of the states of Eastern Europe – have either applied for membership or have stated their intention to do so. However, each enlargement of the EC has posed problems for the Community, as have its attempts to coordinate and harmonize policies in Europe by creating a political union. The disappearance of the Communist regimes of Eastern Europe and the former Soviet Union, and the waning of American interest in Europe, combined to deprive European unity of its two traditional stimuli at the beginning of the 1990s.

The EC achieved further economic integration with the completion of the single European market – removing all barriers to the free movement of goods, people, services and capital across national boundaries – by the end of 1992. There were also signs of movement towards European monetary integration. Having created the European Monetary System (EMS) – which stabilizes exchange rates between the currencies of member states – Community members have proposed a Central Bank and a single European currency, though these further stages are more problematical. Such developments would require an extension of EC authority in some areas, and a transfer of state powers to the EC, as would the development of common defence and foreign policies.

The EC is an economic institution, but its function is also political. It has enabled Germany to play a part in European politics in a manner that has reassured its neighbours and it has given other states, notably France, a bigger world role than they could otherwise expect. Political understanding in foreign policy matters has also progressed, and in security terms the EC may develop its own capabilities in the form of the Western European Union (WEU). However, consensus is lacking on any significant transfer of authority in these fields from national governments to the EC.

---

of southern Europe – Greece, Spain and Portugal – was one of the success stories of the 1970s.

But declarations about self-government and human rights at home were clearly incompatible with the retention of dependent colonies overseas. Postwar Europe dismantled its old empires (⊳ p. 200) from the late 1940s on, though France and Belgium were slow to accept the need for decolonization. Paradoxically, the largest Western European empire, that of the British, experienced the least traumatic upheaval. Disagreements in France over the fate of Algeria (⊳ p. 202) caused the fall of the Fourth Republic and brought de Gaulle back to power.

Political extremism was more or less eliminated as an electoral threat in Western Europe. The extreme right flickered into life a few times in France and in Italy – where it maintained a small presence in the Parliament – but it never achieved substantial support elsewhere. The Communists achieved substantial votes in most West European countries in 1945, but with the onset of the Cold War (⊳ p. 204) they virtually disappeared except as small (but influential) minorities in trade unions and protest movements. Mass Communist parties did survive in Italy, France, Finland and Portugal. However, despite enjoying a brief respite in the 1970s (when they entered or were on the verge of government), they too went into sharp decline in the 1980s. Communist electoral support was concentrated in 'historically doomed' sectors such as heavy industry and peasant agriculture, and the collapse of Communism in Eastern Europe in 1989–90 (⊳ p. 224) accentuated an already emphatic trend.

Postwar Western European politics have been dominated by the parties of the centre – either Social Democrats (centre left) or Christian Democrats (centre right). In practice 'centrism' has meant the maintenance of welfare states and government intervention in the economy, underpinned by a philosophy that has been summarized as 'the market where possible, planning where necessary'. This consensus has been derided as 'corporatist management' by its detractors, but it is, in fact, a distinctively Western European political achievement. The consensus approach to the economy was put under severe strain by the oil crisis and recession of the 1970s. Inadequacies in the redistribution of power and wealth through the political system were increasingly criticized, but centrist governments – many of them coalitions – survived. There were some exceptions. During the early 1980s Britain was polarized between a governing Conservative Party wedded to free-market economic policies, and a Labour opposition temporarily dominated by its socialist left wing, but in most of Western Europe the centre retained power despite increasing strains.

Political challenges

If the centre largely retained the voters' loyalty, there were new forms of political challenge to the status quo. The most spectacular was the student movement of the late 1960s. The 1960s generation was the postwar 'baby boom' come of age, but it was also affluent, educated, and mobilized around issues such as protest against the Vietnam War (⊳ pp. 208 and 216). Its high noon came in France in May 1968 when students took to the barricades, protesting against the government's high defence spending at the expense of education and social services. The student movement came to nothing, but some disillusioned radicals of the generation of 1968 – notably the Marxist-schooled Red Army Faction, a West German terrorist group – concluded that they could make no progress through orthodox channels and turned to terror.

Terrorism has also been used as a weapon by sub-state nationalists. However, despite the fact that no Western European state is without a national minority of some kind, terrorist violence by nationalists has only been widespread in Northern Ireland and Spain's Basque country. Demands by minorities for linguistic and cultural recognition have become a feature of Western European political life. Most states have dealt with nascent sub-state nationalism by devolving government functions and sometimes by federal or quasi-federal concessions.

The future

Western Europe, poised on the brink of a new century, faces an uncertain future. Although socially stable and economically prosperous, it fears competition from the newly industrializing countries and a shift of power to the Pacific (⊳ p. 223). The collapse of Communism revealed Eastern Europe to be in parlous condition (⊳ p. 224), but it greatly reduced the Soviet threat (traditionally a stimulus for European integration; ⊳ box) and reunited Germany. On the threshold of the 21st century the European state system faced the challenge of coping with a powerful undivided Germany once again at its core.   DB

SEE ALSO
● WORLD WAR II: THE WEST p. 190
● DECOLONIZATION p. 200
● THE COLD WAR p. 204

The Great American Dream

The USA emerged from World War II as the most powerful nation on earth. It was also the most prosperous: while Europe's GNP (excluding the USSR) fell by about 25 per cent during the conflict, America's increased by more than 50 per cent in real terms. All this engendered a feeling of tremendous national pride, optimism in the future, and a deep-seated belief that anything was possible.

By the end of the 20th century the USA was still a superpower in terms of military strength, industrial might, and cultural influence. But the great American dream had been soured by a variety of factors, foremost amongst which were the Vietnam War (▷ p. 208), relative economic decline, the persistence of poverty and racism, the Watergate scandal, and an apparently insoluble drugs problem.

The 1950s

World War II fuelled American economic growth and expanded the power of the Federal government. In the decade and a half following the defeat of Germany and Japan, the USA underwent a plethora of important social changes, many of them products both of affluence and of Federal policy. These developments included sub-urbanization of the white middle classes, rising car and TV ownership, and a dramatic baby boom (America's population increased by nearly 30 million during the 1950s). The Cold War engendered a sense of profound insecurity and a comcomitant fear of Communist subversion – a fear exploited by the demagogic Wisconsin Senator, Joseph McCarthy (▷ pp. 204–7). Yet many Americans remained prosperous and content during the eight-year Republican administration of Dwight D. Eisenhower (president 1953–61).

With Americans apparently happier than they had ever been before, only the popularity of rock 'n' roll (a fusion of black and white musical styles accomplished most expertly by a young Mississippian named Elvis Presley) foreshadowed the bitter generational conflict of the next decade.

The eclipse of American liberalism

In 1960 Democratic Senator John F. Kennedy of Massachusetts was elected president. Young, handsome, and extremely wealthy, Kennedy embodied the high hopes of the period, themselves a product of national prosperity. He was, in particular, the darling of American liberals, whose faith in technology and progress convinced them that no problem was insoluble. Though less liberal than many of his backers Kennedy caught the optimism of the hour with his 'can-do' rhetoric. Ambitious plans were laid to destroy the last vestiges of poverty in the country and, prodded by black protesters, the administration continued the reforms (tentatively begun under Eisenhower) in the controversial area of civil rights (▷ box). Kennedy did not live to see these policies come to fruition. He was assassinated in Dallas, Texas, in November 1963.

Liberals feared the worst when Vice-President Lyndon B. Johnson entered the White House. Johnson was a wheeler-dealer Southern Democrat with none of Kennedy's good looks or social graces. To their surprise he embarked on the most ambitious social programme in American history. Pressed by Johnson the US Congress enacted legislation providing federally subsidized medical insurance and medical care for the elderly and persons on welfare. It also passed the Voting Rights Act of 1965 to secure the vote for Southern blacks, and created the Office of Economic Opportunity to promote ways of improving living conditions for the urban poor. Tragically Johnson's 'Great Society' programme became mired in the débâcle of the Vietnam War (▷ p. 208). As Johnson became more and more committed to escalating that conflict, funds needed to promote social reform were diverted to supply the requirements of the Pentagon.

Vietnam proved not only to be Johnson's

THE CIVIL RIGHTS MOVEMENT

National Guardsmen confront angry blacks in Newark, New Jersey, 1967. Despite the dismantling of the formal apparatus of racial inequality by the 1964 Civil Rights Act, discrimination against blacks continued and inter-racial tensions remained high. Black discontent boiled over into violence throughout the mid-1960s, with widespread rioting in the slums of many American cities.

America's civil rights movement had its origins in the modernization of the South's agrarian economy during the middle of the 20th century. Urbanization, mechanization and war-induced prosperity were all beginning to undermine the foundations of the South's racist caste system when, in 1955, the US Supreme Court in the seminal case of Brown v. Topeka issued a mandate for integrated schools across the nation. Shortly afterwards the civil rights movement began in earnest when a dynamic young black Baptist minister, Martin Luther King, Jr, led a successful grass-roots protest against segregated seating on the buses of Montgomery, Alabama.

As hopes rose of an improvement in their condition, blacks across the South abandoned quiescence for activism. From 1960 students played a key role in organizing 'sit-ins' against segregated stores and inter-state transport facilities. Although the Federal government was initially reluctant to act on their behalf, media coverage of the sometimes violent Southern white response enraged the conscience of Northern liberals, forcing Presidents John F. Kennedy and Lyndon B. Johnson to promote reforming legislation. The Civil Rights Act of 1964 was a direct product of King's carefully orchestrated 1963 campaign in Birmingham, Alabama, when non-violent black demonstrators (many of them children) were set upon by white policemen with hoses and dogs.

King's integrationist philosophy and brilliant oratory made him popular with moderates of both races, but by the mid-1960s younger, more radical blacks were becoming critical of his strategy of non-violent direct action. Angered by the US government's failure to protect movement workers in the south, they found the black nationalist philosophy of New York Muslim Malcolm X (1925–65) more appealing. Championing the cause of 'Black Power', groups like the Black Panthers began to call for violent resistance to what they considered to be white oppression.

By the time Martin Luther King was assassinated in 1968 the civil rights movement was in disarray. Internal strife and adverse white reaction to rioting in the depressed ghettos of Northern cities made further gains impossible. The movement had brought important legal and political gains to Southern blacks (not least the vote), but failed to make a dramatic impact on black poverty and the informal segregation practices of the North.

undoing but also that of the liberals. During the mid-1960s increasing numbers of young, middle-class whites became disenchanted with the complacency, conformity and boredom of suburban life – a mood brilliantly captured in Mike Nichols's 1967 film, *The Graduate*. Rejecting the material values of their parents, many young Americans abandoned the pursuit of affluence in favour of student politics, the hippy gospel of love, rock 'n' roll – Bob Dylan, the Beatles and the Rolling Stones were particular favourites – and hallucinogenic drugs. For cosseted, idealistic youth, Vietnam symbolized the bankruptcy of the liberal order in the USA – an order capable of unleashing death and destruction on innocent Indochinese civilians and (as was revealed by the black ghetto riots of 1964–8; ▷ picture) unable (or unwilling) to conquer injustice at home.

The conservative reaction

Student resistance to the Vietnam War and the accompanying draft – conscription of youth for military service – influenced Johnson in his decision not to seek re-election in 1968. But the country as a whole aimed a swingeing blow against 'peaceniks' and rioters by replacing him with Richard Nixon. Nixon, a veteran anti-Communist Republican, promised to end the war, but once in power clandestinely authorized its extension to Cambodia. When news of his action leaked out another wave of anti-war demonstrations began, culminating in the fatal shooting of four student protesters by National Guardsmen at Kent State University in Ohio.

Republican defeats in the 1970 congressional elections finally convinced Nixon that US involvement in Vietnam had to end if he was to be re-elected. But he was to be brought down by a scandal that demonstrated his contempt for the liberal establishment and the Constitution. In 1972 five men were caught breaking into the Democratic National Campaign offices in Washington's Watergate hotel. The men, it was discovered, were agents of Nixon's re-election organization and their aim was to wire-tap Democratic meetings. Attempts by the White House to cover up the affair were exposed by journalists from the *Washington Post*. Irredeemably compromised by his actions, Nixon resigned from office in April 1974 in order to stave off the humiliation of impeachment. The following year South Vietnam, now devoid of American troops, fell to the Communists.

Watergate and the saturation bombing of Cambodia have perhaps obscured the foreign-policy successes of the Nixon years. Agreements with the Soviet Union in the areas of trade and disarmament aided the process of détente (▷ pp. 204–7), while the Communist regime in the People's Republic of China was recognized by the USA as the official government of China.

America after Vietnam

The traumas of Vietnam, urban riots and

Watergate instilled Americans with an uncharacteristic pessimism. The Oil Crisis of the mid-1970s did little to lighten their mood, nor did the Carter administration's botched response to the challenge posed by Islamic fundamentalism in Iran (▷ pp. 210–13). It was therefore with a sense of relief that many Americans, especially evangelicals and blue-collar Republicans, greeted the election to the presidency of Ronald Reagan in 1980.

A conservative Republican and former Hollywood actor who ran initially on a laissez-faire, anti-Communist platform, Reagan charmed his supporters with folksy homilies, low taxes for the rich, and a massive increase in defence spending. But while he did much to restore the confidence of the nation, Reagan proved a relaxed and lethargic President, who failed to coordinate and lead his administration. One result of this was the 'Irangate' scandal, in which it was revealed that White House staff had been involved in secret talks to sell arms to Iran – the profits from which were to be channelled illegally to anti-Communist Contra guerrillas in Nicaragua. More damaging in the long term was Reagan's economic legacy of a US budget deficit ballooning out of control despite cuts in welfare spending. When Reagan was succeeded by his Vice-President George Bush, in 1989, it was clear that a deep sense of public unease underlay the forced euphoria of the previous year's election campaign.

It was not that Americans had nothing to be optimistic about. The collapse of the Soviet economy in the late 1980s (▷ p. 224) made their country the world's only real superpower. American culture – from the glossy, escapist films of Steven Spielberg to the pop music of Madonna, and the proliferation of the MacDonalds' hamburger – continued to exercise an inordinate influence on the world's popular taste. The problem was that neither liberalism nor the conservative reaction to it had fulfilled the promise of the immediate postwar era. Violent crime (often drugs-related) was on the increase; many urban blacks continued to live in poverty (Washington, DC, had the infant mortality rate of a Third World country); the infrastructure of great cities like New York was crumbling; Japanese and German goods were penetrating the home market at an alarming rate; medical insurance had become prohibitively expensive; and proportionately fewer citizens were choosing to participate in the democratic process. The nation's history and underlying dynamism suggested that none of these problems would bring the USA to its knees as some observers predicted. However, there was no denying that for many people, the great American dream remained more a promise than a tangible reality.   RC

The Republican Party Convention at New Orleans, 1988, where delegates chose George Bush as their candidate for that year's presidential campaign. The hype and razzamatazz of American electioneering belie the fact that, at the beginning of the 1990s, proportionately fewer Americans are bothering to participate in the democratic process than ever before.

The Third World
since Decolonization

The term 'Third World' was coined in France in the early 1950s to describe those newly independent states in Africa and Asia that remained outside the camps of the Western alliance and the Soviet bloc (▷ p. 204). Evoking comparison with the 'Third Estate' (or commoners) of pre-revolutionary France (▷ p. 144), the term graphically portrayed the plight of the new states: large in number, but economically weak and lacking political power in the world's financial and trading institutions.

The term is now generally used to refer to Central and South America, the Caribbean, most of Africa, Asia excluding Japan and China, and Oceania excluding Australia and New Zealand. The 'Third World' is, admittedly, an imprecise term; but it is less ethnocentric than expressions such as 'the developing world' and 'the underdeveloped world', and has

On the streets of Calcutta. Unlike most Third World countries India has a sophisticated industrial base, and an advanced administrative and political structure. However, it remains dogged by the problem of how to feed, clothe and house its ever-growing population.

caught the imagination of the peoples of the states to which it applies.

The Third World is mainly but not exclusively non-European, and is largely impoverished, although it includes the affluent oil-rich states of the Persian Gulf. India – in which over one-third of the population is below the official poverty line – is defined as part of the Third World, even though it is one of the ten largest industrial powers in the world. China, on the other hand, is considered to be a 'developed' state, despite displaying many of the characteristics of a Third World country, including low living standards and a lack of technology.

The legacy of imperialism

For all its imprecision, the concept of a 'Third World' conveys certain common features that characterize these countries as a group. The first of these is a shared legacy of European imperialism (▷ pp. 160–3 and 200–3). All Third World states experienced periods of European domination, during which their economies were deliberately refashioned to integrate them into the economy of the Western power to which they were subordinate. The 'development' of these territories was determined by the needs of the colonial powers, for whom the Third World became a supplier of minerals and agricultural products. The producer–consumer relationship between the Third World and the colonial powers tied the colonies firmly to the global system of production and distribution. Since the system was created to suit the needs of the colonial powers, the pattern of international trade remains tilted against the Third World.

All Third World countries bear the deep imprint of European culture. Even where indigenous culture has survived – for example in the Arab world and Southeast Asia – it has been greatly influenced by the experience of colonization. Much so-called modernization has been little more than attempts to imitate either the West or (until 1989–91) the Soviet bloc through industrialization and infrastructure development. Members of the educated Third World elite inherited the intellectual mantle of their colonial masters, and many have been unable to break away from that mental mould. This 'intellectual dependence' is ensured continuity through Western-style education systems imposed by the colonial powers and continued by independent governments. In many countries of Latin America the local languages are virtually extinct, and the colonial language predominates as the official language. Africa was effectively divided into linguistic zones by the colonial powers. For example, Portuguese is the official language in Angola, while in the neighbouring states of Zaïre and Botswana the official languages are respectively French and English.

The social structures of some Third World countries were substantially changed by their colonial rulers, for example through migration. Thus in Fiji, Indian labourers who arrived to work the island's sugar

plantations reduced the indigenous Fijians to a minority; in Latin America, the descendants of Spanish and Portuguese settlers outnumber the native Indians (▷ p. 148).

Western-style political structures may have smothered the indigenous institutions of Third World countries, but they have largely failed to take root in the local soil. Multi-party democracy virtually disappeared from Africa in the 1970s and 1980s. The resurgence of religious fundamentalism in the Third World (both Islamic and Hindu) is directed not against democratic institutions or technological progress, but against the perceived inability of borrowed institutions to bring about a qualitative improvement of life in the Third World. In many cases the imperialism of the West has been replaced by 'internal imperialism'. An alien elite has superseded an indigenous elite that is no less exploitative than the one it replaced.

National identity

The newly emergent states are, on the whole, artificial creations of the imperial powers, and their boundaries – drawn arbitrarily – cut across tribal, ethnic and religious lines. In Africa, for example, only Lesotho, Swaziland and Somalia contain a single ethnic community. Reversion to pre-colonial allegiances is not feasible because of the massive migration and mixing of populations that took place under the impulse of colonial economies. Many Third World states are at best ramshackle groupings of heterogeneous peoples lacking social and political cohesion, and without the ideological and institutional basis necessary for creating successful political structures.

The evanescent unity forged by popular independence movements against colonial rulers did not survive the departure of the latter. Most Third World states have been afflicted by conflicts between social or regional elites jockeying for political power and control of resources. Nigeria, for example, has been troubled by regional rivalry, aggravated by what is perceived by the rest of the country as domination by the more conservative Islamic north. Chad has been torn apart by bitter civil war between the Islamic Arab north and the animist and Christian black African south. The accommodation of rival ethnic and tribal groups is rendered more problematic by the absence of well-developed political parties and institutions. This, in turn, has made it difficult to create a national consensus or to develop an ideology and socio-economic programme acceptable to all sections of the population.

In many cases rapid decolonization put paid to the hopes of national self-determination of smaller ethnic groups and tribes within the newly independent states. By devolving power to the largest group or the dominant tribe, the ex-colonial powers denied the claims of minorities. Having put aside their differences in the struggle against the colonial powers, these minorities resumed their quest for autonomy to safeguard their particular interests. However, once independence had been achieved, the right to self-determination – the most potent rallying-cry in the struggle against foreign domination – was denied them by the ruling elites of the new states. Such 'internal imperialism' has been a persistent source of instability and strife in the Third World.

If aspiring nationalists – other than the Bangladeshis, who successfully broke away from Pakistan in 1971 (▷ p. 201) – have failed to win their independence, it is not because they do not frequently have a strong claim. In most cases secessionist movements – such as the Karen in Myanmar (Burma) – have been coerced by the overwhelming power of the state itself, and an international system that is predisposed towards the maintenance of the *status quo*.

The role of the military

The failure to accommodate the legitimate demands of minorities has fuelled the political instability of the Third World in another way. Monopolization of governmental power has eroded the legitimacy of dominant political groups. Ruling elites have become increasingly reliant on the military to impose their will on disaffected rivals and dissidents. This, in turn, has encouraged the military to capture political power for themselves. There are few states in Africa, Asia or Latin America that have not suffered military intervention at one time or another.

Military interventions, instead of resolving political problems, have tended to aggravate them. By denying civilian populations a voice in government, military regimes have undermined national consensus, and further weakened political institutions. Political instability has thus become endemic in many Third World countries. In Nigeria, Ghana, Pakistan and Bangladesh, repeated military interventions have failed to tackle any of the underlying problems of these

Renamo guerrillas crossing the Zambezi in Mozambique. Military assistance from South Africa enabled Renamo to wage a bloody guerrilla war against the Soviet-backed Frelimo government, which took power when Mozambique achieved independence from Portugal in 1975. Interference by outside powers vying for strategic and political influence on the newly independent states – particularly during the Cold War – has had a destabilizing effect on the Third World. War has hindered economic development.

states. In an earlier period, similar problems afflicted Argentina, Bolivia, and other Latin American states after they achieved independence (▷ p. 149).

The international dimension

In many respects, the international community has taken on a 'global' rather than primarily European character since decolonization. With the assumption of power by local rulers in African, Asian and Caribbean states the 'formal' disabilities formerly afflicting these states have virtually disappeared. They now enjoy diplomatic recognition and UN membership, and participate fully in many international organizations and agreements. The new states have tripled the size of the international system and, as a result, the European states have become the minority. Third World countries have tried to strengthen their influence in international affairs by or-

ganizing themselves in such groups as the Afro-Asian movement, the Non-Aligned Movement (NAM), and the Group of 77 (an unofficial grouping of Third World states). They have also tried to use their majority in the UN to make the international order more equitable. In a world divided by the confrontation between the USA and the USSR, the NAM appeared a sensible alternative for countries that did not wish to be drawn into Cold War rivalry (▷ p. 204).

While the international community has ceased to be specifically European, there is much that has not changed. In terms of technology, power and economy the balance is still heavily weighted against the Third World. Political independence has not brought economic emancipation, and for much of the population of the Third World there has been little discernible improvement in the standard of living. Burgeoning populations consume the benefits of modernization as rapidly as they are delivered in some regions. While the fiction of state sovereignty is preserved, there is little to suggest that the Third World exerts significant influence in the comity of nations. A quarter of a century or more after the formal dismantling of the West's colonial empires, the Third World is still adversely affected by the structure of the world economy and more dependent upon the developed states than in 1945 (▷ box). The gap in technology and economic and political power between the industrial states and the Third World has widened, and the intellectual and cultural penetration of the former colonies by the West is probably deeper than ever before. The Third World has made various attempts to make the international system more responsive to its aspirations. These have varied from demands for minimalist changes in international economic management, to demands for a major restructuring of the entire system – the establishment of a new international economic order.   GR

THIRD WORLD DEBT

Many Third World countries are heavily in debt to the developed world and its banking institutions. These debts involve very large sums, and the interest payments constitute a severe drain on the economies of debtor nations. In the second half of the 1980s, some African countries used more convertible currency in debt repayments than for any other purpose. Large sums are owed to Western commercial banks, some of which – in the 1970s and early 1980s – lent more than their capital bases would normally suggest to be prudent. There is thus no isolated Third World dimension to debt – it involves the banks and the economies of developed nations as well. Unfortunately, because of the link with the 'First World' (the Western capitalist economies), the Third World catches cold every time the developed world sneezes. Increases in interest rates, for example, can be

reflected directly in the interest payments on Third World debt.

Because of reluctance on the part of Western commercial banks to undertake major new loan investments in the Third World, the International Monetary Fund (IMF) acts increasingly as a lender of the first resort. However, the IMF has attached 'packages of conditionality' to its loans, which – while intended to assist Third World countries back to economic health – have often caused major social problems. This has led to the accusation that the IMF has eroded the financial independence of many states. However, despite loans from both private banks and the IMF, development is slow in most Third World countries, and requires even more cash (or easily converted assets) before it can achieve anything like self-sustainable growth.

SEE ALSO

● DECOLONIZATION p. 200
● THE COLD WAR p. 204
● POPULATION AND HUNGER p. 230

Southern Africa in the 20th Century

In 1899–1902 Britain fought a war to capture the gold mines of the Transvaal and bring the states of South Africa together under British control (▷ p. 163). But the Union of South Africa, formed in 1910, became a British dominion very different from Australia or Canada. Its African majority was rendered powerless, and the Union was ruled by a white minority largely consisting of Afrikaners (Boers) with their own language and loyalties.

After the Boer War, the defeated Afrikaners of the Transvaal and Orange Free State won one extremely important concession in the peace treaty of 1902 (▷ p. 163). The British promised not to impose on them the 'colour-blind' franchise of the Cape Colony, which gave the vote to educated and propertied Africans. This meant that in the new Union of South Africa, the black African majority were to become voteless subjects of white rule, controlled by 'Pass Laws' that regulated their employment and restricted their movement. Afrikaners were to enjoy an inbuilt majority in the electorate and therefore in the government.

The price paid for this by the new Union was Britain's insistence that three areas known as the High Commission Territories – Basutoland (Lesotho), Bechuanaland (Botswana) and Swaziland – should not become part of the Union, until the Union had proved the worth of its own 'native policy'.

Gold and maize

The new Union of South Africa appeared economically weak and politically unstable. Its gold mines and other major resources were owned by capitalists overseas, while its government consisted of Afrikaner landowners who were out of sympathy with the country's English-speaking administrators, businessmen and white skilled workers.

The political compromise that emerged – the 'alliance of gold and maize' – was restructured periodically during the course of the 20th century. Once in power, Afrikaner nationalists came to appreciate the crucial importance of gold mining for the national economy and state revenues. The mine owners saw the need for an alliance with Afrikaner landowners to develop commercial agriculture that would feed the mines and towns. The functioning of the 'alliance' can be seen

in the passing of the 1913 Natives Land Act, which set up a system of 'native reserves' in rural areas, from which the mines would draw migrant labourers. At the same time the law aimed to replace self-sufficient African peasants on designated white farms by wage labourers, expelling 'surplus' people to the reserves.

The 'alliance' alienated the more extreme Afrikaner nationalists, who drew their support from poorer Afrikaners, and the English-speaking white workers in the mines. Although a 'job colour-bar' protected white workers from the competition of black workers, white workers rose in protest in the great mine strike (1922), which was crushed with tanks and troops by the government of premier Jan Smuts. In subsequent elections, Smuts was defeated by a coalition of Afrikaner nationalists and white employers led by J.B.M. Hertzog.

The emergence of black African nationalism was voiced by a new elite of skilled artisans, clergymen, teachers, lawyers and journalists. Such people formed the South African Native National Congress in 1912 (renamed the African National Congress in 1923). They petitioned the UK to extend the Cape franchise to the whole Union, but by 1919 the British parliament no longer had jurisdiction over internal matters. Thereafter the ANC withered away until 1940. African aspirations were met instead by trade unions, notably the Industrial and Commercial Workers' Union (ICU), which flourished as a mass movement between 1919 and 1930.

Segregation

South Africa failed to incorporate Southern Rhodesia (Zimbabwe) or the British High Commission territories – Basutoland (Lesotho), Bechuanaland (Botswana) and Swaziland – but gained the mineral-rich territory of South West Africa (Namibia). Captured from Germany in 1915, it was handed over to South Africa as a 'mandate' from the League of Nations in 1919 (▷ p. 182).

The effects of the depression of 1929–33 (▷ p. 184) obliged Hertzog to ally with Smuts – thus re-cementing the old alli-

ance of gold and maize. An unprecedented boom followed for the gold-based South African economy, as the world recovered from the depression on the basis of a guaranteed gold price. Gold production doubled and tripled, drawing in cheap unskilled labour from depressed rural areas as far north as Tanganyika (Tanzania). Hertzog now had the strength to implement a programme of land and labour laws that enforced strict racial segregation throughout South Africa.

A 'purified' Afrikaner nationalism emerged in reaction to the Hertzog–Smuts alliance. In 1938 a great wave of nationalist emotion accompanied celebrations to mark the centenary of the 'Great Trek' (▷ p. 163). New Afrikaner trade unions and business organizations were coordinated by a secret 'Broederbond' (brotherhood) of Afrikaner intellectuals. Meanwhile, increased state revenues were invested in state-owned industries and basic services. The job colour-bar and technical education of whites solved the 'poor white problem' by ensuring that white Afrikaners profited most from the expansion of employment opportunities.

World War II accelerated the development of manufacturing industries to produce goods previously imported. The production of munitions stimulated the mining of other metals besides gold. Urbanization and the renewed growth of the African working class began to break down the checks and balances of the segregation system. The ANC – strengthened by a new generation of young educated people from about 1940 – began to build itself into a mass party and was inspired by the Allied war aims of national liberation and democracy. However, the war was followed by further repression for Africans.

Afrikaner society was bitterly divided by the war. Most Afrikaners, like Hertzog – who was ousted by Smuts as premier – were neutral. Others, like Smuts, backed Britain, but many nationalists were actively pro-German. After the war, 'purified' nationalists campaigned against Smuts on the political platform of *rasse-apartheid* ('race-apartness') – racial segregation reinforced and updated for an

Segregated spectators (right) at a sports stadium in South Africa. Until 1990–1 the policy of apartheid enforced the strict separation of blacks and whites in work, housing, education, religion, sport, marriage and other areas of social life. Racial intermingling in public places was prohibited – trains, buses, beaches and even park benches were segregated.

industrial society. The Nationalist Party of D.F. Malan – a combination of 'purified' and 'reunited' Afrikaner nationalists – defeated Smuts in the 1948 elections.

Apartheid

After 1948 apartheid was enacted in South Africa by new laws that defined racial groups and restricted their residence, employment and education. A plan for the partition of South Africa between massive white areas and small 'Bantu' (black African) Homelands was drawn up, and began to be implemented from 1959. Western economic and defence interests, and English-speaking businesses in South Africa, learned to live with apartheid. In 1950, in response to South African pressure, Britain deposed and exiled Seretse Khama – a young chief in Bechuanaland – because he had married a white woman overseas. Britain also turned a blind eye to South Africa's continued flouting of UN authority over the South West African mandate.

Resistance to apartheid was conducted by the ANC through passive resistance campaigns in 1952–3, 1956 and 1960. In March 1960 the South African police fired on African demonstrators at Sharpeville, south of Johannesburg, killing 67. The outcry abroad resulted in a withdrawal of Western capital and an economic crisis in South Africa. The country was excluded from the Commonwealth on becoming a republic in 1961. The ANC and its PAC (Pan-Africanist Congress) offshoot were banned, driven underground and exiled. Small military wings of these organizations continued to operate underground and periodically tried to sabotage state property. By 1964 all opposition to apartheid, except in the churches, was effectively crushed after brutal police action and detentions without trial.

The South African economy enjoyed a period of unprecedented growth and industrialization in the middle and later 1960s with a great influx of American and European capital. Apartheid was more fully implemented by the forcible removal of millions of people into Bantu Homelands, and by further legislation restricting black residence in the cities. After the independence of the neighbouring black states of Botswana and Lesotho in 1966, and Swaziland in 1968, plans were laid for the Bantu Homelands to become 'independent' republics inside the borders of South Africa – the first being Transkei in 1976.

Discontented industrial employees and urban residents led a revival of African resistance to apartheid during a period of economic recession in the early 1970s. Guerrilla victories over the Portuguese in Mozambique and Angola (1974–5) inspired vigorous new protests among Africans in South Africa. Violence erupted in June 1976 with the shooting by police of hundreds of schoolchildren in Soweto – a sprawling agglomeration of townships near Johannesburg. African protest was guided more by the ideas of 'black consciousness' than by political parties such as the ANC.

The South African government responded to pressure from the growing Afrikaner business community. Minor reforms of apartheid were conceded – to give greater security to the black middle class and skilled working class in the townships. The government proclaimed to the world that it was fighting for capitalism against communism.

The fortunes of the ANC revived in 1980–1, through its influence on the politics of the townships. The government of P.W. Botha used force and guile on neighbouring countries to block ANC guerrillas infiltrating from outside. But the ANC successfully appealed to educated and skilled people in the townships, who founded the United Democratic Front (UDF) in 1985 as a legal mass political party.

Constitutional change

Elaborate changes to the South African constitution in 1983 established a centralized presidential system, diluting parliamentary power into three segregated chambers for whites, Coloureds (mixed race) and Indians. This further alienated the black majority, denied the rights of citizenship. Between 1984 and 1987 the South African government lost control of the townships but attempted to reassert its authority using the army, the police and auxiliaries ('vigilantes' in shantytowns on the edge of the townships). The government also courted Inkatha, the Zulu national movement (led by Chief Gatsha Buthelezi), which had broken with the ANC by 1981.

Repression, rather than reform, once again proved ineffective in containing African nationalist opposition. The South African economy began to suffer severely from sanctions imposed by the USA and other Western states, in particular those exercised by international bankers.

South Africa also became embroiled in an unwinnable war with Cuban forces in Angola, where Namibian nationalists – the South West Africa People's Organization (SWAPO) – had guerrilla bases.

When F.W. de Klerk came to power as president in South Africa (1989), he seized the opportunities presented by the end of the Cold War. A ceasefire was negotiated in Angola, followed by free elections in Namibia. In March 1990 Namibia gained independence under a SWAPO government. Nelson Mandela, the most famous and respected ANC leader, was freed in February 1990 after almost 27 years of imprisonment. The ANC and PAC were unbanned and, for the first time, negotiations began between the government and the ANC, laying down basic principles in the Pretoria Minute of August 1990.

During 1991 the South African government removed basic apartheid laws from the statute book. Full negotiations for the constitution of a 'new' non-racial South Africa began in December 1991. But people still awaited full civil rights, notably 'one person, one vote', as well as affirmative action to redress the imbalances of black and white in South African society.   NP

Nelson Mandela (left) addresses an ANC rally in Soweto. Imprisoned for life on a charge of treason in 1964, Mandela became a potent symbol of black resistance during his years in prison. As vice-president of the ANC he played a leading role in negotiations for constitutional change in South Africa after his release in 1990.

SEE ALSO

- AFRICA TO THE COLONIAL AGE p. 66
- THE PEAK OF EMPIRE p. 160
- DECOLONIZATION p. 200
- THE THIRD WORLD p. 218

NORTH OF SOUTH AFRICA

The white settlers of Southern Rhodesia (Zimbabwe) declined to join the Union of South Africa in 1922, and began to look to a British-oriented future linked with Northern Rhodesia (Zambia) and Nyasaland (Malawi), and even with East Africa. The imposition of apartheid in South Africa after 1948 spurred the formation of an alternative British dominion in Southern Africa. The Central African Federation combined Northern and Southern Rhodesia and Nyasaland (1953). After Angola and Mozambique were proclaimed overseas provinces – rather than colonies – of Portugal, in 1951, white settlement intensified, but Portuguese citizenship was denied to all but a handful of Africans.

World economic recovery in the 1950s boosted the prosperity of white settlers, but also promoted African nationalism. Malawi and Zambia achieved independence under African majority rule in 1964. But Portugal and the whites of the surviving rump of 'Rhodesia' saw no reason to bow before international pressures to follow suit. Southern Rhodesia declared effective though illegal UDI (unilateral declaration of independence) under white minority rule in 1965.

African guerrilla movements began to fight Portuguese rule in Angola and Mozambique in 1961 and 1964 respectively. The African opposition parties in Rhodesia were banned and driven underground in 1964. Portugal and Rhodesia, like South Africa, successfully repressed and fought off insurgents until the early 1970s, when the world energy crisis brought economic problems. Angolan and Mozambican guerrillas intensified their war against Portuguese colonialism in 1971–2, and Zimbabwean guerrillas began to increase their incursions into Rhodesia from Mozambique and Zambia in 1972–3.

Portuguese power in Africa collapsed in 1974, and victorious guerrilla armies came to power in Angola and Mozambique in 1975. Their victory encouraged the guerrillas in Rhodesia. South Africa backed Rhodesia with men and arms until the price became too high. The concession of African majority voting in a state known as Rhodesia–Zimbabwe failed to stop the war. Peace was finally negotiated in 1979, followed by free elections and the independence of Zimbabwe in 1980, under the leadership of Robert Mugabe. The states north of South Africa tried to coordinate their economic and political strategies in the region from 1980 onwards. But South Africa continued to disrupt its northern neighbours by economic sanctions and military incursions, including full-scale war in Angola, until 1989.

The Rise of East Asia

The East Asian region has become an economic powerhouse over the last two decades, helping to shift the world's economic centre of gravity from the Atlantic to the Pacific. Emerging from the destructive effects of World War II, the independence struggles (▷ pp. 200–3), and the Korean and Vietnam Wars (▷ pp. 205 and 208), East Asia has developed into a major centre of manufacturing, commerce and finance.

Japan and the smaller capitalist economies of the region have made East Asia the fastest-growing region in the world during the 1970s and 1980s. Wishing to tap into this economic dynamism, their socialist neighbours, led by China, have begun to experiment with free-market principles.

The massive presence of China as well as the two superpowers has made the regional security order more complex and more fluid than in Europe. Multilateral alliances, such as SEATO (▷ p. 205), have proved ineffective, and not only the USA but also China and the Soviet Union have relied on bilateral ties with key regional allies. The USA has played a significant role in the region's postwar development, first as an aid provider and military guarantor and later as a market for the exports of the industrializing Asian countries. In the early postwar decades, external threats and internal insurgencies stimulated the rise of strong governments. Gradually, however, for the governments of the region, social stabi-

lity and political resilience became inextricably linked to economic growth and industrial development.

Asian economists have described a 'flying geese' pattern of economic development in the region. This 'V' formation sees manufacturing prowess and export dynamism spreading down from its original Asian centre and leader, Japan, to the 'newly industrializing countries' (NICs) of South Korea, Singapore, Taiwan and Hong Kong, and then to the countries of the Association of Southeast Asian Nations (ASEAN) and China. Japan has become the second largest economy in the world after the USA – a huge trader and investor, and the largest aid provider to the Third World. The NICs have attained marked levels of affluence, and all are amongst the world's top twenty trading nations. The resource-rich ASEAN countries are now also beginning to make their mark as exporters of manufactured goods.

'The Japanese Phoenix'

After the defeat of Japan in World War II, its cities lay in ashes and its economy in ruins. The occupying Allied forces under General Douglas MacArthur instituted sweeping economic reforms, and the Korean War procurements by US forces provided a short boost. But the 1950s were predominantly a decade of fierce domestic political strife, particularly over labour rights and the key security relationship with the USA. However, the 1960s opened with a new emphasis on 'income-doubling' and fast economic growth. During the decade, Japan became the first Asian country to join the Organization for Economic Cooperation and Development (OECD), hosted the Tokyo Olympics, and overtook Britain, France and West Germany in the size of its economy.

Because of its heavy dependence on imported oil, Japan was hit hard by the 1973 'oil shock' (▷ p. 212). But concerted efforts to conserve energy and secure

additional import sources restored stable though lower-level growth. Japan was becoming a mature economy, but its sustained export push and – particularly in the 1980s – its growing trade surpluses led to rising tensions with its trading partners, especially the USA and the European Community (EC). Disputes arose successively over exports of textiles, steel, cars, and an increasingly sophisticated range of consumer and office electronic equipment. The USA and the EC retaliated with restrictions on Japanese exports and demands for the wider opening of the Japanese market. At the same time, Japan found itself losing competitiveness in some manufactured products to its East Asian neighbours. As a result, in the late 1980s Japan embarked upon another major economic transformation, stimulating high-technology and service industries and emphasizing the quality of life. The large trade and current-account balances and heavy overseas investing of the second half of the 1980s will not continue through the 1990s, but Japan's adaptability and determination will ensure that it continues to narrow the gap with the USA in economic strength.

Japan has established a reputation for being a dynamic and innovative economic power, but has been hesitant in international political and security affairs. Japan has been ruled since 1955 by the Liberal Democratic Party (LDP), an amalgam of conservative factions preoccupied with domestic interests. The LDP has worked closely with a highly efficient bureaucracy and an adroit business community to chart Japan's economic successes. Japanese foreign policy has been low-key, driven by economics, and overly dependent on the USA. Unlike West Germany, which became reintegrated into the postwar European political and economic order (▷ p. 214), Japan found no settled East Asian order and so became dependent on one alliance – that with the USA. Memories of its past wartime experiences in Asia and the Pacific, together with the security provided by the US nuclear umbrella, persuaded Japan to avoid military entanglements, and to try hard to separate politics from economics. But, as Japan's economic strength has grown, so have demands from the USA for greater burden-sharing in the politico-strategic area. Although – with US encouragement – Japan has built up considerable armed forces (known as the Self-Defence Forces), pacifist public opinion and constitutional limitations still constrain Japan from committing itself to a military role overseas.

New rivals

Following behind Japan are the four NICs – South Korea, Singapore, Taiwan and Hong Kong. Their hallmark has been export-led growth, through making the best use of cheap – but relatively well-educated – labour. Their combined share of world trade grew from only 2% in the mid-1960s to 10% by the end of the 1980s (around the same level as Japan). All four are densely populated, poorly endowed with natural resources and, with the

Hong Kong's thriving business district. Light industry and flourishing foreign trade form the basis of Hong Kong's market economy. Export business is dominated by consumer goods – especially textile and clothing products – whose principal markets are the USA, Britain and Germany.

exception of Singapore, are only 'part-countries' – states which, for political reasons, are separated from nearby cultural entities with which they historically belong. Hong Kong has been described as a classic laissez-faire economy, but in South Korea, Singapore and Taiwan the government has played a strong guiding role. For these nations economic performance has become the touchstone of political legitimacy and national progress. However, sustained economic growth has created a middle class that has called for a greater voice in the political process to match the economic benefits received.

South Korea, handicapped by the psychological and material ravages of the fratricidal Korean War (1950–53; ▷ p. 205), owed its economic take-off to the stability created by Park Chung-hee (president 1961–79). He imposed a firm discipline on the economy and impressed upon the people the need to compete with their neighbours – first with North Korea and later with Japan. Despite occasional hiccups, high growth has continued under his successors; South Korea was the world's fastest growing economy for three successive years (1986–8). North Korea, ruled with an iron grip since 1948 by Kim Il-sung, has prided itself on its own brand of socialist self-sufficiency and has used its own mineral and power resources to finance economic development. In the second half of the 1980s, however, it became increasingly isolated, both ideologically and economically. Mutual suspicions between the two Koreas run deep and the dialogue between the two, since 1972, has been intermittent and unproductive.

Early reunification between the two Koreas does not appear likely; neither does Taiwan–China reunification. Taiwan (the Republic of China) survived military pressure from the mainland in the 1950s but in the early 1970s had to accept Western recognition of its rival, the People's Republic. After decades of stand-off, in the late 1980s Taiwan began to feel economically self-confident enough to develop closer economic, and even political, contacts with China. Taiwan has mirrored much of the South Korean development pattern since the early 1960s, with an efficient technocratic bureaucracy working under Jiang Jie Shi (Chiang Kai-shek; president 1949–75, ▷ p. 196) and then his son, Chiang Chingkuo (1975–88), to push export growth. Despite its economic success, Taiwan's political future still hinges on the attitude of China and the course of the relationship between China and Hong Kong (▷ p. 197).

In the 1960s, Hong Kong was the first of the NICs to become a significant exporter and it still has the highest per capita income. However, since China opened up at the end of the 1970s Hong Kong's economy has become closely interlinked with the Chinese economy and thus its growth record since then has both benefited and suffered from developments within China itself.

Singapore shares with Hong Kong a much greater degree of economic openness than the other two NICs. Its initial industrialization – after independence from Malaysia in 1965 – and subsequent technological upgrading owes much to the input of Western and Japanese multinational companies. Lee Kuan Yew (prime minister 1959–90) worked hard to protect his country's economic base and political independence. His policies, based on the establishment of a virtual one-party state and a free-market economy, remained paternalistic and often heavy-handed.

ASEAN potential

Whereas the NICs began to emerge as exporters of manufactured goods in the early 1970s, the other Southeast Asian countries were long dependent on exports of natural resources before adding, in the 1980s, certain manufactured exports. By the end of the 1980s both Malaysia and Thailand began to be considered close to the 'class of NICs' as their economies boomed and industrialization developed apace. Indonesia and Brunei, both heavily reliant on oil and gas exports, are also slowly diversifying their economies. Despite the traumas of race riots in Malaysia in 1969, a communist coup attempt in Indonesia in 1965, and several military coups in Thailand, these countries have all achieved a broad political stability. The Philippines, however, has not fulfilled its early promise and has failed to recover from the political and economic distortions that Ferdinand Marcos (president 1965–86) introduced through 'crony' capitalism during his corrupt and ruthless dictatorship.

Emerging regional cooperation

Despite the general economic dynamic in East Asia, attempts to create regional organizations comparable to the EC or even the OECD have not borne fruit. The only grouping in the region, ASEAN, was formed in 1967. But it has been more conspicuously successful in the political and diplomatic sphere – notably in coordinating opposition to the Vietnamese occupation of Cambodia after 1979 – than in its initial avowed aim of encouraging intra-regional economic cooperation. A few region-wide business organizations have emerged, but the intergovernmental Asia Pacific Economic Cooperation process, launched by Australia in 1989, has made only slow progress. The diverse ethnic, cultural, and religious backgrounds that typify the countries of East Asia – allied with their differing economic and political systems – have made the creation of institutions for regional cooperation far more difficult than is the case in Europe. **BB**

SEE ALSO

- JAPAN TO THE 20TH CENTURY p. 64
- WORLD WAR II: THE PACIFIC AND FAR EAST p. 194
- CHINA IN THE 20TH CENTURY p. 196
- DECOLONIZATION p. 200
- THE COLD WAR p. 204
- THE WARS IN VIETNAM p. 208

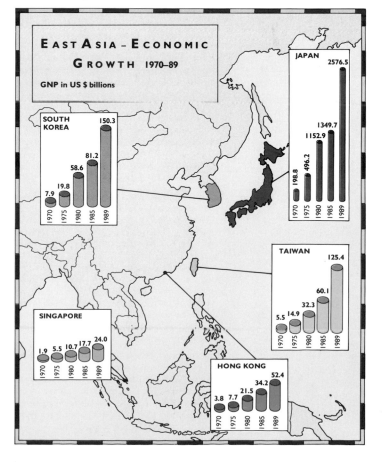

EAST ASIA – ECONOMIC GROWTH 1970–89

GNP in US $ billions

SOUTH KOREA: 7.9 (1970), 19.8 (1975), 58.6 (1980), 81.2 (1985), 150.3 (1989)

JAPAN: 198.8 (1970), 496.2 (1975), 1152.9 (1980), 1349.7 (1985), 2576.5 (1989)

TAIWAN: 5.5 (1970), 14.9 (1975), 32.3 (1980), 60.1 (1985), 125.4 (1989)

SINGAPORE: 1.9 (1970), 5.5 (1975), 10.7 (1980), 17.7 (1985), 24.0 (1989)

HONG KONG: 3.8 (1970), 7.7 (1975), 21.5 (1980), 34.2 (1985), 52.4 (1989)

The Decline of Communism

By the middle of the 1980s, the Soviet Union and the Communist countries of Eastern Europe had reached a profound crisis (▷ p. 199). Their economies were stagnant, and defence expenditure was taking an overlarge share of their budgets. Their industrial regions had suffered considerable environmental damage. Corruption and alcoholism were rife in their societies. But their political system – which had become rigid through attempting to suppress all criticism – was unable to deal with these accumulated problems, and ageing leaderships were increasingly out of touch. The need for change was desperate.

Jubilant East and West Berliners (right) met at the Berlin Wall for an impromptu celebration on the night of 9–10 November 1989, hours after the East German government opened its borders. Individuals began the piecemeal demolition of the Wall with hammers and chisels.

In March 1985, Mikhail Gorbachov became the new general secretary of the Communist Party of the Soviet Union. The choice of Gorbachov represented a belated recognition by the Soviet elite of the serious challenges faced by the system. Gorbachov was a younger leader, a man with a new image and style. He had ideas about how to improve the Communist system. However, the reforms he was to introduce began a process that would lead to the complete collapse of Communism throughout the Soviet Empire.

Glasnost and perestroika

Gorbachov rapidly introduced the policy of *glasnost* ('openness'), which allowed much greater freedom of discussion. At first this was restricted to the mistakes and corruption of the Brezhnev era. But outcry over the failure of the Soviet authorities to tell the truth about the explosion at the Chernobyl nuclear power station in 1986 led to a much greater openness. In the mass media all past

---

THE END OF COMMUNISM IN EASTERN EUROPE

The Communist governments of Eastern Europe were installed when Soviet armed forces liberated the region from Nazi occupation in 1945 (▷ pp. 193 and 198). As none of these regimes had been democratically elected, their power rested on the threat or use of force by the USSR (▷ p. 198). In June 1989, Mikhail Gorbachov announced that the Soviet Union would no longer use force to intervene in the internal affairs of other states. The people of Eastern Europe speedily took the opportunity to deliver their verdict on more than 40 years of Communism. By 1991 it had been utterly rejected. Communist parties throughout the region had either abandoned power voluntarily, or been swept away in a wave of protest.

Poland, always the Soviet satellite where Communism was weakest, was the first regime to fall. Following a perod of unrest, the independent trade union Solidarity, led by Lech Walesa, forced the Polish government to agree to free multi-party elections in August 1989. Solidarity won all but one of the seats in the new upper house of parliament and enough seats in the lower house – where 65% of the seats were reserved for the Communists – to form a coalition government with former allies of the Communists.

In Hungary, private enterprise and foreign investment had been encouraged since the early 1980s. Reformers in the Communist Party gained the upper hand at the end of the decade, and free elections were held in September 1989, resulting in a resounding defeat for the Communist Party.

During the summer of 1989 floods of refugees left East Germany for the West by way of Czechoslovakia and Hungary. In October and November mass anti-Communist demonstrations occurred in many East German cities. This resulted in a change of leadership in the East German Communist Party and the opening of the Berlin Wall (9 November), allowing free movement between East and West Germany (▷ p. 206). Demonstrations in favour of more radical change continued until opposition groups were admitted to the government. When the East German economy collapsed, the drive for German reunification became unstoppable.

Peaceful student demonstrations in Czechoslovakia developed into a mass protest, led by the dissident playwright Vaclav Havel. Faced by overwhelming public opposition, in the last two months of 1989 the Communist Party renounced its leading role and hardline leaders were replaced by reformers. A coalition government was formed and Havel was elected president.

Only in Romania did the revolution take a violent turn. Following the bloody suppression of an uprising in Timisoara by the secret police (Securitate) in December 1989, the army took power and executed the dictator Nicolae Ceaucescu and his wife Elena on charges of genocide and corruption. A National Salvation Front was formed and the Communist Party banned.

Events moved more slowly in Bulgaria where, following popular demonstrations in 1989, the hardline Todor Zhivkov was

replaced as Party leader by reformers. The Communists retained power after elections in 1990 and subsequently as part of a coalition.

In Albania the liberal wing of the Communist Party won an internal power struggle in 1990 and held multi-party elections in 1991. Following public unrest, a coalition government was formed.

Throughout Eastern Europe Communism had collapsed. In free multi-party elections the people rejected a system that had led to economic misery and political humiliation. But the new democratically elected leaders faced appalling economic and social problems – the legacy of more than four decades of Communist mismanagement. By the end of 1991, Communist parties (or their successors) remained in government only in Albania (in coalition) and in two of the six Yugoslav republics.

The end of the authoritarian Communist regimes in Eastern Europe allowed tensions between the various nationalities of the region to resurface. In multi-national Yugoslavia, Serbia forcefully resisted the nationalist aspirations of the Albanian majority in Kosovo province. The northern republics of Slovenia and Croatia declared independence in June 1991. Following reverses in a short campaign, federal forces were withdrawn from Slovenia, but Serb insurgents, backed by the federal army, occupied over one-third of Croatia, initiating a protracted civil war. In January 1992 Slovenian and Croatian independence was internationally recognized.

leaders were criticized, and social problems examined truthfully. Previously banned literature was published. The chief effect of all this was to reveal to the Soviet people the extent of the crisis they faced.

These developments, together with the removal of a number of hardliners from powerful positions in government, enabled Gorbachov to launch a more radical reform, *perestroika* ('restructuring'), in 1987. Perestroika involved far-reaching changes in the Soviet political and economic systems, and in the USSR's relations with the outside world. Many abuses of human rights were ended, and political prisoners were released. Politically, the reforms meant a reduction in the power of the Communist Party. Free multi-candidate elections were held in 1989, when many hardliners were defeated by reformers (some of them non-Communists). Considerable power was transferred to a new parliament, the Congress of People's Deputies, which replaced the rubber-stamp Supreme Soviet. In May 1989 a new executive presidency was created and Gorbachov became the first incumbent. In March 1990 the Communist Party – which had been the only legal political party – renounced its monopoly of power.

In the economic sphere Gorbachov's reforms involved moves to dismantle the inefficient centrally planned system. Factories and collective farms were granted the freedom to make their own decisions, and cooperatives and private enterprises – initially small-scale – were legalized.

Foreign policy too was revolutionized under the new foreign minister, Eduard Shevardnadze. Relations with the West were improved and a number of arms reduction treaties agreed with the USA and its NATO allies (▷ p. 226). The Cold War (▷ p. 204) was effectively ended and in 1989 the last Soviet troops left Afghanistan (▷ p. 207). In the same year the abandonment of the 'Brezhnev Doctrine' (▷ p. 199) – the right of the USSR to intervene in the affairs of Warsaw Pact countries (as it had done in Hungary and in Czechoslovakia; ▷ p. 206) – prompted rapid change in the Soviet satellites. The decision not to defend the Communist regimes of Eastern Europe by force led to their collapse in a series of popular revolutions (▷ box).

Setbacks and reactions

The public perception that – at last – somebody was trying to tackle the crisis initially made Gorbachov's reforms hugely popular in the Soviet Union. But hopes rapidly turned to disappointment. The economic situation continued to worsen as reforms proved inadequate to deal with the accumulated problems. Production fell in many sectors in 1990–1 and severe shortages of food and consumer goods – in part the result of a poor system of distribution – were experienced. In addition, for the first time in years, prices rose rapidly and the value of the rouble plummeted.

During 1989 the power of the central authorities in Moscow waned. The Communist Party was discredited by election defeats and by growing public anger at the abuse of power by party officials who enjoyed special privileges. A wave of strikes, together with moves towards independence from Moscow by a number of republics, further diminished Moscow's authority. Increased nationalist stirrings within the USSR were strongest in the three Baltic republics, where popular movements called for a restoration of the independence they had enjoyed from 1919 to 1940, when they were invaded and annexed by the Soviet Union (▷ box).

By 1990 the political situation had become increasingly polarized. Radicals, led by the newly elected president of the Russian Federation, Boris Yeltsin, accused Gorbachov of not going far or fast enough. Hardliners in the Communist Party, the army and the KGB accused him of abandoning socialism and causing economic chaos and a breakdown of law and order. By the end of the year, Gorbachov had aligned himself with the hardliners in an attempt to restore his flagging authority. Unpopular radical economic reform was rejected and reformers left his government to join forces with Yeltsin. In an apparent retreat from perestroika, armed force was used in an attempt to thwart the drive towards independence in Lithuania and Estonia.

The coup that failed

During 1991, Gorbachov moved back towards the reformers. He agreed to a new

The Moscow statue of Feliks Dzerzhinsky, founder of the Soviet secret police, was one of many potent symbols of the Communist state that were toppled by demonstrators during September 1991.

Union treaty under which power would have been radically decentralized to the 15 Union republics of the USSR. This proved too much for the Communist hardliners, who on 19 August attempted to take control in a military coup. A combination of bungled plans, the courage of street demonstrators led by Yeltsin, and the refusal of sections of the KGB and armed forces to take action against unarmed civilian protesters, led to the collapse of the putsch after only two days.

However, the long-term consequences were huge. The Soviet Union immediately began to disintegrate, with republic after republic declaring independence (▷ box). The Communist Party was banned for its part in the coup. Central authorities became increasingly irrelevant as the republics assumed the powers and responsibilities of the old Soviet government. Left without a function, Gorbachov resigned on Christmas Day 1991.

Power now lay in the hands of republican leaders, in particular Boris Yeltsin and Leonid Kravchuk (newly elected president of Ukraine). They attempted to renegotiate their relationships, forming a new, highly decentralized Commonwealth of Independent States (CIS), although this left many issues unresolved (▷ box, Soviet Disunion). The Soviet Union was formally disbanded on 31 December 1991. Communism had self-destructed, but had left a legacy of economic crisis, rising nationalist tensions, and political chaos. ·MW

SEE ALSO
● THE SOVIET EMPIRE p. 198
● THE COLD WAR p. 204

Nuclear Armament and Disarmament

On 16 July 1945 scientists in America, working on the Manhattan Project, successfully tested the world's first atomic device, at Alamogordo in the New Mexico desert. The fruits of more than three years of intensive research, it was an awesome spectacle, producing an explosion equivalent to thousands of tons (kilotons) of conventional TNT. President Harry Truman had no hesitation in using the new weapon against the Japanese. On 6 August a B-29 Superfortress bomber dropped an atomic bomb on Hiroshima, killing some 80 000 people instantaneously; three days later Nagasaki was hit, killing a further 35 000. These attacks hastened the Japanese surrender and the end of World War II (▷ p. 195). The atomic age had dawned.

SEE ALSO

● WORLD WAR II: THE PACIFIC
   AND THE FAR EAST p. 195
● THE COLD WAR p. 204

These early atom bombs were based on the theory, first propounded by the German chemist Otto Hahn (1879–1968) in 1938, that if the atoms of a heavy element such as uranium were bombarded with neutrons, they would split and create a chain reaction – *nuclear fission* – releasing an enormous burst of energy. The Hiroshima bomb ('Little Boy') achieved this by firing one piece of fissile material (uranium-235) into another; the Nagasaki bomb ('Fat Man') 'imploded' an outer casing of TNT onto the fissile material. The results were the same: heat, blast and a searing flash of light guaranteed to achieve widespread devastation.

The spread of nuclear weapons

Other countries sought to equal the American achievement. In 1949 the Soviets test-exploded a device, followed in 1952 by Britain. France joined the 'atomic club' in 1960 and China in 1964. By then nuclear capability had been taken a stage further with the advent of the thermonuclear (hydrogen) bomb, first tested by the USA in 1952. In the thermonuclear bomb the hydrogen nuclei of deuterium and tritium are fused together – *nuclear fusion* – under the pressure of a fission explosion to release the equivalent of millions of tons (megatons) of TNT. Such an explosion, even if confined to one megaton, would blind people up to 160 km (100 mi) away and devastate anything within 6 km (3.75 mi) of the point of impact.

No one has yet used a thermonuclear device in anger, for possession of such weapons forced a change of attitude towards the concept of war. Traditionally force had been used to achieve a political objective, often after all other methods of persuasion had failed, but now the results of such a policy would be so damaging as to be self-defeating, especially if the opponent also had a means of delivering nuclear weapons. Instead, the nuclear-capable powers began to use their weapons to prevent or deter war, threatening nuclear attack to force an opponent to think twice before embarking on a particular course of action. In the early years of the atomic age this was a one-way process, as the Americans had a monopoly of capability and delivery means, but as the Soviets caught up in the 1960s a situation of rough parity between the superpowers emerged.

MAD and its weaknesses

This led to the development of the theory of MAD (mutual assured destruction), in which each side had the ability to absorb a first-strike surprise attack while retaining sufficient weapons to hit back in a retaliatory second strike of devastating potential. Thus, if the Soviets attacked first, aiming to destroy US landbased ICBMs (intercontinental ballistic missiles), the Americans would probably still have sufficient ICBMs, as well as manned bombers and SLBMs (submarine-launched ballistic missiles) to hit back. As no sane person initiates an assault he knows will lead to his own destruction, so both sides were deterred from offensive action.

But MAD depends on the maintenance of a balance of capability, for if one side gains the means to carry out a devastating first strike that deprives the other of its retaliatory capability, or develops defensive systems that leave it substantially protected against attack, deterrence fails. Both superpowers, for example, have striven to improve the accuracy of their warheads, making them capable of seeking out and destroying more and more targets in a nuclear strike. By the late 1960s the Americans were experimenting with MRVs (multiple re-entry vehicles) which enabled each missile to carry up to five separate warheads. These were soon developed into MIRVs (multiple independently targeted re-entry vehicles), each capable of spinning off to find a separate target. The Soviets followed suit. If each target was, say, an ICBM launch silo, it was now possible to swamp the opposition with so many warheads that its ICBM force would be wiped out, seriously reducing its ability to launch a second strike. As experiments have taken place in America with MARV (manoeuvrable re-entry vehicles), each capable of gauging whether or not a particular target has been hit already and, if it has, of spinning off to a secondary target, the sophistication is awesome.

This would not affect the SLBMs, still the mainstay of second-strike capability. But if either side could successfully track the missile-carrying SSBN (sub-surface ballistic nuclear) submarines as they cruised in deep-ocean areas of the world, they could be targeted in a first strike and destroyed. ASW (anti-submarine warfare) is practised assiduously by the major powers, although as yet no significant breakthrough appears to have been made.

Star Wars

Of far more concern was that if either side developed a substantial defence against incoming missiles or warheads, the balance of MAD would disappear. In the 1960s both superpowers experimented with ABMs (anti-ballistic missiles) – rockets that could intercept and destroy incoming weapons – but this proved both costly and potentially destabilizing. Then, in March 1983, President Ronald Reagan (▷ p. 217) announced his decision to fund a space-based defensive system for the USA, known officially as SDI (the Strategic Defense Initiative) but more popularly as 'Star Wars'. In its most ambitious form – centred upon an elaborate system of laser and charged-particle-beam weapons in space, ready to destroy an incoming Soviet nuclear strike – SDI was likely to be ruinously expensive, and much less than 100% effective. Reagan's view was that, if deployed, it would render nuclear weapons useless as offensive instruments of war. More feasible was a less ambitious system that would protect ICBM sites and key command facilities.

The centre of Nagasaki was destroyed by an atomic bomb dropped by the US Air Force on 9 August 1945. After World War II both Nagasaki and Hiroshima were rebuilt and became spiritual centres for international disarmament groups.

'I have become death, the destroyer of worlds.' These words from the Bhagavadgita were quoted by Robert Oppenheimer, director of the Manhattan Project, on witnessing the first nuclear test in the desert of New Mexico.

Arms control and disarmament

There was, of course, an alternative approach – to negotiate mutual disarmament. Since the 1950s there has been pressure from disarmament groups such as CND (the Campaign for Nuclear Disarmament) in Britain – for unilateral nuclear disarmament, in which one side gives up its nuclear weapons in the hope that the other will follow. But the chances of this happening in a distrustful world affected by the Cold War (▷ pp. 204–7) were poor. Instead, the superpowers approached the problem through arms control, designed to create and maintain the central balance so essential to MAD. In the late 1960s, as ABM technology threatened the balance, the Americans and Russians met to discuss control and in 1972, after three years of negotiation, an ABM Treaty, limiting deployment to two systems only in each superpower homeland, was signed as part of the SALT I (Strategic Arms Limitation Talks) package. This was refined at Vladivostok in 1974 to impose 'ceilings' on the number of nuclear delivery vehicles (bombers, ICBMs and submarines) deployed by each side. The process was taken a stage further by SALT II in 1979, when the ceilings were reduced, but the Russian invasion of Afghanistan in December 1979 prevented ratification by the US Senate.

Further attempts at arms control or disarmament failed as the superpowers entered the 'New Cold War' of the early 1980s (▷ p. 207). The follow-up to SALT, known as START (Strategic Arms Reduction Talks), made slow progress. Similar attempts to extend the principle of control to conventional (non-nuclear) weapons in Europe – MBFR (Mutual and Balanced Force Reduction) – fared worse, and after 15 years of negotiations were stopped and replaced by a new forum, the CFE (Conventional Forces in Europe) talks. It was not until the Soviet government became more flexible under Mikhail Gorbachov (▷ p. 224), after both sides had begun to update and increase their intermediate-range nuclear systems (missiles stationed in and targeted against points in Europe), that a breakthrough occurred. After lengthy negotiation, both superpowers agreed in December 1987 to abolish land-based INF (intermediate nuclear forces), namely Soviet SS-20 and American Pershing II and GLCM (ground-launched cruise missile). The Americans and Soviets, anxious to cut defence spending, continued with START, but little headway was made until July 1991, when a treaty was finally signed in Moscow to cut strategic arsenals to 6000 weapons on each side by 1998. This heralded a new era in superpower relations, but the concurrent breakup of the USSR (▷ p. 225) left the Americans sufficiently worried to retain the option of Star Wars.

Meanwhile, CFE had achieved some success. In November 1990, at the Conference on Security and Cooperation in Europe (CSCE) summit in Paris, 22 NATO and Warsaw Pact countries agreed to substantial cuts in the number of tanks, artillery and combat aircraft deployed in Europe. A follow-up CFE2 treaty, concentrating on troop numbers in the same area, is being negotiated, although the problems are immense. Arms control and disarmament still have some way to go to secure a safer world, particularly as there is now a growing problem of proliferation – the spread of nuclear weapons to states hitherto without them. In the early 1990s, for example, evidence emerged of the pursuit of nuclear capability by Iraq and North Korea. If unstable or aggressive states outside the major powers gain nuclear weapons, START and other agreements may simply be irrelevant. JP

CHEMICAL AND BIOLOGICAL WEAPONS

Chlorine gas was used by the Germans against the Russians in January 1915 and against British and French forces in Flanders three months later. Despite the development of protective gas masks, both sides made widespread use of gas during World War I (▷ p. 177). The Germans replaced chlorine with the more lethal phosgene, and (in 1917) with mustard gas, a blistering agent that was much used by both sides. Disgust at the use of gas led to the international prohibition of chemical weapons (poison and nerve gases) in 1925, but this did not stop the Iraqis using them against Kurdish rebels at Halabja in March 1988.

During the 1991 Gulf War, it was feared that the Iraqis would use chemical and biological weapons (virus gases) against US-led coalition forces or the populations of Saudi Arabia and Israel (▷ p. 213). In the event, the threat did not materialize, but international concern about the spread and possible use of chemical and biological weapons remains. These weapons – often described as the 'poor man's atomic bomb'– are now available to a wide range of states.

Poison gases come in two forms: choking gases such as phosgene, which attack the lungs and restrict breathing; and blistering gases such as mustard gas, which cause horrific burns. Nerve gases – such as tabun and sarin – impair muscle control, making breathing impossible, while biological weapons carry the spores of deadly diseases such as plague or anthrax. Constituent parts of these weapons are relatively easy to manufacture and store in secret; delivery is effected by missiles or bombs.

Attempts have been made to control chemical and biological weapons. In 1972 an international convention banned biological devices, but chemical weapons have proved more difficult to define or identify. Both the USA and the USSR have agreed to reduce their stockpiles in recent years, but a wider international agreement to stop the manufacture, storage and use of all chemical weapons has yet to emerge.

Casualties of a gas attack – blinded by the fumes – lead each other in single file to a dressing station for treatment during World War I.

The United Nations

The world today consists of over 170 states. Each state has a defined territory, a people or peoples and a sovereign government, with the result that humanity is represented politically by numerous individual state governments. Thus humanity lacks a world government, but it does have an international organization where virtually all states can meet around the conference table. That organization is the United Nations.

The United Nations was planned at two conferences held by the Allied powers towards the end of World War II. Earlier in the war, the Allies had agreed to create a new international organization to replace the ill-fated League of Nations (▷ p. 189), and at the Dumbarton Oaks (August–October 1944) and San Francisco (April–June 1945) conferences the Allies worked out what form this new

Soviet president Mikhail Gorbachov addresses the General Assembly of the United Nations in New York in 1988. Speeches and documents are translated into the five official working languages of the UN (Chinese, English, French, Russian and Spanish).

body should take. The institution they created formally came into existence on 24 October 1945. It was called the United Nations Organization (UNO) or simply the United Nations (UN) – a name that had been devised by American president Franklin D. Roosevelt and had been adopted on 1 January 1942 by the anti-Axis (▷ p. 194) nations.

Purposes and principles of the United Nations

The founding fathers of the UN gave their creation three basic purposes, each of which was seen as a counter to the aggressive policy of the Axis powers that had culminated in World War II. The founders determined that the first and principal purpose of the UN should be to maintain international peace and security. Secondly, they decreed that their creation should, 'develop friendly relations among nations based on respect for the principle of equal rights and self-determination of peoples...'. Thirdly, they declared that the UN should 'achieve international co-operation in solving international problems of an economic, social, cultural, or humanitarian character' and promote and encourage 'respect for human rights and for fundamental freedoms for all without distinction as to race, sex, language, or reli-

gion...'. In effect, the founding fathers inserted into the UN Charter (the organization's 'constitution') the liberal-democratic ideals enunciated by the Allied powers – especially the USA – during the war.

The founding fathers gave the UN the authority to discuss disputes, to make recommendations for the settlement of such disputes, and, if necessary, to order collective measures to enforce the peace. This authority was vested primarily in two of the Organization's principal organs, the *General Assembly* and the *Security Council* (▷ box). The Assembly was empowered to discuss disputes and make recommendations on matters of international peace and security. The Security Council could go further, being entitled not only to make recommendations for the peaceful settlement of disputes but also, if these efforts proved ineffective, to direct member-states to impose diplomatic or economic sanctions, or even take military action, against a target government or regime.

The Assembly was also entitled to discuss and make recommendations on virtually any matter falling within the scope of the Charter. It was to be aided in the pursuance of the UN's second purpose by the *Trusteeship Council* and of the third by the *Economic and Social Council* (▷ box).

All UN activities (with the exception of enforcement) were subject to the proviso that the organization should not 'intervene in matters which are essentially within the domestic jurisdiction' of any state. This measure was designed to safeguard the principle of state sovereignty, but it has in practice been subject to differing interpretations by member-states. In the aftermath of the Gulf War (1991; ▷ p. 213), for example, there were differences between member-states on the issue of whether and how they might help the Iraqi Kurds.

The record of the United Nations

The UN's efforts to give effect to its main purpose of keeping the peace have been undermined by deep political divisions, especially those associated with the Cold War (▷ pp. 204–7). The General Assembly's meetings have as often reflected disunity as harmony among nations. The Security Council has similarly been hampered by a lack of unanimity among the great powers, and has rarely exercised its enforcement powers. The first exception was its decision to give military assistance to South Korea in June 1950 (▷ p. 208) – the Soviet delegation was absent from the Council at the time. The imposition of diplomatic and economic sanctions against Southern Rhodesia in December 1966 and an arms embargo against South Africa in November 1977 reflected the great powers' willingness even during the days of the Cold War to authorize collective measures against the 'white-minority' regimes in southern Africa (▷ p. 220). Cooperation between the great powers after the Cold War made

SEE ALSO

- DECOLONIZATION p. 200
- THE COLD WAR p. 204
- THE MIDDLE EAST p. 210
- THE THIRD WORLD p. 218
- NUCLEAR ARMAMENT AND DISARMAMENT p. 226

the Council's decision to authorize economic and military sanctions against Iraq possible in 1990 (▷ p. 213).

However, the UN's contribution to the maintenance of international peace and security extends beyond enforcement. The Security Council has mounted several 'peacekeeping' operations, in which forces drawn from member-states have acted as buffers between warring states or factions, at the request of the government(s) concerned, so as to make a resumption of hostilities less likely. UN peacekeeping forces have been deployed in various combat zones, including Cyprus (from 1964), the Golan Heights (from 1974), and the Lebanon (from 1978).

The General Assembly's debates, though often degenerating into exchanges of propaganda, have at least provided a forum where the states of the world can 'let off steam' – or, to use a phrase of Winston Churchill's, substitute 'jaw-jaw' for 'war-war'.

Successive Secretary Generals (▷ box) have played a significant part in arbitrating various international disputes, and the *International Court of Justice* has also contributed, providing an opportunity for states to take their disputes to legal settlement.

The UN's importance in facilitating the end of armed conflicts and military involvements was most clearly illustrated in 1988 and 1989, when the UN played a significant role in dealing with three long-standing and difficult problems. It helped establish and monitor a ceasefire in the Iran–Iraq war (▷ pp. 210–13); it assisted Soviet military withdrawal from Afghanistan (▷ pp. 204–7); and it played a key role in securing and observing the settlement of the Namibia question (▷ p. 220). These contributions to conflict resolution, like the UN's decision to authorize collective action against Iraq in 1990 (▷ p. 213), were made possible by the increasing degree of co-operation among the five permanent members of the Security Council in the late 1980s.

The UN can also boast of some successes in the pursuance of its other basic purposes. It has helped to accelerate the progress towards self-government of the peoples of former colonies and has done much to make the private cruelties of states a matter for the whole international community. It has also endeavoured to alleviate economic, social, educational, health and related shortcomings in the Third World, particularly through specialized agencies such as the WHO and UNICEF (▷ box). However, the UN has often been criticized for 'selective indignation', that is for denouncing violations of human rights in some states while condoning such violations in others, and for allowing the specialized agencies to waste large proportions of their budgets on unnecessary bureaucracy, to the detriment of the intended recipients.

The UN's overall record, therefore, has been uneven. The organization has not lived up to the ideals of the founding fathers, but it has not failed entirely, and has proved its usefulness in many conflicts. The UN is a free association of states based upon the principle of state sovereignty. In other words the UN can only do as much – or as little – as its member-states allow it to do.

Membership

According to its Charter, applicants for membership of the UN have to satisfy the Security Council and a two-thirds majority of the General Assembly that they are peace-loving states, accept the obligations of the UN Charter, and are able and willing to carry out these obligations. In practice, the UN has granted applicants membership almost as of right, with the result that the organization had grown from an initial complement of 51 member-states to 100 by the end of 1960 and 166 by late 1991. Most of these new members are former colonial or dependent territories.

The Charter also allows for the suspension or expulsion of any member-state that has persistently violated the principles of the organization. The UN has not yet taken such action.

In 1971 the UN decided to accept the government of the People's Republic of China (as opposed to the Republic of China or Taiwan, which had previously held membership) as the representative of the Chinese people. Since then, other than Taiwan, the only states without UN membership are Switzerland, which prefers to maintain its strict interpretation of neutrality, and a number of very small states in the Pacific and Europe. FT

UN troops in southern Lebanon. A UN peacekeeping force (UNIFIL) was deployed in southern Lebanon from June 1978 in an attempt to limit hostilities between warring factions in the area. UN peacekeeping units have only limited powers.

THE UN SYSTEM

The UN has six principal organs. These are listed below, together with an outline of their size and role. All are based in New York, with the exception of the International Court of Justice, which is based in The Hague.

THE GENERAL ASSEMBLY
This is composed of all member-states and can discuss anything within the scope of the Charter. It takes decisions by a qualified majority (two-thirds) of those present on 'important' questions, and by a simple majority on other issues, each member having one vote.

THE SECURITY COUNCIL
This is the main organ for maintaining international peace and security. It has 5 permanent members – China, France, the USSR, the UK and the USA, states that constituted the 'great powers' at the end of World War II – and 10 other seats taken by other member-states in turn. Decisions are reached through 9 out of 15 members voting for a measure. However, any one of the permanent members can invalidate a decision by exercising its right of veto. This system therefore institutionalizes the world authority of the great powers.

THE ECONOMIC AND SOCIAL COUNCIL
This has 54 members. It has acted as a coordinating body for the numerous specialized agencies created by the UN with the aim of achieving international cooperation in the economic, social and related fields.

THE TRUSTEESHIP COUNCIL
This was set up to supervise the progress towards self-government being made by trust territories (mostly colonies lost by Germany after World War I) and any other non-self-governing territories placed under the International Trusteeship System. All but one of the eleven territories placed under this regime have achieved independence, or union with a neighbouring state, and the Council has effectively been wound up.

THE INTERNATIONAL COURT OF JUSTICE
This is the UN's principal judicial organ, available to offer legal rulings on any cases that are brought before it.

THE SECRETARIAT
This acts as a sort of international civil service. Its head is the Secretary General, who combines the task of being the organization's chief administrative officer with that of being an international mediator. The post has had six incumbents so far:
Trygve Lie (Norway) 1946–53
Dag Hammarskjöld (Sweden) 1953–61
U Thant (Burma) 1961–72
Kurt Waldheim (Austria) 1972–81
Javier Perez de Cuellar (Peru) 1982–91
Boutros Boutros Ghali (Egypt) 1992–

THE SPECIALIZED AGENCIES
These are intergovernmental agencies related to the UN and attached to it:
International Labour Organization (ILO)
Food and Agriculture Organization (FAO)
United Nations Educational, Scientific and Cultural Organization (UNESCO)
World Health Organization (WHO)
International Bank for Reconstruction and Development (IBRD, or World Bank)
International Development Association (IDA)
International Finance Corporation (IFC)
International Monetary Fund (IMF)
International Civil Aviation Organization (ICAO)
Universal Postal Union (UPU)
International Telecommunications Union (ITU)
World Meteorological Organization (WMO)
International Maritime Organization (IMO)
World Intellectual Property Organization (WIPO)
International Fund for Agricultural Development (IFAD)
Industrial Development Organization (UNIDO)

In addition to these agencies, which report to the Economic and Social Council, there are two other agencies:
International Atomic Energy Agency (IAEA). This reports to the General Assembly and, as appropriate, to the Security Council.
General Agreement on Tariffs and Trade (GATT). This lays downs rules for international trade.

Among the subsidiary organs set up by the UN are the following:
United Nations High Commissioner for Refugees (UNHCR)
United Nations International Children's Emergency Fund (UNICEF)
United Nations Relief and Works Agency (UNRWA)
United Nations Commission on Criminal Prevention and Criminal Justice (UNCCPCJ)

Population and Hunger

Somewhere between 24 June and 11 July 1987, the human population of the planet Earth reached 5 billion. Yet, two hundred years before that, when the world's population was barely more than one billion, political economists such as Thomas Malthus and David Ricardo were already predicting that the human species would breed itself into starvation. Nevertheless, despite their predictions the human population keeps increasing – but so too does the food supply. Were the prognoses of Malthus and Ricardo wrong? Or, with the inexorable rise in population growth, is it just a matter of time before mass hunger and starvation prove them right? What is the relationship between population and hunger?

Starving Ethiopians in a Sudanese refugee camp in 1991. The 1980s and 1990s have seen large-scale movements of refugees – some driven by war (from, for example, Afghanistan, Cambodia, Ethiopia, Mozambique and Yugoslavia), some by famine (from the Sahel region in Africa), and some by economic deprivation (from Central America, North Africa and the Balkans).

A direct relationship between population and hunger was indicated 1800 years ago by Tertullian, an early Christian writer from North Africa, when he said 'We weigh upon the world; its resources hardly suffice to support us. As our needs grow larger, so do our protests that already nature does not sustain us.' Over the past 200 years this concern has intensified. With more effective means of communication and more accurate record keeping, knowledge about the disparities in living conditions of peoples all over the world has become more accessible. The Chinese famine of 1876–9 claimed approximately 13 million lives, the 1943 Bengal famine 3 million and the Ethiopian famine of 1984 at least 800 000.

Two contending views have emerged concerning the extent to which burgeoning populations affect food supply. The first is that population must be controlled if persistent malnutrition and starvation are not to become the inevitable lot for a substantial portion of the globe. The second is that, even with a projected global population of 10 billion by the year 2070, there is sufficient food to feed everyone.

These views reflect differing assumptions. Those who link hunger directly with overpopulation adhere to the Malthusian principle that in a world of relatively finite resources, increases in human numbers lower the demand for labour. This in turn lowers the wages of labour, leaving large portions of the population without the means to purchase food. Unless human beings seek to restrict their own reproduction through voluntary celibacy, late marriages, abortion and contraception, so, the neo-Malthusians argue, only the natural forces of war, epidemics and starvation will control the balance between population and food availability.

Such assumptions have been challenged by Karl Marx (⇨ p. 168), who believed that the way society was structured and its resources allocated were more important than population and finite resources. Others consider the prevalence of hunger as an issue more related to the way that people are deprived of access to food rather than one of its insufficiency.

Although the debate continues, increasing evidence would seem to support the structural view. Over the past 25 years, increases in food production have outstripped unprecedented global population growth by about 16%. Based upon this figure, it can be deduced that there is sufficient food in the world today to supply every individual with a daily intake of 3600 calories, although 900 million people live on the precipice of malnutrition (2100 calories per day for adult maintenance) or acute hunger (1750 calories per day for short-term adult survival).

Population and poverty

The greatest increases in population continue to occur in countries that are the poorest in terms of their Gross Domestic Product (GDP; the sum of all output produced domestically in a country). The populations of many Third World countries depend upon subsistence agriculture as their principal economic activity. These countries have limited social services and lack most forms of advanced agricultural technology. Under such conditions, rural families tend to have large families, ensuring a degree of labour as well as support for members of the family in their old age. Hence, large families – as was formerly the case in the developed world – continue to be an essential norm for the poor, who represent the majority in most Third World societies (⇨ p. 218).

Ironically, the emphasis placed upon eliminating disease amongst the young – for example through mass immunization programmes – has lowered levels of infant mortality. This has increased the population in many Third World countries, often leaving members of families without prospects for work. Thus towns and cities are seen as havens for alternative employment, although urban centres in underdeveloped countries offer limited job opportunities, and migration to towns and cities has done little to break the poverty cycle.

Hunger and poverty

There is a general belief that the forces of nature are principally to blame for the hunger that threatens much of humanity. Yet the effects of nature cannot be divorced from the issue of man-made poverty. In the USA in 1987, an extensive area in the southeast of the country was stricken by drought. No one died, no lives were threatened. During the same period, drought-affected Ethiopia needed over 1.3 million tonnes (tons) of emergency food to save the lives of over 4 million affected people. The differences between the two situations underscore the relationship between poverty and hunger. In the USA, available resources had been invested in extensive irrigation and water schemes. Food was available, if required, from a well-developed food-reserve system, and farmers were ultimately protected by insurance and loan schemes provided by the federal and state governments. Alternative employment was generally available to those whose assets were not otherwise protected.

In Ethiopia, as in many other Third World countries, the resources required to develop such support systems are generally not available. Without them, people become more and more vulnerable to the

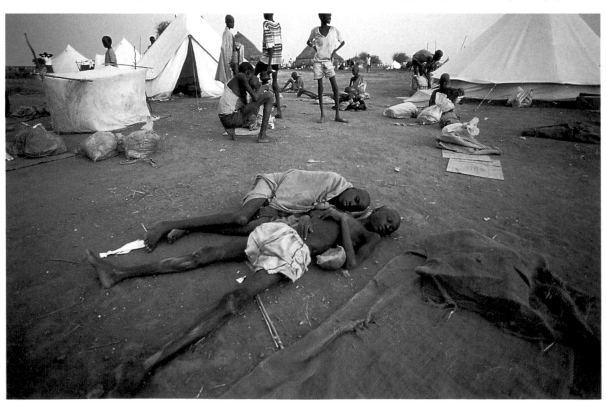

forces of nature, and their poverty intensifies. Ecological degradation demonstrates this well. With few resources, farmers in the Third World must till their fields continuously, leaving no respite for their recovery. Fertilizers are expensive, and therefore not readily available. The topsoil of these lands may have been held in place by trees that have now been felled to be used as fuel for which the poor have no real alternatives. The trees become the victims of poverty as does the land. Rain washes away valuable topsoil and the farmer gets less and less for his efforts. His situation, faced with an inevitably declining income, deteriorates. Subsistence agriculture teeters ever more frequently on the brink of disaster.

Poverty, population and development

If the world produces sufficient food to feed itself but the impoverished are increasingly exposed to threats of malnutrition and starvation, the issue seems to be how best to give the poor access to the food that is clearly available rather than one of population reduction. Greater access can be achieved through effective development. Such development must either help rural families to farm more effectively for profit – so enabling them to purchase a wider variety of foods – or allow them to find alternative means of generating income.

But there are three barriers to effective development that need to be overcome. On the international level, the majority of Third World countries are saddled with international debts (⇨ p. 218) that prevent them from funding the extensive development programmes that they require. Foreign exchange to pay these debts and to seek new loans is often hindered by the trading restrictions of the developed nations, or by the fluctuations in international market prices for the few goods that poor nations may have to sell. And even when development assistance comes from outside donors, all too often it is aid that is tied to the sorts of projects that may benefit the donor and the recipient government, but not necessarily citizens at the grass-roots level.

At the national level, many of the poorest countries are faced with contending demands that cannot be met with their limited resources. The fact that domestic and regional instability is also often prevalent means that a high proportion of national wealth is spent on armaments rather than development. Third World governments also have to expand resources on providing subsidized food for potentially volatile populations in towns and cities – which is often purchased by governments at prices that leave no incentives for farmers. Governments of developing countries, frequently prompted by developed countries, may also view development itself as a 'top-down' process: in other words, more visible large-scale projects such as road and dam construction are pursued, instead of projects that contribute directly to improving the lives of the poor.

It is at local levels that the cumulative

effects of instability and lack of effective development take their hardest toll. These effects are often compounded by a strict adherence to traditions, sometimes reinforced by religions that rationalize but do not necessarily ease the plight of the poor. Lack of education and appropriate technology means that traditional working methods are rarely abandoned, and consequently the poverty of the poor is intensified. Although with increases in family incomes the size of families decreases, this fact does not diminish the more general point that poverty rather than population size lies at the heart of hunger. Whether a population is large or small, there is little evidence that size in itself influences the way societies are structured or the way resources are allocated. In short, population is related to hunger but it is far from being its necessary cause.

The role of the international community

Since the World Food Conference of 1974, the international community has sought to play a greater role in relieving the crises of hunger found in many parts of the world. International organizations such as the United Nations World Food Programme, the Food and Agriculture Organization, the United Nations Children's Fund and the United Nations Development Programme (⇨ p. 229) have all attempted to assist countries where threats of famine and severe malnutrition are rife. These international organizations are supported by the efforts of donor governments (which either give assistance through international organizations or directly to affected countries) or through voluntary non-governmental organizations that are working in affected countries.

These organizations work on two levels. In times of severe food shortages they provide food and medicines for the hungry; frequently they also fund development programmes to stimulate economic growth. Although in the past these development efforts have not always addressed the real causes of hunger, increasingly both Third World governments and members of the international community recognize the need to focus their assistance directly upon the poor.   RK

A family planning poster in India, where large families have traditionally been seen as an insurance against poverty in old age. The Indian government has encouraged birth control and offered incentives for sterilization.

SEE ALSO

● THE THIRD WORLD p. 218
● THE UNITED NATIONS p. 228

POPULATION FACTS

Growth of world population by billion and year

World population	Year	Elapsed years
1 billion	1805	indefinite
2 billion	1926	121
3 billion	1960	34
4 billion	1974	14
5 billion	1987	13
6 billion	1998	11
7 billion	2010	12
8 billion	2023	13
9 billion	2040	17
10 billion	2070	30

The projected slowing down of world population growth to a peak of 10 billion in 2070 is based on the following assumptions: increased use of contraception in developing countries, and an ageing of the global population (with fertile adults making up a smaller percentage of the whole).

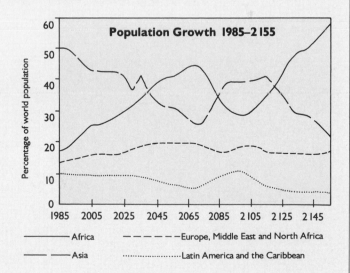

Population Growth 1985–2155

Africa — Europe, Middle East and North Africa — Asia — Latin America and the Caribbean

Population growth by geographic region, 1985-2025

Region	Population (millions)		Growth rate (%)		Birth rate (per 1000)		Death rate (per 1000)	
	1985	2025	1985-90	2020-25	1985-90	2020-25	1985-90	2020-25
WORLD	4,840	8,188	1.71	0.94	26.9	17.6	9.8	8.2
Africa	560	1,495	3.05	1.74	45.0	24.1	14.5	6.7
Asia	2,819	4,758	1.80	0.89	27.4	17.0	9.2	8.1
America	666	1,035	1.58	0.72	23.4	15.3	7.9	8.2
Europe	770	863	0.45	0.15	14.7	13.0	10.3	11.5
Oceania	25	36	1.37	0.59	19.6	15.0	8.2	9.1

The Women's Movement

Although feminist ideas have been voiced in many ages and cultures, the women's movement in its organized form is a comparatively modern development. Over 150 years, organized feminism has flourished in many countries around the world and has been responsible for obtaining significant improvements in the lives of women. Behind a general belief in equality between the sexes lies a history of campaigning for specific political, legal and social rights.

In 1792 the Englishwoman Mary Wollstonecraft wrote one of the great classics of feminist literature, *A Vindication of the Rights of Women*. Her vision of an education for girls that would enable them to fulfil their human potential was to provide inspiration for many future reformers. The emancipation of women was very much part of the liberal and progressive reform movements of the 19th and 20th centuries. In its significance, the emergence of the women's movement can be compared with the abolition of slavery, the rise of nationalism in colonial empires, and the political organization of the working classes (▷ pp. 164–9).

The first wave of feminism

In the first half of the 19th century in the newly industrialized societies of the USA and Britain, the lives of middle-class women were circumscribed by social constraints. Great emphasis was placed on their domestic duties and on voluntary religious and charitable work, but paid employment, particularly outside the home, was discouraged. Working-class women were barred from many of the better paid and traditionally male jobs, and more frequently worked in unskilled sectors of the labour market or in sweatshops (workshops where employees worked long hours in poor conditions for very low wages). All women were denied access to higher education, apprenticeships and professional training, and were legally prevented from the right to suffrage (i.e. the right to vote).

At the Seneca Falls Convention in New York State in 1848 – the first women's rights meeting – the delegates declared that 'all men and women are created equal'. This principle underscored the work of Susan B. Anthony (1820–1906) and Elizabeth Cady Stanton (1815–1902), two of the most prominent campaigners in the powerful American suffrage and equal rights movement. They founded the National Woman Suffrage Association in 1869.

Although in Britain in the 1830s and 1840s, women members of the Owenite socialist movement (▷ p. 166) were actively seeking to spread feminist ideas about marriage, divorce and economic equality, their influence faded with the decline of Owenism. It was not until the 1850s and 1860s that middle-class feminists started to organize what we know today as the Victorian women's movement. Initially they concerned themselves with opening up employment opportunities, improving girls' education, and reforming the property laws. Dr Elizabeth Garrett Anderson qualified as the first

woman medical practitioner in 1865, in spite of strong opposition from the medical profession. In 1878 London University became the first such institution to admit women to all its examinations and degrees. A significant legal reform occurred in 1882 when married women obtained the right to own property.

The suffrage movement in Britain began in 1866 when the radical MP and philosopher John Stuart Mill presented the first female suffrage petition to parliament. By 1900 the National Union of Women's Suffrage Societies, led by Millicent Garrett Fawcett, had become the largest suffrage organization in the country. Its members, called 'suffragists', campaigned for the vote using constitutional and peaceful means. In 1903 a new association of 'suffragettes' was formed – the Women's Social and Political Union – led by Emmeline Pankhurst and her daughter Christabel. Their more militant methods – such as chaining themselves to railings, breaking windows and hunger strikes – were controversial and sometimes outside the law.

By the early 20th century women in organizations like the Women's Cooperative Guild (founded 1883) were also campaigning for social reforms such as birth control information and baby clinics. Women workers tried to improve their economic position through the trade union activities of the National Union of Women Workers, formed in 1906.

In other European countries and in Australia and New Zealand, a strong women's movement also emerged in the mid to late 19th century. French feminists, for example, founded the journal *Le Droit des Femmes* in 1869 and successfully campaigned for entry into the legal profession in 1900 and the right of married women to control their own earnings in 1907. A small but highly effective movement in New Zealand won the vote for women in 1893 – New Zealand thus becoming the first country to grant national women's suffrage.

The force-feeding in prison of British suffragettes who had gone on hunger strike aroused much criticism. The notorious 'Cat-and-Mouse-Act' allowed the release of sick suffragettes but made them liable to re-arrest once they had recovered their health.

THE SPREAD OF WOMEN'S SUFFRAGE			
New Zealand	1893	Ceylon	1932
Australia	1902	(now Sri Lanka)	
Finland	1906	Philippines	1937
Norway[1]	1913	Jamaica	1944
Denmark	1915	France	1945
Soviet Union	1917	Italy	1945
Britain[2]	1918	Japan	1945
Germany	1918	China	1949
Poland	1918	India	1949
Netherlands	1919	Mexico	1952
Canada	1920	Egypt	1956
USA	1920	Kenya	1964
Ireland	1922	Switzerland	1971
Brazil	1934	Jordan	1982

[1] Women in Norway gained partial suffrage in 1907.

[2] Women aged 30 and over were granted the vote in 1918; in 1928 this was extended to women aged 21 and over.

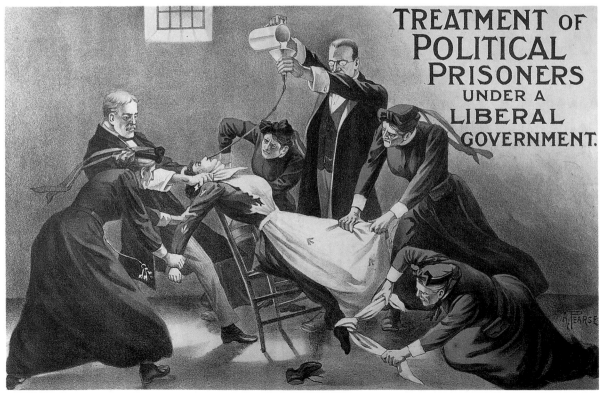

TREATMENT OF POLITICAL PRISONERS UNDER A LIBERAL GOVERNMENT.

Contemporary feminism

Although the first wave of feminism had reached its peak by 1930, the middle decades of the 20th century saw continued efforts to improve the position of women, but on a much reduced scale. The widespread use of female labour during World War II, often in the traditionally male-dominated sectors of agriculture and industry, was to be short-lived. At the end of the war many women gave up the new skills they had learned and returned to the home. In the subsequent 'baby boom' years of the 1950s, traditional ideas about women's role in society regained a strong foothold, particularly in the Western world, and the achievements of the first feminists were largely hidden from history. When Simone de Beauvoir (1908–1986) published her analysis of woman's condition in *The Second Sex* in 1949, her views were regarded by many as being outrageous and even offensive.

The women's movement re-emerged in the late 1960s and early 1970s and was much influenced by radical student politics in North America and Western Europe (▷ pp. 214 and 216). At that time it was frequently referred to as the 'Women's Liberation Movement'. In 1963 the American Betty Friedan (1921–) wrote her classic *The Feminine Mystique*, which together with *The Female Eunuch* (1970) by Australian-born Germaine Greer (1939–) presented a feminist critique of women's subordinate position in society. Women were still conditioned to accept their feminine, domestic and maternal

Women members of the peace movement continuously picketed a USAAF base near Newbury, England, in the 1980s, protesting against the presence on the base of US cruise missiles (▷ p. 227). Their peace camp, an example of the alignment of the women's movement with pacificism and green politics, continued after the removal of the missiles in the early 1990s.

role as paramount. They found it difficult to be active in the men's world of public and political affairs and to enter male-dominated sectors of the economy such as business, industry and banking.

In terms of organization, the women's movement has never been a unified whole, but rather a network of separate campaigns and interest groups. Methods have varied from political lobbying to mass demonstrations and there has been much emphasis on the need for women to work together in separate, women-only groups – for example, the consciousness-raising groups of the 1970s.

Somewhat different in style and aims from the first wave of feminism, the contemporary women's movement has emphasized issues of childcare, sexuality, male violence and the role of men and women in the home. It has raised questions as to how and why men and women are different in the 'nature versus nurture' debate – in other words, apart from physical differences, are women different from men because of their genetic make-up or because of their upbringing? As not all feminists agree on priorities and objectives, division has surfaced since the early 1970s between those who are most concerned with gaining equal rights, those who adopt a 'radical' stance and argue for women's separation from men in political and sexual ways (often adopting lesbianism as a political statement), and those who link feminist aims with other objectives such as socialism.

The international dimension

The women's movement is very much a global phenomenon with organized activity on all continents. Its objectives are often determined by existing conditions and laws in individual countries and cultures.

In the early 20th century nationalist movements sometimes provided women with a liberal framework within which to organize. An Indian Women's Association was founded in 1917 to campaign for suffrage, education and Hindu law reform. In Egypt the Egyptian Feminist Movement, formed in 1923, campaigned for an end to purdah (i.e. the practice of keeping women in seclusion) and the compulsory custom of wearing the veil, as well as for suffrage, better working conditions, and educational opportunities. The movement's leader, Huda Shaarawi (1879–1947), became the first president of the pan-Arab Feminist Union at its foundation in 1944.

More recently, in Eastern Europe and the Soviet Union before the collapse of Communism (1989–91), a small but autonomous women's movement had appeared, quite separate from the official women's organizations that had been run by the state. Although the Communist states provided women with free nurseries and abortion facilities, and encouraged women to work outside the home – often in traditionally male spheres – dissatisfaction remained. Feminists criticized the double burden of housework and employment and a family structure in which the roles of men and women were still traditional.

Although much has been achieved by the women's movement, much remains to be done. In Britain, in spite of campaigns for equal pay since World War I and the Equal Pay Act of 1970, a woman's 'rate for the job' is still less than a man's in many occupations, and women's average earnings on a national scale are approximately only three quarters the average earnings of men. With the exception of the Scandinavian countries, women active in government, in the higher levels of bureaucracy and in the trade unions are in a very small minority. Women are still living in a society largely governed by men.   LW

SEE ALSO
● ECONOMY AND SOCIETY IN THE 19TH CENTURY p. 164
● THE RISE OF MASS POLITICS p. 168

A demonstration in favour of the ERA (Equal Rights Amendment), a proposed amendment to the US Constitution that would have outlawed existing state and federal laws that discriminate against women. The amendment was drafted by the suffrage and equal rights leader Alice Paul (1885–1977) in 1923. Although the ERA was finally approved by the US Senate in 1972, it failed to achieve ratification by enough state legislatures to become the 27th Amendment to the US Constitution.

WOMEN PRESIDENTS AND PREMIERS

Sirimavo Bandaranaike PM of Sri Lanka 1960–5, 1970–7

Indhira Gandhi PM of India 1966–77, 1980–4

Golda Meir PM of Israel 1969–74

Elisabeth Domitien PM of Central African Republic 1975–6

Isabel Perón president of Argentina 1975–6

Margaret Thatcher PM of the United Kingdom 1979–90

Maria de Lourdes Pintassilgo PM of Portugal 1979–80

Vigdis Finnbogadottir president of Iceland 1980–

Eugenia Charles PM of Dominica 1980–

Gro Harlem Bruntland PM of Norway 1981, 1986–9, 1990–

Agatha Barbara president of Malta 1982–7

Milka Planinc PM of Yugoslavia 1982–6

Corazon Aquino president of the Philippines 1986–

Benazir Bhutto PM of Pakistan 1988–90

Violetta Chamorro president of Nicaragua 1990–

Ertha Pascal-Trouillot president of Haiti 1990–1

Kazimiera Prunskiene PM of Lithuania 1990–1 (before Lithuania's independence was internationally recognized)

Mary Robinson president of Ireland 1990–

Edith Cresson PM of France 1991–

Khalida Zia PM of Bangladesh 1991–

Abbasid, a dynasty of Muslim CALIPHS ruling from Baghdad (750–1258). They claimed descent from MUHAMMAD's uncle, Abbas; ⮕ p. 83.

Abdul Hamid II (1842–1918), Ottoman sultan (1876–1909). Crises in foreign affairs and internal disorder disrupted his reign. He was deposed in the YOUNG TURK revolution of 1908.

Abelard, Peter (1079–1142), French philosopher and theologian. After his love affair with Héloïse, he was castrated and became a monk. His provocative theological writings led to a clash with St BERNARD of Clairvaux.

Aberdeen, George Hamilton Gordon, 4th Earl of (1784–1860), British Conservative statesman. He became prime minister of a coalition government in 1852, but resigned in 1855 over his mismanagement of the Crimean War (⮕ p. 155).

Aborigines, the original inhabitants of Australia and Tasmania; ⮕ p. 68.

Aboukir bay, battle of, ⮕ NILE, BATTLE OF THE.

Abraham, Old Testament patriarch whose migration from UR to Harran in Upper Mesopotamia and thence to Canaan is described in the book of Genesis; ⮕ pp. 22 (box) and 82.

absolutism, a political system in which the monarch attempted to centralize power in his own person; ⮕ pp. 119, **122–3**, 135 (box), 144, 150 and 151.

Abu Bakr (c. 573–634), first CALIPH of Islam (632–4). On the death of his son-in-law, the Prophet MUHAMMAD, in 632, he succeeded him as head of the Muslim community (⮕p. 82).

Abyssinia, a former name for ETHIOPIA.

Achaea, an region of ancient Greece in the NW Peloponnese. Its cities were first formed into the **Achaean League** in the 5th century BC. From the early 3rd century BC this was reborn in a greatly extended form as a federal state; ⮕ pp. 31 (map) and 32–3.

Achaemenid, a dynasty that ruled the Persian Empire from the mid-6th to late-4th centuries BC; ⮕ pp. 21 and **26–7**.

Acheson, Dean (1893–1971), US politician, secretary of state (1949–53). He played a key role in promoting the Western Alliance during the early years of the Cold War (⮕ pp. 204 and 205).

acropolis, the hill or citadel that formed the central point of many Greek city-states, often the site of important temples. At Athens the acropolis was developed by a major building programme (c. 449–404 BC), including Athena's temple, the Parthenon; ⮕ p. 30 (box).

Actium, battle of (31 BC), a naval battle ending the Roman civil wars; ⮕ p. 37.

Adams, John (1735–1826), second president of the USA (1797–1801). He pursued a pro-British foreign policy as president and head of the ruling FEDERALIST party in the 1790s.

Adams, John Quincy (1767–1848), sixth president of the USA (1825–9) and eldest son of John ADAMS. His attempts to extend federal powers were opposed by Andrew JACKSON (⮕p. 156).

Addington, Henry, 1st Viscount Sidmouth (1757–1844), British statesman. He succeeded the Younger PITT as prime minister (1801–4). As home secretary (1812–21) he used stern measures against political and economic dissidents.

Aden, a port at the entrance to the Red Sea. A British protectorate until 1957, and a crown colony until 1963, Aden became part of the state of South Yemen in 1967, which merged with North Yemen to form YEMEN in 1990.

Adenauer, Konrad (1876–1976), German statesman. A founder of the West German CHRISTIAN DEMOCRATIC Party, he was the first chancellor of the Federal Republic of (West) GERMANY (1949–63).

Adrianople, battle of (9 August 378), the defeat of a Roman army by VISIGOTH forces W of Constantinople; ⮕p. 78.

Adrianople, Treaty of (1829), a treaty ending the Russo-Turkish War of 1828–9; ⮕ p. 154.

Aegospotami, battle of (405 BC), the final naval victory of the Peloponnesians over the Athenians at the close of the Peloponnesian War; ⮕ p. 31.

Aeolians, the third cultural and linguistic grouping of the ancient Greeks, comprising the Boeotians and Thessalians, and a group of cities on the N coast of Asia Minor (Turkey); ⮕ DORIANS, IONIANS.

Aetolia, an ancient region of NW Greece. From c. 370 BC onwards, its tribes combined into a federal state, the **Aetolian League;** ⮕ p. 33.

Afghanistan, a country in S Central Asia. Afghanistan was ruled by the Persians until the 4th century BC when Alexander the Great invaded (⮕ p. 32), but Greek control was short lived as Afghanistan fell to barbarians from the N. In the 7th century AD Arabs reached the borders, bringing Islam (⮕ pp. 62 and 82). Various Muslim empires followed until 1222 when the country fell under the harsh control of the Mongol Genghis Khan (⮕ p. 54). The rule of TAMERLANE in the 14th century was equally devastating. In the 18th century, the Persians united the country. In the 19th century, rivalry between Russia and Britain, who regarded Afghanistan as the key to India, led to instability. Britain attempted to assert control in two disastrous Anglo–Afghan wars (1839–42 and 1878–81; ⮕ p. 160). Independence was only achieved in 1921 after a third war with the British. A period of unrest followed until a more stable monarchy was established in 1933. A coup in 1973 overthrew the monarchy. A close relationship with the USSR resulted from the 1978 Saur Revolution, but the Soviet invasion (1979) led to civil war (⮕ p. 207). In 1989 the Soviets withdrew, leaving the cities in the hands of the government and Muslim fundamentalist guerrillas controlling the countryside. A guerrilla force captured Kabul in 1992 and installed an Islamic government.

African National Congress, (ANC), a black South African political party founded in 1912. Banned and exiled in 1960, it became a non-racial party in 1969. After a period of guerrilla warfare, it was legalized and began negotiations for a democratic non-racial state in 1990; ⮕ pp. 220–1.

Afrikaners, speakers of the Dutch-derived Afrikaans language in South Africa, also known as Boers; ⮕ pp. 67, 162 and **220–1**.

Agadir crisis (1911), an international dispute that erupted when a German gunboat was sent to Agadir in SW Morocco to protect German interests; ⮕ p. 175.

Aga Khan, ⮕ ISMAILI.

Agincourt, battle of (25 October 1415), an English victory over the French in N France during the Hundred Years War; ⮕ p. 95.

Agricola, Gnaeus Julius (AD 40–93), Roman governor of Britain (78–c. 84). He extended Roman military power into the Highlands of Scotland, as described by his son-in-law TACITUS.

Agricultural Revolution, ⮕ p. 140.

Agrippa, Marcus Vipsanius (c. 64–12 BC), Roman general, lifelong friend and adviser of the emperor Augustus (⮕ p. 38). At the time of his death was virtually co-ruler of the empire.

Ahab, king of Israel (c. 869–c. 850 BC) and son of OMRI; ⮕ p. 23.

Ain Jalut, battle of (1260), the destruction of a Mongol army by Egyptian MAMLUK forces, thwarting an attempted Mongol invasion of Syria and Palestine (⮕ p. 54).

Aix-la-Chapelle, Treaty of (1748), the treaty concluding the War of the Austrian Succession. MARIA THERESA of Austria relinquished Silesia to Frederick the Great of Prussia, the kingdom of Sardinia made gains in N Italy, while in N America the British returned the fortress of LOUISBURG to the French in exchange for the return of Madras in India; ⮕ p. 125.

Akbar (the Great, 1542–1605), Mogul emperor of India (1555–1605); ⮕ p. 63.

Akhenaten (Amenophis IV; d. c. 1362 BC), pharaoh of Egypt (c. 1379–1362 BC); ⮕ pp. 19 and 20 (box).

Akkad, a region of central Mesopotamia, centred on the city of Akkad (or Agade); ⮕ p. 16.

Alamo, the, a mission in San Antonio, Texas, besieged by Mexican troops during the TEXAN Revolution against Mexico (1836). Although the American defenders (led by Colonel Jim Bowie and the frontiersman Davy Crockett) put up a heroic fight, they were finally overwhelmed and massacred in the assault of 6 March 1836.

Alans, groups of mounted warriors who spread across Europe with the Barbarian migrations, settling in Italy, Gaul and N Africa; ⮕ p. 78.

Alaric I (c. 370–410), king of the VISIGOTHS (395–410), who sacked Rome (410); ⮕ pp. 40 and 78.

Alba, Fernando Alvarez de Toledo, Duke of (1507–82), Spanish general. His brutal suppression of Protestant unrest in the Netherlands fuelled the Dutch Revolt; ⮕p. 120.

Albania, a country in SE Europe. The revolt (1444–68) by Skenderbeg (?1403–68) against the Ottoman Turks – who invaded in the 14th century (⮕ p. 114) – is celebrated by Albanians as their national epic. Because most Albanians converted to Islam, they were able to secure autonomy and gain access to high positions in Ottoman service. By 1900, Ottoman enfeeblement encouraged Albanian nationalism, and in 1912, independence was declared. The country was occupied in both the BALKAN WARS and World War I (⮕ pp. 175–9), and the formation of a stable government within recognized frontiers did not occur until the 1920s. Interwar Albania was dominated by Ahmed Zogu (1895–1961), who made himself king (as Zog I) in 1928. He fled when MUSSOLINI invaded in 1939 (⮕ p. 188). Communist-led partisans took power when the Germans withdrew (1944). Under Enver HOXHA, the regime pursued rapid modernization on Stalinist lines, allied, in turn, to Yugoslavia, the USSR and China, before opting (in 1978) for self-sufficiency and isolation. The liberal wing of the Communist Party won a power struggle (1990), instituted social and economic reforms, and held multi-party elections (1991; ⮕ p. 224, box). After the Socialists (former Communists) were defeated in 1992, a new government faced severe economic problems.

Albigensians, ⮕ CATHAR.

Albuquerque, Alfonso de (1453–1515), Portuguese navigator and founder of the Portuguese empire in the east (⮕ p. 116). His conquests of Goa (1510), Malacca (1511; ⮕ p. 63) and Hormuz (1515), laid the basis of Portugal's control of eastern trade routes.

Alcibiades (c. 450–404 BC), Athenian statesman and soldier; ⮕ pp. 30, 31 and 47.

Aleuts, a native people inhabiting the islands of the Bering Sea and adjacent Alaskan coast, related to the Eskimo; ⮕ p. 72.

Alexander I (1777–1825), tsar of Russia (1801–25). The early part of his reign saw widespread reforms, but its middle and later phases were marked by increasingly reactionary policies. Between 1805 and 1815 he was mainly preoccupied with the Napoleonic Wars (⮕ pp. 146–7), and in the following decade with upholding the VIENNA settlement, which led him to support METTERNICH's suppression of national and liberal movements. His 'Holy Alliance' of the Christian monarchs of Europe was short-lived and ineffective; ⫸ p. 180 (box).

Alexander II (1818–81), tsar of Russia (1855–81). His reign witnessed the emancipation of the serfs (1861), reforms of local and provincial government, the legal system and the army, and Russian expansion into Central Asia. He was assassinated in March 1881; ⫸ p. 180 (box).

Alexander III (1845–94), tsar of Russia (1881–94). His reign was characterized by internal repression and the attempts of his ministers to promote economic modernization. In foreign affairs, it saw the conclusion of the Franco-Russian alliance (1892–4) and the consolidation of Russian gains in Asia.

Alexander III (the Great) (356–323 BC), king of Macedon (336–323 BC); ⫸ pp. **32–3** and **44–5**.

Alexandria, the name of six cities founded by Alexander the Great, of which the most successful was Alexandria-in-Egypt. It became the capital of Egypt under the Ptolemies, and flourished as a centre of the arts and sciences and as a commercial city. Under the Romans it was acknowledged as the second city of the empire; ⫸ pp. 19 (box) and 32–3.

Alexius I (Comnenus; 1048–1118), Byzantine emperor (1081–1118) and father of Anna COMNENA. His request for papal help in fighting the SELJUK Turks was one of the causes of the First Crusade; ⫸ pp. 81 and 88.

Alfred (the Great; 849–99), king of WESSEX (871–99), who successfully withstood Viking attacks, and helped to revive English ecclesiastical learning. Building on his achievement, his successors united England; ⫸ p. 86.

Algeria, a country in NW Africa. After the fall of Carthage in 146 BC (⫸ pp. 23 and 36–7), coastal Algeria became Roman. In the 7th century the Arabs brought Islam (⫸ p. 82) despite initial BERBER resistance. Several Berber empires flourished in the Middle Ages (⫸ p. 83). In the 16th century, Turkish corsairs defended Algiers against the Spanish, and placed the region under Ottoman control (⫸ pp. 114–15). During the 18th century, Algeria became a centre for piracy and in 1830 the French invaded on the pretext of protecting trade. Colonization followed, and coastal Algeria was attached to metropolitan France. By 1860 much of the best land was in French hands. (For the history of the Algerian revolution and Algerian independence, ⫸ p. 202, box) The first president of independent Algeria, Ahmed BEN BELLA, was overthrown in 1965 by Colonel Houari BOUMÉDIENNE, who established a one-party socialist state under the Front de Libération Nationale (FLN). After his successor, Colonel Chadli Benjedid (1929–) introduced multi-party democracy (1990), Islamic fundamentalism became a political force. In 1992 the second round of multi-party elections was cancelled when fundamentalists gained a large lead in the first round. The military took power and suspended political activity.

Algonquin, a native North American people, formerly living in the area N of the Great Lakes. The name Algonquin is also used for a wider linguistic grouping.

Ali (?600–61), fourth CALIPH of Islam (656–61) and son-in-law of MUHAMMAD. Ali and his descendants are regarded by SHIITE Muslims as the only true heirs of the authority of Muhammad; ⫸ pp. 82–3.

Allende, Salvatore (1908–73), Chilean Marxist politician, president of CHILE (1970–3). He died in a military coup led by General PINOCHET.

Allied Powers or **Allies, 1.** the countries that fought against the CENTRAL Powers in World War I. The main Allied Powers were France, Britain, Russia, and the USA after 1917 (⫸ pp. 176–9). **2.** the countries that fought against the AXIS POWERS in World War II. The main Allied Powers were Britain, the Commonwealth countries, the USA, the Soviet Union, France, China and Poland (⫸ pp. 190–5).

Almohads, a Muslim dynasty of BERBERS who ruled in N Africa and S Spain in the 12th and 13th centuries, displacing the ALMORAVIDS; ⫸ pp. 83 (box) and 89.

Almoravids, a Muslim dynasty of BERBERS who ruled in N Africa from the second half of the 11th century. In the 1080s they were called into Spain to rescue the Muslim kings from Christian attack. They were overthrown by the ALMOHADS in the mid-12th century; ⫸ pp. 83 (box) and 89.

Alsace-Lorraine, territories in E France annexed after the FRANCO-PRUSSIAN war by the victorious Germans, who claimed that they were historically and ethnically German. They were returned to France by the Treaty of Versailles; ⫸ pp. 174, 176, 178 (map) and 182 (map).

American Civil War (1861–5), ⫸ pp. 156 and **158–9**.

American Federation of Labor (AFL), a federation of North American labour unions, founded in 1886. By 1914 the AFL was a loose alliance of national craft unions with a membership of over two million skilled workers which avoided politics and worked for specific practical objectives; ⫸ p. 166.

American Revolution, ⫸ INDEPENDENCE, AMERICAN WAR OF.

Amerindians, the native people of North and South America; ⫸ pp. 70–3.

Amin, Idi (1926–), ⫸ UGANDA.

Amorites, a Semitic people who settled in Mesopotamia in the early part of the 2nd millennium BC; ⫸ p. 22.

Amritsar massacre (13 April 1919), a massacre of Indians gathered in Amritsar in N INDIA to protest against repressive British legislation. Gurkha troops under Brigadier R.M. Dyer fired on an unarmed crowd, killing 379 and injuring 1200.

Anabaptist, a member of a radical 16th-century Protestant sect; ⫸p. 111 (box).

anarchism, a political theory, first outlined by PROUDHON, advocating the abolition of formal government and the state. Anarchists such as BAKUNIN were particularly influential in Russia during the 1860s and 70s and were hostile to MARXISM. A number of European heads of state were assassinated by anarchists in the 1890s, but the influence of anarchism declined after the Russian Revolution of 1917; ⫸ p. 169.

Anatolia, the Asian part of Turkey, formerly known as Asia Minor.

ancien régime, the social and political system in France, and sometimes by extension elsewhere in Europe, before the Revolution of 1789; ⫸ p. 144.

ANC, ⫸ AFRICAN NATIONAL CONGRESS.

Anderson, Elizabeth Garrett (1836–1917), British physician; ⫸ p. 232.

Andorra, a co-principality in SW Europe, between France and Spain. Since 1278 Andorra has been under the joint sovereignty of a temporal 'prince' (since 1589 the French head of state) and a spiritual 'prince', the Spanish bishop of Urgel. Because of its peculiar constitution, Andorra has found difficulties in obtaining international recognition. In the 1970s and 1980s, however, it has achieved some constitutional and financial reform.

Andrassy, Julius, Count (1823–90), Hungarian statesman. Main negotiator of the AUSTRO-HUNGARIAN *Ausgleich* of 1867, he was prime minister of Hungary (1867–71). As Austro-Hungarian foreign minister (1871–79), he was a creator of the THREE EMPERORS LEAGUE (1873) and a key architect of the Balkan settlement agreed at the Congress of BERLIN in 1878.

Andropov, Yuri (1914–84), Soviet politician, general secretary of the Communist Party (1982–4), president of the Soviet Union (1983–4); ⫸ p. 199.

Angevin, the name given by historians to two dynasties: **1.** the descendants of the early 10th-century Count Fulk of ANJOU, notably HENRY II, RICHARD I and JOHN, who ruled Normandy, England and AQUITAINE as well as ANJOU (the Angevin Empire); **2.** the descendants of CHARLES of Anjou, conqueror of the kingdom of Sicily in 1266, whose successors ruled S Italy (the kingdom of NAPLES) until 1442.

Angles, a Germanic people originating in S Denmark and its islands. In the early 5th century they settled in East Anglia and NORTHUMBRIA as auxiliaries of Britain's sub-Roman rulers; ⫸ pp. 78 (map), 79 (box) and JUTES.

Anglican Church or **Church of England,** the established state Church in England. In 1534 HENRY VIII renounced the supremacy of the pope, founding the Church of England with the monarch at its head. Protestant reforms were instituted during the reign of EDWARD VI. After the reign of the Catholic MARY I, the independent Church of England was re-established in 1558. Conflict between PURITANS and the followers of 'catholicizing' Archbishop LAUD was a contributory factor in the outbreak of the ENGLISH CIVIL WAR. The Church of England was disestablished during the COMMONWEALTH and the PROTECTORATE, but restored at the RESTORATION. The Anglican Church retains many of the Catholic liturgical traditions, but holds most of the tenets of the reformed faith of Protestantism. Its doctrine is based upon the Thirty-Nine Articles (1559), while its liturgy is based upon *The Book of Common Prayer* (1552 and 1662) and its successors. The 18th-century Evangelical Movement emphasized the Protestant tradition (John WESLEY established an independent METHODIST Church in 1791), while the 19th-century Oxford Movement emphasized the Catholic tradition. These two movements continue in the Church of England as the Low Church and the High Church; ⫸ pp. 118–19.

Anglo-Afghan Wars, ⫸ AFGHANISTAN.

Anglo-Burmese Wars (1824–6, 1852, 1885), a series of wars fought between British India and Burma (MYANMAR), during which most of Burma was annexed to British India; ⫸ p. 160.

Anglo-Dutch Wars (1652–4, 1665–7, 1672–4), three naval wars between England and the United Provinces of the Netherlands; ⫸ pp. 121 and 128.

Anglo-Maori Wars, ⫸ NEW ZEALAND.

Anglo-Saxons, ⫸ p. 79 (box).

Angola, a republic in SW Africa. The Kongo and Ndongo kingdoms ruled much of the area when the Portuguese arrived in the late 15th century and developed a major slave trade (⫸ pp. 67, 116 and 129). In the 20th century, forced labour, heavy taxation and discrimination from white settlers helped to stimulate nationalism. Portugal's repression of all political protest led to the outbreak of guerrilla wars in 1961. When independence was finally conceded (1975; ⫸ p. 203), three rival guerrilla movements fought for control of the country. With Soviet and Cuban support, the (Marxist-Leninist) MPLA, under Dr Agostinho Neto (1922–79), gained the upper hand and also managed to repulse an invasion from South Africa (⫸ p. 221, box). In the 1980s, Cuban troops continued to support the MPLA government against the South African-aided UNITA movement in the S. Foreign involvement in the civil war ended in 1990. A ceasefire and multi-party constitution were agreed in 1991.

Anjou, a historic province (or county) of W France. It was ruled by an independent princely house (the ANGEVINS) from the 10th century until conquered by PHILIP II Augustus of France in 1203–5.

Annam, a former kingdom and empire of E INDO-CHINA. It became a French protectorate in 1884 and now forms part of Vietnam; ▷ pp. 60–1.

Anne (1665–1714), queen of England, Scotland and Ireland (1702–7), queen of Great Britain and Ireland (1707–14), the last STUART monarch. She was the daughter of the Catholic JAMES II, but was raised as a Protestant and married the Protestant Prince George of Denmark. Her reign saw England's UNION with Scotland and British success in the War of the Spanish Succession. After the death of her last surviving child the Act of SETTLEMENT (1701) recognized the Protestant HANOVERIANS as successors to the English throne, excluding the Catholic Stuarts; ▷ p. 119.

Anschluss (German, 'connection'), Hitler's annexation of Austria in 1938; ▷ p. 188.

anticlericalism, hostility towards the influence of the Christian clergy in political affairs. In the late medieval period anticlericalism set the scene for the Protestant Reformation (▷ pp. 91 and 110–11). Attacks on the Church gained a new momentum during the 18th-century Enlightenment (▷ pp. 134–5).

Anti-Comintern Pact (1936), an agreement between Germany and Japan declaring their hostility to international communism (▷ p. 188).

Antietam (Sharpsburg), battle of, a battle during the American Civil War in which the North's Army of the Potomac under McCLELLAN stalled LEE'S Confederate drive into Pennsylvania. Over 20 000 men died in fighting on 17 September, the bloodiest day of the war; ▷ p. 158.

Antigonid dynasty, a dynasty descended from Antigonus, one of Alexander the Great's generals; ▷ pp. 32–3.

Antioch, a city formerly in N Syria (now Antakiyah in Turkey). Founded by SELEUCUS I in 300 BC, it rose to prominence in the later Roman and Byzantine periods, and fell to the Arabs in 637. It was taken by Crusaders in 1098 and remained in Christian hands for half a century; ▷ pp. 32, 88 and 103.

antipope, a rival bishop of Rome, in opposition to the lawfully elected pope. In the Middle Ages antipopes were often supported for reasons of political gain by the Holy Roman Emperor, and in the 14th century several antipopes were elected following the Great Schism (▷ p. 90).

anti-Semitism, antagonism towards JEWS; ▷ pp. 169, 186–7 and **192**.

Antonescu, General Ion (1882–1946), Romanian Fascist dictator. He allied Romania with the AXIS Powers in World War II. His regime fell when the Red Army entered Romania in 1944. He was executed as a war criminal.

Antonine Wall, Roman frontier barrier built in 142 BC under the emperor Antoninus Pius. It stretched between the Clyde and the Firth of Forth in Scotland. It was abandoned in AD 196.

Antoninus Pius (AD 86–161), Roman emperor (138–161); ▷ p. 38.

Antony, Mark (Marcus Antonius) (c. 82–30 BC), Roman general; ▷ p. 37.

Anuradhapura, the ancient capital of Sri Lanka; ▷ p. 60.

ANZAC, an acronym for the Australian and New Zealand Army Corps, which fought in World War I. Originally used to denote the Corps which fought in the GALLIPOLI campaign (▷ p. 177), ANZAC was later applied to all Australian and New Zealand servicemen who served together in joint forces.

Anzio, the site of an amphibious landing by Allied forces in central Italy in January 1944; ▷ p. 191.

ANZUS, a Pacific security treaty between Australia, New Zealand and the USA, signed in 1951; ▷ p. 205.

Apache, a native North American people, predominantly nomadic hunter-gatherers. Athapaskan speakers, they moved S from the far N c. 1000 AD, many eventually arriving in the Southwest, where they came into conflict with the PUEBLO Indians; ▷ p. 73.

Apartheid (Afrikaans, *rasse-apartheid*, 'race-apartness'), a doctrine developed by AFRIKANER nationalists in South Africa to reinforce racial segregation after 1948; ▷ pp. **220–1**.

appeasement, a term now used in a pejorative sense to describe the attempts by the British PM CHAMBERLAIN and his French counterpart DALADIER to satisfy what were perceived to be the reasonable demands of the AXIS POWERS from 1936 to 1939; ▷ p. 188.

Appomattox, a village in Virginia, USA, where LEE'S Confederate Army of Northern Virginia surrendered to GRANT'S Army of the Potomac on 9 April 1865, marking the effective end of the American Civil War; ▷ p. 159.

Aquinas, St Thomas (c. 1225–74), Italian DOMINICAN theologian, canonized in 1323. He integrated the ideas of the Greek philosopher ARISTOTLE into Catholic theological thought, making the important distinction between faith and reason; ▷ p. 132.

Aquino, Corazon (1933–), president of the Philippines (1985–92). The widow of an opposition leader murdered by the security forces of Ferdinand MARCOS, she came to power after an uprising that ended the latter's repressive 20-year rule.

Aquitaine, a former province in SW France. Originally the Roman province of Aquitania (▷ p. 37), it was occupied by VISIGOTHS, then conquered by CLOVIS, and subsequently retained a strong separate identity under its own rulers, initially kings (until the 9th century) then dukes (until the 15th century). From 1154 to 1453 the duke of Aquitaine was also king of England; ▷ pp. 78 (map), 85 (map) and 94–5.

Arab conquests, the wars of conquest fought by Muslim Arabs in the century following the death of MUHAMMAD. They created an Arab empire – and spread the Islamic faith – from Spain in the W to Central Asia in the E; ▷ p. 82.

Arab-Israeli Wars (1948–9, 1956, 1967 and 1973), the wars fought between ISRAEL and its Arab neighbours; ▷ pp. **211–12**.

Arab League, an organization formed in 1945 to promote economic and cultural links, and to minimize conflict between, Arab states. It includes all Arab states as well as the PALESTINE LIBERATION ORGANIZATION, which the League regards as the representative of a legitimate and independent state; ▷ p. 212.

Arafat, Yasser (1920–), Egyptian-Palestinian politician, chairman of the PALESTINE LIBERATION ORGANIZATION since 1969 and leader of the al-FATAH movement. He is widely accepted as the leader of the Palestinians-in-exile, although his power has declined in recent years; ▷ p. 212.

Aragon, a kingdom that emerged from a nucleus around the river Aragon during the course of 11th-century wars against the Muslims in N Spain. The marriage of FERDINAND II of Aragon to ISABELLA of Castile in 1469 effectively created a single Spanish monarchy; ▷ pp. 83 (box) and 116.

Arakan, the W coastal area of Burma. A powerful kingdom in the 15th century, it was annexed by Burma in 1784 and was ceded to the British in 1826; ▷ p. 61.

Aramaeans, a group of Semitic-speaking tribes who settled in Syria and along the Euphrates from the 10th century BC; ▷ pp. 20 and **23**.

Arcadia, a mountainous region in the centre of the Peloponnese, Greece. Its city-states were mostly dominated by Sparta until the latter's defeat at Leuctra (▷ pp. 31 and 44), after which Thebes founded in 368 BC a new **Arcadian Confederacy**. This soon lost cohesion, and by 250 BC most of the Arcadians joined the ACHAEAN LEAGUE.

archaeology, ▷ pp. 5, **6–7** and 12–15.

Archaic period, in ancient Greece, the period c. 800–500 BC; ▷ pp. **28–9**.

Ardennes Offensive (or battle of the Bulge) (1944), the last major German advance of World War II. The Germans attempted to capture the Belgian cities of Antwerp and Brussels by splitting the Allied armies; ▷ p. 191.

Areopagus, the earliest council of Athens, with judicial and governing powers. Appointed from a fixed set of aristocratic families, it gradually lost powers to other, more democratic, bodies; ▷ p. 30.

Argentina, a republic in S South America. NW Argentina was part of the Inca Empire (▷ p. 71), while Patagonia and the pampas were home to nomadic Indians. The Spanish arrived in the La Plata estuary in 1516 but early colonization of the region was slow. During the Napoleonic Wars, nationalism grew. SAN MARTÍN helped lead the revolution that ended Spanish rule (▷ pp. 148–9). Independence was declared in 1816, but the war of liberation continued until 1820, and the first national government was only formed in 1826. Although it was reunited under the dictator de Rosas (1835–52), Argentina was wracked by disunity, and the powers of the provincial governments were not curbed until the 1850s. From 1880, large-scale European immigration and British investment helped Argentina to develop a flourishing economy. Prosperity was ended by the Depression, and, in 1930, constitutional rule was interrupted by a military coup. In 1946, a populist leader, Juan PERÓN, came to power with the support of the unions. His wife Eva was a powerful and popular figure, and after her death (1952) Perón was deposed (1955) because of his unsuccessful economic policies. Succeeding civilian governments were unable to conquer rampant inflation, and the military took power again (1966–73). An unstable period of civilian rule (1973–6) included Perón's brief second presidency. In the early 1970s, urban terrorism grew and the economic crisis deepened, prompting another coup. The military junta that seized control in 1976 received international condemnation when thousands of opponents of the regime were arrested or 'disappeared'. In April 1982, President Galtieri ordered the invasion of the FALKLAND Islands and its dependencies, which had long been claimed by Argentina. A British task force recaptured the islands in June 1982, and Galtieri resigned. Constitutional rule was restored in 1983 and financial reforms in the 1990s improved the prospects of the economy.

Argos, an ancient city-state in the NE Peloponnese, Greece. It was repeatedly defeated by Sparta, and in the 5th century BC often allied itself with Athens. In the 390s Argos formed a brief union with Corinth, which was broken up by Sparta, and was itself greatly weakened by civil war c. 370; ▷ p. 31 (map).

Arianism, a heretical form of Christianity practised in the late Roman Empire and in parts of Western Europe until the 8th century, based on the teachings of the Libyan priest Arius 250–336); ▷ p. 91.

Aristides (c. 520s–c. 467 BC), Athenian politician, who was ostracized in 483/2, probably after opposing Themistocles' (▷ p. 29) proposal to develop the Athenian navy. He returned to fight in the Persian Wars, and was responsible from 477 onwards for the first assessment of tribute that the cities of the Delian League (▷ p. 29) were to pay.

Aristotle (384–322 BC), Greek philosopher. What survives of his works are full lecture-notes on his courses, which survey systematically, and develop subtly and profoundly, all known areas of intellectual enquiry, including logic and metaphysics, zoology and physics, politics, ethics, poetics and rhetoric; ⊳ pp. 30 (box) and 32.

Armada, ⊳ SPANISH ARMADA.

Armenia, a country in the Caucasus Mountains of W Asia. Ancient Armenia was incorporated, in turn, into the Persian Empire (⊳ pp. 26–7), the empire of Alexander the Great (⊳ pp. 32–3) and the Seleucid Empire (⊳ pp. 32–3). Independent Armenian states appeared in the 2nd century BC and a united Armenian kingdom was established c. 55 BC. Christianity was adopted c. AD 300. In the 4th and 5th centuries Armenia was divided between the Byzantine Empire (⊳ pp. 80–1) and Persia. An independent kingdom (Greater Armenia) emerged in the 9th century, but was constantly threatened by invasion from the Arabs, Byzantines, Persians and SELJUKS. When Greater Armenia fell to the Mongols (1236–42), many Armenians fled to Cilicia (modern SE Turkey) where a second Armenian kingdom (Little Armenia) flourished until the 14th century, when it was overrun by MAMLUK armies from Egypt. In the 16th century Armenia was fought over by Persia and the OTTOMAN Turks. After 1620 W and central Armenia was ruled by the Ottomans, while E Armenia (the present state) was annexed by Persia. Russia took Persian Armenia between 1813 and 1828. The Armenians under Ottoman rule suffered persecution and, in 1896 and again in 1915, large-scale massacres. During World War I Turkey deported nearly 2 000 000 Armenians (suspected of pro-Russian sympathies) to Syria and Mesopotamia. The survivors contributed to an Armenian diaspora in Europe and the USA. Following the collapse of tsarist Russia, an independent Armenian state briefly emerged (1918), initially as part of a federal Transcaucasian Republic. The Armenian state – which faced territorial wars with all its neighbours – was not finally extinguished until 1922 when it became part of the Transcaucasian Soviet Republic. Armenia became a separate Union Republic within the USSR in 1936. After the abortive coup by Communist hardliners in Moscow (September 1991; ⊳ p. 225), Armenia declared independence and received international recognition when the USSR was dissolved (December 1991). Since 1990 Azeri and Armenian irregular forces have been involved in a violent dispute concerning the status of NAGORNO KARABAKH.

Arminius, chieftain of the Cherusci, and leader of German resistance to Roman efforts to create a province E of the Rhine. He achieved his aim in AD 9 when his forces annihilated three Roman legions in the Teutoburger Forest (⊳ p. 38).

arms control, ⊳ pp. 182–3 and **227**.

Arnhem, battle of (1944), an attempt by the 1st British Airborne Division to secure a bridgehead over the Rhine at Arnhem in the Netherlands to facilitate the Allied advance into Germany; ⊳ p. 191.

Artaxerxes II (c. 436–358 BC), Achaemenid king of Persia (404–358 BC); he defeated the revolt of his brother CYRUS the Younger; ⊳ p. 27.

Arthur, a legendary 6th-century king of Britain. Historically, Arthur may have held back the Saxons for a generation. 'Rediscovered' by the 12th-century chronicler GEOFFREY of Monmouth in his *History of the Kings of Britain* (1136), he became the model of the chivalrous warrior-king for the Middle Ages; ⊳ p. 79 (box).

Arthur, Chester A. (1830–86), twenty-first president of the USA (1881–5). A Republican, he attempted to reform the SPOILS SYSTEM.

Aryans, an Indo-European speaking people who settled in Iran and the Indian subcontinent in ancient times (⊳ pp. 26 and 58). The term was also used in Nazi Germany to describe CAUCASIANS of non-Jewish descent (⊳ p. 186).

Ashanti, a former African kingdom ruling the inland part of modern Ghana. From the mid-18th century it became a major force in W Africa until annexed by Britain in 1901; ⊳ pp. 66 (map) and 67.

Ashikaga, a Japanese noble family, whose members filled the office of shogun 1338–1568; ⊳ p. 64.

Ashoka, Mauryan emperor of India (272–232 BC); ⊳ pp. 58–9.

Ashurbanipal, king of Assyria (668–627 BC). His conquest of Egypt took the empire to its greatest limits, but within 20 years of his death it had fallen apart; ⊳ p. 21.

Ashurnasirpal II, king of Assyria (883–859 BC). Under his rule Assyria reclaimed lost territory and began its expansion; ⊳ p. 21.

Asquith, Herbert Henry (1852–1928), British Liberal statesman, prime minister (1908–16). He backed LLOYD GEORGE over the controversial 'PEOPLE'S BUDGET', and supported the passing of important social legislation, including the introduction of a national insurance scheme in 1911. His HOME RULE Bill provoked violence in the N of Ireland. Asquith formed a coalition with the Conservatives in 1915, but was ousted in 1916 by Lloyd George; ⊳ p. 175 (box).

Assad, Hafiz al- (1928–), president of Syria since 1971. A former air force officer and leading member of the Syrian BA'ATH Party, his rule has often been repressive. In the early 1990s he attempted to improve relations with the West, aligning Syria with the American-dominated coalition during the Gulf War (⊳ p. 213, box).

Association of Southeast Asian Nations (ASEAN), an organization established in 1967 by Indonesia, Malaysia, the Philippines, Singapore and Thailand to promote their mutual economic development; ⊳ pp. 222–3.

Assyria, originally a small area in N Mesopotamia, centred on the ancient capital of Ashur on the Tigris, it expanded from the 9th century BC to become the first Near Eastern empire; ⊳ pp. 16, 19, **20–1**, 23, 26, 43 (box) and 44.

Astyages, the last king of the M˙ DES (585–550 BC; ⊳ p. 26.

Atahualpa (d. 1533), the last emperor of Peru; ⊳ pp. 71 and 116 (box).

Atatürk, Mustafa Kemal (1881–1938), Turkish soldier and statesman, president (1923–38); ⊳ pp. 183 and **210**.

Athapaskan, a group of North American languages spoken by peoples such as the Apache and the Navajo; ⊳ pp. 72–3.

Athelstan (895–939), king of England (925–39). Illegitimate grandson of ALFRED the Great, he consolidated the power of WESSEX, campaigning in NORTHUMBRIA, Cornwall and Wales.

Athens, one of the leading city-states of ancient Greece; ⊳ pp. **28–31**.

Atlantic, battle of the, the struggle for control of the sea routes around the UK and to the USA during World War II; ⊳ p. 190.

Atlantic Charter, a joint statement of liberal-democratic principles for the postwar world signed by CHURCHILL and F.D. ROOSEVELT in 1941. It formed the ideological basis of the United Nations Organization (⊳ p. 228).

Attica, an area of SW central Greece that became the territory of the city-state of Athens in the 8th century BC or earlier; ⊳ p. 31 (map).

Attila (c. 406–53), king of the HUNS (433–53); ⊳ pp. 54 and 78.

Attlee, Clement Richard, 1st Earl (1883–1969), British Labour statesman. He served under Ramsay MACDONALD until the latter formed a coalition government in 1931. Attlee became leader of the Labour Party in 1935 and served as deputy prime minister (1942–5) in CHURCHILL'S wartime government. As prime minister (1945–51) he presided over the extension of the WELFARE STATE.

Auchinleck, Sir John Claude Eyre (1884–1981), British field marshal who commanded the British forces in N Africa 1941–2; ⊳ p. 191.

Augsburg, a Bavarian city that was a major banking and mercantile centre in the 16th century. The Peace of Augsburg (1555) brought a temporary religious settlement to Germany; ⊳ p. 110

Augustine of Canterbury, St (d. 604/5), the first archbishop of Canterbury, who helped to convert the Anglo-Saxons to Christianity; ⊳ p. 79 (box).

Augustine of Hippo, St (354–430), theologian and bishop of Hippo in N Africa. Many of his theological writings were written to defend Christianity against widespread contemporary heresies. His best known works are the *Confessions* and *The City of God*; ⊳ p. 90.

Augustinians, an order of canons; ⊳ p. 91.

Augustus, the title conferred on Octavian (Gaius Julius Caesar Octavianus) (63 BC–AD 14), who was effectively if not technically the first Roman emperor (27 BC–AD 14); ⊳ pp. 37, **38** and 45.

Aurangzeb (1618–1707), Mogul emperor of India (1659–1707); ⊳ p. 63.

Aurelian (Lucius Aurelius Aurelianus; AD 215–75), Roman emperor (270–5), who began the revival continued under Diocletian; ⊳ p. 39.

Aurelius, Marcus (AD 121–180), Roman emperor (161–180). His reign was dominated by wars against Parthia (161–6) and against invading German tribes from across the Danube; ⊳ pp. 38 and *40*.

Austerlitz, battle of, (2 December 1805), a battle fought near the town of Austerlitz in Moravia, in which NAPOLEON defeated larger Austrian and Russian forces, ending the military threat posed to him by the Third Coalition; ⊳ p. 146.

Australia, an island-continent between the Indian Ocean and the Pacific, and an independent member of the COMMONWEALTH. The Aborigines came to Australia around 50 000 years ago (⊳ p. 68). They lived mainly along the N and E coasts and in the Murray Basin until British settlers drove them into the inhospitable interior. The Dutch are credited with the discovery of Australia. Willem de Janesz sighted Cape York Peninsula (1606), Hartog made the first landing in 1616 (in Western Australia), and TASMAN explored the coasts (1642–44). However, the hospitable regions most suitable for colonization were not known to Europeans until Captain COOK landed at Botany Bay (1770), and claimed NEW SOUTH WALES for Britain (⊳ p. 129, box). In 1788, the first settlement was made at Port Jackson (Sydney), with over 700 British convicts and 250 free settlers. Penal settlements at Hobart and Launceston in Tasmania, and Newcastle (NSW) followed (1803–4). Moreton Bay (Brisbane) was established in 1824, Port Phillip (Melbourne) in 1826, and Albany (Western Australia) in 1827. Adelaide (South Australia), a settlement without convicts, was founded in 1837. Free migration was encouraged. The spread of sheep farming, and the discovery of copper (1840s) and gold (1851), attracted large numbers of migrants. The colonists campaigned to end transportation – the last convicts arrived in 1867 – and agitated for participation in government. In 1854, gold miners at Eureka Stockade (Ballarat) rebelled over the lack of representative government. This celebrated incident hastened reform. Between 1855 and 1870, all six colonies gained self-government. By 1900, 3 700 000 people, almost entirely of British and Irish ancestry, were living in Australia. Fear of invasion from

Asia or German New Guinea, and the desire to achieve free trade between the colonies, encouraged federation. In 1901, the Commonwealth of Australia was founded. Australia made an important contribution in WORLD WAR I – one fifth of its servicemen were killed in action. The heroic landing at GALLIPOLI in the Dardanelles (▷ p. 177) is a national day of remembrance in Australia. The DEPRESSION hit the country badly, but the interwar years did see international recognition of Australia's independence. World War II, during which the N was threatened by Japan, strengthened links with America. Australian troops fought in Vietnam (▷ p. 208) and important trading partnerships have been formed with Asian countries. Since 1945, migrants from all over Europe have gained assisted passage to Australia, further diluting the British connection.

australopithecines, hominids of the earliest stage of human evolution; ▷ p. 2.

Austria, a country in Central Europe. The Babenberg family ruled what became Austria from the late 10th century until 1250. Their successor as duke was defeated by Rudolf of HABSBURG, the Holy Roman Emperor, in 1276, and from that date Austria became the heartland of the Empire. With one exception, every Holy Roman Emperor from 1438 to 1806 was a member of the Habsburg family (▷ p. 84). In 1529, and in 1683, Austria repelled the Turks from the walls of Vienna and halted their advance across Europe (▷ p. 114). By the middle of the 16th century, the extent of the Habsburgs' territory had become unmanageable, and CHARLES V divided his inheritance, separating Spain from the Empire in Central Europe (▷ p. 117). In the 18th century, MARIA THERESA and her son JOSEPH II reformed Austria and strengthened the multilingual Habsburg state (▷ pp. 124–5 and 134). This was based on Austria, Hungary and Czech-speaking Bohemia, but it also included Polish, Croat, Slovak, Slovene and Italian areas. Napoleon I abolished the anachronistic Holy Roman Empire (▷ p. 147), but FRANCIS II, foreseeing its dissolution, took the title emperor of Austria. METTERNICH shaped the fortunes of Austria in the early 19th century and attempted to maintain the boundaries drawn by the Congress of VIENNA (1814–15), but the empire was bedevilled by national and ethnic divisions (▷ pp. 150–1). Austria's partnership with the Hungarians – in the Dual Monarchy established in 1867 – did not ease these tensions. Defeat in the AUSTRO-PRUSSIAN WAR (1866) excluded Austrian influence from the German-speaking part of Europe (▷ p. 153), and the Habsburgs were left to dominate unstable S Central Europe (▷ pp. 154–5). In 1914, a Bosnian Serb assassinated the heir to the Austro-Hungarian throne – an event which precipitated World War I (▷ pp. 175 and 176). In 1918–19, the Habsburg empire was dismembered (▷ p. 182). A separate Austrian republic was established despite considerable support for union with Germany. Unstable throughout the 1920s and 1930s, Austria was annexed by Germany in 1938 (the *Anschluss*, ▷ p. 188). Austria was liberated in 1945, but Allied occupation forces remained until 1955 when the independence of a neutral republic was recognized. The collapse of Communism in Eastern Europe in 1989–91 allowed Austria to renew traditional economic links with HUNGARY, CROATIA and SLOVENIA.

Austrian empire (1806–67), a state created in 1804 by the last Holy Roman Emperor FRANCIS II (Francis I of Austria) in anticipation of the end of the Holy Roman Empire (1806). Its boundaries, fixed in 1815, included all the HABSBURG territories and at least 11 nationalities. Under METTERNICH the empire was a bastion of the new European conservatism and a pillar of the system established by the Congress of

VIENNA. It was replaced in 1867 by the AUSTRO-HUNGARIAN EMPIRE; ▷ pp. 151 and 153.

Austrian Succession, War of the, (1740–8), a complex European conflict, fought mainly in Central Europe; ▷ p. 125.

Austro-Hungarian empire, the HABSBURG Dual Monarchy created after Austria's defeat by Prussia and Italy in 1866. The *Ausgleich* (Compromise) of 1867 conceded effective home rule to Hungary. The empire, which was undermined by the aspirations of its minorities for national independence, was partitioned by the Treaty of St Germain (1919); ▷ pp. 175, 176, 178 and 182.

Austro-Prussian War (Seven Weeks War; June–August 1866), a conflict arising from the problematic joint administration of SCHLESWIG-HOLSTEIN after the German-Danish war of 1864 and Prussian proposals to reform the GERMAN CONFEDERATION; ▷ p. 153.

auto-da-fé, a ceremony of the Spanish INQUISITION; ▷ p. 113 (box).

Ava, a former kingdom and capital of Burma; ▷ p. 61.

Avars, a nomadic people found in the Eurasian steppe from the late 6th century. They besieged CONSTANTINOPLE in alliance with the Persians in 626 and went on to found a state in Hungary. After their conquest by Charlemagne in 796 they vanished from history; ▷ pp. 54 and 80.

Averroës (Ibn Rushd; 1126–98), Islamic philosopher whose commentaries on the works of Aristotle had a significant influence on Christian SCHOLASTICISM.

Avignon period, a period during which the popes resided at Avignon in S France (1309–77); ▷ p. 90.

Awami League, a political party in East Pakistan, founded in opposition to the ruling MUSLIM LEAGUE. Under Sheikh MUJIBUR Rahman it led the Bengali movement for independence from Pakistan that culminated in the creation of BANGLADESH.

AWB (Afrikaans, *Afrikaner Weerstansbeweging*, 'Afrikaner Resistance Movement'), a South African neo-Nazi group founded in 1973, advocating violence to maintain APARTHEID or a separate whites-only territory.

Axis Powers, the coalition of Fascist states fighting with Germany against the ALLIED POWERS in World War II. An agreement between Germany and Italy signed in 1936 established a Berlin–Rome 'Axis'. They were joined by Japan after the ANTICOMINTERN PACT, and later by the Nazi-aligned states of Hungary, Slovakia, Croatia, Romania and Bulgaria; ▷ p. 188.

Axum, an ancient city in N Ethiopia, capital of an empire that flourished from the 1st to the 6th centuries AD; ▷ p. 66.

Ayub Khan, Mohammed (1907–74), president of PAKISTAN (1958–69). He came to power in a coup, subsequently attempting to perpetuate his rule through so-called 'basic democracy' which denied the adult franchise. He was overthrown by a popular uprising.

Ayutthaya, the capital of the kingdom of Thailand from the mid-14th century until 1767, when it was destroyed by the Burmese; ▷ p. 61.

Azerbaijan, a republic in the Caucasus Mountains of W Asia. The Azeris were conquered by the Arabs in 632, but, although the region remained under Arab rule until the 11th century, Turkic rather than Arabic language and culture prevailed after the 9th century. The Mongols controlled Azerbaijan from 1236 to 1498, when the Azeris came under Persian rule. In the 18th century tsarist Russia gradually expanded into the Caucasus (▷ p. 127). Russia took N Azerbaijan in 1813, and Nakhichevan and the rest of the present state in 1828. However, the greater part of the land of the Azeris remained under Persian rule. During World War I, a nationalist Azeri movement became allied

with the Turks. After attempts to establish a federal Transcaucasian republic, an independent Azeri state was founded with Turkish assistance (1918), but was invaded by the Soviet RED ARMY in 1920. Azerbaijan was part of the Transcaucasian Soviet Republic from 1922 until 1936 when it became a separate Union Republic within the USSR. Independence was declared following the abortive coup in Moscow by Communist hardliners (September 1991; ▷ p. 225) and was internationally recognized when the USSR was dissolved (December 1991). Since 1990 Azeri and ARMENIAN irregular forces have been involved in a violent dispute concerning the status of NAGORNO KARABAKH.

Aztecs, a native people of Central America; ▷ pp. **71** and 116.

Baader-Meinhof Gang, a terrorist group also known as the Red Army Faction. Led by Ulrike Meinhof and Andreas Baader (both of whom committed suicide after their arrest in 1972), the group was responsible for many bomb outrages and assassinations in the late 1960s and early 1970s; ▷ p. 215.

Ba'athism, a pan-Arab movement, founded in April 1947, and dedicated to the unity and freedom of the Arab Nation. Ba'athist governments are currently in power in IRAQ and SYRIA; ▷ p. 211.

Babi Yar, the scene of a massacre of Jews in the Ukraine by the Nazis in 1941; ▷ p. 192 (box).

Babur (1483–1530), the first Mogul emperor of India (1526–30); ▷ pp. **62–3**.

Babylon, a city of ancient Mesopotamia to the S of modern Baghdad. It was the centre of two major Near Eastern empires (c. 1900–c. 1595 BC and c. 625–539 BC); ▷ pp. **20–1**, 23 and 26.

Bacon, Francis (1561–1626), English politician and philosopher; ▷ p. 133.

Bacon, Roger (c. 1214–92), English Franciscan monk and scientist; ▷ p. 132.

Bactria, a satrapy of the Persian Empire, now largely within N Afghanistan; ▷ p. 32 (map).

Baden, a former margraviate (1362), electorate (1803) and grand duchy (1803) in SW Germany. Baden became part of the German Empire in 1871. The monarchy was overthrown in 1918; ▷ p. 151 (map).

Baden-Powell, Robert Stephenson Smyth, 1st Baron (1857–1941), British soldier who defended Mafeking during the Second Boer War (▷ p. 163, box) and later organized the Boy Scout and Girl Guide movements.

Baghdad Pact, ▷ CENTO.

Bahamas, a group of islands off the coast of Florida and an independent state within the COMMONWEALTH. Columbus landed in the Bahamas when he reached the New World (1492; ▷ p. 109). In the 17th century, English colonists attempted to settle, but development was slow. After the American Revolution, an influx of Loyalists and their slaves established cotton plantations, but the abolition of SLAVERY (1834) ended this activity. Although the first representative assembly met in 1729, internal self-government was not achieved until 1964. Independence was granted in 1973.

Bahrain, an independent emirate in the Gulf. Bahrain – part of the Arab Islamic world since the 7th century – was Persian from 1602 until 1783, when rule by the Sunni al-Khalifa family began. In the 19th century, Bahrain signed a series of treaties under which it became a British protectorate. Bahrain was the first Gulf state to develop its petroleum industry (from 1932). Since independence in 1971, there has been tension between the SUNNI and SHIITE communities. Bahrain joined the coalition forces against Iraq after the invasion of Kuwait (1990–1; ▷ p. 213, box).

Bajezid I (1347–1403), Ottoman sultan (1389–1402).

He brought rival Turkish principalities in W Anatolia into the Ottoman Empire, blockaded Constantinople, and humiliated a crusading army at NICOPOLIS. Defeated and captured by TAMERLANE in 1402, he died in captivity; ⇨ p. 114.

Bakunin, Mikhail (1814–76), Russian anarchist and revolutionary. Hostile to MARX, he advocated the destruction of the centralized state and insurrection by workers and peasants to create a social order based on liberty and equality; ⇨ p. 180 (box).

Balaklava, battle of (25 October 1854), an inconclusive battle during the CRIMEAN WAR; ⇨ p. 155 (box).

Baldwin, Stanley, 1st Earl (1867–1947), British Conservative statesman, prime minister (1923–4, 1924–9, 1935–7). He replaced Bonar LAW as PM in 1923. His terms of office witnessed the General Strike (1926), the crisis over the abdication of EDWARD VIII (1936) and the deterioration of international relations with the rise of the Nazis. He was succeeded as PM by Neville CHAMBERLAIN.

Balfour, Arthur James, 1st Earl (1848–1930), British Conservative statesman, prime minister (1902–3). As foreign secretary (1916–17) under Lloyd George, he issued the BALFOUR DECLARATION (November 1917).

Balfour Declaration, a letter to the World ZIONIST Organization from the British foreign secretary, Arthur BALFOUR, in November 1917. It promised that Britain would 'view with favour' the creation of a Jewish 'homeland' in Palestine in the aftermath of World War I; ⇨ p. 211.

Balkans, a region of SE Europe now comprising ALBANIA, GREECE, BULGARIA, European Turkey, ROMANIA, SLOVENIA, CROATIA, BOSNIA-HERZEGOVINA and YUGOSLAVIA; ⇨ pp. 80, 114–15, 124, **154–5, 175** and **224** (box).

Balkan League, a league formed by several BALKAN states in 1912 to counter Turkish rule in the region; ⇨ p. 175.

Balkan Wars (1912–13), two wars fought between Serbia, Montenegro, Greece, Romania, Bulgaria and Turkey over the remaining Balkan territories of the Ottoman Empire; ⇨ pp. 155 and **175**.

Balliol, John (c. 1250–1313), king of Scotland (1292–6). He was awarded the throne of Scotland by EDWARD I in 1292. When he objected to the English king's high-handed actions, Edward invaded Scotland, and defeated and captured him. In Balliol's absence others, notably William WALLACE, took over the leadership of the Scottish War of Independence.

Ball, John (d. 1381), English priest and rebel. He attacked the wealth of the Church and nobility from the 1360s, resulting in his execution following the 1381 PEASANTS' REVOLT; ⇨ p. 93.

Baltic States, the republics of ESTONIA, LATVIA and LITHUANIA.

Banda, Hastings Kamuzu (c.1902–   ), prime minister of MALAWI (1963–6), president (1966–   ).

Bandaranaike, Solomon West Ridgeway Dias (1899–1959), Sri Lankan politician, prime minister (1956–9). He was succeeded on his death by his wife Sirimavo Bandaranaike (1916–   ), prime minister (1960–5 and 1970–7).

Bandung Conference (18–24 April 1955), the first international gathering of the newly decolonized Afro-Asian states, and the precursor of the NON-ALIGNED MOVEMENT.

Bangladesh, a republic in S Asia. A part of the Mogul Empire from the 16th century (⇨ p. 62), the area came under British rule within India after 1757. On partition in 1947, as the majority of its inhabitants were Muslim, the area became the E province of PAKISTAN (⇨ p. 201, box). Separated by 1600 km (1000 mi) from the Urdu-speaking,

politically dominant W province, East Pakistan saw itself as a victim of economic and ethnic injustice. Resentment led to civil war in 1971 when Indian aid to Bengali irregulars gave birth to an independent People's Republic of Bangladesh ('Free Bengal') under Sheik MUJIBUR RAHMAN. Mujib's assassination in 1975 led eventually to a takeover by General Zia-ur-Rahman, who amended the constitution to create an 'Islamic state'. Zia in turn was assassinated in 1981 and General Ershad took power in 1982. After Ershad was deposed (1990), a parliamentary system was reintroduced.

Bannockburn, battle of (24 June 1314), the defeat of the army of EDWARD II of England by a smaller Scottish army under ROBERT the Bruce.

Bantu, a group of Negroid peoples originating in W Africa; ⇨ p. 66.

Bantustans, an unofficial term used after 1948 for black territories in South Africa, reserved for Bantu-speaking Africans and given a measure of self-government under APARTHEID. Four Bantustans have been declared 'independent' – Transkei (1976) Bophuthatswana (1977), Venda (1979) and Ciskei (1981) – but none are recognized internationally; ⇨ p. 221.

Baptists, a Protestant sect taking its name from the practice of baptism by immersion of adult believers – a ritual established by the Anabaptists during the Reformation (⇨ p. 111, box). Baptist Churches developed within the English and American Puritan movements in the 17th century, and made great strides in the S states of America in the 18th century, where they retain their strongest influence; ⇨ p. 216.

Barbados, an island state in the Caribbean, and independent member of the COMMONWEALTH. Barbados was claimed and settled by the English in the 1620s. Black slaves were imported to work the sugar cane plantations (⇨ p. 128), which, in the 18th century, made the island one of the most profitable parts of the British Empire. SLAVERY was abolished in 1834, but economic and political power remained with a small white minority. Riots in 1937 led to reforms and also greatly increased black political consciousness. As a result, Barbadians became prominent in Caribbean politics. Barbados became independent in 1966.

barbarians, a name used by the Romans to describe the peoples outside their empire whose languages they considered uncivilized; ⇨ pp. 40–1 and **78–9**.

Barbarossa, Khayr ad-Din (c. 1483–1546), Turkish corsair. He drove the Spanish from Algiers in 1516, and became grand admiral of the Ottoman fleet in 1533; ⇨ p. 114.

Barbarossa, Operation, the name used by the German High Command for the German invasion of the Soviet Union in 1941; ⇨ p. 192.

Barons' Wars, the name given to two civil wars in England: **1.** the wars fought between King JOHN and his barons after the former had failed to honour the pledges given in MAGNA CARTA; **2.** the war between HENRY III and baronial opposition led by Simon de MONTFORT.

Basel, Council of (1431–49), a council of the Roman Catholic Church convened to discuss the HUSSITE heresy (⇨ p. 91).

Basil II (the Bulgar-Slayer; c. 958–1025), Byzantine emperor (976–1025). He added Bulgaria and parts of Georgia and Armenia to the Empire; ⇨ p. 81.

Basques, a people of the W Pyrenees living in SW France and N Spain. The Basques of Spain enjoyed virtual independence from the 9th to the 19th centuries, and their provinces have gained limited autonomy within the modern Spanish state; ⇨ pp. 79 and 215.

Bastille, a fortress in Paris, whose storming by the mob in 1789 marked the beginning of the French Revolution; ⇨ p. 144.

Basutoland, ⇨ LESOTHO.

Bavaria, a S German state with strong independent traditions, created an ELECTORATE in 1623 and a kingdom in 1805, a status which it retained within the GERMAN EMPIRE after 1871. Its capital, Munich, became a focus for radical right-wing politics after the suppression of a short-lived soviet republic in 1918; ⇨ pp. 125, 150, 153 and 186.

Bay of Pigs, an attempt by CIA-trained Cuban exiles to overthrow the Communist regime of Fidel CASTRO in CUBA in 1961; ⇨ p. 206.

Beaker cultures, prehistoric cultures named after a characteristic form of drinking vessel found in early Bronze Age burial sites in Central, W and S Europe.

Beaufort, the family name of descendants of John of GAUNT and Katherine Swynford. Several of them played a prominent role in 15th-century English politics. Margaret Beaufort (1443–1509) – who married Edmund TUDOR – was the mother of HENRY VII.

Bechuanaland, ⇨ BOTSWANA.

Becket, St Thomas (1118–70), archbishop of Canterbury (1161–70). He clashed with HENRY II of England over the rights of the English Church, and was murdered in Canterbury Cathedral. After his death he became the focus of one of the most popular saints' cults of the medieval period.

Bede (673–735), English monk and historian, based at Jarrow in NORTHUMBRIA. From 680 he devoted his life to writing the *Ecclesiastical History of the English Peoples* (finished 731); ⇨ p. 2.

Begin, Menachem (1913–92), Polish-born Israeli politician, leader of the right-wing Likud Party and prime minister of Israel (1977–83). He is best remembered for the Israeli–Egyptian peace accord he negotiated with Anwar el-SADAT at CAMP DAVID in 1978. The two men shared a Nobel Peace Prize; ⇨ p. 212.

Belarus, a republic of E Europe. The Belarussian Slavs arrived in the region between the 6th and 8th centuries AD. A number of small Belarussian states flourished after c. 700 but were soon conquered by KIEV RUS (⇨ p. 126). When the TARTARS overran Kiev Rus (1240), the Belarussian lands came under Lithuanian rule. After 1569, when Lithuania and Poland became one state, the area was dominated by a Polish Roman Catholic aristocracy. In 1648–54, the Orthodox Belarussians, who had been reduced to serfdom, rose in revolt against a resented Polish elite that controlled the land, administration and trade. The Belarussians came under Russian rule as a result of the three partitions of Poland (1772, 1793 and 1795; ⇨ p. 127). The region suffered some of the fiercest fighting between Russia and Germany during World War I. Following the Russian Revolutions (⇨ pp. 180–1), a Byelorussian Soviet Republic was proclaimed (1919). The republic was invaded by the Poles in the same year and divided between Poland and the Soviet Union in 1921. Byelorussia was devastated during World War II (⇨ p. 192). In 1945 the Belarussians were reunited in a single Soviet republic. A perceived lack of Soviet concern at the time of the accident at the CHERNOBYL nuclear power station (just over the Ukrainian border) strengthened a reawakening Belarussian national identity (1986). Contamination from Chernobyl affected about 20% of the republic, causing some areas to be sealed off, and necessitating the eventual resettlement of up to 2 000 000 people. Byelorussia declared independence following the abortive coup by Communist hardliners in Moscow (September 1991; ⇨ p. 225) and – as Belarus – received international recognition when the USSR was dissolved (December 1991).

Belgae, a people of NW Gaul, inhabiting the region between the Seine and the Rhine, including modern Belgium. They were conquered by Julius Caesar in

57 BC. SE England was also occupied by groups of Belgae, who migrated there around 100 BC.

Belgium, a country in NW Europe. In the early Middle Ages, the area was divided into counties and duchies subject to the Holy Roman Emperor (▷ p. 84). In the 12th–14th centuries, Bruges, Ghent and other Flemish textile centres were among the most prosperous cities in Europe (▷ p. 99). From 1384, most of modern Belgium was controlled by the rulers of BURGUNDY, whose territories were inherited by the Spanish HABSBURGS in 1504 (▷ p. 95). After the Protestant Dutch United Provinces rebelled and gained independence in the late 16th century, the Catholic south of the Low Countries ('Belgium') remained under Spanish rule (▷ p. 120). By the Treaty of UTRECHT (1713; ▷ p. 123), the Spanish Netherlands passed to AUSTRIA. In the confusion of the French Revolutionary Wars, the Belgians expelled the Austrians (1791), but Belgium was annexed by France in 1793 (▷ p. 146). After the Napoleonic Wars, which ended at WATERLOO in Belgium (▷ p. 147), the Low Countries were reunited as the Kingdom of the Netherlands (1815). In 1830 the Belgians rebelled against Dutch rule and proclaimed their independence (▷ p. 150). Belgian neutrality was recognized by the Congress of London (1831) and the crown was offered to Leopold of Saxe-Coburg Gotha, Queen Victoria's uncle. Belgium's neutrality was broken by the German invasion in 1914 (which led to Britain's declaration of war under the 1831 treaty; ▷ p. 176). The brave resistance of King Albert in 1914–18 earned international admiration; the capitulation of Leopold III when Belgium was again occupied by Germany (1940–5) was severely criticized. The Belgian Congo (Zaïre), acquired as a personal possession by LEOPOLD II (1879), was relinquished amidst scenes of chaos in 1960 (▷ p. 203, box). Belgium is now the main centre of administration of the EC and of NATO, but the country is troubled by the acute rivalry between its Flemish and French speakers and has gradually moved towards a federal system.

Belisarius (505–65), Byzantine general; ▷ p. 80.

Belize, a country of CENTRAL AMERICA. Mayan settlements flourished in Belize (▷ pp. 70–1) until 600 years before the arrival of the Spanish. Although Spain claimed the area, there were no Europeans living in Belize until English pirates and loggers settled in the 17th century. Black slaves were imported to cut timber. In 1862 the area formally became the colony of British Honduras. The colony gained independence as Belize – in 1981, but Guatemala continued to claim it as part of its territory until 1991.

Ben Bella, Ahmed (1916–   ), Algerian nationalist who led his country to independence after a bloody war against France (▷ 202, box). He was prime minister of Algeria (1962–5) and president (1963–5), but was overthrown and imprisoned (1965–79); ▷ p. *200*

Benedictine, a monastic order; ▷ p. 90.

Benedict of Nursia, St (c. 480–c. 550), Italian monk and founder of the Benedictine order; ▷ pp. **90** and **91** (box).

BENELUX, a customs union created by Belgium, the Netherlands and Luxembourg in 1948. All three states are now members of the EUROPEAN COMMUNITY.

Beneš, Eduard (1884-1948), Czechoslovak statesman, president (1935–8 and 1946–8). He worked with MASARYK for Czech independence during World War I. He succeeded Masaryk as president in 1935 but resigned over the partition of Czechoslovakia in the Munich agreement; ▷ pp. 188–9.

Bengal, NE region of the Indian subcontinent, now divided between BANGLADESH and INDIA. A productive lowland area with a distinctive regional culture, it was the first major part of India to be governed by the English EAST INDIA COMPANY; ▷ pp. 62, 63 and 201 (box).

Ben-Gurion, David (1886–1973), Russian-born Israeli politician, prime minister of Israel (1948–53 and 1955–63). A founder-member of the Workers of Zion Party (Mapai) in 1930, he led the struggle for Israeli independence against the British in the 1940s.

Benin, a country of W Africa. Benin was known as Dahomey until 1975. From the 17th to the 19th centuries the kingdom of Dahomey was one of the principal slave trading states of W Africa (▷ p. 67). In the 1890s, the region was conquered by the French. Political turmoil followed independence in 1960, and five army coups took place between 1963 and 1972 when the Marxist-Leninist government of Colonel Kérékou came to power. A multi-party system was restored in 1991.

Benin, kingdom of, a former W African kingdom, based on a city in the S of modern Nigeria. It was the major power among the YORUBA peoples in the 16th and 17th centuries; ▷ pp. 66 (map) and 67.

Bentham, Jeremy (1748–1832), British UTILITARIAN philosopher, economist, and legal theorist. His attempts to solve social problems on a scientific basis had a profound influence on political and social reform in Britain in the 19th century.

Berbers, an indigenous people of the N African hinterland who converted to Islam after the Arab Conquests of the 7th century AD. They were unusual in that they retained their own language, which was not superseded by Arabic; ▷ pp. 66, 79, 83 (box), ALMOHADS and ALMORAVIDS.

Berlin Airlift (1948–9), the supplying by aircraft of food and other necessities to the W sectors of Berlin by the US and British governments; ▷ p. 204.

Berlin, Congress of, a conference of European powers convened to deal with the Eastern Question, presided over by BISMARCK; ▷ pp. 155 and 175.

Berlin Wall, a former barrier between East and West Berlin, built by the German Democratic Republic in 1961; ▷ pp. **206** (box) and 224.

Bernard of Clairvaux, St (c. 1090–1153), French CISTERCIAN monk and abbot of Clairvaux. He turned the Cistercian order into a successful mass movement with about 500 houses by the time of his death (▷ pp. 90–1). He was also involved in the foundation of the Order of Templars (▷ p. 89, box), the Church's attack on Peter ABELARD, and the preaching of the Second Crusade (▷ p. 88).

Bessarabia, a region of E Europe, most of which forms the present-day republic of MOLDOVA; ▷ pp. 127 and 154.

Bevan, Aneurin (1897–1960), British LABOUR politician. As Minister of Health (1945–51) 'Nye' Bevan introduced the NATIONAL HEALTH SERVICE. During Labour's period in opposition in the 1950s he conducted a left-wing campaign against the leadership of Hugh GAITSKELL.

Beveridge, William Henry, 1st Baron, (1879–1963), British economist and civil servant. His report *Social Insurance and Allied Services* (1942) formed the basis of British WELFARE STATE legislation.

Bevin, Ernest (1881–1951), British trade union leader and Labour statesman. He created, and was general secretary of, the Transport and General Worker's Union (1921–1940). He served as Minister of Labour in Churchill's wartime cabinet (1940–5), and as ATTLEE'S foreign secretary (1945–51) was a staunch advocate of US involvement in Europe.

Bhutan, a kingdom in the Himalaya in S Asia. Tibetan influence over Bhutan from the 16th century was followed by Chinese overlordship (1720). Contact with British-dominated India (from 1774) led to border friction and partial annexation in 1865. In 1949 India returned this territory but assumed influence over Bhutan's external affairs. In 1907 the governor of Tongsa became the first king of Bhutan; ▷ p. 200 (map)

Bhutto, Zulfiqar Ali (1928–79), Pakistani politician. He came to prominence as a protégé of AYUB KHAN, but later formed his own Pakistan People's Party and led the movement for Ayub's overthrow. He went on to become prime minister after the secession of BANGLADESH in 1971. He was overthrown by the military in 1977 and later hanged (1979) in dubious circumstances. His daughter Benazir was prime minister of PAKISTAN (1988–90).

Biafra, a province of NIGERIA inhabited mainly by the Ibo people. It seceded as an independent republic in 1967, but was swallowed by government forces in 1970 after a bloody civil war.

Bihar, a region (now a state) of India that was a centre of Magdalha (▷ p. 58) and Mogul (▷ p. 62) power. Bihar came under British rule in the 18th century.

Biko, Steve (1947–77), the main leader of 'black consciousness' among students and young intelligentsia in South Africa in the 1960s and 70s. His murder by secret police shocked the world.

Bill of Rights (1689), an act passed by the English PARLIAMENT guaranteeing the rights of the individual subject – one of the most important instruments of British constitutional law. It incorporated by statute the Declaration of Rights, which stated the terms on which WILLIAM and Mary were to become joint sovereigns of England, Scotland and Ireland; ▷ p. 119.

Bill of Rights (1791), the first 10 amendments to the Constitution of the USA; ▷ p. 143 (box).

Bismarck, Otto von (1815–98), Prussian chancellor (1862–90), German chancellor (1871–90), known as the 'Iron Chancellor'. He united Germany under his Prussian master, WILHELM I, after skilfully exploiting pan-German feelings in a series of wars against Denmark, Austria and France. His successful foreign policy balanced the great powers and he acted as 'honest broker' in the 1878 Balkan Crisis. Stealing the political clothes of the SOCIAL DEMOCRATS, he created Europe's first social security system. He was dropped by WILHELM II in 1890; ▷ pp. **153** and 174.

Black and Tans, an armed auxiliary force sent to IRELAND by the British government (1920–1). Faced with guerrilla attacks by the IRISH REPUBLICAN ARMY, the Black and Tans reacted with great brutality. They were named after the distinctive colours of their uniforms.

Black Death, ▷ pp. 92–3.

Blackfoot Indians, a native North American people, living in the N of the Great Plains. Nomads dependent on the hunting of buffalo, their economy and society was transformed by the use of the horse in the 18th century; ▷ pp. 72 and 73.

Black Hole of Calcutta, a small dungeon in which the Nawab of Bengal incarcerated 146 British prisoners in 1756, most of whom suffocated. Inflated accounts of the incident ensured it a place in British imperial mythology.

Black Power, a movement of black people in the USA aiming to achieve economic, political, and social equality with whites. It stressed the need for a more militant approach to the campaign for CIVIL RIGHTS and for action by blacks alone; ▷ p. 216 (box).

Black Prince, ▷ EDWARD, THE BLACK PRINCE.

Black September, an ad hoc Palestinian terrorist group, recruited from al-FATAH and named after the events of September 1971, when Palestinian militants were forcibly ejected from Jordan. Black September's most notorious action was the assassination of 11 Israeli athletes at the Munich Olympics in 1972.

Blackshirt, the name applied to members of the Italian FASCIST Party before and during World War II; ➪ p. 186.

Blenheim, battle of, (13 August 1704), a military engagement in SW Germany during the WAR OF THE SPANISH SUCCESSION, in which Anglo-Austrian forces under the Duke of MARLBOROUGH and Prince EUGÈNE of Savoy defeated a Franco-Bavarian force marching on Vienna.

Bligh, William, ➪ BOUNTY MUTINY.

Blitz, the systematic night-time bombing of the UK by the German air force (1940–1); ➪ p. 190.

Blitzkrieg (German 'lightning war') a style of military attack used successfully by German generals in the early years of World War II; ➪ p. 190.

Bloody Assizes (1685), the trial and punishment of those who had taken part in MONMOUTH'S rebellion. Judge Jeffreys (1645–89), who presided over the trials, sentenced 300 to death, and 800 to be transported.

Bloody Sunday (22 January 1905), the occasion of a massacre by tsarist troops of peaceful demonstrators in St Petersburg; ➪ p. 180.

Blücher, Gebhart Leberecht von (1742–1819), Prussian field marshal, whose appearance on Napoleon's flank during the battle of WATERLOO was a major factor in the allied victory; ➪ p. 147.

Blum, Léon (1872–1950) French socialist statesman, prime minister (1936–7, 1938, 1946–7). He brought together the anti-Fascist coalition of left-wing parties that came to power in France in 1936; ➪ p. 187 (box).

Boeotia, an ancient region of central Greece, consisting of a number of city-states, of which Thebes was always the biggest and most powerful. The **Boeotian Confederacy** was at its most powerful between c. 378 and 338 BC, when it was defeated by Philip II of Macedon; ➪ p. 31.

Boers, ➪ AFRIKANERS.

Boer Wars, ➪ pp. 160, 162 and **163** (box).

Bohemia, a former kingdom in Central Europe. Settled by Slavs in the 9th century, it was ruled successively by the Premyslids (10th–14th centuries), the house of Luxemburg (1306–1437) – during which time the HUSSITE Reformation took hold – the Czech noble George of Podiebrady (1458–71), the Polish JAGELLION dynasty (1471–1526) and the HABSBURGS (1526–1918). The Bohemian Revolt (1618–21), which marked the opening phase of the Thirty Years War, was suppressed with Spanish help, and was followed by the establishment of greater Habsburg control. Since the breakup of AUSTRIA-HUNGARY after World War I, it has formed part of CZECHOSLOVAKIA; ➪ pp. 113 and 182 (map)

Bohemond of Tarando (c. 1056–1111), Italo-Norman leader of the First Crusade, who established himself as prince of ANTIOCH (1098); ➪ p. 88.

Bokassa, Jean Bédel (1921–), ruler of the Central African Republic (1965–79), president for life from 1972 and self-proclaimed 'emperor' from 1976. He was overthrown in 1979 and sentenced to forced labour for life for murder, cannibalism and embezzlement of public funds; ➪ p. 5 (box).

Boleyn, Anne (1507–36), the second wife of HENRY VIII, and the mother of ELIZABETH I. She was executed on a charge of adultery; ➪ p. 118.

Bolingbroke, Henry of, ➪ HENRY IV.

Bolívar, Simón (1783–1830), South American soldier and statesman who played a key role in the liberation of Venezuela, Colombia, Ecuador, Peru and Bolivia from Spanish rule in the early 19th century. The modern state of Bolivia (formerly Upper Peru) is named after him; ➪ pp. 148–9.

Bolivia, a republic of central S America. Until conquered by Spain in 1535 (➪ p. 116), Bolivia was part of the Inca Empire (➪ p. 71). As Upper Peru, Bolivia was ruled from Lima until 1776, when it became part of a viceroyalty of RIO DE LA PLATA. A revolt against Spanish rule (1809; ➪ p. 149) led to a power struggle between loyalists and nationalists, ending in independence in 1825. The remainder of the 19th century was characterized by political instability. In two devastating wars – the War of the PACIFIC (1879–83), alongside Peru against Chile, and the CHACO War (1932–5) against Paraguay – Bolivia sustained great human and territorial losses. After 1935, political instability continued with a succession of military and civilian governments. Since 1982, however, Bolivia has had democratically elected governments.

Bolshevik (Russian, 'member of the majority'), the faction of the SOCIAL DEMOCRATIC Party in Russia that pursued revolutionary tactics from 1903 under the leadership of Lenin. They changed their name to the Russian Communist Party in 1918; ➪ p. 181.

Bonaparte, ➪ NAPOLEON I.

Boniface VIII (1235–1303), pope (1294–1303). He was captured by PHILIP IV of France after challenging his right to tax the clergy; ➪ p. 90.

Borgia, Cesare (c. 1475–1507), Italian cardinal and politician. During the career of his father, Rodrigo Borgia, as Pope Alexander VI (1492–1503), he rapidly carved out a power base in the PAPAL STATES. Anti-Spanish propaganda, together with his immortalization by MACHIAVELLI as the model for *The Prince*, have made him a byword for cruelty and ruthlessness. His sister Lucrezia (1480–1519) was married four times, largely due to further family ambitions. Her first two marriages were annulled and her third husband was murdered; after her fourth marriage, to the Duke of Ferrara, she became a cultural patron.

Borneo, an island of the East Indies divided between INDONESIA, BRUNEI and the MALAYSIAN states of Sabah and Sarawak; ➪ p. 61 (map).

Bornu, ➪ KANEM-BORNU and p. 67.

Borobudur, a massive Buddhist temple in central Java, built c. 800 AD; ➪ p. 60.

Borodino, battle of (7 December 1812), an engagement fought W of Moscow between Russia and France. The Russians failed to prevent Napoleon's advance on Moscow, but remained strong enough to harass the French on their later retreat from Moscow; ➪ p. 147.

Borromeo, St Charles (1538–84), Italian Counter-Reformation churchman; ➪ p. 112.

Bosnia-Herzegovina, a republic of SE Europe. The SLAV ancestors of the Bosnians arrived in the region in the 7th century AD. From the middle of the 12th century Bosnia came under Hungarian rule. In the 13th century, the local representative of the Hungarian crown in Bosnia founded the autonomous Kotromanić dynasty. Kotromanić rulers conquered Hum (modern Herzegovina) and in the late 14th century established a powerful Bosnian kingdom. In the 1390s a disputed succession and Hungarian and (Turkish) Ottoman invasions led to the decline of Bosnia, which became a Turkish province in the 15th century (➪ pp. 114–15). Under Ottoman rule – during which many Bosnians became Muslims – the region entered a long period of economic stagnation. During the 19th century, several revolts against Turkish rule were put down with ferocity. A major revolt (1875–6) attracted international concern, but the great powers overrode Bosnia's PAN-SLAVIC aspirations at the Congress of BERLIN (1877–8; ➪ p. 155) and assigned an autonomous Bosnia-Herzegovina to Austro-Hungarian rule. In 1908 Austria formally annexed Bosnia to the HABSBURG Empire. In the Bosnian capital Sarajevo in 1914, Gavrilo Princip, a Bosnian student (ethnically a Serb), assassinated Archduke FRANZ FERDINAND, the heir to Habsburg Empire – an event that helped precipitate World War I (➪ p. 176). In 1918, Bosnia became part of the new Kingdom of Serbs, Croats and Slovenes, which was renamed YUGOSLAVIA in 1929. Following the German invasion (1941), Bosnia was included in the Axis-controlled puppet state of Croatia. In 1945, when Yugoslavia was reorganized by Marshal TITO on Soviet lines, Bosnia-Herzegovina became a republic within the Communist federation. After the secession of Slovenia and Croatia and the beginning of the Yugoslav civil war (1991), tension grew between Serbs and Croats in Bosnia. The Muslim Bosnians – the largest ethnic group – reasserted their separate identity. In 1992, a referendum – which was boycotted by the Serbs – gave a majority in favour of Bosnian independence. International recognition of Bosnia-Herzegovina was gained in April 1992, but the Yugoslav civil war spread to Bosnia when Serbs attempted to secure a broad swathe of the republic.

Boston Tea Party (1773), an incident in which a group of American radicals, 'The Sons of Liberty', threw a cargo of tea into Boston harbour; ➪ p. 142.

Bosworth Field, battle of (22 August 1485), the final battle of the Wars of the ROSES, in which RICHARD III was defeated by HENRY VII; ➪ p. 118.

Botany Bay, an inlet on the SE coast of AUSTRALIA, visited by Captain Cook in 1770. Australia's first penal colony was known as Botany Bay, but it was in fact established at Port Jackson, further up the coast of New South Wales; ➪ p. 129 (box).

Botha, Louis, (1862–1919), an AFRIKANER general in the Second Boer War (➪ p. 163, box) and first prime minister of the Union of South Africa (1910–19). He championed the reconciliation of Afrikaner land-owners with British gold-mining capitalists.

Botha, Pieter Willem (1916–), South African prime minister (1978–84), president (1984–9). He was a 'hawk' who used force at home and abroad but baulked at radical constitutional reform.

Botswana, a republic of southern Africa. British missionaries had been active since 1813 in the area, which became the British protectorate of Bechuanaland in 1885. Development was slow, and many Africans had to seek work in South Africa. Nationalism was late to develop, and independence – as Botswana – was granted without a struggle in 1966. Under the first president, Sir Seretse KHAMA, and his successor, Botswana has succeeded in remaining a democracy.

Boudicca ('Boadicea'), queen of the ICENI. After the death of her husband in AD 60 she was badly maltreated by the Romans, and organized a revolt. She and her followers destroyed London, St Albans and Colchester before suffering a crushing defeat somewhere in the Midlands.

Boumédienne, Houari (1927–78), Algerian politician. He overthrew BEN BELLA in 1965, becoming both prime minister and chairman of the revolutionary council until his death.

Bounty Mutiny (April 1789), a mutiny that occurred near Tonga aboard HMS *Bounty*, a British naval ship carrying breadfruit trees from Tahiti to the West Indies. Led by Fletcher Christian, the mutineers – resentful of Captain William Bligh's harsh discipline – cast Bligh and 18 others adrift without maps, but Bligh's navigational skill allowed them to reach Timor six weeks later. The mutineers settled on Pitcairn Island with a number of Tahitian men and women.

Bourguiba, Habib Ben Ali (1903–), Tunisian nationalist politician. After independence he became prime minister (1956) and president (1957). He was elected president for life in 1975, but was overthrown in 1987.

Boxer Rising (1900), a bloody anti-Western uprising in China, so called because its members belonged to a secret society called the Righteous Harmonious Fists; ⇨ pp. 57 and 162.

Boyacá, battle of (1819), the defeat of a Spanish force by Simón BOLÍVAR clinched Colombian independence; ⇨ p. 149.

boyars, the highest order of the Russian nobility in the Middle Ages, ranking immediately below the princes. Their rank and title was abolished by Peter the Great; ⇨ p. 126.

Boyne, battle of the, (1 July 1690), fought near Drogheda in Ireland between the Protestant forces of WILLIAM III of England, and Irish and French forces under the recently deposed JAMES II. William's victory – a major defeat for the STUART cause – ensured the triumph of the GLORIOUS REVOLUTION in England and of English Protestant rule in Ireland; ⇨ p. 119.

Brahe, Tycho (1546–1601), Danish astronomer; ⇨ p. 132.

Brandenburg, a former state in NE Germany. The margrave of Brandenburg became an Elector of the Holy Roman Empire in 1356. Under the HOHEN-ZOLLERNS it became the nucleus of the kingdom of PRUSSIA (1701); ⇨ pp. *85*, 113 (map) and 125.

Brandt Report, the report of the 'North–South Commission' on the state of the world economy, chaired by Willy BRANDT. It put forward a comprehensive plan for confronting the problems of Third World debt and slow development.

Brandt, Willy (Karl Ernst Herbert Frahm; 1913–), German statesman, SOCIAL DEMOCRAT chancellor of the Federal Republic of (West) Germany (1969–74). As a young man he fled Nazi Germany, taking refuge in Norway and assuming the name of Willy Brandt. As chancellor he adopted a policy of détente towards East Germany known as OST-POLITIK. He resigned in 1974 when one of his associates was unmasked as an East German spy. He later chaired an international commission on development issues whose findings were published in the BRANDT REPORT.

Brazil, a country of E South America. In 1500, Pedro CABRAL claimed Brazil for Portugal (⇨ p. 116). Sugar was introduced in 1532. The plantations were dependent upon slaves, at first using native Indians, but gradually replacing them with Africans. In the 17th and 18th centuries, expansion S and W in search of gold and diamonds brought the Portuguese into conflict with Spain over borders. (For details of Brazilian independence, the establishment of the Brazilian monarchy (1822) and of the republic (1889); ⇨ p. 149) The republic was initially stable, but social unrest mounted and, in 1930, Getúlio Vargas seized power. Vargas attempted to model Brazil on Mussolini's Italy, but was overthrown by the military in 1945. In 1950, Vargas was elected president again, but he committed suicide rather than face impeachment (1954). Short-lived civilian governments preceded a further period of military rule (1964–85), during which the economy expanded rapidly, but political and social rights were restricted. Brazil returned to civilian rule in 1985.

Brest-Litovsk, Treaty of (3 March 1918), an agreement between Soviet Russia, Germany and Austria-Hungary, ending Russian involvement in World War I. Russia, weakened by revolution, accepted harsh terms, including the loss of the Baltic provinces, Russian Poland and the Ukraine; ⇨ pp. 178 and 181.

Brétigny, Treaty of (1360), a treaty between England and France; ⇨ p. 94.

Bretton Woods Conference, a United Nations Conference, held in New Hampshire, USA, in July 1944. Representatives discussed the establishment of the INTERNATIONAL MONETARY FUND (IMF) and the International Bank for Reconstruction and Development (World Bank).

Brezhnev, Leonid Ilyich (1906–82). Soviet statesman, general secretary of the Communist Party (1964–82), president of the Soviet Union (1977–82); ⇨ pp. **198–9** and 225.

Brian Boru (?941–1014), king of Munster. He made himself high king of Ireland in the late 10th century. His death at the battle of Clontarf (1014), fighting a rebellion by Leinster and its Scandinavian allies, led to the collapse of Munster's overlordship of Ireland.

Briand, Aristide (1862–1932), French socialist politician, eleven times prime minister of France. A strong advocate of peace and international cooperation in the 1920s, he was an architect of the LOCARNO Treaty and the KELLOGG–BRIAND Pact.

Brigantes, ancient British people inhabiting the Pennine region of N England. They formed a Roman client state and remained nominally independent until AD 69, but were subsequently incorporated into the Roman province under Agricola.

Britain, battle of, an air battle fought between the Royal Air Force and the German air force over S England in summer 1940; ⇨ p. 190.

British Empire, a former empire comprising the United Kingdom and the overseas territories controlled by it. It reached its greatest extent in the late 19th and early 20th centuries, when it accounted for 25% of the world's population and area; ⇨ pp. 160, 161 (map), 162 and 202.

British Expeditionary Force (BEF), a force consisting of four infantry divisions and a cavalry brigade, sent to Belgium in 1914 to counter the German advance. It was virtually wiped out in the early battles of World War I.

British North America Act (1867), legislation passed by the British Parliament uniting the colonies of New Brunswick, Nova Scotia, Canada East (now Quebec) and Canada West (now Ontario) as the DOMINION of Canada.

British Raj, the administration and territories of British India during the period of direct rule by the crown (1858–1947) (⇨ pp. 160 and 201).

Bronze Age, ⇨ pp. 6, **12–13**, 14, 24–5, 44 and 71.

Brownshirt, a member of an early Nazi paramilitary organization, the Sturmabteilung (SA); ⇨ pp. 186–7.

Brunei, a sultanate in SE Asia. In the 16th century the sultans of Brunei ruled all of Borneo; by the 19th century they held a vastly reduced territory that had become a pirates' paradise. The British restored order and established a protectorate from 1888 to 1971. Oil was discovered in 1929. Independence was restored in 1984 under the absolute rule of Sultan Hassanal Bolkiah, allegedly the world's richest man.

Brüning, Heinrich (1885–1970), German chancellor (1930–2). He was forced to resign by HINDENBURG, paving the way for the Nazis; ⇨ p. 186.

Brutus, Marcus Junius (c. 85–42 BC), Roman aristocrat noted for personal integrity and staunch republicanism; ⇨ p. 37.

Buchanan, James (1791–1868), fifteenth president of the USA (1857–61). His term of office was dominated by the growing dispute over the slavery issue. His attempts at compromise between slave-holding and free states led to a split in the Democratic Party, whose Southern candidate lost the 1860 election to LINCOLN (⇨ p. 158).

Buddha ('the Enlightened One'), Prince Siddhartha Gautama (c. 563–c. 483 BC), Indian religious teacher and founder of Buddhism. Born into a Nepalese princely family, he renounced family, wealth and power before experiencing enlightenment at Bodh Gaya c. 528 BC. He spent the rest of his life preaching a message of release from human suffering through right thought and conduct. His religious teaching exerted a powerful influence on Indian society up to c. 500 AD and in that time spread throughout Central and E Asia; ⇨ pp. 58–61.

Bulganin, Nicolai Alexandrovich (1895–1975), Soviet politician. He became prime minister in 1955 after the resignation of Georgii Malenkov, sharing power with KHRUSHCHEV until his removal in 1958.

Bulgaria, a country of SE Europe. The First Bulgarian Empire (681–1018) grew to dominate the Balkans and, under Simeon I (893–927), threatened CONSTANTINOPLE, but was defeated in 1014 by the Byzantine Empire (⇨ p. 81). The Second Bulgarian Empire (1185–1393) succumbed gradually to the Ottoman advance (1362–1393; ⇨ p. 115). Five centuries of Turkish rule reduced Bulgarians to illiterate peasantry, but folk memories of past glories remained. Most Bulgarians remained Christian, and a 19th-century national revival sought to restore an independent Church as the first step towards the restoration of nationhood. Russian intervention produced both a Bulgarian Church (1870) and state (1878; ⇨ p. 155). The latter was an autonomous principality until 1908, and an independent kingdom until 1946. However, the boundaries, established at the Congress of BERLIN (1877–8; ⇨ p. 155), failed to satisfy the Bulgarians, who waged five wars to win the lands they had been promised in the earlier Treaty of SAN STEFANO (1877). Victorious in the first two wars (1885 and 1912), Bulgaria was on the losing side in the final Balkan War (1913; ⇨ p. 175) and in World Wars I and II (1915–18 and 1941–4), and forfeited territory. After the RED ARMY invaded (1944), a Communist regime, tied closely to the USSR, was established and the king was exiled (1946). Following popular demonstrations in 1989, the hardline leader Todor ZHIVKOV was replaced by reformers who renounced the leading role of the Communist Party. Free elections were held in 1990, when the Communists were obliged to enter a coalition, and in 1991, when the Socialists (former Communists) were defeated.

Bulge, battle of the, ⇨ ARDENNES OFFENSIVE.

Bunker Hill, battle of (17 June 1775), the first major engagement of the American War of Independence, fought on the heights commanding Boston harbour. Although the Americans were defeated by the British, their heroic defence and low casualties raised American morale; ⇨ p. 142.

Burgundy, a former duchy in E France; ⇨ p. 95 (box).

Burke, Edmund (1729–97), British WHIG politician and political theorist, born in Ireland. An advocate of gradual reform, he contributed greatly to the evolution of modern Conservative thought. He split with his associate Charles James FOX over the French Revolution; ⇨ p. 145.

Burkina Faso, a republic of the Sahel in W Africa. Mossi kingdoms dominated the area for centuries before French rule began in the 1890s. During the colonial era, the country acted as a labour reservoir for more developed colonies to the S. Since independence in 1960, the country – which kept its French name of Upper Volta until 1984 – has had a turbulent political history, with a succession of military coups.

Burma, ⇨ MYANMAR.

Burundi, a country of E central Africa. Burundi was a semi-feudal kingdom in which the minority Tutsi tribe dominated the Hutu majority. Colonized by Germany in 1890, it was taken over by Belgium after World War I under a LEAGUE OF NATIONS mandate (⇨ p. 202, map). Independence came in 1962, after much conflict throughout the country. Following a military coup in 1966, a republic was established. The killing of the deposed king in 1972 led to a massacre of the Hutu. There have since been further coups and ethnic unrest.

Bushmen, African racial group formerly inhabiting most of Africa S of the Equator. They were mainly confined to the less fertile lands of SW Africa by Bantu expansion in the 1st millennium AD; ⊳ pp. 13 and 66.

Bush, George (1924–), forty-first president of the USA (1989–). A World War II veteran and Texas oil magnate, Bush served as director of the CIA and as Ronald Reagan's vice-president before his election win in November 1988. The Allied victory in the Gulf War (⊳ p. 213) won him many plaudits, but he came under increasing criticism for paying insufficient attention to domestic issues; ⊳ p. 217.

Bute, John Stuart, 3rd Earl of (1713–92), British statesman, prime minister (1762–3).

Buthelezi, Mangosuthu Gatsha (1928–), prime minister of the 'non-independent' Zulu BANTUSTAN of Kwazulu in South Africa since 1972. He is also leader of the Inkatha cultural movement for Zulu revival, which became a political party in 1989.

Buyids, a Persian dynasty of N Iran that ruled in Iraq and W Persia (945–1055); ⊳ p. 83.

Byblos, an ancient trading city on the Lebanese coast; ⊳ pp. 22 and 23.

Byzantine Empire, ⊳ pp. 40, 78–9, **80–1**, 82, 87, 88, 97 (box) and 114.

Byzantium, ⊳ CONSTANTINOPLE.

Cabral, Pedro Alvares (1467–1520), Portuguese navigator. He made landfall on BRAZIL en route to India in April 1500, and claimed the territory for Portugal.

Caesar, Gaius Julius (c. 100 44 BC), Roman general and politician; ⊳ pp. **37** and 45.

Caetano, Marcello (1904–81), Portuguese prime minister (1968–74). SALAZAR'S chosen successor, he decided to maintain the dictatorship and fight to retain the Portuguese empire in Africa, but was overthrown by a left-wing military coup in April 1974.

Cairo Conference (November 1943), an ALLIED conference, codenamed Sextant, at which ROOSEVELT, CHURCHILL and JIANG JIE SHI discussed strategy against both Germany and Japan and decided on a postwar policy for the Far East.

Caledonia, an ancient name for that part of Scotland outside Roman control.

Caligula, Gaius (AD 12–41), Roman emperor (37–41) who succeeded his great-uncle TIBERIUS. After a brief honeymoon period his rule degenerated into outright despotism, and he was eventually murdered. Reports of his cruelty and megalomania, if true, suggest that he was a psychopath.

Caliphate, the governing institution of the Islamic community after the death of MUHAMMAD. 'Caliph' (Arabic, *khalifa*) means 'representative' or 'successor'. Theoretically elective, the caliphate was in practice hereditary. The caliph was both religious and secular head of Islam, but had no power to define Islamic doctrine. The main caliphal dynasties were the UMAYYADS and the ABBASIDS (who were SUNNIS) and the FATIMIDS (who were SHIITES). The caliphate was later claimed by the OTTOMAN sultans, but was abolished by Turkish President Kemal ATATÜRK in 1924; ⊳ pp. **82–3** and 114.

Callaghan, (Leonard) James (1912–), British Labour statesman. As prime minister (1976–9) he faced crises over inflation and British EC membership, and was forced to enter into a pact with the LIBERALS when the slim majority he inherited from Harold WILSON was whittled away. His government, weakened by strikes during the 'Winter of Discontent', was defeated by Margaret THATCHER in the 1979 election. He was succeeded as Labour leader by Michael Foot.

Calvin, John (1509–56), French theologian and leader of the Protestant Reformation in France and Switzerland; ⊳ pp. **110–11**, 113 and 120.

Cambodia, a country of SE Asia. In the early 9th century, the KHMER king Jayavarman II established the Angkorian dynasty, with a new state religion and a spectacular capital, Angkor (⊳ p. 60). By the 12th century, Cambodia dominated mainland SE Asia, but, by the 15th century, Thai and Vietnamese expansion had constricted Cambodia to the Phnom-Penh area. A French protectorate was established in 1863 and continued, apart from Japanese occupation during World War II, until independence in 1953. Throughout the colonial period, Cambodia's monarchy remained in nominal control. In 1955, King (now Prince) Norodom SIHANOUK abdicated to lead a broad coalition government, but he could not prevent Cambodia's involvement in the Vietnam War or allay US fears of his sympathies for the Communists (⊳ pp. 208–9). In 1970 he was overthrown in a pro-US military coup. The military regime was attacked by Communist KHMER ROUGE guerrillas, who sought to create a self-sufficient workers' utopia. The Khmer Rouge were finally victorious in 1975. Under POL POT, they forcibly evacuated the towns and massacred up to 2 000 000 of their compatriots. In 1978 Vietnam – Cambodia's traditional foe – invaded, overthrowing the Khmer Rouge. The hostility between the two countries had been sharpened by the Sino-Soviet split (⊳ p. 197) in which they took different sides. After Vietnamese troops withdrew in 1989, forces of the exiled government coalition invaded. In August 1991 the country's warring factions agreed a peace plan that included free elections and UN supervision and reduction of all Cambodian forces. A large UN peacekeeping force was deployed (1992) and UN participation in the administration of Cambodia was agreed.

Cambyses II, king of Persia (530–522 BC) and son of CYRUS II; ⊳ pp. 19 and 26.

Cameroon, a republic of W central Africa. The area fell victim to Portuguese slave traders in the late 15th century. Germany declared a protectorate over Kamerun in 1884 (⊳ p. 163, map). After World War I, Cameroon was divided between the UK and France. The French Cameroons became independent in 1960. Following a plebiscite (1961), the N of the British Cameroons merged with Nigeria; the S federated with the former French territory (⊳ p. 202, map). A single-party state was established in 1966 and a unitary system replaced the federation in 1972. Political pluralism returned in 1992, when multi-party elections were held.

Campaign for Nuclear Disarmament (CND), a British pressure group founded in 1958 to mobilize public opinion in favour of the unilateral abandonment of British nuclear weapons; ⊳ p. 227.

Campbell-Bannerman, Sir Henry (1836–1908), British Liberal politician, prime minister (1905–8). His premiership saw the granting of self-government to the BOER Republics, and the extension of the ENTENTE CORDIALE to include Russia (1907).

Camp David Accord, the 1978 peace agreement between Egypt and Israel; ⊳ p. 212.

Canaan, the ancient name for the region roughly corresponding to PALESTINE; ⊳ pp. 22 and 23.

Canada, a country of North America and an independent member of the COMMONWEALTH. The ancestors of the Indians came from Asia before 20 000 BC, while those of the Eskimos (INUIT) arrived in around the 6th millennium BC (⊳ p. 72). In the 9th century, Icelanders fished Canadian waters, and after about 1000 short-lived Norse settlements were established in Newfoundland. In 1497, Cabot (⊳ p. 109) explored the Atlantic coast for England, but Canada was claimed for France in 1534 by Cartier. In 1605, the first French colonists

settled on the E coast. French settlement increased after the Company of NEW FRANCE was established (1627) to develop Canada. France and England were, however, in competition in Canada. England claimed Newfoundland in 1583, and, in 1670, the HUDSON'S BAY Company was founded to assert English control of the vast area draining into Hudson's Bay. During European wars (1701–63), the French and English fought in Canada. France lost Acadia (1713) and – after WOLFE took QUEBEC in the battle of the Plains of Abraham (1759) – surrendered the rest of French Canada (1763; ⊳ p. 129). Britain granted toleration for the religion, institutions and language of the French Canadians. Many of the loyalists who left the infant United States (⊳ pp. 142–3) settled in Upper Canada (Ontario), which was separated from French-speaking Lower Canada (Quebec) in 1791. Severe economic problems, and a lack of political rights, led to PAPINEAU'S REBELLION in 1837. After the revolt, Ontario and Quebec were united and granted self-government. Settlement spread rapidly W, but there was no national authority to develop the area between Ontario and British Columbia. Britain, anxious to be rid of responsibility for Canada, encouraged confederation, and in 1867 Ontario, Quebec, New Brunswick and Nova Scotia formed the DOMINION of Canada. Other provinces joined (1870–1905), but Newfoundland did not become part of Canada until 1949. The late 19th century saw important mineral finds, such as the Klondike gold rush, and the W provinces developed rapidly. In World War I, Canadian forces distinguished themselves at VIMY RIDGE, and Canada won itself a place as a separate nation at the peace conferences after the war. The STATUTE OF WESTMINSTER (1931) recognized Canadian independence. The Depression of the 1930s (⊳ pp. 184–5) had a severe impact on Canada – Newfoundland, for example, went bankrupt. Canada played an important role in World War II and the Korean War, and was a founder member of NATO (⊳ p. 204). Throughout the 1970s and 1980s, there was friction over the use and status of the French language. Since 1990 separatist pressure has increased in Quebec, where a referendum on sovereignty is scheduled to be held.

Cannae, battle of, Rome's worst military defeat, on 2 August 216 BC, in Apulia (S Italy). HANNIBAL'S army surrounded and annihilated the Roman forces under the consuls Aemilius Paulus and Terentius Varro. Estimates of Roman losses range from c. 50 000 to over 70 000 men; ⊳ p. 37.

Canning, George (1770–1827), British TORY statesman, foreign secretary (1822–7), prime minister (1827). As leader of the progressive Tories he promoted liberal policies at home and abroad. He was PM for only a few months until his death.

Canossa, the castle in N Italy where Emperor HENRY IV did penance before Pope Gregory VII during the INVESTITURE CONTEST; ⊳ pp. 84–5 and 90.

Canute, ⊳ CNUT.

Capetian, the name of a French royal dynasty reigning from 987 to 1328. Until c. 1200 their authority was restricted to the area of the 'royal principality' around Paris; only from the reign of PHILIP II Augustus did they really dominate their kingdom; ⊳ p. 94.

Cape Province, a province on the S coast of the Republic of South Africa, formerly Cape Colony under British rule until 1910. Under its 'colourblind' franchise limited numbers of blacks (until 1936) and 'coloureds' (until 1955) had the vote; ⊳ p. 220.

capitalism, an economic system based on private ownership of the means of production, to which workers sell their wage-labour. Capitalism is usually seen as a product of a developing urban-industrial society. The word capitalism only began to appear in English from the early 19th century (and almost simultaneously in French and German), but the terms 'capital' and 'capitalist' were present much earlier, along with primitive kinds of capitalist production. However, capitalism as an economic system – MARX'S 'capitalist era' – dates only from the 16th century and did not reach the stage of 'industrial capitalism' until the late 18th and early 19th centuries; ⊳ pp. 4, 121, **130–1**, 140, 141, 150, 157, 164–7, 168, 174, 181, 221, and 222–3.

Capone, Alfonso (1899–1947), US gangster active in Chicago in the prohibition era; ⊳ p. 185 (box).

Caporetto, battle of (October 1917), a battle in which Austro-German forces overwhelmed the Italian army N of Trieste. The defeat effectively took Italy out of World War I; ⊳ p. 176.

Caratacus ('Caractacus') (d. AD 51), British chieftain who led a war of resistance against the Roman occupation in the West Country and Wales. After his defeat he took refuge among the BRIGANTES, but was betrayed and taken to Rome in triumph, where he died.

Carbonari (Italian, 'charcoal burners'), a revolutionary secret society active in France, Spain and Italy in the early 19th century; ⊳ pp. 150 and 152.

Carchemish, battle of (605 BC), a battle in which the Babylonians defeated the Egyptians and the remnants of the Assyrians; ⊳ p. 21.

Caribbean Community and Common Market (CARICOM), an organization of Caribbean states founded in 1973 with the aim of coordinating foreign policy and promoting cooperation in economic, cultural and technological matters.

Carlists, conservative and aristocratic supporters of the claim of Don Carlos (1788–1855) and his descendants to the throne of Spain. Defeated in the First Carlist War (1834–7) against Isabella II (reigned 1833–70), the Carlists persisted in their opposition until their defeat in a further period of unrest and civil war (1870–6).

Carlowitz, Treaty of (1699), a treaty between the Ottomans and HABSBURG Austria; ⊳ p. 124.

Carlyle, Thomas (1795–1881), British essayist and historian; ⊳ p. 5.

Carnegie, Andrew, ⊳ p. 157 (box).

Carolingian Empire, ⊳ pp. 79, **84** and 102.

Carson, Edward Henry, 1st Baron (1854–1935), Anglo-Irish lawyer and Conservative politician. A strong opponent of HOME RULE for Ireland, he raised the ULSTER VOLUNTEERS in 1914.

Carter, Jimmy (1924–), thirty-ninth president of the USA (1977–81). A southern Democrat and committed Baptist who cultivated an informal leadership style, he sought unsuccessfully to convince his compatriots that there were limits to American power and the American dream in the wake of the Vietnam debacle and the 1973 oil crisis. He was a moving spirit behind the CAMP DAVID accord; ⊳ p. 217.

Carthage, an ancient city on the coast of N Africa; ⊳ pp. **23** (box), 37 and 45.

Carthusians, a strict contemplative order, founded by St Bruno of Cologne in 1084 at Chartreuse in E central France.

Casablanca Conference (14–23 January 1943), an Anglo-US conference at which F.D. ROOSEVELT and CHURCHILL agreed that the ALLIED war aim was the 'unconditional surrender' of the AXIS powers.

Cassius (Gaius Cassius Longinus; d. 42 BC), one of the leaders of the conspiracy against Julius Caesar; ⊳ p. 37.

Castile, a kingdom that emerged in central Spain in the 11th century. It acquired the lion's share of the lands conquered from the Muslims in the 12th and 13th centuries, though not until after the marriage

of ISABELLA of Castile to FERDINAND II of ARAGON had effectively created a single Spanish monarchy, did the conquest of Granada (1492) complete the Reconquista; ⊳ pp. 83 (box), and 116.

Castlereagh, Robert Stewart, Viscount (1769–1822), British statesman. His duel with CANNING was a contributory factor in the demise of PORTLAND'S premiership. As foreign secretary (1812–22) he sought lasting peace in Europe through the post-Napoleonic 'Congress system' of diplomacy.

Castro, Fidel (1927–), Cuban revolutionary, president of CUBA (1959–). An opponent of the repressive rule of Fulgencio Batista, Castro was imprisoned in 1953. Released and exiled in 1955, he raised a guerrilla force and, in 1956, landed secretly in the SE of Cuba. By January 1959 Batista had fled, and Castro declared the Cuban revolution. Opposed by the USA, Castro increasingly established diplomatic, economic and military links with the USSR. His defeat of the abortive BAY OF PIGS invasion (1961), and survival of the Cuban Missile Crisis (1962), increased his popularity. The collapse of the Soviet Union in the early 1990s left Castro isolated as a hardline Marxist; ⊳ pp. 206–7.

Catalaunian Fields, battle of the (451), the defeat of Attila by Romans and VISIGOTHS; ⊳ p. 79.

Catalonia, that part of Spain inhabited by Catalan speakers. The area was the county of Barcelona from the 8th century until 1137 when it became part of the kingdom of ARAGON. Catalonia is now an 'autonomous community' of Spain.

Cathars, a heretical medieval sect, also known as Albigensians; ⊳ pp. 89 and **91**.

Catherine II (the Great; 1729–96), empress of Russia (1762–96). She extended Russia's frontiers at the expense of Turkey and Poland, and made important administrative and other changes. She corresponded with Voltaire and other French Enlightenment thinkers; ⊳ pp. 125 (box), 127, *134*, 135 and 154.

Catherine of Aragon (1485–1536), first wife of HENRY VIII and mother of MARY I. Her marriage to Henry was annulled in 1533, against the authority of the Pope; ⊳ p. 118.

Catholic emancipation, full civil and political rights for British and Irish Roman Catholics, including the right to sit in the British Parliament, conceded in 1829 by the Duke of WELLINGTON'S cabinet and GEORGE IV.

Cato the Elder (Marcus Porcius Cato; 234–149 BC), Roman politician who became an outspoken champion of traditional and conservative values. At the end of his life he urged the Romans to destroy Carthage. His great-grandson of the same name, **Cato the Younger** (95–46 BC), tried to follow his political and moral example. A leading opponent of Julius Caesar, he committed suicide after the Republican defeat at Thapsus.

Caucasians (or Caucasoids), the light-skinned racial group of humankind, occupying Europe, Africa N of the Sahara, the Middle East and the Indian subcontinent. They are named after the Caucasus Mountains, and have spread all over the world in the last 500 years.

caudillo, a political-military leader in Spanish America during and after the struggle for independence from Spain, usually possessing a personal and regional ascendancy.

Cavaliers (from the French *chevalier* 'horseman'), the name adopted in the ENGLISH CIVIL WAR by supporters of CHARLES I (who contemptuously applied the term ROUNDHEADS to their Parliamentary opponents).

Cavour, Camillo Benso, Count (1810–61), prime minister of Sardinia-PIEDMONT (1852–9 and 1860–1), and leader of the movement for the unification of Italy; ⊳ p. 152.

Caxton, William (c. 1422–91), English printer, who

set up the first printing-press in England (1476); ⊳ p. 101.

Ceaucescu, Nicolae (1918–1989), Romanian politician, general secretary of the Romanian Communist Party (1969–89), president (1974–89); ⊳ p. 224 (box).

Cecil, William, 1st Baron Burghley (1520–98), English lawyer and statesman, chief adviser to ELIZABETH I. As secretary of state (1558–72) and Lord High Treasurer (1572–98), he dominated English political life for most of her reign.

Celtic Church, a Christian Church that existed in Britain from the Roman period. With the Saxon invasions of the 5th century it was driven out of England to Celtic areas such as Ireland. Members of the Celtic Church were influential in conversion of NORTHUMBRIA. Some practices of the Celtic Church remained at odds with those of the Roman Church until the late 7th century, when they were resolved at the Synod of WHITBY.

Celts, ⊳ pp. 15, **34–5**, 36, 45 and 47.

CENTO, ⊳ CENTRAL TREATY ORGANIZATION.

Central African Federation, (1953–63), a federation joining Southern Rhodesia, Northern Rhodesia and Nyasaland in uneasy 'multi-racial' partnership. It was dissolved when Britain agreed to separate independence for MALAWI (Nyasaland) and ZAMBIA (Northern Rhodesia); ⊳ p. 221 (box).

Central African Republic, a country in central Africa. French influence began in 1889, and the region became the French colony of Oubangi-Chari in 1903. It suffered greatly from the activities of companies that were granted exclusive rights to large areas of the colony. Independence – as the Central African Republic – was gained in 1960. Jean-Bédel BOKASSA took power in a coup in 1965. Revolts by students and schoolchildren helped to end his murderous regime in 1979. Agreement to hold multi-party elections was reached in 1991.

Central America, the isthmus linking North and South America, extending from Mexico's S border to the NW border of Colombia. Under Spanish colonial rule, much of the area belonged to the Captaincy-General of Guatemala. After independence (1821), no region managed to dominate the isthmus and the five provinces emerged as GUATEMALA, EL SALVADOR, HONDURAS, NICARAGUA and COSTA RICA. (PANAMA remained part of COLOMBIA until 1903.) The 19th century saw frequent conflicts between the states and mutual interference in their domestic affairs. US interest in the region increased after the SPANISH–AMERICAN WAR of 1898 and the independence of Panama, with the USA constructing and controlling the PANAMA CANAL. With the exception of Costa Rica, Central America has been long dominated by dictatorships. These have begun to disappear since the 1970s.

Central Intelligence Agency (CIA), the principal intelligence and counterintelligence agency of the USA, established in 1947. A spearhead of America's Cold War effort, the CIA launched covert operations against a wide range of left-wing governments; ⊳ p. 207 (box).

Central Powers, Germany, Austria-Hungary and their allies Turkey and Bulgaria during World War I; ⊳ pp. 176–9, and ALLIED POWERS.

Central Treaty Organization (CENTO), a mutual security organization formed by Britain, Iran, Turkey and Pakistan in 1959. CENTO was based on the Baghdad Pact (formed in 1955 to counter Soviet influence in the Middle East), which was renamed when Iraq withdrew in 1959. The organization became inoperative with the withdrawal of Iran, Turkey and Pakistan in 1979; ⊳ p. 205.

centurion, the principal type of field officer in the Roman army. Each legion had 60 centurions, graded in order of seniority.

Chaco War (1932–5), a conflict fought between

PARAGUAY and BOLIVIA over disputed territory in the Chaco desert. Both sides suffered heavy casualties, especially Bolivia, whose defeat contributed to the radical revolution of 1952.

Chad, a republic in the Sahel of W Africa. Part of the medieval African empire of Kanem-Bornu (▷ p. 67), the area around Lake Chad became French in the late 19th century. The French conquest of the N was not completed until 1916. Since independence in 1960, Chad has been torn apart by a bitter civil war between the Muslim Arab N and the Christian and animist Black African S. Libya and France intervened forcefully on several occasions, but neither was able to achieve its aims. In 1987, an uneasy ceasefire was declared, but, following another civil war, military regimes took power in 1990 and 1991 and unrest continues.

Chaeronea, a city in central Greece, where in 338 BC Philip II of Macedon defeated the Greek allies, resulting in Macedonian domination of Greece; ▷ pp. **31,** 32, 44.

Chalcis, the largest city-state on the island of Euboea in central Greece. During the 'dark ages' (1100–700 BC) Chalcis, with the other chief Euboean city Eretria, was the most prosperous and developed of Greek cities; a war between Chalcis and Eretria c. 730 led to the destruction of the latter; ▷ pp. 29 (box) and 31 (map).

Chalcolithic, a transitional period of prehistory before the Bronze Age, when simple copper objects were used; ▷ p. 15.

Chaldea, a region of S Babylonia inhabited by wealthy tribes of Chaldeans; the original homeland of a line of Babylonian kings of the 8th century BC. The Neo-Babylonian, Chaldean dynasty (625–539 BC), also had its origins there; ▷ p. 21.

Chamberlain, Arthur Neville (1869–1940), British Conservative statesman. He succeeded BALDWIN as prime minister (1937), pursued a policy of AP-PEASEMENT towards Hitler, and negotiated the MUNICH AGREEMENT (1938) which led to the dismemberment of Czechoslovakia. In its aftermath, he recognized the need for war preparation. He resigned in favour of CHURCHILL in 1940; ▷ pp. 5 and **188–9.**

Champa, a former kingdom of Cambodia and central Vietnam; ▷ p. 60.

Champlain, Samuel de (1567–1635), French explorer who founded the colony of Québec (1608) and later played a key administrative role in consolidating his country's North American empire.

Champollion, Jean-François (1790–1832), French scholar who deciphered the Egyptian hieroglyphic inscription on the Rosetta Stone; ▷ p. 17.

Chandragupta, ruler of N India (c. 321–c. 297 BC) and founder of the Mauryan dynasty; ▷ p. 58.

chariot, a two-wheeled horsedrawn vehicle. Before the establishment of cavalry, chariots were used extensively in warfare, for example in Egypt, Assyria and Mycenae, as well as among the Celts; ▷ p. 44.

Charlemagne (c. 742–814), king of the Franks (768–814) and emperor of the West (800–14); ▷ pp. 79, **84,** 85 and 102.

Charles I (1600–49), king of Great Britain and Ireland (1625–49), the son of JAMES I. The 11 years (1629–40) during which he ruled without Parliament, relying on advisors such as Thomas Strafford, created widespread antagonism. His conflict with the LONG PARLIAMENT led to the ENGLISH CIVIL WAR. After his trial and execution in 1649, the COMMONWEALTH was established; ▷ p. 119.

Charles I of Anjou (1226–85), king of Sicily (1266–85); ▷ p. 96.

Charles II (1630–85), king of Great Britain and Ireland (1660–85) following the RESTORATION. The son of CHARLES I, his amorous adventures have

perhaps obscured his achievements in promoting science, commerce and the English navy. His Catholic sympathies – he was secretly converted to Catholicism, married a Catholic and resisted attempts to exclude his Catholic brother James from the succession – provoked widespread distrust; ▷ pp. 119 and 133.

Charles II (the Bald; 823–77), king of the West Franks (843–77), emperor (875–77). The son of LOUIS the Pious, he gained the kingdom of the West Franks by the Treaty of VERDUN; ▷ p. 86.

Charles IV (1316–78), king of Bohemia (1346–78), Holy Roman Emperor (1347–78); ▷ p. 85.

Charles V (the Wise; 1337–80), king of France (1364–80). He put down the JACQUERIE, and regained much of the territory held by the English; ▷ p. 95.

Charles V (1500–1558), HABSBURG king of Spain (1516–56), Holy Roman Emperor (1519–56), by far the most powerful ruler of his day. In America his dominions were extended by the brutal conquests of CORTEZ and PIZARRO. In Europe he organized Christendom against the Turks and successfully defended Spanish and imperial rights in Italy against French aggression. His troops captured FRANCIS I in 1525, sacked Rome in 1527 and Tunis in 1530. But after confronting LUTHER at the Diet of WORMS (1521), he was unable to prevent the spread of Protestantism in Germany and the Netherlands. Worn down by the extent of his responsibilities, he retired to a monastery in 1556; ▷ pp. 85, 97, 110, 114, 117, 120 and 130.

Charles VI (the Mad; 1368–1422), king of France (1380–1422). His mental illness left France without government for long periods and his reign witnessed defeat at Agincourt and English occupation N of the Loire. He married his daughter to HENRY V, declaring the English king to be his heir; ▷ p. 95.

Charles VII (1403–61), king of France (1422–61). During his reign, with the aid of Joan of Arc, the Hundred Years War was brought to a successful conclusion for the French; ▷ p. 95.

Charles X (1757–1836), king of France (1824–30). Brother of LOUIS XVI, he fled to Scotland in 1789, returning to France in 1814 as leader of the ultra-royalists. Reactionary and pro-clerical, his repressive reign provoked the Revolution of 1830; ▷ p. 150.

Charles XII (1682–1718), king of Sweden (1697–1718); ▷ p. 127 (box).

Charles XIV (Jean-Baptiste Jules Bernadotte; 1763–1844), king of SWEDEN and NORWAY (1818–44). A veteran of Napoleon's Italian campaign, and marshal of France (1804), he was elected crown prince of Sweden (1810), in which capacity he allied his adopted country with Britain and Prussia and fought against Napoleon at the battle of LEIPZIG (1813). He succeeded the childless Charles XIII in 1818.

Charles Edward Stuart, ▷ PRETENDER.

Charles Martel (c. 688–741) Frankish leader who stopped the Muslim advance near Poitiers in 732; ▷ pp. 79 and 83 (box).

Charles the Bold (1433–77), duke of Burgundy (1467–77). He failed in his efforts to make Burgundy a kingdom independent of France. When he left no son to succeed him, his territories passed to France and the HABSBURG emperor MAXIMILIAN I; ▷ p. 95 (box) and 120.

Charter 77, a petition signed by a group of Czech dissidents in 1977, outlining their criticisms of the Communist regime of Gustav Husak. Many of the group, including future President Vaclav HAVEL, were persecuted as a result.

Chartism, a British working-class mass movement for political reform, taking its name from the People's Charter (1838). The Charter's six demands

were for annual parliaments, universal male suffrage, equal electoral districts, an end to property qualifications for MPs, voting by ballot, and payment of MPs; ▷ p. 164.

Chattanooga Campaign (1863), a series of operations in the American Civil War. Consisting principally of the battles of Chickamauga and Chattanooga (the latter won by Northern forces under Ulysses S. GRANT), the campaign secured Tennessee for the Union and paved the way for SHERMAN'S decisive thrust towards Atlanta; ▷ p. 159.

Cheka, Soviet secret police agency established by the Bolsheviks (1917–22); ▷ p. 181, NKVD, OGPU and KGB.

chemical warfare, the use of toxic or asphyxiating agents in war; ▷ pp. 177 and **227.**

Chenla, a former KHMER state; ▷ p. 60.

Chernenko, Konstantin (1911–85), Soviet politician, general secretary of the Communist Party and president of the Soviet Union (1984–5); ▷ p. 199.

Chernobyl, the site of a Soviet nuclear power station in the UKRAINE. Its explosion in 1986 caused widespread radioactive pollution; ▷ p. 224.

Cherokee, a native North American people, maize farmers living in a region covering the W Carolinas, Georgia and E Tennessee. One of the 'Five Civilized Indian Nations', they adapted to colonial culture but were forced out of their lands in the 1830s and re-established in Oklahoma; ▷ p. 73.

Cheyenne, a native North American people, living in the central Great Plains. They abandoned settled village life in the 18th century and became nomads dependent on hunting buffalo from horseback; ▷ p. 73.

Chiang Kai-shek, ▷ JIANG JIE SHI.

Chickasaw, a native North American people, maize farmers living in the region of modern Alabama and N Mississippi. One of the 'Five Civilized Indian Nations', they were removed to Oklahoma in the 1830s; ▷ p. 73.

child labour, the employment of children in demanding factory conditions. Children worked long hours and for low wages long before industrialization, but with the Industrial Revolution their cheap and plentiful labour became both more systematic and more prevalent; ▷ pp. 141, 164 and 165.

Chile, a republic on the Pacific coast of S America. During the 15th century the Inca (▷ p. 71) moved into Chile, but were halted by the fierce Araucanian Indians. The Spanish approached Chile from Peru in 1537, and Pedro de Valdivia founded Santiago in 1541. Continuing S, Valdivia was killed by the Araucanians (1554), who were not finally defeated until the late 19th century. In 1810, a revolt – led by Bernardo O'HIGGINS – broke out against Spain. In 1817, troops led by José de SAN MARTÍN crossed from Argentina to aid O'Higgins (▷ p. 149). Chile was liberated in 1818, but O'Higgins offended the powerful landowners and was exiled in 1823. For the next century – during which Chile gained territory in two wars against Peru and Bolivia – conservative landowners held power. Between the late 1920s and the 1940s, Chile was governed by liberal and radical regimes, but social and economic change was slow. The election of the Christian Democrats (1964) brought some reforms, but not until Salvador ALLENDE's Marxist government was elected in 1970 were major changes – including land reform – realized. Chile was polarized between right and left, and political chaos resulted in a US-backed military coup led by General Augusto PINOCHET in 1973. Tens of thousands of leftists were killed, imprisoned or exiled by the junta. Pinochet reversed Allende's reforms, restructuring the economy in favour of landowners and exporters. Pressure on the dictatorship from within Chile and abroad brought the return of democratic rule in 1990.

Chimu, a powerful state centred on the N coast of Peru during the 14th and 15th centuries. It was conquered by the Incas in 1476; ➪ p. 71.

China, a country of E Asia, one of the world's oldest civilizations and home to about one fifth of humanity. China was ruled by imperial dynasties (➪ pp. 52–7) until 1911 when a republic was established. In the 20th century China was wracked by civil war and Japanese invasion until the Communists took power in 1949 (➪ pp. 196–7).

China, Republic of (Taiwan), an island republic off the coast of mainland China. Taiwan was originally inhabited by Malays and Polynesians. The first settlers from China came in the 7th century. Named Formosa ('beautiful') by the Portuguese in 1590, the island was the object of Spanish-Portuguese rivalry and then briefly (1662–83) independent under the Chinese general Koxinga. A period of Chinese rule and renewed migration lasted until a Japanese takeover (1895) began the modernization of agriculture, transport and education. In 1949, the Nationalist forces of JIANG JIE SHI (Chiang Kai-shek) were driven onto Taiwan by the Communist victory on the mainland (➪ pp. 196–7). Under US protection, the resulting authoritarian regime on Taiwan declared itself the Republic of China, and claimed to be the legitimate government of all China. America's rapprochement with the mainland People's Republic of China (➪ p. 197) lost Taiwan its UN seat in 1971 and US recognition in 1978 (➪ p. 229). By the late 1980s Taiwan was moving cautiously towards democracy, and in 1988 a native Taiwanese was elected President. In 1991 Taiwan effectively recognized Communist China, but the island's international status remains problematic (➪ p. 223).

Chindits, Allied forces fighting behind Japanese lines in Burma in World War II. The Chindits were led by Orde Wingate, an exponent of GUERRILLA warfare; ➪ p. 195.

Chinese Civil War (1927–37 and 1946–9), conflicts between Nationalist and Communist forces in China; ➪ p. 196.

Chinese Communist Party (CCP), a Chinese political party, the ruling party in China since the defeat of JIANG JIE SHI'S Nationalists in 1949; ➪ p. 196.

Ch'ing dynasty, ➪ QING.

Chinook, a native North American people, hunters and traders living on the NW coast of modern Oregon and Washington; ➪ pp. 72 and 73.

Chin dynasty, ➪ JIN.

Ch'in dynasty, ➪ QIN.

Chipewyan, a native North American people, living as nomadic caribou hunters SW of Hudson Bay; ➪ pp. 72 and 73.

Choctaw, a native North American people, maize-farmers inhabiting modern SE Mississippi. One of the 'Five Civilized Indian Nations', they were removed to Oklahoma in the 1830s; ➪ p. 73.

Chou dynasty, ➪ ZHOU.

Chou En-lai, ➪ ZHOU ENLAI.

Christian Democrats, the term used to describe a number of conservative European political parties, especially the Christian Democratic Parties of Germany and Italy. Christian Democracy – emphasizing Christian values, a community ethic and social reform – developed after 1945 and remains one of main political forces in Western Europe; ➪ p. 215.

Christianity, ➪ pp 3, 39 (box), **40,** 41, 46, 78–9, 81, 83 (box), 88–9, 90–1, 110–13, JESUS CHRIST, ORTHODOX CHURCH, ROMAN CATHOLIC CHURCH and PROTESTANTISM.

Churchill, Sir Winston Leonard Spencer (1874–1965), British conservative politician, prime minister (1940–5 and 1951–5). Elected to Parliament in 1900 as a Unionist, he switched to the Liberals in 1904 and served in ASQUITH'S and LLOYD GEORGE'S governments. A Conservative again from 1925, he supported rearmament against Nazi Germany during the 1930s and later served in CHAMBERLAIN'S wartime government. He became PM of the wartime coalition in 1940, his morale-boosting oratory making him an immensely popular wartime leader. He lost office to Labour in the 1945 general election, but returned in 1951; ➪ p. 190

Church of England, ➪ ANGLICAN CHURCH.

Cicero, Marcus Tullius (106–43 BC), Roman statesman and orator. He joined Pompey's side in the Civil War (➪ p. 37), but was pardoned by Caesar. He was eventually murdered by Antony and Octavian in 43 BC.

Cid, El, the name given to Rodrigo Díaz de Vivar (c. 1043–99), whose role in fighting the Moors made him a Spanish national hero. In fact, he was also involved in fighting rival Spanish Christians and at one point was in the service of the Muslim ruler of Saragossa.

Cimon (d. 499 BC), Athenian commander; ➪ p. 29.

Circus Maximus, the major racetrack in Rome; ➪ p. 41 (box).

Cistercians, a monastic order; ➪ pp. 90–1.

city-state, the typical unit of political and social organization in ancient Greece, and also in medieval and Renaissance Italy; ➪ pp. **28–31,** 96–7 and 99.

Civil Rights Acts, US legislation extending the civil rights of American blacks. Although the first Civil Rights Act of 1866, later reinforced by the FOURTEENTH AMENDMENT to the Constitution, gave citizenship to all people born in the USA, Southern blacks remained persecuted second-class citizens until the mid-20th century. The Civil Rights Acts of 1957 and 1964 and the Voting Rights Act of 1965 outlawed racial discrimination in all important areas of life; ➪ pp. 159, 216 (box) and DESEGREGATION.

Civil Rights Movement, a US protest movement to end racial segregation and inequality in the Southern states of the USA. Its campaign culminated in the passing by Congress of the 1964 CIVIL RIGHTS ACT and the 1965 Voting Act; ➪ p. 216 (box).

Cixi (or Tz'u-hsi; 1862–1908), Empress Dowager and effective ruler of China (1862–1908); ➪ p. 57.

Classical period, in ancient Greece, the period c. 500–338 BC; ➪ pp. **29–31.**

Claudius (10 BC–AD 54), Roman emperor (41–54), nephew of TIBERIUS and uncle of CALIGULA. Claudius was unexpectedly made emperor by the PRAETORIANS after the murder of Caligula. A conscientious administrator, Claudius was unpopular with the Senate. In AD 43 he organized the conquest of Britain.

Clausewitz, Karl von (1780–1831), Prussian general and philosopher of war. In his most famous work, *On War* (1831), he declared that war was a rational instrument of policy and that – in contrast with 18th-century military strategy – it must be conducted ruthlessly to ensure swift victory. His theories presaged the modern concept of total war (➪ p. 191).

Clay, Henry (1777–1852), US politician, secretary of state under John Quincy ADAMS (1825–9), and later a founder of the WHIG party. He is known as 'The Great Compromiser' because of his efforts at compromise to keep the Union intact on the slavery question.

Cleisthenes (6th century BC), Athenian statesman; ➪ p. 29.

Clemenceau, Georges Benjamin (1849–1929), prime minister of France (1906–9; 1917–20). He was a strong supporter of DREYFUS (1897), and turned back a tide of French defeatism during the later years of World War I. As President of the Paris Peace Conference (1919), he imposed harsh terms on the defeated CENTRAL POWERS; ➪ p. 182.

Clement V (1264–1314), pope (1305–14); ➪ p. 90.

Cleopatra VII (69–30 BC), queen of Egypt. Cleopatra became queen in 51 BC, but was ousted by her co-ruler, Ptolemy XIII, in 48. She was restored in 47 by Caesar, who became her lover and (she claimed) father of her son Ptolemy Caesar. Her affair with Mark Antony began in 41 and continued until their suicides after Actium; ➪ pp. 19 (box), 33 and 37.

Cleveland, (Stephen) Grover (1837–1908), US Democratic politician, twenty-second (1885–9) and twenty-fourth (1893–7) president of the USA. He was an economic conservative and advocate of free trade.

Clive of Plassey, Robert, Baron (1725–74), British general and first governor of Bengal (1757–60 and 1765–7). His defeat of the Indian forces at Plassey (1757) and conquest and administration of Bengal laid the foundations of British rule in India; ➪ pp. *63* and 128.

Clovis I (c. 466–511), king of the FRANKS (482–511) and founder of the Frankish kingdom. He conquered all of N Gaul by 494, but on his death his kingdom was divided between his four sons; ➪ pp. 78–9.

Clovis culture, the earliest clearly defined prehistoric culture of America (c.10 000–8000 BC), characterized by the distinctively shaped points of the stone weapons used in big-game hunting.

Cluny, Abbey of, the mother house of a reformed Benedictine order; ➪ p. 90.

Cnut (Canute; c. 994–1035), king of England (1016–35). He completed his father SWEYN Forkbeard's conquest of England (1016), acquired Denmark (1019), and briefly held Norway (➪ OLAF II). His 'North Sea empire' collapsed on his death; ➪ p. 86.

Cochin China, a former name for the S of VIETNAM. It formed a separate French colony from 1867 to 1949.

Cochrane, Thomas, 10th Earl of Dundonald (1775–1860), British admiral and adventurer, one of the most successful of the British and Irish mercenaries who fought in the wars for South American Independence; ➪ p. 149.

Coercive Acts, repressive legislation passed by the British Parliament against the American colony of MASSACHUSETTS in the wake of the Boston Tea Party. They became known as the 'Intolerable Acts' and led to the CONTINENTAL CONGRESS; ➪ p. 142.

Colbert, Jean Baptiste (1619–83), French statesman. He passed from the service of Cardinal MAZARIN into that of Louis XIV, becoming his chief financial minister (1661). He sought to promote French arts, trade and industry, and to develop a French navy; ➪ p. 122.

Cold War, ➪ pp. 198, **204–7,** 216, 219 and 224.

collectivization, the creation of collective farms imposed in the USSR by Stalin (1929–33). A similar policy pursued by Mao Zedong in Communist China (1953) did not subordinate agriculture to industry as in the USSR, but instead favoured the establishment of peasant communes; ➪ p. 198.

Collins, Michael (1890–1922), Irish nationalist, a leader of SINN FEIN and first commander of the IRISH REPUBLICAN ARMY. He helped to negotiate the Treaty with Britain that established the Irish Free State (1921). He commanded the Free State forces in the Irish Civil War but was assassinated by republican enemies in 1922.

Colombia, a republic of NE South America. The Spanish reached Colombia's N coast in 1500, and founded their first settlement in 1525. Meeting little resistance from the Indians, the conquistadores advanced inland reaching Bogotá in 1538. In 1718 the viceroyalty of NEW GRANADA was established at Bogotá. The struggle for independence from Spain (1809–1819) was fierce and bloody (⇨ pp. 148–9). Almost from Colombia's inception, the centralizing pro-clerical Conservatives and the federalizing anti-clerical Liberals have struggled for control, leading to civil wars (1899–1902 and 1948–1957) in which 400 000 people died. From 1957 until the 1990s there were agreements between the Liberals and Conservatives to protect a fragile democracy threatened by left-wing guerrillas and right-wing death squads. In the early 1990s, a combination of security measures and amnesties has curbed the activities of the powerful drug-trafficking cartels, which had destabilized the country.

Colosseum, the huge stone arena in Rome, inaugurated in AD 80; ⇨ p. 41 (box).

Columba, St (St Columcille; c. 521–97), Irish monk and missionary. Iona, the monastery he founded off the W coast of Scotland, became an important centre of the CELTIC CHURCH, and from there the PICTS were converted to Christianity.

Comanche, a native North American people, nomads dependent after c. 1700 on hunting buffalo from horseback in the Great Plains. They had previously lived in the Great Basin as hunter-gatherers.

Combination Acts, legislation passed by the British Parliament (1799–1800) outlawing the 'combining' of two or more craftsmen for the purpose of bargaining for better wages and working conditions; ⇨ p. 166.

COMECON (Council for Mutual Economic Assistance), an economic organization of the former Soviet bloc, founded in 1948 by Bulgaria, Czechoslovakia, Hungary, Poland, Romania and the USSR. They were later joined by Albania (which left the organization in 1961), East Germany, Mongolia, Cuba and Vietnam. The upheavals of 1989–90 (⇨ pp. 224–5) undermined the principles on which COMECON had been created, and with the establishment of free-market economies in East European countries it was disbanded in March 1991.

Comintern (Communist INTERNATIONAL), international Communist organization formed by Lenin (1919) with the aim of spreading Communist doctrine. Largely a tool for Soviet control over Communist parties in other countries, the Comintern was dissolved by Stalin in order to reassure his non-Communist allies.

Commodus (AD 161–193), Roman emperor (180–192); ⇨ p. 38.

Common Agricultural Policy (CAP), the most important single common policy of the EUROPEAN COMMUNITY, absorbing about a third of the EC's budget. It supports agricultural prices and protects some products with tariffs. Although CAP has increased productivity, guaranteed supplies and stabilized markets, it remains controversial and a cause of disagreement between the EC and other industrial states.

Commons, House of, the lower chamber of the English PARLIAMENT. Representatives of the shires and towns were summoned from the 13th century onwards (and elected on a very narrow franchise before the electoral reforms of the 19th and 20th centuries) to give the consent to national taxation that the nobles alone could not grant. This 'power of the purse', enshrined in the Parliament Act (1911) ensured the gradual eclipse of the House of LORDS by the Commons (who only began to meet separately in the 16th century).

Commonwealth, 1. the English republic established after the execution of CHARLES I and abolition of the monarchy (1649), which lasted until the RESTORATION (1660). Executive power lay with a Council of State and – from 1653 – with the Lord Protector, Oliver CROMWELL (⇨ p. 119), while legislative power was vested in the RUMP Parliament (until 1653), and thereafter in a number of shortlived Parliaments. **2.** an informal grouping of the UK and the majority of its former dependencies. Its roots lie in the 1926 Imperial Conference, which defined the DOMINIONS of the British Empire as 'freely associated . . . members of the British Commonwealth of Nations'. From being a club of Western states, it has been transformed by an influx of newly independent former British colonies in Africa, Asia and the Caribbean into a predominantly Third World association. Its member-states, while independent in every respect, recognize the British sovereign as head of the Commonwealth (⇨ p. 203).

commune, a town in medieval W Europe with a large degree of autonomy, especially one of the city-states of N Italy; ⇨ p. 99.

Commune of Paris, ⇨ p. **153** (box).

Communism, a political ideology – perhaps the most influential of the 20th century – aiming at the overthrow of CAPITALISM, the ownership by the community of the means of production and subsistence, and the creation of a classless society. The primary source of the social and economic doctrine of communism is the COMMUNIST MANIFESTO (1848) written by MARX and ENGELS. Marx's theories, adapted by LENIN as MARXISM-LENINISM, were the guiding force behind the Russian Revolutions of 1917, and the basis of the political system in the Soviet Union from 1917 to 1985. The ideas of Marx and Lenin were adapted to Chinese conditions by Mao Zedong; ⇨ pp. **169**, 178, **180–1**, 185, 186, 189, 191, 192, **196–9**, 200, 201, 204–7, 208–9, 215, 216, 217, 221, 223, 224–5, and 233.

Communist Manifesto, a key document of modern SOCIALISM and COMMUNISM, written by MARX and ENGELS and published in 1848; ⇨ p. 168.

Commynes, Philippe de (c. 1447–1511), French historian whose *Memoires* focus mainly on the reigns of Louis IX and Charles VIII; ⇨ p. 95 (box).

Comnena, Anna (1083–1153), the daughter of the Byzantine emperor ALEXIUS I Comnenus, whose adulatory history of her father's life, the *Alexiad*, is a valuable source for the period.

Comoros, a republic comprising an archipelago between Africa and Madagascar. The four Comoran islands became a French colony in 1912. In a referendum in 1974, three islands voted to become independent, which they declared themselves without French agreement. The fourth island, Mayotte, voted against independence, and remains under French rule. From 1978 to 1990, when free elections were held, the republic was an Islamic single-party state.

Compromise of 1850, a compromise between the Northern and Southern states of the USA on the slavery issue. Promoted by Henry CLAY, it provided for California's admission to the Union as a free state and for a referendum on the slavery question in New Mexico and Utah (⇨ p. 158).

concentration camp, a guarded prison camp for non-military prisoners; ⇨ pp. 163, **192** and 198 (box).

Condé, a French princely family, the junior branch of the house of BOURBON. The name originated with Louis I of Bourbon (1530–69), a Huguenot leader in the FRENCH WARS OF RELIGION. His great-grandson, Louis II of Bourbon (1621–86), known as the 'Great Condé', won notable victories at Rocroi and Lens in the Thirty Years War, and fought first for Louis XIV, then against him, in the FRONDE. A royalist 'army of émigrés', commanded (1796–9) by Louis Antoine Henri de Bourbon-Condé, duc d'Enghien (1772–1804), fought against French Revolutionary forces in Europe from 1793 to 1801.

condottiere, the name given to leaders of bands of mercenaries in the medieval period. Italian city-states were particularly reliant on hired troops to fight their wars. By the 15th century several *condottiere* had ambitions of their own and some became rulers of small territories in central Italy. Francesco SFORZA, for instance, became duke of MILAN.

Confederacy, the 11 Southern states of the USA (Alabama, Arkansas, Florida, Georgia, Louisiana, Mississippi, North Carolina, South Carolina, Tennessee, Texas and Virginia) that seceded from the Union (1860–1). They were reincorporated into the USA after their defeat by the Union in the American Civil War; ⇨ pp. **158–9**.

Confederate States of America, ⇨ CONFEDERACY.

Confederation of the Rhine, an association of German states with a French constitution and Napoleonic legal system established in W Germany by Napoleon in 1806 as a pro-French buffer state. The Confederation failed to survive the withdrawal of the French after Napoleon's defeat at LEIPZIG in 1813; ⇨ pp. 146 and 147.

Conference on Security and Cooperation in Europe (CSCE), an international conference established in 1975 under the Final Act of a security conference held in Helsinki, Finland in 1975. In the Charter of Paris, which officially ended the Cold War (November 1990), the 34 member-states affirmed 'a commitment to settle disputes by peaceful means' and 'a common adherence to democratic values and to human rights and fundamental freedoms'; ⇨ p. 207.

Confucius, ⇨ KONGFUZI.

Congo, a republic of W central Africa. Portuguese slave traders were active in the region from the 15th century. In the 1880s, the explorer Brazza placed the kingdom of the Teke people under French protection, and in 1905 the region became the colony of Middle Congo. Independence was gained in 1960. A Marxist-Leninist state was established in 1963, but a multi-party system was restored in 1991.

Congo Crisis, ⇨ p. **203** (box).

Congress, Indian National, the main political party in INDIA, formed in 1885; ⇨ p. 201.

Congress of the USA, the supreme legislative assembly of the USA. Originating as a unicameral body during the American War of Independence, the Congress became a two-chamber legislature after the ratification of the US Constitution (1788) – the SENATE (or upper house) comprising two delegates from each state, the HOUSE OF REPRESENTATIVES (or lower chamber) made up of Congressmen elected on the basis of a state's population strength; ⇨ pp. 142–3.

Connaught (Connacht), a former kingdom of W Ireland whose rulers were kings of Ireland in the 12th century. Connaught's independence was extinguished from the 13th century.

Connecticut, one of the 13 original states of the USA. English settlers founded colonies in the area in the 1630s. These settlements were united as Connecticut in 1665; ⇨ pp. 156 (map) and 159 (map).

Connolly, James (1868–1916), Irish Marxist trade unionist who was, with Joseph Plunkett, the principal architect of the EASTER RISING (1916). He was captured and shot by the British.

conquistadores (from the Spanish *conquistar,* 'conquer'), the Spanish adventurers (notably Hérnan CORTEZ and Francisco PIZARRO) who conquered the indigenous empires of Central and South America in the early 16th century, and laid the foundations of Spanish power there; ⇨ pp. 71 and **116**.

Conservative Party, a right-wing political party in Britain, descended from the TORY Party. Sir Robert PEEL'S Tamworth Manifesto of 1834 is considered to mark the beginning of the move from old-style

Toryism to moderate reforming Conservatism, though the name Conservative was not formally adopted until later. The split over the repeal of the CORN LAWS kept the Conservatives out of power for much of the period 1846–73, but under DISRAELI they developed into a successful mass party, claiming to represent the 'national tradition'. After 1945 the party tended towards pragmatism in its policies, accepting essentially socialist concepts such as the WELFARE STATE and a measure of state intervention in the economy, but with the accession to the leadership of Margaret THATCHER (1975–90) it embraced a philosophy of economic liberalism and the free market. Electorally it has been the most successful British political party of the 20th century; ⊳ pp. 214 and 215.

Constance, Council of (1414–17), a council of the Christian Church convened to address the problem of heresy and the Great Schism; ⊳ pp. 90 and 91.

Constantine (AD ?285–337), Roman emperor in the West (312–324), and sole emperor (324–337); ⊳ pp. 40 and 80.

Constantinople, a city in Turkey, standing on the BOSPHORUS between the Black Sea and the Mediterranean, and now known as Istanbul. It began life as the Greek city of Byzantium (⊳ p. 31, map). It took its new name from the emperor Constantine in 330, who designed the city as a new Rome and capital of the Eastern Roman Empire (⊳ p. 40). Massive walls defied sieges for centuries until the city fell briefly to the Franks (1204–61), and permanently to the Ottoman Turks (1453); ⊳ pp. 40, 80–1, 89, 90, 97 (box), 114, 131 (box) and 155.

constitutional monarchy, a monarchy in which the power of the sovereign is restrained by institutional checks (for example by a written constitution), in contrast with ABSOLUTE monarchy in which royal authority is theoretically unlimited. The UK, Sweden and the Netherlands are present-day examples of constitutional monarchies.

Constitution of the USA, the written statement of the laws and principles by which the USA is governed; ⊳ p. 143 (box).

Consul, one of two annually elected officials who held the highest authority in the Roman Republic. Under the emperors their power became nominal; ⊳ pp. 36, 38 and 45.

Consulate (1799–1804), the regime, under the first consul Napoleon Bonaparte, that ruled France from the dissolution of the DIRECTORY to Napoleon's coronation as emperor in 1804; ⊳ p. 145.

Continental Congress (1774–89), the assembly composed of representatives of the American colonies that first met in response to the COERCIVE ACTS in 1774. The second Continental Congress (1775–6) proclaimed the Declaration of Independence and declared itself the provisional government of the USA; ⊳ pp. 142–3 and CONGRESS.

Continental System, ⊳ pp. 146 and 149.

Cook, Captain James (1729–79), British naval commander; ⊳ p. 129 (box).

Coolidge, Calvin (1872–1933), US Republican politician, thirtieth president of the USA (1923–9). A vice-presidential nominee, he succeeded to the presidency on the death of HARDING.

Cooperative Movement, trading and social organizations, established from the early 19th century, distributing profits to their membership. Influenced in Britain by Robert OWEN, and in France by Fourier, cooperatives in Europe have generally supported SOCIALIST parties.

Coptic Church, the Egyptian Church, which survived in Upper Egypt after the Arab conquests and persists to this day, with a liturgy and numerous patristic writings in the ancient Coptic language.

Coral Sea, battle of the (7/8 May 1942), a naval battle fought between Australian, US and Japanese forces in World War II; ⊳ p. 194.

Corinth, an important ancient Greek city-state on the isthmus joining the Peloponnese to the mainland. Initially ruled by 'tyrants' and then as a moderate oligarchy, it was a powerful and prosperous state, usually allied to Sparta. Its union with Argos in the 390s was shortlived. In 338 it was defeated, along with its allies Athens and Thebes, by Philip II of Macedon, who based at Corinth his organization for the domination of Greece (the 'League of Corinth'); ⊳ pp. 30 and 31.

Cornwallis, Charles (1738–1805), British soldier and politician best known for his leadership of British forces during the American War of Independence; ⊳ p. 143.

Corn Laws, legislation passed in 1815 which aimed at protecting British agriculture by banning import of foreign grain until the home price had reached 80 shillings a quarter. The effects of the IRISH FAMINE and the influence of the middle-class Anti-Corn Law League led to their repeal by PEEL'S government in 1846; ⊳ p. 151.

Cortez, Hernán (1485–1547), Spanish CONQUISTADOR and conqueror of Mexico. In 1519 he led a private expedition to Mexico, accompanied by 600 volunteers, and marched on the AZTEC capital of TENOCHTITLÁN. They were reluctantly received by the Aztec ruler MONTEZUMA, but the Aztecs revolted, forcing the Spaniards to retreat. Cortez returned and laid siege to Tenochtitlán the following year. On 21 August 1521 the Aztecs, already weakened by smallpox brought by the Spanish from Cuba, surrendered; ⊳ pp. 71 and 116.

Cossacks, peasant-soldiers living chiefly in the Ukraine, originally renegade TARTARS employed by the Grand Dukes of Muscovy to guard their frontiers against the Crimean Tartars from the 15th century. By 1600 the term was also applied to Slavs who fled serfdom in Muscovy, Poland and Lithuania and settled in the Ukraine. Although used as troops by the tsars, they remained independent and troublesome until subjected to Russian rule by Peter I and Catherine II; ⊳ pp. 126–7.

Costa Rica, a republic of CENTRAL AMERICA. Columbus reached Costa Rica during his final voyage in 1502. The area was under Spanish rule – as part of the captaincy-general of Guatemala – until 1821. Although it was part of the Central American Federation (1823–38), Costa Rica developed largely in isolation from its neighbours. Dominated by small farms, Costa Rica prospered, attracted European immigrants and developed a stable democracy. Following a brief civil war in 1948, the army was disbanded. Costa Rica has since adopted the role of peacemaker in Central America.

Côte d'Ivoire, a republic of W Africa, more usually known in the English-speaking world as the Ivory Coast. In the 16th century, Europeans established posts in the area for trading in ivory and slaves. Colonized by France in the 19th century, the Ivory Coast became a relatively prosperous part of French West Africa. Independence was achieved in 1960 under the presidency of Félix Houphouët-Boigny, who has kept close links with France in return for aid and military assistance, and is Africa's longest serving president. After over a decade of single-party rule, multi-party elections were held in 1990.

Council of Europe, an association of mainly West European states. Created in May 1949, it aims to foster greater unity between member-states, and to safeguard their common heritage. It established the European Convention for the Protection of Human Rights in 1950. With 25 member-states it is the largest organization of the European democracies.

Council of Five Hundred, a representative body in ancient Athens; ⊳ pp. 29 and 30.

Counter-Reformation, ⊳ pp. 5, 112–13, 124 and 133.

Courtrai, battle of (11 July 1302), the defeat of the French by Flemish rebels; ⊳ p. 93.

Cranmer, Thomas (1489–1555), English cleric and founding father of the ANGLICAN Church. As archbishop of Canterbury (1533–55), he helped mould the liturgy of the new Anglican Church, revising the *Book of Common Prayer* in 1552. He was tried for treason and burnt as a heretic following the accession of the Catholic MARY I.

Crassus, Marcus (112–53 BC), Roman politician. In 60 BC he formed the First TRIUMVIRATE with Caesar and Pompey, but his attempt to match their military achievements by a war against Parthia ended in disaster at Carrhae in 53 BC; ⊳ p. 37.

Crazy Horse (1849–1877), chief of the Oglala SIOUX Indians who tried to prevent white settlement of Sioux territory. He led Plains Indian forces in their successful assault on CUSTER'S troops at the battle of LITTLE BIG HORN (1876).

Crécy, battle of (26 August 1346), a decisive English victory in the Hundred Years War, fought in N France; ⊳ p. 94.

Cree, a native North American people, living as nomadic hunters S of Hudson Bay; ⊳ p. 73.

Creek (Muskogi), a native N American people, maize farmers living in the Alabama and Georgia flatlands. One of the 'Five Civilized Indian Nations', they were removed to Oklahoma in the 1830s; ⊳ p. 73 (map).

Creole, a native-born descendant of Spanish or other European settlers in the West Indies or Latin America; ⊳ p. 148.

Crimean War, ⊳ p. 155 (box).

Critias (c. 460–403 BC), leader of the 'Thirty Tyrants' in Athens; ⊳ p. 31.

Croatia, a country of S Central Europe. The Croats migrated from UKRAINE in the 6th century and established a kingdom, which, by the 10th century, had occupied most of modern Croatia. In 1102 Croatia passed to the Hungarian crown. After Slavonia (E Croatia) was conquered by the Ottoman Turks (1526), the rump of Croatia came under the rule of the (Austrian) HABSBURGS, who established a Serb military frontier zone (Krajina) against further Ottoman expansion (⊳ p. 115). Dalmatia – the southern coastal region of Croatia – came under Venetian rule in the 15th century (⊳ p. 97, box), was annexed by Napoleon I in 1808 (⊳ p. 147, map), and was ceded to Austria in 1815. Ragusa (Dubrovnik) was an independent city-state from the 9th century to 1808 (⊳ p. 123, map). The Croats strove to preserve their identity within Habsburg Hungary and attempted secession during the 1848–9 Hungarian revolt. By the start of the 20th century a Croat national revival looked increasingly to independent SERBIA to create a South ('Yugo') Slav state. After World War I when the Habsburg Empire was dissolved (1918), the Croats joined the Serbs, Slovenes and Montenegrins in the state that was to become Yugoslavia in 1929 (⊳ p. 182, map). However, the Croats soon resented the highly centralized Serb-dominated kingdom. Following the German invasion (1941), the occupying Axis powers set up an 'independent' Croat puppet state that adopted anti-Serb policies. In 1945 Croatia was reintegrated into a federal Communist Yugoslav state by Marshal TITO, but after Tito's death (1980), the Yugoslav experiment faltered in economic and nationalist crises. Separatists came to power in Croatia in free elections (1990) and declared independence (June 1991). Serb insurgents, backed by the Yugoslav federal army, occupied one third of Croatia including those areas with an ethnic Serb majority – Krajina and parts of Slavonia. The fierce Serbo-Croat war came to an uneasy halt in 1992 after Croatian independence had gained widespread international recognition and a UN peacekeeping force was agreed, but the Yugoslav civil war spread to BOSNIA.

Croesus, king of LYDIA (c. 560–546 BC); ▷ pp. 26, 43 and 47 (box).

Cro-Magnons, ▷ HOMO SAPIENS SAPIENS.

Cromwell, Oliver (1599–1658), English general and statesman, Lord Protector of England (1653–8). A PURITAN country gentleman and opposition member of the LONG PARLIAMENT, he came to prominence as a military leader on the Parliamentary side in the ENGLISH CIVIL WAR, and signed CHARLES I's death warrant. He managed the commanders of the NEW MODEL ARMY, crushed the LEVELLERS, and extended the authority of the COMMONWEALTH to Scotland and Ireland. In 1653 he expelled the RUMP Parliament and, as Lord PROTECTOR, effectively became a dictator. He refused Parliament's offer of the Crown in 1657. He was succeeded as Lord Protector (1658–9) by his son Richard (1626–1712); ▷ pp. *118* and 119.

Cromwell, Thomas, Earl of Essex (1485–1540), English statesman. He became HENRY VIII's chief adviser after WOLSEY's downfall. A Protestant sympathizer, he played a leading part in Henry's breach with Rome and the Dissolution of the MONASTERIES, and also reformed the central administration. He was executed after losing favour; ▷ p. 118.

Crow, a native North American people, living in the central Great Plains. They abandoned settled village life in the 18th century and became nomads dependent on hunting buffalo from horseback; ▷ p. 73 (map).

Crusader states, short-lived Christian kingdoms established in the Levant in the late 11th century; ▷ p. 88.

Crusades, ▷ pp. **88–9.**

CSCE, ▷ CONFERENCE ON SECURITY AND COOPERATION IN EUROPE.

Ctesiphon (modern Baghdad), the capital of the Sassanian Persians; ▷ p. 27 (box).

Cuba, an island-republic in the Caribbean. Indian tribes inhabited Cuba when Columbus claimed the island for Spain (1492). Development was slow until the 18th century, when black slaves were imported to work the sugar plantations. The first war for independence (1868–78) was unsuccessful. The USA intervened in a second uprising (1895–98), forcing Spain to relinquish the island, but independence was not confirmed until after two periods of American administration (1899–1901 and 1906–9). Under a succession of corrupt governments, the majority of Cubans suffered abject poverty. In 1959, the dictatorship of Fulgencio Batista was overthrown by the guerrilla leader Fidel CASTRO, whose revolutionary movement merged with the Communist Party to remodel Cuba on Soviet lines. In 1961, US-backed Cuban exiles attempted to invade at the BAY OF PIGS, and relations with America deteriorated further in 1962 when the installation of Soviet missiles on Cuba almost led to world war (▷ p. 206). Castro encouraged revolutionary movements throughout Latin America, and his troops bolstered Marxist governments in Africa. The upheavals in the USSR and Eastern Europe (1989–91) left Cuba increasingly isolated as a hardline Marxist state.

Cuban Missile Crisis (1962), an international crisis involving the USA and the USSR; ▷ p. 206.

Cuéllar Pérez de, Javier (1920–), Peruvian diplomat, Secretary-General of the United Nations (1982–91); ▷ p. 229.

Culloden, battle of (16 April 1746), the last pitched battle on British soil, fought E of Inverness, Scotland, in which the JACOBITE forces of CHARLES EDWARD STUART were defeated by an English army under the Duke of Cumberland; ▷ p. 119.

Cultural Revolution, ▷ p. 197.

Curzon, George, Nathaniel, 1st Marquis Curzon

of Kedleston (1859–1925), British Conservative statesman, viceroy of India (1899–1905). He later served as foreign secretary under LLOYD GEORGE and BONAR LAW.

Cush, ▷ NUBIA.

Custer, George Armstrong (1839–76), US soldier who served with Union forces during the American Civil War and subsequently commanded troops on the western frontier. Flamboyant and arrogant, he led his men to disaster against the SIOUX Indians at the battle of the LITTLE BIG HORN in 1876.

Cuzco, the capital of the Inca empire; ▷ p. 71.

Cyprus, an island-republic in the E Mediterranean. Greek settlements were established on Cyprus in the middle of the 2nd millennium BC. The island was ruled by the Egyptians (from 323 BC) and was part of the Roman and Byzantine Empires (▷ p. 81). Captured by Crusaders (1191), Cyprus was an independent kingdom until 1489, when VENICE acquired the island. In 1571, the Ottoman Turks took Cyprus (▷ p. 115). British administration was established in 1878. During the 1950s, Greek Cypriots, led by Archbishop (later President) MAKARIOS III (1913–77), campaigned for Enosis (union with Greece). The Turkish Cypriots advocated partition, but following a terrorist campaign by the Greek Cypriot EOKA movement, a compromise was agreed. In 1960, Cyprus became an independent republic. Power was shared by the two communities, but the agreement broke down in 1963. UN forces intervened to stop intercommunal fighting. The Turkish Cypriots set up their own administration. When pro-Enosis officers staged a coup (1974), Turkey invaded the N. Cyprus was effectively partitioned. Over 200 000 Greek Cypriots were displaced from the N, into which settlers arrived from Turkey. Since then, UN forces have manned the 'Attila Line' between the Greek S and Turkish N. Attempts have been made to reunite Cyprus as a federal state.

Cyril, St (c. 827–69), Greek monk, missionary and Bible translator; ▷ p. 81.

Cyrus II (the Great; d. 530 BC), the founder of the Achaemenid Persian empire; ▷ pp. 21 and **26.**

Cyrus the Younger (d. 401 BC), Persian prince, the brother of ARTAXERXES II; ▷ p. 27.

Czechoslovakia, a republic in Central Europe. Slavs first populated the region from the 5th century AD. A Moravian empire flourished in the 9th century, and after its decline in the 11th century, the kingdom of BOHEMIA rose. In the 14th century, the greatest of the Czech kings, CHARLES IV, became Holy Roman Emperor. His support of Church reform eventually led to the Bohemian revolt against Rome known as the HUSSITE movement (▷ p. 91). In 1526 Bohemia fell under HABSBURG rule, and Slovakia was joined to Hungary. The determination of the Catholic Habsburgs to control the mainly Protestant Czech nobility led to the Thirty Years War (▷ p. 113). In 1620, the Czechs were defeated and remained under Austrian rule until 1918 (▷ p. 182). Nationalism grew in the 19th century, and on the collapse of the AUSTRO-HUNGARIAN EMPIRE, the Czechs and Slovaks united in an independent state (1918) – largely due to the efforts of Tomáš MASARYK, who became Czechoslovakia's first president. In 1938, HITLER demanded that Germany be granted the SUDETENLAND, where Germans predominated. Lacking allies, Czechoslovakia was dismembered (▷ pp. 188–9). The Nazi occupation included the establishment of a puppet state of Slovakia, the massacre of the inhabitants of Lidice (1942) and the Slovak Uprising (1944). Following liberation (1945), a coalition government was formed, but the Communists staged a takeover in 1948. In 1968, moves by Party Secretary Alexander DUBČEK to introduce political reforms met with Soviet disapproval, and invasion by Czechoslovakia's Warsaw

Pact allies. In 1989, student demonstrations developed into a peaceful revolution led by the Civic Forum movement. Faced by overwhelming public opposition, the Communist Party renounced its leading role and hardline leaders were replaced by reformers. A coalition government was appointed and Civic Forum's leader – the playwright Vaclav HAVEL – was elected president. Free multi-party elections were held (1990), Soviet forces withdrawn (1991) and Czechoslovakia strengthened ties with Western Europe, for example becoming an associate of the EC. However, Slovak nationalism has increased and the possible secession of Slovakia has become an issue.

Dacia, an ancient region N of the lower Danube, roughly corresponding to Romania. It was conquered by Trajan (AD 101–6) and became a Roman province; ▷ p. 37 (map).

Dáil Éireann (or Dáil), the lower house of the parliament of the Irish Republic.

daimyos, the provincial barons who dominated Japan from the 10th to the 19th centuries; ▷ pp. 64–5.

Dakota Indians, ▷ SIOUX.

Daladier, Edouard (1884–1970), French socialist politician, prime minister (1934 and 1938–40). With CHAMBERLAIN he negotiated the MUNICH AGREEMENT (1938), then took France to war in September 1939; ▷ pp. 188–9.

Danegeld, a term generally used to refer to the individual tributes raised by ETHELRED II to pay off invading Viking armies. Strictly it refers to the 'army tax' levied 1012–51 to pay for the squadron of Danish ships maintained by the English government. The Norman kings revived the tax.

Danelaw, the name given to those parts of E and N England that experienced Scandinavian rule and settlement in the 9th and 10th centuries; ▷ p. 86.

Danton, Georges (1759–94), French revolutionary leader and orator. He dominated the Committee of Public Safety created by the CONVENTION, and was minister of justice (1792–4). His opposition to the Terror led to his downfall and execution; ▷ p. 145.

Danzig, the German name for the Polish city of Gdansk, a free city under the auspices of the LEAGUE OF NATIONS from 1919 to 1939; ▷ p. 182 (map).

Daoism or **Taoism,** a Chinese religious and philosophical system, traditionally set out by Lao Zi in the 4th century BC. Tao – 'the Way' – emphasized the individual's pursuit of the good life and the quiet acceptance of fate.

Dardanelles, the W end of the Bosphorus Straits, linking the Mediterranean to the Black Sea. The 1841 London Convention closed the Straits to warships in peacetime. In April 1915 Anglo-French forces landed at GALLIPOLI, on its N edge, in an unsuccessful attempt to seize the Straits. A new system established at the Paris Peace Conference placed the Straits under an international commission. The Montreux Commission of 1936 restored control of the Straits to Turkey; ▷ pp. 154–5 and 177.

Darius I (d. 486 BC), Achaemenid king of Persia (521–486 BC); ▷ pp. 26–7.

Darius III (d. 330 BC) the last Achaemenid king of Persia; ▷ pp. 27 and 32.

Dark Ages, the period of European history from the 7th to the 10th centuries, once supposed to be an age of barbarism; ▷ pp. 100 and 101.

dating methods, ▷ pp. **7** and 14.

David (d. c. 961 BC), king of Israel (c. 1000–c. 961 BC). A king of the House of Judah, he captured Jerusalem from the Jebusites around 1005 BC and went on to defeat the Philistines. He was anointed at Hebron, but later moved the capital to JERUSALEM.

Under David the kingdom of Israel briefly became an empire dominating Syria and Palestine; ▷ p. 23.

David I (c. 1082–1153), king of Scotland (1124–53). The youngest son of MALCOLM III, he welcomed Englishmen and Frenchmen to his court and adopted a consciously 'modernizing' policy. While he controlled NORTHUMBRIA and Cumbria (1139–53) he was able to face the kings of England on equal terms.

David, St (c. 520–c. 601), the patron saint of Wales. He was revered as a founder of monasteries and for his austere lifestyle.

Davis, Jefferson (1808–89), US politician. He was elected president of the CONFEDERATE STATES OF AMERICA in 1861. During the Civil War he became increasingly unpopular in the South, and narrowly escaped execution for treason when hostilities ended in 1865; ▷ pp. 158–9.

Dawes Plan (1924), a plan for German reparations payments after World War I devised by the US financier Charles G. Dawes; ▷ pp. 185 and 186.

Dayan, Moshe (1915–81), Israeli soldier and politician, recognizable by his black eye-patch. Active in the campaign against the British in Palestine in the 1940s, he led Israeli forces against Egypt in 1956 and was Minister of Defence during the SIX DAY WAR (1967).

Díaz, Porfirio (1830–1915), dictator who governed MEXICO for all but four years (1880–4) between 1876 and 1910. The benefits of his programme of modernization through industrialization and foreign investment were unevenly distributed. Discontent at his dictatorial methods led to the outbreak of the MEXICAN REVOLUTION in 1910.

D-Day (6 June 1944), the first day of the Allied invasion of Western Europe in World War II; ▷ p. 191.

Dead Sea Scrolls, a collection of ancient religious texts discovered in desert caves near the Dead Sea in Israel; ▷ p. 22 (box).

Deccan, the plateau occupying S central India (▷ p. 58).

Decembrists, an early-19th century Russian revolutionary movement, seeking emancipation of the serfs and a constitutional monarchy; ▷ p. 180 (box).

Declaration of Independence (4 July 1776), the declaration of independence from Great Britain by the 13 colonies of North America; ▷ pp. 142–3.

Defence of the Realm Acts (DORA), legislation passed by the British Parliament in World War I to control all aspects of the war effort; ▷ p. 179 (box).

de Gasperi, Alcide (1881–1954), Italian statesman and co-founder of the Italian CHRISTIAN DEMOCRATIC Party, prime minister (1945–53).

de Gaulle, Charles (1890–1970), French general and statesman. The leader of the FREE FRENCH during World War II, he was head of the provisional government (1944–6), but resigned over disagreements on the constitution. He re-entered politics in 1958 during the Algerian Crisis, and became president of the Fifth Republic (▷ FRANCE) in 1959. He granted independence to Algeria, led France in the direction of an independent foreign policy, and resisted Britain's entry into the EEC. His reputation was shaken by the events of 1968 and he resigned in 1969; ▷ pp. 202 (box) and 215.

de Klerk, Fredrik Willem (1936–), South African president (1989–). Succeeding P.W. BOTHA, he negotiated peace with the ANC, released MANDELA from prison, and initiated constitutional negotiations for a non-racial 'New South Africa'; ▷ p. 221.

Delaware, one of the 13 original states of the USA. Delaware was originally Swedish (1638), then Dutch (1655), before coming under English rule in 1664; ▷ pp. 156 and 159.

Delaware Indians, a native North American people, living as maize farmers in the Eastern Woodlands (New Jersey and adjoining areas). They were forced W in the early 18th century following early contact with European settlers.

Delhi Sultanate, a former Indo-Islamic state centred on Delhi; ▷ p. 62.

Delian League, an anti-Persian alliance of the 5th century BC. Dominated by Athens, it became the basis of an Athenian empire; ▷ pp. 29–30.

Delphic oracle, the most important ORACLE in ancient Greece; ▷ pp. 29 (box) and 47 (box).

deme, a geographical unit of local government in Athens and its surroundings; ▷ pp. 29 and 30.

Democratic Party, US political party dating back to the late 18th century when it was known as the Democratic-Republican Party. A vehicle for expansionist and laissez-faire sentiment during the presidency of Andrew JACKSON, it was the dominant political force in the republic before the American Civil War. Traditionally racist and southern-dominated, it emerged as a powerful liberal force in American politics during the 1930s, largely through the growth of its ethnically diverse northern constituency. The party reached its zenith under the guidance of F.D. ROOSEVELT, but its strength as a national force was eroded by the defection of southern whites and blue-collar workers in the 1960s and 1970s; ▷ pp. 156 and 216–17.

Demosthenes (c. 383–322 BC), Athenian statesman and noted orator. He inspired resistance to Philip of Macedon (▷ p. 31), and was forced to commit suicide after the unsuccessful Athenian revolt following Alexander's death.

Deng Xiaoping (1904–), Chinese Communist statesman. A supporter of MAO ZEDONG, he took part in the LONG MARCH (1934–5) and was General Secretary of the Chinese Communist Party (1956–67). He was denounced during the Cultural Revolution (1967), but reinstated in 1973. Denounced for a second time in 1976, he was reinstated in 1977, and remains effective leader of China despite not holding an official government post; ▷ p. 197.

Denmark, a kingdom of Western Europe. Denmark became a distinct state in the 10th century. The Danes participated in the Viking invasions (▷ p. 86), which saw settlers and raiders penetrate much of W Europe, and, under CNUT, a short-lived Anglo-Danish empire was established. Medieval Denmark was beset by territorial wars and dynastic difficulties – the monarchy remained elective until 1660. Norway was acquired in 1380, and under the KALMAR Agreement (1397), Queen Margrethe I united all three Scandinavian kingdoms, but Sweden reasserted its independence in 1583. The Roman Catholic faction was defeated in a civil war (1534–6), and Lutheranism became the state religion. In the 17th century, Denmark was overshadowed by Sweden, its rival for control of the entrance to the Baltic (▷ p. 127). The Danes were defeated by imperial forces in the Thirty Years War (1626; ▷ p. 113), but a decline in Swedish power after 1660 allowed Denmark to reassert itself. Colonial ventures in the 18th century brought prosperity. An alliance with Napoleonic France proved disastrous, and in 1815 Denmark lost Norway to Sweden. The duchies of SCHLESWIG and HOLSTEIN became the subject of a complicated dispute with PRUSSIA (▷ p. 153). After a short war with Prussia and Austria (1864), Denmark surrendered the duchies, but N Schleswig was returned to Denmark in 1920 (▷ p. 183, map). In the 20th century, Denmark's last colonial possessions were either sold (Virgin Islands) or given independence (Iceland) or autonomy (GREENLAND). The country was occupied by Nazi Germany (1940–5), and has since been a member of the Western Alliance (▷ p. 204, box).

Depression, the Great, ▷ pp. 184–5 and 186.

Derby, Edward Stanley, 14th Earl of (1799–1869), British Conservative statesman, prime minister (1852, 1858–9 and 1866–8). The REFORM ACT of 1867 was carried in his last premiership.

Desai, Morarji (1896–), Indian statesman, prime minister (1977–9). He led the newly-created Janata party to victory against Indira GANDHI in 1977.

desegregation, the process by which legal barriers to black equality in the USA (e.g. separate schools and transportation facilities) were broken down by civil rights activists and federal policymakers after World War II (▷ p. 216, box). Although de jure segregation in the southern states was outlawed by the CIVIL RIGHTS ACT of 1964, de facto segregation (i.e. separate housing and schooling produced by economic and social factors) remains a significant issue in American politics.

Desmoulins, Camille (1760–94), French journalist and revolutionary. A supporter of DANTON and his more moderate policies during the Terror, he was executed in April 1794.

Dessalines, Jean Jacques (1758–1806), black emperor of HAITI (1804–6). He achieved the final declaration of Haiti's independence in 1800.

détente, ▷ pp. 206–7 and 216.

de Valera, Eamon (1882–1975), Irish statesman, prime minister (1932–48, 1951–4 and 1957–9), president (1959–73). He was sentenced to death by the British after the EASTER RISING (1916), but reprieved. He fought for Irish independence from Britain in the guerrilla war of 1919–21 as a member of the IRISH REPUBLICAN ARMY. He opposed the Anglo-Irish Treaty which founded the Irish Free State (1921), and led his republicans to defeat in the Irish Civil War. He founded FÍANNA FÁIL in 1926 and won the 1932 election, after which he gradually severed Ireland's remaining constitutional links with Britain.

Devolution, War of (1667–8), one of the wars of Louis XIV; ▷ p. 123 (box).

Dias, Bartholemeu (?1450–1500), Portuguese explorer; ▷ p. 108 (box).

Diaspora, the 'dispersal' of the 10 tribes of Israel in the aftermath of the unsuccessful Jewish revolt against the Romans in AD 135. Since 1948, the same word has been used to denote the movement of Palestinians from the new state of Israel.

dictator, 1. under the Roman Republic, a single leader exercising supreme power appointed for a maximum of six months during an emergency (▷ p. 36). **2.** in modern times, any authoritarian ruler unconstrained by legal or constitutional restrictions, for example, Hitler, Stalin and Mussolini (▷ pp. 186–7 and 198–9).

Dien Bien Phu (1954), a battle in which VIET MINH forces inflicted a major defeat on the French in the First Indochina War; ▷ p. 208.

Dieppe Raid (19 August 1942), a failed assault on German installations in Normandy by Anglo-Canadian forces in World War II; ▷ p. 190.

diet, the name formerly given to the representative assemblies of a number of European states. In the Holy Roman Empire the diet was a meeting of representatives of the German states of the Empire with the emperor himself; it was abolished in 1806. In the 19th century a federal diet was set up in Frankfurt under the GERMAN CONFEDERATION; ▷ pp. 151 and 153, and WORMS, DIET OF.

Diocletian (AD 245–316), Roman emperor (284–305); ▷ pp. 39–40.

Directory, French (1795–9), the regime that ruled France from the end of the JACOBIN Convention to the CONSULATE; ▷ p. 145.

disarmament, ▷ pp. 182–3 and 227.

Disraeli, Benjamin, 1st Earl of Beaconsfield

(1804–81), British Conservative politician and novelist, born the son of a Spanish Jew but baptized a Christian. As a flamboyant young MP his romantic Toryism was expressed through leadership of the Young England group and in political novels. Disraeli served as Chancellor of the Exchequer (1852, 1858–9, 1866–8) under Lord DERBY and was largely responsible for the Second REFORM ACT (1867). 'Dizzy' held the premiership briefly in 1868, then again from 1874 to 1880, when his main interest was in foreign affairs, making Queen VICTORIA Empress of India (1876) and achieving diplomatic success at the Congress of BERLIN (1878).

Dissolution of the Monasteries, ⟶ MONASTERIES.

Djibouti, a republic in E Africa. The area became the colony of French Somaliland in 1888. In 1977, the territory became the Republic of Djibouti, but the new state has suffered ethnic unrest and drought; ⟶ p. 202 (map).

doge, the title of the ruler of the republics of VENICE, GENOA and Amalfi from the 7th to the 18th centuries; ⟶ p. 97 (box).

dollar diplomacy, a US foreign policy of the early 20th century, aiming to serve US business interests abroad; ⟶ p. 160 (box).

Dollfuss, Engelbert (1892–1934), Austrian chancellor (1932–4). He was assassinated by the Nazis in July 1934.

Domesday Book, a record of the possessions of all major landowners in England and their economic resources, produced 1086–7. It provides a unique insight into the society and economy of 11th-century England and the almost complete replacement of Anglo-Saxon by Norman land-holders; ⟶ p. 87.

Dominicans, an order of friars founded by St Dominic (1170–1221); ⟶ p. 91.

Dominican Republic, a republic occupying the E part of HISPANIOLA in the Caribbean. The island of Hispaniola was discovered in 1492 by Columbus. In 1697 Spain ceded the W of the island (HAITI) to France, and from 1795 the whole island was French. Returned to Spanish rule in 1809, the E declared independence as the Dominican Republic in 1821, but was annexed by Haiti (1822–44). The 19th century witnessed a succession of tyrants, and by 1900 the republic was bankrupt and in chaos. The USA intervened (1916–24). Rafael TRUJILLO (1891–1961) became president in 1930 and ruthlessly suppressed opposition. He was assassinated in 1961. Civil war in 1965 ended after intervention by US and Latin American troops. Since then, an infant democracy has faced grave economic problems.

Dominion, the name given to a territory within the BRITISH EMPIRE which, while owing allegiance to the crown, had been granted a measure of self-government.

Domitian (AD 51–96), Roman emperor (81–96); ⟶ p. 38.

Donatism, a breakaway movement of fanatical Christians in North Africa. Although repeatedly condemned by Rome, the Donatist Church survived until the end of the 6th century.

Dönitz, Karl (1891–1980), German admiral, commander-in-chief of the German navy (1943–5). As head of state after Hitler's death he surrendered to the Allies. He was sentenced to 10 years imprisonment for war crimes at the Nuremberg Trials.

Dorians, one of the main cultural and linguistic groupings of the ancient Greeks. The Doric dialect was mainly spoken in the S and E of the Peloponnese, in small parts of mainland Greece, and in Crete, Rhodes and the SW coast of Asia Minor (Turkey). The Greeks believed that the 'Dorians' originally invaded from the N, and destroyed what we call Mycenaean palace-civilization; it is not certain how much truth there is in this account; ⟶ p. 25, AEOLIANS and IONIANS.

Dowding, Hugh Caswell Tremenheere, 1st Baron (1882–1970), British air chief marshal. A pilot in World War I, he rose through the ranks of the RAF to become commander-in-chief of Fighter Command in 1936, contributing much to British success in the battle of BRITAIN in 1940 (⟶ p. 190).

Draco, the first lawgiver of ancient Athens. In 621/20 BC he produced a set of written laws, which were afterwards thought to have been over-severe ('Draconian'), and except for the laws on homicide, were replaced in 594/3 by the laws of Solon (⟶ p. 28).

Drake, Sir Francis (1540–96), English sailor and pirate. He was the first Englishman to sail round the world (1577–80), combining exploration with profitable attacks on Spanish shipping and settlements in the New World. He was one of the commanders of the English naval force that defeated the SPANISH ARMADA.

Dravidians, the people originally inhabiting the Indian subcontinent. They were pushed S by the arrival of the Aryans in the period 2000–1200 BC; ⟶ pp. 58 and 59.

Dreadnought, a class of heavily armed battleship first launched by Britain in 1906; ⟶ p. 175 (box).

Dresden raids (13/14 February 1945), heavy bombing raids by British and US planes on the German city of Dresden. The action, which almost totally destroyed the beautiful baroque city and killed 135 000 people, has come under increasing criticism; ⟶ p. 191.

Dreyfus, Alfred (1859–1935), French army officer of Jewish parentage. He was falsely accused of passing secrets to the Germans in 1894 and sentenced to life imprisonment on Devil's Island. Fresh evidence presented in 1896 suggested his innocence, but ANTI-SEMITISM within the French army prevented a retrial. The ensuing controversy pitted nationalists, militarists and royalists against republicans and socialists. Dreyfus was finally pardoned in 1906; ⟶ p. *169*.

Druids, a priestly order of the CELTS; ⟶ p. 35 (box).

Druze, an unorthodox Muslim sect, centred chiefly in Lebanon. Its followers practice a secret faith, open to men only. Although they revere the Prophet Muhammad, they do not observe Ramadan or go on pilgrimage to MECCA. Druze militias occupied parts of Lebanon during the civil war; ⟶ p. 213.

Dual Alliance (1879), an alliance between Germany and Austria-Hungary; ⟶ p. 174.

Dubček, Alexander (1921–), Czechoslovak statesman. He became leader of the Communist Party in 1968 and launched the reforms of the PRAGUE SPRING. Removed after the Soviet invasion, he became a clerk in a lumber yard, but was to play a crucial role in the 1989 revolution; ⟶ p. *199*.

Dulles, John Foster (1888–1959), US Republican politician and diplomat. As President EISENHOWER's anti-Communist secretary of state (1953–9), he was influential in formulating US foreign policy during the Cold War (⟶ p. 204).

Duma, an elected assembly established by NICHOLAS II of Russia in 1905; ⟶ p. 180.

Dumbarton Oaks Conference (1944), an international conference held in Washington, DC, at which proposals for the foundation of the United Nations were drawn up by representatives from the USA, UK, China and the USSR; ⟶ p. 228.

Dunkirk evacuation (1940), the rescue by sea of British and French troops from the N French port of Dunkirk during World War II; ⟶ p. 190.

Dutch East India Company, a chartered company founded in 1602 by the STATES GENERAL of the Dutch Republic. By the 18th century it had become a large colonial power – but at the expense of its trading competitiveness. It was liquidated in 1799; ⟶ pp. 121 and 128.

Dutch Republic, ⟶ pp. **120–1**.

Duvalier, François (1907–71), dictator of HAITI (1957–71), known as 'Papa Doc'. His son Jean-Claude, or 'Baby Doc' (1951–) was president from 1971 until his overthrow in 1986.

Eastern Front, (in World War I) ⟶ p. 176; (in World War II) ⟶ pp. **192–3**.

Easter Rising (24 April 1916), an Irish rebellion in which nationalists led by Patrick Pearse seized a number of buildings in Dublin and issued a Proclamation of Irish Independence from British rule. Based in the General Post Office in Sackville Street, they held out against superior British forces until 29 April. Sixteen of the leaders were subsequently executed by the British, fuelling the growth of nationalist sentiment in IRELAND.

East Germany, ⟶ GERMANY.

East India Company, English, a chartered company formed by London merchants in 1600 as a monopoly trading company. In defence of its trade in India the Company established a territorial empire there in the 18th century, complete control of which only passed to the British government after the Indian Mutiny (1857); ⟶ pp. 63, 128, 129 and 160.

East Prussia, a former province of Germany on the Baltic Sea. It was separated from the rest of Germany by the POLISH CORRIDOR in 1919. In 1945 the S part went to Poland, and the N part to the USSR; ⟶ p. 182 (map).

East Timor, a Portuguese colony from 1586 until 1975 when it was annexed by INDONESIA; ⟶ p. 202 (map).

East–West Schism, ⟶ pp. **81** and 90.

Ebla, a city-state of ancient Syria; ⟶ p. 22.

ECU (European Currency Unit), a unit of account, based upon a basket of European currencies, used as a reserve asset in the European Monetary System (the system that enables the member-states of the EC to coordinate their exchange rate through the ERM).

Ecuador, a republic on the Pacific coast of S America. By the mid-15th century the Ecuadorian highlands had been incorporated into the Inca Empire (⟶ p. 71). After being conquered by Spain (1532–3), the area was ruled as part of the viceroyalty of Peru. In 1822 Ecuador was liberated by the armies of Antonio José de Sucre (1795–1830) and Simón Bolívar; (⟶ pp. 148–9). Initially federated with Colombia and Venezuela, Ecuador became completely independent in 1830. Throughout the 19th century there were struggles between liberals and conservatives. Since 1895 there have been long periods of military rule, but democratically elected governments have been in power since 1978. Relations with neighbouring Peru have long been tense – war broke out in 1941, when Ecuador lost most of its Amazonian region.

Eden, Robert Anthony, 1st Earl of Avon (1897–1977), British Conservative statesman, foreign secretary (1935–8, 1940–5 and 1951–5), prime minister (1955–7). He resigned after the controversy aroused by the Anglo-French invasion of the SUEZ CANAL zone in 1956.

Edgehill, battle of (23 October 1642), the first battle of the ENGLISH CIVIL WAR, a bloody and indecisive clash between CHARLES I's royalists under Prince RUPERT, and Parliamentary forces under the Earl of Essex, fought at Edgehill near Warwick.

Edo, the capital of the Tokugawa shogunate, now Tokyo; ⟶ pp. 58 and 59.

Edward I (1239–1307), king of England (1272–1307). A masterful ruler, he had a profound effect on the development of English government. He conquered the principality of Wales, but his attempts to dominate Scotland only provoked the Scottish War of Independence; ⟶ pp. 94 and 102.

Edward II (1284–1327), king of England (1307–27). An incompetent ruler, he was discredited by his defeat at BANNOCKBURN and damaged by the excessive confidence he placed in friends such as Piers Gaveston and the Despensers. In 1326 his estranged wife, ISABELLA of France, led the rising which led to his dethronement and murder.

Edward III (1312–77), king of England (1327–77). He claimed the French throne through his mother ISABELLA, thereby provoking the Hundred Years War; ⊳ pp. 94–5.

Edward IV (1442–83), king of England (1461–60, 1471–83). As the son of RICHARD Duke of York, he inherited the YORKIST claim to the throne, and with WARWICK'S help overthrew the LANCASTRIAN HENRY VI. Disagreements with Warwick led to him losing the throne in 1470, but through brilliant generalship he won it back again (1471).

Edward V (1470–?1483), king of England (9 April–25 June 1482). Arrangements for his coronation were in hand when his uncle (later RICHARD III) had him declared illegitimate, deposed and placed in the Tower of London. Since there is no record of him being seen again he was probably murdered.

Edward VI (1533–53), king of England (1547–53). The son of HENRY VIII and Jane SEYMOUR, he succeeded as a minor. Effective power lay first with his uncle, the Duke of Somerset, and then with the latter's rival, the Duke of Northumberland, both of whom continued the Protestant Reformation. He died of tuberculosis at the age of 16; ⊳ p. 118.

Edward VII (1841–1910), king of Great Britain and Ireland, the eldest son of Queen VICTORIA. As Prince of Wales he was virtually excluded from royal duties, partly owing to his leadership of the rakish 'Marlborough House' set, until his long-delayed accession in 1901. He was a popular king but had little political influence.

Edward VIII (1894–1972), king of Great Britain and Ireland (1936), the eldest son of GEORGE V and brother of GEORGE VI. He abdicated in order to marry an American divorcée Mrs Wallis Simpson, causing a constitutional crisis.

Edward, the Black Prince (1330–76), eldest son of EDWARD III, whom he predeceased. His military achievements in the Hundred Years War, notably at the battles of Crécy and Poitiers, won him a great reputation; ⊳ pp. 94 and 103.

Edward the Confessor, St (c. 1003–66), king of England (1042–66), son of ETHELRED II, and founder of Westminster Abbey. The succession of HAROLD Godwinson after Edward's death led to the NORMAN Conquest of England; ⊳ pp. 86 and 87.

EEC, ⊳ EUROPEAN COMMUNITY.

EFTA, ⊳ EUROPEAN FREE TRADE ASSOCIATION.

Egypt, a country of NE Africa. From 3100 to 332 BC, Egypt was ruled by 30 dynasties of pharaohs (⊳ pp. 17–19). The country then formed part of the Ptolemaic kingdom, the Roman Empire (⊳ p. 38) and the Byzantine Empire (⊳ p. 80). The Arabs invaded (639–42), and gradually transformed Egypt into an Arabic Islamic society (⊳ pp. 82–3), a province of the ABBASID caliphate. A rival caliphate was set up by the FATIMID dynasty in Cairo (973–1171). MAMLUK armies – originally Turkish slaves – founded an independent sultanate (1250). In 1517 Egypt became part of the Ottoman (Turkish) Empire (⊳ p. 114). After a French invasion (1798–1801), the Ottoman viceroy Mehemet Ali (⊳ p. 154) made Egypt strong and established a dynasty that lasted until 1953 (⊳ pp. 154–5). (For the history of Egypt from the 19th century; ⊳ pp. 211–12.)

Eichmann, (Karl) Adolf (1902–62), Austrian Nazi official who organized the sending of Jews to Concentration Camps. He was abducted from Argentina by the Israelis and executed (1962).

Eisenhower, Dwight D. (1890–1969), US soldier and thirty-fourth president of the USA (1953–61). Known universally as 'Ike' after his successful career as Allied Commander in Europe during World War II, he was elected president as a Republican in 1952 and served two terms. 'The Eisenhower Doctrine' (1957) offered US economic or military aid to any state in the Middle East threatened by Communist aggression; ⊳ pp. 191 and **216**.

Elamites, an ancient people of SW Iran (modern Khuzistan); ⊳ pp. 16 and 20.

ELAS, a Communist guerrilla group in Greece. ELAS fought against German occupation during World War II, and afterwards fought to replace the monarchy with a Communist state in a bitter civil war (1946–9), but was defeated.

Eleanor of Aquitaine (1122–1204), the most powerful woman of her age. Duchess of AQUITAINE in her own right, she married the CAPETIAN Louis VII, and then – after their 1152 divorce – the ANGEVIN HENRY II. After bearing him eight children, she instigated a revolt against him (1173–4) and was imprisoned until his death (1189), after which she was once again influential; ⊳ p. 94.

elector, a prince of the Holy Roman Empire with the right to participate in the election of the emperor; ⊳ pp. 85, 119 and 125.

Elizabeth I (1533–1603), queen of England and Ireland (1558–1603), the daughter of HENRY VIII and Anne BOLEYN. Her reign was notable for commercial and maritime expansion and high achievement in literature, art and music; ⊳ p. 118.

Elizabeth II (1926–), queen of Great Britain and Northern Ireland, and head of the Commonwealth since 1952. The elder daughter of GEORGE VI, she married her distant cousin Philip Mountbatten in 1947. Since her coronation in 1953, she has visited many countries of the world, particularly those of the COMMONWEALTH.

El Alamein, battle of (October 1942), a major ALLIED victory over German forces in Egypt during World War II; ⊳ p. 192.

El Dorado (Spanish 'the golden one'), a fabled city, rich in gold, sought by the CONQUISTADORES in the early 16th century; ⊳ p. 116.

El Salvador, a republic in CENTRAL AMERICA. Spain conquered the area in 1524 and governed it as part of the captaincy-general of Guatemala. El Salvador was liberated in 1821, but remained in the Central American Federation until 1838. The country has suffered frequent coups and political violence. In 1932 a peasant uprising was harshly suppressed. El Salvador's overpopulation has been partially relieved by migration to neighbouring states. After a soccer match between El Salvador and Honduras in 1969, war broke out because of illegal immigration by Salvadoreans into HONDURAS. Political and economic power is concentrated into the hands of a few families, and this has led to social tension. A state of virtual civil war existed from the late 1970s with the US-backed military, assisted by extreme right-wing death squads, combating left-wing guerrillas. The government and guerrillas signed a peace agreement, which came into effect in 1992.

emirate, a Muslim governorate or principality, from the Arabic *amir*, meaning 'commander'.

Ems Telegram (1870), a dispatch recording a meeting between the French ambassador and WILHELM I of Prussia, sent by the latter to BISMARCK. Bismarck altered the dispatch, inserting a supposed exchange of insults between monarch and diplomat, and then released the amended text to the press, in order to exacerbate tensions between France and Prussia and so provoke a war (⊳ p. 153).

enclosures, the enclosing by landlords of open fields, commons and wastelands. In England it was accelerated by private acts of Parliament in the late 18th and early 19th centuries following the commercial farming improvements of the Agricultural Revolution; ⊳ p. 140.

Encyclopedists, those writers and philosophers of the French Enlightenment who contributed to the *Encyclopédie*; ⊳ pp. 134 and *135*.

Engels, Friedrich (1820–95), German political philosopher who collaborated with MARX on the COMMUNIST MANIFESTO; ⊳ p. 168.

England, a country in NW Europe, part of the UNITED KINGDOM, occupying the larger part of the island of Great Britain. Unified in the 10th century, England was united with WALES in 1536, and with SCOTLAND in 1707 (⊳ pp. 118–19).

English Civil War (1642–9), the conflict between the supporters of CHARLES I and the Parliamentarians, arising from disagreements on constitutional, religious and economic matters between Charles and members of the LONG PARLIAMENT. Charles claimed to rule by divine right, while Parliament asserted its constitutional rights against those of the monarch. Hostilities opened when the king raised his standard at Nottingham in 1642. Parliament's alliance with the Scots enabled it to defeat Charles' forces at MARSTON MOOR (1644), while the creation of the NEW MODEL ARMY – dominated by FAIRFAX and CROMWELL – was followed by decisive Parliamentary victories at NASEBY (1645) and elsewhere. The kings' surrender in 1645 ended the first phase of the war, but his escape in 1647 prompted a brief resumption of hostilities, with Charles now in alliance with the Scots. However, he was soon defeated and captured (1648), and his public execution in 1649 was followed by the establishment of a republican COMMONWEALTH; ⊳ pp. 111 (box) and **118–19**.

Enlightenment, ⊳ pp. 133, **134–5**, 144 and 150.

entente cordiale (1904), an 'understanding' between Britain and France which aimed to counter what was seen as a growing German threat; ⊳ p. 175.

Enver Pasha (1881–1922), Turkish politician and leader of the YOUNG TURKS who seized power in 1909. He took power for himself in 1913 and led Turkey into World War I.

Epaminondas (4th century BC), Theban general; ⊳ p. 31.

Ephesus, an important IONIAN city on the coast of Turkey. It remained a major and prosperous city in Hellenistic and Roman times, best known for its temple of Artemis; ⊳ pp. 31 (map) and *39*.

Ephialtes (assassinated 461 BC), Athenian politician, primarily responsible for the reforms that reduced the powers of the AREOPAGOS; ⊳ p. 30.

Epirus, a region of NW Greece and S Albania, inhabited in Classical times by various tribal groups. They were formed into a kingdom under Alexander I (342–330 BC), supported by Philip II of Macedon. Under PYRRHUS Epirus expanded its power and fought wars in Italy and Sicily.

Equatorial Guinea, a republic of W Africa. The island of Fernando Pó was acquired by Spain in 1778. Río Muni was added in 1856 to create Spanish Guinea. Independence in 1968 began under the dictatorship of Francisco Nguema, who was overthrown by a military coup in 1979.

Erasmus, Desiderius (1466–1536), Dutch humanist; ⊳ pp. 100 and **101** (box).

Erhard, Ludwig (1897–1977), German CHRISTIAN DEMOCRAT statesman, chancellor of the Federal Republic of (West) GERMANY (1963–6).

Eric the Red (?940–?1010), Viking explorer who colonized GREENLAND c. 896; ⊳ pp. 72 and 86.

Eritrea, a country on the Red Sea coast of NE Africa. The region was part of Ethiopia (from the 10th century), but was disputed by the Ottoman

Empire from the 16th century. Eritrea became an Italian colony in 1890 and was the main base for Italian aggression against Ethiopia (1935–9; ▷ p. 188). It was under British administration (1941–52), and was federated with (1952) and then absorbed by (1962) ETHIOPIA. Eritrean Muslims fought for independence from 1975 to 1991, when the Ethiopian authorities recognized Eritrea's right to secede. A referendum on independence is scheduled; ▷ p. 202 (map).

ERM (Exchange Rate Mechanism), a system agreed between 10 of the 12 members of the EUROPEAN COMMUNITY, whereby they limit movement in the value of their currencies. The ERM is not a fixed system; ERM members agree a set of exchange rates against each others' currencies and a margin om either side of these central rates to allow for some daily movement in the markets.

Eskimo, a group of peoples inhabiting northern N America, Greenland and E Siberia; ▷ pp. 72, 73 and INUIT.

Estates-General, ▷ STATES-GENERAL.

Estonia, a republic on the Baltic Sea in NE Europe. Estonia was ruled by Denmark (1227–1346), the (German) TEUTONIC Knights (1346–1558; ▷ p. 85, map) and by Sweden (1558–1712), before becoming part of Russia. Estonian national consciousness increased throughout the 19th century. When the Communists took power in Russia (1917), Estonia seceded, but a German occupation and two Russian invasions delayed independence until 1919 (▷ pp. 181 and 182, map). Estonia's fragile democracy was replaced by a dictatorship in 1934. The Non-Aggression Pact (1939) between Hitler and Stalin assigned Estonia to the USSR, which invaded and annexed the republic (1940). Estonia was occupied by Nazi Germany (1941–4; ▷ p. 192). When Soviet rule was reimposed (1945; ▷ p. 198), large-scale Russian settlement replaced over 120 000 Estonians who had been killed or deported to Siberia. In 1988, reforms in the USSR allowed Estonian nationalists to operate openly. Nationalists won a majority in the republic's parliament, gradually assumed greater autonomy and seceded following the failed coup by Communist hardliners in Moscow (August 1991). The USSR recognized Estonia's independence in September 1991; ▷ p. 225.

ETA, (Basque, *Euzkadi ta Azkatasuna*, 'Homeland and Liberty'), a terrorist organization fighting for an independent BASQUE state (▷ p. 215).

Ethelred II (the Unready; c. 968–1016), king of England (978–1016). When renewed Scandinavian raids became a serious threat after 1000, he attempted to buy the Danes off with DANEGELD. In 1013 he was temporarily deposed by SWEYN FORKBEARD, king of Denmark, but was reinstated on the latter's death in 1014. His nickname means 'without counsel'; ▷ p. 86.

Ethiopia, a country of NE Africa. The kingdom of AXUM flourished in the first millennium AD, accepting Christianity in the 4th century (▷ pp. 66–7). Later, Islam also entered the country. Under MENELIK II, Ethiopia survived the European scramble for empire and defeated an Italian invasion (1896; ▷ p.160). However, the Italians occupied Ethiopia from 1936 to 1941 (▷ pp. 188 and 190). Emperor HAILE SELASSIE played a prominent part in African affairs, but – failing to modernize Ethiopia or overcome its extreme poverty – he was overthrown in 1974. Allied to the USSR, a left-wing military regime instituted revolutionary change, but, even with Cuban help, it was unable to overcome secessionist guerrilla movements in ERITREA and Tigray. Drought, soil erosion and civil war brought severe famine in the 1980s and 1990s (▷ p. 230). The Marxist-Leninist regime was toppled by Tigrayan forces in 1991. The interim authorities recognized the right of Eritrea to secede.

Etruscans, ▷ p. **36** (box).

Eugène of Savoy (1666–1736), French-born Austrian soldier and prince of the House of Savoy. In the service of the Austrian Habsburg Emperors he gained major military successes against the Ottoman Turks (▷ p. 115), and against Louis XIV's forces in the War of the Spanish Succession, fighting with MARLBOROUGH at BLENHEIM, OUDENARDE and Malplaquet; ▷ pp. 123 (box) and 124.

Euphrates, a river of SW Asia, on whose banks a number of important cities of ancient Mesopotamia were built; ▷ p. 16.

Eureka Stockade, ▷ AUSTRALIA.

European Coal and Steel Community, ▷ EUROPEAN COMMUNITY.

European Commission, ▷ EUROPEAN COMMUNITY.

European Community (EC), an organization of West European states. The signing on 1 March 1957 of the Treaties of Rome by Belgium, France, West Germany, Italy, Luxembourg and the Netherlands (which states were all members of the European Coal and Steel Community; 1951) brought into being the European Economic Community (EEC) and the European Atomic Energy Community (Euratom). These three Communities merged their executives and decision-making bodies into a single European Community (EC) in 1967. The EC's principal constituent bodies are: the Council of Ministers, the main decision-making body of the EC; the European Commission, which makes legislative proposals to the Council of Ministers and executes its decisions; the European Parliament, to which the Commission is answerable; and the European Court of Justice, which settles disputes arising out of the application of Community law; ▷ pp. 215 (box), 222 and 223.

European Economic Community (EEC), ▷ EUROPEAN COMMUNITY.

European Free Trade Association (EFTA), an association of West European states formed in 1960 by Austria, Denmark, Norway, Portugal, Sweden, Switzerland and Britain to achieve free trade in industrial products between member-states. EFTA was to lose Denmark, Portugal and the UK to the EC, but it gained Iceland in 1970, and Finland in 1986. Tariffs on industrial goods between EFTA and EC countries were abolished in April 1984. The EC and EFTA have since discussed the creation of a single European trading area.

European Parliament, ▷ EUROPEAN COMMUNITY.

Evans, Sir Arthur John (1851–1941), British archaeologist; ▷ pp. 6 and 24.

evolution, human, the gradual development of modern humans from their ape-like ancestors; ▷ pp. 12–13, AUSTRALOPITHECINES, HOMO ERECTUS, HOMO SAPIENS NEANDERTHALENSIS and HOMO SAPIENS SAPIENS.

excommunication, a sanction used by the Roman Catholic Church, which excluded the excommunicated individual from administering or receiving the Mass. Originally intended as an ecclesiastical sanction, it was occasionally used by the late medieval papacy as a political weapon; ▷ pp. 84–5 and 110.

Exodus, the departure of the Israelites from Egypt under MOSES, as related in the Old Testament; ▷ p. 22 (box).

Fabians, members of the Fabian Society established in Britain in 1884, and one of the groups responsible for the foundation of the LABOUR Party. Fabians rejected revolutionary methods and believed that socialism would be brought about by universal suffrage, legislation and reasoned debate.

Fabius Maximus, Quintus (c. 260–203 BC), Roman senator appointed dictator after Hannibal's victory at TRASIMENE (217 BC). His strategy of avoiding pitched battles earned him the contemptuous nickname *Cunctator* ('the delayer'), which became an honour when his policy was vindicated by the defeat at CANNAE: ▷ p. 37.

Factory Acts, state legislation to protect factory workers, particularly women and children, from long hours and poor conditions, gradually introduced in most industrializing nations during the 19th century, but not always with adequate provision for inspection; ▷ p. 165.

Fairfax, Thomas, 3rd Baron (1612–71), English general. The commander of the Parliamentary forces (1645–50) in the ENGLISH CIVIL WAR. He was later instrumental in the restoration to the throne of CHARLES II.

Faisal I (1885–1933), king of Iraq (1921–33); ▷ p. 210.

Faisal, Ibn Abdul Aziz (1905–75), king of Saudi Arabia (1964–75). Pro-Western in his sympathies, he opposed NASSER's brand of Arab nationalism.

Falange, a Spanish Fascist movement founded in 1933, and adopted by FRANCO in 1937; ▷ p. 189.

Falklands War, a conflict between the UK and Argentina over the Falkland Islands (Spanish 'Islas Malvinas') – a small group of islands in the S Atlantic 12 800 km (8000 mi) from the UK and peopled by 1800 inhabitants of British descent. The islands became a crown colony in 1882 but had long been claimed by Argentina, whose military leader General Galtieri launched a full-scale invasion of the islands on 2 April 1982. After the failure of peace initiatives by the USA and UN, the British government of Margaret THATCHER sent a large naval task force to recover the islands. The ensuing war, which cost the lives of 1000 servicemen, ended in defeat for Argentina.

Farouk (1920–65), king of Egypt (1936–52). Unable to cope with the rising tide of Arab nationalism in Egypt, he was overthrown in a coup led by General Mohammed Neguib and Colonel Gamal Abdel NASSER; ▷ p. 211.

fasces, bundles of rods that symbolized the power of Roman magistrates to inflict corporal punishment. The fasces were revived in the 20th century as a symbol of Italian Fascism; ▷ p. 186.

Fascism, ▷ pp. 185 and **186**–7.

Fashoda Incident (September 1898), an Anglo-French diplomatic crisis; ▷ p. **162** (box).

Fatah, al-, a Palestinian organization formed in the late 1950s and early 1960s to fight for the return of Palestinian Arabs to what is now the state of Israel. It is a dominant element in the PALESTINE LIBERATION ORGANIZATION; ▷ p. **212**.

Fatimids, a dynasty of SHIITE Muslim caliphs of the ISMAILI sect who ruled first in N Africa (from 909) and then in Egypt (969–1171), where they founded Cairo as their capital. Egypt prospered greatly under their rule, though they later declined in power. The Fatimid caliphate was abolished by SALADIN, and Egypt then reverted to its allegiance to the Sunni ABBASID caliphs; ▷ p. 83.

Fawcett, Dame Millicent Garrett (1847–1929), British feminist and pioneering campaigner for women's rights in voting, careers and education; the sister of Elizabeth Garrett Anderson; ▷ p. 232.

Fawkes, Guy, ▷ GUNPOWDER PLOT.

Federal Bureau of Investigation (FBI), the chief investigative agency of the US government, established in 1908 with headquarters in Washington DC. After the appointment of J. Edgar HOOVER as director in 1924 the FBI developed as a highly professional agency with wider powers to investigate cases involving infringement of federal laws.

Federalist Party, an early US political party that evolved in the 1790s under the leadership of George WASHINGTON and Alexander HAMILTON. Conservative and Anglophile, the party lost the watershed election of 1800 to the rival Democratic-Republicans (led by Thomas JEFFERSON) and had disappeared by 1825; ⊳ p. 156.

feminism, ⊳ pp. **232–3.**

Fenian, a member of an Irish revolutionary organization founded in the USA in the 1850s to fight for independence from Britain. In Ireland it was known as the Irish Republican Brotherhood.

Ferdinand II (the Catholic; 1452–1516), king of Castile (1474–1504), king of ARAGON (as Ferdinand II; 1479–1516), king of Sicily (1468–1516) and king of NAPLES (1502–16). His marriage to ISABELLA OF CASTILE (1469) laid the foundations of a united modern Spain. He restored royal authority in Aragon after the disorders of the 15th century and used the resources of Castile to intervene in the Italian wars and in Africa; ⊳ p. 116.

Ferdinand II, (1578–1637) Holy Roman Emperor (1619–37), king of Bohemia (1617–27) and of Hungary (1618–26). A vigorous proponent of Counter-Reformation Catholicism, he crushed the revolt in BOHEMIA (1618) and restored Catholicism there. Despite early successes in the Thirty Years War, he failed to restore imperial power or to eradicate Lutheranism and Calvinism in Germany; ⊳ p. 113.

Ferdinand VII (1784–1833), king of Spain (1808–33). An arbitrary and inept ruler, his abdication at Bayonne in 1810, forced on him by Napoleon, precipitated the wars for Spanish American Independence; ⊳ p. 148.

feudal system, the social and economic system that dominated Western Europe from the 8th to the 13th centuries; ⊳ p. **98.**

Fíanna Fáil (Gaelic, 'soldiers of destiny'), an Irish political party founded by Eamon DE VALERA in 1926 with the aim of creating a united republican IRELAND entirely independent of Britain. It gained power for the first time in 1932 and has held power for long periods since then. It is one of the two most important Irish political parties, along with FINE GAEL.

fief, the estate granted to a vassal by a greater lord under the feudal system; ⊳ p. 98.

Field of the Cloth of Gold (1520), the site of a meeting in N France between HENRY VIII and FRANCIS I of France, marked by lavish entertainments and pageantry.

Fifteen, the (1715), a JACOBITE rebellion in favour of James II's son, the Old PRETENDER James Edward Stuart, which sought to exploit English and Scottish grievances regarding the Act of UNION and the new HANOVERIAN dynasty. It ended in defeat at the battle of Sheriffmuir; ⊳ p. 119.

Fiji, a republic comprising a group of islands in the SW Pacific. Fiji was settled by Melanesians and Polynesians in around 1500 BC (⊳ pp. 68 and *69*). TASMAN reached Fiji in 1643, but Europeans did not settle until the early 1800s. During a period of great unrest, Chief Cakobau, who controlled the W, requested British assistance and ceded Fiji to Britain (1874; ⊳ p. 160). Indian labourers arrived to work on sugar plantations, reducing the Fijians, who retained ownership of most of the land, to a minority (⊳ p. 218). Since independence (1970), racial tension and land disputes have brought instability. A military takeover in 1987 overthrew an Indian-led government and established a Fijian-dominated republic outside the COMMONWEALTH.

Fillmore, Millard (1800–74), US WHIG politician, thirteenth president of the USA (1850–3). He supported the COMPROMISE OF 1850 which attempted to resolve North–South antagonism on the slavery question, but failed to achieve renomination in 1852 when his party split on the same issue.

Fine Gael, (Gaelic, 'United Ireland'), an Irish political party founded in 1923 by supporters of the Anglo-Irish Treaty (which had established the Irish Free State in 1921). The Fine Gael government of 1948–51 severed the last links with Britain by declaring IRELAND to be a republic, but since then the party has held power only intermittently.

Finland, a republic of N Europe. The Swedish conquest of Finland began in the 12th century and was complete by 1634. At the Reformation most Finns became Lutheran. Russia conquered much of the area in the early 18th century and gained complete control in 1809 (⊳ p. 127). Throughout the 19th century Finland was a grand duchy ruled by the Russian tsar. Tension grew as Russia sought to strengthen its political and cultural leverage. In 1906 Finland was allowed to call its own Duma (Parliament), but repression followed again in 1910. After the Russian Revolution of 1917, civil war broke out in Finland. The pro-Russian party was defeated and an independent republican constitution (still in force today) was established (1919). Finland's territorial integrity lasted until the Soviet invasion in 1939 (⊳ p. 192), after which land was ceded to the USSR. The failure of a brief alliance with Germany led to further cession of territory to the Soviet Union in 1944. Finland has, since 1945, retained its neutrality and independence. Following the collapse of the USSR (1991), Finland renegotiated its former close relationship with Russia and applied for membership of the EC.

Finnish-Russian War (or 'Winter War'), conflict between Finland and the Soviet Union 1939–40. The Finns were forced to accept peace on Stalin's terms and to cede their E territories; ⊳ p. 192.

Fire of London, a fire that devastated London in 1666. A number of churches and public buildings – notably St Paul's Cathedral – were rebuilt after the fire by Sir Christopher Wren; ⊳ p. *118.*

First World War, ⊳ pp. **174–9.**

Fitzgerald, Garret (1926–), Irish FINE GAEL statesman and economist, prime minister (1981–2 and 1982–7).

Flanders, a region of NW Europe that is now an autonomous region of BELGIUM. The autonomous county of Flanders rose to prominence in the 10th century and became a major centre of the cloth industry in the Middle Ages (⊳ p. 99). Flanders was ruled by Burgundy (1384–1477; ⊳ p. 95, box), Spain (1477–1714), Austria (1714–90), France (1793–1814), and the Netherlands (1814–31), before becoming part of Belgium.

Flodden Field, battle of (9 September 1513), a battle between the English and Scots following the invasion of England by James V of Scotland in support of his French allies. The Scots were defeated and James killed; ⊳ p. 118

Florence, a former city-state in central Italy. It became economically and then politically predominant in the 13th century. Its alliance with France and the papacy kept it centre-stage during the late Middle Ages. Florence had a series of republican governments until coming under the rule of the MEDICI. In the early 15th century Florence was the first important focus of Humanism and the Renaissance; ⊳ pp. 93, **96–7,** 99 and 101.

Florida, the southernmost state of the USA's E coast. Colonized first by the Spanish in the 16th century, ceded to Great Britain in 1763, and returned to Spain in 1783, Florida finally passed into American hands in 1819 after a controversial campaign led by US General Andrew JACKSON; ⊳ pp. 156 and 157.

Foch, Ferdinand (1851–1929), marshal of France. His victory in the 1st battle of the MARNE (1914) saved Paris. He commanded French forces at the battle of the SOMME, and thereafter concentrated on ensuring Allied cooperation in the war. In March 1918 he was made Allied commander-in-chief, and received the German surrender at Compiègne on 1 November.

Food and Agriculture Organization (FAO), a specialized agency of the United Nations, set up in 1945 to improve the production of agricultural products worldwide, protect the welfare of rural workers and promote conservation; ⊳ pp. 229 and 231.

Ford, Gerald (1913–), thirty-eighth president of the USA (1974–7). A conservative Ohio Republican who succeeded to the presidency after the resignation of Richard NIXON, he proved a stabilizing force in the aftermath of the Watergate scandal (⊳ p. 217). He was defeated by the Democratic candidate Jimmy CARTER in 1976; ⊳ p. 209.

Ford, Henry (1863–1947), US industrialist who pioneered mass production of automobiles. He was the guiding force behind the Ford Motor Company which began production of the cheap and popular Model T in Detroit in October 1908; ⊳ p. 2.

Fort Sumter, a Federal military post in Charleston harbour, South Carolina. Its bombardment by Confederate troops in April 1861 marked the opening of the US Civil War; ⊳ pp. 158 and 159 (map).

Forty-five, the (1745–6), the last JACOBITE rebellion. JAMES II's grandson, the Young PRETENDER Charles Edward Stuart, led an army of Highland Scots into England, but was obliged to retreat to Scotland, where his forces were destroyed at CULLODEN (1746).

forum, the civic centre of a Roman town. The model was the Forum Romanum, the chief public square of Rome, which was the focus of the city's political and commercial activity from before 600 BC.

Founding Fathers, the nickname given to the 55 delegates to the Constitutional Convention of 1787 who drafted the US Constitution; ⊳ pp. 143 and 156.

Fouquet, Nicholas, marquis de Belle-Isle (1615–80), French politician. He was superintendant of finance (1653–61) under Louis XIV, who later had him imprisoned for embezzlement.

Fourteen Points, ⊳ p. **183** (box).

Fourteenth Amendment (1868), an important amendment to the US CONSTITUTION passed by CONGRESS in 1866 and ratified by the states two years later. Designed to protect black rights in the Southern states, it was the basis not only for congressional Reconstruction after the Civil War (⊳ p. 159), but also for the legal assault on segregation in the 1950s and 1960s (⊳ p. 216, box).

Foxe, John (1516–87), English clergyman and historian; ⊳ p. 2.

Fox, Charles James (1749–1806), British WHIG politician. He criticized Lord NORTH's policy towards the American colonies, opposed the Younger PITT's hostility towards the French Revolution and split with BURKE on the same issue. He was an advocate of parliamentary reform and the abolition of slavery; ⊳ p. *145.*

France, a country in Western Europe. The GAULS gradually spread over France from the E about 1500 BC. The ancient Greeks established settlements on the Mediterranean coast from the 7th century BC, and the Romans conquered Gaul from 123 BC (⊳ p. 37). After the Romans departed in the 5th century AD, Germanic tribes invaded, among whom the FRANKS became dominant (⊳ pp. 78 and 79). The Frankish Carolingians built an empire under CHARLEMAGNE, and when his realm was divided in the 9th century, the W part became the ancestor of modern France (⊳ pp. 84 and 85, map). The French nation-state was slow to emerge, however. In medieval times, a series of dynasties sought to extend their power over the area that is now France: the CAROLINGIANS (768–987), the CAPETIANS (987–1328), and the VALOIS (1328–1589). Territorial gains were repeatedly countered by invasion, while the strengthening of the monarchy did not occur without frequent dynastic crises. At the beginning of the Valois period (1328), AQUITAINE, Brittany, BURGUNDY and FLANDERS were still outside the French royal domain, but by the 16th century they had all been included in the French state. For much of the medieval period, the French kings struggled to wrest control of N and W France from the English, particularly in the Hundred Years War (▷ p. 94). By 1453, however, only Calais remained in English hands. The question of frontiers – especially in the E – continued up to the Revolution and beyond. Between the 16th and 18th centuries conflict with Britain and France's other neighbours continued, particularly over colonial possessions and over control of the Low Countries and the Rhineland. Religious conflicts worked against the consolidation of France. The 16th century was scarred by The FRENCH WARS OF RELIGION between Catholics and Protestant HUGUENOTS (▷ p. 111). The Protestant BOURBON Henry of Navarre succeeded the extinct Valois dynasty as HENRY IV. Converting to Catholicism, he granted toleration to the Huguenots, but the 17th century saw the gradual and often brutal suppression of these liberties, and the status of Protestants remained a sensitive issue until the Revolution. Provincial independence also hindered national unity, despite the efforts of the Bourbon monarchs – in particular Louis XIV and his ministers (▷ pp. 122–3) – to weaken them. By the 18th century France had achieved a high degree of centralization, and its glorification of the monarchy – typified by the palace of VERSAILLES – was impressive. However, the Bourbon state was overextended. The national assembly – the STATES-GENERAL – was unsummoned from 1614 to 1789, antagonizing the men of the Enlightenment (▷ p. 134). The Revolution of 1789 (▷ pp. 144–5) sprang from a detestation of heavy and unfair taxes and from a hatred of the economic privileges of the nobility and the Church. However, the Revolutionary regimes that followed the downfall of the monarchy took centralization further, attempting far more than they could achieve – for example, the suppression of Christianity and the implementation of dramatic cultural reforms. The Revolutionary regimes also attempted to spread their ideas throughout Europe, especially under Napoleon (▷ pp. 146–7), whose centralized empire briefly outshone the monarchy of Louis XIV. After Napoleon's defeat at WATERLOO (1815), the less powerful monarchies of the first half of the 19th century – the restored Bourbons (1815–30) and the ORLÉANIST monarchy (1830–48) – were toppled by revolt fed by popular memories of the liberties enjoyed under the Republic (▷ pp. 150–1). The coup of Louis-Napoleon (a nephew of Napoleon I) turned the Second Republic into the SECOND EMPIRE, with himself as NAPOLEON III. However, his reign (1852–70) was brought to an end by defeat in the FRANCO-PRUSSIAN WAR (1870–1; ▷ p. 153). After this defeat, the Third Republic (1871–1940) was established, and immediately faced the revolt of the Paris Commune (▷ p. 153, box). Controversy over the role of religion in the state – particularly the question of religious-based or secular education – did not end until Church and state were finally separated in 1905. At the end of the 19th century the French colonial empire reached its greatest extent, in particular in Africa, SE Asia and the Pacific (▷ p. 160). The Third Republic also saw continuing conflict over France's own boundaries – ALSACE–LORRAINE was lost in 1870 but recovered in 1918 at the end of World War I, during which trench warfare in N France claimed countless lives (▷ p. 176). In World War II (▷ p. 190), Germany rapidly defeated the French in 1940 and completely occupied the country in 1942. Marshal PÉTAIN led a collaborationist regime in the city of VICHY, while General DE GAULLE headed the

FREE FRENCH in exile in London from 1940. After the war, the Fourth Republic (1946–58) was marked by instability, the SUEZ CRISIS of 1956 (▷ p. 211), and nationalist revolts in some of the colonies, notably Vietnam (▷ p. 208) and Algeria (▷ p. 202, box). The troubles in Algeria – including the revolt of the French colonists and the campaign of their terrorist organization, the OAS – led to the end of the Fourth Republic and to the accession to power of de Gaulle in 1959. As first president of the Fifth Republic, de Gaulle granted Algeria independence (1962). While the French colonial empire – with a few minor exceptions – was being disbanded (▷ p. 203), France's position within W Europe was being strengthened, especially by vigorous participation in the EUROPEAN COMMUNITY (▷ p. 215). At the same time, de Gaulle pursued a foreign policy independent of the USA, building up France's non-nuclear armaments and withdrawing French forces from NATO's integrated command structure (▷ p. 204). Although restoring political and economic stability to France, domestic dissatisfaction – including the student revolt of May 1968 (▷ p. 215) – led de Gaulle to resign in 1969. De Gaulle's policies were broadly pursued by his successors as president, Georges POMPIDOU and Valéry GISCARD D'ESTAING. The modernization of France continued apace under the country's first Socialist president, François MITTERRAND.

Franche-Comté, a former province of E France. It was part of the duchy of BURGUNDY (1384–1477) and passed to the Spanish HABSBURGS (1493–1674). It was acquired by France in the Peace of Nijmegen (1678–9; ▷ p. 123 (box).

Franciscans, an order of mendicant friars; ▷ p. 91.

Francis I (1494–1547), king of France (1515–47). His reign was dominated by a prolonged but inconclusive struggle with the emperor CHARLES V for control of Italy. A patron of the arts and scholarship, who presided over a lavishly extravagant court, he is often seen as the archetype of the Renaissance prince; ▷ p. *118*.

Francis II, last Holy Roman Emperor (1792–1806) and first emperor of AUSTRIA (as Francis I; 1804–35). His reign marked the end of enlightened reform in favour of the repressive conservative policies of his chancellor METTERNICH.

Francis of Assissi, St (1181–1226), founder of the Franciscan order of friars; ▷ pp. *90* and 91.

Franco, Francisco (1892–1975), Spanish general and head of state (1939–75). He led the Nationalist forces against the elected Republican government in the Spanish Civil War (1936–9), emerging victorious. In 1939 he became dictator, adopted the FALANGE party and banned all political opposition. Franco maintained Spanish neutrality during World War II. He was succeeded in 1975 by King JUAN CARLOS, whom he had declared his successor; ▷ p. 189 (box).

Franco-Prussian War (1870–1), a conflict between France and Prussia, skilfully engineered by BISMARCK. French defeat at SEDAN was followed by the siege and surrender of Paris in January 1871. The French National Assembly agreed to peace with Prussia, but Parisian radical socialists refused to lay down their arms and established the rebel Commune of Paris. The war culminated in the declaration of the German SECOND EMPIRE; ▷ pp. 153 and 174.

Frankfurt, Treaty of (10 May 1871), the treaty ending the FRANCO-PRUSSIAN WAR. By its terms France ceded ALSACE and much of Lorraine to the Germans, and paid an indemnity of five billion francs.

Franklin, Benjamin (1706–90), American statesman, author and scientist. A tireless promoter of self-improvement, material values and rational

thought, he served as a Pennsylvania delegate to the CONTINENTAL CONGRESS, and helped negotiate the alliance with France during the War of Independence and the Peace of Paris with Great Britain. At the age of 81 he sat in the Constitutional Convention of 1787 (▷ p. 143).

Franks, a Germanic people originating on the lower Rhine. In the 5th century they controlled N Gaul and under Charlemagne carved out a Frankish empire. The word continued to denote a Western European of French culture (though not necessarily language) throughout the Middle Ages; ▷ pp. **78–9**, **84**, 86 and 102.

Franz Ferdinand (1863–1914), archduke of Austria and heir apparent of the Emperor FRANZ JOSEF I. His assassination at Sarajevo on 28 June 1914 was a contributory factor to the outbreak of World War I; ▷ p. 176.

Franz Josef (1830–1916), emperor of Austria (1848–1916). He succeeded to the throne following the abdication of Ferdinand I during the REVOLUTION OF 1848. His attempts to prevent the political modernization and eventual disintegration of the HABSBURG Monarchy were ultimately in vain; ▷ p. 151.

Fraser, (John) Malcolm (1930–), Australian Liberal statesman, prime minister (1975–83).

Frederick I (Barbarossa; c. 1122–1190), king in Germany from 1152, crowned emperor at Rome in 1155. Initially Italy was his prime concern, and this led to conflict with both the papacy and the towns of Lombardy. However, after 1177 he successfully strengthened royal power in Germany. He drowned while crossing a river during the Third Crusade; ▷ pp. **85** and 88 (box).

Frederick II (1194–1250), Holy Roman Emperor (1220–50). He inherited the kingdom of Sicily while still a child, and was crowned king in Germany in 1215 and emperor at Rome in 1220. His marriage (1225) to the heiress to Jerusalem added the Crusader kingdom to his dominions. His attempts to strengthen his authority in Italy led to bitter quarrels with the papacy; ▷ p. 85.

Frederick II (the Great; 1712–86), king of Prussia (1740–86), the son of FREDERICK WILLIAM I; ▷ p. 125.

Frederick William (1620–88), known as the 'Great Elector', HOHENZOLLERN elector of Brandenburg (1640–80); ▷ p. 125.

Frederick William I (1688–1740), king of Prussia (1713–40). The son of Frederick I of Prussia (reigned 1701–13), his reforms established a disciplined and efficient Prussian army and administration; ▷ p. 125

Frederick William IV (1795–1861), king of Prussia (1840–61). He was succeeded by WILHELM I; ▷ p. 151.

Free French, an organization of French exiles in World War II, led by DE GAULLE. Based in London, it continued the war against the Axis Powers after the surrender of France in 1940.

free trade, an economic doctrine advocated by the economist Adam SMITH (1723–90), who argued for a system of international trade without the imposition of tariffs and import quotas by governments. British free-trade landmarks were Huskisson's reduction of tariffs in the 1820s, PEEL'S repeal of the CORN LAWS in 1846 and GLADSTONE'S virtual removal of tariffs by 1860. Free trade was not abandoned in Britain until 1932, with the introduction of 'imperial preference' for the DOMINIONS and a general tariff; ▷ p. 185.

French and Indian Wars (1689–1763), the struggle between Britain and France for colonial supremacy in North America, the final stage of which (1755–63) formed part of the SEVEN YEARS WAR. Naval superiority and an alliance with PRUSSIA gave the English the advantage in terms of supplies and reinforcements. WOLFE'S victory at the Plains of

Abraham led to the surrender of QUÉBEC (1759), and the expulsion of the French from Canada a year later. Britain acquired Canada and LOUISIANA E of the Mississippi in the Treaty of Paris (1763) (⊳ pp. 73 and 129).

French East India Company, a company chartered by Louis XIV in 1664 to compete with the DUTCH and English EAST INDIA COMPANIES. Under Dupleix (governor-general; 1742–54) it attempted to challenge growing British influence in India, but was dissolved after defeat at the hands of Robert CLIVE; ⊳ p. 128.

French Equatorial Africa, a former confederation of French colonies in W central Africa, comprising present-day CHAD, GABON, CONGO and the CENTRAL AFRICAN REPUBLIC.

French Indochina, the former French empire in SE Asia, comprising the protectorates of CAMBODIA, LAOS and ANNAM and the colonies of COCHIN CHINA and Tonkin, all of which were colonized between the late 1850s and 1890s. After a protracted war with the VIET MINH, the French withdrew from Cambodia, Laos and Vietnam in 1954; ⊳ p. 208.

French Indochina War (1946–54), a war fought between French colonial forces and nationalists in VIETNAM, LAOS and CAMBODIA. The war was formally ended by the Geneva Conference in 1954, as was French rule in Indochina; ⊳ p. 208.

French, John Denston Pinkstone, 1st Earl of Ypres (1852–1925), British field marshal and commander of the British Expeditionary Force (1914–15). The BEF sustained heavy losses at the battles of Mons and 1st YPRES, and French was recalled in autumn 1915 to be replaced by HAIG.

French Revolution, ⊳ pp. 5 (box), 123, 131, 135, **144–5,** 146 and 150.

French Wars of Religion (1559–98), a series of religious and political conflicts in France. The clash between Protestant HUGUENOTS and Catholics was caught up in the struggle of noble factions for control of the declining VALOIS dynasty. A more tolerant Catholic tendency emerged after the ST BARTHOLEMEW'S DAY MASSACRE, but from 1576 it was opposed by the extremist Catholic HOLY LEAGUE, led by Henry of GUISE, which was hostile to the conciliatory policies of HENRY III. The League's opposition to the succession of the BOURBON Henry of Navarre – who became heir to the throne in 1584, led to the so-called 'War of the Three Henrys'. After Henry III's assassination in 1589, Henry of Navarre defeated the League and its Spanish allies. As HENRY IV he converted to Catholicism (1593) and established a tolerant religious settlement with the EDICT OF NANTES (1598); ⊳ pp. *110* and *111.*

French West Africa, a former confederation of French territories in W Africa, dissolved in 1959. It comprised present-day BENIN, BURKINA FASO, GUINEA, the CÔTE D'IVOIRE, MALI, MAURITANIA, NIGER and SENEGAL; ⊳ p. 163 (map).

friar, a member of a mendicant order of the Roman Catholic Church; ⊳ p. 91.

friendly society, an association of working men who came together to provide mutual insurance to meet costs of burial or illness. They grew steadily under the patronage of benevolent gentry and, from the 1830s, under the supervision of the state; ⊳ p. 166.

Frisians, a Germanic people from what is now the Netherlands and NW Germany. They were absorbed by the FRANKS c. 800; ⊳ pp. 78 (map) and 79 (box).

Froissart, Jean (c. 1337–c. 1405), French chronicler of the Hundred Years War and of medieval society in general; ⊳ pp. 2, *94* and *103.*

Frondes, (1648–53), two revolts in France during the minority of Louis XIV, primarily a reaction by privileged officials against MAZARIN's measures to finance France's war against Spain, and of nobles resentful of his monopoly of government; ⊳ p. 122.

Front de Libération Nationale (FLN), a radical Muslim independence movement formed in Algeria in 1954, led by BEN BELLA; ⊳ p. 202 (box).

Fuchs, Klaus (1911–88), German-born British nuclear physicist. He passed nuclear secrets to the Soviet Union from 1943; ⊳ p. 207 (box).

Fujiwara, a Japanese noble family, dominant from the late 9th to the late 12th centuries; ⊳ p. 64.

Fulani, nomads of the W African Sahel, originating in the far W, who spread E in the 14th–16th centuries. Strongly influenced by Islam, they undertook JIHADS to establish powerful Muslim states in Senegal and N Nigeria in the 18th and 19th centuries.

Funan, a former state in Cambodia; ⊳ p. 60.

Gabon, a republic of W central Africa. The slave trade developed after the Portuguese arrived in the late 15th century. The French colonized Gabon in the late 19th century. Pro-French Léon M'Ba (1902–67) led the country to independence in 1960 (⊳ p. 202, map). Deposed in a coup (1964), he was restored to power by French troops. Under his successor, Albert-Bernard Bongo, Gabon has continued its pro-Western policies.

Gaiseric (Genseric; 390–477), king of the VANDALS (428–477); ⊳ p. 78.

Gaitskill, Hugh Todd Naylor (1906–63), leader of the British LABOUR Party (1955–63). On the right wing of his party, he clashed with the left over unilateral nuclear disarmament. After his unexpected death he was replaced by Harold WILSON.

Galatia, a region of central Asia Minor (Turkey) inhabited by Celts who migrated there in the 3rd century BC. In AD 25 it became a Roman province; ⊳ p. 37 (map).

Galileo Galilei (1564–1642), Italian mathematician, astronomer and physicist; ⊳ p. **132.**

galleon, a four-masted ship of the late 16th century, probably of Spanish origin. The bulk of the ships of the SPANISH ARMADA were of this type – tall ocean-going vessels capable of mounting a heavy artillery and large numbers of soldiers; ⊳ p. 103.

galley, an ancient warship propelled by oars. Ancient Greek ships (triremes; ⊳ p. 44) were usually manned by free citizens, and those of Carthage by mercenaries; only in the Roman Empire did galley slaves appear, but they were used less widely than is popularly believed. Galleys continued to be the principal type of warship in the Mediterranean until the end of the 16th century; ⊳ p. *117.*

Gallic Wars, ⊳ GAUL.

Gallipoli campaign (1915–16), an abortive attempt by the Allies to seize the DARDANELLES during World War I, with the aim of forcing Turkey out of the war and opening a sea route to Russia. After the failure of a naval expedition in February 1915, a military expedition was sent to the Gallipoli Peninsula in April. It too proved a costly debacle, with ANZAC and British troops sustaining heavy losses; ⊳ p. 177.

Gambia, a republic of W Africa (⊳ p. 202, map). Once part of the Mali empire, the area became involved in the slave trade following the arrival of the Portuguese in the mid-15th century. British traders later supplanted the Portuguese, and a British colony was established in 1843. The Gambia achieved independence in 1965 under Sir Dawda K. Jawara. In 1981 an attempted coup against his rule encouraged efforts to merge with the neighbouring French-speaking country of SENEGAL, but the confederation was dissolved in 1989. The Gambia remains a democracy.

Gandhi, Indira (1917–84), Indian prime minister (1966–77 and 1980–4). The only daughter of Jawaharlal NEHRU, she joined the Indian National CONGRESS and the Indian struggle for independence when still a schoolgirl. She succeeded Lal Bahadur SHASTRI as prime minister in 1964. Her finest hour was the liberation of BANGLADESH in 1971; her worst when she declared a state of emergency and ruled autocratically (1975–7). She was assassinated by her SIKH bodyguards following her decision to storm the Sikh Golden Temple in Amritsar. Her son Rajiv (1944–91), succeeded her as prime minister (1984–9). He looked set to return to power in the 1991 general election but he was assassinated during the campaign; ⊳ INDIA.

Gandhi, Mohandas Karamchand (1869–1948), Indian religious and political leader, known as Mahatma ('Great Soul'). He played a major role in the Indian struggle against British rule, and was imprisoned on a number of occasions for civil disobedience. In his capacity as President of the Indian National CONGRESS from 1928 – he helped negotiate Indian independence in 1947. He was assassinated by a Hindu extremist on 30 January 1948. Gandhi favoured 'non-cooperation', nonviolent resistance (*satyagraha*) and hunger strikes as means of achieving reform, campaigned for the rights of 'untouchables' and tried to unite Hindus and Muslims; ⊳ p. 201 (box).

'Gang of Four', a group of radical Chinese politicians, including MAO ZEDONG's widow, Jiang Qing, who allegedly plotted to seize power on Mao's death in 1976. Arrested and put on trial, the group was found guilty of plotting against the state in 1980.

Garfield, James Abram (1831–81), twentieth president of the USA (1881). A Republican, he was assassinated within months of taking office.

Garibaldi, Giuseppe (1807–82), Italian nationalist and hero of the wars for the unification of Italy; ⊳ p. **152.**

GATT, ⊳ GENERAL AGREEMENT ON TARIFFS AND TRADE.

Gaugamela, battle of (332 BC), Alexander the Great's final victory over the Persians, near the Tigris; ⊳ p. 32.

Gaul, the area covered by modern France and Belgium and extending to the W bank of the Rhine, inhabited in ancient times by Celtic tribes. The S of France became a Roman province in 121 BC; the rest was conquered by Caesar in the Gallic Wars (58–51 BC). Gaul was sometimes referred to as 'Transalpine Gaul', and the area between the Alps and the Apennines (conquered by the Romans in 201–191 BC) as 'Cisalpine Gaul'; ⊳ pp. 37 and 45 (box).

Gaunt, John of (1340–99), duke of Lancaster, and a powerful figure during the reigns of his father EDWARD III and his nephew RICHARD II. Through his first wife Blanche he acquired the Lancaster estates. His third wife was Katherine Swynford, mother of the BEAUFORTS.

Gaveston, Piers (c. 1284–1312), ⊳ EDWARD II.

Gaza, a city and territory – the Gaza Strip – on the Mediterranean coast of SW Asia. Part of PALESTINE, Gaza was occupied by Egypt when the state of Israel was established (1948), and taken by Israel in 1967; ⊳ pp. 211 (map) and 213.

General Agreement on Tariffs and Trade (GATT), an international trade agreement established by the United Nations in 1948, aiming to promote international trade by removing trade barriers, lowering tariffs, and by providing a forum for discussion of trade relations; ⊳ p. 229.

General Assembly of the United Nations, the assembly composed of all member-states of the United Nations; ⊳ pp. 228–9.

General Strike, a strike called by the British TRADES UNION CONGRESS on 5 May 1926 in support of the coalminers, who were threatened with longer hours and lower wages. The strike lasted nine days, during which the government gradually assumed control of key sectors of the economy to ensure food supplies and transport.

Geneva Conference (July 1954), a conference held in Switzerland to negotiate the end of the French Indochina and Korean Wars. It granted independence to LAOS, CAMBODIA and VIETNAM, partitioning the latter; ▷ p. 208.

Geneva Conventions, a series of agreements signed by many countries between 1864 and 1940, providing for the humane treatment of the victims of warfare.

Genghis Khan (c. 1162–1227), the founder of the Mongol Empire; ▷ pp. **54**, 55 and 83.

Genoa, a port in NW Italy. An independent republic from the 10th century, by the 13th century it controlled much of the W Mediterranean trade and some in the E Mediterranean (where it engaged in prolonged rivalry with VENICE). Politically Genoa was unstable, and repeatedly came under outside rule; ▷ pp. 85 (map), 96, 97 (box), 113 (map) and 123 (map).

George I (1660–1727), first Hanoverian king of Great Britain and Ireland (1714–27), elector of HANOVER (1698–1727). Never at home in England and always more interested in Hanover, he was content to give his support to WALPOLE, and thereby contributed to the rise to power of the WHIGS; ▷ p. 119.

George II (1683–1760), king of Great Britain and Ireland and elector of HANOVER (1727–60). The son of GEORGE I, he supported MARIA THERESA in the War of the Austrian Succession. The later part of his reign was marked by British victories in Canada, the Caribbean and India during the SEVEN YEARS WAR.

George III (1738–1820), king of Great Britain and Ireland, (1760–1820) and of HANOVER (1815–20). The grandson of GEORGE II, 'Farmer George' opposed the demands of the American colonists for independence but saw the American colonies lost during his reign. He became insane in 1811, after which his son, later GEORGE IV, acted as regent; ▷ p. 142.

George IV (1762–1830), king of Great Britain and Ireland, and of Hanover (1820–30). The eldest son of GEORGE III, he formed a close association with the WHIG opposition in the 1780s. As regent (1811–20) and as king his dissolute lifestyle undermined the prestige of the crown. A leader of taste and fashion, he gave his name to the REGENCY period.

George V (1865–1936), king of Great Britain and Ireland and emperor of India (1910–36), second son of EDWARD VII. Crises relating to Irish HOME RULE and reform of the House of LORDS, followed closely by World War I, forced him to adapt to fast-changing circumstances. He was succeeded by EDWARD VIII.

George VI (1895–1952), king of Great Britain and Northern Ireland, (1936–52), emperor of India (1936–47). The second son of GEORGE V, succeeding to the throne on the abdication of his brother EDWARD VIII, he is chiefly remembered for helping to sustain public morale during the BLITZ. He was succeeded by his elder daughter, ELIZABETH II.

Georgia, a republic in the Caucasus Mountains of W Asia. Georgian states flourished in the 1st millennium BC, but many fell to the Greeks before being ruled by PONTUS and then Rome from 65 BC. Christianity was adopted c. AD 330. From the 4th to the 7th centuries Georgia was fought over by the Byzantine Empire, the Persians and, later, the Arabs. In the 8th century the Bagratid family established several Georgian kingdoms, and Bagrat II (975–1014) reunited Georgia. His descendants established an empire that included most of the Caucasus region, but from 1220 national unity was destroyed by Mongol invasions and dynastic quarrels. From the 16th to the 18th

centuries Georgia was disputed and overrun by the Ottoman Turks and the Persians. An independent Georgia was reunited in 1762. Russia deposed the Bagratids in 1801, and gradually annexed Georgia (1801–78). Following the Russian Revolution (1918), a Georgian republic was proclaimed, but was invaded by the Soviet Red Army in 1921. It became part of the Transcaucasian Soviet Republic in 1921 and a separate Union Republic within the USSR in 1936. Independence was declared following the abortive coup in Moscow by Communist hardliners (September 1991; ▷ p. 225). Locked into a fierce civil war, Georgia remained outside the Commonwealth of Independent States (▷ p. 225, box). A temporary state council – led by Eduard SHEVARDNADZE – replaced a military council in March 1992.

Georgia, one of the 13 original states of the USA. founded as a colony in 1732; ▷ pp. 156 (map) and 159 (map).

German Confederation (1815–66), an alliance of 39 German states formed at the Congress of VIENNA. Ambassadors of member-states met regularly at the Federal DIET in Frankfurt. The confederation was conceived by the Austrian chancellor METTERNICH.

Germany, a country of Central Europe. Germany has only been unified between 1871 and 1945, and since 1990. However, although for most of their history the German people were divided between a considerable number of states, they played a key role in Europe. Germanic peoples – who displaced Celts in what was to become Germany – helped to destroy the Western Roman Empire (▷ p. 78). Most of the German lands were united under the Frankish Empire, but after the death of CHARLEMAGNE in 814 the inheritance was divided. The Saxon kings – in particular OTTO I – unsuccessfully attempted to reunite the Germans, although most of Germany was nominally within the Holy Roman Empire (▷ p. 84). In the 12th and 13th centuries, the HOHENSTAUFEN Holy Roman Emperors tried to make their mark in Italy as well as N of the Alps (▷ p. 96). This diversion allowed dozens of German princes, dukes, bishops and counts to assert their independence. Their small states formed an astonishing jigsaw on the map of Europe until the 19th century. In 1648 there were no fewer than 343 German states. The HABSBURGS – Emperors for almost the entire period from 1437 to 1806 – were often so concerned with the fortunes of their territories in AUSTRIA, HUNGARY and BOHEMIA, that they were unable to control the subordinate electorates, principalities and bishoprics. The independence of local rulers was reinforced in the 16th century when a number of princes followed the lead of the Protestant reformer Martin Luther (▷ p. 110). The Peace of AUGSBURG (1555) established the principle that a state's religion followed that of its prince. This was soon challenged by both Lutherans and Catholics, and became one of many factors contributing to the Thirty Years War (1618–48; ▷ p. 113). During the 18th century, some small German states – notably Saxe-Weimar under Duke Charles Augustus – became centres of enlightened government and culture (▷ p. 134). Other small territories became involved in the power politics of the major states. For example, after the accession of the elector of HANOVER to the British throne in 1714 as GEORGE I (▷ p. 119), the British sovereign continued to be ruler of Hanover until 1837. The contribution of the small states was, however, overshadowed by the rise of BRANDENBURG-PRUSSIA, under the uncompromising leadership of the HOHENZOLLERN family of electors (kings after 1701). Frederick William, the Great Elector (ruled 1640–88) laid the foundations of Prussia's power. King Frederick William I (ruled 1713–40) expanded the army and did much to give Prussia its military nature, while Frederick II, the Great, (ruled 1740–86) greatly enlarged his kingdom at the

expense of Austria and Poland (▷ pp. 124–5). By the 18th century, Prussia was vying for supremacy in Germany with the Austrian-based Empire. During the NAPOLEONIC WARS (▷ p. 146), France redrew the map of Germany, merging and annexing many territories, establishing new client states, and founding the CONFEDERATION OF THE RHINE. The Napoleonic period saw the upsurge of romantically inspired German nationalist sentiment (▷ p. 150). After the Napoleonic Wars, a GERMAN CONFEDERATION, initially composed of 39 states, was established. Although the Confederation contained important ancient states such as BAVARIA, HANOVER, SAXONY, WÜRTTEMBERG, HESSE, OLDENBURG, BADEN and MECKLENBURG, none could match Prussia or Austria in size or influence. The Confederation did not satisfy the longings of the German people for unity. In 1830, and again in 1848, liberal nationalist movements swept Germany, extracting short-lived liberal constitutions from autocratic princes (▷ p. 151). (For details of German unification; ▷ pp. 152–3). In 1871, a German Empire – of four kingdoms, six grand duchies, five duchies and seven principalities – was proclaimed by the king of Prussia as emperor of Germany (Kaiser). From 1871 to 1918, an expansionist unified Germany attempted to extend its influence throughout Europe, engaged in naval and commercial rivalry with Britain (▷ p. 175), and built a colonial empire (▷ pp. 160 and 163, map). Under the mercurial Emperor WILLIAM II, Germany was a destabilizing force in world politics. Defeat in World War I (1914–18; ▷ pp. 176–9) led to the loss of much territory in Europe (▷ p. 182, map) and the colonies overseas, the end of the German monarchies, the imposition of a substantial reparations and the occupation of the RHINELAND by Allied forces until 1930 (▷ pp. 182–3). The liberal Weimar Republic (1919–33; ▷ p. 186, box) could not bring economic or political stability. In the early 1930s the NAZI Party gained popularity (▷ pp. 186–7), urging the establishment of a strong centralized government, an aggressive foreign policy, 'Germanic character' and the overturn of the postwar settlement, (▷ pp. 188–9). In 1933, Adolf Hitler became chancellor and in 1934 president. His THIRD REICH annexed Austria in 1938 and dismembered Czechoslovakia in 1939 (▷ p. 188) and embarked on the extermination of the Jews and others that the Nazis regarded as 'inferior' (▷ p. 192, box). Invading Poland (1939), he launched Germany into war, defeat, occupation and division (▷ pp. 190–3). In 1945, Germany lost substantial territories to Poland and was divided into four zones of occupation by the Allies – Britain, France, the USA and the USSR (▷ p. 204). Their intention was a united, disarmed Germany, but cooperation between the Allies rapidly broke down, and in 1948–9 the USSR blockaded West Berlin (▷ p. 205). The W zones of Germany were merged economically in 1948. After the merger of the W to form the Federal Republic of (West) Germany, the German Democratic Republic (East Germany) was proclaimed in the Soviet zone (October 1949). The GDR's economic progress suffered by comparison with that of the Federal Republic. Food shortages and repressive Communist rule led to an abortive uprising in the GDR in 1953. West Germany gained sovereignty – as a member of the Western Alliance – in 1955. The division of Germany was only grudgingly accepted in West Germany. Chancellor Konrad ADENAUER refused to recognize East Germany as a separate state and relations with the Soviet Union remained uncertain. Major problems with the Eastern bloc included the undefined status of the areas taken over by Poland in 1945 and the difficult position of West Berlin – a part of the Federal Republic isolated within Communist East Germany. Relations between East and West Germany were soured as large numbers of East Germans fled to the West, and this outflow was stemmed only when the East German leader ULBRICHT ordered the building of the Berlin Wall (▷ p. 206, box). Adenauer strove to gain the acceptance of West Germany back into Western Europe through reconciliation with France and participation in the EUROPEAN COMMUNITY. The economic revival of Germany begun by Adenauer continued throughout the 1960s under his CHRISTIAN DEMOCRAT successors as chancellor – Ludwig ERHARD and Georg KIESINGER. Under SOCIAL DEMOCRAT chancellors in the 1970s – Willy BRANDT and Helmut SCHMIDT – treaties were signed with the USSR (1970) and Poland (recognizing the ODER-NEISSE LINE as Poland's W frontier), and relations with the GDR were normalized (1972). Under Helmut KOHL (chancellor from 1982) West Germany continued its impressive economic growth and enthusiastic membership of the EC. In the late 1980s, West Germany acted as an economic and cultural magnet for much of Eastern Europe. The root causes of the GDR's problems remained, however, and resurfaced in the late 1980s. The ageing Communist leadership led by Erich HONECKER proved unresponsive to the mood of greater freedom emanating from Gorbachov's USSR (▷ p. 224). In 1989 fresh floods of East Germans left the GDR for the West by way of Czechoslovakia and Hungary. Massive public demonstrations in favour of reform resulted in a change of leadership and the opening of the Berlin Wall (November 1989), allowing free movement between East and West Germany. Demonstrations in favour of more radical change continued, and a coalition government, including members of opposition groups, was appointed in the GDR. When the East German economy collapsed, West Germany proposed the monetary union of the two countries, and the call for German reunification became unstoppable. Despite the initial opposition of the USSR, the reunification of Germany as a full member of the EC and NATO took place in October 1990.

Geronimo (c. 1829–1909), APACHE Indian chief who led resistance to white settlement of Arizona.

Gestapo (German, *Geheime Staatspolizei*), Nazi Germany's secret state police, headed by HIMMLER, and notorious for its ruthless methods; ▷ p. 187.

Gettysburg, battle of (1–3 July 1863), a decisive battle of the American Civil War; ▷ pp. *158* and 159 (map).

Ghali, Boutros Boutros (1922–), Egyptian statesman, Secretary-General of the United Nations (1992–); ▷ p. 229 (box)

Ghana, a republic in W Africa. Trade for gold, ivory and slaves led to the establishment of European coastal stations from around 1600 (▷ p. 128, map). Britain ousted the Danes (1850) and the Dutch (1872) to establish the Gold Coast colony in 1874. The great inland kingdom of ASHANTI was not finally conquered until 1898. After World War II, the prosperity of the cocoa industry, increasing literacy and the dynamism of Dr Kwame NKRUMAH, helped the Gold Coast set the pace for decolonization in Black Africa. After independence in 1957 – as Ghana (▷ p. 202, map) – Nkrumah's grandiose policies and increasingly dictatorial rule led to his overthrow in a military coup in 1966. Ghana has since struggled to overcome its economic and political problems. There were six coups in 20 years, including two by Flight Lieutenant Jerry Rawlings (1979 and 1982).

Ghana, kingdom of, a former African kingdom located in modern MALI; ▷ pp. 66 (map) and 67.

Ghent, Treaty of (1814), the treaty ending the War of 1812 between Britain and the USA; ▷ p. 156.

Ghibelline, the pro-imperial faction in Italian politics from the mid-13th century; ▷ p. 96.

Ghurid, a Muslim dynasty ruling in Afghanistan. It established Muslim rule over large parts of N India in the late 12th century; ▷ p. 62.

Gibbon, Edward (1737–94), English historian; ▷ pp. 3 and 41.

Gibraltar, a rocky peninsula on the S coast of Spain, commanding the entrance to the Mediterranean from the Atlantic. Ruled by Britain since the Treaty of UTRECHT in 1714, it is claimed by Spain as Spanish sovereign territory; ▷ p. 123 (map).

Gierek, Edward (1913–), Polish statesman, First Secretary of the Communist Party and de facto ruler of POLAND (1970–80).

'Gilded Age', a term used to describe the decade following the American Civil War, characterized by economic expansion, unrestricted speculation and financial and political corruption; ▷ p. 157.

Girondin, a member of a party of moderate republicans during the French Revolution; ▷ p. 145.

Giscard d'Estaing, Valery (1926–), French independent republican statesman, president of France (1974–81). He was defeated by MITTERRAND in his bid for re-election in 1981.

gladiators, ▷ p. 41 (box).

Gladstone, William Ewart (1809–98), British Liberal statesman, prime minister (1868–74, 1880–5, 1886 and 1892–4). He was a Peelite TORY until 1865, serving as Chancellor of the Exchequer (1852–5, 1859–65, 1865–6) under ABERDEEN, PALMERSTON and RUSSELL. In 1867 he succeeded Russell as leader of the LIBERAL Party. Gladstone's first and second premierships were notable for important reform legislation, but his third (1886) was dominated by an unsuccessful bid for Irish HOME RULE which split the Liberals. His last term saw the passage of a Home Rule Bill through the Commons (1893), but he resigned when it was defeated in the Lords.

glasnost (Russian 'openness'), the policy of greater freedom of discussion introduced by Gorbachov in the Soviet Union from 1985; ▷ pp. 224–5.

Glencoe, Massacre of (1692), the murder by English troops and members of the Campbell clan of members of the Catholic MacDonald clan in the Scottish Highlands, following the Macdonald chief's failure to meet a deadline for declaring his loyalty to WILLIAM III and MARY II.

Glendower, Owen (Owain Glyndŵr; c. 1355–c. 1417), self-styled Prince of Wales whose rebellion against HENRY IV, although unsuccessful, made him a national hero in Wales.

Glorious Revolution, the political events in England in 1688–9, which replaced JAMES II with WILLIAM III and MARY II as joint monarchs, and increased the role in government of the English Parliament; ▷ p. 119.

Gnosticism, a religious movement within the early Christian Church, probably with pre-Christian roots. It emphasized esoteric spiritual truths, the knowledge of which could lead to a freeing of the spirit from the body. It came to be regarded as a heresy. Its sects included MANICHAEISM.

Goa, a former Portuguese colony in India. Captured by Afonso de ALBUQUERQUE in 1510, it became the administrative centre of Portugal's East Indian empire.

Godfrey of Bouillon (c. 1060–1100), a prominent leader of the First Crusade; ▷ p. 88.

Goebbels, Josef (1897–1945), German Nazi politician. From 1933 to 1945 he was Hitler's Minister of Enlightenment and Propaganda, and his control of the press, radio and cinema contributed enormously to the establishment of the totalitarian Nazi state. He committed suicide with his family in Hitler's bunker in 1945.

Goering, Hermann (1893–1945), German Nazi politician. He founded the GESTAPO, and as commander of the German air force built up the Luftwaffe into a formidable fighting force. He was named Hitler's deputy in the early stages of World War II, but lost influence after defeat in the battle of BRITAIN. He was sentenced to death for war crimes at the NUREMBERG TRIALS, but committed suicide in prison.

Golan Heights, a region of SW Syria that was occupied by Israel in 1967. Israel's annexation of the Golan Heights (1981) is not recognized internationally; ▷ pp. 211 (map) and 212.

Golden Horde, the W part of the Mongol Empire; ▷ pp. 54 (map) and 55.

gold rushes, the name given to historic movements of prospectors into recently discovered gold fields. The most famous gold rushes took place in the 19th century: California 1848, Australia 1851–3, Witwatersrand (South Africa) 1884, and Klondike (Canada) 1897–8.

gold standard, a monetary system in which a country's unit of currency was defined in terms of a fixed amount of gold. By 1900 most major countries had adopted it, but could not maintain it during World War I, because of difficulties in the international movement of gold. Britain returned to the gold standard in 1925, abandoning it again in 1931 because of the Depression; ▷ p. 220.

Gomulka, Wladyslaw (1905–82), Polish statesman, First Secretary of the Communist Party and de facto ruler of POLAND (1956–70).

Gonzalez, Felipe (1942–), Spanish socialist statesman. As prime minister (1982–) he dismantled the last remnants of FRANCO'S system, took Spain into the EC and modernized the economy.

Gorbachov, Mikhail Sergeyevich (1931–), Soviet statesman, general secretary of the Communist Party (1985–91), president of the Soviet Union (1989–91); ▷ pp. 207, **224–5**, 227 and *228*.

Gordon, Charles George (1833–85), British soldier and colonial administrator. His defence of Shanghai against the TAIPING rebels earned him the name 'Chinese Gordon'. In 1884 he was sent by the British government to help evacuate Egyptian forces from Khartoum, which was threatened by the MAHDI, but was killed only days before the relief of the city from a ten-month siege; ▷ pp. 161 (box) and 162 (box).

Goths, the Germanic people who invaded large parts of the Western Roman Empire from the 3rd to the 5th centuries. The eastern Goths were known as the OSTROGOTHS, while the western group were known as the VISIGOTHS; ▷ pp. 40 and 78–9.

Gowon, Yakubu (1934–), ▷ NIGERIA.

Gracchus, Tiberius (c. 168–133 BC) and **Gaius** (c. 159–121) (often collectively known as the Gracchi), Roman politicians; ▷ p. 37.

Granada, the last Muslim state in Spain; ▷ pp. 83 (box), 89.

Granicus, battle of the River (334 BC), a victory of Alexander the Great over the Persians; ▷ p. 32.

Grant, Ulysses S. (1822–85), US soldier and eighteenth president of the USA (1869–77). He rose quickly through Union army ranks to assume supreme command of federal operations during the American Civil War. An obvious choice for president in 1868, he served two terms as a Republican; ▷ p. 159

Gravettian culture, a phase of the Upper Palaeolithic period of Eurasian prehistory, named after a cave in the Dordogne, France; ▷ p. 14 (box).

Great Exhibition (1851), an exhibition of industrial products from Britain and the continent, planned and opened by Prince Albert. Held in Joseph Paxton's specially constructed Crystal Palace in Hyde Park, London, it marked the apogee of Britain's supremacy as an urban-industrial, free-trade nation.

Great Leap Forward (1958–9), a programme of industrial and agricultural expansion launched in Communist China; ▷ p. 197.

Great Plague (1664–5), the last of the great bubonic plagues to hit England; it killed about 70 000 people in London alone; ▷ p. *119*.

Great Schism (1378–1417), a period during which rival popes claimed the papacy; ▷ p. **90**.

Great Trek, the northward migration of Afrikaner VOORTREKKERS away from British-administered Cape Colony in the 1830s; ▷ pp. 163 (box) and 220.

Great Wall of China, a series of defensive structures designed to protect China from attack by Central Asian nomads; ▷ pp. 52, *53* and 56.

Greece, a country of SE Europe. The Bronze Age Minoan civilization (c. 2200–1450 BC) was based in Crete (▷ p. 24), while the slightly later Mycenaean civilization (c. 1500–1150 BC; ▷ p. 25) flourished on the Greek mainland. Following a 'dark age', city-states began to emerge in the 8th century BC. (For the history of Archaic and Classical Greece c. 800–338 BC; ▷ pp. 28–31). In the 4th century BC the city-states declined and were conquered by the Macedonians who, under Alexander the Great, spread Hellenistic culture throughout the Middle East (▷ pp. 32–3). From 146 BC Greece formed part of the Roman Empire (▷ pp. 38–41). On the division of the Roman Empire, Greece formed part of the Eastern (Byzantine) Empire based in Constantinople (▷ pp. 80–1). Most of Greece remained under Byzantine rule until 1204, when the Crusaders took Constantinople (▷ p. 89). From 1204 to the 15th century Greece was divided into four states – the Greek kingdoms of Salonika and Epirus in the N, and the Frankish monarchies of Athens and Achaea in the S (▷ p. 85, map). VENICE gained the majority of the Greek islands. From the early 15th century, the Ottoman Turks gradually asserted control over the region (▷ pp. 114–15). However, the continuing vitality of the ORTHODOX CHURCH helped maintain a strong Greek national identity. As early as 1480 there was some resistance to Ottoman rule by klephts (rural bandits). In the 18th century, various European powers, especially Russia, sought to use the Greeks in their quarrels with the Turks. The outbreak of revolution against Ottoman rule in 1821 attracted support throughout Europe. The leaders of the Greek state established in 1830 (▷ pp. 151 and 154) brought Western European constitutional institutions to Greece, but the monarchy established under a Bavarian prince in 1832 was swept away by revolution in 1862. Under a Danish prince – who became King George I in 1863 – Greece gained extra territory in 1863, 1881 and 1913, as Turkish power declined. The 20th century has been marked by great instability. Eleuthérios Venizélos dominated Greek politics from 1910 to 1935, a period of rivalry between republicans and royalists. An attempt by his rival King Constantine I to seize Anatolia from Turkey (1921–2; ▷ pp. 182–3) ended in military defeat and the establishment of a republic in 1924. The monarchy was restored in 1935, but it depended upon a military leader, General Ioannis Metaxas (1871–1941) who, claiming the threat from Communism as justification, ruled as virtual dictator. The nation was deeply divided. The German invasion of 1941 was met by rival resistance groups of Communists and monarchists, and the subsequent civil war between these factions lasted from 1945 to 1949, when, with British and US aid, the monarchists emerged victorious. Continued instability in the 1960s led to a military coup in 1967. King Constantine II, who had not initially opposed the coup, unsuccessfully appealed for the overthrow of the junta and went into exile. The dictatorship of the colonels ended in 1974 when their encouragement of a Greek Cypriot coup (▷ CYPRUS) brought Greece to the verge of war with TURKEY. Civilian government was restored, and a new republican constitution was adopted in 1975.

Greek–Persian Wars, ▷ PERSIAN WARS.

Greek War of Independence (1821–32), the revolt of the Greeks against Ottoman rule, resulting in Greek independence; ▷ pp. 150 and 154.

Greenland, an island mostly within the Arctic Circle, first settled by INUIT by the 10th century AD. It was colonized by Norse from Iceland, Norway and the British Isles in the 980s. Worsening climate conditions after 1200 and the effects of the Black Death led to the abandonment of the Norse settlements by c. 1500. Resettled by Danes from the 1720s, it is now an autonomous dependency of DENMARK; ▷ pp. 72 and 86.

Greens, the name used by a number of political parties dedicated to environmental protection and opposed to nuclear power. 'Green' parties have enjoyed some electoral success in Europe, especially in West Germany in the 1980s.

Gregorian Reform, the period of reform in the Roman Catholic Church instigated by pope GREGORY VII in the late 11th century; ▷ pp. 84 and 90.

Gregory I, St (the Great; 540–604), the first monk to occupy the position of pope (590–604). A successful administrator, monastic founder and theologian, he helped to defend Rome against the invading LOMBARDS and to relieve social distress caused by floods and famine. His work laid the foundations for the future PAPAL STATE. He also encouraged missionary activity, including AUGUSTINE'S mission to England; ▷ p. 90.

Gregory VII (Hildebrand; c. 1021–85), pope (1073–85), a leading exponent of the papal reform movement. 'Gregorian Reform' aimed to enhance the status of the priesthood and to increase the power of the papacy over Western Christendom. His aims caused bitter conflict with the Emperor HENRY IV, who seized Rome in 1084, leaving Gregory to die in exile; ▷ pp. 84–5 and 90.

Grenada, an island in the E Caribbean. Grenada was discovered by Columbus in 1498, colonized by France in 1650 and ceded to Britain in 1783. Independence was gained in 1974. The left-wing New Jewel Movement seized power in a coup in 1979. In 1983 the PM Maurice Bishop was killed in a further coup in which more extreme members of the government seized power. Acting upon a request from E Caribbean islands to intervene, US and Caribbean forces landed in Grenada. After several days' fighting, the coup leaders were detained. Constitutional rule was restored in 1984.

Grenville, George (1712–1770), British statesman, prime minister (1763–5). His STAMP ACT (1765) provoked the American colonists (▷ p. 142). His son, William Wyndham, 1st Baron Grenville (1759–1834), was prime minister (1806–7) of a coalition 'ministry of all the talents', whose most important Act outlawed the slave trade.

Grey, Charles, 2nd Earl (1764–1845), Brtitish WHIG statesman, prime minister (1830–4). His government passed the first great REFORM ACT (1832) and legislation abolishing slavery throughout the British Empire.

Grey, Lady Jane (1537–54), queen of England (10–19 July 1553), great-granddaughter of HENRY VII. Her father-in-law, the Duke of Northumberland, persuaded EDWARD VI to name her his successor to ensure a Protestant succession. The 'Nine Days' Queen' was toppled by the Catholic MARY I, and executed after a rising in her favour.

Griffith, Arthur (1872–1922), Irish journalist and nationalist. A co-founder of SINN FEIN, he was the (unwilling) leader of the Irish delegation in the talks that led to the 1921 Anglo-Irish Treaty, establishing the Irish Free State; ▷ IRELAND.

Gromyko, Andrei Andreyevich (1909–89), Soviet statesman. Appointed foreign minister in 1957, he held the post for 28 years until his replacement by Eduard SHEVARDNADZE in 1985. He was also president of the Soviet Union (1985–8).

Group of Seven (G7), an informal grouping of major Western economic powers – Canada, France, Germany, Japan, Italy, UK and the USA. Since 1975 their leaders have met regularly to discuss major economic, monetary and political problems.

Guadalcanal, a large island in the SW Pacific, occupied by the Japanese from August 1942 to February 1943 during World War II; ▷ pp. 194–5.

Guatemala, a republic in CENTRAL AMERICA. The area was the centre of the Mayan civilization between the 4th and 9th centuries (▷ pp. 70–1). After 1524, Guatemala was the administrative centre of Spanish Central America. Independence was proclaimed in 1821, but the country was part of the Central American Federation until 1839. Guatemala has a history of being ruled by dictators allied to landowners. However, in the 1950s President Jacobo Arbenz expropriated large estates, dividing them among the peasantry. Accused of being a Communist, he was deposed by the army with US military aid (1954). For over 30 years, the left was suppressed, leading to the emergence of guerrilla armies. Thousands of dissidents were killed or disappeared. Civilian government was restored in 1986, but unrest continues.

Guelph, a term derived from the faction (originally the Welf family) opposed to the HOHENSTAUFENS in Germany. In the 13th century it was exported to Italian politics where it became associated with the pro-papal faction; ▷ p. 96.

Guernica, a town in the BASQUE region of Spain, razed by German bombers on 26 April 1937 during the Spanish Civil War; ▷ p. 189 (box).

guerrilla (Spanish, 'little war'), a member of an irregular military force fighting against superior regular forces, using hit-and-run tactics to weaken and demoralize them. The term was first used to describe the Spanish partisans opposing Napoleon in the PENINSULAR WAR.

Guesclin, Bertrand du (c. 1320–80), French military commander; ▷ p. 95.

Guevara, Ernesto 'Che' (1928–67), Argentinian-born revolutionary leader. He fought as a GUERRILLA with CASTRO in the Cuban Revolution, and was rewarded with ministerial rank in Castro's government. In 1967 he led an abortive revolution in Bolivia, during which he was killed. Guevara became a cult figure for radical students in the 1960s and 1970s; ▷ p. 206.

guild, an association of trades or crafts in medieval Europe; ▷ p. 99.

Guinea, a republic in W Africa. Portuguese slave traders visited the coast from the 15th century. The colony of French Guinea was established in 1890. Unlike the rest of French Africa, Guinea voted for a complete separation from France in 1958 (▷ p. 202, map), suffering severe French reprisals as a result. The authoritarian radical leader Sékou TOURÉ isolated Guinea, but he became reconciled with France in 1978. The leaders of a military coup (1984) have achieved some economic reforms.

Guinea-Bissau, a republic in W Africa (▷ p. 200, map). The Portuguese were involved in the slave trade in the area from 1441 but did not establish the colony of Portuguese Guinea until 1879. Failing to secure reform by peaceful means, the PAIGC movement mounted a liberation war (1961–74). Independence was proclaimed in 1973 and recognized by Portugal in 1974. Democratic reforms introduced a multi-party system in 1991.

Guiscard, Robert (c. 1015–85), Norman conqueror; ▷ p. 87.

Guise, one of the leading noble families of 16th-century France. Their power was based on influence at court, estates in E France and military exploits in the service of the crown. Henry (1550–88), the third duke of Guise, led the militant Catholic faction in the FRENCH WARS OF RELIGION.

until his assassination at the behest of HENRY III in 1588; ⇨ p. *110*.

Guizot, François-Pierre Guillaume (1787–1874), French politician. He held important ministerial posts under LOUIS PHILIPPE and was briefly premier (1847–8) before his resignation during the REVOLUTIONS OF 1848; ⇨ pp. 150, 151 and 167.

Gujarat, a region in W India. Its ports developed important trading and cultural links in both westerly and easterly directions. Ruled by Muslims from the late 13th century, it was conquered by the MARATHAS in the mid-18th century before being absorbed by the English EAST INDIA COMPANY; ⇨ p. 62.

Gulag, ⇨ p. **199** (box).

Gulf War (1991), ⇨ pp. **213** (box) and 228.

gunpowder, an explosive mixture of sulphur, charcoal and saltpetre (potassium nitrate), first used in warfare in the 1320s; ⇨ p. 102.

Gunpowder Plot (1605), an English Catholic conspiracy to murder JAMES I and his ministers by blowing up the palace of Westminster during the state opening of Parliament on 5 November 1605. One of the plotters, Guy Fawkes (1570–1606), was discovered and arrested in the cellars beneath Parliament, and later hung, drawn and quartered along with seven other conspirators.

Guptas, a dynasty that ruled from a base in NE India between the mid-4th and 6th centuries. Early Gupta rulers presided over a 'golden age' in religion and the arts during which both Buddhism and Hinduism flourished. Attacks by the HUNS brought about a collapse of Gupta power in the 6th century; ⇨ p. 59.

Gustavus II Adolphus (1594–1632), king of Sweden (1611–32). His reform of Sweden's administration and armed forces, together with his development of mobile field artillery, contributed decisively to Sweden's successes against Poland and in Germany in the Thirty Years War. He died in action at LÜTZEN (1632); ⇨ pp. 113 and 127 (box).

Gutenberg, Johannes (c.1398–1468), German printer; ⇨ p. 101.

Guthrum (d. 890), the leader of a major Danish invasion of Anglo-Saxon England (878). He waged war against ALFRED the Great; ⇨ p. 86.

Guyana, a republic of NE South America. Dutch colonies on the Guyanese coast – established since the 1620s – were captured by the British in 1796 and merged to form British Guiana in 1831. From the 1840s large numbers of Indian and Chinese labourers were imported from Asia to work on sugar plantations. Racial tension between their descendants – now the majority – and the black community (descended from imported African slaves) led to violence in 1964 and 1978. Guyana has been independent since 1966.

Habsburg, a German princely family that became a leading European royal dynasty from the 15th to the 20th centuries. Its power was established by Rudolf I (king of the Romans, 1273–91) who extended the family's rule over Austria. From 1440 to 1806 members of the family held the office of Holy Roman Emperor almost without interruption, and Habsburgs also occupied the thrones of other European states such as SPAIN, HUNGARY and BOHEMIA. After the demise of the Holy Roman Empire (⇨ p. 146) the Habsburgs ruled in AUSTRIA (1806–67) and AUSTRIA-HUNGARY (1867–1918); ⇨ pp. **85**, 113, 115, 117, 120, 123 (box), **124**, 130, 131, *134*, 135, 150, 151 and 153.

Hadrian (AD 76–138), Roman emperor (117–38). His reign was marked by prosperity at home and peace abroad; ⇨ p. 38.

Hadrian's Wall, the wall marking the N limit of the Roman province of Britain; ⇨ p. 38 (box).

Haig, Douglas, 1st Earl (1861–1928), British field marshal, commander of British forces on the Western Front (1915–18) during World War I. His attritional strategy on the SOMME (1916) and at PASSCHENDAELE (1917) has been much criticized; ⇨ p. 177 (box).

Haile Selassie (1892–1975), Ethiopian monarch and the last of its feudal rulers. Exiled in 1935, he returned to ETHIOPIA in 1941 after leading successful resistance against the occupying Italians. In 1955 he introduced a constitution, but his failure to introduce economic reforms and reduce his own political power estranged many of his supporters. The military seized power in 1974 and the emperor, stripped of his power and wealth, died in his palace in 1975.

Haiti, a republic comprising the E of the island of HISPANIOLA in the Caribbean. Columbus discovered Hispaniola in 1492, and in the 17th century the French settled Haiti, which formally became a colony in 1697. Black slaves – who were imported to work plantations – revolted in 1791 and were freed in 1794. TOUSSAINT L'OUVERTURE – a former slave – became governor general (1801), but was unable to defeat a French force sent to restore the old order. Independence was proclaimed in 1804 during a revolt led by Jean-Jacques DESSALINES and Henri Christophe, both of whom reigned as monarchs of Haiti. A united republic was achieved in 1820. Coups, instability and tension between Blacks and mulattos wracked Haiti until the US intervened (1915–35). President François DUVALIER – 'Papa Doc' – (in office 1956–71) and his son Jean-Claude (1971–86) cowed the country into submission by means of their infamous private militia, the Tontons Macoutes. Several coups have followed the violent end to the Duvalier era. A free multi-party election – the first in Haiti's history – took place in 1991, but constitutional government was suspended following a military coup nine months later.

Hallstatt, a burial site in N Austria that has given its name to a Celtic culture of the early Iron Age (900–500 BC); ⇨ pp. 34 and 35.

Hamilcar Barca (c. 270–228 BC), Carthaginian general. After Carthage lost Sicily to the Romans in the First Punic War (⇨ p. 37). Hamilcar conquered S and E Spain. He was the father of HANNIBAL and HASDRUBAL.

Hamilton, Alexander (1755–1804), US politician. An aide to General WASHINGTON in the War of Independence, he served as a New York delegate to the 1787 Constitutional Convention (⇨ p. 143). An advocate of strong central government, he went on to become secretary of the treasury and a leading figure in FEDERALIST party ranks; ⇨ p. 156.

Hamites, a group of N African peoples supposedly descended from Ham, the son of Noah; ⇨ p. 66.

Hammarskjöld, Dag (1915–61), Swedish diplomat, Secretary-General of the United Nations (1953–61). He was killed in a plane crash during the Congo Crisis; ⇨ p. 229.

Hammurabi (d. 1750 BC), king of BABYLON (1792–1750 BC); ⇨ p. 20.

Han, a dynasty that ruled China from 202 BC to AD 220. Founded by the general Liu Bang, its power was consolidated by the emperor Wu Di, who vastly extended the size of the Chinese Empire. The period of Han rule to AD 8 (from a capital at Chang'an) is known as the Western Han, the period from AD 25 to 220 (from a capital at Luoyang) is referred to as the Eastern Han; ⇨ pp. **52–3**, 60 and 65.

Hannibal (247–183 BC), Carthaginian general, son of HAMILCAR BARCA, who according to legend made his son swear eternal enmity to Rome; ⇨ pp. **37** and 45.

Hanover, a former imperial electorate and kingdom in Germany. Briefly part of the kingdom of Westphalia during the Napoleonic Wars, Hanover – whose ELECTOR had succeeded to the British crown as GEORGE I in 1714 (⇨ next entry) – was returned to Britain in 1815, when it also became a kingdom within the GERMAN CONFEDERATION. With the accession to the British throne of VICTORIA in 1837 the crowns of Britain and Hanover were separated, since the laws of succession in Hanover did not allow a woman to inherit the title. It was annexed by Prussia after the AUSTRO-PRUSSIAN WAR in 1866.

Hanover, House of, a British royal dynasty (1714–1901) that took its name from the German princely family that ruled the electorate of HANOVER from 1692 to 1815. In 1714 the elector of Hanover, having married Sophia of the Palatinate, granddaughter of JAMES I, succeeded to the English throne as GEORGE I, in accordance with the Act of SETTLEMENT (1701). The Hanoverian connection ended with the accession of Queen VICTORIA (1837); ⇨ pp. 119 and 125.

Hanseatic League, a former association of towns in N Germany; ⇨ p. 99 (box).

Harappa, the site in present-day Pakistan of a major city of the Indus Valley civilization; ⇨ p. 58.

Hardie, James Keir (1856–1915), British socialist leader, trade unionist, and founding member of the INDEPENDENT LABOUR PARTY.

Harding, Warren G. (1865–1923), twenty-ninth president of the USA (1921–3). A conservative product of the small-town Republican Midwest, he proved a weak and vacillating president. After he died in office, investigations revealed that he had presided over one of the most corrupt administrations in US history.

Harold II (c. 1020–66), king of England (1066); ⇨ p. 87.

Harrison, Benjamin (1833–1901), US Republican politician, twenty-third president of the USA (1889–93). The Sherman Anti-Trust Act (1890) restricting business monopolies (⇨ p. 157) was passed during his presidency.

Harrison, William Henry (1773–1841), US WHIG politician, ninth president of the USA (1841). A veteran of the War of 1812 (⇨ p. 156), he died within a month of taking office.

Harsha (c. 590–647), ruler of an empire in N India; ⇨ p. 59.

Harun al-Rashid (c. 763–809), fifth CALIPH of the Muslim ABBASID dynasty, ruling in Baghdad (786–809). He owes much of his disproportionate fame to his association with the much later stories of the *Thousand and One Nights*.

Hasdrubal (d. 207 BC), Carthaginian general, son of HAMILCAR BARCA. In the Second Punic War (⇨ p. 37) he fought the Romans in Spain (218–208), then went to the aid of his brother Hannibal in Italy, but died in the battle of the river Metaurus.

Hastings, battle of, ⇨ p. 87 (box).

Hastings, Warren (1732–1818), first governor-general of BENGAL (1772–85). He consolidated CLIVE'S gains in India, and further extended British rule there, pursuing a robust policy of reform.

Hatshepsut (c. 1540–c. 1481 BC), daughter of THUTMOSE I and wife of Thutmose II; she was effective ruler of Egypt in the first 20 years of the reign of THUTMOSE III; ⇨ p. 18.

Hattin, battle of (1187), defeat of a Crusader army by SALADIN, leading to the latter's capture of Jerusalem and the collapse of the Crusader kingdoms of the Levant (⇨ p. 88).

Haughey, Charles James (1925–), Irish FIANNA FÁIL statesman, prime minister (1979–81, 1982 and 1989–92). He was succeeded by Albert Reynolds.

Hausa, a W African people of mixed pastoral-agricultural origins, living in N Nigeria. The Muslim cities of Hausaland had major commercial and political influence in W Africa from the 17th century – particularly Sokoto in the first half of the 19th century.

Haussman, Georges Eugène, Baron (1809–91), French civil servant and town planner; ▷ p. 165.

Havel, Vaclav (1936–), Czechoslovak statesman and dramatist, elected president after the fall of the Communist regime in 1989; ▷ p. 224 (box).

Hawke, Robert James Lee (1929–), Australian Labor statesman. 'Bob' Hawke was a successful trade union leader before becoming prime minister of Australia in 1983. He was succeeded by Paul Keating in 1991.

Hawkins, Sir John (1532–95), English naval commander. As treasurer of the navy (1577–89), he played a crucial role in creating the fleet that defeated the SPANISH ARMADA.

Hayes, Rutherford B. (1822–93), US Republican politician, nineteenth president of the USA (1877–81). He ended the process of Reconstruction that followed the American Civil War (▷ p. 159), and withdrew Federal troops from the Southern states.

Heath, Edward Richard George (1916–), British Conservative statesman. As prime minister (1970–4) he took Britain into the EC, but ran into economic difficulties and lost the 1974 election to Labour. He was savagely critical of Margaret THATCHER'S hostility to closer European integration in the late 1980s and early 90s.

Hegel, Georg Wilhelm Friedrich (1770–1831), German idealist philosopher; ▷ pp. **3–4**.

Heian, the capital of Japan 794–1192 AD (modern Kyoto); ▷ p. 64.

Hejaz, a region of SW Asia that contains the main centres of Islamic pilgrimage, MECCA and MEDINA. The area was under Ottoman Turkish rule, nominally from 1517 and definitely from 1845. Hussein, Grand Sharif of Mecca, led a revolt against Turkish rule (1916), declared himself king of Hejaz but was defeated by ibn SA'UD (1924); ▷ pp. 114, 115 (map) and 210.

Heligoland, a tiny island in the German Bight of the N Sea. Originally part of SCHLESWIG-HOLSTEIN, it was seized by Britain (1807) and ceded to Germany (1890) in return for Zanzibar. The island became a major German imperial naval base.

Hellenistic Age, ▷ pp. **32–3** and 45.

Hellespont, the ancient name for the DARDANELLES.

helots, the 'state serfs' of ancient Sparta; ▷ pp. 28 and **42**.

Helsinki Conference (1972–5), a series of meetings of the CONFERENCE ON SECURITY AND COOPERATION IN EUROPE (CSCE), held in Helsinki and Geneva and attended by the leaders of 35 nations. The Helsinki Final Act, whose signatories included the Soviet bloc countries, contained agreements on trade and human rights.

Hengist and **Horsa** (fl. 449–88), the semi-legendary leaders of the first Anglo-Saxon invasion of Britain, and joint kings of Kent.

Henry I (the Fowler; c. 876–936), duke of Saxony (919–36) and father of OTTO I; ▷ p. 84.

Henry I (1068–1135), king of England (1100–35), duke of Normandy (1106–35)). A war of succession lasted until 1106, when he captured his brother Robert of Normandy and imprisoned him for life. The death of his only legitimate son in the White Ship disaster (1120) meant that his last 15 years were darkened by the prospect of an uncertain succession.

Henry II (1133–89), count of ANJOU and duke of Normandy from 1151, duke of AQUITAINE from 1152, king of England (1154–89). The most powerful ruler of his day in W Europe, he pursued expansionist policies, notably against the Bretons, Welsh and Irish; ▷ pp. 94 and 118 (box).

Henry III (1206–72), king of England (1216–72). His mishandling of domestic politics led to a series of crises from 1258, culminating in civil war and his virtual dethronement by Simon de MONTFORT in 1246.

Henry IV (1050–1106), king of Germany (1056–1106). His reign witnessed a bitter struggle with Pope GREGORY VII over the question of lay Investiture; ▷ pp. 84–5 and 90.

Henry IV (Bolingbroke; 1366–1413), king of England (1399–1413). His banishment by RICHARD II prevented him from inheriting the vast estates of his father John of GAUNT. In 1399 he invaded England and deposed Richard. His position as king was never secure, and his reign was marked by war and rebellion, notably the revolt of Owen GLENDOWER in Wales.

Henry IV (1557–1610), king of NAVARRE (as Henry III, 1563–1610) and first BOURBON king of France (1589–1610). A leader of the HUGUENOTS, he ended the FRENCH WARS OF RELIGION by converting to Catholicism (1593), and granted religious and political privileges to the Huguenots in the Edict of NANTES (1598). He obtained peace with Spain by the Treaty of Vervins (1598) and, with his chief minister, SULLY, sought to revive the French economy and royal revenues. He was stabbed to death by a Catholic fanatic.

Henry V (1387–1422), king of England (1413–22) and eldest son of HENRY IV. He conquered Normandy by his daring generalship at Agincourt and by ruthless exploitation of the troubles of the French court. At Troyes he dictated the treaty which, had it not been for a fatal attack of dysentery, would have made him king of France; ▷ pp. 95 and 102.

Henry VI (1165–1197), Holy Roman Emperor (1191–1197). He acquired the kingdom of Sicily through his marriage to the daughter of ROGER II; ▷ p. 85.

Henry VI (1422–71), king of England (1422–61 and 1470–1). He suffered from mental illness from 1453. The Wars of the ROSES broke out when RICHARD Duke of York, who had a better claim to the throne than Henry, was displaced in the order of succession by the birth of an heir to Henry's queen, MARGARET of Anjou. Deposed by EDWARD IV in 1461, he was briefly restored by WARWICK, but was murdered on Edward's return to the throne in 1471.

Henry VII (1457–1509), the first TUDOR king of England (1485–1509). He gained the throne after defeating RICHARD III at BOSWORTH, although his claim to the throne through his mother Margaret BEAUFORT (who was descended from John of GAUNT) was a tenuous one; ▷ p. 118.

Henry VIII (1491–1547), king of England (1509–47), the son of HENRY VII. His divorce of CATHERINE of Aragon marked the beginning of the English Reformation. After the execution of his second wife Anne BOLEYN, he subsequently married Jane Seymour, Anne of Cleves, Catherine Howard and Catherine Parr; ▷ p. **118**.

Henry the Navigator (1394–1460), the son of JOHN I of Portugal; ▷ p. 109.

Heraclius (575–641), Byzantine emperor (610–41); ▷ p. 80.

Herculaneum, a Roman town destroyed along with POMPEII in the eruption of Vesuvius in AD 79.

heresy, doctrines or opinions at variance with the orthodox beliefs of the Christian Church; ▷ pp. **91**, 92, 113 (box), ARIANISM, DONATISM, GNOSTICISM and MANICHAEISM.

hermit, a person living a solitary religious life. Hermits were influential in the early years of the Christian Church, but became rare in the West after the Reformation. They are still found in the ORTHODOX Church; ▷ p. 90.

Herod, a Jewish dynasty ruling as Roman clients in Palestine (47 BC–AD 93). The cruelty of Herod the Great (reigned 37–4 BC) is described in the New Testament account of the Massacre of the Innocents.

Herodotus (?484–?420 BC), the first great historian of ancient Greece; ▷ pp. **2** and 44.

Hertzog, James Barry Munnik (1866–1942), South African prime minister (1924–39). Founder of the (Afrikaner) NATIONAL PARTY, and architect of racial segregation in the 1920s and 30s through his 'Hertzog Bills'; ▷ p. 220.

Herzen, Alexander (1812–70), Russian political thinker. In the 1840s he was a prominent spokesman of the 'Westernizers' but, living abroad after 1847, came to believe that Russia could evolve towards socialism without following the path of Western development; ▷ p. 180 (box).

Herzl, Theodor (1860–1904), ZIONIST (Jewish) leader, founder of the World Zionist Organization, which first met in 1897; ▷ p. 210.

Hesse (Darmstadt), a former landgraviate (1567) and grand duchy (1806) in W Germany. It became part of the German Empire in 1871. The monarchy was overthrown in 1918.

Hesse (Cassel), a former landgraviate (13th century) and electorate (1803) in W Germany. It was annexed by PRUSSIA after the AUSTRO-PRUSSIAN WAR in 1866.

Hess, Rudolf (1894–1987), German Nazi politician, Hitler's deputy and minister of state. He flew alone to Scotland in 1941 to negotiate peace between Britain and Germany. Sentenced to life imprisonment at the NUREMBERG TRIALS, from 1966 until his death he was the sole inmate of Spandau prison in Berlin.

Hezekiah (d. 687 BC), king of Judah (715–687 BC). He revolted against Assyria, ignoring the advice of the prophet Isaiah, and was defeated by SENNACHERIB in 701 BC; ▷ p. 21.

Hidalgo y Costilla, Miguel (1753–1811), Mexican priest and rebel leader; ▷ pp. 148 and 149.

hieroglyphs, the picture signs used in the ancient Egyptian writing system; ▷ p. 17.

hijra (Arabic, 'migration'), the flight of MUHAMMAD from MECCA to MEDINA in 622. The event marks the starting-point of the Islamic calendar; ▷ p. 82.

Himmler, Heinrich (1900–45), German Nazi politician. Leader of the SS from 1929, he became head of all German police forces, including the GESTAPO, in 1936. He supervised the deportation and systematic extermination of the Jews in E Europe. Captured by the Allies at the end of World War II, he committed suicide; ▷ p. 186.

Hindenburg, Paul von (1847–1934), German field marshal. A veteran of the FRANCO-PRUSSIAN WAR, he was recalled at the outbreak of World War I and, with LUDENDORFF, crushed the Russians at TANNENBERG. As chief of the general staff he conducted an effective, but doomed, campaign on the Western Front. As president of Germany (1925–34), he appointed Hitler as chancellor in 1933; ▷ p. 186.

Hinduism, the system of religious beliefs and social customs that developed in India from 1500 BC onwards; ▷ pp. **58–9**, 60, 63, 201, 202 and 218.

Hirohito (1901–89), emperor of JAPAN (1926–89). He became a constitutional monarch after Japan's defeat in World War II.

Hiroshima, Japanese port on the Inland Sea. On 6 August 1945 it was hit by an atomic bomb – the first to be used in warfare – dropped by the US air force, which killed over 75 000 of its inhabitants. A second bomb was dropped on NAGASAKI three days later; ▷ pp. 195 and 226.

Hispaniola, an island in the Caribbean, first discovered by Columbus in 1492. It is now divided between HAITI and the DOMINICAN REPUBLIC.

Hitler, Adolf (1889–1945), Austrian-born German Nazi dictator (1933–45); ▷ pp. 5 (box) and **186–93**.

Hitler Youth, a Nazi youth organization, formed in 1933. From 1936, membership of the Hitler Youth was compulsory for all children aged 10–18. The organization instilled semi-military discipline and Nazi political ideas.

Hittites, an Indo-European people of ANATOLIA, who created a substantial Near Eastern empire in the 2nd millennium BC; ⇨ pp. 19, 20 and **22–3**.

Hobbes, Thomas (1588–1679), English political philosopher; ⇨ p. **135** (box).

Hohenstaufen, a dynasty that ruled the Holy Roman Empire from 1138 to 1254; ⇨ pp. **85** and 96.

Hohenzollern, a dynasty that ruled BRANDENBURG from 1417, PRUSSIA from 1618, and the newly unified German Reich from 1871 to 1918; ⇨ p. 125.

Hojo, the dominant noble family in 13th-century Japan; ⇨ p. 64.

Holinshed, Raphael (d. c. 1580), English chronicler; ⇨ p. 6.

Holocaust, ⇨ p. 192 (box).

Holy League, the name given to a number of alliances and organizations in 15th-, 16th- and 17th-century Europe. Some of the most notable were: the League of 1511, which allied the Pope, Henry VIII, the Swiss, Venice and Ferdinand of Aragon in an attempt to expel the French from Italy (1511); that of 1526, directed by the pope, France, Milan, Florence and Venice against Emperor CHARLES V (1526); that of 1570, which allied the pope, Venice and Spain against the Ottomans (⇨ p. 117); the French Catholic League of 1576, which confronted the HUGUENOTS in the FRENCH WARS OF RELIGION (⇨ p. *110*); and the alliance (1684) of Poland, the Habsburg Emperor, Venice and Pope Innocent XI against the Ottoman Turks (⇨ p. 124).

Holyoake, Keith Jacka (1904–83), New Zealand National Party statesman, prime minister (1957 and 1960–72).

Holy Roman Empire (962–1806), the Western empire created in imitation of the Roman Empire; ⇨ pp. 84–5, 90, 96, 110, 124–5, *134* and 146.

Home of the Hirsel, Alec Douglas-Home, Baron (1903–   ), British Conservative prime minister (1963–4). Chosen by MACMILLAN to succeed him, he resigned his earldom to become PM, but lost the 1964 election to Harold WILSON.

Homer, the Greek poet to whom the *Iliad* and the *Odyssey* are attributed; ⇨ pp. 2 and 44.

Homestead Act (1862), US legislation to promote westward expansion, allowing the purchase of public land for a nominal fee; ⇨ p. 156.

Home Rule, the campaign to repeal the Act of UNION (1801) between Britain and IRELAND and give the Irish their own parliament responsible for domestic affairs. GLADSTONE'S conversion to Home Rule in 1885 led to Joseph Chamberlain's defection to the Conservatives as a Liberal-Unionist and the splitting of the LIBERAL Party.

Homo erectus ('upright man'), an early human type, dating from between 1.6 million and 300 000 years ago. Originating in Africa, they were the first humans to colonize Africa and Asia; ⇨ p. 12.

Homo sapiens neanderthalensis ('wise Neanderthal man'), the human type inhabiting Europe and Asia before modern humans (HOMO SAPIENS SAPIENS). They evolved some time before 100 000 years ago, lasting until 30 000 years ago in Europe; ⇨ pp. 12, **13** and 14.

Homo sapiens sapiens ('wise man'), the modern human type, an early example of which came from the Cro-Magnon cave in France. The time of their first appearance is hotly debated. Although Neanderthals lasted until 30 000 years ago in Europe, recent research shows that modern humans already existed in the Near East 100 000 years ago; ⇨ pp. 12 and **13**.

Honduras, a republic in CENTRAL AMERICA. In 1502

Columbus reached Honduras and in 1523 the first Spanish settlement was established. Honduras gained freedom from Spain in 1821, but was part of the Central American Federation until 1839. Between independence and the early 20th century, Honduras experienced constant political upheaval and wars with neighbouring countries. US influence was immense, largely owing to the substantial investments of the powerful United Fruit Company in banana production. After a short civil war in 1925, a succession of military dictators governed Honduras until 1980. Since then the country has had democratically elected pro-US centre-right civilian governments.

Honecker, Erich (1912–   ), East German Communist politician, general secretary of the Communist Party from 1971, and president from 1976. He was replaced during the anti-Communist revolution of 1989 (⇨ p. 224, box).

Hong Kong, ⇨ pp. **197** and **222**.

Hongwu (1328–98), first emperor (1368–98) of the Ming dynasty in China; ⇨ p. 56.

Hoover, Herbert (1874–1964), US Republican politician, thirty-first president of the USA (1929–33). Renowned for his humanitarian work in Europe after World War I, he sought to streamline American bureaucracy and industry during the 1920s. His failure to solve the problems of the Depression resulted in his crushing defeat by F.D. ROOSEVELT in the election of 1932.

Hoover, J(ohn) Edgar (1895–1972), head of the US Federal Bureau of Investigation (1924–72). Finding the agency in disrepute after scandals during the HARDING administration, he instituted professional standards of selection and training for staff and agents. During the 1960s he was much criticized for his antipathy towards the CIVIL RIGHTS MOVEMENT.

Hopi, a native North American people of the SW, living in NE Arizona; ⇨ pp. 72 and 73.

hoplite, a heavily armed infantryman in ancient Greece; ⇨ pp. 28 and 44.

Hospitallers, a military and religious order of knights; ⇨ p. 89 (box).

Houphouët-Boigny, Félix (1905–   ), first president of the CÔTE D'IVOIRE (1960–   ).

House of Representatives, the lower chamber of the US CONGRESS, which first met in 1789. With delegates apportioned according to the population strength of each state, the House tends to be a more accurate barometer of American public opinion than the SENATE. The CONSTITUTION invests it with the sole right to originate revenue bills.

Howard, Charles, Lord of Effingham (1536–1624), Lord High Admiral of England (1585–1618), commander of the fleet that defeated the SPANISH ARMADA.

Hoxha, Enver (1908–85), Albanian Communist politician, prime minister (1946–54), First Secretary of the Communist Party (1954–85).

Ho Chi Minh (1892–1969), Vietnamese nationalist and revolutionary leader, president of the Democratic Republic of (North) Vietnam (1954–69). A long-term Communist, he led the VIET MINH in the FRENCH INDOCHINA WAR, after which he ruled in Hanoi until his death; ⇨ pp. 161 (box) and **208**.

Hua Guofeng (1920–   ), Chinese Communist politician, prime minister (1976–80). He survived the upheavals of the Cultural Revolution to hold a number of key government posts from 1968 to 1975. He became PM on the death of ZHOU ENLAI, but DENG XIAOPING was the real power behind his administration (⇨ p. 197).

Hudson's Bay Company, a British trading company founded by royal charter (1670) to monopolize the valuable fur trade of the Canadian NW; ⇨ p. 129.

Huguenot, a French Protestant, particularly a follower of CALVIN. Their numbers declined during and

after the FRENCH WARS OF RELIGION, though they were granted toleration by HENRY IV in the Edict of NANTES (1598). Their political privileges were abolished by LOUIS XIII, and their religious rights by Louis XIV in the revocation of the Edict of Nantes (1685; ⇨ p. 122), after which many Huguenots fled abroad; ⇨ pp. 111, 120 and *121*.

Hulagu (1217–65), Mongol prince, a grandson of Genghis Khan, who conquered Iran and Iraq but whose westward advance was checked by the MAMLUKS at the battle of AIN JALUT. His descendants became sovereigns of the division of the Mongol Empire known as the ILKHANATE.

humanism, an important cultural movement during the 15th-century Renaissance, based on the study of classical texts; ⇨ pp. **100–1**.

Humayun (1508–56), second Mogul emperor of India (1530–40, 1554–5), under whose rule Persian influences were introduced into India; ⇨ p. 63.

Humboldt, Alexander von (1769–1859), Prussian naturalist, explorer and polymath; ⇨ p. 148.

Hume, David (1711–76), Scottish philosopher and economist; ⇨ p. 135 (box).

'Hundred Days' (March 20–June 29 1815), the period between Napoleon's return to France from Elba and his abdication after defeat at WATERLOO; ⇨ p. 147.

Hundred Years War (1337–1453), ⇨ pp. 87, 93, **94–5** and **102–3**.

Hungarian Revolution (1956), the first major uprising against Communist rule in Eastern Europe. Its leader Imre NAGY denounced the Warsaw Pact and declared Hungary neutral. The revolution was crushed by a Soviet invasion and its leaders executed; ⇨ p. 198.

Hungary, a country in Central Europe. The MAGYARS colonized the area from the E in the 9th century. The first Magyar king, STEPHEN (reigned 1001–38), encouraged Christianity and West European culture. MATTHIAS CORVINUS (reigned 1458–90) made Hungary a major power and did much to introduce the ideas of the Renaissance to central Europe. In the 16th century Hungary was dismembered by the Austrian HABSBURGS and the Turkish Ottoman Empire (⇨ p. 115, map). The Habsburgs liberated Buda, the capital, from the Turks in 1686, and by the 18th century all the Hungarian lands were within the Habsburg Empire. Lajos KOSSUTH led a nationalist revolt against Austrian rule (1848–9), but fled when Austria regained control with Russian aid. Austria granted Hungary considerable autonomy in the Dual Monarchy (1867) – the AUSTRO-HUNGARIAN EMPIRE. Defeat in World War I led to a brief period of Communist rule under Béla KUN (1919), then occupation by Romania. In the postwar settlement (⇨ p. 182), Hungary lost two thirds of its territory. The Regent Admiral Miklás Horthy (1868–1957) cooperated with Hitler during World War II in an attempt to regain territory, but defeat in 1945 resulted in occupation by the Red Army, and a Communist People's Republic was established in 1949. The HUNGARIAN REVOLUTION in 1956 was a heroic attempt to overthrow Communist rule, but was quickly suppressed by Soviet forces, and its leader, Imre NAGY, was executed. János KADAR – Party Secretary 1956–88 – tried to win support with economic progress. However, in the late 1980s reformers in the Communist Party gained the upper hand, and established a fully democratic, multiparty state. Soviet troops left Hungary in 1990, and the country has taken rapid steps to establish a free-market economy (⇨ p. 224, box).

Huns, a nomadic people of the Volga steppe whose westward movements pushed many Germanic peoples into the Roman Empire in the late 4th century and themselves invaded the Empire in the 4th and 5th centuries; ⇨ pp. 40, 54 and **78**.

Huron (Wyandot), a native North American people, maize farmers living NE of the Great Lakes. Early allies of the French settlers in the area, they suffered a shattering defeat by the IROQUOIS in the mid-17th century; ▷ p. 73.

Hurrians, a non-Semitic people who settled in Syria in the 2nd millennium BC; ▷ pp. 16, 20 (box) and **22.**

Hus, Jan (?1372–1415), Bohemian religious reformer; ▷ p. 91.

Hussein (1935–), king of JORDAN since 1952.

Hussein ibn Ali (1856–1931), Arabian politician, recognized by the Allies as ruler of the HEJAZ (1916–24), and father of FAISAL I of Iraq; ▷ p. 210.

Hussein, Saddam al-Takriti (1937–), president of Iraq since 1976. Leader of the Iraqi BA'ATH Party, he has ruled repressively and embroiled his country in two disastrous wars – one against IRAN (1980–8), the other against a US-led coalition in KUWAIT (1991); ▷ p. 213 (box).

Hussites, followers of Jan Hus; ▷ p. 91.

Hyderabad, the largest PRINCELY STATE of India. It attempted to regain its independence when India became independent; ▷ p. 201 (box).

Hyder Ali (1721–82), Muslim ruler of the Indian state of MYSORE (1761–82), and father of TIPU SULTAN. He won a number of victories against the English EAST INDIA COMPANY.

Hyksos, the 16th- and 17th-dynasty rulers of Egypt, probably originating in the Levant.; ▷ pp. **18–19.**

Ice Ages, a series of colder and warmer phases during which almost all of the Palaeolithic developments in Asia and Europe occurred. During cold phases the polar ice sheets extended as far S as Central Europe and the N American Great Plains. Some of the warmer phases (interglacials) were warmer than at present. The last cold phase ended about 10 000 BC; ▷ pp. **12,** 13, 14 and 70.

Iceland, an island republic in NW Europe. Norwegians settled in Iceland in the 9th century. From 930 Iceland was an independent republic, but Norwegian sovereignty was accepted in 1264 to end a civil war. When Denmark and Norway were united (1381), Iceland became Danish. Nationalism grew in the 19th century, and in 1918 Iceland gained independence, linked to Denmark only by their shared monarchy. In World War II the Danish link was severed and a republic was declared (1944). Disputes over fishing rights in Icelandic territorial waters led to clashes with British naval vessels in the 1950s and 1970s (the 'Cod War').

Iceni, an ancient British tribe of East Anglia. The Iceni were at first allies of Rome, but in AD 60 they rebelled under queen BOUDICCA.

Iconoclastic controversy, a dispute about the role of icons in the Eastern (ORTHODOX) Church; ▷ pp. 80–1.

Idris I (1890–1983), king of LIBYA (1951–69). As head of the Sanusi sect in Cyrenaica (E Libya), he led resistance to Italian colonial rule. Elected king at independence, Idris was deposed by Colonel QADDAFI in 1969.

Ife, a holy city of the YORUBA people in SW Nigeria; ▷ p. 67.

Ilkhanate, the division of the Mongol Empire including Anatolia, Iran and Iraq; ▷ pp. 54 and 55.

Illyria, an ancient region of the NW Balkans. Its non-Greek tribes fought regularly with the Macedonians, and formed a strong, often piratical kingdom in the 3rd century BC, which was gradually absorbed into the Roman Empire; ▷ p. 31 (map).

ILO, ▷ INTERNATIONAL LABOUR ORGANIZATION.

IMF, ▷ INTERNATIONAL MONETARY FUND.

Imhotep, ancient Egyptian architect who designed the Step Pyramid at Saqqara (▷ p. 17).

imperialism, the process whereby one country establishes its rule over other less powerful countries, regions or peoples; ▷ pp. **160–3,** 174 and 200–3.

Incas, a pre-Columbian native people of W South America; ▷ pp. 71 and 116.

Independence, American War of, ▷ pp. **142–3.**

Independent Labour Party (ILP), a British socialist party, founded in 1893. It helped establish the Labour Representation Committee in 1900. Affiliated to the LABOUR Party until 1932, it nevertheless put up its own parliamentary candidates and was often critical of Labour policies.

India, a republic of S Asia. (For the history of the kingdoms and empires of India to the colonial age, and the expansion of Hindu culture and Islam in India; ▷ pp. 58–9 and 62–3). By the middle of the 18th century the English EAST INDIA COMPANY had established itself as the dominant power in India (▷ pp. 63 and 129). After the INDIAN MUTINY (1857–8; ▷ p. 160) was put down, the Company ceded its rights in India to the British Crown. In 1877 the Indian Empire was proclaimed with Queen VICTORIA as Empress. The Empire included present-day Pakistan and Bangladesh, and comprised the Crown Territories of British India and over 620 British-protected PRINCELY STATES, the latter covering about 40% of India. From the middle of the 19th century the British cautiously encouraged Indian participation in the administration of British India. British institutions, the railways and the English language – all imposed upon India by a modernizing imperial power – fostered the growth of an Indian sense of identity beyond the divisions of caste and language. However, ultimately the divisions of religion proved stronger. The Indian National Congress – the forerunner of the CONGRESS Party – was first convened in 1885, and the MUSLIM LEAGUE first met in 1906. Nationalist demands grew after the AMRITSAR MASSACRE (1919). The INDIA ACTS (1919 and 1935) granted limited autonomy and created an Indian federation, but the pace of reform did not satisfy Indian expectations. In 1920 Congress – led by Mohandas GANDHI – began a campaign of non-violence and non-cooperation with the British authorities. (For details of Indian independence and the partition of the subcontinent into predominantly Hindu India and Muslim Pakistan; ▷ p. 201, box) After partition, the frontiers remained disputed. India and Pakistan fought border wars in 1947–9, 1965 (over KASHMIR) and again in 1971 – when Bangladesh gained independence from Pakistan with Indian assistance. Kashmir is still divided along a cease-fire line. There were also border clashes with China in 1962. Under NEHRU – PM 1947–64 – India became one of the leaders of the NONALIGNED MOVEMENT of Third World states. Under the premierships (1966–77 and 1980–4) of his daughter Indira GANDHI India continued to assert itself as the dominant regional power. Although India remained the world's largest democracy – local separatism and communal unrest have threatened unity. The SIKHS have conducted an often violent campaign for an independent homeland – Khalistan – in the Punjab. In 1984 Mrs Gandhi ordered the storming of the Golden Temple of Amritsar, a Sikh holy place that extremists had turned into an arsenal. In the same year Mrs Gandhi was assassinated by her Sikh bodyguard. Her son Rajiv (PM 1984–9) was assassinated in the 1991 election campaign. Tension and violence between Hindus and Muslims has increased since a campaign (1990) to build a Hindu temple on the site of a mosque in the holy city of Ayodha.

India Acts, British legislation relating to the administration of India. The first India Act (1858)

transferred rule of the sub-continent from the English EAST INDIA COMPANY to the crown (▷ p. 160).

Indian Mutiny (1857–8), a rebellion by Indian troops (sepoys) of the English EAST INDIA COMPANY. One of the causes of the revolt was Indian outrage at the issue of cartridges coated in beef and pork fat – offensive to Hindus and Muslims respectively; ▷ p. **160.**

Indian National Congress, ▷ CONGRESS, INDIAN NATIONAL.

Indochina, the area of SE Asia between India and China, consisting of LAOS, CAMBODIA and VIETNAM; ▷ pp. 61 (map), and **208.**

Indonesia, a republic comprising a major archipelago (the East Indies) in SE Asia (▷ p. 200, map). Indian traders brought Hinduism to the East Indies and by the 3rd century AD, Hindu kingdoms had been established in Java and Sumatra. Monks brought Buddhism from India, and both Hindu and Buddhist states flourished in the islands (▷ p. 60). The powerful Buddhist kingdom of Srivijaya on Sumatra (7th–13th centuries) was eclipsed by the Javan Hindu kingdom of Majapahit (13th–15th centuries). Arab traders brought Islam, which took the place of both established religions by the 16th century, while at the same time European incursions began. The struggle between the Portuguese, Dutch, Spanish and British for the rich spice trade ended in Dutch ascendancy in the 1620s (▷ p. 61). The East Indies became the major and most profitable part of the Dutch Empire. Except for a brief period of British occupation (1811–14) and occasional local risings, the Netherlands retained control until 1942 when the Japanese invaded and were welcomed by most Indonesians as liberators from colonial rule (▷ p. 194). Upon Japan's surrender in 1945, Achmed SUKARNO – the founder of the nationalist party in 1927 – declared the Dutch East Indies to be the independent republic of Indonesia. Under international pressure, the Dutch accepted Indonesian independence (1949) after four years of intermittent but brutal fighting (▷ p. 203). Sukarno's rule became increasingly authoritarian and the country sank into economic chaos. In 1962 he seized Netherlands New Guinea, which was formally annexed as Irian Jaya in 1969, although a separatist movement persists. Between 1963 and 1966 Sukarno tried to destabilize the newly-created Federation of Malaysia by armed incursions into N Borneo. General SUHARTO's suppression of a Communist uprising in 1965–6 enabled him to reverse Sukarno's anti-Americanism and eventually to displace him with the support of both the students and the army. Around 80 000 members of the Communist Party were killed in this period. The annexation of Portuguese EAST TIMOR by Indonesia in 1976 is unrecognized by the international community, and guerrilla action by local nationalists continues. International protests followed the killing of unarmed Timorese demonstrators by Indonesian troops in 1991. An ambitious programme of resettlement has been attempted to relieve overcrowded Java, but the Javanese settlers have been resented in the outlying, under-developed islands.

Indo-Pakistan War (September 1965), a border war between India and Pakistan which broke out when Pakistan tried to give military assistance to Muslims opposing Indian rule in KASHMIR. The war was ended by a UN ceasefire. Further fighting occurred in 1971, Indian victory leading to the creation of BANGLADESH; ▷ p. **201.**

indulgence, a method whereby the Roman Catholic Church offered remission of the penance imposed on confessed sinners; ▷ p. 110.

Industrial Revolution, ▷ pp. 119, **140–1** and 164–7.

Indus Valley civilization, an early urban culture in what is now Pakistan; ▷ p. **58.**

Inkerman, battle of (5 November 1854), a clash near SEVASTOPOL during the Crimean War, in which the Russian army under Prince Menshikov was repulsed after launching a surprise attack on an Anglo-French force; ▷ p. 155 (box).

Innocent III (1160–1216), pope (1198–1216). He supported the Fourth Crusade (▷ box, p. 88), instigated Church reform, and launched a crusade against the Cathar heretics in S France (▷ p. 91). He was also an important supporter of the Dominican and Franciscan friars; ▷ p. 91.

Inquisition, ▷ p. 113.

Intermediate Nuclear Forces (INF) Agreement (1987), an agreement between the USA and the Soviet Union to abolish land-based intermediate nuclear forces; ▷ p. 227.

International Brigades, groups of mainly Communist volunteers from outside Spain who fought for the Republicans in the Spanish Civil War; ▷ p. 189 (box).

International Court of Justice, a judicial body established in the Hague by the United Nations to settle disputes brought before it by member-states; ▷ p. 229 (box).

International Labour Organization (ILO), an agency of the United Nations that aims to improve labour conditions and promote social justice; ▷ p. 229 (box).

International Monetary Fund (IMF), a specialized agency of the United Nations founded in 1946 to promote international monetary cooperation, currency stabilization and trade expansion; ▷ p. 229 (box).

Internationals, international organizations of socialist and left-wing political groupings. MARX played a key role in the First International (1864–72). The Second International (established 1889) split with the establishment of the Soviet-controlled Third International in 1919.

Intifada, the Palestinian uprising in the occupied territories from 1987; ▷ p. 213.

Inuit, a native North American people, the dominant group among the Eskimo of the Arctic during the last 1000 years. Their economy depended entirely on the hunting of seals and other marine animals; ▷ pp. 13 and **72.**

Ionians, one of the main cultural and linguistic groupings of the ancient Greeks. The Ionic dialect was mainly spoken in Athens, the islands of the central Aegean, and the cities in the central part of the coast of Asia Minor (Turkey); ▷ AEOLIANS, DORIANS.

IRA, ▷ IRISH REPUBLICAN ARMY.

Iran, a country of SW Asia. The Persian Achaemenid Empire grew under Cyrus II from 539 BC (▷ p. 26). Under DARIUS I and XERXES the Persians ruled from the Danube to the Indus, although their attempts to conquer Greece were eventually unsuccessful (▷ p. 27). Alexander the Great finally defeated the Achaemenids, taking the capital Persepolis in 330 BC (▷ p. 32). Persia was part of the Hellenistic Seleucid Empire (▷ p. 33) until 247 BC, then ruled by the Parthians until 226 AD, when the Sassanians – an Iranian dynasty – established an empire (▷ p. 27, box) that lasted until the coming of the Arabs and Islam in the 7th century. The first Muslim dynasty, the UMAYYADS (▷ p. 82), were based on Damascus, but their successors, the ABBASIDS, (▷ p. 83) moved the capital to Baghdad where Persian traditions predominated. Once Persia had recovered from the ruthless Mongol invasion of the 13th century, a golden age arose under the SAFAVID dynasty. The Safavids were great patrons of the arts, and established SHIITE – rather than SUNNI – Islam as the state religion. The 18th century saw the rise of the Qajar dynasty, who moved the capital from Isfahan to Tehran. In the 19th century, Russia and Britain became rivals for influence in the region. In 1921 an

Iranian Cossack officer, Reza Khan PAHLAVI, took power. Deposing the Qajars in 1925, he became Shah (emperor) himself as Reza I and modernized and secularized Iran. However, because of his pro-German sentiments, he was forced to abdicate by Britain and the USSR (1941) and was replaced by his son Mohammed Reza. The radical nationalist prime minister Muhammad MOSSADEQ briefly toppled the monarchy (1953). On regaining his throne, the Shah tightened his grip through oppression and sought popularity through land reform and rapid development with US backing. (For details of the Shah's overthrow and the creation in 1979 of an Islamic Republic inspired by the Ayatollah Khomeini; ▷ p. 212, box). In the wake of Khomeini's revolution the Western-educated classes fled Iran as the clergy tightened control. Radical anti-Western students seized the US embassy and held 66 American hostages (1979–81). In 1980 Iraq invaded Iran, beginning the bitter Iran–Iraq War, which lasted until 1988 (▷ p. 213, box). Following the death of Khomeini in 1989, economic necessity brought a less militant phase of the Islamic revolution. After the collapse of the USSR (1991), Iran began to look for closer ties with the Islamic former Soviet republics of Central Asia.

Iran Hostage Crisis (November 1979–January 1981), a crisis that arose when militant supporters of the Ayatollah Khomeini seized the US embassy in Teheran, Iran, and took 66 American hostages. President CARTER's unsuccessful attempts to free the hostages – through diplomatic and military means – contributed to his defeat by Ronald Reagan in the 1980 US presidential elections; ▷ pp. 212 and 217.

Iraq, a country of SW Asia. Iraq – ancient Mesopotamia – was the cradle of the Sumerian and Akkadian (▷ p. 16), and Babylonian and ASSYRIAN civilizations (▷ pp. 20–1). In the 7th century BC Iraq became part of Persia's Achaemenid empire (▷ p. 26). Conquered by Alexander the Great (▷ p. 32), Iraq was then fought over by Parthia and Rome until it was absorbed by the Persian Sassanian Empire (▷ p. 27, box). In 637 AD Muslim armies from Arabia defeated the Persians. In 750 the ABBASID dynasty based its caliphate in Baghdad (▷ p. 83), which became the administrative and cultural capital of the Arab world. Abbasid power was ended by the Mongols in the 13th and 14th centuries, and Iraq was absorbed by the Turkish Ottoman Empire in 1534 (▷ p. 114). In World War I the British occupied the area, but Iraqi nationalists were disappointed when Iraq became a monarchy under a British MANDATE (1920). In 1932 Iraq became fully independent. After a pro-German coup in 1941, the British occupied Iraq until 1945. The royal family and the premier were murdered in the 'Free Officers' coup in 1958. A reign of terror against the left followed a further coup in 1963. In 1968 BA'ATHIST officers carried out another coup. Embittered by the Arabs' humiliation in the 1967 war and by US support for the Israelis (▷ p. 210), the regime turned to the Soviets. In 1980 President Saddam HUSSEIN attacked a weakened Iran, responding to Iran's threat to export Islamic revolution. (For details of the Iran–Iraq War, and of Iraq's invasion of Kuwait in 1990 and the ensuing Gulf War between Iraq and a US-led coalition in 1991; ▷ p. 213, box). In the aftermath of Iraq's defeat in the Gulf War, Saddam continued to defy UN demands concerning Iraqi disarmament, despite being forced to accept UN inspection of Iraq's chemical and biological weapons and the country's nuclear capacity.

Ireland, a country of NW Europe. Christianity – traditionally brought by St PATRICK in the 5th century – gave a cultural unity to the kingdoms of Celtic Ireland – CONNAUGHT, Leinster, Meath, Munster and ULSTER. At the end of the 8th century, the

Vikings invaded, settling in E Ireland (▷ p. 86), but were eventually defeated in 1014 by BRIAN BORU, who became effective king of all Ireland. However, throughout the early medieval period, the 'high kings' of Ireland seldom controlled the whole island. (For details of Anglo-Norman and Protestant settlement of Ireland, and the suppression by the English of Catholic Irish rebellions in the 16th and 17th centuries; ▷ p. 119, box.) In 1690 the Catholic JAMES II, having fled England in 1688, attempted to lead a revolt in Ireland. His defeat at the battle of the BOYNE (1690) at the hands of William of Orange (WILLIAM III of England) confirmed Protestant domination and British rule in Ireland. The Protestant ascendancy was, however, split – Anglicans formed the Anglo-Irish ruling classes, while the Presbyterian descendants of Scottish settlers in Ulster were mainly working class. In the 18th century, both Presbyterians and Roman Catholics pressed for the civil rights that they were largely denied. In 1798 the failure of a nationalist revolt led by Wolfe TONE was followed by the amalgamation of the British and Irish parliaments and the establishment of the United Kingdom of Great Britain and Ireland (1801). In the 1840s thousands died in the IRISH FAMINE. Many more were evicted by Anglo-Irish landowners and joined a mass emigration, especially to the USA – between 1845 and 1851 Ireland's population declined by almost 3 000 000. Daniel O'CONNELL led a movement seeking to repeal the Union, and to gain land and civil rights for the Roman Catholic majority. His campaign helped lead to CATHOLIC EMANCIPATION (1829), after which Irish Catholics were able to become MPs in the British Parliament. However, relations between the Protestant and Catholic communities deteriorated, in part owing to increasingly violent actions by nationalist FENIANS whose goal was Irish independence. English policy on Ireland vacillated between conciliation and coercion. GLADSTONE, recognizing the need for reform, disestablished the (Anglican) Church of Ireland and granted greater security of tenure to peasant farmers. In the 1880s Charles Stewart PARNELL led a sizeable bloc of Irish MPs in a campaign to secure Irish HOME RULE. Home Rule Bills were introduced in 1883 and 1893, but after their rejection by Parliament, more revolutionary nationalist groups gained support in Ireland. Fearing Catholic domination, Protestant Unionists in Ulster opposed the Third Home Rule Bill in 1912. Nationalists declared an independent Irish state in the Dublin EASTER RISING of 1916, which was put down by the British. After World War I, Irish nationalist MPs formed a provisional government in Dublin led by Eamon DE VALERA (later PM and president). Except in the NE, British administration in Ireland crumbled and most of the Irish police resigned to be replaced by English officers – the BLACK AND TANS. Fighting broke out between nationalists and British troops and police, and by 1919 Ireland had collapsed into violence. The British response in 1920 was to offer Ireland two Parliaments – one in Protestant Ulster, another in the Catholic S. Partition was initially rejected by the S, but by the Anglo-Irish Treaty (1921) dominion status was granted, although six (mainly Protestant) counties in Ulster – NORTHERN IRELAND – opted to remain British. The Irish Free State was proclaimed in 1922 but de Valera and the Republicans refused to accept it. Civil war broke out between the provisional government – led by Arthur GRIFFITH and Michael COLLINS – and the Republicans. Although fighting ended in 1923, de Valera's campaign for a republic continued and in 1937 the Free State became the Republic of Eire. The country remained neutral in World War II and left the COMMONWEALTH – as the Republic of Ireland – in 1949. Relations between S and N – and between the Republic and the UK – have often been tense during the 'troubles' in Northern Ireland (1968–). However, the Anglo-Irish Agreement (1985) provided for the participation of the Republic in political, legal and security matters in Northern Ireland.

Irgun Zvai Leumi, (Hebrew, 'National Military Organization') a militant Zionist organization formed in 1931 to protect Jewish settlements in Palestine from Arab attack. In the 1940s it conducted a terrorist campaign against the British to force their withdrawal from Palestine; ➪ p. 211.

Irish famine (1845–51), a period of famine in Ireland following a blight that ruined the potato crop, staple diet of the Irish population. It caused the death of about one million Irish people, as well as the emigration of a further million, chiefly to the USA. An inadequate relief programme was exacerbated by absentee landlordism and procrastination by the British government.

Irish Free State, ➪ IRELAND.

Irish Republican Army (IRA), an organization fighting to achieve a united republican IRELAND by means of GUERRILLA warfare. The IRA was formed in 1919 but had roots in earlier anti-British organizations. After British withdrawal from southern Ireland in 1921, the IRA fought and lost a civil war with Irish Free State forces, since when it has been an underground movement. With the renewal of sectarian violence in Northern Ireland in the late 1960s, the IRA split into Official and Provisional wings (1969). The Provisional IRA continues to wage an anti-British terrorist campaign in Northern Ireland and in Britain.

Iron Age, ➪ pp. 6, 12, **13**, **15** and 34.

ironclads, the first wooden battleships with armoured plating. The first 'encounter' between ironclads – *Monitor* v *Merrimac* – took place during the American Civil War; ➪ pp. 158 and 175 (box).

Iron Curtain, a term for the frontier between the former Soviet bloc and the rest of non-Communist Europe; ➪ p. 204.

Ironsides, ➪ NEW MODEL ARMY.

Iroquois, native North American peoples, maize farmers living SE of the Great Lakes. The Iroquois Confederation was formed initially of five tribes in the later 16th century and allied with the British colonists in wars against the French. After the British defeat in the American War of Independence, the bulk of the Iroquois settled in Ontario; ➪ p. 63.

Isabella I (the Catholic; 1451–1504), queen of CASTILE (1474–1504). She was joint ruler of Castile and ARAGON (1479–1504) with her husband FERDINAND; ➪ p. 116.

Isabella of France (1295–1358), queen of England (1308–27), married to EDWARD II in 1308. She became the mistress of Roger Mortimer, with whom she launched an invasion of England (1326) that overthrew her husband. They ruled England together until EDWARD III took over in 1330, and hanged Mortimer.

Isandhlwana, battle of (22 January 1879), a battle between the British and the ZULUS in S Africa. Taken by surprise by Cetshwayo's Impis, the British lost over 1500 men in hand-to-hand fighting.

Islam, ➪ pp. 27 (box), 54, 59, 61, 62–3, 67, 79, 80–1, **82–3**, 87, 88–9, 114–15, 210–13.

Ismailis, one of the branches of the SHIITE form of Islam, which diverged from the major (Twelver) branch, and achieved political dominance in Egypt under the FATIMIDS. A further subdivision became famous in the medieval West as the Assassins. The Aga Khan heads the modern form of that Ismaili branch of Islam.

isolationism, the advocacy of non-participation in the affairs of other nations as the basis of US foreign policy. Isolationism prevented the USA

from joining the League of Nations in 1920 and through the NEUTRALITY ACTS hindered F.D. ROOSEVELT's support for Britain and France before World War II.

Israel, a country on the Mediterranean in the Middle East. Israel (PALESTINE) was occupied by the Hebrews around the 14th century BC. The kingdom of Israel was established about 1000 BC (➪ p. 23). King DAVID made Jerusalem his capital, and under his successor, SOLOMON, the Temple was built and Israel prospered. In the 10th century, the kingdom was divided into Israel in the N and JUDAH in the S, both of which were eventually overrun by the Assyrians (➪ p. 21). In 587 BC Jerusalem was destroyed and many of its people taken into captivity by the Babylonians. The Persians allowed the Jews to return 50 years later. Palestine was then ruled, in turn, by Alexander the Great, the Ptolomies of Egypt and the SELEUCID Empire. Judas Maccabeus revolted against the Seleucids in 141 BC and established a Jewish state that lasted until the Roman conquest in 65 BC. The Zealots – an extreme Jewish sect – were prominent in resistance to Roman rule and led a major revolt in AD 66–70. The Romans destroyed Jerusalem when the revolt was crushed and after a second revolt against the Romans in AD 135, the Jewish population of Palestine was dispersed – the DIASPORA – and the Jews were scattered in small communities across the Middle East, North Africa and Europe. Palestine was part of the Byzantine Empire (➪ p. 80), but in the 7th century an Arab invasion brought the area into the Islamic world (➪ p. 82). In the 12th and 13th centuries the Crusaders unsuccessfully attempted to retake the Holy Land (➪ pp. 88–9). The Turkish Ottoman Empire (➪ pp. 114–15) ruled the area from the early 16th century until 1917–18, when Palestine was captured by British forces (➪ p. 178). The ZIONISTS had hoped to establish a Jewish state, and this hope was intensified following the BALFOUR DECLARATION (1917; ➪ pp. 210–11). However, Palestine came under British administration and it was not until 1948–9 – after the murder of some 6 000 000 Jews in concentration camps by the Nazis (➪ p. 192) – that an explicitly Jewish state emerged. The establishment of a Jewish state met with hostility from Israel's neighbours, leading to a series of Arab–Israeli wars (➪ pp. 211–12). The large-scale influx of Soviet Jews into Israel since 1990 has given extra impetus to the Intifada (Palestinian uprising) against continued Israeli rule in GAZA and the WEST BANK (➪ p. 213). Israel has come under increased international pressure to achieve a Middle East settlement.

Issus, battle of (333 BC), a victory of Alexander the Great over the Persians; ➪ pp. *4*, 27 and 32.

Italy, a country of S Europe. Italy has been united twice – in modern times, since 1861, and in ancient times under the Romans. The Roman Republic was established in 509 BC (➪ p. 36), and by 272 BC all of peninsular Italy had been united under the rule of Rome (➪ p. 37). By 200 BC the foundations of the empire had been laid in the territories conquered from Carthage in N Africa and Spain. For the next five centuries Italy was the centre of the expanding Roman Empire (➪ pp. 38–41). However, by the middle of the 3rd century AD the Roman Empire began to decline, plagued by civil war, economic problems and foreign invasions (➪ p. 41). Rome was sacked by the VISIGOTHS (➪ p. 77) under Alaric (410), but the beleaguered Western Roman Empire lasted until 476 when ODOACER established a Gothic kingdom based in Rome (➪ p. 77). Several centuries of chaotic conditions in Italy followed, during which the PAPACY brought the only stability. The early Middle Ages saw successive waves of invaders – Byzantines, Lombards, Franks, Arabs, Germans, and, in the 11th century, Normans (in the South; ➪ p. 87). The papacy

attempted to strengthen its position in Rome. The supremacy of the Bishop of Rome in the Western Church had been established in 443, but throughout the next thousand years the papacy had to struggle to maintain its position within the Catholic Church and its position as a temporal power in central Italy. Outside the PAPAL STATES, Italy was fragmented into smaller territories. In 800, CHARLEMAGNE conquered Italy and had himself crowned Holy Roman Emperor by the pope in Rome (➪ p. 84). Successive emperors strove to maintain control of Italy, but this brought them into continued conflict with increasingly powerful and independent Italian cities – such as MILAN – and also with the popes who were determined to assert the liberty of the Church (➪ p. 90). Papal disputes with the Holy Roman Empire were common between the 10th and 13th centuries (➪ p. 84), and these conflicts had repercussions throughout Italy. (For the history of Italy from the 12th to the late 15th centuries, including the development of the city-states of Florence, Genoa, Milan and Venice in the N, and the establishment of Spanish power in Sicily and Naples in the S; ➪ pp. 96–7.) In the late 15th century N Italy was invaded by the French. After a bitter struggle for supremacy between the French VALOIS kings and the HABSBURGS (➪ p. 97), the Habsburg Emperor CHARLES V gained control of much of Italy (➪ p. 117). On the division of his empire between the Austrian and Spanish Habsburgs, much of Italy passed to the Austrian branch. French withdrawal from the N was matched by the rise to power of the rulers of PIEDMONT-Savoy, who – after 1720 – also became kings of Sardinia. While some states, felt the effect of the Enlightenment or of more efficient government during the 18th century (➪ p. 134), most of the Italian states saw little development in the 17th and 18th centuries. The kingdom of NAPLES (ruled by Spanish BOURBONS) and the Papal States suffered particularly reactionary and inefficient government. During the Revolutionary and Napoleonic Wars (➪ pp. 146–7), Napoleon annexed part of the peninsula and redrew ancient boundaries. The 'old order' was essentially restored by the Congress of VIENNA (1815) – with the kingdom of Sardinia-Piedmont) and the Austrian provinces of Lombardy-Venetia in the N, the kingdom of the Two SICILIES (Naples) in the S, and the Papal States and minor duchies in the centre (➪ p. 151, map). Napoleon had, however, created a kingdom of Italy (based in Milan) and memories of this short-lived state – and of Napoleonic efficiency and modernization – remained. Revolts against the traditional rulers erupted in 1830 and again in 1848 (➪ pp. 151–2). (For details of Italian unification; ➪ p. 152.) Political development after unification (1861–70) was unsteady. Overseas ventures – such as the attempt to annex parts of ETHIOPIA (1895–6) – were often frustrated. Parliament was held in low esteem and the end of the 19th century saw a series of assassinations, including King Umberto I in 1900. Italy entered World War I on the ALLIED side in the expectation of territorial gains from Austria (➪ p. 176). However, Italy won far less territory than anticipated in the peace treaties after the war (➪ p. 182), when fear of Communist revolution led to an upsurge of Fascism and the accession of Benito MUSSOLINI to power (➪ p. 186). (For details of Italy's alliance with Nazi Germany during World War II; ➪ pp. 190–1.) When Italy was invaded by Allied troops in 1943, Mussolini was dismissed by the king and Italy joined the Allies. In 1946 a republic was proclaimed. Communist influence increased, both at local and national level. However, the dominance of the CHRISTIAN DEMOCRAT Party has kept the Communists out of the succeeding coalitions that have ruled Italy and since 1989–90 the Communists have declined as a political force. Particularly in the 1970s, TERRORIST movements – of both the left and the right – have been active, kidnapping and assassinating senior political and industrial figures (▷ p. 215). Considerable attempts have been made to effect a true unification of the country by encouraging the economic development of the S. However, the political structure of Italy remains unstable, with a succession of short-lived coalitions.

Ivan III (the Great; 1440–1505), grand prince of Muscovy (1462–1505). He claimed the title of 'Ruler of all Russia' in 1497; ▷ p. **126**.

Ivan IV ('the Terrible'; 1530–84), grand prince of Muscovy (1533–47), and first tsar (emperor) of all Russia (1547–84); ▷ p. **126**.

Iwo Jima, battle of (February–March 1945), a prolonged battle between US and Japanese forces for control of the W Pacific island of Iwo Jima in the later stages of World War II; ▷ p. 195.

Jackson, Andrew (1767–1845), US Democratic politician, seventh president of the USA (1829–1837). A self-made frontier aristocrat who led American troops to victory in the Battle of NEW ORLEANS, Jackson personified the democratic and aggressive spirit of the USA as it expanded westwards during the 1830s. He was responsible for introducing the SPOILS SYSTEM into US political life; ▷ pp. 156 and 157.

Jackson, Thomas ('Stonewall', 1824–63), American soldier, one of the most gifted CONFEDERATE generals of the Civil War. The architect of the stunning Shenandoah Valley campaign of 1862, he was accidentally shot and killed by his own troops; ▷ p. 158.

Jacobins, the most radical of the political clubs that flourished during the French Revolution, named after the former Dominican monastery of St Jacques in Paris where it met. They ousted the moderate GIRONDINS in 1793 and, led by ROBESPIERRE, were responsible for the Reign of Terror. The term Jacobin was subsequently used of any extreme left-wing radical; ▷ pp. 144–5, 152 and 153 (box).

Jacobites, supporters of the house of STUART and the claim to the thrones of England, Scotland, and Ireland of JAMES II and his son James Edward Stuart (the Old PRETENDER) after James II's overthrow in the Glorious Revolution of 1688. They took their name from *Jacobus*, the Latin word for James. Drawing most of their support from the Highland clans of Scotland, the Jacobites exerted a significant influence on English politics in the late 17th and early 18th centuries, but their hopes were dashed by the failure of their major rebellions – the FIFTEEN and the FORTY-FIVE; ▷ p. 119.

Jacquerie (May–June 1358), a short-lived peasants' revolt in N France; ▷ p. **93**.

Jagatai Khanate, the division of the Mongol Empire centred on TURKESTAN; ▷ p. 55.

Jagiellon, a Polish dynasty founded by Jagiello, prince of Lithuania (1377–1401), and king of Poland (as Wladislaw I; 1386–1434). His successors ruled Hungary and Bohemia (1471–1526). The dynasty became extinct on the death of Sigismund II Augustus (1548–72).

Jahangir (1569–1627), eldest son of Akbar and Mogul emperor of India (1605–27); ▷ p. 63.

Jainism, an Indian religion founded by the ascetic Mahavira (c. 599–527 BC) in the 6th century BC at about the same time as Buddhism. It remains strong in the W of India; ▷ p. 58.

Jamaica, an island in the Caribbean. Jamaica – which was originally inhabited by Arawak Indians – was sighted by Columbus (1494) and claimed for Spain. It became British in 1655. Black slaves were brought from Africa to work the sugar plantations (▷ p. 129). The abolition of slavery in the 1830s destroyed the plantation system. By the 1930s, severe social and economic problems led to rioting

and the birth of political awareness. Since independence in 1962, power has alternated between the radical People's National Party – led by Michael Manley – and the more conservative Jamaican Labour Party.

James I (1566–1625), the first STUART king of England (1603–25), and, as James VI, king of Scotland (1567–1625). The son of MARY, Queen of Scots, he succeeded ELIZABETH I, with whose death the TUDOR dynasty ended. His refusal to effect PURITAN reform of the ANGLICAN CHURCH, together with his subservient attitude to Spain and insistence on the divine right of kings, contributed to difficulties with PARLIAMENT; ▷ pp. 118–19.

James II (1633–1701) king of England and Scotland (1685–8), the second son of CHARLES I; ▷ p. 119.

James Francis Edward Stuart, ▷ PRETENDER.

Jameson Raid (1895) a raid into the TRANSVAAL led by the British colonial administrator Dr Leander Storr Jameson (1853–1917); ▷ p. 163 (box).

Jamestown, the site on the E coast of Virginia of the first permanent English settlement in North America (1607); ▷ p. 142.

Janissaries, the elite infantry corps of the Ottoman army; ▷ p. 115 (box).

Jansen, Cornelius Otto (1585–1638), Dutch Roman Catholic theologian, the founder of the spiritual movement known as Jansenism. The beliefs of the Jansenists, based on the teachings of St AUGUSTINE on free will, salvation and predestination, in some ways resembled those of CALVIN, and brought them into conflict with the ecclesiastical and secular authorities, who condemned them.

Japan, a country comprising an archipelago in the Pacific off the coast of E Asia. Japanese myth dates the first emperor, Jimmu, to 660 BC. However, the first known emperors reigned in Nara in the 8th century AD. (For details of Japanese history to the late 19th century; ▷ pp. 64–5.) At the end of the 19th century, the MEIJI Emperor overthrew the last shogun and restored power to the throne. He encouraged Western institutions and a Western-style economy, so that by the beginning of the 20th century Japan was rapidly industrializing and on the brink of becoming a world power. By the end of the Meiji era (1912), the Japanese had established an empire. Japan had defeated China (1894–5) – taking Port Arthur and Taiwan – and startled Europe by emerging victorious in the RUSSO-JAPANESE WAR (1904–5) on land and at sea. Korea was annexed in 1910 (▷ p. 65, box). Allied with Britain from 1902, Japan entered World War I against Germany in 1914, in part to gain acceptance as an imperial world power. However, Japan gained little except some of the German island territories in the Pacific and became disillusioned that the country did not seem to be treated as an equal by the Great Powers. The rise of militarism and collapse of world trade led to the rise of totalitarianism and a phase of aggressive Japanese expansion (▷ p. 187). Japan became allied to Nazi Germany and in 1941 Japanese aircraft struck PEARL HARBOR in Hawaii, bringing the USA into World War II (▷ pp. 194–5). An initial rapid Japanese military expansion across SE Asia and the Pacific was halted, and the war ended for Japan in disastrous defeat and the horrors of nuclear attacks on HIROSHIMA and NAGASAKI. Emperor HIROHITO surrendered in September 1945. SHINTOISM – which had come to be identified with aggressive nationalism – ceased to be the state religion, and in 1946 the emperor renounced his divinity. The Allied occupation (1945–52) both democratized politics and began an astonishing economic recovery based on an aggressive export policy. The economy was jolted by major rises in petroleum prices in 1973 and 1979, but Japan nevertheless maintained its advance to become a technological front-runner (▷ pp. 222–3).

Jaruzelski, Wojciech (1927–), Polish soldier and statesman, prime minister (1981–5), president (1989–90). Faced with economic problems and the increasing influence of SOLIDARITY, he imposed martial law (1981–2).

Jaurès, Jean (1859–1914), French socialist politician. He strongly supported DREYFUS and united the French socialists into a single movement. He was assassinated in 1914 by a French nationalist, after advocating a strike by French and German workers against World War I.

Java, the most populous and historically important of the islands of the Indonesian archipelago; ▷ pp. 60–1.

Jefferson, Thomas (1743–1826), third president of the USA (1801–9). A slave-owner, he played a key role in drafting the Declaration of Independence in 1776. He later became governor of Virginia (1779–81) during the War of Independence and served as American minister in Paris and US secretary of state under Washington. After serving as vice-president under John ADAMS, Jefferson led his anglophile Democratic-Republican party to victory in the election of 1800; ▷ p. 156.

Jellicoe, John Rushworth, 1st Earl (1859–1935), British admiral, commander of the Grand Fleet at the battle of JUTLAND; ▷ p. 176.

Jena, battle of (14 October 1806), Napoleon's crushing defeat of a large Prussian force in E Germany. The French victory was followed by Napoleon's occupation of Berlin; ▷ p. 146.

Jenkins's Ear, War of (1739–48), a conflict between Britain and Spain, urged on the British government by merchants resentful of Spanish attempts to exclude English shipping from Spain's overseas empire. They put pressure on a reluctant WALPOLE in Parliament by exploiting Captain Jenkins's claim to have had his ear cut off by Spanish coastguards. The war was later absorbed into the War of the AUSTRIAN SUCCESSION.

Jericho, an ancient city, now in the Israeli-occupied West Bank. Possibly the oldest city in the world, it has been inhabited since c. 8000 BC. In Old Testament tradition, the city fell to Joshua when the walls collapsed at the sound of the Israelite trumpets; ▷ p. 44.

Jerome, St (c. 341–420), Italian theologian. His most important achievement was the production of a standard Latin text of the Bible – the 'Vulgate'. He lived much of his later life as a monk in a cave near Bethlehem.

Jerusalem, a holy city for JEWS (▷ p. 23), Christians and Muslims. As the site of JESUS' teaching and Crucifixion, Jerusalem became increasingly important as a Christian centre from the 4th century AD, and was one of the five PATRIARCHATES of Christendom. The city fell to the Arabs in 637; the Dome of the Rock, the city's holiest Muslim shrine, was built in 691 during the period of Muslim rule. Jerusalem was conquered by Christian Crusaders in 1099 and became part of the Latin Kingdom of Jerusalem, until recaptured by SALADIN in 1187 (▷ p. 88). The city was ruled by the Egyptians and Ottoman Turks until taken by the British in 1917, and remained the capital of the British MANDATE of Palestine until 1948, when it was split between Arabs and Jews in the first Arab–Israeli War. Arab East Jerusalem was annexed by ISRAEL in 1967 (▷ pp. 211 and 212).

Jesuit, ▷ p. 112.

Jesus Christ, religious teacher, regarded by Christians as the Son of God. For historical information about the life and teachings of Jesus we depend almost exclusively on the (late 1st-century) gospel accounts, which are based on an oral tradition preserved by the early Christians, and written by and for believers. Non-Christian sources, such as TACITUS, mention the crucifixion under Pontius

Pilate. Jesus' birth is usually dated before the death of HEROD in 4 BC (the Christian era, starting with the year 1, is based on a miscalculation by a 6th-century monk) and his ministry to the period from c. 28 to 33.

Jews, people of Hebrew descent or those whose religion is JUDAISM. The word Jew is derived from the Latin *Judaeus*, that in turn is derived from the Hebrew *Yehudi*, signifying a descendant of Jacob, the grandson of ABRAHAM. The Exodus of the Jews – which is believed to have occurred c. 1250 BC – was the decisive event in early Jewish history: it resulted in the emergence of Israel as a distinct nation. (For the history of the Jews from the time of King DAVID to the DIASPORA, AD 135; ⊳ ISRAEL.) The dispersed European Jews were the victims of persecution by Christians, partly for religious and cultural reasons and partly because of commercial resentment, and were often confined to ghettoes. Violent ANTI-SEMITISM was common in Europe from the Middle Ages on but reached its most extreme in Nazi Germany where millions of Jews perished in the Holocaust (⊳ p. 192). The idea of a Jewish homeland in PALESTINE was revived in the 19th century and found expression in the establishment of the State of ISRAEL (1948; ⊳ p. 211).

Jiang Jie Shi (Chiang Kai-shek; 1887–1975), Chinese general and statesman, president of China (1928–31 and 1943–9) and of the Republic of China (Taiwan) (1950–75); ⊳ pp. **196** and 223.

Jiangxi Soviet, a Chinese Communist base created in 1931. JIANG JIE SHI's nationalists forced Mao Zedong to withdraw from the base in October 1934; ⊳ p. 196.

jihad, an obligation imposed on Muslims by the QUR'AN to 'strive in the way of God', generally interpreted to mean 'holy war' for the defence or extension of Islam, or of the Muslims' political control over their territories; ⊳ p. 82.

Jimmu, the legendary first ruler of Japan; ⊳ p. 64.

Jin, 1. a N Chinese state established by Juchen nomads from NE MANCHURIA who first gained power over the whole of Manchuria (1119) and then seized N China from the Song Empire (1126), ruling the N until the Mongol invasion of 1210. **2.** ⊳ WESTERN JIN.

Jinnah, Mohammed Ali (1876–1948), Indian Muslim politician, first governor-general of PAKISTAN (1947–8). He became president of the MUSLIM LEAGUE in 1916. Initially willing to compromise with the Hindu Indian National Congress, after 1919 he grew disillusioned with its leadership. By 1940, as leader of the Muslim League, he was campaigning for the partition of INDIA into separate Hindu and Muslim states; ⊳ p. 201.

Joan of Arc (c. 1412–31), French national heroine; ⊳ p. *95*.

Joffre, Joseph Jacques Césaire (1852–1931), marshal of France. As commander-in-chief of the French army (1914–16), he was largely responsible for the decisive Allied victory at the first battle of the MARNE in World War I.

John (1166–1216), king of England (1199–1216). Heir to the whole ANGEVIN empire, by singular incompetence he contrived first to lose ANJOU, NORMANDY and E Poitou in 1203–5 to PHILIP II AUGUSTUS, then to provoke his English barons to rebel. In 1215 they forced him to seal MAGNA CARTA, but by the time he died the realm was once again torn by civil war.

John I (1357–1433), king of Portugal (1385–1433). His victory over CASTILE in the battle of Aljubarotta (1385) ensured Portuguese independence. He then carried the RECONQUISTA across the Straits of Gibraltar in 1415, conquering Ceuta (⊳ p. 123, map).

John VI (1769–1826), king of Portugal (1816–26); ⊳ p. 149 (box).

Johnson, Andrew (1808–75), US Republican politician, seventeenth president of the USA. He served as LINCOLN'S vice-president, assuming the presidency on the latter's assassination in April 1865. His attempts to veto measures for the Reconstruction of the Southern states after the Civil War led to clashes with the Republican majority in Congress; ⊳ p. 159.

Johnson, Lyndon B(aines) (1908–73), US Democratic politician (known as LBJ), thirty-sixth president of the USA (1963–9). As KENNEDY'S vice-president he was sworn in as president when Kennedy was assassinated, and won a sweeping victory in the presidential election of 1964; ⊳ pp. 208, 209, and **216–17**.

John of Austria, Don (1547–78), Spanish general. The illegitimate son of Emperor CHARLES V, he commanded the fleet of the HOLY LEAGUE that defeated the Turkish fleet at LEPANTO (1571) and was governor-general of the Netherlands (1576–8) at a key phase of the DUTCH REVOLT; ⊳ p. *117*.

John Paul II (Karol Wojtyla; 1920–), pope (1978–). A Pole, he became the first non-Italian Pope since 1522 when elected pope in 1978. Anti-Communist and conservative, he became popular in a series of foreign journeys.

Jones, John Paul (1747–92), Scottish-born American seaman whose maritime exploits during the American War of Independence made him one of the founding fathers of the US Navy and a popular hero in America.

Jordan, a kingdom in the Middle East. After being incorporated into the biblical kingdoms of SOLOMON and DAVID, the region was ruled, in turn, by the Assyrian and Babylonian empires (⊳ pp. 20–1), and the Persian (⊳ p. 26) and Seleucid empires (⊳ p. 33). The Nabateans – based at Petra – controlled Jordan from the 4th century BC until 64 BC when the area came under Roman rule. Jordan was part of the Byzantine Empire (⊳ p. 80) from 394 until 636 when Muslim Arab forces were victorious in the Battle of Yarmouk. At first, Jordan prospered under Muslim rule, but declined when the ABBASID caliphs moved their capital to Baghdad (⊳ p. 83). In the 11th and 12th centuries, Crusader states flourished briefly in Jordan (⊳ p. 88). The area was conquered by the Ottoman Empire in the 16th century (⊳ p. 115). In World War I the British aided an Arab revolt against Ottoman rule. The League of Nations awarded the area E of the River Jordan – Transjordan – to Britain as part of the MANDATE of Palestine (1920), but in 1923 Transjordan became a separate EMIRATE. In 1946 the country gained complete independence as the Kingdom of Jordan with Abdullah as its sovereign (⊳ p. 211). The Jordanian army fought with distinction in the 1948 Arab-Israeli War and occupied the WEST BANK territories, which were formally incorporated into Jordan in 1950. In 1951 Abdullah was assassinated. His grandson King Hussein (reigned 1952–) was initially threatened by radicals encouraged by Egypt's President NASSER. In the 1967 Arab-Israeli War (⊳ p. 211), Jordan lost the West Bank, including Arab Jerusalem, to the Israelis. In the 1970s the power of the Palestinian guerrillas in Jordan challenged the very existence of the Jordanian state (⊳ p. 212). King Hussein renounced all responsibility for the West Bank in 1988. A ban on party politics ended in 1991.

Josephine, Empress (Marie Josephine Tascher de la Pagerie; 1763–1814), empress of the French (1804–9) and wife of Napoleon I.

Josephus, Flavius (AD 1st century), Jewish historian. Josephus held a command during the Jewish revolt of AD 66, but was captured and spent the rest of his life in Rome, where he wrote his account of the revolt and his history of the Jews.

Joseph II (1741–90), Holy Roman Emperor (1765–90), effectively joint ruler of Austria with his mother MARIA THERESA to 1780, sole ruler (1780–90); ⊳ pp. 125, *134* and 135.

Joshua, (according to the Old Testament) MOSES' successor as leader of the Israelites; ⊳ p. 23.

Juan Carlos (1938–), king of Spain from 1975. Nominated by FRANCO as his successor, he became king on the latter's death and presided over Spain's transition to a democratic system.

Juárez, Benito (1806–72), Mexican liberal politician who led the resistance to the French-supported Emperor MAXIMILIAN (1862–7).

Juchen, ⊳ JIN.

Judah, the ancient southern Jewish kingdom with its capital at Jerusalem. It was nominally independent until it became part of the Babylonian empire in 587 BC; ⊳ pp. 22 (box) and 23.

Judaism, the oldest of the monotheistic religions. Judaism traces its history back to ABRAHAM's revolt against the idol-worship of his native Mesopotamia (modern Iraq), when he smashed his father's idols and fled to Canaan (modern ISRAEL). The observance of the Passover (*Pesach*) establishes a special relationship between with the One God whose laws Jewish people undertake to observe faithfully. Jewish scripture comprises the same books as the Christian Old Testament (⊳ p. 22). Orthodox Judaism regards all authority as deriving from the Torah (the Pentateuch). Conservative Judaism stands between Orthodoxy and Reformed and Liberal Judaism, which rejects rabbinic authority and holds that Judaism must adapt to changing circumstances.

Jugurtha, king of Numidia (⊳ p. 37, map), who murdered his way to the throne between 118 and 112 BC. He aroused the wrath of Rome by massacring some Italian traders resident in Cirta. The ensuing war lasted until 105 BC, when Jugurtha was defeated and captured by MARIUS.

Julian the Apostate (332–363), Roman emperor (361–3). On becoming emperor he renounced Christianity and proclaimed toleration for all religions, restoring old cults and temples and abolishing Christian privileges; ⊳ p. 40.

July Revolution (1830), a revolution in France that brought about the abdication of the absolutist CHARLES X and the election of LOUIS PHILIPPE as king; ⊳ pp. **150** and 151.

Justinian I (482–565), Byzantine emperor (527–65); ⊳ pp. 78–9 and **80**.

Jutes, a Germanic people originating in Jutland (N Denmark) who settled in Kent and the Isle of Wight in the early 5th century; ⊳ p. 79 (box).

Jutland, battle of (31 May 1916), a naval battle between the British Grand Fleet under JELLICOE and the German High Seas Fleet, fought off the coast of Jutland in the North Sea; ⊳ p. 178.

Kádár, János (1912–89), Hungarian Communist politician. He became party leader after the suppression of the HUNGARIAN REVOLUTION in 1956, dealing ruthlessly with its leaders. He followed a policy of moderate economic reform until his resignation in 1988.

Kadesh, battle of (1285 BC), a clash between Egypt and the Hittites in Syria; ⊳ pp. 17 (map), 19, 22 and 44.

Kalmar, Union of, the union of the crowns of DENMARK, SWEDEN and NORWAY from 1397 to 1523; ⊳ p. 127 (box).

Kamakura, a city SW of Tokyo, where Japan's first SHOGUNATE was set up; ⊳ p. 64.

kamikaze (Japanese, 'divine wind') a tactic used by the Japanese in the later stages of World War II, whereby pilots deliberately crashed aircraft loaded with explosives onto enemy targets; ⊳ p. 195.

Kampuchea, ⊳ CAMBODIA.

Kanagawa, Treaty of (1858), a treaty between Japan and the USA, the first to grant a Western power diplomatic and trading rights in Japan (⊳

p. 65). The terms were extended in the later Treaty of Edo (1858).

Kanem-Bornu, a Central African kingdom located around Lake Chad. Kanem is recorded from the 9th century, Bornu to the W from the 14th century. Bornu annexed Kanem in the late 16th century, forming a powerful Muslim state; ⇨ p. 67.

Kangxi (1654–1722), Chinese emperor of the QING dynasty (1661–1722). During his reign, Taiwan, Tibet and Outer Mongolia were brought under effective imperial control; ⇨ p. 56.

Kansas–Nebraska Act (1854), an Act of the US Congress allowing a referendum on slavery in the territories of Kansas and Nebraska; ⇨ p. 158.

Kapp putsch (March 1920), an attempt by right-wing paramilitaries, led by Wolfgang Kapp (1858–1922), to overthrow the Weimar Republic and restore the German monarchy; ⇨ p. 186.

Karageorge, Petrović (1766–1817), the leader of the first Serbian revolt against the Ottoman Turks (1804–13) and founder of the Karageorgevic dynasty, which ruled SERBIA 1852–8 and 1903–45 (and YUGOSLAVIA from 1929). He was appointed hereditary chief by the Serbian National Assembly (1808), but was defeated by Turkey and driven into exile (1813). He was murdered in 1817 when he re-entered Serbia to assert his authority against the new Serb leadership of Milos OBRENOVIĆ; ⇨ p. 154.

Karnak, the site of the temple of Amun-Ra at THEBES in ancient Egypt; ⇨ pp. 19 and **47.**

Kasavubu, Joseph (1910–69), Congolese politician, first president of the Republic of the Congo (1960–5); ⇨ p. 203 (box).

Kashmir, short for Jammu and Kashmir, a former PRINCELY STATE that attempted to regain independence when India became independent (1947). The state was effectively partitioned – and is still disputed – by INDIA and PAKISTAN; ⇨ p. 201 (box).

Kassites, a dynasty ruling at Babylon (c. 1570–1157) BC; ⇨ p. 20.

Kaunda, Kenneth David (1924–), Zambian statesman. After the independence of Northern Rhodesia (ZAMBIA) in 1964 he became its first prime minister and six months later its first president – an office he held until his electoral defeat in 1991. He was active in the NON-ALIGNED MOVEMENT, and coordinated the policy of the COMMONWEALTH towards the racist regime in South Africa.

Kazakhstan, a republic of Central Asia. The Kazakhs first appear in written history in the late 15th century when they established a nomadic empire in the W and centre of the present republic. Between 1488 and 1518 Kazakh khans controlled virtually all the Central Asian steppe (⇨ p. 55), but before 1600 the Kazakh khanate had split into three separate hordes. In the 17th century the Kazakhs were constantly raided by the Oryats from Djungaria (Xinjiang in China). In the 18th century the Russians began to penetrate the Kazakh steppes and were initially welcomed as overlords in exchange for protection from the Oryats. Revolts against Russian rule were suppressed (1792–4) and what little autonomy the khans still enjoyed was abolished between 1822 and 1848. During the tsarist period there was large-scale Russian peasant settlement on the steppes, but Russian rule was resented and there was a major Kazakh revolt during World War I. After the Russian revolutions (⇨ pp. 180–1), Kazakh nationalists formed a local government and demanded autonomy (1917). The Soviet RED ARMY invaded in 1920 and established an Autonomous Soviet Republic. Kazakhstan did not become a full Union Republic within the USSR until 1936. Widespread immigration from other parts of the Soviet Union became a flood in 1954–6 when the 'Virgin Lands' of N Kazakhstan were opened up for farming. By the time Kazakhstan declared independence – following the abortive coup by Communist hardliners in Moscow (September 1991; ⇨ p. 225) – the Kazakhs formed a minority within their own republic. When the USSR was dissolved (December 1991), Kazakhstan was internationally recognized as an independent republic. The vast new Kazakh state – in theory a nuclear power because of former Soviet nuclear weapons on its territory – occupies a pivotal position within Central Asia.

Keitel, Wilhelm (1882–1946) German field marshal, chief-of-staff of the Supreme Command of the German armed forces (1938–45). A faithful associate of Hitler, he was convicted at the NUREMBERG TRIALS and hanged.

Kekkonen, Urho Kaleva (1900–86), Finnish statesman. As president (1956–82) he promoted his country's neutrality.

Kellogg–Briand Pact (1928), a multilateral agreement condemning war, proposed by the US secretary of state Frank B. Kellogg, and the French foreign minister BRIAND; ⇨ p. 183.

Kennedy, John Fitzgerald (1917–63), US Democratic politician, thirty-fifth president of the USA (1961–3), and the first Roman Catholic to hold that office. His domestic programme involved social reforms and civil rights proposals. In foreign policy he presided over the fiasco of the Bay of Pigs invasion and confronted the USSR in the Cuban Missile Crisis (⇨ p. 206). His presidency saw the start of major US military involvement in Vietnam (⇨ p. 208). He was assassinated in Dallas, Texas, apparently by Lee Harvey OSWALD. His brother Robert F. Kennedy (1925–68) was also assassinated when running for the Democratic presidential nomination in 1968. His brother Edward M. Kennedy (1932–) remains an influential Democratic senator; ⇨ p. 216.

Kenneth I (MacAlpine; d. c. 859), first king of SCOTLAND (843–58). He suppressed the kingdom of the PICTS and imposed Gaelic law and culture on Scotland.

Kenya, a republic of E Africa. Arabs established coastal settlements from the 7th century, and the Portuguese were active on the Kenyan coast from 1498 until the 17th century, when they were evicted by the Arabs. The varied black African peoples of the area were brought forcibly under British rule in 1895 in the East African Protectorate, which became the colony of Kenya in 1920. White settlement in the highlands was bitterly resented by the Africans – particularly the Kikuyu – whose land was taken. Racial discrimination and attacks on African customs also created discontent. Black protest movements emerged in the 1920s and, after 1945, developed into nationalism, led by Jomo KENYATTA, who in 1947 became the first president of the Kenya African Union. When the violent MAU MAU rising – which involved mainly Kikuyu people – broke out (1952–56), Kenyatta was held responsible and was imprisoned on doubtful evidence (1953–61). After the British had crushed the MAU MAU revolt in a bloody campaign, they negotiated with Kenyatta and the other nationalists. Independence, under Kenyatta's KANU party, followed in 1963. His moderate leadership and pro-capitalist policies were continued by his successor, Daniel arap Moi. Considerable restrictions on political activity followed an attempted military coup (1982). From 1989, KANU was the only legal political party, but growing discontent forced the government to permit political pluralism in 1991.

Kenyatta, Jomo (c.1889–1978), first prime minister (1963–4) and president (1964–78) of independent KENYA.

Kepler, Johannes (1571–1630), German astronomer; ⇨ p. 132.

Kerensky, Aleksandr Fyodovich (1881–1970), Russian revolutionary politician, head of the provisional government after the overthrow of NICHOLAS II in March 1917. He continued the war against Germany but failed to implement economic reforms and was ousted by Lenin's BOLSHEVIKS; ⇨ p. 181.

Keynes, John Maynard, Baron (1883–1946), British economist. He criticized the reparations imposed on Germany after World War I as damaging to the international economy. The Depression of the early 1930s led him to argue that unemployment can only be avoided by government spending on public works programmes. Keynes helped to found the INTERNATIONAL MONETARY FUND and the WORLD BANK. His views were central to the establishment of the British WELFARE STATE; ⇨ pp. 183 and 214.

KGB (Russian abbreviation 'Committee of State Security'), the Soviet secret police, formed in 1953 and responsible for external intelligence and internal security. By the 1980s the KGB had over 200 000 men under arms; ⇨ CHEKA, NKVD, OGPU and pp. 199 and **225.**

Khama, Seretse (1921–80), president of Botswana (1966–80). He was exiled to Britain (1949–56) after South African pressure on Britain following his marriage to an Englishwoman. He led Botswana as southern Africa's first prosperous non-racial democracy: ⇨ p. 221.

khanate, a region ruled by a Mongol or Turkic ruler; ⇨ pp. **54–5,** 56, 126 and 127.

Khmers, a people of Cambodia; ⇨ pp. **60–1.**

Khmer Rouge, a Cambodian Communist movement that ruled CAMBODIA 1975–9; ⇨ p. **209.**

Khomeini, Ruhollah (c. 1900–89), SHIITE Muslim leader of the Iranian Revolution of 1979, known as the Ayatollah Khomeini; ⇨ p. 212 (box).

Khrushchev, Nikita Sergeyevich (1894–71), Soviet statesman, First Secretary of the Communist Party (1953–64), prime minister (1958–64); ⇨ pp. **198,** 199 and **200.**

kibbutz, a communal farming settlement in Palestine (later Israel), run by Jews dedicated to the socialist principles first advocated by Theodor HERZL. Self-contained and defensible locations during the early years of Jewish settlement, they are now basically agricultural centres.

Kiesinger, Kurt-Georg (1904–), German CHRISTIAN DEMOCRAT statesman, chancellor of the Federal Republic of (West) GERMANY (1966–9).

Kiev Rus, a state founded in the 9th century, centred on the city of Kiev, which later became divided into a number of principalities. Most of the Kiev Rus fell to the Mongols in the 13th century and later its W and S was overrun by the Lithuanians. Its NE developed into the grand duchy of MUSCOVY. ⇨ pp. 86 and 126

Kim Il-sung (1912–), prime minister of the Democratic People's Republic of (North) KOREA (1948–72), president (1977–); ⇨ p. 223.

King, Martin Luther, Jr (1929–68), US Baptist minister and civil rights activist. Awarded the Nobel Peace Prize in 1964, he was assassinated in Memphis, Tennessee, on 4 April 1968; ⇨ p. 216 (box).

King, William Lyon Mackenzie (1874–1950), Canadian Liberal politician, prime minister (1921–6, 1926–30 and 1935–48). An advocate of Canadian national unity, he governed with the support of Progressives and French Canadians. He promoted Canada's role in NATO after World War II.

Kinnock, Neil Gordon (1942–), leader of the British LABOUR Party (1983–92).

Kirov, Sergei Mironovich (1888–1934), Soviet politician whose murder was used by Stalin to launch his purge of the Communist Party; ⇨ p. 198 (box).

Kissinger, Henry (1923–), German-born US political scientist and statesman who, as National Security Advisor (1969–73) and secretary of state (1973–7), had a major impact on American foreign policy. A one-time hardliner over Vietnam, he won a Nobel Peace Prize (1972) for his role in ending America's involvement in Vietnam. He also helped to end the 1973 Arab-Israeli War; ▷ p. 212.

Kitchener, Horatio Herbert, 1st Earl (1850–1915), British soldier and statesman. His campaign to expel the MAHDI from Sudan ended in victory at Omdurman in 1898. His ruthless policy towards the Boers in the Second Boer War (▷ p. 163), aroused Liberal anger in Britain. He played a crucial role in mobilizing the British army during World War I; ▷ p. 179 (box).

knighthood, a cult of warrior virtues, also known as chivalry, popular in the medieval period. Knights formed a class or 'Order' within medieval society. They entered it through an arming ceremony at about 15 years of age and were expected to be able to ride, fight with lance and sword, and display courtly manners towards women and non-combatants; ▷ p. **100**.

Knights of Labor, a US trade union founded in 1869 by the reformer Uriah S. Stephens. For 20 years he ran a kind of modern industrial unionism, welcoming blacks, women, immigrants and unskilled workers – as well as artisans – into membership; ▷ p. 166.

Knossos, the site of the main palace of the Minoan civilization of Crete; ▷ p. **24**.

Knox, John (1505–72), Scottish Protestant reformer and theologian. He prepared the 'Confession of Faith' adopted by the Scottish Parliament as the foundation of the PRESBYTERIAN Church of Scotland (1560); ▷ p. 111.

Kohl, Helmut (1930–), German statesman. The leader of the CHRISTIAN DEMOCRATS from 1973, he was chancellor of West Germany (1982–90). In elections following German reunification in 1990 he became chancellor of a united Germany, after which he had to contend with problems arising from the integration of the formerly Communist E part of the country into the West German market economy.

Kongfuzi or **Confucius** (551–479 BC), Chinese philosopher; ▷ pp. **52**, 53 and 64.

Königgrätz, battle of (3 July 1866), a battle fought near the Bohemian town of Sadowa, in which the Austrian army was defeated by MOLTKE's Prussians; ▷ p. *153*.

Köprülü, an Albanian family, several of whose members occupied the influential office of grand VIZIER in the Ottoman Empire in the 17th and early 18th centuries; ▷ p. 115.

Koran, ▷ QUR'AN.

Korean War, ▷ pp. 204, **205–6**, and 223–4.

Korea, Democratic People's Republic of, a republic in E Asia – popularly known as North Korea. (For details of Korean history until 1910; ▷ p. 65, box.) Korea – a Japanese possession from 1910 to 1945 – was divided into zones of occupation in 1945. The USSR established a Communist republic in their zone N of the 38th parallel (1948). North Korea launched a surprise attack on the South in June 1950, hoping to achieve reunification by force. The Korean War (1950–3; ▷ pp. 205–6) devastated the peninsula. At the ceasefire in 1953 the frontier was re-established close to the 38th parallel. North Korea has the world's first Communist dynasty, whose personality cult has surpassed even that of Stalin. President KIM IL-SUNG and his son – and anticipated successor – Kim Jong-Il have rejected any reform of the country's Communist system. Since the collapse of Communism in the former USSR and Eastern Europe, North Korea has become increasingly isolated.

Korea, Republic of, a republic of E Asia – popularly known as South Korea. (For details of the history of Korea to 1910; ▷ p. 65, box.) In 1910 Korea fell to harsh Japanese colonial rule. After World War II, the peninsula was divided into Soviet and US zones of occupation. In 1948 the Republic of Korea was established in the American (southern) zone. The surprise invasion of the South by the Communist North precipitated the Korean War (1950–3; ▷ pp. 205–6). The war cost a million lives and ended in stalemate with the division of Korea confirmed. Closely allied to the USA, South Korea underwent an astonishing economic transformation from the 1960s (▷ pp. 222–3). However, the country has experienced long periods of authoritarian rule including the presidencies of Syngman RHEE and PARK CHUNG-HEE. The election of ex-General Roh Tae Woo (1987) introduced the possibility of a more open regime.

Koryo, a former Korean kingdom; ▷ p. 65 (box).

Kossuth, Lajos (1802–94), Hungarian revolutionary who led the revolt against Austria in 1848 (▷ p. 151).

Kosygin, Alexei Nikolaevich (1904–80), Soviet Communist politician. In 1964 he became prime minister following the removal of KHRUSHCHEV. He initially shared power with BREZHNEV, but was eclipsed by him from the late 1960s, resigning in 1980.

Kreisky, Bruno (1911–), Austrian Social Democrat statesman, prime minister (1970–83). In international affairs, Kreisky pursued a policy of 'active neutrality'.

Kremlin, the, (Russian, 'citadel'), the administrative headquarters of the Soviet government (Russian government from 1992). The term was used to describe the central government of the USSR.

Kruger, Stephanus Johannes Paulus (1825–1904), AFRIKANER statesman, president of the TRANSVAAL (1883–1900). His refusal to grant political rights to the *Uitlanders* (non-Afrikaner immigrants in the Transvaal) contributed to the outbreak of the Second Boer War; ▷ p. 163 (box).

Krupp, Alfred (1812–87), German industrialist and armaments manufacturer, nicknamed the 'cannon king' because he sold steel cannon to many nations during BISMARCK's chancellorship. The Krupp dynasty became central to German industrial power and business mythology; ▷ p. 165.

Kublai Khan (1214–94), founder and first emperor (1279–94) of the Yuan dynasty of China, a grandson of Genghis Khan; ▷ pp. 54 (map), **55** and **56**.

Kuchuk Kainardji, Treaty of (1774), a treaty ending the Russo-Turkish War of 1768–74; ▷ pp. 127 and 154.

Ku Klux Klan, the name of two historically distinct white racist organizations. The first was founded in the South in 1867 to obstruct federal Reconstruction policy. The second – anti-Catholic as well as anti-black – emerged during World War I and spread its pernicious doctrines through midwestern and southern states during the course of the 20th century; ▷ p. 159.

Kulak (Russian, 'fist'), a term applied to Russian peasants who were allowed to buy medium-sized farms in STOLYPIN's reforms of 1906; ▷ pp. 180–1 and 198.

Kulturkampf, a dispute between Bismarck's German government and the Roman Catholic Church during the 1870s; ▷ p. 167.

Kun, Béla (1886–1937), Hungarian Communist politician. He overthrew the liberal government and set up a Communist republic in 1919, but was overthrown after only six months by invading Romanian forces.

Kuomintang (or Guomindang, 'National People's Party') a Chinese Nationalist movement founded in 1911. It dominated China from 1928 to 1948 under JIANG JIE SHI. Since 1949 it has been the ruling party of TAIWAN; ▷ pp. 196–7.

Kurdistan, the area inhabited by the Islamic Kurds, which includes parts of the modern states of Iraq, Iran, Turkey, Syria, and Armenia. Kurdistan has never achieved statehood, though at the end of World War I it briefly seemed that it might. Kurdish guerrillas remain active in Iran, Iraq and Turkey; ▷ p. 213 (box).

Kursk, battle of (1943), a decisive tank battle between the Red Army and German forces in World War II; ▷ p. 193.

Kushans, nomads of Iranian origin, who established power over an area stretching from TRANSOXIANA across Afghanistan and KASHMIR to central N India between the 1st and 5th centuries AD; ▷ p. 59.

Kuwait, an EMIRATE on the Persian Gulf. Islam came to Kuwait during the Prophet MUHAMMAD's lifetime. In 1760 the Sabah family created the emirate that has lasted to today, although from 1899 to 1961 Kuwait was a British-protected state. Oil was discovered in 1938 and was produced commercially from 1946. In August 1990 IRAQ invaded and annexed Kuwait (▷ p. 213, box). When Iraq failed to respond to repeated UN demands to withdraw, the UN authorized armed action. Kuwait was liberated by a US-led coalition early in 1991.

Kyrgyzstan (formerly Kirghizia), a republic of E Central Asia. The Kirghiz – a Turkic people – are thought to have migrated to the region in the 12th century. Although nominally subject to UZBEK khans, the nomadic Kirghiz retained their independence until after 1850 when the area was annexed by Russia. Opposition to the Russians – who were given most of the best land – found expression in a major revolt in 1916 and continuing guerrilla activity after the Russian Revolutions of 1917 (▷ pp. 180–1). A Kirghiz Soviet Republic was founded in 1926 and became a full Union Republic within the USSR in 1936. After the abortive coup by Communist hardliners in Moscow (September 1991; ▷ p. 225), Kirghizia declared independence and – under its new name, Kyrgyzstan – received international recognition when the Soviet Union was dissolved (December 1991).

Labour Party, a British left-wing political party founded in 1906 to represent the interests of organized labour. Its 1918 constitution called for democratic control of industry, progressive taxation and the improvement of workers' living conditions. Minority Labour governments held office in 1923–4 and again in 1929–31 (▷ Ramsay MACDONALD). Labour was in opposition after 1931 but entered an all-party wartime coalition in 1940. Under ATTLEE it won a landslide election victory in 1945. The Labour governments of 1945–51 undertook wide-ranging nationalization and extended the WELFARE STATE. Labour lost the 1951 election, remaining in opposition until 1964. The Labour governments of 1964–66, 1966–70 and 1974–79 under WILSON and CALLAGHAN were plagued by mounting economic problems. Since 1979, Labour has been in opposition. The party's sharp move to the left under the leadership of Michael Foot (1980–3) was largely reversed under Neil Kinnock (leader 1983–92).

Lafayette, Marie Joseph, marquis de (1757–1834), French aristocrat and soldier who served in America during the War of Independence. He initially supported the French Revolution, but became disillusioned and fled to Austria in 1792, where he was imprisoned. He was later a leader of the moderates during the JULY REVOLUTION; ▷ p. *143*.

Lancastrian, dynastic name given to the English kings from HENRY IV to HENRY VI, descendants of John of GAUNT, duke of Lancaster. In 1460 their right to the throne was disputed by RICHARD Duke of York; in consequence they became one of the two parties in the Wars of the ROSES; ▷ pp. 95 and 118.

Land League, an organization founded in 1879 by the ex-FENIAN Michael Davitt (1846–1906), with PARNELL as president, to channel Irish agitation over tenant evictions by boycotting unpopular landlords. By 1882 it had given way to the Irish

National League, which put HOME RULE in the forefront of its programme.

Laos, a country of SE Asia. The powerful Lao Buddhist kingdom of Lan Xang was established in the 14th century (⊳ p. 61) and divided into three in 1707. A French protectorate was established in 1893. Japanese occupation in World War II led to a declaration of independence (⊳ p. 201) which the French finally accepted in 1954 (⊳ p. 208), after the colonial war in VIETNAM spilled into Laos. However, the kingdom was wracked by civil war, with royalist forces fighting Communist PATHET LAO. The Viet Cong used Laos as a supply route in the Vietnam War (⊳ p. 209), and US withdrawal from Vietnam allowed the Pathet Lao to take over Laos (1975).

Las Navas de Tolosa (1212), a decisive battle in the Spanish Reconquista; ⊳ p. 89.

La Tène, a site near Lake Neuchâtel in Switzerland that has given its name to a Celtic culture of the late Iron Age; ⊳ pp. 34 and 35.

Lateran Council, a council of the Christian Church summoned by the pope and held at the Lateran Palace in Rome. The most important were the ecumenical or general councils, held in 1123, 1139, 1179, 1215 and 1512–17, whose decrees were binding throughout Western Christendom; ⊳ p. 90.

Lateran Treaties (1929), agreements between MUSSOLINI's government and Pope Pius XI recognizing the VATICAN as an independent state; ⊳ p. 186.

Latimer, Hugh (1485–1555), English Protestant reformer. He was burnt at the stake for heresy with CRANMER and Ridley during the reign of MARY I.

Latin Empire of Constantinople, the Frankish state (1204–61) established by Crusaders after the sack of Constantinople; ⊳ pp. 81 and 89.

Latvia, a republic on the Baltic Sea in NE Europe. Latvia was ruled by the (German) TEUTONIC Knights (⊳ p. 89, box) from 1237 until 1561. The E (Livonia) was Polish until 1629, then Swedish until 1710–21 when it was taken by Russia. The W (Courland) was an autonomous duchy until annexed by Russia in 1795. Latvian national consciousness grew throughout the 19th century. Following the Communist takeover in Russia (1917), Latvian nationalists declared independence (1918). A democratic system lasted until 1936 when General Ulmanis established a dictatorship. The Non-Aggression Pact (1939) between Hitler and Stalin assigned Latvia to the USSR, which invaded and annexed the republic (1940). After occupation by Nazi Germany (1941–4; ⊳ p. 192), Soviet rule was reimposed. Large-scale Russian settlement replaced over 200 000 Latvians who were killed or deported to Siberia. In 1988, reforms in the USSR allowed Latvian nationalists to operate openly. Nationalists won a majority in Latvia's parliament and seceded following the failed coup by Communist hardliners in Moscow (1991; ⊳ p. 225). The USSR recognized Latvia's independence in September 1991.

Laud, William (1573–1645), archbishop of Canterbury (1633–45). He sought to reform the ANGLICAN Church of PURITAN 'corruptions' and restore the power of the clergy. His policies convinced many that he and CHARLES I wished to reintroduce Catholicism, and were a major cause of the ENGLISH CIVIL WAR, during the course of which he was executed; ⊳ p. 119.

Laval, Pierre (1883–1945), French politician, prime minister (1931–2 and 1935–6). After the collapse of France in June 1940 he supported PÉTAIN's VICHY government, becoming effective head of government (1942–4). Arrested as a traitor in 1945, he was tried and executed.

Law, Andrew Bonar (1858–1923), British Conservative politician, prime minister (1922–3). He succeeded BALFOUR as leader of his party in 1910. He

became PM in 1922 when the Conservatives brought down LLOYD GEORGE's coalition government.

Lawrence, Thomas Edward (1888–1935), British scholar and soldier, known as 'Lawrence of Arabia' because of his leadership of the Arab Revolt in 1917–18; ⊳ pp. 178 and 210.

League of Nations, ⊳ pp. **183**, 188 and 228.

Lebanon, a republic on the Mediterranean coast of the Middle East. Lebanon – the home of the ancient Phoenicians (⊳ p. 23) – came, in turn, under Egyptian, Assyrian, Persian, Seleucid, Roman and Byzantine rule. The early Islamic conquests bypassed the Lebanese mountains, leaving important MARONITE Christian enclaves. From the 10th century, SHIITE Islam came to Lebanon, and in the 11th century the DRUZE (a breakaway sect from the Shiites) became a significant force in the region. In the 12th and 13th centuries, the Crusader state of Tripoli (⊳ p. 88) flourished in Lebanon; in the 14th century the area was ruled by MAMLUKS from Egypt. In 1516 the (Turkish) Ottoman Empire took Lebanon (⊳ p. 115, map), administering it as part of Syria, although Druze princes enjoyed considerable autonomy. Intercommunal friction was never far from the surface. A massacre of thousands of Maronites by the Druzes (1860) brought French intervention. After World War I, France received Syria as a League of Nations MANDATE, and created a separate Lebanese territory to protect Christian interests. (For the history of Lebanon from 1945; ⊳ pp. 210 and 212–13.)

Lebensraum (German, 'living space'), a term used by the Nazis to describe those non-German speaking territories to the E of Germany which they intended to settle; ⊳ pp. 186, 188 and 192.

Lechfeld, battle of (955), a battle fought near Augsburg in which a MAGYAR raiding army was defeated by combined German forces under OTTO I; ⊳ p. 84.

Lee Kuan Yew (1923–), prime minister of SINGAPORE (1959–90); ⊳ p. 223.

Lee, Robert E. (1807–70), Virginian-born soldier who commanded CONFEDERATE forces in the E theatre of the American Civil War. Although one of the finest tacticians of that conflict, he was nonetheless responsible for the South's disastrous defeat at Gettysburg in 1863; ⊳ pp. 158–9.

legion, the basic unit of the Roman field army, made up of 60 centuries and containing 4000–5000 infantry. The imperial army amounted to 25–30 legions, commanded by 'legates' of the emperor, and stationed in the frontier provinces; ⊳ pp. 38 (box) and 45.

Leif Eriksson (10th–11th centuries), Norse explorer who reached E Canada (VINLAND); ⊳ pp. 72 and 86.

Leipzig, battle of (also called the 'battle of the Nations', 16–19 October 1813), a decisive defeat of Napoleon by Prussia, Sweden and Austria. Napoleon's army suffered enormous losses and was forced back across the Rhine, allowing the allies to invade France; ⊳ p. 147.

Lemass, Séan Francis (1899–1971), Irish FIANNA FÁIL statesman, prime minister (1959–66).

Lend-Lease Act (1941), US legislation authorizing the supply of equipment and services to Britain and its Allies during World War II; ⊳ p. 190.

Leningrad, siege of, the defence of Leningrad (1941–4), by the RED ARMY in World War II; ⊳ p. 193.

Lenin, Vladimir Ilyich (b. Ulyanov; 1870–1924), Russian revolutionary politician, the leader of the BOLSHEVIKS (from 1903) and founder of the Soviet Union (1922); ⊳ pp. *3*, **180**, **181** and 198.

Leo III (c. 750–816), pope (795–816). He was expelled from Rome by rivals, but reasserted himself with

the help of Charlemagne, whom he crowned emperor; ⊳ pp. 84 and 90.

Leonidas I, king of Sparta (c. 490–480 BC). He commanded the Greek forces at the battle of THERMOPYLAE.

Leopold I (1640–1705), Holy Roman Emperor (1658–1705). His reign witnessed a significant increase in Austrian HABSBURG power; ⊳ p. 124.

Leopold II (1835–1909) king of the Belgians (1865–1909). Chiefly concerned with Belgian colonial expansion, he became king of the Congo Free State (now ZAÏRE) in 1885; ⊳ p. 203 (box).

Lepanto, battle of (7 October 1571), a naval battle off W Greece between the Ottomans and the HOLY LEAGUE; ⊳ pp. 115 and *117*.

Lepidus, Marcus (d. 13 BC), Roman politician, the third member of the Second TRIUMVIRATE; ⊳ p. 37.

Lesotho, a country in southern Africa. Lesotho was founded in the 1820s by the Sotho leader, Moshoeshoe I (c. 1790–1870). The kingdom escaped incorporation in South Africa by becoming a British protectorate (known as Basutoland) in 1868. Since independence (1966; ⊳ p. 202, map), landlocked Lesotho remains dependent on South Africa. Chief Jonathan (PM 1966–86) attempted to limit South African influence, but was deposed in a coup. The Military Council removed the king's powers and (in 1990) placed his son on the throne.

Leuctra, battle of (371 BC), Theban victory over the Spartans in central Greece; ⊳ pp. 31 and 44.

Levant, the coastal region of the E Mediterranean; ⊳ pp. 17, 18 and 20–1.

Levellers, a radical group that enjoyed support within the NEW MODEL ARMY during the ENGLISH CIVIL WAR. They advocated an increase in the electorate, the abolition of the monarchy and House of LORDS, law reform, religious toleration and the abolition of excise taxes and tithes. The Levellers mutinied in 1647 and 1649, but were rooted out of the army, and were a spent force by the 1650s. The 'True Levellers' or Diggers, a more radical group, favoured the communal ownership of land; ⊳ p. 5.

Lewis and Clark expedition (1804–6), a transcontinental journey that explored the territory acquired by the USA in the LOUISIANA Purchase; ⊳ p. *156*.

Lexington and Concord, battle of (19 April 1775), the opening skirmish of the American War of Independence. British forces trying to confiscate a cache of weapons N of Boston were repulsed by armed Massachusetts farmers; ⊳ p. 147.

Leyte Gulf, battle of (1944), a naval battle between US and Japanese forces in World War II; ⊳ p. 195.

liberalism, a political philosophy based on the values of tolerance, freedom of expression and individual liberty. The writings of John LOCKE were an early source of liberal political thought, and many of the principles of political liberalism were enshrined in the Constitution of the USA (⊳ p. 143, box). In the 19th century 'classical liberalism' embraced an economic philosophy insisting on a laissez-faire economy untrammelled by state intervention. In the late 19th century the social inequalities created by unfettered industrial capitalism produced a new type of liberal thinking, given practical expression by the reforming administrations of ASQUITH and LLOYD GEORGE in Britain. Henceforth, however, the cause of political and social reform was to be more successfully championed by the emerging SOCIAL DEMOCRAT and SOCIALIST parties, and Liberal parties went into decline. Traditional 'free-market' economic liberalism enjoyed a revival of influence in the hands of right-wing conservatives such as Margaret THATCHER in Britain and Ronald REAGAN in the USA during the 1980s; ⊳ pp. 150–1 and **168**.

Liberal Democratic Party (LDP), the dominant political party in Japan since World War II; ⇨ p. 222.

Liberal Party, a British political party, the successor to the WHIG party. Associated with FREE TRADE and the growth of civil and political liberty, it flourished from the mid-19th century to the 1920s under such premiers as GLADSTONE, ASQUITH and LLOYD GEORGE. The party split between Asquith's and Lloyd George's factions after World War I, and, with the rise of the LABOUR PARTY, went into decline until the 1960s. Many of the founders of the WELFARE STATE, notably BEVERIDGE and KEYNES, were Liberals. Under David Steel the Liberals forged a pact with CALLAGHAN'S Labour government, and in alliance with the SOCIAL DEMOCRATIC Party (SDP) challenged Labour as the principal opposition party in the 1980s. After their merger with the SDP in 1988, the party became the Liberal Democratic Party, with Paddy Ashdown as leader.

Liberia, a republic in W Africa. Founded by the American Colonization Society in 1821–2 as a settlement for freed slaves, Liberia was declared a republic in 1847. Black American settlers dominated the local Africans and extended their control inland. From 1878 to 1980 power was held by presidents from the True Whig Party, including William Tubman (president 1944–71). Samuel Doe, the first Liberian of local ancestry to rule, took power in a military coup (1980), but was overthrown in a civil war (1990).

Libya, a country of N Africa. In the 7th century BC Phoenicians (⇨ p. 23) settled Tripolitania – which became part of the Carthaginian empire (⇨ p. 23) – and the Greeks founded cities in Cyrenaica. From the 1st century BC coastal Libya came under Roman rule. By the 5th century AD Libya – then part of the Byzantine Empire (⇨ p. 80) – was largely Christian. Arab armies brought Islam to Libya in the 7th century (⇨ p. 82). Tripolitania came under BERBER rule, and Cyrenaica became Egyptian, while the S – Fezzan – remained independent. In the 16th century, the whole of Libya was united under (Turkish) Ottoman rule after a brief period of Spanish rule in Tripoli (⇨ p. 114). Autonomous local dynasties flourished under Ottoman rule and after 1911 when the Italians took Libya. The British Eighth Army defeated the Italians in the Libyan Desert (1942; ⇨ p. 190), and after World War II the country was divided between British and French administrations. Libya gained independence in 1951 (⇨ p. 202, map) under King IDRIS, formerly Emir of Cyrenaica. Although oil revenues made Libya prosperous, the pro-Western monarchy became increasingly unpopular. In 1969 junior army officers led by Muammar al-QADDAFI took power. Gaddafi nationalized the oil industry, but his various attempts to federate with other Arab countries proved abortive. In the 1970s he began a cultural revolution, dismantled formal government, collectivized economic activity, limited personal wealth and suppressed opposition. Libya's alleged support of TERRORISM provoked US air raids on Tripoli and Benghazi in 1986, and UN sanctions in 1992.

Liebknecht, Wilhelm (1826–1900), German politician, a co-founder of the SOCIAL DEMOCRATIC Party.

Liechtenstein, a principality in Central Europe. In 1719 the counties of Schellenberg and Vaduz were united to form a principality for the Austrian Princes of Liechtenstein. Separated from Germany by Austrian territory, Liechtenstein was the only German principality not to join the German Empire in 1871 (⇨ p. 153). Since 1924 the country has enjoyed a customs and monetary union with Switzerland.

Lie, Trygve (1896–1968), Norwegian politician and first Secretary-General of the United Nations (1946-53); ⇨ p. 229.

Lin Biao (Lin Piao; 1908–71), Chinese Communist general and politician. Designated Mao's successor in 1969, he was apparently killed in a plane crash while fleeing to the USSR after organizing an abortive coup against Mao.

Lincoln, Abraham (1809–65), sixteenth president of the USA (1861–5). His election as Republican president on an anti-slavery programme led to the secession of the CONFEDERATE states and to the American Civil War. His salvation of the Union in that conflict, together with his emancipation of the slaves (1862) and his championing of American democracy have ensured him almost legendary status in US history; ⇨ pp. **158–9.**

Lithuania, a country on the Baltic Sea in NE Europe. The Lithuanians were first united c. 1250. Their 'grand princes' greatly enlarged the country, annexing Byelorussia (now BELARUS) and most of UKRAINE. The marriage of grand prince JAGIELLO to the queen of Poland (1386) united the crowns of the two countries, although Lithuania retained autonomy until 1569. Lithuania was annexed by Russia in 1795 when Poland was partitioned (⇨ p. 125, box). Lithuanian national consciousness increased throughout the 19th century and Lithuanians rose with the Poles against Russian rule in 1830–1 and 1863. German forces invaded in 1915 and encouraged the establishment of a Lithuanian state. After World War I, the new republic faced invasions by the RED ARMY from the E and the Polish army from the W (1919–20). Internationally recognized boundaries were not established until 1923. The dictatorship of Augustinas Voldemaras (1926–29) was followed by that of Antonas Smetona (1929–40). The Non–Aggression Pact (1939) between Hitler and Stalin assigned Lithuania to the USSR (⇨ p. 189), which invaded and annexed the republic (1940). Lithuania was occupied by Nazi Germany (1941–4; ⇨ p. 192). When Soviet rule was reimposed (1945), large-scale Russian settlement replaced over 250 000 Lithuanians who had been killed or deported to Siberia. In 1988, reforms in the USSR allowed Lithuanian nationalists to operate openly. Nationalists won a majority in the republic's parliament, but their declaration of independence (1990) brought a crackdown by Soviet forces in Lithuania. Following the failed coup by Communist hardliners in Moscow (August 1991; ⇨ p. 225), the USSR recognized Lithuania's independence.

Little Big Horn, battle of (25 June 1876), the defeat of General CUSTER's forces by the SIOUX under CRAZY HORSE. Over 200 men of the US 7th cavalry died in Custer's last stand.

Litvinov, Maksim Maksimovich (1876–1951), Soviet politician and diplomat; a firm supporter of the LEAGUE OF NATIONS and an advocate of collective security against the rising tide of Fascism in the 1930s; ⇨ p. *198*.

Liverpool, Robert Banks Jenkinson, 2nd Earl of (1770–1828), British TORY politician, prime minister (1812–27). His government's repressive measures were mitigated after 1822 by the more liberal influence of PEEL and CANNING.

Livingstone, David (1813–73), Scottish missionary and explorer whose discoveries included the Zambezi River (1851), the Victoria Falls (1855) and Lake Malawi (1859). His famous meeting with STANLEY took place at Ujiji in 1871.

Livy (Titus Livius; c. 59 BC–AD 17), Roman historian; ⇨ p. 2.

Lloyd George, David, 1st Earl of Dwyfor (1863–1945), British Liberal politician, prime minister (1916–22). He served as Chancellor of the Exchequer (1908–15) under ASQUITH, his 'PEOPLE'S BUDGET' causing a constitutional crisis. He became PM of a coalition government after Asquith's overthrow in 1916, proving an energetic leader during World War I. He strove for a more moderate settlement at

the PARIS PEACE CONFERENCE. Known as the 'Welsh wizard', he was an eloquent orator, but his perceived opportunism led to a split in the LIBERAL Party from which it never recovered; ⇨ p. 182.

Llywelyn (the Great; 1195–1240), king of Gwynedd. He established a powerful Welsh principality based on N Wales. Taking advantage of the civil war at the end of JOHN's reign, he was able to bring the English crown to recognize his achievement.

Locarno, treaties of (1925), a series of agreements, signed by various European powers, guaranteeing the German frontiers in the W and, by treaties of mutual guarantee between France, Czechoslovakia and Poland, safeguarding borders in the E; ⇨ p. 183.

Locke, John (1632–1704), English philosopher and political theorist; ⇨ p. **135** (box).

Lodi, Peace of (9 April 1454), a treaty between warring Italian states; ⇨ p. 97.

Lollards, followers of the late 14th-century English religious reformer John Wyclif; ⇨ p. **91.**

Lombardy, a region of N Italy, taking its name from the Lombards whose invasion of Italy in the 6th century finally ended Justinian's reconquest. Independent until conquered by the Franks in the 8th century, the cities of the plain of the River Po developed a high material culture and became important financial centres from the 12th century; ⇨ pp. 79, 80 and 96.

London dockers' strike (August 1889), a spontaneous strike by London dockers. Socialists such as Tom Mann and John Burns assisted union leader Ben Tillett in organizing the demand for sixpence an hour – 'the docker's tanner' – which was achieved after the intervention of Cardinal Manning (1808–92); ⇨ p. 166.

Long March (1934–5), the epic journey undertaken by Chinese Communists from SE to NW China after repeated KUOMINTANG attacks on the JIANGXI SOVIET; ⇨ p. 196.

Long Parliament, the Parliament called by CHARLES I in November 1640. Despite periodic purges of its members and the frequent changes of regime between 1649 and the RESTORATION, it was not legally dissolved until March 1660.

longship, the long, narrow, double-pointed warship of the Vikings, propelled by oars and sails. Crews varied from 20 to 80 oarsmen and warriors. Its excellent sea-going qualities made possible the ambitious Viking voyages, while its shallow draught allowed deep penetration of European river basins; ⇨ pp. 86 and 103.

López, Francisco Solano (1827–70), Paraguayan dictator (1862–70). His devastating PARAGUAYAN WAR with Brazil, Uruguay and Argentina (1865–70) reduced the male population of Paraguay by as much as nine-tenths.

Lords, House of, the upper chamber of the English PARLIAMENT. Composed of unelected hereditary peers (until the addition of life peers in the 20th century) and the heads of a number of monastic houses (until the Reformation, after which they were replaced by a number of bishops), it was for long the more important of the two chambers. It was temporarily abolished during the COMMONWEALTH and, although restored in 1660, its power vis-à-vis the COMMONS has gradually declined since the 17th century.

Louis I (the Pious; 778–840), king of the Franks, emperor of the Romans (814–40) and son of CHARLEMAGNE; ⇨ pp. 84 and 86.

Louis IX, St (1214–70), king of France (1226–70). His piety – he led two crusades – sense of honour and justice did much to reconcile the French people to the massive expansion of the power of central government that had characterized the reigns of both his father Louis VIII and grandfather PHILIP II.

Louis XI (1423–83), king of France (1461–83). He consolidated the remarkable territorial gains made by his father CHARLES VII. At the treaty of Picquigny (1475) he bought off an English invasion. He later exploited the death of CHARLES THE BOLD (1477) to acquire Picardy and the duchy of BURGUNDY.

Louis XIII (1601–43), king of France (1610–43). The eldest son of HENRY IV, he was greatly influenced by his chief minister RICHELIEU from 1624; ⇨ p. 122.

Louis XIV (1638–1715), king of France (1643–1715); ⇨ pp. 119, **122–3**, 124, 131 and 133.

Louis XV (1710–74), grandson of Louis XIV and king of France (1715–74). His reign saw disastrous defeats abroad during the SEVEN YEARS WAR, increasing political conflict with the sovereign courts (*parlements*), and a loss of prestige by a monarchy increasingly seen by its opponents as despotic.

Louis XVI (1754–93), the last king of France (1774–92) before the French Revolution; ⇨ pp. **144–5**.

Louis XVIII (1755–1824), king of France (1814–15 and 1815–24). The brother of LOUIS XVI, he assumed the title of king while in exile in 1795; ⇨ p. 147.

Louisburg, a former French fortress in Nova Scotia in Canada. Built in 1720, it was captured by the British in 1745, returned to the French in 1748 and finally taken and destroyed by WOLFE in 1758; ⇨ pp. 128 (map) and 129.

Louisiana, 1. a state of the USA admitted to the Union in 1812. **2.** a former French province encompassing much of the present-day S and midwestern USA, purchased by President Thomas JEFFERSON from Napoleon in 1803 (⇨ pp. 129, 156 and 157, map).

Louis Philippe I (1773–1850), king of the French (1830–48), elected to that position after the JULY REVOLUTION of 1830. However, the 'citizen king' became ever more repressive as dissent, fuelled by agricultural and industrial depressions, grew. He was overthrown by the REVOLUTION OF 1848, fleeing to England as 'Mr Smith'; ⇨ pp. 150–1.

Loyola, St Ignatius (1491–1556), Spanish Catholic reformer and founder of the Jesuits; ⇨ p. 112.

Ludendorff, Erich von (1865–1937), German general and politician. Chief-of-staff to HINDENBURG, he planned the battle of TANNENBERG and stabilized the German line on the Western Front after 1916. He planned the last major German offensive of World War I and fled to Sweden after Germany's defeat. He took part in the KAPP PUTSCH (1920) and assisted Hitler in the abortive MUNICH PUTSCH.

Lumumba, Patrice (1925–61), Congolese politician, first prime minister of the Democratic Republic of the Congo (now Zaïre); ⇨ p. 203 (box).

Lusitania, British transatlantic liner sunk by a German submarine on 7 May 1915 with the loss of 1195 lives, some of them citizens of the neutral USA.

Luther, Martin (1483–1546), ⇨ pp. **110** and 111.

Luthuli, Albert John, (1898–1967), black South African politician, president of the ANC (1952–67). Representing the Christian liberal element in the ANC, he advocated passive resistance to APARTHEID and received the Nobel Peace Prize in 1960.

Lützen, battle of (1632), an engagement during the Thirty Years War in which the Protestant forces of the Swedish king, GUSTAVUS II ADOLPHUS (who died in the battle), defeated the Catholic imperial forces under WALLENSTEIN; ⇨ p. 113.

Luxembourg, a country in NW Europe. Luxembourg has changed hands many times through inheritance and invasion. In 1443, Luxembourg passed to the dukes of Burgundy, and was inherited by the Spanish HABSBURGS in 1555–56. In 1713 the country came under Austrian rule, but was annexed by France during the Napoleonic Wars. In

1815 Luxembourg became a Grand Duchy with the Dutch king as sovereign, but in 1890 it was inherited by a junior branch of the House of ORANGE. Occupied by the Germans during both World Wars, Luxembourg concluded an economic union with Belgium in 1922 and has enthusiastically supported European unity.

Luxemburg, Rosa (1870–1919), German revolutionary leader, founder (with Karl Liebknecht) of the Communist Spartacist Movement. She and Liebknecht were murdered by right-wing irregulars during the SPARTACIST revolt of 1919 (⇨ p. 186).

Lydia, a kingdom that flourished in W Anatolia in the 1st millennium BC; ⇨ pp. 26, 43 and 47 (box).

Lynch, John Mary (1917–), Irish FIANNA FÁIL statesman. 'Jack' Lynch – a leading Gaelic football player – was prime minister 1966–73 and 1977–9.

Lysander, (c. 456–395 BC), Spartan admiral who did most to win the naval victories that won the Peloponnesian War for Sparta (⇨ pp. 30–1).

MacArthur, Douglas (1880–1964), US general. He conducted a brilliant campaign in the SW Pacific in World War II and was commander of the Allied occupation forces in Japan (1945–51). He commanded UN forces in Korea (1950–1), but was sacked for advocating attacks on China, ⇨ pp. **194–5** and 222.

McCarthy, Joseph Raymond (1908–57), ⇨ pp. **205** (box) and 216.

Macaulay, Thomas Babington, 1st Baron (1800–59), English historian and politician; ⇨ p. 6.

Macbeth (d. 1057), king of Scotland (1040–54). He became king after killing his predecessor (Duncan I). In 1054 he was defeated by Earl Siward of Northumbria at Dunsinnan Hill, but was able to hold on in Moray until he was killed in 1057.

Maccabees, a Jewish family who led a revolt against the Syrian rulers of Israel (168–142 BC). The semi-independent state they created lasted until the capture of Jerusalem by the Romans in 63 BC.

Maccabeus, Judas, ⇨ ISRAEL.

McClellan, George B. (1826–85), US soldier who commanded the Union Army of the Potomac during the early years of the American Civil War. His apparent reluctance to engage the enemy after the battle of ANTIETAM led to his dismissal in November 1862; ⇨ p. 158.

MacDonald, James Ramsay (1866–1937), British LABOUR statesman, prime minister (1924 – the first Labour PM – and 1929–35). His second Labour government (1929–31) collapsed over a cabinet split on employment benefit cuts. MacDonald's decision to form a coalition National Government (1931–5) split the Labour party, which expelled him in 1935.

Macdonald, Sir John Alexander (1815–91), Canadian politician, the first prime minister of the Dominion of Canada (1867–73 and 1878–91) after the passing of the BRITISH NORTH AMERICA ACT.

Macedon, a kingdom in the N of ancient Greece; ⇨ pp. 31 (map) and 32.

Macedonia, the name adopted in 1945 by a constituent republic of YUGOSLAVIA for a region that had, in part, been within the ancient kingdom of MACEDON. The area became Slavic in the 9th century and was ruled by the Byzantine Empire and then by SERBIA before falling to the Ottoman Empire in the 1370s. In the 20th century, the region was disputed in two Balkan Wars and in World War I, after which it was ceded to Serbia. During the Yugoslav Civil War (1992; ⇨ p. 224) Macedonia effectively seceded from Yugoslavia.

Machel, Samora, (1933–86), first president of independent MOZAMBIQUE (1976–86). Continuing civil war defeated his plans for socialist transformation of his country

Machu Picchu, a well-preserved city of the Incas (⇨ p. 71) in the Andes of Peru. It escaped destruction at the hands of the conquistadors and was only rediscovered in 1911; ⇨ pp. *50–51*.

McKinley, William (1843–1901), twenty-fifth president of the USA (1897–1901). He was elected president as an orthodox Republican in the watershed election of 1896. The SPANISH-AMERICAN WAR was fought during his presidency. Elected to a second term in 1900, his career was cut short by an anarchist's bullet in 1901.

Macmillan, Harold, 1st Earl Stockton (1894–1987), British Conservative politician, prime minister (1957–63). He succeeded EDEN after the SUEZ crisis. His term as PM was one of prosperity, Macmillan himself saying, 'You've never had it so good'. His government dismantled the British Empire in Africa, and strengthened Anglo-US collaboration, but failed to take Britain into the EEC when DE GAULLE vetoed British membership in 1963; ⇨ p. 202.

Madagascar, an island-republic off the SE coast of Africa (⇨ p. 202, map). The first inhabitants were POLYNESIANS from Indonesia in the early centuries AD, and were later joined by mainland Africans and by Arabs. In the early 19th century, the island was united by the Merina kingdom. The Merina sovereigns attempted to modernize Madagascar but the island was annexed by France in 1896, although resistance continued until 1904. Strong nationalist feeling found expression in a major rising (1947–8) that was suppressed with heavy loss of life. Independence was finally achieved in 1960. Since a military coup in 1972, Madagascar has had left-wing governments. Mounting public pressure brought economic and political reforms after 1990.

Madero, Francisco Indalécio (1873–1913), a leader of the MEXICAN REVOLUTION and president of Mexico (1911–13).

Madison, James (1751–1836), US politician, fourth president of the USA (1809–17). Initially a defender of federal power over STATES' RIGHTS, he played a major role in drafting the US Constitution and Bill of Rights. His presidency was dominated by the WAR OF 1812; ⇨ p. 143.

Magdalenian, the final phase of the Upper Palaeolithic period of European prehistory; ⇨ p. 14 (box).

Magdalha, a centre of ancient kingdoms of NE India on the middle Ganges; ⇨ pp. 58 and 59.

Magellan, Ferdinand (c.1480–1521), Portuguese navigator; ⇨ p. 109.

Magenta, battle of (4 June 1859), French victory over Austria during the wars for the unification of Italy; ⇨ p. 152.

Maginot Line, fortifications built by the French to protect their border with Germany before World War II. Since it was not continued along the Franco-Belgian border to the coast, the Germans were able to outflank the line and advance into France from Belgium (spring 1940) (⇨ p. 190).

Magna Carta, a charter that rebel barons forced the English king JOHN to seal at Runnymede (15 June 1215) – in effect the first written constitution in European history. It granted rights and liberties 'to all freemen of the realm and their heirs for ever' and by the mid-13th century was generally regarded as a fundamental statement of English liberties – hence the term 'Great Charter'. But John had no intention of abiding by its terms and civil war soon broke out again.

Magyars, nomadic raiders who occupied the area W of the Carpathians in the 890s and terrorized much of Central and S Europe in the following decades. But as they gave up nomadism so they gradually became less of a threat; the raid that ended at LECHFELD was probably a last throw before they settled down as Hungarians; ⇨ pp. 54 and 84.

Mahdi, the name given by SUNNI Muslims to a Messiah whose coming before the Last Day will bring a reign of justice on Earth. Of the many who have claimed the title, the most notable was the Sudanese Muhammad Ahmad bin Abdallah (1843–85), who revolted against Anglo-Egyptian rule and besieged General GORDON in Khartoum; ▷ pp. 161 and 162.

Mahican or **Mohican,** a native N American people, living as maize farmers in the Eastern Woodlands (upper New York state). They were dispersed by the Dutch in the mid-17th century.

Mahmud of Ghazni (969–1030), Muslim ruler of the Ghaznavid dynasty of Afghanistan; ▷ p. 62.

Majapahit, a former Hindu kingdom centred on Java; ▷ p. 60.

Major, John (1943–), British Conservative politician. He became prime minister in November 1990 after Margaret THATCHER was persuaded to stand down, and led the Conservatives to their fourth consecutive election victory over Labour in April 1992.

Makarios III (1913–77), Greek Cypriot Orthodox archbishop and politician. Originally a supporter of the union of Cyprus with Greece (ENOSIS), he became the first president of the Republic of CYPRUS (1960–74 and 1974–7).

Malacca, a former city-state on the SW coast of the Malay peninsula. Its Muslim rulers controlled the spice trade through the Straits of Malacca in the 15th century. Capture by the Portuguese in 1511 marked the beginning of European dominance in the area; ▷ pp. 60 and 61.

Malan, Daniel François (1874–1959), South African National Party statesman, prime minister (1948–54); ▷ p. 221.

Malawi, a republic of central Africa. David LIVINGSTONE and other British missionaries became active in the area from the 1860s. A British protectorate, later called Nyasaland, was declared in 1891. In 1915 the Rev. John Chilembwe led a violent rising in the fertile S where Africans had lost much land to white settlers. Federation with the white-dominated CENTRAL AFRICAN FEDERATION (1953–63) was resented. The nationalist leader Hastings Banda (later president) helped to break the Federation. Since independence as Malawi in 1964, Banda has provided strong rule and – despite criticism – maintained close relations with South Africa.

Malaya, a region of SE Asia, now the peninsular part of the state of MALAYSIA.

Malaysia, a country of SE Asia. Malaysia's ethnic diversity reflects its complex history and the lure of its natural wealth and prime trading position. Most of the area was part of the Buddhist Sumatran kingdom of Srivayaja (▷ p. 60) from the 9th century to the 14th century, when it fell to the Hindu Javanese. From the 15th century, Islam came to the region and the spice trade attracted Europeans. The trading post of Malacca was taken by the Portuguese in 1511 and then by the Dutch in 1641. The British established themselves on the island of Penang (1786), founded SINGAPORE (1819), and in 1867 established an administration for the Straits Settlements – Malacca, Penang and Singapore. Ignoring Thai claims to overlordship in the peninsula, the British took over the small sultanates as protected states. The British suppressed piracy and developed tin mining with Chinese labour and rubber plantations with Indian workers. Sarawak became a separate state under Sir James Brooke – the 'White Raja' – and his family from 1841, and was ceded to the British Crown in 1946. Sabah became British – as British North Borneo – from 1881. The Japanese occupied the whole of Malaysia during World War II (▷ p. 192). A Federation of Malaya – the peninsula – was

established in 1948, but was threatened by Communist insurgency until 1960. Malaya became independent in 1957 with a constitution protecting the interests of the Malays who were fearful of the energy and acumen of the Chinese. Sabah, Sarawak and Singapore joined the Federation – renamed Malaysia – in 1963 (▷ p. 200, map). Singapore left in 1965 but the unity of the Federation was maintained, with British armed support, in the face of an Indonesian 'confrontation' in Borneo (1965–6). Tension between Chinese and Malays led to riots and the suspension of parliamentary government (1969–71), but scarcely hindered the rapid development of a resource-rich economy. During the 1980s, the growth of Islamic fundamentalism led to a defensive re-assertion of Islamic values and practices among the Muslim Malay ruling elite.

Malcolm III (Canmore; c.1031–93), king of Scotland (1058–93). He defeated MACBETH in 1054, and killed him in battle in 1057. After 1066 he welcomed English exiles (including Margaret – later St Margaret – whom he married) to his court. He was killed at Alnwick while raiding NORTHUMBRIA.

Malcolm X (1925–65), US militant black activist, a leading spokesman of the Black Muslim movement in the 1950s. He was assassinated by a rival in 1965; ▷ p. 216 (box).

Mali, a republic in the Sahel of W Africa (▷ p. 202, box). Mali is named after an empire in the area (12th–14th centuries). Conquered by France (1880–95), it became the territory of French Sudan. Mali became independent in 1960. A radical socialist government was toppled in 1968, since when Mali has been ruled by military governments.

Mali, kingdom of, a W African kingdom located in the S of modern MALI. It was the centre of a Muslim empire in the later 13th and 14th centuries; ▷ pp. 66 (map) and 67.

Malta, an island-republic in the central Mediterranean Sea. Malta was ruled, in turn, by Rome (218 BC–394 AD), the Byzantine Empire (until 870), the Arabs (until 1091) and Sicily (until 1530). From 1530 to 1798, Malta was in the hands of the Knights of St John or HOSPITALLERS (▷ p. 89, box), who repelled a Turkish siege in 1565. The French held Malta from 1798 to 1800, provoking the Maltese to request British protection (1802). As a British colony (from 1814), Malta became a vital naval base, and the island received the George Cross for its valour in World War II. Malta gained independence in 1964.

Malthus, Thomas Robert (1766–1834), British economist and population theorist. In his *Essay on the Principle of Population* (1798) he argued that populations increase at a higher rate than their means of subsistence, and that disastrous overpopulation is only prevented by disease, famine and war; ▷ p. 230.

Mamluk or **Mameluke,** a word denoting a slave, specifically a military slave, in Islamic societies; Turks from beyond the E frontier of Islam in Central Asia were imported to serve in this capacity from the 9th century. They were favoured because of their fighting qualities and their (sometimes uncertain) loyalty to their masters. Military slavery was not regarded as shameful in any way, and Mamluks were able to form regimes of their own in Egypt (the Mamluk sultanate, 1250–1517) and India (the Delhi Sultanate, 13th–16th centuries); ▷ pp. 62 and 83.

Manchu, a nomad people of Altaian origin (▷ p. 54), who took over MANCHURIA and then China, establishing the QING dynasty; ▷ pp. 55 and 56.

Manchukuo, the name given by the Japanese to the puppet-state they established in Manchuria, after occupying it in 1932 (▷ pp. 187 and 188). The area was placed under the nominal control of Pu Yi, the

last QING emperor of China. Soviet forces liberated Manchukuo in 1945, after which it reverted to its more familiar name.

Manchuria, the NE part of modern China. The SW was sometimes incorporated in Chinese empires but the rest was under nomad control. The last of its nomad rulers, the Manchus, brought Manchuria within the Chinese state when they took control of the empire in 1644; ▷ pp. 56, 65, 187 and 188.

mandate, the name given to former territories of the Ottoman Empire and former German colonies administered by the ALLIED states under the trusteeship of the League of Nations after World War I; ▷ pp. 182 and 210.

Mandela, Nelson Rolihlahla (1918–), black South African politician, president of the ANC (1991–). A lawyer and ANC activist from the 1940s, he became the symbolic leader of all black South Africans during his imprisonment from 1962. He was freed by DE KLERK in 1991 and headed ANC negotiations with the government; ▷ p. 221.

Manfred (1232–66), king of Sicily (1258–66), the last HOHENSTAUFEN ruler of Sicily (▷ p. 96).

Manichaeism, a GNOSTIC sect started by Mani (AD 216–77), a Babylonian living in Sassanid Persia. His teachings offered redemption to a chosen few who renounced all worldly possessions, and saw the universe as a battleground for a constant struggle between good and evil. The sect spread to the West, and survived into the 10th century.

Manifest Destiny, a 19th-century slogan used to advocate US expansion across the N American continent. Employed mainly by Jacksonian Democrats, it served to justify wars of aggression against Mexico and native American Indians in the 1840s; ▷ p. 156.

maniple, in the Roman army, a small unit of 120–200 footsoldiers; ▷ p. 45.

Mannerheim, Baron Carl Gustav Emil von (1867–1951), Finnish soldier and politician, president (1944–6). He commanded non-Communist 'Whites' against the Communist 'Reds' in the civil war following Finland's declaration of independence. He was commander-in-chief in the FINNISH-RUSSIAN WAR (1939–40; ▷ p. 192).

Manzikert, battle of (1071), a battle in which the Byzantines were defeated by the SELJUK Turks; ▷ pp. 54 and 81.

Maoris, the Polynesian people living in New Zealand; ▷ p. 69.

Mao Zedong (Mao Tse-tung; 1893–1976), Chinese revolutionary politician, founder of the People's Republic of China and chairman of the Chinese Communist Party until his death; ▷ pp. 196–7.

Maquis, a French underground resistance movement in World War II; ▷ p. 190.

Marathas, Hindu clan-leaders who established a powerful military position in central India (the Deccan) in the mid-17th century under the leadership of Sivaji. They ruled the area until defeated by the British in the early 19th century, when they accepted British protection of their PRINCELY STATES; ▷ p. 63.

Marathon, battle of (490 BC), a battle in E Attica in which Athens and Plataea defeated the invading Persian forces of Darius I; ▷ pp. 29, 31 (map), 42 and 44.

Marat, Jean Paul (1743–93), French journalist and revolutionary. He was assassinated in his bath by Charlotte Corday, a GIRONDIN sympathizer; ▷ p. 145.

marches, areas of disputed land between states during the medieval period; ▷ p. 102.

March on Rome (1922), the convergence of squads of Fascists on Rome, after which MUSSOLINI took power in Italy; ▷ p. 186.

Marcos, Ferdinand (1917–1989), president of the PHILIPPINES (1965–86); ▷ p. 223.

Margaret of Anjou (1430–82), queen of England (1445–61). The incapacity of her husband HENRY VI meant that she played an unusually dominant political role. This contributed to the outbreak of the Wars of the ROSES, in which she took an active part on the LANCASTRIAN side until captured after the battle of TEWKESBURY.

Mari, a trading city of ancient Mesopotamia; ⊳ pp. **20** and **43**.

Maria Theresa (1717–80), ruler of the HABSBURG hereditary lands and queen of Hungary (1740–80); ⊳ pp. **124–5**.

Marie Antoinette (1755–93), queen of France, the daughter of Maria Theresa and the Holy Roman Emperor Francis I; ⊳ pp. **125** and **144–5**.

Marius, Gaius (157–86 BC), Roman general and politician. His military achievements included his defeat of JUGURTHA and important reforms of the army; ⊳ p. **37**.

Marlborough, John Churchill, 1st Duke of (1650–1722), English general and statesman. He commanded the allied forces in the War of the Spanish Succession (1701–13), his spectacular victories at BLENHEIM, RAMILLIES, OUDENARDE and Malplaquet contributing greatly to the defeat of Louis XIV; ⊳ p. **123** (box).

Marne, battles of the, two battles fought on the River Marne in World War I. In the first battle (September 1914), French and British forces turned back the German assault on Paris; in the second battle (July 1918), they repelled a similar assault, the last German offensive of the war; ⊳ pp. **176**, **177** and **178**.

Maronite, a follower of John Maron (or Maroun), a 7th-century Christian patriarch who preached that Christ had both a human and a divine nature but a single divine will. Persecuted for heresy, the Maronites fled to what is now LEBANON, where they became the dominant sect; ⊳ p. **212**.

Marshall Plan, US aid programme to assist recovery in Europe after World War II; ⊳ p. **204**.

Marston Moor, battle of (2 July 1644), a key battle of the ENGLISH CIVIL WAR, fought in Yorkshire. The rout of Prince RUPERT's Royalists by CROMWELL's Parliamentary forces left most of the N of England in Parliamentary hands.

martyr, a Greek word meaning 'witness', which came to be applied to victims of religious persecution who preferred to face death rather than to renounce their faith. The earliest martyrs were Jews opposed to Hellenism (⊳ p. **32**), but under the Roman Empire martyrdom became a feature of early Christianity; ⊳ p. **40**.

Marx, Karl Heinrich (1818–83), German political philosopher and founder of modern COMMUNISM; ⊳ pp. **3–4**, **5**, **168–9**, **180** (box), **181** and **186**.

Marxism-Leninism, the revolutionary philosophy of Lenin and guiding doctrine of the USSR; a modification of MARXISM asserting that imperialism is the highest form of CAPITALISM; ⊳ p. **181**.

Mary I (1516–58), queen of England (1553–58). The daughter of HENRY VIII and CATHERINE of Aragon, her marriage to her cousin PHILIP II of Spain failed to produce children. The execution of Protestants during her reign earned her the nickname 'Bloody Mary'; ⊳ p. **118**.

Mary II (1662–94), queen of England (1689-94) jointly with WILLIAM III. She was the eldest daughter of James II by his first wife; ⊳ p. **119**.

Mary, Queen of Scots (1542–87), queen of Scotland (1542–67). The daughter of James V of Scotland and Mary of Guise, she was brought up in France as a Catholic. A rising of anti-Catholic nobles led to her deposition in favour of her son James VI (later JAMES I of England) in 1567. She fled to England where, after years of imprisonment, she was executed at Fotheringay for plotting against ELIZABETH I; ⊳ p. **118**.

Maryland, one of the 13 original states of the USA, founded in 1632 as a haven for persecuted English Roman Catholics; ⊳ pp. **156** (map) and **159** (map).

Masada, a fortress in Judaea. It was captured by the ZEALOTS at the start of the Jewish revolt in AD 66. Besieged by the Romans, the rebels held out until 73, when they destroyed the fort and committed mass suicide.

Masaryk, Tomáš Garrigue (1850–1937), Slovak politician, first president of Czechoslovakia (1919–35). He worked with BENEŠ for Czech independence during World War I, raising a Czech Legion to fight against the CENTRAL POWERS. He gained power when the Austro-Hungarian Empire collapsed, resigning in 1935 in favour of Beneš.

Mason-Dixon line, the state boundary between Pennsylvania and Maryland surveyed by Charles Mason and Jeremiah Dixon (1763–7). It is popularly regarded as the line dividing the Northern and Southern states of the USA.

Massachusetts, a state on the NE coast of the USA and one of the original 13 colonies. It was founded by the Puritan Massachusetts Bay Company in 1630; ⊳ pp. **142**, **157**, and **216**.

Matabele, ⊳ NDEBELE.

Matilda (or Maud; 1102–67), the daughter of HENRY I, she married the German emperor Henry V in 1114 and was subsequently known as the Empress. In 1127 Henry I made her his heir and from 1135 she and her second husband, Geoffrey PLANTAGENET, fought STEPHEN for the throne of England. Her son HENRY II succeeded Stephen as king.

Matthias Corvinus (1440–90), king of Hungary (1458–90). It took years of struggle before his election as king was generally recognized. An active defender of his kingdom against the Turks, he was later able to take the initiative against the Holy Roman Emperor, capturing Vienna in 1485.

Mauritania, a republic in NW Africa. The French arrived on the coast in the 17th century, but did not annex the Arab emirates inland until 1903. Mauritania became independent in 1960 (⊳ p. **202**, map). When Spain withdrew from the Western Sahara in 1976, Morocco and Mauritania divided the territory between them, but Mauritania could not defeat the Polisario guerrillas fighting for West Saharan independence and gave up its claim (1979). Tension between the dominant Arab N and black African S led to violence in 1989.

Mauritius, an island-republic in the S Indian Ocean. Known to the Arabs and the Portuguese, the island was settled by the Dutch in 1638. Mauritius was French from 1715 until 1814, when it became British. Black slaves were imported, followed in the 19th century by Indian labourers whose descendants are the majority community. Independence was gained in 1968.

Mauryan Empire (c. 325–185 BC), the first major Indian empire; ⊳ pp. **58–9**.

Mau Mau, a secret organization founded in KENYA in 1950, centred on the Kikuyu tribe, dedicated to the expulsion of white settlers by acts of terrorism and the withdrawal of the British from the colony.

Maximian (Marcus Aurelius Valerius Maximianus; d. 310) co-emperor with Diocletian (286–305); ⊳ pp. **39–40**.

Maximilian (1832–67), Austrian archduke who was installed by Mexican conservatives and NAPOLEON III of France as emperor of MEXICO (1864–7).

Maximilian I (1459–1519), Holy Roman Emperor (1493–1519). A HABSBURG, he created significant new prospects for the family in the Low Countries by his marriage to Mary of Burgundy, daughter of CHARLES THE BOLD (1477). He achieved a further dynastic coup by marrying his son Philip to the daughter of FERDINAND and ISABELLA, thereby uniting Spain and the Habsburgs; ⊳ p. **120**.

Maya, the name given to a pre-Columbian culture of Meso-America, centred on the tropical lowlands of SE Mexico (Yucatán) and Guatemala. Maya culture reached its peak during the Classic phase of Meso-American prehistory (300–900 AD) and was characterized by extensive temple-cities built around stepped pyramids; ⊳ pp. **70–1**.

Mayflower, the ship in which the PILGRIM FATHERS sailed from Plymouth to Cape Cod, Massachusetts, in 1620; ⊳ p. **142**.

mayors of the palace, lords of the royal household under the MEROVINGIAN dynasty who came to wield effective political power; ⊳ p. **79**.

Mazarin, Jules (1601–61), Italian cardinal. He left the papal diplomatic service for that of Cardinal RICHELIEU, becoming first minister to Anne of Austria, widow of LOUIS XIII and regent during the minority of Louis XIV; ⊳ p. **122**.

Mazzini, Giuseppe (1805–72), Italian nationalist, republican and founder of YOUNG ITALY; ⊳ p. **152**.

Mecca, the holy city of Islam, now in Saudi Arabia. A pilgrimage to Mecca once during a lifetime – if possible – is an obligation on Muslims; ⊳ p. **82**.

Mecklenburg, two former duchies – from 1815, grand duchies – in N Germany. Mecklenburg-Schwerin (the larger) and Mecklenburg-Strelitz became part of the German Empire in 1871. The Mecklenburg monarchies were overthrown in 1918.

Medes, a people of ancient Iran; ⊳ p. **26**.

Medici, a family that ruled Florence from the 15th to the 18th centuries. Immigrants to Florence in the 13th century, they became eminent bankers with international connections. Cosimo 'Il Vecchio' (1389–1464) ruled Florence unofficially from 1434 to 1464; he and his grandson Lorenzo 'The Magnificent' (ruled 1469–92) were famed as patrons of artists and humanists. After a period of exile the Medici returned in 1512, and ruled as dukes, then grand-dukes, from 1530 to 1737; ⊳ pp. *96* and 97.

Medici, Catherine de (1519–89), wife of Henry II of France (1547–59). She sought to protect the interests of her sons, Francis II, Charles IX, and Henry III in the difficult circumstances of the FRENCH WARS OF RELIGION. Her alliance with the Catholic GUISE faction led to the ST BARTHOLOMEW'S DAY MASSACRE (1572); ⊳ p. **111**.

Medina, an Arabian city about 450 km (280 mi) NE of Mecca, to which MUHAMMAD emigrated or fled (the HIJRA) in 622, where he is buried; ⊳ p. **82**.

megalith, a large stone structure of the Neolithic and early Bronze Age, found in many parts of the world; ⊳ p. **15**.

Mehemet Ali (1769–1849), Albanian-born soldier in the service of the Ottoman Turks, and pasha of Egypt (1805–49); ⊳ pp. **154–5**.

Mehmet II (the Conqueror; 1430–81), Ottoman sultan (1451–81). He greatly improved the Turkish army and navy, and used them to extend Ottoman rule in the Balkans, the Aegean and the Mediterranean; ⊳ pp. **81** and **114**.

Meiji restoration (1867–9), the restoration of imperial government in Japan under Mutsuhito; ⊳ pp. **64** (box), **65** and **167**.

Meir, Golda (Goldie Mabovitch; 1898–1979), Israeli politician, prime minister (1968–74). Born in Russia, she was educated in the USA and emigrated to Palestine in 1921. She founded the Israeli Labour Party in 1967.

Melbourne, William Lamb, 2nd Viscount (1779–1848), British Whig statesman, prime minister (1834 and 1835–41). He was a close adviser of Queen VICTORIA in her early years as sovereign.

Melanesians, the peoples of the SW division of Oceania, including New Guinea, New Caledonia and the New Hebrides; ⊳ pp. **68** and **69** (map).

Memphis, the ancient capital of Egypt, traditionally founded by Menes; ⊳ pp. **17–19**.

Mendès-France, Pierre (1907–82), French socialist politician, prime minister (1954–5). He became PM after the French defeat at DIENBIENPHU, taking France out of INDOCHINA and granting independence to Tunisia, but was brought down by an economic crisis.

Menelik II (1844–1913), emperor of Abyssinia (ETHIOPIA) (1889–1913). He kept his country in-dependent during the European SCRAMBLE FOR AFRICA, inflicting a humiliating defeat on the Italians at Adowa (1896).

Mennonites, a radical Protestant sect that emerged in the 16th century; ▷ p. 111 (box).

Menshevik (Russian, 'member of the minority') a member of the moderate wing of the SOCIAL DEMOCRATIC Party in Russia, which advocated gradual reform to achieve socialism; ▷ p. 181.

Mentohotep II, the first Theban pharaoh of Egypt (2060–2010 BC); ▷ p. 18.

Menzies, Sir Robert Gordon (1894–1978), Australian statesman. He was prime minister as head of the United Australia Party (1939–41) and again (1949–66) as head of the Liberal Party.

mercantilism, ▷ p. 128.

Merchant Adventurers, English businessmen dealing principally in general imports and the export of cloth. The associations that they formed to protect their interests both at home and abroad were especially prominent in the 15th and 16th centuries; ▷ p. 99.

Mercia, the central kingdom of Anglo-Saxon England, which achieved its greatest power in the 8th century, and was partitioned by the Danes in 878; ▷ p. 79 (box).

Meroë, the capital of the African kingdom of NUBIA (on the Nile in modern Sudan) from the 6th century BC to the 4th century AD. It was a major point of contact and trade between Mediterranean civilizations and central Africa.

Merovingians, a dynasty of Frankish kings (c. 500–751) founded by CLOVIS I; ▷ pp. 78–9.

Mesolithic, ▷ p. 13.

Mesopotamia, an area of SW Asia between the TIGRIS and EUPHRATES rivers; ▷ pp. **16, 20, 22,** 27 (box), 32 (map), 44, 80, 114 and 178.

Methodism, English evangelical Protestant movement, originally developed by John Wesley (1703–91) and his followers in the 18th century. Methodism was hostile to liberalism and science, and emphasized religion as an emotional experience rather than a system of thought. It broke away from the ANGLICAN Church in 1791 and thereafter gained many adherents in both Britain and America.

Metternich, Clemens Wenzel Nepomuk Lothar, Prince (1773–1859), Austrian foreign minister (1809–21) and chancellor (1821–48). The arch-conservative architect of Restoration Austria and Europe at the Congress of VIENNA. He was removed from office during the REVOLUTIONS OF 1848; ▷ p. 151.

Mexican-American War (1846–8), a conflict between Mexico and the USA, easily won by US forces under Generals Zachary TAYLOR and Winfield Scott. It was ended by the Treaty of Guadelupe Hidalgo; ▷ p. 156.

Mexican Revolution, a period of violent upheaval and political reform in MEXICO (1910–40). In 1910 Porfirio DÍAZ's long rule was ended by a movement of democratic protest led by Francisco MADERO. However, Madero's brief presidency unleashed pent-up discontents. In the central state of Morelos, ZAPATA led an agrarian revolt of villagers deprived of their lands by the expansion of sugar estates. The N of Mexico produced a series of revolutions that brought about the collapse of the old centre. Madero was murdered by the counter-revolutionary General Huerta in 1913, but fighting

during the rest of the decade saw the triumph of revolutionary forces of the N. Combining many forces besides peasants and workers, the Mexican Revolution was a genuine social revolution, achieving land and other reforms unprecedented in Latin American history. However, it also ushered in a long period of single-party rule.

Mexico, a republic in the N of Central America. When the Spanish arrived in Mexico in 1519, the Mayan civilization in Yucatán was in decline (▷ p. 71) but Aztec power, centred on TENOCHTITLÁN (Mexico City), was flourishing (▷ p. 72). In 1519–21, the mighty Aztec empire was overthrown by a small band of Spanish invaders under CORTEZ. For the next 300 years Mexico was under Spanish rule, its economy largely based on silver and gold mining and the produce of large estates owned by Spanish grandees. The first revolt against Spanish rule broke out in 1810 (▷ p. 148), but Mexican independence was not gained until 1821 after a guerrilla war led by Vicente Guerrero. Initially an empire – under Agustín Itúrbide – Mexico became a republic in 1823, but conflict between federalists and centralists erupted, developing into civil war. In 1836 TEXAS rebelled against Mexico, declaring independence. When the USA annexed Texas in 1845, war broke out, resulting in the loss of half Mexico's territory – Texas, New Mexico and California (▷ pp. 156 and 157, map). A period of reform began in 1857, with a new liberal constitution. A civil war (1858–61) between reformists and conservatives was won by the reformists under Benito JUÁREZ, but the economy was shattered. After Mexico failed to repay debts, Spain, Britain and France invaded in 1863. Although Spain and Britain soon withdrew, France remained, appointing Archduke MAXIMILIAN of Austria as emperor (1864). Under US pressure and Mexican resistance, the French withdrew in 1867. Maximilian remained in Mexico City and was captured and executed. Juárez re-established the republic. The authoritarian rule of General Porfirio DÍAZ (1876–80 and 1884–1910) brought peace, but wealth was concentrated into a few hands. The MEXICAN REVOLUTION against the power of the landowners erupted in 1910. The reformist policies of President Francisco MADERO were supported by the outlaw Pancho VILLA, but revolutionary violence continued, and in 1916–17 a US expeditionary force was sent against Villa. From 1924 the revolution became anticlerical and the Church was persecuted. Order was restored when the Institutional Revolutionary Party came to power in 1929. In the 1930s the large estates were divided and much of the economy was nationalized. Political opposition has been tolerated, although the ruling party is virtually guaranteed perpetual power.

Michael VIII (Palaeologus; 1224–82), Byzantine emperor (1259–82). A successful soldier in the NICAEAN EMPIRE, he reconquered CONSTANTINOPLE from the Latins in 1261 (▷ p. 81).

Micronesians, the peoples of the NW division of Oceania, including the Mariana, Marshall and Gilbert islands; ▷ pp. 68 and 69 (map).

Middle Ages, the period of European history usually dated from the fall of the last Western Roman emperor in the late 5th century to the 15th-century Italian Renaissance; ▷ pp. **78–103.**

Middle East, ▷ pp. **210–13.**

Midway, battle of (1942), ▷ p. **194.**

Milan, a former Italian state ruled by the VISCONTI family from 1395 to 1535. In 1535 Milan was absorbed into HABSBURG Lombardy and was ruled by Spain (1535–1714), Austria (1714–97), the French-dominated Cisalpine Republic (1797–1805), the Napoleonic kingdom of Italy (1805–14) and Austria (1814–59), before becoming part of the kingdom of Italy.

Miletus, the most important of the ancient IONIAN

cities on the coast of Asia Minor. Miletus founded more than 60 colonies in the ARCHAIC period, most in the Black Sea area; ▷ pp. 29 (box) and 31 (map).

MI5 and MI6 (abbreviations for Military Intelligence, sections five and six), respectively the internal security and counter-intelligence agency and the intelligence and espionage agency of the British government; ▷ p. 207.

Mill, John Stuart (1806–73), British philosopher and UTILITARIAN social reformer; ▷ p. 232.

Minamoto Yoritomo (1147–99), military ruler of Japan (1185–99) and first shogun; ▷ p. 64.

Ming dynasty (1368–1644), an imperial dynasty of China; ▷ pp. **56,** 65 (box) and 108.

Minoan civilization, ▷ pp. **24–5** and 46.

Mirabeau, Honoré Gabriel Riqueti, vicomte de (1749–91), French aristocrat and revolutionary. A leading figure in the early stages of the French Revolution, his efforts to prevent the complete erosion of royal power discredited him in the eyes of the radicals.

Mississippi culture or **Temple Mound Culture,** a North American culture that predominated in the Mississippi basin, c. 700–1500 AD. It was characterized by the building of large earthen mounds or pyramids supporting wooden temples, tombs and elite residences; ▷ p. 73.

Missouri Compromise (1820–1), legislation passed by the US Congress to resolve disagreement over the extension of slavery in the territories beyond existing state boundaries. Maine entered the Union as a free state and Missouri as a slave state, while slavery was banned in the N part of the Louisiana purchase; ▷ p. 158.

Mitanni, a kingdom of ancient N Syria; ▷ pp. 20 (box) and 22.

Mithras, a god of Persian origin who became the object of a cult among soldiers of the Roman army during the late Empire; ▷ p. 39 (box).

Mitterrand, François (1916–), French socialist statesman. He held ministerial posts under the Fourth Republic and sought to unite the parties of the left in the 1960s. He became leader of a unified Socialist Party in 1971 and president in 1981, defeating GISCARD D'ESTAING. A strong advocate of the French nuclear bomb, he weathered economic and political crises and profited from disunity on the right to secure a second term in 1988.

Mixtec, a Meso-American people who established an important regional state in central Mexico before they were conquered by the Aztecs in the late 15th century; ▷ p. *70.*

Mobutu, Seko Sese (1930–), president of ZAÏRE (1965–); ▷ p. 203 (box).

Moguls, a Muslim dynasty that ruled India from 1526. The last nominal Mogul 'king of Delhi' was deposed by the British in 1857; ▷ pp. **62–3.**

Mohammed, ▷ MUHAMMAD.

Mohawk, a native North American people, the easternmost of the five tribes of the IROQUOIS confederation, living in the Eastern Woodlands (E New York State).

Mohenjo-daro, the most important site of the ancient Indus Valley civilization, located in the province of SIND in modern Pakistan; ▷ p. 58.

Mohican, ▷ MAHICAN.

Moldavia, ▷ MOLDOVA and ROMANIA

Moldova, a republic of SE Europe. Known as BESSARABIA, the area was ruled by KIEV RUS (10th–12th centuries; ▷ p. 126) and the TARTARS (13th–14th centuries) before becoming part of the Romanian principality of Moldavia – within the (Turkish) Ottoman Empire (▷ p. 115, map) – in the 15th century. Bessarabia was intermittently occupied by Russia in the 18th century before being ceded to the Russians in 1812 (⊏> p. 127). Bessarabia – which has an overwhelming ethnic Romanian majority – was briefly restored to Moldavia (1856–78), but otherwise remained Russian until World War I. An autonomous Bessarabian republic was proclaimed in 1917, but was suppressed by a Russian BOLSHEVIK invasion (1918). The Russians were removed by Romanian forces and Bessarabia was declared, in turn, an independent Moldavian republic and a part of the kingdom of ROMANIA (1918). When Romania entered World War II as a German ally, the USSR reoccupied Bessarabia, which was reorganized as the Moldavian Soviet Republic in 1944. Following the abortive coup by Communist hardliners in Moscow (September 1991; ⊏> p. 225), Moldavia declared independence but affirmed its intention of eventual reunion with Romania. As Moldova, the republic received international recognition when the Soviet Union was dissolved (December 1990), but the Russian and Ukrainian minorities of Transdnestr and the Gagauz (Turkic) minority in the S continue to agitate for secession.

Molly Maguires, a secret Irish-American organization active in the 1860s and 1870s; ⊏> p. 166.

Molotov, Vyacheslav Mikhailovich (1890–1986), Soviet politician, foreign minister (1939–41 and 1953–6), in which capacity he negotiated the NAZI-SOVIET PACT. After the death of Stalin in 1955, Molotov joined Beria and Malenkov in a ruling triumvirate, but was ousted by KHRUSHCHEV in 1957.

Moltke, Helmuth, Count von (1800–91), Prussian field marshal, chief of the imperial German general staff (1871–88). He won victories for Prussia against Denmark (1864), Austria (1866) and France (1870–1), in the latter two cases using railways for swift mobilization (⊏> p. 153).

Moluccas, ⊏> SPICE ISLANDS.

Monaco, a principality on the Mediterranean coast of France. The Grimaldi family has ruled Monaco since 1297. Monaco was annexed by France in 1793 but restored in 1814, under the protection of the king of Sardinia. The greater part of the principality was lost – and eventually annexed by France – in 1848. Since 1861 Monaco has been under French protection. Prince Rainier III granted a liberal constitution in 1962.

Monasteries, Dissolution of the (1536–40), the systematic abolition of MONASTICISM during the English Reformation, following a survey of monastic wealth organized by Thomas CROMWELL. The lesser monasteries were dissolved in 1536, the rest two years later. By 1539 more than 500 had been suppressed. The crown gained substantial lands and income, some of which was used to establish new dioceses. Successive monarchs sold off these lands, mainly to the advantage of the gentry and nobility; ⊏> p. 118.

monasticism, the lifestyle of monks or nuns living in secluded communities. Monasticism is found in various religions, especially Christianity, Buddhism and Jainism; ⊏> pp. 90–1 and 100.

monetarism, an economic doctrine emphasizing the role of the money supply in the functioning of an economy. Unlike KEYNESIAN economists, monetarists believe that with the exception of managing the money supply, governments should not intervene in the economy; ⊏> p. 215.

Mongol Empire, ⊏> pp. 53, **54–5,** 56, 61, 83 and 114.

Mongolia, a country of E Central Asia. Mongolia was the home of the HUNS – who ravaged both the Chinese and Roman empires (1st–5th centuries AD; ⊏> p. 54) – and of the strong Uighur state in the 8th and 9th centuries. In the 13th century the Mongol dynasty of Genghis Khan created an immense but short-lived Asian empire (⊏> pp. 54–5). In the 17th century, Mongolia was annexed by China, but 'Outer' Mongolia – the N – retained autonomy as a BUDDHIST monarchy. In 1921, Outer Mongolia broke away from China with Soviet assistance and in 1924 the Mongolian People's Republic was established. Pro-democracy demonstrations led to a liberalization of the regime in 1990. The Communists won the first multi-party elections.

Mongoloids, the racial group of humankind including most of the peoples of Asia, and the INUITS and ALEUTS of N Canada. AMERINDIANS are sometimes classed as Mongoloids.

Monmouth's Rebellion (1685), the attempt by CHARLES II's illegitimate son, James, Duke of Monmouth (1649–85), to seize the throne from JAMES II. His largely peasant army was defeated at the battle of Sedgemoor. Monmouth's supporters were savagely punished in the BLOODY ASSIZES.

Monnet, Jean (1888–1979), French economist and administrator. As author of the SCHUMAN Plan for the European Coal and Steel Community, and president of the latter (1952–5) he was a 'founding father' of the EUROPEAN COMMUNITY (⊏> p. 215).

Monroe Doctrine (1823), a US foreign policy doctrine enunciated by President MONROE; ⊏> p. 157.

Monroe, James (1758–1831) fifth president of the USA (1817–25). The USA acquired FLORIDA from Spain during his two-term presidency. A moderate Democratic-Republican, he lacked imagination, but his warning against European involvement in American affairs (the Monroe Doctrine) has won him a lasting place in US history; ⊏> p. 157.

Mons, a people of S Burma and Thailand, related to the Khmers of Cambodia; ⊏> pp. 60 and 61.

Montenegro, a former kingdom of SE Europe that was never subjugated by the Turkish Ottoman Empire. It was ruled by prince-bishops (1516–1851), became a secular principality (1851; ⊏> p. 151, map), was recognized as independent at the Congress of Berlin (1878; ⊏> p. 155), and became a kingdom (1910). After occupation by Austria-Hungary during World War I, Montenegro was absorbed by SERBIA (1918). In 1992, it formed – with Serbia – the new smaller Yugoslav Federation.

Montesquieu, Charles, baron de la Brède et de (1689–1755), French political philosopher; ⊏> p. 135.

Montezuma (1466–1520), the last Aztec emperor (1502–20). He was overthrown by CORTEZ, and killed either by the Spaniards or by his own people.

Montfort, Simon de, Earl of Leicester (c. 1208–65), leader of the baronial opposition to HENRY III from 1258, despite being the latter's brother-in-law. After defeating Henry at the battle of Lewes (1264), he was de facto ruler of England until killed in battle at Evesham.

Montgomery, Bernard Louis, 1st Viscount of Alamein (1887–1976), commander of the British 8th army in the N African, Italian and Normandy campaigns of World War II; ⊏> p. 191.

Moor, a term used by Europeans for the Muslim inhabitants (of Arab, Berber or mixed stock) of N Africa and Spain. The word derives from ancient Mauretania (roughly equivalent to modern Morocco); ⊏> pp. 83 (box) and 89.

More, Sir Thomas (1478–1535), lord chancellor of England (1529–32). A humanist, author of *Utopia* (1516), and critic of abuses in the Church, More nevertheless opposed the Reformation. Refusing to recognize HENRY VIII as head of the ANGLICAN CHURCH, he was tried and executed.

Morelos, José María (1765–1815), Mexican priest and revolutionary; ⊏> p. 149.

Moro, Aldo (1916–78), Italian CHRISTIAN DEMOCRAT statesman, prime minister (1963–8 and 1974–6). He was kidnapped and murdered by the RED BRIGADES in 1978.

Morocco, a kingdom of NW Africa. The region became a Roman province in 46 AD. In the 7th century Morocco became Islamic. In the 11th and 12th centuries the ALMORAVID (BERBER) empire – which included Muslim Spain (⊏> p. 83, box) – was based in Marrakech. Morocco was ruled by the ALMOHAD dynasty who ruled a N African empire from 1147 until 1269. The Sharifian dynasty – descended from the Prophet MUHAMMAD – rose to power in the 16th and 17th centuries, and still retains the throne. In the 19th century Spain confirmed control of several long-claimed coastal settlements. In the 'Moroccan Crises' (1905–6 and 1911; ⊏> p. 175), French interests in Morocco were disputed by Germany. Under the Treaty of Fez in 1912 France established a protectorate over Morocco, although the Spanish enclaves remained. The 1925 Rif rebellion stirred nationalist feelings, but independence was not gained until 1956. King Hassan II (reigned 1961–) has survived left-wing challenges through strong rule and vigorous nationalism – as in his 1975 'Green March' of unarmed peasants into the then Spanish (Western) Sahara (⊏> p. 202, map). Morocco still holds the Western Sahara despite international pressure and the activities of the Algerian-backed Polisario guerrillas fighting for the territory's independence. A ceasefire was agreed in 1991 and a UN-sponsored referendum on the disputed Western Sahara was scheduled for 1992.

Mortimer, Roger, 1st Earl of March (1287–1330), English nobleman; ⊏> ISABELLA OF FRANCE.

Morton, John (c. 1420–1500), English cleric. As bishop of Ely he reputedly helped to organize the overthrow of RICHARD III in 1485. HENRY VII made him archbishop of Canterbury in 1486 and chancellor in 1487.

Moses, the leader of the Israelites at the time of the EXODUS; ⊏> p. 22 (box).

Mosley, Sir Oswald Ernald (1896–1980), British politician, founder of the British Union of Fascists in 1932. He was interned during World War II and never recovered political credibility.

Mossadeq, Muhmammad (1880–1967), Iranian politician, leader of a nationalist-populist front that ruled IRAN 1951–3.

Mountbatten, Louis, 1st Earl Mountbatten of Burma (1900–79), British naval commander, Chief of Combined Operations (1942–3), Supreme Commander in SE Asia (1943–5) and last viceroy of India (1947). He was assassinated by the IRISH REPUBLICAN ARMY in 1979; ⊏> p. 201 (box).

Mozambique, a republic of SE Africa. The coast attracted Arab settlements from the 9th century AD. The Portuguese founded coastal trading posts from 1531, but only gained control of the whole country at the end of the 19th century. Forced labour and minimal development fuelled nationalist feelings, and in 1964 the Frelimo movement launched a guerrilla war against Portuguese rule. Independence was achieved in 1975, and a Marxist-Leninist state was established. The pressures of poverty and the destabilization of the country by South Africa – through support for the Renamo guerrilla movement (⊏> p. *218*) – led to renewed ties with the West, and Marxism was abandoned by Frelimo in 1989. Political pluralism has been permitted since 1990.

Mugabe, Robert Gabriel (1924–), first prime minister (1980–8) and then president (1988–) of independent ZIMBABWE; ⊏> p. 221 (box).

Muhammad (c. 570–632), the Prophet and founder of Islam; ⊏> pp. 82–3.

Mujibur Rahman, Sheikh (1920–75), first prime minister (1972–5) and president (1975) of BANGLADESH. Co-founder of the AWAMI LEAGUE, he opposed discrimination against the BENGALIS by the PUNJABI-dominated government of PAKISTAN. He was assassinated by a group of army officers.

Mukden Incident (18 September 1931), the seizure of the Manchurian city of Mukden (now Shengyang) by Japanese troops. Although ordered to stop by Tokyo, the Japanese army proceeded to occupy the whole of MANCHURIA; ▷ pp. 187 and 188.

Mulroney, (Martin) Brian (1939–   ), Canadian Progressive Conservative statesman, prime minister (1984–   ).

Munich Agreement (29 September 1938), an agreement between Britain, France, Germany and Italy, compelling Czechoslovakia to cede the SUDETENLAND to Germany; ▷ pp. **188–9**.

Munich 'beer-hall' putsch (8 November 1923), an abortive uprising by the Nazis; ▷ p. 186.

Müntzer, Thomas (1489–1525), a rebel leader in the German Peasants' War; ▷ p.111 (box).

Murad I (1360–89), Ottoman sultan (1362–89); ▷ p. 114.

Murat, Joachim (1767–1815), marshal of France. He was created king of Naples (1808–15) by Napoleon, but deserted him during the retreat from Moscow, and conspired with the Austrians to protect his own throne. He rallied to Napoleon in 1815 during the HUNDRED DAYS, but was later captured and shot by the Austrians.

Muscovy, grand duchy of, a former Russian principality (13th–17th centuries), the nucleus of the modern Russian state; ▷ p. 126.

musketeer, a soldier armed with a long-barrelled muzzle-loading firearm or musket, aimed from the shoulder. The term came into use in the 16th century when the weapon was large and heavy, needing a cumbersome forked rest to support it when firing; ▷ p. 102.

Muslim, a follower of Islam; ▷ pp. 82–3.

Muslim League, a political party representing the interests of Indian Muslims; ▷ p. 201.

Mussolini, Benito (1883–1945), Italian dictator, known as 'Il Duce' (the leader). He was appointed prime minister by King Victor Emanuel III after the MARCH ON ROME. He assumed dictatorial powers in 1925, annexed Abyssinia in 1936 (the year in which he allied Italy with Germany) and took Italy into World War II in 1940. He was deposed after the Allied invasion of Sicily, and was shot by Italian partisans after briefly heading a puppet regime in German-occupied N Italy; ▷ pp. 5 (box), 186, 188, 189, 190 and 191.

Mutsuhito (1852–1912), emperor of Japan (1867–1912); ▷ p. 65.

Myanmar (Burma), a republic of S Asia. The Burman kingdom of PAGAN was founded in the 9th century AD (▷ p. 61). Burman supremacy over the Irrawaddy valley was first claimed in 1044 by King Anawratha, who adopted Buddhism from the rival MON people. Chinese conquest (1287) allowed a reassertion of Mon power until the 16th century. After 1758 the Konbaung dynasty expanded Burman territory until British counter-expansion led to total annexation (1826–85). Separated from British India in 1937, Burma became a battleground for British and Japanese forces in World War II (▷ p. 195). In 1948, Burma left the COMMONWEALTH as an independent republic, keeping outside contacts to a minimum, particularly following the coup of General NE WIN in 1962. Continuing armed attempts to gain autonomy by non-Burman minorities have strengthened the role of the army, which retained power following multi-party elections in 1990 and detained leaders of the winning party.

Mycenaean civilization, ▷ pp. 25, 28, 44 and 46.

Mysore, a former regional state of SW India. Under HYDER ALI and his son, TIPU SULTAN, it was a major force in the area during the second half of the 18th century until defeated by the British in 1799.

Nabonidus, the last CHALDEAN king of Babylon; ▷ p. 21.

Nagasaki, a port on Kyushu island in Japan. It was hit by an atomic bomb dropped by the US air force on 9 August 1945, three days after the first atomic bomb attack on HIROSHIMA; ▷ pp. 195 and 226.

Nagorno Karabakh, a predominantly Armenian enclave within AZERBAIJAN, formed in 1923 on the orders of Stalin. It declared itself part of ARMENIA in 1987, leading to anti-Armenian pogroms in Azerbaijan and hostilities between the two republics.

Nagy, Imre (1896–1958), Hungarian Communist politician. He became prime minister in 1953 and introduced a programme of economic and political liberalization. When the HUNGARIAN REVOLUTION broke out in 1956 he promised free elections and an end to Soviet domination, but was overthrown by Soviet tanks and executed by the regime of János KÁDÁR in 1958.

Najd or **Nejd,** a former sultanate of central Arabia, ruled by the Sa'ud family from the early 19th century. The Sa'udis extended their territory by conquest to found SAUDI ARABIA (1932); ▷ p. 210.

Namibia, a republic of SW Africa. A German protectorate of South West Africa – excluding Walvis Bay, which had been British since 1878 – was declared in 1884 (▷ p. 163, map). Seeking land for white settlement, the Germans established their rule after great bloodshed – over three quarters of the Herero people were killed in 1903–4. South Africa conquered the territory during World War I, and (after 1919) administered it under a League of Nations MANDATE. In 1966, the UN cancelled the mandate, but South Africa – which had refused to grant the territory independence – ignored the ruling. The main nationalist movement SWAPO began guerrilla warfare to free Namibia, the name adopted by the UN for the state. South Africa unsuccessfully attempted to exclude SWAPO's influence. After a ceasefire agreement in 1989, UN-supervised elections were held in November 1989 for a constituent assembly. Independence, under the presidency of SWAPO leader Sam Nujoma, was achieved in March 1990 (▷ p. 221).

Nanak (1469–1539), Indian religious teacher, the founder and first Guru of the SIKH faith. Coming from a Hindu background, he settled in PUNJAB and taught a faith that was neither Hindu nor Muslim, emphasizing personal devotion to God and strict personal morality.

Nanjing, Treaty of (1842), a treaty between Britain and China, ending the first OPIUM WAR. China ceded Hong Kong to Britain and opened five 'Treaty Ports' – including Guangzhou (Canton) and Shanghai – to overseas traders, who were given immunity from Chinese law (▷ pp. 57 and 162).

Nantes, Edict of (1598), a decree by HENRY IV terminating the FRENCH WARS OF RELIGION and defining the religious and political rights of the HUGUENOTS. The latter were granted freedom of worship and control of 200 cities. This last condition was incompatible with the centralizing policies of RICHELIEU and Louis XIV, the latter revoking the Edict in 1685; ▷ pp. 111 and 122.

Naples, kingdom of, a former state in S Italy, with Naples as its capital. Founded by Greek colonists around 600 BC (▷ p. 29, map), the city fell to Rome in 326 BC, but retained its Greek culture. Naples was under Byzantine rule from the 6th to the 8th centuries, and survived as an independent duchy until it became part of the Norman kingdom of Sicily in 1139. The kingdom passed to the HOHENSTAUFEN in the late 12th century (▷ p. 85, map). As part of the kingdom of the TWO SICILIES, it passed successively to the ANGEVINS, to the ARAGONESE, to Spain (from 1504), to Austria (during the War of the Spanish Succession), to the BOURBONS in 1734, to Napoleon in 1799, and to the Bourbons again in 1816. It fell to Garibaldi in 1860, when the kingdom was united with the rest of Italy; ▷ pp. 96–7, 113 (map), 123 (map), 123, 131, 146, 150 and 151 (map).

Napoleonic Code, ▷ p. **147** (box).

Napoleonic Wars (1796–1815), ▷ pp. **146–7**, 148, 152, and 154.

Napoleon I (Napoleon Bonaparte; 1769–1821), emperor of the French (1804–14); ▷ pp. 3 (box), 5 (box), 102, 144, 145, **146–7**, 148–9, 152 and 154.

Napoleon III (Charles-Louis Napoléon Bonaparte; 1808–73), emperor of France (1852–70). He came to power by election to the presidency of the Second Republic (1848). He became emperor in 1852 following a coup of the previous year which established an authoritarian pseudo-democracy. Captured at SEDAN (1870) during the FRANCO-PRUSSIAN WAR, he spent the rest of his life in exile in England; ▷ pp. 5 (box), 151 and 165.

Nara, the first capital of Japan (710–784); ▷ p. 64.

Naseby, battle of (1645), a decisive victory for the Parliamentary forces in the ENGLISH CIVIL WAR. The NEW MODEL ARMY under FAIRFAX and CROMWELL routed the Royalist forces under Prince RUPERT near Naseby in Northamptonshire, hastening the final defeat of CHARLES I.

Nassau Agreement (1962), an agreement between the USA and Britain in which the USA supplied Britain with Polaris missiles for its nuclear submarines. The agreement displeased DE GAULLE, who vetoed British entry into the EEC, claiming Britain was not sufficiently orientated towards Europe.

Nasser, Gamal Abdel (1918–70), president of Egypt (1956–70); ▷ pp. *200* and **211–12**.

Natal, a province on the E coast of the Republic of South Africa, a British colony until 1910. It includes numerous small areas of Zulu BANTUSTAN; ▷ p. 163.

Natchez, a native North American people, maize farmers of the Southeast (SW Mississippi). They preserved many features of MISSISSIPPI CULTURE into the period of European contact until dispersed by the French in the early 18th century.

National Health Service (NHS), the system of national health care (financed by taxation) introduced in Britain by Aneurin BEVAN in 1948. The principal of totally free health care lasted only three years; ▷ WELFARE STATE.

nationalism, a feeling of common identity shared by a group of people with the same language, culture, ethnic origins and history. It manifests itself in a sense of loyalty to a 'mother country', particularly where that country has not yet become a state in its own right. Nationalist sentiment can lead to movements for national independence or secession. FASCISM contains elements of extreme nationalism; ▷ pp. **150–1**, 152–3, 154–5, 175, *180*, 183, 186, 210 and 224–5.

National Party, an AFRIKANER political party in South Africa, originally founded in 1914. It lapsed in 1934, but after 1940 'original' and 'purified' nationalists allied to win power in 1948; ▷ pp. 220–1.

National Socialism, ▷ NAZI.

Nations, battle of the, ▷ BATTLE OF LEIPZIG.

NATO (North Atlantic Treaty Organization), a military alliance of the USA, Canada, the UK and 13 other countries, established in 1949; ▷ pp. **204** (box) and 214–15.

Navajo, a native N American people of the SW (Arizona and adjoining areas). Originally Athapascan migrants from the far N, they abandoned nomadic hunting-gathering c. 1700 and adopted farming techniques; ▷ p. 73.

Navarino, battle of (20 October 1827), a key battle of the Greek War of Independence; ▷ p. 154.

Navarre, a former kingdom of SW France and N Spain. It was ruled by the kings of France from 1284 to 1316 and again after 1589 when Henry III of Navarre became HENRY IV of France, and united with France in 1620. The S (greater) part of Navarre was annexed by the Spanish kingdom of CASTILE in 1515.

Navigation Acts (1651, 1662 and 1696), English legislation aimed at destroying Dutch trade; ▷ pp. 128–9.

Nazca, a pre-Columbian South American culture centred on S Peru, at its peak during the Classic phase of South American prehistory (1–800 AD).

Nazi, a member of the National Socialist German Worker's Party (NSDAP), which was founded by Hitler in 1919 and took power in Germany in 1933; ▷ pp. 186–7 and 188–9.

Nazi–Soviet Pact (23 August 1939), a non-aggression pact between Nazi Germany and the Soviet Union; ▷ pp. 189 and 192.

Ndebele or **Matebele,** a people of S Africa. Pushed northward in the 1820s by both ZULU and BOER pressure, many eventually settled in Matebeleland (in modern Zimbabwe) from the mid-1830s, dominating the local SHONA peoples.

Neanderthals, ▷ HOMO SAPIENS NEANDERTHALENSIS.

Nebuchadnezzar II (d. 562 BC), king of Babylon (604–562 BC); ▷ p. 21.

Necker, Jacques (1732–1804), Swiss Protestant banker and chief finance minister to Louis XVI (1777–81 and 1788–9). His use of loans rather than taxation to finance government contributed to his popularity at the beginning of the French Revolution (▷ p. 144).

Nefertiti, the wife of the Egyptian pharaoh AKHENATEN.

Negroids, a racial group originating in W Africa S of the Sahara. Bantu speaking Negroid peoples spread out to dominate much of S and E Africa S of the Equator in the first millennium AD; ▷ p. 66.

Nehru, Jawaharlal (1889–1964), Indian statesman. He became a leader of the Indian National CONGRESS and worked with GANDHI in campaigns of civil disobedience from the 1920s, for which he was imprisoned several times by the British. As the first prime minister of independent India (1947–64) he worked for a secular democratic state, embarked on a path of industrialization, and attempted to tackle the poverty problem with a series of five-year economic plans. He had to face conflicts with Pakistan over KASHMIR (1948) and with China over the N borders (1962). His daughter Indira GANDHI became Indian PM in 1966; ▷ p. 201.

Nelson, Horatio, Viscount (1758–1805), the most successful British admiral of the Napoleonic wars. He abandoned the tactics of 18th-century naval warfare (mostly exchanges of broadsides between two opposing lines of ships), preferring – as at the battle of TRAFALGAR – to break the enemy line at right angles and then engage in destructive fighting at close quarters; ▷ p. 146.

Neolithic, ▷ pp. 12, **13,** 15 and 44.

Nepal, a Himalayan kingdom in S Asia. The Kathmandu Valley supported a Hindu-Buddhist culture by the 4th century AD (▷ p. 58). In 1768 the ruler of the principality of Gurkha in the W conquered the Valley, and began a phase of expansion that ended in defeat by the Chinese in Tibet (1792) and the British in India (1816). From 1846 to 1950 the Rana family held sway as hereditary chief ministers of a powerless monarchy. Their isolationist policy preserved Nepal's independence at the expense of its development. A brief experiment with democracy was followed by a re-assertion of royal autocracy (1960). Violent pro-democracy demonstrations (1990) forced the king to concede a democratic constitution. Multi-party elections were held in 1991.

Nerchinsk, Treaty of (1689), a treaty between Russia and Qing China, fixing the Sino-Russian border to the N of the River Amur; ▷ p. 56.

Nero (AD 37–68), Roman emperor (54–68), stepson of Claudius. His reign began well, but later degenerated into a catalogue of crimes (including the murder of his mother), extravagance and irresponsibility, leading to disaffection, conspiracies and revolts. Deserted by all, he committed suicide.

Nerva (c. AD 30–98), Roman emperor (96–98); ▷ p. 38.

Nestorian Church, a Christian sect established by the followers of Nestorius (d. c. 451), who was ousted from the PATRIARCHATE of Constantinople for his heretical views on the nature of Christ and the Virgin Mary. The Church survived in Persia until the Mongol invasions of the 14th century.

Netherlands, a kingdom of NW Europe (often referred to as Holland). In medieval times a patchwork of duchies, bishoprics and cities ruled the Netherlands. In the 15th century most of the area was governed by the dukes of Burgundy (▷ p. 95, box) and in the 16th century control of the Netherlands – the present kingdom, plus BELGIUM and LUXEMBOURG – passed to the Spanish HABSBURGS (▷ p. 117). The Spanish attempted to suppress Dutch Protestantism (▷ p. 120), and this provoked a revolt – initially led by the Prince of ORANGE, WILLIAM I (the Silent) – that became a lengthy struggle for independence. (For details of the Dutch Revolts, the formation of the independent United Provinces of the Netherlands, and Dutch commercial power in the 17th century; ▷ pp. 120–1.) Dutch power declined in the 18th century. In 1795 the French invaded and ruled the country as the Batavian Republic (1795–1806) and the Kingdom of Holland (1806–10, under Louis Bonaparte). The Dutch lost important colonies to the British in the Napoleonic Wars, but kept an empire in INDONESIA and the West Indies. The Congress of VIENNA (1815) united all three Low Countries in the Kingdom of the Netherlands under the House of Orange, but Belgium broke away in 1830 and Luxembourg in 1890. The Dutch were neutral in World War I, but suffered occupation by the Germans 1940–5. Following a bitter colonial war, the Dutch accepted that they could not reassert control over Indonesia after World War II (▷ p. 203). The Dutch have shown enthusiasm for European unity, and, with the other Low Countries, founded BENELUX, the core of the EC.

Neutrality Acts (1935–9) US legislation designed to prevent the USA from becoming embroiled in a European war. The first act (1935) banned loans and shipments of war materials to belligerents. The ISOLATIONIST impulse behind the legislation was undermined by F.D. Roosevelt's policy of LEND-LEASE.

Neville, Richard, ▷ WARWICK, EARL OF.

New Amsterdam, ▷ NEW YORK.

Newcastle, Thomas Pelham-Holles, Duke of (1693–1768), English WHIG prime minister (1754–6 and 1757–62). His second premiership, in coalition with the Elder PITT, was marked by English success in the SEVEN YEARS WAR.

New Deal (Works Project Administration), an economic and social programme launched by F.D. ROOSEVELT to help the USA recover from the Depression; ▷ p. **185.**

New Economic Policy (NEP), a policy introduced in the USSR by Lenin in 1921 permitting some private ownership of industries; ▷ p. 181.

New England, a region of the NE USA comprising the present-day states of CONNECTICUT, MAINE, MASSACHUSETTS, NEW HAMPSHIRE, RHODE ISLAND and VERMONT.

Newfoundland, an island province of Canada. First discovered by Europeans in 1497, it was a focus for Anglo-French rivalry until sovereignty was granted to Britain in the Treaty of Utrecht (1713–14); ▷ pp. 128 and 129.

New France, the collective name for the French empire in continental North America (1534–1763). Initially embracing the shores of the St Lawrence River, NEWFOUNDLAND and Acadia (NOVA SCOTIA), the territory expanded W under the impetus of the fur trade to include much of the Great Lakes region. Designated a royal province in 1663, the area became a focal point for Anglo-French rivalry in the 18th century and was ceded to Great Britain after the Seven Years War (1763); ▷ p. 129.

New Granada, a former Spanish colony comprising present-day Colombia. It became a viceroyalty in 1717.

New Hampshire, one of the 13 original states of the USA. The New England state of New Hampshire was settled by English colonists in the 1620s and was originally part of MASSACHUSETTS; ▷ pp. 156 (map) and 159 (map).

Ne Win (1911–), Burmese soldier and statesman. After seizing power in March 1962 he abrogated the 1948 constitution, disbanding political parties and promulgating a constitution to strengthen the military's political control. He retired from the presidency in 1981 but continued to wield considerable power behind the scenes.

New Jersey, one of the 13 original states of the USA. European colonization began in 1609 with the arrival of Henry Hudson, but the colony was originally disputed by England and the Dutch. Many QUAKERS settled in the state in the 17th century; ▷ pp. 156 (map) and 159 (map).

New Model Army, the Parliamentary army created in 1645 during the ENGLISH CIVIL WAR. The New Model Army, whose members were known as 'Ironsides', itself became a powerful – and often radical – political force until the RESTORATION; ▷ p. 119.

New Orleans, battle of (8 January 1815), a British defeat at the hands of American forces led by General Andrew JACKSON. Although the battle was fought after the Treaty of GHENT had concluded the War of 1812, it catapulted Jackson to national fame and was an important factor in his 1828 presidential election victory; ▷ p. 156.

New Right, an informal and diffuse conservative movement that exercised a major influence on US politics during the late 20th century. Essentially a reaction to the liberal statist reforms of the 1960s, it drew its strength from a number of sources, notably fundamentalist Christians and alienated white middle class voters. The REAGAN presidency represented the high point of New Right influence (▷ p. 217).

New South Wales, the original British colony in AUSTRALIA (1788). It once included all of E Australia.

New Spain, a former Spanish viceroyalty comprising present-day Mexico and large parts of what are now the SW states of the USA; ▷ p. 148.

Newton, Sir Isaac, ▷ p. 133.

New York, one of the original 13 states of the USA. Originally the Dutch colony of the New Netherlands (whose capital New Amsterdam was on the site of present-day New York City), the region passed into British hands in 1664 and was the scene of important military operations during the War of Independence; ▷ p. 142.

New Zealand, a country in the S Pacific and an independent member of the COMMONWEALTH. The Maoris migrated from Polynesia to New Zealand during the 8th century (▷ p. 69). Although the Dutch explorer Abel TASMAN discovered the W coast of South Island in 1642 (▷ p. 129, box), European settlement in New Zealand dates only from the end of the 18th century, in part because of the hostility shown by the Maoris towards the intruders. Captain James Cook circumnavigated both main islands (1769–70), and his descriptions of the country encouraged colonization (▷ p. 129, box). By the beginning of the 19th century, a number of whaling stations had been established in New Zealand by Australian interests. As colonization increased, Britain determined to annex New Zealand. North Island was ceded to the British Crown by Maori chiefs under the Treaty of WAIT-ANGI (1840), while South Island was claimed by right of discovery. New Zealand was governed as a part of New South Wales until a separate colonial government was established in 1841. The 1840s were marked by fierce armed resistance to British settlement by the Maoris, the majority of whom live in North Island. Relations between the Maoris and the white settlers deteriorated further during the 1850s as the colonists sought more land and Maori chiefs increasingly refused to sell it. When troops were used to evict Maoris from disputed lands in Waitara, war broke out (1860). Fighting continued for most of the decade in North Island, and guerrilla action in the King Country – the centre of North Island – was not suppressed until 1870. The Maori Wars retarded the European settlement of North Island, while – in the last quarter of the 19th century – the discovery of gold and the introduction of refrigerated ships to export meat and dairy products greatly stimulated the colonization and economy of South Island. However, by the beginning of the 20th century, North Island was dominant again, and by 1911 migrants from Britain had boosted the country's population to one million. Subsequent immigration has remained overwhelmingly British, although there are sizeable communities of Samoans, Cook Islanders and Yugoslavs. Liberal governments (1891–1912) pioneered many reforms and social measures, including votes for women (1893) and the world's first old-age pensions (1898). Dominion status was granted in 1907, although the country did not formally acknowledge its independent status until 1947. In World War I, New Zealand fought as a British ally in Europe, achieving distinction in the disastrous Allied expedition to the GALLIPOLI peninsula during the campaign against Turkey (1915; ▷ p. 177). When Japan entered World War II in 1941, New Zealand's more immediate security was threatened. The major role played by the USA in the Pacific War led to New Zealand's postwar alliance with Australia and America in the ANZUS pact, and the country sent troops to support the Americans in Vietnam (▷ p. 208). The entry of Britain into the EC in 1973 restricted the access of New Zealand's agricultural products to what had been their principal market. Since then New Zealand has been forced to seek new markets, particularly in the Far and Middle East. Under Labour governments (1972–75 and 1984–90), the country adopted an independent foreign and defence policy. A ban on vessels powered by nuclear energy or carrying nuclear weapons in New Zealand's waters placed a question mark over the country's role as a full ANZUS member.

Ney, Michel, duc d'Elchingen (1769–1815), marshal of France. He served with distinction in the Napoleonic Wars, earning the epithet 'bravest of the brave' at BORODINO in 1812. He joined the restored Bourbon army in 1814 but defected to Napoleon in the Waterloo campaign. He was shot for treason following Napoleon's defeat and abdication; ▷ p. 146 (box).

Nez Perce, a native North American people, living in the Plateau area of the West (Idaho and adjoining areas). Originally semi-nomadic hunter-gatherers, they adopted a horse-riding, buffalo-hunting way of life after c. 1750.

Ngo Dinh Diem (1901–63), president of South Vietnam (1955–63). He began military action against VIET CONG guerrillas, but his repressive regime was brought down, and Diem killed, in a US-backed coup in November 1963 (▷ p. 208).

Nguyen Van Thieu (1923–), South Vietnamese soldier and politician, president (1967–75). His period of rule was dominated by the Vietnam War (▷ p. 208).

Nicaean Empire (1204–61), a Greek empire based on Nicaea (modern Iznik in Turkey), which became a centre of Byzantine resistance after the capture of CONSTANTINOPLE by Crusaders (1204) and the establishment of the LATIN EMPIRE.

Nicaragua, a republic of CENTRAL AMERICA. In 1502 Columbus landed in Nicaragua, which remained a Spanish possession until independence was gained in 1821. Independent Nicaragua witnessed strife between conservatives and liberals. Early in the 20th century, the political situation deteriorated, provoking American intervention – US marines were based in Nicaragua from 1912 to 1925, and again from 1927 until 1933. General Anastasio SOMOZA became president in 1937. Employing dictatorial methods, members of the Somoza family, or their supporters, remained in power until overthrown by a popular uprising led by the SANDINISTA guerrilla army in 1979. Accusing the Sandinistas of introducing Communism, the USA imposed a trade embargo on Nicaragua, making it increasingly dependent on Cuba and the USSR. Right-wing Contra guerrillas, financed by the USA, fought the Sandinistas from bases in Honduras. A ceasefire between the Contras and Sandinistas was agreed in 1989. In free presidential elections in February 1990, the Sandinista incumbent Daniel Ortega was defeated by Violeta Chamorro.

Nicholas I (1796–1855), tsar of RUSSIA (1825–55). His reign was characterized by unrelenting repression of dissent. Nicholas' foreign policy was formed by his hatred of revolution and support of the Restoration settlement of 1815.

Nicholas II (1868–1918), last tsar of RUSSIA (1894–1917). Autocratic and incompetent, his loss of control of his country precipitated the Russian Revolutions. In March 1917, when the revolution began, he abdicated, and in July 1918 he and his family were murdered by the BOLSHEVIKS, ending the ROMANOV dynasty; ▷ pp. 180–1.

Nicopolis, battle of (23 September 1316), the defeat of a Crusader army under SIGISMUND, king of Hungary, by the Ottoman Turks; ▷ pp. 88 and 114.

Niger, a republic of the Sahel in W Africa. From the 15th century, the area was dominated in turn by the sultanate of Agadès, HAUSA kingdoms and the Nigerian empire of Sokoto. The French territory of Niger was proclaimed in 1901, but much of the country was not pacified until 1920. Independence was gained in 1960 (▷ p. 202, map). After the economy was wracked by a prolonged drought, the military took power in a coup (1974). Civilian rule was restored in 1989. Following pro-democracy demonstrations (1990–91), it was announced that multi-party elections would be held in 1992.

Nigeria, a republic in W Africa. The KANEM empire flourished in N Nigeria from the 11th to the 14th centuries, during which time Islam was introduced. Various HAUSA kingdoms rose in the NW, which from the early 19th century contained the FULANI empire. YORUBA kingdoms and the Kingdom of BENIN (▷ p. 67) occupied the SW, and Ibo kingdoms the SE. European intervention in the coastal region began with Portuguese explorers in the 15th century. From 1713 the slave trade in Nigeria came to be dominated by Britain. After British slave trading ended in 1807 (▷ p. 129, box), British traders and explorers penetrated the interior. In 1861, Lagos was acquired, and in 1885 a British protectorate was established on the coast. In the scramble for empire, the commercial Royal Niger Company colonized the interior from 1886, and in 1900 its territories were surrendered to the British crown as the protectorate of Northern

Nigeria. In 1914 the coast and the interior were united to form Britain's largest African colony. An unwieldy federal structure introduced in 1954 was unable to contain regional rivalries after independence (1960). In 1966, the first PM, Sir Abubakar Tafawa Balewa (1912–66), and other prominent politicians were assassinated in a military coup. After a counter-coup brought General Yakubu Gowon to power, a bitter civil war took place (1967–70) when the Eastern Region – the homeland of the Ibo – attempted to secede as BIAFRA. Although the E was quickly re-integrated once Biafra was defeated, Nigeria remained politically unstable. The number of states was gradually increased from 3 to 30 in an attempt to prevent any one region becoming dominant. A military coup overthrew Gowon in 1975, and an attempt at civilian rule (1979–83) also ended in a coup. Another coup brought Major General Ibrahim Babangida to power in 1985. It is planned to reintroduce civilian rule before the end of 1992.

Nightingale, Florence (1820–1910), British nurse, popularly known as the 'Lady with the Lamp'. Her work in organizing hospitals for the British wounded during the Crimean War (1854–6) brought her immense public acclaim.

'Night of the Long Knives' (30 June 1934), the liquidation by Hitler's SS of the leadership of the BROWNSHIRTS; ▷ p. 187.

nihilism, a doctrine rejecting all traditional values and institutions and advocating the violent overthrow of the latter, especially as held by Russian revolutionary extremists in the late 19th century.

Nijmegen, Peace of (1678–9), the series of treaties ending Louis XIV's Dutch War; ▷ p. 123 (box).

Nile, battle of the (also called the battle of Aboukir Bay; 1 August 1798), a naval battle in which the British commander NELSON destroyed the fleet that had carried the French army to Egypt; ▷ p. 146.

Nilo-Saharans, a group of black African peoples who originated in the Nile Valley and spread W into W Africa and S into present-day Kenya and Tanzania; ▷ p. 66.

Nimeiri, Gaafar Mohammed Al- (1930–), Sudanese soldier and statesman. He led a successful coup in May 1969 and subsequently elevated himself to the presidency. He fled to Egypt after his overthrow in a coup in 1985.

Nimitz, Chester William (1885–1966), commander of the US Pacific fleet from 1941. He played a large part in the defeat of Japan in World War II; ▷ p. 194.

Ninety-five Theses, the criticisms of the Roman Catholic Church nailed to the door of the castle church at Wittenberg by Martin Luther in October 1517 (▷ p. 110). Luther's action is traditionally regarded as the starting point of the Reformation (▷ p. 110).

Nineveh, a city of ancient ASSYRIA; ▷ pp. 16 (map), 21 and 27 (map).

Nine Years War (1688–97), one of the wars of Louis XIV; ▷ p. **123** (box).

Nixon, Richard Milhous (1913–), thirty-seventh president of the USA (1969-74). A conservative Republican, he is chiefly remembered for the Watergate scandal which led to his resignation in 1974; ▷ pp. 208–9 and **217**.

Nkomo, Joshua Mqabuko Nyongolo, (1917–), Zimbabwean politician; ▷ ZIMBABWE.

Nkrumah, Kwame (1909–72), Ghanaian statesman, prime minister of the Gold Coast (1952–7) and first prime minister of independent GHANA (1957–60). He was president from 1960 until his deposition in 1966.

NKVD (Russian acronym for 'People's Commissariat of Internal Affairs'), Soviet secret police agency created in 1934 from the former OGPU, with the purpose of overseeing all internal security in the USSR as well as coordinating foreign intelligence gathering; ⇨ p. 199 (box).

Nok culture, the earliest identifiable Iron Age culture of W African sculpture; ⇨ p. 66.

Non-Aligned Movement (NAM), a conference meeting every three years to promote world peace, to reject the system of world power blocs and help bring about a more even distribution of the world's wealth; ⇨ p. 219.

Normandy, a former independent duchy in NW France. It was finally conquered by PHILIP II AUGUSTUS of France in 1204; ⇨ pp. 87 and 94.

Normandy Landings (June 1944), the start of the Allied invasion of Western Europe in World War II; ⇨ p. 191.

Norman Conquest, ⇨ p. 87.

Norsemen, ⇨ VIKINGS.

North, Frederick, Lord (1732–92), British prime minister (1770–81). His early successes were obscured by his mishandling of the American War of Independence. Although supported by GEORGE III, he lost the confidence of Parliament after the British defeat at YORKTOWN, and resigned.

North African campaigns, series of military campaigns in Africa in World War II in which the Allies fought to gain control of the S coast of the Mediterranean as a springboard for an invasion of S Europe; ⇨ pp. **190–1.**

North Atlantic Treaty Organization, ⇨ NATO.

North Carolina, one of the 13 original states of the USA. It was the site of the earliest attempted English settlement of North America (⇨ ROANOKE ISLAND). The area was resettled by English colonists in the 1650s; ⇨ pp. 156 (map) and 159 (map).

Northern Ireland, a province of the UNITED KINGDOM in the NE of Ireland. The kingdom of ULSTER flourished in what is now Northern Ireland before the Vikings began to raid the region about 800. The Danes founded several coastal towns but were finally defeated c. 1014. Anglo-Norman adventurers began their involvement in Ulster in the 12th century, but Ulster remained a centre of unrest and resentment of English rule. After a major revolt at the end of the 16th century, a plantation of Scottish Protestant settlers was made in Ulster under James I (⇨ p. 119, box). These settlers were the ancestors of Ulster's large Protestant population. Ireland was united with England in 1801 in the United Kingdom, but Ulster's non-Roman Catholic majority stood apart from the growing nationalist movement throughout the 19th century. When the Irish Free State (the forerunner of the Republic of IRELAND) was established in 1922, the six counties of Northern Ireland remained part of the United Kingdom. In the 1970s and 1980s bitter conflict resurfaced in the province as Roman Catholics – seeking unity with the Republic of Ireland – clashed with Protestant Loyalists intent upon preserving the link with Britain. British troops were stationed in Northern Ireland to keep order and to defeat the terrorist violence of the IRA.

Northern War (1700–21), a conflict in which Sweden on one side opposed Russia, Denmark and Poland on the other; ⇨ p. 127 (box).

Northern Wei, a dynasty of nomad origins, ruling N China 386–533 AD; ⇨ pp. 53 and 54.

North German Confederation, a Prussian-dominated association of N German states formed after the AUSTRO-PRUSSIAN WAR of 1866; ⇨ p. 153.

North Korea, ⇨ KOREA, DEMOCRATIC PEOPLE'S REPUBLIC OF.

Northumbria, the northern kingdom of Anglo-Saxon England. Settled by the ANGLES during the period of Anglo-Saxon invasions, Northumbria became a kingdom and was Christianized by St Aidan and his successors in the mid-7th century. Viking invaders overran the kingdom in 867. Although reconquered by WESSEX in the 10th century, and remaining a distinct earldom, it never regained its previous independence. It was disputed between England and Scotland for several centuries; ⇨ p. 79 (box).

Northwest Frontier, the strategically important mountainous region of N Pakistan between Afghanistan and KASHMIR, inhabited mainly by the PATHANS. It was under British control 1849–1947 and is now a province of Pakistan.

Northwest Passage, the route to Asia around the N coast of North America, proposed by Sir Humphrey Gilbert (1572), and unsuccessfully attempted by the English explorers Martin Frobisher (1576–8) and John Davis (1585–7) and others.

Norway, a kingdom of NW Europe. The period from the 9th to the 11th centuries was marked by the vigorous expansion of the Vikings from their Scandinavian homelands (⇨ p. 85). Vikings from Norway plundered N Europe, settled in the British Isles, Iceland and Greenland and explored the Atlantic coast of North America. Norway itself was divided into a number of warring small kingdoms and was not united until 1015–28 under OLAF II Haraldsson, who converted many Norwegians to Christianity and later became the country's patron saint. However, the instability and civil wars that had preceded his rule returned in the 12th century, and unity under a strong monarch was not experienced again until the reign of Haakon IV (reigned 1217–63). The marriage of Haakon VI (reigned 1355–1380) to the future Queen Margrethe I of Denmark united the destinies of Norway and Denmark. Danish kings – who ruled Norway as a part of their own realm until 1814 – ensured the early adoption of the Lutheran religion by Norwegians. At the end of the Napoleonic Wars, Norway attempted to regain autonomy, but the country came under the rule of the kings of Sweden, although a separate Norwegian Parliament was allowed a considerable degree of independence. Growing nationalism in Norway placed great strains upon the union with Sweden, and in 1905 – following a vote by the Norwegians to repeal the union – King Oscar II of Sweden gave up his claims to the Norwegian crown to allow a peaceful separation of the two countries. After a Swedish prince declined the Norwegian throne, Prince Carl of Denmark was confirmed as King of Norway – as Haakon VII – by a plebiscite. Norway was neutral in World War I, and declared neutrality in World War II, but was occupied by German forces (1940) who set up a puppet government under Vidkun QUISLING. After the war, Norway joined NATO and agreed in 1972 to enter the EC, but a national referendum rejected membership.

Nova Scotia, a maritime province of E CANADA that was the scene of bitter Anglo-French rivalry until Great Britain's sovereignty was confirmed under the Treaty of PARIS (1763). It was the first Canadian colony to achieve 'responsible' government (1848) and acceded to confederation in 1867; ⇨ p. 128 (map)

Novgorod, city-state of medieval Russia. It bowed to Mongol overlordship only in the later Middle Ages. After years of struggle with Muscovy, it was incorporated into the grand duchy of MUSCOVY by IVAN III in 1478; ⇨ p. 86.

Nubia, an ancient region of NE Africa in the N of modern Sudan, known as 'Cush' by the ancient Egyptians; ⇨ pp. 17, 18, 19, **66** and 67.

Nuclear Test Ban Treaty (1963), an international agreement, signed by the USA, UK and USSR, prohibiting the testing of nuclear devices in the atmosphere or in outer space or under water. In 1974 the USA and USSR agreed not to test devices on earth larger than 150 kilotons; ⇨ p. 227.

Nujoma, Sam (1929–), first president of independent NAMIBIA (1990–). He helped found SWAPO in 1959, and was active as a guerilla leader during his period in exile in Zambia and Angola until 1990.

Numidia, an ancient kingdom in N Africa to the W of Carthage. From the time of Hannibal it was ruled by native kings who supported Rome and enjoyed its protection. Under the empire it became a Roman province; ⇨ p. 37 (map) and JUGURTHA.

Nuremberg Laws (1935), laws passed by the Nazis depriving Jews of citizenship rights; ⇨ p. 187.

Nuremberg rallies, open-air conventions held annually by the Nazi Party in the 1930s in Nuremberg, Bavaria, used by Hitler to deliver major political speeches; ⇨ p. 187.

Nuremberg Trials (1945–6), trials held in Nuremberg after World War II, in which Nazi leaders were convicted by an Allied tribunal of WAR CRIMES, and crimes against peace and humanity, several of them being sentenced to death. Japan's wartime leaders were convicted in similar trials in Tokyo.

Nyasaland, ⇨ MALAWI.

Nyerere, Julius Kambarage (1922–), Tanzanian statesman. He was first prime minister (1961) and president (1962) of independent Tanganyika (1961), and – following the union of Tanganyika and Zanzibar president of TANZANIA (1964–85).

Nystad, Treaty of (1721), the treaty ending the NORTHERN WAR; ⇨ p. 127 (box).

OAS, ⇨ ORGANIZATION OF AMERICAN STATES.

OAU, ⇨ ORGANIZATION OF AFRICAN UNITY.

Obote, Milton (1924–), Ugandan statesman, prime minister (1962–6), president (1966-71 and 1980–5). He was deposed by Idi Amin in 1971, but returned from exile to take up the presidency again after Amin's downfall. He was overthrown by the military in 1985; ⇨ p. 203 and UGANDA.

Obrenović, a Serbian dynasty founded by Milos Obrenovic I (1780–1860). It ruled Serbia 1817–42 and 1858–1903, alternating with the rival KARA-GEORGEVIĆ dynasty.

O'Connell, Daniel (1775–1847), Irish nationalist and barrister who founded the Catholic Association in 1823 to mobilize support for CATHOLIC EMANCIPATION. Although unable to take his seat as he was a Catholic, he was elected MP for Co. Clare in 1828. Catholic Emancipation was conceded in the following year. O'Connell later campaigned for the repeal of the Act of UNION of 1801.

Octavian, ⇨ AUGUSTUS.

October Revolution, the seizure of power in Russia by Lenin's BOLSHEVIKS in November (October according to the Julian calendar) 1917; ⇨ p. 181.

Oder-Neisse Line, the present-day border between Germany and Poland, formed by the Oder and Neisse rivers, agreed at the Potsdam Conference in July 1945 (⇨ p. 204).

Odoacer (c. 433–93), Gothic king who became effective ruler in Italy when he overthrew the last Roman emperor in 476; ⇨ p. 40.

Odo Nobunaga (1534–82), military ruler of Japan (1578–82), who ruthlessly fought his way to supreme power between 1559 and 1578. He was assassinated before his rule over the whole of Japan could be consolidated; ⇨ p. 64.

OECD, ⇨ ORGANIZATION FOR ECONOMIC COOPERATION AND DEVELOPMENT.

Offa (d. 796), king of MERCIA (757–96), who constructed the earthwork known as Offa's dyke between England and Wales.

Ogdei (1185–1241), the son and successor of Genghis Khan, whose policy of conquest he continued; ⇨ p. 54.

OGPU (Russian acronym for 'United State Political Administration'), the Soviet secret police agency from 1923 to 1934, when it was succeeded by the NKVD.

O'Higgins, Bernardo (1778–1842), Chilean revolutionary, born of an Irish father. He led the struggle for independence from Spain and was the first president of CHILE (1817–23); ▷ p. 149.

Okinawa, an island between Taiwan and Japan. Strategically a vital location with bases commanding the approaches to Japan, Okinawa was captured from the Japanese by US forces after fierce resistance in June 1945; ▷ p. 195.

Olaf II, St (Haraldsson; c. 995–1028), king of Norway (1015–28), where he attempted to stamp out paganism. Driven out by CNUT, he died in battle attempting to regain his kingdom from the Danes.

Oldenburg, a former county (12th century), duchy (1774) and grand duchy (1829) in N Germany. Oldenburg became part of the German Empire in 1871. The monarchy was overthrown in 1918.

Oldowan, the earliest stone tool-making tradition, named after the OLDUVAI Gorge, and starting contemporary with *Homo habilis* (▷ p. 12). Simple flakes were struck from pieces of stone for cutting various materials.

Olduvai Gorge, the best-known early human fossil site in Africa, part of the Great Rift Valley System in Tanzania; ▷ p. *12*.

oligarchy, rule by a small group of people, especially in ancient Greece; ▷ p. 28.

Olmec, a pre-Columbian Meso-American culture, centred on lowland E Mexico. Olmec culture was a major influence during the Formative phase of Meso-American prehistory (1000 BC–300 AD).

Olympia, a plain in the W Peloponnese, Greece. From the 8th century BC it was the site of the Olympic Games, which grew to become the most important of the four Panhellenic athletic games.

Oman, a SULTANATE of SW Asia. Persia ruled Oman from the 4th century AD until Muslim armies invaded, bringing Islam in the 7th century (▷ p. 83). The area's flourishing trade with the E attracted the Portuguese (1507), who founded Muscat and occupied the coast until 1650. Ahmad ibn Sa'id, who became Imam in 1749, founded the present dynasty. His successors built an empire including the Kenyan coast and Zanzibar, but in 1861 Zanzibar and Oman separated. A British presence was established in the 19th century and Oman did not regain complete independence until 1951. Sultan Qaboos – who came to power in a palace coup in 1970 – has modernized and developed Oman. In the 1970s South YEMEN supported left-wing separatist guerrillas in the S province of Dhofar, but the revolt was suppressed with military assistance from the UK.

Omri, king of Israel (c. 876–c. 869 BC). He established his capital at SAMARIA; ▷ p. 23.

OPEC, ▷ ORGANIZATION OF PETROLEUM EXPORTING COUNTRIES.

Opium Wars (1839–42 and 1856–60), two wars fought between Britain and China; ▷ pp. 57 and 162.

oracle, in the ancient world, a divine prophesy mediated through a priest or priestess. The Greeks had a large number of oracular shrines, of which the most famous was Apollo's at Delphi; ▷ pp. 29 (box) and 47 (box).

Orange Free State, an inland province of the Republic of SOUTH AFRICA, a former independent AFRIKANER (Boer) republic (1854–1900) and British colony (1900–10); ▷ pp. 163 (box) and 220.

Orange, house of, a European princely family whose territories were originally centred on Orange in S France. William of Nassau succeeded to the title of Prince of Orange in 1544, and as WILLIAM THE SILENT played a leading role in the DUTCH REVOLT against Spain. His successors were prominent both in Dutch domestic politics and in wider European affairs, WILLIAM III of Orange becoming king of England in 1689. The Princes of

Orange became hereditary monarchs of the new kingdom of the Netherlands in 1815; ▷ pp. 119, **120–1** and 123 (box).

Oregon Boundary Dispute (1843–6), a dispute between Britain and the USA over territory in the NW previously jointly occupied by the two states. Compromise was reached in 1846, when the USA received a large portion of the disputed territory (now the US states of Oregon, Washington, Idaho and parts of Montana and Wyoming); ▷ .p. 157.

Organization for Economic Cooperation and Development (OECD), an organization founded in 1961 to replace the Organization for European Economic Cooperation, which had been established in connection with the US Marshall Aid Plan in 1945 (▷ p. 205). It aims to encourage economic and social welfare in member-states and to stimulate aid to Third World countries. Its membership has grown from the original 20 to 24 states; ▷ p. 223.

Organization of African Unity (OAU), an organization of 32 African states founded in 1963. Chief among its objectives have been the eradication of colonialism (▷ p. 200), and the promotion of economic and political cooperation between member-states. Since foundation the OAU has grown to include all the African states except South Africa. Morocco, a founder-member, withdrew in 1985.

Organization of American States (OAS), an organization established in 1948 to promote solidarity amongst the states of the Americas. Its 32 members include the USA as well as Latin America and Caribbean states.

Organization of Petroleum Exporting Countries (OPEC), an organization founded in Baghdad, Iraq, in 1960 with the aim of coordinating the petroleum-producing and exporting policies of its 13 member-states: Algeria, Ecuador, Gabon, Indonesia, Iran, Iraq, Kuwait, Libya, Nigeria, Qatar, Saudi Arabia, the United Arab Emirates and Venezuela. It sprang to prominence during the 1973 Arab–Israeli War, when members restricted the supply and quadrupled the price of their oil exports, causing serious economic problems for the consumer nations of the West; ▷ p. 212.

Orkhan (1326–60), the son of OSMAN I and 'Bey' of the Ottoman Turks (1326–60); ▷ p. 114.

Orléans or **Bourbon-Orléans,** the junior – and (after 1883) only surviving – branch of the French royal house of BOURBON. The Orléanist Louis-Philippe reigned from 1830 to 1848; ▷ p. 150.

Orphic mysteries, a religious cult of ancient Greece, believed by its adherents to have been established by Orpheus, the legendary poet and musician. It flourished in the 6th century BC.

Orthodox Church, a family of Christian churches in Eastern Europe under the general primacy of the PATRIARCHATE of Constantinople. From 1453 the Russian Church has been its largest member. The Orthodox Church developed from the Greek Church of the Byzantine Empire. The Greek Church finally broke with Rome in 1054 after centuries of controversy over the issues of papal primacy and the wording of the Creed. Veneration of icons plays an important part in worship; ▷ pp. 81, 90 and 155 (box).

Osman I (1258–1326), the founder of the Ottoman Empire; ▷ p. 114.

Ostpolitik (German 'eastern policy'), West German foreign policy introduced from 1969 by Willy BRANDT. The policy normalized relations between West and East Germany through direct talks, trade, treaties and mutual recognition of frontiers, and helped reduce East–West tension in the 1970s.

ostracism, an institution in ancient Athens for banishing politicians; ▷ p. 29.

Ostrogoths, the eastern Goths, a people originating in the Don basin. They became vassals of the HUNS

in Pannonia c. 375–454 after being displaced by the latter's westward movement. Under THEODERIC the Great they overthrow ODOACER in 488 and became rulers of Italy c. 493–523. They were eventually overwhelmed by Justinian's reconquest between 536 and 552; ▷ pp. 40 (map), **78–9** and 80.

Oswald, Lee Harvey (1939—63) the alleged assassin of President KENNEDY in 1963. Oswald himself was gunned down by a nightclub owner, Jack Ruby, before he could stand trial. The Warren Commission set up to investigate Kennedy's assassination rejected allegations of a wider conspiracy, concluding that Oswald had acted on his own.

Ottawa Agreements (1932), a series of economic agreements between Britain and its DOMINIONS, establishing a system of 'imperial preferences' to counter the effects of the DEPRESSION. The agreements imposed high tariffs on imports into Britain from countries outside the COMMONWEALTH and provided for duty-free imports of quotas of goods from the Dominions. The USA raised tariffs in response.

Otto I (the Great; 912–73), king of Germany (936–73), emperor (962–73); ▷ p. **84**.

Otto II (955–83), king of Germany (961–83), emperor (973–83) and son of OTTO I; ▷ p. 84.

Otto III (980–1002), king of Germany (983–1002), emperor (996–1002), and son of OTTO II; ▷ p. *84*.

Ottoman Empire, ▷ pp. 55, 81, 83, **114–15**, 117, 124, 126, 127, **154–5**, 175, 178 (map), 182 and 210.

Ottonian dynasty, the German dynasty founded by HENRY I, duke of Saxony; ▷ p. 84.

Oudenarde, battle of (July 1708), a victory of EUGÈNE of Savoy and MARLBOROUGH over the French during the War of the Spanish Succession (▷ p. 123). The French had outflanked Marlborough and occupied Ghent and Bruges, threatening the Allies' hold on the S Netherlands and the security of the Dutch Republic.

Owen, Robert (1771–1858), British manufacturer and socialist visionary. Owen built a model environment for his workers in the New Lanark mills and put his cooperative theories into practice at various experimental communities, such as New Harmony, Indiana (1825); ▷ pp. 166 and 168.

Oxenstierna, Axel Gustaffson, Count (1583–1654), Swedish chancellor (1612–54). A brilliant reforming administrator under GUSTAVUS II ADOLPHUS, he directed Swedish foreign policy during the Thirty Years War.

Oyo, kingdom of, ▷ pp. 66 (map), 67, and YORUBA.

Pacific campaigns, the naval and amphibious engagements fought between Japanese and Allied forces in the central and SW Pacific during World War II; ▷ pp. **194–5**.

Pacific, War of the (1879–83), a war fought between Chile on one side and Bolivia and Peru on the other for control of the nitrates of the N Atacama desert. Enjoying command of the sea, Chilean forces eventually captured Lima in 1881. By the treaty of Ancón (1883) Peru lost two S provinces, while Bolivia was deprived of access to the Pacific.

Pagan, a former kingdom of Burma based on the central Irrawaddy and founded c. 849 AD; ▷ p. 61.

Pahlavi, Reza Khan (1877–1944), Shah of Persia (Iran) (1926–41). Rising through the ranks of the Persian army, he led a coup in 1921 and proclaimed himself Shah five years later. His son Mohammed Reza (1919–80) became Shah on his father's abdication in 1941, ruling Iran until his overthrow in KHOMEINI'S Islamic Revolution of 1979; ▷ p. **212** (box).

Paine, Thomas (1737–1809), English radical political theorist. His pamphlet *Common Sense* (1776) defended the case of the American colonists against Britain. *The Rights of Man* (1790) defended the French Revolution against the attacks of BURKE; ▷ p. 145.

Pakistan, a republic of S Asia. The Indus Valley was the seat of the ancient Harappan civilization (2300–1700 BC; ⇨ p. 58), but by 1500 BC the Ganges Basin had become the driving force in the subcontinent. The area was ruled by a succession of kingdoms and empires before the colonial age (⇨ pp. 58–9 and 62–3), and from the 8th century Pakistan was converted to Islam. From the 18th century the region came under British rule (⇨ p. 160). Pakistan as a nation was born in August 1947 when British INDIA was partitioned as a result of demands by the MUSLIM LEAGUE for an Islamic state in which Hindus would not be in a majority (⇨ p. 201, box). Pakistan had two 'wings' – West Pakistan (the present country) and East Pakistan (now BANGLADESH) – separated by 1600 km (1000 mi) of Indian territory. A number of areas were disputed with India. KASHMIR – the principal bone of contention – was effectively partitioned between the two nations, and in 1947–9 and 1965 tension over Kashmir led to war between India and Pakistan. The problem of Kashmir is unsolved with fighting continuing intermittently along parts of the ceasefire line. The Muslim League leader Muhammad Ali JINNAH was the first governor general, but Jinnah, who was regarded as 'father of the nation', died soon after independence. Pakistan – which became a republic in 1956 – suffered political instability and periods of military rule, including the administrations of General Muhammad AYUB KHAN (1958–69) and General Muhammad Yahya Khan (1969–71). Although East Pakistan contained the majority of the population, from the beginning West Pakistan held political and military dominance. In elections in 1970, Sheikh MUJIBUR Rahman's AWAMI LEAGUE won an overwhelming majority in East Pakistan, while the Pakistan People's Party (PPP) won most of the seats in West Pakistan. Mujibur Rahman seemed less interested in leading a new Pakistani government than in winning autonomy for the East. In March 1971, after abortive negotiations, the Pakistani army was sent from the West to East Pakistan, which promptly declared its independence as BANGLADESH. Civil war broke out and India supported the new state, forcing the Pakistani army to surrender by the end of the year. The leader of the PPP, Zulfiqar Ali BHUTTO (PM 1972–7), was deposed in a military coup led by the Army Chief of Staff, Mohammed ZIA UL-HAQ. Bhutto was imprisoned (1977) for allegedly ordering the murder of the father of a former political opponent, sentenced to death (1978) and, despite international protests, hanged (1979). In 1985 Zia lifted martial law and began to return Pakistan to civilian life. Zia was killed in a plane crash (1988). Following elections in 1988, Bhutto's daughter and the PPP's new leader, Benazir, became the first woman prime minister of an Islamic state. She was dismissed by the president in 1990, and subsequent elections were won by the Islamic Democratic Alliance.

Palaeolithic, ⇨ pp. 12–14.

Palatinate, a former German state whose prince was one of the ELECTORS of the Holy Roman Empire, comprising the Lower Palatinate on the Rhine and the Upper Palatinate between Bavaria and Bohemia; ⇨ p. 113.

Pale, the area around Dublin that was the effective extent of English authority in Ireland before ELIZABETH I and her Stuart successors imposed their rule; ⇨ p. 119 (box).

Palestine, the area of land between the Jordan River in the E and the Mediterranean coast in the W, and the GOLAN HEIGHTS in the N and the borders of Egypt in the S, which has become the modern state of ISRAEL. In the process, the indigenous Arab population has been largely displaced; ⇨ pp. 21, 22–3, 39 (box), 40, 83, 81, 88, 155 (box), 178, 182, 192 (box) and **210–13.**

Palme, Olaf (1916–86), Swedish SOCIAL DEMOCRAT statesman, prime minister (1969–76 and 1982–6). He was assassinated by a gunman.

Palmerston, Henry John Temple, 3rd Viscount (1784–1865), British statesman, prime minister (1855–8 and 1859–65). He entered the Commons as a TORY in 1806 but served in WHIG governments as foreign secretary (1830–41 and 1846–51), supporting British interests and liberal and national causes abroad. As PM he presided over the conclusion of the CRIMEAN WAR and kept Britain neutral during the American Civil War.

Pan-Africanist Congress (PAC), a black South African political party that broke away from the AFRICAN NATIONAL CONGRESS in 1959; ⇨ p. 221.

Panama, a republic of CENTRAL AMERICA. Panama was discovered in 1501, and became part of Spanish NEW GRANADA (COLOMBIA). In the 1880s a French attempt to construct a canal through Panama linking the Atlantic and Pacific Oceans proved unsuccessful. After Colombia rejected US proposals for completing the canal, Panama became independent (1903), sponsored by the USA. The PANAMA CANAL eventually opened in 1914. The USA was given land extending 8 km (5 mi) on either side of the canal – the Canal Zone – complete control of which will be handed to Panama in 2000. From 1983 to 1989 effective power was in the hands of General Manuel Noriega, who was deposed by a US invasion and taken to stand trial in the USA, accused of criminal activities.

Panama Canal, a waterway across the isthmus of PANAMA in Central America built by the USA (1904–14) on territory leased from the republic of Panama. The Canal Zone, under US control since 1903, will revert to Panama by 2000, but the Canal's perpetual neutrality is assured.

Pankhurst, Emmeline (1858–1928), British feminist and leader of the suffragettes. The militant methods she used in her campaign for universal women's suffrage led to her being imprisoned on eight occasions. Her daughters Christabel (1880–1958) and Sylvia (1882–1960) were also suffragettes; ⇨ p. 232.

Panmunjom Armistice (27 July 1953), a ceasefire agreement signed in the demilitarized zone between North and South Korea by representatives of the United Nations Command and the North Koreans and Chinese, ending the Korean War (⇨ p. 206).

Pan-Slavism, a 19th-century movement for a confederation of all Slavic peoples under the leadership of Russia; ⇨ p. 155.

papacy, the office of, or system of government by, the pope in the Roman Catholic Church; ⇨ pp. 84, **90–1,** 110 and 112.

Papal States (or 'Patrimony of St Peter'), lands in central Italy under the rule of the pope. In 756 the LOMBARD king ceded territory in central and N Italy to the pope, who became a temporal as well as a spiritual ruler. The Papal States comprised the territories of Latium (the area around Rome), Umbria, Marche and Romagna. Papal control – hampered by disputes with the Holy Roman Emperors throughout the Middle Ages – remained ineffectual until the 1350s. The Papal States reached their greatest extent under Pope Julius II (reigned 1503–13), but by the 18th century the pope's temporal power was weak. During the Revolutionary and Napoleonic Wars the Papal States were variously annexed by their neighbours and absorbed into the French Empire. They were restored in 1815, but were lost to the new kingdom of ITALY during Italian unification; ⇨ pp. 85 (map), 96, 97, 113 (map), 123 (map), 150 (map).

Papen, Franz von (1879–1969), German chancellor (1932). He made concessions to the Nazis, and after resigning persuaded HINDENBURG to appoint Hitler chancellor in January 1933 (⇨ p. 186).

Papineau's Rebellion (1837), an abortive French Canadian republican uprising against British authority in CANADA.

Papua New Guinea, a country of the S Pacific and an independent member of the COMMONWEALTH. The first inhabitants of New Guinea came from Indonesia around 50 000 BC (⇨ p. 68). European colonization began in 1828 when the Dutch claimed W New Guinea. A British protectorate, established in the SE in 1884, was transferred to Australia (1906) and renamed Papua. NE New Guinea came under German administration in 1884, but was occupied by Australian forces in 1914. From 1942 to 1945 Japanese forces occupied New Guinea and part of Papua (⇨ p. 194). In 1949 Australia combined the administration of the territories, which achieved independence as Papua New Guinea in 1975 (⇨ p. 200, map). Bougainville island, a major source of copper, declared independence unilaterally in 1990, but a central government economic blockade has isolated the island.

Paracelsus (1493–1541), Swiss-German physician and alchemist; ⇨ p. 132 (box).

Paraguay, a republic of central South America. The Spanish reached the area in the 1520s. Jesuit missionaries to the Guaraní Indians dominated the country from 1609 until 1767, when they were expelled. Since independence in 1811, Paraguay has suffered many dictators, including General José Francia, who totally isolated Paraguay (1814–40). War against Argentina, Brazil and Uruguay (1865–70) cost Paraguay over one half of its people and much territory. The CHACO Wars with Bolivia (1929–35) further weakened Paraguay. General Alfredo STROESSNER gained power in 1954, ruling with increasing disregard for human rights until his overthrow in a military coup in 1989.

Paraguayan War (1864–70), a war fought by Argentina, Uruguay and Brazil against the Paraguay of Francisco Solano LÓPEZ, whose ambitious diplomacy antagonized all his neighbours at once. López led a tenacious resistance, resulting in heavy loss of life and the ruin of his country. This 'War of the Triple Alliance' was the most prolonged international conflict in Latin American history.

Paris, Congress of (1856), a conference that negotiated the end of the Crimean War; ⇨ p. 155.

Paris, Treaty of (1763), the treaty that ended the SEVEN YEARS WAR. It confirmed Britain's maritime and colonial supremacy at the expense of France and Spain; ⇨ pp. 125 and **129.**

Paris Peace Conference (1919–20), ⇨ pp. **182–3,** 184, 186 and 188.

Park Chung-Hee (1917–79), president of the Republic of (South) Korea (1961–79); ⇨ p. 223.

Parliament, a representative assembly summoned by the monarch in England from the 13th century to give advice and agree to taxation; it has since become the legislative body of the United Kingdom. Composed of the crown, the House of LORDS and the House of COMMONS, only since the GLORIOUS REVOLUTION has the latter become the most important of the two chambers and its sessions a regular rather than occasional event. Originally drawn from very narrow social groups, the size of the electorate has greatly increased in the 19th and 20th centuries.

Parnell, Charles Stewart (1846–91), Irish nationalist leader. A Protestant Anglo-Irish landowner, he became leader of the Irish MPs supporting HOME RULE in 1878. In 1881 he was imprisoned in Kilmainham gaol for inciting agrarian violence. From 1886 Parnell supported the Liberal leader GLADSTONE, a convert to home rule, but was forced to resign the Irish party leadership in 1890, after being cited in the O'Shea divorce case; ⇨ IRELAND.

Parthia, ⇨ pp. 27 (box) and 32 (map).

Pascal, Blaise (1623–32), French mathematician, scientist and philosopher. His *Lettres provinciales*

(1656–7) defended the JANSENISTS against their Jesuit enemies.

Passchendaele, battle of (31 July–21 November 1917), a British attack in Flanders (officially the third battle of YPRES), in World War I. The combined British, Australian and Canadian offensive became bogged down in 'a porridge of mud'. The British suffered over 240 000 casualties for no gain in a battle whose name has become synonymous with the horrors of trench warfare; ⊳ pp. 176 and 179.

Pathan, a people living in Afghanistan and NW Pakistan. Pathan uprisings on the NORTHWEST FRONTIER led to a British military occupation of the area in the late 1890s.

Pathet Lao, a Laotian Communist organization. It took power in 1975 in the wake of US withdrawal from Vietnam; ⊳ p. 209 and LAOS.

Patriarchate, the title given in the early Middle Ages to the five chief bishoprics of Christendom – Rome, Alexandria, Antioch, CONSTANTINOPLE and JERUSALEM. Rome was to become pre-eminent in the Western Church, and Constantinople in the Eastern (ORTHODOX) Church.

patricians, the hereditary elite in ancient Rome; ⊳ p. 36.

Patrick, St (c. 390–c. 460), the patron saint of Ireland. Born in Britain, he came to Ireland as a missionary (c. 435), establishing the see of Armagh.

Patton, George Smith (1885–1945), US World War II general. He led the 3rd Army in the invasion of France in 1944, breaching the German defences in Normandy, taking Paris and reaching the Moselle; ⊳ p. 191.

Paul, St (Saul of Tarsus; d. c. AD 65), early Christian apostle and the author of 13 Epistles in the New Testament. Formerly a persecutor of Christians, he was converted to Christianity on the road to Damascus, and went on to carry out missionary work in Greece, Anatolia and elsewhere. He died a martyr's death under Nero.

Pawnee, a native North American people, living in the Great Plains (Nebraska). They mixed settled farming with the seasonal hunting of buffalo.

Pearl Harbor, a US naval base in Hawaii. A surprise Japanese attack on the base in December 1941 brought the USA into World War II; ⊳ p. 194.

Pearse, Pádraic (1879–1916), Irish poet and nationalist who proclaimed Irish independence in the EASTER RISING (1916). He was court-martialled and shot by the British.

Peasants' Revolt (1381), an English rebellion led by Wat TYLER and John BALL; ⊳ p. 93.

Peasants' War (1525), a revolt of the German peasantry during the Reformation. Believing they were supported by Luther's teachings, the rebels sought the restoration of customary rights and a reduction of the demands of ecclesiastical and lay lords; ⊳ pp. 110 and 111 (box).

Pedro I (1798–1835), first emperor of Brazil (1822–31); ⊳ p. 149 (box).

Pedro II (1812–91), emperor of Brazil (1831–89); ⊳ p. 149 (box).

Peel, Sir Robert (1788–1850), British Conservative statesman, prime minister (1834–5 and 1841–6). As home secretary (1822–7 and 1828–30), he set up the Metropolitan Police Force (1829). His second premiership saw the passage of some significant reforms, but his repeal of the CORN LAWS in 1846 split the Conservative Party and he was compelled to resign.

Peisistratos (c. 600–527 BC), tyrant of Athens; ⊳ p. 29.

Pelham, Henry (1695–1754), British WHIG statesman, prime minister (1743–6 and 1746–54). He was succeeded by his brother and close political associate, the Duke of NEWCASTLE.

Pelopidas (c. 410–364 BC), Theban general; ⊳ p. 31.

Peloponnese, the large peninsula in S Greece, dominated in the 8th–4th centuries BC by Sparta, which formed the **Peloponnesian League** in the 6th century; ⊳ pp. 28–31.

Peloponnesian War, ⊳ pp. 2 and 30–1.

Peninsular War (1807–14), one of the Napoleonic Wars, fought in the Iberian Peninsula between France on one side and British, Spanish and Portuguese forces on the other. The conflict, which arose from Napoleon's efforts to control Spain and Portugal, ended in defeat for France. The future duke of WELLINGTON quickly recovered Portugal, but was obliged to fight a lengthy campaign against Napoleon's generals in Spain before achieving ultimate victory at the battle of VITORIA (1813); ⊳ p. 147.

Pennsylvania, a colony and state of the E USA, one of the original 13 colonies. Founded by the Quaker William Penn (1644–1718) in 1681, the colony remained a fiefdom of the Penn family until the American War of Independence. Ethnically heterogeneous and dominated by the great commercial centre of Philadelphia (the national capital during the revolutionary period), it swiftly became one of the most politically significant states in the Union; ⊳ pp. 142, 143, 157 and 159.

Penn, William, ⊳ PENNSYLVANIA.

Pentagon, the Department of Defense building and headquarters of the US armed forces at Arlington, Virginia.

'People's Budget' (1909), a budget introduced in Britain by LLOYD GEORGE, introducing tax on high incomes and a land tax to finance social reforms such as pensions and national insurance. The rejection of the budget by the House of Lords – a breach of constitutional convention – led to legislation curtailing their powers.

Pepin III (the Short; 715–768), king of the Franks (751–768); ⊳ pp. 79 and 84.

Pepys, Samuel (1633–1703), English administrator and president of the ROYAL SOCIETY. His diaries provide a colourful picture of contemporary social and political life.

Perceval, Spencer (1762–1812), British TORY politician. He succeeded the Duke of PORTLAND as prime minister (1809–12) and remains the only British PM to have been assassinated.

Percy, a noble family of medieval England. As earls of Northumberland from 1377 to 1670, they were pre-eminent in N English society. The Percy rebellion of 1403–8 posed serious problems for HENRY IV.

perestroika (Russian, 'reconstruction'), the policy of economic and political reform instituted in the Soviet Union by Gorbachov from 1987; ⊳ p. 225.

Pergamum or **Pergamon,** a Hellenistic city in W Asia Minor (Turkey), and the centre of a powerful independent kingdom ruled by the Attalid dynasty until 133 BC, when it became a Roman province. ⊳ p. 33.

Pericles (c. 495–429 BC), Athenian statesman and general; ⊳ p. 30.

Per-Ramesses, an ancient Egyptian capital; ⊳ p. 19.

Perry, Matthew Calbraith (1794–1858), US naval officer, the leader of an expedition to Japan (1853–4) that forced the shogunate to open two Japanese ports to US trade in the treaty of KANAGAWA, ending Japan's isolation; ⊳ p. 65.

Persepolis, a ceremonial centre of ancient Persia; ⊳ pp. 26–7.

Persia, a region of SW Asia, modern Fars in Iran; the area in which the Iranian Persian tribe settled in the 1st millennium BC. The term is also applied to the Persian Achaemenid Empire, and was the name

used for IRAN until 1935; ⊳ pp. 19, 21, **26–7**, 29, 31, 32, *42*, 43, 44, 80, 82, 83 and 114.

Persian Wars, ⊳ pp. 27 and 29.

Peru, a republic on the W coast of South America. When the Spanish arrived in Peru in 1531 the Inca Empire was at its peak (⊳ p. 71). Inca resistance was quickly subdued by Pizarro (⊳ p. 116, box) and Peru became one of Spain's most valuable possessions (⊳ p. 148). Much of South America was governed from Lima as the Spanish viceroyalty of Peru. Independence was proclaimed in 1821 after the Argentine SAN MARTÍN took Lima, but Spanish forces did not leave until 1824 (⊳ p. 149). Independent Peru saw political domination by large landowners. Progress was made under General Ramon Castilla (1844–62) and civilian constitutional governments at the beginning of the 20th century, but instability and military coups have been common. Defeat in the War of the PACIFIC (1879–83) – in which Peru fought in alliance with Bolivia against Chile – resulted in the loss of nitrate deposits in the S, while victory against Ecuador (1941) added Amazonian territory. From 1968 a reformist military government instituted a programme of land reform, attempting to benefit workers and the Indians, but faced with mounting economic problems the military swung to the right in 1975. In 1980 elections were held, but owing to the economic crisis and the growth of an extreme left-wing guerrilla movement – the Sendero Luminoso ('Shining Path') – Peru's democracy remained under threat. In 1992, the president effected a coup, suspending the constitution and placing opposition leaders under arrest.

Pétain, Henri-Philippe (1856–1951), French general and head of state. A hero of World War I, he was appointed PM in 1940 and concluded an armistice with the Germans, surrendering three-fifths of France to German control. He set up the VICHY Government which administered unoccupied France, and collaborated with the Germans. With the ALLIED invasion of France, he retreated into Germany, but returned to be tried for treason and condemned to death. The sentence was commuted by DE GAULLE to life imprisonment.

Peter I (the Great; 1672–1725), tsar of Russia (1682–1725); ⊳ pp. 126–7.

Peter, St (Simon Peter; d. c. AD 64), the leader of the apostles who followed JESUS, regarded by Roman Catholics as the first pope; ⊳ p. 90.

Peterloo Massacre (16 August 1819), a clash between demonstrators and the local yeomanry at a mass meeting for parliamentary reform at St Peter's Fields, Manchester. Troopers tried to arrest the chief speaker, the reformer Henry Hunt, resulting in 11 civilians dead and hundreds injured. The name given to the incident by its critics is an ironic reference to the battle of Waterloo (1815).

phalanx, the basic infantry unit of the ancient Greeks; ⊳ pp. **33** (box) and 44.

Pharaoh, the title used by the kings of ancient Egypt, derived from *Per'ao,* meaning 'the Great House' or palace; ⊳ pp. **17–19**, 22, 42, 43 and 44.

Pharsalus, battle of (9 August 48 BC), a battle in Thessaly (N Greece) where POMPEY was completely defeated by Caesar; ⊳ p. 37.

Philby, Harold (known as 'Kim'; 1912–88), British double agent; ⊳ p. 207 (box).

Philip II (382–336 BC), king of MACEDON (359–336), brought all Greece under his domination. His son, Alexander the Great, continued his conquests; ⊳ pp. **31**, 32, 33 (box) and 44.

Philip II (Augustus; 1165–1223), king of France (1179–1223). The most successful of all French kings, his administrative developments and his conquests, notably of NORMANDY and ANJOU, more than doubled the resources of the French monarchy; ⊳ p. 94.

Philip II (1527–98), king of Spain, Naples and Sicily

(1556–98), and of Portugal (as Philip I, 1580–98). The son of Emperor CHARLES V, his four wives included MARY I of England; ▷ pp. 111, **112–13**, 114, **117**, 118, 120 and 130.

Philip IV (the Fair; 1268–1314), king of France (1285–1314). A high-handed and highly controversial ruler, he launched attacks on FLANDERS and AQUITAINE, arrested Pope BONIFACE VIII and ordered the suppression of the TEMPLARS; ▷ p. 94.

Philip V (1683–1746), king of Spain (1700–46); ▷ p. 123 (box).

Philip of Hesse (1504–67), German prince who played a prominent role in establishing Protestantism in Germany during the Reformation. He created the Schmalkaldic League to defend Lutheranism against the Emperor CHARLES V, and helped suppress the PEASANTS' WAR and the Anabaptist experiment at Münster; ▷ p. 111 (box).

Philippi, battle of (42 BC), a battle in which the Republican forces of Brutus and Cassius were defeated by Mark Antony (accompanied by Octavian, who played little part in the battle); ▷ p. 37.

Philippines, a republic comprising an archipelago in the Pacific off the E coast of Asia. Magellan discovered the islands in 1521 (▷ pp. 61 and 109), naming them after Philip II of Spain. Spanish rule spread through the archipelago from the middle of the 16th century, but was harassed by the Dutch and by Moro pirates from Mindanao. The Spanish colonial regime was harsh, and although trade grew, economic growth was not matched by political development. The islands' administration was archaic and Jesuit influence was strong. Eventually a combination of rising nationalism and resentment at economic injustice led to an unsuccessful revolt (1896) against Spanish rule. The islands were ceded to the USA after the SPANISH-AMERICAN WAR (1898; ▷ p. 157), but American rule had to be imposed by force and resistance continued until 1906. A powerful American presence had a profound effect on Filipino society, which bears the triple imprint of Asian culture, Spanish Catholicism and American capitalism. US policy in the Philippines wavered between accelerating and delaying Filipino self-rule. In 1935 the nationalist leader Manuel Quezon became president of the semi-independent 'Commonwealth' of the Philippines. The surprise Japanese invasion of 1941 traumatized the islands' American and Filipino defenders (▷ p. 194). Japan set up a puppet 'Philippine Republic', but, after the American recapture of the archipelago, a fully independent Republic of the Philippines was established in 1946. Between 1953 and 1957 President Ramon Magsaysay crushed and conciliated Communist-dominated Hukbalahap guerrillas, but his death ended a programme of land reforms. Coming to power in 1965, Ferdinand MARCOS inaugurated flamboyant development projects, but his administration presided over large-scale corruption. Marcos used the continuing guerrilla activity as a justification for his increasingly repressive rule. When he attempted to rig the result of presidential elections in 1986, Marcos was overthrown in a popular revolution in favour of Corazon AQUINO. Her government faced several attempted coups. Insurgency by groups including Communists and Islamic nationalists remains a problem.

Philippine Sea, battle of the (19/20 June 1944), a naval battle between US and Japanese forces in World War II; ▷ p. 195.

Philip the Bold (1342–1404), duke of Burgundy (1363–1404); ▷ p. 95 (box).

Philip the Good (1396–1467), duke of Burgundy (1419–67); ▷ p. **95** (box and text).

Philistines, the descendants of the Peleset, one of the 'Sea Peoples' who settled the area around Gaza early in the 1st millennium BC, and ultimately gave their name to the whole region of PALESTINE; ▷ p. 23.

Phoenicians, ▷ pp. **23**, 29 (map), 43 and 46.

Phoenix Park murders, the assassination in Dublin, on 6 May 1882, of the new Chief Secretary for Ireland, Lord Frederick Cavendish, and his Permanent Undersecretary, Thomas Burke, by members of an extreme Irish nationalist group.

Phoney War, the period of inactivity between the start of World War II and Hitler's assault on the West in April 1940; ▷ p.190.

Physiocrats, a group of 18th-century French economic thinkers; ▷ p. 135 (box).

Picts, a Celtic people living in what is now Scotland, who conducted raids into N England in the 4th and 5th centuries. Gradually confined by pressure from the SCOTS to the NE, they were absorbed by KENNETH I MacAlpine to create the kingdom of Scotland in the 9th century; ▷ p. 79 (box).

Piedmont, a former kingdom of N Italy. From 1718–20 its rulers – the dukes of Savoy – were also kings of Sardinia. In the 19th century Piedmont, under its prime minister Cavour, played a central role in the movement for Italian unification. The Piedmontese king, VICTOR EMMANUEL II, became the first king of Italy; ▷ pp. 151 and 152.

Pierce, Franklin (1804–69) fourteenth president of the USA (1853–7). His alienation of the Northern wing of the Democratic Party through his support for the KANSAS-NEBRASKA Act cost him the chance of renomination in 1856.

Pilgrim Fathers, a 19th-century term for the original settlers of New PLYMOUTH, the first permanent British colony on the NE coast of N America (▷ p. 142).

Pilsudski, Józef Klemens (1867–1935), Polish soldier and president (1918–21). He led Polish troops against Russia between 1914 and 1917. In 1919, having changed sides to support the ALLIES, he was appointed head of state of the newly recreated POLAND. He fought a successful war against the BOLSHEVIKS (1919–20), and was virtual dictator of Poland from 1926 until his death.

Piltdown Man, the supposed fossil remains of an early hominid found in Sussex, England, in 1911. Research in the 1950s discovered it to be a hoax, consisting of the carefully modified jaw of a chimpanzee and a modern human skull.

Pinochet, Augusto (1915–), Chilean soldier and politician. He led the CIA-backed coup that overthrew ALLENDE in 1973 (▷ p. 206), becoming president himself in 1974. After 16 years of repressive rule, he allowed elections to be held in 1989, handing over to Patricio Aylwin as head of a coalition in March 1990.

Pitt, William, 1st Earl of Chatham (Pitt the Elder; 1708–78), British WHIG politician, prime minister (1756–7, 1757–61 and 1766–8). His leadership (in coalition with NEWCASTLE) took Britain to victory in the SEVEN YEARS WAR, and his vigorous foreign policy helped lay the foundations of Britain's imperial power.

Pitt, William (Pitt the Younger; 1759–1806), British politician. He became prime minister at the age of 24 in 1783 and occupied the post until 1801, carrying out important economic reforms. From 1793 his premiership was dominated by the Revolutionary and Napoleonic Wars. He resigned over GEORGE III's opposition to CATHOLIC EMANCIPATION, but was PM again from 1804 to 1806.

Pizarro, Francisco (1475–1541), Spanish CONQUISTADOR; ▷ pp. 71 and 116 (box).

Plaid Cymru (Welsh 'party of Wales'), a political party, founded in 1925, seeking to achieve autonomy for Wales within the UK in cultural, linguistic and economic matters.

Plantagenet, the name by which HENRY II's father, Geoffrey of Anjou (1113–51), was known. Since the 15th century the name has been used to identify the dynasty of kings of England descended from him, beginning with HENRY II and ending with RICHARD III. The first three Plantagenet kings are usually referred to as ANGEVINS.

plantation, an estate for the cultivation of crops such as tobacco and sugar in the S colonies of North America and the British West Indies; ▷ p. 129 (box).

Plassey, battle of (13 June 1757), the victory in W Bengal of Robert CLIVE over Nawab Siraj ud-Daula, which established British dominance in Bengal; ▷ p. 129.

Plataea, battle of (479 BC), victory of the Greek infantry forces led by Pausanias the Spartan, over the Persian forces of Xerxes I, at Plataea, a Boeotian city-state in central Greece. This was the final battle of the Persian Wars; ▷ pp. **29**, 31 (map) and 44.

Plate, battle of the River (13 December 1939), a naval battle between British and German forces in the S Atlantic early in World War II; ▷ p. 190.

Plato (428/7–348/7), Athenian philosopher. In his many philosophical dialogues, and his teachings in his Academy, he set out, from SOCRATES' starting position, a constantly developing range of new ideas and theories, including the so-called 'Theory of Forms', and the proposed radical reorganization of society and politics in his *Republic*.

plebeians, in ancient Rome, all citizens apart from the elite patricians; ▷ p. 36.

Plekhanov, Georgi (1856–1918), Russian political philosopher and politician. The most influential Russian interpreter of Marxism, he helped formulate the programme of the Russian SOCIAL DEMOCRATIC Party. When the party split, he sided with the MENSHEVIKS.

Plutarch (AD c. 46–120), Greek biographer and philosopher; ▷ p. 2.

Plymouth Colony, the first permanent British colony on the NE coast of N America, settled by the PILGRIM FATHERS in 1620. It joined the New England Confederation in 1643 and became part of MASSACHUSETTS in 1691; ▷ p. 142.

Pocahontas (c. 1595–1617), ALGONQUIN princess; ▷ p. 72 (box).

pogrom, (Russian 'destruction'), a word used to describe organized massacres of, or attacks on, Jews which took place in Russia from the 1880s onwards.

Poincaré, Raymond Nicolas Landry (1860–1934), French politician, prime minister (1912–13, 1922–4, 1926–9), president (1913–20). He provided strong leadership in World War I, and supported severe reparations against Germany in 1919. As PM in the postwar years, he ordered, with Belgium, the occupation of the RUHR (1923–5; ▷ pp. 183).

Poitiers, battle of (19 September 1356), an encounter between the French and English during the Hundred Years War; ▷ pp. 94 and 102.

Poland, a country of E Europe. Small Polish states united to form a single nation in the 11th century. Kings Wladyslaw I and Casimir III (the Great) strengthened Poland, encouraged trade, codified laws and founded the country's first university at Kraków. In 1386 Queen Jadwiga married Jagiello, the grand duke of LITHUANIA, uniting the two realms. The union of Lublin (1569) established full political ties between the two countries, and at its height the 'Commonwealth of Two Nations' extended from the Baltic to the Black Sea. In 1572 the last of the JAGIELLONS died, leaving no heir. The monarchy became elective, and the power of both the sovereign and the parliament declined. The country became involved in numerous wars –

against Muscovites, Turks, Tartars, Cossacks and Swedes. At the end of the 18th century Poland was too weak to prevent a partition of its territory by Russia, Prussia and Austria (⊳ p. 125). In the 19th century the greater part of Poland was within imperial Russia, against which the Poles revolted unsuccessfully in 1830, 1848 and 1863 (⊳ pp. 150 and 155). National feeling also grew in the areas ruled by Austria and Prussia. After World War I, Poland was restored to statehood (1919; ⊳ p. 182, map), but the country was unstable. Marshal Józef PILSUDSKI staged a coup in 1926, and became a virtual dictator. During the 1930s relations with Hitler's Germany became strained (⊳ p. 189). An alliance with Britain was not enough to deter Hitler from attacking Poland, and thus precipitating World War II (1939; ⊳ p. 192). Poland was partitioned once again, this time between Nazi Germany and the USSR. Occupied Poland lost one sixth of its population, including almost all the Jews, and casualties were high after the ill-fated WARSAW RISING (1944). Poland was liberated by the RED ARMY (1945; ⊳ p. 193), and a Communist state was established. The new Poland lost almost one half its territory in the E to the USSR, but was compensated in the N and W at the expense of Germany. A political crisis in 1956 led to the emergence of a Communist leader who enjoyed a measure of popular support, Wladyslaw GOMULKA. In 1980, following the downfall of Gomulka's successor, Edward GIEREK, a period of unrest led to the birth of the independent trade union SOLIDARITY, led by Lech WALESA. Martial law was declared by General Wojciech JARUZELSKI in 1981 in an attempt to restore Communist authority. Solidarity was banned and its leaders were detained, but public unrest and economic difficulties continued. In 1989 Solidarity was legalized and agreement was reached on political reform. (For details of the collapse of the Communist system in Poland; ⊳ p. 224.) Lech Walesa became president in 1990.

Poland, partitions of, ⊳ p. **125** (box).

polis, Greek term for city-state; ⊳ p. **28.**

Polish Corridor, a strip of territory ceded by Germany to Poland in the Versailles Peace Settlement (1919) to allow Poland access to the Baltic. It was retaken by Germany in 1939; ⊳ pp. 182 (map).

Polish Succession, War of the (1733–38), a conflict arising from the rival claims to the Polish throne of Augustus of Saxony and Stanislas Leszczynski. These were used by France and Spain as an excuse to attack the Austrian HABSBURGS in Italy and the Rhineland to obtain Lorraine for France.

politburo, the most important decision-making body of the COMMUNIST party under all Marxist regimes.

Polk, James Knox (1795–1849), the eleventh president of the USA (1845–9), a Jacksonian Democrat and devotee of MANIFEST DESTINY. His term was marked by the acquisition of California and New Mexico after US victory in the MEXICAN–AMERICAN War and the settlement of the OREGON BOUNDARY DISPUTE with Britain.

Polonnaruwa, a former capital of Sri Lanka; ⊳ p. 60 (box).

Pol Pot (1925–), Cambodian Communist politician, prime minister (1976–9). His brutal 'reconstruction' of CAMBODIA left more than a million dead; ⊳ p. 209.

Polybius (c. 210–c. 129 BC), Greek historian who spent much of his life in Rome. His work chronicled the rise of the Roman Empire from 220 to 146 BC, and sought to analyse its causes and effects; ⊳ pp. 35 (box) and 42.

Polynesians, the peoples of the islands of the central Pacific, including Hawaii, Samoa, Tonga and New Zealand; ⊳ pp. **68–9.**

Pombal, Sebastiao José de Carvalho e Mello,

Marquis of (1699–1778), first minister of king José I (1750–77) of Portugal. He was responsible for the rebuilding of Lisbon after the earthquake of 1755, the expulsion of the Jesuits from Portugal (1759) and efforts to improve the Portuguese economy.

Pompeii, a Roman town in Campania, destroyed by the eruption of Vesuvius in August AD 79. Excavations since the 18th century have provided a unique glimpse of the life of a 1st-century Roman town; ⊳ p. 6.

Pompey (Gnaeus Pompeius Magnus; 106–48 BC), Roman general and statesman who conquered much of the Middle East for the Roman Empire in the 60s BC. In 49 he led the Republican forces against Caesar, his former ally, but was defeated at Pharsalus in 48. Pompey fled to Egypt, where he was murdered; ⊳ p. 37.

Pompidou, Georges (1911–1974), French statesman, prime minister (1962–8), president (1968–74). He lifted DE GAULLE's veto on British entry into the EC.

Pontius Pilate, prefect of Judaea from AD 26 to 36 who ordered the crucifixion of JESUS.

Pontus, an ancient region of N Asia Minor, extending along the S Black Sea coast. It became a Roman province after POMPEY'S victory over its king Mithridates VI in 63 BC; ⊳ p. 37 (map).

Poor Laws, English legislation to provide relief for the poor. Parish relief for the rural poor had been available since the 16th century. The UTILITARIAN-influenced Poor Law Amendment Act of 1834 abolished the Speenhamland system of outdoor relief (1795); henceforth paupers were forced for relief into the deliberately harsh conditions of the workhouses.

Popish Plot (1678–81), a supposed Catholic plot to murder CHARLES II, invented by the Anglican cleric Titus Oates. It exploited and fuelled English fears of Catholicism and led to a major political crisis in England, with attempts to oust the king's brother, the Catholic JAMES II, from the succession.

Popular Front, the name given to various coalitions of moderate and left-wing parties committed to the defence of democratic government from Fascism in the 1930s, especially those forming governments in France, Spain and Chile; ⊳ p. **187** (box).

population, ⊳ p. **230.**

Populist Movement, an agrarian socialist movement in 19th-century Russia; ⊳ p. 180 (box).

Populist Party, a short-lived US political party that sought to articulate the views of hard-pressed farmers in the southern and midwestern states during the 1890s. The party was dissolved after agreeing to merge with the DEMOCRATS in 1896; ⊳ p. 157.

Portland, William Henry Cavendish Bentinck, 3rd Duke of (1738–1809), British statesman, prime minister (1783 and 1807–9). In both his ministries he was only nominal head of the government, his first term being dominated by the strange alliance of FOX and NORTH, the second by CANNING and CASTLEREAGH.

Portsmouth, Treaty of (5 September 1905), a peace treaty ending the RUSSO-JAPANESE WAR (⊳ pp. 65 and 180), signed at Portsmouth, New Hampshire, USA, following mediation by US President Theodore ROOSEVELT. Japan gained a protectorate over Korea and railway rights in S Manchuria, as well as the Liaodong Peninsula (including Port Arthur, now Lüshun) and the S part of Sakhalin island.

Portugal, a country of W Europe. The N of Portugal resisted the Muslim conquests in the Iberian peninsula in the 8th century. Reconquest of Portuguese territory from the Muslims was slow (⊳ p. 89), but Portugal – a kingdom from 1139 – established its present boundaries in 1270. In the 15th

century Portugal became a dynamic trading nation. Prince Henry the Navigator (⊳ p. 109) became a leading patron of Portuguese exploration, which in the 15th century had mapped much of the W African coast. By the middle of the 16th century Portugal had laid the foundations of a vast colonial empire in Brazil, Africa and Asia (⊳ p. 116). On the extinction of the Aviz dynasty in 1580, the thrones of Spain and Portugal were united, until a revolution in 1640 led to the accession of the Portuguese Braganza family. In the 17th and 18th centuries Portuguese power declined, but the country retained major colonies. In 1807 the royal family fled to Brazil to escape a Napoleonic invasion. King John VI did not return from Brazil until 1821 (⊳ p. 149, box), and in his absence the Portuguese had established a liberal constitution. Dynastic problems began when John VI's son Pedro declared Brazil independent (1822), and they continued in a crippling civil war (1832–4) between liberal constitutionalists supporting Queen Maria II (Pedro's daughter) and absolutists under the rival King Miguel (Pedro's brother). Instability continued for much of the 19th century. Portugal's African empire was confirmed, although the country lacked the power to gain more territory in the scramble for Africa (⊳ p. 163, map). The monarchy was overthrown in 1910, but the Portuguese republic proved unstable and the military took power in 1926. From 1932 to 1968, under the dictatorship of António SALAZAR, stability was achieved but at great cost. Portugal became a one-party state, and expensive colonial wars dragged on as Portugal attempted to check independence movements in Angola and Mozambique. In 1974 there was a left-wing military coup whose leaders granted independence to the African colonies (1974–5; ⊳ p. 221, box), and initially attempted to impose Marxism on the country. However, elections in 1976 decisively rejected the far left. Civilian rule was restored as Portugal effected a transition from dictatorship to democracy, and simultaneously – through the loss of empire and membership of the EC – became more closely integrated with the rest of Europe.

Potemkin, the battleship whose crew mutinied in the Black Sea during the Russian Revolution of 1905 (⊳ p. 180).

Potsdam Conference (17 July–2 August 1945), a meeting of the USA, UK and USSR at Potsdam, outside Berlin. The conference confirmed the decision made at the YALTA Conference to divide Germany and Austria into zones of Allied military occupation, outlawed the Nazi Party, broke up large German business monopolies, and redistributed certain German territories to Poland and the USSR; ⊳ p. 204.

Powhatan, ALGONQUIN chief; ⊳ p. 72 (box).

Praetorians, the elite unit of the Roman army, established as a permanent force in the early Empire. The Praetorian Guard played an important part in political events (⊳ CLAUDIUS) and its commander, the Praetorian Prefect, was the most powerful official in the empire.

Pragmatic Sanction (1713), the decree promulgated by the Emperor Charles VI to ensure that his territories passed undivided to his eldest daughter; ⊳ pp. **124–5.**

Prague, Defenestration of, the ejection by Bohemian Protestant aristocrats of two imperial representatives from a window of the Royal Palace in Prague; ⊳ p. 113.

Prague Spring (1968), the name given to the period of reform in Czechoslovakia under the Communist regime of Alexander DUBČEK, involving greater freedom of speech and moves towards multi-party democracy. It was crushed by tanks of the WARSAW PACT in August 1968; ⊳ p. *199.*

prehistory, ⊳ pp. **12–15.**

Presbyterians, anti-Episcopalian Protestants who – influenced by CALVIN – favoured a form of Church government in which each church was governed by its minister aided by lay elders within a national structure headed by a synod. During the Reformation the HUGUENOTS organized such a Church in France, while John KNOX founded the Presbyterian Church of Scotland; ⇨ p. 111.

pretender, any claimant to a throne from which he or his ancestors were ejected, particularly the JACOBITE 'Old Pretender', James Edward Stuart (1688–1766), son of JAMES II by his second wife, and his son the 'Young Pretender', Charles Edward Stuart (Bonnie Prince Charlie; 1720–88), who attempted to make good their claims in the FIFTEEN and the FORTY-FIVE; ⇨ p. 119.

primary elections, preliminary elections in the USA in which voters elect party candidates for election to public office.

Primo de Rivera y Orbaneja, Miguel (1870–1930), Spanish general and dictator (1923–30); ⇨ SPAIN.

primogeniture, the principle by which property or title descends to the eldest child, usually the eldest son. It became a characteristic feature of English property law in the 12th century.

Princely States, the 629 British-protected states in India whose rulers enjoyed varying degrees of autonomy. The principal states (in order of precedence) were HYDERABAD, MYSORE, Baroda, (Jammu and) KASHMIR, Gwalior, Bhopal, Travancore, Kolhapur, Udaipur (Mewar) and Indore. Some of the princely states were coerced into joining India at independence and three seriously attempted to regain their independence; ⇨ p. 201 (box).

printing, the mass production of text and illustrations by mechanical devices. Movable type was invented in Europe around 1450, but woodblock printing dates back to 8th-century China; ⇨ p. 101.

privateering, the activity of armed, privately owned ships commissioned for action against those of hostile states by governments or sovereign princes (particularly English, French and Dutch). It was an important component of naval warfare before the emergence of large, state-controlled navies.

procurator, an administrative official under the Roman Empire; ⇨ p. 38.

Progressive Movement, a multifaceted movement working to achieve social and economic reforms appropriate to a modern industrial economy in the USA (c. 1900–20). Committed to free trade and the control of monopolistic 'trusts', the movement drew support from a wide range of groups.

Progressive Parties (1912, 1924 and 1948), the label assumed by three short-lived 20th-century US political parties. The first, a vehicle for the renewed presidential ambitions of Theodore ROOSEVELT, unsuccessfully fought the election of 1912. The second sought to convince the electorate of the need for public control of natural resources and railroads but won only 17% of the popular vote in 1924. The third represented a dissident left-liberal faction united behind the abortive presidential candidacy of former Democratic vice-president Henry Wallace in 1948.

Prohibition (1920–33), ⇨ p. **185** (box).

Protectorate, English (1653–9), the regime established by Oliver CROMWELL after the dissolution of the RUMP Parliament, during which he ruled as Lord Protector. After his death, the Protectorate was brought to an end by army intervention, and the monarchy restored; ⇨ pp. *118* and 119.

Protestantism, the religion of those churches that broke with the Roman Catholic Church at the Reformation, whose doctrines are based on the principles of reformers such as Luther, CALVIN, ZWINGLI and others. Movements rejecting Roman authority established reformed national forms of Christianity in the various states of N Europe, such as Lutheranism in Sweden and parts of Germany, Calvinism in Switzerland and Scotland (⇨ PRESBYTERIANS) and ANGLICANISM in parts of England. The 18th century saw movements for spiritual reform in Protestant countries – Pietism in Germany, and the Evangelical revival in Britain and North America. European emigration brought all the Protestant traditions to America, Canada, Australia and elsewhere; ⇨ pp. 91, **110–11,** 112–13, 117, 118, 119 (box); 120–1 and 122.

Proudhon, Pierre Joseph, (1809–65), French political writer and revolutionary, most famous for his assertion that 'property is theft'. His belief that ANARCHY was the most just form of social organization partly inspired the Paris Commune of 1871.

Prussia, a former state in N and central Germany. By the early 18th century BRANDENBURG-Prussia had developed into a powerful Protestant state. Its territories were expanded by FREDERICK the Great, under whom it became a great power. In the 19th century Prussia vied with Austria for dominance within the GERMAN CONFEDERATION, emerging as the victor in 1866 and becoming the nucleus of the German state created in 1871. Prussia was abolished as a distinct entity by the Allied powers after WORLD WAR II; ⇨ pp. **125,** 127 (box), 131, 146, 147, 151, 152, **153** and 174.

Ptolemy, the family name of the Macedonian dynasty that ruled Egypt from 304 BC, when Ptolemy Soter, one of Alexander's generals, proclaimed himself king, to the death of CLEOPATRA, the last of the line, in 30 BC; ⇨ pp. 19 (box), **32–3** and *47*.

Pueblo (Spanish, 'small town'), the name used to describe the maize-growing cultures of the North American Southwest; ⇨ pp. 72–3.

Punic Wars, three wars between Rome and Carthage; ⇨ pp. **37** and 45.

Punjab, a region of S Asia that was ruled by the SIKHS until 1849 when it was annexed by the British. In 1947 it was divided between India and Pakistan on a religious basis; ⇨ p. 201 (box).

Puritans, those English Protestants in the later 16th and early 17th centuries who sought to 'purify' the ANGLICAN Church of its imperfections, and who emphasized the importance of independent judgement based upon conscience and the Bible. Attempts by Parliament to impose such changes on the Crown contributed to the tensions that led to the ENGLISH CIVIL WAR. After the RESTORATION some Puritans were absorbed into the Anglican Church while others joined Nonconformist denominations; ⇨ p. 118.

Pygmies, racial group of central Africa, hunter-gatherers now mainly inhabiting the rainforest of the Congo basin; ⇨ p. 66.

Pym, John (1583–1643), English politician, one of the leaders of the opposition to CHARLES I in the LONG PARLIAMENT. His administrative and financial measures (and alliance with the Scots) helped ensure the final success of the Parliamentary forces in the ENGLISH CIVIL WAR.

pyramids, monumental tombs built by the pharaohs of the Egyptian Old Kingdom; ⇨ p. 17.

Pyramids, battle of the (1798), Napoleon's victory over the MAMLUKS in Egypt was intended to be the prelude to French colonization of the East and an attack on British India, but these plans were overturned by NELSON's victory at ABOUKIR BAY.

Pyrrhus (c. 318–272 BC), king of EPIRUS (307–303, 297–272 BC). A cousin of Alexander the Great, his ambition was to revive the latter's empire. His campaigns in Italy involved some costly ('Pyrrhic') victories, and he was finally defeated by the Romans in 275 BC.

Qaddafi, Muammar al- (1942–), Libyan politician, president of Libya from 1971. A Bedouin, he led a military coup to overthrow King IDRIS I in 1969.

Qatar, an emirate in the Persian Gulf. By the 8th century AD Qatar was Islamic and had developed as a trading centre. In the 1860s Britain intervened in a dispute between Qatar and its Bahraini rulers, installing a member of the Qatari ath-Thani family as sheik. Qatar was part of the OTTOMAN EMPIRE from 1872 until 1914. Its ruler signed protection treaties with Britain in 1916 and 1934, and did not regain complete independence until 1971.

Qianlong (1710–96), Chinese emperor of the QING dynasty (1736–96). The Chinese Empire reached its greatest extent in his reign, with conquests in TURKESTAN, Xinjiang and Nepal; ⇨ p. 56.

Qin or **Ch'in,** the first imperial Chinese dynasty (221–206 BC); ⇨ pp. 52 and *53*.

Qing or **Ch'ing,** the last Chinese imperial dynasty (1644–1911); ⇨ pp. 56–7.

Quadruple Alliance, the alliance of Britain, Prussia, Austria and Russia against Napoleon in 1813, also known as the Fourth Coalition; ⇨ p. 147.

Quakers, a radical sect – the Society of Friends – founded by George Fox (1624–91). They rejected a formal church, admitting only the authority of divine revelation, and advocated pacifism.

Quebec, a Canadian province and historic centre of French-Canadian political power. First settled during the 17th century, it remained in French hands until 1763, when sovereignty was transferred to Great Britain by the Treaty of PARIS. During the 19th century Quebec was riven by tensions between the French-speaking rural majority and British merchants in Montreal, which prompted the outbreak of PAPINEAU'S REBELLION in 1837. The BRITISH NORTH AMERICA ACT of 1867 made Quebec a separate province within the Dominion of CANADA; ⇨ pp. 128 and 129.

Quebec Liberation Front (FLQ), a French-Canadian terrorist organization seeking independence for the Canadian province of QUEBEC. Its terrorist campaign of the late 1960s and early 1970s was unpopular and the constitutional Parti Québécois proved a more successful vehicle for French-Canadian separatism.

Quesnay, François (1694–1774), French economist and leader of the Physiocrats; ⇨ p. 135 (box).

Quetzalcóatl, a legendary hero and god of pre-Columbian Meso-America, traditionally associated with the foundation of the cities of Tula and Chichén Itzá and the establishment of TOLTEC power. He allegedly sailed eastward, promising to return, a legend exploited by the Spanish CONQUISTADORES.

Quisling, Vidkun (1887–1945), Norwegian Fascist politician. He declared himself head of state after the German invasion of NORWAY in 1940. His name is now used pejoratively to describe a traitor who aids an occupying enemy force.

Qur'an or **Koran,** the holy book of Islam; ⇨ p. 82.

Raffles, Sir (Thomas) Stamford (1781–1826), British colonial administrator who established a settlement at SINGAPORE.

Raglan, Fitzroy James Henry Somerset, 1st Baron (1788–1855), British soldier and diplomat. As commander-in-chief during the Crimean War (⇨ p. 155) he was widely blamed for his mismanagement of the campaign.

Rajputs, members of a Hindu landowning caste who established a powerful military position in W India (modern Rajasthan) in the 17th century. The various Rajput states, notably Jodhpur and Jaipur, retained a measure of autonomy as PRINCELY STATES under British rule; ⇨ p. 63.

Raleigh, Sir Walter (1552–1618), English explorer and courtier. A favourite of ELIZABETH I, he made the first – unsuccessful – attempt to colonize VIRGINIA (1584). Imprisoned by JAMES I on trumped-up treason charges, he was executed after an unsuccessful mission to find gold in South America.

Ramesses II, a pharaoh of the 19th dynasty of ancient Egypt (c. 1304–1237 BC); ▷ pp. 19, 22 and 44.

Ramillies, battle of (23 May 1706), an important victory of MARLBOROUGH over a Franco-Spanish army during the War of the Spanish Succession (▷ p. 123). It was followed by the virtually bloodless conquest of much of the Spanish Netherlands.

Ranke, Leopold von (1795–1886), German historian; ▷ p. 3.

Rapallo, Treaty of (1922), a treaty of friendship between Germany and the Soviet Union, renewing diplomatic relations between the two states after their severance during World War I. It was the first international agreement to recognize the Soviet Union.

Rasputin, Grigor Efimovich (1871–1916), Russian mystic and religious fanatic, popularly known as the 'Mad Monk'. He came to wield undue influence at the Court of St Petersburg in the years before the Revolution, gaining a disastrous hold on the Tsarina (Empress) Alexandra Feodorovna, who believed he could cure her son's haemophilia. He was assassinated by a group of noblemen in 1916; ▷ pp. 180–1.

Rastadt, peace of (1714), a treaty between the Emperor Charles VI and Louis XIV, putting an end to the former's attempt to continue the War of the Spanish Succession; ▷ p. 123 (box).

Reagan, Ronald W. (1911–), fortieth president of the USA (1981–9). He won landslide election victories against Democratic challengers Jimmy CARTER in 1980 and Walter Mondale in 1984; ▷ p. 217.

Reconquista, the Christian reconquest of Spain; ▷ pp. 89 and 116.

Reconstruction Acts (1867–8), legislation passed by the US Congress reorganizing the defeated CONFEDERATE states of the South after the US Civil War; ▷ p. 159.

recusant, a term used for those in England (primarily Catholics) who would not attend the services of the ANGLICAN Church as laid down by the law, and who were fined for their non-attendance.

Red Army, the land forces of the USSR, originally created by TROTSKY to defend the BOLSHEVIK revolution. It may have lost as many as 10 million men in World War II; ▷ p. 181.

Red Brigades, Italian anarchist organization. It conducted a campaign of bombings, kidnappings and murders in the 1970s, the most notorious being that of Aldo MORO in 1978; ▷ p. 215.

Red Cross Society, an international humanitarian agency established in 1863 by Henri Dunant, who was also responsible for the first of the GENEVA CONVENTIONS. Based in Switzerland, it is dedicated to caring for the victims of war. The Red Cross (known as the Red Crescent in Islamic countries) now has over 100 national societies and its work has expanded to include disaster relief.

Red Guards, militant student supporters of Mao Zedong during the Cultural Revolution; ▷ p. 197.

Reform Acts, three far-reaching measures for electoral reform in 19th-century Britain. In 1832 the WHIGS increased the electorate by nearly a half, enfranchising mainly prosperous middle-class voters. The Conservative administration of Lord DERBY gave the vote to many urban working men in the Reform Act of 1867. In 1884 the LIBERALS extended the household franchise to agricultural workers in the counties, increasing the total electorate from about three to about five million male voters.

Reformation, ▷ pp. 5, 91, 101, **110–11**, 112–13 and 118.

Regency, in general the rule of any Regent during the incapacity of the legal monarch on grounds of age or health; in England, specifically, the period of government of the Prince of Wales, the future GEORGE IV, from 1811 (when GEORGE III was finally declared insane) to 1820.

Reichstag (German, 'imperial parliament'), the legislative assembly of the German SECOND EMPIRE and the Weimar Republic. The Reichstag building was burnt on 27/28 February 1933, probably by agents of the Nazis, who claimed the fire was part of a Communist plot; ▷ p. 186.

reparations, compensation payments exacted from a defeated enemy by the victors, especially those demanded of Germany by the ALLIES after World War I; ▷ pp. 183 and **184–5**.

Representatives, House of, the lower house of the US CONGRESS.

Republican Party, a US political party originating in the mid-1850s. Committed to preventing the spread of slavery into the W territories, the party was victorious in the presidential election of 1860 which prompted the secession of the states of the CONFEDERACY. Republicans played a key role during the Civil War, suppressing the rebellion against federal authority and subsequently formulating a plan of Reconstruction for the conquered South. During the late 19th and early 20th centuries the party moved away from its antislavery roots to become a strong ally of American corporate capital. Long recognized as the more conservative of America's two major parties, it has enjoyed unbroken success in presidential elections since 1980, but has failed to maintain a majority over the DEMOCRATS in CONGRESS during that period; ▷ pp. 158–9 and 216–17.

resistance movements, the underground organizations that fought against the AXIS occupiers in World War II; ▷ p. 190.

Restoration (1660), the re-establishment of the English STUART monarchy after the PROTECTORATE, largely brought about by General Monck. Few former supporters of the Protectorate were punished, although the restoration of the ANGLICAN Church meant the expulsion of some clergy. In an attempt to prevent further conflict, the king was given a fixed revenue and a small standing army; ▷ p. 119.

Revere, Paul (1735–1818), an American patriot who rode out from Boston on the night of 18 April 1775 to warn Concord farmers of the approach of British troops (▷ p. 142). Although his exploits were immortalized by the 19th-century poet Henry Wadsworth Longfellow, Revere was in fact captured by the redcoats and never reached his destination.

Revolutionary Wars (1792–1802), ▷ p. 146.

Revolutions of 1848, ▷ pp. 151 and 152.

Rhee, Syngman (1871–1965), Korean statesman. He became first president of the Republic of (South) KOREA in 1948. Popular unrest forced his resignation in 1960.

Rhineland, an area of Germany surrounding the banks of the Rhine and bordering France and the Low Countries. It was 'demilitarized' under the Treaty of Versailles and occupied by Allied forces until 1930. Hitler's troops reoccupied the area in 1936; ▷ pp. 182 and 188.

Rhode Island, one of the 13 original states of the USA. Rhode Island was founded in 1636 by dissident Protestant settlers from MASSACHUSETTS; ▷ pp. 156 (map) and 159 (map).

Rhodes, Cecil (John) (1853–1902), British colonial administrator in South Africa, often seen as the quintessential 19th-century British imperialist. He amassed a fortune from diamond mining and defended British interests against the BOERS, playing a key role in the acquisition of Bechuanaland and the territories that are now Zimbabwe. He was

prime minister of Cape Colony (1890–6), but resigned after the JAMESON RAID.

Rhodesia, ▷ ZIMBABWE.

Ribbentrop, Joachim von (1893–1946), German Nazi politician. As German foreign minister (1938–45), he negotiated the Nazi-Soviet Pact and the Tripartite Pact between Germany, Italy and Japan (1940). He was executed as a war criminal.

Ricardo, David (1772–1823), English economist and advocate of FREE TRADE. He recognized the pitfalls of an unregulated market, but believed that government intervention was a greater evil.

Ricci, Matteo (1552–1610), Italian Jesuit resident at the Chinese imperial court; ▷ p. 56.

Richard I ('Coeur de lion' or 'the Lionheart'; 1157–99), king of England (1189–99). He spent most of his reign in the continental lands of the ANGEVIN empire and on Crusade, leaving England to be governed by ministers; ▷ p. 88.

Richard II (1367–1400), king of England (1377–99). He kept his head during the PEASANTS' REVOLT (1381), but thereafter governed much less effectively, and he was dethroned by Bolingbroke (HENRY IV) in 1399. He died in prison, presumably murdered.

Richard III (1452–85), king of England (1483–5). After years of loyal service to his brother EDWARD IV, he proclaimed the illegitimacy of his nephew EDWARD V and seized the throne in June 1483. It was widely believed that he had ordered the murders of Edward V and his brother in the Tower of London. Although Richard successfully suppressed the rebellion of October 1483, less than two years later he was defeated by Henry Tudor at BOSWORTH, and died in the fighting; ▷ p. 118.

Richard of York, ▷ YORK, RICHARD, 3RD DUKE OF.

Richelieu, Armand-Jean du Plessis, duc de (1585–1642), French cardinal, chief minister to LOUIS XIII (1624–42). He completed the political subjugation of the HUGUENOTS, and made enormous efforts – in alliance with Protestant Sweden – to defeat the Spanish Habsburgs; ▷ p. 122.

Rights of Man and the Citizen (1789), the statement of the principles of the French Revolution, incorporated as the preface to the French Constitution of 1791; ▷ p. 144.

Riot Act, an act passed by the English PARLIAMENT in 1714, intended in part to protect the new Hanoverian regime from JACOBITE demonstrations. It required any unlawful gathering of 12 or more people to disperse within one hour of the reading of the Act by a Justice of the Peace. The act was frequently invoked in the 19th century, notably at the PETERLOO massacre (1819).

Rio de la Plata, a Spanish viceroyalty established in 1776, comprising present-day ARGENTINA, URUGUAY and PARAGUAY; ▷ p. 149.

Risorgimento (Italian 'resurrection'), the period of and movement for Italian unification in the 19th century; ▷ p. 152.

Roanoke Island, the site (off the coast of modern North America) of the earliest English settlement in the New World (1585). Unfortunately for Walter RALEIGH, the organizer of the venture, the first settlers failed to establish a viable colony and the island was abandoned by English adventurers in favour of VIRGINIA; ▷ p. 142.

'robber baron', the archetype of the ruthlessly aggressive businessman of the USA's GILDED AGE in the 1870s and 1880s; ▷ p. 157 (box).

Robert I (the Bruce; 1274–1329), king of Scotland (1306–29). After years of indecision, in 1306 he had himself crowned to provide a rallying-point for the Scottish nation against English domination. Victory over EDWARD II at BANNOCKBURN (1314) ensured Scottish independence.

Robert II (1316–90), king of Scotland (1371–90), the

first king of the Stewart (STUART) dynasty. He was active in the government of Scotland from the 1330s, but by the time he eventually succeeded to the throne he was a spent force.

Robespierre, Maximilien François Marie Isidore (1758–94), French revolutionary and leader of the JACOBINS. He played a crucial role in the overthrow of the GIRONDINS and, as a member of the Committee of Public Safety, helped unleash the reign of Terror. He was himself executed in the coup of 9 Thermidor (1794); ➤ p. 145.

Rockefeller, John D. (1839–1937), American industrialist and philanthropist whose financial genius made him a fortune as head of the giant Standard Oil Company. A deeply devout Baptist as well as a ruthless entrepreneur, he ploughed vasts amounts of money into charitable endeavours.

Rockingham, Charles Watson-Wentworth, 2nd Marquis of (1730–82), British statesman, prime minister (1765–6 and 1782). As leader of the Whig opposition (the 'Rockingham Whigs'), he opposed Britain's war against the American colonists.

Roger II (Guiscard; c. 1095–1154), king of SICILY (1130–54). He ruled a powerful centralized state, dominating the central Mediterranean, which tolerated and combined its Latin, Greek and Islamic elements; ➤ p. 87.

Rokossovsky, Konstantin Konstantinovich (1896–1968), Polish-born Soviet field marshal. He played a major role in the battles of Stalingrad and Kursk during World War II. In 1944 his forces failed to intervene to assist the WARSAW RISING against the occupying German forces (➤ p. 193).

Rollo (c. 860–931), a Viking leader who invaded NW France and in 912 was recognized as Duke Robert of NORMANDY by Charles III of France; ➤ pp. 86–7.

Romania, a country of SE Europe. Romanians claim descent from the DACIANS, a Thracian people, who were Romanized in the 2nd and 3rd centuries AD. They survived as a Latinate population by retreating to the highlands, and emerged to found the principalities of WALLACHIA and MOLDAVIA in the 14th century. Although compelled to accept Ottoman overlordship in the 15th century (➤ p. 115), they were never subjected to direct Turkish rule. Oppressive rule by Greek princes imposed by the Turks in the 18th century stimulated Romanian nationalism. Unity was achieved when Alexander Cuza was elected prince of both Wallachia and Moldavia (1859; ➤ p. 155). A German dynasty was chosen in 1866, and Romania's independence was internationally recognized in 1878. When both the Russian and Austro-Hungarian Empires collapsed at the end of World War I, Romania won additional territory with substantial Romanian populations from both. 'Greater Romania' was beset with deep social and ethnic divisions, which found expression in the rise of the Fascist Iron Guard in the 1930s. King Carol II suppressed the Guard and substituted his own dictatorship, but he was forced by Germany to cede lands back to Hungary (1940), while the USSR retook considerable territories, including the present republic of MOLDOVA. Carol fled and Romania – under Marshal Ion ANTONESCU – joined the AXIS powers (1941), fighting the USSR to regain lost territories. King Michael dismissed Antonescu and declared war on Germany as the RED ARMY invaded (1944), and a Soviet-dominated government was installed (1945). The monarchy was abolished in 1947. From 1952, under Gheorghe Gheorghiu-Dej (1901–65) and then under Nicolae CEAUȘESCU, Romania distanced itself from Soviet foreign policy while maintaining strict Communist orthodoxy at home. The harsh, corrupt and nepotistic rule of Ceaucescu and his wife Elena was overthrown in 1989 (➤ p. 224). An international team of monitors judged multiparty elections in 1990 to be 'flawed' but not fraudulent. Romania has sought Western aid to overcome severe economic and social problems.

Roman Catholic Church, the Western Church founded by the apostle St PETER, comprising Christians in communion with the PAPACY. In the early medieval period Christians from Ireland to the Carpathians came to acknowledge the bishop of Rome as pope (from the Vulgar Latin *papa*), and used Latin for worship, scripture reading and theology. The Eastern (ORTHODOX) Church finally broke with Rome in 1054. In the 16th century most of N Europe broke away from the primacy of Rome to form reformed Churches (➤ p. 110). This division of Western Christianity led to the terms 'Protestant' for these N churches and 'Roman Catholic' for Latin Christianity. After the Reformation, the Catholic Church continued to develop new religious orders such as the Jesuits (➤ p. 112). Supreme in S Europe, Catholic Christianity was later extended to the Americas and parts of Asia and Africa; ➤ pp. 85, **90–1**, **110–11**, **112–13**, 118–19, 120, 122, 124, 133, 151, 155 (box) and 169.

Roman civil wars, the period of turmoil in the 1st century BC leading to the breakdown of the Republic; ➤ p. 37.

Roman Empire, 1. the territories ruled by ancient Rome (➤ pp. 36–41). **2.** Rome and its territories under the rule of the emperors, beginning in 27 BC (➤ pp. 38–41).

Romanov dynasty, the dynasty that ruled Russia from the accession of Michael Romanov in 1613 to the abdication of NICHOLAS II during the Revolution of February 1917; ➤ p. 126.

Roman Republic, the period (509–27 BC) when Rome was ruled as a republic; ➤ pp. 36–7.

Rome, the capital of the Roman Empire (➤ pp. 36–41), traditionally founded in 753 BC (➤ p. 36); subsequently the seat of the PAPACY, and capital of modern Italy from 1871.

Rome, Treaties of, ➤ EUROPEAN COMMUNITY.

Rommel, Erwin (1891–1944), German field marshal whose brilliant command of the Afrika Korps in N Africa in World War II earned him the name 'the Desert Fox'. He was accused of plotting to kill Hitler in 1944 and forced to commit suicide by the Gestapo; ➤ p. 190.

Romulus, the traditional founder of Rome; ➤ p. 36.

Romulus Augustulus (b. c. AD 461), the last Roman emperor in the West (475–6); ➤ p. 40.

Roosevelt, Franklin Delano (1882–1945), thirty-second president of the USA (1933–45). He overcame a crippling bout of polio to become Democratic governor of New York and then leader of his country during one of the most critical phases of its history. Essentially a pragmatist, Roosevelt was a driving force behind the NEW DEAL and America's decisive contribution to the ALLIED cause in World War II. At times arrogant and insensitive to the plight of the powerless (notably blacks and Japanese-Americans), he was nonetheless an inspirational leader whose infectious optimism lightened the burdens of economic depression and war for a generation of Americans; ➤ pp. 185 and 204.

Roosevelt, Theodore (1858–1919), twenty-sixth president of the USA (1901–9). A bluff progressive Republican, he succeeded to the presidency after the assassination of MCKINLEY. He pursued an imperialistic foreign policy and sought to limit the power of the huge corporations that dominated the US economy. He fought an unsuccessful presidential campaign in 1912 on a PROGRESSIVE Party ticket.

Rosebery, Archibald Philip Primrose, 5th Earl of (1847–1929), British Liberal politician. A keen imperialist, he succeeded GLADSTONE as prime minister (1894–5).

Roses, Wars of the, the name give to the intermittent English civil wars of the later 15th century.

The name is a slightly misleading one, since by the time the dynastic struggle between YORKISTS and LANCASTRIANS started, three battles, beginning with the first battle of St Albans (1455) – the result of disastrous incompetence of Henry VI's government – had already occurred. But from the moment that RICHARD OF YORK asserted his claim to the throne (October 1460), the quarrels and ambitions of men like RICHARD III and the earl of WARWICK were acted out within the framework of dynastic rivalry. After the battle of BOSWORTH one contemporary remarked that the Lancastrian red rose (HENRY VII) had avenged the Yorkish white rose (i.e. the sons of EDWARD IV); by the 17th century this symbolism was being applied to the whole series of wars; ➤ pp. 95 and 118.

Rosetta Stone, a bilingual inscription of 196 BC, written in three scripts – hieroglyphic, Egyptian demotic and Greek, and found at the village of Rosetta in Egypt in 1799. It was deciphered by CHAMPOLLION; ➤ p. 19 (box).

Rothschild, a family of Jewish bankers. Lionel (1808–79), an Anglo-Jewish financier and politician, was one of the first Jews to serve as a British MP. In 1875 he loaned £4 million to the British government to enable it to purchase substantial shares in the SUEZ CANAL, ➤ p. 169.

Roundheads, the supporters of PARLIAMENT during the ENGLISH CIVIL WAR, so called on account of their close-cropped heads.

Rousseau, Jean-Jacques (1712–78), Swiss-born French philosopher and political theorist; ➤ p. 135 (box).

Roxane, the wife of Alexander the Great; ➤ p. 32.

Royal Society, a scientific society founded in Britain in 1660 and chartered by CHARLES II in 1662; ➤ p. 133.

Rubicon, a stream in N Italy flowing into the Adriatic near Rimini, important because it marked the boundary of the province of Cisalpine GAUL. When Caesar crossed it in 49 BC he was entering Italy in arms and therefore starting a civil war (➤ p. 37).

Ruhr, the principal industrial region of W Germany. It was occupied by France in 1921 when Germany defaulted on REPARATIONS; ➤ pp. 183, 185 and 186 (box).

Rump Parliament, the remnant of the LONG PARLIAMENT following the expulsion of some of its members by Colonel Thomas Pride of the NEW MODEL ARMY (1648). It ordered CHARLES I'S execution in 1649.

Rupert, Prince (1619–82), the son of Frederick V, elector of the PALATINATE, and the nephew of CHARLES I. He served as a royalist commander in the ENGLISH CIVIL WAR, suffering defeats at MARSTON MOOR and NASEBY.

Russell, John, 1st Earl (1792–1878), British statesman, prime minister (1846–52 and 1865–6). A WHIG MP from 1813, he was largely responsible for drafting the 1831 Reform Bill. His first ministry was troubled by CHARTIST agitation, and failed to gain the support of the Whig aristocracy. He succeeded PALMERSTON to become PM for a second time (1865–6) until the defeat of his last franchise bill.

Russia, a country of E Europe and Central and N Asia. The earliest known homeland of the SLAVS is thought to lie in the N foothills of the Carpathians from whence the eastern Slavs migrated towards the Dnieper valley during the first millennium BC. (For details of the foundation of Russia's 'ancestor' state (KIEV RUS), the rise of MUSCOVY and the expansion of the Russian Empire under the ROMANOV dynasty; ➤ pp. 127–8.) ALEXANDER I (reigned 1801–25) dabbled with constitutional ideas, but was absorbed with the struggle against Napoleon, who occupied Moscow in 1812 (➤ p. 147). Under NICHOLAS I (reigned 1825–55) – the champion of autocracy, the ORTHODOX CHURCH and Russian nationalism – a fierce reaction set in. ALEXANDER II (the 'Tsar Liberator'; reigned 1855–81) emancipated the serfs, but suppressed the Polish rising of 1863–64 with severity. Throughout the 19th century, the Russian Empire's frontiers were extended into Central Asia, the Caucasus and the Far East, and at the same time Russia attempted to increase its influence in SE Europe at the expense of the declining Turkish OTTOMAN Empire. These imperial tendencies sometimes led to confrontation with Western European powers. ALEXANDER III (reigned 1881–94) combined repression at home with restraint abroad. Under NICHOLAS II (reigned 1894–1917), Russia saw rapid industrialization, rising prosperity, and (after 1906) limited constitutional reform, but his reign was cut short by World War I (▷ pp. 176–8) and the Revolutions of 1917. (For details of the Russian Revolutions, the establishment of the SOVIET UNION and the careers of Lenin and Stalin, ▷ pp. 180–1 and 198–9.) In World War II – in which up to 27 million Soviet citizens may have died – the Union at first concluded a pact with Hitler (1939), and invaded Poland, Finland, Romania and the Baltic states, annexing considerable territory. However, in 1941 the Germans invaded the USSR (▷ pp. 192–3). In victory the Soviet Union was confirmed as a world power, controlling a cordon of satellite states in Eastern Europe and challenging the West in the Cold War (▷ pp. 198–9 and 204–7). However, the economy stagnated and the country was drained by the burdens of an impoverished and overstretched empire. Leonid BREZHNEV (1964–82) reversed the brief thaw that had been experienced under Nikita KHRUSHCHEV (1956–64), and far-reaching reform had to await the policies of Mikhail GORBACHOV after 1985. (For details of the introduction of reforms under Gorbachov, the renunciation of Communism in E Europe, the decline of Communism in the USSR, the abortive coup by Communist hardliners in Moscow and the dissolution of the Soviet Union; ▷ pp. 224–5.)

Russian Civil War (1918–21), a conflict in Russia between anti-Communist 'Whites' (with Western support) and the Soviet RED ARMY after the Russian Revolution, ending in victory for Lenin's BOLSHEVIKS; ▷ p. 181.

Russian Revolutions (1905, March 1917 and November 1917), ▷ pp. 4, 141, 169, 178, 182 and **180–1**.

Russo-Japanese War (1904–5), a conflict between Russia and Japan for ascendancy in MANCHURIA and Korea. The Russian naval base of Port Arthur and the Manchurian capital, Mukden, both fell to the Japanese, while the Russian Baltic fleet was destroyed in the Straits of Tsushima (May 1905) after a epic 28 000 km (18 000 mi) journey from its base. The war was ended by the Treaty of PORTSMOUTH. Russia's humiliating defeat – the first defeat of a Western power by Japan – caused unrest that led to the 1905 Revolution; ▷ pp. 65 and 180.

Russo–Turkish Wars (1768–74, 1787–92, 1806–12, 1828–9, 1853–6 and 1877–8) a series of wars fought between Russia and Turkey over disputed territories in the Balkans, the Crimea and the Caucasus. The wars steadily reduced the European territories of the Ottomans; ▷ pp. 127 and **154–5**.

Rwanda, a country of E central Africa. The feudal kingdom of Rwanda was a German possession from 1890 until it was taken over by Belgium after World War I. The monarchy – of the dominant minority Tutsi people – was overthrown by the majority Hutu population shortly before independence in 1962. Tribal violence has continued intermittently. In 1990–1 an army of Tutsi refugees occupied much of the N.

Ryswick, Treaty of (1697), the treaty ending the Nine Years War; ▷ p. 123 (box).

SA, ▷ BROWNSHIRT.

Saar (Saarland), a region of Germany on the French border. As the Saar, it was administered by France under the auspices of the League of Nations from 1919 until 1935 (▷ p. 182) when it was returned to Germany following a plebiscite. As Saarland, it was again occupied by France after 1945 – and (from 1948) part of the French customs union – until 1957 when it became a German Land.

Sabah, a state of MALAYSIA, formerly British North Borneo (1882–1963); ▷ p. 200 (map).

Sadat, Anwar el- (1918–81), Egyptian statesman. he succeeded Nasser as president in 1970 and remained in office until his assassination in 1981; ▷ p. 212.

Sadowa, battle of, ▷ KÖNIGGRÄTZ.

Safavids, a dynasty – probably of Kurdish descent – that ruled Iran from 1501 to 1722. They were originally a SUFI order, founded in NW Persia in the early 14th century. Under their rule Iran became officially SHIITE. Isfahan became the capital under their greatest ruler, Shah Abbas I (ruled 1587–1629); ▷ p. 114.

Saigo Takamori (1827–77), one of the leaders of the Meiji restoration in Japan (▷ p. 65). He later turned against Meiji policy, particularly the destruction of SAMURAI influence, and led a rebellion (1877), committing suicide when it failed.

St Bartholemew's Day Massacre (23/4 August 1572), a massacre of Protestant HUGUENOTS by Catholic mobs during the FRENCH WARS OF RELIGION. The massacre was ordered by the French queen mother, Catherine de MEDICI, who was strongly influenced by the Catholic GUISE faction. Some 3000 Protestants were killed in Paris, and many more in the provinces; ▷ pp. *110* and 111.

St Germain, Treaty of (10 September 1919), a treaty between the Allied Powers and Austria, part of the Paris Peace Conference after World War I; ▷ p. **182**.

St John, Knights of, the Knights Hospitallers; ▷ p. 89 (box).

Saint-Just, Louis de (1767–94), French revolutionary. A member of the Committee of Public Safety during the Terror (▷ p. 145), he denounced DANTON, and was later executed with ROBESPIERRE.

St Laurent, Louis Stephen (1882–1973), Canadian Liberal politician. As a reforming prime minister (1947–57) he promoted good relations between English- and French-speaking Canadians.

Saint-Simon, Claude (1760–1825), French nobleman and early theorist of SOCIALISM. He advocated an industrial society controlled by industrialists dedicated to ameliorating the condition of the poor, and the spiritual guidance of society by scientists.

Saite, the 26th and last great native dynasty of ancient Egypt (664–525 BC); ▷ p. 19.

Sakharov, Andrei (1921–89), Soviet nuclear scientist and dissident; ▷ p. 199 (box).

Saladin (Salah al-Din; ?1137–93), Kurdish soldier who seized power in Egypt and Syria, defeated the armies of the Crusader states at HATTIN (1187), and was the adversary of RICHARD I of England and PHILIP II AUGUSTUS of France during the Third Crusade; ▷ p. 83 and 88.

Salamis, battle of, (480 BC), naval battle in which the Greek fleet defeated the Persian fleet in the narrows between the island of Salamis and the coast of Attica. This, crucially, gave the Greeks control of the sea, and was the decisive battle of the Persian Wars; ▷ pp. **29** and 44.

Salazar, António de Oliveira (1889–1970), Portuguese prime minister (1932–68). Effectively a dictator, he established a neo-Fascist state in which political opposition was strictly repressed. He was succeeded by CAETANO.

Salians, 1. a group of FRANKS who settled in the Netherlands in the 4th century. **2.** a dynasty of

German emperors of the 11th and 12th centuries; ▷ p. 84.

Salic Law, the legal code of the SALIAN Franks. It was most notably invoked during the dispute between CHARLES VI of France and EDWARD III of England, the French claiming that it excluded Edward from inheriting their throne since he was a descendant in the female line.

Salisbury, Robert Arthur Talbot Gascoyne-Cecil, 3rd Marquess of (1830–1903), British Conservative statesman, prime minister (1885–6, 1886–92, 1895–1900 and 1900–2) and the last British PM to lead the government from the House of LORDS. He succeeded DISRAELI as Conservative leader in 1881. His first two premierships saw the imperialist SCRAMBLE FOR AFRICA, and his third and fourth terms were dominated by the Second Boer War.

Sallust (c. 86–35 BC) Roman historian. His *Histories*, which survive only in fragments, cover the events from 78 to c. 60 BC.

SALT, ▷ STRATEGIC ARMS LIMITATION TALKS.

Samaria, the capital of the northern kingdom of Israel, founded by OMRI in the 9th century BC.

Samnite Wars, the series of conflicts between Rome and the peoples of the S central Apennines, known collectively as Samnites, between 343 and 290 BC, which led to the Roman conquest of the region; ▷ p. 45.

samurai, the Japanese warrior class; ▷ pp. **64** (box), 65 and 194.

Sandinistas, the Sandinista Liberation Front, a Nicaraguan guerrilla army named after Augusto César Sandino, a Nicaraguan guerrilla leader killed by government forces in 1934. The Sandinistas overthrew the regime of Anastasio SOMOZA in July 1979 but were defeated in elections in 1990.

San Francisco Conference (25 April–26 June 1945), an international meeting held in San Francisco, USA, which established the United Nations Organization (UN). Altogether, 51 states signed the UN Charter on 26 June; ▷ p. 228.

San Marino, a small S European republic surrounded by Italian territory. Established as an independent COMMUNE by the 12th century, San Marino retained its autonomy because of its isolation and by playing off powerful neighbours against each other. Its independence was recognized by Napoleon (1797), the Congress of VIENNA (1815) and the new Kingdom of ITALY (1862). In 1957 a bloodless 'revolution' replaced the Communist-Socialist administration that had been in power since 1945.

San Martín, José de (1778–1850), South American revolutionary soldier who played a major role in the liberation of Argentina, Chile and Peru from Spanish rule; ▷ p. 149.

sans culottes, the revolutionary Paris mob during the French Revolution between 1789 and 1795; ▷ p. 145.

San Stefano, Treaty of (March 1878), a treaty ending the Russo-Turkish War of 1877–8; ▷ p. 155.

Santa Anna, Antonio López de (1795–1876), Mexican soldier and politician. His defeat at the battle of San Jacinto (1836) resulted in Mexico's loss of TEXAS. As commander of Mexican forces he was defeated again in the war of 1846–8, which saw further loss of territory to the USA.

Saracen, a term used by medieval Europeans, especially during the Crusades, for Arabs and Middle Eastern Muslims. The derivation of the word is uncertain.

Sarajevo, ▷ BOSNIA-HERZEGOVINA.

Saratoga, battle of (7 October 1777), a decisive battle between British and American forces in the American War of Independence. The British defeat ended General Burgoyne's attempt to isolate NEW ENGLAND from the other American colonies; ⇨ p. 143.

Sarawak, a state of MALAYSIA occupying the NW part of Borneo; ⇨ p. 200 (map)

Sargon I (c. 2370–2315 BC), Akkadian conqueror of Sumer; ⇨ pp. **16** and 44.

Sargon II (d. 705 BC), king of Assyria (721–705 BC); ⇨ p. 21.

Sassanians, ⇨ pp. **27** (box), 39, 80 and 82.

Sa'ud, Abd al-Aziz ibn (c.1880–1953), king of Saudi Arabia from 1932 until his death. Proclaimed Sultan of NAJD in 1921, he overthrew Ibn Ali HUSSEIN, king of HEJAZ, five years later to gain control of Mecca. In 1932 he created the kingdom of SAUDI ARABIA; ⇨ p. 210.

Saudi Arabia, a kingdom of SW Asia. The Prophet MUHAMMAD was born in the early 7th century AD in MECCA where he received revelations from God and proclaimed Islam. Arabia quickly became Muslim, but, following the Prophet's death, the political focus of Islam moved, first to Damascus, then to Baghdad (⇨ pp. 82–3). The unity of Muslim Arabia collapsed and gave way to tribal rivalries. Early in the 16th century the Ottoman Turks established their authority over much of the peninsula. In 1744 a Muslim preacher – Muhammad ibn abd al-Wahhab – and the ancestor of the country's present rulers, the Sa'udis, formed an alliance that was to spearhead the Wahhabi political-religious campaign. In the 20th century the Wahhabis united most of Arabia under ibn SA'UD. In 1902 ibn Sa'ud took Riyadh and in 1906 defeated his rivals to control central Arabia (NAJD). Between 1912 and 1927 he added the E, the SW (Asir) and the area around Mecca (HEJAZ). In 1932 these lands became the kingdom of Saudi Arabia (⇨ p. 210). Although the country has been pro-Western, after the 1973 Arab-Israeli War, Saudi Arabia put pressure on the USA to encourage Israel to withdraw from the occupied territories of PALESTINE by cutting oil production (⇨ p. 213). Saudi Arabia has not escaped problems caused by religious fundamentalism and the rivalry between SUNNI and SHIITE Islam. Saudi Arabia found itself bound to support Iraq in its war with Shiite Iran (1980), but played a major role in the coalition against Iraq in the Gulf War (1991; ⇨ p. 213).

Saul, first king of the Israelites (c. 1020–1000 BC); he fought successfully against the Philistines; ⇨ p. 23.

Saxons, the name used by the Romans to describe the tribes living between the Elbe and Weser in N Germany and S Denmark. They raided Britain from before 300 and settled there in the 5th century; ⇨ p. 79 (box).

Saxony, a former duchy (9th century), electorate (1432) and kingdom (1806) in Germany. Because of its alliance with Napoleon I, Saxony lost half its area at the Congress of VIENNA. Saxony became part of the German Empire in 1871. The monarchy was overthrown in 1918; ⇨ p. 151 (map).

Scapa Flow, a British naval base in the Orkney Islands, enjoying easy access to both the Atlantic and North Sea. In 1919 the German High Seas Fleet, interned at the end of World War I, scuttled itself there.

Schleswig-Holstein, a province (Land) of N Germany. The duchies of Schleswig and Holstein were inherited by the king of Denmark in 1460 and held by Denmark – despite their mainly German population – until 1866 when they were seized by Prussia and Austria (⇨ p. 153). North Schleswig – which has a Danish majority – was returned to Denmark in 1920; ⇨ p. 182 (map).

Schlieffen Plan, a plan prepared in 1905 by Count Alfred von Schlieffen (1833–1913) to counter the Franco-Russian alliance in the event of war. The plan – involving violation of Belgian neutrality to outflank French defences followed by an attack on Russia – was the basis of Germany's attack in 1914; ⇨ p. 176.

Schliemann, Heinrich (1822–90), German archaeologist; ⇨ pp. 7 and 25.

Schmidt, Helmut Heinrich Waldemar (1918–), German SOCIAL DEMOCRAT statesman. As chancellor of West Germany (1974–82) he continued BRANDT'S policy of OSTPOLITIK and grappled with economic problems of the mid-1970s. He was unseated as chancellor when the Liberal Free Democratic Party withdrew support from his coalition government.

scholasticism, a style of philosophical learning based on ARISTOTLE and his Arabic commentators (⇨ p. 83, box) combined with Christian doctrine. It was characteristic of European universities from the 13th to the 16th century. When it fell out of fashion it came to be misunderstood and despised; ⇨ p. 100.

Schuman, Robert (1886–1963), French politician, prime minister (1947–8). As foreign minister (1948–52) he put forward the 'Schuman Plan' proposing the creation of the EUROPEAN COAL AND STEEL COMMUNITY.

Schuschnigg, Kurt von (1897–1977), Austrian chancellor (1934–8). He could do little to prevent the German takeover of Austria and resigned under pressure from Hitler in 1938; ⇨ p. 188.

Scientific Revolution, ⇨ pp. 132–3 and 134.

Scipio Aemilianus, Publius Cornelius (c. 185–129 BC) adopted grandson of SCIPIO AFRICANUS, who commanded the Roman forces in the third Punic War (⇨ p. 37) and destroyed Carthage in 146 BC.

Scipio Africanus, Publius Cornelius (236–183 BC) Roman general who defeated the Carthaginians in Spain in the Second Punic War, and then led an expeditionary force to Africa, where he defeated HANNIBAL at Zama in 202 BC; ⇨ p. 37.

Scotland, a country of NW Europe, part of the UNITED KINGDOM, occupying the N of the island of Great Britain. Pre-Roman Scotland was inhabited by the Celts (⇨ p. 34). Only S Scotland was included within the Roman sphere of influence. The N – beyond the ANTONINE WALL – was largely untouched by Romanization. The Scots from NE Ireland invaded N Britain in the 5th and 6th centuries and when their king (KENNETH I MacAlpine) also became king of the PICTS (843) the foundations of a Scottish state were laid. The early Scottish kingdom was unstable owing to the power of the nobles and a system of succession by which the king was usually succeeded by the eldest member of a collateral branch of the royal family – a system that usually produced a king of age but which led to endless dynastic squabbles and the assassination of the majority of the early monarchs. PRIMOGENITURE cannot be said to have been established until the reign of the reforming king DAVID I (reigned 1124–53), under whom English influence greatly increased. Scotland came steadily within the English sphere of influence from the 11th century, and EDWARD I of England attempted to dominate Scotland at a time of disputed succession in the 13th century. After the battle of BANNOCKBURN (1314), Scottish independence was asserted by ROBERT the Bruce (reigned 1306–29), whose grandson was the first Stewart (STUART) king of Scotland. After 1371, Scotland suffered a succession of long minorities, weak Stewart kings, conspiracies by overmighty nobles and continuing border wars with England. Threatened by England, Scotland entered the 'Auld Alliance' with France for protection. The Reformation in Scotland – during the turbulent reign of MARY, Queen of Scots (reigned 1542–67) – took on a CALVINIST character. The succession of James VI of Scotland as JAMES I of England in 1603 united the crowns of the two realms, although full integration did not occur until Scotland's Parliament was abolished by the Act of UNION in 1707 (⇨ p. 119).

Scottish National Party (SNP), a political party dedicated to achieving Scottish independence from the UK. Originally founded in 1928, it enjoyed some electoral success in the 1970s, fell away in the 1980s, then attracted strong support in the early 1990s for its demands for an independent Scotland within a federal Europe.

'Scramble for Africa', ⇨ pp. 160 and **162**.

Scythians, a nomadic people of the STEPPES; ⇨ p. 54.

SDI, ⇨ STRATEGIC DEFENSE INITIATIVE.

Sea Peoples, ⇨ pp. 22, **23** and PHILISTINES.

SEATO, ⇨ SOUTHEAST ASIA TREATY ORGANIZATION.

Second Empire, a term variously used to describe both the regime of NAPOLEON III in France (1852–70; ⇨ p. 151) and the German Empire or 'Reich' created in 1871 (⇨ pp. 153 and 174). The first German Reich implicit in the title was the Holy Roman Empire (⇨ p. 84).

Second Front, the popular name for Anglo-American plans to attack Germany from the W in World War II (⇨ p. 191).

Security Council, a permanent organ of the United Nations, established for the maintenance of international peace and security ⇨ pp. 206 and **228–9**.

Sedan, battle of (1 September 1870), French defeat by Prussia in the FRANCO-PRUSSIAN WAR which precipitated the fall of NAPOLEON III's Second Empire and the proclamation of the Third Republic.

Sedgemoor, battle of, ⇨ MONMOUTH'S REBELLION.

Seleucid dynasty, the dynasty descended from Seleucus, one of Alexander the Great's generals; ⇨ pp. 32–3.

Selim I (the Grim; 1470–1520), Ottoman sultan (1512–20); ⇨ pp. 114 and 115 (map).

Seljuks, a Turkish dynasty that conquered large areas of the E part of the Middle East in the first half of the 11th century. They routed the Byzantines at MANZIKERT (1071) and later harried Christian pilgrims on their way to Jerusalem. They were eclipsed by the Mongols in 1243; ⇨ pp. 54, **83** and 88.

Semites, peoples of the Middle East speaking one of the Semitic languages, such as Akkadian, Aramaic, Phoenician and Hebrew; ⇨ p. 22.

Senate, 1. (in ancient Rome) an aristocratic body of c. 300 (later 600) lifelong members whose function was to advise the CONSULS. It had immense prestige and in practice was the governing body of the Roman Republic. Under the Empire it lost its real power, but remained a repository of traditional aristocratic values, and was the main source of political opposition to the emperors (⇨ pp. **36** and 38). **2.** the name given to other assemblies and legislatures in various countries, notably the upper house of the US CONGRESS.

Seneca, a native N American people, the westernmost of the five tribes of the IROQUOIS Confederation, living in the Eastern Woodlands (W New York state).

Seneca, Lucius Annaeus (c. 4 BC–AD 65), Roman senator, playwright and philosopher. Seneca was one of Nero's chief advisers during the early years of his reign, but was later ousted and eventually forced to commit suicide on suspicion of involvement in a conspiracy.

Senegal, a republic of W Africa (⇨ p. 202, map). The region was part of the medieval empire of MALI. The coast was explored by the Portuguese in the 15th century and gradually came under French control from the 17th century. A national political awareness developed early in the 20th century, and the country contributed substantially to the nationalist awakening throughout French Africa. After independence in 1960 – under the poet Léopold Sedar Senghor – Senegal maintained close relations with France, and received substantial aid. Attempted federations with MALI (1959–60) and GAMBIA (1981–9) were unsuccessful. Senghor retired in 1980, having re-introduced party politics.

Sennacherib (d. 681 BC), king of Assyria (704–681 BC); ⇨ p. 21.

Serbia, a country of SE Europe. Serbia threw off allegiance to the BYZANTINE EMPIRE c. 1180 and flourished as an independent state. In 1345 Stefan Dusan declared himself emperor of Serbia, but the Serbian empire was destroyed by (Turkish) Ottoman conquest, symbolized by the battle of Kosovo in 1389 (⇨ p. 114). Led by KARAGEORGE, the Serbs rose against Turkish rule between 1804 and 1813 (⇨ p. 154). (For the history of the establishment of an independent Serbian kingdom, the unity of the southern Slavs under Serb leadership as Yugoslavia, and the disintegration of Yugoslavia in the 1990s; ⇨ YUGOSLAVIA).

serf, a word deriving from the Latin *servus*, meaning a slave. However, the serf was not a slave but a property-holding VILLEIN, a characteristic figure in Western European society after the demise of slavery there between the 10th and 12th centuries; ⇨ p. 98.

Servius Tullius, semi-legendary king of Rome; ⇨ p. 45.

Settlement, Act of (1701), an act of the English Parliament assigning the English Crown to the House of HANOVER in the event of Queen ANNE dying without children.

Sevastopol, a Russian port and naval base on the Crimean peninsula, besieged during the Crimean War; ⇨ p. 155 (box).

Seven Weeks War, ⇨ AUSTRO-PRUSSIAN WAR.

Seven Years War (1756–63), a complex struggle between Britain and Prussia on one side and France and Austria on the other; ⇨ pp. **125**, 127 and **129**.

Severus, Alexander (AD 208–35), Roman emperor (222–235); ⇨ p. 38.

Severus, Lucius Septimius (c. AD 145–211), Roman emperor (193–211), who fought his way to the throne in the civil war (192–7); ⇨ p. 38.

Sèvres, Treaty of (August 1920), a treaty between the Allies and Turkey, part of the Paris Peace Conference after World War I; ⇨ pp. **182** and 210.

Seychelles, an archipelago in the Indian Ocean. The islands became a French colony in the middle of the 18th century, were ceded to Britain in 1814 and gained independence in 1976. The PM – Albert René – led a coup against President James Mancham in 1977, and established a one-party socialist state. Attempts to overthrow René, including one involving South African mercenaries (1981) have been unsuccessful. The government conceded the principal of multi-party elections in 1991.

Seymour, Jane (1509–37), the third wife of HENRY VIII, and mother of EDWARD VI; ⇨ p. 118.

Sforza, a family that ruled MILAN (1450–1535). Francesco Sforza (1401–66), a Romagnol mercenary, was invited by the Milanese to become their duke shortly after the end of the rule of the VISCONTIS. He and his son Lodovico 'il Moro' (1451–1508) held Milan at the centre of Italian politics and culture; Lodovico was partly instrumental in encouraging the French invasion of 1494 (⇨ p. 97).

Shaftesbury, Anthony Ashley Cooper, 7th Earl of (1801–85), British reformer. A prominent evangelical Christian, as Lord Ashley he was leader of the 'ten-hour movement' (1832–3) for restricting factory working hours, and an active campaigner behind successive FACTORY ACTS; ⇨ p. 165.

Shah Abbas I, ⇨ SAFAVIDS.

Shah Jahan (1592–1666), Mogul emperor of India (1628–57). During his reign the boundaries of the empire continued to expand, particularly in central India. He was the patron of such major works as the Red Fort and the Taj Mahal; ⇨ pp. *62* and 63.

Shaka, ⇨ ZULUS.

Shamir, Yitzhak (1915–), Israeli politician, leader of the right-wing Likud Party and prime minister of Israel from 1988. As a member of the STERN GANG, he was involved in the campaign to oust the British from Palestine in the 1940s.

Shan, a people of SE Asia, closely related to the Thai. They moved from SW China to their present territory in NE Burma by the 13th century. The Shan states have belonged to the unified Burmese states since the 16th century; ⇨ p. 61.

Shang, the first historical Chinese dynasty (1480–1050 BC); ⇨ p. 52.

Sharpeville, a segregated black township outside Vereeniging, S of Johannesburg. It was the scene of a massacre by police of 69 PAN-AFRICANIST CONGRESS demonstrators in March 1960; ⇨ p. 221.

Shastri, Lal Bahadur (1904–66), Indian statesman. He was chosen to succeed NEHRU as a stop-gap prime minister in 1964, but died in Tashkent hours after signing the peace treaty ending the 1965 war with Pakistan.

Sheridan, Philip (1831–88), US soldier who served with distinction as a Union commander during the Civil War, noted particularly for his offensive operations in the Shenandoah valley (⇨ p. 159).

Sherman, William Tecumseh (1820–91), US soldier renowned for his campaigns against the CONFEDERACY in the American Civil War. While his famous 'March to the Sea' through Georgia in 1864 presaged the onset of 'total war', his subsequent drive N to link up with GRANT effectively terminated Confederate resistance; ⇨ p. 159.

Shevardnadze, Eduard (1928–), Soviet foreign minister (1985–90), acting president of GEORGIA (1992–); ⇨ p. 225.

Shi Huangdi (259–210 BC), the first ruler of all China and founder of the Qin dynasty. The famous terracotta army of 6000 life-size warriors and horses, found in 1974, guards the approach to his as yet unexcavated tomb; ⇨ p. 52.

Shiite, a follower of the smaller of the two main divisions of Islam, taking its name from the *Shi'at 'Ali*, the 'party of ALI', the son-in-law of MUHAMMAD. Shiites, unlike the majority SUNNIS, believe that Ali and his descendants are the sole true heirs to the authority of Muhammad. Shiitism has produced a variety of sects, including the ISMAILIS. The Shiites are dominant in IRAN, where they make up 93% of the population; ⇨ pp. **82–3**, 212 (box) and 213.

Shimonoseki, Treaty of (17 April 1895), the treaty ending the SINO-JAPANESE WAR of 1894–5; ⇨ p. 65 (box).

Shinto, the principal native religious philosophy of JAPAN: 'the Way of the Gods'. Its major features are worship of the spirits present in nature, loyalty to the emperor as descendant of the sun-goddess, and an emphasis on ritual purity; ⇨ p. 64.

ship money (1635–8), a tax levied from English seaports by CHARLES I; to finance his government in England independently of PARLIAMENT. The LONG PARLIAMENT declared it illegal in 1641.

shoguns, the hereditary military dictators who ruled Japan from the late 12th to the 19th century, during which time the emperors retained a purely notional supremacy; ⇨ pp. 64–5.

Shona, a SE African people of Bantu origin, living in the area of modern Zimbabwe and Mozambique. From the 13th century they were ruled by powerful states controlling the export of gold to the E coast.

Shoshone, a native North American people, hunter-gatherers living in the Great Basin region (modern Nevada); ⇨ pp. 72 and 73 (map).

Sicilian Vespers (1282), a popular revolt ending ANGEVIN rule in Sicily, so called because it took place at the time of the evening service on Easter Tuesday 1282; ⇨ pp. 93 and **96**.

Sicilies, Kingdom of the Two, a term used to describe S Italy during the periods when NAPLES and Sicily were under common rulership. The first occasion of this was Norman rule; ROGER II styled himself King of Sicily and Italy from 1130. After periods of NORMAN, HOHENSTAUFEN and ANGEVIN rule the unity was broken by the Sicilian revolt of 1282 (the SICILIAN VESPERS), after which the island came under ARAGONESE control. Naples eventually became Aragonese in 1442, and under Alfonso the Magnanimous (ruled 1442–58) the two kingdoms were reunited; ⇨ pp. 87 and 96.

Siegfried Line, the line of defensive fortifications built by Germany along its W frontier with France before and during World War II. It proved incapable of stopping Allied advances in 1944–5.

Sierra Leone, a republic of W Africa (⇨ p. 202, map). Freetown was founded by British philanthropists (1787) as a settlement for former slaves and became a British colony in 1808. The interior was added in 1896. Independence was gained in 1961. A disputed election led to army intervention (1967), and Dr Siaka Stevens – who came to power in a coup in 1968 – introduced a one-party state. The military took power in 1992.

Sigismund (1368–1437), as king of Hungary (1387–1437) he led resistance to the Turks; as Holy Roman Emperor (1411–37) he presided over the reunification of the Latin church at the Council of CONSTANCE; as king of BOHEMIA (1419–37) he had to cope with the HUSSITE rebellion; ⇨ p. 90.

Sihanouk, Norodom (1922–) Cambodian politician, king of CAMBODIA (1941–55), prime minister (1955–60), head of state (1960–70). After his abdication in 1955, he dominated Cambodian political life until 1970, when he was overthrown in a US-backed military coup. He was nominal head of state (1975–6) following the victory of the KHMER ROUGE in the civil war; ⇨ p. 209.

Sikh, a follower of the Indian religious teacher NANAK. Sikhism originated in the PUNJAB, where it is still the majority religion. In recent years militant Sikhs have pursued a violent campaign for an autonomous state of 'Khalistan' (⇨ INDIA).

Sikh Wars (1845–9), a series of wars fought between the English EAST INDIA COMPANY and the Sikhs of NW India, which resulted in British annexation of the PUNJAB; ⇨ p. 160.

Sikkim, a former PRINCELY STATE that retained virtual independence from British India. It was an Indian protectorate until 1975 when it became part of India.

Silesia, a major industrial region in N Central Europe (⇨ p. 113, map). Silesia was Polish (from 989/92), was settled by Germans (from the 11th century), and then passed, in turn, to Bohemia (1335), Hungary (1469), Bohemia (1490) and the Austrian HABSBURGS (1526). Prussia fought and won two wars for possession of Silesia in the 18th century (⇨ p. 125). Silesia was partitioned between Poland, Germany and Czechoslovakia after World War I (⇨ p. 182). Since 1945 most of Silesia has been in Poland.

Silk Route, ⇨ p. **52** (box).

Simnel, Lambert (c. 1477–c. 1500), a boy coached to pose as Edward, earl of Warwick, who was imprisoned by HENRY VII as a potential rival for the throne of England. His supporters launched an unsuccessful invasion of England in 1487, and

Lambert was captured and given a menial post in Henry's household.

simony, the practice, widespread in the medieval Church, of buying and selling ecclesiastical benefits or offices. It was one of the abuses criticized by Luther and others during the Reformation (▷ p. 110).

Sind, a region occupying the lower Indus Valley, the site of one of the world's earliest urban civilizations. The area increasingly fell under Islamic influence after an Arab invasion in 711. A province of British India from 1843, it became a province of SE Pakistan in 1947; ▷ pp. 58 and 62.

Singapore, a city-state of SE Asia. Singapore was a trading centre until destroyed by the Javanese in the 14th century. The city was revived by Sir Stamford RAFFLES for the British EAST INDIA COMPANY (1819), and developed rapidly as a port for shipping Malaya's tin and rubber. It acquired a cosmopolitan population and became a strategic British base. Occupied by the Japanese (1942–5; ▷ p. 194), it achieved self-government (1959), and joined (1963) and left (1965) the Federation of MALAYSIA. Since independence it has become wealthy under the strong rule of prime minister LEE Kuan Yew; ▷ pp. 200 (map) and 223.

Sinhalese, a people of Sri Lanka who arrived by sea from N India c. 550 BC and soon adopted Buddhism. They remain the majority population of SRI LANKA, outnumbering the later Hindu arrivals, the Tamils; ▷ p. 59.

Sinn Fein (Gaelic 'ourselves alone') an Irish political party, founded in 1905, whose goal is a united republican IRELAND. Sinn Fein MPs won a majority of the Irish seats in the 1918 general election, and proclaimed Irish independence from Britain in 1919. The party split over the creation of the Irish Free State and the partition of Ireland in 1922. Most Sinn Fein members were absorbed into DE VALERA's new FÍANNA FÁIL party in 1926. In 1969 it split into 'official' and 'provisional' wings, as did the IRISH REPUBLICAN ARMY, with which it is closely connected.

Sino-Japanese Wars, two conflicts between China and Japan. The war of 1894–5 was fought in Korea over the future of that state, which had long been a Chinese vassal, but was increasingly a focus for Japanese expansionism. The Chinese were soon defeated by superior Japanese forces, and by the Treaty of SHIMONOSEKI agreed to Korean independence and ceded Formosa (Taiwan) to Japan (▷ pp. 57 and 65). The war of 1937 arose from the Japanese army's seizure of MUKDEN (1931) and subsequent annexation of MANCHURIA. The Japanese, although opposed by JIANG JIE SHI's Nationalists as well as the Communists, quickly overran N China. Beijing fell on 7 August 1937, closely followed by Shanghai and Nanking. With Japan's entry into World War II, the war became absorbed into that wider conflict (▷ pp. 194 and 196).

Sioux or **Dakota Indians,** a group of native North American peoples living in the Great Plains. They were the first major group of Plains Indians to abandon settled agricultural village life in the 18th century to become nomads dependent on the hunting of buffalo from horseback. The western Sioux mounted fierce resistance to white encroachment on their lands under leaders such as SITTING BULL and CRAZY HORSE until the late 19th century; ▷ p. 73.

Sitting Bull (c.1834–90), Dakota SIOUX chief. His resistance to white encroachment on Plains Indians' hunting grounds culminated in the Sioux victory at LITTLE BIG HORN in 1876. He settled on a Dakota reservation after an amnesty (1881), but was killed in further hostilities in 1890.

Six Acts, British parliamentary statutes passed after the PETERLOO Massacre (1819), designed to suppress radical and reform agitation.

Six Day War, the name given by the Israelis to the 1967 Arab–Israeli War; ▷ pp. **211–12.**

Sixteen States, a period of Chinese history (317–420 AD) when the area of the Chinese Empire – particularly the N – was split into small states, some ruled by dynasties of nomad origins, none of which was powerful enough to reunite China.

slavery, ▷ pp. 28, 29, 39, **42,** 98, **129** (box), 156 and 158–9.

Slavs, the peoples who settled E Europe in ancient times, first referred to by this name in the mid-6th century. They were initially subject to the AVARS, whose westward migration pushed the southern Slavs into the Balkans, but became increasingly independent. After Charlemagne's destruction of the nomads c. 800, they converted to Christianity and became part of the Byzantine orbit, though they often constituted a threat to CONSTANTINOPLE; ▷ pp. 80, 154–5 and 175.

Slovenia, a republic of S Central Europe. The Slovenes arrived in the W Balkans in the 6th and 7th centuries. In the 9th century, the area was divided between several German rulers and only the Slovenes in the S (Carniola) resisted Germanization. Carniola became a HABSBURG (Austrian) province in 1335 and, although it remained under Habsburg rule almost continuously until 1918, the Slovenes managed to preserve their national identity. Official encouragement of the Slovene language under Napoleonic French rule (1809–14) gave impetus to a Slovene national revival in the 19th century. When the Habsburg Empire collapsed (1918), the Slovenes joined the Serbs, Croats and Montenegrins in the new state that was renamed YUGOSLAVIA in 1929. When Yugoslavia became a Communist federal state in 1945, the Slovene lands were reorganized as the republic of Slovenia. After the death of Yugoslav President TITO (1980), the federation faltered in nationalist crises. Slovenia, the wealthiest part of Yugoslavia, edged towards democracy and its traditional close relationship with Austria. In free elections in 1990, nationalists gained a majority in the Slovene Assembly, which declared independence in June 1991. Following reverses in a short campaign, Yugoslav federal forces were withdrawn from Slovenia, whose independence gained widespread diplomatic recognition in 1992 (▷ p. 224, box).

Smith, Adam (1723–90), Scottish economist and philosopher; ▷ p. **135** (box).

Smith, Ian Douglas (1919–), prime minister of (Southern) Rhodesia (ZIMBABWE) 1964–78. He led the white settler electorate to declare independence (UDI) in 1965, finally conceding power to Robert MUGABE in 1979–80 (▷ p. 221, box).

Smith, John (1580–1631), one of the founders of the Jamestown colony in Virginia; ▷ pp. 72 (box) and 142.

Smuts, Jan Christian (1870–1950), South African prime minister (1919–24 and 1939–48). His active support for Britain in World War II cost him the 1948 election; ▷ pp. 220–1.

Soares, Mário Lopés (1924–), Portuguese socialist statesman, prime minister (1976–8 and 1983–5), president (1986–).

Sobieski, John III (1629–96), king of Poland (1674–96). In response to an appeal from the pope, he joined Austrian and German forces to compel the Turks to lift their siege of Vienna in 1683, and also joined the HOLY LEAGUE of 1684 against the Turks.

social contract, a term used by political theorists such as HOBBES, LOCKE and ROUSSEAU to describe the agreement by which the individual sacrifices some of his liberty in return for the protection of the state; ▷ p. **135** (box).

Social Darwinism, a theory applying the principles of evolution to the development of human society; ▷ p. 161 (box).

Social Democrat, a term used to describe a number of left-of-centre political parties. Before the establishment of the Third INTERNATIONAL in 1919, the term described socialist political parties usually subscribing to a MARXIST analysis of society. Between 1919 and 1945, the label described those left-wing parties – such as the German Social Democratic Party (SDP) – which, whilst often avowedly Marxist, rejected the leadership of the SOVIET UNION. In the postwar period, the term has come to be applied to democratic left-wing parties committed to redistribution of wealth, extension of welfare and social security schemes, and limited state management of the economy. In Britain, a Social Democratic Party (SDP) was formed in 1981 by four LABOUR dissidents, who formed an alliance with the LIBERAL party. The majority of the party merged with the Liberals in 1988, but a minority persisted as the SDP until the 1992 elections; ▷ pp. 169, 180 and 215.

Social Democratic and Labour Party (SDLP), a Northern Irish political party of the moderate left, seeking to achieve a united Ireland by constitutional means. It has been led by John Hume since its foundation in 1970.

Social Democratic Party (SDP), ▷ SOCIAL DEMOCRAT.

socialism, a political and economic theory advocating the ownership and control of the means of production, distribution and exchange by the entire community or by the state, and the equal distribution of wealth. The term was first used in France and Britain by SAINT-SIMON and Robert OWEN. Parties describing themselves as 'socialist' range from extreme left-wing COMMUNIST parties advocating political change by violent revolution, to moderate SOCIAL DEMOCRAT or LABOUR parties embracing the institutions of representative democratic government; ▷ pp. **168–9,** 181, 185, 186, 189 (box), 198, 211, 215 and 233.

Society of Friends, ▷ QUAKERS.

Socrates (470–399 BC), Athenian philosopher. He founded no formal school and wrote nothing, but spent his life debating in Athens with other philosophers and wealthy young men, some of whom stayed as devoted adherents, while others like Critias and Alcibiades went into politics. He professed only a unique awareness of his own ignorance, and everyone else's, and sought to demonstrate the moral confusions of others, and to found ethical conduct on more satisfactory rational definitions of the virtues. He was successfully prosecuted after the end of the Peloponnesian War for corrupting the young and introducing new gods, and was executed by the administration of hemlock; ▷ p. **30** (box) and 31.

Solferino, Battle of (25 June 1859), the second bloody battle (three weeks after MAGENTA) of the Franco-Piedmontese campaign to expel Austria from Lombardy. Although Austria was defeated, French casualties were so high that NAPOLEON III concluded a separate peace with Austria at VILLA-FRANCA; ▷ p. 152.

Solidarity, (Polish, *Solidarnosc*) an independent trade union movement that emerged from unrest in the Lenin shipyard in Gdansk, Poland, in 1980, under the leadership of Lech WALESA; ▷ p. 224 (box).

Solomon (d. c. 922 BC), king of Israel (c. 961–c. 922 BC) and son of David, traditionally famous for his wisdom. His policies, which included organized tax and labour – from which his own tribe of Judah was omitted – led to the division of the kingdom shortly after his death; ▷ pp. 23 and 43.

Solomon Islands, an archipelago in the S Pacific. Settled by MELANESIANS about 2500 BC (▷ p. 69, map), the islands were briefly colonized by Spain (1568–1606). The islanders were exploited as a workforce for plantations in other Pacific islands before Britain established a protectorate in 1893. Occupied by the Japanese (1942–5), the Solomons were the scene of fierce fighting, including a major battle for Guadalcanal (▷ pp. 194–5). Independence was gained in 1978.

Solon (7th–6th centuries BC), Athenian statesman and lawgiver; ▷ pp. 28–9.

Somalia, a republic of E Africa. Muslim traders established trading posts along the Somali coast from the 7th century. In 1886 Britain established a protectorate in the N of the region, while the Italians took the S. In World War II the Italians briefly occupied British Somaliland. In 1960 the British and Italian territories were united as an independent Somalia (▷ p. 202, map). In 1969 the president was assassinated and the army – under Major-General Muhammad Siad Barre – seized control. Barre's socialist Islamic Somalia became an ally of the USSR. In 1977 Somali guerrillas – with Somali military support – drove the Ethiopians out of the largely Somali-inhabited Ogaden. Somalia's Soviet alliance was ended when the USSR supported Ethiopia to regain the Ogaden. Barre was overthrown in 1991, since when a bitter civil war has been fought over the capital, local leaders have taken control of many districts of the countryside and Somalia has collapsed into anarchy and famine.

Somme, battle of the (July–November 1916), a 20-week British and French offensive to smash the German hold on N France; ▷ pp. 176 and 177 (box).

Somoza, a family that dominated Nicaraguan politics from the 1930s to 1979. Anastasio Somoza Garcia (1896–1956) ruled NICARAGUA 1936–56, his road to power opened by the assassination of Augusto César Sandino in 1934. On his own assassination he was succeeded by his sons Luis (1956–63) and then Anastasio (1966–79). Anastasio was ousted by the SANDINISTA revolution of 1979.

Sonderbund, an association of seven conservative Roman Catholic cantons in Switzerland, formed in 1845; ▷ p. **151**.

Song or **Sung,** an imperial dynasty of China (960–1127); ▷ p. 53.

Songhay, a people and kingdom of the W African Sahel (in modern MALI). In the 15th and 16th centuries, Songhay formed a powerful Muslim empire controlling trans-Saharan trade. It was conquered by Moroccans in 1590; ▷ p. 67.

South Africa, a country of southern Africa. Black African peoples were long established in what is now South Africa when white settlement began in the Dutch colony of Cape Town (1652; ▷ p. 67). Slaves were imported, but the conquest of the local African societies – only completed late in the 19th century – provided an alternative source of labour. Britain acquired the Cape (1814), abolished slavery (1833), and annexed NATAL (1843). The Boers (or AFRIKANERS) – of Dutch and French HUGUENOT descent – moved inland on the GREAT TREK (1835–7) to found the republics of the TRANSVAAL and ORANGE FREE STATE. (For details of the Boer Wars between Britain and the Afrikaner republics, ▷ p. 163, box; for details of South Africa in the 20th century, ▷ pp. 220–1.)

South Carolina, one of the 13 original states of the USA. The area was visited by the Spanish in 1521 and twice briefly settled by them in the 16th century. The first permanent English settlement was established in 1670; ▷ pp. 156 (map) and 159 (map).

Southern Rhodesia, ▷ ZIMBABWE.

South Korea, ▷ KOREA, REPUBLIC OF.

South Sea Bubble (1720–1), a speculative boom in the stock of the South Sea Company, caused by the granting to the Company of a monopoly of the trading privileges in Spanish America ceded to

Britain in 1713. The 'bubble' burst, ruining many and threatening – temporarily – the position of the House of HANOVER.

soviet (Russian, 'council'), a council elected by the workers or soldiers of a particular district in Russia, created under Communist leadership to act as the basic organizational structure of the 1917 Revolution (▷ p. 181). Delegates from each soviet met at an all-Russian Congress in June 1917. In the Soviet Union soviets existed at local, regional and national level, the highest governing council being the Supreme Soviet.

Soviet Union, the Union of the Soviet Socialist Republics (USSR), a Communist federal state of Eastern Europe and Central and N Asia founded by Lenin in December 1922. It was dissolved following the abortive coup in Moscow by Communist hardliners in December 1991; ▷ pp. 192–3, **198–9**, 204–7 and **224–5**.

Soweto (South-Western Townships), a segregated black residential area SW of Johannesburg, the scene of police shootings of school children demonstrating in June 1976; ▷ p. 221.

Spain, a kingdom of Western Europe. In the 8th century BC Greek settlements were founded on the Mediterranean coast, and in the following century Celtic peoples settled in the Iberian peninsula. In the 6th century BC the Carthaginians (▷ p. 23) founded colonies in Spain including Barcelona, Cartagena and Alicante, but from the time of the Second PUNIC WAR (218 BC) the Romans gradually annexed Iberia (▷ p. 37). Roman rule in Spain lasted until the Germanic invasions of the 5th century. By the 7th century almost all of the Iberian peninsula was controlled by the VISIGOTHS and Christianity had been introduced (▷ p. 78). Muslim invaders from Morocco rapidly conquered most of the peninsula rapidly (711–14) and a powerful emirate – later a caliphate – was established at Córdoba, which became one of the most important cities in the Islamic world (▷ p. 83, box). From the 11th century, a lengthy struggle began as small Christian kingdoms in the N of Spain began to expand S into Muslim areas (the Reconquista; ▷ p. 89). Asturias was the first Spanish Christian kingdom to defeat the Moors – at Covadonga (722) – but by 1035 CASTILE, ARAGON and NAVARRE were the leaders of the reconquest. By the 13th century only Granada remained in Muslim hands. Unity was achieved following the marriage in 1469 of FERDINAND II of Aragon to ISABELLA I of Castile. (For details of 16th- and 17th-century Spanish history, notably the growth of the Spanish Empire in Europe, the Americas and the East, the reigns of CHARLES V and PHILIP II, and the division of the HABSBURG lands between Spain and Austria; ▷ pp. 116–17.) Spanish power in the 17th and 18th centuries was probably overextended. The wealth of the Latin American possessions was not used to power economic development in Spain. The 17th-century Spanish Habsburgs were not as gifted as their ancestors and were unable to override strong provincial loyalties and institutions that hindered the development of a centralized state. In 1700, the Habsburg line ended and a grandson of Louis XIV of France, became the first BOURBON king of Spain as Philip V (1683–1746). In the subsequent War of the Spanish Succession (1701–14; ▷ pp. 123 and 124), Spain lost further possessions – including Belgium, Luxembourg, Lombardy, S Italy and Sardinia – and ceded GIBRALTAR to Britain. However, Spain's Bourbon rulers brought a measure of reform and enlightenment to a deeply conservative country. In 1808 Napoleon placed his brother Joseph on the throne of Spain, but Spanish resistance was spirited and in 1814 the British and Spanish armies forced the evacuation of the French (▷ p. 147). King FERDINAND VII (1784–1833) – restored in 1814 – was an absolutist who rejected a liberal constitution introduced in his absence. He

lost the Latin American empire when the Spanish possessions in Central and South America made good use of Spain's weakness to take their independence (▷ pp. 148–9). During the first half of the 19th century, Spain saw a series of struggles between liberal and monarchist elements, with radical republicans poised to intervene from the left and army officers from the right. In the CARLIST WARS (1833–39, 1849 and 1872–76) the supporters of Queen Isabella II (1830–1904) – Ferdinand VII's daughter – countered the rival claims of her uncle Don Carlos and his descendants. Isabella was deposed in the revolution of 1868, which was followed by a short-lived liberal monarchy under an Italian prince (1870–3) and a brief republican experiment in 1873–4. In the last decades of the 19th century, the political situation became increasingly unstable, with the turmoil of labour disturbances, pressure for provincial autonomy, and growing anti-clericalism. As a result of the SPANISH-AMERICAN WAR of 1898 the last significant colonial possessions – CUBA, the PHILIPPINES, Guam and PUERTO RICO – were lost. The end of Spain's empire inflicted a severe wound to Spanish pride and led to doubts as to whether the constitutional monarchy of Alfonso XIII (1886–1941) was capable of delivering the dynamic leadership that Spain was thought to require. Spain remained neutral in World War I, during which social tensions increased. A growing disillusionment with parliamentary government and political parties led to a military coup in 1923 led by General Miguel Primo de Rivera (1870–1930). Primo was initially supported by Alfonso XIII, but in 1930 the King withdrew that support. However, the range of forces arrayed against the monarchy and the threat of civil war led Alfonso to abdicate (1931). The peace of the succeeding republic was short-lived. Neither of the political extremes – left nor right – was prepared to tolerate the perceived inefficiency and lack of authority of the Second Spanish Republic. In 1936, the army generals rose against a newly elected republican government and the Spanish Civil War began (▷ p. 189, box). After the civil war, under General FRANCO, political expression was restricted, and from 1942 to 1967 the Cortes (Parliament) was not directly elected. Spain remained neutral in World War II, although it was beholden to Germany. After 1945, Franco emphasized Spain's anti-Communism – a policy that brought his regime some international acceptance from the West during the Cold War. In 1969, Franco named Alfonso XIII's grandson JUAN CARLOS as his successor. The monarchy was restored on Franco's death (1975) and the King eased the transition to democracy through the establishment of a liberal constitution in 1978. In 1981 Juan Carlos played an important role in putting down an attempted army coup. In 1982 Spain joined NATO and elected a socialist government. Since 1986 the country has been a member of the EC. Despite the granting of regional autonomy (1978), Spain continues to be troubled by campaigns for provincial independence – for example in CATALONIA – and by the violence of the BASQUE separatist movement ETA.

Spanish–American War (1898), a war between Spain and the USA. Cuba's second war of independence against Spain, begun in 1895, gradually drew in the USA. The explosion of the battleship USS *Maine* in Havana harbour precipitated direct US intervention in the conflict. Spain lost Cuba, while the USA gained Puerto Rico and the Philippines, and a quasi-protectorate over Cuba; ▷ p. 157.

Spanish Armada, the large military and naval force sent by PHILIP II of Spain to invade England in 1588. Defeated in the English Channel by the English fleet under the Lord High Admiral, Howard of Effingham, it tried to escape round Scotland and Ireland, suffering further losses by storm and shipwreck. Of the 130 Spanish ships that originally set out, only 86 returned; ▷ pp. 117 and 118.

Spanish Civil War (1936–9), ▷ p. **189** (box).

Spanish Inquisition, ▷ p. **113** (box).

Spanish Main, the area of Spanish settlement and trading activity in the Caribbean between the 16th and 18th centuries, whose wealth and trading opportunities attracted the attention of foreign pirates, PRIVATEERS and traders.

Spanish Netherlands, the S provinces of the Netherlands ceded to Spain by the Union of Arras (1579), including modern BELGIUM, LUXEMBOURG and part of N France. The region later passed to the Austrian HABSBURGS in the Treaty of UTRECHT; ▷ pp. **120** and 123 (box).

Spanish Succession, War of the (1701–13), a war fought for the succession to the throne of Spain; ▷ pp. 117, 121, **123** (box) and 124.

Sparta, one of the leading city-states of ancient Greece; ▷ pp. **28–31**.

Spartacist Rising (1919), an attempted revolutionary uprising by the German Communist Party in Berlin led by Rosa LUXEMBURG and Karl Liebknecht; ▷ p. 186.

Speer, Albert (1905–81), German Nazi politician. The official architect of the Nazi party, he designed the massive stadium at Nuremberg. Minister of armaments during World War II, he was imprisoned at the NUREMBERG Trials.

Spice Islands, the Moluccas, between the Indian and Pacific Oceans, highly valued as a source of profitable spices (▷ p. 81, map). The Portuguese established settlements there in the 16th century but were ousted in the early 17th century by the DUTCH EAST INDIA COMPANY, which established a more complete monopoly of the local spice trade.

Spinoza, Baruch (1632–77), Dutch Jewish philosopher; ▷ p. 120.

spoils system, a system of patronage widespread in 19th-century US politics, whereby a victorious party rewarded its backers with public appointments.

Sri Lanka, an island of S Asia, formerly known as Ceylon. In the 6th century BC Sinhalese invaders from N India arrived in Ceylon (▷ p. 59). They established a capital at Anuradhapura, which became a key centre of Buddhist learning (▷ p. 60, box). In the 12th century Tamil invaders from S India established a kingdom in the N where they displaced the Sinhalese. Spices drew Arab traders. Trading settlements were founded by the Portuguese in the 16th century, and then by the Dutch, who were invited by the king of Kandy to oust the Portuguese in the 17th century. From 1796 British rule replaced the Dutch, uniting the entire island for the first time. Nationalist feeling grew from the beginning of the 20th century, leading to independence in 1948, and a republican constitution in 1972. The country has been bedevilled by Tamil-Sinhalese ethnic rivalry which led to major disorders in 1958, 1961 and since 1977. In 1971 a Marxist rebellion was crushed after heavy fighting. Sri Lanka elected the world's first woman prime minister, Sirimavo BANDARANAIKE (PM 1960–5 and 1970–7). In the 1980s separatist Tamil guerrillas fought for an independent homeland (Eelam). Fighting between rival Tamil guerrilla groups, Sinhalese extremists and government forces reduced the NE to near civil war. An Indian 'peace-keeping' force intervened (1987), but this aggravated an already complex situation. The Tamil NE is scheduled to achieve autonomy, but unrest continues.

Srivijaya, a former empire based on S Sumatra; ▷ p. 60.

SS (abbreviation for *Schutzstaffel*, German 'protection squad'), a Nazi organization run by HIMMLER as a powerful and ruthless military elite. It was used by Hitler to suppress the SA in the NIGHT OF THE LONG KNIVES (1934), and controlled the concentration camps. The GESTAPO was one of its subdivisions; ▷ pp. 187, 192 and 193.

Stalin, Josef Vissarionovich (b. Dzhugashvili; 1879–1953), Soviet Communist politician and dictator; ▷ pp. 3 (box), 181, 189, 192, **198** and 199.

Stalingrad, battle of (1942–3), ▷ p. **193**.

Stamford Bridge, battle of (25 September 1066), English victory over the Vikings; ▷ p. 87.

Stamp Act (1765), a British taxation measure designed to increase the American contribution to the costs of defending the North American colonies; ▷ p. 142.

Stanley, Sir Henry Morton (1841–1904), Anglo-American explorer and journalist. He was sent by the *New York Herald* to find David LIVINGSTONE, whom he met at Ujiji on Lake Tanganyika (10 November 1871). He later helped the Belgian king LEOPOLD II to establish the Congo Free State; ▷ p. 161 (box).

START, ▷ STRATEGIC ARMS REDUCTION TALKS.

Star Wars, ▷ STRATEGIC DEFENSE INITIATIVE.

States-General or **Estates-General,** the name given to two historical assemblies: **1.** in the United Provinces of the Netherlands, a permanent assembly of deputies from the estates of the seven provinces of the Dutch Republic (▷ p. 120); **2.** in France, the periodic meeting of deputies of the three estates of clergy, nobility and commons, as in 1614 and 1789 (▷ p. 144).

states' rights, a US political doctrine upholding the rights of individual states against the central power of the federal government.

Stephen I, St (c. 975–1038), first king of Hungary (1001–38). He established the Christian church in his realm and campaigned energetically to convert his subjects.

Stephen of Blois (c. 1096–1154), king of England (1135–54). He seized the crown after the death of his uncle HENRY I, but spent his reign fighting to retain England (more or less successfully) and Normandy (unsuccessfully) against the claims of the Empress MATILDA and her son, the future HENRY II.

Steppes, the grasslands of Eurasia, stretching from the Ukraine in the W to SW Siberia in the E; ▷ pp. **54** and **55**.

Stern Gang, a Zionist terrorist group, an offshoot of the IRGUN ZVAI LEUMI, dedicated to ousting the British from Palestine in the 1940s. Officially called *Lohamei Heruth Israel* ('Fighters for the Freedom of Israel'), it was led by Avraham Stern until his death in 1942.

Stolypin, Peter Arkadievich (1862–1911), Russian politician. As prime minister (1906–11), he combined a policy of agricultural reform with political repression, ruthlessly punishing activists in the 1905 Russian Revolution; ▷ p. 180.

Stone Age, ▷ pp. 12 and 13.

Stonehenge, a prehistoric ritual site in Wiltshire, England, a circular earth bank with internal stone settings. It was started in the Neolithic period (about 3000 BC). The present monument was built around 1500 BC.

Strategic Arms Limitation Talks (SALT), a series of meetings (1969–72 and 1974–9) between the USA and USSR with the aim of limiting the number of nuclear weapons deployed by both sides; ▷ pp. 207 and 227.

Strategic Arms Reduction Talks (START), negotiations between the USA and USSR during the 1980s to reduce stockpiles of strategic nuclear weapons, ▷ pp. 225 and 227.

Strategic Defense Initiative (SDI or 'Star Wars'), a space-based US defence system against nuclear attack; ▷ p. 226.

Stresemann, Gustav (1878–1929), German politician. As foreign minister (1923–9) during the Weimar Republic, he pursued conciliatory policies towards Germany's former enemies. He accepted the DAWES and YOUNG Plans for reparations, negotiated the Treaties of LOCARNO and Germany's entry into the League of Nations; ▷ p. 186 (box).

strips, the smallest units held by individual farmers in medieval village fields; ▷ p. 98.

Stroessner, Alfredo (1912–), president of PARAGUAY (1954–89).

Stuart or **Stewart, House of,** the royal dynasty that ruled in Scotland (1371–1714), and in England from the accession of JAMES I (1603) to the death of Queen ANNE (1714), apart from the period of the COMMONWEALTH and the PROTECTORATE (1649–60). The first Stuart king of Scotland was ROBERT II, a descendant of the hereditary stewards of the kings of Scotland. After 1714 the Old and Young PRETENDERS unsuccessfully maintained the Stuart claim to the thrones of England and Scotland against the House of HANOVER; ▷ p. 119.

Sudan, a republic of NE Africa. N Sudan – once known as NUBIA – was strongly influenced by Egypt (▷ pp. 17 and 19), and was later the seat of the kingdom of Cush (600 BC–AD 350; ▷ p. 66). Medieval Christian kingdoms fell to Muslim invaders from the 13th century. In 1820–1 Sudan was conquered by the Egyptians, who were challenged in the 1880s by an Islamic leader who claimed to be the MAHDI. The Mahdists took Khartoum, killed Sudan's Egyptian-appointed governor, General GORDON (1885), and created a theocratic state. Britain intervened, and – after the Fashoda Incident (▷ p. 162, box) – Sudan was administered jointly by Britain and Egypt. Nationalism developed strongly after World War I, but independence was only given in 1956 (▷ p. 202, map). Sudan remains politically unstable, alternating between civilian and military regimes. The civil war between the Muslim N and the animist-Christian S that began in 1955 remains unresolved.

Sudetenland, a region of CZECHOSLOVAKIA, bordering Germany, annexed by Hitler as part of the THIRD REICH in 1938. It was returned to Czechoslovakia in 1945, the POTSDAM Agreement authorizing the expulsion of most of its German-speaking inhabitants; ▷ pp. 188–9.

Suetonius (c. AD 69–c. 140), Roman biographer; ▷ p. 2.

Sueves, a term denoting the German tribes of the Upper Danube: the Alemanni, Marcomanni and Quadi. They entered Gaul in 406, and with the Asding VANDALS set up a kingdom in NW Spain (409) that survived until it was absorbed by the VISIGOTHS in 584; ▷ pp. 78 (map) and 79.

Suez Canal, an international waterway linking the E Mediterranean to the Red Sea, built through Egyptian territory by the French engineer Ferdinand de Lesseps and opened in 1869. Control of the Canal was shared by Britain and France between 1875 and 1956. NASSER'S nationalization of the Canal in 1956 provoked the Suez Crisis; ▷ pp. 202 and 211.

suffragette, a member of the Women's Social and Political Union, a militant British feminist movement founded by Emmeline Pankhurst in 1903 to campaign for the right of adult women to vote in general elections. The suffragettes' militant tactics were suspended on the outbreak of World War I; ▷ p. **232**.

Sufi, a Muslim mystic. From the 12th century Sufis began to be organized into a number of orders (Arabic, *tariqa*), many of which still survive and remain influential; ▷ p. 82 (box).

Suharto (1921–), INDONESIAN soldier and politician, president (1967–). He overthrew SUKARNO in a bloody coup (1967) in which tens of thousands of supposedly Communist sympathizers were killed.

Sui, a Chinese imperial dynasty (589–618 AD); ▷ p. 53.

Sukarno, Achmed (1901–70), Indonesian statesman

and nationalist. He declared INDONESIA a republic in 1945 and opposed the return of Dutch colonial power after World War II. He was president until his overthrow and arrest in 1966.

Suleiman I (the Magnificent; 1494–1566), Ottoman sultan (1520–66); ⇨ pp. 114 and 115 (map).

Sulla, Lucius Cornelius (c. 138–78 BC), Roman dictator, opponent of MARIUS in the civil war of the 80s; ⇨ p. 37.

sultanate, an institution of government in the Islamic world, prominent since the 11th century, when the SELJUK Turks were granted the title of sultan (in Arabic the word originally meant 'power') by the ABBASID caliph. In effect, though not in theory, the Seljuk sultan exercised secular power, while religious authority was left to the CALIPH. Sultanates arose throughout the Islamic world: the largest and most long-lived was that of the Ottomans (late 13th–early 20th centuries); ⇨ pp. 62, 82–3, 88, 114 and 154.

Sumatra, the westernmost island of INDONESIA; ⇨ pp. 60–1.

Sumer, the S part of ancient Mesopotamia, where the earliest cities developed; ⇨ pp. **16** and 20.

Sung, ⇨ SONG.

Sunni, the majority sect within Islam, followers of the *sunna* or tradition of the prophet Muhammad. Sunnis regard the first four CALIPHS as legitimate heirs to the Prophet MUHAMMAD, but the minority SHIITES accept only the fourth caliph, ALI, as his true successor; ⇨ pp. 83 and 213 (box).

Sun Yat-sen (Sun Zhong Shan; 1866–1925), Chinese politician. As leader of the KUOMINTANG he overthrew the MANCHU dynasty in 1911 and was briefly president of the republic (1912) before resigning in favour of YUAN SHIKAI. In the period of civil strife following Yuan's death, he led a series of governments controlling small areas of S China. He reorganized the Kuomintang with Russian help and cooperated with the Chinese Communist Party. He is seen as the father of modern China by both Nationalists and Communists; ⇨ p. 196.

Suppiluliumas I, Hittite ruler (c. 1380–1350 BC); ⇨ p. 22.

Supremacy, Acts of, English parliamentary legislation confirming the supreme authority of HENRY VIII (1534) and ELIZABETH I (1559) over the ANGLICAN Church.

Suriname, a republic of S America. Dutch settlement began in 1602 and the area was confirmed as a Dutch colony in 1667. Suriname has a mixed population, including American Indians, and the descendants of African slaves and of Javanese, Chinese and Indian plantation workers. Since independence in 1975, racial tension has contributed to instability and there have been several coups.

SWAPO, (South West African People's Organization), a Namibian political party founded in 1959; ⇨ p. 221 and NAMIBIA.

Swaziland, a kingdom of southern Africa. The Swazi kingdom was formed early in the 19th century, and came under British rule in 1904. The country resisted annexation by the BOERS in the 1890s and by South Africa during the colonial period. Following independence (1968; ⇨ p. 202), much of the traditional royal authority was restored (1973). A bitter power struggle within the royal family followed the death of King Sobhuza II (1982).

Sweden, a kingdom of N Europe. Sweden became Christian in the 10th and 11th centuries, and a stable monarchy dominated much of the Middle Ages. In 1397, the crowns of Sweden, Norway and Denmark were united, and for just over a century Sweden struggled for independence and then with Denmark for dominance of Scandinavia. Stability

returned with the accession in 1523 of GUSTAVUS I (reigned 1523–60), who founded the Vasa dynasty and confiscated Church lands, an act that led to the Reformation in Sweden. Under the Vasas, Sweden's role in N Europe expanded considerably, particularly during the reign of GUSTAVUS ADOLPHUS; reigned 1611–32) when Sweden played a major part on the Protestant side in the Thirty Years War (⇨ p. 113). Sweden was a great power and the able chief minister Axel OXENSTIERNA helped win a Baltic empire, but the military adventures of Charles XII in the Great Northern War (1700–21) ended in defeat at the battle of Poltava (1709) – a turning-point in European history (⇨ p. 127, box). Throughout the 18th century Sweden was troubled by internal struggles between the monarchy and the aristocracy. Involvement in the NAPOLEONIC WARS was Sweden's last conflict, and since then the country has enjoyed neutrality. The founder of the present Swedish dynasty, Jean-Baptiste BERNADOTTE, was elected crown prince to the childless king (1810), and succeeded in 1818. In 1814 Sweden lost Finland and the last possessions S of the Baltic, but gained Norway from Denmark in compensation. The union of Norway and Sweden was dissolved in 1905 when King Oscar II gave up the Norwegian throne upon Norway's vote for separation. In the 20th century neutral Sweden has developed a comprehensive WELFARE STATE under SOCIAL DEMOCRATIC governments. The country assumed a moral leadership on world issues but was jolted by the (unclaimed) assassination of PM Olaf Palme (1986). In the 1990s economic necessity has obliged Sweden to dismantle aspects of the welfare state. The country has also become a candidate for EC membership.

Sweyn Forkbeard (d. 1014), king of Denmark (987–1014) and father of CNUT. He was involved in several raids on England before attempting its conquest (1013–14). He gained considerable support there, becoming king in 1014 when ETHELRED II fled to Normandy, but died soon afterwards.

Switzerland, a republic of W Central Europe. Switzerland occupies a strategic position, but the Swiss have used their remarkable position to withdraw from, rather than participate in, European power politics. In the 11th century, what is now Switzerland became part of the Holy Roman Empire. In 1291, three local territorial units – the 'Forest Cantons' of Schwyz (which gave its name to the country), Unterwalden and Uri – joined together in a League against the (Austrian) HABSBURG Emperors. Other similar cantons joined the infant League throughout the later Middle Ages, and by 1513 the League included 13 cantons and a variety of dependent territories. Intense religious rivalries in the 16th century – with Zürich, Basel, Berne and Schaffhausen becoming Protestant – resulted in a civil war that tested but did not destroy the League. At the end of the Thirty Years War (1648; ⇨ p. 113), Switzerland's independence was finally recognized. The French Revolutionary Wars saw the creation of a Helvetian Republic in 1798, but in 1803 Napoleon dismantled this unitary state and returned the country to a confederation (⇨ p. 147, map). At the Congress of VIENNA (1815) Swiss neutrality was recognized and the country gained its present boundaries. Continuing tensions in the early 19th century saw attempts by some cantons to secede and set up a new federation – the SONDERBUND (⇨ p. 151) – but the compromises of a new constitution in 1848 – which is still the basis of Swiss government – balanced cantonal and central power. As a neutral country Switzerland proved the ideal base for the RED CROSS (1863), the League of Nations (1920) and other world organizations, but Switzerland avoids membership of any body it considers might compromise its neutrality – a national referendum in 1986 voted against Swiss membership of the UN.

syndicalism, a movement related to SOCIALISM, advocating the overthrow of CAPITALISM and the ownership of industry by industrial workers; ⇨ p. 169.

Syracuse, a seaport in Sicily, founded by Greek colonists in the 8th century BC, and absorbed into the Roman Empire in 212 BC. The Athenian expedition to capture it during the Peloponnesian War was a major disaster; ⇨ pp. 29 (map) and 30.

Syria, a republic of SW Asia. Syria was an important part of the Hittite, Assyrian and Persian empires (⇨ pp. 21, 22–3 and 26–7), before being conquered by Alexander the Great (332 BC; ⇨ p. 32). From 305 BC Syria was the centre of the Seleucid Empire (⇨ p. 33), and in 64 BC the area became a Roman province based on ANTIOCH (⇨ p. 37, map). The Byzantine Empire ruled the area (300–634; ⇨ p. 80) until the Muslim armies of Khaled ibn al-Walid invaded the country. Most Syrians accepted Islam rapidly. In 661 Mu'awiyya, the founder of the UMAYYAD dynasty (⇨ p. 82), established his capital in Damascus, and the city reached the zenith of its power. When the Umayyads were overthrown by the ABBASID dynasty from Baghdad (750) Damascus' pre-eminence ended (⇨ p. 83). From the 12th to the 14th century parts of coastal Syria were ruled by Crusader principalities (⇨ p. 88). The MAMLUKS ruled Syria from the 13th century until 1516 (⇨ p. 83) when the area was annexed by the Ottoman Empire (⇨ p. 115, map). Ottoman rule was not ended until 1917 when a combined British-Arab army was led into Damascus by Prince Faisal ibn Hussein. In 1920 independence was declared, but the victors of World War I handed Syria to France (1920) as a trust territory. Since independence in 1946 Syria has suffered political instability. The pan-Arab, secular, socialist BA'ATH Party engineered Syria's unsuccessful union with Egypt (1958–61; ⇨ p. 211). Syria fought wars with Israel in 1948–49, 1967 and 1973, and in the 1967 Arab–Israeli War Israel captured the strategic GOLAN HEIGHTS from Syria (⇨ pp. 211–12). A pragmatic Ba'athist leader Hafiz al-ASSAD came to power in 1970 and allied Syria to the USSR. Assad's popularity has been challenged by Syria's increasing involvement in Lebanon since 1976 and by SHIITE fundamentalism. Since 1989–90, economic pressures have lessened Syria's dependence upon the USSR. Syria's participation in the coalition against Iraq (1990–91; ⇨ p. 213, box) gained greater international acceptance for Syria, which had attracted criticism for sympathizing with TERRORISM.

Tacitus (c. AD 55–120), Roman senator and historian, famed for his acute analysis of despotism and its effects; ⇨ p. 2.

Taft, William Howard (1857–1930), twenty-seventh president of the USA (1909–13). A conservative Republican, he sought re-election in 1912, but was well beaten by the Democrat Woodrow WILSON, the Republican vote being split by Roosevelt's decision to run on a PROGRESSIVE Party ticket.

Tahiti, an island of French Polynesia in the S Pacific. Claimed by British and French navigators in the 18th century, Tahiti became a French protectorate in 1842 and a colony in 1880; ⇨ pp. 69 (map) and 129 (box).

Taiping Rebellion (1851–64), a Chinese peasant rebellion; ⇨ p. **57**.

Taira Kiyamori, military dictator who seized power in Japan in the mid-12th century; ⇨ p. 64.

Taiwan, ⇨ CHINA, REPUBLIC OF.

Taizong (T'ai-tsung; 596–649), the second TANG emperor of China (627–49); ⇨ p. 53.

Tajikistan, a republic of Central Asia. The Tajiks, an Iranian people, were included in the Persian Empire until the 8th century AD when the Arabs extended their influence over most of the area.

From the 10th century, the Tajiks were also subject to Turkic influences from the N. In the 13th century the Tajiks were overrun by the Mongols (▷ p. 54). The area was, in turn, part of the Mongol Empire, the JAGATAI Khanate and the empire of TAMERLANE and his descendants (▷ p. 55). A period of UZBEK rule was ended when the Afghans invaded in the 18th century. In the 19th century most of the Tajiks owed allegiance to the (Uzbek) khan of Bukhara. The area was annexed by tsarist Russia (1860–68). After the Russian revolutions (▷ pp. 180–1), the area was reoccupied by the Soviet RED ARMY (1920), but Tajik revolts simmered from 1922 to 1931. Tajikistan became a Union Republic within the USSR in 1929, declared independence after the abortive coup by Communist hardliners in Moscow (September 1991; ▷ p. 225), and was internationally recognized when the Soviet Union was dissolved (December 1991).

Talleyrand-Périgord, Charles Maurice de (1754–1838), French foreign minister (1799–1807 and 1814–15). He negotiated secretly with the allies to depose Napoleon after 1807, and represented France at the Congress of VIENNA.

Tamerlane ('Timur the Lame'; 1336–1405), Mongol conqueror of an area extending from the Mediterranean to Mongolia in the 14th century, ruling (after 1369) from his capital at Samarkand; ▷ pp. **55, 83** and **114.**

Tamil, a people of S India and Sri Lanka; ▷ p. 59.

Tang, a Chinese imperial dynasty (618–907) under which the Chinese empire was extended into Central Asia and Korea. The dynasty is noted for its technological and artistic achievements, including the invention of printing and manufacture of gunpowder; ▷ p. 53.

Tanganyika, ▷ TANZANIA.

Tannenberg, battle of, 1. the defeat of the TEUTONIC KNIGHTS by the Poles in 1410 (▷ p. 89, box). **2.** a series of actions fought in East Prussia (now Poland) between Germany and Russia in August 1914. Two Russian armies advancing towards Königsberg (now Kaliningrad), were respectively defeated and forced to retreat by Generals von HINDENBURG and LUDENDORFF. The Russians never again entered German territory in World War I (▷ p. 176).

Tanzania, a republic of E Africa (▷ p. 202, box). The coast was explored by Arabs from the 8th century and the Portuguese from the 16th century. Zanzibar was an Omani possession from the 18th century, became an independent sultanate in 1856 and then a British protectorate (1890–1963). After independence in 1963 the sultan of Zanzibar was deposed in a radical left-wing coup. The mainland became the colony of German East Africa in 1884 (▷ p. 163, map), the British trust territory of Tanganyika in 1919 and an independent state in 1961. In 1964 Tanganyika and Zanzibar united to form Tanzania. President Julius Nyerere's policies of self-reliance and egalitarian socialism were widely admired, but proved difficult to implement and were largely abandoned by the time he retired as president in 1985.

Taoism, ▷ DAOISM.

Tariq ibn Zaid (fl. 700–12), Berber general who led the first Islamic invasion of Spain; ▷ p. 83 (box).

Tarquin the Proud, the last king of Rome; ▷ p. 36.

Tartars or **Tatars,** the name given to the westernmost group of nomads of Turkish and Mongol origin. They moved into the area N of the Black and Caspian Seas with the 13th-century Mongol advance, establishing the Khanate of the Golden Horde (▷ p. 55). Most Tartars came under Russian rule in the 16th century, although the Tartar Khanate of the Crimea survived until 1783; ▷ p. 126.

Tasman, Abel (1603–61), Dutch explorer; ▷ p. 129 (box).

Taylor, Zachary (1784–1850), twelfth president of the USA (1849–50). A hero of the MEXICAN–AMERICAN WAR, he was nominated by the WHIGS as their presidential candidate in 1848. He opposed concessions to the South on the issue of the extension of slavery to the new states gained from Mexico (▷ pp. 156 and 158).

Tecumseh (c.1768–1813), Shawnee Indian chief who sided with the British in the War of 1812 (▷ p. 156), dying in the battle of the Thames (1813).

Teheran Conference (28 November–1 December 1943) the first meeting between CHURCHILL, STALIN and F.D. ROOSEVELT during World War II. The 'Big Three' discussed the opening of a SECOND FRONT in W Europe, future Soviet influence in E Europe, and the establishment of the United Nations after the war.

Templars, a military and religious order of knights; ▷ p. 89 (box).

Temple Mound Culture, ▷ MISSISSIPPI CULTURE.

Tennis Court Oath (20 June 1789), the declaration by commoners (the Third Estate) of the French STATES GENERAL that they would not disperse until LOUIS XVI had agreed to a written constitution. (They had met in one of the royal tennis courts after they were shut out of their usual meeting place.)

Tenochtitlán, the ancient island capital of the Aztecs, on the site of present-day Mexico City. Its capture by CORTEZ in 1521 led to the capitulation of the Aztec empire; ▷ p. 71.

Teotihuacán, an early temple-city of Meso-America near Mexico City; ▷ pp. 70–1.

Teresa of Avila (1515–82), Spanish nun and mystic. She reformed the Carmelite order, returning it to older, more austere rules. Her account of her mystical experiences brought her – briefly – before the Inquisition. She was canonized in 1622.

Terror, Reign of, the period during the French Revolution, when the CONVENTION pursued a ruthless policy of liquidating all those who were seen as a threat to the regime; ▷ p. 145.

Terrorism, violent activity intended to achieve a political objective. In modern parlance the term is generally used to denote acts of terror carried out by clandestine organizations against non-combatant groups to force a national government to accede to a demand. As such it has been used by extremists of both left and right (notably the BAADER-MEINHOF Gang), and by groups representing national minorities (notably the Provisional wing of the IRISH REPUBLICAN ARMY). Political terrorism has been used by totalitarian regimes to liquidate opposition, as under Hitler and Stalin; ▷ pp. 180 (box), 186, 212 and 215.

Test Acts (1673 and 1678), English legislation making the holding of public office conditional upon a denial of the transubstantiation in the mass (as believed by Roman Catholics) and a certificate of attendance at ANGLICAN communion. The Acts were not repealed until 1829.

Tet Offensive (29 January–25 February 1968), an offensive launched by the North Vietnamese army and the Vietcong against US, Allied, and South Vietnamese forces; ▷ pp. **208** and 209 (box).

tetrarchy, the 'rule of four' established by Diocletian; ▷ pp. 39–40.

Teutoburger Forest, battle of the (AD 9), the annihilation of three Roman legions by German tribesmen; ▷ p. 38.

Teutonic Knights, a German military and religious order; ▷ pp. 85 (map) and 89 (box).

Tewkesbury, battle of (4 May 1471), a battle fought between EDWARD IV and the Lancastrian forces of MARGARET of Anjou during the Wars of the ROSES.

Texas, Republic of (1836–45) a short-lived independent republic in the SW USA established when American settlers in the Mexican province of Texas staged a successful revolt (1835–6). It was extinguished in 1845, when the USA annexed it as a slave state; ▷ p. 156.

Thailand, a kingdom of SE Asia, known before 1939 as Siam. The Thais originated in Yunnan (China) and moved S after the Mongol destruction of their kingdom, Nanchao (1253). For details of the emergence of the Thai principalities and the rise of Thailand to become the most powerful state in SE Asia (▷ p. 61). The adroit diplomacy of its rulers enabled it to remain free of European colonization. Rama I (reigned 1782–1809), founder of the present dynasty, moved the capital to Bangkok. His successors were forced to cede their claims over neighbouring lands to Britain and France. A constitutional monarchy was established by a bloodless coup (1932), whose Westernized leaders (Pibul Songgram and Pridi Phanomyang) struggled for political dominance for the next quarter of a century. During World War II Thailand was forced into an alliance with Japan (▷ p. 194). Since then Thailand has made a decisive commitment to the US political camp, which has brought major benefits in military and technical aid. Despite continuing army interventions in politics, Thailand has prospered. However, the stability of the country was compromised by the wars in Vietnam (▷ pp. 208 9) and by continuing Cambodian conflict (until 1991), as Cambodian refugees and guerrillas remained in Thai border regions.

Thatcher, Margaret (1925–), British Conservative politician, prime minister (1979–90). Europe's first woman PM, and a vigorous advocate of the free-market philosophy of the NEW RIGHT, she applied a rigid MONETARIST economic policy, reduced government intervention in industry, curbed trade union power, privatized major industries, cut taxes, and called into question the values of the WELFARE STATE. The defeat of Argentina in the 1982 FALKLANDS WAR secured her an overwhelming victory over Labour in the 1983 election, and the short-lived boom of the mid-1980s brought her a third term in 1987. Growing economic problems together with her strident opposition to greater European integration led to her replacement by John MAJOR in November 1990; ▷ pp. 214 and 233.

Thebes, 1. the most important city of ancient BOEOTIA in central Greece. It gained steadily in power after the Peloponnesian War, but was defeated by Philip II of Macedon at Chaeronea in 338 BC, and was sacked by Alexander after it had revolted against him in 336 (▷ pp. **31** and 32). **2.** a city of ancient Egypt (▷ p. 19 and KARNAK).

Themistocles (c. 523–c. 458 BC), Athenian general and statesman; ▷ p. 29.

Theoderic (the Great; c. 450–526), king of the OSTROGOTHS (474–526). He was recognized as king of Italy in 497 and as king of the VISIGOTHS from 511. Ruling in Roman imperial style, he was the most successful barbarian ruler of his era; ▷ p. 78.

Theodosius I (349–95), Roman emperor (378–395), the last to rule over both halves of the Empire (▷ p. 40). Prompted by St Ambrose, Bishop of Milan, Theodosius, a fervent Christian, persecuted heretics and banned pagan worship.

Thera, ▷ p. 24 (box).

Thermopylae, battle of (480 BC), the first land battle of the Persian Wars. The small Greek forces under the Spartan king LEONIDAS held up the Persian invading force at the narrow pass at Thermopylae in central Greece, until Phocian guards treacherously revealed a mountainous route round the the back. Leonidas, the Spartans and the Boeotians remained to die heroically, while the rest of the Greeks withdrew; ▷ p. 29.

Thessaly, a region in NE Greece, south of Macedonia. A **Thessalian Confederacy** had developed by the 6th century BC, but was only briefly a major power in Greece in the mid-4th century, before falling under the domination of Philip II of MACEDON; ⇨ p. 31 (map).

Thiers, Louis Adolphe (1797–1877), French politician. As head of the first government of the Third Republic he was responsible for the suppression of the Paris Commune; ⇨ p. 153 (box).

Third Estate, the class of commoners in a society divided into social groups known as estates (particularly in France before the Revolution. The other estates were the nobility and the clergy; ⇨ pp. 144, 218 and STATES-GENERAL.

Third Reich, the name used by the Nazis to describe the regime they established in Germany (1933–45) (⇨ pp. 186–91). In Nazi parlance the First Reich was the HOLY ROMAN EMPIRE (962–1806), and the Second Reich the empire founded by Bismarck after the defeat of France (1871–1918).

Third World, ⇨ pp. 148, 203, **217–18** and 230–1.

Thirteen Colonies, the 13 British colonies of North America that rebelled against Great Britain (1775–83) and surrendered elements of their sovereignty to form the United States of America: i.e. Massachusetts, New Hampshire, Rhode Island, Connecticut, New York, New Jersey, Pennsylvania, Delaware, Maryland, Virginia, North Carolina, South Carolina and Georgia. Of these states only Rhode Island was unrepresented at the Constitutional Convention that met in Philadelphia in 1787. The designation 'Thirteen Colonies' distinguishes them from other New World colonies such as Nova Scotia and Barbados, which remained loyal to the crown during the American War of Independence; ⇨ pp. **142–3.**

Thirty-Nine Articles, the doctrines of the ANGLICAN Church, drawn up in the 16th century by CRANMER and Ridley; ⇨ p. 118.

Thirty Tyrants, a brutal oligarchy that ruled Athens 404–403 BC; ⇨ p. 31.

Thirty Years War (1618–48), ⇨ pp. **113**, 117, 120, 124 and 130.

Thrace, a region comprising what is now S Bulgaria and European Turkey. Its Indo-European tribes warred and traded with each other and the Greek cities. Much of Thrace was overcome by PHILIP II of Macedon, and later became part of a Hellenistic kingdom.

Three Emperors' League (German, *Dreikaiserbund*), an alliance between Germany, Austria-Hungary and Russia in 1873; ⇨ p. 174.

Three Kingdoms, a period of Chinese history (220–265 AD) after the fall of the Han empire, when power was contested by three regional states: Wei in the N, Shu in the W and Wu in the E; ⇨ p. 53.

Thucydides (c. 455–c. 400), Athenian aristocrat and historian; ⇨ pp. **2** and 30.

Thule Culture, an early Eskimo culture; ⇨ p. 72.

Thutmose I, pharaoh of Egypt (c. 1525–1512 BC) and father of HATSHEPSUT; ⇨ p. 18.

Thutmose III, pharaoh of Egypt (c. 1504–1450 BC) and nephew of HATSHEPSUT. He re-established Egyptian control over Syria and Nubia, and undertook new building work at KARNAK (⇨ p. 19).

Tiahuanaco, the most important temple-city of pre-Columbian South America, on the shore of Lake Titicaca; ⇨ pp. 70–1.

Tiberius (42 BC–AD 37), Roman emperor (AD 14–37). He was the stepson of Augustus, who chose him as successor only after he had run out of alternatives. Tiberius' rule was prudent and cautious, but was marred by treason trials and became a reign of terror; ⇨ p. 38.

Tiglath-Pileser III, king of Assyria (745–727 BC); ⇨ p. 21.

Tigris, the fast-flowing river to the E of the EUPHRATES. Great centres such as Hellenistic Seleucia and Ctesiphon, a capital of the Parthians and Sassanians, were built on its banks; ⇨ p. 16.

Tilsit, Treaty of (7 and 9 July 1807), the agreements between France and Russia following Napoleon's defeat of Russia at the battle of Friedland (June 1807) and of PRUSSIA at JENA. Russia gained much of Poland, while Prussia lost a third of its territory and half its population. Tsar ALEXANDER I promised to mediate between Britain and France and, if unsuccessful, to join an anti-British coalition.

Timur, ⇨ TAMERLANE.

Tipu Sultan (1750–99), ruler of the Indian state of MYSORE (1789–99). His attempts to continue the policy of his father, HYDER ALI, in building a powerful and militarily effective state ended in defeat by the British and death in battle at his capital of Seringapatam.

Tirpitz, Alfred von (1849–1930), German admiral, secretary of state for the navy (1897–1916); ⇨ p. 175 (box).

tithe, a tenth part of all agricultural produce or personal income, paid as a tax by the laity to the clergy for the upkeep of the Church. The tithe system – operated on a parochial basis to sustain the parish clergy – was abolished in England in 1936.

Tito (Josip Broz; 1892–1980), Yugoslav guerrilla leader and statesman, prime minister (1945–53), president (1953–80). A Croat, he founded the Yugoslav Communist Party, organizing partisans against occupying German forces (1941–4) in World War II. As PM of YUGOSLAVIA he split with Moscow in 1948 (⇨ p. 204) and adopted a policy of NON-ALIGNMENT in the Cold War. He established a collective government with rotational leadership to succeed him.

Tobruk, siege of (1941–2), German siege of British and Commonwealth troops in the Libyan port of Tobruk in World War II. Tobruk surrendered to German and Italian forces in June 1942 but was recaptured by MONTGOMERY in November 1942; ⇨ p. 191.

Tocqueville, Alexis, comte de (1805–59), French historian; ⇨ p. 5.

Togo, a republic in W Africa (⇨ p. 200, map). Colonized by Germany in 1884, Togoland was occupied by Franco-British forces in World War I, after which it was divided between them as trust territories. British Togoland became part of GHANA; the French section gained independence as Togo in 1960, and subsequently relations with Ghana have been strained. Togo has experienced great political instability and several coups.

Tojo, Hideki (1884–1948), Japanese general and politician. As prime minister (1941–4), he gave the order to attack PEARL HARBOR, and turned Japan into a virtual military dictatorship. He resigned after repeated Japanese defeats by the USA in the Pacific and was hanged as a war criminal in 1948; ⇨ p. 187.

Tokugawa, the last Japanese shogunate (1603–1867), founded by Tokugawa Ieyesu; ⇨ pp. **64–5.**

Tokugawa Ieyesu (1542–1616), the founder of the Tokugawa shogunate (1603–1867); ⇨ p. 64.

Tolpuddle martyrs, the name given to six Dorset farm workers who were transported to Australia in 1834; ⇨ p. 166.

Toltecs, a former people of N Mexico; ⇨ pp. *70* and 71.

Tone, (Theobald) Wolfe (1763–98), Irish Protestant and nationalist. He was joint founder (1791), with the Catholic Lord Edward Fitzgerald, of the Society of United Irishmen, a movement seeking the independence of IRELAND from Britain. He sought French support for an Irish revolt, and was

arrested in the abortive rebellion of 1797–8, later committing suicide.

Tonga, a kingdom in the S Pacific. Inhabited by Polynesians for over 3000 years (⇨ p. 69), Tonga has been ruled by kings since the 10th century. European intervention began when Captain COOK visited Tonga (1773–7). Civil war in the first half of the 19th century was ended by King George Tupou I (reigned 1845–93) who reunited Tonga, preserved its independence and gave it a modern constitution. From 1900 to 1970 Tonga was a British protectorate.

Topa Inca (d. 1493), the ruler responsible for the expansion of Inca power (⇨ p. 71).

Tordesillas, Treaty of (7 June 1494), an agreement between Spain and Portugal dividing between them the new lands discovered by the late 15th-century voyages of exploration; ⇨ p. 116.

Torquemada, Tomás de (1420–98) the first Grand Inquisitor of the Spanish Inquisition; ⇨ p. 113 (box).

Tory, a British political party. The name was originally applied to those royalists opposed to the WHIGS' attempts to exclude JAMES II from the succession to the English throne after the POPISH PLOT. They were generally supporters of the divine right of kings and sometimes of absolutist theories of government. Hostile to the GLORIOUS REVOLUTION and tainted by JACOBITE associations, they were excluded from power by the monarchs of the House of HANOVER for most of the 18th century. Toryism revived with the Younger PITT in the 1780s, and gained further impetus from opposition to the French Revolution in the 1790s. Under Sir Robert PEEL, the Tory Party developed into the modern CONSERVATIVE Party in the 1830s.

totalitarianism, government by a centralized authoritarian single-party regime that closely regulates all aspects of life, as in Hitler's Germany or Stalin's Soviet Union; ⇨ pp. 186–7 and 198–9.

total war, ⇨ pp. 179 (box) and **191** (box).

Toulouse, Kingdom of, a VISIGOTHIC kingdom founded in AQUITAINE in 418; ⇨ p. 78.

Touré, Sékou (1922–84), first president (1958–84) of the Republic of GUINEA.

Toussaint l'Ouverture (?1744–1803), a former slave and the greatest of the leaders of HAITI's revolt against the French (⇨ p. 148). He was governor-general of Haiti from 1801, but was betrayed when Napoleon sent troops to restore French control.

Toyatomi Hideyoshi (1536–98), military ruler of Japan (1582–98). He consolidated military rule over the whole of Japan and invaded Korea in 1592; ⇨ p. 64 and 65 (box).

Trades Union Congress (TUC), a British trade union organization. It was founded in 1868 by members of 'trades' who established a national congress to secure legal status for unions, which was finally achieved in 1871. The Parliamentary Committee of the TUC lobbied governments in the interest of unions and was transformed into a General Council in 1921. The TUC has had close links with the LABOUR Party since the early 20th century; ⇨ p. 166.

trade unions, ⇨ pp. *165*, **166–7** and 168.

Trafalgar, battle of (21 October 1805), a naval clash between a combined Franco-Spanish fleet and the British fleet under NELSON off the Spanish port of Cadiz. Nelson's victory ended Napoleon's hopes of an invasion of Britain, but he was fatally wounded in the battle; ⇨ pp. 146 and 148.

Trajan (AD 53–117), Roman emperor (AD 98–117). His reign saw the conquest of Dacia and a less successful war against Parthia; ⇨ p. 38.

Transjordan, ⇨ JORDAN.

Transoxiana, an area of Central Asia between the Amu Darya and Syr Darya rivers (the ancient Oxus and Jaxartes; ⇨ p. 32, map). Crossed by the Silk Route, it was the place where European/Near Eastern culture met the nomad world of Central Asia.

Transvaal, a province in the NE of the Republic of SOUTH AFRICA, a former independent AFRIKANER (Boer) republic (1852–1900) and British colony (1901–10). Transvaal forms the heartland of South Africa, including the administrative capital Pretoria and gold mining areas around Johannesburg; ⇨ pp. 163 and 220.

Trasimene, battle of Lake (217 BC), Hannibal's defeat of the Romans in central Italy; ⇨ p. 37.

treaty ports, the Chinese ports opened to Western trade by the 'Unequal Treaties' in the mid-19th century; ⇨ pp. 57 and 162.

Trenchard, Hugh Montague, 1st Viscount (1873–1956), British soldier and airman, and creator of the Royal Air Force (RAF). He became Chief of the Air Staff with the formation of the RAF in 1918. He was a strong advocate of strategic bombing.

Trent, Council of, ⇨ p. **112.**

Trianon, Treaty of (4 June 1920), a treaty between the Allied Powers and the new republic of Hungary, part of the Paris Peace Conference after World War I; ⇨ p. **182.**

tribune, an official representing the PLEBEIANS in ancient Rome; ⇨ p. 36.

Trinidad and Tobago, a republic in the E Caribbean. Trinidad was inhabited by Arawak Indians and Tobago by Carib Indians when Columbus discovered them in 1498. Trinidad was neglected by Spain and became British in 1797. Tobago was claimed by the Spanish, Dutch and French before being ceded to Britain in 1802. African slaves were imported to work sugar plantations, but after the abolition of slavery in the 1830s, labourers came from India. The islands merged as a single colony in 1899 and gained independence in 1962. The country – which has been a republic since 1976 – witnessed a Black Power revolt in 1970 and an attempted coup by Islamic fundamentalists in 1990.

Triple Alliance (1882), an alliance between Germany, Austria and Italy; ⇨ p. 174.

Triple Entente, the alliance between Britain, France and Russia during World War I; ⇨ pp. 175 and 176.

trireme, an ancient Greek war galley; ⇨ p. 44.

triumvirate, a group of three ruling collectively. In ancient Rome the First Triumvirate comprised Pompey, Caesar and Crassus, and the Second Triumvirate Mark Antony, Octavian and Lepidus; ⇨ p. 37.

Trotsky, Leon (Lev Davidovich Bronstein; 1879–1940), Russian revolutionary. He played a major role in organizing the OCTOBER REVOLUTION, after which he became Commissar for Foreign Affairs (1917–18). As Commissar for War (1918–24) he created the RED ARMY. He lost influence as Stalin's power increased and was expelled from the Communist Party in 1927. He was assassinated in Mexico in 1940; ⇨ pp. 3 and 181.

Troy, an ancient city of Asia Minor; ⇨ pp. 7 and 25 (box).

Troyes, Treaty of (1420), a treaty between England and France; ⇨ p. 95.

Trucial States, ⇨ UNITED ARAB EMIRATES.

Trudeau, Pierre Elliott (1919–), Canadian Liberal statesman, prime minister (1968–79 and 1980–4). His most significant accomplishment was to take the heat out of QUEBEC'S francophone separatist movement by promoting substantive constitutional reforms. Canada achieved final constitutional independence from the UK parliament during his second period in office.

Trujillo (Molina), Rafael (Léonidas) (1891–1961),

dictator of the DOMINICAN REPUBLIC (1930–61). His dictatorship established complete control of all aspects of Dominican life. Isolated by CASTRO'S revolution in Cuba and democratic revolution in Venezuela, he was assassinated in 1961.

Truman, Harry S. (1884–1972), thirty-third president of the USA (1945–53). A southern-born 'New Deal' Democrat, Truman succeeded to the presidency when F.D. ROOSEVELT died shortly before the end of World War II. In office he consented to the use of the atomic bomb against Japan. His policy of containment of Communism led the USA to commit itself firmly to Western Europe, Japan and the Republic of Korea; ⇨ pp. 195, 204 and 205.

Tshombe, Moise (1920–69), Congolese politician. Under his 'presidency' the province of Katanga seceded from the newly independent Congo in 1960; ⇨ p. 203 (box).

Tubman, Harriet (c. 1821–1913) black American abolitionist and social reformer. A fugitive slave she was a leading figure in the informal 'Underground Railroad' network that spirited Southern blacks to freedom before the American Civil War.

Tudor, House of, a royal dynasty that ruled England from the accession of HENRY VII in 1485 to the death of ELIZABETH I in 1603, when the throne passed to JAMES I of the House of STUART; ⇨ pp. 101 and 118

Tughluqs, a Muslim dynasty ruling the Indian sultanate of Delhi (1320–1413); ⇨ p. 62.

Tunisia, a country of N Africa. The Phoenicians founded Carthage (near Tunis) in the 8th century BC (⇨ p. 23). The Carthaginian Empire fell to Rome in the PUNIC WARS (⇨ p. 37). The area passed to the Byzantine Empire (⇨ p. 80) in 533 AD. In 647 an Arab invasion won Tunisia for the Islamic world (⇨ p. 82) and for over 900 years the area was disputed by a variety of Muslim dynasties. From 1574 to 1881 Tunisia was part of the (Turkish) Ottoman Empire (⇨ p. 115). In 1881 France established a protectorate, although the bey (monarch) remained the nominal ruler. Nationalist sentiments grew in the 20th century. Tunisia was occupied by the Germans (1942–3). Independence was gained under Habib BOURGUIBA in 1956 and the monarchy was abolished (1957). In the late 1980s the regime became increasingly unpopular and intolerant of opposition. Since Bourguiba's deposition by his PM (1988) – because of 'incapacity' – multi-party politics have been permitted.

Tupac Amarú, José Gabriel (1740–81), the leader of the largest Indian rebellion of the colonial period in South America (1780–1), which affected Peru and Bolivia directly and had echoes elsewhere in Spanish America. A descendant of the INCA, he was defeated and executed in May 1781; ⇨ p. 149.

Turkestan, an area of S Central Asia dominated since the middle of the 1st millennium by nomads speaking Turkic languages: Kazakh, Kirghiz, Turkmen, Uighur and Uzbek. The area came under Russian and Chinese rule in the 18th and 19th centuries; ⇨ pp. 55 and 56.

Turkey, a country of SE Europe and Asia Minor. The Hittite empire was founded around 1650 BC (⇨ p. 22), and quickly gained control of all of Anatolia (present-day Turkey). By the 6th century BC (Persian) Achaemenid power was expanding into Anatolia (⇨ pp. 26–7). However, in 334 BC Alexander the Great crossed into Asia and destroyed the Achaemenid Empire (⇨ p. 32). Anatolia was divided into several Hellenistic states until the Roman Empire took control of the area (⇨ p. 37). In AD 330 Emperor Constantine established the new city of CONSTANTINOPLE (now Istanbul) which became capital of the Byzantine Empire (⇨ pp. 40 and 80). In the 11th century the Muslim SELJUK Turks occupied most of Asia Minor. In the 13th century the Seljuks were replaced by the

Ottoman Turks, who by the end of the 14th century had conquered most of the Balkans. (For details of the rise and decline of the Ottoman Empire; ⇨ pp. 114–15 and 154–5.) In 1908 the YOUNG TURKS revolt attempted to stop the decline, but defeat in the Balkan Wars (1912–13; ⇨ p. 175) virtually expelled Turkey from Europe. Alliance with Germany in World War I ended in defeat and the loss of all non-Turkish areas (⇨ pp. 176–9). The future of Turkey in Asia itself seemed in doubt when Greece took the area around Izmir and the Allies defined zones of influence. General Mustafa Kemal – later known as ATATÜRK ('father of the Turks') – led forces of resistance in a civil war and went on to defeat Greece. Turkey's present boundaries were established in 1923 by the Treaty of Lausanne (⇨ p. 182). With the abolition of the sultanate (1922) Turkey became a republic, which Atatürk transformed into a secular Westernized state. Islam was disestablished, Arabic script was replaced by the Latin alphabet, the Turkish language was revived, and women's veils were banned. Soviet claims on Turkish territory in 1945 encouraged a pro-Western outlook, and in 1952 Turkey joined NATO. PM Adnan Menderes was overthrown by a military coup in 1960 and hanged on charges of corruption and unconstitutional rule. Civilian government was restored in 1961, but a pattern of violence and ineffective government led to a further army takeover in 1980. In 1974, after President MAKARIOS was overthrown in CYPRUS by a Greek-sponsored coup, Turkey invaded the island and set up a Turkish administration in the N (1975). Differences with GREECE over Cyprus have damaged the country's attempts to join the EC, as has the country's record on human rights. In 1983 civilian rule replaced the military government. Since then Turkey has drawn as close as possible to Western Europe, although the emergence of Islamic fundamentalism in the late 1980s has raised doubts concerning Turkey's European identity. Since the dissolution of the USSR (December 1991) Turkey has forged economic and cultural ties with the former Soviet republics of Central Asia, most of which are Turkic in language and tradition.

Turkmenistan, a republic in Central Asia. The Turkmens are a nomadic Turkic people who were conquered by the Mongols in the 13th century (⇨ p. 54) and were then ruled by the GOLDEN HORDE and the JAGATAI Khanates (⇨ pp. 54–5), before becoming nominally subject to Persia, or the (Uzbek) khans of Khiva and Bukhara. The area came under Russian rule between 1869 and 1881. The Turkmens fiercely resisted the Russians and rose in revolt in 1916. An autonomous Transcaspian government was formed after the Russian revolutions (⇨ pp. 182–3), and the area was not brought under Soviet control until the RED ARMY invaded in 1919. The Turkmen territories were reorganized as the Republic of Turkmenistan in 1924 and admitted to the USSR as a full Union Republic in 1925. Independence was declared following the abortive coup by Communist hardliners in Moscow (September 1991; ⇨ p. 225) and the republic received international recognition when the USSR was dissolved (December 1991).

Turks, a nomad people of Central Asian, Altaian origins. They periodically dominated surrounding, settled peoples and, from the 11th century, under SELJUK and – later – Ottoman leadership, established their power over SW Asia and the Near East, many eventually settling in Anatolia (modern TURKEY); ⇨ pp. 54, 83 and 114.

Tuscany, a former state of central Italy. The MEDICI family – who had been leaders of the Florentine republic for most of the Middle Ages – became dukes of Florence in 1531 and grand dukes of Tuscany in 1569. Tuscany passed to the Duke of Lorraine – the husband of MARIA THERESA of Austria – when the Medici became extinct in 1737, was absorbed into Napoleonic states (1801–14) and was incorporated in the kingdom of Italy (1860).

Tutankhamun, pharaoh of Egypt (c. 1361–1352 BC). He is famous for his burial site, discovered by Howard Carter in 1922, but was in fact an insignificant king; ▷ p. 19.

Tyler, John (1790–1862) tenth president of the USA (1841–5). As WHIG vice-president he succeeded to the presidency after the premature death of William Henry HARRISON. His defence of STATES' RIGHTS lost him the support of his cabinet.

Tyler, Wat (d. 1381) English rebel. He emerged as leader of the Kentish insurgents in 1381, presenting their demands to RICHARD II at Smithfield. After he was stabbed to death in a quarrel, the rebels dispersed; ▷ p. 93.

Tyndale, William (1494–1535), English Protestant and Bible translator. Exiled in the Habsburg Low Countries, he set up a printing press at Antwerp, producing Protestant literature, including Bibles, for export to England. A victim of CHARLES V'S repression of heresy, he was strangled to death at Louvain.

tyrant, in ancient Greece, a sole ruler, usually a usurper; ▷ p. 28.

Tyre, a Phoenician city. Loyal to the Persian king, it was besieged for months by Alexander the Great, who captured it after a lengthy siege in 332 BC; ▷ pp. **23**, 27 (map) and 32 (map).

Tyrol (Tirol), an Alpine province of Austria. Tyrol was under Habsburg rule from 1363 until 1918 except during the Napoleonic Wars, when it was ceded to Bavaria (1805–15), causing the Tyrolese to rise in a major revolt (1809). South Tyrol was ceded to Italy after World War I (▷ p. 182, map).

Tyrone, Hugh O'Neill, 2nd Earl of (1540–1616), Ulster chieftain; ▷ p. 119 (box).

Tz'u-hsi, ▷ CIXI.

U-boat (German, *Unterseeboot),* German submarine used to attack shipping in both World Wars to cut off trade and resources to Britain. Protected convoys of merchantmen were organized in response; ▷ pp. 176 and 190.

UDI, the Unilateral Declaration of Independence by the white settler government under Ian Smith in Southern Rhodesia in 1965; ▷ p. 221 (box).

Uganda, a republic of E Africa (▷ p. 202, map). The British protectorate of Uganda – established in 1894 – was built around the powerful African kingdom of Buganda, whose continuing special status contributed to the disunity that has plagued the country since independence in 1962. Dr Milton OBOTE, who suppressed the Buganda monarchy in 1966, was overthrown in a coup by General Idi Amin in 1971. Amin earned international criticism when political and human rights were curtailed, opponents of the regime were murdered and the Asian population was expelled. The army took over in 1979, supported by Tanzanian troops. Obote was restored but was ousted in a military coup in 1985, since when instability and guerrilla action have continued.

Ugarit, an ancient Canaanite city on the N Syrian coast; ▷ pp. 7 and 22.

Ukraine, a republic of Eastern Europe. The earliest known homeland of the SLAVS is thought to be in the N foothills of the Carpathians in Ukraine, whence the eastern Slavs migrated towards the Dniepr valley during the first millennium BC. Greek colonies flourished on the Crimean coast from about the 7th century BC. The state of Rus (▷ p. 126) – centred on KIEV – is the common ancestor of both Russia and Ukraine. Kiev was wrecked by the invasion of the TARTARS (1237–41), but other powerful centres grew up in Galicia in the W and the Vladimir area in the NW. These centres came under Polish rule in the 14th century when both Poland

and Lithuania extended S and E into the steppes on their border (*u krajina*, on the border). Polish influence increased in Ukraine, particularly after the formal union of Poland and Lithuania (1569), but Polish landowners and administrators were resented by the Ukrainians who were reduced to serfdom. In the 16th century, Poland encouraged the foundation in Ukraine of autonomous colonies of COSSACKS – Slavic warrior-peasants who formed mercenary cavalry forces – to act as buffers against Tartar invasions. However, the Cossacks grew overstrong and challenged the Poles, most seriously in the 1648–51 rebellion led by Bohdan Khmelnytsky, who requested assistance from the Russian tsar (1652). Two Russo-Polish wars followed (▷ p. 126) and in 1660–7 Ukraine was partitioned between Poland and Russia. The Ottoman Turks occupied Polish Ukraine from 1672 to 1699. Tsarist Russia suppressed the autonomy of the Cossacks and reunited most of Ukraine under Russian rule (1793) in the second partition of Poland (▷ p. 125, box). In 1878 Russia banned the use of the Ukrainian language in schools and in print. However, the Ukrainian nationalist movement continued in the more liberal atmosphere of Galicia in the W, which had been annexed by Austria in the first partition of Poland (1772). The Ukrainians in Russia took the opportunity afforded by World War I and the Russian revolutions (▷ pp. 180–1) to proclaim independence (January 1918), but a Ukrainian Soviet government was proclaimed in Kharkov. Ukraine united with Galicia when the Austro-Hungarian Empire collapsed (November 1918). The new state was invaded by Poland in pursuit of territorial claims and by the Soviet RED ARMY in support of the Kharkov Soviet. The Red Army prevailed and in 1922 Ukraine became one of the founding republics of the USSR, but the Lvov district of Galicia remained in Polish hands. From 1928, Soviet leader Joseph Stalin instituted purges in Ukraine and a new programme of Russification. After World War II – when Ukraine was occupied by Nazi Germany (▷ p. 192) – Soviet Ukraine was enlarged by the addition of Lvov (from Poland), Bukovina (from Romania) and Ruthenia (from Czechoslovakia) and, finally, Crimea (from Russia) in 1954. Ukrainian nationalism was spurred by the perceived Soviet indifference to Ukraine at the time of the nuclear accident at CHERNOBYL, N of Kiev, in 1986. Ukrainian politicians responded to the restructuring of the USSR in the late 1980s by seeking increased autonomy. The decision of the republic to declare independence following the abortive coup by Communist hardliners in Moscow (September 1991) hastened the demise of the USSR. Ukraine gained international recognition in December 1991 when the Soviet Union was dissolved, but tension remained between Moscow and Kiev concerning the allegiance of Soviet forces in Ukraine, and the status of Crimea and the Black Sea fleet.

Ulbricht, Walter (1893–1973), East German Communist politician. As party leader (1950–71) he implemented a policy of 'sovietization' of East Germany.

Ulm, battle of (October 1805), Napoleon's defeat of a large Austrian force was followed by the French occupation of Vienna; ▷ p. 146.

Ulster, a former kingdom and province in the N of Ireland. Six of its nine counties fall within NORTHERN IRELAND (which is often referred to as Ulster), while the remaining three are in the Republic of IRELAND; ▷ p. 119 (box).

Ulster Unionist Party, a political party supported by Northern Ireland's Protestant majority, dedicated to preserving the Union between Great Britain and NORTHERN IRELAND. It ruled the province from the partition of Ireland in 1922 to the reimposition of direct rule from London in 1972.

Since 1969 it has had to contend for the Unionist vote with the Revd Ian Paisley's more extreme Democratic Unionist Party.

Ulster Volunteers, a paramilitary force raised by CARSON in January 1913 to exclude ULSTER from the Third HOME RULE Bill. By 1914 over 100 000 men were under arms, but civil war between Ulster Volunteers and Irish nationalists was averted by the outbreak of World War I.

Umar ibn al-Khattab (c. 581–644), second caliph of Islam (634–44). Under his rule the Muslim Arab conquest of the Middle East began.

Umayyad, a dynasty of Muslim CALIPHS ruling from Damascus (661–750). A later Umayyad dynasty ruled in Spain (928–1031); ▷ pp. **82** and 83 (box).

Union, Acts of, the laws creating the political union of Great Britain and Ireland. An act passed by HENRY VIII in 1536 formally incorporated WALES into the English crown, though the region had been subjugated by England since the late 13th century. The thrones of England and Scotland were united with the accession of JAMES I in 1603. The Act of Union between England and SCOTLAND (1707) abolished the Scottish Parliament, the Scots henceforth sending MPs and peers to the Westminster PARLIAMENT, but retained the separate Scottish legal system and PRESBYTERIAN Church and allowed Scotland to trade with England's colonies. The United Kingdom of Great Britain and IRELAND was established with the amalgamation of the British and Irish parliaments in 1801; ▷ pp. 118–19.

United Arab Emirates, a federation of seven EMIRATES on the Persian Gulf. The Gulf tribes were converted to Islam in the 7th century AD. When the Portuguese occupied some ports in the 16th century, the region was prosperous, but economic decline followed, coinciding with the (Turkish) OTTOMAN conquest. A political vacuum in the mid-18th century was filled by the British, who saw the region as a link in the trade route to India. Treaties ('truces') were signed with local rulers during the 19th century, bringing the Trucial States under British protection. In 1958 oil was discovered in Abu Dhabi. When the British withdrew in 1971 the Trucial States formed the United Arab Emirates.

United Arab Republic, the unsuccessful union of Egypt and Syria (1958–61); ▷ p. 211.

United Democratic Front (UDF), a non-racial South African political party founded in 1983. It was incorporated into the ANC in 1991; ▷ p. 221.

United Empire Loyalists, the term applied to those Americans who remained loyal to the British crown during the War of Independence and who migrated to CANADA in the wake of their side's military defeat in 1783.

United Kingdom, the union of England, Scotland, Wales and Northern Ireland. Pre-Roman Britain was inhabited by the Celts (▷ p. 35). Julius Caesar invaded Britain in 55–54 BC, although wholesale conquest and Romanization did not occur until after AD 43 (▷ p. 37). The Roman province of Britannia – covering the area S of Hadrian's Wall (▷ p. 38, box) – lasted until the 5th century AD. The Scots from NE Ireland invaded N Britain in the 5th and 6th centuries, and when their king also became king of the PICTS (843) the foundations of a Scottish state were laid. From the 6th century Wales was divided into small kingdoms, which by the 12th century had been reduced to Gwynedd (in the N), Powys (centre) and Deheubarth (the S). (For details of the the Anglo-Saxon invasions of England; ▷ p. 79, box.) In the 950s King EDGAR of Wessex united England. (For details of the Viking raids and the Norman conquest; ▷ pp. 86–7.) At first England was just part of the Anglo-Norman state, but soon became the dominant force in an empire that included much of

France. Throughout the Middle Ages England waged war to retain possessions in France – the Hundred Years War (⊳ pp. 94–5). Scotland came increasingly under English influence from the 11th century, and EDWARD I (reigned 1272–1307) attempted to dominate Scotland at a time of disputed succession. After the Battle of BANNOCKBURN (1314), Scottish independence was asserted by ROBERT THE BRUCE (reigned 1306–29), whose grandson was the first Stewart (STUART) king of Scotland. HENRY II of England (reigned 1154–89) became overlord of Ireland in 1171, but English control of the N was limited until Protestant settlers arrived in great numbers in the 16th and 17th centuries (⊳ p. 119, box). Wales was gradually absorbed by England, despite the attempt by LLYWELYN II of Gwynedd to establish an independent Welsh nation in the 13th century. In the Middle Ages succession to the English throne was often contested, most notably in the civil war between the Houses of YORK and LANCASTER (the Wars of the ROSES). The development of the English state was aided by the emergence of the Houses of PARLIAMENT, but conflicts between the Crown and overmighty nobles were common. In 1215 King JOHN (reigned 1199–1216) was forced to grant considerable powers to the nobles. By the time HENRY VII (reigned 1485–1509) seized the throne to establish the TUDOR dynasty the numbers and strength of the nobility were diminished, and England was poised to emerge as a leading power. (For details of the Tudor dynasty, the English Reformation and the reign of Elizabeth I; ⊳ p. 118). The succession of James VI of Scotland as JAMES I of England in 1603 united the crowns of the two realms under the Stuarts, although full integration did not occur until Scotland's Parliament was abolished by the Act of UNION in 1707. (For details of the conflicts between the Stuarts and Parliament, the ENGLISH CIVIL WAR of 1643–9 and the Glorious Revolution of 1688–9, which resulted in the establishment of a parliamentary monarchy; ⊳ pp. 118–19). WILLIAM III (reigned 1688–1702) and his successor Queen ANNE (reigned 1702–14) fought the ambitions of Louis XIV of France, and an involvement in European wars continued after the (German) HANOVERIAN monarchs came to the throne in 1714. Colonial wars against the Dutch in the 17th century and the French in the 18th century saw a notable expansion of the British Empire (⊳ pp. 128–9). The American colonies were lost in 1783 (⊳ pp. 142–3), although Canada and some West Indian islands were retained. As if to compensate for the loss, British interest turned almost simultaneously to India, where much of the subcontinent had come under the sway of the EAST INDIA COMPANY (⊳ pp. 128 and 160). The United Kingdom – formed in 1801 through the union of Great Britain and Ireland – fought almost continuous wars against Revolutionary and Napoleonic France (1789–1815; ⊳ pp. 146–7), and emerged from the wars with further colonial gains. The reign of Queen VICTORIA (1837–1901) witnessed the height of British power. Britain – the first country to undergo an Industrial Revolution (⊳ pp. 140–1) – dominated world trade. British statesmen – including PMs Sir Robert PEEL, Lord PALMERSTON, William Ewart GLADSTONE and Benjamin DISRAELI – dominated the world stage. The British Empire included much of Africa, the Indian subcontinent and Australasia (⊳ pp. 160–3). Parliamentary democracy increased with the gradual extension of the right to vote, starting with the REFORM ACT of 1832. Representative government was granted to distant colonies, beginning with CANADA and AUSTRALIA, but was denied to IRELAND, where nationalist sentiment was stirring. By 1900 Britain's economic dominance was being challenged by the USA and, more particularly, by Germany (⊳ p. 174). Rivalry with imperial Germany was but one factor contributing to World War I (⊳ pp. 176–9). PM Herbert ASQUITH led a reforming Liberal Government from 1908 to 1916 but – after criticism of his conduct of the war – was replaced by David LLOYD GEORGE, who as Chancellor of the Exchequer had introduced health and unemployment insurance. The 'old dominions' – Canada, Australia, New Zealand and South Africa – emerged from the war as autonomous countries, and their independent status was confirmed by the STATUTE OF WESTMINSTER (1931). The EASTER RISING in Ireland (1916) led to the partition of the island in 1922. Only NORTHERN IRELAND – the area with a Protestant majority – stayed within the United Kingdom. In World War II Britain – led by PM Sir Winston CHURCHILL, who had strenuously opposed APPEASEMENT in the 1930s – played a major role in the defeat of the AXIS powers, and from 1940 to 1941 the UK stood alone against an apparently invincible Germany (⊳ pp. 190–1). After the war, the Labour government of Clement ATTLEE established the WELFARE STATE. At the same time, the British Empire began its transformation into a COMMONWEALTH of some 50 independent states, starting with the independence of India in 1947 (⊳ p. 201). By the late 1980s Britain was no longer a world power, although a British nuclear deterrent was retained. By the 1970s the UK was involved in restructuring its domestic economy and, consequently, its welfare state – from 1979 to 1990 under the Conservative premiership of Margaret THATCHER. The country has also joined (1973) and has attempted to come to terms with the EUROPEAN COMMUNITY (⊳ p. 215).

United Nations (UN), an international organization formed in 1945 to promote international peace and security; ⊳ pp. 203, 206, 211, 212, 213, **228–9** and 231.

United Provinces of the Netherlands, ⊳ pp. 111, 113, 117, **120–1**, 123 (box), 128, 130–1 and NETHERLANDS.

United States of America, a republic of North America. The earliest human settlement in America was probably around 10 000 BC, when descendants of hunters from Siberia moved S (⊳ p. 70). Nearly all the native peoples of North America spring from this ancestry (⊳ pp. 72–3). The Vikings may have reached Maine and even Cape Cod (⊳ p. 86), but the first recorded European landing was by the Spaniard Juan Ponce de León in Florida (1513). (For details of early white settlement of North America, the American War of Independence and US territorial and economic growth; ⊳ pp. 142–3 and 156–7). Although the 19th century witnessed the transformation of the USA into an industrial giant, strains appeared between the increasingly industrial N and the plantation S over the issue of slavery. This led to the Civil War (⊳ pp. 158–9) under the presidency of Abraham LINCOLN. The N was victorious, but after federal troops were withdrawn from the S (1877) racial segregation returned to the S until after World War II. Interest in world trade increased American involvement abroad. The Cuban revolt against Spanish rule led the USA into a war against Spain (1898) and brought US rule to the Philippines, Puerto Rico and Guam. American participation in World War I from 1917 hastened the Allied victory (⊳ p. 178), but the idealistic principles favoured by President Woodrow WILSON were compromised in the postwar settlement (⊳ p. 183, box). After the war the USA retreated into ISOLATIONISM and protectionism in trade. The imposition of Prohibition (⊳ p. 185, box) increased the activities of criminal gangs, but the 1920s were prosperous until the Depression began in 1929 (⊳ pp. 184–5). Federal investment and intervention brought relief through the NEW DEAL programme of President F.D. ROOSEVELT. The Japanese attack on PEARL HARBOR brought the USA into World War II (1941; ⊳ pp. 194–5). American involvement in the European and Pacific theatres of war was decisive and committed the USA to a world role as a superpower in 1945. US assistance was instrumental in rebuilding Europe (through the Marshall Plan) and Japan. From the late 1940s to the end of the 1980s, the USA confronted the Soviet Union's perceived global threat in the Cold War (⊳ pp. 204–7). As the leader of the Western alliance, the USA established bases in Europe, the Far East and the Indian and Pacific Oceans, so encircling the Soviet bloc. The USA was involved in the Korean War (1950–3) against Chinese and North Korean forces (⊳ pp. 205), and in direct military intervention in Guatemala (1954), Lebanon (1958 and 1983–5), the Dominican Republic (1965), Panama (1968 and 1989) and Grenada (1983). The greatest commitment, however, was in Vietnam, where from 1964 to 1973 US forces attempted to hold back a Communist takeover of Indochina (⊳ pp. 208–9), but a growing disenchantment with the war forced an American withdrawal. (For details of US domestic affairs since 1945; ⊳ pp. 216–17). Growing economic problems in the 1970s led to the election of a MONETARIST president, Ronald Reagan, in 1981. The USA continued to support movements and governments perceived as being in the Western interest – for example, backing Israel in the Middle East (⊳ pp. 210–19), providing weapons to the Unita guerrillas in ANGOLA and the Contra guerrillas in Nicaragua, and leading the coalition against Saddam Hussein's Iraq (⊳ p. 213, box). However, the increasing economic challenge from Japan, and the collapse of Communism in Eastern Europe (1989) and the USSR (1991), raised questions about the USA's future world role.

Ur, a city of ancient Sumer; ⊳ pp. 16 and 20.

Urartu, a state that flourished in E Anatolia from the 9th to the 7th centuries BC; ⊳ p. 21.

Urban II (c. 1042–99), pope (1088–99). He urged the sending of the First Crusade and was also a notable reformer; ⊳ pp. 88 and 90.

Urnfield cultures, a group of Bronze Age cultures originating in E Central Europe in the 2nd millennium BC and spreading across much of the rest of Europe. They were characterized by cemeteries in which the ashes of the dead were buried in urns.

Uruguay, a republic on the E coast of South America. The Spanish landed in Uruguay in 1516, and for much of the colonial era Uruguay was disputed between Spain and Portugal. In 1808 independence was declared from Spain, but Uruguay had to repulse successive Brazilian and Argentinian armies (1811–27) before independence was achieved (1828). Until 1903 Uruguay was ruled by dictators and wracked by civil war. However, prosperity from cattle and wool, and the presidencies of the reformer José Battle (1903–7 and 1911–15), turned Uruguay into a democracy and an advanced welfare state. A military dictatorship held power during the Depression. By the late 1960s economic problems had ushered in a period of social and political turmoil, and urban guerrillas became active. In 1973 a coup installed a military dictatorship that made Uruguay notorious for abuses of human rights. In 1985 the country returned to democratic rule.

Uruk, a city of ancient Sumer; ⊳ p. 16.

USSR, ⊳ SOVIET UNION.

Uthman (c. 574–656), third caliph of Islam (644–56). His murder led to the outbreak of the first civil war in Islamic history; ⊳ p. 82.

Utilitarianism, the philosophical belief that the highest good is the greatest happiness of the greatest number of people. Most fully articulated by BENTHAM and later also in a modified form by John Stuart MILL, it greatly influenced 19th-century reform activity.

Utrecht, Peace of (1713), the treaty ending the War

of the Spanish Succession between Louis XIV's France and the European grand alliance; ⇨ pp. **123** (box) and 129.

Uzbekistan, a republic of Central Asia. The region was overrun by the Persians (6th century BC; ⇨ p. 27), the Arabs (8th century AD; ⇨ p. 82) and the Mongols (13th century; ⇨ pp. 54–5), before becoming the centre of the empire of TAMERLANE and his descendants (⇨ p. 55; who established their capital at Samarkand. The Uzbek khanates of Bukhara and Khiva were established in the 15th and 16th centuries respectively. Persia ruled part of the area during the 18th century. Tsarist Russia first attempted to invade the region in 1717 but the Uzbeks did not finally come under Russian rule until the khans of Bukhara and Khiva became vassals of the tsar (1868–73). After the Russian revolutions (⇨ pp. 180–1), the Basmachi revolt (1918–22) resisted Soviet rule, but the khans were eventually deposed (1920) and Soviet republics established (1923–4). Uzbekistan was created when the USSR reorganized the boundaries of Soviet Central Asia. Independence was declared after the abortive coup in Moscow by Communist hardliners (September 1991; ⇨ p. 225) and international recognition was achieved when the USSR was dissolved (December 1991).

Uzbeks, Central Asian nomads of Altaian origins, speaking a Turkic language. They moved S into TRANSOXIANA in the late 15th century and have been the dominant group in the area since.

U Thant (1909–74), Burmese statesman, Secretary-General of the United Nations (1961–71); ⇨ p. 229.

Valerian (d. AD 260), Roman emperor (253–260); ⇨ p. 39.

Valley of the Kings, the desolate valley on the W bank of the Nile near Thebes, where the pharaohs of the ancient Egyptian New Kingdom were buried in rock-cut tombs.

Valois, a dynasty that ruled France from 1328 to 1589. EDWARD III's decision to dispute the right of Philip of Valois to inherit the CAPETIAN throne precipitated the Hundred Years War, but Philip's descendants retained the crown until HENRY III was stabbed to death in 1589 during the FRENCH WARS OF RELIGION; ⇨ pp. 94–5

Van Buren, Martin (1782–1862), eighth president of the USA (1837–41). His close association with Andrew JACKSON secured him the posts of secretary of state and then vice-president under the latter's presidency, and ensured his own election to the presidency in 1836.

Vandals, a Germanic people who raided Roman provinces in the 3rd and 4th centuries. Under pressure from the HUNS they crossed the Rhine, ravaged Gaul and Spain and founded a kingdom in N Africa (429), destroyed in 533 by the Byzantines; ⇨ pp. 40 (map) and 78.

Vargas, Getúlio (1885–1954), Brazilian statesman; ⇨ BRAZIL.

Varus (d. AD 9), Roman commander; ⇨ p. 38.

vassal, a tenant holding land (a fief) in return for services owed to a greater landlord under the feudal system; ⇨ p. 98.

Vatican City, a tiny sovereign state that is all that remains of the once extensive PAPAL STATES in Italy. When the French troops protecting the Pope were withdrawn in 1870, Italian forces entered Rome, which became the capital of the new kingdom of Italy (⇨ p. 152). Pope Pius IX (reigned 1846–78) protested at the loss of his temporal power and retreated into the Vatican, from which no Pope emerged until 1929, when the LATERAN TREATIES provided for Italian recognition of the Vatican City as an independent state. Since the 1960s the Papacy has again played an important role in international diplomacy, particularly under Popes Paul VI (reigned 1963–78) and JOHN PAUL II (1978–).

Vauban, Sébastien le Prestre de (1633–1707), French military engineer serving under Louis XIV. He planned 160 bastion fortresses and conducted some 50 sieges during his long career; ⇨ p. 103.

Vedas, the ancient sacred texts of Hinduism; ⇨ p. 58.

Veneti, ancient people settled around the area of modern Venice, later absorbed by the Romans; ⇨ p. 97 (box).

Venezuela, a republic of N South America. Venezuela was originally inhabited by Arawak and Carib Indians. Although the first permanent Spanish settlement was established in 1520, Spain did not begin to develop Venezuela until the 17th century. (For details of Spanish colonial rule and of the wars of independence; ⇨ pp. 148–9.) Initially united with Colombia and Ecuador, Venezuela seceded in 1830. Independence was followed by a series of military coups, revolts and dictators, including Juan Vicente Gómez, whose harsh rule lasted from 1909 to 1935. Since General Marcos Peréz Jiménez was overthrown in 1958, Venezuela has been a civilian democracy.

Venice, a former republican city-state in NE Italy; it became a great commercial and maritime power in the later medieval period. Its power declined from the 16th century, and it came under Austrian control after the French invasion of 1797. It was absorbed into the Kingdom of Italy after the AUSTRO-PRUSSIAN WAR of 1866; ⇨ pp. 84 (map), **97** (box), 113 (map), 115, *117*, 123 (map), 131 (box), 151 (map) and 152.

Vercingetorix (d. 46 BC), chief of the Arverni, a tribe of central Gaul, and the leader of a great revolt against Caesar in 52 BC. He was eventually defeated and besieged at Alésia. He was later paraded at Caesar's triumph and executed shortly afterwards; ⇨ p. 45 (box).

Verdun, battle of (1916), a lengthy engagement between French and German forces around the fortress town of Verdun in World War I; ⇨ pp. 176, 177 and **179** (box).

Verdun, Treaty of (August 843), a treaty between the three grandsons of Charlemagne. After 13 years of intermittent civil war the three sons of LOUIS THE PIOUS – Lothar, Louis the German and CHARLES THE BALD – agreed to a three-way partition of the empire; ⇨ p. 84.

Vereeniging, Treaty of (31 May 1902), the treaty ending the Second Boer War; ⇨ pp. 163 (box) and 222.

Versailles, ⇨ p. 122 (box).

Versailles, Treaty of (June 1919), a treaty between the ALLIED POWERS and Germany, part of the Paris Peace Conference after World War I; ⇨ p. **182**.

Verwoerd, Hendrik Frensch (1901–66), South African prime minister (1958–66). He was the main architect of APARTHEID, initially as minister of 'Bantu affairs'.

Vespasian (AD 9–79), Roman emperor (69–79). He was commanding the Roman forces against the Jewish revolt at the time of Nero's death. Proclaimed by his army, he emerged as the victor of the ensuing civil wars. His peaceful reign was marked by financial stringency and administrative efficiency; ⇨ p. 38.

Vespucci, Amerigo (1454–1512), Florentine explorer whose published accounts of his voyages to the New World (1499–1500; 1501–2) helped ensure that the new continent was called 'America'.

Vestal Virgins, six priestesses who tended the perpetual sacred fire in the temple of Vesta in the Roman Forum. Chosen at the age of 6, they served for 30 years, during which they had to remain virgins. Transgressors were buried alive.

Vichy Government, the semi-Fascist French government established after the fall of France in World War II, named after the town in unoccupied France where it was set up by PÉTAIN.. Dominated by LAVAL and Darlan, it was opposed by the FREE FRENCH and by the French Resistance, and collapsed in 1945; ⇨ pp. 190 and 210.

Vicksburg Campaign (1863), a decisive campaign of the AMERICAN CIVIL WAR waged for control of a Confederate stronghold on the Mississippi River; ⇨ p. **159**.

Victor Emmanuel II (1820–78), king of PIEDMONT and Sardinia (1849–61) and first king of Italy (1861–78). A key figure of the RISORGIMENTO, he supported his liberal Prime Minister, Camillo di Cavour, both in his domestic and his Italian policy; ⇨ p. 152.

Victoria (1810–1901), queen of Great Britain and Ireland (1837–1901) and empress of India (1876–1901). The only child of George III's fourth son, she succeeded WILLIAM IV as the last sovereign of the House of HANOVER and became the longest reigning British monarch. She married her cousin, Albert of Saxe-Coburg Gotha, who exerted considerable influence over her until his death in 1861 – an event from which she never fully recovered. Her popularity was mirrored in her Golden Jubilee (1887), and Diamond Jubilee (1897) celebrations. Her death in 1901 marked the end of an era in English history; ⇨ UNITED KINGDOM.

Vienna, Congress of (1814–15), the international peace conference held following the defeat of Napoleon I. METTERNICH, the dominant figure of the Congress, established as its guiding principle the restoration of the rule of hereditary monarchs; ⇨ pp. **147**, 150, 152 and 154.

Viet Cong, the name used by its opponents to describe the National Front for the Liberation of South Vietnam, a Communist guerrilla organization active in South Vietnam (1959–75); ⇨ pp. **208–9**.

Viet Minh, a Vietnamese Communist guerrilla organization founded by HO CHI MINH in 1941 with the aim of expelling the Japanese and the French from Vietnam; ⇨ p. **208**.

Vietnam, a country of SE Asia. (For details of the early history of Tongking – the N of Vietnam – and Annam – the centre; ⇨ p. 60.) In 1802 Nguyen Anh united Tongking, Annam and Cochin China (the S), and made himself emperor of Vietnam. The French intervened in the area from the 1860s, established a protectorate in Vietnam in 1883 and formed the Union of Indochina – including Cambodia and Laos – in 1887. Revolts against colonial rule in the 1930s marked the start of a period of war and occupation that lasted for over 40 years. (For the history of Vietnam from 1939 to 1975; ⇨ pp. 208–9.) Since the Communist takeover of the S (1975) and the reunification of Vietnam, reconstruction has been hindered by a border war with China (1979) and the occupation of Cambodia (1979–89) by Vietnamese forces. Lack of Western aid and investment has hindered economic development, and this, combined with political repression, has led to large numbers of refugees (the 'Boat People') fleeing the country.

Vietnam War (1959–75), ⇨ pp. 207, **208–9**, 216 and 217.

Vijayanagar, a former Hindu empire of S India (14th–16th centuries); ⇨ p. 59.

Vikings (also called the Norsemen), the Danish, Swedish and Norwegian seafarers and traders who raided and settled parts of N and W Europe between the 8th and the 11th centuries; ⇨ pp. 79 (box) and **86–7**.

Villa, Francisco ('Pancho', b. Doroteo Atango; 1878–1920), Mexican revolutionary. A former bandit, he led some of the northern forces in the MEXICAN REVOLUTION from 1911 until his defeat by rivals in 1915. He was assassinated in 1920.

Villafranca di Verona, Treaty of (1859), an agreement concluding the Franco-Piedmontese war against Austria. In the subsequent Peace of Zürich (1859) Austria retained Venetia and ceded Lombardy to France.

Villanovan Culture, an Iron Age culture from which the Etruscan civilization probably developed; ⇨ p. 36 (box).

villein, a tenant holding property from a manorial lord in medieval Europe. From the 12th to the 15th centuries villeins were regarded as 'unfree' (and thus often called SERFS), on the grounds that they were denied access to the public courts (jurisdiction over the villein belonging to his landlord); ⇨ p. 98.

Vimy Ridge, battle of (9 April 1917), a successful Allied attack on a key German position on high ground N of Arras in World War I.

Vinland, the Viking name for an area of E Canada, possibly N Newfoundland, which was discovered accidentally by Norse from Greenland c. 1000; ⇨ pp. 72 and 86.

Virginia, one of the 13 original states of the USA. The 'Old Dominion' dates from the establishment of an English colony at Jamestown in 1607. The original charter of Virginia included most of the SE of what is now the USA in its boundaries. Virginia played a leading role in the American Revolution and called the first CONTINENTAL CONGRESS. Four of the first five US presidents were Virginians. In the US Civil War, the state was the centre of the CONFEDERACY, whose capital was Richmond, Virginia; ⇨ pp. 156 (map) and 159 (map).

Virginia Campaigns (1861–5), a series of important operations fought in the E theatre of the American Civil War. Union forces experienced early setbacks, amd the effective generalship of Robert E. LEE and 'Stonewall' JACKSON enabled the Confederates to hold Union forces at bay for much of the war. GRANT'S murderous drive towards the Confederate capital in 1864–5 (the Petersburg campaign) ultimately decided the outcome of the conflict in the North's favour; ⇨ pp. **158–9.**

Virginia Plan, a plan advocating strong federal government for the USA, presented to the Constitutional Convention in 1787; ⇨ p. 143.

Visconti, Giangaleazzo (1351–1402), duke of Milan; ⇨ p. 97.

Visigoths, the western Goths, a people who migrated to the Danube delta from NE Europe in the 3rd century. They defeated and killed the Roman emperor Valens at ADRIANOPLE in 378. Under Alaric they invaded Italy (401) and sacked Rome (410). In 418 they established a kingdom based on Toulouse in S France until expelled by the FRANKS (507). Their kingdom in Spain lasted until the Muslim invasion of 711; ⇨ pp. 40 and **78–9.**

Vitoria, battle of (21 June 1813), WELLINGTON'S final victory in the PENINSULAR WAR, fought in N Spain, ousting the French from the Iberian peninsula and clearing the way for an allied invasion of S France; ⇨ p. 147.

Vittorio Veneto, battle of (27 October 1918), the final battle on the Italian Front in World War I in which ALLIED troops defeated weakened Austro-Hungarian forces. Three days later Austria asked for an armistice; ⇨ p. 178.

vizier, a leading court official in the Ottoman Empire; ⇨ p. 115.

Voortrekkers, pioneer AFRIKANER migrants who 'trekked' into the interior from Cape Colony in the 1830s; ⇨ pp. 163 (box) and 220.

Vorster, Balthazar Johannes (1915–1983), South African prime minister (1966–78). The architect of the state security system, he was forced to resign in the aftermath of the 1976 SOWETO uprising.

Vyshinsky, Andrei (1883–1954), Soviet politician

and diplomat, foreign minister (1949–53). As public prosecutor (1935–8) he presided over Stalin's show trials (⇨ p. 198, box).

V-2, a rocket-powered ballistic missile used by the Germans to bombard London in late World War II.

Wagram, battle of (5/6 July 1809), a victory of Napoleon over the Austrians, who had sought to exploit his difficulties in the PENINSULAR WAR.

Waitangi, Treaty of (1840), a treaty between the British government and NEW ZEALAND Maori chiefs (⇨ p. 69). Britain obtained sovereignty over New Zealand and – in exchange – guaranteed Maori rights over tribal lands. Breaches of the treaty led to intermittent warfare over the next 30 years.

Waldheim, Kurt (1918–), Austrian diplomat and politician, Secretary-General of the United Nations (1972–81), president of Austria (1986–).

Wales, a principality of the UNITED KINGDOM, in the W of the island of Great Britain. Wales was incorporated into the English crown in 1536 (⇨ p. 118).

Walesa, Lech (1943–), Polish politician. Underground trade union organizer in the Gdansk shipyard in the 1970s, he led the wave of strikes in August 1980 that led to the creation of the free trade union SOLIDARITY. He was imprisoned after the declaration of martial law in November 1981. In 1989 he negotiated the historic agreement ending Communist rule in Poland. He became president in 1990; ⇨ p. 224 (box).

Wallace, William (c. 1270–1305), leader of a Scottish revolt against English domination. He defeated the English at Stirling Bridge in 1297, but was himself defeated and captured at Falkirk in 1298 by EDWARD I, who had him executed.

Wallachia, a former principality of SE Europe, now part of ROMANIA; ⇨ pp. 85 (map), 151 (map) and 155.

Wallenstein, Albrecht Wenzel Eusebius von (1583–1634), Czech nobleman and general. His ability to raise troops and money was crucial for HABSBURG success in the first half of the Thirty Years War (⇨ p. 113). His increasing attempts to build up his own personal power worried the Emperor FERDINAND II, who had him assassinated.

Wall Street Crash, ⇨ p. 184.

Walpole, Sir Robert (1676–1745), English WHIG politician. As 'Prime Minister' (1721–42), his power was based in part on a system of bribing MPs to ensure the winning of votes in Parliament, and on the support of the crown. Committed to low taxation and a peaceful foreign policy, he refused to enter the War of the POLISH SUCCESSION. His opposition to the War of JENKINS' EAR contributed to his downfall; ⇨ p. 119.

Walsingham, Sir Francis (1530–90), English politician, secretary of state to ELIZABETH I from 1573. A Puritan, he favoured an aggressive anti-Spanish and anti-Catholic foreign policy (in contrast with the moderate CECIL), and exposed a number of plots against Elizabeth, including that of MARY, Queen of Scots.

Warbeck, Perkin (1474–99), a pretender to the English throne. From 1492 onwards he claimed to be Richard of York, the younger of the princes last seen in the Tower of London in 1483 (⇨ EDWARD V). He was captured in 1497 and executed two years later.

war crimes, acts committed in wartime that breach the accepted rules and customs of war. At the NUREMBERG TRIALS, Nazi politicians and soldiers were charged with 'crimes against humanity' and with 'waging aggressive war' by international tribunals from the victorious Allied powers.

warlord, ruler of a region owing his power to the command of military force rather than legitimate civil authority or hereditary right. Warlords were a

prominent feature of Chinese history in periods of imperial decline; ⇨ p. 196.

War of 1812 (1812–14), a conflict between Britain and the USA fought mainly on the US–Canadian border; ⇨ pp. 146 and **156.**

Warring States, a period of Chinese history (481–221 BC); ⇨ p. 52.

Warsaw Ghetto, a ghetto of 400 000 Jews established during the German occupation of Warsaw. In 1943 its 100 000 survivors staged an uprising against the Germans, after which they were put to death; ⇨ p. *192.*

Warsaw Pact, a military treaty and alliance of the USSR and seven East European countries; ⇨ p. **204** (box).

Warsaw Rising (1944), Polish insurrection in Warsaw during World War II. The uprising was brutally put down by the Germans – the advancing Soviet forces outside the city failing to give help to the insurgents; ⇨ p. 193.

Warwick, Richard Neville, Earl of (1428–71), English nobleman active during the Wars of the ROSES. Later known as 'kingmaker', owing to his prominent role in helping EDWARD IV to win the crown in 1461 and in restoring HENRY VI to the throne in 1470, he was killed at the battle of Barnet.

Washington Conference (1921–2), an international conference that discussed political tensions in the Far East and naval disarmament. The nine participating countries – including the USA, Britain, France, China and Japan – guaranteed China's independence and territorial integrity. In addition ratios of naval strength between the major powers were laid down; ⇨ p. 183.

Washington, George (1732–99), first president of the USA (1789–97). A wealthy Virginia slaveholder, he proved an able commander of American forces in the War of Independence. Fearful of social unrest, he was a strong supporter of the federal Constitution and in 1788 was a popular choice for chief executive of the new republic. His presidency saw the growth of the USA's first political parties in the 1790s. As father of his country, Washington was anxious to adopt a neutral stance in politics, but he himself was identified with FEDERALIST policies; ⇨ pp. 143 and 156.

Watergate scandal, a major US political scandal during the 1972 presidential campaign; ⇨ p. **217.**

Waterloo, battle of (18 June 1815), a battle in which British and Prussian forces under WELLINGTON and BLÜCHER defeated Napoleon, following the latter's return to France from exile on the island of Elba and invasion of the S Netherlands; ⇨ p. *147.*

Wavell, Archibald Percival, 1st Earl (1883–1950), British field marshal. He was commander in chief in the Middle East (1940–1), defeating the Italians in N Africa. As viceroy of India (1944–7) he took part in the negotiations for Indian independence; ⇨ p. 201 (box).

Webster, Daniel (1782–1852), US lawyer and politician, a leader of the WHIG Party in the 1830s and 1840s. As secretary of state (1841–3) he negotiated the Maine–New Brunswick border in the Webster–Ashburton Treaty.

Weimar Republic (1919–33), the German republic formed after World War I; ⇨ p. **186** (box).

Weizmann, Chaim (1874–1952), Polish-born Zionist leader and first President of independent Israel in 1948. He was instrumental in persuading the British government to issue the BALFOUR Declaration in 1917.

welfare state, a system whereby the state protects the social and economic well-being of the population through a variety of measures paid for by general taxation, such as unemployment benefit, old-age pensions and free comprehensive health care. The postwar British welfare state was based on the BEVERIDGE Report, which outlined a social insurance scheme 'from cradle to grave'. Similar systems exist in most West European countries. From the 1980s the system has come under increasing attack from the radical right, which claims that welfare provision fosters a culture of dependency.

Wellington, Arthur Wellesley, 1st Duke of (1769–1852), Anglo-Irish soldier and statesman. Sent to Portugal with English troops to exploit the uprising there against the French (1809), he expelled the French from Portugal, and advanced into Spain. Subsequent victories, notably at VITORIA (1813), were followed by his invasion of France. His greatest success was the defeat of Napoleon at WATERLOO (1815). An unpopular TORY prime minister (1828–30), he reluctantly abolished the TEST ACTS and vehemently opposed the reform of PARLIAMENT; ➪ pp. 146–7.

Wenceslas (c. 907–29), Christian prince of BOHEMIA killed by his pagan brother Boleslav during the course of a struggle for power. He was subsequently canonized and is regarded as the Czech national saint.

Wessex, the kingdom of the West Saxons, consisting of lands S of the Thames and W as far as Dorset. In the 9th century Wessex, under ALFRED the Great, led the resistance to the Vikings, and remained the centre of English political power until the Norman conquest in 1066; ➪ pp. 79 (box), 86 and 87.

West Bank, a region of PALESTINE W of the River Jordan, occupied by Israel since 1967. The West Bank was administered by Jordan from 1948 to 1967. Jordan renounced all legal responsibility for the West Bank (in favour of the PLO) in 1980; ➪ pp. 211 (map) and 213.

Western European Union (WEU), an organization formed on 17 March 1948 with the original intention of collaborating in 'economic, social and cultural matters and for collective self-defence'. These functions have gradually been transferred to the EC, the Council of Europe and NATO. However, in 1984 the WEU was reactivated to improve military cooperation between members and to strengthen their contributions to NATO. Its members are Belgium, France, Germany, Italy, Luxembourg, the Netherlands, Portugal, Spain and the UK; ➪ p. 215 (box).

Western Front, ➪ pp. 176–9.

Western Jin, a Chinese dynasty (265–316 AD) founded by Sima Yan, ruler of Wei, the most northerly of the THREE KINGDOMS. It briefly reunited China before losing the N to nomad invaders in 316, surviving in the S (as the Eastern Jin) until 420; ➪ p. 53.

Western Samoa, a state in the S Pacific. Samoa was settled by Polynesians about 300 BC (➪ p. 69). From the 1870s the USA, UK and Germany became active in Samoa. In 1899 the three rival powers divided the group, giving the western islands to Germany. New Zealand occupied the German islands in 1914, and administered Western Samoa until independence in 1962.

West Germany, ➪ GERMANY.

Westminster, Statute of (1931), British declaration granting self-government and self-determination to all DOMINIONS within the British Commonwealth – Canada, Australia, New Zealand, the Union of South Africa and the Irish Free State. All could now determine their own foreign and economic policies, though the constitutional question of the status of the British crown in the dominions was left unresolved.

Westphalia, Peace of (1648), the agreement ending the Thirty Years War, comprising the treaties of Münster (between the United Provinces of the Netherlands and Spain) and Osnabrück (between Sweden, the Holy Roman Emperor and France). The treaties, which represented a blow to HABSBURG

imperial ambitions, confirmed Dutch independence, split Germany into over 300 states, and gave territories in Germany to Sweden. It also checked Habsburg ambitions in Germany and gave important territorial gains to BRANDENBURG-Prussia; ➪ pp. 113, 120, 124 and 127.

Whig, a British political party opposed to the TORIES. The name was originally applied to those who, following the POPISH PLOT, sought to exclude CHARLES II'S Catholic brother, JAMES II from the succession. Broadly, the Whigs wished to limit the authority of the monarch in accordance with the social contract theories of John LOCKE that triumphed in the Glorious Revolution of 1688–9 (➪ p. 119). They engineered the accession of the House of HANOVER, monopolizing power and office after 1714. Increasingly oligarchical and aristocratic, the movement broke down in the changed social and political conditions in the 19th century, but contributed men and ideas to the new LIBERAL Party.

Whig Party, a US political party active from the late 1830s to the mid-1850s. Led by some of the most famous statesmen in American history (notably Daniel WEBSTER and Henry CLAY), the Whig party campaigned vigorously in favour of economic nationalism, but was eventually destroyed by the sectional tensions of the pre-Civil War period.

Whitby, Synod of, a meeting held at Whitby in NORTHUMBRIA in 664 that effectively brought the CELTIC CHURCH under the control of Rome.

White House, the official residence of the president of the USA in Washington DC. The term is also used to denote the US president and his advisers; ➪ pp. 216 and 217.

White Russians, those Russians who fought against and were defeated by the RED ARMY during the Civil War following the Russian Revolution. They were named after the royalist opponents of the French Revolution who adopted the white flag of the BOURBON dynasty; ➪ p. 181.

Whitlam, (Edward) Gough (1916–), Australian Labor statesman, prime minister (1972–5). Whitlam was dismissed by the governor-general, Sir John Kerr, when he refused to call a general election during a financial crisis.

Wilberforce, William (1759–1833), British politician. The leader of a group of evangelical Christian MPs who championed moral reform at home and abroad, his efforts resulted in the abolition of the slave trade (1807) and of slavery (1833) in Britain and its colonies; ➪ p. 129 (box).

'Wild West', a romantic designation for the final stage of US frontier settlement in the late 19th century. Characterized in the popular mind by gunfighters, golddiggers, cowboys and Indians, the 'Wild West' was a much harsher place than the myth implied, 'colourful' characters such as Billy the Kid and Wyatt Earp being pathological killers, and the 'savage' Native Americans helpless (if sometimes cruel) victims of modern western civilization. Although frontier conditions were certainly fluid, the historical West was the more humdrum (and substantial) creation of farm families and ranchers (➪ p. 156).

Wilhelm I (1797–1888), king of Prussia (1861–88) emperor of Germany (1871–88). He used arms to suppress the 1848 revolution in BADEN and was regent for his insane brother FREDERICK WILLIAM IV of Prussia from 1858. He appointed BISMARCK as chancellor in 1862 and thereafter supported his policy of strengthening the power of Prussia; ➪ pp. 153 and 175.

Wilhelm II (1859–1942), emperor of Germany and king of Prussia (1888–1918), a grandson of Queen VICTORIA of Britain. He dropped BISMARCK in 1890, took control of Germany himself and set about strengthening the country's military and naval

forces. His support of AUSTRIA-HUNGARY against Serbia led to the outbreak of World War I. He abdicated on Germany's defeat in 1918; ➪ pp. 174–5, 178 and 179.

William (the Lion; c. 1142–1214), king of Scotland (1165–1214). Invading England in pursuit of his claim to NORTHUMBRIA, he was captured (1174) and forced to cede Edinburgh and other castles. However, RICHARD I allowed him to buy them back in 1189.

William I (the Conqueror; 1028–87), the first Norman king of England (1066–87); ➪ pp. 87 and 94.

William I (the Silent; 1533–84), Prince of ORANGE and Count of Nassau; ➪ p. 120.

William II (Rufus; c. 1056–1100), king of England (1087–99). He suppressed baronial revolts and consolidated the Norman conquest. His premature death, which has led to fanciful theories, was probably a hunting accident.

William III (1650–1702), king of England (1689–1702) with his wife MARY II following the Glorious Revolution. He was also effective ruler of the United Provinces of the Netherlands (1672–1702); ➪ pp. 119, 121 and 123 (box).

William IV (1765–1837), king of Great Britain and Ireland and dependencies overseas, and king of HANOVER (1830–7). The third son of GEORGE III, he succeeded his childless brother GEORGE IV.

Wilson, Harold James (1916–), British Labour prime minister (1964–70 and 1974–6). He succeeded GAITSKELL as Labour leader, defeating Alec Douglas-HOME in the 1964 election. In his first period in office he faced balance-of-payments and sterling crises, but his administration passed some important reforming legislation, notably the introduction of comprehensive education, and changes in the law on homosexuality, divorce and abortion. He was defeated in the 1970 election by Edward HEATH. His last minority administration confirmed Britain's membership of the EEC after a referendum. He was succeeded as Labour leader and PM by James CALLAGHAN.

Wilson, Woodrow (1856–1924), twenty-eighth president of the USA (1913–21). He won the watershed election of 1912 as a reform-minded Democrat, taking the USA into World War I on the side of the Allies and masterminding the creation of the League of Nations. A moralist in politics, he outlined his programme for a peaceful postwar world order in the Fourteen Points. ISOLATIONISTS in the US Senate dealt him a massive blow by rejecting American entry into the League in 1920; ➪ pp. 182 and 183.

Windsor, House of, the dynastic name adopted by the British royal family in 1917, when GEORGE V dropped all his German titles – derived from the marriage of VICTORIA to Prince Albert of Saxe-Coburg-Gotha – because of World War I.

witchcraft, the use of supernatural powers – supposedly acquired through a pact with the devil – for evil purposes. It was first declared a heresy by Pope Innocent III in 1484. The religious struggles of the Reformation stimulated even further the obsession with witchcraft, and between 1580 and 1650 the number of witch trials in Europe rocketed throughout Western Europe. Both Roman Catholic and Protestant theologians identified witchcraft with active heresy. The witch craze died down in Western Europe after 1650.

Wolsey, Thomas (1473–1530), English cardinal and Lord Chancellor. He served as HENRY VIII'S chief minister until discredited by his failure to secure from Pope Clement VII the king's divorce from CATHERINE of Aragon; ➪ p. 118.

women's liberation, a movement campaigning to improve the status of women in society that emerged in the 1960s and early 1970s; ➪ p. 233.

women's suffrage, the right of women to vote in elections. The cause of women's suffrage was taken up by 19th-century feminists, and – most famously – by the British suffragettes in the early 20th century; ▷ pp. 168 and 232.

World Bank (International Bank for Reconstruction and Development), a specialized agency of the United Nations set up in 1945 to aid development – particularly in poorer member-countries – through capital investment; ▷ p. 229.

World Health Organization (WHO), a specialized agency of the United Nations, established in 1945 with the aim of promoting the attainment by all peoples of the highest possible standards of health ▷ p. 229.

World War I (1914–18), ▷ pp. 162, 169, **174–5**, **176–9**, 180, 182, 183, 184 and 186.

World War II (1939–45), ▷ pp. 188–9, **190–5**, 198, 201, 204, 211, 214, 216, 220, 222, 226, 228 and 235.

Worms, Diet of (1521), a meeting of the DIET of the Holy Roman Empire, at which Luther defended his teachings in the presence of the Emperor CHARLES V. Having heard Luther, the Diet condemned his teaching.

Wounded Knee, massacre of (1890), the last major 'battle' of America's Indian Wars, fought in South Dakota. US 7th cavalry gunned down some 200 Sioux men, women and children who were resisting attempts to disarm them.

Württemberg, a former county (1153), duchy (1495), electorate (1802) and kingdom (1806) in S Germany. Württemberg became part of the German Empire in 1871. The monarchy was overthrown in 1918; ▷ p. 151 (map).

Wyclif, John (?1330–84), English theological reformer; ▷ p. 91.

Xenophon (c. 435–354 BC), Greek soldier, who led 10 000 Greek mercenaries in a heroic retreat during a civil war in the Persian Empire. He recounted this exploit in his great work, the *Anabasis*.

Xerxes I (c. 519–465 BC) king of Persia (486–465 BC) and son of DARIUS I; ▷ pp. 27 and 29.

Xhosa, a cattle-farming people of southern Africa. The eastward push of British settlers from the early 19th century led to wars in 1834–5, 1846–53 and 1877–9. Today the Xhosa live mainly in the BANTUSTANS of the Transkei and the Ciskei.

Xia, traditionally the first dynasty to rule China (c. 21st–16th centuries BC); ▷ p. 52.

Yalta Conference (4–11 February 1945), the second meeting of the 'Big Three' Allied leaders at which STALIN, CHURCHILL and ROOSEVELT discussed the final stages of World War II and the postwar division of Europe; ▷ p. 204.

Yamashita, Tomoyuki (1885–1946), Japanese general known as the 'Tiger of Malaya'. He commanded the forces that overran Malaya (1941–2) and Singapore (1942), and was defeated in the Philippines in the campaign against the Americans (1944–5). He was executed for war crimes in 1946.

Yeltsin, Boris Nikolayevich (1931–), president of Russia (1990–). He led the opposition to the Soviet coup of August 1991, and after the collapse of the Soviet Union became the dominant politician in post-Communist Russia; ▷ p. 225.

Yemen, a country of SW Asia. From the 8th to the 1st century BC the N was the home of the Sabaeans. In AD 628 the area became Islamic. The Ottoman Turks first occupied the area in 1517 (▷ p. 115) and were not finally expelled from the N until 1911, when Imam Yahya secured Yemen's independence. Britain took Aden as a staging post to India (1839) and gradually established a protectorate over the S. In 1963 an armed rebellion began against British rule in the S which gained independence in 1967 after a civil war between rival liberation movements. A republican revolution broke out in the N

in 1962, and from 1963 until 1970 a civil war was fought, with President NASSER's Egypt supporting the victorious republicans and Saudi Arabia supporting the royalists. Relations between North Yemen and Marxist South Yemen were difficult. The collapse of South Yemen's Communist trading partners (1989–90) undermined the country's weak economy, and the two countries merged in May 1990.

Yom Kippur War, the name given by the Israelis to the 1973 Arab–Israeli War; ▷ p. 212.

Yongle (1359–1424), Ming emperor of China (1403–24), who extended the Chinese Empire with campaigns in Central Asia and Annam (modern Vietnam), and sent out the voyages of discovery of Zheng He; ▷ p. 56.

York, Richard, 3rd Duke of (1411–60), heir to the throne of England until 1453. He claimed the throne in 1460, in opposition to HENRY VI of the house of LANCASTER. Despite his death at the battle of Wakefield (1460), and the YORKIST defeat at the second battle of St Albans (1461), Richard's son gained the throne as EDWARD IV shortly afterwards.

Yorkist, the dynastic name given to the English kings from EDWARD IV to RICHARD III, descendants of RICHARD, 3rd Duke of York. In 1460 Richard claimed their right to the throne in opposition to the LANCASTRIAN HENRY VI; in consequence they became one of the two warring parties in the Wars of the ROSES; ▷ pp. 95 and 118.

Yorktown, battle of (1781), the final battle of the American War of Independence; ▷ p. 143.

Yoruba, a people living in the SW of modern NIGERIA; the focus of early cultures such as Ife and the development of kingship and urbanism in W Africa. The Yoruba kingdom of Oyo was a major force in 18th-century W Africa (▷ p. 67).

Young Italy, an Italian nationalist organization founded during the Risorgimento; ▷ p. 152.

Young Plan (1929), a plan for German reparations payments after World War I. Devised by a committee under US financier Owen D. Young, it replaced the DAWES Plan; ▷ p. 185.

Young Turks, Ottoman patriots dedicated to the Westernization of Turkey, who forced constitutional change in 1908 by allying themselves to elements of the Turkish army. In 1909 they forced Sultan ABDUL HAMID II to abdicate in favour of his son and effectively seized power.

Ypres, battles of, three battles fought on a salient in the British line near the Belgian town of Ypres in World War I. The first (October 1914) defeated the German attempt to reach the Channel ports. The second (April–May 1915) saw the first use of poison gas on the Western Front. The third (July–November 1917) is known as PASSCHENDAELE; ▷ pp. 176 and 177.

Yuan, the Mongol dynasty (1271–1368) established in China by Kublai Khan; ▷ pp. 55 and 56.

Yuan Shikai (Yuan Shih-K'ai; 1859–1916), Chinese soldier and politician. He became president of the new Chinese republic in 1912 after the fall of the QING dynasty (▷ p. 196), but his suppression of Sun Yat-sen's KUOMINTANG and submissive attitude to an increasingly expansionist Japan provoked further unrest. China was left divided between rival WARLORDS after his death.

Yucatán, a tropical lowland peninsula of E Mexico, a major centre of pre-Columbian Meso-American civilization, particularly at the height of Maya culture (300–900 AD); ▷ p. 71.

Yugoslavia, a country of SE Europe. The SLAV ancestors of the Serbs arrived in the W Balkans in the 6th and 7th centuries AD and created a large kingdom that was destroyed by (Turkish) Ottoman conquest, symbolized by the battle of Kosovo in 1389 (▷ pp. 114–5). Only mountainous MONTENEGRO managed to preserve any autonomy. Led by

KARAGEORGE, the Serbs rose against Turkish rule between 1804 and 1813. Under his rival Miloś OBRENOVIĆ, the Serbs rose again in 1815 and became an autonomous principality, but the country was destabilized by rivalry between the Karageorge and Obrenović dynasties. Both Serbia and Montenegro were recognized as independent in 1878 (▷ p. 155). By the start of the 20th century a Croat national revival within the Austro-Hungarian HABSBURG Empire looked increasingly to Serbia to create a South ('Yugo') Slav state. After Serbia gained MACEDONIA in the Balkan Wars (1912–13; ▷ p. 175), Austria grew wary of Serb ambitions. The assassination of the Habsburg heir (1914) by a Serb student provided Austria with an excuse to quash Serbian independence. This led directly to World War I (▷ p. 176) and the dissolution of the Habsburg Empire, whose South Slav peoples united with Serbia and Montenegro in 1918. The interwar Kingdom of Serbs, Croats and Slovenes – renamed Yugoslavia in 1929 – was run as a highly centralized 'Greater Serbia'. The country was wracked by nationalist tensions, and Croat separatists murdered King Alexander in 1934. Attacked and dismembered by Hitler in 1941, Yugoslavs fought the Nazis and each other. The Communist-led partisans of Josip Broz TITO emerged victorious in 1945, and re-formed Yugoslavia on Soviet lines. Expelled by Stalin from the Soviet bloc in 1948 on account of their indiscipline, the Yugoslav Communists rejected the Soviet model, and pursued policies of decentralization, workers' self-management and non-alignment. However, after Tito's death in 1980, the Yugoslav experiment faltered in economic and nationalist crises. (For details of the Yugoslav Civil War, and the breakup of Yugoslavia in the early 1990s; ▷ p. 224, CROATIA, SERBIA and SLOVENIA.) International recognition of Slovenia, Croatia and BOSNIA–HERZEGOVINA reduced Yugoslavia to a small Serb-dominated state. MACEDONIA also declared sovereignty (1991) but (up to June 1992) was denied international recognition, although it had effectively seceded from the federation.

Zaïre, a republic of central Africa. The African Luba and Kuba kingdoms flourished from the 16th to the 18th centuries. The region was ravaged by the slave trade, and in 1885 became the personal possession of King LEOPOLD II of the Belgians. (For details of Zaïre's colonial history and independence; ▷ p. 203, box.) Colonel Mobutu twice intervened in the troubled affairs of the Congo and in 1965 made himself head of state. He renamed the country Zaïre, gradually restored the authority of the central government, and introduced a one-party state (1967). Mobutu's strong rule attracted international criticism, and, following unrest, he was obliged to concede a multi-party system (1991).

Zama, battle of (202 BC), the defeat of Hannibal by SCIPIO AFRICANUS in N Africa, ending the Second Punic War; ▷ p. 37.

Zambia, a republic of central Africa. The area was brought under the control of the British South Africa Company of Cecil RHODES in the 1890s. (For details of Zambia's history until independence; ▷ p. 221, box). Kenneth KAUNDA led Zambia to independence and ruled the country as a one-party state from 1973 to 1990, when he was defeated in free elections.

Zanzibar, ▷ TANZANIA.

Zapata, Emiliano (1879–1919), an agrarian rebel and guerrilla leader during the MEXICAN REVOLUTION. He dominated the sugar-growing state of Morelos from 1911 until his assassination in 1919.

Zealots, a militant Jewish sect involved in the anti-Roman revolt of AD 66; ▷ ISRAEL, MASADA.

zeppelin, a generic term for German airships, principally in World War I, named after their designer Graf Ferdinand von Zeppelin.

Zheng He (Cheng Ho; died c. 1433), Chinese admiral and explorer; ▷ pp. 56, 108 and 109.

Zhivkov, Todor (1911–), Bulgarian Communist politician, First Secretary of the Communist Party (1954–89), prime minister (1962–71), president (1971–89); ▷ p. 224 (box).

Zhou, the second historical Chinese dynasty (1122–256 BC); ▷ p. 52.

Zhou Enlai (Chou En-lai; 1898–1976) Chinese Communist politician, prime minister (1949–76), foreign minister (1949–58). A founder member of the Chinese Communist Party, in 1949 he became the first PM of the People's Republic. He exercised a moderating influence on extremist elements during the Cultural Revolution (▷ p. 197). The best-known and best-regarded of China's leaders on the international stage, he played a major role in the Sino–US détente of the early 1970s.

Zhukov, Georgi Konstantinovich (1896–1974), Soviet field marshal. The architect of the Soviet Union's campaigns in World War II, he defeated the Germans at Stalingrad, lifted the siege of Leningrad, and led the final assault on Germany and capture of Berlin; ▷ p. 193.

Zia ul-Haq, Mohammed (1924–88), Pakistani soldier and politician. He overthrew Z.A. BHUTTO in a coup (1977). As president of PAKISTAN from 1978 he banned political parties, introduced an Islamic legal code, and played the role of US surrogate in the Afghan civil war. He did not relinquish the presidency until his death in an air crash in 1988.

Zimbabwe, a republic of S central Africa. The region was the location of the ancient kingdom of Zimbabwe (▷ p. 67, box). The area was gradually penetrated by British and Boer hunters, missionaries and prospectors from the 1830s, and was occupied by the British South Africa Company of Cecil RHODES in the 1890s. The highlands of what became Southern Rhodesia were settled by White farmers, who deprived Africans of land and reduced them to a cheap labour force. (For details of Zimbabwean independence; ▷ p. 221, box.) Independent Zimbabwe – under Robert MUGABE – has effectively become a one-party state.

Zimbabwe, Great, an ancient palace-city of SE Africa; ▷ p. **67** (box).

Zimmermann note (January 1917), a secret telegram from German foreign minister Alfred Zimmermann to the German minister in Mexico City, stating that should the USA join the ALLIES, Germany would help Mexico to recover Texas, New Mexico and Arizona (lost to the USA in 1848). Revelation of the telegram accelerated the decline of US-German relations which led to US entry into World War I on 6 April.

Zinoviev, Grigory Yevseyevich (1883–1936), Soviet politician. A letter allegedly written by Zinoviev urging British Communists to revolt may have contributed to the LABOUR government's defeat in the 1924 general election.

Zionism, the Jewish national liberation movement, founded in the 1890s by Theodor HERZL. It was dedicated to the creation of a national home for the Jews, free from the ANTI-SEMITISM rife in parts of Europe. It became the political creed of the Jewish settlers in Palestine and the driving force behind the creation of Israel in 1948; ▷ p. 210.

Zizka, John (?1370–1424), Bohemian priest and soldier who led the Hussite rebellion; ▷ p. 91.

Zog I, ▷ ALBANIA.

Zollverein (German, 'customs union'), a customs union abolishing economic barriers between the various German states in 1834; ▷ p. 153.

Zoroastrianism, the religion of the ancient Iranians and their rulers, particularly the Sassanians; ▷ p. 27 (box).

Zulus, a Bantu people (▷ p. 66) of SE Africa (modern NATAL). They became the dominant military force in the area under the leadership of Shaka (1818–28), their expansion to secure grazing land for their cattle precipitating the migration of surrounding peoples. They remained powerful until defeated by Britain in the Zulu War (1879). Zululand was annexed by Britain in 1894. Today the Zulus live mainly in the BANTUSTAN of Kwazulu; ▷ pp. 67, 162 and 221.

Zuni, a native North American people of the Southwest, living in New Mexico; ▷ pp. 72 and 73.

Zwingli, Ulrich (1484–1531), the leader of the Reformation in Switzerland. He broke with Luther over differences between them on the nature of the Eucharist. After his death in battle against the Swiss Catholic cantons, the leadership of the Swiss Reformation passed to Calvin; ▷ pp. 110–111.

PICTURE ACKNOWLEDGEMENTS

The Publishers would like to thank the following for permission to reproduce pictures in the Encyclopedia:

Ancient Art & Architecture Collection, pp. 15, 16, 18 (top), 20, 30, 33, 34, 35 (top and bottom), 39 (top), 58, 59 (top and bottom), 62 (bottom), 69, 70 (top and bottom), 78, 95 (bottom).
Archiv für Kunst und Geschichte, pp. 7 (top), 14 (top and bottom), 18 (bottom), 19, 21, 22, 26, 36, 38, 41, 80, 84, 85, 87, 93, 95 (top), 96, 104/105, 109, 116, 118 (bottom), 121, 122, 124, 125, 126, 130, 132, 134 (top), 135, 136/137, 141 (top), 143, 144 (top and bottom), 146, 147, 148, 150, 152, 153, 154, 164, 165, 168, 169 (top), 177 (top), 181 (top), 184, 190, 192, 193, 194, 206 (top), 226.
Bettmann Archive, p. 209 (top).
Bibliothèque Nationale (Paris), p. 103.
Bodleian Library (Oxford), p. 108.

Bridgeman Art Library, pp. 4, 65, 103.
British Museum, p. 67.
Christie's Colour Library, pp. 160, 161, 180.
Culver Pictures Inc., p. 131.
E.T. Archive, p. 57 (top).
Mary Evans Picture Library, pp. 140, 141 (bottom), 149, 167, 169, 186, 198.
Explorer, pp. 7 (bottom), 23, 27, 28, 53, 56, 60, 62 (top), 73, 82, 118 (top), 119, 133 (top and bottom).
Gamma Presse Images, pp. 170/171, 197, 199 (top and bottom), 204, 206 (bottom), 207, 209 (bottom), 213, 217, 218, 219, 220, 221, 222, 224, 226, 228, 229, 230, 231.
Sonia Halliday Photographs, pp. 88, 114.
The Robert Harding Picture Library, p. 72.

The Hulton Picture Company, pp. 57 (bottom), 142, 166, 177 (bottom), 195, 196, 201, 202, 203, 210.
Images Colour Library, pp. 39 (bottom), 61.
Image Select, pp. 179 (top), 181 (bottom), 188, 227.
India Office Library, p. 63.
David King Collection, p. 3.
Museum of London, p. 6.
Scala, pp. 2, 74/75, 83, 97, 98, 99, 100, 101, 117.
Spectrum Colour Library, pp. 31, 48/49.
Syndication International, pp. 66, 68, 71.
Roger-Viollet (Paris), pp. 40, 94, 110, 111, 155, 174, 175, 176, 187, 189.
Werner Forman Archive, p. 67.
Zefa Picture Library, pp. 53 (top), 64, 156.